Short Story Criticism

Guide to Gale Literary Criticism Series

For criticism on	Consult these Gale series
Authors now living or who died after December 31, 1999	*CONTEMPORARY LITERARY CRITICISM (CLC)*
Authors who died between 1900 and 1999	*TWENTIETH-CENTURY LITERARY CRITICISM (TCLC)*
Authors who died between 1800 and 1899	*NINETEENTH-CENTURY LITERATURE CRITICISM (NCLC)*
Authors who died between 1400 and 1799	*LITERATURE CRITICISM FROM 1400 TO 1800 (LC)* *SHAKESPEAREAN CRITICISM (SC)*
Authors who died before 1400	*CLASSICAL AND MEDIEVAL LITERATURE CRITICISM (CMLC)*
Authors of books for children and young adults	*CHILDREN'S LITERATURE REVIEW (CLR)*
Dramatists	*DRAMA CRITICISM (DC)*
Poets	*POETRY CRITICISM (PC)*
Short story writers	*SHORT STORY CRITICISM (SSC)*
Literary topics and movements	*HARLEM RENAISSANCE: A GALE CRITICAL COMPANION (HR)* *THE BEAT GENERATION: A GALE CRITICAL COMPANION (BG)*
Asian American writers of the last two hundred years	*ASIAN AMERICAN LITERATURE (AAL)*
Black writers of the past two hundred years	*BLACK LITERATURE CRITICISM (BLC)* *BLACK LITERATURE CRITICISM SUPPLEMENT (BLCS)*
Hispanic writers of the late nineteenth and twentieth centuries	*HISPANIC LITERATURE CRITICISM (HLC)* *HISPANIC LITERATURE CRITICISM SUPPLEMENT (HLCS)*
Native North American writers and orators of the eighteenth, nineteenth, and twentieth centuries	*NATIVE NORTH AMERICAN LITERATURE (NNAL)*
Major authors from the Renaissance to the present	*WORLD LITERATURE CRITICISM, 1500 TO THE PRESENT (WLC)* *WORLD LITERATURE CRITICISM SUPPLEMENT (WLCS)*

ISSN 0895-9439

Volume 60

Short Story Criticism

Criticism of the
Works of Short Fiction Writers

Janet Witalec
Project Editor

GALE®

THOMSON
GALE

Detroit • New York • San Diego • San Francisco • Cleveland • New Haven, Conn. • Waterville, Maine • London • Munich

THOMSON

GALE

Short Story Criticism, Vol. 60

Project Editor
Janet Witalec

Editorial
Anja Barnard, Jenny Cromie, Kathy D. Darrow,
Justin Karr, Julie Keppen, Joseph Palmisano

Research
Michelle Campbell, Tracie A. Richardson

Permissions
Margaret A. Chamberlain

Imaging and Multimedia
Dean Dauphinais, Lezlie Light, Luke
Rademacher

Composition and Electronic Capture
Carolyn Roney, Kathy Sauer

Manufacturing
Stacy L. Melson

LIBRARY OF CONGRESS CATALOG CARD NUMBER 88-641014

ISBN 0-7876-7017-0
ISSN 0895-9439

Printed in the United States of America
10 9 8 7 6 5 4 3 2 1

Contents

Preface vii

Acknowledgments xi

Literary Criticism Series Advisory Board xiii

Preface

Short Story Criticism (*SSC*) presents significant criticism of the world's greatest short story writers and provides supplementary biographical and bibliographical materials to guide the interested reader to a greater understanding of the authors of short fiction. This series was developed in response to suggestions from librarians serving high school, college, and public library patrons, who had noted a considerable number of requests for critical material on short story writers. Although major short story writers are covered in such Gale series as *Contemporary Literary Criticism* (*CLC*), *Twentieth-Century Literary Criticism* (*TCLC*), *Nineteenth-Century Literature Criticism* (*NCLC*), and *Literature Criticism from 1400 to 1800* (*LC*), librarians perceived the need for a series devoted solely to writers of the short story genre.

Scope of the Series

SSC is designed to serve as an introduction to major short story writers of all eras and nationalities. Since these authors have inspired a great deal of relevant critical material, *SSC* is necessarily selective, and the editors have chosen the most important published criticism to aid readers and students in their research.

Approximately eight to ten authors are included in each volume, and each entry presents a historical survey of the critical response to that author's work. The length of an entry is intended to reflect the amount of critical attention the author has received from critics writing in English and from foreign critics in translation. Every attempt has been made to identify and include the most significant essays on each author's work. In order to provide these important critical pieces, the editors sometimes reprint essays that have appeared elsewhere in Gale's Literary Criticism Series. Such duplication, however, never exceeds twenty percent of an *SSC* volume.

Organization of the Book

An *SSC* entry consists of the following elements:

- The **Author Heading** cites the name under which the author most commonly wrote, followed by birth and death dates. Also located here are any name variations under which an author wrote, including transliterated forms for authors whose native languages use nonroman alphabets. If the author wrote consistently under a pseudonym, the pseudonym will be listed in the author heading and the author's actual name given in parentheses on the first line of the biographical and critical introduction. Uncertain birth or death dates are indicated by question marks. Single-work entries are preceded by the title of the work and its date of publication.

- The **Introduction** contains background information that introduces the reader to the author and the critical debates surrounding his or her work.

- A **Portrait of the Author** is included when available.

- The list of **Principal Works** is ordered chronologically by date of first publication and lists the most important works by the author. The first section comprises short story collections, novellas, and novella collections. The second section gives information on other major works by the author. For foreign authors, the editors have provided original foreign-language publication information and have selected what are considered the best and most complete English-language editions of their works.

- Reprinted **Criticism** is arranged chronologically in each entry to provide a useful perspective on changes in critical evaluation over time. All short story, novella, and collection titles by the author featured in the entry are printed in boldface type. The critic's name and the date of composition or publication of the critical work are given at the beginning of each piece of criticism. Unsigned criticism is preceded by the title of the source in which it appeared. Footnotes are reprinted at the end of each essay or excerpt. In the case of excerpted criticism, only those footnotes that pertain to the excerpted texts are included.

- Critical essays are prefaced by brief **Annotations** explicating each piece.

- A complete **Bibliographical Citation** of the original essay or book precedes each piece of criticism. Source citations in the Literary Criticism Series follow University of Chicago Press style, as outlined in *The Chicago Manual of Style,* 14th ed. (Chicago: The University of Chicago Press, 1993).

- An annotated bibliography of **Further Reading** appears at the end of each entry and suggests resources for additional study. In some cases, significant essays for which the editors could not obtain reprint rights are included here. Boxed material following the further reading list provides references to other biographical and critical sources on the author in series published by Gale.

Indexes

A **Cumulative Author Index** lists all of the authors that appear in a wide variety of reference sources published by the Gale Group, including *SSC*. A complete list of these sources is found facing the first page of the Author Index. The index also includes birth and death dates and cross references between pseudonyms and actual names.

A **Cumulative Nationality Index** lists all authors featured in *SSC* by nationality, followed by the number of the *SSC* volume in which their entry appears.

An alphabetical **Title Index** lists all short story, novella, and collection titles contained in the *SSC* series. Titles of short story collections, separately published novellas, and novella collections are printed in italics, while titles of individual short stories are printed in roman type with quotation marks. Each title is followed by the author's last name and corresponding volume and page numbers where commentary on the work is located. English-language translations of original foreign-language titles are cross-referenced to the foreign titles so that all references to discussion of a work are combined in one listing.

In response to numerous suggestions from librarians, Gale also produces an annual paperbound edition of the SSC cumulative title index. This annual cumulation, which alphabetically lists all titles reviewed in the series, is available to all customers. Additional copies of this index are available upon request. Librarians and patrons will welcome this separate index; it saves shelf space, is easy to use, and is recyclable upon receipt of the next edition.

Citing *Short Story Criticism*

When citing criticism reprinted in the Literary Criticism Series, students should provide complete bibliographic information so that the cited essay can be located in the original print or electronic source. Students who quote directly from reprinted criticism may use any accepted bibliographic format, such as University of Chicago Press style or Modern Language Association (MLA) style. Both the MLA and the University of Chicago formats are acceptable and recognized as being the current standards for citations. It is important, however, to choose one format for all citations; do not mix the two formats within a list of citations.

The examples below follow recommendations for preparing a bibliography set forth in *The Chicago Manual of Style,* 14th ed. (Chicago: The University of Chicago Press, 1993); the first example pertains to material drawn from periodicals, the second to material reprinted from books:

Morrison, Jago. "Narration and Unease in Ian McEwan's Later Fiction." *Critique* 42, no. 3 (spring 2001): 253-68. Reprinted in *Short Story Criticism.* Vol. 57, edited by Janet Witalec, 212-20. Detroit: Gale, 2003.

Brossard, Nicole. "Poetic Politics." In *The Politics of Poetic Form: Poetry and Public Policy,* edited by Charles Bernstein, 73-82. New York: Roof Books, 1990. Reprinted in *Short Story Criticism.* Vol. 57, edited by Janet Witalec, 3-8. Detroit: Gale, 2003.

The examples below follow recommendations for preparing a works cited list set forth in the *MLA Handbook for Writers of Research Papers,* 5th ed. (New York: The Modern Language Association of America, 1999); the first example pertains to material drawn from periodicals, the second to material reprinted from books:

Morrison, Jago. "Narration and Unease in Ian McEwan's Later Fiction." *Critique* 42.3 (spring 2001): 253-68. Reprinted in *Short Story Criticism.* Ed. Janet Witalec. Vol. 57. Detroit: Gale, 2003. 212-20.

Brossard, Nicole. "Poetic Politics." *The Politics of Poetic Form: Poetry and Public Policy.* Ed. Charles Bernstein. New York: Roof Books, 1990. 73-82. Reprinted in *Short Story Criticism.* Ed. Janet Witalec. Vol. 57. Detroit: Gale, 2003. 3-8.

Suggestions are Welcome

Readers who wish to suggest new features, topics, or authors to appear in future volumes, or who have other suggestions or comments are cordially invited to call, write, or fax the Project Editor:

Project Editor, Literary Criticism Series
The Gale Group
27500 Drake Road
Farmington Hills, MI 48331-3535
1-800-347-4253 (GALE)
Fax: 248-699-8054

Acknowledgments

The editors wish to thank the copyright holders of the excerpted criticism included in this volume and the permissions managers of many book and magazine publishing companies for assisting us in securing reproduction rights. We are also grateful to the staffs of the Detroit Public Library, the Library of Congress, the University of Detroit Mercy Library, Wayne State University Purdy/Kresge Library Complex, and the University of Michigan Libraries for making their resources available to us. Following is a list of the copyright holders who have granted us permission to reproduce material in this volume of *SSC*. Every effort has been made to trace copyright, but if omissions have been made, please let us know.

COPYRIGHTED MATERIAL IN *SSC*, VOLUME 60, WAS REPRODUCED FROM THE FOLLOWING PERIODICALS:

COPYRIGHTED MATERIAL IN *SSC*, VOLUME 60, WAS REPRODUCED FROM THE FOLLOWING BOOKS:

Literary Criticism Series Advisory Board

Rick Bass
1958-

American short fiction writer, novelist, and essayist.

The following entry presents an overview of Bass's short fiction career through 2002.

INTRODUCTION

Bass is recognized as one of the foremost nature writers in America today. He is celebrated as both a skillful storyteller and outspoken advocate of wilderness preservation. Bass has established himself as a regional fiction and nonfiction writer of the American South, Southwest, and Pacific Northwest, setting his stories in the mountains, rivers, forests, swamps, and valleys of these areas. His stories express an admiration for nature, alarm at the forces of development that are altering America's landscape, and nostalgia for memories of wilderness and wildlife. His narrators are usually men engaged in traditional masculine activities—such as hunting, fishing, and ranching—while they also exhibit a sensitivity to human relationships as well as a respect for nature that is at times spiritual. Bass's prose is lyrical, descriptive, and punctuated by striking images. Many of his narratives include elements of magical realism, as well as characteristics of the tall tale, fable, or folk myth. Bass's short story and novella collections include *The Watch* (1989), *Platte River* (1994), *In the Loyal Mountains* (1995), *The Sky, the Stars, the Wilderness* (1997), and *The Hermit's Story* (2002).

BIOGRAPHICAL INFORMATION

Bass was born March 7, 1958, in Fort Worth, Texas, where his mother was a schoolteacher and his father a geologist. Bass's childhood experiences of deer hunting with his grandfather in south Texas became the basis for his first book of essays *The Deer Pasture* (1985). Bass graduated with a bachelor of science degree in petroleum geology from Utah State University in 1979. From 1979 to 1987, he worked as a petroleum geologist in Jackson, Mississippi. This experience is recounted in his nonfiction book *Oil Notes* (1989). Bass's first story to be published, "Where the Sea Used to Be," appeared in the *Paris Review* in 1987. Bass is married to Elizabeth Hughes, an artist who has illustrated some of his books, with whom he has two daughters. In 1987 the couple moved to a ranch in northern Montana, in the remote Yaak Valley, which is part of the Kootenai National Forest. The struggles of their first winter living in Montana are captured in Bass's *Winter: Notes from Montana* (1991). After this experience, Bass has become an outspoken environmental activist, particularly concerning the preservation of Yaak Valley. The relationship between his fiction-writing and environmental activism is expressed in his essay collection *Brown Dog of the Yaak: Essays on Art and Activism* (1999). His concern with wildlife conservation is also expressed in *The Ninemile Wolves* (1992), *The Lost Grizzlies* (1995), and *The New Wolves* (1998). Bass's personal connection with animals is further illustrated in a memoir recounting the life of his favorite dog, *Colter: The True Story of the Best Dog I Ever Had* (2000). Bass's first novel, *Where the Sea Used to Be,* based on his novella of the same name, was published in 1998.

MAJOR WORKS OF SHORT FICTION

Bass's first collection of short stories, *The Watch,* concerns characters in various stages of transition. Central themes of this volume include love, friendship, and the passage of youth. In the title story, an old man leaves his family to live in a swamp, where he kills alligators with his bare hands and soon attracts several women seeking refuge from their abusive husbands. Eventually, the man's son captures him from the wilderness and chains him to the front porch like a dog. In "Mexico," two men, friends since childhood, try to cultivate a prize-winning fish in the swimming pool of a home in suburban Houston, Texas. Meanwhile, one of the men, the narrator, observes the marital dynamics between his friend Kirby and Kirby's wife, Tricia. These characters also appear in three of Bass's other stories. In "Redfish," the two friends spend a winter evening trying to catch a fish after Kirby and Tricia have had a quarrel. "Ironwood" and "The Wait" find the two friends several years later, struggling with the disappointments of separation and divorce. In "Ruth's Country," set in Utah, a Mormon woman and a cattle rancher fall in love, forcing the woman to choose between her community and her relationship with the young rancher. Bass's next story collection, *Platte River,* comprises three novellas. These pieces demonstrate Bass's increasingly experimental narrative technique and the maturing of his themes and style. "Mahatma Joe" and "Field Events" both include elements of magical realism, as well as elements of the tall tale, fable, and folk myth. In "Mahatma Joe," set in Montana, an aging, married evangelist falls in love with his twenty-year-old neighbor. In "Field Events," three young men train for athletic competition and find love over the course of a summer vacation. The title novella, "Platte River," is a Hemingway-esque tale of three men fishing for steelhead bass on the Platte River in Michigan. *In the Loyal Mountains* includes stories written in a more traditional narrative style, rather than the magical realist style of many of Bass's earlier fiction. "Days of Heaven" and "The Valley" both reflect Bass's efforts to preserve the Yaak Valley. "Swamp Boy" and "The Wait" explore humanity's relationship to the urban wildlife in Houston. Other stories in the volume express a sense of nostalgia for a past American wilderness. "The History of Rodney" concerns a young couple living in the forgotten town of Rodney, Mississippi, and addresses the conflict between the desire for permanence and the awareness of life's unceasing changes. *The Sky, the Stars, the Wilderness* is another collection of three novellas. While sharing the settings and themes of Bass's previous fiction, these novellas express mystical connection between the protagonists and the natural environments they inhabit. In the title novella, a middle-aged woman recalls her childhood on a west Texas ranch and the death of her mother when she was eight years old. "The Myth of Bears," set in the American West during the early 1900s, concerns a trapper named Trapper and his wife Judith. One night, Judith mysteriously sneaks out of their cabin to live in the nearby woods. From a hidden vantage point, she observes as Trapper continues to search for her over the course of several seasons. In the novella "Where the Sea Used to Be," a young geologist looks for oil in the Appalachian foothills of Alabama. His uncanny ability to find hidden oil takes on a mystical quality. When he meets and falls in love with a young woman, the geologist must struggle between his passion for finding oil and his passion for the woman. Bass's volume of short stories entitled *The Hermit's Story* was published in 2002. In the title story, a man and woman on a hunting exercise with six dogs discover a dry basin beneath the frozen surface of a lake. In "Swans," the narrator describes the physical decline and death of an Idaho homesteader whose wife sets fires on the shore of a frozen pond in order to warm the swans that live there. In "The Cave," a pair of lovers strip naked and descend into an abandoned coal mine in West Virginia. In "Eating," a wild owl finds itself in a roadside diner in North Carolina.

CRITICAL RECEPTION

Bass is critically acclaimed for his compelling stories, well-crafted prose, unique narrative voice, and lyrical, sometimes haunting tales of human encounters with the endangered American wilderness. Bass receives mostly high praise for his three collections of short stories and

two volumes of novellas. Many critics laud his skills as a regional writer whose vivid descriptions of the natural landscapes in which his stories are set express a strong sense of place and intimate knowledge of the wilderness. Other commentators comment on the mysterious, spiritual quality of Bass's stories, expressing a mystical element to the relationship between humans and nature. Environmentalists acclaim the intersection of fiction and environmental activism in Bass's stories, many of which express a pro-environmental message in the context of fictional narrative. Critics also comment on Bass's insightful representations of American men, portraying their struggles with their own ideals of masculinity and their efforts to resolve personal relationships through encounters with nature. Some scholars, however, find Bass's male characters to be unappealing and loutish, while others similarly feel that his female characters are underdeveloped.

PRINCIPAL WORKS

Short Fiction

The Watch: Stories 1989
Platte River 1994
In the Loyal Mountains 1995
The Sky, the Stars, the Wilderness 1997
The Hermit's Story: Stories 2002

Other Major Works

The Deer Pasture (essays) 1985
Wild to the Heart (essays) 1987
Oil Notes (nonfiction) 1989
Winter: Notes from Montana (nonfiction) 1991
The Ninemile Wolves: An Essay (essay) 1992
The Lost Grizzlies: A Search for Survivors in the Wilderness of Colorado (nonfiction) 1995
The Book of Yaak (nonfiction) 1996
*Fiber [illustrated by Elizabeth Hughes Bass] (nonfiction) 1998
The New Wolves (nonfiction) 1998
Where the Sea Used to Be (novel) 1998
Brown Dog of the Yaak: Essays on Art and Activism (essays) 1999
Colter: The True Story of the Best Dog I Ever Had (nonfiction) 2000

*The short story "Fiber" was published in *Mississippi Review* (spring 1997).

CRITICISM

Christopher Merrill (essay date winter 1989)

SOURCE: Merrill, Christopher. "Reclaiming the Frontier: New Writings from the West." *New England Review and Bread Loaf Quarterly* 12, no. 2 (winter 1989): 208-19.

[*In the following excerpt, Merrill compares Bass's* The Watch *with further books about the American West, arguing that they re-imagine the traditional frontier myth.*]

> "Try this for openers: the art of a region begins to come mature when it is no longer what we think it should be."
>
> William Kittredge

It is no secret we are a nomadic people. The average American, according to the latest statistics, moves every two years; a questionnaire I recently received from my college alumni office *begins* with queries about the number of job changes and moves I have made since graduation, underscoring the idea that for many of us mobility has become a central feature of our lives. Rarely do we spend our adult years in the same town or city in which we were born and raised—a fact not lost on writers, who from the earliest days of our history have charted this restlessness, this drive to settle one unknown landscape after another.

For a long time, of course, the movement was westward, the dream of a frontier firing our collective imagination. The writings of the first explorers fueled this migration and helped shape our national identity: what Czeslaw Milosz calls "the great soul of the people" finds new expression in such classics as *The Journals of Lewis and Clark,* John Wesley Powell's *Down the Colorado,* and John Muir's *The Mountains of California*—all of which were soon eclipsed in the popular imagination by the hundreds of Westerns Hollywood produced. How the West was won remains one of our most powerful (and often destructive) myths, influencing everything from fashion to foreign policy. Those who censured Ronald Reagan for sending American troops into Grenada and Central America were probably not surprised to learn his favorite author is Louis L'Amour: we are who we read.

Serious writers, however, have worked since before the official closing of the frontier in 1890 to articulate a different vision of the West. As Thomas J. Lyon, one of the most astute critics of Western literature, has remarked:

> There's always been a strong, romantic fascination with the wilds in America. And that's made the West romantic territory. But it's time for that romantic fasci-

nation to end. The frontiers have been explored now. 'Westering' is over. In America we think in terms of endless expansion, in 'growth is health.' But Western writers have been saying the idea doesn't work anymore. Recognizing limits, recognizing the frontier era is over *now* is the key. That's what makes the best Western literature serious, as opposed to the cowboy, pulp Western things. And that insight is important for the whole world. If Western writers can make a contribution to Euro-American civilization, it's in the recognition that there *are* limits.

Such a recognition, which for Western writers is both a function of form and a practical necessity, distinguishes their best work. These writers have little choice but to reclaim the frontier *in imaginative terms,* resettling it in their poetry, fiction, and nonfiction in a spirit exactly opposite to that in which it was first divided up: only reverence and humility before the land and its indigenous peoples may counter the generations of abuse we have heaped on them. Wallace Stegner, Gary Snyder, Edward Abbey and many others continue the discussion begun by writers like Robinson Jeffers and John Steinbeck, Willa Cather and Mary Austin, about the importance of recognizing and defining limits on our belief in the frontier mentality.

. . . . .

[Bass] reveals in his first collection of stories, **The Watch,** a genuine affinity for life in the West. Born and raised in Texas, he has lived in Utah, Arkansas, and Mississippi, and now caretakes a ranch in northwestern Montana; his stories are set in a similar variety of places, roughly half in the South, half in the West. He is by turns a petroleum geologist and environmental activist, which must give him a broad view of one of the thornier issues facing Westerners—the development of natural resources versus the preservation of wilderness areas. In like manner, his fiction is informed by the sympathy he generates for a wide range of characters. Rooted in the storytelling tradition of the South, he is equally at home spinning tales about the West; his Mississippi stories are as concerned with what [William] Kittredge calls "a necessary wildness" as almost anything found in Montana. That his work has been included in both *New Stories from the South* and *The Best of the West* will surprise no one who reads **The Watch**: his "emotional ownership" of various landscapes is destined to enrich our literary life.

Like Kittredge, Bass probes the limits of possibility, discovering "nothing will get you into trouble so deep or as sad as faith." His characters are at once damned and redeemed by their faith—in loyalty, in love, in a simpler way of life, in the belief that at certain times trouble "was so far away that it seemed it would never return." But trouble is often closer than we think. For the narrator of **"Mississippi"** it takes the form of daily reminders that he was responsible for the failure of his relationship with Leanne, "the fat girl who asked (him) to marry her." When he said no, she moved to California, leaving him with thousands of bottles of original-brand Coca-Cola, "because she didn't like the new formula." Like her brother, Hector, who believes their farm is sitting on top of an oil well but who will never get around to drilling for it, the narrator prefers to live in a world of possibility: *if* Hector strikes it rich, Leanne will use her share of the money to lose weight and he'll get an education . . . But since he couldn't make a commitment, all he has now are the Coke bottles, three or four of which he smashes "against the rocks in the back pasture" after a bad day of work, and the vain hope that Leanne will return. "If she comes back and asks me again," he says at the end of the story, "this time I will marry her."

Oil plays a leading role in the trilogy of stories set in Houston—**"Mexico," "Juggernaut,"** and **"Redfish."** The nameless narrator and his best friend, Kirby, grew up when "there weren't any wars, and there wasn't any racism, not in [their] lives, and [they] weren't hungry," realize in their senior year of high school that theirs is a privileged moment in our history. Houston is oil-rich, so rich in fact that it can support not one but two hockey teams; and the boys spend their nights watching aging athletes from the Juggernauts, the seedier of the two teams, fight it out on a rink at the edge of town. **"Juggernaut"** closes with a paean to that time:

> This was back in those first days when Houston was clean and just growing, not yet beginning to die or get old. Houston was young, then, too. You cannot imagine how smooth life was for you, if you were in high school, that one spring, when oil was $42 a barrel, and everyone's father was employed by the petroleum industry, and a hero for finding oil when the Arabs wouldn't sell us any. Anything was possible.

But Houston, like so many Western cities, has a boom-and-bust economy. Bass is particularly adept at charting the social effects of such an economy on the skids. In **"Mexico"** and **"Redfish"** we find the narrator and Kirby trying to make sense of their lives *after* high school. Something has gone wrong. The oil boom is over, the hockey teams are gone, and Houston is growing old:

> Hell will come here first, when it opens. Everyone here's already dead. The heat killed them or something. People don't even fall in love anymore: it's just the pelvic thrust, and occasionally children as the result. There's no love, and that's the surest sign of death.

To combat their sense of doom, they keep a large bass in Kirby's swimming pool (along with "stumps, gravel, old trees," and a broken-down Volkswagen!), drink too many beers and an exotic concoction of rum, Diet Coke, and lime juice called a Cuba Libre, or drive to the Gulf to fish—in a freak snowstorm. And they hope something will change: "Maybe there will be a bad hatch of mosquitoes. A thunderstorm. Perhaps the Astros lose. We go to Mexico. The flights cost seventy-nine dollars, one way."

Odds are, though, nothing will change. The recognition that we live in a world of dwindling possibilities is what unifies this collection. Galena Tom Ontz may have "two girlfriends and a key to Canada," but he also has a bad heart. And while the narrator of **"Choteau"** believes Ontz—"the wild man" of Montana's Yaak Valley—still has choices, still has freedom, it soon becomes clear that time is running out for him, as it is for so many characters in these stories, Rick Bass's flair for dramatizing an individual's confrontation with his own mortality makes **The Watch** a wise and wonderful book.

Mark Kamine (review date 6 February 1989)

SOURCE: Kamine, Mark. "The Macho Myth Unmasked." *New Leader* 72, no. 3-4 (6 February 1989): 19-20.

[*In the following review of* The Watch, *Kamine cites the volume as impressive and praises Bass's well-crafted prose.*]

Over the past two years Rick Bass has published short fiction in the *Paris Review, Esquire, GQ,* and the *Quarterly.* His work has been anthologized in *Best American Short Stories* and *New Writing from the South,* and his was the opening story in *The Pushcart Prize XIII.* **"The Watch,"** the title piece of this first collection, will appear in the upcoming *O'Henry Awards* volume. All told, as impressive a record as any young writer of the '80s has compiled—and these have been boom years for young writers.

The book is equally impressive. Bass gives us more than well-crafted prose and the glimmerings of a voice; several of the stories are fully achieved, free from all residue of apprenticeship.

The 10 stories in **The Watch** are set in the heart of the country: Texas, Utah, the woods of Mississippi and the hills of Montana. They are dominated by their male figures, and thus full of fishing and hunting and drinking. But Bass does not glamorize these American male pastimes, he realizes how easy it is to hide behind them, to use them to avoid confronting the more substantial challenges presented to us in living with ourselves and among others.

In **"Choteau,"** the chief figure is Galena Jim Ontz, a man with "two girlfriends and a key to Canada." He's one of those fearless, hard-drinking, hard-driving frontiersmen out of America's legendary past, and the nameless first-person narrator follows wherever Galena Jim leads. The narrator understands Jim better than he understands himself, however, as we soon learn:

"[Jim]'s got black hair, an old lined-looking face—he's forty—and light blue eyes, a kid's grin. . . . He loves to hunt. I do not know how he got the key [to the gate leading to Canada]. Some sort of charm or guile somewhere, I'm sure. People only see that side of him. Though surely Patsy, who has been his girlfriend ever since she left Oklahoma with him, sees the other part. I do, too. He is still a boy, still learning to be a man, this in the fortieth year of his life."

Jim's nickname harks back to the night he stole a cement-mixer, filled it with the luminous blue ore called galena, then poured the mixture of ore and cement onto the streets and sidewalks and main plaza of his town, creating galena-speckled surfaces: "Your car or truck headlights will pick up sudden, flashing blue-bolt chunks and swatches in the road, blazing like blue eyes, sunk down in the road—the whole road glittering and bouncing with that weird blue galena light, if you are driving fast." It's the kind of mythic incident Bass' characters seem to exist for. (In **"Mexico,"** the protagonist is trying to raise the world's largest bass—in his swimming pool.)

But by the end of **"Choteau"** the myth is shattered, the vulnerability of the legendary figure is revealed. On a hunting trip, Galena Jim tries to ride a moose. He's thrown, the moose comes after him, and he is reduced to "running and scrambling, diving around rocks and rolling under logs, clutching his heart." Jim has what appears to be a mild stroke, and suddenly the mask falls away: "He didn't have any color, and for a moment, broken and hurt like that, almost helpless, he seemed like my friend rather than a teacher of any sort; and he seemed young, too, like he could have been just anybody, instead of Galena Jim Ontz, who had been thrown by a moose; and we sat there all afternoon, he with his eyes closed, resting, saving up, breathing slowly with cracked ribs."

There is always, in these stories, a moment when the hero is brought low, when the dream is surrendered and all that's left is the memory of glory. In **"Mexico,"** the bass in the swimming pool is caught by high-school kids who have snuck into the yard. The rugged, alligator-wrestling Buzbee of **"The Watch"** ends up chained to the porch of the general store run by his bachelor son, who only wants someone to talk to. Women leave the odd, stubborn, obsessed narrators of **"Mississippi"** and **"In Ruth's Country"** for safer, more conventional alternatives.

Yet despite the consistency of theme, the stories sometimes fail to hit their marks because Bass' influences overwhelm him. Barry Hannah is a kind of presiding deity here—a brave choice for a mentor in these days when the goal of many young writers seems to be a muting of voice, but a dangerous one, too.

Two of the stories disappear under Hannah's weight. **"Mississippi"** and **"Cats and Students, Bubbles and Abysses"** are too full of the kind of extended nominative groupings he has perfected—"the wild big fairway of pumping and producing oil wells" is an example from **"Mississippi."** Other Hannahisms compound the problem, including frequent interjections of commentary on the narrative ("That is what my state is about"; "Another desperate Southerner, done escaped at his first chance") and a similar narrative pointing used to introduce an episode or a descriptive passage ("This is how we discovered Robby"; "Summers in Mississippi are like this"). Although Bass does Hannah well, he is better when he eases up on the verbal accelerator and moves us along at a pace more in line with the secret yearnings of his characters who, for all of their exploits with cars and trucks and horses, with guns and fishing poles, are less after perfect sporting moments than a little bit of human contact.

We know we are a long way from the manly heroics of a character out of Hemingway when we find that the narrator and his friend Kirby in **"Redfish"** have gotten what little knowledge they have about fishing from their reading, and even their drinks are new to them. "It was our first time to drink Cuba Libres, and we liked them even better than margaritas. We had never caught redfish before either, but had read about it in a book." Given the newness of it all to them, there is just the right amount of clumsiness in those sentences—the awkward use of the infinitive in the first, the not quite secure antecedent of the "it" in the second. And the more we learn about the narrator and his friend, the more apt these effects become. (Bass excels at subtly adjusting syntax to aid his characterizations.)

Before long we see what's at stake here, what in essence has been at stake throughout. The narrator and Kirby wander along the beach. It's windy and cold and they haven't caught any fish. When they decide to drag a lifeguard tower back to their camp but can't get it to budge, their hopes for living out even one successful night of mythic American malehood begin to crumble. Kirby admits he misses his wife. "We were a long way from our fire, and it looked a lot smaller, from where we were. . . . Kirby started crying and said he was going home to Tricia but I told him to buck up and be a man. I didn't know what that meant or even what I meant by saying that, but I knew I did not want him to leave." The narrator is lonely, and his friend Kirby is lost. The fishing trip—and the whole macho ethos, it seems—is only their excuse to stay close, to comfort each other (they never do catch any fish, though when Bass leaves them, they are still trying).

Throughout *The Watch* Bass' characters have a yearning for the old achievements. They want to catch the biggest fish, make the fastest time, regain their youth, their lovers, their belief in legends. Yet only when they give up these pursuits, or at least gain some perspective on them, do they achieve something important: intimacy, recovery, wisdom.

At the end of **"Wild Horses,"** one of the longer, more powerful stories in the book, Bass leaves us with the image of a boy training a horse to pull a sled. "The egrets hopped and danced, following at a slight distance, but neither the boy nor the horse seemed to notice. They kept their heads down, and moved forward." It's an image of dedication and progress, both in abundant evidence in *The Watch.*

Meredith Sue Willis (review date 26 March 1989)

SOURCE: Willis, Meredith Sue. "Stories With a Sense of Place." *Washington Post Book World* (26 March 1989): 11.

[*In the following review, Willis compares* The Watch *with two other short story collections, all depicting a strong sense of regional place, and discusses the symbolic significance of animals in Bass's stories.*]

Will Weaver's short story collection, *A Gravestone Made of Wheat,* is dominated by landscape and the relationships between men. Weaver is a crafter of sentences and paragraphs, and his loving, familiar, crucial descriptions of machines are beautiful—sometimes more vivid than his characters. In "Going Home," he writes, "I began to think about the engine, about how the spark plugs and cylinders and camshaft and transmission and running gear all worked together; about how one small thing—a loose wire, a short, an oil seal—could break that whole rhythm that propelled us up these mountains, I began to hear engine noises. But the noise was only my own heartbeat drumming in my ears."

Occasionally, these stories suffer from a self-conscious symbolism, as in one called "Gabriel's Feathers," in which a boy, torn between his parents, is made to freeze "exactly halfway between his father and mother." But in the best of them, all literary pretentiousness is dropped and a wonderful weirdness rolls. In "Cowman," for example, getting rid of a recalcitrant cow outweighs the importance of separating from a wife. And in a few of the stories, even the obsessions and disconnections are transcended as laconic men find ways to speak with each other. Two boy cousins collude to hide their grandfather's failing eyesight from the family in "From the Landing." After the secret is revealed, the

old man deteriorates rapidly. The boys, grown to men with little in common, go fishing together and come to an understanding of their responsibility toward their grandfather. This is an excellent story with natural suspense and a genuine breakthrough between the two men.

Rick Bass' collection, *The Watch,* is even more imbedded in place and in the bonds between men. In these stories, the Texas Gulf Coast, Mormon Utah, malaria bayou country and Montana near the Canadian border have the stature of pagan gods. They seem to create the people and cause the events. Like landscape, animals possess great power for Bass. In some of the shorter stories, the animals are perhaps fraught too heavily with meaning—for example, the enormous fish that lives in the shadowy depths of a suburban swimming pool in the story **"Mexico."** But when Bass' animals work for him as both symbols and real creatures, and when his people are aware of themselves as animals, then we read some superb fiction.

Perhaps the best single story in any of these collections under review is Bass' **"Wild Horses."** The situation is that a man gets drunk on the eve of his wedding and jumps off a bridge to his death. The buddy who was with him drinking and talking (the quintessential human interaction for Bass) goes on to form an attachment to the jilted bride: "Once a month—at the end of each month—Sydney would stay over on Karen's farm, and they would go into her big empty closet, and he would let her hit him . . . until . . . the palms of her hands hurt too much to hit him any more."

The working through of this strange and wonderful relationship is given depth and context by the woman's job with an aged veterinarian who treats horses and mules, mostly for free. Old Dr. Lynly makes house calls to people like a group of poverty-stricken, mutilated loggers who keep driving their wretched mule even though its right knee "buckled," and "dried blood ran down in streaks to the mule's hoof, to the mud." The mule, of course, is not unlike Sydney, who keeps getting his bones broken by the wild horses he trains and his heart broken by Karen. The mule works as an emblem in the story because Sydney sees himself as a dumb animal, and because part of Karen's personal healing is through the healing of animals. The claustrophobia of the relationship between the man and woman is relieved and enriched by its place in human society, in the animal kingdom, in the landscape.

People in their context, in their social setting, are Bobbie Ann Mason's great strength in her new collection of stories, *Love Life.* Her stories are crowded with women, men and children, and all their friends, relatives and chattering television sets. There is relatively little in the way of cows that refuse to stand up or suppurating mule knees here, but neither is there any hint of sentimentalizing what happens between people.

Mason has a reputation as a regional writer, but what she is really writing about is the numerous Americans whose dreams and goals have been uplifted and distorted by popular culture. Mason would be worth reading if only for her clearly delineated view of what Americans do with their lives. And her people do act: they are not passive. A man goes looking for a daughter given up for adoption at birth; a restless young woman decides to join the army; an aging drugstore cowboy goes to Nashville and cuts a record, but his wife chooses to stay home. Each situation feels real; each character stands in the round, well-lit. There is flexible, wiry writing even in the stories that mistake termination for conclusion.

But the best of Mason's stories satisfy the reader's desire for closure. In the powerful piece "Big Bertha Stories," a damaged Vietnam veteran frightens his son with tales of an enormous, anthropomorphized strip mining machine. The son has nightmares, and the mother, at first cheerful and determined to keep everyone's upper lip stiff, succumbs to nightmares too. It is a satisfying, honest conclusion for this story. There is no hiding from the stresses that tear apart families. The political analogies are understated but unmistakable.

In their best stories, these three authors build on their considerable natural strengths—the gift of voice to objects and laconic men for Weaver; the intense interplay between the natural world and human beings in Bass; the flow and rapids of human intercourse for Mason. But all three writers are capable of going further. Weaver and Bass can explode out of the sealed bell jars of their obsessions; Mason knows how to narrow the broad beam of her vision into searing insight. All three transcend the limitations of their strengths.

Perry Glasser (essay date September 1989)

SOURCE: Glasser, Perry. "Purer Than Everything Else." *North American Review* 274, no. 3 (September 1989): 69-72.

[*In the following excerpt, Glasser chronicles* The Watch *as a promising collection by a young author, but criticizes the stories for their predictability and superficiality.*]

Writers alternately understand themselves to be engaged in a futile, irrelevant dalliance, or they understand themselves to be engaged in the most vital and necessary of human activities: the articulation, formation and preservation of the human spirit.

That's if they think about themselves at all—which probably shouldn't be so very often.

If the first political act of the writer is mastery of the self, the discipline that applies buttocks to chair, then the second act is to convince someone—*anyone*—that this stuff is worth reading. It's easy to get readers if one resorts to emotional blackmail, a political act most of us learn at our mother's knee. All sorts of generous critics can be shanghaied into reading a writer's work. Like water from the rock struck by Moses, praise can gush forth from parents, siblings, teachers, pastors. But that kind of ego-nurturing doesn't last long for the neurotically compulsive artist, for whom wide-spread praise and oxygen are equivalent necessities.

For the writer who requires a wider audience, the third political act, the one that in most of our minds separates the amateur from the professional, is to attain publication. A Xerox machine will do (hence the appeal of university writing programs). Better than photocopy is a chapbook. Better than a chapbook is a magazine. Better than a magazine is a book.

But there are magazines, and then there are *magazines*. Books and *books*. Appearance and circulation have a lot to do with the placement of a publishing medium in the hierarchical rankings. You might wistfully hope that attaining publication is exclusively a matter of quality. Every editor *swears* this to be true, especially for *his* journal/press/house. Most readers, if they think about it at all, just assume editors publish what they believe to be best. Veteran writers know such a fairy tale is for tyros. Novices nurture their ambitions with faith in a pure system, the faith that allows them to write and write again in the face of frequent rejection. However, the first awful moment a writer believes that the cause of rejection is not inadequacy in the work itself but a system that jealously guards entry, that moment marks the writer's departure from Art. The gradual suspicion that no amount of revision, self-flagellation, course enrollment or perseverance is as effective as a little schmoozing eats away at the pursuit of quality. The effects of this knowledge on dozens and dozens of writers accounts for the tide of mediocrity that rises on the swell of intrigue and networking.

The jaded reader of this column will smile and ask just why I expect writing to be any different from any other social endeavor. Well, Art *ought* to be purer than everything else. Good Art should be rewarded amply, but for being good Art.

. . . . .

Rick Bass's fiction has won a number of awards, and this collection is his first. Seen all at once, Bass's book gives us an insight into the development of a young writer. Bass acknowledges "helpful advice" from Carol

Houck Smith, Tom Jenks, Rust Hills and Gordon Lish, as well as James Linville and the staff of *The Paris Review.* The collection contains Houston stories, Mississippi stories and Utah/Montana stories. Not surprisingly, Rick Bass has lived in all of these places, but though many of these stories share locales and characters, they are separated from each other in the book. This seems less a collection than an aggregation of Bass's early work. Reading ***The Watch,*** we witness a young writer wrestling with his material, trying to order his experience, searching for his voice, and discovering what works and what does not.

When Bass's fiction works well, it works very well indeed—but a few of these stories seem generated by a young writer's desire to write well, rather than a young writer who urgently needs to tell a story. The former isn't a *bad* point of generation, of course, but when unaccompanied by the latter, the consequent fiction falls flat. Reading Bass's first book is like watching a newborn thorough-bred learn to stand; you smile at the awkwardness, hoping that at some future date you'll see the awesome power and speed of a champion.

One has to hope Bass will resist any who'd urge him to publish too much too soon, to capitalize on the moment. They will necessarily move on to next season's discovery, discarding last year's writer like a pet rock or a hula hoop. It's possible to publish too early.

Take **"Mexico,"** for example, the first story in the collection. It is over-worked, coy in its resolution and use of imagery. The same is true of **"Cats and Students, Bubbles and Abysses,"** which from the title down puts a reader on notice to prepare for work that will be profound and cute all at once, a regular *tour de force,* so you'd better sit up and pay attention. It's a student's work, a very good student, but still a student. Too much attention to craft overwhelms whatever story lurks behind the prose, and characters over-trimmed for the sake of linguistic dexterity and some trendy idea of art eventually are reduced to stereotypical caricatures. In **"Cats and Students,"** we read,

> I guess the most weight I've ever lifted is the back end of Slater's car. Robby and Slater and I took it up to Oxford to look at Faulkner's old house out in the country one Sunday. We got sort of lost and sort of stuck in the mud. We had a couple of dozen watermelons and a keg of beer in the back, and it was a hot Mississippi summer, and we were going to have a picnic, and the jack sank down in the mud and got lost, but I lifted the back end up anyway . . .

Familiar stuff. Good ol' boys on a muddy road, a six-pack of beer, watermelons, ingenuous language. The reference to Faulkner, of course, is supposed to make us know that the characters are a cut above the ordinary red-neck. Too many of Bass's southern grotesques or

executives in the "awl bizness" are simply clichéd characters whose obsessions fill us with neither delight nor insight, but leave us wondering why we're reading about people habitually feeble-minded. And there isn't a single female character who serves as anything other than an ideal object for the males in the book.

In too many of the stories, Bass relies on the newest typographical boost to profundity, the isolated paragraph. Designed to make each paragraph seem chiseled and finely honed, a work of art in and of itself, the page design rivets our eyes to each block of narrative, and only incidentally fills a book with white space.

It's an illusion.

Seeing such paragraphs, we believe we are reading short fiction dedicated to compression. We can only pray such mannerisms soon go the way of dialogue introduced with dashes, poetry typed without employing the shift key. Trendy writing *looks* smart but says nothing special.

Bass constructs whole stories whose point is to equate a character with an animal, the hunter's mentality. We acquire the qualities of that which we stalk, capture, or kill. Wear the fetish, be the creature. Eat its heart. Beside each other, stories such as **"The Government Bears," "Red-fish,"** and **"Wild Horses,"** become obvious as soon as we read their titles, though separately they read well, even brilliantly, especially **"Red-fish."**

Once he gets out of his own way, Bass writes wonderfully lucidly, able to tell a sensitive, well-observed, moving tale that has at its core a mystery. **"Juggernaut"** is such a story. The middle-aged, slope-shouldered Mr. Odom, a high school teacher whose seeming only claim to fame is a forest green Corvette, is discovered to be Larry Loop, the "goon" for a Texas ice hockey team, the Juggernauts. "You could tell he was not from the north. You could tell he had not grown up with the game, but had discovered it, late in life. He was big, and the oldest man on the ice, grey-headed, tufts of it sticking out from behind his savage, painted goalie's mask—though he was not a goalie—and more often than not when he bumped into people, they went over." When the narrator and his friend see one of their high school classmates, Laura, waiting after a game in a parking lot for Mr. Odom, the rhapsodic Conrad-esque ending is completely earned.

> . . . in two months she would be graduating, and what she was doing would be okay then, . . . and for the first time we saw the thing, in its immensity, and it was like coming around a bend or trail in the woods and seeing the hugeness and emptiness of a great plowed pasture or field, when all one's life up to that point has been spent close to but never seeing a field of that size . . . it was very clear to us that the whole rest of our

lives would be spent in a field like that, and the look Laura gave us was sweet and kind, but also wise, and was like an old familiar welcome.

No gimmicks here. No elaborate gyrations to draw a simple equation between character and animal, just a story that is plainly felt and honestly told. As Rick Bass grows as a writer, and he clearly will, he will develop the authority that comes with trusting his material and his reader. Who knows? Maybe he'll stop taking so much advice from New York mandarins and listen more intently to his own very fine muse.

Jon Saari (review date fall 1989)

SOURCE: Saari, Jon. Review of *The Watch,* by Rick Bass. *Antioch Review* 47, no. 4 (fall 1989): 499-500.

[*In the following review, Saari praises the stories in* The Watch, *depicting them as mesmerizing.*]

These ten stories [in ***The Watch***] introduce a writer of originality who possesses a sense of the bizarre in everyday life. In three of the stories an unnamed narrator recounts his experiences with his best friend, Kirby. Kirby has inherited hundreds of small oil wells from his father, which he is selling off one by one and using the money to live a wayward life of trips to Mexico full of drink and aimless celebration. Kirby has a large bass named Shack living in his swimming pool in the deep end where Kirby has submerged a Volkswagen bug. Neighborhood children try to catch Shack, who takes on symbolic import for the narrator. In another story, **"Juggernaut,"** the narrator returns to high school to write about his and Kirby's high school geometry teacher, a man who tells outlandish, obviously untrue stories, a club hockey team called the Juggernauts whose play is full of buffoon performances, and a petite, olive-skinned high school temptress the boys lust after. All of these plot lines come together into an absurd, farcical conclusion.

Other stories in this collection are just as bafflingly delightful in their conclusions about experience today. In the novella-length title story, an old man named Buzbee retreats to malaria-infested Mississippi swampland where he recruits town women to revel in his harem. He wrestles alligators and holds the women in seductive awe. His son forms an allegiance with an unlikely partner to capture his father, attaching a ball and chain to the old man's ankle and throwing away the key. Conventional in their construction, these stories are mesmerizing in their power to shock and persuade.

John Mort (review date 1 February 1994)

SOURCE: Mort, John. Review of *Platte River,* by Rick Bass. *Booklist* 90, no. 11 (1 February 1994): 993.

[*In the following review of* Platte River, *Mort comments that Bass writes beautifully, but that the three novellas included in this volume are spare and thematically unrelated.*]

The Montana environmentalist (*The Ninemile Wolves* [1992]) here [in ***The Platte River***] offers three spare, unrelated stories. **"Platte River,"** the weakest, is about an ex-football player who journeys from Montana to speak at a small college in northern Michigan. It effectively evokes the sadness of a life in which dreams were realized early, and then nothing else happened; it might make a good reading for men's consciousness meetings. **"Mahatma Joe,"** about a Canadian evangelist who is near death, and who manages one last convert in an embittered young woman trying to find herself in a wilderness valley, has a lilting, seductive charm about it, however, and an understated humor. The most appealing by far of these tales is the amusing **"Field Events,"** about two overgrown teenage boys who spend every spare moment discus throwing. They spot an even bigger man, a man so big he partakes of myth, wandering naked in a field, and recruit him to their cause. The gentle giant can hurl a discus far enough to break the Olympic record, but, alas, he's moonstruck over his friends' lonely sister. Bass writes beautifully, but this is such a slender book that readers may feel a bit cheated.

Sam Walker (review date 8 March 1994)

SOURCE: Walker, Sam. "Author's Tall-Tale Novellas Push Envelope of the Plausible." *Christian Science Monitor* (8 March 1994): 13.

[*In the following review, Walker declares that the stories in* Platte River *stretch the boundaries of realist fiction and resemble myth, fable, and the tall-tale.*]

Imagine a man so muscular he can lift up a car, throw a discus 300 feet, and carry a cow on his shoulders. A character in Rick Bass's new book ***Platte River*** accomplishes these feats.

But in his seventh work of fiction, the author—who some consider one of America's most promising—has undertaken a task no less Herculean: gripping contemporary fiction by the trunk and shaking its branches.

Bass bends the code of realism to which most of his colleagues adhere. The three novellas collected here are full of events that push the envelope of the plausible, and his mythical narrative style harks back to a time when most men sat in hunting lodges telling tall tales.

"Platte River," the title novella, is the book's finest. It's the story of Harley, a former football player who lives in a remote cabin in Montana with his girlfriend, Shaw. When Shaw announces her decision to leave and begins the slow process of packing, Harley flies to northern Michigan to visit an old friend named Willis.

In one of the book's most memorable scenes, Harley, Willis, and two other men go fishing after midnight. The scene, described from an omniscient viewpoint, pits Harley against a struggling steelhead salmon that, like Shaw, eludes him.

"In the dark like that, Harley hasn't really seen anything, just the fish's huge silver form leaping once, right before it broke the leader. . . . And he stands there with the loose line, the empty rod, and swears, swears in his heart, that he can feel the fish (a part of himself now) still running, out to the lake already—out to the lake."

The elements are strikingly simple here: man and fish, possession and loss. There's no labored description of reeling techniques, steelhead spawning, or even Harley's thought process. Harley, like most of Bass's characters, is defined less by what he thinks than by what he feels.

"Mahatma Joe," the first novella, is set in an isolated corner of northern Montana. In this Edenic valley, "moose grazed in the fertile river meadow during the summer, and ducks floated on the slow blue waters. Elk, with their antlers in velvet, slept in people's yards in the high heat of the afternoon, and tried to get into the hay barns at night. . . . Small children would walk out and touch the elk's antlers and feed them sugar cubes during those warm spells when rules dissolved."

The story revolves around two characters: Leena, a "hardy" young woman from the South who moved to the valley to escape a failed love affair, and Mahatma Joe, an evangelical preacher who worries that his power to save souls is waning.

In a last grand effort at divine servitude, Mahatma Joe plants an immense vegetable garden to feed the starving in Africa. He enlists the help of his wife, Lily, and later, Leena.

Accounts of ice skating by moonlight, swimming in a cold river, and working the soil will attract readers' senses as much as their literary sensibilities to this story.

"Field Events," the book's second and least resonant novella, is the story of A.C., a modern-day Sampson who is befriended by a family in upstate New York. Accounts of A.C.'s incredible (yet plausible) strength might cause some readers to snap the book shut; but those who finish this story will recognize what Bass has accomplished.

A.C.'s almost superhuman qualities give the story a larger-than-life quality—like a fable. In this context, A.C.'s equally large desire to be loved is intensified, as is the story's theme of emotional rescue. All of Bass's stories evoke a naturalistic world in which people's importance is measured not by the Proustian intricacies of their intellect, but by their familiarity with raw emotions and the forces of nature.

With his book *Platte River,* Bass creates a clear and luminous world where legends are still told.

Christopher Tilghman (review date 13 March 1994)

SOURCE: Tilghman, Christopher. "Floating Down the River." *Los Angeles Times Book Review* (13 March 1994): 3, 11.

[*In the following review of* Platte River, *Tilghman praises Bass's strong sense of place and lyrical voice, but contends that some of his stories lack a strong focus.*]

People who admire Rick Bass' resplendent 1989 story collection, **The Watch,** as well as his several intervening nonfiction books on what the publishers call "the outdoors," have been looking forward to his new book of fiction with unusual interest. Some may be gunning for him, a writer who makes his reputation all too easily with a single book, but most of us are simply eager. We want to see where Bass' jumpy, oddly lyrical voice—a voice entirely his own—takes him a year or two down the road; we want to see if he's getting deeper to the truths of his slightly fractured sense of reality, whatever those truths may be. We want to see if he's still putting it all on the line, risking all, every time he writes.

Platte River, a collection of three long stories, has now arrived, and it's a fine book; it is a strong, visual, American book, enlivened by an unstudied masculine sensibility that this male reader, for one, finds distinctly refreshing. The title story is stunning; in my view, it's the best single piece Bass has written to date, more plainly and empathetically told than most of his work, a very moving story about an old football player named Harley (how's that for maleness?).

But perhaps the larger questions about Bass' career and the direction of his thinking remain unanswered in this book. Huge themes—the wilderness, purification and redemption, the use of sacrament—are planted all through these stories, but at this point Rick Bass still seems to be sowing more than he is reaping. His argument with the world can feel a little incoherent. He's got plenty of time and he's given us a thoroughly enjoyable evening of reading, but under the smooth flow of his marvelous prose, *Platte River* sometimes loses its way.

Many of the large themes are put in play by the opening story, **"Mahatma Joe."** Mahatma Joe Krag is a churlish old evangelist, who came to a remote valley in Montana years ago looking for converts. Though he failed totally in his primary mission, he has remained in this little Eden largely to take the fun out of life for everyone else. Bass is wonderful about the valley, "a park, green and forever," and about the vivid assortment of types and pilgrims that it attracts. Mahatma Joe, one of those types, is nevertheless determined to wreck it: "He wanted the town to have rules, ever more rules"; he writes venomous letters and drafts ordinances, imagining the valley as "a new place to get it right."

With his lyrical sense of place and his fierce protectiveness of the wild, Bass is on home ground here. The conflict, with all its comedies and magical turns, is nicely conceived. But I have to say that as the story evolves, I don't know who or what is winning the battle. Joe's final dizzy project, carried out in moonlight, is to plant vegetable gardens on some of the valley's creek banks. "What was once a meadow was now a cultivated garden, ordered and perfect," the narrator tells us, but is this more rule making, or has Joe's mission been finally subverted by the rich soil of the valley?

What the story lacks is the focused passion of Bass' splendidly raw essay on many of the same themes, "The Ninemile Wolves." There's also a large serving of theological images here—baptism, Calvary—but no examination of what they mean for either the faithful or the faithless. Instead, **"Mahatma Joe"** ends, for me, in confusion.

Vastly more successful are the other two stories, **"Field Events"** and **"Platte River."** The former opens with a black-bearded giant of a man emerging primevally from a frigid river, while two hulking and athletic brothers spy from behind the protection of a boulder. The giant, named A.C. (the initials could stand for a lot of things, but I like Allis-Chalmers) happens to be swimming naked, miles upstream to his house, with the painter of a canoe in his teeth. The brothers, high school track and field stars, decide, wonderfully, that A.C. is the discus thrower of their dreams.

"Field Events" turns into a lovely fable about vigor and youth. "So young! So young!" exclaims the narrator about these boys, the brothers and A.C., and about the sister, Lory, whom A.C. falls in love with. Through one year A.C. trains at the discus, and he throws farther and farther, as if finally, to give it one last toss around the circumference of the earth. "That's over 126,720,000 feet," one of the brothers exclaims. "How far'd you throw today, A.C.?"

From the water came A.C., and to the water he returns. "In the spring . . . after the snows melted and the rivers began to warm . . . he began to swim again, but with Lory this year." Water—cold spring runoff water—has mystical qualities for Bass, and here he is quite certain of himself. It's a motif from **"Mahatma Joe,"** and from **"Platte River,"** being lost and drowned, a sinner, then swimming for the air; being purified by the shock of icy water; finding answers in the secrets below the surface.

Thus in **"Platte River,"** the former pro football player, Harley, living in isolation on the Canadian border with a woman who is about to leave him, finds himself doing a two-day lecture gig at a small rural art college. It's a scam cooked up by the running back Harley used to block for in college, who now teaches English. Bass gives us the dispirited faculty at this college in the woods, the sad marriages, the suicidal colleague, the rusted-out Toyotas they all drive, and by the end of the predictable evening, the men end up in perhaps the only place on earth that they trust: on the banks of the Platte River casting for steelhead salmon. Maybe it's silly, but that's what they do.

Perhaps none of these men can be saved: Harley, or the suicidal English prof, or the former running back with his failing marriage. Perhaps manhood, as a positive value, cannot be saved, in this century anyway. But I liked the men in this story and the dogged efforts they were making, and if I had my choice, I'd choose fishing with them over a lot of fussier alternatives. I feel the same way about this book. I'm not satisfied by it, totally, but I liked it, I felt comfortable with it, and I'd choose Rick Bass over just about any other writer at work today.

Robert Buffington (essay date fall 1994)

SOURCE: Buffington, Robert. "Tolerating the Short Story." *Sewanee Review* 102, no. 4 (fall 1994): 682-88.

[*In the following essay, Buffington discusses various short fiction collections in terms of the principles of the short story form and comments that the three stories in* Platte River *should be categorized as long stories rather than as novellas.*]

I may as well say at once that I am no cousin of Mr. Poe.

> Were we bidden to say how the highest genius could be most advantageously employed, . . . we should answer, without hesitation—in the composition of a rhymed poem, not to exceed in length what might be perused in an hour. . . . In almost all classes of composition, the unity of effect or impression is a point of the greatest importance. . . . This unity cannot be thoroughly preserved in productions whose perusal cannot be completed at one sitting. . . .
>
> Were we called upon, however, to designate that class of composition which, next to such a poem, . . . should best fulfil the demands of high genius, . . . we should unhesitatingly speak of the prose tale. . . . We allude to the short prose narrative, requiring from a half-hour to one or two hours in its perusal. The ordinary novel is objectionable, from its length.
>
> —Edgar Allan Poe, "*Twice-Told Tales,* by Nathaniel Hawthorne: A Review," 1842

Poe's premise, that unity of effect or impression is the major literary consideration, makes a very large nostrum to swallow. To take one undisputed example of high genius, it puts Shakespeare's best sonnets above his best plays. And Poe's ranking of genres puts "The Minister's Black Veil" above *Lear.*

But take the ordinary objectionable novel. Consider what goes on in the typical novel written by one leading contemporary writer:

1. A is in love with B, who, however, is in love with C, who is in love with D, who is in love with A. The resulting action is both funny and sad.

2. There are surprises for both the characters and the reader in some of the ultimate pairings. None, or at best two, have their hearts' desires.

3. There are other surprises.

4. Characters, numerous and of various classes, conditions, and ages, are biographical, psychological, and moral entities.

5. In the form of a physical trial, a central character undergoes a trial of the soul.

6. There are supranatural or mystical experiences.

7. There is much witty and often philosophical conversation.

8. There are set pieces of nature description—"word painting"—which I am inclined to skim. But nature as a specific locus is a constant presence, often a threat.

God's own plenty is here. This is the sort of novel that one settles down with. At the end, reached reluctantly, the reader's feeling is akin to seeing or reading one of Shakespeare's tragicomedies. No unity of effect—but there is the unity embraced by "the mysterious limits of form," in Allen Tate's phrase—surely enough unity to satisfy most mortals. And the abundance within those limits is, needless to say, far beyond the short story's scope.

Poe presides over *The Culture and Commerce of the American Short Story,* an informal history that Andrew Levy has limned in neutral tones and tentative strokes; but he has provided us with some interesting information nevertheless. Poe was the patron saint of the American short story from about 1885 until the mid-twentieth century.

Poe's high valuation of the genre was tied, in Levy's view, to his ambition to found and edit a magazine of the highest quality in both content and format and of the highest profitability as well. "I perceived," Poe envisioned for a prospective backer, "that the whole energetic, busy spirit of the age tended wholly to the Magazine literature—to the curt, the terse, the well-timed, and the readily diffused." A magazine boom did ensue in the last two decades of Poe's century, helped by cheaper printing and by burgeoning corporate advertising budgets. Between 1885 and 1905 the number of

magazines with circulations of 100,000 or more increased almost eightfold—from 21 to 159. They and the newspapers competed for short stories (a paper advertised "one hundred short stories by one hundred authors in one hundred days"). About this time apparently began the notion, which persists, that the short story is the quintessentially American art form.

In response to the large cash market for the short story came a flood of handbooks on how to write it: *The Art and Business of Story Writing; The Plot of the Short Story; Stories You Can Sell; Breaking into Fiction.* Flourishing from about 1910 into the 1950s, when the serious money from magazines began to dry up, they almost all began with Poe's premise that unity of effect is the thing.

Incomprehensibly—I almost said *fatuously*—Levy drags in the critical anthology *Understanding Fiction* (1943) as an example of the short-story handbook. This is one of those backhanded slaps at "the New Critical movement," obligatory apparently in academic criticism, that assumes the reader has no firsthand knowledge of the so-called New Critics and evinces no firsthand knowledge on the writer's part either—only the approved attitude toward the recent literary past as some sort of broad conspiracy. *Understanding Fiction* was a sequel to Cleanth Brooks's and Robert Penn Warren's *Understanding Poetry* (1938) and, like their earlier textbook, instructed the student in the reading, not the writing, of a literary art (including the novel).

The short-story handbooks sound more than anything else like present-day books and tapes on investing in real estate—how to build a fortune, without capital, in your spare time. Just as writing about real estate may be more profitable than investing in it, so the author of *A Guide to Fiction Writing* (1940) could point to several students who published their own short-story handbooks before ever publishing a story.

As the handbook industry has declined, the number of writers' workshops has grown. As of 1989 American universities were offering 250 writing programs. These have created a market for fiction-writing textbooks, cousins to the do-it-yourself handbooks (I believe that the author of at least one of the textbooks has never published fiction).

The value of writers' workshops is continually debated. Nelson Algren in 1973 declared that the Iowa Writers Workshop in thirty-five years had not produced a single work worth rereading. The stories of Flannery O'Connor alone give the lie to that. But Levy recounts the story—"probably fictitious"—that O'Connor politely listened to the savage attacks of workshop students and the advice of her thesis director without blotting a line.

Himself a former student in the Johns Hopkins writing program, Levy devotes his postscript to a four-day visit to the Iowa Writers Workshop, the oldest and best known graduate workshop. Although Levy is interested only in the Fiction Workshop, there is also the Poetry Workshop at Iowa, and the two are quite different, or were during the year I spent there. The difference I think has something to do with the genre of the short story.

The genius behind the Writers Workshop and still its head in 1958-59 was Paul Engle, a poet but not a fictionist. He was an old friend of Robert Frost, whom he got out to Iowa City that winter for a memorable public reading—the cultural event of the year in that snowbound little town. I listened to several rebroadcasts of it on WSUI ("the oldest station west of the Mississippi, this is WSUI in Io*way* City"). But, though I had had a remarkably cordial correspondence with Mr. Engle before going up to Iowa, I never met him and never even saw him set foot in the Fiction Workshop.

Our workshop, which had more students than the Poetry Workshop, was handled that year by several instructors, including Vance Bourjaily, Donald Justice (who did double duty between the two workshops), and, during the summer, George P. Elliott. They gave students' efforts flatteringly serious attention, but the tone of the class meetings was set by the students, and it was far from serious. Most of the students were just out of college and seemed to be killing time while trying to decide what to do with the rest of their lives. Why not take a stab at authorship in the meantime? In the general sessions they competed at getting the biggest laughs at the expense of the story being discussed. (I can imagine the risibility inspired by Flannery O'Connor's "grotesques.") None seemed to be doing novels—only short stories. These seemed hastily written and were devoid of style, except for some bald imitations of Faulkner and Hemingway and recent winners of Nobel prizes.

My two office-mates in the Communications Skills Department (God forgive the committee that named it), where we had teaching fellowships, were like me a few years out of college. Vern Rutsala had been in the U.S. Army in Germany and was married. Martin Robbins had worked on a weekly newspaper and for a public-relations firm in New York. Although they were taking the fiction as well as the poetry workshop, their talents lay in poetry. Some of the poems Vern was writing were included in the excellent collection he published five years later in the Wesleyan poetry series, then the best series in the country. Marty, though a gregarious bachelor then, worked at his poetry almost daily. If he didn't have a new poem going, he revised old ones; I never knew him to give as much care to his prose. Both of these poets, I suspect, were just slumming in the Fiction Workshop.

That summer, free of teaching, I made several visits to the Poetry Workshop. Conducted mainly by Donald Justice, a very fine poet who could do things like sestinas and villanelles (Paul Engle would pop in and out), the Poetry Workshop was much more technical and serious than the rambunctious Fiction Workshop. Poetry was accorded more respect.

The difference between the two workshops bears out Levy's theme that since Poe the American short story has been regarded as a "disposable artifact," more easily produced than others. One of its best practitioners, John Cheever, called the short story "a bum."

"Reading it . . . with a perfect contempt for it, one discovers in it after all"—as Marianne Moore wrote of poetry—"a place for the genuine." But another problem emerges with the short-story collection. As William Dean Howells observed, the reader "can read one good short story in a magazine with refreshment, and a pleasant sense of excitement . . . but if this is repeated in ten or twenty stories, he becomes fluttered and exhausted." Collections have traditionally been difficult to market.

Of 17 short story collections that I have read or sampled in the past two years, however, only one was published by a university press and only one by a small independent press—the mainstays of poetry publishing. The other 15 were published by major trade houses. The annual *Best American Short Stories* in a recent five-year period doubled its sales. The publishing renaissance of the American short story has resulted, by Levy's calculations, from the increasing number of readers enrolled in the proliferating workshops.

After reading a good amount of recent short fiction, I have two general observations. First, the eighteenth- and nineteenth-century term *sketch* could be revived usefully, for many "stories" are not really stories, even in the Joycean sense (Poe remarked of Hawthorne's collection that many were not *tales,* but "pure essays"). Second, it is a shame that the "beautiful and blest *nouvelle,*" as Henry James called it, still has little currency in the United States. The short novel, despite its relative economy, can approach the richness that I attempt to summarize above in the typical novel of Dame Iris Murdoch. Even Poe, in allowing up to two hours' reading time for the prose narrative, leaves some room for the novella.

Rick Bass's ***Platte River*** is billed as a collection of three novellas, but each is just a long story, with a story's pace, the longest taking only about 15,000 words. Still these *are* stories. The first two, which I like better than the title story, are in fact almost tall tales, with something of the arbitrarily fabulous quality of Garcia Marquez. I say "arbitrarily" because this is something the writer turns on and off at whim. For example, in **"Field Sports"** a man of fabulous strength (his favorite recreation is dancing in the grass with one of his cows slung over his shoulders) is too large to fit in his friend's VW and must ride standing on the rear bumper. But later, to drive his girl friend, he gets behind the wheel of the same VW.

A true novella is featured in Susan Engberg's fine collection. From the beginning of "Sarah's Laughter" we have the luxurious sense that the author has a full canvas to fill (in this case about 30,000 words). A reclusive retired newspaper book-page editor of seventy-seven is amazed to find himself becoming friends again with the woman who divorced him twenty years ago and is happily remarried. Sarah; their daughter Martha, who is in town visiting and has something to tell him; and even Sarah's husband are engaged in dragging this ingenuously difficult man toward life, which he fears. "Sarah's Laughter" is by far the best piece of short fiction that I have read in the past two years.

That is the only true novella that turned up in seventeen volumes. Joseph Epstein's nine stories in *The Goldin Boys,* however, are longer than average and typically cover almost all of a character's life. The typical character is Jewish and a native of Chicago by several generations. He owns a retail business, to which he enjoys going early in the morning before the help arrives, so that he can collect his thoughts and plan his day. Or his father owns such a business, and he himself has become a doctor or lawyer or accountant or a professor at the University of Chicago. There are also mobsters, a Polish count, a magazine publisher, and two novelists who exploit friends to make characters. (The author of this first collection may well have a novella in him.) The title story is predictable. The best stories are "Kaplan's Big Deal," "The Count and the Princess," and "Marshall Wexler's Brilliant Career" (though I feel cheated at the end by a death by car accident).

Of William Hoffman's fiction I have been aware since 1971, when I reviewed his novel *A Walk to the River.* By now Hoffman has published ten novels and, with *Follow Me Home,* three collections of stories. He is the best pure storyteller I have read in these two years. He writes adventure, as in "Tides," an initiation story told from the point of view of a father rather than his son, both of whom are confronted by a sinister-pathetic villain who suddenly appears as from the pages of Joseph Conrad. He writes broad social comedy, as in "Abide with Me." His endings are unpredictable but right—even when they are shocking, as in "Night Sport," a story about a sociopathic Vietnam amputee. His world is the South—specifically Virginia—but he labors in no one's long shadow within that dense fictional tradition. Hoffman's Virginia is not yet a classless society, though the best class is fraying at the edges; and his characters range from farmhands to the hunt-club set.

False Gods by the prolific novelist Louis Auchincloss consists of five long stories. The abstract "Ares, God of War" is an outline of a novel, covering thirty years; the protagonist's heart attack at the end is a deus ex machina (another false god). "Hephaestus, God of New Fangled Things" and "Polyhymnia, Muse of Sacred Song" treat the conflict between art and life. Auchincloss handles the social scene and dialogue in the manner of James, but with sometimes startlingly concrete detail.

Best known for *Hiroshima* and *A Bell for Adano,* John Hersey published one volume of short stories, and that not long before his death. It displays an impressive range of settings. "Fling," "The Announcement," and "The Captain" are very good. "Requiescat" rests on a fussy notion of guilt (like that which admonishes a citizen to feel responsible for a riot at the other end of the continent).

The title story of Elizabeth Tallent's *Honey* I like better than her *New Yorker* and *Best American Short Stories* exhibit, "The Prowler." But the title (like the impoverished titles of Bass's tales) is inadequate for this story.

There are also good stories in a collection by Hilary Masters (especially "Trotsky's House" and "Touching Down") and good stories in a collection by R. B. Binstock, none of which appear to have had magazine publication—another sign of trade-house hospitality to the genre. Whether you are devoted to the genre or only occasionally tolerant thereof, you will find in the eight volumes cited here the genuine article.

A postscript: Last week, on going to vote in a sleepy Georgia August primary run-off, I was struck by the book an elderly poll worker had brought with him to while away the hours—a recently published library book on how to write fiction.

James LeMonds (review date November 1994)

SOURCE: LeMonds, James. Review of *Platte River,* by Rick Bass. *English Journal* 83, no. 7 (November 1994): 105-06.

[*In the following review, LeMonds praises* Platte River, *commenting that Bass is one of the finest American writers today.*]

I picture Rick Bass huddled in front of his wood stove in the Yaak Valley of Montana, writing with gloves on in the dead chill of winter. Maybe he's just back from the Dirty Shame Saloon, headquarters to the Valley's thirty residents and the home of Dirty Burgers and Shameful Fries. An expatriate of sorts, Bass lived in

Utah, Arkansas, and Mississippi before giving up on malls and subdivisions and settling on the isolation of the Yaak. It is a story of restlessness and discovery which sweeps like a chinook wind through the three novellas in his fine new book, *Platte River.*

While place dominates his nonfiction, most recently in *Winter* and *The Ninemile Wolves,* people come to the fore in these stories. They are loners, even when surrounded by friends and comforted by lovers, cast adrift from the past, running to something they can see but can't quite define. It is a loneliness that matches the desolation of the landscape Bass selects for his settings, unpeopled places capable of turning characters inward to wanderlust or despair, and in some instances, capable of healing them as well.

The pairings of characters are quirky; often the couples are seeming incompatibles who need each other to stave off the loneliness but aren't certain the relationship can truly fill their needs. Despite it all, there is hope, the sense that somewhere there is a place and a person that will fit if they just keep looking.

"**Mahatma Joe**" is the story of a failed evangelist who has left an Eskimo village in Alaska and come to the remote Grass Valley of northwestern Montana. Mahatma Joe has brought Lily, previously his housekeeper and now his wife. His soul-saving days over, Joe turns his attention to securing his own salvation by sending canned goods and preserves to starving Africans. Leena appears in Grass Valley from somewhere in the South, having gone through three men in six years, and desperate for escape. She works at the local mercantile and sleeps in a tent by the river where she bathes and swims in the icy water. Lily and Leena are pushed toward radical departures from the straight-and-narrow by Joe's dream to plant one last garden that will attract God's attention. Bass takes us into the hearts of all three characters, and we learn that they have connected, not to exchange love or emotion, but to find a place where they can belong. The outcome is tenuous, perhaps temporary, but each character finds a degree of satisfaction.

"**Field Events**" features the surreal A. D., discovered and informally adopted by the discus-throwing Irons brothers as he swims naked upstream in the Sacandaga River of northeastern New York, towing a loaded canoe. Like Mahatma Joe and Leena, A. D. has moved away from a painful past and finds a glimmer of a future in his acceptance by John and Jerry, whose late night pastimes include lugging their Volkswagen beetle around the block. Larger even than the muscle-bound brothers, A. D. is too massive to fit in the VW and must ride on the back bumper. His hobbies include pirouetting across fields with adult cows across his shoulders and bear-hugging statues in the town square which he brings home to deposit in John and Jerry's back yard.

The brothers' parents, Heck and Louella, and sister Lindsay accept A. D. as one of their own, in a way that goes beyond courtesy or kindness. When Louella first saw A. D.:

> She stopped drying dishes and was alarmed at the size of him, standing there among her children, shaking hands, moving in their midst. She had had one miscarriage, nearly twenty years ago. This man could have been that comeback soul.

By the end, A. D.'s prowess with the discus, which he tosses three hundred feet despite uneven form (the current world record is 234 feet), takes a back seat to the love he finds with Lory, John and Jerry's diminutive sister, an unhappy teacher, 34, still living at home and painfully self-conscious about the dimensions of her overly large breasts.

The title story is a fitting finish, as characters tumble together in an overlapping cycle of escape, loss, depression, and hope. Ex-professional football player Harley finds that Shaw, the woman he loves, may leave him for good this time. Meanwhile, Harley is invited to speak at a school in northern Michigan where his former college teammate, Willis the Wolverine, teaches English. He stays only one night, but this brief time spent fishing for steelhead on the Platte River with Willis' buddies and conversing with their wives, while not erasing his pain, brings Harley to an understanding of the complexity, uneasiness, and perpetual search for place that afflicts us all:

> And he had the feeling, as the men walked in silence ahead of him, that each of them knew, somehow intuitively, what Harley was going through, the tremble and terror of Shaw's packing, one box at a time, leaving . . . He had the feeling that not only was his secret being read, but these men had gone through the very same thing—had chased their wives before, lost them, caught them, let them go, chased them, found them—and that the reason no one was saying anything as they walked, with the stars scattered bright around them, was that they were all the same. There was no need to speak.

Rick Bass' imagery is consistently fresh, the voice passionate and unpretentious. *Platte River* merely adds to his reputation as one of the finest American writers going today.

***Publishers Weekly* (review date 1 May 1995)**

SOURCE: Review of *In the Loyal Mountains,* by Rick Bass. *Publishers Weekly* 242, no. 18 (1 May 1995): 43.

[In the following review, the critic positively evaluates In the Loyal Mountains, *claiming that there is a solid thematic cohesion to the collection.]*

In this moving and self-assured collection of 10 stories [*In the Loyal Mountains*] (some of them linked, others not), Bass (*Platte River*) captures two very different regions of the country. A handful of the selections are set in an isolated Montana valley, a place inhabited by cougars and bears and the occasional pedestrian who gets pulled off the road and mauled. Others are set in the deep South, including **"The Legend of Pig-Eye,"** in which a Mississippi boxer recounts the bizarre training rituals of his instructor, which include outswimming a crazed horse named Killer. All of the stories are told in the first person, and all the narrators are men. Often looking back at important moments in their lives, they never waver in their love for their environments: "I wake up smiling sometimes because I have all my days left to live in this place," says the unnamed narrator of **"The Valley."** For that love, the men often pay a price measured in human isolation, but they pay it willingly. The protagonist of **"Swamp Boy"** speaks for most of Bass's men when he says: "My heart was wild and did not belong among people." Between the opening story, **"The History of Rodney"** (a Southern-gothic tale about the denizens of a pig-infested Mississippi ghost town), and the close of the title story (a nostalgic riff on Texas, suicide and golf) Bass achieves a solid thematic cohesion and an irrational sort of communion among the stories that give this collection something like the heft of a wonderfully layered novel.

Dan Cryer (review date 19 June 1995)

SOURCE: Cryer, Dan. "A Natural Background for the Mysteries of Life." *Newsday* (19 June 1995): B6.

[*In the following review, Cryer applauds Bass's depiction of natural landscape as a setting for deeper explorations of life's mysteries in* In the Loyal Mountains.]

Rick Bass' stories immerse the reader in a dreamy, languid ocean of mystery. Set in Texas, Mississippi and Montana, and told by male narrators, they probe warily around some deep, unsayable truth as if pinpointing it would break a spell. Written with a fluid, unpretentious lyricism, they are vivid and original testimonies to life's enduring strangeness. Bass emerged on the literary scene in 1989 with *The Watch,* a story collection that immediately marked him as an accomplished practitioner of the genre. *Platte River,* published last year, solidified his reputation. Meanwhile, Bass has written a series of nonfiction books—including *Winter, The Ninemile Wolves* and the forthcoming *The Lost Grizzlies*—that demonstrate his prowess as an observer of the natural world.

In the 10 stories that make up Bass' superb new book, *In the Loyal Mountains,* the beauty and vitality of the out-of-doors is a given. The book teems with fish and game, with owls hooting, bears hiding in the woods and deer silently stalking. Mountains and lakes offer refuge from city stresses. Yet nature is not only powerful, as mighty, irresistible force or as incomparable source of spiritual sustenance, but also fragile, as victim of a sometimes ignorant and merciless humankind.

"Days of Heaven," told by a caretaker at a Montana ranch owned by wealthy outsiders eager to "develop" it, is one of the less memorable stories because of its too obvious pro-environmental agenda. Much more persuasive is a story like **"The History of Rodney,"** in which a random shifting in the course of the Mississippi River has turned a once thriving southern village into a ghost town. In Bass' magical rendering, the river becomes a symbol for unpredictable undercurrents that are mirrored in the narrator's love affair.

"Swamp Boy" neatly captures the modern world's simultaneous awe before nature and its desire to subdue it. The narrator looks back to a Houston boyhood when he and his buddies would beat up a fat, bespectacled youth who spent his days picking berries and flowers and collecting specimens for his aquarium. Throughout, the narrator insists that he went along with these rituals of humiliation—including stringing the kid upside-down in a tree—only as an observer. Then at the end of the story we learn that he was the swamp boy, thus embodying the larger culture's ambiguity.

In **"Antlers,"** the inhabitants of a remote Montana valley partake in another odd ritual. At Halloween, they gather at the local tavern to drink, dance and carouse while wearing antlers. All this takes place in a context of men who hunt and the woman who serially beds them. Her sole refusal is to a man she finds cruel because his bow-and-arrow hunting results in a slow, painful death for the animal. Here the juxtapositions of love and death, humans and animals, and humans dressed like animals, work to expose human emotions, to display them in their raw, "uncivilized" clarity.

"Fires," which seems to be set in the same valley, is about the friendship that develops between a local man and a world-class runner spending a summer there for high-altitude training. His job is to trail her during her runs on a bicycle, as a gun-toting guard against bears. He has no mate and she is temporarily separated from her boyfriend. Their relationship is intense—she asks him to feel her heart after every run—and largely wordless and altogether chaste. In the background are the fires the government uses to manage forest growth. One last fire before her departure, like their non-affair, nearly explodes out of control.

In **"The Legend of Pig-Eye,"** an aspiring young boxer trains amid rural Mississippi splendor and then heads out to broken-down bars to drum up fights. Mack's trainer-manager hopes to prime him for the big time. But whether he has the goods, despite his nearly 100 victories, is suspect, as is his desire. Bass makes his after-practice lake swims symbolize those question marks. For Mack knows that what he calls **"The Lake of Peace"** may also have been the place where a previous protege, Pig-Eye, committed suicide once his ring career began to decline.

The title story is a middle-aged Texan's retrospective on a big-spending, high-spirited uncle who treated him like a son and ended up a crook and a suicide. Uncle Zorey flew the teenaged Jackie off to hunt and fish; he supplied him with a girlfriend (in fact a hooker); he drove them all into the hill country for picnics and swims. The story conveys Jackie's gratitude to a terribly flawed man as well as his dismay that it took so long to appreciate the subtler virtues of his father, a golf pro regarded in the papers as a class act.

Even in this story, in which divided human loyalties are more central than nature's revelations, one sees the subtle Rick Bass magic at work. As the writer noted in an interview with this paper last year, "You never say the thing the story's about. Just go all around the edge until, like one of those glass cutters, you cut a circle in the glass and the glass falls out—until you capture it, and walk away." Readers will walk away amazed.

David Long (essay date 26 June 1995)

SOURCE: Long, David. "Rick Bass: Lessons from the Wilderness." *Publishers Weekly* 242, no. 26 (26 June 1995): 83-4.

[*In the following essay, Long highlights the development of Bass's writing career, his writing process, and the intersection of his fiction and the author's environmental activism.*]

Montana has bred, or attracted, more than its share of writers, but few have craved its isolation or valued its wildness with the passion of Rick Bass. "Do I want more society or less? I think the question is going in the wrong direction," he says. "In our society it's going to be hard to get *enough* remoteness, or enough time with one's self. I wouldn't be so cornball as to say I think all the great lessons that lie ahead of us are to be found in the woods, but the more time I spend here, the more I'm impressed with the way we *ignore* what's in the woods."

It's a cool spring day when *PW* tracks him down in the Yaak Valley, a remote pocket of northwestern Montana where he and his wife, the artist Elizabeth Hughes, have lived since 1987. He's waving from the porch of a

handsome new house they've just moved into. Two weeks ago, Elizabeth gave birth to their second daughter, Lowry; Mary Katherine was born in 1991. Bounding around the woods are the two pups, Ann and Homer, whom readers will recall from *Oil Notes,* now in their middle years; also his bird dog, a young German shorthair named Colter. Bass himself is compact and muscular. His eyebrows bunch as he talks, his gaze narrows into a squint as if he were eyeing something far across the meadow. He laughs readily, and to *PW*'s northern ears his Texas accent has a softly pleasing cadence.

Bass's life is awash with writing projects. This month, Houghton Mifflin will publish his second collection of short stories, **In the Loyal Mountains** followed in November by *The Lost Grizzlies,* his longest nonfiction book. Meantime, he produces a relentless flow of personal essays on natural history and environmental issues for magazines such as *Audubon, Men's Journal* and *Outside.* And there are more stories, more novellas and the novel he's been amassing for years, *Where the Sea Used to Be.*

The 10 short stories in the new book will be familiar to Bass's faithful—they've been turning up regularly in the major story venues for several years, including *Best American Short Stories, The Pushcart Prize* and *New Stories from the South.* Though Bass is dead-serious about Montana's wilderness debate, only four of the stories are located in this region of the country; the rest come from the Deep South of his past. If there's a common thread, he explains, it has to do with hanging onto things worth hanging onto, deciding where to stand and fight.

All are told from the first-person, and like the novellas in **Platte River** (1994), they feel nearly mythological. Often his narrators find themselves chronicling the life and times of a small, good-hearted band of citizens. As the narrator of **"The Valley"** says, "I wake up smiling sometimes because I have all my days left to live in this place." Bass shares this sentiment, though for him it is tempered by a deep foreboding. "I'm scared to death that these woods and this valley will get trashed," he says.

From Geology to 'Paris Review'

For generations, Bass's family lived in Texas. Born in Fort Worth in 1958, raised in Houston, Bass trained as a scientist, studying wildlife biology and geology at Utah State, then worked several years as an oil and gas geologist in Mississippi. His passion for the mysteries of finding oil fills the pages of *Oil Notes* (1989). A sneaky book in some ways, amiable and journal-like at the surface, its bigger concerns pool abundantly below: how to act on the unseen, how to cope with plenty and scarcity, how to respect one's work, how to love.

But he had no formal education as a writer. He began to write on his lunch breaks while working as a geologist. "I didn't know there was a publishing world out there, I just wrote." These pieces eventually became *The Deer Pasture.* Later, he wrote essays and travel pieces for the Sierra Club, which were collected in his second book, *Wild to the Heart.* And he began writing fiction. His early efforts were routinely rejected, but gradually editors offered more and more feedback. "It was like going to school through the mail. I'd focus for a week or two on one mysterious little line. *Lacks depth,* for instance. Then I'd address the problem in the next draft."

In the mid-1980s, Bass frequented the Lemuria bookstore in Jackson, Mississippi. Its staff kept urging him to read Jim Harrison's *Legends of the Fall,* and he kept shutting them off. The jacket called Harrison an outdoorsman. *I don't want to read about deer hunting and that stuff,* Bass thought, but finally relented. "It threw a mental switch, a big door just swung open." The next story he wrote was published in the *Paris Review.*

Readers will find echoes of Barry Hannah's zaniness in Bass's plots, and he credits Eudora Welty's writing for teaching him how elegant orthodox storytelling could be (a photo of Bass and Welty conversing graces a table in his living room). He's indebted as well, he feels, to Thomas McGuane and fellow Texan John Graves. And not only as craftsmen. "It's who they are as people. I need to learn to live with being a writer as much as learning *how* to write. When times get tough artistically, those models, those forebears give you support and confidence."

These days, Bass writes in a cabin some distance from the new house. No electricity, no distractions. He attends to his fiction first thing, before the day intrudes, writing in longhand in notebooks, perhaps five pages on a good morning. "I used to get my work done in a couple of hours," he says. "Now it takes four or more, same amount of work." He expects the novel will take a year to finish drafting, another to edit. It's a massive manuscript, over 1300 pages at present, his most complex and structured work of fiction to date.

"When you're really in love with something you're working on," he says, "90% of the time you think: Man, this is it, this is the only thing in the world. It takes on its own light and magic. The other 10% you have this huge despair—you saw the way you wanted it, but you just missed it. You're the only one who sees it; it's invisible, it's vaporous."

Later in his typical work day, he turns to the environmental work that has increasingly commanded his time—newspaper editorials, letter-writing campaigns, essays. He used to write two or three magazine pieces a year, which felt about right to him. Lately, taking on environmental degradation in the West, he's producing

15 or 20. "It's like a war effort," he says. "It feels enormous trying to still do fiction with this—it's not sustainable, but then neither is what's being done to land up here. I'm going berserk, just lobbing these essays, trying to publicize what's going on." A piece on deforestation he did for *Scholastic Scope* brought him some 2000 responses from schoolkids. "Such beautiful letters," he says. He handwrote each one an answer.

His work day typically ends in physical labor. Lately he's been hauling slabs of rock for a wall along the road and building a slew of wire cages to keep the deer out of his aspen saplings. And at least once a week, he drives 45 miles to the gym in Libby for a session of power-lifting, which he views as another form of meditation.

ART AND ACTIVISM

He and Elizabeth passed their first winters in the Yaak caretaking the Fix Ranch—not far, as it turns out, from their new property. He wrote about this period of acclimatization in a memoir called *Winter.* W.W. Norton had already published his first collection of stories, **The Watch** (1989), and he was under contract for two more works of fiction, but they declined his nonfiction projects. Bass's agent at the time, Tim Schaffner, sold *Winter* and *Oil Notes* to Seymour Lawrence at Dutton, who shortly thereafter took those manuscripts with him to Houghton Mifflin. For a time, it appeared that Bass would continue to split his fiction and nonfiction between the two houses, but he was eventually released from the contract with Norton. Houghton Mifflin is now his sole hardback publisher. His present agent is Bob Datilla of the Phoenix Literary Agency.

Bass is lavish in his praise for his editors. His magazine editors, among them Gordon Lish and Rust Hills; Carol Houck Smith at Norton; and his editors at Houghton Mifflin—the legendary Sam Lawrence, along with Leslie Wells, Camille Hykes, Larry Cooper and Hilary Liftin. "I was *very lucky.* I needed a lot of editing and still do. It's not just lip service, I mean they're literally life savers. It's a triangle, me doing the grunt work, and them refining it, and then the resting time out in the woods. Those three anchor points."

The only recent project Houghton Mifflin did not release is *The Ninemile Wolves* (1992), which Bass decided to publish with Clark City, a Montana press. In it, he tracks the largely unhappy fate of each wolf in one small Montana pack, making a passionate defense of wolf reintroduction in the Northern Rockies. It's a deeply heartbreaking story, one of dueling bureaucracies and incompatible myths. (And a footnote Bass finds sadly ironic: Clarke City has since had to shut its doors.)

In *The Ninemile Wolves,* and in a manuscript of environmental pieces called *The Book of Yaak,* Bass's anger becomes palpable. "Traditionally," he says, "the literature of protest, if it's going to be called literature, has been gentlemanly, restrained. But when you turn the flame up, the water's going to boil, and the West is on fire, environmentally. Corporate industry has taken and taken until there's this last fragment of wildness left and now they're coming after that. They'll come and take the last owl, they'll come and take the last owl's habitat, the last bear, by rifle or bulldozer. I mean, if you don't yell now you're going to miss your chance."

For all that, Bass is determined not to mix his activism and his art. Political agendas corrupt a fiction writer's choices, he's convinced. Even so, questions of ownership and land stewardship *do* surface in his new stories. **"Days of Heaven"** begins bluntly: "Their plans were to develop the valley, and my plans were to stop them." The narrator, caretaker of a ranch, holds emotional title to the place but is ultimately at the owner's mercy and hates to jeopardize his tenancy. The story ends in a profoundly elegiac mood, the narrator wondering whether, if he keeps still, the would-be developers will simply go away. He knows they won't. A metaphor for the Yaak, Bass readily admits.

Bass's characters are at their best—generous, tolerant of one another's foibles—when residing in the smallest communities. In this, too, there's slippage between his fiction and nonfiction. "Well, it's a kind of crisis for me as a writer," he says, "because I'm trying hard to keep those themes separate, but they really want to merge— the social history of the stories, and the natural or biological history I'm writing about in my nonfiction. Basically, a community of people that has a large respect for each other's differences is just an expression of the beauty of the natural world—what they call species diversity."

As it happens, Bass speaks with *PW* the week after the bombing of the federal building in Oklahoma City. The newspapers are full of reports about paramilitary cabals in Montana's backwoods. But there's none of this in the Yaak, Bass says with a note of optimism. "People wouldn't tolerate it here. The hate groups establish themselves where they can drown out everybody else, and they couldn't do that here. They couldn't drown out the communal acceptance. There are no loose seams; we've woven our lives together here and they can't disrupt that social fabric."

Elaine Kendall (review date 27 June 1995)

SOURCE: Kendall, Elaine. "Two Lands Linked by a Mystical Quality." *Los Angeles Times* (27 June 1995): E4.

[*In the following review, Kendall praises Bass's sense of regional place in the stories of* In the Loyal Mountains.]

Impelled by a profound love of the land, the 10 stories in *In the Loyal Mountains* are a reminder that American literature draws its unique strength from a powerful sense of place. Here, author Rick Bass concentrates on two distinct and contrasting regions, the Delta country of Mississippi and a remote valley in Montana, areas linked only by a mystical quality common to both.

In **"The History of Rodney,"** the narrator and his wife have rented a ramshackle house in a ghost town where they are the only white inhabitants. Rodney was a thriving river port until the Mississippi flooded and shifted its course, leaving cotton barges stuck on a sea of mud and the ruined houses of the townspeople surrounded by dying fish.

The population fled to more hospitable environments, but after the mud became a meadow, a few descendants of slaves drifted back and stayed. Once Rodney was home to 16,000; now the population stands at 12.

A huge pig lives under the narrator's house, producing a litter each year, and "like the bad toughs in a Western, they own the town," running wild until they're needed for food. Daisy, the narrator's nearest neighbor, has told him that the pigs were created by her mother, whose powers were legendary. According to Daisy, marauding Union soldiers were marched into the church and transformed into swine by the force of her mother's will.

"I'm glad Elizabeth and I have found this place," the narrator says. "We have not done well in other places. Cities—we can't understand them. In a city everything seems as though it is over so fast: minutes, hours, days, lives." That will not be their problem in Rodney.

"Swamp Boy" is another bayou tale, less Gothic and chillingly realistic; a reminiscence of a school year when the narrator passively joined in tormenting a classmate. "I was that boy, and I was the other one too. I was at the edge of fear, the edge of hesitancy, and had not yet—not then—turned back from it."

"The Legend of Pig-Eye" takes the reader on a jaunt through the low-down bars of the Delta, looking for prizefights. The fighter is a literate young man, perfectly, if only temporarily, happy to be tooling around the South, taking on all contenders.

The atmosphere is gritty and authentic, but the drama of the story comes from Don's highly original method of training his protégés by chasing them through the woods on horseback. The unorthodox regimen works brilliantly, ending only when the trainee plunges into a lake with the raging horse following; a story for dreamers, naturalists and fight fans, who seldom have much in common.

"Fires" is a departure from the fantastic tone of the other stories; it's almost a romance. Here the writer is living in the Montana wilds, a settlement of two dozen souls. A woman runner, the sister of one of the inhabitants, comes for high-altitude training, and the writer is engaged to bicycle along behind her with a pistol, just in case a bear strays out of the hills and attacks. "Every valley had its bear stories, but we thought ours was the worst, because the victim had been a woman."

The connection between the man and the woman deepens, but the summer ends and the runner returns to her usual life, leaving the man who has come so close to her thinking "about fears, all the different ones, and the things that could make a person run."

"The Valley" is set in the same northwest village, a place where the writer has come "to start small. I have to get it right." There is a mysterious cemetery in those woods, where only women are buried, their photographs framed and set into the headstones. No one knows who they are or how they came to be there, but the popular theory is that the women died during the horrific winters, were frozen, and were then brought out on pack-horses in the spring to be buried. But how to explain the newest monuments? The springs are muddy, but there are never any hoof prints.

The riddle remains unsolved, but one thing is certain. This particular country still belongs to men, and only the most extraordinary women can survive there.

It's a lesson emphasized again in **"Antlers"** and touched upon in **"Days of Heaven,"** both of which take place in the hidden Montana hills and are told from the viewpoint of a writer whose love for this harsh and lonely landscape determines his themes and pervades every phrase.

Rick Bass and K. C. Johnson (interview date 7 February 1996)

SOURCE: Bass, Rick, and K. C. Johnson. "What the Woods Would Expect of You: An Interview with Rick Bass." In *Delicious Imaginations: Conversations with Contemporary Writers,* edited by Sarah Griffiths and Kevin J. Kehrwald, pp. 142-49. West Lafayette, Ind.: Purdue University Press, 1998.

[*In the following interview, which took place on 7 February 1996, Bass discusses the art of the short story, his nonfiction writing, and his environmental activism.*]

Rick Bass is the author of the noted fiction collections **The Watch, Platte River,** and **In the Loyal Mountains.** He is also the author of seven books of non-fiction: The

Deer Pasture, Wild to the Heart, Oil Notes, Winter, The Ninemile Wolves, The Lost Grizzlies, and, most recently, *The Book of Yaak* (Houghton Mifflin, 1996). In 1997, Houghton Mifflin published his collection of novellas entitled **The Sky, the Stars, the Wilderness.**

Born in Houston in 1958, Bass studied at Utah State University and then worked for several years as a petroleum geologist in Jackson, Mississippi. Bass and his wife, Elizabeth Hughes, moved to a remote ranch in the Yaak Valley of northern Montana in the fall of 1987. Preserving the valley—considered by many to be the wildest in the continental United States—and fighting to protect the area as wilderness now consumes much of Bass's energy and writing. Currently, not one acre of the Yaak is protected, and the U.S. Forest Service continues to authorize clear-cutting and build roads in the area.

Bass is currently working on his first novel, *Where the Sea Used to Be.*

K. C. Johnson is a journalist working in the sports department of the *Chicago Tribune.* He graduated magna cum laude from Beloit College in 1989 and has devoted much of his time since both to reading about and backpacking in the outdoors.

This interview took place on 7 February, 1996 in Evanston, Illinois, after Bass had given two readings from *The Lost Grizzlies.*

[Sycamore Review]: *I read an interview in* Poets & Writers Magazine *where you were quoted as saying short stories are a young person's form.*

[Rick Bass]: Did I say that? A lot of people say that. Not to say an old person can't write a story, but I do think it is a young person's form. The energy profile would be a good way to think of it. The word you hear most often about short stories is "compression." I don't even think it's so much compression as just the energy paths. Each sentence carries more energy in a story than it does in a novel. And it carries a different kind of energy that is quite often a more youthful kind of energy. What do I mean by youthful? It's still growing. It just has a . . . I don't know what a young sentence would be.

There's also so much mystery in short stories, so much that is unresolved. Sentences can have more amplitude in a short story. A sentence can also carry more certainty—or uncertainty—and more mystery in a short story than in a novel. A similar sentence in a novel is not a writer's voice but almost a speaker's tone of voice, like the way you can recognize a young person by the voice on the phone. It's almost that elemental.

I think as I get older, my works get longer. I'll have a story that I think is going to be twelve pages and it'll end up being one hundred pages.

Was that the case with **Platte River,** *your collection of novellas?*

Yeah, I thought that the novella **"Platte River"** was going to be an eight-pager. I think—I know—as I get older and I write a sentence, my mind wanders more and I make more connections than I made when I was younger. *This* reminds me of *this* reminds me of *this* reminds me of *this.*

Anyway, as I'm writing now I go laterally a lot of times in my mind for connections and thoughts rather than that pounding straight ahead with a directness that I might have had in earlier short stories. Back then, I wrote a sentence and did not look left or right, and did not think, okay, this could connect to something out here. I just went down the line.

You published a non-fiction book, The Ninemile Wolves, *in 1992, followed by* **Platte River** *in 1993. Most recently, you've published* **In the Loyal Mountains,** *a collection of short stories, and then* The Lost Grizzlies, *a book of non-fiction. Is it difficult for you to switch from writing fiction to non-fiction?*

Yeah, very.

What process do you need to go through to make the switch? Is that something you can put into words?

I'll try. It's a good question. I could write an essay about it. I don't know if I could put it into words. But it has to do with creating internal space and settling into rhythms. I do prepare for a run or a spell at fiction the way, you know, you would for an athletic event. You train for it mentally. I don't mean you do exercises, thinking, okay, what would the best point of view be on that or how would I describe that color. But, definitely, I'm always aware of when I'm getting ready and settling in for a run at fiction. It's almost a blood rhythm. I can *feel* it. I can really, really feel it when I'm ready to get into fiction. It's very much like settling in, like digging a hole in the ground and settling inside it.

I remember I had been away from fiction for a long time and I was on this beach walking in Honduras—it was with Dennis Sizemore on a Round River project on the Mosquito Coast—and something in my blood made me realize I was ready for fiction. It's just a rhythm. I try not to fight it. If I'm not in it, then I just do the best I can with my non-fiction.

But I feel the approach of this space that I can duck down into and work fiction—that's the best I can explain it. Which is not very good.

Can you put a ratio on the number of pages of fiction writing you do compared to non-fiction writing?

Again, I get in these pits, these troughs where I work fiction. In those, sometimes it's fifty-fifty. But then when I'm out of that pit, it's probably more like nine-to-one weighted toward non-fiction and advocacy. But once or twice every couple years, I'll be in a fiction frame of mind. And I'll really try to make hay when I'm in it, write as much as I can for however long it lasts. Boy, I love it. You know, the thing about absence making the heart grow fonder: I just love fiction writing more and more every year.

Each time I write a short story I think, oh, it's going to be my last one, because I'm getting so brittle with rage. I don't have the tolerance, I don't have the compassion, I don't have any of those qualities that you need for fiction. I'm just an old grouch and cynic, and I don't have time for fiction. I don't have that generosity of spirit, I don't have any of that stuff. I don't have that tolerance for mystery. I just want change affected now. I want results achieved now. And so I'm not in a fiction mode, but when I do get back to it, it's just so great. I'm in one right now, and it's really, really great.

Fiction is still more rewarding for you?

Oh, yeah, far and away. It's not even comparable. When fiction works.

Why, because you invest more of yourself?

No, because I don't invest more of myself. I invest everything I have in my non-fiction, or I try to. If anything, I pull back in my fiction and invest other people's selves. I invest my imaginary characters' selves in my fiction, which is fun, really fun. I guess, if I really had to be pinned down on it, I'd say I discover more in fiction. I'm surprised more in fiction. I don't learn as much about something when I write non-fiction. Not to say I don't learn from non-fiction, but just not as much. I learn things about the human heart when I write fiction. I can learn that in non-fiction, too, but not with that cleft, the feeling of surprise.

Again, it's not to say non-fiction can't illuminate something about someone's heart and that falling-away-surprise feeling, but just something about the feel of fiction I like better. It's like, you know, do you like fruit or do you like meat? You can't say one's better than the other, you just have a taste.

You mentioned that you're writing fiction now. Are you still working on your novel, Where the Sea Used to Be?

Oh, I've been banging on that for the last two years non-stop.

The dust jackets of your books keep saying that the novel is coming . . .

(Laughs.) That's funny. It's true. Because I keep working on it.

Will it be your next published book?

(Laughs) No, now I never promised. I just said I'm working on it. I didn't say when it was going to be done.

Do you still write out everything in longhand first?

Yeah, everything.

Why? For the physical act of it?

I guess that's most of it. A lot of it is just what I'm used to. I write a lot of letters on word processors, so it's not like I'm unfamiliar with keyboards. But I just like the way my hand feels on the page.

How frustrating is it for you to see your art being sapped by political causes?

Oh, it's frustrating all right. But it is really important to remember, even though fiction is very important to me and I love the challenge and the craft of it, that it's still just one person. There are a lot of writers in the world; there are a lot of artists in the world; there are a lot of bricklayers in the world; there are a lot of everything. As writers, we spend so much time alone and banking so much of our emotion on the story, working on our art. There's very much the tendency to think that it is the most important thing in the world, not just to us but to everybody else, and that's not so. Even if you have the most faithful readers in the world, you may only have several thousand of them. That's not a very large percentage of the world. And so it's not the biggest deal in the world if I don't get back to the short story. A lot of people go through their lives never getting to do the thing they love even once, so I can't complain. And yet I do.

Did you have any idea when you moved to the Yaak Valley that you would get so involved in efforts to protect it?

Oh, gosh no.

Do you think you would've moved there if you had known?

No, I don't think so. I went up there just to find a remote place to write fiction. And I actually did write a story the first week I was there. I felt like in Mississippi my stories were starting to repeat themselves: the characters were starting to act the same, the same colors—

green and yellow—were coming up an awful lot, a lot of the same imagery, a lot of the same scenes. And I was homesick for the mountains, so I just left and found this beautiful valley and settled in there and started writing. And then through the years, as the blinders were lifted and I saw what was going on in this world, I decided to get active and use whatever tools I could to expose the wrongs and lean all of my hopes on the possibility that if people know what's going on there, they'll take steps and action to stop it.

Are there other voices besides yours fighting for the Yaak?

Yeah, there are. The Montana Wilderness Association has been working hard to protect the Yaak. Some other organizations are starting to put it on their list of priorities.

Are you the only one living in the valley, though, that's speaking out?

Well, I have a forum to do so. A lot of people are talking in the bar, the hunters, a lot of people are reaching a consensus that something needs to be done, that the thing we most treasure about the valley is being taken from us. It's almost like being in Japan, though. It's very much a cultural taboo to speak against the timber industry because for so long they employed so many people in that part of the world. They didn't employ many people in Yaak; they employed people in the mill towns of Libby and Troy. Now they've cut their timber and left. They cut all the timber off their land. They cut most of it off federal lands and have left. It's really just mop-up right now. So there is a period of transition. There is potential for change in attitudes.

We saw a little bit of the emotion behind the Yaak for you at the talk tonight. Your hands are tied. But can you describe what that does to you? Like you said, there are greater injustices in the world. But for you, this is your greatest injustice.

Exactly. It destroys my inner peace. But again, there are a lot of people who don't have inner peace. It's not the end of the world. Again, little Ricky is not happy with the world. Big deal. A lot of people aren't happy with their lives, a lot of people aren't happy with the world. That's all it is. Period. I think it's wrong. I think it's unjust. It destroys my inner peace. It hampers my ability to make really good art. But it's important to keep it in perspective. I don't think what it does to me is the important question. The important question is, what is it doing to the land? It's not that big a deal for one person to be unhappy because of an injustice. But to take an entire ecosystem, the incredible grace and magic of an entire ecosystem and erase it from the face of the earth? That is evil. And that is much more significant than whether I am made a bit somber or unhappy by a clear-cut. I don't mean to diminish your question, but that's the answer to it.

And you'll keep fighting until when?

Until I can't. Or until it gets better, until it gets fixed. Hopefully, that won't be too long.

Do you still hold out any hope?

Oh, yeah.

Or else you wouldn't be doing it, I guess.

Well, I don't know about that. But I still hold out hope. I'd still be doing it even if I didn't have hope. Just because it's what's right and because it's what the woods would expect of you.

Kirkus Reviews (review date 15 September 1997)

SOURCE: Review of *The Sky, the Stars, the Wilderness,* by Rick Bass. *Kirkus Reviews* (15 September 1997): 1402.

[*In the following review, the commentator praises* The Sky, the Stars, the Wilderness, *calling the stories appealing, thoughtful, and captivating.*]

Two appealing short stories and an exquisite novella [*The Sky, the Stars, the Wilderness*] from Montana essayist and storyteller Bass (*The Book of Yaak,* 1996; *In the Loyal Mountains,* 1995, etc.).

The title novella revels in the rugged beauty of bluffs and thickets in Texas hill country, where three generations preserve the family ranch as a haven for wild animals and the wild at heart. The narrator, a middle-aged woman living alone on the ranch with her memories, recalls her formative influences: iron-willed Grandfather, whose battle cry ("the natural history of Texas is still being sacrificed upon the altar of generalization") was stifled by a stroke, then reemerged when the old man relearned speech using the cadences of birdsong; his Mexican right-hand, Chubb, who was afraid of the dark but a tireless worker and fiercely loyal by day; Father, the country agent, who fought in vain to end overgrazing and protect eagles from his sporting, good-old-boy neighbors; and especially Mother, who died when the narrator was still a girl, but whose limestone-bluff resting place ensured that her presence remained, even as the family dwindled one by one. These ties to the past, binding the mother to the daughter and the daughter to the land, prove more durable than any link with potential mates. In **"The Myths of Bears,"** another Texan, Judith, breaks free of the increasing lunacy of her longtime partner, Trapper, outwitting him and enduring winter in the Alaskan wilderness alone, only to be tripped up later by her concern for him; in **"Where the Sea Used to Be,"** an Alabama man breaks away from his cold-blooded rich boss to show a knack for finding oil from the air that makes him legendary, but also introduces him to a rival passion: Sara.

As thoughtful and captivating as his previous work: stories that can only increase Bass's reputation as a writer remarkably able to put people in nature in a way that enhances our understanding of both.

Publishers Weekly (review date 15 September 1997)

SOURCE: Review of *The Sky, the Stars, the Wilderness,* by Rick Bass. *Publishers Weekly* 244, no. 38 (15 September 1997): 48.

[*In the following review of* The Sky, the Stars, the Wilderness, *the critic applauds Bass's graceful prose and the mythological quality of his stories.*]

"Spirit world, my butt," thinks one hard-bitten character in the first of these three splendid novellas, but it is exactly that—a spirit world—that Bass grasps in his tales of people in the Western wilderness [in *The Sky, the Stars, the Wilderness*]. In the first, a mentally ailing trapper goes after a troublesome quarry: his wife. In the second, a wildcat oil man, who has never once picked a dry well, finds his rewards not in the money or in his perfect record but in his own enchantment with the land. In the title piece, the longest and most powerful of the three, a 44-year-old woman returns to her family's huge Texas ranch and remembers how she communed with her dead mother's spirit in the nature all around her, She wonders what part of her character is due to "bloodline" and what part "has been sculpted by the land," and how, indeed, she has failed the land by not producing children to continue the legacy. Bass (*In the Loyal Mountains*) takes a number of breathtaking turns and apparent digressions in this moving story, and readers will encounter a bounty of meditations on time and memory that showcase his graceful, precise, almost musical language, and his magical way of making nature animate. His innate sense of shaping a story brings to these tales the transcendence of myth.

Donna Seaman (review date 15 October 1997)

SOURCE: Seaman, Donna. Review of *The Sky, the Stars, the Wilderness,* by Rick Bass. *Booklist* 94, no. 4 (15 October 1997): 385.

[*In the following review, Seaman contends that all three novellas in* The Sky, the Stars, the Wilderness *are "beautifully mystical."*]

Bass has delved deeply into his love of nature and written three beautifully mystical novellas [in *The Sky the Stars, the Wilderness*]. These long stories are disorienting at first, so imbued are they with the slow, perfect rhythm of wilderness rather than the measure of clocks and artificial busyness of human existence. His characters, too, are unfamiliar, even exotic in their intimacy with wilderness, their disconnection from society. In **"The Myth of Bears,"** a shimmering tale as mysterious as the northern lights, a man and a woman live deep in the woods of the Yukon, their isolation rendering them wolf- and bearlike, a transformation echoing Native Americans' profound connection to animals, a theme also explored in Linda Hogan's *Solar Storms* and Robert Stone's *Bear and His Daughter*. In the lyrical title story, a young girl senses the spirit of her dead mother in the living rock, the sky, trees, and birds, a gorgeous and resonant metaphor for Mother Earth that Bass uses with great skill and noble purpose, leaving us enthralled yet quietly appalled at our desecration of the "church of the wild."

Andy Solomon (review date 30 November 1997)

SOURCE: Solomon, Andy. "The Scientist is a Romantic." *Boston Globe* (30 November 1997): G2.

[*In the following review of* The Sky, the Stars, the Wilderness, *Solomon extols Bass's expression of love for and understanding of the natural landscape in which the writer's stories are set.*]

Rick Bass embodies a fortunate confluence of virtues. From his earliest story collection, *The Watch,* he's professed a devout love for the land. As a petroleum geologist, he also possesses a scientific comprehension of the land. And as a writer of superb descriptive gifts, he has few equals in describing it.

Bass the storyteller weds art to understanding. More than a writer, he is an interpreter. But petroleum geologists bore into their ground obliquely. That's what Bass does in the two long stories and novella constituting his luminous new book [*The Sky, the Stars, the Wilderness*]. "The Myth of Bears" is a contemporary fable set in Montana after the turn of the century. Trapper had met Judith when they were 18. After nearly two decades together, he thought she was tame, but he was wrong. "He'd not understood she was the wildest, most fluttering thing in the woods." That's where she's fled now, having run away from Trapper, the only person who ever loved her. It's an equivocal kind of flight, however. On the one hand, she wants freedom: "It's not that he is a bad man, or that I am a bad woman, she thought. It's just that he is a predator, and I am prey. . . . If I am to survive, I have to run." The night she escaped, she believes, "was the first night of her life."

Yet she wants to entice as much as elude Trapper. When she sees him tracking her to bring her back, "she watched as if it were her wedding day; she felt that much love for him, and that much relief that he was missing her." Although his pursuit feels oppressive— "Why won't he leave me alone? . . . All I want is my life"—when she thinks he's quit his hunt she despairs: "It is terrible without the thought of him out there chasing her, hunting her. It's horrible. There's too much space." Love is both security and entrapment. She wants to run, yet not run away.

In the forests Judith runs through, life is primal. She is never more than two days from starvation. Trapper is incapable of abstraction, wholly absorbed by the direct, sensual need for his woman: "There is no spirit world, he thinks. There is just her, whom he wants to capture. . . . If he can capture her . . . all will be made new again."

This is basic Rick Bass, usually at his most articulate when rendering inarticulate people, people who feel more than think and sense more than speak, less reduced than purified to their most elemental drives, moving darkly through a misty landscape, as though Bass were perfecting the silhouette as a literary form.

His cast is more cluttered, his plot more snarled in **"Where the Sea Used to Be,"** making that story less engaging. Yet it, too, echoes the quest for freedom of the first story, as one wildcat oil man insists "that it was better to belong to yourself and have one acre in a drilling well than to belong to another man, even if that man had a hundred." Again, Bass conveys his passion for the land, which his characters find they cherish more than they can any woman.

Deep in Rick Bass runs a quixotic, eccentric vein. For years, he's lived on a ranch in northwestern Montana's Yaak Valley, a half-hour from the nearest phone. One Christmas, he sent a Manhattan friend a 6-foot Douglas fir tree through the mail. In *Oil Notes,* a 1989 memoir, he described his first date with his wife, taking her to the park for a picnic lunch of BLT sandwiches, lugging a microwave and extension cord in his trunk to plug into the tennis court lights outlet to grill the bacon.

His love for and knowledge of the land, his quixoticism, and his deepening in the years since *Oil Notes* all combine in the hauntingly beautiful title novella.

A 44-year-old woman returns to the West Texas ranch where she grew up. After her mother's death when the girl was 8, she lived there with three generations of men: her grandfather and the old Mexican hand Chubb, her father, and her younger brother. Now, all are gone.

But she is not alone. Her mother was not buried but "planted" on the land, and both the land and the daughter are alive with her presence. The daughter feels both mother and soil are deep inside her: "I am not the land itself, neither am I a clone of my family. But the magnitude of my attachment to these things—and the stability it affords—staggers me."

The men in her life did not teach her this love for the land; that seems to have sprung in her fully grown. They enhanced and balanced that love. Her grandfather knew all the constellations, loved the sky, suggested it's where heaven was, while she suspects it might lie in the earth, her home, the wellspring of luck and grace. Together, their views form the sky god/earth mother complement that gave rise to Greek myth. In contrast, her father fought to defend the aquifer beneath their ranch, even as she was finding blessings in the eagles soaring above it. Between the grandfather and Chubb, too, lay oppositions that were really complements. Chubb saw on the land countless sources of his people's myths and legends; the grandfather felt it could only be understood and preserved by those who practiced empirical, systematic reason. The daughter herself will later eschew his science for its lack of "sacred awe."

The duality of romantic and scientist have always existed in Bass himself, but they blend into a unity. He writes of the land with that kind of love only profound understanding can bring. And, as numinously as he describes its points of focus, the love itself proves ineffable, breathing between the lines, an active, not a verbal quality.

That's the lesson his 44-year-old narrator leaves with us: "I have seen what it is we do best, and that is to love and honor one another: to love family, and to love friends, and to love the short days." Whatever we love, she insists, we keep alive.

Thomas Curwen (review date 18 January 1998)

SOURCE: Curwen, Thomas. "The Call of the Wild." *Los Angeles Times Book Review* (18 January 1998): 5.

[*In the following review, Curwen discusses central themes within the three novellas of* The Sky, the Stars, the Wilderness.]

At 9,100 feet, Yovimpa Point sits on the edge of the Earth. From here the world falls away in a succession of unspoiled plateaus and cliffs that drop nearly 5,000 feet before rising again to the north rim of the Grand Canyon, leaving Yovimpa with a clear shot over forests of piñon and ponderosa pines to a horizon more than 100 miles away. The view takes you back in time as well: The gravel and dust at your feet were laid down nearly 50 million years ago, while the sediments that form the distant Vermilion Cliffs go back to the age of the dinosaurs.

Such perspectives fascinate Rick Bass, who might feel at home in this faraway place. The three novellas that constitute *The Sky, the Stars, the Wilderness* resonate with the myriad links, like perceptions of space and time, that connect viewer and viewed, subject and object, and persistently complicate such points of view. Each link is only relative, but each represents on an elemental level an attempt to bridge the gap between the ineffable awe and apartness that nature invokes. Bass wastes no time charting this distance. In **"The Myth of Bears,"** the first story in this collection, the premise—a man's yearlong pursuit of a woman bent on escaping him—is simple enough, but Bass strips away subtlety to amplify loss and need.

> . . . He wants her back worse than he ever wanted a pelt. Judith has been gone now almost a year.
>
> She broke through the cabin's small window on a January night during a wolf moon when Trapper was having one of his fits. At such times something wild enters him.

So it begins: their cat-and-mouse through the Yukon woods. It's winter, 40 below zero. She sleeps at the base of a fire-hollowed cedar; he methodically encircles her, crying and howling as he meticulously sets traps in the drifting snow. Bass complicates this strange little disquisition on love and obsession by entering the psychological wilderness of both hunter and prey. "I am no longer running from anything. I am running to something," she thinks, desperate at one moment to be left alone, and yet, "without the thought of him out there chasing her, hunting her . . . it's horrible. There's too much space." Like an echo, the drama reverberates in the emptiness of nature that Bass has carved out. Voices call out across an empty clearing. Indians believe bears are human. Men and women hope their differences reconcilable, their apartness transccnd-able.

Apartness, both humbling and exasperating, sublimates desire into flights of poetry or depredations of greed. Bass knows these impulses: They frame his fiction, provide its moral core. In *The Book of Yaak,* his story of the Yaak valley in Montana where he, his wife and children live, he ascended the pulpit to denounce the timber industry; only his lyricism for the place sweetened his bitter invectives. In *The Sky, the Stars, the Wilderness,* however, the blend is more masterful, guided seemingly less by anger than by possibility.

In **"Where the Sea Used to Be,"** Bass returns to the Mississippi Delta to write about Wallis Featherston, a petroleum engineer who, with his dog, Dudley, travels the back roads of Alabama and circles its forests in his plane looking for signs of oil. (Before his first stories were compiled and published in *The Deer Pasture* [1985], Bass worked as an oil and gas geologist in Mississippi and, later this year, will explore the region more thoroughly in his first novel, also titled *Where the Sea Used to Be*.) Again, something more mythic lies beneath Bass' simple story line:

> People waved at Wallis and Dudley when they saw them driving, and yet he remained a mystery, unlike other things in the country. Their lives were simple and straight and filled with work and the talk about crops and the grocery store, and ever, pleasurably, hatefully, always with emotion, the weather; but he was outside these things.
>
> 'He's got to be that way,' an old man said, spitting, when they talked to him at the gas station. 'He's looking for the hardest thing to find in the world. Shit, it's buried: It's invisible.'

Wallis succeeds—he has never drilled a dry well—because of his innate connection to the land, a connection forged by his respect for its people, his sense of its past and his shamelessly romantic imagination. "When he walked through the woods and it was quiet, he tried to imagine the sound the old waves had made"—a sound 300 million years old, made by the ancient ocean that covered this basin and supported thousands of varieties of sharks that lived in its warm waters. It's a sound that his competition, an older man who buys up huge tracks of land, hires others to prospect and dreams of building a company like a Shell or a Phillips, will never know. More the solitary idealist, an Adam in the wilderness, Wallis has a different passion.

> He flew: long, lazy circles over towns and woods, flying low and slow: peeling an apple as he flew, sometimes. Looking for the thing, the things no one else knew to look for yet, though he knew they would find it, and rip it into shreds. He considered falling in love.

The narrator of **"The Sky, the Stars, the Wilderness"** doesn't consider falling in love; she has already found it with her family and the land they own in west Texas: "a 10,000-acre oasis of forest and woodland, with mountains full of blooming mountain laurel and cliffs bearing petroglyphs from 500 years ago—rock etchings of Spaniards with guns and swords and iron helmets, horses and banners—but civilization passed through like only a thin breeze."

Middle-aged now, she lives with the memories of growing up with her father; grandfather; an old friend, Chubb; and Omar, her younger brother. Mother died when she was a girl and is buried on a bluff above the Nuece River beneath an oak that stood when Cabeza de Vaca crossed the land.

History, as timeless as the migrations of birds, as irrevocable as conquistadors and republicans, as colloquial as the broadcast of a baseball game, fills these pages in a slow, nearly hypnotic paean to a place that will assuredly evanesce. Since her mother's death, the narrator, who remains bravely nameless, almost transient herself, admits to her confusion. ". . . [B]eing torn in two directions by the richness of life, is what it felt like—the richness of the past, the promise of the future—and always wondering, How much of me is really me? What part has been sculpted by the land, and what part by my blood legacy, bloodline? What mysterious assemblage is created anew from those two intersections?"

In nothing less than time, she discovers her connections to this place, not the least of which are her memories: running with Omar at night down the ghostly white caliche road, past the dark sweet smelling cedars, past the ancient headstone, past Chubb's cabin with its light on and through the river, feeling with bare feet ancient wagon wheel ruts cut in the submerged stone. "There is no true fence, no stone wall, between the present and the past," she begins to understand. Her education, however, never slips into sentimentality; Bass never loses sight of its relevance. Anything that breaks with the past disrespects the future, a lesson that angrily drives the polemic of *Yaak* [*The Book of Yaak*] and is the heart and soul of **"The Sky"** [**"The Sky, the Stars, the Wilderness"**]. Here the villains are the Catfish Man and Predators Club: a man who drains the aquifer and ranchers who poison the eagles, actions that change the lives of the narrator and her family.

In this poignant meditation, Bass has carved a curious and meaningful niche for himself among nature writers. Though the world has irrevocably changed and degraded for the narrator, memory and hope—two parties for which Emerson had a unique fondness—rather than fostering bitterness and regret invoke love and respect. It is a picture of innocence surviving experience, perhaps as Judith will survive Trapper's snare. But even if the hunt is successful, the bridge to the wild transgressed, as these three stories prove possible, Bass is wise to remind us that everything pursued, whether in our dreams, our relationships or our backyards, develops a response appropriate to the pursuit.

Stare out at the Earth and sky at Yovimpa, try to comprehend this incomprehensible view and know that it will change—if not for reasons of history and time then for another that may give Bass pause. Sites close to Yovimpa and not far beyond are being eyed for their oil and gas reserves, perhaps giving us reason to cry and howl at the loss.

Rick Bass and Bonnie Lyons and Bill Oliver (interview date 1998)

SOURCE: Bass, Rick, and Bonnie Lyons and Bill Oliver. "Out of Boundaries." In *Passion and Craft: Conversations with Notable Writers,* edited by Bonnie Lyons and Bill Oliver, pp. 72-84. Chicago: University of Illinois Press, 1998.

[In the following interview, Bass recounts his literary influences, major themes in his fiction, and his first volume of short stories.]

A committed environmental activist, essayist, and fiction writer, Rick Bass has two reading audiences. To those primarily concerned with the natural world and the preservation of natural resources, Bass is the prolific, persuasive author of seven highly regarded nonfiction books: *The Deer Pasture* (1985), *Wild to the Heart* (1987), *Oil Notes* (1989), *Winter: Notes from Montana* (1991), *The Ninemile Wolves* (1992), *The Lost Grizzlies: A Search for Survivors in the Wilderness of Colorado* (1995), and *The Book of Yaak* (1997). For readers of fiction, he is most importantly the author of ***The Watch*** (1989), ***Platte River*** (1994), ***In the Loyal Mountains: Stories*** (1995), and ***The Sky, the Stars, and the Wilderness*** (1997). His stories have been described as "true and desperate and full of longing," as "weirdly lyrical," and as "complex, compelling, and expressed in a unique and powerful voice."

A petroleum geologist by education and an environmental activist by bent, Bass nine years ago left the oil business and most of humanity behind by moving to an area in the northwest corner of Montana called the Yaak. This was much more than a geographical change; Bass has called Montana "the state of my rebirth." When we interviewed him, Bass was living in a cabin on a dirt road near the "village" of Yaak itself, which consists of a mercantile (general store) and a saloon, The Dirty Shame.

His house was difficult to find, but when we finally tracked him down, Bass proved to be a remarkably direct interview subject. In the following comments, he often uses geological metaphors in talking about his stories and essays and in describing his attitudes toward nature.

[*Bonnie Lyons and Bill Oliver*]: *In* Oil Notes *you say, "There's a deceit in writing, you're trying to pull all the clever elements together and toss out the dull and round-edged ones." Is there more deceit in fiction than in essays?*

[Rick Bass]: When I write fiction I'm trying to see the characters so clearly there doesn't seem to be any question of it *being* fiction. I don't feel like there's any deceit in it. In nonfiction, I think I'm trying for more sleight of hand. It feels more technical to do a good job in nonfiction. When I'm writing the first draft of a story it feels less technical, more emotional. I'm watching for seams and fissures.

Seams and fissures?

If a story's going well, if I've got the force of it moving all in the same direction, then it's almost like water rushing down a canyon, or a culvert. More like a culvert, because it's contained all around and there's only one direction for it to go, where gravity is taking it. The

danger then is I have this mass of story, all going the same way, and it might become very predictable. So that's when I start looking for side cracks or seams, fissures, where I can get some of the story to go, to keep it from all rushing down that culvert to the bottom.

Are there times you can't find those fissures?

Sometimes I don't see any, or I don't make any. Those are real hard stories to work with. But with almost any story, even failed ones, I will later see where the fissures were and where I didn't have my head up enough to exploit them.

So you're resisting a kind of inevitability when you're writing? That is, you feel from the start where the story is going, but you don't want it to go there in a predictable way?

Yes, I can sense the shortest way for it to go, or I guess you could say the easiest way, and I have to fight that. I like that word "inevitability," it's a good way to put it. I'm looking for surprises as I tell a story. I've talked to other writers about this, and my favorite writers say that in their best stories they didn't have any idea they'd turn out the way they did. It's a good lesson, a hard lesson for me, not to plan a story ahead of time but just to gather what's important and start out on it.

Why is that a hard lesson for you?

My inclination is to try to control what I'm doing. Even to be talking about it like this is to assert a kind of self-conscious control over it. Later on I will really downplay everything I say here and the occupancy it took up in my mind.

Is that because you're afraid that talking about the writing process and its techniques will distract you from the storytelling itself?

Exactly. Shoot, the technical stuff is what editors are for. I like to get my first draft down, then deal with questions of plot and motivation. For me, there are two entirely different mindsets—creating the story and then fixing it. What we're talking about now feels like fixing the story.

As one who writes both essays and stories, how do you decide whether particular material will be treated in one form or the other?

The question of timeliness comes into it. If I feel it's not urgent for anybody to know it, if I'm writing primarily for myself and nobody else, I will think in terms of fiction. If, on the other hand, the subject bears a certain urgency, I tend to put it in nonfiction so people will be more inclined to act on it. I realize this way of thinking is flawed because great fiction can sometimes motivate people much more strongly than a piece of nonfiction. But I think it comes back to the question of urgency. If I'm going to issue a bulletin saying the woods are on fire, I'm not going to sit back and say, "In 1930 when he was seventeen years old Joe first began playing with matches."

Don't some ideas just naturally seem more appropriate to one form or the other—fiction or nonfiction? You don't always make a deliberate decision about it, do you?

I didn't used to, but recently I've been seeing things in double vision. I can see the same material handled either way. Since I'm more interested in writing fiction now, I'm trying to discipline myself to put the nonfiction away and save the best material for stories. I'm doing a lot of research on endangered species—wolves, grizzlies, caribou—and I'm seeing these things in terms of nonfiction, but I'm also trying to put some of the material away to write about later, more slowly and with less urgency, in fiction. I'm also doing research on J. Frank Dobie. My inclination is that it's a subject for nonfiction because he was a real person, but at the same time I can imagine a wonderful story about a character like him. I'm going to try as hard as I can to do the fiction first, even though I've got a lead for the Dobie piece in my mind and a theme and all sorts of facts for a nonfiction treatment. I'm trying to hold all that at bay.

How did you start writing professionally?

I wrote hunting and fishing articles just out of college, but I wasn't having much luck publishing them. I published several in a row and then the magazine stopped buying them because they were always the same: I went on a trip, I never killed a deer, I never caught a fish, I just looked around at mountains or felt the wind or something. They bought it a few times, then they said, "Look, you got to start killing stuff." I felt constricted by that formula, so I started looking to travel essays, then to fiction.

In Wild to the Heart, *you write, "If it's wild to your heart protect [it], focus on it." Is that how you feel about your writing? If so, what is the nature of its wildness?*

I certainly try to focus on it. By "it" I mean the stories and characters rather than my success or failure in the marketplace, the attention or lack of attention paid to my work, or the technique of it. When I write I want to preserve something that matters to me. That's how I feel about writing. It's something that can get away from you. A story is something that can be lost, just like natural resources. There's Hemingway's advice about storing up material or turning down the flame,

letting it get crusty with the barnacles of time. That's a fine idea, but I feel many people just let stories get away. They'll hold onto a story for years, then another story comes up and the first one never gets written. I'll listen to people tell me great stories that they mean to write. After two or three years, if they haven't done it, I'll say, "Can I write that story? I really want it." They'll say, "No, I'm going to write it." But finally I just wear them down. They realize they're never going to write it, so then I'll write it. When I do, it feels just like it was my own.

You say you prefer to disregard the attention or lack of attention paid to your writing. **The Watch** *got a great deal of notice. Was that a mixed blessing?*

It made me self-conscious. For about a year after it came out, I was looking at all the reviews and I got real aware of people watching what I was doing. I started to have trouble with the fiction. But I got it figured out. The way I did it was with a kind of belligerence. I constructed an anger or defiance about people reading my work—I didn't give a damn what they thought, good or bad. I held that attitude as a sort of callus for a couple years and finally it fell away. In its place, now I truly don't care if some people dislike my work, because I know that as long as I like it some others will, too. That sounds simple, but starting out it was not that simple for me. Everybody had to love my work or I thought it wasn't good enough. I'm pleased I got out of that trap as soon as I did.

How did you happen to turn to fiction writing?

I read *Legends of the Fall* by Jim Harrison. It's a collection of three novellas, and when I read the third one, *Legends of the Fall,* I thought, boy, this is what I need to be trying to do. It was a quantum leap for my enjoyment of fiction—some of the devices used, the mixture of language, and the force of the story. It has a sort of breathlessness about it that carries you along. It's a great, great novella.

Has Harrison continued to be an important influence on you?

Yes. Lately he's been influencing me with his reading capacity; he reads everything and retains it. His striving not to repeat himself also impresses me, and I would like to follow his example in that. His determination to enjoy life, not just to be a writer but to enjoy life in great quantities, has been a real inspiration. So I've learned and continue to learn from him.

Your fiction has been compared to Richard Ford's and Raymond Carver's. Do you see any similarities?

I see no similarities with Carver's stories, to my great regret, but I do see similarities with Ford's. I used to model a lot of stories after his *Rock Springs* collection.

It's a very powerful book. I remember the end of the title story, "Rock Springs," where the narrator asks the reader all these questions beginning, "Would you think . . ." I never heard of such a thing. We're always told it's bad to put rhetoric in a story. To put it at the *end* of a story, what kind of stunt is that? All of a sudden, five or six stories in a row, and he's ending them with questions. There was an opening of boundaries. Also, I like his roundabout way of telling a story, that air of relaxation mixed with immediacy. It's a fine tension, a fine ambivalence. That reflective tone can really get you in trouble, but you can also use it as a great tool with which to injure the reader, to get your point across.

"Injure" the reader?

Yeah, rough him up, bring him around to the truth. A lot of Ford's stories are bringing home unhappy truths which will make you more whole if you accept them. Sometimes the narrator grabs the reader by the collar at the end and says, "Did you ever think this, well, did you?"

In The Deer Pasture *you describe your father as a great storyteller. Does some of your interest in fiction come from him?*

Without a doubt. And my mother, too. She's a great observer. If somebody does something funny or there's some peculiar clash of personalities, she's going to notice that and she'll tell us about it when she gets home. My father will take something that's happened and he'll tell it in a way that's not quite the truth though you couldn't get him in a court of law. He takes something that needs telling and makes it larger and better. In different ways both my parents are a great help to my storytelling. When I go home there's always another story.

How is it, working on your nonfiction books with Elizabeth [his wife]? Did you meet her because she was your illustrator?

I knew her before I wrote the books. We've known each other for a long time. She's not only a good illustrator but a good editor. She's got excellent instincts. She either likes something or she doesn't, and if she doesn't, it's probably not good. She's a tough reader and that's the best editor to have. You know, it's great to have editors who can help structurally or with line editing, but the most important thing is to cut through all the nonsense and say this works or it doesn't.

So she's your first editor?

When I'm in trouble she is. If I know something is working, I'll just wait and surprise her with it when it comes out in a book or magazine. But if I'm in trouble, she's my first editor.

You say in Winter, *"The writing was more important than anything could ever be—which is sad, but the way it has to be." Why sad? Why the way it has to be?*

Writing is inevitable to me because that's what I do, it's what I am. It's in the definition, a writer writes. It's sad because there are so many other things I want to do. I wish I were compelled only to hike. I want to see every one of these peaks and side drainages and mountains and ridges. I want to know every tree in this valley and then the valley next to it and the one north of here, over in Canada where I don't have any maps. The days aren't long enough and I can't cover enough ground in the day, so that's sad. I'd like to read every book I own, it's very sad because I never will. A couple years ago I finally figured that out. Writing takes time from things I want to do. Every writer thinks, What if I didn't write? What if I didn't know there was such a thing as writing? Would I enjoy life more? Would I look at life differently? And of course you would, you would look at it with a cleaner, more innocent perspective. You wouldn't always be putting these double and triple spins on everything that comes to your eyes. You might be a little more rested. But this is a kind of self-pity. Whatever you do, if you do it fully, you're going to be running close to exhaustion all the time.

You say writing is inevitable because that's what you do. When you were working as a petroleum geologist, did that work also feel inevitable?

Not to the same degree. And it might have been something as simple as the fact that I did it in an office, more or less in daylight hours, and got regularly paid for it. When I was looking at the logs, moving my pencil across the maps, certainly I felt a kind of inevitability about catching the oil. It's the same as when we're talking about fiction being almost a kind of nonfiction—you believe in it, you see it so clearly. Mapping for oil had that same kind of inevitability. If I mapped it so that there was oil there on the map, then it was there. It was icing on the cake to drill and find out it actually was there. There were so many things I wanted to do, geology was probably borderline. If you're going to assign numbers to it, with writing being eight or nine, then everything else is fours and fives.

What might a ten be?

I don't know, I'd be dead.

But you leave open the possibility there's something you might be drawn to even more than writing?

I'm not looking for anything else. Maybe it's just something as simple as better writing. I think I have a fear of boundaries.

You come across in your essay as a happy person. Most of your fictional characters are much darker. Any ideas why?

I try to make the essays positive because I get tired of hearing the doom and gloom story of the environment and I know everybody else does, too. It's not going to change anything to say how bad things are; we know how bad they are. If you start droning on about increasing populations and present land-use practices, you turn into what Jim Harrison calls an "ecobore." So the only other tack I can think of is to try to celebrate what's good, help readers to treasure certain things, so they will say, "Yeah, it would kill me if that was ever gone." In fiction there's not that same pressure to celebrate the good.

Would you talk a little about the organization of **The Watch***?*

My editor for that book, Carol Smith, and I organized the stories for meaning and for development of attitudes, and also we paid attention to length, not wanting to put too much burden on the reader, because it's hard to read two or three long stories in a row. We didn't want successive stories with similar themes either. We wanted to have some diversity and also a cumulative effect that would lead toward the general theme of the book: time's passage and the acknowledgment of it, and the race to stay ahead of it or to hide out from it. The last story in the book, **"Redfish,"** does, I think, have a closed, resolute ending, more so than the other stories. I think the resolution of that story could speak for any of the others. Arranging the collection was like putting a puzzle together. It was fun. A lot easier than writing the stories.

Why did you use the title of "The Watch" as the title of the entire collection? Do you think it's the strongest story?

I don't know that it's the strongest, but it seemed good. I was originally going to call that story **"Field Events"** because everything seemed to be taking place either at the edge of the woods or out in a field or meadow. I was living in Mississippi among some meadows, and a lot of that imagery crept into the story. Anyway, when we were putting the collection together, Carol suggested **The Watch** and it suited me fine.

At the end of that story, Jesse's got a stopwatch and is timing himself on the bicycle. What about other watches or kinds of watching in the story?

Jesse has his little pocket watch, and that was a big part of it. But also Hollingsworth was standing out on the porch through much of the story watching for Jesse to come riding by. So "watching" becomes a metaphor for

loneliness. Jesse's also watching for Buzbee out there. The collection is going to be published in France and the title is driving the translator nutty, because there are all these different words in French that mean "pocket watch" or "to look out for" or "to look at." I think the one we're going to use is "to watch out for."

Doesn't "The Watch" suggest that freedom, as exemplified by Buzbee and as opposed by Hollingsworth, is the ultimate good?

Yes, and I'm most moved in that story by Buzbee's courage, his defiance. Would you rather be safe or happy? That's an old question. I'm doing this research on wolves. This federal biologist caught this old wolf who'd been suspected of killing some calves. The plan was to relocate the wolf where he wouldn't get into so much trouble, but he'd injured his foot in a trap and they didn't know if he could survive with the bad foot. If they kept him in a cage he'd get acclimated to humans and would be no good in the wild. So they let him go, and sure enough he starved to death. The biologist defended his decision rather eloquently, saying that, for the wolf, any period of survival in the wild is preferable to time spent in captivity. I think that's true.

Hollingsworth appears to represent all those debilitating forces that sap us of life, and not coincidentally, he's a big talker. Buzbee says about women, too, they "always wanted to talk," as if talk "could be used to keep something else away, something big and threatening." That echoes something you said in your essays, that actions are better than words. Isn't that a curious position for a writer to take? Logically extended, wouldn't it lead to silence?

For a couple hours a day you believe so strongly in your stories that they truly are actions, not words but actions. I'm not much on speaking, it's been abused so badly. It is so easy to lie when speaking aloud. It's much harder to lie when writing.

The opening sentences of the first two stories, "Mexico" and "Choteau," play off each other. In "Mexico": "Kirby's faithful. He's loyal: Kirby has fidelity. He has one wife, Tricia." And in "Choteau": "Galena Jim Ontz has two girlfriends and a key to Canada." Don't the opening sentences define Kirby and Jim as opposites, in a sense?

If you'd been editing these stories and mentioned that to me I would have gone nutty and never would have finished the collection. That's interesting what you say. But I really get paranoid about that sort of thing. I'll have to go back and look at that.

Why would that make you paranoid?

Well, I have the idea each story should be unique, a different mineral or gem, not different shapes of one mineral.

Of the stories in the collection, only **"The Watch"** *and* **"Wild Horses"** *are not in the first person. Why did you use third person for those?*

When I start a story in third person it's got something mythic or Biblical about it. With first person, it's like I'm down in the dirt just scratching the story out, trying to earn or create it. But the third-person stories simply are meant to be told. It's like that new age stuff, channeling.

At the end of **"Redfish"** *the narrator imagines his friend Kirby and him riding horses into the surf and he talks about the horses' fear "of going down under too heavy a load, and of all the things unseen, all the things below." Is that a metaphor for what all the characters in the stories fear?*

Yes. The stories tend to be about the characters' attempts to control whatever they're afraid of. Like Hollingsworth tried to control Jesse and Buzbee. But in **"Redfish"** Kirby and the narrator go get the horses and they start riding out into the water, further and further. It's dark and it's snowing but they keep going into the deeper water, into the Gulf, which opens up into infinity. Maybe that's why the story has more resolution, because the characters confront their fears instead of trying to put up a screen and block them out.

Three stories in the collection focus on Kirby and his friend, the unnamed first-person narrator. Are these stories autobiographical?

Yes, though I'm not the narrator. That's where the fiction comes in.

Since there are real-life sources for at least some of your characters, do you ever worry that the small number of people in this part of the country will prove a hindrance?

That's a good question, one that I asked myself when I first moved up here. But there are a lot of good characters in this vicinity. And here I'm speaking like a map guy. There's a greater density of good characters up here than anywhere else I've been. By "good characters" I mean people things happen to or who go out and make things happen, people who don't just accept life rushing at them. Interesting, lively people. I don't mean eccentric. They just feel *full*. They interest me.

You've called Montana "the state of my rebirth." Why?

It's like being a newborn when you come into a place about which you know nothing. It's an invigorating, almost giddy feeling.

Was it hard for you to make the decision to give up your career as a petroleum geologist and come out here?

No, it wasn't hard. It was hard work but it wasn't a hard decision. I mean, it was hard physical work and emotional work, saying, "Okay, I'm just going to write now. I'll do some geology but I probably won't make any money at it, being on my own." I had only published one story at the time. That part of it was hard, but the decision to try it was not hard. There was no decision at all. It just had to be done.

You suggest in your essays that happiness is within the individual's grasp. You write that "a state of mind, if you mold it right, is as real and durable as anything else capable of being retained in this world. Good things last longer than bad." That sounds a lot like Walden. *Is such an attitude on your part congenital or learned, or is it an expression of some kind of faith or philosophy?*

It feels to me like a learned attitude. In science there are theories about cell memory, and in weightlifting there's a theory: if your muscles have done a movement before, if they've lifted a certain weight or been a certain size, then they're going to "remember" that. If your muscles have reached certain boundaries, even if they get smaller or weaker later on, they'll be able to achieve that expansion again, and more easily than the first time. I think happiness is that same way. If you're unhappy and you work to be happy, then it doesn't matter if you become unhappy again because with effort you can be happy. If you've done it once, you can do it again. Maybe even a little easier. It just gets to be a habit. This is not to say happiness can ever be a constant state, but you can pursue it as a goal with more confidence, having achieved it before.

When you came to live here were you retreating from civilization, giving up on it?

Yes.

In Winter, *you say, "Decay in our nation is frustrating. We truly are becoming senile. I feel as if we are very near the end." Do you really feel that way?*

Well, at that point, I lost my resolve to celebrate. I mouthed off. But I do feel that way. Again, using the metaphor of boundaries and cell memory and muscle memory, I'd have to say we're losing our elasticity. We're becoming more crowded and therefore less tolerant of other people's space and other people's beliefs and values. It's ultimately a function of population— too many people in too small a space. I guess the definition of elasticity is movement, the ability to move in a certain space. We're getting old and brittle as a nation. We can't run as fast as we could and can't be as generous. I don't think people were meant to live as closely together as they do. We didn't evolve that way. You can plot population curves and in the mid-range, before the exponential climb that all populations take, things are normal. But when the curve starts to kick up, all the rules fall apart. They fall apart for bacteria and for rats, and I think they fall apart for people, too. We develop shorter tempers, shorter lives. If we are really doomed as a nation, and as a human race, I don't think that includes nature—only humans' place in the scheme of things. Nature will never end. If we fry from a nuclear war, some bacteria will survive and life will go on. But selfishly speaking, my primary concern is how people can survive in the world. And the way to do it is to keep things in the mid-range, keep the fluctuations from getting out of hand, from reaching highs and lows humans can't survive. Whether it's something as simple as air or water quality or something as complex as human sociology.

Do you love nature more than people?

These days that's probably closer to the truth than I would like to realize. I love my friends more than I love deer or elk, but I love the general condition of deer and elk more than I love the general condition of cities. So I guess my answer to your question depends on whether we're talking about the abstract or the specific.

Is your relationship to nature a spiritual one?

There's more country realism than Emersonian transcendentalism in it. But at the same time it *is* spiritual. I'm hesitant even to speak about it because I feel that only now am I being allowed to look at nature. I'm trying to learn more, if nature will have me. There's an incredible spirituality in these woods. When I go up into them the question is, will they have me or will they not have me? If I just relax, I see incredible things out here. Animals come up to me, bears wanting to play, deer and elk not the least bit afraid. Other times they'll run from me. I don't want to be like Emerson and say I know what's going on because I have a sense that would offend the spirituality I find here, that nature would turn its back on me. I'm cautious. I like to be in nature, and I figure when it's time to kick me out it will, and if it's time to take me apart it will.

Have you actually had wild animals wanting to play with you?

Yes, young bears. Coyotes and ravens, too. These are animals that folklore and history attribute spirits to—there's something to it. Those aren't just old wives' tales. Almost without fail science proves them. Sometimes I hike to some incredibly high spot that takes me all afternoon to get to and some storm will come blowing in and these ravens will be playing. They'll be diving and swooping at me and ripping right at the side of my head; they'll be spiraling around and showing off

because nobody can see it; there's nobody around except me and the ravens. I was on a hunt one time and a coyote came right up to me and sat down and looked at me. I had a gun, so how did he know I wasn't going to shoot him? I made these dog noises to him, and he just sat there watching me, and every now and then he walked to the left or the right. Finally I started talking to him. I said, "Hey, puppy," like I would to one of my dogs, and he turned and ran and was gone. When I get into the woods, amazing things happen, if I just take off and start walking, not knowing where I'm going, not having a plan. I feel very much like a guest up here.

In one of your essays you talk about a snake acting embarrassed. Do you think animals can be understood in such human terms, or were you just being whimsical?

No, I believe that. We say animals feel cold or hot, pleasure or discomfort. It's not that much more of a step to say they can feel embarrassed or can feel pride.

In your writing there's a special value placed on youth and the intensity of feeling that often accompanies it. In Oil Notes *you say, "You have to fight to stay young. Everybody, no exceptions, has to do that." One of the most admirable things about Galena Jim (**"Choteau"**) and Buzbee (**"The Watch"**) is that they retain energy, youthfulness, intensity of feeling. Is there no value, or at least are there no consolations, in aging?*

The important thing is vitality. Youth most often possesses vitality but it's not always directly proportionate. Many of the stories I write are about characters losing vitality or fighting not to lose it.

You've been working on a novel. Would you care to talk about it?

It's a long novel. What I first thought was the end of it turned out to be only the end of the first section. I've got over two thousand pages now. It's about a wolf biologist and her father who is this old eccentric geologist oil millionaire. And it's about her boyfriend who is a student of the old man. The narrator is a young man from the Texas hill country who comes up to Montana and learns about wolves from the biologist and then goes down to Houston and learns about oil and gas from the biologist's boyfriend and the old man. Then he goes off on his own and becomes a geologist. It's fun. I really like the characters a lot.

What other writing are you doing?

I'm doing a long, book-length essay called "The Afterlife," about this valley. It's nonfiction, though it's starting to turn into fiction. It deals with seasons and age and youth, what happens when you go into the woods and what is man's place between animals and the afterlife. I'm also working on the text for a photo book about the wildlife in the northern Rockies. I'm finishing up a book about wolves. I'm also doing short stories, a couple collections of novellas that are either finished or in stages of being finished. I'm doing a series of essays about hunting. I'm doing a collection of oral histories of old people in this valley. There are fourteen or fifteen things I'm working on.

How many hours a day do you write?

I used to write just two hours a day, but I write four hours now.

With all these projects, how do you decide which one to work on?

I used to try to get it lined up before I went to bed so I could work on it subconsciously while I slept, and then I'd get up and go with it. But that was too constraining. So in the morning when I wake up, I decide while I'm eating breakfast. I put in my four hours, then it's over—and I go hiking.

Rick Bass (essay date 1998)

SOURCE: Bass, Rick. "Why the Daily Writing of Fiction Matters." In *Why I Write: Thoughts on the Craft of Fiction,* edited by Will Blythe, pp. 74-83. Boston: Little, Brown and Company, 1998.

[*In the following essay, Bass asserts that fiction writing is important because it sharpens the perceptions and imagination of both the emotional and physical senses, and concludes that fiction has a healing effect on the world.*]

I live in a remote valley deep in the woods, and I must confess that when I go into town and encounter someone who asks where I live and what I do, for the longest time it was not entirely with pride that I would tell him or her I was a writer, and a thing I especially did not enjoy admitting was that I was a fiction writer. It seemed to me to be like answering, "Oh, I breathe," or "I'm a yawner," or "I look at air a lot." Hunch-shouldered over a one-dimensional sheet of paper, scowling and frowning at the patterns of ink, sometimes laughing, I might as well have answered, it seemed to me then, "I'm invisible" or "I don't do anything."

For a long time there was a shadow to my movements, and to my life, that asked, How real is this thing that I do? Writing was invisible and airy enough, vaporous an act as it was—one trafficked in ideas as one might traffic in smoke, or scent, or memory—but then even worse, it seemed, was the writing of fiction: invisible ideas about things that had never even happened. A layer of the invisible laid crossways on another layer of the invisible: a grid, a subworld, of nothing. The black hole into which one disappeared for three, four, five hours a day, where everything was within arm's reach and where it all moved very slowly. Even in those rare moments when the pen raced full tilt across the page, left to right, the hand took roughly ten to fifteen seconds to traverse that eight-inch span.

It's such a slow world down there—the invisible second basement below the invisible first basement—that when you emerge, blinking and pulse-stilled, later in the day, and walk up the path from your writing cabin to your real life in your real house, even the most mundane movements of the earth seem to split your mind with onrushing speed. Simple conversation, thought, numerical gymnastics, even a seemingly easy task such as making a phone call or peeling a potato—anything of the regular nature of the world conspires to race past you like a Roger Clemens fastball; you open your mouth to respond, you raise your hand, but by that point the world has moved again. The electric sight of a butterfly dancing over tall green grass causes your brow to furrow, and you watch it with a thing like exhaustion. Things were so slow and controlled just a few minutes ago, back in your writing! Very carefully, then, you begin to ease back into humanity. You walk carefully, as if on ice, disbelieving, perhaps, if your immersion or submersion has been deep enough, that this is the real world, or rather, that you have any business in it.

You make a conscious commitment to try to enjoy the physicality of that part of the day that's left. You can't help but think (even if only with your body, like a kind of echo) about the world you're trying to remake, or protect, or attack, or celebrate—the one you left behind. And when you have a good day, a good *physical* day, in that second part of the day, you sometimes feel like a traitor when you encounter joy or pleasure, or anything else deeply felt.

Which brings me, I think, to the reason writing is important (the reason any kind of art is important), and especially fiction writing. Art is an engagement of the senses; art sharpens the acuity with which emotions, and the other senses, are felt or imagined (and again, here, it challenges reality: What is the difference between feeling happy and really *being* happy? What is the difference between imagining you can taste something and really tasting it? A hair's breadth; a measurement less than the thickness of a dried work-skein of ink on paper).

The reading of good writing can engage the senses, can stretch them and keep them alive in the world—that is, sensate, rather than numb. Above all, in the reading of good fiction, the reader is called upon not only to believe in the thing being described, but to feel it deeply even while knowing full well on some conscious level going in that *it ain't true*—that it's made up. This is a double stretching, one that can require of the reader's mind an extraordinary suppleness. I think that almost everyone would posit that this is a good thing. To put it bluntly, I remember a football coach's arguing with some players whom he wanted to begin lifting weights. They were afraid of becoming muscle-bound and losing their speed and flexibility. The coach was desperate, spitting flecks of saliva in his inarticulate rage. Finally he understood how to explain it: "It'll make you faster and *more* flexible," he said. "You can stretch muscle. You can't stretch fat."

Fiction, by its very nature—being about a thing that, at best, at its most realistic, has not quite happened that way *yet*—is about a stretching and widening of borders, about options and possibilities of energy and character. Near a story's end, of course, as in life, all this possibility funnels into only one seemingly foregone, inescapable conclusion, but in the beginning, anything is possible—anything can be woven out of the elements at hand.

Good fiction, to my mind, breathes possibility, which is to say also that it breathes a kind of diversity, into every assemblage of characters, energies, and ideas. Reading it makes our minds supple, able to go two ways with equal strength rather than just one way: to consider the "real" but also equally to consider and feel the life of the story we're reading.

Fiction has always mattered because of its ability, its mandate, to reach across the borders and boundaries of reality, to give one the feeling, with each paragraph read, of new territory—but if you believe, as I do, that despite the stitchwork lacing of fiberoptic cables and such, the world is becoming more fragmented and more brittle, then anything that retains the ability to leap across those ever-encroaching and constricting borders is only going to become more important, particularly as we, the hungry, benumbed mass of us, continue swelling at the seams, funneling toward a conclusion that has felt inevitable all along: what my liberal friends call a loss of cultural diversity and what my right-wing friends (way right) call "one world order."

My beloved valley—the Yaak Valley of extreme northwestern Montana—is but a perfect example of and metaphor for every other finely crafted and specific system that is breaking down or being swallowed whole and assimilated, made general (and hence weak). The Yaak is the wildest place I've ever seen—ice-carved twelve thousand years ago into a magic little seam between the Pacific Northwest and the northern Rockies. It's a land a writer could love easily, a showcase of giant predators—grizzly bears, black bears, wolves, wol-

verines, golden eagles, coyotes, bald eagles, mountain lions, lynx, owls, bobcats—consuming big prey such as moose, deer, elk, even caribou.

Almost everything eats something else up here: so much tooth-and-claw, so much tension and remaking, so much chase and pursuit—so much like a writer stalking and following a story. Even the insects in the old-growth forests up here are largely carnivorous, consuming each other rather than preying on the forest itself, in which case they would devour the very thing that gives them nourishment.

If the forest in the Yaak, with its seething, *specific* characters, its incredible richness of diversity, and hence possibility, is so very much like the mind of a fiction writer, then understand, too, that the politics and human influences on the valley, the corporate designs on it, are also so very much like the mind of generalized, homogeneous, world-merge society. You do not need to be a scientist—or a reader or writer of fiction—to take a walk in the Yaak and know that, beautiful and mysterious though it is (seething with mosquitoes and black flies and steamy summer rain), the forest stands at the edge of some kind of loss.

Giant square and rectangular and triangular clearcuts are carved out of the valley yearly, stamped onto the sides of the steep mountains, baking and drying to arid lifeless moonscapes, on land that was previously a rich, diverse jungle. Roads rip through these old, secret corridors, old, secret paths of wolves and grizzlies, bringing light and heat into a place that was previously cool and dark.

Everything in the Yaak is being cut off from every other thing. The roads and clearcuts reduce the living, pulsing whole into a series of isolated, machinelike parts. William Kittredge has said, "As we destroy that which is natural, we eat ourselves alive."

In the face of such loss, such pain, one can enter shock. Numbness becomes a defensive mechanism, as does denial.

Fiction can be like a salve or balm to reverse this encrustation. Like sweating on a good hike, or building a stone wall, it can reengage the senses. It can reconnect isolated patches, islands of dulling senses and diminishing imagination, diminishing possibilities.

The other day, I was in my cabin working on fiction through a long green summer morning. Earlier a lion had caught a fawn, and the fawn's bleats had shaken me, as had, when I got up and went out to investigate, the sight of the lion leaping up from its hiding spot in the willows and running away. After that, it was a slow day for me, one in which I had trouble focusing. I've been using mostly analogies of lateral movement in discussing the travels on which fiction takes you, as if it were some horizontal surface along which you moved when going from the physical to the imagined; but I think it can also be described as travel along a vertical path. It often feels as if you were descending from the rock world, the real world, into the imagined one; and on a good day as if you could slip down into that chute, that shaft, into the below-place, easy as pie, like some subaqueous diver weighted with lead ankle wraps, or like some scientist suited up in an iron bathysphere: a quick descent, a gentle bump on the bottom, and you're there, and you can begin writing. Other days, though, it is as if you were full of air and could not sink beneath the surface—and certainly, on that day I heard the squawling and got up from my desk and walked out and flushed the lion up from out of those willows, the day turned raggedly (though wonderfully) into one of those days on which there can be no escape from the deep physical, no journeying across that gap into the deeply imagined. It was perhaps like being caught in a leghold trap.

I kept trying—working on a sentence, scratching it out. Trying it from another angle, scratching it out.

It was like a joke. My cabin's right at the edge of a vivid green marsh, full of life and rot. A south summer wind was blowing hard, sweeping laterally across the marsh, flattening the tall grass and slamming mountain-scent in through the open screened windows as I tried to descend, still juiced from the lion and juiced, too, now, from this, the incredible gusting wind, and the scents it brought, and all that green, green waving light. A wall of thundercloud came moving up the valley, rising like some wave larger than anything seen at sea, and it rolled in over the marsh and brought hail and then slashing rain, a drumming, shouting sound against my tin roof, deepening, in all that moisture, the smells of the marsh, crushing flowers, releasing the scent of wild strawberries after the sun came back out; and I had to just sit there, pen in hand, and float on the surface, unable even to get my head beneath the water.

Is there a story—are there stories—so important to tell that you could descend beneath this fury, such a day's *tempest,* find them, and deliver them to the reader? *Yes*; I believe there are.

Are such stories as real as the storm-lash itself—those precious few stories? *Yes. Or maybe. Yes.*

And then the kicker is this: in passing from the real to the imagined, in following that trail, you learn that both sides have a little of the other in each, that there are elements of the imagined inside your experience of the "real" world—rock, bone, wood, ice—and elements of the real—not the metaphorical, but the actual thing it-self—inside stories and tales and dreams. You write a sentence about a hawk's swooping on a swallow and have no sooner finished it and looked up than you see feathers falling from the sky.

But still, for the most part, each resides in its own country: the real and the imagined; the actual and the possible. And it's important to keep the path, the trail, between the two open; important to keep the brush at least somewhat beaten back, to allow relative ease of passage between the two. Which brings us finally to the notion of why the daily doing of it is important—the writing of fiction, if that's what you do, and to a lesser extent, the reading of it. You've got to keep the grass worn down between the two worlds, or you'll get lost as shit; and sometimes you get a little disoriented, even with daily passages and explorations of the two further territories. You can't help but remember what Faulkner is alleged to have said when asked whether he wrote daily or only when the inspiration hit him. It's said he replied that he wrote only when the inspiration came, but that he made sure it came every morning at ten o'clock sharp when he sat down at his desk.

Another of these kinds of smart sayings I remember is one in which some prolific writer was asked how he'd managed to publish so many books. He said that it was quite easy: a page a day equaled a book a year. I've been working on my first novel for over twelve years now, and such statements give me encouragement and remind me that it's not just books that are important but also the sentences within them. It should be an obvious realization, but its implications become clear only when you do the math. The present draft of my novel is about 1,400 pages, which parses out to approximately one paragraph a day over those twelve years. The novel is, of course (I hope), nothing so boring as one paragraph from each day of my life over that twelve-year span, but rather a paragraph per day of a parallel and imagined life—which, after a dozen years of daily entering into and exiting from it, can make a writer increasingly a little goofy and also a bit tired, as if he or she were working one long stretch of double overtime, or had two families, or two lives.

We write fiction, I think, for very nearly the same reasons that we read it: to sharpen our senses and to regenerate those dead or dying places and parts within us where the imagination has been lost or is trying to be lost. Pine trees lose their needles every three years, and bears enter the earth, the dream-world, and float in sleep for five or six months at a time, but we humans are fragile and almost hairless, shivering on the earth, and our cells are dying and being reborn daily; we must eat often, and sleep nightly, pulled out each day by the sun. Almost all of our rhythms are compressed into parameters of one single earth's rotation. It is the rhythm into which we have evolved; it fits our bodies, physically, and it fits our minds and our imaginations. We can accumulate the days and their imaginings and then craft and create things beyond a day's work, but the days are our basic building blocks—a day's work is like a paragraph. To leave too many gaps in the thing being crafted or imagined, to work too erratically, is to run the risk, I'd think, of weakening with gaps and absences of rhythm the foundation and structure of the thing one is attempting to make real, or attempting to make be felt as deeply as if it *were* real.

That famous advice of Hemingway's is repeated often, about how a writer should leave a day's work slightly unfinished and at a point where he or she knows something of what will be in the next paragraph, to help facilitate the ease with which the rhythm may be resumed the next day. The descent of the bathysphere, vertically, or the morning trek into the woods, horizontally. The passage from here to there. The practice of staying supple rather than becoming brittle.

The daily doing of it is nothing less than a way to rage against constriction and entrapment, fragmentation and isolation, the poisonous seeds of our monstrous success in terms of our biomass and our effect upon the world, but at this cost: the erosion of the individual, the erosion of the specialist, the unique, the crafted.

The stories we tell in fiction—stories of warning or celebration, stories of illustrative possibility—are important. When the shit really hits the fan for a civilization, artists can become more important than ever, in helping to bend a culture back to another direction, away from the impending and onrushing brick wall.

I believe this. I believe that by crossing the path back and forth enough times, as if weaving something, fiction can become as real as iron or wood; that it can rust, rot, or burn; that it can nurture and nourish, or inflame. I believe that it can decide actions and shape movements, sculpt us more securely or intelligently (as well as more passionately) into the world, just as the continents on whose backs we are riding sculpt our cities, towns, and cultures.

I believe fiction can heal things, and I think we would all agree, now more than ever, that we can use some healing, and that we need it daily.

J. P. Steed (essay date fall 2000)

SOURCE: Steed, J. P. "Bass's 'Fires' and 'Elk.'" *Explicator* 59, no. 1 (fall 2000): 54-6.

[In the following essay, Steed discusses the importance of the biblical mythos of fire to Bass's short stories "Fires" and "Elk."]

In Judeo-Christian mythology, fire is associated with divinity and, more specifically, with the simultaneous acts of destruction and creation, or "renewal." There is the pillar of fire leading the Israelites out of Egypt (Exodus 13.21), which is expressly personified and identified as "the Lord"; it is associated with renewal in that it is the means by which the Israelites are saved, or led out of the wilderness. And there is Isaiah's use of fire when he says, "the fire devoureth the stubble, and the flame consumeth the chaff" (5.24). Such personification can be seen as further association with a form of divinity, and although destruction is in the foreground here, the association of fire with renewal is implied by the metaphor, for the burning of stubble by the harvester is more pointedly an act of regeneration, because the ash from the stubble and chaff fertilizes new growth.

Rick Bass's **"Fires,"** from *In the Loyal Mountains* (1995), is a story about renewal that uses the mythos of fire to inform its meaning. The story takes place throughout the summer months, while the forest service is burning trees they have cut on the slopes of the mountains, prior to planting seedlings. When Glenda, near the end of the story, comes to say good-bye to the narrator, she sets fire to his field and the two take refuge in the lake, surrounded by the fire, as Glenda says over and over, "Please, love" (50).

Without the mythos of fire, the story may seem to be about loss. Glenda's plea takes on a mournful tone, and as the fire burns the narrator holds her tightly in the water and tells the reader, "I thought about luck and about chance. I thought about fears, all the different ones, and the things that could make a person run" (50). Eventually the grass fire burns out and Glenda gets out of the lake and runs away. The narrator watches as "[h]er feet raised puffs of dust in the road" (50).

But the presence of fire (and Bass's emphasis on it in the title of the story) signifies renewal, not loss. That Bass is familiar with fire as both destroyer and creator is clear. The narrator comments on the fact that the soil in these mountains is "rich from all the many fires" (37), and the fires set by the forest service recall Isaiah's burning the stubble. But clearly it is the fire set by Glenda that is most significant. Early in the story, the narrator tells us, "I haven't lived with a woman for a long time. Whenever one does move in with me, it feels as if I've tricked her, caught her in a trap, as if the gate has been closed behind her, and she doesn't yet realize it" (38). Taking this into consideration, we might read Glenda's fire as signifying the destruction of this pattern of failed relationships—a destruction of the narrator's old life—and thus the creation of a new, potentially more successful one. Glenda and the narrator do not end up together, but although Glenda runs away, their relationship destroys the narrator's old pattern.

Also, with the theme of fire informing the way we read Glenda's plea, "Please, love" takes on a new tone, a new meaning. Before, it might have been read as mournful, as signifying loss, with "love" read as an epithet for the narrator, and what is being requested remaining unknown or unarticulated—in effect, lost. But "love" is not capitalized, and the reader realizes that it is the verb itself that Glenda is requesting: As the catalyst for change and the minister of renewal, she is pleading with the narrator to put an end to his old life and to, from this point on, "[p]lease, love."

The fact that the narrator describes Glenda as leaning back on a shelf of ice and spreading her arms "as if she were resting on a cross" (42) only substantiates the reading of Glenda as savior or redeemer. As a Christ-figure, Glenda then sets a fire that is associated simultaneously with divinity and renewal.

In the short story **"Elk,"** one of Bass's newer stories, the biblical mythos of fire informs the reading in a similar fashion. Two men canoe "across the Yaak River and [go] into the wilderness" (80). They shoot an elk and the rest of the story is about their journey home: packing the quartered elk on their backs through the snow, lighting dead trees on fire to prevent hypothermia and frostbite. Like Glenda, Matthew in **"Elk"** is the "savior." It is Matthew to whom the narrator turns for guidance on the hunt, and it is Matthew who lights the first tree on fire, saving the narrator from freezing to death. At one point the narrator remarks that Matthew "seemed to have a fire and a hardness in him" (81), suggesting that Matthew himself is fire personified. Because Matthew is the Christ-figure, fire is thus again associated with divinity and renewal.

Bass associates fire with renewal in other ways: For example, when the men kill the elk, they build a fire near which they can clean and skin the animal, and the narrator describes how "the orange light danced against the elk's hide and against his antlers, making it seem as if he had come back to life" (80). Fire here is associated with the animating force—that which can make the dead live again. The most significant use of fire in **"Elk,"** as in the story **"Fires,"** occurs at the end, when the dead trees are burned to give life to the narrator. Fire is destroyer and creator, making life out of death. Perhaps most significant, though, is that the association with divinity—and the allusion specifically to the biblical myth—is re-emphasized as the two men go from one dead tree to the next, lighting each on fire, until they are safely home: These burning trees, still standing upright, recall the pillar of fire that leads the Israelites out of the wilderness. The narrator comments on the "crooked, wandering path" of burnt trees (82), recalling the wanderings of the Israelites. The story is in fact about the journey out of the wilderness, because the men cross into the wilderness and shoot their elk by paragraph three. When the men reach civilization and the bar, it is the end of their journey. They have reached a sort of "promised land," and the narrator, who before was not competent enough to get an elk on his own, who "knew next to nothing" (80), has been redeemed from his ignorance.

Works Cited

Bass, Rick. *In the Loyal Mountains.* New York: Houghton, 1995.

———. "Elk." *New Yorker* 1 Dec. 1997: 80-83.

Robert H. Brinkmeyer, Jr. (essay date 2000)

SOURCE: Brinkmeyer, Robert H., Jr. "Regeneration through Community." In *Remapping Southern Literature: Contemporary Southern Writers and the West*, pp. 66-105. Athens, Ga.: University of Georgia Press, 2000.

[*In the following excerpt, Brinkmeyer discusses Bass along with several other Southern writers who have written stories that take place in the American West and utilize narratives which begin with their characters' flight from the South, and end with the creation of a sense of community that resolves personal and interpersonal conflicts.*]

Recent Southern writers who write about the contemporary West represent a wide cross section of Southern fiction. Despite their diverse styles and interests, almost all of these authors utilize and revise the American myth of flight westward toward freedom. Driving the narrative in almost all of their work is the dream of stepping free from the confining nets of culture and of starting over with the past left tidily behind. Almost all of these works, in the end, make it clear that this dream is indeed just that—a dream, and one that taken to its extreme becomes a nightmare, calling to mind Bernard DeVoto's observation, as restated by Wallace Stegner, "that the only true individualists in the West had wound up on one end of a rope whose other end was in the hands of a bunch of cooperators."[1] A number of the works explicitly explore the terrifying manifestations that the quest for radical freedom can take. . . . . Even when the lesson is not so dramatic, the message in these works remains clear: the desire for radical individual freedom leads down dangerous and self-destructive paths. For all their apparent turning from the traditional Southern ideals of place and continuity, Southerners writing about the contemporary West in the end embrace something very close to those very ideals, even if the place where their characters finally settle is often far from Dixie.

Structuring almost all of these works is a tension between the desire to bolt for freedom, a centrifugal force flying outward, and the desire to settle in a community, a centripetal force pulling inward. If most of these works begin with a straight line heading west, the tension between these two forces characteristically pulls that line back into a circle, the two forces now taut and balanced around a center point of home and community. The completed circle represents not enclosure but balance—balance between freedom and responsibility, conscience and selfishness, remembering and forgetting. And so, as much as these works center on flight and escape, they end up being most fundamentally about settling in and establishing communities. Not that the flights westward are meaningless; they are almost always necessary for breaking away from rigid and confining lives, but in almost every case they are finally abandoned for a life in place, not space.

. . . . .

Rick Bass, the contemporary Southern writer who has most enthusiastically embraced the wilderness as a guiding force in life and art, is much more positive than Betts and Offutt about the value of individual freedom. In the end, though, he too embraces a circling back, a balance between home and solitude, responsibility and freedom. For Bass, moving west is a stepping free in every sense of the word, a move toward independence and a commitment to live by the elemental wildness embedded within us all. As suggested by the title of his collection of autobiographical essays, *Wild to the Heart* (1987), Bass believes that all people carry within them a fundamental wildness—a spirit of joy, wonder, and hope that mirrors the rhythms of the natural world and that is being crushed by the demands and routines of everyday contemporary life. *Wild to the Heart* chronicles Bass's efforts to keep that wildness vital. Although he feels most alive when he is camping in the Utah mountains, Bass eventually comes to see that wildness and freedom depend more on vision than on location. "If you focus on the right things, and ignore the others," Bass writes, "you can find wildness and freedom anywhere."[2] Armed with this Weltyesque knowledge of sight and insight, Bass makes a stirring call for others to embrace and nurture the wilderness of their interior lives: "If it's wild to your own heart, protect it. Preserve it. Love it. And fight for it, and dedicate yourself to it, whether it's a mountain range, your wife, your husband, or even (heaven forbid) your job. It doesn't matter if it's wild to anyone else: if it's what makes your heart sing, if it's what makes your days soar like a hawk in the summertime, then focus on it. Because for sure, it's wild, and if it's wild, it'll mean you're still free. No matter where you are" (*WH* [*Wild to the Heart*] 158).

Although here downplaying place in his celebration of vision, Bass in his later works celebrates a particular place—the wilderness West—as imperative for him to maintain his joy and freedom. Vision and focus are of course still important, but the West, specifically Montana's Yaak Valley, nourishes and grounds the wholeness and insight Bass seeks. In *Winter: Notes from Montana* (1991), Bass describes himself and his wife, Elizabeth, as modern-day pioneers, made world-weary by the routines of modern life, gripped by the dream of renewing themselves in the West. Merely getting in the car to drive west makes Bass feel "freer and fresher and more daring, more hopeful than I can ever remember feeling."[3]

Later, when Elizabeth arrives, Bass declares the break with the past complete. "All the rest of our old life fell away into the past," he writes, adding that "it was intoxicating to have nothing behind us anymore, and to have everything ahead of us" (*W* [*Winter: Notes from Montana*] 15). In a hopeful and unironic dismissal of the past, rare in Southern writing, Bass here wholeheartedly embraces the American dream of leaving history behind, of fleeing west into a new world of possibility and potentiality. It is the dream that, as Bass notes in *The Book of Yaak* (1996), "seems to be the genetic predisposition in our country's blood—the handwriting of it telling us to move across the country from right to left, always farther from some echo of England, perhaps, or farther from everything."[4]

When Bass first drives into Montana's Purcell Mountains, he says that it was like "wading into cold water on a fall day" (*W* 7). Here and elsewhere, Bass characterizes moving to the West as a bracing immersion in a frigid lake or stream, a shocking bodily awakening from the enervating life left behind in modern society. Bass typically depicts modern urban life in terms of incarceration, people locked away in "high-rise jails" and ensnared in smothering routines.[5] "Sometimes I feel," the narrator of Bass's story **"Swamp Boy"** says, "as if I've become so entombed that I have *become* the giant building in which I work—that it is my shell, my exoskeleton, like the seashell in which a fiddler crab lives, hauling the stiff burden of it around for the rest of his days" (*ILM* [*In the Loyal Mountains*] 27-28). While Bass has little good to say about modern life in any region, he finds that life in the South is particularly grim, since not only has the region embraced New South corporatism and boosterism but it also has remained shackled by an overwhelming sense of history. "Nothing is forgotten," the narrator of Bass's short story **"Mississippi"** comments, characterizing Southern history's stranglehold upon the region.[6]

So strong is history's grip that Bass suggests that history even permeates the South's natural world. The narrator of **"Government Bears"** notes the lingering presence of the Civil War in Southern woods:

> I don't care if it was a hundred and twenty years ago, these things still last and that is really no time at all, not for a real war like that one, with screaming and pain. The trees absorb the echoes of the screams and cries and humiliations. Their bark is only an inch thick between the time then and now: the distance between your thumb and forefinger. The sun beating down on us now saw the flames and troops' campfires then, and in fact the warmth from those flames is still not entirely through traveling to the sun. The fear of the women: you can still feel it, in places where it was strong.
>
> (*TW* [*The Watch*] 172-73)

In contrast to the Southern woods, Bass conceives the Western wilderness as being free from history, a point underscored in his conceptualization of his move to Montana as a crossing from the historical (modernity and linear time) into the natural (nature and lunar cycles). In this regard, Bass's image of plunging into frigid water implies not only the cleansing that comes in moving West—to enter the wilderness is to wash off the grime of civilization, bodily as well as spiritually—but also the invigoration of being freed from the burden of history.

Immersion also suggests, even more significantly, regeneration. For Bass, moving to the West involves the shedding of the burdensome and confining shell of modern identity. As he puts it in *Winter*: "I felt like I'd wanted my entire life to peel off my city ways, city life, and get into the woods—molting, like an insect or a snake (160). To live in the Western wilderness is to embrace humanity's "natural" state of being; it is to reorient one's life according to the cycles of the natural world, what Bass calls "the blood-rhythms of wilderness" (*BY* [*The Book of Yaak*] 13). Masked and repressed by modern culture, these rhythms live deep within the hearts of humanity, ready to be drawn out and nurtured. Early in *The Book of Yaak*, Bass asks "is it too much to imagine that the pulsings of our blood, and our emotions, follow the rough profile of the days of light in this valley?" (3). He goes on to describe how his body has been slowing adapting to the wilderness patterns: "My blood began to learn new rhythms. My body became increasingly fluent in the language of cycles. . . . Small cycles radiated into larger ones. I kept following them—noticing different ones each day—and continue to." Bass comes to realize these reorientations are fitting him to the wilderness, giving him his place. He is, he notes, "being reshaped and refashioned, to better fit it in spirit and desire" (*BY* 5-6).

Bass elsewhere depicts these transformations in terms of a positively configured devolution, a descent that by his yardstick is actually an ascent—a far cry from the

bestiality into which characters in Cormac McCarthy's work frequently devolve—toward the primal state of the animal. "I'm falling away from the human race," Bass writes in *Winter*. "I don't mean to sound churlish—but I'm liking it. It frightens me a little to recognize how much I like it. It's as if you'd looked down at your hand and seen the beginnings of fur. It's not as bad as you might think" (*W* 73). In *The Book of Yaak* he experiences an initial uneasiness about his growing adaptation to the wilderness, feeling himself "a misanthrope, turning back and away from the human race." "I was more ape than man," he writes. "I had shaken off old human loyalties." After a time, however, the uneasiness gives way to joyful acceptance, since "the truth is the truth, and after a while it didn't matter" (*BY* 21). At the end of *Winter* Bass is at his most definitive regarding his transformations: "I admire the weasels, the rabbits, and the other wild creatures that can change with the seasons, that can change almost overnight. It's taken me a long time to change completely—thirty years—but now I've changed. I don't have any interest in turning back. I won't be leaving this valley" (*W* 162).

Bass's falling away from the human, of course, does not carry him entirely into the animal realm—animals do not embark on quests to understand themselves, nor do they write books. Moreover, in the Montana woods Bass does not live alone, without human connection; he is there with Elizabeth and their two sons—and his home is clearly his gravitational center. Less the misanthrope than the family man, Bass in his efforts at psychological wholeness resembles Chris Offutt in *The Same River Twice*: both seek to balance the urge toward wilderness freedom with the pull toward home. Like Offutt's, Bass's solitary walks into the woods are not flights from but lessons in community. Bass sees modern life as a "lost-gyroscopic tumble" (*BY* xv) of greed and rapacity, with the wilderness as a counterforce of stability, a place of "unrelenting order and complexity, unrelenting grace" (*BY* 181). Rather than seeing the natural world as a bloody Darwinian battlefield, which is what modern corporate society has become, Bass sees it as the model of the self-supporting community by which he structures his own life. A triple-trunked larch tree, standing only with the help of its neighbors, becomes for Bass the image of nature's community: "Trees of different species formed a circle around it—fir, aspen, lodgepole, even cedar. Their branches, as it was growing, must have helped to shelter and stabilize it, hold it up, as though they were friends, or at the very least—and in the sense of the world that I think we must turn to the woods to relearn—like community" (*BY* 181).

The issues that Bass foregrounds in his nonfiction about living in the West—particularly matters involving self-renewal and regeneration—profoundly shape his fiction. Bass's stories characteristically explore the conflicting urges toward settling down in a community and lighting out into a space of individual freedom. Although Bass typically valorizes the compulsion to break through the nets of conformity and standardization, to move psychologically if not literally to the West, he makes it clear that both compulsions at their extremes push one toward self-destruction: living within a community, one can become rigid and repressed; living with complete individual freedom, one can become isolated and misanthropic.

Those characters in Bass's fiction who take flight from confinement—usually manifested in a smothering marriage or relationship—typically enjoy a life of unfettered freedom for only so long. After being alone for a while, they usually find themselves drawn back toward others, sometimes into new relationships, sometimes to the very situation from which they bolted. In **"The Myth of Bears,"** for instance, Judith flees into the wilderness to escape her husband, Trapper, only to realize her need to feel connected to Trapper even as she flees him. As much as she likes to be on the run, she realizes that she enjoys her freedom only when she knows that Trapper is pursuing her. "It's terrible without the thought of him out there chasing her, hunting her," the narrator reports her thinking. "It's horrible. There's too much space."[7] After Trapper eventually catches up with Judith, they return to home together, quickly settling into their old routines. At the end, Judith remains caught between her conflicting pulls of settling in and escaping, though at least for now the tension is no longer so wrenching as to be destructive. "She feels cut in half," the narrator observes, "but strangely, there is no pain" (*SSW* [*The Sky, the Stars, the Wilderness*] 45). The challenge facing characters such as Judith is to find a way to live independently—to feel free—while at the same time being involved with another person and/or other people. Negotiating this space between freedom and confinement—his psychological frontier—is the task with which most of Bass's characters struggle.

Truly lost are those characters in Bass's fiction who do not respond to the challenge to integrate freedom within community. They remain paralyzed, frozen in place by the security and comfort of inertia. Not only destructive to themselves, they frequently seek to hold back others, psychologically, if not literally, in their little worlds. Hollingsworth, for instance, in **"The Watch"** ends up chaining his father to the porch of their home to keep the old man from taking off to live in a community of runaways deep in the swamp. Some characters, like Hollingsworth, never come to understand the destruction they inflict as they strive to keep things fixed and unchanging. Others come to see their failings, like Har-

ley in **"Platte River,"** who in the end understands that he has always been constrained by the past, that he has never been able to let anything go or to live without restraint. Living as he has, he sees, has turned him "into a fucking *crustacean*," burdened and burdensome.[8] At the story's end, he stands at the Pacific coast and feels for the first time the urge to take flight, imagining the joyous possibilities of hopping aboard an outbound ship and riding it to wherever it is going. It is just such a freedom that Bass everywhere celebrates; it is the joyful wildness buried deep within humanity, the wildness that is nowhere more outwardly manifested than in Bass's beloved Montana wilderness, the wilderness that he, in his role as environmental activist, is working tirelessly to save.

Richard Ford's Montana has little of the joy that Rick Bass's does. Although sharing with Bass a poignant awareness of the need for human connection, Ford depicts a West that is the inverse of Bass's, a negative of his photograph. For the most part Ford's West is cheerless and enervating, less a place of new beginnings and rebirth than of boredom and gloom. Most of his stories take place either in late fall, with winter looming, or in the dead of winter; there is a sense of winding down toward death or, even more depressingly, of living a death-in-life. Ford's West might be encapsulated in the opening of his short story "Great Falls": "This is not a happy story. I warn you."[9]

Notes

1. See Stegner, "Thoughts in a Dry Land," in *Where the Bluebird Sings,* 50.

2. Rick Bass, "River People," in *Wild to the Heart* (New York: W. W. Norton, 1987), 143. All subsequent citations from essays in this collection, hereafter *WH,* are documented within the text.

3. Rick Bass, *Winter: Notes from Montana* (Boston: Houghton Mifflin/Seymour Lawrence, 1991), 7. All subsequent citations from this work, hereafter *W,* are documented within the text.

4. Rick Bass, *The Book of Yaak* (Boston: Houghton Mifflin, 1996), 2. All subsequent citations from this work, hereafter *BY,* are documented within the text.

5. Rick Bass, "The Wait," in *In the Loyal Mountains* (Boston: Houghton Mifflin, 1995), 114. All subsequent citations from stories in this collection, hereafter *ILM,* are documented within the text.

6. Rick Bass, "Mississippi," in *The Watch: Stories* (New York: W. W. Norton, 1989), 126. All subsequent citations from stories in this collection, hereafter *TW,* are documented within the text.

7. Rick Bass, "The Myth of Bears," in *The Sky, the Stars, the Wilderness* (Boston: Houghton Mifflin, 1997), 33. All subsequent citations from stories in this collection, hereafter *SSW*, are documented within the text.

8. Rick Bass, "Platte River," in *Platte River* (Boston: Houghton Mifflin/Seymour Lawrence, 1994), 140.

9. Richard Ford, "Great Falls," in *Rock Springs: Stories* (New York: Atlantic Monthly Press, 1987), 29. All subsequent citations from stories in this collection, hereafter *RS,* are documented within the text.

Donna Seaman (review date 1 May 2001)

SOURCE: Seaman, Donna. Review of *The Hermit's Story,* by Rick Bass. *Booklist* 98, no. 17 (1 May 2001): 1443.

[*In the following review, Seaman comments that the stories in* The Hermit's Story *are among the best Bass has written.*]

Bass, a passionate, versatile, and increasingly lauded author acutely attuned to the wild and our conflicted relationship with nature, is especially gifted as a short story writer. His newest collection [*The Hermit's Story,*] is his most pristine, tender, and transporting yet. Bass uses simple, solid language, building sentences that preserve breathing space around each word like a stacked stonewall reveals the contours of each stone. Beautiful in their magical imagery, dramatic in their situations, and exquisitely poignant in their insights, these stories of awe and loss are quite astonishing in their mythic use of place and the elements of earth, air, fire, and water. In **"Swans,"** a woman lights fires along the shore of a freezing pond to warm the five swans living there, while the once robust fire in her aging mate's mind slowly turns to ash. In the title story, a woman, a man, and a half-dozen hunting dogs lost in a blizzard find miraculous shelter beneath what they feared was the frozen surface of a deep lake. Bass evinces a fascination with vision and its diminishment and how the world is transformed when sight is regained. He portrays a man suffering from a detached retina, a fireman who experiences a strange form of tunnel vision while surrounded by flames, and a crazy pair of lovers who descend naked into an abandoned mine, exchanging the incandescence of the sun for utter darkness. Marriage, too, begins in radiance but is often driven into the dark underworld as love flickers and fails. Bass' characters endure near-entombments and other in-the-dark rites of passage, struggling toward the light, toward the recognition that they must love each other, the earth, and all its creatures.

***Publishers Weekly* (review date 27 May 2002)**

SOURCE: Review of *The Hermit's Story,* by Rick Bass. *Publishers Weekly* 249, no. 21 (27 May 2002): 34.

[*In the following review, the critic maintains that* The Hermit's Story, *as a whole is uniformly excellent and that each story is both lovely and satisfying.*]

★ Nature is as otherworldly as a line of bright birds frozen stiff, and as prosaic as a patch of grass, in this uniformly excellent collection. In the title story [of *The Hermit's Story*], a dog trainer and her companion, a man called Gray Owl, take six dogs out on a hunting exercise. Toward the end of their trip, Gray Owl falls through the ice of a lake, but instead of drowning, winds up on at the bottom of a dry basin covered with a layer of ice. He is joined by the trainer and the dogs, and together they cross the lake under the ice, an adventure that forces the trainer to examine her perspective, since every step presents a fresh challenge to the senses. **"The Fireman"** relates the dissolution of the title character's first marriage through the metaphor of fire, with Bass skillfully juxtaposing the blaze of human relationships and the searing, organic power of fire. The volume dips into humor with the pseudo-fantastical **"Eating,"** in which an owl trapped in a canoe lashed to the top of a car initiates a memorable episode in a North Carolina diner; the ensuing gastronomical feats both amaze and amuse. The jewel of this collection, **"Swans,"** introduces Billy, who has a preternatural connection with the trees on his Idaho homestead, and describes his idyllic life with his wife, a soulful baker. As the story progresses, Billy grows ill and slowly wastes away, even as the unnamed narrator eloquently and simply chronicles his decline. Billy's life takes on a stirring quality of pathos, and his graceful death leaves the reader deeply satisfied yet yearning for more. That sentiment might be extended to each of the lovely stories gathered here.

Jim Coan (review date 1 June 2002)

SOURCE: Coan, Jim. Review of *The Hermit's Story,* by Rick Bass. *Library Journal* 127, no. 10 (1 June 2002): 198.

[*In the following review, Coan praises the stories of* The Hermit's Story, *which he describes as entertaining and thought-provoking.*]

In his new collection [*The Hermit's Story*], novelist and nature writer Bass (e.g., *Colter*) focuses a naturalist's eye not only on the frozen lakes and interplay of predator and prey often found in his work but also on the ebb and flow of human emotions and relationships. Among several selections set in a remote region of northern Montana is the title story, in which a couple and a pack of dogs, lost in a winter storm, almost miraculously find refuge beneath the ice on a frozen lake. Failed or troubled marriages figure throughout, and the male characters often ponder lost love while deeply involved in more immediate tasks, like fighting fires or helping a friend after an eye operation. In an especially strong story, **"The Distance,"** a man recalls his first visit to Jefferson's Monticello as a teenager while touring the estate with his wife and daughter. His critical view of both Jefferson and the tour guide gives Bass a chance to quote from Jefferson's writings, which show that he was a dedicated and radical environmentalist. Thought-provoking and entertaining, these stories move along quickly but continue to resonate long after the reader is done; several have been anthologized in award collections. Recommended for all libraries.

Chris Solomon (review date 5 July 2002)

SOURCE: Solomon, Chris. "*Hermit's Story* Goes Underground to Reveal the Light." *Seattle Times* (5 July 2002): H41.

[*In the following review, Solomon lauds* The Hermit's Story *for its use of natural landscape settings as integral components to the stories.*]

You might say that Rick Bass' sense of direction is all turned around. In the general cosmology, "up" is the direction with good connotations. There's heaven, the warm sun, mountaintop enlightenment. Underground? That's home to Hades. The dirt nap.

Yet frequently in the stories of Bass, a former petroleum geologist whose 17 books include the memoir *Oil Notes,* much wonder lies just beneath the Earth's skin. Going underground means probing something more elemental, a literary wildcatting in which characters—and Bass—tap into the essence of things. "Landscape—geology—is all there is," the author has said. "I can write (different) stories, but if landscape's not a character, I'm not much interested in them. It fascinates me, to start at the bottom, and work up."

That oilman's impulse is very obviously present in two of the more memorable stories in his new collection, *The Hermit's Story.* In **"The Cave,"** a former coal miner and his new girlfriend find an old adit in West Virginia, strip down and descend into the mine. In the blackness, their eyes "as large as eggs," they are somehow more attuned than ever to their surroundings. Time seems to stretch like taffy.

Something similar happens in the book's title story, in which a dog trainer and an older Indian man escape a blizzard by crawling through a hole in a lake that is frozen on top but is drained underneath. Under the ice is a blue world, protected, so vivid that the trainer can smell the adrenaline of the hunting dogs, "a scent like damp, fresh-cut green hay."

Bass' best stories often have a moment of it-could-happen magical realism, and **"The Cave"** is no exception: The couple climbs aboard an old pumpjack boxcar and races through the mine as the screaming steel wheels illuminate them with orange sparks, "as if they had been painted or even created by that light." They finally emerge like some sooty Adam and Eve. "They could taste the green light on their bodies," Bass writes.

And yet in these stories, the wonder characters feel, and the gratefulness for that wonder, is repeatedly tempered by the sadness of knowing that nothing lasts. Decay always comes, so "that even an afternoon such as that one could become dust."

The story **"Swans"** is filled with familiar, outsized mountain people influenced by Bass' life in northwest Montana's rural Yaak Valley. "I have seen men here lift the back ends of trucks and roll logs out of the woods that a draft horse couldn't pull," says the narrator, who lives in a fictional valley. "Dogs live to be 20, 25 years old."

Of these people, the narrator most admires Amy and her husband, a Bunyanesque logger named Billy. Amy and Billy's life together is so in tune with nature's rhythms that time seems to stand still for them. The flawed, burdened narrator can only wonder at their lives, and enjoy its reflected light. They are as mythic and magical as the wild place they call home. Yet in time, even strongmen like Billy are as fragile as these few remaining special places.

Time has taken a toll on all of the marriages in these stories. Husbands muse on moribund relationships, sometimes hoping to kiss life into them, with varying levels of success. The same could be said of Bass' explorations of this theme.

The standout, however, and the collection's best story, is **"The Fireman."** In it, a volunteer firefighter finds that the dangerous, adrenaline-infused moments inside a burning house mysteriously reinvigorate his relationship with his wife. The fire captain compares the conflagrations to rivers of magma in the Earth, "rivers of the way things used to be and might some day be again—true but mysterious, and full of power."

FURTHER READING

Criticism

Coleman, Ancilla F. "Rick Bass: Contemporary Romantic." *Publications of the Mississippi Philological Association* (1990): 53-8.

Discussion of Bass's fiction in the tradition of Romantic literature.

Ruiter, David. "Life on the Frontier: Frederick Jackson Turner and Rick Bass." *JASAT: Journal of the American Studies Association of Texas* (26 October 1995): 66-73.

Treats the myth of the American West in Bass and Turner.

Additional coverage of Bass's life and career is contained in the following sources published by the Gale Group: *American Nature Writers*; *Contemporary Authors*, Vol. 126; *Contemporary Authors New Revision Series*, Vols. 53, 93; *Contemporary Literary Criticism*, Vols. 79, 143; *Contemporary Southern Writers*; *Dictionary of Literary Biography*, Vols. 212, 275; and *Literature Resource Center*.

Cyberpunk Short Fiction

The following entry presents criticism on the representation of cyberpunk in world short fiction literature; for discussion of cyberpunk literature in the twentieth century, see *TCLC,* Volume 106.

INTRODUCTION

According to *Merriam-Webster's Encyclopedia of Literature* (1995), cyberpunk is defined as: "A science-fiction subgenre comprising works characterized by countercultural antiheroes trapped in a dehumanized, high-tech future."

In the periodical *Amazing Science Fiction Stories* (1983), Bruce Bethke published a story entitled "Cyberpunk," coining the phrase from an amalgam of the words cybernetics—the art of replacing human body parts with computerized ones—and punk—the musical and cultural youth movement of the 1970s and 1980s. The editor of *Isaac Asimov's Science Fiction Magazine,* Gardner Dozois, is credited with first using this term to designate a new literary offshoot of the science fiction genre. Cyberpunk's literary roots date back to the technological fiction and hardboiled crime writing of the 1940s and 1950s (especially the rough, urban idiom of Raymond Chandler), to the subversive fantasies of William S. Burroughs and J. G. Ballard, and to the visionary prose of Samuel R. Delany and Philip K. Dick who took up themes of alienation in a mechanized future. During the 1970s, author and critic Bruce Sterling called for a modernized science fiction, one that reflected contemporary social and scientific concerns, and cyberpunk was often seen as an exemplar of this demand. Important cyberpunk short fiction writers include Sterling, John Shirley, Lewis Shiner, Rudy Rucker, William Gibson, and Pat Cadigan.

Cyberpunk fiction generally focuses on the effects of advanced technology—particularly computers—on individual and collective human psychology and behavior. More specifically, cyberpunk came to describe a cultural movement, which included not only fiction but also music, film, print and online magazines, and scholarly theory, that sought to come to terms with the post-industrial Age of Information by confronting it with punk subculture rebelliousness. Characterized by a self-conscious style and dystopian themes, cyberpunk reached the height of its popularity in the 1980s alongside the deconstructive and postmodernist theories of

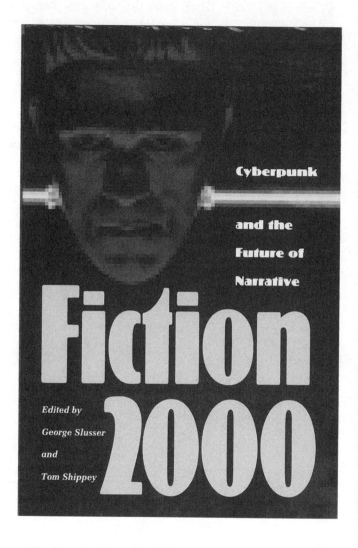

Noted essayists Gregory Benford, Istvan Csicsery-Ronay, Jr., David Porush, and Lewis Shiner examine current cyberpunk literature as well as the subgenre's future course in Fiction 2000.

thinkers such as Jacques Derrida and Jean-François Lyotard, who emphasized subjective interpretation and denied the existence of central meaning in literature and society. These ideas coincided with the rise of Internet culture, a phenomenon that moved the personal computer from the workplace to the home, where it became entrenched in daily human life. Cyberpunks imagined a world devoid of human contact, where robots and cyborgs—hybrids of humans and machines—ruled and human consciousness was usually detached from the body. While the cyberpunk movement explored valid fears about the encroachment of machines into human life, it was strongly criticized by feminists, who believed that it promoted the needs and desires of white middle-class males. Consequently, a branch of cyberpunk arose that addressed the concerns of women, homosexuals, and people of color in the technological era. Cyberpunk began dying off as a literary subgenre in the early 1990s, as acceptance of cyberculture and computers increased among the public. Critical assessment of cyberpunk ranges from those who approach it with scorn to those who view it as a legitimate literary exploration of life in the post-humanist age.

In 1986, Sterling published *Mirrorshades,* a collection of cyberpunk short fiction. In his preface to *Mirrorshades,* Sterling provided the definitive explanation of cyberpunk's nature and ambitions: "Technical culture has gotten out of hand. The advances of the sciences are so deeply radical, so disturbing, upsetting, and revolutionary that they can no longer be contained. . . . And suddenly a new alliance is becoming evident: an integration of technology and the Eighties counterculture. An unholy alliance of the technical world and the world of organized dissent—the underground world of pop culture, visionary fluidity and street-level anarchy. . . . For the cyberpunks . . . technology is visceral. . . . Not outside us, but next to us. Under our skin; often, inside our minds. . . . Eighties tech sticks to the skin, responds to the touch: the personal computer, the Sony Walkman, the portable telephone, the soft contact lens."

REPRESENTATIVE WORKS

Anthologies

Mirrorshades: The Cyberpunk Anthology [edited by Bruce Sterling; contributors include Pat Cadigan and William Gibson] (anthology) 1986

Storming the Reality Studio: A Casebook of Cyberpunk and Post-Modern Science Fiction [edited by Larry McCaffery; contributors include Kathy Acker, J. G. Ballard, William S. Burroughs, Don DeLillo, and Thomas Pynchon] (anthology) 1992

Kathy Acker
Blood and Guts in High School (novel) 1982

J. G. Ballard
The Atrocity Exhibition (short stories) 1969

Alfred Bester
The Stars My Destination (novel) 1956

Bruce Bethke
"Cyberpunk" (short story) 1983

William S. Burroughs
Naked Lunch (novel) 1959

Pat Cadigan
"Rock On" (short story) 1984
"Angel" (short story) 1987
Patterns (short stories) 1989
"True Faces" (short story) 1992

Raymond Chandler
The Big Sleep (novel) 1939

Samuel R. Delany
Nova (novel) 1969
"Among the Blobs" (short story) 1988

Philip K. Dick
Do Androids Dream of Electric Sheep? (novel) 1968

William Gibson
"The Gernsback Continuum" (short story) 1981
Burning Chrome (short stories) 1987

William Gibson and Bruce Sterling
"Red Star, Winter Orbit" (short story) 1986

Rob Hardin
"Fistic Hermaphrodites" (short story) 1988
"Microbes" (short story) 1988
"nerve terminals" (short story) 1988

Harold Jaffe
"Max Headroom" (short story) 1988

James Patrick Kelly
"Solstice" (short story) 1985

Marc Laidlaw
"400 Boys" (short story) 1983

Tom Maddox
"Snake-Eyes" (short story) 1986

Misha
"Wire for Two Tims" (short story) 1983
"Wire Movement #9" (short story) 1983

Thomas Pynchon
Gravity's Rainbow (novel) 1973

Rudy Rucker
"Tales of Houdini" (short story) 1983

Lewis Shiner
"Till Human Voices Wake Us" (short story) 1984

John Shirley
"Freezone" (short story) 1985
"Wolves of the Plateau" (short story) 1988

Olaf Stapledon
Last and First Men (novel) 1937

Bruce Sterling
Crystal Express (short stories) 1990

Bruce Sterling and Lewis Shiner
"Mozart and Mirrorshades" (short story) 1985

Robert Stone
Dog Soldiers (novel) 1973

James Tiptree, Jr.
The Girl Who Was Plugged In (novella) 1973

*These works are considered important cyberpunk influences. Source: Kadrey, Richard. "Cyberpunk 101 Reading List." *Whole Earth Review* (summer 1989): 83.

OVERVIEWS AND GENERAL STUDIES

Bruce Sterling (essay date 1986)

SOURCE: Sterling, Bruce. Preface to *Mirrorshades: The Cyberpunk Anthology,* edited by Bruce Sterling, pp. ix-xvi. New York: Arbor House, 1986.

[*In the following introduction to his seminal anthology* Mirrorshades, *Sterling introduces and elucidates the defining characteristics of the genre of cyberpunk.*]

This book showcases writers who have come to prominence within this decade. Their allegiance to Eighties culture has marked them as a group—as a new movement in science fiction.

This movement was quickly recognized and given many labels: Radical Hard SF, the Outlaw Technologists, the Eighties Wave, the Neuromantics, the Mirrorshades Group.

But of all the labels pasted on and peeled throughout the early Eighties, one has stuck: cyberpunk.

Scarcely any writer is happy about labels—especially one with the peculiar ring of "cyberpunk." Literary tags carry an odd kind of double obnoxiousness: those with a label feel pigeonholed; those without feel neglected. And, somehow, group labels never quite fit the individual, giving rise to an abiding itchiness. It follows,

then, that the "typical cyberpunk writer" does not exist; this person is only a Platonic fiction. For the rest of us, our label is an uneasy bed of Procrustes, where fiendish critics wait to lop and stretch us to fit.

Yet it's possible to make broad statements about cyberpunk and to establish its identifying traits. I'll be doing this too in a moment, for the temptation is far too strong to resist. Critics, myself included, persist in label-mongering, despite all warnings; we must, because it's a valid source of insight—as well as great fun.

Within this book, I hope to present a full overview of the cyberpunk movement, including its early rumblings and the current state of the art. *Mirrorshades* should give readers new to Movement writing a broad introduction to cyberpunk's tenets, themes, and topics. To my mind, these are showcase stories: strong, characteristic examples of each writer's work to date. I've avoided stories widely anthologized elsewhere, so even hardened devotees should find new visions here.

Cyberpunk is a product of the Eighties milieu—in some sense, as I hope to show later, a definitive product. But its roots are deeply sunk in the sixty-year tradition of modern popular SF.

The cyberpunks as a group are steeped in the lore and tradition of the SF field. Their precursors are legion. Individual cyberpunk writers differ in their literary debts; but some older writers, ancestral cyberpunks perhaps, show a clear and striking influence.

From the New Wave: the streetwise edginess of Harlan Ellison. The visionary shimmer of Samuel Delany. The free-wheeling zaniness of Norman Spinrad and the rock esthetic of Michael Moorcock; the intellectual daring of Brian Aldiss; and, always, J. G. Ballard.

From the harder tradition: the cosmic outlook of Olaf Stapledon; the science/politics of H. G. Wells; the steely extrapolation of Larry Niven, Poul Anderson, and Robert Heinlein.

And the cyberpunks treasure a special fondness for SF's native visionaries: the bubbling inventiveness of Philip José Farmer; the brio of John Varley; the reality games of Philip K. Dick; the soaring, skipping beatnik tech of Alfred Bester. With a special admiration for a writer whose integration of technology and literature stands unsurpassed: Thomas Pynchon.

Throughout the Sixties and Seventies, the impact of SF's last designated "movement," the New Wave, brought a new concern for literary craftsmanship to SF. Many of the cyberpunks write a quite accomplished and graceful prose; they are in love with style, and are (some say) fashion-conscious to a fault. But, like the punks of '77, they prize their garage-band esthetic. They love to grapple with the raw core of SF: its ideas. This links them strongly to the classic SF tradition. Some critics opine that cyberpunk is disentangling SF from mainstream influence, much as punk stripped rock and roll of the symphonic elegances of Seventies "progressive rock." (And others—hard-line SF traditionalists with a firm distrust of "artiness"—loudly disagree.)

Like punk music, cyberpunk is in some sense a return to roots. The cyberpunks are perhaps the first SF generation to grow up not only within the literary tradition of science fiction but in a truly science-fictional world. For them, the techniques of classical "hard SF"—extrapolation, technological literacy—are not just literary tools but an aid to daily life. They are a means of understanding, and highly valued.

In pop culture, practice comes first; theory follows limping in its tracks. Before the era of labels, cyberpunk was simply "the Movement"—a loose generational nexus of ambitious young writers, who swapped letters, manuscripts, ideas, glowing praise, and blistering criticism. These writers—Gibson, Rucker, Shiner, Shirley, Sterling—found a friendly unity in their common outlook, common themes, even in certain oddly common symbols, which seemed to crop up in their work with a life of their own. Mirrorshades, for instance.

Mirrored sunglasses have been a Movement totem since the early days of '82. The reasons for this are not hard to grasp. By hiding the eyes, mirrorshades prevent the forces of normalcy from realizing that one is crazed and possibly dangerous. They are the symbol of the sun-staring visionary, the biker, the rocker, the policeman, and similar outlaws. Mirrorshades—preferably in chrome and matte black, the Movement's totem colors—appeared in story after story, as a kind of literary badge.

These proto-cyberpunks were briefly dubbed the Mirrorshades Group. Thus this anthology's title, a well-deserved homage to a Movement icon. But other young writers, of equal talent and ambition, were soon producing work that linked them unmistakably to the new SF. They were independent explorers, whose work reflected something inherent in the decade, in the spirit of the times. Something loose in the 1980s.

Thus, "cyberpunk"—a label none of them chose. But the term now seems a fait accompli, and there is a certain justice in it. The term captures something crucial to the work of these writers, something crucial to the decade as a whole: a new kind of integration. The overlapping of worlds that were formerly separate: the realm of high tech, and the modern pop underground.

This integration has become our decade's crucial source of cultural energy. The work of the cyberpunks is paralleled throughout Eighties pop culture: in rock video; in the hacker underground; in the jarring street tech of hip-hop and scratch music; in the synthesizer rock of London and Tokyo. This phenomenon, this dynamic, has a global range; cyberpunk is its literary incarnation.

In another era this combination might have seemed far-fetched and artificial. Traditionally there has been a yawning cultural gulf between the sciences and the humanities: a gulf between literary culture, the formal world of art and politics, and the culture of science, the world of engineering and industry.

But the gap is crumbling in unexpected fashion. Technical culture has gotten out of hand. The advances of the sciences are so deeply radical, so disturbing, upsetting, and revolutionary, that they can no longer be contained. They are surging into culture at large; they are invasive; they are everywhere. The traditional power structure, the traditional institutions, have lost control of the pace of change.

And suddenly a new alliance is becoming evident: an integration of technology and the Eighties counterculture. An unholy alliance of the technical world and the world of organized dissent—the underground world of pop culture, visionary fluidity, and street-level anarchy.

The counterculture of the 1960s was rural, romanticized, anti-science, anti-tech. But there was always a lurking contradiction at its heart, symbolized by the electric guitar. Rock technology was the thin edge of the wedge. As the years have passed, rock tech has grown ever more accomplished, expanding into high-tech recording, satellite video, and computer graphics. Slowly it is turning rebel pop culture inside out, until the artists at pop's cutting edge are now, quite often, cutting-edge technicians in the bargain. They are special effects wizards, mixmasters, tape-effects techs, graphics hackers, emerging through new media to dazzle society with head-trip extravaganzas like FX cinema and the global Live Aid benefit. The contradiction has become an integration.

And now that technology has reached a fever pitch, its influence has slipped control and reached street level. As Alvin Toffler pointed out in *The Third Wave*—a bible to many cyberpunks—the technical revolution reshaping our society is based not in hierarchy but in decentralization, not in rigidity but in fluidity.

The hacker and the rocker are this decade's pop-culture idols, and cyberpunk is very much a pop phenomenon: spontaneous, energetic, close to its roots. Cyberpunk comes from the realm where the computer hacker and the rocker overlap, a cultural Petri dish where writhing gene lines splice. Some find the results bizarre, even monstrous; for others this integration is a powerful source of hope.

Science fiction—at least according to its official dogma—has always been about the impact of technology. But times have changed since the comfortable era of Hugo Gernsback, when Science was safely enshrined—and confined—in an ivory tower. The careless technophilia of those days belongs to a vanished, sluggish era, when authority still had a comfortable margin of control.

For the cyberpunks, by stark contrast, technology is visceral. It is not the bottled genie of remote Big Science boffins; it is pervasive, utterly intimate. Not outside us, but next to us. Under our skin; often, inside our minds.

Technology itself has changed. Not for us the giant steam-snorting wonders of the past: the Hoover Dam, the Empire State Building, the nuclear power plant. Eighties tech sticks to the skin, responds to the touch: the personal computer, the Sony Walkman, the portable telephone, the soft contact lens.

Certain central themes spring up repeatedly in cyberpunk. The theme of body invasion: prosthetic limbs, implanted circuitry, cosmetic surgery, genetic alteration. The even more powerful theme of mind invasion: brain-computer interfaces, artificial intelligence, neurochemistry—techniques radically redefining the nature of humanity, the nature of the self.

As Norman Spinrad pointed out in his essay on cyberpunk, many drugs, like rock and roll, are definitive high-tech products. No counterculture Earth Mother gave us lysergic acid—it came from a Sandoz lab, and when it escaped it ran through society like wildfire. It is not for nothing that Timothy Leary proclaimed personal computers "the LSD of the 1980s"—these are both technologies of frighteningly radical potential. And, as such, they are constant points of reference for cyberpunk.

The cyberpunks, being hybrids themselves, are fascinated by interzones: the areas where, in the words of William Gibson, "the street finds its own uses for things." Roiling, irrepressible street graffiti from that classic industrial artifact, the spray can. The subversive potential of the home printer and the photocopier. Scratch music, whose ghetto innovators turn the phonograph itself into an instrument, producing an archetypal Eighties music where funk meets the Burroughs cut-up method. "It's all in the mix"—this is true of much Eighties art and is as applicable to cyberpunk as it is to punk mix-and-match retro fashion and multitrack digital recording.

The Eighties are an era of reassessment, of integration, of hybridized influences, of old notions shaken loose

and reinterpreted with a new sophistication, a broader perspective. The cyberpunks aim for a wide-ranging, global point of view.

William Gibson's *Neuromancer,* surely the quintessential cyberpunk novel, is set in Tokyo, Istanbul, Paris. Lewis Shiner's *Frontera* features scenes in Russia and Mexico—as well as the surface of Mars. John Shirley's *Eclipse* describes Western Europe in turmoil. Greg Bear's *Blood Music* is global, even cosmic in scope.

The tools of global integration—the satellite media net, the multinational corporation—fascinate the cyberpunks and figure constantly in their work. Cyberpunk has little patience with borders. Tokyo's *Hayakawa's SF Magazine* was the first publication ever to produce an "all-cyberpunk" issue, in November 1986. Britain's innovative SF magazine *Interzone* has also been a hotbed of cyberpunk activity, publishing Shirley, Gibson, and Sterling as well as a series of groundbreaking editorials, interviews, and manifestos. Global awareness is more than an article of faith with cyberpunks; it is a deliberate pursuit.

Cyberpunk work is marked by its visionary intensity. Its writers prize the bizarre, the surreal, the formerly unthinkable. They are willing—eager, even—to take an idea and unflinchingly push it past the limits. Like J. G. Ballard—an idolized role model to many cyberpunks—they often use an unblinking, almost clinical objectivity. It is a coldly objective analysis, a technique borrowed from science, then put to literary use for classically punk shock value.

With this intensity of vision comes strong imaginative concentration. Cyberpunk is widely known for its telling use of detail, its carefully constructed intricacy, its willingness to carry extrapolation into the fabric of daily life. It favors "crammed" prose: rapid, dizzying bursts of novel information, sensory overload that submerges the reader in the literary equivalent of the hard-rock "wall of sound."

Cyberpunk is a natural extension of elements already present in science fiction, elements sometimes buried but always seething with potential. Cyberpunk has risen from within the SF genre; it is not an invasion but a modern reform. Because of this, its effect within the genre has been rapid and powerful.

Its future is an open question. Like the artists of punk and New Wave, the cyberpunk writers, as they develop, may soon be galloping in a dozen directions at once.

It seems unlikely that any label will hold them for long. Science fiction today is in a rare state of ferment. The rest of the decade may well see a general plague of movements, led by an increasingly volatile and numerous Eighties generation. The eleven authors here are only a part of this broad wave of writers, and the group as a whole already shows signs of remarkable militancy and fractiousness. Fired by a new sense of SF's potential, writers are debating, rethinking, teaching old dogmas new tricks. Meanwhile, cyberpunk's ripples continue to spread, exciting some, challenging others—and outraging a few, whose pained remonstrances are not yet fully heard.

The future remains unwritten, though not from lack of trying.

And this is a final oddity of our generation in SF—that, for us, the literature of the future has a long and honored past. As writers, we owe a debt to those before us, those SF writers whose conviction, commitment, and talent enthralled us and, in all truth, changed our lives. Such debts are never repaid, only acknowledged and—so we hope—passed on as a legacy to those who follow in turn.

Other acknowledgments are due. The Movement owes much to the patient work of today's editors. A brief look at this book's copyright page shows the central role of Ellen Datlow at *Omni*, a shades-packing sister in the vanguard of the ideologically correct, whose help in this anthology has been invaluable. Gardner Dozois was among the first to bring critical attention to the nascent Movement. Along with Shawna McCarthy, he has made *Isaac Asimov's Science Fiction Magazine* a center of energy and controversy in the field. Edward Ferman's *Fantasy and Science Fiction* is always a source of high standards. *Interzone,* the most radical periodical in science fiction today, has already been mentioned; its editorial cadre deserves a second thanks. And a special thanks to Yoshio Kobayashi, our Tokyo liaison, translator of *Schismatrix* and *Blood Music,* for favors too numerous to mention.

Now, on with the show.

Gerald Jonas (essay date 18 January 1987)

SOURCE: Jonas, Gerald. Review of *Mirrorshades: The Cyberpunk Anthology,* edited by Bruce Sterling. *New York Times Book Review* (18 January 1987): 33.

[*In the following review, Jonas characterizes the stories comprising the cyberpunk anthology* Mirrorshades.]

Mirrorshades is subtitled "The Cyberpunk Anthology." The editor, Bruce Sterling, explains in a brief preface that, "cyberpunk" is a new science-fiction esthetic for our time, born of "an unholy alliance of the technical world and the world of organized dissent—the under-

ground world of pop culture, visionary fluidity, and street-level anarchy. . . . Cyberpunk comes from the realm where the computer hacker and the rocker overlap, a cultural Petri dish where writhing gene lines splice." A few pages of this word-hype and it is a relief to turn to the stories themselves, 12 in all, the earliest originally published in 1981, the most recent in 1986.

What we find is a science fiction that takes the runaway power of science and technology for granted, that plays paranoia straight and finds comic relief in anarchy, and that gives center stage to characters who ask of the future not, "What's new under the sun?" but "What's in it for me?" The best known exponent of cyberpunk is William Gibson, whose 1985 novel *Neuromancer* (a computer hacker's power fantasy) won every major prize in science fiction. Unfortunately, Mr. Gibson is represented in *Mirrorshades* by a minor story (circa 1981) and a pedestrian collaboration with Mr. Sterling. The sense of on-the-edge excitement that made *Neuromancer* so popular is captured here in a long story called "Freezone" by John Shirley. Ignore the first three pages of background synopsis, which is as unconvincing as it is unnecessary; the rest of the story offers a funny yet affectionate portrait of the artist as a hard-core rock "classicist" who cannot stand the "new" artificial music and who is drawn into an assassination plot because he likes the looks of one of the plotters: "Bare breasts, nipples pierced with thin screws. . . . Her makeup looked like a spin painting. Her teeth were filed. Rickenharp swallowed hard, looking at her. Damn, she was *his type.*"

Rudy Rucker, a mathematician by trade, contributes a breezy "Tales of Houdini" that tickles the imagination and then vanishes without a trace. In a zany collaboration called "Mozart in Mirrorshades," Lewis Shiner and Mr. Sterling see time travel as opening the door for exploitation of the earth's resources on a scale undreamed of by today's most ruthless corporate polluters; the serious-slapstick style of this tale reminded me of the movie *Brazil*.

There are also some good, if unremarkable, stories by Tom Maddox, Pat Cadigan, Mr. Shiner solo, James Patrick Kelly and Paul Di Filippo, any of which could have appeared in science fiction magazines any time in the last 25 years without benefit of the "cyberpunk" label. Mirrorshades are, of course, mirrored sunglasses that hide the wearer's eyes from the gaze of passers-by.

Larry McCaffery (essay date 1991)

SOURCE: McCaffery, Larry. "Introduction: The Desert of the Real." In *Storming the Reality Studio: A Casebook of Cyberpunk and Postmodern Science Fiction,* edited by Larry McCaffery, pp. 1-16. Durham, N.C.: Duke University Press, 1991.

[*In the following introduction to his* Storming the Reality Studio, *McCaffery explores "the way in which cyberpunk and other innovative forms of SF are functioning within the realm of postmodern culture generally."*]

But how could we know when I was young

All the changes that were to come?

All the photos in the wallets on the battlefield

And now the terror of the scientific sun?

        —The Clash, "Something About England"

It is the real, and not the map, whose vestiges subsist here and there, in the deserts which are no longer those of the Empire, but our own. The desert of the real itself.

  —Jean Baudrillard, "The Precession of the Simulacra"

i haven't fucked much w/ the past but i've fucked plenty w/ the future.

        —Patti Smith, "babelogue"

In gathering together the materials contained in *Storming the Reality Studio,* I hope to create a context that will illuminate and broaden our understanding of two enormously exciting topics that have broad significance for postmodern culture generally. The first of these has to do with the recent evolution of what I will call "postmodern science fiction." This evolution was spurred on within genre SF by the "cyberpunk controversy" during the 1980s. Sparked initially by the publication of William Gibson's *Neuromancer* in 1984, this controversy spawned numerous critical debates in SF fanzines and at SF conferences and ultimately had the effect of opening up a dialogue within the field that encouraged even cyberpunk's most hardened opponents to examine the nature and roles of the genre, especially as these have been changing in response to postmodern culture. Equally significant in SF's recent transformations has been the development of experimental, quasi-SF works created by a number of major "mainstream" literary innovators (Pynchon, Burroughs, Ballard, Mooney, DeLillo and many others) that featured themes, motifs, and other elements that would previously have been associated with SF.

The nature and background of these parallel developments are discussed by a number of the critical essays included here as well as being schematically introduced in the Kadrey/McCaffery "Cyberpunk 101" text that follows this introduction. I have also aimed at presenting a range of stories, novel excerpts, poems, and other materials that can suggest something of the richness of theme and variety of stylistic innovation that characterizes contemporary SF and its many hybrid forms. A number of recurrent issues that emerge from the inter-

action of primary and secondary sources here—particularly those having to do with the meaning of artistic "realism" in our postfuturist age, the concepts of literary "authenticity" and "originality," and the paradoxes involved in artistic rebellion when "rebellion" is now a commodifiable *image* that is regularly employed as a "counterculture" marketing strategy—can all be shown to reflect and relate to similar issues being debated by nearly all artists and critics associated with postmodernism.

Indeed, the central topic addressed by this casebook is the way in which cyberpunk and other innovative forms of SF are functioning within the realm of postmodern culture generally: that is, the broader significance of SF's relationship to the complex set of radical ruptures—both within a dominant culture and aesthetic and also within the new social and economic media system (or "postindustrial society") in which we live. These are the ruptures and dislocations associated with postmodernism, as that term is used in this volume by critics such as Jean-François Lyotard, Fredric Jameson, Brian McHale, Dave Porush, Arthur Kroker and David Cook, and Jean Baudrillard, as well as by other critics not included here, such as David Bell, Gilles Deleuze, O. B. Hardison, and Kate Hayles.

THE DESERT OF THE REAL: A BRIEF HISTORY OF THE POSTMODERN UNIVERSE

To one degree or another, all the critics cited above closely tie the evolution of postmodern culture to technological developments. *Storming the Reality Studio* specifically explores this connection, for it is my conviction that the myriad features and tendencies associated with the slippery term "postmodernism" can be understood best by examining what is unique about our contemporary condition. And it seems undeniable that this condition derives its unique status above all from technological change. Almost inevitably, those artists who have been most in touch with these changes, intuitively as well as intellectually, have relied on themes and aesthetic modes previously associated with SF. Some of these artists have naturally been genre SF writers working within the relatively insular SF publishing scene. Others have arrived at SF modes from without—from "mainstream" postmodernist experimentalism, including fictional forms, but also poetry, drama, rock music, television and video art, performance art, and many other modes. In a basic sense, then, this book is dedicated to the proposition that the interaction between genre SF and the literary avant-garde—two groups historically segregated (at least in the United States) and, hence, not influencing one another directly—needs to be noted, discussed, and encouraged.

It is to be expected that critics seeking to account for the central features of postmodern culture exhibit considerable differences in the nature and scope of their inquiries, as well as their particular emphases. But underlying most of their investigations—which are grounded less in literary criticism than in economics, philosophy, political science, semiology, and cultural anthropology—is a view that the past several decades have seen the evolution of a new network of political and economic systems, a global movement away from local, nationalistic sources of economic and political control (and other forms of power wielding) toward multinational ones. This shift is intimately connected with the arrival of what Ernest Mandel (in his influential study, *Late Capitalism*) has termed the "Third Stage" in capitalist expansion—that of "postindustrial capitalism," which has followed the earlier stages of market capitalism and the monopoly (or imperialist) stage. This new stage, emerging roughly in the years immediately following WWII, has produced our own postmodern world by expanding capitalism's operations, by eliminating those areas of pre-capitalist organizations previously tolerated and exploited, and, as Fredric Jameson summarizes, by creating "a new and historically original penetration and colonization of Nature and the Unconscious" (1984a:78). This unprecedented expansion, made possible specifically by the exponential growth of technology, has profoundly altered not only the daily textures of the world(s) we inhabit but the way we think about the world and ourselves in it. The new economic and political systems responsible for multinational capitalism are highly dependent upon rapid technological advancements that will allow them to compete successfully for global resources and further expansion. Because competition among the multinationals is so intense and because success within this competition depends so much upon gathering highly specialized marketing information (including political and social information for insurance and investment purposes, etc.), the development of highly sophisticated methods of information gathering and data storage has been a key priority in technological research and production—so much so that one can say now that the key "global resource" is the *information itself* rather than the oil, farm goods, or other resources usually associated with capitalist market systems.

These technological advancements have introduced a broad range of new "high-tech" products into postmodern society, such as sophisticated offensive and defensive military weaponry and surveillance to protect the resources and markets of the multinationals; increasingly complex (and expensive) medical equipment and supplies, including a new array of prosthetic devices; and a whole host of consumer products, from automobiles to chain saws, cellular phones, trash compactors, microwave ovens, and so forth.

But even more significant than these "tangible products" has been the rapid proliferation of technologically mass-produced "products" that are essentially *reproduc-*

tions or *abstractions*—images, advertising, information, memories, styles, simulated experiences, and copies of original experiences. Particularly notable in this regard has been the prodigious expansion in the past several decades of three industries: advertising, information, and what is referred to as "the media (or culture) industry." As Greil Marcus has noted, in different ways all three industries have "turned upon individual men and women, seized their subjective emotions and experiences, changed those once evanescent phenomena into objective, replicable commodities, placed them on the market, set their prices, and sold them back to those who had, once, brought emotions and experiences out of themselves—to people who, as prisoners of the spectacle, could now find such things only on the market" (1989:101). Created for consumers by other products (TVS and film projectors, VCRS, CDS, computers, instacams, cameras, xerox and fax machines), these commodities can be reproduced (and then consumed) more easily than previous, unwieldy consumer products (cars, shoes, tanks); increasingly, they have thoroughly interpenetrated our daily lives with their "virtual realities," and begun to inhabit and colonize our imaginations and desires, even our unconscious, in a manner whose full implications are only now beginning to be recognized.

Overall, of course, such developments have enormously benefited the multinational system, for they have created a huge expansion of the *realm* in which the "dance of biz" (Gibson) can now whirl and infiltrate the desires of the soul. Together with the collective failure of communism to provide a viable alternative, the expansion of capitalism into its third stage has consolidated multinationalism's position so that virtually every corner of the globe is being successfully colonized by, for example, American popular culture. Thus, even in China, where these developments have met with massive political and cultural resistance, rock music is flourishing, Mickey Mouse and Donald Duck are national icons, and Rambo and Marlboro Men stalk the imaginations of the public. Even before the startling political events in China and Eastern Europe in 1989 (surely a pivotal year in this century's history), it seemed only a matter of time before the entire world would become united as one huge consumer market for the "free enterprise system." But as Greil Marcus notes, the success of this particular system of "freedom" has paradoxically created new forms of social control: "This was the modern world; to the degree that the real field of freedom had expanded, so had the epistemology, the aesthetics, the politics and the social life of control" (1989:101).

Although the general results of these developments are evident globally, the specific effects have inevitably been most far-reaching in those countries where technological advancement, together with social and economic pressures, are most intense—particularly the United States and Japan, but also Western Europe. The routine introduction of high-tech artifacts into these countries provides their citizens with a host of stimulating possibilities—but an equal number of troubling psychological, moral, and epistemological quandaries, as well. Many of these quandaries can be framed within age-old, venerable terminologies that go back as far as Plato and Eastern mysticism: What is real and what is illusion? What does it mean to be "alive" or "dead"? to be "conscious"? to be "immortal"? But in many cases, terms that were previously purely speculative abstractions ("immortality," "illusion") whose "existence" was tied to matters of semiotics and definition have now suddenly become literalized. Throughout history, for example, people have debated the nature of "life" and "death," and have argued about how one might go about achieving "immortality." Despite their vast emotional and psychological resonances, however, such discussions had little practical relevance until we began to develop technologies that allowed us to keep brain-damaged (or otherwise physically impaired people) "alive" indefinitely, or to replace our body parts with organ transplants, or to create computer and robotic systems that can "talk" and otherwise simulate the features of a "conscious" human being.

Such technological systems and artifacts that people can interface with (physically and imaginatively) or that can recreate experiences and "realize" desires, illusions, and memories have created vast new "areas" of sensory experience with their own spatial and temporal coordinates, their own personal and metaphysical dimensions. These new realms of experience—theorized by Guy Debord's "Society of the Spectacle," Baudrillard's "precession of simulacra," and Cook and Kroker's "hyper-reality," and metaphorized perhaps most vividly by Gibson's "cyberspace"—have become integrated so successfully into the daily textures of our lives that they often seem more "real" to us than the presumably more "substantial," "natural" aspects. Indeed, these reproduced and simulated realities, whose objective forms serve as a disguise for their subjective content, have begun subtly to actually *displace* the "real," rendering it superfluous. Even as early as the 1950s, Guy Debord theorized this obsolescence of the real by describing contemporary life as now belonging to the "Society of the Spectacle" where "everything that was directly lived has moved away into a representation" (1977:1). Similarly, Jean Baudrillard, borrowing an image from Borges, has summarized this process as the replacement of the territory by the map so that the postmodern realm is now "the desert of the real." This is the postmodern desert inhabited by people who are, in effect, consuming *themselves* in the form of images and abstractions through which their desires, sense of identity, and memories are replicated and then sold back to them as products.

The psychological and metaphysical implications of such developments are explored by most of the fiction writers included in this volume, many of whom take already extant technological realities and push them (often only slightly) into more extreme possibilities. Similar extrapolative approaches can be found in many recent popular films (*Robocop* [1987], *The Terminal Man* [1974], *Videodrome* [1983], *Total Recall* [1990]), music (Sonic Youth's *Daydream Nation* [1988] or the performance art and albums by Laurie Anderson), and in the "mechanized, industrial sculptures" created by Mark Pauline and the Survival Research Lab. But even much more ordinary, familiar examples demonstrate the striking ways in which technology is transforming our perceptions of our relationship to time, memory, self-identity, and "reality." Consider the relatively mundane example of the effect that photography has had on our relationship to memory, a theme richly explored by Philip K. Dick in *Do Androids Dream of Electric Sheep?* (1968) and in Ridley Scott's adaptation of Dick's novel in the film *Blade Runner* (1982), and by Don DeLillo's *White Noise* (1985). Basically, our memories of many of the key events of our past are now recollections not of "actual" past events, but of the photographs or videos we have taken of them. In a sense, people now often use the "real experience"—a trip to the Grand Canyon, our daughter's wedding—primarily as a "pretext" for the more "substantial" later experience of "reliving" these experiences through reproduced sounds and images that magically conjure up for us our past, a conjuration that seems more "substantial" precisely because it can be endlessly reproduced.

Clearly these developments in technology and critical theory require some radical rethinking of several of the basic paradigms and metaphors through which West Europeans have viewed themselves since the time of the ancient Greeks. As noted earlier, these concepts are as fundamental as the nature of "consciousness" and "desire," or the familiar set of categorical oppositions that we rely upon to understand ourselves and our relationship to the universe: male/female, organic/inorganic, artifice/nature, reality/illusion, originality/duplication, life/death, human/inhuman. The breakdown of these concepts and distinctions, as well as the rise of new metaphors and categories of perception, is obsessively explored (often with startling and provocative results) by nearly all the critics and fiction writers included in this volume. In a basic sense, then, the works contained in this volume continually return to the same questions: What does it mean to be *human* in today's world? What has stayed the same and what has changed? How has technology specifically changed the answers we supply to such questions? And what does all this suggest about the future we will inhabit?

These are obviously important questions that not only have no simple answers, but that also are difficult (maybe impossible) to formulate within the conventions of so-called "traditional realism." The nature and sources of this difficulty are varied and complex. For one thing, the scientific, economic, and metaphysical principles producing these massive transformations often require specialized knowledge and intellectual skills not readily accessible to most artists. While railroads, steel mills, and assembly lines were fundamentally altering America's landscapes and mind-sets during the nineteenth century, it was still possible for the average American to grasp the mechanisms and principles responsible for such changes. Today, an analogous understanding of what is taking place in computer technology, astronomy, biology, and chemistry is simply too difficult. Consider the following list of some of the recurrent political, philosophical, moral, and cultural issues that postmodern sf and cyberpunk have been exploring: the far-reaching implications of the recent breakthroughs in cybernetic and genetic engineering, organ transplants, virtual reality, and artificial intelligence research; the equally significant developments involving information storage, and, in particular, the ways in which computerized data, microstorage, and data bank development are controlled and owned by multinationals (in short, the increasing monopolization of information by private business for the purposes of wielding power and control over nation-states and individuals); the social, psychic, political, and behavioral impact resulting from the shift away from the older industrial technologies to the newer information and cybernetic ones; the massive expansion of the "culture industry," an industry indiscriminately seeking profits from the sale of everything from "lite" beer to presidential images, detox centers, napalm, famine relief, invasion, and salvation; the assistance given to this expansion by technology's greater facility to introduce media images, print, and other informational sources directly into our homes, cars, and offices—and consequently, into the most intimate reaches of our imaginations, our self-definitions, our desires; the resulting "new and historically original penetration and colonization of Nature and the Unconscious" (Jameson 1984a:76).

Issues such as these, which are so massive, troubling, and profoundly disruptive, are rarely dealt with by mainstream "realistic" writers, not only because of the specialized knowledge required, but also because they challenge the normative bedrocks upon which the fantasies of "realism" are grounded. Thus, with only a handful of exceptions, most contemporary American authors continue to write novels as if these key issues (and the forces that produced them) do not exist. With the gap between the future and the present narrowing every day—and, paradoxically, with the growing recognition that if we move even "twenty minutes into the future" (à la *Max Headroom* [1985]), we will encounter a world as unimaginably transformed as what we find in Bruce

Sterling's *Schismatrix* (1985)—the potential importance of informed, aesthetically innovative sf becomes obvious; here we have a form whose maximal level of artifice and focus on the future permit it to jettison the familiar, "correct" images, narratives, and implications that combine to produce the realistic illusions projected in most art. Freed from the requirements of "realism," and sensitive to the ways in which the "real" and the "true" are being systematically replaced (even *excluded*) by the "hyperreal" of images, statistics, and other abstractions whose role is to "stand in" for reality, postmodern sf has recently produced the only art systematically exploring this "desert of the real(s)."

SF AND THE LITERARY AVANT-GARDE

As I have just summarized, the challenge of finding a suitable means to examine the "postmodern condition" has produced a vigorous and highly energized response from a new breed of sf authors who combine scientific know-how with aesthetic innovation. But because much of this writing *is* so radical and formally experimental, and because writing which bears the imprint of "sf" has been so commonly relegated to pop-culture ghettos, it has remained until recently largely ignored, except within its own self-contained world. Examples of important, aesthetically radical sf exhibiting many of the features associated with postmodernism are evident as early as the mid-1950s and early 1960s, when literary mavericks like Alfred Bester, William S. Burroughs, J. G. Ballard, Philip K. Dick, and Thomas Pynchon began publishing books that self-consciously operated on the fringes of sf and the literary avant-garde.

During the 1970s and 1980s, a few other authors working at the boundaries of sf and postmodern experimentalism continued to borrow the use of motifs, language, images—as well as the "subject matter"—of sf. Important examples would include Don DeLillo's *Ratner's Star* (1976) and *White Noise,* Ted Mooney's *Easy Travel to Other Planets* (1981), Joseph McElroy's *Plus* (1976) and *Women and Men* (1986), Denis Johnson's *Fiskadoro* (1985), Margaret Atwood's *The Handmaid's Tale* (1985), William T. Vollmann's *You Bright and Risen Angels* (1987), Kathy Acker's *Empire of the Senseless* (1988), and Mark Leyner's *My Cousin, My Gastroenterologist* (1990). While writing outside the commercial sf publishing scene, these writers produced works that perfectly fulfill the generic task of sf, described by Vivian Sobchack as "the cognitive mapping and poetic figuration of social relations as these are constituted by new technological modes of 'being-in-the-world'" (1987:225). As is true of the cyberpunk novels that began appearing in the early 1980s, these mainstream works (recently dubbed "slipstream" novels by cyberpunk theoretician Bruce Sterling) typically portrayed individuals awash in a sea of technological change, information overload, and random—but extraordinarily *vivid*—sensory stimulation. Personal confusion, sadness, dread, and philosophical skepticism often appeared mixed with equal measures of euphoria and nostalgia for a past when centers could still hold. The characters and events in these works typically exist within narrative frameworks that unfold as a barrage of words, data, and visual images drawn from a dissolving welter of reference to science and pop culture, the fabulous and the mundane, a tendency that reaches its most extreme expression in William Burroughs's hallucinatory mid-1960s novels.

A few of these "mainstream" postmodern writers have drawn very self-consciously from genre SF for specific tropes and narrative devices. This is very obvious in, for example, Burroughs's use of the motifs of the 1930s space opera works he read as a youth, in DeLillo's borrowing of dystopian elements in *White Noise,* in Vollman's improvisational treatment of a much wider range of SF modes in *You Bright and Risen Angels,* or Kathy Acker's borrowing of specific passages from *Neuromancer* in *Empire of the Senseless.* But typically one gets less a sense of these authors consciously borrowing from genre SF norms than of their introducing these elements simply because the world around them demands that they be present.

WHAT BECOMES A MIRRORSHADE MOST?
ENTER CYBERPUNK

Not surprisingly, however, it has been within the realm of genre SF that technology's role in the evolution of postmodern life has been most frequently scrutinized and transformed into narratives and metaphors. One way to view the mid-1980s cyberpunk phenomenon is to suggest that it represented a synthesis of SF with postmodern aesthetic tendencies and thematic impulses. This synthesis could be loosely paralleled with the much-documented integration of "modernism" and SF during the 1960s, when SF experienced its last series of major formal disruptions during its "New Wave" period. Such a summary is misleading in several respects. For instance, while SF's New Wave self-consciously adopted specific modernist devices—Brian Aldiss's borrowing of Joyce (*Barefoot in the Head* [1969]), John Brunner's use of Dos Passos (*Stand on Zanzibar* [1968]), or Gene Wolfe's and Gregory Benford's employment of Faulkner (*The Fifth Head of Cerberus* [1972] and *Against Infinity* [1983])—it also produced a number of works as fully grounded in "postmodernist" impulses as those appearing in the 1980s (cyberpunk or otherwise). These would include several of the major works by SF innovators such as Samuel R. Delany, Joanna Russ, Thomas Disch, Ursula K. Le Guin, and Philip K. Dick. Nor does this cyberpunk-as-postmodernism equation provide much information about cyberpunk's *particular* aesthetic and thematic orientations. Books such as Le Guin's *Always Coming*

Home (1985), Russ's *Extra(Ordinary) People* (1985), and Delany's *Triton* (1976) or his Nevèrÿon series are every bit as "postmodern" in their formal innovations and thematic concerns as anything written by the cyberpunks. Nevertheless, the premise that cyberpunk represents one particularly intriguing example of the "postmodernization" of SF generally suggests one of the theses governing this casebook.

The cyberpunk SF "movement" first came into prominence in 1984, when William Gibson's *Neuromancer* was published to considerable popular and critical success (it was the first SF novel to garner all three of SF's major awards, winning the Hugo, Nebula, and Philip K. Dick awards). But the seeds of its development were actually planted several years earlier, when Gibson and other writers later associated with cyberpunk began publishing stories and novels that had a different edge from other SF works dealing with similar issues. Cyberpunk was written by a generation of authors once-removed from the 1960s New Wave innovators, and this ten- or fifteen-year age difference was evident in their work in several ways. (The same point can be made about the differences between the "mainstream" innovators of the 1960s [Coover, Barth, and Gass] and their 1980s counterparts [Leyner, Vollmann, and Ann Beattie].) For one thing, the cyberpunks were the first generation of artists for whom the technologies of satellite dishes, video and audio players and recorders, computers and video games (both of particular importance), digital watches, and MTV were not exoticisms, but part of a daily "reality matrix." They were also the first generation of writers who were reading Thomas Pynchon, Ballard, and Burroughs as teenagers, who had grown up immersed in technology but also in pop culture, in the values and aesthetics of the counterculture associated with the drug culture, punk rock, video games, *Heavy Metal* comic books, and the gore-and-spatter SF/horror films of George Romero, David Cronenberg, and Ridley Scott.

In their works and in numerous, highly contentious public debates that took place at SF conferences and conventions, the cyberpunks presented themselves as "techno-urban-guerilla" artists announcing that both the technological dreams and nightmares envisioned by previous generations of SF artists were already in place, and that writers as well as the general public needed to create ways of using this technology for our own purposes before we all became mere software, easily deletable from the hard drives of multinationalism's vast mainframe. Cyberpunk, then, became a significant movement within postmodernism because of its ability to present an intense, vital, and often darkly humorous vision of the world space of multinational capitalism—and to render this vision both formally (through a style appropriate to its age) and concretely (through the dominant cultural imagery). Like their avatars Pynchon, Ballard, Dick, and Burroughs, cyberpunk authors constructed works that moved seamlessly through the realms of hard science and pop culture, realms that included chaos theory and Madonna, dada and punk rock, MTV and *film noire,* Arthur Rimbaud and Lou Reed, Arnold Schwarzenegger and Oliver North, instant reruns and AI. Decked out in mirrorshades and leather jackets, the cyberpunks projected an image of confrontational "reality hacker" artists who were armed, dangerous, and jacked into (but not under the thumb of) the Now and the New.

The overall effect of cyberpunk within SF is analogous to what occurred within rock music in the mid-1970s when punk music rudely and crudely deconstructed nearly everyone's relationship to popular music. When the slam dancers cleared out, and the pieces of amps, guitars, and vocal sounds were once again rejoined into something that seemed vaguely recognizable, there was a certain sense of sane clarity (or clear insanity) in the air. In the case of both punk and cyberpunk, however, this sense did not produce a constricting attitude of conformity among ambitious writers and musicians. While inevitably there were artists in both fields who were merely blindly mimicking the successful patterns of more creative counterparts, truly imaginative artists hardly felt that they were now required to narrowly imitate, say, punk and cyberpunk's emphasis on sensationalized, S & M surface textures, its Benzedrine-rush pacings, or its parodically nonconformist stance. Rather, there was a feeling in both the rock and SF communities that *whatever direction* these forms were now taking, they could be reconstructed afresh so that priorities could once again be recognized. With music there was an immediate series of healthy mutations, as with the Clash's incorporation of reggae and jazz, the cool, funky minimalism of Talking Heads (who later ventured into more complex arrangements influenced by African rhythms and Brian Eno), the cowpunk sounds of the Meat Puppets (whose name Gibson uses as a central motif in *Neuromancer*), and the speed-metal transformations of punk and blues elements.

Similarly, cyberpunk writers soon began producing works that defy easy categorization. It is precisely at this point of transformation and mutation that cyberpunk's evolution within genre SF begins to interact with the world outside—with the literary world of Don DeLillo, for instance, or of William S. Burroughs, Ted Mooney, Kathy Acker, William T. Vollmann, J. G. Ballard, Harold Jaffe, and Mark Leyner. At this point, it also becomes clear that the cyberpunk phenomenon is important for reasons that lie far outside its impact on the recent direction of SF. These reasons, as I have already suggested, are related to a series of broad issues pertaining to postmodernist art in general: the breakdown of genre distinctions, for example, and the increasingly arbitrary separation of pop art from "serious

art" (or art from advertising, image from referent, the natural from the conventionalized, originality from imitation, fiction from criticism, man-made from machine-made, live from Memorexed) and to the vital artistic interactions resulting from these interminglings. But most centrally these reasons involve the shared perception among a significant number of postmodern artists that art which fails to come to grips, formally or thematically, with these changes is irrelevant or (less harshly) out of sync with the times.

Thus, this casebook presents cyberpunk and related "mainstream" forays into quasi-SF forms as the inevitable result of art responding to the technological milieu that is producing postmodern culture at large. The critical debate spawned by postmodernism which has emphasized the semiological, *conventional* bases of all fictional forms (including the "natural" forms of realism) makes it easier to recognize the common aesthetic grounds shared by cyberpunk (and all SF) and other highly stylized forms. In this respect, SF's aesthetics can be seen as extending the implications of the surfictionist, metafictionist, and fabulist experiments of the 1960s in using its highly stylized codes and conventions to produce textual "meaning" in a manner as fully distinctive as the linguistic systems that give rise to meaning in a Shakespearean sonnet, a medieval morality fable, or a postmodernist story by Coover or Barth. Once the complex nuances of these codes and conventions are recognized, however, cyberpunk's narrative strategies can be shown to unfold in a typically postmodernist way: mixing together genres, borrowing devices from the cinema, computer systems, and MTV, infusing the rhythms of its prose with those of rock music and TV advertising, pastiching prior literary forms and otherwise playing with literary elements, and, above all, adopting the familiar postmodernist device of developing familiar "mythic" structures and materials which can then be undercut and exploited for different purposes.

It is this latter device that has been perhaps the most misunderstood and misrepresented by cyberpunk's critics, who have constantly pointed toward cyberpunk's appropriation of devices and materials associated with other genres—the use of hard-boiled detective formulas in *Blade Runner* and in Gibson's *Neuromancer,* the analogous use of gothic horror in *Alien* (1979) and of cop formulas in *Robocop* and *The Terminal Man*—as exhibiting its superficiality and collective failure of imagination. What such criticism ignores, however, is cyberpunk's postmodernist spirit of free play (*jouissance*) and collaboration, its delight in creating cut-ups and collages (à la Burroughs) in which familiar objects and motifs are placed in startling, unfamiliar contexts. To take an obvious example, when Gibson relocates hundreds of semiological fragments within the dissolving, surreal electronic nightworld he invents for his cyberspace trilogy, a new discourse is established, different messages conveyed. Yes, *Neuromancer*'s hero, Case, is a computer "cowboy" and "detective," and his mission is the familiar "Big Heist" with all the plot trappings, Molly is a "moll" out of a 1940s *film noire,* and Case's psychological motives center on his desire to seek revenge against the forces who fucked him over. True, the "messages" occasionally bear similarities to what we find in Chandler and Hammett: the hero lost in a society of criminal and impersonal forces, a nostalgic longing for a more authentic, uncorrupted past. But Gibson is also using the framework of *Neuromancer* to introduce his own agenda, which is a veritable case-book of postmodern SF concerns: the contrast between the human "meat" and metal, the relationship betwen human memory and computer memory; the denaturing of the body and the transformation of time and space in the postindustrial world; the increasingly abstract inter-action of data and images in this world; the primacy of information in the "dance of data" that comprises so much of life today (a "dance" which Gibson employs as a metaphor for everything from the interaction of sub-atomic particles to the interactions of multinational corporations); the ongoing angst and paranoia (evident, as well, in the works of Burroughs, Dick, Pynchon, and DeLillo) that some overarching demiurge is manipulat-ing individuals and international politics; the mystical sense that our creation and re-creation of data and im-ages produces systems capable of merging with one an-other into new intelligences; and the spectre haunting nearly all postmodern SF—the uneasy recognition that our primal urge to replicate our consciousness and physical beings (into images, words, machine repli-cants, computer symbols) is *not* leading us closer to the dream of immortality, but is creating merely a pathetic parody, a metaexistence or simulacra of our essences that is supplanting us, literally taking over our physical space and our roles with admirable proficiency and without the drawbacks of human error and waste, with-out the human emotions of love, anger, ambition, and jealousy that jeopardize the efficiency and predictability of the capitalistic exchange—without, in short, the messy, unruly passions which also make the brief move-ment from conception to death so exhilarating and so frightening. And so human.

Near the end of "Postmodernism, or the Cultural Logic of Late Capitalism," Fredric Jameson announces the need for contemporary artists to invent "radically new forms" capable of responding to the complexities and textures of our historical moment. These new forms, he argues, would contain the possibilities for a new kind of "political art" that does more than either long for the past or merely represent our current "world space of multinational capital." This world space would indeed be represented in such art, Jameson notes, but it would achieve "a breakthrough to some as yet unimaginable new mode of representing this last, in which we may

again begin to grasp our position as individual and col-lective subjects and regain a capacity to act and struggle which is at present neutralized by our spatial as well as our social confusion" (1984a:92).

I hope to establish that Jameson's eloquent and timely call for new art forms capable of assisting us in clarify-ing the nature and meaning of our lives has in fact al-ready begun to be answered by some of the artists and critics who are represented here. Their work represents the most concerted effort yet by artists to find a suitable means for displaying the powerful and troubling tech-nological logic that underlies the postmodern condition. Mixing equal measures of anger and bitter humor, tech-nological know-how and formal inventiveness, post-modern SF should be seen as the breakthrough "realism" of our time. It is an art form that vividly represents the most salient features of our lives, as these lives are be-ing transformed and redefined by technology. It also seeks to empower us by providing a cognitive mapping that can help situate us in a brave new postmodern world that systematically distorts our sense of who or where we are, of what is "real" at all, of what is most valuable about human life.

Brian McHale (essay date spring 1992)

SOURCE: McHale, Brian. "Elements of a Poetics of Cyberpunk." *Critique* 33, no. 3 (spring 1992): 149-75.

[*In the following essay, McHale delineates the relation-ship between the "postmodernist poetics of fiction and cyberpunk poetics."*]

Cyberpunk science fiction is clearly on the postmodern-ist critical agenda. If it had not been already, it surely is now with the appearance of the new book on postmod-ernism by Fredric Jameson, whose contribution to the setting of that agenda can hardly be overestimated. In the new book's first endnote, Jameson laments the ab-sence of a chapter on cyberpunk, "henceforth, for many of us, the supreme *literary* expression if not of post-modernism, then of late capitalism itself" (Jameson [1991] 417). If I understand the tenor of this somewhat enigmatic note and the other scattered allusions to cy-berpunk (28, 286, 321), Jameson seems to be identify-ing cyberpunk as *the* literary manifestation of postmod-ernism, otherwise predominantly a nonliterary, visual, and spatial cultural phenomenon, whose preferred me-dia is architecture, photography, art installations, film, video, and the like. He seems even to be implying that cyberpunk is somehow the direct expression of late capitalism, almost as though it were unmediated by in-herited literary forms or historical genres. This would be an extraordinary position for someone who has taught us so much about the mediating function of genre (but perhaps I have misunderstood him here). In any event, it is an especially untenable position in the case of cyberpunk, which can hardly be properly "placed" in its cultural-historical context without taking into account its relations to two bodies of writing and their respective poetics, namely the poetics of the science fiction (SF) genre and the poetics of "elite" postmodernist fiction. Although cyberpunk may be (and doubtless is) a number of things—including a school phenomenon in the community of SF readers and writers, a generational phenomenon in the history of SF, a barefaced marketing device, and even, perhaps, the "supreme literary expression of late capitalism"—one thing that it surely must be is a convenient name for the kind of writing that springs up where the converging trajectories of SF poetics and postmodernist poetics finally cross (McHale, 1991).

As far as cyberpunk's relation to the SF tradition is concerned, there are few, if any, absolute novelties in cyberpunk SF; all the motifs that I document below have precedents in earlier SF, and some are very widely attested, to the point of constituting routine SF formulas or clichés. Cyberpunk's critics sometimes have adduced this fact as counter-evidence to excessive claims for the novelty and "breakthrough" character of cyberpunk by its propagandists. Perhaps there is something to be said for this point of view, nevertheless, cyberpunk, in an important sense is innovative despite the familiarity or formulaic character of its SF motifs. What is new in cyberpunk, first of all, is the conspicuousness of certain selected motifs and their foregrounding relative to other motifs from the SF repertoire; and second, the co-occurrence of certain motifs in the same texts, the solidarity among these motifs, the way they mutually corroborate and reinforce each other to create a motif complex that is distinctive of the cyberpunk wave of SF—even if every individual item in the complex can be traced back to earlier SF phases. The novelty of cyberpunk, in other words, lies not in the absolute newness of any particular component, but in a shift of dominance or center of gravity reflected in the combination of components and their relative conspicuousness in cyberpunk texts.

Cyberpunk's relation to "elite" postmodernist poetics is rather different. In this paper I will undertake to demonstrate and substantiate the overlap between the postmodernist poetics of fiction and cyberpunk poetics. The shared motifs I will identify occur at different levels of the text in postmodernism and cyberpunk; that is, what typically occurs as a motif of narrative structure or a pattern of language in postmodernist fiction tends to occur as an element of the fictional world in cyberpunk. Cyberpunk, one might say, translates or transcodes postmodernist motifs from the level of form (the verbal continuum, narrative strategies) to the level of the projected world.[1] To put it differently, cyberpunk tends to

"literalize" or "actualize" what occurs in postmodernist fiction as metaphor—metaphor not so much in the narrow sense of a verbal trope (though that is also a possibility), but in the extended sense in which a textual strategy or a particular use of language may be understood as a figurative representation of an "idea" or theme. In this respect, too, cyberpunk practice is clearly a continuation or extension of SF practice generally, for SF often generates elements of its worlds by literalizing metaphors from everyday discourse or mainstream fiction and poetry.[2] The three large bundles or complexes of motifs that cyberpunk SF shares with mainstream postmodernist fiction are motifs of what might be called "worldness"; motifs of the centrifugal self; and motifs of death, both individual and collective.

I. COWBOYS AND SUNDOGS

> Isn't this an "interface" here? a meeting surface for two worlds . . . sure, but *which two*?
>
> —Thomas Pynchon

Both science fiction and mainstream postmodernist fiction possess repertoires of strategies and motifs designed to raise and explore ontological issues; this is the basis for the overlap between the poetics of postmodernist fiction and SF poetics in general and cyberpunk poetics in particular. That is, SF, like postmodernist fiction, is governed by an ontological dominant, by contrast with modernist fiction or, among the genres of "genre" fiction, detective fiction, both of which raise and explore issues of epistemology and thus are governed by an epistemological dominant. Thus, whereas epistemologically oriented fiction (modernism, detective fiction) is preoccupied with questions such as, what is there to know about the world? who knows it and how reliably? how is knowledge transmitted, to whom, and how reliably? ontologically oriented fiction (postmodernism, SF) is preoccupied with questions such as, what is a world? how is a world constituted? are there alternative worlds, and if so how are they constituted? how do different worlds and different kinds of worlds differ? and what happens when one passes from one world to another? (McHale [1987] 9-11, 59-72, and passim; Calinescu 267).

To explore such ontological issues, both SF and postmodernist fiction use and adapt the resources common to all varieties of fiction, in particular the universal fictional resource of presentation of virtual space. If all fictional texts project virtual spaces, not many of them foreground and exploit the spatial dimension to the degree that SF and postmodernist texts do.[3] This shared poetics of space is partly to be explained by the common historical origins of SF and postmodernist fiction in romance. In medieval romance the category of "world," normally the unrepresentable, absolute horizon of all experience and perception, is itself made an object of representation through a particular metaphorical use of enclosed spaces *within* the romance world: castles, enchanted forests, walled gardens and bowers. Such symbolic enclosures, functioning as scale models or miniature analogues of worlds, bring into view the normally invisible horizons of world, the very "world-ness" of world. In other words, in medieval romance, space becomes an all-purpose tool for "doing" ontology—a means of exploring ontology *in* fiction, as well as (potentially at least) the ontology *of* fiction (Jameson [1975] 135-163, [1981] 103-105).

This is true not only of medieval romance itself, but of its "heirs" including SF and postmodernist fiction. SF in particular has developed in the course of its history as a genre repertoire of microworlds, scale-model worlds designed to bring into view the "worldness" of the category "world" itself. Ultimately derived from the castles, forest, and bowers of medieval romance, these SF microworlds—domed space colonies, orbiting space stations, subterranean cities, "cities in flight,"—recur throughout the genre's history. They recur yet again in cyberpunk SF, but with a new intensity of emphasis, sharpness of focus, and functional centrality.

The typical cyberpunk microworld uses the familiar motifs of outer-space fiction as building blocks: orbiting space stations or platforms, as in Tom Maddox's "Snake-Eyes" and William Gibson and Bruce Sterling's "Red Star, Winter Orbit" (both in *Mirrorshades* 1986), Gibson's *Neuromancer* (1984) and *Count Zero* (1986), Sterling's *Schismatrix* (1985), John Shirley's *Eclipse* (1985), Walter Jon Williams' *Hardwired* (1986), and Michael Swanwick's *Vacuum Flowers* (1987); or off-world colonies, whether domed, as in Rudy Rucker's *Software* (1982) and Lewis Shiner's *Frontera* (1984), or subsurface, as in Swanwick's *Vacuum Flowers* and Rucker's *Wetware* (1988). However, if the basic construction materials are SF clichés, the treatment of these materials in the cyberpunk context is typically revisionist or parodic. Where space stations and space colonies of traditional SF are glamorous showcases of high technology (think of Kubrick's *2001*), those of cyberpunk SF are likely to be orbiting slums—shabby, neglected, unsuccessful, technologically outdated (e.g., "Red Star, Winter Orbit," *Frontera, Eclipse, Vacuum Flowers*). Alternatively, for the miniature egalitarian democracies of traditional SF (think of *Star Trek*), cyberpunk substitutes off-world havens of privilege, orbiting penthouses to which the wealthy and powerful withdraw to escape the poverty and danger of the planet surface (e.g., *Neuromancer, Count Zero, Hardwired*).

Moreover, the cyberpunk adaptations of these familiar motifs heighten precisely the "worldness" of outer-space microworlds. This tendency is particularly conspicuous in Sterling's *Schismatrix,* Swanwick's *Vacuum Flowers,* and Williams' *Voice of the Whirlwind* (1987).

These texts extrapolate a future in which the human race, having evacuated planet Earth (partially in Williams, totally in Sterling and Swanwick), lives dispersed throughout the solar system in artificial planets and space colonies (on asteroids, the moons of other planets). Not only do these orbiting city-states differ from one another in the ways that nations differ in our world—in language, culture, political systems—but they also differ in more basic, indeed ontological, ways—in light, gravity, temperature, strains of bacteria. They differ, in other words, as worlds differ, and their differences heighten the world-modeling function of these enclosures.

Another cyberpunk variant brings these microworlds down out of orbit to the terrestrial surface and superimposes them on the current map of the world. In Marc Laidlaw's *Dad's Nuke* (1985) and Williams' *Hardwired,* for example, the United States of the near future has been balkanized (or, I supposed, "lebanonized"); that is, it has disintegrated into self-contained, warring enclaves sustained (in Laidlaw, less so in Williams) by disparate and competing ideologies and epistemologies. In Lucius Shepard's *Life During Wartime* (1987) and Lewis Shiner's *Deserted Cities of the Heart* (1988) Mexico and Central America have disintegrated in this way; in Shirley's *Eclipse,* Europe. These extrapolated near futures literalize a familiar metaphor in the sociology of knowledge (Berger & Luckmann 1966), that of the multiple, competing "subuniverses" or "enclaves" of meaning into which complex (post)modern societies have diversified. Here the diversification of knowledge is literal and geographical, and Berger and Luckmann's epistemological enclaves have erected barbed-wire perimeter fences and armed themselves with the latest military hardware against their epistemological competitors.

Alternatively, microworlds appear as islands: the artificial island of Freezone in Shirley's *Eclipse* (neatly mirroring and balancing the orbiting space station FirStep in the same text), or the islands of Sterling's *Islands in the Net* (1988). Some of Sterling's islands, such as Galveston Island in the opening episodes, are, as his title has it, "in the net," that is, integrated into the global communications and information network; but others, both literal islands (Grenada, Singapore, Turkish Cyprus) and figurative ones (a renegade submarine, motorized North African nomads, pocket dictatorships), remain defiantly outside the net. These latter islands—disparate, marginalized, renegade, resisting integration into the homogenizing world-system—strongly foreground the "worldness" of island microworlds.

Especially with these enclave and island microworlds cyberpunk SF returns to its distant historical roots in the kinds of romance world spaces that Jameson has described. Cyberpunk also returns to its romance roots through its use of wandering adventurer-heroes as a device for foregrounding its microworlds. "Worldness" in medieval romance (and in later subliterary derivatives, such as the Western) was heightened by the narrative device of the conventional knight errant's itinerary, which took him from microworld to microworld—from castle to enchanted forest to cave to bower to another castle, and so on. Freely crossing world boundaries, the knight errant thus served to expose the differences among (micro)worlds.

How conscious cyberpunk is of the adventurer-hero tradition is suggested by the nickname of Williams' hero in *Hardwired,* who smuggles contraband across the internal frontiers of what used to be the United States: he is (what else?) Cowboy. Space-traveling versions of the knight errant or cowboy abound in cyberpunk; Swanwick's Rebel Mudlark (*Vacuum Flowers*) is one, Sterling's Abelard Lindsay (*Schismatrix*) another, Williams' Etienne Steward (*Voice of the Whirlwind*) yet another. Sterling even coins a name for them: they are "sundogs" (by analogy, I suppose, with "seadogs," another adventurer-hero model), and the interplanetary spaces they traverse on their itineraries from microworld to microworld are "sundog zones."

IN THE ZONE

When Sterling calls these interplanetary spaces "sundog zones," he alludes to similar multiple-world spaces projected by postmodernist texts, in particular the "Zone" of Pynchon's *Gravity's Rainbow* and William Burroughs's "Interzone." All these spaces, cyberpunk and postmodernist alike, are instances of what Michel Foucault called "heterotopia," the impossible space in which fragments of disparate discursive orders (actualized in cyberpunk as disparate microworlds) are merely juxtaposed, without any attempt to reduce them to a common order.

In its terrestrial versions, this cyberpunk zone typically takes one of two forms. One form is that of the war zone, the familiar spaces of our world fragmented and "reconfigured," (*Gravity* 520) sometimes literally, by the impact of war—whether guerrilla war, as in Shepard's *Life During Wartime* and Shiner's *Deserted Cities,* tactical nuclear war, as in Shirley's *Eclipse,* or unconventional forms of so-called "conventional" warfare, as in Williams' *Hardwired.* The model of Pynchon's zone of postwar occupied Germany is a strong presence in some of these texts (e.g., *Eclipse*); in others, especially those involving tropical jungle warfare (*Life During Wartime, Deserted Cities*), the model is rather Michael Herr's Vietnam War journalism in *Dispatches* (1978), or the fictionalized version in his screenplay for Coppola's *Apocalypse Now.*

The other typical cyberpunk zone, and the source of what is perhaps the most characteristic cyberpunk imagery, is the urban zone. This is, so to speak, an "imploded" zone: instead of microworlds spaced out along a narrative itinerary, here they have been collapsed together in the heterotopian space of a future megalopolis where "fragments of a large number of possible orders glitter separately in the dimension, without law or geometry, of the *heteroclite*" (Foucault xviii). The most characteristic and most influential example of this cyberpunk zone is the "Sprawl," the near-future cityscape—that of the Boston-Atlanta Metropolitan Axis (the "Sprawl" proper) but also its Japanese equivalent, Tokyo/Chiba City—of Gibson's stories ("Johnny Mnemonic," "New Role Hotel," "Burning Chrome") and novels (*Neuromancer, Count Zero, Mona Lisa Overdrive*). Similar urban zones occupy the backgrounds (e.g., in Pat Cadigan's *Mindplayers* or Williams' *Hardwired* and *Voice of the Whirlwind*) and sometimes the foregrounds (e.g., L.A. in Richard Kadrey's *Metrophage* or the island-city Freezone in Shirley's *Eclipse*) of many other cyberpunk novels. They have even been projected into outer space to become the slummy asteroid-belt "tank towns" and the "cislunar sprawl" of "orbital hongkongs" in Swanwick's *Vacuum Flowers.*

The compositional principle of the Sprawl and its cognates, terrestrial and extraterrestrial, is maximally intimate juxtaposition of maximally diverse and heterogeneous cultural materials (Japanese, Western, and Third World, high-tech and low-tech, elite and popular, mainstream "official" culture and youth or criminal subcultures). The Sprawl is an image of the carnivalized city, the city as permanent carnival. Kadrey makes this explicit when, in *Metrophage,* he places in the background of his narrative a literal carnival, that of the Dia de los Muertos, its literally carnivalesque structure mirroring *en abyme* the carnivalesque structure of the "reconfigured" Los Angeles of Kadrey's near-future world.

At the center of this imploded multiple-world space—though "center" is a rather infelicitous term for a space whose organizational principle is precisely centerlessness—one typically finds an even more compact zone of cultural heterogeneity and juxtaposition, a kind of dense node of collapsed micro-worlds. This zone-within-the-Zone—red-light district, ghetto or barrio, sometimes a single building—can be read as a synecdoche (*pars pro toto*) or *mise en abyme* of the broader zone that surrounds it. Examples include the multistorey flea-market, the Hypermart, of Gibson's *Count Zero*; OmeGaity, the homosexual cruising warren on Shirley's island-city Freezone, with its "strange vibe of stratification: claustrophobia layered under agoraphobia" (129); the Iron Barrio prison-camp of Shepard's *Life During Wartime*; and the Golden Age of Hollywood Pavilion of Kadrey's *Metrophage,* an "enormous tented structure" housing reconstructions of classic Hollywood movie sets, left over from a world's fair and now home to a population of vagrants and squatters.

CYBERSPACE

All the strategies of "worldness" described so far have involved juxtapositions among microworlds occupying the same ontological plane and arranged along the same horizontal axis. It is also possible, however, to foreground the "worldness" of world by juxtaposing worlds not, as in all these cases, in series, on a horizontal axis, but rather *in parallel,* on a *vertical* axis; that is, it is possible to juxtapose worlds occupying *different* ontological planes—worlds and metaworlds, or worlds and inset worlds (worlds-within-worlds).

The characteristic cyberpunk form of inset world is "cyberspace" (Gibson's coinage), the computer-generated space mentally experienced by computer operators whose nervous systems are directly interfaced with the computer system. According to the fictitious history developed in cyberpunk novels, cyberspace evolved from the "virtual worlds" of military simulations, but its real origin (as Gibson has cheerfully admitted in an interview) is less glamorous, namely, contemporary video-arcade games and computer-graphics programs (McCaffery [1990] 138). More generally, the cyberspace motif arises from the potent illusion, experienced (I suppose) by all computer users, sophisticated and unsophisticated alike, of gazing into (or even moving around inside) some space lying somehow "within" or "behind" the flat screen of the computer monitor. And of course, apart from its immediate experiential source in illusions of this kind, cyberspace also has a long SF pedigree, including all the many variations on the SF motif of "paraspace": parallel worlds, other "dimensions," worlds of unactualized historical possibility.

Gibson's cyberspace, also called the "matrix," is a three-dimensional grid, "a 3-D chessboard, infinite and perfectly transparent" (*Burning Chrome* 168) in which concentrations of data (those stored by corporations, government agencies, the military) are represented by color-coded geometrical shapes: "the stepped scarlet pyramid of the Eastern Seaboard Fission Authority burning beyond the green cubes of Mitsubishi Bank of America, and high and very far away . . . the spiral arms of military systems" (*Neuromancer* 52). The user of this system has the illusion of moving among these representations as through a landscape, but a landscape entirely mental and virtual. The matrix is a "consensual hallucination," that is, exactly the same hallucinatory landscape is experienced by everyone who "jacks into" one of the system's terminals.

Apart from this second plane of shared cyberspace reality, parallel to the primary reality plane, Gibson's fictional world also incorporates a number of "private" paraspaces, limited-access worlds-within-the-world. The billionaire Virek, for instance (*Count Zero*), whose sickly body is kept alive in a vat, has had a private mental reality constructed for himself, one that simulates the city of Barcelona, while Bobby Newmark (*Mona Lisa Overdrive*) is permanently jacked into a unit that contains its own separate cyberspace world-construct ("an *approximation of everything*" [128]). These private paraspaces are not, however, hermetically sealed but may be entered not only from the primary reality plane but even, in extraordinary circumstances, from other inset worlds. Bobby Newmark, for instance, penetrates Virek's world-construct from the cyberspace matrix at the climax of *Count Zero*. It is possible, in other words, to adventure from parallel world to parallel world on the vertical axis, just as one can from microworld to microworld on the horizontal axis of the primary reality plane.

Other cyberpunk versions of the cyberspace motif (e.g., Laidlaw's in *Dad's Nuke,* Cadigan's in *Mindplayers*) have more or less close affinities with Gibson's. But if cyberspace (whether on Gibson's model or some other) is the most characteristic cyberpunk variant on the paraspace motif, it is nevertheless not the only one. Where texts such as *Neuromancer, Mindplayers,* and *Dad's Nuke* construct a two-tier ontology[4] by juxtaposing a primary reality plane with an inset cyberspace world, other cyberpunk texts do so by juxtaposing the primary reality plane with a parallel realm of mythic archetypes. Examples include Shiner's *Frontera,* whose protagonist, Kane, acts out the hero "monomyth" simultaneously in the real world and the myth world to which he has access in dreams and hallucinations; Shiner's *Deserted Cities of the Heart,* where the myth being reenacted is the Mesoamerican one of Kukulcan/Quetzlcoatl; and Shepard's *Green Eyes* (1984), where the parallel myth world is that of voodoo divinities. In other words, these texts literalize or actualize the kinds of mythological materials that function metaphorically in modernist texts such as *Ulysses* and *Doktor Faustus.* While Joyce's Leopold Bloom "is" Odysseus only figuratively, in a kind of extended metaphor, Shiner's Kane *really* is the Hero with a Thousand Faces on a different but parallel plane of reality.[5]

The paraspace motif, including cyberspace and its functional equivalent, the myth world, not only serves to bring into view the "worldness" of world; it also offers the possibility of reflecting on world making itself, and on science fiction world making in particular. Paraspace is, at least potentially, a scale model of the fictional world itself, a fictional-world-within-the-fictional-world, or, in other words, a *mise en abyme* of the text's fictional world. It offers, in other words, the possibility of metafiction.

Cyberpunk texts often exploit the metafictional potential of paraspace. This metafictional dimension is foregrounded when, for instance, in Shepard's *Green Eyes,* the paraspace myth world first manifests itself in stories (fictions-within-the-fiction) written by the novel's protagonist. Inset stories and *mise en abyme* proliferate in Shepard's second, and more properly cyberpunk novel, *Life During Wartime,* which is heavily influenced by Latin-American "magic realist" poetics. The text incorporates paraphrases of stories by one Juan Pastorín that echo elements of the novel's real world, and Shepard's protagonist, Mingolla, comes finally to believe that he has been written into one of Pastorín's stories (359-360). There is also an elaborate description (324-331) of a mural, "The Mechanics Underlying Superficial Reality," which duplicates *en abyme* many of the novel's features.

In Gibson's *Mona Lisa Overdrive,* the artificial intelligence Continuity, who intervenes in this novel's cyberspace world, is described as "writing a book . . . *always* writing it" (42). A similar self-reflexive, metafictional potential can sometimes be discerned in microworlds on the horizontal axis; for instance, the scale model of an ocean ecology constructed at a research station in Cuernavaca in Shiner's *Deserted Cities* readily lends itself to interpretation as a *mise en abyme* of SF world modeling.

II. SIMSTIM

Which world is this? What is to be done in it? Which of my selves is to do it?

—Dick Higgins

Postmodernism's shift of focus to ontological issues and themes has radical consequences for literary models of the self. A poetics in which the category "world" is plural, unstable, and problematic would seem to entail a model of the self that is correspondingly plural, unstable, and problematic. If we posit a plurality of worlds, then conceivably "my" self exists in more than one of them; if the world is ontologically unstable (self-contradictory, hypothetical, or fictional, infiltrated by other realities) then so perhaps am "I." Dick Higgins' first question would seem to entail his last: if we can ask, "Which world is this?," then it follows that eventually we must also get around to asking, "Which of my selves . . . ?"

Modernist perspectivism (e.g., *Ulysses, The Sound and the Fury, To the Lighthouse, Les Faux-monnayeurs*) multiplied points of view on the world, but without, for the most part, undermining the underlying unity of the self. Though in modernist fiction the perspectives on the world are many, and each differ from all the others, nevertheless each perspective is lodged in a subjectivity that is itself relatively coherent, relatively centered and stable; and this is true even of those modernist texts (e.g., *A la Recherche du temps perdu, La coscienza di Zeno, Die Mann ohne Eigenschaften*) in which the unity and continuity of the self is problematized. Still, perspectivism does exert considerable centrifugal pressure on the self, and there are tendencies in modernism toward fragmentation and decentering. Never brought to full fruition during the modernist period, these centrifugal tendencies could not be realized until the emergence of a postmodernist poetics that explores and problematizes the ontologies of worlds and texts.[6]

For the most part, fragmentation and dispersal of the self occurs in postmodernist fiction at the levels of language, narrative structure, and the material medium (the printed book), or between these levels, rather than at the level of the fictional world. In other words, postmodernist fiction prefers to represent the disintegration of the self figuratively, through linguistic, structural, or visual metaphors, rather than literally, in the persons of characters who undergo some kind of literal disintegrative experience. There are exceptions. Both Pynchon and Sukenick, for instance, have texts in which characters fracture or disintegrate, not metaphorically (psychologically) but ontologically. In *Gravity's Rainbow,* for instance, Pirate Prentice is literally a medium, a "fantasist-surrogate" possessed by alternate selves, while the novel's supposed hero, Tyrone Slothrop, undergoes disassembly and "scattering," entirely disappearing from the world by the closing episodes. Similarly, Sukenick has characters who, before our eyes, so to speak, "peel off" from other characters (Roland Sycamore in *Out*), "split" into two (Boris Ccrab in *Blown Away*), infiltrate and take possession of other characters by "a kind of psychic osmosis" (*Blown Away*), and so on.

Ontologically oriented like postmodernist fiction, science fiction has also developed a repertoire of strategies for asking, "Which world is this?," yet it has for the most part managed to avoid asking the corollary question, "Which of my selves?" It has, in other words, appeared to evade the consequences of its ontological pluralism and experimentalism for its model of the self. Or rather, SF has tended to neutralize the issue of the (re)presentation of self by keeping characterization generally "thin," "shallow," and impoverished, strictly subordinated to the foreground category of "world." In this respect we might even say, paradoxically, that traditional SF, otherwise so "premodernist" in its orientation, has always been postmodernist. "The disappearance of character (in the traditional sense) from contemporary ('postmodern') fiction," writes Christine Brooke-Rose, "is one of the ways in which SF and the more 'serious,' experimental fiction have come together" (102); character, newly absent from "serious" fiction, has always been absent from SF!

Cyberpunk practice is to actualize or literalize what in postmodernist poetics normally appears as a metaphor at the level of language, structure, or the material medium. Where postmodernism has figurative representations of disintegration, cyberpunk texts typically project fictional worlds that include (fictional) objects and (fictional) phenomena embodying and illustrating the problematics of selfhood: human-machine symbiosis, artificial intelligences, biologically engineered alter egos, and so on.

Since cyberpunk handles the centrifugal self at the level of fictional world rather than at one or more of the formal levels of the text, as postmodernist fiction prefers to do, its motifs of dispersion and decentering fall naturally into categories based on the types of fictional objects and phenomena represented. Here we can turn to Sterling's fiction for a convenient taxonomy. In a series of stories culminating in his 1985 novel *Schismatrix,* Sterling projects a future history in which humankind divides into two "posthuman" species in competition with one another, each species employing a different range of technologies to enhance and transform itself so as to improve its own chances for success. The "Mechanists," or "Mechs," use electronic and biomechanical means to augment themselves; prostheses to enhance the body, but with the side effect of violating its integrity; brain computers interfacing to extend the mind, but with the side effect of attenuating and dispersing it. Their rivals, the "Shapers," use bio-engineering techniques—cloning, genetic engineering—to achieve the same ends, and with similar side effects: who am "I" if I am a member of a "congenetic clan" of identical cloned individuals? These two technological options— the Mech option and the Shaper option—define alternative ranges of representational motifs of the centrifugal self.[7] Swanwick, in *Vacuum Flowers,* offers a parallel future history and an alternative pair of categories; in his version, the division is between the "wettechnic civilization" (roughly, the Mech option) of the solar system proper and the bioprogramming technologies (roughly, the Shaper option) of the comet worlds. We might call the first set, corresponding to the Mech option, cyberpunk proper, and the second set, corresponding to the Shaper option, "bio-punk."

RIDING THE EYE-FACE

The traditional SF iconography of the humanoid robot, as developed by Capek, Binder, Asimov and others, is relatively rare in cyberpunk; only Rudy Rucker (*Software, Wetware*) has exploited it in any very ambitious way. More typical of cyberpunk are its artificial intelligences (AIs), software surrogate humans, i.e., programs, rather than the hardware robots (or "wetware" androids) of traditional SF. Examples include Gibson's Wintermute and Neuromancer, who merge at the end of *Neuromancer,* but by the time of its sequel, *Count Zero,* have already broken up into multiple software "selves." All of these variants on the robot motif serve to raise the classic SF question, who (or what) is human? At what point does a machine cease being a "mere" machine and begin to count as a human being?

This same question is also raised, but in inverted form, by the cyberpunk motif of prosthesis: at what point does a human being cease to be a human being and begin to count as a machine? Sterling's Mechanists (*Schismatrix*) present an entire range of prosthetic possibilities, from biomechanical arms and legs, through remote-control "waldos" that enable human beings to extend their presence into unliveably hostile environments (deep space, ocean abysses), to "wireheads" who, abandoning their organic bodies entirely, survive as software ghosts in electronic machines. Less total prostheses are recurrent motifs in Gibson, Kadrey (*Metrophage*) and Williams (*Hardwired, Voice of the Whirlwind*), especially artificial eyes and surgically implanted weapons (knife-blades under the fingernails, a microfilament garotte in the thumb, a murderous "cybersnake" prosthetic weapon in the throat), even, in Kadrey, prosthetic genitalia!

Prosthetic augmentation is possible for mental capacities as well as for the body's physical capacities. There are minimal forms of this mental-augmentation motif, in which units ("microsofts," "augs") introduced permanently or temporarily into the nervous system supply specialized knowledge or preprogrammed technical skills when needed (Gibson, Shirley's "Wolves of the Plateau"). In Swanwick's *Vacuum Flowers,* maximum mental augmentation takes the form of the temporary programming of individuals with any of a range of useful or desirable personality constructs ("personas"), either for the sake of the specialized skills that these latter possess (doctor, police, skilled worker, weapons operator), or simply for reasons of entertainment and fashion. Exploring the possibility of multiple "personas" overlaid one on top of the other and occupying the same brain, this maximal form of the motif (also to be found in a somewhat different version in Cadigan's *Mindplayers*) captures in a particularly arresting way the cyberpunk theme of the plurality and fragmentation of the self.

At some hard-to-define point prosthetic augmentation shades off into a complete human-machine symbiosis or fusion, and the borders of the self blur and erode. The image of a human being coupled with a machine— "jacked-in," "riding the eye-face" (i.e., the "I-face," or human-machine interface)—recurs in many variations throughout cyberpunk; it is, indeed, the most characteristic piece of cyberpunk iconography. In these postures of fusion, the human partner in the symbiosis may experience an exhilarating expansion of self, as does Williams' protagonist Cowboy when he plugs into his armored vehicle, or, alternatively, an identity-threatening dilution or attenuation, as with Reno, Williams' part-human, part-prosthetic character, or the "wirehead" Ryumin in *Schismatrix.* In extreme cases, the human self may be entirely absorbed into the machine. Williams' Reno, who begins as part prosthetic, ends by being a literally centrifugal self, diffused throughout the worldwide information network. Similarly, Rucker's Cobb Anderson persists as disembodied, taped "software" capable of being booted up in a variety of "hardware" vehicles, custom-made bodies as well as machines. Both in Rucker's two cyberpunk novels and in Swanwick's *Vacuum Flowers,* renegade cybernetic systems aspire to absorb the entire human race into a collective group-mind incorporating human and machine intelligences alike—the ultimate form of human-machine symbiosis.

Zombies

The "biopunk" subvariety of cyberpunk SF makes available an entirely different, though complementary, range of motifs of the centrifugal self. Where machine-oriented cyberpunk produces electronic and mechanical surrogates of human beings (robots, AIs), the biopunk variety "grows" new human individuals in vats, or clones identical multiples of the "same" individual, literally pluralizing the self (*Schismatrix, Wetware, Vacuum Flowers, Dad's Nuke, Voice of the Whirlwind*). Where the machine-oriented variety augments and extends human capacities through mechanical means (prostheses, "waldos"), biopunk accomplishes the same thing through bio-techniques, engineering new, reconfigured human types: "angels" (*Schismatrix, Wetware*), mermaids/mermen (Shiner's "Till Human Voices Wake Us"). Finally, where the machine-oriented variety threatens the individual human self with diffusion throughout an electronic network, biopunk threatens bodily fusion with other individuals (the effect of the drug "merge" in *Wetware*) and, ultimately, physical diffusion and loss of differentiation (the woman grotesquely reconfigured as a wall of undifferentiated tissue, the "Wallmother," in *Schismatrix,* the planet-wide biomass in Greg Bear's *Blood Music*).

It is not hard to see that these biopunk motifs revise, update, and rationalize classic gothic-horror motifs of bodily invasion and disruption. This is especially the case with the biopunk variations on the classic B-movie gothic-horror motif of the zombie. The traditional zombie, of course, is a corpse reanimated by powerful voodoo magic to do the magician's will. In its various biopunk adaptations, the zombie is rarely a corpse, more often a living human being "possessed" by some alien self, or under the irresistible control of some other human being. The technologies of possession and control vary.

One variant, for instance, extrapolates from the familiar capacity of present-day drugs to induce in the drug user temporary personality changes of a regular and to some extent predictable kind, changes in effect "coded" in the chemical structure of the drug. These extrapolated "designer drugs" of the future temporarily efface the "real"

self and induce, for instance, a prostitute-self (Gibson's "meat puppets"), or a soldier self (Shepard's "samurai"—the name both of the drug and the personality it induces; Williams' "hardfire"). In one sophisticated version, found in Sterling's *Islands in the Net,* the capacity for transformation into an assassin personality is chemically preprogrammed into the individual, requiring only an enzyme trigger to activate it: merely eating a carton of yogurt turns a personable Rastafarian into a "killing machine." Clearly, this military use of drugs to induce a soldier personality is functionally equivalent to the motif of human-machine symbiosis in which the pilot directly interfaces with his weapons system (Maddox's "Snake-Eyes," Swanwick and Gibson's "Dog-fight," Shepard's *Life During Wartime*, Williams' *Hardwired* and *Voice of the Whirlwind,* Kadrey's *Metrophage*).

A second biopunk variant on the zombie motif extrapolates from a classic paranoid theme, what Pynchon calls "the old Radio-Control-Implanted-In-the-Head-At-Birth problem" (542). In other words, this variant involves biotechnological devices, such as surgically implanted radio receivers that subject the individual self to some irresistible remote control by others. Shiner's hero Kane, in *Frontera* is subjected to just this sort of biotechnological control, and Shepard (*Life During Wartime*) has an entire radio-controlled zombie army. Rucker (*Wetware*) elaborates a range of horrible baroque variations on this control motif, including a "zombie box" that, affixed to the spine, turns a human being into a remote-controlled zombie; a miniaturized "robot rat" that replaces the right half of the human brain, transforming a human being into a puppet-like "meatie"; and a robot "Happy Cloak" that, draped around a vat-grown, mindless cloned body, is capable of animating it and inducing in it a semblance of sentience. The distinction here between machine-oriented cyberpunk motifs and biopunk motifs is obviously a purely artificial one, and biotechnological control devices such as those found in *Wetware* shade imperceptibly into the range of techniques for superimposing personalities that we have already mentioned (*Vacuum Flowers* and *Mindplayers*). Also related is the motif of telepathic mind-control, a much more conventional SF motif, to be found in Shepard's *Life During Wartime* alongside the more distinctively cyberpunk variants of the drug-induced personality and the radio-controlled zombie.

Finally, closest of all in some ways to the traditional zombie of horror fiction and movies, is what might be called the motif of the cellular-level self. In *Green Eyes,* Lucius Shepard's self-conscious revision of the zombie myth, a particular strain of bacteria introduced into the brain of a fresh corpse generates there a short-lived ersatz personality (a "Bacterially Induced Artificial Personality"). Under these bizarre circumstances, the self is plural and decentered, literally "a disease in a borrowed brain" (89).[8] The ultimate elaboration of this variant of the centrifugal self is to be found in Greg Bear's *Blood Music* (1985), in which the cells of the human body acquire their own collective intelligence, like that of an ant hill, wholly independent of the intelligence of their human "host." Seizing control of their "environment"—first the bodies of their hosts and ultimately the entire planet—and reshaping it to their needs, they transform Earth into a vast, constantly metamorphosing biomass, possessing a single collective selfhood. Simultaneously the one and the many, centripetal and centrifugal Bear's cellular-level intelligence mirrors the world-spanning symbiotic human-machine intelligences of Rucker and Swanwick.

SIMSTIM

The theme of the centrifugal self, and the representational motifs through which it is manifested in cyberpunk SF, are essentially incompatible with the perspectivist narrative strategies of modernist fiction. Modernist strategies such as multiple limited points of view and "parallax" of perspectives rest on the assumption of relatively centered, relatively stable subjectivities. Recognizing this, postmodernist writers have either sought to "background" these strategies, relegating them to a subordinate and ancillary role, or have, like Pynchon in *Gravity's Rainbow,* deployed them in ways that undermine the modernist assumptions upon which they rest—in effect parodying modernist perspectivism. But Pynchon's is a difficult precedent to emulate, and cyberpunk writers have all too often ended up falling back on perspectivist structural clichés inherited from modernist poetics (either directly, or indirectly by way of SF's own modernist generation, the so-called "New Wave" SF of the 1960s). This is true, for instance, of Shiner's *Frontera,* Shirley's *Eclipse,* Gibson's *Count Zero* and *Mona Lisa Overdrive,* and other cyberpunk novels composed on the modernist model of multiple, shifting points of view.

But the modernist assumptions underlying perspectivism can be countered, and in ways that are distinctively cyberpunk rather than weak imitations of Pynchon's postmodernism. How this can be achieved is demonstrated by two texts, Sterling's *Islands in the Net* and Gibson's *Neuromancer.* These texts share, among other things, the motif of "simstim" (Gibson's coinage), that is, "simulated stimulus." In Gibson's world, simstim is an extrapolated communications and entertainment medium involving not only audio and visual sensory channels, as television presently does, but the entire range of senses, the full human sensorium. As an entertainment medium, Gibson's simstim is a cross between the "feelies" of Huxley's *Brave New World* and American commercial television's egregious *Life Styles of the Rich and Famous*: simstim stars (Tally Isham in "Burning Chrome," Neuromancer, and Count Zero, Angie Mitchell at the end of *Count Zero* and in *Mona Lisa Overdrive*) travel, interview celebrities, and enjoy the good life while wearing equipment that records the full range of their sensory experience for broadcast (appropriately edited, of course) to consumers who vicariously re-experience through simstim receivers at home what the stars have directly experienced in real life. Typical SF extrapolated technology, in other words—but with interesting implications for literary perspectivism.

Exactly *what* implications can be clearly seen in Sterling's *Islands.* In the world of Sterling's novel there is no "simstim" in the sense of Gibson's entertainment medium; here the technology behind simstim is still cutting-edge, too expensive for the average consumer, and reserved for corporate communications uses only. David and Laura, about to undertake a risky diplomatic mission to Grenada for the Rizome multinational corporation, of which they are "associates," are custom-fitted with videocam sunglasses, as well as audio pickups, microtransmitters, and earpieces for audio reception. Transmitted through satellite links to Rizome's communications center, their sensory input (audio and visual channels only, not, in this case, the full sensory range) is made available to Rizome associates throughout the worldwide communications "Net."

Thus, the episodes in Grenada unfold on two "planes" or in two "locations" simultaneously. At the same time that we follow Laura (through whom this text is focalized) and David as they make their way around the island, Rizome associates throughout the world are also following them, and occasionally intervening over their audio links: these interventions, audible only to David and Laura, not to the Grenadians around them, are indicated in the text by square brackets:

> At that moment a new voice came online. ["Hello Rizome-Grenada, this is Eric King in San Diego. . . . Could you give me another look at that distillation unit. . . . No, you, Laura, look at the big yellow thing—"]
>
> "I'll take it," Laura shouted to David, putting her hand over her ear. "Eric, where is it you want me to look?"
>
> ["To your left—yeah-Jeez, I haven't seen one like that in twenty years. . . . Could you give me just a straight, slow scan from right to left. . . . Yeah, that's great."] He fell silent as Laura panned across the horizon.
>
> (82-83)

As this passage indicates, feedback from their Rizome "eavesdroppers" back home literally shapes how and what David and Laura perceive—where they turn their attentions, how long they spend looking, from what angles. Negatively, their consciousness of being eavesdropped upon also determines what gets "edited out" of their behavior: for example, they refrain from sexual byplay except when their transmission rigs have been removed, in effect practicing self-censorship.

So Rizome's corporate self, unified but also dispersed by the "Net," can and does freely occupy the point of view of Laura and David. These latter can be seen (at least when they are wearing their videocam rigs) as the corporate self's sense organs, its feelers probing the outside world. Here, in other words, a perspectivist strategy (focalization through a limited point of view) has been reinterpreted and freshly re-motivated in terms of a characteristic cyberpunk motif of the centrifugal self. Rizome's corporate self is a relatively benign version of the more threatening biological (*Blood Music*) and human-machine collectivities (*Vacuum Flowers, Wetware*) with which we are already familiar. Nevertheless, it *is* a version of them, and here it serves to turn a structural cliché into a novel means of representing the submergence of the individual self in the collective.

Even more radical, perhaps, is Gibson's use of the simstim motif to remotivate perspectivism in *Neuromancer.* While she breaks into the Sense/Net corporate headquarters, and again during her raid on the Tessier-Ashpool refuge of Villa Staylight, Molly the female ninja wears a simstim broadcast rig, enabling her partner Case to accompany her on the raid vicariously, as it were. Using simstim technology, Case can occupy Molly's point of view at will, literally at the flip of a switch. As in the Grenada episodes of *Islands in the Net,* the action unfolds simultaneously on two "planes," three if one counts cyberspace, for Case shifts back and forth among his own point of view on the primary reality plane, Molly's point of view, and the secondary, cyberspace reality plane. The effect is that of "split-screen" cinema or television—or indeed, that of multiple-point-of-view fiction.

This is, in one sense, a purely formal solution ingeniously motivated by a representational motif at the level of the fictional world. The text of *Neuromancer* is consistently focalized through Case, but in these episodes Case is not at the center of the action, or rather he does not occupy its only center; the action involving Molly is at least as important and engaging. The simstim motif allows Gibson to introduce Molly's experience without violating the basic point of view convention of the text.

Ingenious though it may be, this is not, however, *only* a characteristically cyberpunk solution to a formal problem. It is also a subversive gesture, implicitly undermining the model of the centered, centripetal self upon which modernist perspectivism rests. With the flip of a switch Case is able to experience another's body, "other flesh," *from within.* He experiences another's physical pain when he shifts into Molly's sensorium a moment after she has had her leg broken (64). He even has the opportunity to see himself from another point of view, literally as another sees him:

> [He] found himself staring down, through Molly's one good eye, at a white-faced, wasted figure, afloat in a loose fetal crouch, a cyberspace deck between its thighs, a band of silver [elec]trodes above closed, shadowed eyes. The man's cheeks were hollowed with a day's growth of dark beard, his face slick with sweat.
>
> He was looking at himself.
>
> (256)

Finally, and perhaps most radically, when Case flips the switch that displaces him into Molly's point of view, he literally *changes gender*: he inhabits, if only temporarily, a woman's body. "So now you get to find out just how tight those jeans really are, huh?" wisecracks the Finn after he finishes explaining the simstim hook-up to Case (53), and this witty, subversive literalization of male clichés of sexual conquest ("I wouldn't mind getting into *her* pants!") suggests just how disorienting—at least potentially—this motif can be. A comparable instance of literalizing a typical modernist structure through some representational motif of extrapolated future technology occurs in Kadrey's *Metrophage.* Here the protagonist, one Jonny Qabbala, is fitted with prosthetic eyes capable of recording and playing back whatever passes through their visual field. Before he has fully mastered his new prosthesis, Jonny inadvertently triggers playbacks of scenes that had passed before his eyes some time earlier: "As Jonny looked at the animals, a frozen image of the bodysheathed Swedes imposed itself on his vision, the street by La Poupée clear in the background. Then it was gone. Jonny blinked, tensing the muscles around his eyes. The image of the Swedes flashed back. He held it this time, made it move slowly, forward and backward" (185). Later Jonny will deliberately play back images of his dead lover. In other words, this technological motif motivates typical modernist structures of memory, whether that of involuntary memory in Proust, or obsessive memory-loops such as those in Benjy's and Quentin's monologues in Faulkner's *The Sound and the Fury.* As a vehicle for imagining what it would be like to *be* a centrifugal self—to be in two places at once, to occupy two different points of view and two different bodies simultaneously, to change genders at the flip of a switch—the characteristic cyberpunk motif of simstim gives fresh, concrete, and radical meaning to Dick Higgins' question, "Which of my selves is to do it?"

III. The Final Frontier

> His whole psychology, his point of orientation, is to dabble with death and yet somehow surmount it.
>
> —Philip K. Dick

The ultimate ontological boundary, the one which no one can help but cross, is, of course, the boundary between life and death, between being and not-being. It is only to be expected, then, that an ontologically oriented poetics such as that of postmodernist fiction should be preoccupied with death. Perhaps it would be more accurate to put this the other way around and to say rather that the ontologically oriented poetics of postmodernism is the latest, renewed manifestation of our culture's protracted struggle to represent, and thus symbolically to master, death. Either way, postmodernist fiction might somewhat reductively be characterized as one long, resourceful, highly diversified, obsessive meditation on the intolerable fact of personal extinction—your death, my death, our collective death (McHale [1987] 227-35).

Thomas Pynchon remarks, in the controversial introduction to his short-story collection *Slow Learner* (1984), that in science fiction "mortality is . . . seldom an issue," and that this is a mark of the genre's immaturity and helps explain its appeal for immature readers (5). This is unfair; there are a number of SF writers (one thinks of Philip K. Dick and Thomas Disch, among others) who have been as seriously preoccupied with mortality as any "mainstream" writer, and who have used SF conventions and formulas to explore death in ways not open to writers outside the SF genre. Nevertheless, it could be argued that no generation or group of SF writers has made the exploration of death its special province until the emergence of the cyberpunk "wave" in the 1980s.

One important exception to this generalization, one that deals with a particular variant of the theme of death has been a special province of SF writing in general since 1945 (and in fact before): the theme of nuclear holocaust. If late-twentieth-century literature in general, including postmodernist fiction, has turned with renewed attention to the perennial human preoccupation with death, it is no doubt in part because for the first time in history human beings feel threatened with "double" death: inevitable personal extinction, as always, but also the probable global self-destruction of the race and its posterity through nuclear war (or, alternatively, some ecological disaster). To SF writing in particular has fallen the task of feeding our imaginations with images and scenarios of our impending global extinction.[9] This task has been inherited in due course by the cyberpunk generation of SF writers, who have stamped their own distinctive mark and emphases on the theme of nuclear war.

DAD'S NUKE

A distinguishing mark of cyberpunk SF, writes Bruce Sterling, is its "boredom with Apocalypse" (*Chrome* xi), which does not mean that cyberpunk disregards the nuclear war theme but rather that, like its SF and postmodernist precursors, it seeks ways of renewing and defamiliarizing it.

Thus, for instance, John Shirley prefaces his *Eclipse* (1985) with an alarming and enigmatic "note from the author":

This is not a post-holocaust novel.
Nor is this a novel about nuclear war.
It may well be that this is a *pre*-holocaust novel.

Distancing himself in this way from familiar SF nuclear war motifs (such as the "post-holocaust novel"), Shirley prepares us for his revisionist treatment of nuclear war; what follows is a representation of the nuclear apocalypse as a long drawn-out agony, a tactical nuclear war of attrition in Europe. In other words, Shirley challenges the image of apocalypse as an instantaneous, transformative, irreversible event, substituting for it an image of "slow-motion" apocalypse, an endlessly protracted "pre-holocaust" from which the world never emerges into a transformed, post-holocaust future.

Bruce Sterling's *Islands in the Net* (1988) defamiliarizes the nuclear threat in a particularly powerful and subtle way. Projecting a near-future world from which nuclear weapons have supposedly been abolished, Sterling has his heroine Laura, the quintessentially normal citizen of this world, uncover a cabal of renegades armed with atomic weapons and intent on nuclear blackmail. Before our eyes, as it were, her nuclear-free world is shockingly transformed into our own brink-of-apocalypse world. The effect is that of a double defamiliarization: Laura's nuclear-free world, alien to us but familiar to her, is abruptly transformed into a state of affairs utterly alien to her but only too familiar with us. Because we view this familiar state of affairs through Laura's eyes and from her alien perspective it jolts us with a shock of defamiliarized recognition: "On some deep unconscious level," Laura reflects, "people liked the political upheaval, the insecurity, the perverse tang of nuclear fear. The fear was an aphrodisiac, a chance to chuck the long-term view and live for the moment. Once it had always been like that. Now that she was living it, hearing people talk it, she knew" (334). "Once it had always been like that," indeed, but the experience passes for routine unless we deliberately adopt an alienated point of view, such as that of Sterling's woman from the future.

Another powerful defamiliarizing strategy of cyberpunk nuclear war fiction is what might be called the motif of "backyard apocalypse." The nuclear threat is literally reduced to backyard dimensions in Marc Laidlaw's satirical *Dad's Nuke* (1985), where suburban neighbors in an embattled neighborhood enclave compete over who possesses the most advanced family arsenal. When the neighbor across the street acquires his own backyard tactical nuclear missile system, Dad responds by installing a miniature nuclear reactor in the garage! Sterling exploits a version of this same motif in *Schismatrix* (1985), where he defamiliarizes nuclear war by reducing its dimensions and making it a universally available option. In a future in which "world" has been reduced to the dimensions of orbiting "microworlds," the threat of annihilation becomes correspondingly small scale: every orbital microworld is vulnerable to instant micro-apocalypse through the simple puncturing of its airtight outer shell. Furthermore anyone, even a crew of pirates, can possess technology sufficient to destroy such a world.

> *Worlds could burst.* The walls held life itself, and outside those locks and bulkheads loomed utterly pitiless darkness, the lethal nothingness of naked space. . . . There was no true safety. There had never been any. There were a hundred ways to kill a world: fire, explosion, poison, sabotage. . . . The power of destruction was in the hands of anyone and everyone. Anyone and everyone shared the burden of responsibility. The specter of destruction had shaped the moral paradigm of every world and every ideology.
>
> (79-80)

Scaling it down to microworld proportions in this way restores to the motif of nuclear apocalypse its power to shock and haunt: Sterling's microworlds are transparently scale models of our world, his micro-apocalypses displaced versions of the collective death we face.

Critics have suggested that the literary representation of nuclear war is itself a displacement, that, in fact, every image of collective death is only a kind of metaphor for personal death.[10] Perhaps so; in any case, it is striking that in cyberpunk SF motifs of apocalypse and motifs of personal extinction co-occur, mutually corroborating and reinforcing each other. If anything, though, it is at the level of personal extinction, rather than that of collective disaster, that the cyberpunk meditation on death is most innovative, most resourceful, and most persistent. "The spectre haunting all c[yber]-p[unk]," as Larry McCaffery has observed, is *the* Spectre, the spectre of death ("Desert" 15).

EXCLUDED MIDDLES

Life and death form a binary opposition, of course. As Pynchon reminds us in his recent novel *Vineland* (1990), returning to a metaphor from his earlier *The Crying of Lot 49* (1966), ours is "a world based on the one and zero of life and death" (72). Between life and death there is no third option, no middle state; the law of the excluded middle applies. But, as we know from *The Crying of Lot 49,* excluded middles are "bad shit, to be avoided" (36), so in *Vineland* Pynchon tries to imagine a middle state of "mediated death" (218) occupied by beings called Thanatoids who, because of some "karmic imbalance" (173), are not permitted fully to die but must linger on in an ambiguous condition "like death, only different" (170). Pynchon's is one version of the postmodernist modeling of the ontological frontier between life and death. Other, parallel versions are to be found in SF, for instance the "half-life" state upon which Dick's *Ubik* (1969) is premised, and the many other SF variations on the theme of suspended animation.

Fusing the SF and postmodernist strategies for modeling death, cyberpunk seeks to imagine some middle state beyond or outside biological life—not a state of nonbeing, not death. Here, as in the case of other cyberpunk motifs, the range of motifs for exploring this middle or half-life state divides along the lines laid down in Sterling's future history of the "posthuman" race: on one side, the "Mechanist" options, or cyberpunk proper, that is, electronic means of resurrection and persistence beyond death; on the other side, the "Shaper" or "bio-punk" options, that is, bio-engineered means of "posthumous" survival.

The paradigm of cyberpunk motifs of death and machine-mediated resurrection might be a cinematic rather than a literary example: the death of the policeman Murphy and his resurrection as the hybrid RoboCop in Paul Verhoeven's film of that name (1987). In this extraordinary sequence, Murphy's death on the operating table is represented from his subjective point of view. Emergency procedures fail to save him; the doctors declare him dead; the screen goes black. Then, after a moment of darkness, the subjective camera-eye perspective returns, this time framed as in a camera viewfinder, with LED numbers flashing in one corner of the screen. Murphy has been revived as RoboCop, part human being, part machine.[11] This same interior perspective on the experience of dying and being posthumously "booted up" in a machine, so graphically represented in the *RoboCop* sequence, is persistently explored by Rudy Rucker in *Software* and its sequel *Wetware.* Throughout these texts, intelligences, both human and machine, face death and experience the disorienting transition to a new mechanical or biological body and the limbo state between existing in one body and existing in another. This is, in a sense, the focus or dominant of Rucker's poetics, and he is relentless in his experimentation with means of representing the subjective experience of death and resurrection.

If Rucker seems particularly obsessive in his exploration of this theme, his preoccupation with death is by no means unique in cyberpunk writing. "She didn't know she had died," runs the opening sentence of Swanwick's *Vacuum Flowers.* "She had, in fact, died twice. . . ." Having thus established the keynote of his novel, Swanwick goes on to explore what it means, subjectively, to have died, indeed to have died twice, in a world possessing the technological capacity to retrieve and preserve the personalities of the dead, and to program a new personality over a former personality, obliterating and in effect "killing" the former self in the process. Rebel Mudlark, the "she" of the opening sentences, has survived her first death thanks to her personality having been taped, and has "died" a second time when that taped personality was superimposed over another personality—or was it the other who died? The former personality (called Eucrasia) has not, in any case, been wholly obliterated but persists under the Rebel-personality as a kind of "ghost" self, "haunting" Rebel from within. Similar variations on the motif of the "ghost" self and "haunting" from within recur throughout Cadigan's *Mindplayers,* where residues of the personalities of the dead persist within the minds of the living, thanks to mind-to-mind contact mediated by machines.

In fact, "ghosts" of various kinds, both in and out of machines, abound in cyberpunk. There are, for instance, the "wireheads" of Sterling's *Schismatrix* and Williams' *Hardwired,* human selves persisting outside their natural bodies as configurations of information in computer and communication networks; and the "personality constructs" of Gibson's trilogy, ROM units preserving the selves of deceased characters. In both these variants, the dead manifest themselves to the living as uncanny posthumous voices like those of certain postmodernist texts (e.g., Flann O'Brien's *The Third Policeman,* 1940/1967; Russell Hoban's *Pilgermann,* 1983; Thomas Disch's *The Businessman,* 1984); this effect is exploited particularly powerfully by Williams in *Hardwired.* Gibson even has beings actually called "ghosts." These, however, are not posthumous selves but constructs, computer-simulated selves who have never existed as biological organisms, but spring full-grown from artificial-intelligence programs—ghosts from the machine. Another version of the ghost from the machine appears in Swanwick's *Vacuum Flowers,* in the form of "interactive ALIs," or Artificial Limited Intelligences, short-lived computer simulations of human beings. In one of its formats, the ALI is agonizingly aware of its brief life span and imminent death; in another, however, its memories are recorded and made available to a successor ALI, ensuring "a kind of serial immortality" (242).

At the end of his trilogy, in the closing pages of *Mona Lisa Overdrive,* Gibson assembles representatives of all his posthumous or out-of-body types in the cyberspace world: a computer-simulated "ghost," a posthumous ROM personality construct, three human beings who have "died into" the cyberspace matrix. As early as the end of *Neuromancer,* we had had intimations of the possibility of posthumous survival in cyberspace, but here the association is confirmed: cyberspace is the machine-mediated version of the World to Come, and in this function bears a certain resemblance to some of the postmodernist variations on the World-to-Come *topos* (e.g., Christine Brooke-Rose's *Such,* 1966; Alasdair Gray's *Lanark,* 1981; and especially the double-agents' Hell of Pynchon's *Gravity's Rainbow* [537-548]). "There's dying, then there's dying," as one of Gibson's characters somewhat unhelpfully explains (*Mona Lisa* 252); there's dying the death of the organic body, then there's dying into the half-life of cyberspace.

The "bio-punk" versions of the death and half-life motif do not figure so conspicuously in cyberpunk writing as do the machine-mediated versions. Nevertheless, it is striking that several of the essentially machine-oriented treatments of this theme have a strong body-oriented component, a strain or undercurrent of gothic-horror imagery of the disrupted, exploded, or dismembered body. This is the case, for instance, with Cadigan's *Mindplayers,* where, in one episode, the heroine must make contact with the mind of a deceased poetess whose brain has been extracted and preserved in "stay-juice"—a typical gothic-horror image. It is also true of Kadrey's *Metrophage,* where the crime-boss Conover maintains, in an off-limits precinct of his house, a grisly "farm" of multiple clones of his own body, alter egos from whom he "harvests" transplant organs in order to keep himself alive. ("Suicide and murder all rolled into one package" [215].) Rucker's two cyberpunk novels, also, abound in gothic-horror imagery of dismemberment, cannibalism, necrophilia; *Wetware* in particular alludes explicitly, and appropriately, to Edgar Allan Poe.

Specifically bio-punk equivalents of the various machine-oriented motifs are to be found in Williams' *Voice of the Whirlwind,* Sterling's *Schismatrix,* Bear's *Blood Music,* and Shepard's *Green Eyes.* Thus, for instance, in the world of *Voice of the Whirlwind,* as well as among the Shaper bio-engineers of *Schismatrix,* cloning serves the same function that booting up a software self in a new body does in the machine-mediated variants; it ensures "serial immortality." Thus Steward, at the beginning of *Voice of the Whirlwind,* is already a "Beta," i.e., the clone of his dead "Alpha" self, later on dying and "returning" yet again as his own "Gamma"; a character who dies in the first pages of *Schismatrix* similarly "returns" near its close, many decades later, as a cloned *Doppelgänger* of herself. Sterling also exploits the familiar SF motifs of suspended animation and extreme longevity, especially the latter. In the course of *Schismatrix,* only one natural death is recorded; other characters either die by violence or, in extreme old age, "fade" into an ambiguous half-life state.

The bio-punk equivalent of "wirehead" survival, i.e., posthumous existence as a configuration of information in a cybernetic system, occurs in Bear's *Blood Music.* Here human selves are encoded as information at the level of the component cells of their own bodies; thus, when the body is dissolved and its component cells dispersed, the original self can nevertheless be posthumously reconstituted from the information encoded at the cellular level. This, eerily, is what happens late in *Blood Music* to an entire family who are physically dissolved into undifferentiated tissue and then reconstituted as "themselves," returning to "haunt" (benignly) the surviving family member.

If Bear thus gives a distinctively bio-punk twist to the ghost motif, Shepard does the same with the zombie motif. In his *Green Eyes,* posthumous life is induced in corpses through the introduction of a strain of bacteria. The life span of these bacterially induced artificial personalities ranges from a norm of a few minutes or hours, to several months in extraordinary cases, so-called "slow-burners." Shepard, especially in the early parts of the novel, explores the subjective experience of posthumous life in "slow-burners": their struggles to gain control of their new bodies, their growing awareness of the imminence and inevitability of their own second deaths. He gives us, in other words, the bio-punk version of the death and half-life of Verhoeven's RoboCop.

In its preoccupation with the representation of death, both in its machine-oriented and its bio-punk forms, cyberpunk shows to what degree it has converged with mainstream postmodernist fiction, and how far it has outstripped all the earlier "waves" of science fiction, where the representation of death, even in the boldest and most sophisticated New Wave examples (e.g., Dick's *Ubik,* Disch's *On Wings of Song*), seems somewhat primitive and flatfooted by comparison. The cyberpunk writers—and filmmakers—demonstrate that conventional "old-wave" science fiction of the *Star Trek* type has it all wrong: death, not space, is the final frontier.

Notes

1. Underlying my rather casual use of "levels" here is Harshav's three-dimensional model of the text; see Benjamin Hrushovski [Harshav], "The Structure of Semiotic Objects: A Three-Dimensional Model," *Poetics Today* 1:1-2 (1979) 365-76; rpt. in *The Sign in Music and Literature* Ed. Wendy Steiner (Austin: U of Texas P, 1981).

2. See Joanna Russ, "Speculations," *Extrapolations* 15 (1973), 55-6; Samuel Delany, "Shadows," in *The Jewel-Hinged Jaw: Notes on the Language of Science-Fiction* (Elizabethtown, N.Y.: Dragon, 1977) 88-98; and Stanislaw Lem, "Todorov's Fantastic Theory of Literature" in *Microworlds: Writings on Science Fiction and Fantasy* (San Diego, New York, London: Harcourt, 1984) 209-232. Lem's account of how SF discourse literalizes metaphor occurs in a pugnaciously negative review of Todorov's *Introduction à la littérature fantastique.* Lem's example, "A black cloud swallowed the sun" (218-219), while metaphorical in everyday discourse, could be taken literally in a SF text such as Fred Hoyle's *The Black Cloud.* In fact, though this particular example belongs to SF, the principle of literalized metaphor has actually been borrowed by Lem, without acknowledgments, from Todorov's account of the fantastic; see Tzvetan Todorov, *The Fantastic: A Structural*

Approach to a Literary Genre, trans. Richard Howard (Ithaca: Cornell UP, 1975) 76-77.

3. See Jameson on the "spatial turn" of postmodernism, *Postmodernism,* 16, 154-57, 364-376 and passim; and, on the spatial dominant in SF, see his "Science Fiction as a Spatial Genre: Generic Discontinuities and the Problem of Figuration in Vonda McIntyre's *The Exile Waiting.*" *Science-Fiction Studies* 14:1 (March 1987), 44-59, especially 53-58. On space in postmodernist fiction, see also Carl D. Malmgren, *Fictional Space in the Modernist and Postmodernist American Novel* (Lewisburg: Bucknell UP, 1985).

4. See Thomas Pavel, "Narrative Domains," *Poetics Today* 1:4 (Summer 1980), 105-114, rpt. in his *Fictional Worlds* (Cambridge: Harvard UP, 1986).

5. Literalization of modernist-style mythic archetypes is also a motif of postmodernist writing: see, e.g., Donald Barthelme, *Snow White* (1967), *The Death Father* (1974), and *The King* (1990), Robert Coover, *Pricksongs and Descants* (1969), Italo Calvino, *The Castle of Crossed Destinies* (1969/1973), Gunter Grass, *The Flounder* (1977), Angela Carter, *The Bloody Chamber* (1979), John Fowles, *Mantissa* (1982), and especially the fiction of John Barth, including *Giles Goat-Boy* (1966), *Lost in the Funhouse* (1968), *Chimera* (1972), and *The Tidewater Tales* (1987). Barth puts the case for literalizing mythic archetypes in quite explicit terms: "to write realistic fictions which point always to mythic archetypes is in my opinion to take the wrong end of the mythopoeic stick, however meritorious such fiction may be in other respects. Better to address the archetypes directly"; *Chimera* (New York: Fawcett, 1973) 207-08.

6. See Thomas Docherty, *Reading (Absent) Character: Towards a Theory of Characterization in Fiction* (Oxford: Oxford UP, 1982) and Uri Margolin, "Dispersing/Voiding the Subject: A Narratological Perspective," *Text* 5 (1986).

7. See Tom Maddox, "The Wars of the Coin's Two Halves: Bruce Sterling's Mechanist/Shaper Narratives." *Mississippi Review* 47/48, 237-244.

8. It seems likely that Shepard's motif of bacterially induced personality owes something to Thomas Disch's New Wave SF novel *Camp Concentration* (1968), in which, in a medical experiment on prison inmates, a strain of syphillis is introduced which produces a temporary heightening of intelligence.

9. See W. Warren Wagar, *Terminal Visions: The Literature of Last Things* (Bloomington: Indiana UP, 1982); David Dowling, *Fictions of Nuclear Disas-*

ter (London: Macmillan, 1987); and Brian McHale, "The (Post)Modernism of *The Name of the Rose*," *Hebrew University Studies in Literature and the Arts* 17 (1989), 24-30. I am indebted throughout the following section to my student Tamar Hager, who is researching fictions of nuclear war.

10. See Susan Sontag, "Imagination of Disaster," in *Against Interpretation and Other Essays* (New York: Dell, 1966), 223-225; Wagar, *Terminal Visions*, 70.

11. There is a close analogy to *RoboCop* in the premise of the *Max Headroom* television series (in the United States, ABC, spring 1987), though, as usual, the impact has been watered down for the TV audience: the supposedly dead Edison Carter has been "resurrected" as his manic alter ego, the computer simulation Max Headroom, but then it transpires that Carter isn't really dead after all, so that Max doesn't replace but merely mirrors (however distortedly) his human "original". A postmodernist analogue is McElroy's *Plus* (1976), in which the supposedly deceased human protagonist, who has allowed his brain to be reused as the control system for an orbiting satellite, feeds on cosmic radiation and gradually regenerates "himself," recovering piece by piece his supposedly "lost" memories and identity.

Works Cited

Bear, Greg. *Blood Music.* 1985; New York: Ace Science Fiction, 1986.

Berger, Peter L. and Thomas Luckmann. *The Social Construction of Reality: A Treatise in the Sociology of Knowledge,* Garden City, NY: Doubleday, 1966.

Brooke-Rose, Christine. *A Rhetoric of the Unreal: Studies in Narrative and Structure, especially of the Fantastic.* Cambridge and New York: Cambridge UP, 1981.

———. *Such,* 1966; in *The Christine Brooke-Rose Omnibus: Four Novels,* Manchester and New York: Carcanet, 1986.

Cadigan, Pat. *Mindplayers.* Toronto, New York, London: Bantam, 1987.

Calinescu, Matei. "From the One to the Many: Pluralism in Today's Thought." *Innovation/Renovation: New Perspectives on the Humanities.* Ed. Ihab Hassan and Sally Hassan. Madison and London: U of Wisconsin P, 1983. 263-288.

Dick, Philip K. *Ubik.* Garden City, NY: Doubleday, 1969.

Disch, Thomas M. *The Businessman: A Tale of Terror.* New York: Harper and Row, 1984.

Foucault, Michel. *The Order of Things: An Archeology of the Human Sciences.* New York: Pantheon, 1970.

Gibson, William. *Burning Chrome* [stories]. 1986; New York: Ace Science Fiction, 1987.

———. *Count Zero.* 1986; New York: Ace Science Fiction, 1987.

———. *Mona Lisa Overdrive.* Toronto, New York, London: Bantam, 1988.

———. *Neuromancer.* New York: Ace Science Fiction, 1984.

Gibson, William, and Bruce Sterling. "Red Star, Winter Orbit." *Mirrorshades: The Cyberpunk Anthology.* Ed. Bruce Sterling, New York: Arbor, 1986. 202-222.

Gibson, William, and Michael Swanwick. "Dog Fight." *Burning Chrome.* New York: Ace Science Fiction, 1987. 142-167.

Gray, Alasdair. *Lanark.* New York: Braziller, 1981.

Herr, Michael. *Dispatches.* New York: Avon, 1978.

Hoban, Russell. *Pilgermann.* New York: Summit Books, 1983.

Jameson, Fredric. "Magical Narratives: Romance as Genre." *New Literary History* 7:1 (Autumn 1975): 135-163.

———. *The Political Unconscious: Narrative as a Socially Symbolic Act.* Ithaca: Cornell UP, 1981.

———. *Postmodernism, or, The Cultural Logic of Late Capitalism.* Durham, NC: Duke UP, 1991.

Kadrey, Richard. *Metrophage.* 1988; London: Gollancz, 1989.

Laidlaw, Marc. *Dad's Nuke.* 1985; London: Gollancz, 1986.

Maddox, Tom. "Snake Eyes." *Mirrorshades: The Cyberpunk Anthology.* Ed. Bruce Sterling. New York: Arbor, 1986. 12-33.

McCaffery, Larry. "The Desert of the Real: The Cyberpunk Controversy." *Mississippi Review* 47/48 (1988): 7-15. Reprinted in *Storming the Reality Studio: A Casebook of Cyberpunk and Postmodern Science Fiction.* Ed. Larry McCaffery. Durham and London: Duke UP, 1991. 1-16.

———. "An Interview with William Gibson." *Across the Wounded Galaxies: Interviews with Contemporary American Science Fiction Writers.* Urbana and Chicago: U of Illinois P, 1990.

McElroy, Joseph. *Plus.* 1976; New York: Carroll and Graf, 1987.

McHale, Brian. "POSTcyberMODERNpunkISM." *Storming the Reality Studio: A Casebook of Cyberpunk and Postmodern Science Fiction.* Ed. Larry McCaffery. Durham and London: Duke UP, 1991. 308-323.

———. *Postmodernist Fiction.* New York and London: Methuen, 1987.

O'Brien, Flann. *The Third Policeman.* 1940; New American Library, 1967.

Pynchon, Thomas. *The Crying of Lot 49,* 1966; New York: Bantam, 1967.

———. *Gravity's Rainbow.* New York: Viking, 1973.

———. *Slow Learner: Early Stories.* Boston and Toronto: Little, Brown, 1984.

———. *Vineland.* Boston, Toronto and London: Little, Brown, 1990.

Rucker, Rudy. *Software.* 1982; Harmondsworth: Penguin, 1985.

———. *Wetware.* New York: Avon, 1988.

Shepard, Lucius. *Green Eyes.* New York: Ace Science Fiction, 1984.

———. *Life During Wartime.* Toronto, New York, London: Bantam, 1987.

Shiner, Lewis. *Deserted Cities of the Heart.* 1988; Toronto, New York, London: Bantam, 1989.

———. *Frontera.* New York: Baen, 1984.

———. "Till Human Voices Wake Us." *Mirrorshades: The Cyberpunk Anthology.* Ed. Bruce Sterling. New York: Arbor House, 1986. 125-138.

Shirley, John. *Eclipse.* 1985; New York: Popular Library/Warner Books, 1987.

———. "Wolves of the Plateau," *Mississippi Review* 47/48 (1988): 136-150.

Sterling, Bruce. *Islands in the Net.* New York: Arbor House/William Morrow, 1988.

———. *Schismatrix,* 1985; New York: Ace Science Fiction, 1986.

Swanwick, Michael. *Vacuum Flowers.* New York: Arbor House, 1987.

Verhoeven, Paul, dir., *RoboCop,* 1987.

Williams, Walter Jon. *Hardwired.* 1986; London and Sydney: Futura, 1988.

———. *Voice of the Whirlwind.* 1987; London and Sydney: Futura, 1989.

Thomas Foster (review date spring 1999)

SOURCE: Foster, Thomas. "The Rhetoric of Cyberspace: Ideology or Utopia?" *Contemporary Literature* 40, no. 1 (spring 1999): 144-60.

[*In the following review, Foster analyzes* Cyberspace/Cyberbodies/Cyberpunk: Cultures of Technological Embodiment *and* Virtual Realities and Their Discontents, *in terms of rhetorical and ideative content.*]

As I write this review, in the fall of 1998, it is almost impossible to avoid encountering the rhetoric of "cyberspace" or electronic communications networks, if only in the form of television commercials, most notably for AT&T's and MCI's Internet services. Over the course of the last year, these multinational telecommunications companies have begun to produce advertisements celebrating computer-mediated communication in explicitly utopian terms. Typically, such advertisements stress the obsolescence of physical appearance and bodily markers of difference: cyberspace, the imaginary site of social interactions conducted through networked computers, is a "place" where gender, race, and physical disability cease to matter, we are told.

At the same time, MCI's most recent ads, for its Worldcom system, end by announcing that "now the world is *officially* open for business." These ads also boast of MCI's proprietary ownership of a world-spanning segment of the Internet, celebrating the fact that users can now depend on one company to connect them to any place on the globe. This assertion of ownership, however, contradicts the more utopian claims of the virtual communitarians (such as Howard Rheingold), who argue that the decentralized infrastructure of the Internet translates into decentralized and therefore non-hierarchical and more democratic social structures. More accurately, MCI's assertion of ownership of the network contradicts the communitarian assumption that decentralized forms of communication as the basis for new forms of social interaction are incompatible with the institutions of monopoly capitalism.[1] This second set of commercials fairly blatantly reveals the self-interest motivating MCI's promotion of Internet technocultures, as implied by the way the ads link their utopian rhetoric to a rhetoric of capitalist expansion and neocolonialism ("now the world is *officially* open for business").

I cite these developments because they confirm the continuing relevance of the 1996 essay collection *Virtual Realities and Their Discontents*, edited by Robert Markley, a collection based on a 1994 special issue of the science and literature journal *Configurations* (all but one of the six essays in the book originally appeared in the special issue). As essay collections go, this one is remarkably cohesive. All the contributions offer much-needed critiques of the utopian and promotional function with which the concept of cyberspace has become associated in American popular culture. As my example of the MCI and AT&T commercials suggests, this tendency to drop a utopian veil over commercial interests has only intensified since these essays were initially written and published.

In his introduction to the volume, Markley defines this book's project as the restoration of "the histories that cyberspace seeks to deny or transcend" (10). This transcendence of history is accomplished, in Markley's view, by the abstraction of "cyberspace" as a concept from specific "virtual technologies," defined as "the hardware and software that intervene in our bodies" (2). Summarizing his own contribution to the collection, Markley argues that the utopian rhetoric about cyberspace depends upon interpreting it in a very traditional way, as "a fundamental reality of form underlying our mundane existence" and urged upon us "because it offers us a world more aesthetically pleasing, more beautiful, than the one we inhabit" (8). Markley here strikes a recurrent theme in these essays: cyberspace understood as a utopia produced by this kind of formal abstraction from the "mundane" or physical world of embodied existence reproduces Platonic and Cartesian dualisms, though Markley's essay itself argues for an even more direct connection to Leibniz's theory of the monad.

Identifying another common thread among these essays, Markley's introduction also links the utopianism of popular discourses on cyberspace with an uncritical investment in the ideology of scientific progress, what Markley calls "the metanarrative of technological development" and "the rhetoric of the 'new' that is endemic to both academic and popular writing on cyberspace, postmodernism, and late capitalism" (7, 9). Finally, the essays in *Virtual Realities and Their Discontents* share a common interest in contesting what Arthur and Marilouise Kroker call the trope of the disappearing body in postmodern culture.[2] As Markley puts it, too often virtual reality is represented as or assumed to be "the fulfillment of a quest for a postindustrial, postmodern transcendence, the ascent to a Leibnizian future in which the body (suitably dematerialized) becomes indistinguishable from its idealized simulation" (6).

All of these points are absolutely valid, and their recognition is more urgently needed today than ever before. And while I may have described the volume as remarkably cohesive, it is equally remarkable for the range and diversity of its six essays, which offer six very different historical contexts in which to reimagine cyberspace, or rather virtual reality technologies (VR), in more productive ways. For instance, N. Katherine Hayles provides an account of the three main waves or stages in the development of cybernetics, ending with virtual reality systems, in order to demonstrate how the utopian rhetoric of cyberspatial disembodiment is grounded in a "skeuomorph," or the persistence in both the popular imagination and scientific discourse of an anachronistic mode of theorizing information. Specifically, Hayles argues that the early cybernetic "move" of "conceptualizing information as a pattern distinct from the physical markers that embody it" has made it possible to conceptualize cyberspace "as a disembodied realm of information that humans enter by leaving their

bodies behind," even though this definition of information has been at least complicated by the more recent shift to systems theory and to concepts of self-organization and reflexivity that tend to emphasize relationships between bodies and environments (34). The effect of these more recent developments, as Hayles reads them, is to reveal how much more advanced our bodies already are, even when understood purely as information-processing systems, than any technological system or computer interface that is likely to be available any time soon. This essay is especially noteworthy for defining both the continuing influence of earlier moments in the development of information theory and also alternative theories of embodiment that might be generated by more recent developments in cybernetics. In other words, to contest the rhetoric of disembodiment in cyberspace, Hayles argues, it is necessary to understand the history of cybernetics better than most of us probably do, rather than to reject cybernetics as essentially linked to the devaluation of embodied existence.

Richard Grusin's essay similarly critiques the "trope of dematerialization" in the discourse on cyberspace (51), but rather than defining this trope in terms of representations of embodiment, Grusin discusses how it appears in the debates about the relation between print culture and electronic media, as well as debates about the relation of electronic media to poststructuralist redefinitions of textuality and writing. Grusin's essay links the tendency of cyberspace rhetoric to personify technology itself as an agent of change (41) with cyberspace rhetoric's tendency to interpret electronic media as *de*contextualizing rather than *re*contextualizing print culture (53).

Markley offers an account of Platonic tendencies within the history of mathematics as a historical framework for understanding cyberspace, while David Brande situates not only the rhetoric of cyberspace but also cyberpunk science fiction and cyborg imagery in the context of post-Fordist economies. Brande reads the figure of the cyborg as a fantasy of a perfect late-capitalist form of subjectivity, perfectly adapted to the economic imperatives of an information economy (98), while cyberspace is understood as a capitalist dream, a limitless space for commercial expansion, freed from the limits of geography, and therefore a perfect way to manage capitalism's ever-present crisis of accumulation (100-101). This is precisely the fantasy expressed in MCI's Worldcom commercials.

David Porush also draws on cyberpunk fiction, in an essay that explores the relevance of mystical traditions and discourses of transcendence to the concept of cyberspace as it is popularly represented. Porush's essay very usefully distinguishes between the negative and positive consequences of this historical context. On the one hand, representing cyberspace in terms of a desire for transcendence is another example of the tendency to associate cyberspace with fantasies of disembodiment, dematerialization, and flight from history. On the other hand, such representations also allow cyberspace to be associated with irrationality and therefore with postmodern critiques of Enlightenment reason. As Porush puts it, "We cannot emigrate to cyberspace until we accept the inherent irrationality of any model that can succeed in fooling our brain into thinking it is an alternative space" (119). In developing this second line of argumentation, about irrationality, Porush also has recourse to the history of mathematics and the theory of irrational or absurd numbers.

Finally, Michelle Kendrick turns to a different philosophical tradition, in order to offer an alternative account of cyberspace and virtual reality technologies and to avoid what she sees as the traps of cyberspace rhetoric—that is, the tendency for the concept of cyberspace to erase "the material effects of virtual technologies on subjectivity," and the tendency for accounts of cyberspace to present it as a technology that allows us to *consciously* control the way in which our subjectivities are mediated technologically (146). Kendrick uses David Hume's skeptical philosophy, and specifically his theory of the fictive nature of identity, to argue instead for an understanding of subjectivity "not as stable, coherent, or knowable but always as process, a kind of ongoing technoproject," whose very technologial mediation implies that the subject is "contingent on the experience of embodiment" (160).

These arguments are powerful and persuasive on their own terms; moreover, in the context of the pervasive rhetoric exemplified by the AT& T and MCI commercials, the interventions that the contributors make in that rhetoric are necessary and urgent. Nevertheless, it seems to me important to recall that cyberpunk science fiction, the other main cultural site for rhetorics of "cyberspace," attracted academic attention from students and critics of postmodernism precisely because cyberpunk fiction seemed to offer a way to restore both a utopian dimension and a social critique to theories of postmodern culture. It is for this reason that the collection *Cyberspace/Cyberbodies/Cyberpunk: Cultures of Technological Embodiment,* edited by Mike Featherstone and Roger Burrows, makes a good comparison with *Virtual Realities and Their Discontents.* The Featherstone and Burrows collection is also based on a special issue of a journal, in this case the British journal *Body and Society.* But more importantly, this collection contains essays by some of the writers who are specifically discussed in the Markley collection (such as Michael Heim and Mark Poster), and the openness of Featherstone and Burrows's book to more utopian approaches to the topic of cyberspace indicates some of the limitations that result from Markley's emphasis on

revealing the ideological self-interest behind the rhetoric of cyberspace.

Featherstone and Burrows begin their introduction by pointing out that one of the commonplaces of postmodern theory and criticism is the rejection of modernism's utopian impulse to "make it new," in favor of an aesthetics of pastiche, camp, cultural recycling, or "image scavenging." Featherstone and Burrows argue that the "recent upsurge of interest in cyberspace, cyberbodies and cyberpunk" results from an increasing uneasiness with this conception of postmodernism and even a sense that such formulations are reaching a dead end in *"fin de millênnium* pessimism, with the assumption that there are no new moves in the game and that we are confronted by a future which 'has already happened'" (1). In this context, of discontents with postmodernism rather than virtual realities, both cyberpunk and popular rhetorics of cyberspace can be understood as sites of tension between "those who wish to recover [cyberpunk and cyberspace] into postmodernism" and those who see them as "breaking down the boundaries of this [postmodern] framework to revive utopian impulses" (1). Featherstone and Burrows's collection attempts to stage this tension and these debates by including examples of both sides, resulting in a much less cohesive collection than Markley's, and one that lacks Markley's ambition to intervene and alter the terms of popular discourse and critical conversation. Featherstone and Burrows, however, seem to offer a more complex and contradictory depiction of the topic.

On the relatively utopian and celebratory side, David Tomas offers a reading of "the human body's reconceptualization" in Norbert Wiener's early writings on cybernetics, as a context for the emergence of the concepts of the "cyborg" and "cyberspace" (22). In contrast to the authors in Markley's volume, Tomas tends to present this "reconceptualization" without negatively evaluating its consequences, as either a fact to be accepted or even an opportunity to be embraced. British author Sadie Plant's writing represents a very intriguing attempt to define a "cyberfeminist" discourse, and her essay in this collection suggests that the rhetoric of cyberspace literalizes Luce Irigaray's French feminist metaphors for sexual difference, including mimicry. This essay is valuable for its suggestions of how cyberspace rhetoric might not only require but also facilitate feminist interventions; by the same token, however, the essay tends to reproduce Irigaray's own dehistoricizing tendencies, such as the repeated references to "woman" in general rather than specific, historically situated women (58-59).

On the more critical side, Kevin Robins argues that cyberspace is a fantasy in which the pain of real-world identity crises can be reimagined as pleasurable, so that the rhetoric of cyberspace represents merely a "banal utopia" whose function is regressive and defensive rather than progressive or critical (142, 153). Vivian Sobchack offers a remarkable, personalized critique of the very reconceptualization of the human body that Tomas tends to celebrate. Sobchack's essay reflects on her prosthetic limb and imagines what it would feel like to invest in her prosthesis and describe it to herself in the utopian terms that critics like Tomas use to describe cyborgs more generally. The essay ends by rejecting any claim to be a cyborg as necessitating a devaluation of Sobchack's organic embodiment (210).

Both Robins and Sobchack offer more aggressive and at times even dismissive critiques of the rhetoric of cyberspace and cybernetic or virtual embodiment than any of the contributors to Markley's volume, while Tomas and Plant are far less critical of that same rhetoric than any of Markley's contributors. More typical of the essays in Featherstone and Burrows's collection, however, is their tendency to both acknowledge and criticize the "bad utopian" rhetoric around cyberspace and to offer positive alternatives to that rhetoric. For example, Deborah Lupton explicitly analyzes the "central utopian discourse around computer technology"—that is, "the potential offered by computers for humans to escape the body" (100). She also focuses on the same tendency to anthropomorphize computers as agents of cultural change that Richard Grusin reviews. But for Lupton, this anthropomorphizing rhetoric is read not as an abdication or mystification of human agency but instead as signifying an intimacy between humans and computers that exposes our own sense of embodied "vulnerability" (110-11). In a reading of cyberpunk fiction's representations of virtual embodiment, Nigel Clark argues that cyberpunk represents cyberspace as a fantasy of escape from embodiment but also, paradoxically, as demanding "a constant attentiveness to the flesh that comes with the capacity to retune the body's signifying surfaces from one moment to the next" (127). This collection also reprints Anne Balsamo's important reading of the novel *Synners* by Pat Cadigan, the only woman writer included in the initial group of cyberpunk writers. Balsamo offers a taxonomy of four modes of virtual or technologically mediated embodiment, of which the "disappearing body" is only one (220-24).

Mark Poster and Michael Heim are two of the writers included in Featherstone and Burrows's book who are also the subject of critiques in Markley's collection for promoting rather than demystifying cyberspace. Poster's essay primarily updates his earlier work on redefinitions of subjectivity in "the mode of information" to include virtual reality technologies, but Heim actually revises the work for which he is criticized in Markley's collection. Heim begins his essay by asserting, "Life's body is becoming indistinguishable from its computer prosthesis" (65). The relatively celebratory or at least affirmative nature of Heim's rhetoric becomes apparent

in contrast to Hayles's comments on this same claim in her essay in Markley's book. Hayles points out that "taken to the extreme, the awareness of the mediated nature of perception that VR technologies provide can be taken to signify that the body itself is a prosthesis," and she goes on to ask, "is it necessary to insist, once again, that embodiment is not an option but a necessity in order for life to exist?" (35-36). Apparently it is.

Heim is more specifically criticized by Markley for another famous statement. In an earlier essay, Heim wrote, "Cyberspace is Platonism as a working product," Platonism literalized, concretized, and *marketed* in technological form.[3] Heim thereby associates cyberspace with an ideal realm of form that is to be privileged over the world of matter and bodies and reinscribes cyberspace within a dualistic philosophical framework (Markley 67). Heim's essay in Featherstone and Burrows, however, explicitly rewrites and complicates his earlier work in precisely the way that Markley calls for in his introduction—that is, by turning from the abstraction of cyberspace to the specifics of virtual technologies. Heim distinguishes two forms of virtual reality. One uses head-mounted displays to visually immerse users in a virtual world through which they move or navigate in a purely virtual manner, without having to move physically, or only in very rudimentary ways. The other form of virtual reality (the CAVE system) creates a virtual environment, a literal room within which computer simulations are displayed, thereby encouraging users to physically move their own bodies through the virtual displays (71-74). The first virtual reality system encourages identification with a virtual point of view distinct from the user's physical body, while the second system requires users to simultaneously experience both physical and virtual perspectives, to experience VR without transcending their own bodies.

I do not mean to suggest that the contributors to Markley's collection completely dismiss cyberspace or fail to define alternatives. The alternatives they offer to the decontextualizing, utopian rhetoric of cyberspace tend, however, to be subordinated to their critiques, and sometimes to seem appended almost as afterthoughts. Markley himself ends his essay by asserting that "the imaginary realm of cyberspace . . . is a fantasy based on the denial of ecology and labor." This emphatic assertion tends to overwhelm the suggestion in the next paragraph that it might be possible to create "a reconfigured cyberspace" which would recognize that "there are no frictionless systems" or perfect worlds (77). But given Markley's demonstration of how the rhetoric of cyberspace is embedded in idealist dualisms between form and matter, it is difficult to see exactly how cyberspace could be reconfigured in this way. Similarly, Grusin ends his essay by arguing, as noted earlier, that "electronic information technologies do not *de*contextualize the texts of Western culture, they *re*contextualize them," so that "we need to analyze the cultural work" of electronic writing (53). Brande locates the value of cyberpunk fiction "not in the possibilities it constructs but in the vividness of its *staging* of a seemingly intractable logic of the market" (88; emphasis added), a restaging of capitalist ideology on the level of narrative form that has the critical potential to teach readers to decode capitalist ideology as it is encoded and mystified by the rhetoric of cyberspace (99). For Brande, this critical restaging of capitalist ideology is the only alternative cyberpunk offers to the banal utopia of cyberspace rhetoric.

In Markley's collection, it is the essays by Hayles, Porush, and Kendrick that are most concerned to define positive alternatives to the target of the volume's critique. Hayles is explicitly concerned with "the overlapping patterns of replication [of the past] and innovation that have brought us" to the verge of a "posthuman era" (37). Porush insists that cultural critics accept and embrace the irrationality of cyberspace precisely as an alternative to "the rationalism of utopian vision" and what he sees as its assumptions about the perfectibility of humanity (124). Kendrick argues that virtual technologies are not particularly new, since subjectivity has always been mediated by what she calls the "technological real." The overall impression created, however, is one of negation and an insistence on critical and historical distance from the rhetoric surrounding these new technologies, rather than a fully elaborated articulation of more positive rhetorics (which some of these authors, such as Hayles, have done elsewhere in their work; Hayles's forthcoming book *How We Became Posthuman* is eagerly awaited and will undoubtedly address the concerns I am raising here). The preferred methodology of Markley's collection, historical contextualization, is its strength, but that same methodology has its limitations, as well.

From the perspective of the Featherstone and Burrows collection, then, Markley sometimes seems to overstate his critique, as when he claims that any utopia is necessarily associated with fetishizing the new rather than offering any critical perspective on the present ([9]; Porush offers a similar reading of utopia as necessarily invested in a concept of human perfectibility and therefore again with ideologies of progress [122]). I would agree that utopian rhetoric is always risky; the use of utopian discourse to generate critical reflection on the present can easily slide into fantasies of transcendence and escape from the limits of history. But the question raised by reading these two book collections together is whether that risk might not be worth taking, at least sometimes. What do we lose, if anything, when we decide in advance never to take this risk?

Markley does acknowledge, at least parenthetically, that "the literature of cyberspace," in its utopian and traditionally metaphysical aspects, is "distinct from the cultural criticism of cyberpunk" science fiction (57). But I tend to agree with Featherstone and Burrows that this potential for critique in cyberpunk's representations of cyberspace and cybernetic embodiment is indistinguishable from a reading of cyberpunk as "prefigurative social theory," as "a *theoretically* coherent vision of a very near future" (8). Markley's collection usefully raises the question of whether the utopian rhetoric of cyberspace has been so hopelessly appropriated and contaminated by multinational corporations that it is necessary for cultural critics to abandon that rhetoric entirely. Featherstone and Burrows's collection raises the equally urgent question of what we will lose if the utopian dimension of cyberspace has been foreclosed. To what extent, if any, can the utopian rhetoric of cyberspace still represent "liberatory fantasies that surround new technologies" and whose "source to some extent lies in real popular needs and desires," needs and desires that it would be "a mistake to dismiss . . . as false consciousness?"[4]

One of the more intriguing suggestions that Markley makes is that raising "political questions about power, knowledge, and experience" is necessary in order to create "a more productive, if no less heated, debate between the practitioners and critics of cyberspace," between the developers and ideologues of cyberspace and its cultural analysts (66). I am left, however, with a real question in my mind as to what kind or kinds of politics Markley has in mind, and what kinds of political contexts end up being left out of *Virtual Realities and Their Discontents* precisely because this collection tends to reject utopian thought in any form as dehistoricizing. It might be useful here to recall socialist feminist Sheila Robotham's work on the "prefigurative political forms" associated with the new social subjects of the 1960s and 1970s, including feminism, gay and lesbian movements, and racial and ethnic liberation struggles. To the extent that this kind of politics depends upon "the transformation of values and relationships in the process of making the new world," on trying to live now as we would like to be able to live in a more just and equitable society, Robotham's suggestion is that foreclosing on utopian thought in favor of ideological critique privileges a particular concept of politics and history.[5] It seems to me possible that a similar point could be made about Markley's collection: its understanding of the politics of cyberspace is both enabled and limited by its refusal of the utopian.

In this context, it might seem significant that Featherstone and Burrows's collection contains more explicitly feminist essays (by Plant, Lupton, and Balsamo) than Markley's. More importantly, as a group, the essays in Featherstone and Burrows's collection go further than any of the essays in Markley's in moving beyond the abstract rhetoric of "the body" to considerations of specific, historical forms of embodied existence, since invoking an abstract concept of "the body" is the necessary precondition for imagining cyberspace as a transcendence of "the body." Michelle Kendrick's essay in Markley's book explicitly thematizes the fact that "[t]he most appropriate critical response to those approaches that celebrate the displacement of historical bodies into 'the body' is to ask, . . . 'Which one?'" (150). In Featherstone and Burrows's book, Anne Balsamo's identification of at least four separate types of virtual embodiment and her attention to the relation between gendered and racial bodies and technobodies is the most obvious example of an essay which actually does what Kendrick is here calling for. Kendrick's own turn to Hume seems to reinstate an abstraction of "the body" by using Hume to argue for "a primacy of the body which is inescapable" (153) and for "the absolute necessity of the body in producing and maintaining [the] foundational perceptions" on which our "narratives of identity" are based (160).

I am suggesting here that there is still a relatively high degree of abstraction to the Markley volume's critique of cyberspace as an abstraction. On the one hand, *Virtual Realities and Their Discontents* cannot be expected to do all the work of dispelling the utopian rhetoric of cyberspace that celebrates virtual technologies precisely as mechanisms of abstraction from material bodies. On the other hand, it also seems possible that to fully carry out the critique of abstraction that Markley's book initiates might require returning to modes of utopian thought that the book is intent on resisting. I was struck, for example, by the level of abstraction at which capitalism is invoked as a historical context for cyberspace. Markley refers to a "logic of alienation" (70), while Brande criticizes both Haraway's cyborg feminism and Hayles's concept of the "posthuman era" for ignoring how postmodern "processes of denaturation" are "provoked by larger historical and economic processes" (82). The rhetoric here seems depressingly familiar, with Marxism being invoked as the final determining instance, the "larger" process, within which questions of gender, sexuality, or race should be subsumed. It is precisely this type of Marxism that Robotham was contesting by insisting on the value of prefigurative forms of politics. I agree with Brande that processes of capital development can be understood as processes of virtualization, as Henri Lefebvre suggests in his Marxist account of the transition from the "absolute space" imagined by precapitalist societies to the "abstract space" of modern financial and communications networks.[6] But surely it is possible to combine such an analysis with consideration of how these processes affect constructions of embodied experiences in ways that do not simply reflect the imperatives of late capitalism.

Is it possible to historicize cyberspace without abandoning its utopian possibilities, including possibilities for reimagining embodiment that might coincide with the political projects of feminism, queer theory, or critical race studies? Allucquère Rosanne Stone's book on virtual systems theory suggests that the history of the national public sphere and its construction of the "citizen" might provide a model that combines history and utopia. Stone argues that the history of the public sphere is characterized by mechanisms of abstraction, disembodiment, and the textualization of subjectivity which long precede the invention of virtual reality computer interfaces but which might be understood as necessary steps in producing "the subjectivity that could fairly unproblematically inhabit the virtual spaces of the nets."[7] More specifically, she suggests that the construction of "the socially apprehensible citizen" depends upon a process of coupling the physical space of embodiment with the virtual or discursive spaces which give meaning to bodies (40-41). At issue here is how to map the distinction between virtual point of view and physical body onto other types of cultural and philosophical dualisms. Stone insists that "the physical/virtual distinction is *not* a mind/body distinction," and that "the virtual component of the socially apprehensible citizen is not a disembodied thinking thing, but rather a different way of conceptualizing a *relationship* to the human body" (40). From this perspective, Markley often seems to have recourse to a more simplistic mapping of the structure of virtual embodiment onto Platonic and Cartesian dualisms, as when he claims that "the division between cyberspace and virtual technologies reflects and reinscribes the oppositions of mind/body, spirit/matter, form/substance, and male/female that have structured Western metaphysics since Plato" (2). Are these dualistic structures actually isomorphic?

It is particularly significant that Stone's definition of the socially apprehensible citizen also emphasizes the performative aspects of embodiment, specifically Judith Butler's work on gender performativity and alternative sexual practices.[8] Stone's book gives much more attention to the relationship between cyberspace or virtual systems and queer theory or transgender issues than any of the essays in either the Markley or the Featherstone and Burrows collection. Kendrick in fact criticizes Stone for this interest (with reference to an earlier essay of Stone's rather than to her book), because for Kendrick transgender performance in cyberspace means only "that users can consciously construct what 'else' they would be" (Markley 159), rather than that practices of virtual embodiment might usefully be historicized in relation to practices of drag or butch-femme. Markley argues that the split between physical and virtual, between "lived experience" and cyberspace as "the idealized, symbolic realm of general equivalents" only reinscribes a capitalist "logic of alienation" (70). But instead of theorizing the distinction between physical and virtual as a *splitting,* it seems equally possible to theorize it in terms of the enforced, performative *repetition* of identity categories, which in their very repetition create opportunities for intervention and resignification, as Butler has argued occurs with gender categories in drag or butch-femme practices.

I have argued elsewhere for using theories of transgender performativity as a framework for understanding virtual reality, through readings of how feminist and lesbian science fiction writers have appropriated the representational framework of cyberpunk fiction, including the thematics of cyberspace.[9] One of the issues raised by reading Markley's collection in relation to Featherstone and Burrows's is how to read cyberpunk fiction and its theoretical or critical relevance, with Markley associating cyberpunk with critique rather than utopian celebration and Featherstone and Burrows associating it with "prefigurative social theory," by which they seem to mean some combination of critique and utopian thought. Both of these readings beg the question of differences between types of cyberpunk texts and between cyberpunk and other related forms of contemporary science fiction narrative. It is important to note that Anne Balsamo's essay in Featherstone and Burrows is the only essay in either book to build its argument around an example of feminist cyberpunk. The other essays in Featherstone and Burrows that turn to cyberpunk rather than the popular rhetoric of cyberspace tend to depend either on William Gibson's writing or on film rather than print fiction. In the Markley collection, only William Gibson and Neal Stephenson are cited. I point out this absence not to argue for token representation of women and minority writers, but to suggest that their absence structurally affects the kinds of arguments that the contributors to these books are able to make. How would these accounts of cyberspace and its proper historical contexts be altered if Maureen McHugh's or Melissa Scott's narratives about VR were taken as the starting point or the test ground for analyzing cyberspace?[10]

The same question might be posed in terms of race and cyberspace, a topic that has received far less attention than issues of gender and sexuality in cyberspace, and cyberpunk (indeed, the entire science fiction field) offers far fewer resources for correcting this neglect, given the even smaller number of "ethnic" or "minority" writers working within the genre compared to feminist science fiction writers. Stone's attempt to recontextualize virtual systems in terms of the history of modern citizenship seems especially useful for opening onto racial histories. To what extent does the historical construction of "whiteness" and especially white masculinity as an unmarked racial norm function as a context for cyberspace and modes of cybernetic embodiment? I would point out that science fiction film and especially the subgenre of films about cyborgs and human-machine hybrids, often involving narratives about white men becoming cyborgs, seem to provide an especially rich field for developing these issues, as Samantha Hol-

land's and Alison Landsberg's contributions to the Featherstone and Burrows collection suggest.

Finally, the contributors to the Markley volume, with the exception of N. Katherine Hayles, often seem to overlook or minimize any utopian content within what Hayles calls the "posthuman era" (37). As part of their critiques of the utopian rhetoric around cyberspace or other technological forms of embodiment, both Markley and Sobchack cite Don Ihde's theory of the "doubled desire" that often structures attitudes toward technology (Markley 72; Sobchack 209-10). Ihde argues that people often want technology to be both *transparent* and *transformative*. By "transparent," Ihde means "a wish . . . for the technology to truly 'become me,'" to be fully assimilated to our already existing organic bodies and sensoria—that is, for the technology to function *naturally*. On the other hand, Ihde argues that we desire technology as the enhancement and improvement of our "naked capacities," as a transformation of our physical capabilities and modes of embodiment.[11] Both Markley and Sobchack emphasize how this "doubling" of desire functions as ideological mystification, allowing us to naturalize the ways in which technology transforms us, and to represent such transformations optimistically as involving no real loss to ourselves. Hayles's notion of the posthuman, however, seems to imply a shift in this ideological relation to technology, in which relatively radical forms of transformation are accepted and even sought out. Ihde's work might equally well be read as implying that it is only by accepting such transformations, as both gain and loss, that the "posthuman" can function as a critique of humanism, including its elevation of particular (white, male) bodies to the level of the generically human.

The necessary resistance of *Virtual Realities and Their Discontents* to the multinational utopia of borderless and bodiless communication in cyberspace threatens to slide into the suggestion that any work on cyberspace ultimately plays into the hands of the telecommunications companies. On the other hand, the willingness to consider cyberpunk and other posthuman narratives of cyberspace and cybernetic embodiment as "prefigurative social theory," in Featherstone and Burrows's collection, threatens to slide into a dehistoricized celebration, as the critical value of utopian thought slides into escapism. These two books demonstrate the difficulties of sustaining these analytic distinctions in technocultural contexts. The research agenda they define involves a return to popular narratives and theoretical models capable of articulating critical negation and utopian possibility. At the same time, the challenge defined by these two books is to combine these approaches, methodologies, and critical rhetorics without eliminating the conflicts, "friction," and different political stakes they bring with them.

Indiana University

Notes

1. Howard Rheingold, *The Virtual Community: Homesteading on the Electronic Frontier* (New York: HarperPerennial, 1993).

2. Arthur and Marilouise Kroker, "Theses on the Disappearing Body in the HyperModern Condition," *Body Invaders: Panic Sex in America,* ed. Arthur and Marilouise Kroker (New York: St. Martin's, 1987) 24.

3. Michael Heim, "The Erotic Ontology of Cyberspace," *Cyberspace: First Steps,* ed. Michael Benedikt (Cambridge, MA: MIT P, 1991) 68.

4. Constance Penley and Andrew Ross, "Introduction," *Technoculture* (Minneapolis: U of Minnesota, P, 1991) xiii.

5. Sheila Robotham, "The Women's Movement and Organizing for Socialism," *Beyond the Fragments: Feminism and the Making of Socialism,* ed. Sheila Robotham, Lynne Segal, and Hilary Wainwright (London: Merlin, 1979) 132-44, 121.

6. Henri Lefebvre, *The Production of Space,* trans. Donald Nicholson-Smith (Cambridge, MA: Basil Blackwell, 1991) 234, 266.

7. Allucquère Rosanne Stone, *The War of Desire and Technology at the Close of the Mechanical Age* (Cambridge, MA: MIT P, 1995) 97.

8. See Judith Butler, *Gender Trouble: Feminism and the Subversion of Identity* (New York: Routledge, 1990).

9. See Thomas Foster, "'Trapped By the Body?': Telepresence Technologies and Transgendered Performance in Feminist and Lesbian Rewritings of Cyberpunk Fiction," *Modern Fiction Studies* 43 (1997): 708-42.

10. Maureen McHugh, "A Coney Island of the Mind," *Isaac Asimov's Cyberdreams,* ed. Gardner Dozois and Shelia Williams (New York: Ace, 1994) 83-90; Maureen McHugh, "Virtual Love," *Nebula Awards 30,* ed. Pamela Sargent (San Diego: Harcourt, 1996) 99-110; Melissa Scott, *Trouble and Her Friends* (New York: Tor, 1994).

11. Don Ihde, *Technology and the Lifeworld: From Garden to Earth* (Bloomington: Indiana UP, 1990) 75.

MAJOR WRITERS OF CYBERPUNK FICTION

Tom Maddox (essay date fall 1988)

SOURCE: Maddox, Tom. "The Wars of the Coin's Two Halves: Bruce Sterling's Mechanist/Shaper Narratives." In *Storming the Reality Studio: A Casebook of Cyberpunk and Postmodern Science Fiction,* edited by Larry McCaffery, pp. 324-30. Durham, N.C.: Duke University Press, 1991.

[In the following essay, which was originally published in 1988, Maddox provides a thematic overview of Sterling's Mechanist/Shaper stories.]

Cyberpunk, science fiction's new movement of the 1980s, continues the style and spirit of the 1960s' New Wave: literary, insurgent, contemptuous of the genre's prevailing standards. As critics have remarked, however, the new writers differ in not being repulsed by technology; rather, they use hard science and technology as the stone on which to hone their aesthetic edge.

Bruce Sterling is one of the movement's most visible and characteristic figures, its leading pamphleteer, provocateur, promoter, and critic; also one of its most accomplished and influential novelists and short story writers. As "Vincent Omniaveritas," editor of the mimeoed *Cheap Truth,* Sterling stirred up argument and self-examination within SF's typically self-congratulatory community through inciting and publishing rude, pseudonymous voices. In prefaces to William Gibson's *Burning Chrome* (1986b) and the *Mirrorshades* (1986a) anthology—edited by Sterling—he mapped a territory and challenged writers and critics to occupy or dispute it. Restless, quarrelsome, and energetic, he has become SF's Ezra Pound—an ardent voice for new literature, arbiter of its standards, artistic explorer of its terrain.

However, Sterling is a c-p writer, not a literary modernist, and his vision is biological more than aesthetic, grounded in post-Darwinian conceptions of life and information evolving to ever greater levels of complexity. The emergence of these new levels occurs as a series of ruptures of the present order—intrusions of different and frightening modes of being—and thus, more so than any SF writer with whom I am familiar, Sterling has explored the Other as the future of our becoming.

The Mechanist/Shaper narratives can provide an introduction to this aspect of Sterling's work. After *Involution Ocean* (1977), a short novel that can be viewed as juvenilia, and "Man-Made Self," a story Sterling rejected in its published form because it was garbled by the press, the Mechanist/Shaper sequence begins in 1982 with the story "Swarm." It continues through the stories "Spider Rose," "Cicada Queen," "Sunken Gardens," and ends in 1985 with "Twenty Evocations" and the novel *Schismatrix*. These stories are collected in *Crystal Express* (1990). (All page numbers from these stories refer to this collection.)

Shaper and Mechanist name the primary posthumanist modes of being—binary opposites in the dialectic of mankind's fate. Technopolitical fusions, they manifest polar strategies of human evolution:

The Shapers . . . had seized control of their own ge-
netics, abandoning mankind in a burst of artificial evolution. Their rivals, the Mechanists, had replaced flesh
with advanced prosthetics.

("Sunken Gardens," 89-90)

Creating themselves anew, the Shapers (also known as
the Reshaped) possess high intelligence and beauty. Internally and externally, they differ from us. Simon Afriel, protagonist of the first Mechanist/Shaper story, can
serve as a model:

His hormonal balance had been altered slightly to compensate for long periods spent in free fall. He had no
appendix. The structure of his heart had been rede-
signed for greater efficiency, and his large intestine had
been altered to produce the vitamins normally made by
intestinal bacteria. Genetic engineering and rigorous
training in childhood had given him an intelligence
quotient of one hundred and eighty.

("Swarm," 4)

Though the Mechanists can prolong life virtually indefinitely through replacing or augmenting flesh by mechanical devices, the ultimate result, known as a "Senior Mechanist" or "wirehead" is a most peculiar entity:

"With the loss of mobility comes extension of the
senses. If I want I can switch out to a probe in Mercu-
rian orbit. Or in the winds of Jupiter. I often do, in fact.
Suddenly I'm there, just as fully as I'm ever anywhere
these days. The mind isn't what you think. . . . When
you grip it with wires, it tends to flow. Data seem to
bubble up from some deep layer of the mind. This is
not exactly living, but it has advantages."

(*Schismatrix*, 1985:179)

Like two species struggling to fill the same ecological
niche, Shapers and Mechanists in these narratives
struggle to dominate post-humanity.

As Sterling himself would quickly point out, these concerns do not constitute innovation within SF. Early on,
in Olaf Stapledon's bloodless sagas, later in Arthur C.
Clarke's *Childhood's End* (1953) and *2001* ([1968]
which Sterling glancingly cites at the end of
Schismatrix) and on through the interminable manifestations of Frank Herbert's Dune novels, SF has concerned itself with just such themes as humanity's transformations and consequent strange destinies. However,
no one before Sterling has imagined these metamorpho-
ses with such intensity and realized them so completely,
or extrapolated them with so much style.

"Swarm," the first Mechanist/Shaper narrative, evokes
many of the characteristic themes of later stories: fac-
tional struggle as the primary field of conflict; the fa-
naticism thus engendered; the high evolutionary stakes.
More important, the central dynamic of the whole
Mechanist/Shaper universe is stated. The Swarm's
agent—an intelligent being representing a hive organism—says,

"This urge to expand, to explore, to develop, is just
what will make you extinct. You naively suppose that
you can continue to feed your curiosity indefinitely. It
is an old story, pursued by countless races before you.
Within a thousand years—perhaps a little longer—your
species will vanish. . . .

"Knowledge is power! Do you suppose that fragile
little form of yours—your primitive legs, your ludi-
crous arms and hands, your tiny, scarcely wrinkled
brain—can *contain* all that power? Certainly not! Already your race is flying to pieces under the impact of
your own expertise."

(25)

Afriel will stay with Swarm, kept alive through the hive
organism's means, his essential being the subject of an
existential wager: Afriel's belief that he and his descendants can maintain their post-humanity—"that fragile
little form of yours"—against Swarm's belief that it can
absorb and transform him and his kind into one of its
agents. "Swarm" ends ambiguously: the only certainty
is the uncertain posthuman future.

Then comes "Spider Rose," the story of a Mechanist
woman living in isolation, starved for human emotion,
maintained in a biochemical "sanity" of dubious worth
and perceiving the world through mechanical means:

She watched through eight telescopes, their images col-
lated by computer and fed into her brain through a
nerve-crystal junction at the base of her skull. . . . Her
ears were the weak steady pulse of radar, listening, listening.

("Spider Rose," 29)

Trading with the Investors—an alien species interested
only in wealth—she acquires a creature, "a genetic artifact, able to judge the emotional wants and needs of an
alien species and adapt itself to them in a matter of
days." She loves the creature, but in the aftermath of an
attack by a Shaper enemy, must eat it in order to survive; after being rescued by the Investors, she undergoes a metamorphosis revealing that the creature's properties have become incarnated in her. At the story's end,
she bursts from a cocoon in the insectlike form her In-
vestor rescuers prefer.

These first two stories thus use the Mechanist/Shaper
context as the ground for rather conventional SF.
"Swarm" conjures its power through its convincing presentation of the alien hive organism. "Spider Rose" succeeds both in its Grand Guignol presentation of the
Mechanist woman's initial altered state and the trump
card play of her final transformation.

With "Cicada Queen," the trope of posthumanism acquires symbolic depth, and the Mechanist/Shaper sequence its own higher level of complexity. Here Ster-

ling presents ideas abducted from Ilya Prigogine—Nobel Prize-winning theorist of dissipative systems—and transformed under the rubric "Prigoginic Levels of Complexity":

> Every level of Prigoginic complexity was based on a self-dependent generative catalyst: space existed because space existed, life was because it had come to be, intelligence was because it is.
>
> (55)

First level is the primordial ur-cosmos ("de Sitter space"); second level, the universe of space and time; third level, life; fourth level, intelligence; fifth level, merely postulated, "as far beyond intelligence as intelligence is from amoebic life, or life from inert matter" ("CQ").

A host of ideas and images accompanies these artificial and ironic intellectual constructs. The reader is rushed into perplexity from the first page, where words such as "dogs" and "defection" and "initiation" obviously have special meaning; within the next few hundred words a whole forest of semiotic constructs will emerge, from "Queen" to "Kosmosity" to "Polycarbon Clique," and so on.

As a result, reading "CQ" is both challenging and exhilarating. Sterling has provided the necessary materials for understanding all the story's most arcane elements, but he demands that the reader participate actively in understanding them. Readers of William Gaddis's novels—*The Recognitions, JR,* and *Carpenter's Gothic*—will recognize the technique: the author presents the reader with a fragment of bone and forces the reader to envision the dinosaur.

Next comes "Sunken Gardens." It states the penultimate theme of the Mechanist/Shaper universe: futility is absolute, and so is freedom. In it, the Regals of Terraforming-Kluster sit in orbit and supervise the transformation of Mars; on the planet itself, factions live—both Shaper and Mechanist—that have failed economically and been banished. They can escape only through ecological competitions in which each faction presents innovation in technique and taste, and the winners become Regals themselves.

Mirasol, the Shaper protagonist of "SG," learns in one of the competitions that a group of humans exists on the planet in a state of savagery; it contains the survivors of a group that was nearly annihilated by the Regals for discovering the Investors' technique of starflight. The Regal leader admits the action and says,

> "If humanity's efforts turned to the stars, what would become of terraforming? Why should we trade the power of creation itself to become like the Investors?"

"But think of the people," Mirasol said. "Think of them losing their technologies, degenerating into human beings. A handful of savages, eating bird meat."

"Our game is reality," the Regal said. . . . "You can't deny the savage beauty of destruction."

"You defend this catastrophe?"

The Regal shrugged. "If life worked perfectly, how could things evolve? Aren't we posthuman? Things grow; things die. In time the cosmos kills us all. The cosmos has no meaning, and its emptiness is absolute. That's pure terror, but it's also pure freedom. Only our ambitions and our creations can fill it."

"And that justifies your actions?"

"We act for life," the Regal said.

(100)

The Regal preaches a posthuman acceptance of the meaninglessness and futility of human action and consequent absolute freedom. As Hassan i Sabbah, the "Old Man of the Mountain" and leader of the cult of Assassins, said, in words William Burroughs is fond of quoting, "Nothing is true. Everything is permitted."

Schismatrix reveals that this philosophy can be attributed only ambiguously to Sterling. A young boy near the novel's end says to Abelard Lindsay, "Posthumanism! Prigoginic levels of complexity! Fractal scales, bedrock of space-time, precontinuum ur-space!" Then, seemingly innocent and unaware of the implications of his question, he asks, "Have I got it right?" These ideas, felt by many of the novel's characters as ontological bedrock, are shown as mere slogans, semiotic constructs through which humanity can manifest its will.

Schismatrix unironically presents ideas that move beyond these and complete them. "Life moves in clades," says Wells/Wellspring, a particularly interesting character in both "Cicada Queen" and *Schismatrix,* who then explains:

> "A clade is a daughter species, a related descendant. It's happened to other successful animals, and now it's humanity's turn. The factions still struggle, but the categories are breaking up. No faction can claim the one true destiny for mankind. Mankind no longer exists."
>
> (*Schismatrix,* 183)

Thus, the last section of *Schismatrix* is titled "Moving in Clades," as mankind moves on.

Dialectician that he is, Sterling uses the terms Mechanist and Shaper to generate new ideas, new tensions. For instance, some Mechanists become "Lobsters," who live "exclusively within skin-tight life support systems," flanged here and there with engines and input-output jacks, who never eat or drink and have sex only through cranial plugs ("Cicada Queen"); while some Shapers transform into aquatic "Angels":

The skin was smooth and black and slick. The legs and pelvic girdle were gone; the spine extended to long muscular flukes. Scarlet gills trailed from the neck; the rib cage was black openwork, gushing white, feathery nets packed with symbiotic bacteria.

(*Schismatrix*, 282)

And in the ultimate transformation, Abelard Lindsay transfers across a fundamental boundary of being through an insubstantial Presence:

He stretched his arms out toward it. It came over him in a silver wave. Stellar cold, a melting, a release.

And all things were fresh and new.

He saw his clothes floating within the hallway. His arms drifted out of the sleeves, prosthetics trailing leashes of expensive circuitry. Atop its clean white ladder of vertebrae, his empty skull sank grinning into the collar of his coat.

(*Schismatrix*, 287)

Mechanist and Shaper manifest dominant fields of post-humanity, then, but these fields are neither inclusive nor permanent.

Schismatrix sustains the complexity we noted in "Cicada Queen" for its entire length and, thus, is in some ways a very demanding book. A well-known editor in SF, one sympathetic to Sterling's work, commented to me when the book came out that the narrative was without necessary transitions between episodes. A friend of mine, when asked for a single comment on Sterling's fiction, said, "Too many moving parts."

Both statements point to an essential fact of Sterling's work: organic profusion. The Mechanist/Shaper stories ultimately become so rich in detail and concept that one can choke on them . . . or develop a taste for them. For these stories, as for living things, one can only guess at their long-term chances. Intricacy that alarms in the present quite often proves a sustaining virtue over the long run. For Sterling, the Mechanist/Shaper universe served as an aesthetic and philosophical laboratory, where he has honed his craft and dramatized the issues he believed crucial to humankind's evolution. Like the proliferating organisms of the Mechanist/Shaper narratives, his fiction to date represents a series of adaptations to a universe of constant change: thus, he presents not one style and set of themes but a multiplicity of them, dynamically evolving.

SEXUALITY AND CYBERPUNK FICTION

Thomas Foster (essay date fall 1997)

SOURCE: Foster, Thomas. "'Trapped by the Body'?: Telepresence Technologies and Transgendered Perfor-

mance in Feminist and Lesbian Rewritings of Cyberpunk Fiction." *Modern Fiction Studies* 43, no. 3 (fall 1997): 708-42.

[*In the following essay, Foster analyzes the predominance of "themes of gender and sexual performativity or cross-identification in these narratives about cyberspace."*]

What we have in today's virtual-reality systems is the confluence of three very powerful enactment capabilities: sensory immersion, remote presence, and teleoperation.

—Brenda Laurel, *Computers as Theatre*

In cyberspace the transgendered body is the natural body.

—Allucquère Rosanne Stone, *The War of Desire and Technology*

Virtual reality, it turned out, was nothing but air guitar writ large.

—Robert J. Sawyer, *The Terminal Experiment*

Andrew Ross once rather notoriously described the cyberpunk fiction of William Gibson, originator of the cyberspace metaphor, as "the most fully delineated urban fantasies of white male folklore" (145).[1] In Ross's reading, cyberpunk representations of virtual realities and human-computer interfaces do indeed turn out to be "nothing but air guitar writ large," not only commercialized hype (as Robert Sawyer suggests) but specifically adolescent male commercialized hype.[2]

This essay uses Allucquère Rosanne Stone's recent work on the status of embodiment in virtual systems to account for the existence of a significant number of popular narratives by women writers about virtual reality, despite Ross's characterization of cyberpunk fiction as inherently masculinist. In particular, Stone's work helps explain the predominance of themes of gender and sexual performativity or cross-identification in these narratives about cyberspace. I have written elsewhere about the relevance of theories of performativity to narratives of cyborg embodiment,[3] but this essay considers the relevance of those theories to virtual reality computer interfaces and computer simulations, which tend to be represented popularly as technologies of disembodiment.[4] To what extent do theories and practices of subversive mimicry and performativity, such as drag or butch-femme, function as a cultural framework for constructing the meaning of virtual reality and telepresence technologies?[5]

I will focus on three examples of narratives that use practices of gender cross-identification to conceptualize cyberspace and virtual reality: Maureen F. McHugh's short stories, Melissa Scott's novel *Trouble and Her Friends,* and Laura Mixon's novel *Glass Houses.* I will end by using Caitlin Sullivan and Kate Bornstein's novel *Nearly Roadkill* to raise some questions about the dominance of gender and sexual performance in these narratives and about the remarkable absence of popular attention to the way that cyberspace might facilitate modes of racial performance such as passing and black-face. While Stone's comment that "in cyberspace the transgendered body is the natural body" (180) seems intended primarily to articulate the challenge posed by virtual systems to existing constructions of gender identity, the same statement might also be read as articulating a new set of emergent gender norms. Transgendered bodies and performances do in fact seem to be increasingly naturalized in computer-mediated communication and in popular narratives about it, in ways that transracial bodies and performances are not.[6]

Both text-based and graphic virtual interfaces make possible the decoupling of public persona from the physical space of the body. This detachment certainly lends itself to a traditional Cartesian dualism between mind and body, and therefore can also reproduce the gendered hierarchy that equates masculinity with universal rationality and femininity with embodied particularity.[7] However, this same detachment of public persona from physical location can also have the effect that Judith Butler famously attributes to gay performance styles such as drag or butch-femme—that is, the detachment of public persona from physical body can reveal that sex and gender are not related as cause and effect and that sex and gender do not necessarily exist in a one-to-one expressive relation to one another.

This critique of expressive subjectivity has received less attention than Butler's arguments about subcultural practices of gender masquerade, but it is that critique which best defines the mutual relevance of virtual reality and theories of performativity. Butler argues, for example, that the categories of the "inner" and the "outer," upon which expressive subjectivity depends,[8] "constitute a binary distinction that stabilizes and consolidates the coherent subject." But in situations where "the 'inner world' no longer designates a *topos*, then the internal fixity of the self and, indeed, the internal locale of gender identity, become similarly suspect" (*Gender Trouble* 134). Virtual systems represent just such a situation, where the "inner world" of subjectivity is no longer simply located within the subject's physical body. Virtual reality computer interfaces or telepresence technologies both restage and disrupt the distinction between inner and outer worlds. Virtual personae or body images become relatively more detached from any "internal fixity" or "locale"—specifically, bodies as material bounded spaces. If the process of virtualization itself involves the progressive "dissociation of space from place," as Mitsuhiro Yoshimoto suggests, then the "locale of gender identity" also becomes dissociated from any fixed location (115). The question is: to what

extent can such personae, and the challenges they pose to traditional notions of the relation between sex and gender, be ideologically recontained as mere secondary projections of a securely interiorized self?

In the popular discourse on virtual reality computer interfaces, the disappearance of this expressive relation between body and gender identity is perhaps most clearly demonstrated in Howard Rheingold's notorious speculations about the sexual uses of these interfaces, which he calls "teledildonics." Rheingold imagines a technology that will allow computer users to map their body images into computer-simulated graphic environments in cyberspace, along with feedback devices that will translate actions in cyberspace into physical sensations in the user's body; if the user's image or avatar in cyberspace reaches its hand to "touch" another person's image or is "touched" by someone else's virtual hand, then an approximation of those sensations will be transmitted to the user's actual body (350). Rheingold takes this scenario a step further by raising the possibility that users would map their physical bodies onto their virtual images *non-mimetically,* and it is the implications of this dissociation of virtual image from a one-to-one relationship with any physical body that have been generally overlooked in responses to this scenario. Rheingold suggests that "there is no reason to believe you won't be able to map your genital effectors to your manual sensors and have direct genital contact by shaking hands. What will happen to social touching when nobody knows where anybody else's erogenous zones are located?" (353).

Let's put aside for the moment the question of whether we really know now where anybody else's erogenous zones are located, or even our own. What this passage from Rheingold's popular introduction to virtual reality implies is the breakdown of the binary relationship between sex and gender which mandates, among other things, that there are only as many genders as there are biological sexes. By contrast, in virtual environments, the relationship between body and social presence can no longer be taken for granted.

The conceptualization of this potential breakdown of expressive relationships between embodiment and social identity in terms of "teledildonics," however, also has other implications. The figure of the dildo invokes lesbian sexual practices, and in contemporary lesbian criticism it is not uncommon to find the dildo invoked as "an especially embarrassing affront to normative heterosexuality" which suggests "its (possibly postmodern) subversion" (Lamos 91), or as a means by which "lesbians have turned techno-culture's semiotic regime of simulation and the political economy of consumer culture back against the naturalization of masculinist hegemony" in a reading of how "the reproduction of the penis as dildo" exposes the phallus as merely a "simulacrum," a copy without an original (Griggers 121). Lisa Moore, in fact, has adopted Rheingold's terminology to analyze Jeannette Winterson's lesbian fiction.

Given this reading of "dildonics," tele- or otherwise, as a subversive imitation of the phallus which reveals it to be only an idealized copy of itself and not a secure source of cultural authority, it is only a short step to the reading that Theresa Senft proposes, which moves from the use of the dildo as sexual prosthesis to a reading of sexual identity itself as prosthetic; as Senft puts it "a *transgendered woman . . .* lives a prosthetic sexuality—she points to the fact that *all* gender is a strap on that you can't strap off" (23). And the context for this claim is Senft's attempt to define a model for sexual and gender performances in cyberspace, in what Stone calls the "spaces of prosphetic communication" (36).

The result is a chain of associations, which moves from imagining how virtual images or personae might be differently mapped onto physical bodies to a notion of teledildonics to lesbian sexual practices and prostheses to a theory of sexual and gender identities and performances as prosthetic. One effect of this chain of associations, however, is to conceptualize virtual performativity in exclusively sexual and gendered terms, rather than in terms of transracial performance, which is equally implicit in the initial rejection of one-to-one mappings of bodies and social identities, as I read Rheingold's teledildonics scenario. Lauren Berlant has identified the problem with applying a model of "prosthetic identity" to minoritized subjects, especially the mulatta or women whose bodies are also racially marked. Such women find themselves in the dilemma of figuring over- or hyper-embodiment, and therefore the inability to transcend their particular bodies, for "a culture that values abstraction" and the ability to identify with the universalized national body of the American citizen, a body that Berlant argues functions as a prosthesis necessary for participation in the national public sphere (113). In other words, to consider the articulation of gender and race is to immediately problematize the model of "prosthetic identity" that Senft proposes for virtual embodiment. The association of virtual technologies with forms of teledildonics or prosthetic sexual identities has the positive effect of denaturalizing binary gender identities, but that association has not encouraged consideration of the effects of virtual embodiment on racial identities and histories. What would it mean to think of race as well as sexuality as a prosthesis? That question is one that any attempt to apply theories of sexual performativity to the analysis of cyberspace must also consider.

Rheingold's teledildonics scenario has also been taken up by at least one feminist science fiction writer, Maureen F. McHugh, in a story entitled "A Coney Island of the Mind." This story is a rather programmatic translation of Rheingold's speculations into a fictional narrative, with a twist that Rheingold doesn't envision. In McHugh's story, an adolescent male protagonist uses a commercial virtual reality system designed to immerse the operator in a virtual environment through the use of head-mounted displays, datagloves to translate the movements of the hands into movements of the virtual image of the operator's body, and a treadmill to facilitate the illusion of movement within the computer-generated graphic. This virtual environment, the "Coney Island" of the title, can be accessed simultaneously by multiple participants who can interact virtually. The literary allusion in the title, to a poem (and book of poems) by Beat poet Lawrence Ferlinghetti, is important for at least two reasons. First, the allusion emphasizes the application of a literary metaphor to the representation of cyberspace, though the allusion is also to a literary movement, the Beats, which attempted to return poetry and print culture in general to a model of performance. Second, the allusion also invokes Ferlinghetti's use of the phrase "Coney Island of the Mind," which Ferlinghetti uses as a metaphor of both poetry and the American public sphere, both understood as a kind of carnivalesque space that is simultaneously a social and a textual space.

The main character of the story has invested considerable time and expense customizing a virtual body image for himself that he refers to as "Cobalt," and a body image that makes deliberate though superficial use of the non-mimetic possibilities of virtual embodiment by rendering his eyes and hair a bright blue (84-85), in an attempt to separate himself from users who simply adopt a more generic and preprogrammed simulation of a body. As Cobalt, this character encounters the virtual image of a young woman with "yellow snake eyes and brown skin" (87). While they are holding hands on the virtual boardwalk, he realizes that she is having an orgasm and that she has taken "a hotsuit and re-wire[d] the crotch so the system thinks it's a hand," just as Rheingold imagined (89).

The young man is at first embarrassed to have been tricked in this manner (89), a response that is especially interesting given that it distinguishes this rewiring of erogenous zones from simple cross-dressing or the creation of alternative personae in virtual reality. Earlier in the story, Cobalt is solicited by a group of "queens (who are mostly black and tall and female and camp, that being the current fashion in queens)" (86). He dismisses their suggestive comments as "white noise," but goes on to remark that they are "not what he's looking for anyway although who's to say what he'd be looking for if he had the option?" (86). On one level, the "option" that Cobalt doesn't have is to experience the sexual options made possible by a full-body "hotsuit" with sexual feedback mechanisms, an "option" to which minors are denied access. But on another level, it is clear that the "option" is also the choice to explore alternative identity practices, such as flirting or having cybersex with someone who has chosen to appear as a black drag queen. But in the context of this virtual environment, the story clearly indicates that such modes of cross-identification and border-crossing are both encouraged and safe because they are perceived as having no real consequences for the world outside cyberspace. This reading is reinforced when Cobalt gets a sexual thrill from the thought that the person he's met, who appears as an attractive woman in virtual reality, might actually be someone completely different. It makes his heart pound to think that she might be "ugly, or fat, or old. Maybe she is blind, or deformed. Wild thought that this beautiful girl can be anything" (88). In this passage, Cobalt's virtual experience is presented as progressive, as he steps beyond the expected heterosexual prejudices of a boy his age by not only imagining but also enjoying the thought that he is flirting with a woman who doesn't meet normal standards of physical beauty. At the same time, it is clear that such moments of stepping outside the pressures of social conventions for gender and sexuality are also ideologically recontained by the assumption of a clear distinction between cyberspace and "real life," with virtual experiences having no particular effect on who Cobalt is outside virtual reality.

Cobalt's ability to maintain this distinction momentarily breaks down, when this other person goes a step further by telling Cobalt that he has not only been tricked into having sex without knowing it but that he's been tricked into having sex with a gay man without knowing it. The other character asks Cobalt if he's a girl, and then reveals that "she" is glad he's not, because "she" is "'not into girls. I just like wearing girl bodies because I like you righteous boys, you sweet straight boys'" (89-90). Cobalt's reaction to this revelation is beyond embarrassment. His first thought is that "he'll have to change his look, never look like this again, abandon Cobalt, be something else" (90). The implication of this moment of homosexual panic is that Cobalt is so mortified that he momentarily assumes either that his virtual image is somehow legible to others as a gay style of embodiment, leading to encounters like this one, and therefore revealing something about who he really is; or, alternately, that this encounter has somehow marked his virtual persona for other people, in the same way that a rumor about his sexuality in real life would affect his social identity in ways that he could not control. At this point, it seems that Cobalt both collapses the distinction between virtual experiences and "real life" and, for that very reason, imagines using the resources of virtual reality to literalize the typical adolescent fantasy of escaping an embarrassing situation by becoming someone else. But, of course, Cobalt's previous attitude toward virtual reality simulations was that they had no

such effect on who he really is, that encounters with "queens" in VR were incapable of invoking the "real life" response of homosexual panic, and that the social meaning of his presence in cyberspace remained in his authorial control, no matter how far he walked on the wild side in VR. By the end of the story, this attitude reemerges, with Cobalt imagining how he can renarrate and edit the story to claim bragging rights among his friends.

McHugh's version of Rheingold's teledildonics scenario then identifies the difference between modes of cyber-cross-dressing, "wearing girl bodies," that only reinforce normative gender and sexual identities and modes of virtual embodiment that more fundamentally subvert such identities by more fully utilizing the potential of virtual technologies to disrupt the expressive or one-to-one mapping of social identities and meanings onto bodies. By the same token, this narrative suggests that teledildonics also makes possible acts of cyber-transracialization: is the "brown skin" of this female body image assumed as a calculated element in the seduction, or is the gay male operator also brown-skinned? Significantly, this question and the issues it raises about the extent to which exoticizing racial stereotypes might be implicated in transgendered or drag performances tends to be overwhelmed by the spectacular nature of the gender and sexual cross-identifications in the story.[9]

This implicit distinction between what Lisa Nakamura calls virtual "identity tourism" and more truly unsettling forms of virtual cross-dressing becomes particularly important in the context of the gay character's statement about wearing girl bodies. That phrase suggests an extension of Judith Butler's comments on drag as "the mundane way in which genders are appropriated, theatricalized, worn, and done; it implies that all gendering is a kind of impersonation and approximation" ("Imitation" 21). For the characters in McHugh's story, virtual reality seems to be imagined as the mundane way in which sexed bodies are appropriated, theatricalized, worn, and done. In other words, McHugh's story suggests that virtual reality might foreground Butler's argument that both bodies and genders must be understood as constructed through frameworks of cultural intelligibility, that in turn must themselves be continually produced and reproduced through repeated performances of those interpretive frameworks. At the same time, this reference to "wearing girl bodies" also evokes the problem of distinguishing theatrical modes of performance, which maintain a strict dualistic hierarchy between performer and role, from the kind of discursive performativity that Butler privileges as subversive in its repetition and undoing of the originality of the performer's identity.[10] Conceptualizing virtual cross-dressing as an act of "wearing girl bodies" can be read as a reinscription of the Cartesian mind/body dualism, in which the body functions as a mere receptacle for the mind or self.

The gay male character's statement about "'wearing girl bodies because I like you . . . sweet straight boys'" also suggests an inversion of Butler's famous reading of lesbian femme performances through the comment of one femme that she likes "her boys to be girls" (*Gender* 123); the character in McHugh's story likes to be a girl in order to have virtual sex with straight men. One of the main questions the story implicitly poses is whether this sexual act was a heterosexual or a homosexual one. Or is it an example of what Jodi O'Brien calls "uncoded desire" (63), a form of sexual practice for which there is, as yet, no category? Allucquère Rosanne Stone's recent book on virtual systems theory offers the best theorizations to date of these new possibilities and of the relationship between virtual embodiment and theories of performativity. Stone's book focuses primarily on sexuality and gender but also provides an opportunity to consider how the experience of telepresence might affect racial identities as well.

For Stone, virtual reality technologies make visible what she calls "location technologies"—that is, techniques for mapping cultural meanings and representations onto physical bodies. Her work attempts to account for the ways in which "the accustomed grounding of social interaction in the physical facticity of human bodies is changing" (17). Stone uses the term "virtual systems theory" to encompass not only the new relationships between physical and virtual bodies in cyberspace but also older forms of "warranting," one of the key terms Stone introduces, defined as "the production and maintenance of this link between a discursive space and a physical space" (40). This process of warranting is not unique to cyberspace but has always functioned "to guarantee the production of what would be called a citizen," since "this citizen is composed of two major elements": the "collection of physical and performative attributes that Judith Butler and Kobena Mercer in separate works call the culturally intelligible body" and "the collection of virtual attributes which, taken together, compose a structure of meaning and intention for the first part," primarily through discursive means (40). These two sets of attributes compose what Stone calls "the socially apprehensible citizen" (40), and the process of becoming such a citizen means acquiring a new, virtual body. (It is important to note that the "physical" body, in Stone's model, is, therefore, no more purely natural or organic than is the body in Butler's work; instead the physical body is constituted and experienced through discursive and performative means.)

For Stone, then, as for critics like Michael Warner and Lauren Berlant, the production of the "citizen" has always involved a process of abstraction from the particularity of the body, and this history provides the context in which to understand the changes introduced by virtual reality and new technologies of computer-mediated communication. Berlant describes this traditional process of forming the universalized body of the citizen by transcending particular forms of embodiment as the nation's promise to provide "a kind of prophylaxis for the person, as it promises to protect his privileges and his local body in return for loyalty to the state" (113). Berlant adds, "American women and African-Americans have never had the privilege to suppress the body" that this process of citizenship requires (113). In some narratives about cyberspace, virtual technologies are imagined precisely as a means of mediating and resolving this dilemma. Several of the characters in Caitlin Sullivan and Kate Bornstein's novel *Nearly Roadkill* argue that cyberspace is liberating for women in particular because it protects them in the way that the more traditional "prophylaxis" of public discourse has not: "And for women! Whoa! Suddenly they can tell assholes to fuck off without getting killed, or be really sexy in a way they would never be normally, and just enjoy it" (10-11). In this passage, through the mediation of text-based virtual communities, women are able to go public *and* still safely assert their differences from men, both through performing their sexualities and through verbal confrontation. In this version of virtual reality as public sphere, it is not necessary for women to transcend their sexual and gendered particularities in order to become part of the general public.

Virtual technologies also tend to make it much more difficult than it used to be to impose a one-to-one relationship between a single body and a single discursive identity, or in Stone's terms to warrant, to guarantee or ground, social identity in a physical body, and it therefore becomes more difficult to limit discursive identities to one per body, or by extension to limit genders and sexual orientations to one per sexed body. It is this intervention in already existing cultural techniques of abstraction and disembodiment that invalidates or at least qualifies the popular association of VR and cyberspace with a Cartesian desire to escape embodiment entirely, to be free of the "meat," as one of William Gibson's characters might put it. In Stone's words, "the virtual component of the socially apprehensible citizen is not a disembodied thinking thing, but rather a different way of conceptualizing a *relationship* to the human body" (40).

In virtual systems, it is no longer necessary for this relationship to be expressive in order for bodies to be culturally intelligible. Like drag performances, virtual reality technologies have the potential to, in Butler's words, "mock . . . the expressive model[s] of gender" and "compulsory heterosexuality" (*Gender* 137), which assume "that there is first a sex that is expressed through a gender and then through a sexuality" ("Imitation" 29).

In another story by McHugh, "Virtual Love," a woman narrator and a male character learn to recognize and become attracted to one another in virtual reality because of their skill in creating and operating multiple, alternative personae, both male and female, including a black woman persona for the white woman narrator (101). The story hinges around the revelation that both these characters are physically confined to wheelchairs, which leads the male character to explain their unusual skill in constructing virtual personae in terms of how everyone else in VR is "'projecting something. But I'm not. I'm not projecting myself at all'" (109). To realize the full potential of virtual reality, it is necessary to recognize, as Butler puts it, that "the distinction between expression and performativeness is crucial" (*Gender* 141).

The narrator ends the story by rejecting the essentialism of the other character's explanation: "I don't think I'm less likely than anyone else to project, any more objective than anyone else. But maybe people like Sam and me, we spend more time. We refine our art" (110). This comment could be read as reasserting an expressive model of subjectivity, associated with artistic expression. But it is equally possible to read the narrator here as generalizing the need to critique expressive assumptions about virtual embodiment to include everyone, not just the differently abled, especially since the scenes that reveal the physical bodies of the characters seem designed to shock readers and make us aware of how our reading of the story might have performed a similar act of expressive "projection." That is, readers would be shocked if we began by assuming that there was a general correspondence, at least, between the various body images we see the characters take on and their actual physical forms. At the same time, the narrator's final comment also suggests a critique of technological determinism, which would locate the disruption of expressive assumptions in the technology itself, rather than in the cultural frameworks in which the technology is made to mean and which structures the ways in which the technology gets used.

As I just suggested, the scenes in which the characters' physical forms are revealed seem designed to enact within the reading process the necessity of unlearning expressive assumptions about the relationship between virtual and physical space, which is thematized in the story as a central problem for users of virtual reality. In fact, the revelation scenes are deliberately staggered, so that first the narrator describes how she is no longer able to "forget" her physical body and "come alive" through the mediation of a virtual persona. She loses this ability to "come alive" in cyberspace because her romance with the other character is becoming too serious and she feels proceeding as if her virtual persona were real would be deceiving him and only frustrating herself. At this point, the narrator tells us that "I know myself, a tiny woman in a chair, held in by seat re-straints, wearing a VR visor and gloves. . . . Flipper babies they call us when we are little, seal babies" (107). Her virtual lover later tracks her down and appears to her in his physical form: "the little man in the wheelchair is all head, head with a sharp, pointed chin and thinning hair and quick eyes. He's not really all head, he has a body, and short stick legs, short muscular arms. Like something out of a Valasquez painting, a dwarf" (109). The narrator is then able to accept a romance in virtual reality and also, perhaps even more importantly, to overcome her tendency to privilege her physical body as her "real" or "true" self. When she meets her lover again in virtual reality at the end of the story, her virtual persona takes over, and she finds herself behaving like the character would, "kind of in your face" (110). The narrative's refusal of any clear distinction between actor and role, face and mask, is underscored by the fact that the story never gives the "true" names of the characters; they are only identified by the names of their personae.[11]

These scenes of revelation are all the more disturbing given the contrast between them and the narrator's detailed and loving descriptions of both her personae and her lover's various body images, which take up a significant portion of the story. The point of this deliberate shock is to demonstrate how the form of the story, in a print medium, is capable of incorporating some characteristics of virtual technologies and providing an experience for readers that approaches those made possible by virtual reality. McHugh's "Virtual Love" invokes and revises a traditional understanding of narrative point of view, which implies an embodied perspective on the actions of the narrative. But, as N. Katherine Hayles has argued in an important essay on the characteristics of printed "info-narratives," "in cyberspace point of view does not emanate from the character; rather, the pov literally *is* the character" ("Flickering" 82-83). That is, in narratives set in virtual environments, the characters' points of view are detached from any direct connection to a specific body, and those points of view or personae function themselves as narrative agents.[12] It is precisely this transformation in the narrative function of point of view, this formal encoding of technological change, that McHugh's "Virtual Love" retroactively makes readers self-conscious about. We realize in retrospect that the narrator's point of view was much more dissociated from her physical body, through the mediation of virtual technologies, than we had initially realized before that physical embodiment was revealed to us. The story not only thematizes this process of dissociation for the characters, but also transfers it to readers of the story. And that process is precisely one of interrogating the naturalness of expressive assumptions.

Butler emphasizes that all forms of gender are performative, with the expressive model becoming the norm only through "the repeated stylization of the body, a set of repeated acts . . . that congeal over time to produce the appearance of substance, of a natural sort of being" (*Gender* 33). For Butler, drag constitutes a disruptive repetition of these gender norms, one that foregrounds the arbitrary relation between sex and gender by, for instance, juxtaposing a recognizable performance of femininity against the background of a culturally intelligible male body. I would argue that virtual reality constitutes another form of disruptive repetition, with the user's physical body repeated and reiterated as an image or representation in cyberspace. In effect, virtual systems spatialize the repeated performance of gender norms over time and thereby reveal the gap between embodiment and the performance of it, which allows for subversion, intervention, and the critical rearticulation of that relationship.[13] It is this spatialization of a gender identity that is normally produced as a "social temporality" that allows virtual systems to reveal "the imitative structure of gender itself," the extent to which gender is an imitation without an original (*Gender* 141, 137). In Stone's model of virtual systems, this point is made when she defines both the physical body and the discursive persona as having performative elements, so that the experience of virtual embodiment can potentially lead to a rethinking of physical embodiment as well (41).

Sue-Ellen Case has recently critiqued Butler's theory of performativity, which Case reads as a project that aims "to recuperate writing at the end of print culture," by appropriating to writing the qualities of live or visual performance that are threatening to make print media obsolete. At the same time, for Case, the project of theories of performativity also amounts to the devaluation of theatrical performance for its dependence upon an essentialist distinction between the actor and the role (17). "The use of performance" in theories of queer performativity, Case argues, "is to challenge writing to become performative. The contradiction between performance as mutable and nonreproductive," or nonrepeatable, "and writing as stable and reproductive, motivates writing to somehow perform 'mimicry' and 'to discover a way for repeated words to become performative utterances'" (21). In Case's view, the result for lesbian theory has been to create a double bind between "the two strategies of lesbian visibility and queer performativity" (20).

This critique then makes two main claims, which my reading of feminist narratives about virtual reality and performativity in cyberspace at least problematize. First, theories of performativity surreptitiously reinstate the privilege of writing over visual media by endowing writing "with the seductive pleasurable qualities of performance and . . . relegating bodily performances to a prior, essentialized mode of production" (23). As I suggested above, however, in my reading of McHugh's "Virtual Love," print media does seem capable of incor-

porating or textually performing the transformations in the experience of point of view which are made possible by virtual technologies, suggesting a reversal of the hierarchy that privileges writing, since virtual technologies have become the model for literary form. Second, Case argues that the importance of imitation, iteration, and repetition in Butler's theory of gender performativity tends to privilege writing over "bodily performances," which are understood as relatively unique and "nonreproductive" events. My reading of virtual reality computer interfaces as performative technologies argues for exactly the opposite understanding of how iteration and repetition might function in such technologies. Precisely through their spatializing of the process of iteration, virtual technologies make it possible to visualize the kind of discursive performativity that Butler privileges over theatrical performativity and therefore to bridge and potentially resolve the dichotomy Case identifies between lesbian visibility and queer performativity.[14]

At the same time, virtual performativity, as I have described it so far, also promises to overcome Carole-Anne Tyler's critique of "camp theory," which she criticizes for assuming a "gay sensibility" that is capable of recognizing the difference between subversive performances that unsettle gender norms and normative performances that reproduce and confirm those norms (54-56). This critique again focuses on how the subversion of gender becomes visible, with Tyler suggesting that subcultural practices of gender masquerade are only preaching to the converted, because they assume a queer framework of reception, such as a gay bar, where the audience is already prepared to read the discrepancies between sex, gender, and sexual practice rather than to assume an expressive relation between them. Virtual technologies, as they are represented in the texts I have been discussing, promise the possible generalization of this queer framework of reception and its greater imbrication in processes of everyday life and communication, with one result being increased possibilities for gender masquerade and mimicry to function subversively.[15]

Melissa Scott's 1994 novel *Trouble and Her Friends* launches a more explicit and fully developed lesbian feminist revision of cyberpunk fiction than McHugh's stories. The novel focuses on a circle of gay and lesbian computer hackers, all of whom have had an invasive procedure which allows them to interface their nervous systems directly with cyberspace computer networks through the use of an neural implant called a "brainworm" that allows for full-body processing, translating information into bodily sensations.

The novel sets up a complex relationship between alternative sexualities and hacking. *Trouble and Her Friends* begins as the cyberspace networks are finally coming under direct government regulation, with the result that hackers in general are faced with the challenge of "going straight, moving out of the shadows into the bright lights of the legal world, the legal nets" (33-34). But what does it mean for these gay and lesbian hackers to "go straight"? Is this the equivalent of coming out of the closet, as the rhetoric of "moving out of the shadows into the bright lights" suggests? Or is it the equivalent of going back into the closet, by assimilating to heterosexual norms as well as to the middle-class norms of legitimate computer users, as the phrase "going straight" suggests?[16]

The novel's deployment of the rhetoric of the closet associates being closeted with the use of cyberspace as an escape from oppressive social relations in the urban spaces represented in the novel. That desire for escape is thematized precisely in terms of performative possibilities: one of the main characters thinks of the cyberspace "nets" as a place "where a woman could easily be as hard and tough as any man" (210). Cyberspace therefore represents a temptation for these gay and lesbian characters as a space of liberation from the constraints of living in a more homophobic "real" world, though this liberatory function is qualified by the way in which the novel represents the prejudices other computer hackers still possess about women and gay computer users. The novel also suggests, however, that the liberation made possible by computer interfaces may be purchased only at the cost of ghettoizing or recloseting subversive gay performances in cyberspace, where they will have no effect on social relations more generally. In other words, the thematics of the "closing of the electronic frontier" functions not only as a critique of cyberpunk's tendency to romanticize outlaw hackers[17]; this same thematics also emphasizes the necessity of establishing connections between cyberspace and the world outside the Nets, of setting up a feedback loop between those two kinds of spaces and therefore between virtual and the physical bodies. In this sense, Scott's novel supports Stone's claim that "the virtual component of the socially apprehensible citizen" is not an escape from embodiment but instead represents a "different way of conceptualizing a *relationship* to the human body" (40). *Trouble and Her Friends* might then be read not as an elegy for the unregulated anarchy of the Internet, as it might initially appear, but instead as one of the first narratives exploring the preconditions for virtual citizenship.

Rather than offer a more extended reading of Scott's novel than this, I want to focus on one specific passage that attempts to explain the attraction of cyberspace for marginalized groups in general, especially since this passage insists on conceptualizing the value of virtual technologies in terms that include, but are not limited to, the modes of gender and sexual performance such technologies permit. One of the main lesbian characters, whose handle in cyberspace is "Trouble," speculates that

> maybe that was why the serious netwalkers, the original inhabitants of the nets, hated the brainworm [or neural interface]: not so much because it gave a different value, a new meaning, to the skills of the body, but because it meant taking that risk, over and above the risk of the worm itself. Maybe that was why it was almost always the underclasses, the women, the people of color, the gay people, the ones who were already stigmatized as being vulnerable, available, trapped by the body, who took the risk of the wire.

(128)

Other computer hackers are presented in the novel as being prejudiced against people who use this brainworm implant rather than a more traditional keyboard or graphic interface, and the distinction made in this passage between two possible reasons for this prejudice is a difficult, but important, one. The passage suggests two reasons why historically marginalized groups might be attracted to a VR technology that permits the body to be used as a computer interface and why white men might hate this same technology. On the one hand, this technology holds the promise of giving "a different value, a new meaning" to the experience of embodiment, a refiguring of embodiment that is especially attractive to people who have been historically "stigmatized as . . . trapped" by bodies that mark them as marginal. In other words, these peoples are presented as having reasons to want to intervene in the construction of embodiment that straight white men do not.

It is interesting to note that gay people are associated here with women and racialized groups, as occupying marked or stigmatized bodies. While it is true that the history of homosexuality's pathologizing by medical and psychiatric discourse constitutes a material, historical stigma, that stigma is not usually immediately culturally visible or legible in the anatomical features of homosexuals, in contrast to women and racial groups. The assimilation of gay people to these other stigmatized bodies only seems valid for gay people who are already out and perhaps marked by a recognizable performance style, like the women who see the Nets as a place where they can "easily be as hard and tough as any man" (210). The suggestion seems to be that cyberspace permits a kind of spectacularized gayness. But if cyberspace functions in this novel as a privileged gay performance space, a space where "the transgendered body is the natural body," for that very reason cyberspace also potentially functions as a kind of closet or escape valve that confines gay performance to cyberspace only.

This same passage from *Trouble and Her Friends* also argues that it is not just the process of revaluing embodiment as the basis for using computers that repulses anyone who has not been historically "trapped by the body." The passage refers to another risk, besides having to relearn the "meaning" and "value" of the body as computer interface. This other "risk" is associated with giving one's body "over to pure sensation," or becoming just a body under the control of "a stranger's hand," during the process of having the neural implant installed (128). This second risk seems to invoke the historical experiences of women, people of color, and gay people prior to cyberspace, with the suggestion that these subjects' relations to their bodies might always have been understood as virtual, as mediated through cultural technologies of representation. This reading is similar to Lauren Berlant's analysis of the specific relation of women and African-Americans to the "peculiar dialectic between embodiment and abstraction in the post-Enlightenment body politics" and therefore to what Berlant calls the "prosthetic body" of the abstract citizen (113, 114). That is, for women and African-Americans, that prosthesis has never seemed natural, given their relative exclusion from the category of the universally human which that prosthetic body represents. That social body has then always appeared as a prosthesis rather than as a natural extension or expression of themselves for these marginalized groups. In other words, in this passage from Scott's novel, virtual reality technologies are represented as promising to disrupt the Cartesian mind/body dualism and the categories of immanence and transcendence that organize the mind/body dualism along gendered and racial lines.

The suggestion in Scott's novel that cyberspace might lend itself to gay styles of embodied performance is made more explicit in Laura Mixon's 1992 novel *Glass Houses*. This novel is narrated in the first person by Ruby, a lesbian character who suffers from agoraphobia, but who luckily possesses a neural implant that allows her to run a salvage business by remotely operating various robot bodies or "waldos" through telepresence—that is, through a device that transmits the sensory impressions of the robots into Ruby's mind, replacing her own sensorium, but which also allows her to use the robots as remote extensions of her own body. Jon McKenzie has discussed the significance of Scott Fisher's recent insistence (at the 1993 SIGGRAPH conference on computer graphics and simulations) on reconceptualizing immersive virtual reality computer interfaces in terms of telepresence (87). The point of such a shift in terminology, McKenzie notes, is to reintroduce the question of human performance or "experience design" into a technical discourse that sometimes focuses more exclusively on perfecting hardware and software; the result is to foreground the interrelationship between human and technological performance in such technologies (88).[18]

The machine Ruby uses most often is referred to as Golem; she's constructed it from salvaged parts, including an arm from a military robot called a "schwarzenegger." The narrative genders these robots, with Golem being referred to as "he" and a smaller robot (Rachne, short for Arachne) being referred to as "she." It's difficult not to read this as a technological version of butch-femme roleplaying. Ruby comments on how she always prefers to negotiate with her salvage clients "in waldo," talking to them through a robot stand-in, because "they can't read me that way" (119). In other words, the robot body elicits a different set of social responses from other people who cannot as easily "read" Ruby's gender expressively from her physical appearance. Similarly, Ruby speculates that "it's easier to love" the city "when your awareness is encapsulated in a metal body that puts nothing of you at risk" (78). The risk in this passage is precisely the risk of having a body that can be read too easily through the frameworks of cultural intelligibility that Butler has analyzed.

When operating the Golem robot, Ruby refers to it throughout the novel as "my-his" body. The only exception comes at a moment when Ruby is using the robot body to carry her own physical body, and she watches herself being carried by herself:

> I-Golem looked down at the woman in my arms. It was Ruby-me, of course, and her-my eyes were closed, fluttering a little. She-I curled with her-my cheek against Golem's chassis.
>
> She-I looked so young and vulnerable from the outside, not ugly and scrawny like me. I was terrified that I wouldn't be able to keep her from harm; I wished she were back home, safe, right this very minute
>
> (60-61).

It is important to note that Ruby here seems to identify more completely with the robot body, in feeling terrified that "I" wouldn't be able to protect "her" physical body, a shift marked by the abandonment of the hybrid pronoun forms, as Karen Cadora has pointed out in a reading of this novel as an example of "feminist cyberpunk" (360-61).[19] It is also important to note that this passage thematizes the disjunction between Ruby's inner and outer perspectives on her physical body, her view of herself as "she/I" and her view of herself as "me": "she/I looked so young and vulnerable from the outside, not ugly and scrawny like me." In other words, Ruby's more positive self-image comes from being split into "she" and "I" through the medium of telepresence. But when she refers to herself as "me," I would argue, she is attempting to unify these two perspectives into a single coherent subjectivity with the result that she only internalizes the split subjectivity that has been externalized through telepresence technology, in a kind of rewriting of the mirror stage.[20] But this passage associates this internalizing of split subjectivity with Ruby's internalizing of a negative social judgment about her femininity and appearance. This passage also demonstrates how such technologies might both literalize and disrupt what Butler calls "the binary distinction between inner and outer," demonstrating Butler's argument that when "the 'inner world' no longer designates a topos, then the internal fixity of the self and, indeed, the internal locale of gender identity, become similarly suspect" (*Gender* 134).

The passage quoted above, in which Ruby looks at her own body through the eyes of one of her robots, exemplifies the main narrative impulse of *Glass Houses*. The plot of the novel concerns Ruby's becoming aware of a plot to cheat another character out of an inheritance, with the result that she organizes a group of counter-conspirators, in typical cyberpunk fashion. But the real story of the novel concerns Ruby's process of overcoming her agoraphobia. At the beginning of the novel, Ruby deals with this problem by spending all her time "'junked out on your stupid machines,'" as her roommate and lover puts it (65). As in *Trouble and Her Friends,* telepresence represents a temptation to escape embodiment or to use this technology to acquire a safer form of embodiment as an interface with the outside world. It is in this way that the novel intervenes in the traditional gender narrative that associates women with domesticity, though it is also clear that Ruby's agoraphobia represents precisely a kind of "female malady," in which she is only able to go beyond the limits of her home through surrogates. She is not exactly confined to her home, but she is not exactly free to come and go, either.

By the end of the novel, however, Ruby's involvement in the events of the plot necessitate her joining her robots in the outside world, in a doubling of her subjectivity and physical location. Ruby learns to use both her physical and her robot bodies. In this narrative, then, the robot bodies are not simply supplements or prostheses for the physical body; when Ruby learns to use her own body, she does not give up the use of the robot bodies. The use of telepresence does *not* require the abandonment of the physical body. This doubling of Ruby's embodiment is summed up very nicely in the double meaning of the title of the novel. The chapter in which Ruby first goes out to function in both her physical and her robot bodies is entitled "People Who Live in Glass Houses." There is a literal referent for this phrase, since what Ruby is doing is breaking into a house designed to include prominent windows and "glass-covered walkways" (153). But it seems equally clear that this same phrase is used as a metaphor for the way that Ruby inhabits her body. The telepresence technology that she uses makes her body transparent, in the sense that she can project her consciousness outside that body. Her body no longer exactly functions as a limit or a receptacle for her mind, or if it is a receptacle, then it is one whose boundaries are permeable and unstable. At the same time, this figure of the glass

house also thematizes the continuing importance of embodiment, in part by invoking the continuing vulnerability of Ruby's body: people who live in glass houses shouldn't throw stones. Ruby's belief in the invulnerability of her robot body, as a means of negotiating urban space more safely, does not mean that she has escaped the effects of physical embodiment. In other words, the narrative of *Glass Houses,* aside from its plot, also demonstrates Ruby's acceptance of this vulnerability as a form of value as well as risk or danger.

Caitlin Sullivan and Kate Bornstein's novel *Nearly Roadkill* seems like a suitable place to conclude, since it explores the possibilities for transgendered performances in actually existing computer technologies, specifically text-based roleplaying on the Internet. This novel goes much further than any of the other texts I've discussed in its treatment of cyberspace as a space of liberation from gender norms and especially from the assumption that gender identities are expressive of biological sex and sexual identities. This novel focuses on two characters, Winc and Scratch, who enjoy what they call "splattering" or the often simultaneous performance of multiple, differently sexed and gendered personae in various chat rooms and bulletin boards. It is not until the middle of the novel that the two meet F2F (face-to-face), and it is only then that readers learn Winc is a male-to-female transsexual and Scratch is a self-identified lesbian with butch tendencies. The pair become celebrities when they refuse to register their identities with the government, which is attempting to regulate use of the Internet in response to corporate pressure; registering the identities of users will make it possible for companies to gather demographic data and to tailor advertisements to the specific interests of computer users, based on tracing the kinds of information individual users access.

Winc and Scratch regard the Internet as "a place where there's no fear," where "it doesn't matter" if users are "women. They could be black, Latino, the little guy in the wheelchair outside our building. The Asians getting off the boat in California. Gays. Lesbians. Children. Anyone who can't speak up because they were always afraid of being put in their place" (134-35). This sense of liberation from imposed places and identities is, however, almost exclusively developed in terms of the liberation of online gender and sexual performances from any necessary mimetic or expressive relation to the physical bodies and appearances of the performers. There is almost no consideration of how this technology might be used by blacks, Latinos, or Asians, despite their inclusion in the list of social subjects who might share this attitude toward the Internet.

There is one episode in the novel, however, where questions of racial masquerade intrude on the freewheeling genderbending of the main characters. Winc gets into a debate about the politics and ethics of this kind of on-line performance with a character named Leilia whose online persona is feminine, and who turns out to be Winc's lover Scratch, who is white, in disguise. This character notes that "she" finds it "hard to talk" about possibilities for subverting gender norms online "without a context" (72). The example "she" offers of such a context is an annual civil rights march where suddenly "the colors of our skin don't matter . . . because it's *that* day, that march" (74). At this point, Winc decides that "she" has probably been talking to a black person, and they open a discussion of how whiteness functions as an unspoken norm, with Scratch (as Leilia) noting "wearily" that "one of the cool things for black folks online is that they are assumed to be white, too. Not that they want to be white, but they're assumed to be 'in the club,' without having to prove credentials at the door" (74).

It is important to note how Scratch, who later describes herself as prone to bouts of depression in which she wishes she "were black because I hate my skin" (195), becomes mistaken as "black" by Winc not only because she refers to civil rights marches but also because she questions the limits of sexual and gender role-playing online when she is in character as Leilia. "Race" figures primarily as a limit or an obstacle to the free play of performativity in cyberspace, and this representation of racial questions seems to me to oversimplify the relationship of racial identities to virtual modes of embodiment.

The exchange between Winc and Scratch-as-Leilia does, however, raise two questions that open up a more complex and productive consideration of race in cyberspace, although those questions are immediately dropped in the novel itself, as it turns back to an exclusive consideration of gender and sexuality for the next 300 pages or so. First, the passage suggests that the bracketing of physical characteristics online may only reproduce the logic of the modern public sphere, by allowing "black folks" to assimilate more easily to white norms. In that sense, online racial performance seems to amount to nothing more than another form of passing, though in this case all black people can potentially pass on the Internet, not just those with sufficiently light skin. Second, this passage also suggests that the supposed subversiveness of sexual, gender, *or* racial performativity can easily be recontained within a particular "context" or interpretive framework. The question this character raises is how to articulate such spaces of performativity where gender or racial norms can be relaxed, whether this occurs online or during special marches and holidays, with social spaces where those norms are rigorously enforced. In other words, the question is how gender or racial subversion moves beyond preaching to the converted, or how changes on the level of the virtual might affect the physical.[21]

Throughout this essay, I have been focusing on how feminist and lesbian science fiction writers have begun to create narratives of virtual embodiment that situate these technologies in the context of the historical experiences of women and homosexuals, specifically the relative exclusion of both groups from the universalizing categories of the human and the citizen and their resulting relegation to the particularity of "the body." These popular narratives tend to imply progressive uses of virtual reality and other computer interface technologies and to locate those progressive uses in the possibilities for subversive gender and sexual performance that the technologies make possible. But it is important, I think, to note that these narratives tend to ignore or minimize possibilities for racial performances online and in cyberspace. This may simply reflect the political underdevelopment of the discourse on the cultures emerging around new computer technologies. But the dominance of sexual and gender performativity over racial masquerade in these narratives of virtual reality can also be explained theoretically, by noting Fredric Jameson's use of camp as a way to conceptualize the general postmodern loss of depth, which he argues transforms the world into "a glossy skin, a stereoscopic illusion, a rush of filmic images without density"—that is, a virtual reality computer simulation (34). The result of such transformations is to make social presence dependent upon social style, in the same way that virtual reality equates presence and style. In McHugh's "A Coney Island of the Mind," the main character notes that "the streets are all full of programming, of nonplayer characters, and kids without style, which is to say that this night Coney Island is empty" (87). Camp seems to provide a ready-made model for such a situation, but camp as a model for virtual embodiment has tended to privilege the performance of sexuality and gender over race.

This reading suggests that racial performativity may not be subversive in a way that is analogous to gender and sexual performativity. Histories of racial performance in the U.S., such as blackface minstrelsy, suggest in fact that racial norms are often installed and reproduced precisely through modes of racial cross-identification which are not mimetic or expressive in the same way that gender norms have been historically, so that such modes of racial performativity are much less likely to possess a subversive meaning than modes of gender cross-identification such as drag.[22] A recent article in *Emerge* magazine on the presence of white supremacist organizations on the Internet noted their promotion of modes of virtual blackface as part of a smear campaign against African-Americans, including posing as African-Americans to post material supporting the legalization of pedophilia (Sheppard 38). If, as Stone suggests, transgendered bodies and performances are in the process of becoming naturalized in virtual systems, it may be necessary to keep a critical perspective on that process.

Notes

1. In *Neuromancer,* Gibson defines cyberspace as a "consensual hallucination" (5) and as a "graphic representation of data abstracted from the banks of every computer in the human system" (51).

   Originally written as an internal document for the Autodesk company, one of the earlier designers of virtual reality equipment, and collected in Brenda Laurel's *The Art of Human-Computer Interface Design,* John Walker's essay "Through the Looking Glass" exemplifies how the literary metaphor of cyberspace was taken up by computer researchers and programmers. Walker cites *Neuromancer* to argue for changing the dominant metaphor of the human-computer interface. Walker wanted to replace the metaphor of interfacing as carrying on a conversation with the computer, with the metaphor of interfacing as entering another space on the other side of the computer screen (443).

   The concrete results of this shift in metaphors were attempts to design hardware and software that would produce this sensation of entering a "cyberspace," such as the head-mounted display, which produces an immersive effect by filling the user's entire field of vision, and the dataglove, which maps the movements of the user's hand as a kind of 3-D cursor. New software was also needed to map the movements of the head or the user's point of view into the simulation, for instance.

   To gain a sense of the history of these kinds of responses to the cyberspace metaphor, see Benedickt's *Cyberspace: First Steps* collection; Laurel's *Computers as Theatre,* especially the second edition which updates the final chapter on virtual reality; and Stone's *The War of Desire and Technology.*

2. The most thoroughgoing critique of the rhetoric around cyberspace is Robert Markley's collection *Virtual Reality and Its Discontents.* In his introduction, Markley specifically argues that this rhetoric reproduces "the metanarrative of technological development" as an unquestioned good (7) and that the globalizing use of cyberspace to refer to all forms of virtual technologies renders those technologies in an abstract and dehistoricized form: "the division between cyberspace and virtual technologies reflects and reinscribes the oppositions of mind/body, spirit/matter, form/substance, and male/female," Markley writes (2). Despite the argument that cyberspace "does not transcend the problems of materiality, embodiment, or capital," this collection pays little attention to specifically gendered and racialized modes of virtual embodiment or disembodiment, with the exception of Hayles's "Boundary Disputes," which is reprinted in the collection, and to a lesser extent, Kendrick's essay.

   See also Stone's argument about how the term "cyberspace" has functioned as a globalizing or abstract metaphor for a diverse "network of electronic communication prostheses" (35).

3. See Foster, "'The Sex Appeal of the Inorganic'" (297-300). Fuchs also uses Butler's theory of performativity to analyze cyborg imagery (114-15).

4. It is important to note, however, that there has always been a strong counter-discourse among designers and programmers of virtual systems, a discourse that associates such systems with concepts of full-body processing that incorporate embodied modes of processing information. For example, Randal Walser, a researcher at Autodesk, claims that "Print and radio tell. Stage and film show. Cyberspace embodies" (60).

   One of the central debates in work on cyberpunk fiction and technocultures more generally concerns whether cyberspace and virtual systems should be read primarily as another example of what Arthur and Marilouise Kroker call the "disappearing body" in postmodern culture or whether these new technologies might instead (or also) make it possible to intervene in the construction of embodiment. To quote Scott Bukatman, if there is increasing acceptance that "the body must become a cyborg to retain its presence in the world," there is little agreement about whether this reconceptualization of embodied existence "represents a continuation, a sacrifice, a transcendence, or a surrender of 'the subject'" (245).

   For critiques of this trope of the disappearing body and the association of cyberspace with disembodiment or escape from what Gibson calls "the meat," especially in narratives by male cyberpunk authors, see Morse; Nixon; Stockton; Kendrick; Lang; chapter 1 of Springer's book, "Deleting the Body"; and Dery, *Escape Velocity,* chapter 6, on "obsolete bodies and posthuman beings."

   Work that attempts to offer an alternative to this trope of disembodiment, or to read in such narratives a more complex history, would include Tomas; Hayles's essays, especially "Boundary Disputes," which places this trope more firmly in the history of cybernetics and systems theory; the rest of Springer's book, which argues that "speculation about the bodily obsolescence" is combined with "a desire to preserve bodily pleasures" (161); Balsamo's reading of Pat Cadigan's feminist cyberpunk novel *Synners* in Balsamo's chapter 6 (140-46); Foster; most of the essays in Featherstone and Burrows's *Cyberspace/Cyberbodies/ Cyberpunk* collection, especially Lupton, Clark, and Sobchack; and some of the recent work on text-based virtual communities, such as Cherny, Lang, and Argyle and Shields.

5. For work on sexual or gender performativity and virtual embodiment see Case; Fraiberg; Woodland; and Senft and Horn's special issue of *Women and Performance* on "Sexuality and Cyberspace: Performing the Digital Body," especially Senft's introduction and the essays by O'Brien and Ehrlich.

6. For reasons that I will discuss at the end of this essay, much less work has been done of the topic of race and performativity. Nakamura's essay is a groundbreaking application of Butler's theory of performativity to questions of racial passing and masquerade or minstrelsy in cyberspace. See also Dery's comments about "afrofuturism" in his introduction to the interview with Samuel R. Delany, Greg Tate, and Tricia Rose (Dery, "Black to the Future" 736-43); Mexican-American performance artist Guillermo Gómez-Peña's "Virtual Barrio"; Hayles's intriguing suggestion that cyberspace and narratives about it demonstrate the themes of "marked bodies" and "invisibility" associated with African-American literary texts such as Ralph Ellison's *Invisible Man* ("Seductions" 183); Shohat and Stam's speculations of the possibility of using virtual reality as part of a "multicultural or transnational pedagogy" (165-66); and the section of Case's book that focuses on Chicana lesbian writer Cherie Moraga and her concept of "queer Aztlan" (Case 161-64).

7. McKenzie similarly notes that virtual reality combines two paradigms of performance, human and technological (the latter defined in terms of efficiency and input/output ratios), into a new configuration that both "heightens the oppositions that structure it—presence/absence, originality/ derivativeness, organic/inorganic, authenticity/ inauthenticity, immediacy/mediation—while also exposing a certain cohabitation" between them (101).

There has been less attention to the ways in which such mind-body dualisms have historically structured concepts of sexual, gender, and racial differences, which might therefore also carry over into the construction of cyberspace and which might, alternatively, be disrupted by the development of cyberspace. Stone is one of the main exceptions to this tendency (40-41).

8. See also Jameson's argument that "the very concept of expression presupposes . . . a whole metaphysics of the inside and outside" (11) and therefore a "conception of the subject as a monadlike container" (15). In Jameson's view, of course, postmodernism's cultural logic involves the disappearance of such "depth models" of subjectivity (12).

9. Tyler's critique of Butler's account of drag performance raises similar questions (53-58). Tyler points out that drag performances often depend upon stereotypes about racialized or lower-class women in order to mark the difference between a "subversive" or denaturalizing drag performance and a naturalizing performance of gender. That is, drag performances often mark their excess or their ironic distance from white, middle-class norms of femininity by reproducing stereotypes about women who do not conform to those white, middle-class norms (Tyler's example is Dolly Parton, who Tyler suggests may appear "campy" from a middle-class perspective but who might appear to epitomize feminine norms from a different class perspective).

10. I'm alluding here to Eve Sedgwick's critique of Butler's *Gender Trouble,* where Sedgwick argues that gender performances are as likely to be essentializing as subversive, to the extent that they depend on a clear distinction between performer and performance. See also Butler's response to this charge, in *Bodies That Matter* (226-33 and 282-83, n. 11).

11. This withholding of the characters' "real" names seems particularly suggestive in relation to Ralph Ellison's similar strategy in *Invisible Man,* and therefore seems to support Hayles's suggestion that cyberspace narratives often demonstrate, in some more or less displaced form, the themes of "marked bodies" and "invisibility" found in African-American literary traditions ("Seductions" 183; see note 6 above).

12. In his most recent work, Bolter has begun to similarly theorize immersive virtual reality computer interfaces as a medium that works primarily through the manipulation of point of view ("Ekphrasis" 267-69). This argument is perhaps more forcefully articulated in a short piece Bolter published in *Wired* magazine, in which he claims that "computer graphics is showing itself to be a technology for generating points of view" and that this medium is not "just about morphing objects" but more importantly "about morphing the view and the viewer" ("You Are" 113).

Bolter also defines the medium of virtual reality as non-expressive: "you don't 'express' yourself in defining your computer graphic identity. Instead, you occupy various points of view, each of which constitutes a new identity" (114).

While Bolter draws a very strong distinction between print and visual media, like virtual reality

("Ekphrasis" 256-57), I tend to agree with Hayles's analysis of the interaction between print narrative and virtual technologies, especially around issues of redefining point of view.

13. See Fuch's suggestion that cyborg body images that combine organic and mechanical elements might be read in a similar way. Fuchs quotes Butler's argument that "if every performance repeats itself to institute the effect of identity, then every repetition requires an interval between the acts, as it were, in which risk and excess threaten to disrupt the identity being constituted" (Butler, "Imitation" 28); Fuchs then goes on to define these "intervals" as the "breaks in cyborg identity encoded by their 'divided' selves" (Fuchs 114).

14. Sonnega raises a similar issue, in the context of a critique of the computer graphic technique of morphing as a favored mode of racial representation on MTV. Sonnega points to the difficulty performance techniques, with their emphasis on the visual, have in accounting "for the sensations of spatial 'inbetweenness' that mark the lives of so many actual people" in postmodern culture (46-47). He goes on to critique morphing for construing "intercultural performance not as a contestation of the normative patterns that maintain cultural boundaries, but as an escape from them" (55). Morphing then functions as a painless form of border-crossing or identity tourism, much like the modes of cross-identification that initially excite Cobalt in McHugh's "A Coney island of the Mind."

15. Similarly, O'Brien distinguishes between sexual performances coded as fiction that only reconfirm the knowledge of "our 'physical reality'" (such as "a white 40-something male middle-manager who goes online" as a woman and has text-based cybersex with a black man) and performances that more successfully resist such categorization (her example being a "self-identified lesbian" who has anal sex with a gay man using a dildo) (62-63).

O'Brien also notes that current "nettiquette" involves the assumption that any Internet user identified as a woman who is also "cruising for sex" and "hypergendered" is actually "a guy trying to 'trick' other men into having sex" (60). This assumption clearly functions as a strategy for reinstating a clear hierarchy between "real life" and virtual personae, in particular by ruling out possibilities for female-female impersonation.

I am trying to define the ways that these narratives of virtual reality imagine what O'Brien ends by calling for, more "cross-over between those in queer and straight spaces" online (66).

16. O'Brien's essay begins with an analysis of an ad for online services in the *Advocate,* which uses the slogan "There are no closets in Cyberspace" and which claims that online chat rooms are "meeting places so free and open and wild and fun they make Castro Street look Victorian" (55). Scott's novel and its more complex mapping of connections between cyberspace and the closet can be read as an intervention in this kind of popular discourse.

17. There is nothing particularly new about his critique of the romanticized outlaw hacker in cyberpunk fiction. As early as 1988 (that is, almost as soon as cyberpunk started to become popular), cyberpunk writers themselves began to question this figure. Examples would include Bruce Sterling's novel *Islands in the Net* and Gibson's *Virtual Light.*

18. Brenda Laurel's book *Computers as Theatre* also clearly participates in this attempt to foreground questions of human performance modes within VR technologies.

19. Harper also offers a reading of Ruby's "hybridized subjectivity" (413-15). Both Harper and Cadora draw primarily on Haraway's "Cyborg Manifesto" as a theoretical model for reading *Glass Houses,* with the result that they overlook the performative aspect of the novel's representation of telepresence technologies—that is, they both read Ruby as a feminist cyborg, rather than as a user of virtual reality, as theorized by Stone.

20. On a more theoretical level, Hayles argues that technocultures informed by cybernetic models require a reconceptualization of Lacan's mirror stage, in which the dialectic of presence and absence is presumed to have been denaturalized and demonstrated to be specious and is instead replaced by a dialectic between randomness and pattern ("Seductions" 186).

21. Butler raises the question of "what will constitute a subversive or deinstituting repetition" ("Imitation" 25) given that all identities are constituted through acts of repetition, imitation, and impersonation (27).

Tyler's essay is one of the best elaborations of the problems involved in making such a distinction and especially on the problems involved in using drag as a model. She specifically elaborates on the question of how to distinguish subversive from naturalizing gender performances.

22. For such histories, see Lott's and Rogin's books on blackface minstrelsy in the U.S. Rogin critiques Lott for overstating the transgressive implications of blackface as cross-racial performance, as part of a more general "postmodern recuperation of blackface" that tends to assimilate it to

forms of cross-dressing such as drag or butch-femme (Rogin 30).

Nakamura argues that cross-racial performances in text-based virtual communities often have the effect of reproducing racial stereotypes by defining what kinds of performances count as Asian or African-American (190).

I have written at greater length about questions of racial performance within technoculture contexts in "The Souls of Cyberfolk': Performativity, Virtual Embodiment, and Racial Histories," a chapter in my work-in-progress, *Incurably Informed: Posthuman Narratives and the Rescripting of Postmodern Theory.*

Works Cited

Argyle, Katie, and Rob Shields. "Is there a Body in the Net?" *Cultures of Internet: Virtual Spaces, Real Histories, Living Bodies.* Ed. Rob Shields. Thousand Oaks, CA: SAGE, 1996. 58-69.

Balsamo, Anne. *Technologies of the Gendered Body: Reading Cyborg Women.* Durham: Duke UP, 1996.

Benedikt, Michael, ed. *Cyberspace: First Steps.* Cambridge, MA: MIT P, 1991.

Berlant, Lauren. "National Brands/National Body: *Imitation of Life." Comparative American Identities: Race, Sex, and Nationality in the Modern Text.* Ed. Hortense J. Spillers. New York: Routledge, 1991. 110-40.

Bolter, Jay David. "Ekphrasis, Virtual Reality, and the Future of Writing." *The Future of the Book.* Ed. Geoffrey Nunberg. Berkeley: U of California P, 1996. 253-72.

———. "You Are What You See." *Wired* January 1997: 113-14.

Bukatman, Scott. *Terminal Identity: The Virtual Subject in Postmodern Science Fiction.* Durham: Duke UP, 1993.

Butler, Judith. *Bodies That Matter: On the Discursive Limits of "Sex".* New York: Routledge, 1993.

———. *Gender Trouble: Feminism and the Subversion of Identity.* New York: Routledge, 1990.

———. "Imitation and Gender Insubordination." *Inside/Out: Lesbian Theories, Gay Theories.* Ed. Diana Fuss. New York: Routledge, 1991. 13-31.

Cadora, Karen. "Feminist Cyberpunk." *Science-Fiction Studies* 22 (1995): 357-72.

Case, Sue-Ellen. *The Domain-Matrix: Performing Lesbian at the End of Print Culture.* Bloomington: Indiana UP, 1996.

Cherny, Lynn. "'Objectifying' the Body in the Discourse of an Object-Oriented MUD." Stivale 151-72.

Clark, Nigel. "Rear-View Mirrorshades: The Recursive Generation of the Cyberbody." Featherstone and Burrows 113-33.

Dery, Mark. "Black to the Future: Interviews with Samuel R. Delany, Greg Tate, and Tricia Rose." *South Atlantic Quarterly* 92 (1993): 735-78.

———. *Escape Velocity: Cyberculture at the End of the Century.* New York: Grove P, 1996.

Ehrlich, Michael. "Turing, My Love." Senft and Horn 187-203.

Featherstone, Mike, and Roger Burrows, eds. *Cyberspace/Cyberbodies/Cyberpunk: Cultures of Technological Embodiment.* London: SAGE, 1995.

Ferlinghetti, Lawrence. *A Coney Island of the Mind.* New York: New Directions, 1958.

Foster, Thomas. "Meat Puppets or Robopaths?: Cyberpunk and The Question of Embodiment." *Genders* 18 (1993): 11-31.

———. "'The Sex Appeal of the Inorganic': Posthuman Narratives and the Construction of Desire." *Centuries' Ends, Narrative Means.* Ed. Robert Newman. Stanford: Stanford UP, 1996. 276-301, 371-78.

Fraiberg, Allison. "Electronic Fans, Interpretive Flames: Performing Queer Sexualities in Cyberspace." Stivale 195-207.

Fuchs, Cynthia J. "'Death is Irrelevant': Cyborgs, Reproduction, and the Future of Male Hysteria." *Genders* 18 (1993): 113-33.

Gibson, William. *Neuromancer.* New York: Ace, 1984.

Gómez-Peña, Guillermo. *The New World Border.* San Francisco: City Lights, 1996.

———. "The Virtual Barrio the Other Frontier (or The Chicano Interneta)." *Clicking In: Hot Links to Digital Culture.* Ed. Lynn Hershman Leeson. Seattle: Bay P, 1996. 173-79.

Griggers, Cathy. "Lesbian Bodies in the Age of (Post)Mechanical Reproduction." *The Lesbian Postmodern.* Ed. Laura Doan. New York: Columbia UP, 1994. 118-33.

Harper, Mary Catherine. "Incurably Alien Other: A Case for Feminist Cyborg Writers." *Science-Fiction Studies* 22 (1995): 399-420.

Hayles, N. Katherine. "Boundary Disputes: Homeostasis, Reflexivity, and the Foundations of Cybernetics." *Configurations* 2 (1994): 441-67.

———. "The Seductions of Cyberspace." *Rethinking Technology.* Ed. Verena Andermatt Conley. Minneapolis: U of Minnesota P, 1993. 173-90.

————. "Virtual Bodies and Flickering Signifiers." *October* 66 (1993): 69-91.

Jameson, Fredric. *Postmodernism, or, The Cultural Logic of Late Capitalism.* Durham: Duke UP, 1991.

Kendrick, Michelle. "Cyberspace and the Technological Real." Markley, *Virtual Reality* 143-60.

Kroker, Arthur and Marilouise. "Theses on the Disappearing Body in the Hyper-Modern Condition." *Body Invaders: Panic Sex in America.* Ed. Arthur and Marilouise Kroker. New York: St. Martin's, 1987. 20-34.

Lamos, Colleen. "The Postmodern Lesbian Position: *On Our Backs.*" *The Lesbian Postmodern.* Ed. Laura Doan. New York: Columbia UP, 1994. 85-103.

Lang, Candace. "Body Language: The Resurrection of the Corpus in Text-Based VR." Stivale 245-58.

Laurel, Brenda. *Computers as Theatre.* 2nd ed. Reading, MA: Addison Wesley, 1993.

Lott, Eric. *Love and Theft: Blackface Minstrelsy and the American Working Class.* New York: Oxford UP, 1993.

Lupton, Deborah. "The Embodied Computer/User." Featherstone and Burrows 97-112.

Markley, Robert. "Introduction: History, Theory, and Virtual Reality." Markley, *Virtual Reality* 1-10.

————, ed. *Virtual Reality and Its Discontents.* Baltimore: Johns Hopkins UP, 1996.

McHugh, Maureen F. "A Coney Island of the Mind." 1992. *Isaac Asimov's Cyberdreams.* Ed. Gardner Dozois and Sheila Williams. New York: Ace, 1994. 83-90.

————. "Virtual Love." 1994. *Nebula Awards 30.* Ed. Pamela Sargent. New York: Harcourt Brace, 1996. 99-110.

McKenzie, Jon. "Virtual Reality: Performance, Immersion, and the Thaw." *TDR: The Drama Review* 38.4 (1994): 83-106.

Mixon, Laura J. *Glass Houses.* New York: Tor, 1992.

Moore, Lisa. "Teledildonics: Virtual Lesbians in the Fiction of Jeanette Winterson." *Sexy Bodies: The Strange Carnalities of Feminism.* Ed. Elizabeth Grosz and Elspeth Probyn. New York: Routledge, 1995. 104-27.

Morse, Margaret. "What Do Cyborgs Eat?: Oral Logic in an Information Age." *Culture on the Brink: Ideologies of Technology.* Ed. Gretchen Bender and Timothy Druckrey. Seattle: Bay P, 1994. 157-89.

Nakamura, Lisa. "Race In/For Cyberspace: Identity Tourism and Racial Passing on the Internet." Stivale 181-93.

Nixon, Nicola. "Cyberpunk: Preparing the Ground for Revolution or Keeping the Boys Satisfied?" *Science-Fiction Studies* 19 (1992): 219-35.

O'Brien, Jodi. "Changing the Subject." Senft and Horn 54-67.

Penney, Simon. "Virtual Reality as the Completion of the Enlightenment Project." *Culture on the Brink: Ideologies of Technology.* Ed. Gretchen Bender and Timothy Druckrey. Seattle: Bay P, 1994. 231-48.

Rheingold, Howard. *Virtual Reality.* New York: Summit, 1991.

Rogin, Michael. *Blackface, White Noise: Jewish Immigrants in the Hollywood Melting Pot.* Berkeley: U of California P, 1996.

Ross, Andrew. *Strange Weather: Culture, Science, and Technology in the Age of Limits.* New York: Verso, 1991.

Sawyer, Robert J. *The Terminal Experiment.* New York: Harper Prism, 1995.

Scott, Melissa. *Trouble and Her Friends.* New York: Tor, 1994.

Sedgwick, Eve Kosofsky. "Queer Performativity: Henry James's *The Art of the Novel.*" *GLQ* 1.1 (1993): 1-16.

Senft, Theresa. "Introduction: Performing the Digital Body—A Ghost Story." Senft and Horn 9-33.

————, and Stacy Horn, eds. *Sexuality and Cyberspace: Performing the Digital Body.* Special issue of *Women and Performance* 9.1 (1996).

Sheppard, Nathaniel, Jr. "Trashing the Information Superhighway: White Supremacy Goes Hi-Tech." *Emerge* July-August 1996: 34-40.

Shohat, Ella, and Robert Stam. "From the Imperial Family to the Transnational Imaginary: Media Spectatorship in the Age of Globalization." *Global/Local: Cultural Production and the Transnational Imaginary.* Ed. Rob Wilson and Wimal Dissanayake. Duke: Durham UP, 1996. 145-70.

Sobchack, Vivian. "Beating the Meat/Surviving the Text, or How to Get Out of This Century Alive." Featherstone and Burrows 205-14.

Springer, Claudia. *Electronic Eros: Bodies and Desire in the Postindustrial Age.* Austin: U of Texas P, 1996.

Sterling, Bruce. *Islands in the Net.* New York: Ace, 1988.

Stivale, Charles J., ed. *CyberSpaces: Pedagogy and Performance on the Electronic Frontier.* Special issue of *Works and Days* 13.1-2 (1995).

Stockton, Sharon. "'The Self Regained': Cyberpunk's Retreat to the Imperium and the Responses of Feminism." *Contemporary Literature* 36 (1995): 588-612.

Stone, Allucquère Rosanne. *The War of Desire and Technology at the Close of the Mechanical Age.* Cambridge, MA: MIT P, 1995.

Sullivan, Caitlin, and Kate Bornstein. *Nearly Roadkill:An Infobahn Erotic Adventure.* New York: High Risk Books/Serpent's Tail, 1996.

Tomas, David. "Old Rituals for New Space: *Rites de Passage* and William Gibson's Cultural Model of Cyberspace." Benedikt 31-47.

———. "The Technophilic Body: On Technicity in William Gibson's Cyborg Culture." *New Formations* 8 (1989): 113-29.

Turkle, Sherry. *Life on the Screen: Identity in the Age of the Internet.* New York: Simon & Schuster, 1995.

Tyler, Carole-Anne. "Boys Will Be Girls: The Politics of Gay Drag." *Inside/Out: Lesbian Theories, Gay Theories.* Ed. Diana Fuss. New York: Routledge, 1991. 32-70.

Walker, John. "Through the Looking Glass." *The Art of Human-Computer Interface Design.* Ed. Brenda Laurel. Reading, MA: Addison Wesley, 1990. 439-47.

Walser, Randal. "Spacemakers & the Art of the Cyberspace Playhouse." *Mondo 2000* 2 (1990): 60-63.

Warner, Michael. "The Mass Public and the Mass Subject." *Habermas and the Public Sphere.* Ed. Chris Calhoun. Cambridge, MA: MIT P, 1992. 377-401.

Woodland, J. Randal. "Queer Spaces, Modem Boys, and Pagan Statues: Gay/Lesbian Identity and the Construction of Cyberspace." Stivale 221-40.

Yoshimoto, Mitsuhiro. "Real Virtuality." *Global/Local: Cultural Production and the Transnational Imaginary.* Ed. Rob Wilson and Wimal Dissanayake. Durham: Duke UP, 1996. 107-18.

ADDITIONAL PIECES

Veronica Hollinger (essay date spring 1990)

SOURCE: Hollinger, Veronica. "Cybernetic Deconstructions: Cyberpunk and Postmodernism." *Mosaic* 23, no. 2 (spring 1990): 29-44.

[In the following essay, Hollinger views cyberpunk in its relation to postmodernism, genre science fiction, and literary realism.]

If, as Fredric Jameson has argued, postmodernism is our contemporary cultural dominant ("Logic" 56), so equally is technology "our historical context, political and personal," according to Teresa de Lauretis: "Technology is now, not only in a distant, science fictional future, an extension of our sensory capacities; it shapes our perceptions and cognitive processes, mediates our relationships with objects of the material and physical world, and our relationships with our own or other bodies" (167). Putting these two aspects of our reality together, Larry McCaffery has recently identified science fiction as "the most significant evolution of a paraliterary form" in contemporary literature (xvii).

Postmodernist texts which rely heavily on science-fiction iconography and themes have proliferated since the 1960s, and it can be argued that some of the most challenging science fiction of recent years has been produced by mainstream and vangardist rather than genre writers. A random survey of postmodernist writing which has been influenced by science fiction—works for which science-fiction writer Bruce Sterling suggests the term "slipstream" ("Slipstream")—might include, for example, Richard Brautigan's *In Watermelon Sugar* (1968), Monique Wittig's *Les Guérillères* (1969), Angela Carter's *Heroes and Villains* (1969), J.G. Ballard's *Crash* (1973), Russell Hoban's *Riddley Walker* (1980), Ted Mooney's *Easy Travel to Other Planets* (1981), Anthony Burgess's *The End of the World News* (1982), and Kathy Acker's *Empire of the Senseless* (1988).

Not surprisingly, however, the specific concerns and esthetic techniques of postmodernism have been slow to appear in genre science fiction, which tends to pride itself on its status as a paraliterary phenomenon. Genre science fiction thrives within an epistemology which privileges the logic of cause-and-effect narrative development, and it usually demonstrates a rather optimistic belief in the progress of human knowledge. Appropriately, the space ship was its representative icon during the 1940s and '50s, the expansionist "golden age" of American science fiction. Equally appropriately, genre science fiction can claim the realist novel as its closest narrative relative; both developed in an atmosphere of nineteenth-century scientific positivism and both rely to a great extent on the mimetic transparency of language as a "window" through which to provide views of a relatively uncomplicated human reality. When science fiction is enlisted by postmodernist fiction, however, it becomes integrated into an esthetic and a world-view whose central tenets are an uncertainty and an indeterminacy which call into question the "causal interpretation of the universe" and the reliance on a "rhetoric of believability" which virtually define it as a generic entity (Ebert 92).

It is within this conflictual framework of realist literary conventions played out in the postmodernist field that I want to look at cyberpunk, a "movement" in science fiction in the 1980s which produced a wide range of fictions exploring the technological ramifications of experience within late-capitalist, post-industrial, media-saturated Western society. "Let's get back to the Cyberpunks," Lucius Shepard recently proposed in the first issue of *Journal Wired* (1989), one of several non-academic periodicals devoted to contemporary issues in science fiction and related fields; "Defunct or not, they seem to be the only revolution we've got" (113).

* * *

Cyberpunk was a product of the commercial mass market of "hard" science fiction; concerned on the whole with near-future extrapolation and more or less conventional on the level of narrative technique, it was nevertheless at times brilliantly innovative in its explorations of technology as one of the "multiplicity of structures that intersect to produce that unstable constellation the liberal humanists call the 'self'" (Moi 10). From this perspective, cyberpunk can be situated among a growing (although still relatively small) number of science-fiction projects which can be identified as "anti-humanist." In its various deconstructions of the subject—carried out in terms of a cybernetic breakdown of the classic nature/culture opposition—cyberpunk can be read as one symptom of the postmodern condition of genre science fiction. While science fiction frequently problematizes the oppositions between the natural and the artificial, the human and the machine, it generally sustains them in such a way that the human remains securely ensconced in its privileged place at the center of things. Cyberpunk, however, is about the breakdown of these oppositions.

This cybernetic deconstruction is heralded in the opening pages of what is now considered the quintessential cyberpunk novel—we might call it "the c-p limittext"—William Gibson's *Neuromancer* (1984). Gibson's first sentence—"The sky above the port was the color of television, tuned to a dead channel" (3)—invokes a rhetoric of technology to express the natural world in a metaphor which blurs the distinctions between the organic and the artificial. Soon after, Gibson's computer-cowboy, Case, gazes at "the chrome stars" of shuriken, and imagines these deadly weapons as "the stars under which he voyaged, his destiny spelled out in a constellation of cheap chrome" (12). Human bodies too are absorbed into this rhetorical conflation of organism and machine: on the streets of the postmodern city whose arteries circulate information, Case sees "all around [him] the dance of biz, information interacting, data made flesh in the mazes of the black market . . ." (16). The human world replicates its own mechanical systems, and the border between the organic and the artificial threatens to blur beyond recuperation.

If we think of science fiction as a genre which typically foregrounds human action *against* a background constituted by its technology, this blurring of once clearly de-

fined boundaries makes cyberpunk a particularly relevant form of science fiction for the post-industrial present. Richard Kadrey, himself a (sometime) cyberpunk writer, recently noted the proliferation of computer-based metaphors—"downtime," "brain dump" and "interface," for example—which are already used to describe human interaction ("Simulations" 75). We can read cyberpunk as an analysis of the postmodern *identification* of human and machine.

Common to most of the texts which have become associated with cyberpunk is an overwhelming fascination, at once celebratory and anxious, with technology and its immediate—that is, *unmediated*—effects upon human being-in-the-world, a fascination which sometimes spills over into the problematizing of "reality" itself. This emphasis on the potential interconnections between the human and the technological, many of which are already gleaming in the eyes of research scientists, is perhaps the central "generic" feature of cyberpunk. Its evocation of popular/street culture and its valorization of the socially marginalized, that is, its "punk" sensibility, have also been recognized as important defining characteristics.

Sterling, one of the most prolific spokespersons for the Movement during its heyday, has described cyberpunk as a reaction to "standard humanist liberalism" because of its interest in exploring the various scenarios of humanity's potential interfaces with the products of its own technology. For Sterling, cyberpunk is "post-humanist" science fiction which believes that "technological destruction of the human condition leads not to futureshocked zombies but to hopeful monsters" ("Letter" 5,4).

Science fiction has traditionally been enchanted with the notion of transcendence, but, as Glenn Grant points out in his discussion of *Neuromancer,* cyberpunk's "preferred method of transcendence is through technology" (43). Themes of transcendence, however, point cyberpunk back to the romantic trappings of the genre at its most conventional, as does its valorization of the (usually male) loner rebel/hacker/punk who appears so frequently as its central character. Even Sterling has recognized this, concluding that "the proper mode of critical attack on cyberpunk has not yet been essayed. Its truly dangerous element is incipient Nietzschean philosophical fascism: the belief in the Overman, and the worship of will-to-power" ("Letter" 5).

It is also important to note that not all the monsters it has produced have been hopeful ones; balanced against the exhilaration of potential technological transcendence is the anxiety and disorientation produced in the self/body in danger of being absorbed into its own technology. Mesmerized by the purity of technology, Gibson's Case at first has only contempt for the "meat" of the human body and yearns to remain "jacked into a custom cyberspace deck that projected his disembodied consciousness into the consensual hallucination that was the matrix" (5). Similarly, the protagonist of K.W. Jeter's *The Glass Hammer* (1987) experiences his very existence as a televised simulation. The postmodern anomie which pervades *The Glass Hammer* demonstrates that Sterling's defense of cyberpunk against charges that it is peopled with "futureshocked zombies" has been less than completely accurate.

* * *

"In virtual reality, the entire universe is your body and physics is your language," according to Jaron Lanier, founder and CEO of VPL Research in California; "we're creating an entire new reality" (qtd. in Ditlea 97-98).

Gibson's *Neuromancer,* the first of a trilogy of novels which includes *Count Zero* (1986) and *Mona Lisa Overdrive* (1988), is set in a near-future trash-culture ruled by multi-national corporations and kept going by black-market economies, all frenetically dedicated to the circulation of computerized data and "the dance of biz" (16) which is played out by Gibson's characters on the streets of the new urban overspill, the Sprawl. The most striking spatial construct in *Neuromancer,* however, is neither the cityscape of the Sprawl nor the artificial environments like the fabulous L-5, Freeside, but "cyberspace," the virtual reality which exists in simulated splendor on the far side of the computer screens which are the real center of technological activity in Gibson's fictional world. Scott Bukatman describes cyberspace as "a new and decentered spatiality . . . which exists parallel to, but outside of, the geographic topography of experiential reality" (45). In a fascinating instance of feedback between science fiction and the "real" world, Autodesk, a firm researching innovations in computerized realities in Sausalito, California, has recently filed for trademark protection of the term "cyberspace" which it may use as the name for its new virtual reality software (Ditlea 99). Jean Baudrillard's apocalyptic commentary seems especially significant here: "It is thus not necessary to write science fiction: we have as of now, here and now, in our societies, with the media, the computers, the circuits, the networks, the acceleration of particles which has definitely broken the referential orbit of things" ("The Year 2000" 36).

Along with the "other" space of cyberspace, *Neuromancer* offers alternatives to conventional modalities of human existence as well: computer hackers have direct mental access to cyberspace, artificial intelligences live and function within it, digitalized constructs are based on the subjectivities of humans whose "personalities" have been downloaded into computer memory, and human bodies are routinely cloned.

This is Sterling's post-humanism with a vengeance, a post-humanism which, in its representation of "monsters"—hopeful or otherwise—produced by the interface of the human and the machine, radically decenters the human body, the sacred icon of the essential self, in the same way that the virtual reality of cyberspace works to decenter conventional humanist notions of an unproblematical "real."

As I have noted, however, cyberpunk is not the only mode in which science fiction has demonstrated an anti-humanist sensibility. Although radically different from cyberpunk—which is written for the most part by a small number of white middle-class men, many of whom, inexplicably, live in Texas—feminist science fiction has also produced an influential body of anti-humanist texts. These would include, for example, Joanna Russ's *The Female Man* (1975), Jody Scott's *I, Vampire* (1984), and Margaret Atwood's *The Handmaid's Tale* (1985), novels which also participate in the postmodernist revision of conventional science fiction. Given the exigencies of their own particular political agendas, however, these texts demonstrate a very different approach to the construction/deconstruction of the subject than is evident in the technologically-influenced post-humanism of most cyberpunk fiction.

Jane Flax, for example, suggests that "feminists, like other postmodernists, have begun to suspect that all such transcendental claims [those which valorize universal notions of reason, knowledge, and the self] reflect and reify the experience of a few persons—mostly white, Western males. These transhistoric claims seem plausible to us in part because they reflect important aspects of the experience of those who dominate our social world" (626). Flax's comments are well taken, although her conflation of all feminisms with postmodernism tends to oversimplify the very complex and problematical interactions of the two that Bonnie Zimmerman has noted. Moreover, in a forthcoming essay for *Extrapolation,* I have argued that most feminist science fiction rather supports than undermines the tenets of liberal humanism, although "changing the subject" of that humanism, to borrow the title of a recent study by Nancy K. Miller.

We can also include writers like Philip K. Dick, Samuel R. Delany and John Varley within the project of anti-humanist science fiction, although these writers are separated from cyberpunk not only by chronology but also by cyberpunk's increased emphasis on technology as a constitutive factor in the development of postmodern subjectivity. Darko Suvin also notes some of the differences in political extrapolation between cyberpunk and its precursors: "in between Dick's nation-state armies or polices and Delany's Foucauldian micropolitics of bohemian groups, Gibson [for example] has—to my mind more realistically—opted for global economic power-wielders as the arbiters of peoples [sic] lifestyles and lives" (43).

* * *

In "Prometheus as Performer: Toward a Posthumanist Culture?" Ihab Hassan writes: "We need first to understand that the human form—including human desire and all its external representations—may be changing radically, and thus must be re-visioned. We need to understand that five hundred years of humanism may be coming to an end, as humanism transforms itself into something that we must helplessly call posthumanism" (205).

Sterling's *Schismatrix* (1986) is one version of "posthumanity" presented as picaresque epic. Sterling's far-future universe—a rare construction in the cyberpunk "canon"—is one in which countless societies are evolving in countless different directions; the Schismatrix is a loose confederation of worlds where the only certainty is the inevitability of change. Sterling writes that "the new multiple humanities hurtled blindly toward their unknown destinations, and the vertigo of acceleration struck deep. Old preconceptions were in tatters, old loyalties were obsolete. Whole societies were paralyzed by the mind-blasting vistas of absolute possibility" (238). Sterling's protagonist, a picaresque hero for the postmodern age, "mourned mankind, and the blindness of men, who thought that the Kosmos had rules and limits that would shelter them from their own freedom. There were no shelters. There were no final purposes. Futility, and freedom, were Absolute" (273).

Schismatrix is a future history different from many science-fiction futures in that what it extrapolates from the present is the all-too-often ignored/denied/repressed idea that human beings will be different in the future and will continue to develop within difference. In this way, *Schismatrix* demonstrates a familiarly post-structuralist sensibility, in its recognition both of the potential anxiety *and* the potential play inherent in a universe where "futility, and freedom, [are] Absolute."

Sterling's interest in and attraction to the play of human possibility appears as early as his first novel, *Involution Ocean* (1977). In this story (which reads in some ways like a kind of drug-culture post-*Moby-Dick*), the protagonist falls into a wonderful vision of an alien civilization, in a passage which, at least temporarily, emphasizes freedom over futility: "There was an incredible throng, members of a race that took a pure hedonistic joy in the possibilities of surgical alteration. They switched bodies, sexes, ages, and races as easily as breathing, and their happy disdain for uniformity was dazzling. . . . It seemed so natural, rainbow people in the rainbow streets; humans seemed drab and antlike in comparison" (154).

This is a far cry from the humanist anxieties which have pervaded science fiction since the nineteenth century. Consider, for example, the anxiety around which

H.G. Wells created *The Time Machine* (1895): it is "dehumanization," humanity's loss of its position at the center of creation, which produces the tragedy of the terminal beach, and it is, to a great extent, the absence of the human which results in the "abominable desolation" (91) described by Wells's Time Traveller. Or consider what we might term the "trans-humanism" of Arthur C. Clarke's *Childhood's End* (1953), in which a kind of transcendental mysticism precludes the necessity of envisioning a future based on changing technologies, social conditions and social relations. Greg Bear's more recent *Blood Music* (1985) might be read, from this perspective, as a contemporary version of the same transcendental approach to human transformation, one based on an apocalyptic logic which implies the impossibility of any change in the human condition *within history*. *Blood Music* is especially interesting in this context, because its action is framed by a rhetoric of science which would seem to repudiate any recourse to metaphysics. Darko Suvin has noted, however, that it functions as "a naïve fairytale relying on popular wish-dreams that our loved ones not be dead and that our past mistakes may all be rectified, all of this infused with rather dubious philosophical and political stances" (41).

* * *

"Certain central themes spring up repeatedly in cyberpunk," Sterling points out in his preface to the influential short-fiction collection, *Mirrorshades: The Cyberpunk Anthology*. "The theme of body invasion: prosthetic limbs, implanted circuitry, cosmetic surgery, genetic alteration. The even more powerful theme of mind invasion: brain-computer interfaces, artificial intelligence, neurochemistry—techniques radically redefining the nature of humanity, the nature of the self" (xiii).

The potential in cyberpunk for undermining concepts like "subjectivity" and "identity" derives in part from its production within what has been termed "the technological imagination"; that is, cyberpunk is hard science fiction which recognizes the paradigm-shattering role of technology in post-industrial society. We have to keep in mind here, of course, that the Movement has become (in)famous for the adversarial rhetoric of its ongoing and prolific self-commentary which, in turn, functions as an integral part of its overall production as a "movement." We should be careful, for this reason, not to confuse claims with results. The anti-humanist discourse of cyberpunk's frequent manifestoes, however, strongly supports de Lauretis's contention that "technology is our historical context, political and personal" (167). As I have suggested, this context functions in cyberpunk as one of the most powerful of the multiplicities of structures which combine to produce the postmodern subject.

Thus, for example, the characters in Michael Swanwick's *Vacuum Flowers* (1987) are subjected to constant alterations in personality as the result of programming for different skills or social roles—metaphysical systems grounded on faith in an "inner self" begin to waver. Human bodies in Gibson's stories, and even more so in Sterling's, are subjected to shaping and reshaping, the human form destined perhaps to become simply one available choice among many; notions of a human nature determined by a "physical essence" of the human begin to lose credibility (for this reason, many behavioral patterns defined by sexual difference become irrelevant in these futures). Thus Rudy Rucker can offer the following as a chapter title in *Wetware*: "Four: In Which Manchile, the First Robot-Built Human, Is Planted in the Womb of Della Taze by Ken Doll, Part of Whose Right Brain Is a Robot Rat."

We must also recognize, however, that "the subject of the subject" at the present time has given rise to as much anxiety as celebration (anxiety from which the postmodernist theorist is by no means exempt). The break-up of the humanist "self" in a media-saturated post-industrial present has produced darker readings which cyberpunk also recognizes. Fredric Jameson, whose stance *vis-à-vis* the postmodern is at once appreciative and skeptical, has suggested that fragmentation of subjectivity may be the postmodern equivalent of the modernist predicament of individual alienation ("Cultural Logic" 63). Pat Cadigan's "Pretty Boy Crossover" (1985), for example, raises questions about the effects of simulated reality upon our human sense of self as complete and inviolable. In her fictional world, physical reality is "less efficient" than computerized simulation, and video stars are literally video programs, having been "distilled . . . to pure information" (89, 88) and downloaded into computer matrices. Cadigan's eponymous Pretty Boy is tempted by the offer of literally eternal life within the matrix and, although he finally chooses "real" life, that reality seems to fade against the guaranteed "presence" of its simulation. Bobby, who has opted for existence as simulation, explains the "economy of the gaze" which guarantees the authenticity of the self in this world: "If you love me, you watch me. If you don't look, you don't care and if you don't care I don't matter. If I don't matter, I don't exist. Right?" (91).

* * *

"Pretty Boy Crossover" offers this succinct observation about the seductive power of simulated reality: "First you see video. Then you wear video. Then you eat video. Then you *be* video" (82).

In K.W. Jeter's *The Glass Hammer*, being is *defined* by its own simulation. *The Glass Hammer* is one of the most self-conscious deconstructions of unified subjectivity produced in recent science fiction, and one which dramatizes (in the neurotic tonalities familiar to readers of J.G. Ballard) the anxiety and schizophrenia of the (technologically-produced) postmodern situation. In *The Glass Hammer* the break-up of the "self" is narrated in a text as fragmented as its subject (subject both as protagonist and as story). Jeter's novel is a chilling demonstration of the power of simulated re-presentation to construct "the real" (so that it functions like a cyberpunk simulacrum of the theories of Jean Baudrillard). It "narrates" episodes in the life of Ross Schuyler, who watches the creation of this life as a video event in five segments. There is no way to test the accuracy of the creation, since the self produced by memory is as unreliable a re-presentation as is a media "bio." As Schuyler realizes: "Just because I was there—that doesn't mean anything" (59).

The opening sequence of *The Glass Hammer* dramatizes the schizophrenia within the subjectivity of the protagonist:

> Video within video. He watched the monitor screen, seeing himself there, watching. In the same space . . . that he sat in now. . . .
>
> He watched the screen, waiting for the images to form. Everything would be in the tapes, if he watched long enough.
>
> (7)

Like Schuyler himself, the reader waits for the images to form as s/he reads the text. Episodes range over time, some in the past(s), some in the present, some real, some simulated, many scripted rather than "novelized," until the act of reading/watching achieves a kind of temporary coherence. It is this same kind of temporary coherence which formulates itself in Schuyler's consciousness, always threatening to dissolve again from "something recognizably narrative" into "the jumbled, half-forgotten clutter of his life" (87).

What takes place in *The Glass Hammer* may also be read as a deconstruction of the opposition between depth and surface, a dichotomy which is frequently framed as the familiar conflict between reality and appearance. Jeter reverses this opposition, dramatizing the haphazard construction of his character's "inner self" as a response to people and events, both real and simulated, over time. The displacement of an "originary" self from the text places the emphasis on the marginal, the contingent, the re-presentations (in this case electronically produced) which actually create the sense of "self." Jeter's technique in *The Glass Hammer* is particularly effective: the reader watches the character, and watches the character watching himself watching, as his past unfolds, not as a series of memories whose logical continuity guarantees the stability of the ego, but as an entertainment series, the logical continuity of which is the artificial re-arrangement of randomness to *simulate* coherence.

* * *

Near the outset of Case's adventures in *Neuromancer,* Gibson's computer cowboy visits the warehouse office of Julius Deane, who "was one hundred and thirty-five years old, his metabolism assiduously warped by a weekly fortune in serums and hormones." In Deane's office, "Neo-Aztec bookcases gathered dust against one wall of the room where Case waited. A pair of bulbous Disney-styled table lamps perched awkwardly on a low Kandinsky-look coffee table in scarlet-lacquered steel. A Dali clock hung on the wall between the bookcases, its distorted face sagging to the bare concrete floor" (12).

In this context, it is significant that the "average" cyberpunk landscape tends to be choked with the debris of both language and objects; as a sign-system, it is overdetermined by a proliferation of surface detail which emphasizes the "outside" over the "inside." Such attention to detail—recall Gibson's nearly compulsive use of brand names, for example, or the claustrophobic clutter of his streets—replaces the more conventional (realist) narrative exercise we might call "getting to the bottom of things"; indeed, the shift in emphasis is from a symbolic to a surface reality.

In a discussion of *Neuromancer,* Gregory Benford observes that "Gibson, like Ballard, concentrates on surfaces as a way of getting at the aesthetic of an age." This observation is a telling one, even as it misses the point. Benford concludes that Gibson's attention to surface detail "goes a long way toward telling us why his work has proved popular in England, where the tide for several decades now has been to relish fiction about surfaces and manners, rather than the more traditional concerns of hard SF: ideas, long perspectives, and content" (19).

This reliance on tradition is perhaps what prevents Benford, whose own "hard science fiction" novels and stories are very much a part of science fiction's humanist tradition, from appreciating the approach of writers like Gibson and Jeter. The point may be that, in works like *Neuromancer* and *The Glass Hammer,* surface *is* content, an equation which encapsulates their critique—or at least their awareness—of our contemporary "era of hyperreality" (Baudrillard, "Ecstasy" 128). In this context, the much-quoted opening sentence of *Neuromancer,* with its image of the blank surface of a dead television screen, evokes the anxiety of this new era. Istvan Csicsery-Ronay, for example, sees in cyberpunk the recognition that "with the computer, the problem of identity is moot, and the idea of reflection is transformed in to [sic] the algorithm of replication. SF's computer wipes out the Philosophical God and ushers in the demiurge of thought-as-technique" (273).

Like much anti-humanist science fiction, cyberpunk also displays a certain coolness, a kind of ironically detached approach to its subject matter which precludes nostalgia or sentimentality. This detachment usually discourages any recourse to the logic of the apocalypse, which, whether positive (like Clarke's) or negative (like Wells's), is no longer a favored narrative move. Jameson and Sterling (representatives of "high theory" and "low culture" respectively?) both identify a waning interest in the scenarios of literal apocalypse: Jameson perceives in the postmodern situation what he calls "an inverted millennnarianism, in which premonitions of the future . . . have been replaced by the senses of the end of this or that" ("Cultural Logic" 53); in his introduction to Gibson's short-story collection, *Burning Chrome,* Sterling comments that one "distinguishing mark of the emergent new school of Eighties SF [is] its boredom with the Apocalypse" (xi).

This is supported by Douglas Robinson, in his *American Apocalypses,* when he concludes that "antiapocalypse—not apocalypse, as many critics have claimed—is the dominant topos of American postmodernism" (xvi). In a discussion of Derrida's discourse on apocalypse, Robinson argues that "the apocalyptic imagination fascinates Derrida precisely as the 'purest' form, the most mythical expression or the most extreme statement of the metaphysics of presence" (251n1).

One reason for this tendency to abandon what has been a traditional science fiction topos may be the conviction, conscious or not, that a kind of philosophical apocalypse has already occurred, precipitating us into the dis-ease of postmodernism. Another reason may be the increased commitment of anti-humanist science fiction to the exploration of changes that will occur—to the self, to society and to social relations—in time; that is, they are more engaged with historical processes than attracted by the jump-cuts of apocalyptic scenarios which evade such investment in historical change. Cyberpunk, in particular, has demonstrated a keen interest in the near future, an aspect of its approach to history which discourages resolution-through-apocalypse.

* * *

In a discussion of "the cybernetic (city) state," Scott Bukatman has argued that as a result of the tendency in recent science fiction to posit "a reconception of the human and the ability to interface with the new terminal experience . . . terminal space becomes a legitimate part of human (or post-human) experience" (60). In many cases, however, science-fiction futures are all too often simply representations of contemporary cultural mythologies disguised under heavy layers of futuristic make-up.

The recognition of this fact provides part of the "meaning" of one of the stories in Gibson's *Burning Chrome* collection. "The Gernsback Continuum" humorously ironizes an early twentieth-century futurism which could conceive of no real change in the human condition, a futurism which envisioned changes in "stuff" rather than changes in social relations (historical distance increases the ability to critique such futures, of course). In Gibson's story, the benighted protagonist is subjected to visitations by the "semiotic ghosts" of a future which never took place, the future, to borrow a phrase from Jameson, "of one moment of what is now our own past" ("Progress" 244). At the height of these "hallucinations," he "sees" two figures poised outside a vast city reminiscent of the sets for films like *Metropolis* and *Things to Come*:

> [the man] had his arm around [the woman's] waist and was gesturing toward the city. They were both in white. . . . He was saying something wise and strong, and she was nodding. . . .
>
> . . . [T]hey were the Heirs to the Dream. They were white, blond, and they probably had blue eyes. They were American. . . . They were smug, happy, and utterly content with themselves and their world. And in the Dream, it was *their* world. . . .
>
> It had all the sinister fruitiness of Hitler Youth propaganda.
>
> (32-33)

Gibson's protagonist discovers that "only really bad media can exorcise [his] semiotic ghosts" (33) and he recovers with the help of pop culture productions like *Nazi Love Motel*. "The Gernsback Continuum" concludes with the protagonist's realization that his dystopian present could be worse, "it could be perfect" (35).

Gibson's story is not simply an ironization of naive utopianism; it also warns against the limitations, both humorous and dangerous, inherent in any vision of the future which bases itself upon narrowly defined ideological systems which take it upon themselves to speak "universally," or which conceive of themselves as "natural" or "absolute." David Brin's idealistic *The Postman* (1985), for example, is a post-apocalyptic fiction which closes on a metaphorical note "of innocence, unflaggingly optimistic" (321), nostalgically containing itself within the framework of a conventional humanism. Not surprisingly, its penultimate chapter concludes with a re-affirmation of the "natural" roles of men and women:

> And always remember, the moral concluded: Even the best men—the heroes—will sometimes neglect to do their jobs.
>
> *Women, you must remind them, from time to time.* . . .
>
> (312)

Compare this to Gibson's description of the Magnetic Dog Sisters, peripheral characters in his story, "Johnny Mnemonic" (1981), also collected in *Burning Chrome*: "They were two meters tall and thin as greyhounds.

One was black and the other white, but aside from that they were as nearly identical as cosmetic surgery could make them. They'd been lovers for years and were bad news in a tussle. I was never quite sure which one had originally been male" (2).

Another story in the same collection, "Fragments of a Hologram Rose," uses metaphors of the new technology to express the indeterminate and fragmented nature of the self: "A hologram has this quality: Recovered and illuminated, each fragment will reveal the whole image of the rose. Falling toward delta, he sees himself the rose, each of his scattered fragments revealing a whole he'll never know. . . . But each fragment reveals the rose from a different angle . . ." (42).

Gibson's rhetoric of technology finally circumscribes all of reality. In his second novel, *Count Zero* (1986), there is an oblique but pointed rebuttal of humanist essentialization, which implicitly recognizes the artificiality of the Real. Having described cyberspace, the weirdly real "space" that human minds occupy during computer interfacing, as "mankind's unthinkably complex consensual hallucination" (44), he goes on to write the following:

> "Okay," Bobby said, getting the hang of it, "then what's the matrix? . . . [W]hat's cyberspace?"
>
> "The world," Lucas said.
>
> (131)

It is only by recognizing the consensual nature of sociocultural reality, which includes within itself our definitions of human nature, that we can begin to perceive the possibility of change. In this sense, as Csicsery-Ronay suggests (although from a very different perspective), cyberpunk is "a paradoxical form of realism" (266).

Csicsery-Ronay also contends that cyberpunk is "a legitimate international artistic style, with profound philosophical and aesthetic premises," a style captured by films such as *Blade Runner* and by philosophers such as Jean Baudrillard; "it even has, in Michael Jackson and Ronald Reagan, its hyperreal icons of the human simulacrum infiltrating reality" (269).

* * *

Lucius Shepard concludes his "requiem for cyberpunk" by quoting two lines from Cavafy's "Waiting for the Barbarians": "What will we do now that the barbarians are gone? / Those people were a kind of solution" (118).

Cyberpunk seemed to erupt in the mid-80s, self-sufficient and full-grown, like Minerva from the forehead of Zeus. From some perspectives, it could be argued that this self-proclaimed Movement was nothing

The 1982 cult classic Blade Runner *was a cinematic adaptation of Philip K. Dick's 1968 cyberpunk novel* Do Androids Dream of Electric Sheep?

more than the discursive construction of the collective imaginations of science-fiction writers and critics eager for something/anything new in what had become a very conservative and quite predictable field. Now that the rhetorical dust has started to settle, however, we can begin to see cyberpunk as itself the product of a multiplicity of influences from both within and outside of genre science fiction. Its writers readily acknowledge the powerful influence of 1960s and '70s New Wave writers like Samuel R. Delany, John Brunner, Norman Spinrad, J.G. Ballard and Michael Moorcock, as well as the influence of postmodernists like William Burroughs and Thomas Pynchon. The manic fragmentations of Burroughs's *Naked Lunch* and the maximalist apocalypticism of Pynchon's *Gravity's Rainbow* would seem to have been especially important for the development of the cyberpunk "sensibility." Richard Kadrey has even pronounced *Gravity's Rainbow* to be cyberpunk *avant la lettre*, "the best cyberpunk novel ever written by a guy who didn't even know he was writing it" ("Cyberpunk" 83). Equally, Delany has made a strong case for feminist science fiction as cyberpunk's "absent

mother," noting that "the feminist explosion—which obviously infiltrates the cyberpunk writers so much—is the one they seem to be the least comfortable with, even though it's one that, much more than the New Wave, has influenced them most strongly, both in progressive and in reactionary ways . . ." (9).

Due in part to the prolific commentaries and manifestoes in which writers like Sterling outlined/analyzed/defended their project(s)—usually at the expense of more traditional science fiction—cyberpunk helped to generate a great deal of very useful controversy about the role of science fiction in the 1980s, a decade in which the resurgence of fantastic literature left much genre science fiction looking rather sheepishly out of date. At best, however, the critique of humanism in these works remains incomplete, due at least in part to the pressures of mass market publishing as well as to the limitations of genre conventions which, more or less faithfully followed, seem (inevitably?) to lure writers back into the power fantasies which are so common to science fiction. A novel like Margaret Atwood's *The Handmaid's Tale,* for instance, produced as it was outside the genre market, goes further in its deconstruction of individual subjectivity than do any of the works I have been discussing, except perhaps *The Glass Hammer.*

Gibson's latest novel, *Mona Lisa Overdrive,* although set in the same universe as *Neuromancer* and *Count Zero,* foregrounds character in a way which necessarily mutes the intensity and multiplicity of surface detail which is so marked a characteristic of his earlier work. Sterling's recent and unexpected *Islands in the Net* (1988) is a kind of international thriller which might be read as the depiction of life *after* the postmodern condition has been "cured." Set in a future after the "Abolition" (of nuclear warfare), its central character, Laura Webster, dedicates herself to the control of a political crisis situation which threatens to return the world to a global state of fragmentation and disruptive violence which only too clearly recalls our own present bad old days. Sterling's "Net" is the vast information system which underlies and makes possible the unity of this future world and his emphasis is clearly on the necessity for such global unity. Although, in the final analysis, no one is completely innocent—Sterling is too complex a writer to structure his forces on opposite sides of a simple ethical divide—the movement in *Islands in the Net* is away from the margins toward the center, and the Net, the "global nervous system" (15), remains intact.

As its own creators seem to have realized, cyberpunk—like the punk ethic with which it was identified—was a response to postmodern reality which could go only so far before self-destructing under the weight of its own deconstructive activities (not to mention its appropriation by more conventional and more commercial writers). That final implosion is perhaps what Jeter accomplished in *The Glass Hammer,* leaving us with the image of a mesmerized Schuyler futilely searching for a self in the videoscreens of the dystopian future. It is clearly this aspect of cyberpunk which leads Csicsery-Ronay to conclude that "by the time we get to cyberpunk, reality has become a case of nerves. . . . The distance required for reflection is squeezed out as the world implodes: when hallucinations and realia collapse into each other, there is no place from which to reflect" (274). For him, "cyberpunk is . . . the apotheosis of bad faith, apotheosis of the postmodern" (277). This, of course, forecloses any possibility of political engagement within the framework of the postmodern.

Here cyberpunk is theorized as a symptom of the malaise of postmodernism, but, like Baudrillard's apocalyptic discourse on the "condition" itself, Csicsery-Ronay's analysis tends to underplay the positive potential of representation and re-visioning achieved in works like *Neuromancer* and *Schismatrix.* Bukatman, for example, has suggested that the function of cyberpunk "neuromanticism" is one appropriate to science fiction in the

postmodern era: the *reinsertion* of the human into the new reality which its technology is in the process of shaping. According to Bukatman, "to dramatize the terminal realm means to somehow insert the figure of the human into that space to experience it *for us.* . . . Much recent science fiction stages and restages a confrontation between figure and ground, finally constructing a new human form to interface with the other space and cybernetic reality" (47-48).

The postmodern condition has required that we revise science fiction's original trope of technological anxiety—the image of a fallen humanity controlled by a technology run amok. Here again we must deconstruct the human/machine opposition and begin to ask new questions about the ways in which we and our technologies "interface" to produce what has become a *mutual* evolution. It may be significant that one of the most brilliant visions of the potential of cybernetic deconstructions is introduced in Donna Haraway's merger of science fiction and feminist theory, "A Manifesto for Cyborgs: Science, Technology, and Socialist Feminism in the 1980s," which takes the rhetoric of technology toward its political limits: "cyborg unities are monstrous and illegitimate," writes Haraway; "in our present political circumstances, we could hardly hope for more potent myths for resistance and recoupling" (179).[1]

Note

1. An earlier version of this essay was presented at the 1988 Conference of the Science Fiction Research Association, Corpus Christi, Texas. I would like to thank the Social Sciences and Humanities Research Council of Canada for their generous support. I would also like to thank Glenn Grant, Editor of *Edge Detector: A Magazine of Speculative Fiction,* for making so much information and material available to me during the process of revision.

Works Cited

Acker, Kathy. *Empire of the Senseless.* New York: Grove, 1988.

Atwood, Margaret. *The Handmaid's Tale.* Toronto: McClelland, 1986.

Ballard, J.G. *Crash.* 1975. London: Triad/Panther, 1985.

Baudrillard, Jean. "The Ecstasy of Communication." *The Anti-Aesthetic: Essays on Postmodern Culture.* Ed. Hal Foster. Trans. John Johnston. Port Townsend, WA: Bay, 1983. 126-34.

———. "The Year 2000 Has Already Happened." *Body Invaders: Panic Sex in America.* Ed. Arthur Kroker and Marilouise Kroker. Trans. Nai-Fei Ding and Kuan Hsing Chen. Montreal: New World Perspectives, 1987. 35-44.

Bear, Greg. *Blood Music.* New York: Ace, 1985.

Benford, Gregory. "Is Something Going On?" *Mississippi Review* 47/48 (1988): 18-23.

Brautigan, Richard. *In Watermelon Sugar.* New York: Dell, 1968.

Brin, David. *The Postman.* New York: Bantam, 1985.

Bukatman, Scott. "The Cybernetic (City) State: Terminal Space Becomes Phenomenal." *Journal of the Fantastic in the Arts* 2 (1989): 43-63.

Burgess, Anthony. *The End of the World News.* Markham, ON: Penguin, 1982.

Burroughs, William. *Naked Lunch.* New York: Grove, 1959.

Cadigan, Pat. "Pretty Boy Crossover." 1985. *The 1987 Annual World's Best SF.* Ed. Donald A. Wollheim. New York: DAW, 1987. 82-93.

Carter, Angela. *Heroes and Villains.* 1969. London: Pan, 1972.

Clarke, Arthur C. *Childhood's End.* New York: Ballantine, 1953.

Csicsery-Ronay, Istvan. "Cyberpunk and Neuromanticism." *Mississippi Review* 47/48 (1988): 266-78.

Delany, Samuel R. "Some *Real* Mothers: An Interview with Samuel R. Delany by Takayuki Tatsumi." *Science-Fiction Eye* 1 (1988): 5-11.

de Lauretis, Teresa. "Signs of Wo/ander." *The Technological Imagination.* Ed. Teresa de Lauretis, Andreas Huyssen, and Kathleen Woodward. Madison, WI: Coda, 1980. 159-74.

Ditlea, Steve. "Another World: Inside Artificial Reality." *P/C Computing.* November 1989: 90-102.

Ebert, Teresa L. "The Convergence of Postmodern Innovative Fiction and Science Fiction: An Encounter with Samuel R. Delany's Technotopia." *Poetics Today* 1 (1980): 91-104.

Flax, Jane. "Postmodernism and Gender Relations in Feminist Theory." *Signs: Journal of Women in Culture and Society* 12 (1987): 621-43.

Gibson, William. *Count Zero.* New York: Arbor House, 1986.

———. "Fragments of a Hologram Rose." 1977. *Burning Chrome.* New York: Ace, 1987. 36-42.

———. "The Gernsback Continuum." 1981. *Burning Chrome.* 23-35.

———. "Johnny Mnemonic." 1981. *Burning Chrome.* 1-22.

———. *Mona Lisa Overdrive.* New York: Bantam, 1988.

———. *Neuromancer.* New York: Berkley, 1984.

Grant, Glenn. "Transcendence Through Détournement in William Gibson's *Neuromancer.*" *Science-Fiction Studies* 17 (1990): 41-49.

Haraway, Donna. "A Manifesto for Cyborgs: Science, Technology, and Socialist Feminism in the 1980s." 1985. *Coming to Terms: Feminism, Theory, Politics.* Ed. Elizabeth Weed. New York: Routledge, 1989. 173-204.

Hassan, Ihab. "Prometheus as Performer: Toward a Posthumanist Culture?" *Performance in Postmodern Culture.* Ed. Michel Benamou and Charles Caramello. Madison, WI: Coda, 1977. 201-17.

Hoban, Russell. *Riddley Walker.* 1980. London: Pan, 1982.

Hollinger, Veronica. "Feminist Science Fiction: Breaking Up the Subject." *Extrapolation* 31 (1990): forthcoming.

Jameson, Fredric. "Postmodernism, or The Cultural Logic of Late Capitalism." *New Left Review* 146 (1984): 53-94.

———. "Progress versus Utopia, or Can We Imagine the Future?" *Art After Modernism: Rethinking Representation.* Ed. Brian Wallis. New York: The New Museum of Contemporary Art, 1984. 239-52.

Jeter, K.W. *The Glass Hammer.* New York: Signet, 1987.

Kadrey, Richard. "Cyberpunk 101 Reading List." *Whole Earth Review* 63 (1989): 83.

———. "Simulations of Immortality." *Science-Fiction Eye* 1 (1989): 74-76.

McCaffery, Larry. "Introduction." *Postmodern Fiction: A Bio-Bibliographical Guide.* Ed. McCaffery. Westport, CT: Greenwood, 1986. xi-xxviii.

Miller, Nancy K. "Changing the Subject: Authorship, Writing, and the Reader." *Feminist Studies/Critical Studies.* Ed. Teresa de Lauretis. Bloomington: Indiana UP, 1986. 102-20.

Moi, Toril. *Sexual/Textual Politics: Feminist Literary Theory.* New York: Methuen, 1985.

Mooney, Ted. *Easy Travel to Other Planets.* New York: Ballantine, 1981.

Pynchon, Thomas. *Gravity's Rainbow.* 1973. New York: Bantam, 1974.

Robinson, Douglas. *American Apocalypses: The Image of the End of the World in American Literature.* Baltimore, MD: Johns Hopkins UP, 1985.

Rucker, Rudy. *Wetware.* New York: Avon, 1988.

Russ, Joanna. *The Female Man.* New York: Bantam, 1975.

Scott, Jody. *I, Vampire.* New York: Ace, 1984.

Shepard, Lucius. "Waiting for the Barbarians." *Journal Wired* 1 (1989): 107-18.

Sterling, Bruce. *Involution Ocean.* 1977. New York: Ace, 1988.

————. *Islands in the Net.* New York: Arbor House, 1988.

————. "Letter from Bruce Sterling." *REM* 7 (1987): 4-7.

————. Preface to *Burning Chrome.* ix-xii.

————. Preface to *Mirrorshades: The Cyberpunk Anthology.* New York: Ace, 1988. ix-xvi.

————. *Schismatrix.* New York: Ace, 1986.

————. "Slipstream." *Science-Fiction Eye* 1 (1989): 77-80.

Swanwick, Michael. *Vacuum Flowers.* New York: Arbor, 1987.

Suvin, Darko. "On Gibson and Cyberpunk SF." *Foundation* 46 (1989): 40-51.

Wells, H.G. *The Time Machine.* 1895. *The Time Machine and The War of the Worlds.* New York: Fawcett, 1968. 25-98.

Wittig, Monique. *Les Guérillères.* 1969. Trans. David Le Vay. Boston: Beacon, 1985.

Zimmerman, Bonnie. "Feminist Fiction and the Postmodern Challenge." *Postmodern Fiction: A Bio-Bibliographical Guide.* Ed. McCaffery. 175-88.

Keith R. A. DeCandido (review date 1 November 1991)

SOURCE: DeCandido, Keith R. A. Review of *Storming the Reality Studio: A Casebook of Cyberpunk and Postmodern Science Fiction,* edited by Larry McCaffery. *Library Journal* 116, no. 18 (1 November 1991): 99.

[*In the following review, DeCandido cites* Storming the Reality Studio *as "an important work."*]

Editor McCaffery here [in *Storming the Reality Studio*] collects over 50 essays, short stories, novel excerpts, literary criticism, poetry, artworks, and a comic strip that illustrate the influences on and of the cyberpunk subgenre of science fiction and its distinctive sensibility. Most of the space goes to the two godfathers of cyberpunk, William Gibson (whose *Neuromancer,* Berkley, 1984, won the science fiction triple crown—Hugo, Nebula, and Philip K. Dick awards) and Bruce Sterling, but most other major cyberpunk writers are represented.

McCaffery does not limit cyberpunk to science fiction but puts it in the context of postmodern literature and 1980s popular culture. The only flaw is that Sterling's preface to *Mirrorshades,* often considered a cyberpunk manifesto and constantly referred to in the essays, is not presented until the end of the nonfiction section. An important work; highly recommended for all sf, literature, and pop culture collections.

Dana Polan (review date 1993)

SOURCE: Polan, Dana. Review of *Storming the Reality Studio: A Casebook of Cyberpunk and Postmodern Science Fiction,* edited by Larry McCaffery. *Poetics Today* 14, no. 4 (1993): 771-72.

[*In the following review, Polan calls* Storming the Reality Studio *"a wonderful introduction to the cyberpunk phenomenon."*]

It may seem strange to find reviewed in a journal of poetics a book devoted to fiction, half of which is made up of primary works in that genre. But as the foremost genre of "cognitive estrangement" (in Darko Suvin's nice description), science fiction has always raised compelling questions of and for poetics—questions about the relations between standard and alternative language systems, about the nature of textual representation, about formula and its subversion, and so forth. Not for nothing did *Poetics Today* editor Brian McHale devote a major portion of his *Postmodernist Fiction* (1987) to science fiction; not for nothing does he have a follow-up essay in *Storming the Reality Studio.*

And in the branch of science fiction with which this anthology is concerned in particular—cyberpunk—the relation to poetics can become even more explicit. To a large degree, cyberpunk is a literature of what French writer Guy Debord termed "the society of the spectacle," a universe in which we experience reality through, and as, a series of signs, messages, texts—life itself rendered as pure semiosis. Many of the cyberpunk writers themselves are theory-literate, and their works are filled with references to new critics, new discursive modes of investigation, and new branches of the human sciences (for example, one of the leading conspirators in William Gibson's *Neuromancer* has taken courses in semiotics). At the same time, many of today's critical theorists adopt a virtually science-fictional approach to the order of things (take, for instance, Jurij Lotman's idea of literature as a "secondary modelling system") and thereby create their own forms of cognitive estrangement. Indeed, the notion that literature is primary, while criticism is secondary gets blasted away in much of today's discursive practice, which can be at once poetics and poetic.

In fact, the writings in *Storming the Reality Studio* all seem to have been picked to exemplify new, widely shared modes of thinking, writing, and representing. If, for instance, a passage from Derrida's *Of Grammatology* shows up here in close proximity to an excerpt from Pynchon's *Crying of Lot 49*, it is not because the former offers critical tools with which to understand the latter, but because both are indicative of a new discursive moment. The most apt term available to describe this moment is "postmodernism," and one function of *Storming the Reality Studio* is to bring together some of the most famous articulations of postmodernism (hence selections by Jameson, Lyotard, and Baudrillard, among others) with equally famous examples of its discursive practice (hence excerpts from Pynchon, Burroughs, and Kathy Acker).

Within literary postmodernity, cyberpunk is a privileged genre. It images a world of semiotic simulations, of rampant commodification, of an informational society run wild, of emotion turned into superficial affect; a world where the body and the mind are rendered mutable (by electronic and mechanical prostheses, by mind alteration, by memory implantation, and so on). Imaged as well are the consequences of this world for a society (still) made up of self-willed individuals, whose lives make for gripping narrative.

Storming the Reality Studio is a wonderful introduction to the cyberpunk phenomenon. It offers a range of fiction, poetry, and graphics from cyberculture and allied traditions, such as works by Burroughs, Pynchon, De-Lillo, and Acker, as well as critical/theoretical pieces on and of postmodernism by Jameson, Baudrillard, Derrida, and Arthur Kroker. The essays specifically on cyberpunk traverse a vast array of issues, from feminist possibilities in the new fiction (Joan Gordon) to the relation of cyberpunk to new experiments in literary forms other than science fiction (Veronica Hollinger, Brian McHale); from the possible superseding of a specifically literary cyberpunk by an emergent multimediaism (Brooks Landon) to cyberpunk's relationship to philosophies of rebellion (Timothy Leary—yes, *that* Timothy Leary); from cyberpunk's ambiguous position in the marketplace of late capitalism (Istvan Csicsery-Ronay, Jr.) to cyberpunk and the new sounds in rock (Larry McCaffery); from cyberpunk's reputation in postmodern Japan (Takayuki Tatsumi) to the ideology of cyberpunk (Darko Suvin). The anthology also offers a superb interview (by editor McCaffery) with William Gibson, an extremely comprehensive bibliography, and a captivating annotated reading list (not just of cyberpunk, but also of its influences and allegiances).

FURTHER READING

Criticism

Butler, Andrew M. *The Pocket Essential Cyberpunk.* London: Harpenden, Pocket Essentials, 2000, 96 p.
> Offers an entry-level primer on cyberpunk.

"Johnny Mnemonic: Cyberpunk William Gibson Gets the Hollywood Treatment." *Cinefantastique* 26, no. 3 (April 1995): 44, 46.
> Discusses the cinematic adaptation of Gibson's short story "Johnny Mnemonic."

Kelly, Kevin. "Cyberpunk Era: Interviews with William Gibson." *Whole Earth Review* 63 (summer 1989): 78-83.
> Collage of seven interviews with cyberpunk author Gibson.

Leblanc, Lauraine. "Razor Girls: Genre and Gender in Cyberpunk Fiction." *Women and Language* 20, no. 1 (31 March 1997): 71-6.
> Examines the construction of gender with the cyberpunk genre through a reading of three fictional works by Gibson, Pat Cadigan, and Laura J. Mixen.

Stockton, Sharon. "'The Self Regained': Cyberpunk's Retreat to the Imperium." *Contemporary Literature* 36, no. 4 (1995): 588-612.
> Investigates the relationship between capitalism, gender issues, and cyberpunk.

Wolmark, Jenny. "Cyberpunk, Cyborgs, and Feminist Science Fiction." *Feminist Contributions to the Literary Canon: Setting Standards of Taste,* edited by Susanne Fendler, pp. 139-79. Lewiston, N.Y.: Mellen, 1997.
> Evalutes cyberpunk in feminist terms.

Additional coverage of cyberpunk and general science fiction literature is contained in the following sources published by the Gale Group: *St. James Guide to Science Fiction Writers*; *Science Fiction Writers*; and *Twentieth-Century Literary Criticism,* Volume 106.

Gustave Flaubert
1821-1880

French novelist, short story writer, playwright, and letter writer.

The following entry presents criticism of Flaubert's short fiction works from 1992 to 2001. For criticism of Flaubert's short fiction career published prior to 1992, see *SSC,* Volume 11.

INTRODUCTION

Among the most influential French writers of the nineteenth century, Flaubert is remembered primarily for the stylistic precision and dispassionate rendering of psychological detail found in his masterpiece *Madame Bovary* (1857; *Madame Bovary*). A meticulous craftsman, Flaubert diligently researched his subjects and infused his works with psychological realism with the goal of achieving a prose style "as rhythmical as verse and as precise as the language of science."

BIOGRAPHICAL INFORMATION

Flaubert was born in Rouen, where his father was chief surgeon at the city hospital and his mother was a respected woman from a provincial bourgeois family. As a child, Flaubert attended school at the Collège Royal de Rouen. During a summer vacation with his family in Trouville, Flaubert met Elisa Schlésinger, a married woman for whom he harbored a lifelong infatuation. Upon receiving his baccalaureate degree, Flaubert honored his parents' wishes and reluctantly registered for law school in Paris, despite his stronger interest in literature. In 1844, however, he experienced an attack of what is now believed to have been epilepsy; he subsequently abandoned his law studies and devoted himself entirely to writing. In 1845, Flaubert completed the first draft of *L'éducation sentimentale* (1869; *Sentimental Education*). Following the death of both Flaubert's father and sister in 1846, Flaubert moved to the family home at Croisset, near Rouen, with his mother and infant niece. Flaubert was occupied with the writing of *Madame Bovary* from 1851 to 1856. After the first publication of the novel in serial form in *Revue de Paris,* Flaubert was charged with offenses against public and religious morals and an obscenity trial ensued. Flaubert's defense argued successfully that the novel was in-

deed a moral work, and Flaubert was acquitted. Published in book form two months after the trial, *Madame Bovary* enjoyed widespread sales and significant critical commentary. Towards the end of his career, Flaubert wrote his short fiction collection *Trois contes* (1877; *Three Tales*). With the exception of occasional trips abroad and to Paris, Flaubert lived at his family's home in Croisset until his death in 1880.

MAJOR WORKS OF SHORT FICTION

Although Flaubert is remembered for his novels, he produced a collection of short fiction, *Three Tales,* towards the end of his career. This work presents three stories—"Un Coeur simple," "La légende de Saint Julien l'Hospitalier," and "Hérodias"—ranging in setting from contemporary France to classical antiquity, each of which explores the concept of sainthood and the Christian idea of the Holy Trinity. The first tale,

"Un Coeur simple," chronicles the story of a French peasant woman, Félicitié, who works for the same employer as a servant for her entire life. A loyal, kind-hearted, devout woman, Félicitié is left or forgotten by her closest family members and friends. However, her life takes a turn when she inherits a parrot that becomes her constant companion. After the bird's death, she cannott bear to part with it and has it stuffed. Associating its image with the Holy Spirit, she begins to pray to the stuffed body of the parrot. In "Saint Julien," a young man inadvertently fulfills a prophecy that he will one day kill his parents. As a result of this tragedy, he becomes a reclusive hermit. The final tale in the collection, "Hérodias," is based on the story of the death of John the Baptist. Many of the characters in the tale are based on Roman and biblical history.

CRITICAL RECEPTION

While some critics have interpreted the stories in *Three Tales* as moralistic, others have argued that the volume demonstrates Flaubert's belief that history can be divided into three distinct phases: paganism, Christianity, and *muflisme,* which refers to Flaubert's conception of the nineteenth century as an era marked by the petty values and lifestyles of the bourgeoisie. The role of religion has been identified as the unifying thematic concern of the three stories of the collection, particularly Flaubert's interest in such issues as transcendence, faith, and redemption. Commentators have consistently praised the technical virtuosity of Flaubert's writing—his use of style, structure, imagery, and symbolism. In recent years, some critics have been concerned with the order of the stories in *Three Tales,* as they do not appear in the order in which they were written. Another area of critical interest has been the presence, or lack thereof, of satire in his short fiction.

PRINCIPAL WORKS

Short Fiction

Trois contes [Three Tales] 1877
Oeuvres complètes. 8 vols. 1885
Oeuvres complètes. 23 vols. 1910-33
Oeuvres. 2 vols. 1946-48
Early Writings of Gustave Flaubert (short stories and essays) 1991

Other Major Works

Madame Bovary [Madame Bovary] (novel) 1857
Salammbô [Salammbô] (novel) 1863

L'éducation sentimentale: Histoire d'un jeune homme [Sentimental Education: A Young Man's History] (novel) 1869
Lettre à la Municipalité de Rouen (letters) 1872
Le candidat: Comédie en 4 actes [The Candidate: A Humorous Political Drama in Four Acts] (play) 1874
La tentation de Saint Antoine [The Temptation of Saint Anthony] (novel) 1874
Bouvard et Pécuchet [Bouvard et Pécuchet] (unfinished novel) 1881
Novembre [November] (novel) 1885
Par les champs et par les grèves: Voyages en Bretagne [Over Strand and Field: A Record of Travel through Brittany] (travel essay) 1885
Mémoires d'un fou (novel) 1901

*This collection contains the stories "Un Coeur simple," "La légende de Saint Julien l'Hospitalier," and "Hérodias."

CRITICISM

Ann L. Murphy (essay date February 1992)

SOURCE: Murphy, Ann L. "The Order of Speech in Flaubert's *Trois Contes." The French Review* 65, no. 3 (February 1992): 402-14.

[*In the following essay, Murphy identifies speech as a unifying element of the stories in* Trois contes.]

In his study of **Trois Contes** Michael Issacharoff argues that unlike the novelist who requires from his reader at least an *initial* linear reading of his work, the author of a collection of short stories implicitly grants to his reader the freedom to read the stories in any order he chooses (40). Accordingly, as Issacharoff reasons, the reordering to which Flaubert submitted his three tales prior to their definitive compilation in a single volume—**"La Légende de Saint Julien L'Hospitalier,"** written first, appears second after **"Un Cœur simple"**—constitutes an explicit invitation to undertake such a non-linear reading (42). The "problem of non-linearity" mentioned in Issacharoff's title is linked to that of discerning unity in the volume. Since there is no way to guarantee that the stories will be read in order, the unity of the whole must somehow be located independently of the order in which its parts are read. Issacharoff finds this unity in the recurrence in each of the stories of specific symbols, and of the dialectic between inside and outside.

Issacharoff's argument for a unity to *Trois Contes* seems an appropriate response to critics who treat one of the tales and neglect the others, or to those who would deny any unity whatsoever to the triptych.[1] Yet his linking the question of unity to that of non-linearity does not appear to address sufficiently the possible significance of Flaubert's reordering of his works for publication. One must indeed wonder about the significance of this gesture, for in switching the positions of **"Saint Julien"** and **"Un Cœur simple,"** Flaubert does not totally destroy the order in which the tales were written, since **"Hérodias"** retains its third position. Thus, rather than viewing it, following Issacharoff, as the disordering of an original order, whereby Flaubert would be communicating to his reader that order does not matter, I prefer to consider it as an ordering of an original disorder, signifying that order is important.

The result of this reordering most underscored by critics is the creation of a temporal regression, a movement back in time from the modern France of **"Un Cœur simple,"** to the medieval period of **"Saint Julien,"** and finally to the pre-Christian era of **"Hérodias."**[2] I would like to argue as well that a less obvious result of this reordering, and one which was perhaps less consciously intended by Flaubert, is a progressive enlargement of the spatio-temporal realm in which an increasingly complex relationship between word and event or act is established. Indeed, a careful examination of *Trois Contes* reveals that each of the tales places emphasis on a different aspect of speech, and puts forth a specific relationship between word and event of which this aspect of speech is, in turn, a reflection. Tracing, therefore, what is no longer the order of writing (the order of composition), but rather the order of speech, it is possible to show, as I wish to do here, that the linear movement from one tale to the next, in the order in which they are juxtaposed in the definitive volume, creates an "economy" based on an incremental increase, in both breadth and complexity, of the trajectory linking the moment speech is uttered to the moment it acquires meaning, however vague and relative this meaning may be. The aspect of speech highlighted in each tale and the reflection of this aspect in the tale's events describes the unity of the tales taken individually, and the progressively expanding speech trajectory contributes to the coherence of the volume as a whole.

In **"Un Cœur simple"** emphasis is placed on speech in its iterative and imitative form. This aspect of speech is represented, indeed incarnated, by Loulou, the parrot which the servant Félicité receives from her employer Mme Aubain. The last of the series of objects/people which Félicité, as Flaubert describes, "aime successivement,"[3] Loulou is at the same time different from his antecedents. He is, as Michal Ginsburg observes, a "synthetic figure" of the whole series of those who have previously peopled Félicité's affections (171-72). I

maintain as well that Loulou duplicates Félicité herself as the locus of certain psychic tics that shape her experience: the first, what Raymonde Debray-Genette, after Freud, has identified as the compulsion to repeat ("Figures" 351), placing the servant at the center of a series of repeated "events," and the second, her tendency to imitate her surroundings or the experience of those who surround her. Loulou is a metaphoric projection of Félicité as repetition and imitation.

The formula equating Loulou and Félicité is developed precisely when the connection between Loulou and speech is established. Teaching the bird to speak, or rather to imitate her speech, Félicité places him in the same apprentice position that she herself held with respect to Virginie, Victor, and others. Once apprentice, now "master," Félicité is for Loulou the source of what is to be absorbed and reproduced, repeated and imitated: "Elle entreprit de l'instruire; bientôt il répéta 'Charmant garçon! Serviteur, Monsieur! Je vous salue, Marie!'" (66)—a repertory which repeats the daily and religious preoccupations of the servant. In this way, Loulou absorbs and reproduces on the verbal level the "experience" of Félicité, just as she absorbed and reproduced her understanding of Virginie's First Communion and Victor's experience at sea. The identification between Félicité and Loulou is reinforced when a later allusion to the parrot's repertory of imitated speech serves as a point of departure for the description of how the bird and the servant duplicate each other physically:

> Ils avaient des dialogues, lui, débitant à satiété les trois phrases de son répertoire, et elle, y répondant par des mots sans plus de suite, mais où son cœur s'épanchait. Loulou, dans son isolement, était presque un fils, un amoureux. Il escaladait ses doigts, mordillait ses lèvres, se cramponnait à son fichu; et, comme elle penchait son front en branlant la tête à la manière des nourrices, les grandes ailes du bonnet et les ailes de l'oiseau frémissaient ensemble.
>
> (70)

Moreover, if, like Félicité, Loulou attaches himself to one source of "language" and repeats it—here Félicité herself—he, again like Félicité, detaches himself from this source as a *single* source and reattaches himself to others. Loulou eventually imitates, repeats on the verbal level, several fragments of the aural environment which surrounds him:

> Comme pour la distraire, il reprodusait le tic-tac du tournebroche, l'appel aigu d'un vendeur de poisson, la scie du menuisier qui logeait en face; et aux coups de la sonnette, imitait Mme Aubain: "Félicité! la porte! la porte!"
>
> (70)[4]

Loulou's voice as the locus of a collection of repeated and imitated sounds joins the less banal and more substantially figured description of Félicité's room, repository of fragments of the life she spent in the Aubain household. Like the bird whose voice is the instrument by which aural reality is reproduced, Félicité—via her fetichistic imagination—is the instrument by which the Aubain household is reproduced. It is significant that both the bird's collection of sounds and Félicité's bedroom eventually become all that remains for the servant of the "reality" they represent: deaf, Félicité's hearing will capture no more the noises which surround her, but will hear only their imitation in Loulou's voice; alone, following the death of Mme Aubain and the sale of the Aubain house, Félicité will live, and eventually die, in its facsimile, among the relics of the past. The original reality disappears, but through Loulou, as through Félicité herself, its repetition, its imitation remains. Absence is transformed into presence.

When Félicité has the dead parrot stuffed, it is the symbol of this repetition, the figure which totalizes this representation, which is itself repeated. It is possible that the parrot's name, being the repetition of two identical sounds—Lou-lou—as well as reproducing, on the level of the signifier, his status as embodiment of repetition and imitation, indicates his "re-embodiment," in a second life, as a stuffed bird and then as symbol of the Holy Spirit. The stuffed Loulou represents the repetition of the bird's physical being; his identification with the Holy Spirit recapitulates this resurrection of the physical—Félicité finds that the dove which conventionally portrays the Holy Spirit "était vraiment le portrait de Loulou" (75)—and adds to it. In identifying Loulou with the Holy Spirit, Félicité corrects what she views as a flaw in the dove-Holy Spirit connection, and this precisely on the basis of the parrot's capacity to speak: "Le Père, pour s'énoncer, n'avait pu choisir une colombe, puisque ces bêtes-là n'ont pas de voix, mais plutôt un des ancêtres de Loulou" (75). The equation parrot speech = the Word of God, by sanctifying the parrot, grants transcendence as well to repetition and imitation, and to that shrine to both, Félicité's room, over which the stuffed bird presides.

Thus, repetition having become idealized, or sacred, Loulou, the objects in Félicité's room, and Félicité herself all acquire a meaning beyond and superior to the inertness of their existence as matter, as material reality. From this perspective, Félicité's obsession, throughout the tale, with the celebration of Corpus Christi (la Fête-Dieu) acquires a special significance. Echo of Virginie's First Communion and of the street altar she and Félicité make together, allusions to Corpus Christi and to this "moment des reposoirs" punctuate the surface of Flaubert's text through the last page, where the final procession coincides with Félicité's death. Celebrated in honor of the Eucharist, this re-enactment consisting precisely of the symbolic consecration of bread and wine *as* the body and blood of Christ is itself a figure of repetition and transcendence. Thus, despite the objections of Félic-

ité's neighbors for whom placing Loulou on the reposoir "n'était pas convenable" (79), and despite the irony underlying the description of the entire scene, Loulou's presence on the final street altar of the tale is undeniably appropriate.

In **"Un Cœur simple,"** therefore, speech is the intersection of repetition/imitation and their continuation in a transcendent mode. Through this speech as sort of pivotal phenomenon, Félicité succeeds, albeit imperfectly and unconsciously, in assigning a unity and meaning to her life of devotion, self-effacement, and loss. If the final beat of this "cœur simple," this space in which are played out successive efforts to create a presence from what is past or lost can coincide with a vision of "un perroquet gigantesque planant au-dessus de sa tête" (83), it is because, as we have seen, speech also fulfills the function of granting presence to what is absent. Notwithstanding the discursive ambiguity conveyed by the much commented "elle *crut* voir" through which Flaubert introduces this vision and so casts doubt on Félicité's "apotheosis," the mere possibility that Félicité's last moment of life corresponds to the sight of a parrot-become-God confers unity onto the tale.

In **"Un Cœur simple"** repeated and imitated speech mirrors repeated and imitated events, the dominant figure of the *same* reducing the tale's temporality to the timeless present of the identical. In the second of the *Trois Contes,* **"La Légende de Saint Julien l'Hospitalier,"** the first tale's unity of presence is fragmented and differed by multiple instances of prophetic language which, while it repeats or summarizes the present, also negates it by surpassing it. In this tale, prophetic speech, by announcing a future, creates a distance between the proferring of speech and its resolution; this distance represents, as compared to **"Un Cœur simple,"** an enlargement of the word's trajectory. In other words, synchronic repetition in **"Un Cœur simple"** gives way to diachrony and *différance* in **"Saint Julien."**

The diachronic movement in **"Saint Julien"** is evident from the beginning of the tale. The immediate focus of the description is the universe inhabited by Julien's parents: "Le père et la mère de Julien habitaient un château au milieu des bois, sur la pente d'une colline" (85). Julien's introduction at his birth is delayed by a lengthy and detailed description of the castle and the parents. This structure of delay is reflected and repeated by the two prophetic utterances pronounced, one to the mother and one to the father, soon after Julien's birth. Furthermore, just as allusion to Julien followed the description of his parents, a prophecy addressed to him will join, following a delay, those addressed to his parents. After the pronouncement of the prophecy directed to Julien, the remainder of the text, pushed forward by the future orientation of the prophecies, concerns the closing of the distance which prophetic speech creates between word and event.

The world into which Julien is born is one in which the two dominant, and potentially contradictory values of medieval European society, religion and chivalry, coexist harmoniously. The text's announcement of his birth—"A force de prier Dieu, il lui vint [à la mère] un fils" (87)—repeats this harmonious synthesis of values: praying to God evokes the religious value; the child's maleness, the value of chivalry. However, Julien's birth, while it recapitulates this synthesis of values, is also the event which occasions the utterance of the first two prophecies. The prediction to his mother that her son will be a saint corresponds to her religious preoccupations at the same time that it hyperbolizes them. To the father, it is announced that Julien will be a conqueror, linked somehow to an emperor's family—a prophecy which corresponds to the father's chivalrous values while clearly surpassing them. These prophecies taken together restate the synthesis of religion and chivalry. Taken separately in the manner in which they are actually uttered, however, they fragment this synthesis because neither parent discloses to the other what was heard. Furthermore, in the extraordinary extension of the values from which they emanate, the prediction of sainthood and that of military glory render apparent the latent opposition between religion and chivalry. Thus, the present of harmony and synthesis opens up onto a future of conflict and contradiction.

The third prophecy, addressed to Julien himself, functions in the same manner as those addressed to his parents. Consequently, at the same time that it indicates his future parricide it stands as a recapitulation or as an interpretation of the present, here, of the behavior which Julien has introduced into, and which is incompatible with, the framework of the two values which have thus far shaped him. I am referring here to Julien's wanton and obsessive destruction of animal life, the first example of which takes place in the chapel, seat of the religion represented by the mother, when Julien kills the little mouse. The subsequent occurrence may be considered the result of Julien's perverse disdain for the conventions of gentlemanly hunting into which his father had just initiated him. Julien's obvious rejection of the values of his parents may of course be homologous to his murder of them. Furthermore, the immediate situation surrounding the utterance of this third prophecy projects Julien's future murder of his parents. Julien has just shot arrows which have killed a doe and a faun, and which will kill the patriarchal stag, pronouncer of the prophecy. This deer "family" reflects Julien's own, and by killing the doe and the stag, he has already symbolically killed his mother and his father.

The stag's prophecy, the last of the tale, becomes, as Carla Peterson points out, "the turning point in the plot as it prepares the fulfillment of the earlier prophecies" (248). "Saint Julien" may therefore be considered as divided into two large sections: while the first section is devoted to the presentation of prophetic speech which repeats the present, divides it, and announces a future, the tale's second half focuses on the realization of Julien's destiny as predicted, as alternately conqueror, parricide, and saint, and presents a gradual reconstitution of the original synthesis of chivalry and religion. The relationship between the two halves of this tale, between the speech uttered in the first half and the events described in the second, is one of repetition and imitation. This recalls the imitative relationship between event and word in "Un Cœur simple"; yet, whereas in that tale such a relationship is maintained in a seemingly timeless and changeless present, in "Saint Julien" the future orientation of prophecy introduces a temporal protraction which must come to a close before a complete coextension of speech with event is achieved.

The narrative space, or the temporal dimension of the tale, created by prophetic language is enlarged throughout most of the second half, diminished toward the end, and finally disappears altogether. First, the numerous feats listed among Julien's accomplishments as soldier-conqueror, and the geographical distances he must travel to realize them, attest to the passing of a considerable amount of time between the moment he flees his parents' home and marries the Emperor's daughter. Moreover, his parents tell Julien's wife that they had been searching for him "depuis plusieurs années" (112). Then, the time which elapses between Julien's departure from his wife, following the act of murdering his parents, and the moment he contemplates drowning himself is sufficient for him to become an old man. Finally, still more time passes between that moment and Julien's death/apotheosis which itself conflates with the very end of the story.

An attenuation of the temporal distance between word and event or act occurs in the final situation of the tale where Julien hosts Christ, who has appeared to him in the form of a leper. Here, it is no longer a question only of the fulfillment of a prophecy—that of sainthood—but also of acts performed in obedience to commands which, like prophetic speech, indicate a future, however near. Thus, Julien's immediate compliance with the leper's requests for food, drink, and warmth, and with the imperatives by which the leper specifies acts meant to meet his need for warmth, and Julien's for self-sacrifice, mirrors the perfect commensurability between speech and event which has regulated the entire tale—and Julien's destiny. In this scene, the near one-to-one correspondence between word and act matches the total identity established in death between Julien and the leper—"Julien s'étala dessus complètement, bouche contre bouche, poitrine sur poitrine" (130)—and between the end of Flaubert's story and the fulfillment of the last prophecy for the saint: "et Julien monta vers les espaces bleus, face à face avec Notre-Seigneur Jésus, qui l'emportait dans le ciel" (130-31).

In **"Hérodias,"** the last of the trilogy, speech figures prominently as both repetition, which dominates in **"Un Cœur simple,"** and prophecy, dominant in **"Saint Julien,"** and both aspects combine to produce speech as weapon. The status of speech as weapon reflects the essentially conflictual relationship binding the central characters—Iaokanann, the future saint John the Baptist, who repeats the speech of earlier Hebrew prophets to denounce the current socio-political *status quo* and to announce a new order; the ambitious Hérodias whose present goal is to have the man killed; and Antipas, her indecisive and ineffectual husband whom she cannot convince to do just that. This power struggle is translated into a linguistic dynamic based on the dialectic between speaking and silencing.

This dynamic is most evident in two passages where Iaokanann's speech is either alluded to or is actualized. The situation contextualizing the first passage involves the voice of Iaokanann, imprisoned under the palace floor, interrupting Antipas's thoughts. The voice fades, Antipas summons the prisonkeeper/executioner Mannaei and inquires abut Iaokanann. Finally, Hérodias appears and restates her demand that Iaokanann be killed, to which Antipas responds with sarcasm and feigned laughter. This passage begins with Hérodias reacting to this laughter and, seizing the word from her husband with an angry "Tais-toi!," she then recounts in her own words her recent humiliation by Iaokanann:

> "Des gens, au bord du fleuve, remettaient leurs habits. Sur un monticule, à côté, un homme parlait. . . . Dès qu'il m'aperçut, il cracha sur moi toutes les malédictions des prophètes. . . . Impossible de fuir! les roues de mon char avaient du sable jusqu'aux essieux; et je m'éloignais lentement, m'abritant sous mon manteau, glacée par ces injures qui tombaient comme une pluie d'orage."

(142)

With respect to Antipas, whose speech she has silenced, Hérodias clearly has the upper hand. Yet in her own discourse, what she relates is the ability of Iaokanann's words to overpower her, her story ending with the image of her momentary immobilization and near-paralysis.

At this point the passage changes from Hérodias's direct discourse to the free indirect style where the narrative records her speech indirectly but without subsuming it totally. "Iaokanann l'empêchait de vivre" both states to what extent Iaokanann has become an obstacle for Hérodias and, in its form, constitutes a reduction of Hérodias's power of speech and power *over* speech. The next paragraph begins as a continuation of

Hérodias's speech in free indirect discourse, and then yields to discourse of ambiguous status. Neither entirely free indirect nor wholly descriptive, it is a combination:

> Ses discours [ceux d'Iaokanann], criés à des foules, s'étaient répandus, circulaient; elle les entendait partout, ils emplissaient l'air. Contre des légions, elle aurait eu de la bravoure. Mais cette force plus pernicieuse que les glaives, et qu'on ne pouvait saisir, était stupéfiante.

(142-43)

Here, allusion is to the tendency of Iaokanann's words to spread, to disperse, to circulate via their subsequent repetition by members of the listening crowds to whom they are addressed, which constitutes a force greater than a weapon. Against this capacity of Iaokanann's speech to propagate itself beyond its initial utterance, Hérodias is defenseless since, as the passage implies, she is potent only when speech is wielded as a weapon. Thus, in the last part of the passage, presented as mere narrative description, Hérodias is indeed disarmed, reduced to speechlessness: "et elle parcourait la terrasse, blême par sa colère, manquant de mots pour exprimer ce qui l'étouffait" (143).

Traced here is the gradual linguistic dispossession of Hérodias who, while initially able to suppress her husband's speech and impose her own, is herself, at the end, silenced by the mere evocation of Iaokanann's speech. The second key passage is based on the actualization of Iaokanann's speech and illustrates a similar dynamic. Here before a waiting crowd, the door covering the view of Iaokanann in his underground prison has been opened to satisfy the curiosity of visiting Roman pro-consul Vitellius. In direct discourse, Iaokanann develops his diatribe, recognized as "les paroles des anciens prophètes" which he utters forth "comme de grands coups, l'une après l'autre" (160). Words functioning as blows cause Antipas to react bodily: when hearing Iaokanann's summoning of the "fils de David," he "se rejeta en arrière," interpreting here as a real danger what he so coolly laughed off in the first passage. At this point, it is he who, in indirect discourse clearly echoing the direct discourse of Hérodias in the previous passage, takes action to silence Iaokanann, but to no avail:

> Antipas brisa la cordelette du cachet suspendu à sa poitrine, et le lança dans la fosse, en lui commandant de se taire.
>
> "Je crierai comme un ours, comme un âne sauvage, comme une femme qui enfante!"

(160-61)

Not to be silenced, Iaokanann continues his attack, this time targeting directly Antipas and Hérodias by alluding to their "incest," and to Antipas's sterility, clearly a homologue to his present linguistic ineffectiveness. Indeed, Iaokanann's victims are silenced; listening, "[Antipas] haletait, pendant qu'[Hérodias] observait béante le fond du puits" (161).

Continuing to view this second passage as an echo, a re-presentation in the form of an illustration, of the first, we can draw still more parallels between several of their segments. Illustrating Hérodias's direct "Dès qu'il m'aperçut, il cracha sur moi toutes les malédictions des prophètes" is the following narration of Iaokanann's taking notice of Hérodias and his subsequent insult of her:

> L'homme effroyable se renversa la tête; et empoignant les barreaux, y colla son visage, qui avait l'air d'une broussaille, où étincelaient deux charbons:
>
> "Ah! c'est toi, Iézabel!"
>
> (161)

Later, interrupting the wave of insults is the description of Hérodias's helplessness and defenselessness—"Elle chercha du regard une défense autour d'elle" (162)—and echoing the "Iaokanann l'empêchait de vivre" of the first passage, we find "Antipas paraissait mourir," the interchangeability of the Herods in the face of the baptist becoming once again apparent. Finally, again an allusion to the reproduction and dissemination of Iaokanann's discourse:

> La voix grossissait, se développait, roulait avec des déchirements de tonnerre, et, l'écho dans la montagne la répétant, elle foudroyait Machaerous d'éclats multipliés.
>
> (162)

Eventually, Iaokanann's voice is silenced solely by virtue of the fact that the door to his pit is again closed; Hérodias disappears and Antipas's attempts at self-justification do not succeed in convincing anyone of the legitimacy of his marriage.

My focus thus far has been on how speech in **"Hérodias"** repeats a situation without advancing it or opening it up beyond itself. Here, the linguistic dispossession of character Hérodias is equivalent to a temporary immobilization of the text **"Hérodias."** Yet other forms of utterance are also working on the text, forcing it away from a position of stasis resembling that of the entirety of **"Un Cœur simple,"** and into a dynamics of forward movement which characterized **"Saint Julien."** Just as prophetic speech in this latter expanded narrated time and enlarged narrative space, by announcing a future beyond the present, so, too, in **"Hérodias"** prophecy functions to move the story beyond the situation just described.

Amid all the prophetic utterances proferred by the baptist in **"Hérodias,"** one in particular stands out. Near the beginning Mannaei tells Antipas of having overheard Iaokanann utter, "Pour qu'il croisse, il faut que je diminue" (138), and on the last page, Phanuel, another seer of sorts, is described as having understood the sense of these words. Framing the text in this fashion, this utterance announces a future and, similarly to the prophecies directed to Julien and his parents, summarizes the present. To see how this utterance summarizes the present, it is necessary to decontextualize it, applying these words, for a moment, not to Iaokanann, but rather to Hérodias. It is through her weakening that Iaokanann gains strength; it is his speech belittling her both linguistically and otherwise which circulates and grows. However, through her weakening, she herself gains strength. Thus, the necessity for someone to weaken in order that someone grow stronger functions as a textual imperative and orients the power struggles shaping the relationship between the three main characters.[5]

The movement from the banquet scene to Salomé's dance and then to the beheading of the baptist links Hérodias's weakening to her strengthening. The banquet scene, a chaotic depiction of the association eating/drinking/speaking, has, at moments, Iaokanann as its focus. From all the cacophanous disorder emerges discourse which suggests the possibility that the baptist is the resurrected prophet Elijah, for the Hebrews, the precursor of the long-awaited Messiah. This situation, in terms of the dynamic Hérodias-Iaokanann, represents a continuation of her weakening—absent from the banquet, she is herself silenced absolutely—and his force, here gaining a certain momentum from the possible equation Iaokanann = Elijah. Yet from her weakened position of silence, Hérodias herself will experience a relative triumph. This will occur at the introduction of Salomé onto the banquet scene and with Salomé's dance itself.

With the entry of Salomé, the loud discussions of the guests are muted, transformed into the "buzzing of surprise and admiration" (177-78). Silencing the crowd which watches her, Salomé dances in silence; she is compared to the pantomime Mnester, effecting communication not with language but with her body. Her silent sensuality has as result the total disarming of Antipas who impulsively promises her anything. Salomé prolongs her silence, momentarily disappears, and then returns, armed with her terrible request:

> Elle ne parlait pas. Ils se regardaient.
>
> Un claquement de doigts se fit dans la tribune. Elle y monta, reparut; et en zézayant un peu prononça des mots, d'un air enfantin:
>
> "Je veux que tu me donnes dans un plat, la tête. . . ." Elle avait oublié le nom, mais reprit en souriant: "La tête de Iaokanann."
>
> Le Tétrarque s'affaissa sur lui-même, écrasé.
>
> (180-81)

It is thus from her weakened position of silence, or rather, *through* her silence that Hérodias derives new-found strength. From the silence of her daughter's dance, embodiment of her own silence here rendered efficacious; passing through a tenuous relationship to language suggested by Salomé's lisping and stuttering, Hérodias, source of the snapping fingers and—even the text itself is silent on this (Genette 199-200)—of the request, emerges empowered. Antipas, himself weakened by his own impulsive utterance, is powerless to refuse her the baptist's head.

Hérodias's triumph thus corresponds both to her husband's capitulation and Iaokanann's decapitation. Yet her overtaking of her adversaries corresponds as well to the fulfillment of half of the prophecy. Considering once again the words "Pour qu'il croisse il faut que je diminue," and recontextualizing them to apply to the situation of the character who actually pronounces them—Iaokanann—we may now equate the weakening of the baptist with his beheading. Literally reduced to his head, he is at the same time reduced to the source of his now-silenced voice, and, in death, as a head on a platter, will follow the circuit taken by his words in life. Thus, Iaokanann's head, like his speech among members of his audiences, circulates from table to table and from banquet guest to banquet guest. The following day, the head will be transported out of the palace, out beyond the city gates, and, significantly, beyond the outer border of Flaubert's text. The second half of the prophecy which regulated the forward movement of **"Hérodias"**—"il croisse"—will be fulfilled only after its ending. Breaking through textual limits in this fashion, Iaokanann's words are free to disperse and circulate in an infinitely expanded time and space. There, the prophet's diminishment will join the growth of a new order which will eventually reward his martyrdom with sainthood.

To conclude, the order of the stories collected in **Trois Contes** describes a movement based on an increasingly complex relationship between utterance and event, in turn established on an increasingly enlarged spatio-temporal grid. From the immediate simplicity of the relationship between imitated/repeated speech and imitated/repeated actions and events (**"Un Cœur simple"**), the volume passes through utterance which is divided within itself and separated from the events it announces, but which eventually reintegrates in a final fusion (**"Saint Julien"**), and arrives, finally, at speech which is fractured, fragmented, and uncontrollably expended, and whose significance is only partially realized within the bounds of Flaubert's writing (**"Hérodias"**). In short, the movement from parroting to prophecy translates into a certain tripartite illustration of the ways language is assigned meaning, the components of which may be identified as imitation, interpretation, and dissemination. Corresponding to the "saint-making" process evident in each tale, therefore, is a "sign-making" one, and religion, which the tales establish in this fashion as a creative process, becomes homologous to art. Finally, an articulation of this movement with the regressive temporality also traced by the order of the tales finds that speech uttered in the most distant past, since it extends into the most expansive time and space, is subject to the most extensive dispersion. This dispersion at the chronological beginning marked by **"Hérodias"** gestures toward the absence of an originary full meaning, a void at the origin which that tale only partially resolves, and which **"Saint Julien"** and **"Un Cœur simple,"** each in its own specific way, attempt first to mask and then to fill.

Notes

1. Critics have indeed approached *Trois Contes* from many different angles. Several studies do treat only one of the tales, a practice which seems wholly justified by the fact that Flaubert at first had each tale published separately, and, significantly, in the order in which they appear in the definitive volume: "Un Cœur simple" in *Le Moniteur Universel,* 12-19 April 1877; "Saint Julien" in *Le Bien Public,* 19-22 April 1877; "Hérodias" in *Le Moniteur Universel,* 21-27 April 1877. The tales' presentation in a single volume has prompted critics to uncover their possible interrelationship(s). René Jasinski, for example, finds that sainthood is the unifying theme of the collection. Frederic Shepler specifies that each of the tales links sainthood to sacrifice and locates the volume's unity in "un rythme alternatif de déclin et de croissance" (407). Marc Bertrand considers each tale as a particular way of resolving the tension between social discourse and the inner speech of the individual. For John R. O'Connor, the structure of each of Flaubert's stories is regulated by the figure of the double cone as described by W. B. Yeats: as empirical, objective reality undergoes shrinkage or depletion, subjective or spiritual reality expands. Carla Peterson discusses *Trois Contes* as both a representation of the Christian Trinity and as a Nietzschean subversion of the tripartite conception of history. Finally, some critics are clearly ambivalent on this question of unity. Raymonde Debray-Genette, for example, has insisted that the volume exists only because Flaubert had written enough stories to constitute a collection ("Re-présentation" 348). Elsewhere, however, Debray-Genette suggests that the stories may be linked by the fact that in each, utterance is "always characterized by a specific kind of disorder, which is in turn either the product or the cause of a more general disintegration of the relationship of the individual to the world" ("Profane" 13).

2. Studies treating the unity of the volume do address, though not always, the question of their order. Jasinski links the theme of sainthood to the temporal regression described by their definitive order: "De la sainte moderne, en passant par le saint médiéval, on remontait à saint Jean-Baptiste, donc aux origines même du christianisme" (119). In his discussion of death and redemption, Shepler begins with "Hérodias" and ends with "Un Cœur simple"—thereby beginning with the end of the volume and ending with its beginning—showing how sacrifice and rebirth are coextensive only in "Saint Julien," the Biblical times of "Hérodias" being too early for perfect redemption, and the modern period of "Un Cœur simple" too late. Though both Bertrand and O'Connor treat the tales in the order in which they appear, neither discusses his understanding of the volume's unity in terms of this order. For Carla Peterson, the regressive temporal order is a necessary component of Flaubert's deconstruction of history, and emphasizing it is essential to her argument. Finally, Debray-Genette bases her discussion on the order in which the stories were composed, finding that this order develops repetition and contrast in an increasingly complex manner ("Profane" 14-15).

3. "[Félicité] aime successivement un homme, les enfants de sa maîtresse, un neveu, un vieillard qu'elle soigne, puis son perroquet" (From a letter to Mme Roger des Genettes, 19 June 1876 [Flaubert, *Correspondance* 234]).

4. For Shoshana Felman, this passage illustrates how the parrot symbolizes a "second-degree repetition": "Loulou ne reproduit pas seulement la répétition des amours et des pertes, ou la répétition linguistique des clichés; il reproduit, avant tout, la répétition des répétitions. Non seulement le perroquet répète les répétitions de Félicité, mais encore il reproduit des sonorités qui sont déjà, en elles-mêmes, répétitives" (165).

5. It is in the generalization of this relationship between growth and decline which Shepler locates the unity of the entire volume.

Works Cited

Bertrand, Marc. "Parole et silence dans les *Trois contes* de Flaubert." *Stanford French Review* 1 (1977): 191-203.

Debray-Genette, Raymonde. "Les Figures du récit dans 'Un Cœur simple.'" *Poétique* 3 (1970): 348-64.

———. "Profane, Sacred: Disorder of Utterance in *Trois Contes*." Trans. Susan Huston. *Flaubert and Postmodernism*. Eds. Naomi Schor and Henry Majewski. Lincoln: U of Nebraska P, 1984. 13-29.

———. "Re-présentation d' 'Hérodias.'" *La Production du sens chez Flaubert. Colloque de Cerisy*. Ed. Claudine Gothot-Mersch, Paris: 10/18, 1975. 328-57.

Felman, Shoshana. "Illusion réaliste et répétition romanesque." *La Folie et la chose littéraire*. Paris: Seuil, 1978. 159-69.

Flaubert, Gustave. *Trois Contes*. Paris: Garnier Flammarion, 1965.

———. *Correspondance*. Vol. IV. Paris: Charpentier et Fasquelle, 1893.

Genette, Gérard. "Demotivation in 'Hérodias.'" Trans. Marlena Corcoran. *Flaubert and Post-modernism*. Eds. Naomi Schor and Henry Majewski. Lincoln: U of Nebraska P, 1984. 192-201.

Ginsburg, Michal Peled. *Flaubert Writing*. Stanford: Stanford UP, 1986.

Issacharoff, Michael. "*Trois Contes* et le problème de la non-linéarité." *L'Espace et la nouvelle*. Paris: Corti, 1976. 39-59.

Jasinski, René. "Le Sens des *Trois Contes*." *Essays in Honor of Louis Francis Solano*. Eds. Raymond J. Cormier and Urban T. Holmes. Berkeley: U of California P, 1970. 117-28.

O'Connor, John R. "Flaubert: *Trois Contes* and the Figure of the Double Cone." *PMLA* 95 (1980): 812-26.

Peterson, Carla. "The Trinity in Flaubert's *Trois Contes*: Deconstructing History." *French Forum* 8 (1983): 243-58.

Shepler, Frederic. "La Mort et la rédemption dans les *Trois Contes* de Flaubert." *Neophilologus* 56 (1972): 407-16.

Nathaniel Wing (essay date fall-winter 1992-1993)

SOURCE: Wing, Nathaniel. "Reading Simplicity: Flaubert's 'Un Coeur simple.'" *Nineteenth-Century French Studies* 21, nos. 1-2 (fall-winter 1992-1993): 88-101.

[*In the following essay, Wing explores Félicité's metonymic relationship to the world in "Un Coeur simple."*]

> Cen'est pas une petite affaire que d'être simple."
>
> —Flaubert, letter to Louise Colet, 20 Sept, 1851

It has become commonplace in modern readings of Flaubert to observe that the protagonists of his texts are themselves readers, represented as interpreters of the world of the fiction and that the realization of their desires depends upon the ability to understand and manipulate the codes that constitute the intelligible world.

From Emma Bovary, whose sensibility and understanding have been formed by the stereotypes of Romantic literature, to the minor characters of *L'Education sentimentale,* whose intelligence is represented as a Babel of borrowed nineteenth century aesthetic and political theories, to the mythic figures of Salammbô and Mathô, who struggle to interpret an opaque world in terms of only partially intelligible religious systems, the protagonist's consciousness is defined in relation to interpretive discourses brought to bear on the world represented by the text. Since knowledge and desire for Flaubert's protagonists are set forth in terms of the already said or the already experienced, their relation to the world is profoundly mystified and a constant source of irony. While irony demystifies the protagonist's efforts at interpretation by revealing the gap that separates desire and knowledge from the language available to the subject, Flaubert's irony does not allow the *reader* to establish a stable, secure interpretive vantage point, itself exempt from the mystifications that inevitably befall the protagonists. In short, Flaubert's irony implicates our own interpretations of the interpretive failures of the protagonists in the fiction. Our reading of the character's attempts to make sense of their world constantly calls into question the validity of our own efforts to make sense of the texts, as I have shown elsewhere in a discussion of *Madame Bovary;* irony leads not to a stable and authoritative decoding, but to a continual process of interpretation.[1]

If this mirror play of interpretation is a constant in Flaubert's texts, and I believe it is, should our reading be given over entirely to tracing the shifting supplementarity of meanings, allegorizing our interpretations, locating figure upon figure of figuration? While neither language nor "experience" can ever be understood simply, available to proper and unmediated expression, there are telling moments in Flaubert's texts that might be called moments of simplicity.[2] These instances, all the more powerful for their rarity, are not transcendent moments of synthesis beyond difference, but rather instances of effective communication within an ironic relationship to language. In the passages that I am thinking about, the resources of language are said to be strained to excess and to yield a fleeting moment that is represented as the possibility of shared emotion or truth. The very commonplace experience of the limits of language and the disjunction between expressive intention and its result yield . . . a common-place, a locus of communality of language and subject.[3] The famous passage in *Madame Bovary* about the stars, cracked cooking pots, dancing bears and the language of love is an obvious example. Rodolphe, Emma's first lover, cannot respond without irony to her passionate declarations of love, since he has heard so often the same expressions in the service of the same desires from many different lips.

Il s'était tant de fois entendu dire ces choses, qu'elles n'avaient point pour lui rien d'original. Emma ressemblait à toutes les maîtresses; et le charme de la nouveauté peu à peu tombant comme un vêtement, laissait voir à nu l'éternelle monotonie de la passion, qui a toujours les mêmes formes et le même langage. Il ne distinguait pas, cet homme si plein de pratique, la dissemblance des sentiments sous la parité des expressions. Parce que des lèvres libertines ou vénales lui avaient murmuré des phrases pareilles, il ne croyait que faiblement à la candeur de celles-là; on en devait rabattre, pensait-il, les discours exagérés cachant les affections médiocres; comme si la plénitude de l'âme ne débordait pas quelquefois par les métaphores les plus vides, puisque personne, jamais, ne peut donner l'exacte mesure de ses besoins, ni de ses conceptions, ni de ses douleurs, et que la parole humaine est comme un chaudron fêlé où nous battons des mélodies à faire danser les ours, quand on voudrait attendrir les étoiles.[4]

As a naive ironist, Rodolphe has completely missed the point, which is, I believe, that while there is no such thing as a proper language equal to desire and knowledge, there is nonetheless within the alienating figures of discourse ("comme si . . .") the possibility of a common place, an excess of language, which runs over, spills ("déborder") beyond the limits of received ideas and cliché.

A passage remarkably similar to this one occurs in **"Un Coeur simple,"** when Félicité, who has become deaf, engages in tender dialogues with Loulou, her parrot: "Ils avaient des dialogues, lui, débitant à satiété les trois phrases de son répertoire, et elle, y repondant par des mots sans plus de suite, mais où son coeur s'épanchait. Loulou, dans son isolement, était presque un fils, un amoureux."[5]

Once again, this passage must be read for its simplicity, beyond, though not outside irony. The objective absurdity of the situation is hardly difficult to discern. The language that provokes Félicité's passionate responses is mechanical, quite literally alien to its "speaker," a bird; Félicité herself, being deaf, is incapable of receiving and interpreting it. Like the overflowing of meaning and sentiment beyond the ordinary limits of discourse that remains inaccessible to a naive ironist, like Rodolphe, or a naive reader of **"Un Coeur simple,"** for that matter, this passage suggests the fleeting possibility of a place in language for "the heart." The same excess as that alluded to in *Madame Bovary* is said to occur, simply, without syntax "les mots sans plus de suite, mais où son coeur s'épanchait."

The simplicity of this meaningful excess is akin to the ageless and impossible ideal of a pure, proper expression in which emotion and truth could be transmitted directly, without mediation or figural translation, as though there were recourse to the imperfection of which Mallarmé speaks: "Les langues imparfaites en cela que plusieurs, manque le suprême: penser étant écrire sans accessoires, ni chuchotement, mais tacite encore l'immortelle parole, . . ."[6] The relation to simplicity in Flaubert is not outside the "incidental" properties of language, outside of difference and repetition, but, rather, lodged unequivocally in figuration, yet accidentally, unexpectedly it produces an excess ("déborder," "épancher").

This fortuitous inconsistency is succinctly asserted in the title of Flaubert's famous short tale: **"Un Coeur simple."** In a letter of June 19, 1876, Flaubert described the subject of the story:

> L'Histoire d'un coeur simple est tout bonnement le récit d'une vie obscure, celle d'une pauvre fille de campagne, dévote mais mystique, devouée sans exaltation et tendre comme du pain frais. Elle aime successivement un homme, les enfants de sa maîtresse, un neveu, un vieillard qu'elle soigne, puis son perroquet; quand le perroquet est mort, elle le fait empailler et, en mourant à son tour, elle confond le perroquet avec le Saint-Esprit. Cela n'est nullement ironique comme vous le supposez, mais au contraire très sérieux et très triste. Je veux apitoyer, faire pleurer les âmes sensibles, en étant une moimême.[7]

The passage insists upon the tacit understanding between the narrator of the tale and the reader that produces an emotional effect upon the reader, "a performative program ("Cela n'est nullement ironique . . .") implying illocutory understanding between the *destinaires* ("apitoyer, faire pleurer les âmes sensibles") and *destinateur* ("en étant une moimême")," as Ross Chambers notes in his *Story and Situation*.[8] The effect that results is outside of conventional irony: "Cela n'est nullement ironique, comme vous le supposez, mais au contraire très serieux et très triste." Chambers maintains that the emphasis here on the effects of the narration is accompanied in the text itself by an effacement of the grammatical apparatus of narration; the suppression from the title of the word *histoire* eliminates generic self-reference, and in the body of the text the writing strives to conceal indices that might point too clearly to the act of narration. The story appears to be telling itself. Chambers' remarks are pertinent, I believe, but they do not account for the features of narrative logic and, more generally, of the central protagonist's understanding of the symbolic that produce the effect of simplicity; in what follows, I examine those features and their profound importance to an understanding of the characterization of Félicité. What, then, is the rhetoric of narative simplicity?

The title itself, with the term *histoire* eliminated, provides some useful indications; it produces that particular relation to figuration that does not blindly dismiss difference in favor of a mythical proper meaning, but inscribes the possibility of the "simple" within the fig-

ural. The title asserts a "simple," and also banal, figure of language: the heart, quite commonly, is a figure for the entire person, and more precisely for the emotions. Specifically, *coeur* functions as a synecdoche, a form of metonymy, or association of terms according to the contiguity of their signifieds (from the Greek *metonymia,* meaning a transfer of a name), here the part, *coeur,* for the whole, "une pauvre fille de campagne." The term *simple* suggests naivete, frankness, innocence, spontaneity, modesty, even a profound mysticism going beyond ordinary religious experience, yet it also suggests credulity or even simple-mindedness. As a figural expression, even though commonplace, the title is anything but uncomplex. Simple is opposed to complex, in other words, to the sorts of transfers, derivations, and differences which are the very stuff of figuration.[9] The protagonist of the story, consequently, can be interpreted not only as signifying a naive emotional relation to the world but as representing a particular relation to language. Impossibly, this relation is represented as both figural *and* uncomplex, metonymic and simple. The name of the servant, Félicité, as has been often noted, is derived from Latin *felicitas,* from *felix,* happy, and is associated not just with contentment but with religious beatitude. Felicity, then, enjoys a particular relation to meaning, that is both banal, simple, and, in Flaubert's and our desacralized world, virtually inconceivable. We needn't take recourse in a "neo-Wordsworthian celebration of imbecility and nonconsciousness" to explain this character, as Jameson contends in an essay on *Trois contes.*[10] Things are not that simple, since the reader must be available to understanding in ways that are not circumscribed by the antinomy, naive/ironic, and this is "nullement ironique comme vous le supposez . . ."

Considerable effect is derived in the story from metonymy. This trope is linked from the outset to simplicity, to immediacy of emotion, and to the absence of abstract reflection; it figures the immediacy of the protagonist's relationship to the world of the fiction and to language in general. I certainly do not want to suggest here that there is any interest in reviving the well-known typology proposed by Roman Jakobson, that identifies the master trope of realist fiction as metonymy, and that of symbolism as metaphor. When pressed by readings as subtle, for example, as those of de Man on Proust it is clear that the two figures upon which the typology is based merge and interact.[11] It is doubtful at best whether the trope of metonymy is better suited than metaphor to mimetic, realist writing. In a certain sense, of course, as many critics have noted, **"Un Coeur simple"** is an ongoing reflection and implicit critique of the realist project. Félicité's relation to signs and objects appears to allow for no difference whatsoever, thus actualizing the realist's desire for the *mot juste,* the perfect representation. Loulou, furthermore, can be read as representing the collapse between signifier and signified, between visual sensual signifiers and textual, linguistic signifiers. Félicité, especially in her association with Loulou, can thus be interpreted as a figure of a certain logic of literary representation according to which words are not distinct from the experience of a fictive, sensual reality. While this reading is not without validity, I think that we must look as well for other effects of metonymy. Flaubert's tale systematically uses that figure to characterize Felicité's sentimental and cognitive relations to the world and this is invariably presented as a most *un*complex way of relating to things. I would like to consider two aspects of this metonymic relationship to the world represented in the story. The first has to do with the way in which Félicité understands the sequence of events in her life, that is, how the protagonist interprets narrative. The second concerns how Félicité makes associative connections, how she relates to people and objects, to a parrot and to the Holy Ghost.

Félicité's relation to narratives of desire and social order, referred to as *histoire,* is established in the beginning of chapter two in which the story of her first and only love affair is recounted. The story serves as a paradigm of all of Félicité's subsequent sentimental attachments; it is the narrative of separation and loss and it thematizes Félicité's subordination and her alienation from social order. "Her own" story of desire is a pure repetition of other narratives of disappointments in love: "Elle avait eu, comme une autre, son histoire d'amour . . ." The story, of course, is about misplaced faith, deception and betrayal. From the outset of the tale there is no active role for her in narratives of socially effective action, of *histoire,* considered in the broad senses of the term, as knowing how or being able to do ("savoir" or "pouvoir faire") in any arena other than that of domestic time and space.

A remarkable thing about Félicité's awareness of the world of others is that she understands various events only as they have an immediate impact upon her, not as linked to any overriding past or future pattern integrating the personal and the social. This indifference to history, social and moral, is exemplified by a second passage in chapter 2. She accompanies Madame Aubain and her children on a trip to the seashore, driven by M. Liébard in his cart. Liébard recounts the lives of the people who own the properties adjacent to the road: "La jument de Liébard, à de certains endroits s'arrêtait tout à coup. Il attendait patiemment qu'elle se remit en marche; et il parlait des personnes dont les propriétiés bordaient la route, ajoutant à leur histoire des réflexions morales. Ainsi, au milieu de Touques, comme on passait sous des fenêtres entourées de capucine, il dit, avec un haussement d'épaules: 'En voilà une Mme Lehoussais, qui au lieu de prendre un jeune homme . . .' Félicité n'entendit pas le reste; . . ." (28-9). Because Félicité assumes no place in social and moral anecdotes, and

implicitly, in the narrative order in which they are recounted these stories hold no interest for her at all. This indifference prevails even in a context that recalls her former love, for the Mme Lehoussais alluded to here is the rich widow whom Théodore had married after his brief encounter with Félicité. Her logic of narrative, in the words of one passage, is "naturel": after her mistress dies of pneumonia, Félicité too is diagnosed as having the disease: "'Ah! comme Madame,' trouvant naturel de suivre sa maîtresse" (57). Earlier in the story, Mme Aubain's excessive grief at the absence of her daughter seems to Félicité as *tout simple.* (39). *Simple* and *naturel* signify the same ignorance of complexity and lack of interpretive distance on events. Similarly, the episode in which Félicité saves the children and her mistress from an enraged bull, whom they surprise in a pasture as they return from an outing, is never associated in Félicité's mind with any transcendent significance; her action does not take its place metaphorically in a general scheme of social values: "Cet événement, pendant bien des années, fut un sujet de conversation à Pont-l'Evêque. Félicité n'en tira aucun orgueil, ne se doutant même pas qu'elle eut rien fait d'héroique" (28). An event impresses itself upon the protagonist because of the intensity of its emotive impact upon her, and, by and large, events remain unassimilated by any more complex interpretation. While this logic is implicit throughout the story, it is most clearly suggested in this passage that serves the technical function of a narrative "summary:"

> Puis des années s'écoulèrent, toutes pareilles et sans autres épisodes que le retour des grandes fetes: Pâques, l'Assomption, la Toussaint. Des événements intérieurs faisaient une date, où l'on se reportait plus tard. Ainsi, en 1825, deux vitriers badigeonnèrent le vestibule; en 1827, une portion du toit, tombant dans la cour, faillit tuer un homme, L'été de 1828, ce fut à Madame d'offrir le pain bénit; Bourais, vers cette époque s'absenta mystérieusement; et les anciennes connaissances peu à peu s'en allèrent: Guyot, Liébard, Mme Lechaptois, Robelin, l'oncle Gremanville, paralysé depuis longtemps.

> (45)

What is missing in this passage, of course, is a summation from Félicité's point of view of the meaning of events or the representation of such a point of view by a narrator. Narrative meaning for Félicité is not arrived at through metaphoric synthesis, in which the protagonist groups like events according to their similarities at a higher level of significance.[12] Félicité's relationship to history remains within the uncomplex schema of the chronicle; there is no evaluation of the relative importance of events and there is no representation from her point of view of a general social context, forming the background against which the specific occurrence is assessed.[13] The logic of narrative connectives is reduced to its most elementary form; it is the logic of the list.

Rather than sequence and causality merging, as they do in traditional narrative, with prior events assuming the logical role of motivating subsequent actions simply because they occur earlier in the story, as Barthes and others have remarked, sequence remains in Félicité's mind strictly temporal. Narrative sequence is divided into discrete episodes in which the overriding significance of events is never theorized as part of the narration itself. For Felicité the personal is not distinct from the universal for the simple reason that she does not perceive the difference; the meaningful event is *naturel* or *tout simple.*

There is one moment in the story in which Félicité does reflect upon the important events of her past and links them according to the feelings of sadness and loss that they have inspired in her. After the death of her parrot she takes the bird's remains to Honfleur where she will have Loulou stuffed. Being deaf, as she approaches Honfleur she fails to hear a coach that overtakes her rapidly from behind and she is thrown into a ditch by a lash of the angry coachman's whip. As she takes up her journey again, she sees the town from above and pauses: "Arrivée au sommet d'Ecquemauville, elle aperçut les lumières de Honfleur qui scintillaient dans la nuit comme une quantité d'étoiles; la mer, plus loin, s'étalait confusément. Alors une faiblesse l'arrêta; et la misère de son enfance, la déception du premier amour, le départ de son neveu, la mort de Virginie, comme les flots d'une marée, revinrent à la fois, et, lui montant à la gorge, l'étouffaient" (52). *Misère, déception, départ, mort,* all indicate separation and loss, and although the emotions arise in a moment of retrospection, that moment is uncomplicated by any meditation on causality or ultimate purpose.

Just as the past for Félicité merges seamlessly with the present, she has absolutely no conception of the future. The obsession with predictive narratives that characterizes the restless desires of so many of Flaubert's characters, notably an Emma Bovary, or Frédéric Moreau, and in a quirky way, Bouvard and Pécuchet, is absolutely lacking in Félicité; she is unable to project the future according to any interpretive schema based on an understanding of a narrative pattern derived from past events.

Félicité's understanding of the world, her interpretations of places, things and signs, is given over almost exclusively to metonymic relations, presented by the text in the simplest forms. When told that the ship on which her nephew, Victor, set sail has arrived in Havana, Félicité wishes to know what the place is like; she imagines only that the city is filled with cigar smoke: "A cause des cigares, elle imaginait la Havane un pays où l'on ne fait pas autre chose que de fumer, et Victor circulait parmi les nègres dans un nuage de tabac."

She asks M. Bourais, the pharmacist who represents the voice of science, for further information:

> Il atteignit son atlas, puis commença des explications sur les longitudes; et il avait un beau sourire de cuistre devant l'ahurissement de Félicité. Enfin, avec son porte-crayon, il indiqua dans les découpures d'une tache ovale un point noir, imperceptible, en ajoutant: "Voici." Elle se pencha sur la carte; ce réseau de lignes coloriées fatiguait sa vue, sans lui rien apprendre; et Bourais l'invitant à dire ce qui l'embarrassait, elle le pria de lui montrer la maison où demeurait Victor. Bourais leva les bras, il éternua, rit énormément; une candeur pareille excitait sa joie; et Félicité n'en comprenait pas le motif,—elle qui s'attendait peut-etre à voir jusqu'au portrait de son neveu, tant son intelligence était bornée.

(40)

For Félicité, word and thing must show an immediate and necessary relationship; since cigars come from Havana, the city is heavy with cigar smoke. The abstractions of a map mean nothing to her unless there is a possible visual similarity, what semioticians call an iconic relation, between the representation and the object it signifies, hence her concern for the location of Victor's house. In a more general sense, she is represented as having a unique capacity to experience the similarity of related objects as though without difference. At the funeral of Virginie, she imagines that her nephew is being buried at the same time: "Elle songeait à son neveu, et, n'ayant pu lui rendre ces honneurs, avait un surcroît de tristesse, comme si on l'eût enterré avec l'autre" (44). It is important to stress the general significance and prevalence of metonymy in Félicité's simplified associative system. The extensive passages in which this figure comes into play, those concerning the Holy Ghost and the parrot, should not be seen as somehow different in kind from others in which there is doubtless less at stake than there is in Félicité's visions of the Holy Spirit. The conflation of the parrot and the Holy Ghost is not a singular occurrence, an example of the stunning immediacy of the sacred, or of a dotty hallucination; it partakes of the simplicity that is inscribed throughout the tale.

The confusion between the Holy Ghost and the parrot occurs in chapter 4, but it is prepared by the patterns that I have discussed, disseminated throughout the text and more immediately by a passage in chapter 3 in which Félicité listens to stories of the Bible and transposes them "literally" into daily events of her own existence. The suppression of the difference between the everyday and the sacred in her interpretation of the story is made possible by her associations with the material objects and events spoken of in the story with those present in her own life. "Les semailles, les moissons, les pressoirs, toutes ces choses familières dont parle l'Evangile, se trouvaient dans sa vie; le passage de Dieu les avait sanctifiées; et elle aima plus tendrement les agneaux par amour de l'Agneau, les colombes à cause de Saint-Esprit." In this passage, the abstraction required to imagine the Holy Ghost, at once bird, fire and breath, puts this figure provisionally beyond her. She can only make conjectural associations with her immediate and material world: "C'est peut-être sa lumière qui voltige la nuit aux bords des marécages, son haleine qui pousse les nuées, sa voix qui rend les cloches harmonieuses . . ." (34). The priest's interpretive narratives of the holy stories are a matter of profound indifference to her: "Quant aux dogmes, elle n'y comprenait rien, ne tacha même pas de comprendre." As noted before, Félicité lacks the capacity to process narratives metaphorically. The ability to imagine the holy Ghost will await the fortuitous arrival of the parrot Loulou, who furnishes the material component that will eventually enable her to assimilate the divine as real.

In a passage immediately preceding that in which Félicité conflates the Holy Ghost with Loulou, there is a description of a bizarre collection of objects that she assembles in her room to preserve the past: in this strange collection, the profane and the sacred intermix and merge so that the distinction between them loses all value. The objects represent perfectly for her the person with whom they are associated, linked for her in an unmediated relation. Unlike the fetishist, who acknowledges that his favored object is a substitute, Félicité makes no such derived associations. The negative component of the fetish, which as Freud has noted, is both a denial as well as an affirmation of the presence of the lost object, falls away; the object for Félicité is pure affirmation, an impossibly literal figure.

> Cet endroit, où elle admettait peu de monde, avait l'air tout à la fois d'une chapelle et d'un bazar, tant il contenait d'objets religieux et de choses hétéroclites.
>
> Une grande armoire gênait pour ouvrir la porte. En face de la fenêtre surplombant le jardin, un oeil-de-boeuf regardait la cour; une table, près du lit de sangle, supportait un pot à l'eau, deux peignes, et un cube de savon bleu dans une assiette ébréchée. On voyait contre les murs: des chapelets, des médailles, plusieurs bonnes Vierges, un bénitier en noix de coco; sur la commode, couverte d'un drap comme un autel, la boite en coquillages que lui avait donnée Victor; puis un arrosoir et un ballon, des cahiers d'écriture, la géographie en estampes, une paire de bottines; et au clou du miroir, accroché par ses rubans, le petit chapeau de peluche! Félicité poussait même ce genre de respect si loin, qu'elle conservait une des redingotes de Monsieur . . .
>
> (53)

The archeological museum in Flaubert's *Bouvard et Pécuchet,* which this collection resembles in condensed form, has been studied by Eugenio Donato.[14] The museum is based on certain epistemological assumptions, the most important of which is that the display of artifacts can be ordered as a representation of human reality and history. This display presumes that each object can be linked to an integral object and that all be included in a narrative reconstruction of history. Félicité, however, short circuits the process of abstraction, to arrive at the presence of the past in the fragment itself; her relation to the objects in the collection is fundamentally a-historical. As in the case of her relation to narrative, she does not translate discrete components into a metaphoric schema.

The stuffed parrot assumes a prominent place in this collection: "Au moyen d'une planchette, Loulou fut établi sur un corps de cheminée qui avançait dans l'appartement. Chaque matin, en s'éveillant, elle l'apercevait à la clarté de l'aube, et se rappelait alors les jours disparus, et d'insignifiantes actions jusqu'en leurs moindres détails, sans douleur, pleine de tranquillité" (53-4).

The passage in which Félicité assimilates the Holy Ghost to her parrot is unusual in the story: it describes in detail Félicité's translation of meaning from one object to another; the process passes through the abstractions that metaphorically link representations perceived as different, and arrives finally at the metonymic assimilation of each component. She first sees the stained glass window representing the Holy Ghost, notes a resemblance to Loulou, which is later reinforced by her viewing a naive engraving of the Spirit, an "image d'Epinal," that she recognizes as an "authentic" portrait of Loulou. "A l'église, elle contemplait toujours le Saint-Esprit, et observa qu'il avait quelquechose du perroquet. Sa ressemblance lui parut encore plus manifeste sur une image d'Epinal, représentant le baptême de Notre-Seigneur. Avec ses ailes de pourpre et son corps d'émeraude, c'était vraiment le portrait de Loulou" (54).

Quite exceptionally, the passage remains within the logic of representation, in which the similarity between terms is perceived as a likeness within difference. It is not until Félicité buys the "image d'Epinal" and places it adjacent to Loulou that parrot and spirit are assimilated, and then, seeing them together: "Ils s'associèrent dans sa pensée, le perroquet se trouvant sanctifié par ce rapport avec le Saint-Esprit, qui devenait plus vivant à ses yeux et intelligible. Le Père, pour s'énoncer, n'avait pu choisir une colombe, puisque ces bêtes-là n'ont pas de voix, mais plutôt un des ancêtres de Loulou. Et Félicité priait en regardant l'image, mais de temps à autre se tournait un peu vers l'oiseau."

The representation of Félicité's action "literalizes" the metonymic process; contiguity of association is accompanied by literal contiguity of the objects, as the engraving of the Holy Ghost is placed *next* to Loulou. While there remains something incomplete in her mind about metaphoric likeness ("il avait quelque chose du perroquet . . ."), incomplete and imbued with figural difference, the assimilation of the representation and the object becomes possible when the two are placed next to one another. Two pages later in the same chapter, following the death of her mistress and the announcement that the house is to be sold at auction, there is no longer any trace of figural difference in Félicité's perception of the parrot-Holy Ghost: "Ce qui la désolait principalement, c'était d'abandonner sa chambre,—si commode pour le pauvre Loulou. En l'enveloppant d'un regard d'angoisse, elle implorait le Saint-Esprit, et contracta l'habitude idolâtre de dire ses oraisons agenouillée devant le perroquet. Quelquefois, le soleil entrant par la lucarne frappait son oeil de verre, et en faisait jaillir un grand rayon lumineux qui la mettait en extase" (56).

In the final chapter of the tale just before her death, Félicité is taken by delirium and, in the end hallucinates. She has given the parrot to the celebration of the Fête Dieu, Corpus christi, the festival of the Eucharist, to be placed on the altar in the procession. As she dies she believes she sees a giant parrot in the heavens: "et, quand elle exhala son dernier souffle, elle crut voir, dans les cieux entrouverts, un perroquet gigantesque, planant au-dessus de sa tête" (61).

The ending makes possible an entirely superfluous rational interpretation of Félicité's vision; it could be said to be the effect of her hallucination. This is of course true, but utterly beside the point, since Félicité has made such associations throughout the text on a daily basis; for her the supernatural is "tout simple." Representing the death of the protagonist, the ending of **"Un Coeur simple"** is quite traditional, but it does not provide the reader with a secure understanding of how to interpret the event. The final episode is both an exalted moment of religious ecstasy and the last delirium of a blind, deaf and dotty old woman. We must read simultaneously in the register of irony, with an acute awareness of both the aptness and the incongruities of the word made parrot, and beyond irony, accepting the possibility of both complex and simplified interpretation . . . "nullement ironique comme vous le supposez." The reading of **"Un Coeur simple"** that I have proposed here would accommodate ironic doubleness of meaning, yet make a place for the possibility of the simple. If Félicité represents the inevitable failures of certain aspects of the realist project, that interpretation of the tale is complicated by the necessity of reading figures simply. This is a complex interpretation that does not deny ironic duplicities and the workings of discursive mediation, but also, and paradoxically, makes a place for simplicity, a figure that we know to be an impossible immediacy. While we remain wary of the aporia of language and of the duplicities specific to realist representation, we need also to acquiesce to in-

stances of immediacy, of felicity, which are produced throughout Flaubert's text.

Notes

1. N. Wing, "Emma's Stories: Narrative, Repetition, and Desire in *Madame Bovary*," in *The Limits of Narrative: Essays on Baudelaire, Flaubert, Rimbaud and Mallarmé.* (Cambridge and New York: Cambridge University Press, 1986) 41-77.

2. See Gérard Genette, "Silences de Flaubert," in *Figures* (Paris: Seuil, 1966) 223-243. Genette discusses the interruption of narrative by silence, quietness that overcomes the protagonists and a pause in action, in moments represented as intense subjective experiences. This is clearly one way that the text subverts its own ironic duplicities. See also, Marc Bertrand, "Parole et silence dans les *Trois contes* de Flaubert," *Stanford French Review* 1.2 (Fall, 1977):191-204.

3. This commonplace, as I will show, is radically different from the effects produced by cliché in Flaubertian *bêtise*, the unconscious citation, in which a protagonist unwittingly reproduces as his/her own a discourse belonging to the doxa, parroting as individual what is recognizably in general circulation. For a recent and excellent discussion of cliché and stupidity in Flaubert, see Christopher Prendergast, "Flaubert: The Stupidity of Mimesis," in *The Order of Mimesis: Balzac, Stendhal, Nerval, Flaubert* (Cambridge and New York: Cambridge University Press, 1986) 180-211. See also Jefferson Humphries, "Aphorism and Criticism: Deconstruction and the Commonplace Tradition," in *The Puritan and the Cynic: The Literary Moralist in America and France.* (New York, Oxford: Oxford University Press, 1987) 56-74.

4. Flaubert, *Madame Bovary* (Paris: Garnier, 1961) 178-9.

5. Flaubert, "Un Coeur simple," *Trois contes* (Paris, Gallimard, "Folio," 1966) 51. All references to "Un Coeur simple" are to this edition.

6. S. Mallarmé, "Crise de vers," *Œuvres complètes* (Paris: Gallimard, "Editions de la Pléiade," 1945) 363-4.

7. Quoted in *Préface à la vie d'écrivain: Extraits de la correspondance de Gustave Flaubert.* G. Bollème, ed. (Paris: Seuil, 1963) 272-3.

8. Ross Chambers, *Story and Situation: Narrative Seduction and the Power of Fiction* (Minneapolis: University of Minnesota Press, 1984) 127.

9. We can assume that Flaubert was well aware of the resonances of the term *simple* in classical and medieval rhetoric and in medieval theology. *Sim-*

plicitas is both a figure of rhetoric, the artful use of common speech, and a religious practice whereby the imitation of Christ's rectitude facilitates salvation. In rhetoric, simplicitas is an artifice designed to imitate simplicity, calculated to convince the listener by imitation of common, everyday speech. See Quintilian, *Institutio oratoria,* ed. H. Butler (Cambridge, Massachusetts: Harvard University Press, Loeb Classical Library, 1976) 81, 521, on the "felicissimus sermo," the happiest use of ordinary language. E. Gilson, *La Philosophie au moyen-âge* (Paris: Payot, 1963) discusses Saint Pierre Damien's *De sancta simplicitate* and the critique of philosophical discourse and reasoning as a means of access to salvation and the privileging of the exemplary lives of the simple. Clearly one must distinguish between the protagonist Félicité's unironic relation to the world of signs, in which the naive, the un-rational and the mystical merge, and Flaubert's rhetorical use of the figure of simplicity. The language of Flaubert's text, however, does not artfully feign an immediate relation to the simple, and this is the crucial issue, since the reader is drawn into a language that must be read as both "literal" and figurative, the literal being derived as supplementary to the figural. I wish to thank my colleague, Alexandre Leupin, for pointing out to me precise textual references to the figure *simplicitas.*

10. See F. Jameson, "Flaubert's Libidinal Historicism," in Flaubert and Postmodernism, N. Schor and H. Majewski, ed., (Lincoln and London: University of Nebraska Press, 1984) 82.

11. See P. de Man, "Semiology and Rhetoric," in *Allegories of Reading* (New Haven and London: Yale University Press) 3-19.

12. Chambers, *Story and Situation,* notes the absence of hierarchy in narrative in this story, 127.

13. See H. White, "The Value of Narrativity in the Representation of Reality," in *On Narrative,* W. J. T. Mitchell, ed. (Chicago and London: University of Chicago Press, 1981) 1-24.

14. E. Donato, "The Museum's Furnace: Note Toward a Contextual Reading of *Bouvard et Pécuchet,*" in *Textual Strategies,* J. Harari, ed. (Ithaca: Cornell University Press, 1979) 213-238. See also my "Detail and Narrative Dalliance in Flaubert's *Bouvard et Pécuchet,*" in *French Forum* 13.1 (1988): 47-56.

Karen L. Erickson (essay date 1992)

SOURCE: Erickson, Karen L. "Prophetic Utterance and Irony in *Trois contes.*" In *Modernity and Revolution in Late Nineteenth-Century France,* edited by Barbara T. Cooper and Mary Donaldson-Evans, pp. 65-73. Newark: University of Delaware Press, 1992.

[In the following essay, Erickson examines the role of both prophecy and irony in Trois contes.]

Prophecy is a recurrent voice in Flaubert's collection of tales, and provides a parabolic narrative model for a kind of textual transmission rooted in historical social commentary—the visionary challenge to a community through the voice of a prophet.[1] In this [essay], I will examine the role of the prophet in *Trois contes,* the ways in which prophetic utterances affect narrative structure, and the role of irony in the process of challenging the characters continually to reinterpret the meaning of prophecy and of their very nature. I use the term "irony" here to mean the progressive revelation to a character of a misunderstanding or limitation, often involving a recognition of hubris. Looking at irony this way, we see parallels between prophecy and irony. Prophetic discourse points ahead to a textual "future," and implies an external authority, the source of the prophecy. Irony also invokes a more complete knowledge, a different narrative perspective, in its disclosure of the dissonance between reality and appearance. The use of these devices complicates issues of narrative coherence and voice, and reveals in the text elements of social criticism.

Prophecy in *Trois contes* presents a variable presence, but in all three tales there are voices of revelation which share certain characteristics, evoke similar reactions in those hearing the voices, and set in motion a progression from misinterpretation to correction to new interpretation. The prophetic voice is most apparent in the third tale, **"Hérodias,"** which recounts the events surrounding the death of the biblical figure of John the Baptist, Iaokanann. His diatribes follow the model and evoke the wrath of the ancient Hebrew prophets. He is imprisoned in the depths of Hérode's citadel; nonetheless his voice travels freely and mystically. It reveals the crimes of incest, murder, and assassination, and predicts continued sterility and impending deaths. The fact that nothing can stop this unusual voice distinguishes it from the efforts of Phanuel and Hérodias, who show considerable powers of divination in their attempts to read the inevitable in signs and stars. Phanuel's messages, one of which is that an important man will die that night, are continually interrupted, which adds to the suspense of the story. The tale develops suspense, as well, in the theme of departure and return, through its portrayal of debates about the resurrection, the return of the prophet Elijah, the coming of the Son of David. Prophecy is central to the main intrigues: the possible renunciation of Hérodias and Salomé's consequent training and dance, the political attacks on Hérode's power, the death of Iaokanann.

In **"Hérodias,"** prophecy is not a private, potentially imaginary or hallucinatory incident but a social interaction. The prophet's message is repeated, translated, free to spread beyond its context, beyond the citadel, beyond its own narrative. This enrages Hérodias, terrifies Hérode, frustrates Mannaëi, entrances the Romans, seduces Phanuel, revives the people's image of their exile; it functions in different ways in the characters' various private dramas. The classical containment of time and place in this story contributes to the pressure on the various events, desires and subplots. The overabundance of narrative possibilities and potential outcomes is illustrated in the reactions to Iaokanann's voice. The narrative suggests, through Hérode's search for a scapegoat, that one single death could satisfy everyone and fulfill the various elliptical statements repeated throughout the story. The characters expect certain results from the prophecy, and from the death of this man, but such expectations bring narrative silence, not freedom, for those who sought to cut off prophetic language at its source, or at what they thought was its source. The many factions and enemies present at the banquet are represented as members of an antique world which is passing. At the end of the tale, the characters are divided into those who believe and those who do not. The latter are left within the citadel, the isolated and solitary place of the story. For the believers, there is an escape or departure, as the disciples leave carrying Iaokanann's head with them. In representing this remnant, Flaubert shows in an understated manner the profound compulsion to save something from the death of time's passing and the resolution of endings, though no key is offered for how one escapes decline, or fate, or death.

In the second tale, **"La Légende de saint Julien l'Hospitalier,"** the prophetic voice has a more legendary, mystical character. Three voices offer prophecies: A hermit speaks to Julien's mother during the night and has the unearthly character of a supernatural speaker, both in his words and in his presence and disappearance—he predicts her son will be a saint. A gypsy outside the castle speaks to the father, predicting worldly glory. The mother says nothing of the prediction of sainthood for fear of being seen as proud; the father says nothing of the prediction of worldly power for fear of being ridiculed. Yet they both await the outcome of their separate predictions. The words of the black stag, who addresses Julien in the forest, become the foundation for the central scene of the tale (central in structure as well as plot). His pronouncement, "Maudit! Maudit! Maudit! Un jour, coeur féroce, tu assassineras ton père et ta mère!"[2] ("Accursed! Accursed! Accursed! One day, cruel heart, you will kill your father and mother!") introduces the specific threat of parricide, as well as the underlying preoccupation with damnation and salvation. This is the legend of a *saint*; Julien must absolutely reach sainthood. The title, like the prophetic messages, informs the progress of the story, as it introduces expectations of a certain kind of fulfillment.

In contrast to the social character and repeated quotation of Iaokanann's prophetic utterances in **"Hérodias,"** the predictions in **"La Légende"** remain (with one significant exception) within the individual experience of the different characters, who keep hidden from each other their potentially mystical encounter with prophetic speakers. The lack of communication in this realm contributes both to the suspense of the intrigue and to the actual working-out of the narrative. When Julien finally confides in his wife, telling her of the stag's words and of his fear of fulfilling them, a prophetic utterance is passed on to a third party for the first time. Her reaction is to reason with him, to analyze the utterance within a logical context:

> [. . .] enfin, un jour, il avoua son horrible pensée.
>
> Elle la combattait, en raisonnant très bien: son père et sa mère, probablement, étaient morts; si jamais il les revoyait, par quel hasard, dans quel but, arriverait-il à cette abomination? Donc, sa crainte n'avait pas de cause, et il devait se remettre à chasser.[3]
>
> ("But at last one day he told her of his dreadful fear. She fought against it, reasoning very soundly: his father and mother were probably dead; but if he were ever to see them again, what chance or purpose could possibly lead him to commit such a horrible crime? His fear was completely groundless, and he ought to take up hunting again.")

When Julien's parents arrive in an unlikely and (to the wife's logical reasoning) unpredictable meeting of principals, he is in fact out on a solitary hunt. In his absence, his wife becomes the intermediary in establishing identity and in interpreting the appropriate response to the prophetic utterance. She renders possible the realization of the prophecy in part by placing them in her own bed, as a mark of honor, in part by not communicating in turn her knowledge of Julien's fear: "Ils firent mille questions sur Julien. Elle répondait à chacune, mais eut soin de taire l'idée funèbre qui les concernait."[4] ("They asked her countless questions about Julien. She answered every one, but was careful not to mention the gloomy obsession in which they were concerned.") Julien arrives in the darkness before dawn to feel two bodies asleep in his bed. He thinks his wife is with another man, kills his parents in a murderous rage, thus fulfilling the prophecy.

When Julien's wife appears at the door with a lighted candle, "elle comprit tout" ("she took everything in"), and in horror drops the candle which Julien picks up. By its light he recognizes his parents. His wife contributes both to the fulfillment of the crime and to his realization of its nature, participating in the progressive and therefore partial revelation of the prophetic utterance. Though this scene seems to fulfill the prophecy, the tale continues as Julien recounts his story and seeks salvation. This comes finally in the form of a mystical leper—with an uncanny voice, glowing eyes, compelling demands—who asks the sacrifice of Julien's life. He provides an answer, not to the prediction of assassination, but to the threat of damnation. Julien becomes a saint.

At first reading, **"Un Coeur simple"** presents no prophet figure. However, in comparison with these other voices, we see that the kinds of speech, linguistic problems, and misinterpretations presented in *Trois contes* are introduced and find a first voice in Loulou, the parrot. The prophetic speakers in the last two tales are characterized by voices with unusual volume, character and attraction, blazing eyes, a solemn stance. In **"La Légende,"** the hermit speaks "sans desserer les lèvres" ("without opening his lips"), the gypsy has "les prunelles flamboyantes" ("blazing eyes"), the stag also speaks "les yeux flamboyants, solennel comme un patriarche et comme un justicier" ("with blazing eyes, solemn as a patriarch or a judge"). The Leper's voice reaches Julien across a great distance and through a storm; he is described thus: "la figure pareille à un masque de plâtre et les deux yeux plus rouges que des charbons" ("his face like a plaster mask and his two eyes redder than burning coals"); at the end of the legend, the Leper's eyes "tout à coup prirent une clarté d'étoiles" ("all at once his eyes took on the brightness of the stars"). In **"Hérodias,"** Iaokanann also is portrayed with blazing eyes and roaring voice: "Ses prunelles flamboyaient; sa voix rugissait" ("His eyes flashed, his voice roared"), and his voice defies containment. For example, his long diatribe begins with a sigh audible throughout the citadel: "Ce fut d'abord un grand soupir, poussé d'une voix caverneuse. Hérodias l'entendit à l'autre bout du palais. Vaincue par une fascination, elle traversa la foule; et elle écoutait" ("First, in a sepulchral voice, there came a great sigh. Herodias heard it at the other end of the palace. Yielding to an irresistible urge, she made her way through the crowd and bent forward to listen"). As the diatribe continues, Iaokanann's face "avait l'air d'une broussaille, où étincelaient deux charbons" ("looked like a mass of brushwood in which two live coals were glowing"). Finally, the voice completely escapes realistic bounds: "La voix grossissait, se développait, roulait avec des déchirements de tonnerre, et, l'écho dans la montagne la répétant, elle foudroyait Machaerous d'éclats multipliés" ("The voice grew louder and stronger, rolling and roaring like thunder, and as the mountains sent it back, it broke over Machaerus in repeated echoes").

In comparing Flaubert's portrayal of Loulou, we see that the parrot shares the uncanny volume and attraction of his voice and a peculiar light in his eye, as if Loulou

were a lesser version of a prophetic speaker: "Les éclats de sa voix bondissaient dans la cour, l'écho les répétait" ("his shrieks rang round the courtyard, the echo repeated them"). After Loulou's death and return as a stuffed parrot, his glass eye interacts with the light and with Félicité's devotion: "Quelquefois, le soleil entrant par la lucarne frappait son oeil de verre, et en faisait jaillir un grand rayon lumineux qui la mettait en extase" ("Sometimes the sun, as it came through the little window, caught his glass eye, so that it shot out a great luminous ray which sent her into ecstasies").[5] Though it is a caricature, the parrot comes to represent the voice of God which speaks in the descent of the Spirit in Félicité's deformed theology. She can hear this voice long after she is deaf to human speech, and attends to his utterances with reverence. The parrot, capable of repeating meaningful sounds, is almost by definition a figure for unusual or random revelation, ironic disclosure, comical misinterpretation, and speaks as if in parody of the prophetic voices which follow in the collection. This simple voice, however, is profoundly appropriate for the nature of crime and belief set forth in the first tale.

Loulou's prophetic utterance is linked to the irony that reveals the reality, the human limitations beneath appearances. In the tradition of Merlin's laughter (the laughter of the prophet who sees through pretense to recognize secret plots and future events, and who signals his prophetic insight through laughter[6]), the parrot laughs at Bourais (Mme. Aubain's financial advisor) long before any question of his propriety is raised in the story:

> La figure de Bourais, sans doute, lui paraissait très drôle. Dès qu'il l'apercevait, il commençait à rire, à rire de toutes ses forces. Les éclats de sa voix bondissaient dans la cour, l'écho les répétait, les voisins se mettaient à leurs fenêtres, riaient aussi; et, pour n'être pas vu du perroquet, M. Bourais se coulait le long du mur, en dissimulant son profil avec son chapeau, atteignait la rivière, puis entrait par la porte du jardin; et les regards qu'il envoyait à l'oiseau manquaient de tendresse.[7]

> ("Bourais's face obviously struck him as terribly funny, for as soon as he saw it he was seized with uncontrollable laughter. His shrieks rang round the courtyard, the echo repeated them, and the neighbors came to their windows and started laughing, too. To avoid being seen by the bird, M. Bourais used to creep along the wall, hiding his face behind his hat, until he got to the river, and then come into the house from the garden. The looks he gave the parrot were far from tender.")

The narrator does not give an authoritative interpretation of the seemingly inexplicable laughter; the explanation, "Bourais's face obviously struck him as very funny" is limited by "sans doute"—"probably, obviously." Like Julien's wife, the narrator reasons with this odd voice and seeks a reasonable explanation. Something in this scene is peculiar, and unresolved. Bourais hides from Loulou, slinking around "en dissimulant son profil avec son chapeau" ("hiding his face behind his hat") just as Hérodias hides her face when Iaokanann sees her:

> Dés qu'il m'aperçut, il cracha sur moi toutes les malé-dictions des prophètes. Ses prunelles flamboyaient; sa voix rugissaient; il levait les bras, comme pour arracher le tonnerre. Impossible de fuir! [. . .] je m'éloignais lentement, m'abritant sous mon manteau, glacée par ces injures qui tombaient comme une pluie d'orage.[8]

> ("As soon as he saw me, he spat all the curses of the prophets at me. His eyes flashed, his voice roared, and he raised his arms as if to pluck thunder out of the sky. It was impossible to get away from him. [. . .] I moved off slowly, cowering under my cloak, my blood running cold at the insults that were raining down on me.")

The repetition of vocabulary ("Dès qu'il l'apercevait / Dès qu'il m'aperçut") and descriptive detail reinforces the correspondence between the two scenes. Characters are drawn to listen to the voice in spite of themselves; like the people in the citadel, the neighbors come to laugh along with Loulou, without understanding why they are laughing. When Bourais commits suicide upon the discovery of his fraud and wrongdoing, the narrative explains implicitly the reason for Loulou's laughter. This is also the work of a kind of irony, a peripeteia, reversal of fortune, that reveals the pettiness of the self-important human dimension. Through its laughter and through its decay, the bird signals the future material downfall of the household, as the stag and Iaokanann each predict the end of a family line. Though the narrative resolution of Loulou's prophetic utterance appears quite simple (the parrot laughs at Bourais; Bourais is unmasked as an unsavory character in contradiction with his image and standing in the bourgeois household and community), Loulou also plays a more and more central role in Félicité's problematic spiritual development, not unlike the Leper and Iaokanann in the other tales. The description of the parrot, his ambiguous relation to divinity, and his role in unveiling a hidden element or coarseness beneath the appearance of gentility and grace, the weakness hidden by a position of power, announce the more elaborate prophetic voices in the other tales.

When a narrative contains a prophecy of some future occurrence, there is an implicit narratological leap, an anticipation by the listener of the fulfillment of the prophecy. The suspense of waiting for the other piece of the puzzle, the scene of completion, can and often does dominate the narrative. In stories containing prophecies, from "Sleeping Beauty" to the Oedipus myth, the characters try to bring about or hinder the realization—to deflect, soften, or avoid altogether the prophesied outcome. Other narratives move without clearly recognizable prophecy, and only at the second scene are we aware that an anterior scene was indeed prophetic. It is this way that Loulou's laughter becomes prophetic, for only when Bourais is disgraced do we understand why the parrot laughed. Julien's wife understands, after the parricide, why her reasoning was powerless. Her understanding of her own participation in the event is ironic. In the final scene of **"Hérodias,"** Phanuel can interpret an obscure statement that Iaokanann made ("Pour qu'il croisse, il faut que je diminue" ["If he is to wax, then I must wane"]) only in the wake of the prophet's death, and with the unspecified news brought in from the outside. But even then, the tales refrain from any final judgment.

The multiplicity of possible interpretations indicates the ambiguity inherent in this type of expectation. Thinking that one interpretation resolves the prophecy, that one outcome verifies and dispenses with the prophecy, is the fundamental error[9]; Loulou's laughter refers to Bourais, but also to the stupidity of those who trust him. The work of repetition, quotation, interpretation of both the prophecy and its apparent fulfillment suggests that prophetic discourse is not an equation between pronouncement and realization but a continual reevaluation of potential. The citadel in **"Hérodias"** becomes a figure for the story itself, a place preparing to respond, but not yet ready to answer the riddle of its meaning. In the story of the Gordian knot, Alexander chose to cut the knot with his sword to answer the riddle. This may have led to domination, but the riddle contained in the knot was lost in the process. Prophecy in fiction offers this kind of mystery or riddle.

Prophecy and irony both depend upon perspective. Like the chorus in Greek tragedy, or an omniscient narrator, or the voice of irony, prophetic speech points to and challenges the limitations of narrative. In a sacred text, the authority of a divine source of prophecy (implied by the context of belief) calls for and guides interpretation. The authority of a prophetic voice in fiction lies partly within the narrator's scope, but partly beyond. The invocation by the prophet of an authority which knows a larger context and communicates in this parabolic fashion is a vehicle then for a kind of criticism, the revelation of truth; Flaubert's ironic portrayals of *"bêtise,"* the comparatively lucid powers of the prophetic voices, the urgency of harkening to this voice and the consequences of remaining deaf to it follow the tradition of Western prophetism. The prophetic perspective is linked ultimately with the external voice of commentary, with interpretation, and in many cases, with lament. Both prophecy and irony make explicit in the separation between utterance and revelation the desire for resolution and coherence, and challenge the characters', or the reader's, interpretation of a given event or statement. In the multiplicity of potential itineraries that prophecy ushers in, and in the progressive rejection of possible interpretations, these tales illustrate the ambiguity of meaning, the lack of control, the inevitable downfall of the proud. Flaubert's use of prophecy in **Trois contes** is evidence of a profound exploration of the potential of language.

Notes

1. Gustave Flaubert, *Trois contes,* ed. Edouard Maynial (Paris: Garnier Frères, 1969). All quotations from *Trois contes* will refer to this edition. All English translations are from Robert Baldick's translation (*Three Tales,* Baltimore, Maryland: Penguin, 1961).

   Numerous critics have studied the religious aspects of the tales, most often through general concepts like sainthood or the Trinity. Two articles have a particular relevance to the question of prophecy: Carla Peterson, "The Trinity in Flaubert's *Trois contes*: Deconstructing History" (*French Forum,* 8 [1983], 243-58) and Ian Reid, "The Death of the Implied Author? Voice, Sequence and Control in Flaubert's *Trois contes*" (*Australian Journal of French Studies,* 23 [1986], 195-211). Raymonde Debray-Genette explores certain aspects of the subject in "Profane, Sacred: Disorder of Utterance in *Trois contes*" (in *Flaubert and Postmodernism,* ed. Naomi Schor et al. [Lincoln: University of Nebraska Press, 1984], 13-29). Susan Selvin's study, "Spatial Form in Flaubert's *Trois contes*" (*Romanic Review,* 74 [1983], 202-20) contains pertinent remarks that can be directly transposed from their slightly different context; the notion of epiphany is outlined by Emily Zants in "*Trois contes*: a New Dimension in Flaubert" (*Nottingham French Studies,* 18 [1979], 37-44). I discuss the characteristics of prophecy in secular texts in my doctoral dissertation, "Prophecy and Fulfillment in Flaubert's *Trois contes*" (Yale University, 1987). A fundamental study of the notion of prophecy as it is used here is Erich Auerbach's essay "Figura," in *Scenes from the Drama of European Literature* (Gloucester, Mass.: Peter Smith, 1973), especially 29-60.

2. *Trois contes,* 98.

3. Ibid., 108-9.

4. Ibid., 111. This type of narrative suspension is similar to the interrupted or marginalized speech of Phanuel and Hérodias, and characterized by its limitation. Throughout *Trois contes* the tension between speech and silence becomes implicated in the tension between power and impotence.

5. Ibid., 66.

6. Paul Zumthor writes of this laughter: "Le trait est digne de remarque, car c'est dans le folklore universel un thème très répandu: le sorcier éclate de rire au milieu des opérations magiques [. . .]. [Merlin] rit de la désillusion de ses compagnons et de la vanité de leurs efforts; dans la Vita, c'est qu'il a, seul des assistants, la prescience d'un ridicule caché, d'une situation paradoxale qui va se découvrir." ("The trait is worthy of note, for it is a widely spread theme in universal folklore: The sorcerer bursts out laughing in the middle of magic operations [. . .]. [Merlin] laughs at the disillusionment of his companions and at the vanity of their efforts; in the *Vita,* he is the only one who has the foreknowledge of a hidden folly, or a paradoxical situation which is going to be revealed.") *Merlin le prophète* (Geneva: Slatkine Reprints, 1973), 45-46.

7. *Trois contes,* 53.

8. Ibid., 150-51.

9. Cf. Flaubert's remark in a letter to his friend Louis Bouilhet: "L'ineptie consiste à vouloir conclure" ("Stupidity consists in wanting to reach a conclusion"); as presented in *Préface à la vie d'écrivain: Extraits de la correspondance,* ed. Geneviève Bollème (Paris: Seuil, 1963), 52.

Christopher Wise (essay date spring 1993)

SOURCE: Wise, Christopher. "The Whatness of Loulou: Allegories of Thomism in Flaubert." *Religion and Literature* 25, no. 1 (spring 1993): 35-49.

[*In the following essay, Wise investigates how the philosophical thought of Thomas Aquinas infused Flaubert's fiction, especially "Un Coeur simple," and rejects his classification as a postmodern author.*]

It is well known that the philosophy of Thomas Aquinas had a significant impact upon James Joyce, especially in shaping Joyce's earliest published fiction, *Dubliners* (1914) and *A Portrait of the Artist as a Young Man* (1916); and, it is equally well known that Joyce was profoundly influenced by the novels of Gustave Flaubert, especially *L'éducation sentimentale* (1869), of which Joyce claimed to have memorized entire chapters. However, the corresponding relationship between Aquinas and Flaubert has been passed over in silence by literary scholars, when not prematurely obviated as either theoretically untenable or historically groundless.[1] In the essay to follow, while I will not suggest that Aquinas in any way directly "influenced" the writings of Flaubert, it will be my contention that Thomist thought not only permeates the attitudes and notions which shape Flaubert's fictional discourse, especially **"Un coeur simple"** (1877) and *L'éducation sentimentale,* but that its presence also testifies to the ontotheological character of Flaubert's aesthetic vision. Furthermore, it will be my intention to create yet more obstacles to recent attempts at periodizing Flaubert as a "postmodern" writer. Also the quasi-mythical depiction of Flaubert as a writer "at odds with language" will be criticized here as largely overstated and ideologically misdirected. I will argue instead that Flaubert's interest in language, far removed from the linguistic preoccupations of the late twentieth century, hinged rather on his nearly religious belief that the fixation of *le mot juste* could lead to the revelation of essence, a notion summarily rejected in most postmodern thought.

Perhaps no other text has influenced contemporary scholarship on Flaubert as much as Roland Barthes's *Le degré zéro de l'écriture* (1953; translated into English as *Writing Degree Zero,* 1968). Though not really characteristic of Barthes's later "post-structuralist" phase, *Writing Degree Zero* contains many of the germinal ideas which would come to dominate American literary scholarship in the late seventies and eighties. In the specific case of Flaubert, titles such as Jonathan Culler's *Flaubert: The Uses of Uncertainty* (1975), Naomi Schor's *Flaubert and Postmodernism* (1984), and Vaheed K. Ramazani's *The Free Indirect Mode: Flaubert and the Poetics of Irony* (1988) all illustrate the extent to which linguistic and deconstructive readings of Flaubert have gained precedence in the academy over the last two decades. In much contemporary scholarship on Flaubert, questions posed by Barthes in *Writing Degree Zero,* as well as the deconstructive philosophies of Jacques Derrida, have largely shaped the ground rules for critical inquiry into Flaubert's writing today. In a recent article in *PMLA,* for example, Ramazani has argued that "Flaubert's entire aesthetic project consisted in the effort to define an authentic self from within the voice of the other" ("Cliché" 121); or that Flaubert's alienation from his reading public was so severe that he had no choice but to aggressively subvert the "dominant discourse" of his public while still hopelessly imbedded within it.

Ramazani's argument, like many other similar ones, is predicated upon Barthes's earlier and now widely embraced thesis that at some point in the mid-nineteenth century, older, more classical modes of writing somehow "disintegrated" and, thereafter, "the whole of Literature, from Flaubert to the present day, became the problematics of language" (Barthes 3). In other words, literature underwent a "paradigmatic fall," and this fall is most clearly evident in the writings of Flaubert (Sontag xix). Though the later Barthes might reject the Husserlian character of his earlier thesis, in *Writing Degree Zero* he nevertheless speaks of this momentous "event" in terms of a "phenomenon which owed its existence to consciousness, not to revolution" (73). Following this event, and the subsequent "Flaubertization" of writing, nothing would ever be the same, Barthes ar-

gues, in part because writers had now forever abandoned any notion that language could authentically mirror or reflect reality. Henceforth, irony, sarcasm, wordplay, parody, pun, and so on would increasingly proliferate as the preferred means of subverting or deconstructing a now-exhausted bourgeois discourse.

Though more accurately periodized in terms of "post-structuralism" rather than "postmodernism," Jacques Derrida's philosophy of the "trace" has also significantly influenced contemporary criticism of Flaubert. While Derrida's "overturning" of western metaphysics is too well known (and too complex) to be rehearsed again here, it is nevertheless worthwhile to briefly outline what is at stake in the question of Flaubert's "entire aesthetic project" from a Thomist perspective, as opposed to a Derridean one. First, as Susan A. Handelman has argued in *The Slayers of Moses: The Emergence of Rabbinic Interpretation in Modern Literary Theory* (1982),[2] one consequence of the Derridean move to displace ontology in favor of textuality is an ultimate (and unavoidable) refusal of the Johannine doctrine of Logos as Incarnate Word (175). In other words, from a Derridean perspective, religious belief in Christ as the "Logos made flesh" finally amounts to a crass literalization of a Jewish metaphor, a reification of a Hebraic symbol for the benefit of Greco-Roman culture (168-69). Thus, as Handelman also affirms, "[t]he central doctrine of the Church—Incarnation—celebrates not the exaltation of the word, but its transformation from the linguistic order into the material realm, its conversion into flesh" (4). Even more to the point, Handelman demonstrates that Derrida's attack on the onto-theological basis of Western thought is finally coterminous with an attack on the Christian faith itself, or on "the son [who] dreams himself to be his own father, born into the flesh and elevated above all texts and written discourses" (169).

Secondly, the deconstructive philosophy of Derrida directly undermines the orthodox Thomist position that there is finally something irreducible about things. In other words, for Aquinas, as we will discuss below, there is ultimately an objective quality to reality, an actuality that substantiates the external world. For Derrida, on the other hand, the "real" is always socially constructed for us through the pre-existing layers of previous interpretation. Reality for Derrida therefore comes to us as "always already" read, or as previously inscribed by the infinitesimal "traces" of preceding readers: hence the centrality of the image of the palimpsest for Derrida and his followers.

While such questions are obviously beyond the scope of the present essay, they relate to recent debates on Flaubert in many far-reaching and unavoidable ways. To cite but a few cases, in a deconstructive commentary entitled "Point of View in 'Un coeur simple,'" Ben

Stoltzfus has argued that Félicité's mystical vision of the parrot Loulou at the climax of **"Un coeur simple"** was "sheer irony" on the part of Flaubert, "an extraordinary joke that its author had played on the faithful" (23-24). Though typical of contemporary criticism on Flaubert, Stoltzfus's argument ignores the fact that Flaubert's often excessive religiosity was both well known and even debated within Flaubert's own lifetime. In fact, Flaubert himself once wrote in a letter to a friend that the culminating "epiphany" of Félicité was "not at all ironic . . . but [was] on the contrary very serious and sad" (*Correspondence* 7.307).[3] Similarly, Fredric Jameson has dismissed Félicité's vision, as well as the transfiguration of Saint Julien at the climax of **"La légende de St. Julien,"** as "sham endings" (80); and in his book on Flaubert, Culler has argued that Flaubert's work constitutes a "cosmic joke" to demonstrate the absence of God, or the ultimate "nothingness" at the heart of all existence (73-74).[4] While provocative, and even illuminating on occasion, all of these readings demonstrate the relative helplessness of contemporary criticism in its attempts to account for descriptions of the transcendent in Flaubert.

The prejudices of contemporary culture have often led to a critical dismissal of Thomist aesthetics on the basis of Aquinas's "inability" to differentiate categorically between aesthetic and non-aesthetic objects. In fact, the medieval mind generally has been criticized in modern times as simplistic, primitive, and even "neurotic" on the basis of its allegorical world view (Eco, *Aquinas* 138). For a long time, medievalists have challenged such preconceptions, but too often they have met with little success. As Charles S. Singleton demonstrates in his seminal article "The Irreducible Dove" (1957), even professional medievalists often have difficulty overcoming post-enlightenment prejudices against the "obscurantist" and "superstitious" attitudes of medieval readers (133). However, more recently scholars have begun to consider the possibility that Aquinas's "ineptitude" may in fact point to a more problematic development within our own cultural history: namely, our own ineptitude in recognizing the aesthetic within the ordinary.

For Aquinas, as for many other medieval thinkers, no existing thing can be divorced from the beautiful because "every being is beautiful and God creates nothing that is not beautiful" (Eco, *Aquinas* 44); or, as Gerald B. Phelan has commented, "All things are beautiful [for Aquinas] because they exist, and the degree of their beauty is in precise proportion to the perfection of their being" (160). Accordingly, in Thomism even monsters are perceived as beautiful, as well as those things that evoke a sense of horror or terror in the viewer, by virtue of the fact that they meet the criteria of being.

In the case of Flaubert, the medieval "failure" to differentiate between aesthetic and non-aesthetic objects pre-

vails throughout much of his writings.[5] However, the parrot Loulou, from **"Un coeur simple,"** is the most obvious example of the aesthetic potential of the ordinary in Flaubert: that a moth-eaten, stuffed parrot could serve as an authentic symbol of the Holy Ghost has perplexed readers since the story's initial publication in 1877. However, the writings of Flaubert abound with similar examples, from the sundry objects of Madame Arnoux's boudoir to the mud-speckled shoes of Emma Bovary. The headgear of Charles Bovary, which has provoked endless annotation and discussion, might also be clarified when considered in light of the medieval delight in finding beauty in the monstrous, or the aenigmate.

For Aquinas, form is the locus of essence and content, or form assumes reality by being "reified" in content. Form is not then, as in Aristotle, "the structural principle of beings, but rather those very structural beings" (Eco, *Aquinas* 69). Thus, everything is beautiful in Thomism insofar as it "is" and, conversely, everything "is" insofar as it is beautiful: that is Aquinas's notion of integrity (Callahan 58). However, the goal of Thomist aesthetics is ontological, rather than epistemological. Aquinas is more interested in the "fullness of being" than in the mere identification of essence: a dialectic of sorts between essence and existence. While abstract in theory, the experiential thrust of Aquinas's aesthetics is made less obscure in the fiction of Flaubert. In *L'éducation sentimentale,* for example, Frédéric's failed "dreams of love" constitute the failure inherent in any merely epistemological recognition of the aesthetic object (in this case the object being Madame Arnoux), whereas Félicité's ontological experience of the aesthetic object (the parrot Loulou) constitutes an essential realization of the object's being, its very "createdness." In other words, Félicité does not merely recognize Loulou's being, she experiences it.[6]

However, the most famous aspects of Thomist aesthetics—in Joyce's *Portrait,* Stephen discusses them with Lynch—are the notions of the three formal criteria of beauty, all principles which may be observed in the work of Flaubert: *consonantia, integritas,* and *claritas,* or proportion, integrity, and clarity. For our purpose, the most important of these principles in Flaubert is that of *claritas,* or radiance, though all three criteria must be understood in terms of process, not unlike the unfolding of creation by Yahweh within the Genesis account (Maurer 50-51). Proportion, the first property of the aesthetic object, refers to the ontological beauty of a thing which is beautiful simply because it is. As we have seen, no thing in the Thomist universe can exist which is not beautiful because the very fact of its existence points to its suitability for receiving a form (Maurer 14). Integrity, the second property, is also a type of proportion, though it differs in that "integrity" refers to the very fitness of the thing to receive its form, some things being more perfect than others. Perfection, in this sense, means "the complete realization of form: a thing is perfect when it fully conforms to a given mode of perfection" (Eco, *Aquinas* 67). However, proportion is often the most difficult type of beauty to recognize because of its very abundance and obviousness. On the other hand, when a thing has integrity, it is more visible, and thus easier to recognize. Clarity, the final of the three properties, has four complementary significations, according to Eco: *claritas* can mean "light and physical color"; it can mean the *lumen manifestans,* "the light of reason that makes things known"; "the shining forth of earthly renown"; and the "celestial glory of the glorified body of the blessed [saints], Christ's transfigured body, and objects" (104).

The notion of *claritas* becomes a hallmark of the Flaubertian epiphany. In **"La légende de St. Julien,"** for example, the Leper who visits the hut of Julien is possessed of a beauty which only a saintly figure can recognize: certainly he has no earthly *claritas*. His body is covered with "scaly pus-covered sores" and his breath is "thick and nauseous as fog" (79). Julien first overcomes his hesitation at encountering him by recognizing a "royal majesty" in the Leper's bearing. He then clothes, feeds, and gives up his bed to the Leper before physically surrendering his very body to provide warmth for the sick man. When Julien lies on top of the Leper to keep him from freezing to death, "mouth to mouth, breast to breast," we are told that "[the Leper's] eyes assumed the brightness of stars, his hair lengthened out like the rays of the sun. . . . The roof flew off, the firmament unrolled—and Julien ascended towards the blue expanse, face to face with Our Lord Jesus, who bore him to Heaven" (81). Finally, the epiphany of *claritas*—light, breath, and the body of Christ—brings the tale to a close.

The narrator of **"La légende de St. Julien"** claims that the source of his tale is the stained glass window of a medieval cathedral, not unlike Félicité's stained glass window in **"Un coeur simple."** The medieval tale of Saint Julien as "radiant light" is thus refracted to us through a *claritas* of glass. As a homage to the French Catholic tradition in which he was raised, this story aptly demonstrates the extent to which Flaubert's cultural heritage is rooted in the Thomist world view.

The fallacy inherent in most readings of the parrot in **"Un coeur simple"** stems from the merely symbolic approach taken by the majority of Flaubert's critics. Rather, Loulou is best understood in terms of allegory rather than symbol. In the medieval world, "everything speaks of something else"; or, in the language of John Scotus Erigena, "There is nothing among visible and corporeal things which does not signify something incorporeal and intelligible" (Eco, *Aquinas* 139). Félicité, whose life is marked by the cycle of the great Catholic festivals, exists primarily within the medieval cosmos. In a world shaped by the ideas of theologians such as Aquinas—where the divine becomes manifest in concrete reality, or where form itself is defined as the meeting place of essence and content—it should not surprise us that the ordinary medieval person did not distinguish between aesthetic and "ordinary" phenomena. Nor should it surprise us that a similar incapacity exists in Félicité, whose provincial life remains as yet unaffected by post-enlightenment skepticism and empiricism.

As Northrop Frye reminds us, all interpretation is allegorical insofar as it attaches ideas to the structure of poetic imagery (89). However, the key to allegorical interpretation is community. The problem for many modern writers like Flaubert is that there no longer exists any community to address, outside the bourgeois community which Flaubert regards as profane and even nauseating. And yet the possibility of overcoming the deadening effects of bourgeois culture latently survives for Flaubert in the figures of Saint Julien and Félicité. These characters stand as strong warnings against our interpreting the failures of Emma Bovary and Frédéric Moreau as pure "cynicism" or "perversity" on the part of Flaubert.

As we have seen in **"La légende de St. Julien,"** in serving the Leper, Julien encounters the "radiant" body of Christ whose eyes take on "the brightness of stars" and whose breath emits "the sweetness of roses" (81). And as we have also seen, for Aquinas, clarity assumes the qualities of light, or of the radiant body of Christ. At the death of Félicité, before her final vision of the parrot, the service of Corpus Christi is being performed in the courtyard outside her window. Flaubert begins the last paragraph with the description of an "azure vapor" which Félicité inhales "sensuously [and] mystically." On the altar below, where the stuffed parrot sits, a "mass of brilliant color" descends, and the golden sun of the priest "shines forth upon them all" (81).

Besides Félicité's "epiphany," there are many other examples in **"Un coeur simple"** where radiant light plays a central role. Earlier, Flaubert tells us that Félicité "found it difficult to imagine the Holy Ghost in person, for it was not only a bird but a fire as well and, at times, a breath. She thought it might be its light . . . its breath" (28). "She formed the idolatrous habit of kneeling in front of the parrot when she prayed. Sometimes the sun came through the little window and caught his glass eye, when a great luminous ray would shoot from it, and she would be in ecstasies" (47). In another instance, when Félicité sorts through the now-grown Virginie's old clothes, "[t]he sunshine streamed in upon these poor little things, bringing out their stains and creases made by the child's movements" (39). Here we see aptly illustrated the Thomist thesis that (in Joyce's Stephen's phrase) "radiance . . . is *quidditas* [the "whatness" of a thing] (213). At this particular moment, the clothes reveal their very essence to Félicité; thus the radiant light shines forth and "a deep peace [seems] to reign over every living thing" (39).

The influence of Aquinas on Dante has been discussed for centuries, and there have been many critics who have similarly discussed Dante's influence on Flaubert, especially in *L'éducation sentimentale*.[7] Frédéric Moreau's first encounter with Madame Arnoux is "like a vision," an "almost religious stirring of the heart" (6). Flaubert tells us that "[a] woman's face used to shine in [Frédéric's] poetic paradise, so that, the first time he had seen her, he had promptly recognized her" (270). Henceforth, Madame Arnoux becomes Frédéric's "Beatrice" whose very presence lends meaning to his existence: she becomes the sole "object of his being," even his "vocation," and the "aim and center" of his life and thoughts (48). Even more specifically, Flaubert comments that Frédéric's "dreams had raised her to a position outside the human condition. Beside her, he felt less important on earth than the scraps of silk which fell from her scissors" (174). Later in the novel, Frédéric assures Madame Arnoux that he "can no more live without [her] than without the air of heaven." Frédéric demands, "Do you not feel the yearnings of my spirit mounting towards yours? Do you not feel our souls must mingle?" (257).

That Flaubert gives Madame Arnoux the Christian name of "Marie" is, of course, no accident; Flaubert exploits Frédéric's "Mariolatry" by describing how the young man worships Madame Arnoux's very name, "breathing it in ecstasy, [for it] contains clouds of incense and trails of roses" (271). In the final love scene, Frédéric tells Madame Arnoux how he often repeated her name, how he "tried to kiss it . . . [because it] contained all the joys of the flesh and soul" (391).

Frédéric's idolatry of Madame Arnoux, and all her material possessions, reaches extremes unrivaled even in Petrarch and Dante: the words that fall from her lips seem to Frédéric new objects, "creation[s] exclusively hers" (47). Madame Arnoux's work basket fills Frédéric with amazement, "as though it were an object from another world."[8] He "longs to know the furniture of her room, the dresses she had worn" (6). Later, when these same dresses are sold in a public auction, Frédéric nearly swoons "as if he had seen crows tearing her corpse to pieces" (384). Flaubert tells us that "[a]s each thing disappeared, he felt as if a part of his heart had been taken from him; and the monotony . . . numbed him with fatigue afflicting him with a deathly torpor, dissolving his very being" (384). Near the end of the novel, Madame Dambreuse maliciously purchases a silver box of Madame Arnoux's, and Frédéric is so infuriated with her that he breaks off their relationship, sacrificing a large fortune to avenge the "sacrilege" (242).

Flaubert also uses radiant light to describe Madame Arnoux at nearly every appearance she makes within the novel. In the opening scene, for example, she becomes "the focal point of light at which the totality of things converged" (10). In another scene, Madame Arnoux is described as standing "[behind the] eastern horizon, growing pale with a fiery, orange light" (78). Flaubert tells us that "[her] room looked peaceful. Bright sunshine poured through the window panes and glittered on the corners of the furniture. Madame Arnoux was seated by the window, and a great sunbeam, falling on the little curls at the nape of her neck, flooded her amber skin with liquid gold" (127). Again, in a chair next to Madame Arnoux, "[t]here was a circle of white light on the ceiling above the lamp, while the shadows lay in the corners like many thicknesses of black gauze" (157). Hard and bright light is "reflected by the low white ceiling . . . [where Madame Arnoux's] lapis lazuli locket was fastened to her waist by a thin gold chain" (8). (Lapis lazuli often symbolizes for Flaubert the colors of heaven or eternity: he also exploits its radiance in his climactic descriptions of the parrot Loulou in **"Un coeur simple"** when the parrot's blue forehead scintillates "like a plaque of lapis lazuli" [50]). And, finally, in the countryside, Frédéric sits enraptured by the light which streams through Madame Arnoux's hands and fingers:

> Sometimes sunbeams streaming through the Venetian blinds would hang from ceiling to floor like the strings of a lyre; motes of dust would float and whirl in these bars of light. She liked to pass her hand through them: Frédéric would seize it gently, and gaze at the tracery of her veins, the grains of her skin, the shape of her fingers.
>
> (253)

Frédéric's fascination with Madame Arnoux's hands passes beyond mere fetishization of the aesthetic object; his wonder is nothing if not religious in nature. Throughout *L'éducation sentimentale,* Madame Arnoux's eyes are also fantastically described: Frédéric feels her glance "penetrate his soul, like those great sunbeams that go right down to the bottom of water" (79). Her face, which is described as an "oval," radiates "an extraordinary splendor. An infinite sweetness [pours] forth from her lovely eyes" (242).

Though Frédéric is blinded in the radiance of her beauty, we must not forget that even he considers himself to have "failed" in his "dreams of love" (395). Flaubert emphasizes the failure of Frédéric, who remains paralyzed by the sheer force of his narcissistic infatuation for Madame Arnoux. Frédéric fails in his dreams of love because his realization of her "essence" does not lead any further than the threshold of "epiphany"; this is to say, Frédéric's education is only sentimental, not cognitive. It does not grasp the full extent of *claritas.*

Nor has Frédéric's vision the clarity of Saint Julien's. During their last meeting, when Frédéric observes the protruding shoe of Madame Arnoux, he feels disturbed, even disgusted. Throughout the novel, the shoes and feet of Madame Arnoux assume erotic proportions, especially apparent when Frédéric constructs a shrine of sorts to one of Madame Arnoux's slippers (275). The inability of Frédéric to overcome his disturbance at the sight of Madame Arnoux's foot is indicative of his larger inability to come to terms with feminine sexuality itself. Near the end of the novel, Madame Arnoux takes off her hat, and the sight of her white hair strikes Frédéric "like a blow full in the chest" (421). Though fully able to recognize the "divinity" of Madame Arnoux, Frédéric is paralyzed by her more terrifying earthiness, her mortality and sexuality as a woman.

Frédéric's visit to the brothel, which is the final epiphany of the novel, appropriately brings an end to Flaubert's tale because it is yet another illustration of Frédéric's stupefaction before the sexuality of woman, his paralysis at the "shrine of the feminine deity" (396-97). Showing up with his handful of flowers, Frédéric "turns pale and stops dead at seeing so many women at his disposal." The fact that the adult Frédéric considers this occasion "the best time [he] ever had" tells us something of the retardation of his emotional and sexual maturity by the close of the story: in this regard, *L'éducation sentimentale* can be described as a "failed" *bildungsroman,* in which the hero attains no authentic maturity or character development: his epistemological appreciation of Madame Arnoux never ascends to the ontological. At the opposite extreme, Félicité in **"Un coeur simple,"** with no formal education or religious instruction, reaches the apex of spiritual development through her final, even "idiotic," realization of the "whatness" or "being" of the parrot Loulou.

Critics such as Roland Barthes and Jonathan Culler have made much of the question *"qui parle?"* in Flaubert, but in doing so they have largely transposed late-twentieth century ideas onto an edifice which was constructed in another era, with another set of criteria and assumptions. The point then is not that Flaubert was "really" or "secretly" Thomist, but that Flaubert had by no means made any quantitative leap towards "post-metaphysical" thought, as many contemporary scholars would have it. In discussing *le mot juste,* Flaubert himself once wrote that he was attempting to find the word that would express a thing "as it always is, in itself, in its essence, freed of all ephemeral contingencies" (*Correspondance* 2.462). This search for the true "essence" of a thing ("in itself") corresponds to Joyce's doctrine that "the artist reveals the 'signature' of each thing, [or] the word that captures its *quidditas* or whatness" (Cross 185). Hence, in a letter to George Sand, Flaubert comments that "[f]eelings and images are governed by the laws of numbers, and what seems to be

outward form is actually essence" (*Correspondance* 7.294). It is difficult to comprehend how a writer who believed in ideal forms to the extent that he considered his artwork to be "governed by the laws of numbers" could be interpreted today as an early "postmodernist" novelist, in league with a mode of thinking which is characterized by its radical denial of "essence" and older notions of mimesis and representation.

On the contrary, as Aquinas before him, Flaubert considered form to be equivalent to essence, an orthodox scholastic position. In this sense, the search for *le mot juste* is coterminous with the search for the precise word which will release the *quidditas,* the "whatness," of a thing. In the Thomist four-level hermeneutic, as inherited from Origen and Augustine, the final interpretive phase beyond allegorical interpretation is the anagogic phase. In *Anatomy of Criticism,* Northrop Frye likens anagogic criticism to Christian notions of the Incarnate Word, the Logos, or the "word that is all words" (122). Not unlike Frye's interest in Logos, Flaubert's interest in *le mot juste* significantly transcends a merely linguistic fascination with the way sentences are put together.

In an essay entitled "Flaubert and the Status of the Subject," Victor Brombert has also problematized the older Barthean notion that "concrete detail in Flaubert remains resistant to any structure or meaning" (110). Brombert reminds us instead that art, in Flaubert's own words, "is representation"; and that Flaubert emphatically believed that "[w]e must think of nothing but representing" (111). Brombert points out that, during the composition of **"Un coeur simple,"** Flaubert kept a stuffed parrot on his desk "so as to paint from life." He says, "[t]he eye, the mirror, the mime—all preside over the Flaubertian doctrine of reproduction. . . . Seeing sharply comes first [for Flaubert], the contemplation of the object" (110). However, what Brombert does not go on to say is that there is nothing very original about Flaubert's "contemplative" approach to aesthetic phenomena, or that in orthodox Thomist aesthetics "the operation of the mind apprehending the beautiful is also termed *contemplation*" (Callahan 42).

Hence, in answer to Germaine Brée's question posed in the opening pages of *Flaubert and Postmodernism*—"Will [the new] generation find a contemporary in Flaubert?" (8)—my own critical response, alongside Brombert's, must be an emphatic *no.* Instead, I would extend Charles Singleton's earlier and more pertinent observation that there is in far too much contemporary scholarship a reactionary sense of repugnance "at the notion that anyone, in this latter day of enlightenment, should be asked to adopt a 'reader's attitude' which looks so like superstition or obscurantism, or at least to require an act of 'faith' which one is not at all disposed to make" (133).

To this end, Singleton also raises a revealing question for our purposes here, first posed by Aquinas at the end of the *Summa Theologica* (3.39.7), concerning the dove which appears at the baptism of Christ:

> Shall the reader, as he reads of Christ's baptism, understand that the dove which descends to alight upon His head is a *real* dove, or not. It is granted that this *is* the Holy Ghost or an appearance of the Holy Ghost. But what of the *dove*? Is it a real dove (*"verum animal"*) or is it merely the semblance of a dove? [Singleton's emphases]

(133)

For Aquinas, of course, the dove is both the Holy Ghost (or a "visitation" of the Holy Ghost), and it is a "real" dove. Accordingly, Singleton argues that we must be careful to distinguish a form of allegory which is able to differentiate image and reality in a this-for-that relationship, or what Dante calls the "allegory of poets," from a form of allegory which can coalesce them in a this-and-that relationship, or the "allegory of theologians" (131). While centered in the writings of Dante, Singleton's distinction has important epistemological and literary reverberations for Flaubert, as does Aquinas's discussion of the "irreducibility" of the dove at the baptism of Christ. The central issue for Flaubert was not then "the problematics of language," as Barthes would have it (3), although Flaubert was fascinated by syntax to be sure, but rather the creative articulation of an essentially theological, "both/and" (or "this-and-that") approach to objective reality.

Another way of saying this might be that the parrot Loulou, which Félicité "idiotically" mistakes for the dove of the Holy Ghost, is also "irreducible" for Flaubert, like its prototype at the baptism of Christ for Thomas Aquinas (Singleton 135). For this reason, and many others, we may not think of Flaubert as a "postmodern" novelist.[9]

Notes

1. In *Flaubert and Joyce,* for example, Richard K. Cross argues that "there would be little value in a summary rehearsal of connections [between Aquinas and Flaubert]" (185), largely on the basis of his earlier assertion that Joyce's notion of "epiphany" is indistinguishable from "common symbol formation" (22n); or, because Joyce is not really "Thomist" in the first place. While few scholars of the *Summa Theologica* would argue that Joyce does not in some way misread Aquinas, Cross's assertion points to a more problematic assumption underlying his entire book: namely, that an "influence study" is somehow valuable in and of itself, or that the literary scholar's most important task is to verify authorial originality. Umberto Eco in his *The Aesthetics of Chaosmos* and Will-

iam T. Noon in his *Joyce and Aquinas* (the only book-length comparisons of Joyce and Aquinas to date) both acknowledge that Joyce himself "probably never read directly from the texts of Aquinas" (Eco 6). Nevertheless, such comparative studies of Joyce and Aquinas have proven worthwhile and valuable, though the scholars who have ventured in this direction have often found it necessary to proceed on the grounds of homology or analogy rather than through any proof of direct influence. For example, Noon states plainly that "Joyce's 'Thomism' is for the most part a matter of thematic correspondences and general categories or affinities of outlook" (xi). Further, he suggests that "the Thomism in Joyce invites attention to notions and attitudes which could have become operative . . . only to the extent that they were part of the air [Joyce] breathed, which he accepted . . . because they were there, like the mountains around Dublin" (3). The same approach, I believe, can be used fruitfully to study the presence of Thomistic ideas in the work of Gustave Flaubert.

2. Also see my forthcoming review of Susan A. Handelman's *Fragments of Redemption: Jewish Thought and Literary Theory in Benjamin, Scholem, and Levinas* in *Christianity and Literature.*

3. In *The Dossier of Flaubert's "Un Coeur Simple"* (1976), George Willenbrink, editor of the dossier, states "It is quite clear that [Flaubert] was serious about Félicité, about her virtues, about her vision—and did not mean them to be understood in any ironic sense. . . . I find it difficult to understand how anyone can read 'Un Coeur Simple' to the end and still maintain that the parrot is an ironic symbol. There is irony in the story, but not against religion or the church—primarily because Félicité's faith is free of dogma. . . . To be sure, it is a religious statement" (244-47).

4. In the case of Culler, it should not surprise us that a critic who would take *"Down with the priests!"* as his motto for the study of comparative literature would have considerable difficulty understanding the function of the transcendent in Flaubert.

5. The same is also true for Joyce, who will take this medieval notion—that everything in creation has aesthetic potential—to an ultimate extreme when Stephen Dedalus's "green snot" in *Ulysses* serves as an occasion for an epiphany, to name but one example. In his "Pola Notebook" of 1904, Joyce states theoretically what his fictional work only implies: that "every object is beautiful . . . be it a flower, a monster, a moral act, a stone, a table" (Eco, *Chaosmos* 27).

6. Compare Joyce's *Dubliners* and *A Portrait of the Artist as a Young Man,* which were modeled upon

L'éducation sentimentale. In these texts by Joyce, the moment of epiphany has two faces: epistemological realization, leading towards an even more deadening paralysis, or ontological realization leading towards a deeper maturity and spiritual growth.

7. See Cross (65-66).

8. Compare Joyce's use of the basket in *A Portrait of the Artist as a Young Man,* when Stephen Dedalus is discussing Aquinas's aesthetic theories (211-12).

9. Special thanks to Thomas Werge, Robert Griffin, and Reinhold Grimm, who all made helpful comments on earlier versions of this essay.

Works Cited

Barthes, Roland. *Writing Degree Zero.* New York: Hill and Wang, 1968.

Brombert, Victor. "Flaubert and the Status of the Subject." Schor 108-15.

Callahan, John Leonard. *A Theory of Esthetic according to the Principles of St. Thomas Aquinas.* Washington: Catholic U of America P, 1947.

Cross, Richard. *Flaubert and Joyce.* Princeton: Princeton UP, 1971.

Culler, Jonathan. "Comparative Literature and the Pieties." *Profession 86.* New York: MLA, 1986. 30-33.

———. *Flaubert: The Uses of Uncertainty.* Ithaca: Cornell UP, 1975.

Eco, Umberto. *The Aesthetics of Chaosmos.* Tulsa, Oklahoma: U of Tulsa P, 1982.

———. *The Aesthetics of Thomas Aquinas.* Cambridge: Harvard UP, 1988.

Flaubert, Gustave. *Correspondance,* 9 vols. Paris: Louis Conard, 1926-33.

———. *L'éducation sentimentale.* Paris: Garnier, 1964. Cited translation: Anthony Goldsmith, *Sentimental Education.* London: Dent, 1956.

———. *Trois Contes.* Paris: Larousse, 1973. Cited translation: John Gilmer, *Tales from Flaubert.* London: Eveleigh Nash & Grayson, 1928.

Frye, Northrop. *Anatomy of Criticism.* Princeton: Princeton UP, 1957.

Handelman, Susan A. *The Slayers of Moses: The Emergence of Rabbinic Interpretation in Modern Literary Theory.* Albany: SUNY P, 1982.

Jameson, Fredric. "Flaubert's Libidinal Historicism." Schor 76-83.

Joyce, James. *Dubliners.* New York: Viking, 1982.

———. *A Portrait of the Artist as a Young Man.* New York: Viking, 1985.

Maurer, Armand A. *About Beauty: A Thomistic Interpretation.* Houston: Center for Thomistic Studies, U of Saint Thomas P, 1983.

Noon, William T. *Joyce and Aquinas.* New Haven: Yale UP, 1957.

Phelan, Gerald B. "The Concept of Beauty in St. Thomas Aquinas," *G. B. Phelan: Selected Papers.* Toronto: Pontifical Institute of Mediaeval Studies, 1967.

Ramazani, Vaheed K. "Historical Cliché: Irony and the Sublime in *L'éducation sentimentale.*" *PMLA* 108 (1993): 121-35.

———. *The Free Indirect Mode: Flaubert and the Poetics of Irony.* Charlottesville: U of Virginia P, 1988.

Schor, Naomi, ed. *Flaubert and Postmodernism.* Lincoln: U of Nebraska P, 1984.

Singleton, Charles S. "The Irreducible Dove." *Comparative Literature* 9 (1957): 129-35.

Sontag, Susan. Preface. *Writing Degree Zero.* By Roland Barthes. New York: Hill and Wang, 1968.

Stoltzfus, Ben. "Point of View in *Un coeur simple.*" *French Review* 35 (1961). 20-25.

Willenbrink, George, ed. *The Dossier of Flaubert's "Un Coeur Simple."* Amsterdam: Editions Rodopi, 1976.

Nicholas Cronk (essay date fall-winter 1995-96)

SOURCE: Cronk, Nicholas. "Reading 'Un Coeur Simple': The Pleasure of the Intertext." *Nineteenth-Century French Studies* 24, nos. 1-2 (fall-winter 1995-96): 154-61.

[*In the following essay, Cronk explores the function of the allusions associated with the names of the children, Paul and Virginie, in Flaubert's tale "Un Coeur simple."*]

> *So, they took the curator to where they kept the reserve collection. You want a parrot? they said. Then we go to the section of the birds. They opened the door, and they saw in front of them . . . fifty parrots. "Une cinquantaine de perroquets!"*
>
> ———Julian Barnes, *Flaubert's Parrot*

Flaubert's use of *Paul et Virginie* as an element in the structure of **"Un Cœur simple"** is well known. The names of Mme Aubain's children, Paul and Virginie, are explicit pointers to a wide range of implicit allusions: the families in both works live in isolation and are dominated by two women of different social standing; and both works have significant motifs in common: departure by ship; departure to the convent; separation leading to death; a backdrop of sea and storms; and so forth.[1]

Before considering the function of these allusions, it is important to recognize that Flaubert's use of Bernardin de Saint-Pierre in **"Un Cœur simple"** is not confined to *Paul et Virginie,* and that commentators have undervalued the equally important presence in Flaubert's *conte* of *La Chaumière indienne.* Published in 1791, this *conte philosophique* tells the tale of an English doctor who travels the world in search of truth and books. He is disappointed at every turn; he is journeying home from India, by now thoroughly disillusioned, when a violent storm obliges him to seek refuge in the isolated "chaumière indienne" of an outcast. The obvious contentment of the pariah, shunned by his fellow men, but living peacefully with his wife and baby, astonishes his English visitor, who questions him about the path to truth and happiness: "Je pense que tout homme est obligé de chercher la vérité pour son propre bonheur" (287).[2] But since our senses are so liable to mislead us, how should we seek for truth? asks the doctor.

> Je crois, répondit le paria, que c'est avec un cœur simple. Les sens et l'esprit peuvent se tromper; mais un cœur simple, encore qu'il puisse être trompé, ne trompe jamais.
>
> (287-88)

The idea of "un cœur simple" is thus, literally, at the heart of the *conte,* and Bernardin de Saint-Pierre drives it home relentlessly. The phrase occurs eleven times in the central section of the text (287-91), and is repeated once more in the concluding lines of the work (315).

In adopting the key phrase of Bernardin's *conte* as the title of his own, Flaubert seems to be signalling to the reader both the similarities and the differences between Félicité and the pariah. Both protagonists attain a state of wisdom and grace through suffering and unhappiness: "Instruit par le malheur," says the pariah, "jamais je ne refuse mon secours à un plus malheureux que moi" (286), and again, "Je me trouvais moins misérable en voyant que je pouvais faire quelque bien" (295). Where he is articulate and reflective, Félicité appears as "une femme en bois, fonctionnant d'une manière automatique" (45),[3] but she is shown none the less to become more loving as successive blows are dealt to her happiness (her miserable childhood, the betrayal of Théodore, the successive deaths of Victor, Virginie, Loulou, and her mistress): "La bonté de son cœur se développa" (66). They both ultimately achieve a sense of inner happiness by keeping themselves at a distance from human society, Félicité becoming deaf and then

blind, the pariah living in his isolated home: the echoes of Rousseau are unmistakable. There is one crucial difference between them, however: Félicité ends her life completely isolated from all human contact, whereas the pariah lives with his wife and child, a point reiterated in the closing sentence of the *conte:*

> "Il faut chercher la vérité avec un cœur simple; on ne la trouve que dans la nature; on ne doit la dire qu'aux gens de bien." A quoi il ajoutait: "On n'est heureux qu'avec une bonne femme."
>
> (315-16)

Both perform acts of charity: the pariah not only offers hospitality to the Englishman but also gives firewood and food to the latter's entourage, even though they despise him:

> "Homme vertueux, lui dit l'anglais, vous valez beaucoup mieux que moi, puisque vous faites du bien à ceux qui vous méprisent."
>
> (283)

Félicité is similarly charitable and, bearing out a remark of the pariah's to the effect that greater misery brings greater enlightenment, she becomes increasingly selfless in her devotion to others: her initial acts of generosity are towards Victor and Virginie, and after they are taken from her, she helps cholera victims, offers protection to Polish refugees, and finally cares for le père Colmiche, horribly disfigured by cancer and living in a pigsty.

Both characters live in close harmony with nature: Félicité protects her mistress and children from a bull, the pariah protects his family from the dangers of the forest; and both are closely attached to an animal, Félicité to the parrot, the pariah to his dog, "un compagnon inséparable" (305). Since both Félicité and the pariah are illiterate, both are invulnerable to the noxious influence of books such as those that the English doctor is so busy collecting; and both experience Rousseauesque disappointment in their encounters with town or city: for the pariah, Delhi is associated with religious superstition and political terror; for Félicité, frenzied visits to Honfleur presage the departure of Victor and later the death of Virginie. The seemingly innocent remark at the beginning of **"Un Cœur simple"** that in all seasons Félicité wears "un mouchoir d'indienne" (44) is a sure clue to her literary parentage.[4]

Flaubert's knowledge and strategic use of *La Chaumière indienne* should not surprise us. He was interested in the genre of the *conte philosophique,* and in the years 1845-54 had meditated writing a "conte oriental" about seven sons of a dervish each in search of happiness.[5] Flaubert was an admirer of Voltaire's *contes,* and *Bouvard et Pécuchet,* begun before **"Un Cœur simple"** and finished after it, is, in his own phrase, a "roman philosophique" that has clear echoes of *Candide.*[6] *La*

Chaumière indienne was obviously well known to Flaubert, and, more to the point, it was very well known to the first readers of **"Un Cœur simple."** When Flaubert writes to Ernest Chevalier, "Je crois, comme le Paria de Bernardin de Saint-Pierre, que le bonheur se trouve avec une bonne femme . . ." (9 April 1851),[7] he knows there is no need to explain the allusion to his correspondent. *Paul et Virginie,* constantly reprinted in the nineteenth century, was frequently published together with *La Chaumière indienne,* the two titles conjoined on the title-page: thus Flaubert's first readers would have automatically associated the two texts.[8] In the twentieth century, *La Chaumière indienne* has hardly ever been reprinted, and it has disappeared from the canon; modern readers—and editors—are no longer receptive to allusions that for the readers of 1877 were transparent.

The critics who have acknowledged the presence of *Paul et Virginie* in **"Un Cœur simple"** have said little about Flaubert's underlying purpose. Showalter contents himself with describing **"Un Cœur simple"** as an "ironic reply" to Bernardin de Saint-Pierre; Gevrey rightly contests this view, and describes with much greater subtlety the range of links between the two texts. Her conclusion, though, is disappointing:

> On voit donc comment Flaubert reprend et transforme des scènes ou des motifs essentiels de *Paul et Virginie.* . . . Les marges des scénarios qui appellent des distinctions, les abandons de scènes trop proches, prouvent que Flaubert était conscient de ces ressemblances harmoniques.
>
> (278, 284)

Flaubert could hardly have been unaware of the similarities between the two works: his choice of the names Paul and Virginie for the children of Mme Aubain is a deliberate allusion, as is his use of the pivotal phrase of *La Chaumière indienne* as the title of his story. What is interesting here is not Flaubert's treatment of Bernardin as a "source," but his appropriation of Bernardin as a means to prod and manipulate the reader, a strategy which is only possible because Flaubert could be certain that his readers could not fail to recognize the allusions to (among other works . . .) *Paul et Virginie* and *La Chaumière indienne.*

There may be some doubt about how a nineteenth-century reader would have responded to Virginie (though Emma Bovary's reaction when she reads *Paul et Virginie*—at the age of twelve—is possibly more typical than some critics are willing to admit). But there is precious little ambiguity about *La Chaumière indienne* (which is one reason why, unlike *Paul et Virginie,* it has not retained its place in the canon): the pariah is presented as an unproblematic paragon of virtue, and there is nothing in the text to undermine either his be-

liefs or his actions. The second half of the story, the part that deals with the pariah, is utterly devoid of irony. This affects directly our response to Félicité: the parallels between her and the pariah are so carefully built up that our knowledge of his character colors our reading of hers. Is she too being proposed to us as an unambivalent model of piety?

The interpretation of Félicité's character is at the heart of any reading of the text, and is connected with the long-standing critical debate about the function of irony in the work. Flaubert famously remarked in a letter to Mme Roger des Genettes that his intentions in **"Un Cœur simple"** were anything but ironic:

> Cela n'est nullement ironique comme vous le supposez, mais au contraire très sérieux et très triste. Je veux apitoyer, faire pleurer les âmes sensibles, en étant une moi-même.
>
> (19 June 1876)

Many commentators have expressed skepticism about this claim, and the intertextual link between Félicité and the pariah only complicates the question further: in underscoring the similarities, is Flaubert emphasizing or denying the differences?

Intertextual resonances will always resist the attempts of the reader to control and contain them: thus if Félicité echoes the pariah, she also echoes other fictional characters, among them la Grande Nanon in *Eugénie Grandet* (1833) and Geneviève in Lamartine's *Geneviève: Histoire d'une servante* (1851). The opening sentence of **"Un Cœur simple"**—"Pendant un demi-siècle, les bourgeoises de Pont-l'Evêque envièrent à Mme Aubain sa servante Félicité" (45)—is already a quotation of Balzac's novel:

> La Grande Nanon était peut-être la seule créature humaine capable d'accepter le despotisme de son maître. Toute la ville l'enviait à M. et à Mme Grandet.
>
> (1041)[9]

Nanon, like Félicité, lives a frugal and pious life in the service of others; she has no husband (until the end); she loves children; she has a close empathy with animals (1069); and she is described as having "le cœur simple" (1043).

Geneviève similarly leads a life of exemplary self-sacrifice and devotion to others. Like Félicité, she loses one by one the human beings who care for her most: her brother is taken away by the army, her invalid mother, to whom her entire childhood is sacrificed, dies; her father dies of grief; she has, like Félicité, a close attachment to her nephew, and like her she has "son histoire d'amour," but sacrifices her fiancé for the sake of her young sister; she later finds contentment serving a parish priest, who dies young. Both women outlive the mistress or master they have served faithfully, and witness the dismantling of the house they have cared for. At a time of grief, her life is described as "une vie machinale" (82),[10] recalling the description of Félicité, "fonctionnant d'une manière automatique" (45); both women are described as being ageless. Both lead lives of simple piety, both perform signal acts of charity, Geneviève tending the sick in the same way as Félicité. *Paul et Virginie* is invoked as a work of moral edification (31) and, in a clear echo of *La Chaumière indienne,* the narrator declares the need to write for "les simples de cœur" (36), and applies to Geneviève variously the phrases "simplicité du cœur" (112), "le cœur simple" (188), "ce cœur simple" (309), and "ces coeurs simples" (355). Like Félicité, Geneviève is portrayed as a child of nature with a close understanding of animals, and a number of details prefigure Félicité's attachment to Loulou: Mlle Reine Garde, the "real" servant whose visit to Lamartine is described in the framing narrative, writes a poem about her sense of loss on the death of her pet goldfinch (23); Geneviève, working for a miser (a descendant of Grandet), finds solace in a pet lamb and a dog whose name, Loulou, shows him to be a direct ancestor of Félicité's parrot (255).

By the second half of the century, the virtuous and devoted servant—"La servante au grand cœur dont vous étiez jalouse" of Baudelaire's "Tableaux parisiens"—had become a literary topos; Flaubert had already exploited it in *Madame Bovary* in the character of Catherine Leroux.[11] But the existence of these various intertexts complicates our reaction to Félicité. Nanon, who devotes her life to her miserly master, and Geneviève, who endures social humiliation for the sake of her dead sister's honor, are in no sense ironized. Their exemplary lives of self-denial, like that of the pariah, generate an aura of Rousseauesque sentiment, and like him, both servants end up living in the society of a family, and so may be said to reap the reward ultimately for their sacrifices. This makes our understanding of Félicité all the more problematic. The manifest parallels with Nanon and Geneviève serve on the one hand to underline the fundamental piety of the character; and on the other to throw into relief the unprecedented solitude in which Félicité finds herself at the end of her life.

Similar intertextual challenges beset the parrot, of course, and they further complicate, and enhance, our reading of the conte. Readers of the 1870s would have been well acquainted with Gresset's *Ver-Vert* (1734) and Parny's *La Guerre des Dieux anciens et modernes* (1799), two works that, like *La Chaumière indienne,* were constantly reprinted in the nineteenth century, and that have both since vanished from the canon. *La Guerre des Dieux,* quoted drunkenly by M. Bovary *père* at Berthe's baptism to antagonize the priest, is an anti-Christian satire that features the Holy Ghost as a "divin pigeon"; *Ver-Vert,* a comic-heroic poem, tells the story

of a parrot, "un perroquet dévot," lovingly nurtured by the nuns of Nevers, who on a boat trip to Nantes learns some shockingly earthy vocabulary from his fellow passengers and has to be punished: the scene recalls the efforts of the butcher's boy Fabut to teach swear-words to Loulou (68). The only direct speech attributed to Loulou are the words taught him by Félicité: "Charmant garçon! Serviteur, monsieur! Je vous salue, Marie!" (68); Ver-Vert's only reported utterance is "Ave, ma sœur," taught him by the nuns. Ver-Vert is killed by the devotion of the sisters who overfeed him, and the description of his ascent to join the ranks of other "héros perroquets" in the sacred groves of Elysium is described with a religious fervor that anticipates, in a different register—or is it?—, the closing lines of **"Un Cœur simple."** Félicité's parrot would surely have put Flaubert's early readers in mind of these satirical eighteenth-century predecessors. They might even have remembered a remark of the pariah in *La Chaumière indienne*: "Les hommes s'instruisent comme les perroquets" (293).

These intertexts further complicate our response to Félicité, for even if her literary forebears are all exemplary models of unironized virtue, we can hardly discount the relevance of the parrot's pedigree in Enlightenment anti-Christian satire. And there are, of course, other intertexts for the parrot: for example, the motif common in painting of woman and parrot as a symbol of erotic desire (already used by Banville in "La Femme au perroquet," one of the *Camées Parisiens* published in 1873) gives a particular slant to Félicité's emotional isolation.[12]

The problematic presence of irony in **"Un Cœur simple"** is connected with the debate about whether or not Flaubert conceived the *conte* as a response to the criticisms of George Sand. It is probably relevant that Flaubert's denial of ironic intent (cited above) is followed in the very next sentence by a description of his grief at George Sand's funeral a few days earlier. Shortly before her death, Flaubert wrote to Sand:

> Vous verrez par mon *Histoire d'un cœur simple* où vous reconnaîtrez votre influence immédiate que je ne suis pas si entêté que vous le croyez. Je crois que la tendence morale, ou plutôt le dessous humain de cette petite œuvre vous sera agréable!
>
> (29 May 1876)

And to her son Maurice Sand, after her death, he wrote:

> Vous me parlez de votre chère et illustre maman! Après vous, je ne crois pas que quelqu'un puisse y penser plus que moi! Comme je la regrette! Comme j'en ai besoin!
>
> J'avais commencé **"Un Cœur simple"** à son intention exclusive, uniquement pour lui plaire. Elle est morte, comme j'étais au milieu de mon œuvre.

Il en est ainsi de tous nos rêves.

(29 August 1877)

Not all commentators even agree that Flaubert was, as he here claims, writing for George Sand.[13] The couple's differences over the moral function of literature, like their differing estimations of Rousseau,[14] had been well aired over the years: "Toi à coup sûr, tu vas faire de la désolation," she wrote to him, "et moi de la consolation" (18 and 19 December 1875). Yet if any reader was likely to be so sensitive to the parallels between Félicité and the pariah that he or she might overlook more potentially satirical intertexts, it was surely George Sand, and for a specific reason: she herself had made Bernardin de Saint-Pierre a pivotal intertext of *Indiana* (1832), the first novel published under her own name, and the novel that had established her reputation. The heroine of this work is stifled by Europe and by marriage, and a string of references to *Paul et Virginie* operate as a kind of emotional and cultural counterpoint to the central theme.[15] A reference to "les parias" (322) evokes Bernardin's *conte*, reinforced by the closing words of the novel:

—Adieu, me dirent-ils, retournez au monde; si quelque jour il vous bannit, souvenez-vous de notre chaumière indienne.

(344)

George Sand could only be flattered by the fact that Flaubert, in making *La Chaumière indienne* the starting point of his own story, was imitating her example.

"Un Cœur simple" thus has a curiously complex intertextual relationship with *Indiana*. Both works are steeped in the writing of the eighteenth century, though in different and rival traditions: *Indiana* evokes Rousseauesque feeling and looks back to *La Nouvelle Héloïse* in its portrayal of an emotional triangle, while **"Un Cœur simple,"** with its echoes of Gresset and Parny, is closer to the satirical tradition of Voltaire; yet notwithstanding these differences, both narratives rely crucially on allusion to *Paul et Virginie* and *La Chaumière indienne*.

Flaubert famously disliked didactic writing, and in a letter to the author Ernest Feydeau, he cites Rousseau and George Sand as examples of writers who "preach":

Tu tiens à établir tes idées, et tu prêches souvent. Tu me diras que c'est exprès, tu as tort, voilà tout; tu gâtes l'harmonie de ton livre, tu rentres dans la manie de presque tous les écrivains français, Jean-Jacques, George Sand; tu manques aux principes, tu n'as plus en vue le Beau et l'éternel Vrai.

(4 January 1859)[16]

Intertextuality is a powerful (dialogic) means of correcting this tendency of literature to preach (to be monologic). "L'intertextualité est donc une machine

perturbante," writes Laurent Jenny: "Il s'agit de ne pas laisser le sens en repos—de conjurer le triomphe du cliché par un travail transformateur" (279). Flaubert, whose use of intertextuality unsettles our commonplace responses both to his text and to his intertexts, alludes to this dilemma, and by implication to the necessity of intertextuality, in a well-known letter to George Sand: "Tout le problème est là. Être troubadour sans être bête. Faire beau tout en restant vrai" (3 June 1874).

Notes

1. For more detailed comparisons, see Françoise Gevrey, "*Paul et Virginie* et *Un Cœur simple*: résonances d'une 'humble pastorale' dans un conte 'bonhomme'" 267-84. See also English Showalter, Jr., "*Un Cœur simple* as an Ironic Reply to Bernardin de Saint-Pierre" 47-55; and Phillip A. Duncan, "Paul and Virginie/Flaubert and Bernardin" 436-38.

2. References to *La Chaumière indienne* are to Bernardin de Saint-Pierre's *Œuvres complètes,* Vol. 6.

3. References to *Un Cœur simple* are to the Garnier-Flammarion edition of the *Trois Contes* by Pierre-Marc de Biasi.

4. The present article is concerned specifically with *Un Cœur simple*; but it would be fruitful to read *Une Chaumière indienne* as an intertext for the *Trois contes* as a whole.

5. See Jean Bruneau, *Le "Conte oriental" de Flaubert.*

6. See Helen G. Zagona, *Flaubert's "Roman philosophique" and the Voltairian Heritage. Bouvard et Pécuchet,* like *Un Cœur simple,* may similarly be read as a response to *Paul et Virginie*: see Normand Lalonde, "*Bouvard et Pécuchet,* poème bucolique" 162, note 13.

7. Quotations of correspondence are from Gustave Flaubert, *Œuvres complètes,* and *Gustave Flaubert-George Sand: Correspondance,* edited by Alphonse Jacobs.

8. See the list of editions in the Classiques Garnier edition of *Paul et Virginie,* edited by P. Trahard, revised by E. Guitton 263-83; they identify over thirty joint editions of *Paul et Virginie* and *La Chaumière indienne* in the years 1823-1877. The pairing of the two works makes particular sense in the light of the suggestion that they need to be read in juxtaposition: see Roseann Runte, "*La Chaumière indienne*: counterpart and complement to *Paul* et Virginie" 774-80.

9. References to *Eugénie Grandet* are to the Pléiade edition of *La Comédie humaine,* Vol. 3.

10. References to Lamartine's *Geneviève: Histoire d'une servante* are to the first edition (Paris: Lévy, 1851).

11. Flaubert had also created a servant figure, Berthe, in his unpublished *Rage et impuissance* (written in 1836). Other examples of the topos of the devoted servant include, from Louise Colet's *Le Poème de la femme, La Paysanne* (1853) and *La Servante* (1854), and the Goncourt brothers' *Sœur Philomène* (1861) and *Germinie Lacerteux* (1865). Millet's much-acclaimed *Les Glaneuses* and *L'Angélus* date from the late 1850s. On the intertextual connections between the works cited above and *Un Cœur simple,* see Un Cœur simple, edited by Silvia Douyère 33-42; Alison Fairlie, "La contradiction créatrice: quelques remarques sur la genèse d'*Un Cœur simple*" 203-31; M. F. Daví Trimarchi, "Lamartine, Balzac, Flaubert: una serva" 293-309; and Raymonde Debray Genette, "Simplex et Simplicissima: de Nanon à Félicité" 229-46.

12. The erotic topos of woman and parrot originated in seventeenth-century art, and was used by, for example, G. B. Tiepolo in the eighteenth century; in the nineteenth century it is found in famous paintings by Delacroix, Courbet and Manet, as well as in countless less famous portraits (for example, by Alexandre Cabanel); there is an erotic daguerreotype, c. 1855, on the same theme (see Stefan Richter, *The Art of the Daguerreotype* 95). Philippe Bonnefis considers this motif in "Exposition d'un perroquet" 59-78; see also the discussions on this topic in *French Studies Bulletin,* Nos 35 (1990), 36 (1990), 39 (1991), 40 (1991) and 47 (1993).

13. For example: "Après coup seulement, son plan déjà bien établi et la première partie de la texte écrite, il se rend compte de la joie que doit éprouver sa 'chère maître' à la lecture de cette tendre histoire" (Jacobs 12).

14. See Joachim Merlant, *Un Entretien inconnu de Flaubert et de George Sand sur Rousseau.*

15. See George Sand, *Indiana,* ed. by Béatrice Didier, 77, 94, 101, 256, 318, 319, 320 and 342.

16. In the Pléiade edition of the *Correspondance,* Jean Bruneau corrects the date of this letter to 28 December 1858.

Works Cited

Balzac, Honoré de. *Eugénie Grandet. La Comédie humaine.* Ed. Pierre-Georges Castex. Biblithèque de la Pléiade. Vol. 3. Paris: Gallimard, 1976. 12 vols.

Bernardin de Saint-Pierre, Jacques-Henri. *La Chaumière indienne. Œuvres complètes.* Vol. 6. Paris: Méquignon-Marvis, 1818. 12 vols.

———. *Paul et Virginie.* Ed. P. Trahard, revised by E. Guitton. Classiques Garnier. Paris: Bordas, 1989.

Bonnefis, Philippe. "Exposition d'un perroquet." *Revue des Sciences Humaines* 53 (1981): 59-78.

Bruneau, Jean. *Le "Conte oriental" de Flaubert.* Paris: Denoël, 1973.

Daví Trimarchi, Maria Francesca. "Lamartine, Balzac, Flaubert: una serva." *Flaubert e il Pensiero del suo Secolo.* Messina, 1985. 293-309.

Debray-Genette, Raymonde. "Simplex et Simplicissima: de Nanon à Félicité." *Mimesis et Semiosis, littérature et représentation: miscellanées offertes à Henri Mitterand.* Eds. Philippe Hamon and Jean-Pierre Leduc-Adine. Paris: Nathan, 1992. 229-46.

Duncan, Phillip A. "Paul and Virginie/Flaubert and Bernardin." *Studies in Short Fiction* 24 (1987): 436-38.

Fairlie, Alison. "La contradiction créatrice: quelques remarques sur la genèse d'*Un Cœur simple*." *Essais sur Flaubert: En l'honneur du professeur Don Demorest.* Ed. Charles Carlut. Paris: Nizet, 1979. 203-31.

Flaubert, Gustave. *Œuvres complètes.* Paris: Club de l'Honnête homme, 1971-75. 15 vols.

———. *Trois Contes.* Ed. Pierre-Marc de Biasi. Paris: Flammarion, 1986.

———. *Un Cœur simple.* Ed. Silvia Douyère. Paris: Pensée universelle, 1974.

French Studies Bulletin. Nos 35 (1990), 36 (1990), 39 (1991), 40 (1991) and 47 (1993).

Gevrey, Françoise. "*Paul et Virginie* et *Un Cœur simple*: résonances d'une 'humble pastorale' dans un conte 'bonhomme'." *Travaux de littérature* 5 (1992): 267-84.

Jacobs, Alphonse, ed. *Gustave Flaubert—George Sand: Correspondance.* Paris: Flammarion, 1981.

Jenny, Laurent. "La stratégie de la forme." *Poétique* 27 (1976): 257-81.

Lalonde, Normand. "*Bouvard et Pécuchet,* poéme bucolique." *French Studies* 49 (1995): 155-63.

Lamartine, Alphonse. *Geneviève: Histoire d'une servante.* Paris: Lévy, 1851.

Merlant, Joachim. *Un Entretien inconnu de Flaubert et de George Sand sur Rousseau.* Montpellier: Coulet, 1912.

Richter, Stefan. *The Art of the Daguerreotype.* Harmondsworth: Viking, 1989.

Runte, Roseann. "*La Chaumière indienne*: Counterpart and Complement to Paul et Virginie." *Modern Language Review* 75 (1980): 774-80.

Sand, George. *Indiana.* Ed. Béatrice Didier. Folio. Paris: Gallimard, 1984.

Showalter, Jr., English. *"Un Cœur simple* as an Ironic Reply to Bernardin de Saint-Pierre." *French Review* 40 (1966): 47-55.

Zagona, Helen G. *Flaubert's "Roman philosophique" and the Voltairian Heritage.* Lanham: UP of America, 1985.

Ron E. Scrogham (essay date April 1998)

SOURCE: Scrogham, Ron E. "The Echo of the Name 'Iaokanann' in Flaubert's 'Hérodias.'" *The French Review* 71, no. 5 (April 1998): 775-84.

[*In the following essay, Scrogham emphasizes the concept of naming in the tale "Hérodias," citing specifically how it functions as a device of echo, identity, and reciprocity.*]

Flaubert's **"Hérodias"** closely follows the Gospel-record of the events that precede and culminate in the decollation of saint Jean-Baptiste, with the notable exception of the form of the saint's name. While Hérode Antipas surveys Machærous and its environs from the terrace of his palace, a voice rings out, breaking the silence of the early dawn:

> —Où est-il? demanda le Tétrarque.
>
> Mannaëi répondit, en indiquant avec son pouce un objet derrière eux:
>
> —Là! toujours!
>
> —J'avais cru l'entendre!
>
> Et Antipas, quand il eut respiré largement, s'informa de Iaokanann, le même que les Latins appellent saint Jean-Baptiste.
>
> (4: 255)

Although the narrator of **"Hérodias"** explicitly identifies this thoroughly familiar figure, who appears in a virtual reproduction of one of the most famous biblical stories, as saint Jean-Baptiste, this character persists throughout **"Hérodias"** with the unfamiliar name "Iaokanann." Flaubert insists upon this conspicuous name in order to represent the reflexivity that the process of naming entails. The utterance of "Iaokanann" acts as an echo, simultaneously identifying the character Iaokanann and, reciprocally, those who name him, as an echo simultaneously identifies its source and itself.

Naming reciprocally identifies the one who names and the one who is named. If a name reflects, at its most basic level, an assignment of a category of knowledge, then a name reveals both the nature of the one who belongs to this category—the named—and that of the one whose thinking uses such a category—the one who names. The name that a parent gives to a newborn child exemplifies a conscious reciprocity in naming. Except for the indication of gender, the name reflects the parent more than the child, inasmuch as it continues a family tradition, honors some dear person or principle, or expresses an expectation for the future. The pharmacist Homais in *Madame Bovary* chooses for his children names which "rappelaient un grand homme, un fait illustre ou une conception généreuse" (1: 125). For Homais, the names of his children: Napoléon, Franklin, Irma, and Athalie, serve as deliberate emblems to the world of his own character. However, when no acknowledgment of self-identification occurs in the process of naming, a self-alienation follows which results in misdirected actions bringing about undesired ends—a condition endemic to **"Hérodias."**

The form of the name "Iaokanann," which focuses this process of reciprocal identification, receives scant treatment among the commentators. Benjamin Bart, when speaking of **"Hérodias,"** reports that "Flaubert always referred to it as 'Saint John,' or 'Iaokanann,' the Semitic form which it amused him to use" (699); a suggestion which reveals the novelty of the name, but not its significance. Helen Zagona considers it to be a "particular adaptation of the Hebrew spelling (Yohanan) . . . preferred by Flaubert as the one which would contribute most to the evocation of Judaic atmosphere" (72, note 15). For Zagona, this form of the name acts as a "Parnassian device" that evokes an exoticism and an ancient past which flavor the tale in much the same way as the elaborate descriptions of architecture, dress, and food (72, note 15). John O'Connor describes the name as a device that distances the tale from any certain interpretative framework. According to O'Connor, when the narrator identifies Iaokanann as "'le même que les Latins appellent saint Jean-Baptiste,' . . . the narrator, by specifically identifying himself as a non-Latin, characterizes his point of view as innocent of any Christian intent, perhaps of any identifiable frame of interpretative reference whatsoever" (822). The name serves to distance this Iaokanann of **"Hérodias"** from that saint Jean-Baptiste in the Gospels of Mark and Matthew, leaving the reader to make any interpretative superposition of the referent character onto the tale. Although these glosses of the name do go far in identifying its Semitic form, its contribution to the atmosphere of **"Hérodias"** and its functional value in distancing the tale from its referent, they do not adequately explain the conspicuous form of this name and its function within the tale.

The conspicuousness of this name results from its dissimilarity from models of the name in the sources for **"Hérodias"** and from the evolution of the name through the manuscripts to the published version. Flaubert does not follow Renan, who, in *La Vie de Jésus,* a source for **"Hérodias"** (Burns 324), describes "un certain Iohanan ou Jean, jeune ascète plein de fougue et de passion"

(Zagona 75). Although "Iohanan" is the transliterated Hebrew word for "Jean," Flaubert modifies this name; his "Iaokanann" more closely, but not exactly, resembles "Iochanan," another form of "Iohanan." C. A. Burns notes that in the last manuscript of **"Hérodias"** written in Flaubert's hand and in the version prepared by a copyist, both have the name as "Ioakanam"; whereas, the first edition of **Trois Contes** has it as "Iaokanann" (314). That earlier form does approximate "Iochanan"; however, in the final edition Flaubert presents a form of the name seemingly crafted for an original effect.

Any possible nuance of meaning, which would favor one form of the name over another, finds no etymological support. "Iohanan" and its derivative "Iochanan" both mean "Yah has shown favor"; a meaning which persists in the transliterated Greek form of "Jean" 'Ioannes,' which appears in the Gospels. If "Iaokanann" does etymologically differ from these Semitic and Greek forms of "Jean" the text does not illustrate that difference. Iaokanann appears as "favored by Yah": he speaks as one of his prophets (4: 266); Jacob, whose daughter has been miraculously healed by Jésus, identifies Iaokanann as Élie, the one who announces the Messiah (4: 271); the jailers find the serpents dead that they introduced into Iaokanann's cell, while he remains unharmed (4: 258). The character of Iaokanann functions in the tale in a manner consistent with the etymology of his name, and, therefore, the significance of "Iaokanann" lies within its form rather than its meaning.

In the choice of proper names, a concern for euphony has precedence in **"Hérodias,"** as Zagona confirms: "A letter from Clermont-Ganneau indicates that his [Flaubert's] search for desired rhythmic effects led him at times to inquire into Hebrew and Arabic names with an interest principally in the number of syllables they contained" (78). The sound of **"Hérodias,"** as it is read aloud, interests Flaubert greatly. Israel-Pelletier, referring to Flaubert's correspondence concerning **"Hérodias,"** states that Flaubert "did praise its quality as a great *gueulade,* a term by which he meant that the tale read well out loud, a quality that he always attributed to the superior work of art" (104). Euphony alone does not determine the final form of "Iaokanann," whose pronunciation and rhythm hardly vary from the "Ioakanam" of the copyist's version, except for the final syllable. This modification from "am" to "ann" indicates the significance of the final form of the name.

The name "Iaokanann," in contrast to the other possible names, exhibits the formal quality of an echo. Within the name "Iaokanann," an "an" repeats in the penultimate and ultimate syllables, followed by the repetition of the consonant "n." This "echo" of the sound [an] appears deliberate based on the evidence of the changed spelling of the name from "Ioakanam" in the manuscripts to "Iaokanann" in the final edition. The possible

Semitic forms from which Flaubert may have derived this name do end in "anan" ("Iohanan" and "Iochanan"); however, none end in that final termination "nn." The repetition of the consonant "n" (a visual "echo") prevents any possible nasalization that might occur with the French pronunciation of the transliterated "Iohanan" or "Iochanan." The "anann" of "Iaokanann" ensures an exact reproduction of sound and, thereby, formalizes an echo.[1]

The name "Iaokanann" associates audibly the phenomenon of an echo to the character Iaokanann. The pronunciation of "Iaokanann" builds at the plosive consonant "k," after which follows the repeated sound "an"—an overall effect which onomatopoetically evokes the thunderclap and echo that Iaokanann's voice resembles: "La voix grossissait, se développait, roulait avec des déchirements de tonnerre, et, l'écho dans la montagne la répétant, elle foudroyait Machærous d'éclats multipliés" (4: 267). On the terrace of Antipas's palace, the voice repeats itself, either from Iaokanann crying out again, or from the echo of his cry, or from Hérode's tormented imagination: "Tout à coup, une voix lointaine, comme échappée des profondeurs de la terre, fit pâlir le tétrarque. Il se pencha pour écouter; elle avait disparu. *Elle reprit* [emphasis added]" (4: 254). The delay ("elle avait disparu"), that separates the initial outburst from its repetition gives the effect of an echo, no matter the source of the repeated cry.

The name "Iaokanann" does not sound without being echoed by those who hear it. When Mannaëi removes the cover of the subterranean cell so that Vitellius may see "le trésor d'Hérode": "La voix s'éleva:—Malheur à vous, Pharisiens et Sadducéens, race de vipère, outres gonflées, cymbales retentissantes! On avait reconnu Iaokanann. Son nom circulait" (4: 265). The crowd repeats his name, as the mountains echo the thunderclap. In the same diatribe, as Iaokanann unleashes his torrent of curses against Antipas, the interpreter for Vitellius "d'un ton impassible, redisait, dans la langue des Romains, toutes les injures que Iaokanann rugissait dans la sienne. Le Tétrarque et Hérodias étaient forcés de les subir deux fois" (4: 266). Unlike Vitellius, Antipas and Hérodias understand both the original expression of Iaokanann's imprecations and its translation. They suffer doubly because the translation echoes these insults.

Salomés fatal demand of the head of the prophet appears as an echo of her mother's utterance of his name. Gérard Genette notices that the exchange between mother and daughter, which appears in the Gospel of Mark as: "'What shall I ask?' And she [Hérodias] said, 'The head of John the baptizer'" (6: 24-25), remains conspicuously absent from **"Hérodias"** (199-201). Instead, a "claquement de doigts" (4: 275) summons Salomé to Hérodias on the fringes of the banquet hall. The location of this scene offstage delays the sounding of Iaokanann's name before the expectant gathering. Salomé's inability to remember Iaokanann's name when demanding his head of Antipas ("Elle avait oublié le nom, mais reprit en souriant: 'La tête de Iaokanann!'" [4: 275]), prolongs even more this delay. The reader familiar with the Gospel account already knows which name has been spoken, but it doubly tarries in reaching the ears of Antipas, just like an echo delays sounding when its source is far removed from those who eventually hear it.

"Iaokanann" exemplifies reflexivity by the audible and figurative echoes heard in the name's utterance. The repetition of sound in the name formalizes the self-identification of a physical echo. Unlike the mirror, which spatially inverts the reflected object, the echo, indistinguishable from its source-sound, does not disorient its reflection. It has a dual existence: an independent one, as a sound itself, and a dependent one, as a representation of a sound. The echo, *qua* echo, necessarily refers to some source (which, too, can be an echo), which is, nonetheless, identical to the echo. A self-identification ensues from this forward and backward reference from the sound to the echo and from the echo to the sound.

The self-identification of the physical echo serves as an analogy of the reciprocal identification inherent in naming. The name "Iaokanann" identifies both the character bearing it—echo as a sound itself—and those characters who pronounce this name—echo as representation of a sound. When the characters in **"Hérodias"** say "Iaokanann," they make both a literal and figurative echo. The figurative echo represents the relationship between the one who names and the one who is named. The self-effacement of Iaokanann, consistent with his role as messenger of the divine, contrasts with the diverse and definite representations of his identity by others. The naming of Iaokanann elicits various associations that "echo" the multiple perspectives of those who name, the otherwise monotone, Iaokanann. The identifications of Iaokanann and the reciprocal identifications are no more separable than the thunder from its echo.

When Iaokanann curses the Pharisees and Sadducees, when he complains of the licentiousness of the people, when he prophesies the impending judgment, "On avait reconnu Iaokanann. Son nom circulait" (4: 265). The people realize that: "C'étaient les paroles des anciens prophètes" (4: 266). Iaokanann repeats quite literally the words of the ancient prophets as Joyce Cannon reports: "In addition to the Gospels Flaubert studied the Prophets and the Psalms, mostly for the purpose of putting into John's mouth the abuse which he directs at Hérodias. In fact John's language reproduces whole passages of the Bible, and particularly of Isaiah" (333). As Old Testament prophet to these people, Iaokanann complains in a familiar fashion of their obstinacy, at-

tacks the godlessness of their oppressors, and promises a prosperous future. The reciprocal identification which follows from Iaokanann being one of the ancient prophets is that these people must be that stiff-necked, idolatrous people of old. Vitellius, a non-partisan observer of the religious practices of the Jews confirms this atavistic identification of these people: "Leur dieu pouvait bien être Moloch, dont il avait rencontré des autels sur la route" (4: 274). Iaokanann cannot be Elijah or Isaiah for them, unless the reciprocal be true as well—they are the exiled, subjugated, and oppressed Israelites.

The people do not see themselves as Iaokanann and Vitellius see them. As Iaokanann recites the words of the prophets of old, "Le peuple revoyait les jours de son exil, toutes les catastrophes de son histoire" (4: 266). This nostalgic reminiscence seems paradoxical, inasmuch as the current occupation of their homeland, and their status as oppressed subjects of Rome, differ little from those exiles of the past. Perhaps the current situation becomes even more bitter because the Jews remain exiles in their own land. Furthermore, the internecine conflict, concerning the right to the "sacrificature" (4: 261), and the quick desertion of this ancient prophet when his influence causes too much discomfort: "—Il dérange tout! dit Jonathas.—On n'aura plus d'argent, s'il continue! ajoutèrent les Pharisiens. Et des récriminations partaient . . ." (4: 273), mirror that feckless people of old. By identifying Iaokanann as one of the ancient prophets, the people identify themselves as well. By failing to acknowledge this self-identification, they reprise the role of the ancient people, while remaining unaware of their complicity in the situation in Machærous.

The further identification of Iaokanann as Elie resonates particularly for Antipas and Hérodias. At the feast of Antipas, during a discussion among the guests about the coming of the Messiah, Éléazar contends that the Messiah cannot have appeared in the person of Jésus because ". . . il devait être précédé de la venue d'Élie;" to which "Jacob répliqua:—Mais il est venu, Élie! . . .—Son nom? Alors, il cria de toutes ses forces:—Iaokanann!" (4: 271). While weighing Salomé's request for the head of Iaokanann and remembering Phanuel's ominous prophecy of the impending death "d'un homme considérable" (4: 268) that night in Machærous, Antipas entertains the possible consequences of Iaokanann being Élie: "Si Iaokanann était véritablement Élie, il pourrait s'y soustraire; s'il ne l'était pas, le meurtre n'avait plus d'importance" (4: 276). If, however, Iaokanann is Élie, then Antipas and Hérodias fail to notice the consequence of this identification; namely, that they are respectively Achab and Iézabel—two of the most infamous characters in the Old Testament.

Iaokanann attacks Antipas and his position as ruler thus: "Iaokanann l'invectiva pour sa royauté.—'Il n'y a pas d'autre roi que l'Éternel!' et pour ses jardins, pour ses statues, pour ses meubles d'ivoire, comme impie Achab!" (4: 266). Similarly, upon seeing Hérodias, Iaokanann cries out: "Ah! c'est toi, Iézabel!" (4: 266). In this instance, the reflexivity of the process of identification, as exemplified by the echo, becomes apparent. If Iaokanann names Antipas and Hérodias as Achab and Iézabel respectively, then, reciprocally, he is Élie. Like the echo, the identifier and the identified exchange roles, and, thus, simultaneously identify each other.

Antipas's reaction to the identification of Iaokanann with Élie demonstrates his inability to assume a posture of reflexivity and, hence, of self-identification before Iaokanann. The banquet begins with Antipas reclining on a couch of ivory, flanked by Vitellius and Aulus. When he hears Iaokanann's name: "Antipas se renversa comme frappé en pleine poitrine" (4: 271). Referring to this scene, Maurice Delcroix notes that ". . . Hérodias est peut-être le seul texte de Flaubert où la parole, et pas même la parole de celui dont dit le nom, mais la parole d'un autre, est efficace comme la matière" (Debray-Genette 355). This name in particular exhibits a formal materiality because of its manifestation of a physical echo. When Salomé requests "La tête de Iaokanann!", as reward for her dance, "Le Tétrarque s'affaisa sur lui-même, écrasé" (4: 276). Antipas reacts here as he does with the identification of Iaokanann as Élie, suggesting that it is this name which levels him, as well as the request. Antipas cannot stand up to the name of Iaokanann, as do the mountains, which echo the outburst of that voice (4: 267). The mountains stand before, receive, and echo the name of Iaokanann, whereas Antipas falls back and even collapses at its utterance.

The physical flattening of Antipas, who "était las de réfléchir" (4: 255), before the naming of Iaokanann represents his inability to make a reciprocal self-identification. This inability for reflection, shows itself in the conflict between Antipas's constant dread and timidity before his enemies, both real and imagined, and his complicity in the death of someone with whom he has no quarrel. Antipas's basic question in the opening passage, "Où est-il?" (4: 255), reveals such a self-alienation. The Tetrarch has no reason to doubt the whereabouts of Iaokanann, who remains jailed in his subterranean cell, under Antipas's orders. The jailer, Mannaëi, jealously guards Iaokanann out of personal motives of hatred, which exceed in zeal his obedience to Antipas: "Sans avoir reçu ces ordres, Mannaëi les accomplissait; car Iaokanann était Juif, et il exécrait les Juifs comme tous les Samaritains" (4: 255). Contrary to evidence, the Tetrarch does doubt the whereabouts of Iaokanann who poses an unnamed threat to him. Antipas's desire to keep that threat unnamed and impersonal expresses itself in the use of the pronoun *il*, rather than the name "Iaokanann." The content of the question rec-

ognizes Iaokanann as an enemy to be feared, but the impersonal form of the question denies this very recognition.

Iaokanann's incarceration proves to be ineffectual in allaying the fears of Antipas because Iaokanann threatens him with his spirituality. Aimée Israel-Pelletier points out that "Iaokanann's voice, and his words, are meant to express the absolute proximity of an ideal and divine presence. . . . As if, in accordance with the Aristotelian and medieval Christian thinking, among all forms of expression, the voice came closest to nature, to mind, to soul, to truth" (94). The real terror Antipas experiences at the sound of Iaokanann's voice manifests an intuition against evidence that the state of enmity between them lies outside of the sphere of familiar political conflict and, instead, in the spiritual arena. He never brings this intuition to the level of consciousness and at last orders the death of whom he confesses: "Malgré moi, je l'aime!" (4: 259). This self-alienation, expressed by "Malgré moi," results from the inability of Antipas to make the reciprocal self-identification in relation to Iaokanann; the consequences of which are paradoxically undesired, yet intended.

The process of self-identification becomes as problematic for the reader as for the characters of **"Hérodias."** In that initial identification of "Iaokanann as "le même que les Latins appellent saint Jean-Baptiste" (255), the narrator appears in an unusually explicit manner and makes a reference that has relevance to neither the atmosphere nor the events of the tale. The reference to "saint Jean-Baptiste" is an anachronistic one, given that only in the early Church (long after the events of this tale), do such titles of veneration become common. This anachronism differs from the mention of the disgrace of Agrippa, which "n'eut lieu qu'après la mort de Jésus" (*Société des Études* 4: 254, note 2), in that the latter furthers the action, whereas the former seems solely directed to the reader.

O'Connor, speaking of the non-identifiable interpretive frame of reference within **"Hérodias,"** exhibited by the narrator's stated distance from those who know Iaokanann as saint Jean-Baptiste and by the oblique identification of Jesus in the tale, places the burden of identification upon the reader:

> It is the reader, therefore, who—in the face of the text's refusal to declare itself—must supply the identity of Jesus. It is true that Jesus is later identified, but the point of view is again non-partisan and secular, and if, by Iaokanann's own declaration and the plot of the tale, **"Hérodias"** bears witness to the waning of an entire civilization, the intimacy and portentousness of that civilization's relation to the waxing spiral of the Christian civilization to come is left entirely to the reader to supply.

(822)

A reflexive identification takes place with the reader in relation to Iaokanann, analogous to that of the people of Machærous, Antipas, and Hérodias. If this Iaokanann is saint Jean-Baptiste for the reader, then who is the reader?

Margaret Lowe's approach to the question of the relation of **"Hérodias"** to its reader analyses the currents of belief, in the Catholic Church, that Flaubert found particularly dangerous to late nineteenth-century France. According to her, the readers contemporary with Flaubert no longer identified with the faith of saint Jean-Baptiste and "all he stands for traditionally—the desert, asceticism, intransigence, selflessness, fearlessness" (552) and had given themselves over to a "culte de la mère," which finds its most pronounced expression in the marioltary of the French neo-Catholicism (556). The readers, who know the story of the beheading of saint Jean-Baptiste sufficiently well to provide the off-stage conversation between Salomé and Hérodias, and who can easily identify the *il* in the formula; "Pour qu'il grandisse, il faut que je diminue" (4: 255), can deduce their complementary identity to Iaokanann. Following Lowe, the reflection of Iaokanann's identity upon the readers reveals them as wanderers, who have strayed far from the faith, in pursuit of heresies which are redolent of the Machærous of **"Hérodias."**

Flaubert is not, however, exhorting the reader to Christian practice. On the contrary, in a less parochial sense, he compels the reader to make the necessary self-identification, which follows as a consequence of the reader's interaction with the text. The reader participates in the telling of the tale, by supplying information that may or may not have been intended to be absent from it, or by echoing "saint Jean-Baptiste" every time "Iaokanann" appears. The identification of Iaokanann as saint Jean-Baptiste draws the reader into the very same posture of reflexivity in which the other characters of **"Hérodias"** find themselves. Thus, this seemingly anachronistic reference to saint Jean-Baptiste makes immediate to the reader the experience of the characters of the tale. By participating in identifying Iaokanann, the reader identifies him or herself as well. Such participation demands conscious awareness in order to avoid the self-alienation of Antipas, who, after all the guests depart from the banquet hall, sits, ". . . les mains contres ses tempes, et regardant toujours la tête coupée . . ." (4: 277). Genette imagines Antipas, in our final look at him, as having been ". . . led to sacrifice Jokanann [sic], without exactly knowing why or how" (200).

The name "Iaokanann" functions as an attractive force, which draws the reader and the characters of **"Hérodias"** to a posture of reflexivity and self-identification, much in the same way that, upon hearing his voice from afar, Hérodias "vaincue par une fascination, . . . traversa la foule . . ." (4: 265) and that Anti-

pas, in spite of himself, loves Iaokanann. Flaubert persists in calling his saint Jean-Baptiste "Iaokanann" in order to attract all the participants of **"Hérodias"** to Iaokanann, so that they may hear themselves in his echo. The failure to recognize themselves in Iaokanann results in a self-alienation; although, not the salutary one, whereby the reader recognizes and transcends the familiar roles in life, which soon become confused with the identity of self. Instead, the self-alienation of **"Hérodias"** divorces action from understanding, leaving only a deafness, whose silence no voice can break.[2]

Notes

1. Flaubert uses a similar technique of forming a name to reflect the idea of echo and repetition in "Un Cœur simple." Ann Murphy points out that: "It is possible that the parrot's name, being the repetition of two identical sounds—Lou-lou—as well as reproducing, on the level of the signifier, his status as embodiment of repetition and imitation, indicates his 'reembodiment,' in a second life, as a stuffed bird and then as symbol of the Holy Spirit" (404).

2. I am grateful to Professor Gilbert Chaitin of the University of Indiana at Bloomington for this observation concerning the prevention of nasalization that the added "n" effects.

Works Cited

Bart, Benjamin. *Flaubert*. Syracuse: Syracuse UP, 1967. 698-704.

Burns, C.A. "The Manuscripts of Flaubert's *Trois Contes*" *French Studies*. 8 (1954): 297-325.

Cannon, Joyce H. "Flaubert's Documentation for *Hérodias*." *French Studies* 14 (1960): 325-39.

Debray-Genette, Raymonde. "Re-présentation d'*Hérodias*." *La Production du sens chez Flaubert*. Ed. Claudine Gothot-Mersch. Centre culturel International de Cerisy-La-Salle. Paris: Union Générale d'Étitions, 1975. 345-57.

Flaubert, Gustave. *Œuvres complètes de Gustave Flaubert*. Ed. Société des Études littéraires françaises. 16 vols. Paris: Club de l'Honnête Homme, 1971-75.

Genette, Gérard. "Demotivation in *Hérodias*." *Flaubert and Postmodernism*. Eds. Naomi Schor and Henry F. Majewski. Lincoln: Nebraska UP, 1984. 193-201.

Israel-Pelletier, Aimée. "Reading the Language of Desire and Writing." *Flaubert's Straight and Suspect Saints: The Unity of* Trois Contes. Amsterdam: Benjamins, 1991. 89-107.

Lowe, Margaret. "'Rendre plastique . . .': Flaubert's Treatment of the Female Principle in *Herodias*." *Modern Language Review* 78 (1983): 551-58.

Murphy, Ann L. "The Order of Speech in Flaubert's *Trois Contes.*" *French Review* 65 (1992): 402-14.

O'Connor, John, R. "Flaubert's *Trois Contes* and the Figure of the Double Cone." *PMLA* 95 (1980): 812-26.

Zagona, Helen Grace. "A Historical, Archaeological Approach: Flaubert's *Hérodias.*" *The Legend of Salome and the Principle of Art for Art's Sake.* Paris: Minard, 1960. 69-88.

Marie Josephine Diamond (essay date 1998)

SOURCE: Diamond, Marie Josephine. "Flaubert's 'Quidquid Volueris': The Colonial Father and the Poetics of Hysteria." *SubStance* 85, no. 1 (1998): 71-88.

[*In the following essay, Diamond finds parallels between Flaubert's "Quidquid volueris" and Mary Shelley's* Frankenstein.]

> It is generally admitted that with woman the powers of intuition, of rapid perception, and perhaps of imitation, are more strongly marked than in man; but some, at least of these faculties are characteristic of the lower races, and therefore of a past and lower state of civilization.
>
> —*Charles Darwin*

> We have trained and bred one kind of qualities into one half of the species, and another kind into the other half. And then we wonder at the contradictions of human nature! . . . We have bred a race of psychic hybrids, and the moral quality of hybrids is well known.
>
> —*Charlotte Perkins Gilman*

> The mechanism of poetry is the same as that of hysterical fantasies.
>
> —*Sigmund Freud*

Written in October 1837 when Flaubert was not yet seventeen, **"Quidquid volueris"** articulates a peculiarly modern version of the grotesque. During a visit to South America, a French anthropologist, Paul de Monville, mates a Brazilian slave and an orangutan as an interspecies experiment. The woman dies a horrific death in childbirth. Sixteen years later, the scientist sends for her monstrous offspring, Djalioh, to live with him in France. The hybrid, described as excessively sensitive and imaginative but mute, falls in love with Adèle, his "father's" fiancée. Two years after the wedding, he kills their child, rapes and kills Adèle and kills himself. The anthropologist has him stuffed and exhibited as a zoological curio and soon forgets the entire episode. Through a colonial rewriting of the Oedipal plot, Flaubert thus dramatizes the dilemma of the anachronistic Romantic in a positivistic world.

Like Mary Shelley's *Frankenstein,* **"Quidquid volueris"** describes the creation of a monster through scientific experimentation. However, written a generation after *Frankenstein,* the context of Flaubert's story is explicitly colonial, and Shelley's idealistic scientist of the Enlightenment has become the racist apologist. Unlike Frankenstein who is tormented by the product of his hubris and is ultimately destroyed, Flaubert's scientist blithely walks over the corpses produced by his experiment (including his wife and child) and is rewarded with scientific and social recognition.

The obvious villain of the piece, the second-generation Frankenstein, is the anthropologist, representative of positivism and materialism. Like many of his generation, the young Flaubert railed against the brave new world of science and, within the context of the opposition between science and its devalued counterpart, a vaguely defined "poetry," between analysis and the imagination, he often made his affiliation very clear. Thus he wrote to Ernest Chevalier, June 27 1837:

> Il y a des jours où je donnerais toute la science des bavards passés, présents et futurs, toute la sotte érudition des éplucheurs, équarisseurs, philosophes, romanciers, chimistes, épiciers, académiciens, pour deux vers de Lamartine ou de Victor Hugo. Me voilà devenu bien anti-prose, anti-raison, anti-vérité car qu'est-ce que le beau sinon l'impossible, la poésie si ce n'est la barbarie—le coeur de l'homme. . . .
>
> (*Correspondance,* 25)

> (There are days when I would give up all the science of the babblers of the past, present and future, all the stupid erudition of the dissecters, knackers, philosophers, novelists, chemists, grocers, academicians, for two lines of Lamartine or Victor Hugo. I have become very anti-prose, anti-reason, anti-truth, for what is beauty if not the impossible, what is poetry if not the barbarous—the heart of man.)[1]

What is obvious in this letter is that the lines between science and poetry have been drawn. On the one side are knowledge, facts, analysis, prose; on the other, beauty, the impossible, savagery and poetry. In a further illustration of the destructiveness of science, Flaubert brings out the gender distinction implicit and obvious in the opposition science/poetry: all that remains of a beautiful woman, he writes, after she has been dissected by a scientist, is a repulsive heap of body parts. Thus, woman is a general metaphor for the beauty and wildness ("*barbarie*") of poetry and of emotion conceived as the repressed other of the scientific and rational enterprise of civilization.

However, Flaubert's hatred of science and love of poetry is by no means as simple as might appear from the letter to Chevalier. This is obvious in his early short stories, particularly in **"Quidquid volueris."** The expansiveness of reveries and the imagination, the longing for a pantheistic communion with the totality of nature that was part of Romantic philosophy at its inception, still exists in his early works but is countered by a bitter, mordant and annihilating irony that both reflects and attacks the reifications and commodifications of scientific materialism. Flaubert is at times as critical of romantic clichés and themes as the most cynical positivist. Like Musset in his *Confession d'un enfant du siècle,* like the Baudelaire of the "Spleen" poems, Flaubert's narrator of the short stories represents himself as moribund and obsessed with the paraphernalia of death. The Gothic, reduced to its brac-a-brac, returns in the early works as the sign of Romanticism's demise. **"Quidquid volueris"** is by no means an unambiguous representation of poetry victimized by science.

Paradigmatic readings of the story have interpreted Flaubert's ambivalence towards Romanticism as a manifestation of his own unresolved Oedipal struggles with his father. In his psycho-biography of Flaubert, *L'Idiot de la famille,* Sartre reads **"Quidquid volueris"** as an aggressive acting out of an Oedipal fantasy, in the guise of a battle between poetry and logic, that includes an inevitable self-punishment (Vol. 1, 274-275). In his *Uses of Uncertainty,* Jonathan Culler relates the theme of the transgressive son, embodied in Djalioh, to the social thematics of the Chatterton type of Romantic hero, the young poet crushed by the forces of capitalism (39-41). Like Sartre, he highlights the failure of Djalioh's revolt. And he interprets the excesses of this literally monstrous signifier as a sign of unassimilability, a surplus of signification and source of power that Flaubert neutralizes by means of his deadening irony. Thus, Djalioh signifies self-destruction, the failed Romantic self projected as monstrous cliché. From a postmodernist perspective, Leyla Perrone-Moisés in her "Quidquid volueris: Scriptural Education," reaches a similar conclusion. Taking Djalioh as a signifier for Flaubert's writing in general, she deconstructs a progressive, evolutionist reading of his work that would view this early text as a youthful excess corrected and civilized in the later, mature works (138-158). **"Quidquid volueris,"** from this deconstructive perspective, represses the alterity represented by Djalioh—the madness and excess that is positivism's other—through narrative distancing and mockery of Romantic clichés. From the beginning, she maintains, Flaubert's Romanticism is rotten to the core; like Djalioh, it can only be varnished and put on show in a museum: ". . . the romantic will remain fossilized in the archeological strata of the Flaubertian domain" (Moisés, 152). Thus, the apeman embodies both Romanticism and "*bêtise*" as an alterity that persists in Flaubert's writings. All three readings, from different points of departure, emphasize Flaubert's denial or reification of alterity—his own alterity to his father, his excessive alter ego, his Romantic madness.

These psycho-aesthetic perspectives on **"Quidquid volueris"** quite justifiably read the figure of Djalioh as a metaphor for Flaubert's own Oedipal problematic within the ideological struggle between Romantic ideal-

ism and scientific positivism. However, they take little account of the determining context of the story, namely its colonialism. Moreover, to reduce Djalioh to a fetishized Romanticism risks reproducing the gesture of Paul de Monville; and to deconstruct an evolutionary perspective on Flaubert's writings risks blurring the importance of the evolutionary ideology that informs the story and produces Djalioh in the first place. Such emphases displace and occlude the colonial context of otherness in the story, beginning with the Brazilian slave woman who gives birth to the monster. And while it may be true that Romantic platitudes are mocked in **"Quidquid volueris,"** the narrator has a double vision: he makes generalizations that echo the cynical materialism of Paul de Monville but he fully identifies, at times, with the Romantic longings of Djalioh. This doubleness is repeated in Djalioh himself in his ambiguous psychic sexuality and species hybridity. Despite its platitudes and clichés, Romanticism identified as feminine and wild persists as an embodiment of Djalioh. From the fetishizing and evolutionary perspective of the colonial anthropologist, Djalioh is at the bottom of the hierarchy of the human species. However, he most resembles his scientific progenitor when he rapes and kills, but this identification with the father and the destruction of feminine alterity permits of no successful Oedipal resolution. In effect, Djalioh configures the poetics of hysteria that will dominate Flaubert's work and preoccupy writers of the second half of the century: the impasse of the (feminine) poet-son of a colonizing father caught in a psycho-sexual and aesthetic double bind.

Paul de Monville's profession as anthropologist is crucial to the plot. His object of research is, by definition, civilization's other. In France of the 1830's, anthropology—the word had been introduced in France in 1788 by Alexandre Chavanne in his *Anthropologie ou science de l'homme*—was an extension of the physical sciences whose aim was to catalogue, control and master nature (Cohen, 210-62). The discipline was founded on the biological sciences and heavily influenced by physiologists such as Cabanis and Florens. When the Société d'anthropologie de Paris was founded in 1859 (twenty years after the publication of **"Quidquid volueris"**), sixteen of the founding members were physicians and there was still scant interest in the specificity of "other" cultures or in ethnographic studies. On the contrary, anthropology was directly implicated in the construction of racial classifications, primarily through the measurement of skulls. "Skeletomania" was the order of the day. Bory de Saint Vincent, for example, divided man into fifteen races, the lowest being the Hottentot who, it was commonly believed, could not speak but could only articulate guttural sounds. (This description of the Hottentot's difficulty in speaking corresponds to that of Djalioh.) Malte-Brun characterized African languages in general as consisting of "Barely articulated yells, many strange sounds, roars, whistling sounds imitated from the animals" (Cohen, 241). Just below the Africans, in this schema, were the animal species, led by the orangutan. The affinity between Africans and apes was thought to be so strong that it was rumored that the Institut de France at the beginning of the century had requested an explorer to "make the experiment of a connection between a male orangutan and an African woman" (Cohen, 242). Of course, while it was assumed that the African woman was sexually rapacious and wanted nothing more than to fulfill her sexual desires, especially with a white man, intercourse between an African man and a white woman was considered against nature and the worst of crimes. Such was the "scientific" anthropological discourse that provided the background for **"Quidquid volueris"** and the conception of Paul de Monville and his monstrous creation.

Scientific anthropology thus rationalized the denigration and commodification of otherness—defined as feminine, sexual, savage—in the context of colonialism. It was an extension, through the use of the notion of race, of the biological study of the body to the study of cultural differences hierarchically conceived. In the various chains of being created by biologists, ending in social Darwinism, the European, white male as analytical thinker was placed at the top and the African, associated with the feminine, the emotions, sexuality, dancing and singing, at the bottom. The polarization of masculine and feminine, human and animal, civilized and savage was to become ever more rigid as science provided the ideology for the expansion of the capitalist Market and colonization. Flaubert shatters the authority of such hierarchical and dualistic paradigms in **"Quidquid volueris"** by contextualizing the opposition science/poetry, civilized/savage, masculine/feminine as a production of the European psyche, a subjective phenomenon whose origin is in repression rather than in any objective reality, and by dialectically linking the Law of the colonial scientist father with a poetics of hysteria in which the male and the female are in a deadly, unresolvable conflict.

From the beginning, the creation of Djalioh, like that of Frankenstein's monster in Shelley's novel, is introjected as a psychological phenomenon. The subtitle and genre definition of **"Quidquid volueris"** is "Etudes psychologiques," and Flaubert explicitly defines his bizarre tale as a product of his narrator's night fantasies. Like Shelley, he originates his story in a dream world on the borders of the unconscious, but the narrative tone of the two stories is completely different. Shelley's tale is unrelieved in its tragic unfolding whereas Flaubert distances himself from the horrors of his plot through a narrator who indulges in ironic and mocking interruptions. This is apparent in the introductory paragraphs where the first-person narrator invites the demons of his unconscious to inspire a macabre tale—*"une de vos folies, de vos rires étranges"* (103) ("one of your follies,

your strange jokes")—and to spare him the conventions of invoking the muse or of writing a preface. The winged, bearded, multi-colored, "little devils" in long overcoats who enter through the keyhole, warm their clawed hands at the hearth, and shake the walls and doors of the bedroom are both macabre and comic. Although they disrupt the narrator's sleep and mimic madness and hysteria with their antic behavior, these goblins are the "children" of his brain—and prefigure the confused identification between the monstrous father and son to which they give birth. The narrator is complicitous with the transgressive fantasies that enter his locked room and shake the foundations of his sleep and his sanity. Thus, if he identifies with the idealistic, feminized Djalioh, his imagination also anticipates the cold sadism of the scientist who generates the events of the ensuing story as well as the brutality of the unnatural and victimized son who momentarily shatters his civilized cage. Often ambiguous, his interventions nevertheless express on the narrative level the hysterical impasse and failure of the Oedipal resolution that is the fate of the feminized and savage Djalioh.

From the beginning, Flaubert destabilizes and demystifies the confident hierarchies of the racist scientist. Paul de Monville's interspecies experiment takes place in Brazil, the locus of a tradition of French travel writings, beginning in the sixteenth century with Jean de Léry and Montaigne, for example, which represents the savage from a positive, even utopian perspective.[2] More significantly, the narrator exposes a desire for power over the animal/female body behind the façade of scientific objectivity. Although the Académie des Sciences, in Flaubert's story, had inspired interest in interspecies breeding, Paul de Monville undertakes his experiment on a gamble with a planter friend, the prize for its successful completion being an African slave girl. The desire for sexual domination over the colonized other is thus implicated in the scientific/anthropological project. Moreover, revenge and sexual frustration determine the object of the experiment: an African slave who, negating the conventional stereotyping of the African woman as lascivious and desirous of white men, had previously rejected the scientist's sexual advances. Although, in his narration to his friends of the origins of Djalioh, de Monville jocularly dismisses this rejection with the ironic quip that she perhaps found him "uglier than a savage," such ironic reversals effect a displacement of the negative meaning of savage from the colonized other to the colonizing master that operates—albeit flippantly—throughout the text. Thus, the narrator interprets the pet monkeys in Adèle's house, supposedly related to Djalioh, as caricatures of civilized man— "mêmes sentiments, mêmes appétits brutaux, un peu moins d'orgeuil—et voilà tout" (111) ("same feelings, same brutal appetites, a little less pride—and that's all"). The European master is the brute, the orangutan who violates the African woman and almost tears her apart is merely his transparent surrogate. For his "successful" experiment resulting in the birth of Djalioh, whose mother dies in torment, De Monville receives "la croix d'honneur." Thus, Flaubert ironically exposes the civilized European scientist as the real monster of the story—a father whose law masks an unrelieved brutality and a denial of otherness. Such ironic juxtapositions and reversals are typical of the narrator's attacks on positivism, and radically undermine the assumption of neutrality and superiority of the European scientist. The sexual rapaciousness conventionally projected onto the African woman by contemporary racist science is here clearly located in the European man. The African woman's rejection of him exposes his impotence, and the orangutan functions as his surrogate in his need to violate her recalcitrant body. Once his superiority is established, he takes pride in his mediation of the reproductive process and in his generation of his quasi-offspring, whom "he raises like a son."

Although Djalioh can be read as a surrogate for Flaubert himself, the poet who felt more empathic identification with animals than with the patriarchal representatives of the modern social order,[3] he represents a more general figure of otherness. As a semi-animal hybrid on the margins of human evolution,[4] he embodies the oppressed alterity of the colonized other, especially of the female slave, and is literally inconceivable without the violent mediations of his colonial father. And this otherness of a repressive civilized order returns as hysteria—a prefiguration of the crisis of the bourgeois order at the end of the century that founds Freudian analysis. Incompatible with the established symbolic code and the rigid binary oppositions of gender and racist ideology, the male incorporation of what is socially identified as the "feminine"—which also embodies the threat of homosexuality—permits of no positive Oedipal resolution. The hysterical impasse is resolved here only in death and the reenactment of the destruction of the feminine that begins the story. The colonial context and repositionning of female alterity in **"Quidquid volueris"** present the possibility of a rereading of hysteria both in its relation to bisexuality and its destabilizing of the bourgeois family.

The colonial context of the story establishes a nexus between poetry, the feminine, and the savage that gives an original and crucial twist to the Oedipal plot. In effect, the colonial scene of open brutality against the "savage" woman is dialectically connected to the civilized scene of Paul de Monville's courtship and marriage and, in particular, to the violence that destroys his family, the restaging on a different level of his surrogate rape of the female slave. His own savagery generates the return of the savage that finally disrupts his home and shatters its image of docile domesticity represented by his angelic wife and child. Adèle, however, is less an angel than a domestic prisoner whose marriage ends

a life of activity and imagination and occasions a paralyzing neurosis:

> . . . elle qui, quelque temps auparavant était si folle, si pensive, qui courait dans les prairies, qui lisait les romans, les vers, les contes, qui galopait sur sa jument à travers les allées de la forêt, qui aimait tant à entendre le bruissement des feuilles, le murmure des ruisseaux, elle se trouvait tout à coup une dame,—c'est à dire quelque chose qui a un grand châle et qui va seule dans les rues.
>
> (107)

> (. . . she who, a short time before was so wild, so pensive, who ran through the meadows, read novels, poetry, stories, who galloped her mare through the paths in the forest, who so loved to hear the rustle of leaves, the murmur of streams, found herself a woman,—that is, something that wears a shawl and can walk unaccompanied in the street.)

Indeed, Adèle's marriage turns sensitivity into neurasthenia and she spends much of her time confined to her couch which no longer serves, as the narrator regretfully comments, as the privileged place of eighteenth-century gallantry and erotic pleasure. (By the end of the century the hysterical woman will continue to recline on her couch as she begins her talking cure.) As Barbara Ehrenreich and Deirdre English point out in *For Her Own Good,* this conception of woman as the opposite or negation of masculine virtues and activities "necessarily romanticizes the moribund woman and encourages a kind of paternalistic necrophilia" (109). The narrator ironically deprecates the blond, vaporous and angelic physical type represented by Adèle and invokes her antithesis, the passionate, dark Andalusian with eyes burning like volcanoes. In effect, Djalioh, whose desire is also characterized as volcanic, contains this image of the passionate woman and embodies the repressed other of Adèle.

The figure of Djalioh includes the repressed feminine, the African woman physically destroyed because of her resistance to the violence of the colonizing white man and the white woman reduced to a shadow existence and neurotic passivity. He is sexually ambiguous. Even in appearance he is not the hulking ape-like monster one might expect from his paternity. He is small, thin and yellowish in color (a common description of the Hottentot in racist classifications) and his body is a mixture of weakness and lassitude (in this he resembles Adèle) and physical strength located in his hands and chest. His response to nature expresses the same mixture of conventionalized male and female responses:

> Souvent, en présence des forêts, des hautes montagnes, de l'océan . . . toute son âme se dilatait devant la nature comme une rose qui s'épanouit au soleil; et il tremblait de tous ses membres, sous le poids d'une volupté intérieure, et la tête entre ses deux mains, il tombait dans une léthargie mélancolique. Alors, dis-je, son

âme brillait à travers son corps, comme les beaux yeux d'une femme derrière un voile noir.

(105)

(Often, in the presence of forests, high mountains, the ocean, . . . his entire soul would dilate before nature like a rose blossoming in the sun; and he trembled with every limb under the weight of an inner voluptuousness and, his head in his hands, he would fall into a melancholic lethargy. Then, I declare, his soul would shine through his body like the beautiful eyes of a woman behind a black veil.)

In this description, in which his violent, masculine sexual desire is identified with the feminine image of a dilating rose and his melancholy with the black veil hiding the beautiful eyes of a woman, he exemplifies Freud's description of the psychic bisexuality of the hysteric—"An hysterical symptom is the expression of both a masculine and a feminine unconscious sexual fantasy" ("Hysterical Fantasies," 151)—which must be resolved before a woman (hysteria being gendered as female) can assume her rightful passive femininity as wife and mother. Without this resolution the hysteric remains paralyzed, often by a somatic pathological formation. Djalioh is tortured by desire and longing to which he cannot give expression—he literally cannot speak.

Nor can he satisfy his sexual desire. When his "father" takes him to a brothel, he runs away, like Frédéric in L'Education sentimentale,[5] and takes with him a rose and a mirror. Perrone-Moisés interprets the rose and mirror here as images of irreconcilable need and desire, nature and culture, the two sides of Djalioh, and she suggests that he does not speak because his relationship to his imago (his mirror stage) is blocked (147-49). However, both the rose and the mirror are associated with the feminine. The conventional symbol of female sexuality, roses are consistently associated with Adèle, but as we have seen, Djalioh's own sexuality is also compared to a dilating rose. The mirror is also a conventional sign of female vanity and narcissism. Djalioh's identification with the feminine inhibits sexual possession of a woman and traps him in idealizations. Within the order represented by Paul de Monville, socially sanctioned sexual initiation takes place through the commodification of the female body and, in taking Djalioh to the brothel, repeats—in the context of civilization—the gesture of introducing the orangutan to the African slave. As the partial embodiment of his African mother who, in the nineteenth-century imagination, is as much other to civilization as nature, Djalioh runs away from identification with both his animal and civilized father. He is trapped in structures of the imaginary and his wild, poetic fantasies never achieve any social expression, but this prereflective formation is absorbed into an Oedipal configuration that postdates the mirror stage. Djalioh's crisis occurs at puberty, at the threshold

of the Oedipal resolution. His imaginary includes both the inarticulate semiotic and the daydreams that characterize the adolescent imagination—the origin, according to Freud both of poetry and hysteria.[6] His mutism is a sign for the impossibility of carrying over the imaginary into the culturally symbolic, typically the situation of the female hysteric denied access to the socially symbolic because of her gender and of the savage because of a presumed racial inferiority. One recalls G. Eichtal and I. Urbain's comparison between the feminine and the savage united, among other things by their common passion for "jewelry, dancing and singing" (15-16). Thus Gobineau, in his racist ideology, relates the passion and spontaneity attributed to Africans to the creation of art only, however, when crossed with the cerebrality of Europeans, and expressed the belief that all art in civilizations such as Egypt came into being through the mediating influence of the white man (but not through miscegenation) (Gobineau, 317-20). By making Djalioh's mutism a constituent part of his being, an irreversible phenomenon, Flaubert points to the absolute irreconcilability of the repressed feminine-savage-poetic within the order of colonizing civilization.

The focus of Djalioh's Oedipal fantasies is Adèle, and Djalioh reaches a climax of frustration at the celebration of her wedding to Paul. Tortured and intoxicated by the giddy eroticism of the dance, he takes a violin and attempts to play it. His rending, inexpressible cries—"as if a weight were crushing his chest"—are translated into discordant and fragmented sounds and sudden changes of tempo and harmonics:

. . . et tous ces sons, tout ce bruit de cordes et de notes qui sifflent, sans mesure, sans chants, sans rythme, une mélodie nulle, des pensées vagues et coureuses qui se succédaient comme une ronde de démons, des rêves qui passent et s'enfuient, poussés par d'autres, dans un tourbillon sans repos, dans une course sans relâche.

(108)

(. . . and all these sounds, all this noise of strings and notes that wheeze, without measure, without songs, without rhythm, vague and fleeting thoughts following each other like a demons' rondo, dreams that pass and disappear, urged on by others, in a whirl without rest, in a race without relief.)

Baudelaire's description of hysteria in his extraordinary article on Madame Bovary is especially relevant to a reading of this hysterical crisis:

L'hystérie! Pourquoi ce mystère physiologique, ce mystère que l'Académie de médecine n'a pas encore résolu, et qui, s'exprimant dans les femmes par la sensation d'une boule ascendante et asphyxiante (je ne parle que du symptôme principal), se traduit chez les hommes nerveux par toutes les impuissances et par toutes les aptitudes à l'excès.

(649)

(Hysteria! Why this physiological mystery, this mystery that the Academy of Medicine has not yet resolved, and which, expressed in women as the sensation of an ascending and suffocating ball (I refer only to the principal symptom), is manifested in nervous men through every kind of impotence and aptitude for excess.)

Baudelaire, of course, was one of the first critics to point to Madame Bovary's psychic bisexuality. In effect, Djalioh experiences both the "asphyxiating ball" ascribed to the female hysteric and the impotence and excesses ascribed to the male hysteric that converge in the musical equivalent of a psychic explosion.

The description of an unmelodic, dizzying whirl is familiar in Flaubert's work and is identifiable with an epileptic and hysterical crisis that incorporates the semiotic inarticulateness of the imaginary associated with the pre-mirror stage. Djalioh's mutism, impotence and excesses originate in the structure of paternal mastery and brutality and the oppression of the feminine—a structure replicated in the anthropologist's bourgeois home. Nor can Djalioh resolve the impulses in himself towards masculine oppression and female submission. Thus, in an Oedipal fantasy provoked by the wedding, he pictures himself tearing off Adèle's clothes and carrying her across oceans to the shade of tropical palm tree where, reassuming his passive female sexuality, he imagines submitting to her sexual embrace—a graphic instance of his sexual ambivalence.[7] The impossibility of a resolution of this psychic bisexuality results in somatic conversion symptoms of dizziness and extreme pressure in the head and veins, relieved only at the dénouement of the text when he finally acts out his desires in an orgy of rape, murder and suicide. Such acting out remains continuous with the structure of hysteria. As Freud notes, ". . . of practical importance too is the case of hysterical persons who may not express their fantasies as symptoms, but consciously realize them in action and thus imagine and consciously bring about assaults, attacks, or sexual transgressions" ("Hysterical Fantasies," 148).

The final scene repeats the primal scene of Djalioh's conception. As with Mary Shelley's monster, his first victim is a child, in this instance the child of his unnatural father and Adèle. Through this murder he attacks the very act of paternal generation by a retroactive annihilation of his own birth. The rape of Adèle is prefaced by the apparently gratuitous information that, when Djalioh first approaches her, she is reading a novel by Balzac. Given the similarity between the name Paul de Monville and Paul de Manerville, the accomplice of the sadistic hero of Balzac's *La Fille aux yeux d'or*, it is likely that this is the novel of Balzac that Flaubert indirectly points to as an influence on his own bizarre work. Indeed, in his story of interspecies hybridity he outdoes the "monstrous" theme (homosexuality) of *La Fille aux yeux d'or*, and the brutality of the rape and murder of Adèle is more shocking than the murder of Paquita, the Creole slave of Balzac's novel. The rape of Adèle, which, like that of Djalioh's own mother, takes place in a locked room, represents a closure on the scene of his conception: Adèle dies; he does not escape like the orangutan but kills himself. The explosion of violence that breaks the hysterical impasse in this acting-out destroys the image of the passive female angel, the icon of nineteenth-century colonial ideology. Djalioh literally tears off the veils of Adèle, and her negated sexuality is violently parodied in her death throes:

> Tout à coup Djalioh sentit sous lui les convulsions d'Adèle, ses muscles se raidirent comme le fer, elle poussa un cri et un soupir plaintifs, qui furent étouffés par des baisers. Puis il la sentit froide, ses yeux se fermèrent, elle se roula sur elle-même et sa bouche s'ouvrit.
>
> (113)

> (Suddenly Djalioh felt beneath him Adèle's convulsions; his muscles stiffened like iron; she let out a plaintive cry and sigh that he stifled with kisses. Then he felt her become cold; her eyes closed; she rolled over and her mouth fell open.)

In a frenzy, Djalioh kills himself by smashing his head against a marble chimney piece. The story closes with a summary of platitudinous reactions to the event, which is soon forgotten. As in the case of de Marsay of *La Fille aux yeux d'or*, who walks away from an equally brutal murder as though it had never happened, the event leaves no impression on Paul de Monville who remarries and continues to amuse himself in society. Stuffed and varnished, Djalioh is exhibited in the museum of zoology.

What Flaubert stages in **"Quidquid volueris"** is a hysteria defined as a conflicted bisexuality that permits of no social resolution. The monster of Shelley's *Frankenstein* has been interpreted as an embodiment of female anger at cultural marginalization, his destruction of the children and women in the paternal home as a revolt against the reduction of women to the passive role of angel in the house.[8] From the perspective of the male writer, the hysterical monster is obsessed by the representation of male/female relations as violent and oppressive. As the living embodiment of that reality, he lives the masculine and feminine in himself as a constant battle. Whereas the hysterical woman, in Freud's paradigm, has difficulty giving up her bisexuality to assume the passive position of wife and mother, Djalioh can assume the position of the father only by brutally destroying his feminine self, defined as primitive and poetic. In effect, when he does imitate his father—whose paternity was established through the mediation of brute force over the colonized slave woman, he becomes murderer and rapist. Djalioh's self-destruction for what is apparently an enactment of a murderous Oedipal fantasy is also a destruction of the father in himself and a re-identification with the feminine. As murderer and rapist, he is a caricature of Paul de Monville whom the narrator calls "the monster of civilization," the representative of institutionalized authority, science and Law, the cultural symbolic defined in its monstrosity. Thus, the impasse of hysteria Flaubert describes in **"Quidquid volueris"** is structurally dialectical to a cultural order represented as violent, oppressive and emotionally dissociated. On the side of hysteria is an unresolvable bisexuality, imagination without symbolic expression, and passion without fulfillment; on the side of the Law is the destruction of the feminine, the negation of emotion and poetic expression in the name of power, calculation and science. The embodiment of the relation between the two orders is the stuffed and varnished corpse of Djalioh. The scientist deals with alterity by fetishizing and collecting it—as in nineteenth-century skeletomania, the collection of thousands of skulls of "other" racial types, and the exhibition and autopsy of the alien body of the Hottentot woman. The positivist Law of the Father represses the order of the imaginary—the unconscious, the psychically bisexual, dreams and fantasies—through a similar reification. The inherent and unresolved tensions between the hysteric and legitimate patriarchal Law recur throughout Flaubert's writings. Like Madame Bovary, a precursor of Freud's female hysterics, who could find no solace in assuming the passive role of an Adèle, Flaubert's male hysterics can see no way out in assuming the prescribed paternal role of master of the house and representative of the Law. **"Quidquid volueris"** exposes this dilemma by taking the Oedipal problematic outside of the confines of the bourgeois home and contextualizing it within a larger structure of social and cultural domination. Its irresolution is replicated in the oscillations of the narrator, who alternately assumes the voice of the ironic and reifying father and the hysterical son.

In one of those generalizations that was common currency in nineteenth-century thought, Eichtal and Urbain distinguish between the white and the black view of the world in the following way: "Tandis que le blanc est panthéiste et s'absorbe dans la contemplation de l'infiniment grand, le noir est fétichiste et adore la puissance infinie dans ses manifestations infiniment petites" (22). ("Whereas the white man is a pantheist and devotes himself to the contemplation of the infinitely great, the black man is a fetishist and adores infinite power in its smallest manifestations.") This observation could be reversed in **"Quidquid volueris."** The Romantic pantheism Eichtal and Urbain associate with whites is Djalioh's psychically feminized domain; and, while Paul de Monville cannot be said to adore anything, he fetishizes power, especially the state power embodied in the cross of honor. He fetishizes his wife, who represents the acquisition of a considerable fortune

and whom he metonymizes as "des cachemires à payer, une petite poupée à habiller," (105) ("cashmere shawls to pay for, a little doll to dress"); and he literally makes a fetish of Djalioh. The narrator empathically identifies with Djalioh, but also assumes a perspective analogous to that of the materialistic de Monville.

Despite his use of worn-out Romantic similes, the narrator describes Djalioh's soul and his love for Adèle in the idealistic language of Romantic pantheism:

> Son âme se prenait à ce qui était beau et sublime, comme le lierre aux débris, les fleurs au printemps, la tombe au cadavre, le malheur à l'homme . . . où l'intelligence finissait, le coeur prenait son empire; il était vaste et infini, car il comprenait le monde dans son amour. / Aussi il aimait Adèle, mais d'abord comme la nature entière, d'une sympathie douce et universelle; puis peu à peu cet amour augmenta, à mesure que sa tendresse sur les autres diminuait.
>
> (105)
>
> (His soul clung to what was beautiful and sublime, like ivy to ruins, flowers to springtime, the tomb to the corpse and unhappiness to man . . . where intelligence ended, the heart established its empire; it was vast and infinite because it embraced the world through its love. / Also he loved Adèle, but first like nature in its entirety, with a gentle and universal sympathy; then little by little this love increased as his tenderness for others diminished.)

The identification of the narrator with Djalioh becomes transparent when he describes him walking deep in dreams in the chateau, and suddenly assumes the present tense to speak for him:

> Qu'il est doux de rêver ainsi, en écoutant avec délices le bruit de ses pas sur les feuilles sèches et sur le bois mort que le pied brise, de se laisser aller dans des chemins sans barrières, comme le courant de la rêverie qui emporte votre âme!
>
> (109)
>
> (How sweet it is to dream this way, listening with delight to the sound of your steps on dry leaves and on twigs that snap underfoot, to wander down open paths, like the current of daydreams that transport your soul.)

However, the other side of Djalioh's frustrated longings is rage, and the narrator's nihilistic damning of civilization repeats, on a different level, both Djalioh's final destructiveness and de Monville's reduction of all value to material profit. Through his use of clichés and platitudes, through ironic descriptions of violence and horror, the narrator participates in rhetorical reifications of the same order as the cruelties of Paul de Monville. Thus he addresses woman in a sado-masochistic, nineteenth-century version of the Renaissance poetic mode of the "carpe diem," and, in an uncanny prefiguration of Baudelaire's necrophiliac "La Charogne," invokes her disintegration and death:

Hélas! c'est triste, mais c'est vrai . . . cet ange de
beauté mourra, et deviendra un cadavre, c'est-à-dire
une charogne qui pue,—et puis un peu de poussière, le
néant, de l'air fétide emprisonné dans une tombe.

(111)

Alas, it's sad but true . . . this angel of beauty will die
and become a corpse, a dead body that stinks, and then
a bit of dust, nothing, some fetid air imprisoned in a
tomb.

The other side of frustrated Oedipal desire is hatred of
the forbidden woman and the fantasy of necrophilia so
common to the nineteenth-century male imagination, in
which reification of the feminine is both a reaction
against and continuous with the masculinist order of
materialism, negation of alterity and pseudo-idealization
of the virginal mother. Thus, the narrator doubly kills
Adèle, as it were, by describing her body, exhumed for
reburial two years after her death, as a stinking corpse.
Rage against the inhibiting father is thus displaced onto
rage against the forbidden object of the desexualized
mother. In assuming the position of necrophiliac, the
son identifies with the father with a vengeance and, in a
sado-masochistic act, destroys the feminine in himself.
Unlike the female, African, or Creole protagonists of
Mme de Staël, Mme de Duras, and George Sand, who
destroy themselves before destroying another, the annihilation of the "other" women in paradigmatic male Romantic writers is a structural premise of their fiction.
The figure of Djalioh, who embodies the masculine and
feminine in conflict provides some understanding of
this phenomenon. His killing of Adèle literalizes the legal and social negation of the feminine veiled by bourgeois sentimentality, and replicates the destruction of
the African slave woman (and feminized male slaves)
by European colonizers. Thus he grotesquely imitates
and takes the place of his father. The narrator of
"Quidquid volueris" similarly veers between the order
of the father and the order of the son. As we see in the
introductory evocation of his diabolical imagination, his
devils are both fathers and sons—ambiguous tricksters,
playful and sadistic, disruptive and destructive. They
stage Flaubert's personal drama that was also to be the
dominant drama of the nineteenth-century bourgeoisie—the confrontation and stalemate between hysteria
and patriarchal Law. In his hysteria, the narrator, like
Djalioh, embodies both the destructive father and the
repressed feminine—hence the narrative duality of
scathing generalizations and mockery of Romanticism,
on the one hand, and sympathetic identification with
Djalioh's poetic aspirations on the other. It seems that
the male hysteric in particular cannot avoid being implicated in the sado-masochistic structures more commonly associated with the paranoid imagination.[9] In effect, Flaubert finally sacrifices the feminine to
patriarchal law, but his sacrifice is prototypically mediated by the internalized father and the brutal destruction
of his own feminine sensibility. The hysteria and un-

stable sexuality of the male/poet/savage without a viable social or symbolic context collapses into such sado-
masochism. The poetic equivalent of Flaubert is
Baudelaire, where the dream of an exotic feminine otherness similarly alternates with cutting irony and necro-
philic fantasies. In the staging of the hysterical impasse,
Flaubert anticipates the crisis of the nineteenth-century
colonization of feminine alterity that will shatter the
1880s and 1890s. Not until the emergence of
Salome—in Flaubert's **"Hérodias,"** Mallarmé's
"Hérodiade" and Moreau's symbolic paintings—will
the threatening "other" woman—the "Great Hysteric,"
in Huysmans's formula—return. Salome, however, is a
sado-masochistic fantasy of male writers; she represents
the logical return of the repressed when, casting off her
veils, she finally asks for the patriarchal head.

Notes

1. Unless otherwise indicated, all translations are my
   own.

2. Brazil has continued to be a significant locus in
   French representations of the other. Lévi-Strauss,
   who situates himself in the tradition (among many
   others) of Montaigne and Rousseau, transformed
   twentieth-century anthropological theory with
   Tristes Tropiques, an account of his field experience in Brazil.

3. Such identifications, often described in Flaubert's
   notes and letters, play an important thematic role
   in his fiction. Most relevant to the matter of
   "Quidquid volueris" is a dream he describes in
   which he is walking with his mother when he is
   surrounded by laughing monkeys. The passage is
   worth quoting in its entirety:

   > Ils nous entouraient comme dans un cercle; un a
   > voulu me caresser et m'a pris la main, je lui ai
   > tiré un coup de fusil à l'épaule et je l'ai fait
   > saigner; il a poussé des hurlements affreux. Ma
   > mère m'a dit alors: "Pourquoi le blessestu ton
   > ami? qu'est-ce qu'il t'a fait? ne vois-tu pas qu'il
   > t'aime? comme il te ressemble!" Et le singe me
   > regardait. Cela m'a déchiré l'âme et je me suis
   > réveillé . . . me sentant de la même nature que
   > les animaux et fraternisant avec eux d'une com-
   > munion toute panthéiste et tendre

   ("Voyages en Italie et en Suisse, avril-mai 1845,"
   in *Flaubert: Oeuvres complètes,* 460).

   (They surrounded us as in a circle; one wanted to
   caress me and took my hand; I shot him in the
   shoulder and made him bleed; he began to howl.
   Then my mother said to me: "Why do you wound
   your friend? What has he done to you? Can't you
   see that he loves you? How much like you he is!"
   And the monkey looked at me. My soul was torn
   and I woke up . . . feeling that I was of the same
   nature as the animals, fraternizing with them in a
   pantheistic and tender communion.)

Despite the conclusion of the dream in which Flaubert asserts his tender and pantheistic communion with animals, his relation to the monkeys reveals the same kind of ambivalence that traps Djalioh in an ambivalent sexuality. The other side of the pantheistic identification (a feminine positioning) is the sadist who shoots and wounds the animal. This pattern will reach its most sophisticated expression and resolution in "La légende de Saint Julien l'hospitalier."

4. For a summary of Europe's fascination with the ape-man see Perrone-Moisés, "Quidquid volueris," 141-42.

5. Flaubert's *Education sentimentale* deconstructs the binary opposition between prostitution and idealized love by showing them to be specular images of each other.

6. See Freud, "The Relation of the Poet to Day-dreaming."

7. In "Hysterical Fantasies and their relation to Bisexuality," (151) Freud gives a similar example of this bisexual impasse: . . . for instance, in one case I observed, the patient pressed her dress to her body with one hand (as the woman) while trying to tear it off with the other (as the man).

8. See, for example, Mary Poovey, *The Proper Lady.*

9. In "Hysterical Fantasies and Their Relation to Homosexuality," (148), Freud compares hysterical fantasies to the delusions of paranoiacs which, however, do achieve direct access to consciousness. Based on the sado-masochistic component of the sexual instinct, paranoid delusions also represent, according to Freud, a defense mechanism against homosexual desire.

Works Cited

Baudelaire, Charles. *Curiosités esthétiques.* Paris: Garnier, 1962.

Cohen, William B. *The French Encounter with Africans.* Bloomington: University of Indiana Press, 1980.

Culler, Jonathan. *The Uses of Uncertainty.* London: Elek, 1974.

Darwin, Charles. *On the Origin of Species by Means of Natural Selection.* New York: Appleton, 1860.

Ehrenreich, Barbara and Deirdre English. *For Her Own Good.* Garden City: Anchor Books, 1979.

Eichtal, Gustave, and Ismael Urbain. *Lettres sur la race noire et la race blanche.* Paris, 1839.

Flaubert, Gustave. *Correspondance 1830-1851.* Ed. Jean Bruneau. Paris: Gallimard, Bibliothèque de la Pléiade, 1973.

———. "Quidquid volueris" in *Flaubert: Oeuvres complètes.* Ed. Jean Bruneau. Paris: Seuil, 1964. Vol. 1, 102-113.

Freud, Sigmund. "Hysterical Fantasies and their Relation to Bisexuality." *Dora: An Analysis of a case of Hysteria.* Ed. Philip Rieff. New York: Macmillan, 1963.

———. "The Relation of the Poet to Daydreaming" in *On Creativity and the Unconscious.* New York: Harper, 1958. 44-55.

Gilman, Charlotte Perkins. *The Living of Charlotte Perkins Gilman: An Autobiography.* New York: Harper Collophon, 1975.

Gobineau, Arthur de. *Essai sur l'inégalité des races humaines* (1854). Paris: Pléiade, 1983.

Moisés, Leyla Perrone. "Quidquid volueris: Scriptural Education." *Flaubert and Postmodernism.* Eds. Naomi Schor and Henry F. Majewski. Lincoln: University of Nebraska Press, 1984.

Poovey, Mary. *The Proper Lady and the Woman Writer: Ideology as Style in the Works of Mary Wollstonecraft, Mary Shelley and Jane Austen.* Chicago: University of Chicago Press, 1984.

Sartre, Jean-Paul. *L'Idiot de la famille.* Paris: Gallimard, 1974.

Leonard Marsh (essay date spring 2000)

SOURCE: Marsh, Leonard. "Of Walls and the Window: Charting Textual Markers in Flaubert's 'Légende de Saint Julien l'Hospitalier.'" *Modern Language Studies* 30, no. 1 (spring 2000): 157-65.

[*In the following essay, Marsh offers a stylistic analysis of Flaubert's "La légende de Saint Julien l'Hospitalier."*]

The **"Légende de Saint Julien l'Hospitalier"** is quite different in origin from its two adjacent tales in Flaubert's *Trois Contes.* Whereas the story of Félicité in **"Un Coeur simple"** is a fictional narrative and the subject of John the Baptist in **"Hérodias"** is already documented in the scriptures, the story of Julien is a hagiographic legend, an accretion of details and events over the centuries. As such, it is an admixture of various strains of stories containing personages with similar names and biographical details, both real and fictive. While recognizing the patchwork development of the legend, one critic posits Flaubert's own imposition of a certain order of stylistic and thematic repetition in the tripartite narrative structure of his tale (Selvin 206). Another critic, while admitting to the radical non-linearity of the legend, does see another order, one beneath the apparent order of the text, a system of interrelations within a symbolic network that extends across all three stories of Flaubert's volume (Issacharoff 29). On the surface the tale can indeed be measured linearly, for it is divided into three parts following a progressively chronological order. But beyond that measurement there exists a reality that defies clear calibration and operates on an axis different from linear or horizontal progression. That axis is vertical, a path that shows no linear progression but rather a buildup or thickening of symbol. Thus, while the text's tripartite structure warrants a linear reading across its boundaries, it is also appropriate to read the tale vertically as if turning it inside out, reading through its boundaries and reading the textual markers on which the boundaries are built.

It is my purpose to demonstrate a reading of the text which reveals a harmonious interaction between both axes: the linear, chronological progression along the horizontal axis and the thickening of symbol on the vertical axis as evidenced in textual markers. Chronological or linear progression across the boundaries of its three parts is marked principally by a change in Julien's place of habitation. On the vertical axis, on the other hand, the text is populated with markers that are linked to Julien's successive habitations and these markers point as signs to the eternal issues of the conflict between peace and hostility as well as the sacred and the profane. These markers that pop up in the text are the wall and the window, the host, the nave, and most interestingly the basil plant.

Reading the text simultaneously at the beginning, before the narrative starts, and at the end, after the narrative finishes, reveals a point at which both axes intersect. Such a reading both respects the temporal and physical boundaries of the text and contravenes them in that the text has both a title and a tag, each containing more than it says on the surface and each pointing to the other. The title capsules the narrative as story and the tag documents it. The title tells us the story is a legend, literally from the Latin *legendum,* something to be read, but also an appendant which, when read, will aid in the interpretation of the text, like the legend of a map (Felman 55). This latter meaning directs our attention simultaneously to the story's closing authorial tag which Flaubert appends to tell his reader that this story is "telle à peu près qu'on la trouve, sur un vitrail d'église, dans mon pays" (648).[1] This uncharacteristic intrusion of Flaubert is compounded by his first person reference in "mon pays," which identification between person and homeland redirects us to the title in the characterization of Julien as "hospitalier" (Felman 52). In fact, both the title and the closing tag modulate the story's matrix of hospitality, that principle on which the whole story is built and which explains its fundamental bipolar energy, the rival and competing forces of peace and hostility and the sacred and the profane. The title

and the tag each function independently as icon of the whole tale, the title containing the legend in word and the tag resuming the legend in illustration through its reference to the stained glass window. Together they frame the story by delimiting its boundaries for the reader (Knight 73).[2]

Within the confines of the title and the tag, the tale is physically divided into three parts. The first part situates Julien in his family with the attendant three mysterious predictions: the first that he would be a saint, the second that he would be connected by blood and glory to the family of an emperor and the third that he would be a parricide. The second part situates Julien married in the family of an emperor and unwittingly committing parricide. The third part presents Julien the saintly anchorite dedicated to the charitable work of ferrying passengers across a dangerous river. The architecture of the narrative is clean and measured. The first part sets the stage; the second shows the fulfillment of the second and third predictions and the third part shows the fulfillment of the first prediction. But within this symmetrical and syntagmatic structure on the horizontal axis operates the text's matrix of hospitality which is less measured, less on the surface, less chronological and less sequential. It is this matrix of hospitality that accounts for the paradigmatic development of textual markers on the vertical axis. These markers, without respect to any of the particular parts of the tale in which they are plotted along the text's horizontal axis, demonstrate the pull between the inhospitable forces of peace and hostility and the sacred and the profane. Yet, at the same time, the matrix of hospitality is sustained throughout the legend along its horizontal axis by that which is intrinsic to hospitality, namely successive places of Julien's habitation. Thus, the text becomes an icon of its subject in that it is a map which charts on a vertical axis the signs of opposing forces and at the same time explains its signs on a horizontal axis, the narrative of the legend.

On the horizontal axis the first of Julien's habitations is the castle compound where he is born. It is the locus of Edenic peace: "On vivait en paix depuis si longtemps que la herse ne s'abaissait plus . . . (623)." In fact, the peace is a religious peace, for the archer patrolling the bastion's curtain would retreat to his watchtower in the heat of the day and fall asleep "comme un moine" (623). Later we are told that Julien's mother kept her household "réglé comme l'intérieur d'un monastère" (624) and that baby Julien "ressemblait à un petit Jésus" (626). All of these similes move the text to its vertical axis by representing the castle as church, a sacred place, and an edifice of Romanesque design heavy with walls and ramparts. Beneath the text there exists even more subtle evidence of the castle as church. The "herse" (portcullis) and "courtine" (that wall called a curtain joining two bastions) are both devices designed to protect the castle, yet they are at peace stage, open and un-protected. But they are also words that function in liturgical code. The "herse" is a candleholder or funeral pall and the "courtine" is a drape behind the liturgical altar. Both words now have a religious dimension on the vertical axis and foreshadow what is on the horizontal axis the eventual funeral of Julien's parents. What are secular devices denoting protection from the enemy become elements of a religious ritual.

The castle compound is a series of concentric circles comprising "quatre tours aux angles" (623) and then "[u]ne seconde enceinte, faite de pieux" (623). Within this second enclosure are found an orchard, then a garden, then a trellis and then an area for playing mall. The description continues to take the reader inside the castle by displaying ironwork, tapestries, and cupboards. Clearly the progression spirals from outside to inside along a horizontal path, for the castle tour ends deep within, so deep that the place is indiscriminate and mentioned as if just in passing: "Il y avait même, dans un endroit écarté, une étuve à la romaine; mais le bon seigneur s'en privait, estimant que c'est un usage des idôlatres" (624). This place is a Roman sauna, the very antithesis of the outside world, and the brief commentary notes that it represents for the castle lord the very antithesis of the sacredness of Christianity, idol worship. The sauna is rejected by the castle lord and this is the narrative's way of converting the last vestige of the castle's profane properties to its Christian properties as church. This place deep within functions as an icon of the text's matrix of hospitality, for it is at the very core of this habitation. At the same time, it iconizes the radical inhospitality between interior and exterior, peace and hostility, the sacred and the profane. Immediately after this castle tour ending in the sauna, the reader is told that the lord has married. Here is where the lady's household is described in terms of a monastery and immediately upon this description she gives birth. But how?: "A force de prier Dieu, il lui vint un fils" (624).

This birth is the very first event in the story and it is the very first *passé simple*. All previous verbs were in the *imparfait* of description or habitual action. As such, this event is textually flagged for special attention. The impersonal rendering of "il lui vint un fils" juxtaposed to "Dieu" in a causal relationship is none other than a rewriting of the first Christian event of salvation, namely the virgin birth of Jesus brought about by no human intervention.[3] The pagan sauna has been transformed here into a sacred human sauna, the virgin mother of Jesus, whose body becomes a church, a habitation in itself, housing the divinity deep within. It is this conversion in the text that resolves the paradox of the Roman sauna iconizing both hospitality and inhospitality. In addition, the account of the first two predictions made to Julien's parents by "un vieillard en froc de bure" (625) is clearly a rewriting of the Lucan account of the ritual presenta-

tion of the infant Jesus in the temple. In this account the aged Simeon predicted Jesus as light of the nations and glory of the people of Israel (Lk 2:22-35). Julien then as a "petit Jésus" has entered the castle, risen up from within it and made it sacred. A schema of rival inhospitable forces has been established. On one level what is exterior to the castle is profane and hostile and on another level what is interior is sacred and peaceful. Julien's sanctity will rest on reconciling, making hospitable, those inhospitable forces.

The window is the gap in the wall that breaches the boundary between these forces and it is the window-wall relationship that pops up as a marker at the beginning of the text along the horizontal axis. Romanesque architecture is such that the window was scarce and narrow so as not to compromise the supportive power of its heavy walls. In the opening paragraph of the tale, Flaubert does a literal vertical scan of the outside of the strong-walled castle. He stops and focuses on one detail and this detail will serve as a textual marker that will move the text again to the vertical axis by identifying the castle as church and by representing the rival forces of sacred and profane. Flaubert notes that "sur le bord des fenêtres, à tous les étages, dans un pot d'argile peinte, un basilic ou un héliotrope s'épanouissait" (623). The Greeks associated the basil plant with hate, anger and misfortune (Grieve 85) and as such this textual marker acts as a presage to the third prediction and its subsequent fulfillment in the parricide. In addition, the noun "basilic" is associated with the Greek "basileus" (king) and it is here that we see this textual marker as a metonym in kernel form of the Romanesque church. The Greeks originally used the word "basilica" for the building or court in which the king-archon meted out justice in Athens and, as early as the second century B.C., the Romans began to use that term for their courts of justice (Fanning). By the ninth to the twelfth centuries, that period we call Romanesque and during which no doubt the legend of St. Julien flourished, churches began to be modeled on the rectangular Roman basilica, or law court, and this is the architectural style that art historians call "basilican" ("Romanesque"). This concept of regal church, a meeting of the secular and the sacred, is brought into Flaubert's description of Julien's birth castle at the point just before the castle tour ends at the innermost Roman sauna: ". . . la chapelle était somptueuse comme l'oratoire d'un roi" (624). But, as we have seen, the contamination of the sacred by the secular was rejected by the castle lord, Julien's father. Yet Julien's father does have a place in the secular side of this basilica as law court, for the text styles him as a judge: "Toujours enveloppé d'une pelisse de renard, il se promenait dans sa maison, rendait la justice à ses vassaux, apaisait les querelles des ses voisins" (624). Thus, the text's representation of Julien's father problematizes for Julien the dichotomous interrelation between secular and sacred. Once again, it will be Julien's task to resolve this dichotomy.

The basil plant that marks the text also marks, then, the castle of Julien's birth as a Romanesque church. It is also a marker that points to another character in Flaubert's tale. It must be stated here that Julien is the only character in the tale that has a name; this is not unusual in a hagiographic account that aims to highlight the sanctity of one single person. Yet a different St. Julien of the fourth century who, because he and his wife opened their home as a charitable hospital for the poor, was time and again confused with and assimilated into the legend of Flaubert's St. Julien. And this fourth-century Julien's wife was named Basilissa (Butler 56). The significance of her name will become apparent at the moment of the discovery of the parricide.

The next castle Julien is to inhabit is the one given to him upon his marriage to an emperor's daughter. In contrast to his family castle, it is built on a high ridge overlooking a gulf rather than on the slope of a hill in the middle of a forest. "[B]âti à la moresque" (635), everything is light and airy:

> Les chambres, pleines de crépuscule, se trouvaient éclairées par les incrustations des murailles. De hautes colonnettes, minces comme des roseaux, supportaient la voûte des coupoles, décorées de reliefs imitant les stalactites des grottes.
>
> (636)

In short, there were found "mille délicatesses d'architecture" (636). Essentially estranged from his heavy-walled and dark Romanesque castle, Julien is out of his element now in this Moorish-like castle where windows abound and columns rather than walls are the important structural elements. This castle is also a metaphor for an abrupt change in Julien's life, for here he even meets a different culture: "Julien ne faisait plus la guerre. Il se reposait, entouré d'un peuple tranquille; et chaque jour, une foule passait devant lui, avec des génuflexions et des baisements à l'orientale" (636). Here we find Julien gazing out a window in a state of mental escapism; he is "accoudé dans l'embrasure d'une fenêtre, en se rappelant ses chasses d'autrefois" (636). It is through the window that he hears the noise and light footsteps of a fox that eventually will entice him to re-enter the woods, take up his hunt again, and unwittingly kill his parents. While he is on the hunt, his wife lets in his parents looking for their long-lost son and she puts them to bed. When Julien returns, he finds them in bed and, thinking them to be his wife with another man, he slays them both. The point is that the window functions as the breach in the wall between the two inhospitable forces of peace and hostility. It has led Julien out of the arena of peace and into the arena of

hostility. In a very real way the window contributes here to bring peace and hostility together in a clash with the ensuing victory of hostility over peace. It is precisely because of the window that when Julien returns, he mistakes his parents for his wife and a lover: "Les vitraux garnis de plomb obscurcissaient la pâleur de l'aube . . ." (641) (Felman 56).

The noise of the murder had brought Julien's wife to the room where he saw "le fantôme de sa femme, une lumière à la main. . . . D'un large coup d'oeil, elle comprit tout, et s'enfuyant d'horreur laissa tomber son flambeau" (642). Julien's wife provides the light both literally and figuratively and he thus discovers that he has murdered his parents. What is important here is that it is his wife's glance that seals his fate, and that glance, extended in the light of the torch, shows him his parricide. The unnamed wife, Basilissa in some accounts, becomes identified with her glance and, as such, functions as an eponym of the mythical reptile, the basilisk, that kills with its own glance. She also functions as a synonym of the basil plant that signifies anger and misfortune. For this reason Flaubert has his Julien summon his wife after the parricide and command her "premièrement de ne pas lui répondre, de ne pas l'approcher, de ne plus même le regarder . . ." (642).

After the parricide Julien's life takes a different course. During his parents' funeral an unidentified monk, whom the reader knows is Julien, followed the procession from afar without anyone approaching him. During the mass the monk remains "à plat ventre au milieu du portail, les bras en croix, le front dans la poussière" (643). Here is Julien, the former "petit Jésus," now marked as the crucified Christ, half inside and half outside the church. Interior and exterior have meshed, peace and hostility have joined, the sacred and the profane have been reconciled, all in the person of Julien. Here Julien's cruciform position is an emblem of the text since we are at a veritable crossroads in the legend. In addition, his prostrate position at the entrance to the church's nave establishes his own body as a metonym of the church, reinforces him as the Jesus figure, and, by virtue of the etymological link between nave and boat, marks the text in preparation for his new life as ferryman.

This new integrity directs Julien to lead the life of a mendicant. It is now that he experiences inhospitality vis à vis humanity. Everyone flees from him, doors are closed in his face, he is stoned and derided so that finally "[r]epoussé de partout, il évita les hommes . . ." (643). Here is where the text's matrix of hospitality defines Julien. Julien is *hospes,* a stranger, an outsider, in one sense of the Latin word. That is why he becomes *hospes* in the other sense of the word, one who entertains a stranger, an insider, a host. And this he becomes with the aid of the river. Having transformed his life, he lives close to the river in a simple hut whose architecture is nothing more than its assimilation with the nature that surrounds it in the style of the Romantics' sacred grotto. The walls of Julien's successive habitations have become progressively lighter in order to blur the distinction between interior and exterior and neutralize the rivalry between peace and hostility. Julien dedicates himself to ferrying needy passengers across the river without asking for any retribution. The text has prepared the reader for this. Julien as nave of the church in his prone, cruciform position now becomes another "navis," the church that is the bark in which he ferries his travelers across the river. It is interesting to note that his mendicant life and hospitality here form a re-writing in reverse of what his parents had experienced as they spent years looking for their son:

> [I]ls marchaient depuis plusieurs années, sur de vagues indications, sans perdre l'espoir. Il avait fallu tant d'argent au péage des fleuves et dans les hôtelleries, pour les droits des princes et les exigences des voleurs, que le fond de leur bourse était vide, et qu'ils mendiaient maintenant.

(638)

One night Julien was awakened by the sound of someone calling his name three times, an echo of the triple prediction. The sound came "de l'autre bord, ce qui lui parut extraordinaire, vu la largeur du fleuve" (646). Here the text prepares us for a surreal climax. Julien goes to meet his passenger, finds a leper and succeeds in ferrying him across despite a raging storm which would have capsized any boat if the scene were an account of reality. Through it all "il apercevait les prunelles du Lépreux qui se tenait debout à l'arrière, immobile comme une colonne" (647). Here Julien has clearly already passed through the breach in the wall of reality. Indeed the discourse of the text has shifted from *discours réaliste* to *discours fantastique*. He shelters the leper in his own hut and answers to his triply expressed needs of food, drink, and warmth. In answer to the leper's cry for warmth, Julien removes his clothes so the leper may feel the warmth of his body and the two lie down on the bed: ". . . et il sentait contre sa cuisse la peau du Lépreux, plus froide qu'un serpent et rude comme une lime" (648). The shape of a snake and the rigidity and movement of a file both suggest the psychosexual embrace common to accounts of mystical rapture. It is the point at which the traditionally conceived boundary between body and soul is dissolved and at which creation and God are united. The text goes on to telescope this synesthetic experience of mystical rapture and in this way it redeems Julien and legitimizes him as saint:

> Alors le Lépreux l'étreignit; et ses yeux tout à coup prirent une clarté d'étoiles; ses cheveux s'allongèrent comme les rais du soleil; le souffle de ses narines avait la douceur des roses; un nuage d'encens s'éleva du

foyer; les flots chantaient. Cependant une abondance de délices, une joie surhumaine descendait comme une inondation dans l'âme de Julien pâmé. . . .

(648)

With this account of Julien ravished Flaubert now depicts the surreal dissolution of Julien's final abode. Without any walls or roof, Julien's abode now emblematizes the reconciliation of the opposing forces of interior and exterior, peace and hostility. The leper's body expands "touchant de sa tête et de ses pieds les deux murs de la cabane. Le toit s'envola, le firmament se déployait" (648) and the two ascend to heaven in the ultimate Christian union only a saint can merit.

Here ends the narrative but the text continues. In Flaubert's authorial tag of one sentence the reader is ostensibly presented with the tale's source, namely the depiction of the legend of Julien in a stained glass window in the cathedral of Rouen, Flaubert's hometown. But this window is more than an occasion for Flaubert to establish the veracity of his tale. As a window in the wall of a cathedral, it iconizes the tale's matrix of hospitality by opening a gap in the wall that separates the outside secular and hostile world from the sacred and peaceful world within. The window functions also now not only as the summation of the narrative in its chronological order on the horizontal axis but also as a replica of all that is window throughout the narrative, namely the negative space of what is wall, and this is the content of window on the vertical axis.

This reading of the **"Légende de Saint Julien l'Hospitalier"** has endeavored to show how certain textual markers function to add symbolic depth to the breadth of a narrative which is known for its simplicity of content and structure. While he has preserved the hagiographic legend that has endured in the permanence of the oral tradition and in the stained glass of the Rouen cathedral, Flaubert has recast the legend into a rich nexus of signs that point to the eternal questions of peace and hostility, the sacred and the profane.

Notes

1. All quotes from the tale are from Gustave Flaubert, *Oeuvres Complètes*. 2 vols. Paris: Gallimard, 1952. Vol. 2.

2. Knight continues to note that "[b]y telling us that the story is contained in a stained glass window, an effect is achieved whereby the story contains the window, but the window contains the story, and so on *ad infinitum*" (73).

3. It is not an allusion to the Immaculate Conception as Felman mistakenly notes (43).

Works Cited

Butler, Alban. *Lives of the Saints*. Ed. Herbert Thurston and Donald Attwater. 4 vols. New York: Kenedy, 1956. Vol. 1.

Fanning, Ralph. "Basilica." *The Encyclopedia Americana*. 1997 ed.

Felman, Shoshana. "La Signature de Flaubert: *La légende de saint Julien l'Hospitalier*." *Revue des sciences humaines* 53.181 (1981): 39-57.

Flaubert, Gustave. *Oeuvres Complètes*. 2 vols. Paris: Gallimard, 1952. Vol. 2.

Grieve, Maude. *A Modern Herbal*. New York: Dover, 1971.

Issacharoff, Michael. "'Trois Contes' et le problème de la non-linéarité." *Littérature* 15 (1974): 27-40.

Knight, Diana. *Flaubert's Characters: The Language of Illusion*. Cambridge: Cambridge UP, 1985.

"Romanesque Art and Architecture." *The Encyclopedia Americana*. 1997 ed.

Selvin, Susan Cauley. "Spatial Form in Flaubert's *Trois Contes*." *Romanic Review* 74 (1983): 202-220.

Lewis J. Overaker (essay date winter 2001)

SOURCE: Overaker, Lewis J. "Manifestations of the Holy Ghost in Flaubert's 'Un Coeur simple.'" *Renascence* 53, no. 2 (winter 2001): 119-48.

[*In the following essay, Overaker suggests that in Flaubert's story "Un Coeur simple," through the character of Félicité and the parrot named Loulou, one is witness "to a serious and triumphant spiritual journey in which the workings of the Holy Ghost are disclosed."*]

> Do you not know that your body is a temple of the Holy Spirit within you, which you have from God? You are not your own; you were bought with a price. So glorify God in your body.
>
> —1 Corinthians 6.19-20[1]

The variously interpreted character of Félicité continues to inspire—and to frustrate—the many readers of Flaubert's popular story, most of whom remain puzzled by what seems like a jarring incongruity in the fundamental terms and imagery of the narrative. The title figure in her moving unsophistication enjoys a saintly relationship with the third Person of the Holy Trinity, yet the prominent symbol of that relationship is the nearly absurd one of a decaying stuffed parrot named Loulou.[2] In the quasi-satirical world of Félicité's spirituality, the pervasive richness and indwelling timelessness of the Paraclete have been comically reduced to the vulgar artifices and none-too-permanent craft of the taxidermist. Even while the parrot is still alive, Flaubert refuses to spare us the bird's less than endearing animal habits such as his biting his perch, his pulling out is own

feathers, his scattering his droppings indiscriminately, and his spilling of his bath water (218/44).[3] In short, the tale presents us with a Loulou problem. How can we take seriously a story about sainthood and the Holy Ghost when an illiterate maidservant and the wormy carcass of an exotic bird are the vehicles of such a putatively theocentric narrative? The purpose of this essay is to argue that the reason for which Félicité deserves the title of saint is not in spite of the impact Loulou has upon her life, but rather because of it, and that in re evaluating the role of the parrot in the tale, we find ourselves witnesses to a serious and triumphant spiritual journey in which the workings of the Holy Ghost are disclosed.

Before proceeding with detailed analysis of **"Un Coeur simple,"** however, it may be helpful to refamiliarize readers with the tale by offering a brief synopsis. The title figure, Félicité, an illiterate maidservant, selflessly devotes most of her life to Mme. Aubain and her household, becoming attached in turn to various people—an unworthy fiancé, the children of her mistress (especially the daughter Virginie), her nephew, and an old man dying of cancer. All these persons desert her by going away or by forgetting her or by dying, thus causing her increasingly to turn to religion as an anodyne for physical and emotional loss. Eventually she acquires a pet, the parrot Loulou, who serves as a beloved surrogate for the close attachments of which her desolate life has deprived her; but when the parrot also dies, Félicité has him stuffed and keeps him near her as an icon of the Holy Spirit. Finally, on her own deathbed, the servant has a vision of God the Holy Ghost in the form of an immense parrot looming over her. Flaubert's story constitutes the introductory unit of a trilogy of tales all of which explore religious themes and two of which, **"La Légende de Saint Julien"** and **"Hérodias,"** feature canonical saints (Saint John the Baptist in the latter instance) as characters.

As a point of departure in their search for the true meaning of **"Un Coeur simple,"** scholars often consult Flaubert's correspondence for clues. Although we certainly cannot afford to ignore the author's own statements, we must be wary of encumbering our reading of the story with too many preconceived notions. The danger of doing so is that Flaubert often contradicts himself or seems inconsistent in his expressions of religious opinion. Arguing that the author was a natural skeptic and even a scoffer in sacred matters, readers sometimes point to his remark on the pilgrims to Lourdes, whom he viewed as victims of superstition, as in his letter of 5 October 1872 to Mme. Roger des Genettes: "What are your feelings about the pilgrims to Lourdes and of those who abuse them? Oh, wretched humanity!" (*Correspondance* 15. 167). Alternatively, they cite his comment on **"Hérodias"** in a letter of 19 June 1876 to the same recipient, "The story . . . , as I understand it, has nothing to do with religion" (*Correspondance* 15. 458), or his observation concerning our tale in the same letter that Félicité's final vision simply portrays her befuddlement: "when her time to die comes, she confuses the parrot with the Holy Ghost" (*Correspondance* 15. 458). There are, however, in Flaubert's correspondence just as many observations that reveal a wholly different religious orientation. In a letter of 30 March 1857 to Mlle. Leroyer de Chantepie, for instance, Flaubert writes, "religion attracts me above all else. . . . All dogmas are particularly repulsive to me . . . but I consider the sentiment that invented them as the most natural and poetic known to mankind" (*Correspondance* 13. 570). To the same lady in June 1857 he writes, "All piety attracts me, Catholic piety above all other kinds" (*Correspondance* 13. 587), and to his niece Caroline on 9 March 1868, "The only important thing . . . is religion" (*Correspondance* 14. 404). The natural and poetic nature of Christian faith and sentiment, made more attractive by the absence of dogma, describes very closely the basis of Félicité's spiritual journey. Finally, it is important to remember that on 19 June 1876 Flaubert makes it abundantly clear, again addressing Mme. Roger des Genettes, just how he wishes us to react to the life of Félicité: "Being a sensitive soul myself, I want to move others like me to pity and to tears" (*Correspondance* 15. 458); and a few weeks later (7 August) he expresses to Caroline his intention to conclude the story on a high note: "But above all, I must end my *Félicité* in a magnificent way!" (*Correspondance* 15. 481)—this latter hardly consistent with a concept of Félicité dying alone, hallucinating and duped, no matter how ironically gaudy and crudely circus-like the scene in the street below may be.

Whatever his personal religious attitudes, Flaubert could hardly have isolated himself from the spiritual climate of his age. Nineteenth-century France witnessed a Catholic revival and the recrudescence of a certain personalism in Christian faith. As early as 1762 Rousseau, rejecting the deism of his own century, could write through the voice of his Savoyard Priest, "I serve God in the simplicity of my heart. . . . As to those dogmas which have no effect upon action or morality, dogmas about which so many men torment themselves, I give no heed to them" (*Emile* 272). Chateaubriand in his *Génie du christianisme* (1802) professed a similar revulsion toward dogma: "The Gospel has been preached to the poor in spirit. . . . Its doctrine is not to be found in the workings of the intellect but in the heart; it does not teach one to argue, but to live well" (1.72).[4] Although clearly associated with the mind-set of Catholic royalists and Romantics, Chateaubriand nevertheless continued to exert broader cultural influences in France throughout the century, and, as Philip Spencer has noted (165), these extended to writers such as Flaubert, who were in obvious sympathy with the earlier writer's scorn of prescriptive dogma.

In searching for traces of the author's attitude toward Félicité, we must continually bear in mind his writerly principle of self-exclusion and non-intervention in the imaginary experiences he sought to represent, although, in fact, numerous elements from the creator's own biography—characters, places, emotions—enter the tale entirely unaltered or but thinly disguised.[5] Perhaps Flaubert's most illuminating words on the role of the author in his fiction appear in a letter of 6 February 1876 to George Sand, written just after the completion of **"La Légende de Saint Julien"** and only days before he commenced **"Un Coeur simple"**:

> As for revealing my personal opinion regarding the characters I create, I say no, no, a thousand times no! I do not have the *right* to do so. If the reader does not draw from a book the moral which is to be found there, it is either because he is an imbecile or because the book is *false* in the precision of its artistry.
>
>   (*Correspondance* 15. 435)

Flaubert's preference for the "*survol*" or "overview" technique is a highly sophisticated approach to composition; but it also presents many challenges to interpretation. William VanderWolk describes the on-going task Flaubert sets for us as readers: it is as if the author, "cognizant of the importance of memory, looked one hundred years into the future and called out to us to comb our own experience in order to find the key to the mysteries he presents us" (184). Confronted by an author who seems to relish ambiguity (Paul Kran describes any effort to decipher Flaubert's true feelings about religion as "doomed to failure," [42]), we will undoubtedly find our best access to the spiritual marrow of the stories in the texts themselves—armed, but not burdened, with the knowledge of Flaubert's biography and his statements on spirituality, but nevertheless free to let the fictions come to us as the author invites us to do. Flaubert warns us indeed that unlocking the door to his deeper significances will be far from easy and that any formulations in this realm will tend to be inconclusive. In a letter of 7 April 1848 to Maxime du Camp he affirms his allegiance to ambiguity: "I have a need to say incomprehensible things" (*Correspondance* 13. 622). And recognizing that Flaubert, like several of his contemporaries, sometimes employs irony as a means of veiling his own deepest feelings and beliefs, we must guard ourselves from being pushed too decisively in the direction either of cynicism on the one hand or of sentimentality on the other. If we accept Flaubert's invitation to allow his fictions to speak for themselves, we shall find that, finally, we can be comfortable in regarding Félicité without qualification as a saint, and in being able to understand the importance of Loulou in fresh perspective as an essential component of, rather than an obstacle to, the hagiographic profile offered us.

A brief review of the critical perspectives on Loulou in the scholarship of **"Un Coeur simple"** may be useful at this point. As early as 1922, Albert Thibaudet elevated

Félicité to the ranks of Flaubert's *"vies gagnées,"* i.e., characters whose lives are ultimately successful and even exemplary; he regards the life of Flaubert's heroine as one *"qui a mérité d'être"*—one not lived in vain (212). Félicité's classification as a saint, however, which is now almost universally accorded (though often grudgingly), has been the result of a long, hard labor. Of course, there are those who continue to deny Félicité sainthood. One such is Ben Stoltzfus, who sees in Loulou Flaubert's "supreme mockery" (23) of the solace available to the faithful, and who regards Félicité as "merely the dupe of religious faith" (20). Martin Bidney shares this cynical point of view, evaluating Loulou's function as follows: Félicité's "faith has been nourished by ecstasies brought on by rays of light rebounding from the glass eye of an idolatrously worshipped, worm-eaten stuffed parrot. . . . With all his respect for the sincerity of Félicité's simple heart, Flaubert cannot resist the temptation of playing ironic tricks on her," tricks which approach "the point of semi-parody" (215-16). Victor Brombert, another critic of the skeptical persuasion, can declare that, although Flaubert's "compassionate account of this simple woman *at times comes close* to hagiography" (*Novels* 238, emphasis mine), the "old servant," a near saint, "lives *a meaningless existence* in a disconsolate world of which she herself is unable to make any critical assessment" (*Novels* 245, emphasis mine). Obviously Loulou creates a problem for these writers, even those who affirm Félicité's saintly status, since their principal difficulty lies in coming to terms with the awkward symbolism of the parrot. Enid Starkie, for instance, acknowledges the presence of "holiness" in each of the **Trois Contes,** but because "Félicité has perfect innocence and goodness," her "sainthood might then not be considered of the highest" (*Master* 273-74). Ultimately, Starkie can offer only a negative assessment of the effect upon readers of Félicité's problematic icon: "the tale is basically as pessimistic as anything [Flaubert] ever wrote. In his view, all of us here below, metaphorically speaking, have only a moth-eaten stuffed parrot to represent the Holy Ghost" (*Making* 300). Stirling Haig, who allows that the life of Félicité progresses from the profane to the sacred on account of the presence of Loulou in her life, seems ultimately to recant his own assertion by declaring that the link between the two is nothing more than "a result of the well-known confusion" (305). Aimée Israel-Pelletier, also adamant in her asseveration of Félicité's saintliness, is equally unable to reconcile the role of Loulou with the religious basis of her interpretation. She grants that Félicité achieves a "mystical reunion with the Holy Spirit" (22) at the end of her life, but concludes by apparently denying that the parrot can embody any authentic spiritual meaning in its owner's existence: "what [Félicité], and Flaubert, expose through Loulou is the wholly contrived, arbitrary, mobile, and, here, comical and pathetic nature of representation, in particular, of religious representation" (49). Other responses to Loulou as a central figure in the tale range from the patronizing words of Jonathan Culler, who implies that we exaggerate the bird's significance ("We *allow* the arbitrary connection between the parrot and the Holy Ghost and *permit* the potentially sentimental to pass over into the sacred" [211, emphasis mine]), to the reaction of Karen Erickson, who finds the embarrassing emblem of Félicité's religious pilgrimage inadequate: "Though it is a caricature, the parrot comes to represent the voice of God which speaks in the descent of the Spirit in Félicité's deformed theology" (69). By thus suggesting that Flaubert has set up a dichotomy between the presence and the absence of God in the tale, Erickson merely voices, as have so many before her, a sense of impasse or irreconcilable conflict in the fundamental import of Flaubert's work—a conflict that continues to plague readers.

The Loulou problem, then, persists in erecting a barrier between our wish to grant sainthood to Félicité for the right reasons and our capacity for integrating her story of sanctification into a tale of the workings of the Holy Spirit, ironically objectified by a physically tawdry symbol. For it is not enough to award Félicité the status of "saint" simply on the basis of her many acts of service and sacrifice nor because of her loving and forgiving nature. Even if Félicité had undergone three times as much suffering at the hands of insensitive and ungrateful persons as that depicted in the tale, she would hardly qualify as a saint. Legions of headstones in innumerable cemeteries, actual and fictitious, commemorate lives not dissimilar to Félicité's with such inscriptions as "Well done, thou good and faithful servant." The graves these headstones mark are usually those, as Benjamin Bart suggests, of Montaigne's "innocents," those who, because their lives are "completely unreflective" (Starkie's phrase for Félicité [*Master* 274]), do not have to struggle heroically or vigorously with sin and are therefore "always and effortlessly good" (697). Such "innocents" must be carefully distinguished from saints.

True saints come in all shapes and sizes and in all degrees of physical activity and inactivity. They may lead armies into battle or may never leave the confines of the cloister. They may be blatant sinners most of their lives or may exemplify purity from their earliest days. They live in fiction and in real life today. But active intervention of the Holy Spirit is a vital component of true sainthood. The lives of saints reveal an identifiable presence of grace betokening an intimate relationship with God, a relationship almost always marked by a vision, by an encounter with the divine, or by a miracle. In Flaubert's own work one has only to instance the lives of Saint Anthony or Saint Julian to grasp the distinction between "innocents" and "saints."

Loulou, I wish to argue, supplies that additional ingredient in Félicité's life that separates her from a mere "innocent." For as long as we deride or ignore Loulou, keeping the parrot at a distance or treating him as a loose metaphor for religion in general rather than as a serious and successful representation of the Holy Ghost, we fail also to accept Félicité's saintliness without reservation, and also to perceive the profoundest meaning of her life. Culler speaks of the tension that the reader experiences by facing up to the deliberately unresolved significance of the story: "to state explicitly [Félicité's] saintliness and the sacred character of her suffering and vision would be to expose oneself to multiple and inescapable ironies; but to draw the line across the very threshold . . . is to leave an uncompleted structure which the reader must complete if he is to feel satisfied" (211). Culler points clearly to the absolute necessity of redefining the role of Loulou if one is ever to find unity and connectedness in the tale: "we can take the ending as finally transcending irony only if we have come to postulate a kind of order which makes the identification of the parrot and the Holy Ghost worthy and appropriate" (210). Anthony Thorlby employs similar threshold imagery: "the resolution of such suffering and love as Félicité's is made in heaven, and across the very threshold Flaubert draws his most daring line" (58-59). Similarly, Robert Griffin, stressing Flaubert's theoretically ambiguous relationship between the sacred and the profane, and following in Culler's traces, remarks that we often feel invited to collaborate "with the text and thus corrupt . . . it by averring a circumscribed but unauthorized meaning" (18). Nevertheless Israel-Pelletier, not content with interpretive indeterminacy, has recently encouraged us not to back away from what some might regard as a "singular or subversive" reading of the tale; for to "refuse to do so . . . is . . . to opt for aesthetic contemplation over responsibility" (12).

It would appear, then, that if we are to cross the "daring line" and commit ourselves to a responsible reading of the story, we must wholeheartedly engage the Loulou problem by entertaining the idea that the Holy Ghost is truly fundamental to the narrative—intimately and crucially associated with the mystery of Félicité's entire life. References to the Holy Ghost in scripture can throw light on the question of whether or not Loulou may serve as an appropriate representative of the Holy Spirit and whether Félicité may be properly regarded as a uniquely blessed recipient of His gifts as we experience them in mundane life. Here we may consider passages in the Christian Bible from both the Old and New Testaments.

Even in the Old Testament, Isaiah, Ezekiel, and Joel foretell the coming of the Holy Spirit. Isaiah (32.15) images the Spirit of God being poured upon all Israel like rain transforming a wilderness into a fruitful field. Félicité's farm background may be loosely, though perhaps unconsciously, relevant here. Flaubert makes it

clear in **"Un Coeur simple"** that her early life has been associated with farming, ploughed fields, crops, and pastures—with *"la campagne"* (202/19), *"les récoltes"* (203/20), and *"la troisième pâture"* (205/24)—and that, when she is dying, "The scents of summer came up from the meadows . . ." (224/54). Flaubert adds at one point that Félicité was impressed and moved by the Gospel references to sowing, reaping, and wine-making: "The sowing of the seed, the reaping of the harvest, the pressing of the grapes—all those familiar things of which the Gospels speak had their place in her life. God had sanctified them in passing . . ." (209/29-30). The narrator also associates Loulou with thunderstorms and heavy rain, which agitate the parrot disturbingly, perhaps because they remind him of the sudden downpours of his native forests (220/47). Ezekiel echoes Isaiah's imagery of the Spirit being poured out (39.29) but also introduces the idea of the Holy Ghost as the means by which God enlivens the valley of the dry bones: "Behold, I will open your graves, and raise you from your graves, O my people. . . . And you shall know that I am the Lord. . . . And I will put my Spirit within you, and you shall live . . ." (Ezekiel 37.12-14). The mention of graves in this passage suggests a kind of subterranean relevance to the incident of Virginie's burial in **"Un Coeur simple"** (215-16/40-41); Flaubert makes a special point of Félicité's faithfulness in tending and visiting the girl's grave. Whereas Mme. Aubain's initial reaction to the death of her daughter is despair and rebellion against God, Félicité humbly accepts the loss and, strengthened by the Holy Spirit, helps to console and fortify her mistress. A passage from Joel, however, probably relates more closely to Félicité's spiritual career, speaking as it does of visions and servants: And it shall come to pass afterward, that I will pour out my spirit on all flesh; your sons and your daughters shall prophesy, your old men shall dream dreams, and your young men shall see visions. Even upon the menservants and maidservants in those days, I will pour out my spirit. (Joel 2.28-29)

New Testament writings on the coming of the Holy Ghost (also commonly referred to as the "Holy Spirit," "Advocate," or "Counselor" and related to the Greek word, *parakletos*) include passages from all four Gospels, the Acts of the Apostles, and several of Saint Paul's epistles. Taking up the earthly life of Jesus first, we recall from the story of the Incarnation that the Blessed Virgin Mary "was found to be with child of the Holy Spirit" (Matthew 1.18); compare **"Un Coeur simple"**: "In one of the stained-glass windows in the apse the Holy Ghost looked down on the Virgin" (209/29). The Holy Ghost then makes His entrance into Christ's physical life at the time of His baptism, the account of which appears in all the Gospel accounts. John the Baptist proclaims that he has been baptizing with water but that soon the Messiah will appear, the one who, in John's words, "will baptize . . . with the Holy

Spirit and with fire" (Luke 3.16). In John's Gospel it is the dove resting on Jesus' head that enables John the Baptist to identify the Son of Man in the crowd (John 1.32-33), whereas in the other three Gospels, the Spirit of God descends upon Jesus *after* His baptism but always in the form of a dove (Matthew 3.16; Mark 1.10; Luke 3.22). Mention of this episode also occurs in **"Un Coeur simple"** when Félicité observes the dove—the emblem of "the Holy Ghost . . . in a colour-print depicting the baptism of Our Lord" (221-22/50). Additional Gospel references to the Holy Ghost provide a deeper understanding of His nature and function. He is often associated with the giving of strength and protection and with the ability to act without fear. Mark records Jesus' words to the Apostles: "And when they bring you to trial and deliver you up, do not be anxious beforehand what you are to say; but say whatever is given you in that hour, for it is not you who speak, but the Holy Spirit" (Mark 13.11). Here we might recall Félicité's early embarrassed encounter with Théodore after she had screamed in fright at his attempt to assault her sexually. When Théodore tries to excuse his behavior as the result of drunkenness, "She did not know what to say in reply and felt like running off" (**"Un Coeur simple,"** 203/20). A moment later, however, she finds her voice and responds to his enquiry about her marriage plans with considerable aplomb and self-composure: "She answered with a smile that it was mean of him to make fun of her" (203/20). It is the power of the Holy Ghost which sustains Jesus during His long fast and confrontation with Satan: "And Jesus, full of the Holy Spirit, returned from the Jordan, and was led by the Spirit for forty days in the wilderness, tempted by the devil" (Luke 4.1-2). Flaubert tells us that Félicité "copied all Virginie's observances, fasting when she did and going to confession with her" (**"Un Coeur simple,"** 209/30). And Jesus credits the Holy Ghost, for example, as His source of power in being able to cast out evil spirits: "But if it is by the Spirit of God that I cast out demons, then the kingdom of God has come upon you" (Matthew 12.28).

Even though the Holy Ghost does not become fully manifest in the Bible until after the crucifixion, He enters several Gospel narratives at earlier points and in a variety of ways. It is because of the promise and intervention of the Holy Ghost, for example, that Simeon is led to the temple to meet Jesus: "it had been revealed to [Simeon] by the Holy Spirit that he should not see death before he had seen the Lord's Christ. And inspired by the Spirit he came into the temple" (Luke 2.26-27). Speaking to a crowd after denouncing the Pharisees, Jesus warns them that they will be forced to acknowledge Him before the rulers and authorities of the synagogues; but He allays their fears by saying, "for the Holy Spirit will teach you in that very hour what you ought to say" (Luke 12.12). Again, Félicité's response to Théodore comes to mind. The Holy Ghost is also

portrayed as a great provider of human needs. Jesus speaks of God's loving generosity by telling the disciples: "Ask, and it will be given you; seek, and you will find; knock, and it will be opened to you. . . . If you then, who are evil, know how to give good gifts to your children, how much more will the heavenly Father give the Holy Spirit to those who ask him!" (Luke 11.9-13).

In the Book of John, Jesus speaks of the real nature and function of the Holy Ghost, foretells the day of Pentecost, and, in a post-resurrection appearance, bequeaths the Holy Ghost to the disciples. John records Jesus' words regarding the knowledge and peace that the Holy Ghost will bring them: "But the Counselor, the Holy Spirit, whom the Father will send in my name, he will teach you all things, and bring to your remembrance all that I have said to you. Peace I leave with you; my peace I give to you . . ." (John 14.26-27). Again addressing the disciples, Jesus gives them a further definition of the Holy Ghost: "And I will pray the Father, and he will give you another Counselor, to be with you forever, even the Spirit of truth, whom the world cannot receive, because it neither sees him nor knows him; you know him, for he dwells with you, and will be in you" (John 14.16-17). Many English translations use the word "Advocate" (for "Counselor") in this context; in the French Bible of 1830 (translated by Father Bouhours), which Flaubert undoubtedly knew, the word is rendered as "consolateur" (comforter). Then, after the crucifixion, at the time of Jesus' appearance to the downhearted disciples, the gift of the Spirit is actually bestowed. Coming upon them suddenly, Jesus says, "'Peace be with you. As the Father has sent me, even so I send you.' And when he had said this, he breathed on them, and said to them, 'Receive the Holy Spirit. If you forgive the sins of any, they are forgiven; if you retain the sins of any, they are retained'" (John 20.21-23). A commentator in *The Interpreter's Bible* paraphrases the core message of these words to the Apostles as follows: "by ourselves" the difficulty of rising above our own sinful natures "cannot be done at all. But then, Christ does not ask impossibilities from his people. He gives what makes it possible"—namely the gift of the Holy Spirit. "And with something of Christ within them, all things spiritual [come] within their reach"; "ordinary people, once Christ's Spirit has touched and inspired and quickened them, can live and do live, can serve God and the cause and do serve God and the cause, as they could not do before" (8.797).

Theologians sometimes retitle the entire Book of Acts "The Acts of the Holy Spirit"; but the most familiar passage involving the Holy Ghost deals with the day of Pentecost, which in liturgy commemorates the birthday of the Church: "And suddenly a sound came from heaven like the rush of a mighty wind, and it filled all the house where [the Apostles] were sitting. And there appeared to them tongues as of fire, distributed and resting on each one of them. And they were all filled with the Holy Spirit . . ." (Acts 2.2-4). Finally, Paul, particularly in his letters to the Romans and the Corinthians, sheds additional light on how the Holy Ghost functions ideally in human lives. To the Corinthians Paul makes it clear that the gift of the Holy Ghost was bequeathed to all: "Now there are varieties of gifts, but the same Spirit; and there are varieties of service, but the same Lord; and there are varieties of working, but it is the same God who inspires them all in every one. To each is given the manifestation of the Spirit for the common good" (1 Corinthians 12.4-7). In Romans Paul relates the Holy Ghost to suffering and prayer. As regards suffering, Paul writes, "For all who are led by the Spirit of God are sons of God . . . and if children, then heirs, heirs of God and fellow heirs with Christ, provided we suffer with him in order that we may also be glorified with him" (Romans 8.14-17). As for prayer, Paul observes: "Likewise the Spirit helps us in our weakness: for we do not know how to pray as we ought, but the Spirit himself intercedes for us with sighs too deep for words. And he who searches the hearts of men knows what is the mind of the Spirit, because the Spirit intercedes for the saints according to the will of God" (Romans 8.26-27).

What the biblical accounts tell us of the Holy Ghost, then, can be seen as specifically relevant to Félicité's own experience, although, of course, she is too ignorant to rationalize the connections theologically or to articulate them in a conscious way. In Flaubert's words, "Of dogma she neither understood nor even tried to understand anything," "her religious education" having "been neglected in her youth" (209/30). To sum up, we learn that although the Holy Ghost generally cannot be seen, He did actually reveal himself briefly during Jesus' earthly life in visual form as a dove. We discover also that the Holy Ghost casts out fear, providing both the strength and protection needed to serve God; that He functions chiefly as a source of comfort for those who suffer; that He acts as an intermediary between God and our needs, responding even to our feeblest prayers; and that He empowers us to forgive. It is clear, too, from scripture that He exists in the minds and hearts of true believers as a constant reminder of God's presence in human life, and that, armed with His power, believers are led to righteous actions. The Nicene Creed, recited or sung at Mass, sums up the Holy Spirit in the understanding of the Church as the power through whom the Incarnation became possible—"the giver of life, who proceeds from the Father and the Son," with whom He "is worshiped and glorified," and who "has spoken through the Prophets." And the gifts of the Holy Ghost are available to all, but perhaps especially so to the simple and the outcast. The annals of saints and martyrs, indeed, are replete with persons who would have led seemingly insignificant lives had they not been cho-

sen by God, and aided by the Holy Ghost, for a special task. Saint Joan of Arc, for instance, was a peasant, Saint Bernadette of Lourdes was illiterate, and Saint Felicity was a slave. The last of these has a certain interest for Flaubertians since Saint Felicity and her companion Saint Perpetua were both martyred at Carthage, the setting of Flaubert's earlier novel *Salammbô*, and since both were also tossed by a savage cow before being killed in the arena by gladiators—an incident conceivably related to that of the charging bull in **"Un Coeur simple"** (see *Butler's Lives of the Saints* 1.498).

Reminded then of how the Comforter, as revealed in scripture and the teachings of the Church, can enter and affect individual lives, we can better understand Félicité's close relationship with this unique Person of the Trinity—a divine and all pervasive force of which Loulou (from Félicité's naive and uneducated angle of vision) provides a suitable, if also ironic, representation.

To know a successful relationship with the Holy Ghost is not something many believers, even the most learned and prayerful, achieve easily. We have seen that the Holy Ghost is commonly invisible and speechless, so that any immediate or dramatic connection one might experience with Him is likely, by definition, to be exceptional, even extraordinary and non-traditional. But if we recall that the Holy Ghost was bequeathed to all followers of Christ and that the gift is not restricted by any need for theological knowledge or any requirement, or even conception, of dogma, it follows that Félicité's potential for a rare bond with the Holy Ghost is entirely valid. All we need do is trust the insights of scripture and, in the light of these, accept that **"Un Coeur simple"** is written to make vital to the reader what can actually occur within the believing heart of a very simple woman. And we need also to lay aside the idea that the story reflects Flaubert's own spiritual odyssey and, with it, Professor Stoltzfus' misguided contention "that Loulou is Flaubert's symbol rather than Félicité's" (23). Nor need we regret that the inherent theodicy represented in the tale lacks scholarly or intellectual persuasiveness. Rather, what Flaubert would have us encounter is exclusively Félicité's religious experience; and we must begin with her if we are to free ourselves to consider her uniqueness in a serious way. Not to do so is both arrogant and theologically maladroit. Regarded within this admittedly restrictive framework, Félicité's story becomes a microcosm of the process by which the true believer grows slowly, often incognizantly, into a relationship with the most elusive and difficult-to-define Person of the Holy Trinity.

In the opening paragraphs of the tale, Flaubert imparts a view of Félicité's going to daily Mass and sleeping in front of the hearth with her rosary beads in her hands—the very portrait of a believer. It is not important that her supplications lack sophistication or that her prayer-life consists, in all likelihood, only of the words heard at Mass or of the rote petitions of the Angelus, which she probably understands but vaguely. Félicité, no matter how unlettered, impresses us as one who has embraced the faith unquestioningly and for whom traditional Catholic values are vitally important, even if she is almost totally unaware of the high and special gift of faith she has received. This gift is clearly that of the Holy Ghost as a working partner in her life, a gift which affords her a sense of God's presence even as she performs the most humdrum chores. Her life, work, and feelings are all irradiated by a penumbra of the sacred—that quality that the Holy Ghost is uniquely empowered to supply. Apart from the assumption of Félicité's living in intimate relationship with the Holy Spirit, no matter how obscure or even superstitious that relationship might appear to outsiders, it would be virtually impossible to account for the almost incredible resilience and courage that characterize her life.

Despite her simple faith and at times almost risible naiveté, however, Félicité possesses a keen moral sense and is not without skills that earn our admiration. The tale's opening paragraphs establish her as a treasure among domestics whose ceaseless diligence and varied capacities—sewing, washing, ironing, cooking, butter-churning, barnyard care, etc.—excite the envy of Mme. Aubain's bourgeois counterparts in Pont-l'Évêque (201/17). Nor are her talents limited to the performance of household chores. We learn early on, for instance, that Félicité is a shrewd bargainer at local markets (202/18) and no-one's fool when it comes to outwitting the visiting sellers of hens and cheeses who would take unfair advantage; these latter always go away "full of respect for her" (204/22). Only once does Flaubert suggest any failure of intellect in his heroine. When Félicité asks her mistresses' solicitor, M. Bourais, to help her understand where Havana is (knowing that her nephew Victor resides there), she is surprised to discover that the map contains no likeness of the young man: her "intelligence was so limited that she probably expected to see an actual portrait of her nephew" (213/36). Though unlettered and totally unfamiliar with books, she is far from helpless or easily duped in practical affairs. Also in ethical and sexual matters her instincts are sound, as becomes clear in her refusal to be seduced by Théodore, who had briefly pursued her when she was only eighteen: "She was not ignorant of life as young ladies are, for the animals had taught her a great deal; but her reason and an instinctive sense of honour prevented her from giving way" (203/20). In addition Félicité displays considerable social expertise in regularly managing to get rid of the drunken Marquis de Gremanville, Mme. Aubain's improvidently comic uncle, whose unwelcome visits disrupt household order: "[She] used to push him gently out of the house, saying politely: 'You've had quite enough, Monsieur . . . See you another time!' and shutting the door on him" (204/22). Félicité's dis-

missal of the undesirable but nobly-born uncle finds a humorous parallel toward the end of the story. Loulou, for the moment endowed with human characteristics, laughs derisively at the face of Bourais when the solicitor approaches the house: "[it] obviously struck him as terribly funny, for as soon as he saw it he was seized with uncontrollable laughter" (218/45). In perhaps the most comic episode of the tale, Bourais, humiliated before the neighbors by Loulou's outbursts of ridicule, is forced to enter by a circuitous route through the garden, hiding his face with his hat; and the looks he gives the troublesome parrot "were far from tender" (218/45). Here Flaubert seems to fortify the bond between Félicité and Loulou, enhancing their shared sense of partnership and common experience. In both episodes social inferiors—an illiterate maidservant in one case, a talking bird in the other—invert traditional hierarchy by dominating a situation in which guests who regard themselves as superior to others are humbled.

Although Flaubert describes Félicité early in the narrative as lacking in distinctive features—as a kind of *"femme en bois"* (202/18) or wooden doll in appearance and manner, he deliberately fails to sustain this caricature. Her behavior, for instance, is sometimes unpredictable. When Mme. Aubain's friend Liébard counsels her to assuage her grief for Victor's death by visiting the young man's mother at Trouville, she reacts with anger, dismissiveness, and a judgmentalism that, for the moment at least, excludes forgiveness: "It doesn't matter a bit, not to them it doesn't" (213/37). But Félicité is not immune to growth and change. After Virginie has died and Mme. Aubain finally lets down her guard, permitting herself to weep in communion with her servant, Félicité is so grateful for the embrace and so moved by the common bond of suffering, that she feels a totally dependent loyalty to her mistress from that point on: she cherishes her indeed "with dog-like devotion and religious veneration" (217/43). Yet immediately after characterizing his title figure as servile and blindly loyal to Mme. Aubain, Flaubert in the following sentence certifies that his *"femme en bois"* is far from being rigid or unable to evolve: "Her heart grew softer as time went by" (217/43).

In addition to domestic skills, social aplomb, and righteous impulses, Félicité can claim a certain degree of self-awareness. While she is trudging to Honfleur with the dead Loulou in her basket, an angry coach-driver whips her savagely for having startled his horses. Bleeding from the wound but still clutching the parrot that has become the center of her life, she reaches the summit of a hill, feels faint, then experiences a moment of expanded consciousness (221/48). The sudden violence of her trauma has jolted her into a new psychological and spiritual dimension. The painful reverses that seem to have composed her life collect in her mind and well up in her throat stiflingly—her miserable childhood, the unhappiness of her first love affair, the successive losses of her nephew and of Virginie. At this point of crisis we see her for the first time grasping as a whole the significance and value of her life rather than simply being immersed in and overwhelmed by its quotidian minutiae. Haig would undoubtedly interpret the incident as an example of Flaubert's narrative complexity, a stylistic means of providing the illusion of Félicité's interior growth while keeping her still at arm's length—and thus remotely ambiguous; from such a critical perspective, "Félicité is for observation, not for absorption" (315). But an impression of the character's dignity, based on her hard-won cognizance that life is composed of choices, is inescapable, to which Flaubert adds the pathos of an old woman looking back over the long years of an existence that might have been different. Even if Félicité were wholly stupid and uninsightful, even if she responded to every eventuality in the same way, loving and forgiving indiscriminately, and even if she were incapable of self-knowledge, she would still be a child of God eligible to receive the gifts of the Holy Spirit. But her story would then be uncompelling. Rather, Flaubert is careful to surround his heroine with a framework of anecdotal details that encourages the reader to respect her and to respond seriously to the totality of her life—and this in spite of the simplicity and naiveté, even the existential flatness, that appear to define it. If we re-examine the profile that emerges from Flaubert's artfully selected particulars, applying to them some knowledge of how the Holy Ghost can enter and affect human lives, we may begin to recognize that **"Un Coeur simple"** is the fictional account of a genuine saint, of a woman whose inner strength and power to serve others elevates her far above the level of mere "innocents," and for whom the presence of the divine in the most mundane experiences becomes an urgent reality.

We have seen already that the manifold gifts of the Holy Ghost specifically include the courage to act righteously without fear or hesitation and the ability to forgive others. It is clear also that among His other functions are the readiness to assist prayer and the provision of comfort in discouraging circumstances. Danger, separation, privation, misunderstanding, fatigue, and loneliness are Félicité's constant companions, yet she always picks herself up and returns to the task of loving and serving others without a hint of self-pity or any sense of sacrifice. When she saves the life of her mistress and the children by blinding a stampeding bull with clods of earth, the townspeople are awe-struck with admiration and tell of her extraordinary bravery and resourcefulness for many years afterwards; yet the unassuming maidservant regards the matter as quite inconsequential: "Félicité never prided herself in the least on what she had done, as it never occurred to her that she had done anything heroic" (206/25). In the context of Félicité's belief system, it is difficult to attribute such fearless vir-

tue and selfless humility to merely natural traits, unassisted by higher powers. And many years later we see our heroine offering cider to soldiers as they pass through town, caring for the victims of cholera, tending Polish refugees, and dressing the wound of the cancer-ridden Père Colmiche who is dying in a pig-sty. For the latter, who holds out his trembling hands whenever she leaves him, Félicité is like a savior: "The poor old fellow would thank her in a faint whisper, slavering and trembling all the while, fearful of losing her and stretching his hands out as soon as he saw her moving away" (217/43). Stepping in to assure the safety of those in danger and ministering to the needs of the suffering, Félicité becomes, in Flaubert's ordering of her life, an agent of the Holy Ghost.

It is, however, in her capacity to forgive those who have wounded her that Félicité shows herself uniquely blessed by the power of the Holy Spirit; for Flaubert presents her as almost the incarnation of this virtue, exploring that aspect of her character in rich particularity. At one painful juncture Félicité feels distraught because six months have passed since she has heard from Victor, her nephew who has gone abroad. Mme. Aubain cruelly waves her concerns away, suggesting that worries about a forgettable ship-lad are far less upsetting than her own failure to receive a letter from Virginie within the space of a mere four days: "'Oh, your nephew!' And Mme. Aubain started pacing up and down again, with a shrug of her shoulders that seemed to say: 'I wasn't thinking of him—and indeed, why should I? Who cares about a young, good-for-nothing cabinboy? Whereas my daughter—why, just think!'" (212/35). At first naturally indignant, Félicité, presumably operating under the grace of her divine mentor, is able to do more than forgive these slurs; she completely forgets them, rationalizing that such hurtful behavior might only be the understandable reaction of a mother, momentarily losing her head over a beloved child. Flaubert gives us a second instance of forgiveness when Félicité, now on her deathbed, sends for Fabu, who had toyed with Loulou and tried to teach him to swear. Having suspected the butcher's assistant of having poisoned her beloved parrot with parsley, she now wishes to cleanse her soul by confessing that she has harbored ill thoughts of him: "'Forgive me,' she said, making an effort to stretch out her arm. 'I thought it was you who had killed him'" (224/53). We are never told whether her suspicions have any basis in fact; very probably they do not. But Fabu's guilt or innocence is beside the point. What Flaubert wishes to dramatize is Félicité's extraordinary ability, even in semi-delirium, to forgive a man she believes has deprived her of her most precious companion and, as an extension of the Holy Spirit's universal embrace, to try to bring him within the compass of her love by weakly extending her arm.

Because of her habit of living exclusively for others, however, Félicité can experience the virtue of forgiveness at higher levels than the merely personal. Listening to the priest at Virginie's catechism lesson, she identifies tearfully with the pain of Christ in the story of the Passion, then extends her feelings of affection to the animal world—to lambs and doves because of their association in her mind with the Lamb of God and the traditional avian emblem of the Holy Ghost (209/30). Fortified by her love of Christ and companioned by the Holy Ghost, she is also almost uniquely able to love those around her and to orient herself psychologically toward their lives. Usually she focuses on a single person at a time, on Virginie or Victor for instance, preoccupying herself almost exclusively with that person's joys, sorrows, and needs. At Virginie's first communion, Félicité participates vicariously in the sacramental experience with unusual intensity, identifying almost physically with the little girl who has been her charge, and nearly fainting when she watches her receive the host (209-10/30-31). Her own private communion the following morning lacks the rapture she had felt the previous day, chiefly because it lacks the element of close emotional identification with the child she has come to adore. After Victor has left for Havana, she experiences an even higher degree of identification with a loved one: "From then on Félicité thought of nothing but her nephew" (212/34). Her concern for Victor's welfare reaches an absurd level of intensity when she worries that the same hot sun or buffeting wind that afflicts Pont-l'Évêque on a given day might cause her nephew discomfort in far-away Cuba. The effect nevertheless is only mildly satirical, dominated as it is by our sense of Félicité's all pervasive love for someone who is absent from her. Félicité even understands her own mortality in relation to another human being, for she feels it contrary to the natural order of life that Mme. Aubain should predecease her: "That Madame should die before her upset her ideas, seemed to be contrary to the order of things, monstrous and unthinkable" (222/51). Leading a life of almost total self-abnegation, Félicité gets used to rebuffing slights and so resists taking umbrage; she accustoms herself to spontaneously pardoning those who thoughtlessly wound her. She develops in short the God-inspired talent for giving freely of herself and of exposing herself to pain without expectation of solace or reward. Ordinary magnanimity is a recognizable and attractive quality in persons of good will; but the generosity of heart embodied in Félicité belongs to a higher order. Unrelated to self-interest and utterly unconscious of itself, this higher capacity for forgiveness is Christlike in nature and, at least from Flaubert's point of view, cannot possibly be willed into existence without divine assistance or intervention.

Even Flaubert's pregnant silences reinforce the concept of Félicité as a perpetual forgiver of others. Curt dismissals, abandonments by those to whom she has committed herself, and simply being forgotten become a pattern in her life. At these times we can assume that she offers pardon without realizing that she does so; for Félicité, the capacity to forgive is innate and spontaneous, and Flaubert often marks the nature of this special gift by refraining from any overt mention of her reactions, leaving the matter entirely to inference. Thus, although Félicité's heart is grieved to the quick by Virginie's departure for the Ursuline convent at Honfleur, Flaubert provides us with only the externalities of the scene—the arrival of the carriage, the loading of the baggage, instructions to the driver, the giving of provisions and parting gifts, the sobbing of the passenger, the mother's kiss—all of which poignantly exclude Félicité's profound feelings of loss and regret though she is explicitly present (210/31). Then the carriage pulls away, Mme. Aubain breaks down in sorrow and is consoled by numerous friends, while Félicité is left to suffer in silence and, in the imagination of the reader, to forgive those who have ignored her. The narrative reticence, sometimes referred to as a blank, is more powerful emotionally than any words could possibly be because, as readers, we are already becoming aware of the sanctity that empowers and sustains the character who, though mute, is the heart of the scene's pathos. A similarly telling exclusion in the life of Flaubert's heroine occurs near the end of the tale when Paul and his vulgarly aggressive wife come to the house after Mme. Aubain's death to collect their inheritance; drawers are ransacked, furniture is sold, pictures are removed, and the setting in which Félicité had come to love and serve her mistress for many years past is brusquely disrupted. The author, with the ironic precision that so often characterizes his prose, refers to the invasive couple merely as "the heirs" (222/51), failing even to name them. But the point of the scene is that Félicité must play the role of silent and impotent observer as Mme. Aubain's memory is desecrated and what she has come to think of as her own home is virtually destroyed. Yet, again, we are invited to imagine that Félicité's habitual spirituality triumphs—that the Holy Ghost strengthens her to absorb the new pain and then to forgive those who have caused it with no particular consciousness of altruism or heroic conflict.

As must by now be clear, Félicité's extraordinary capacity to forgive is linked indissolubly in the tale to her faculty for perseverance. Often she is denied the solace of intimate moments of personal contact—a final goodbye, a last embrace, for instance—that in most human lives fortify the sufferers of loss, helping them to bear their grief and come to closure. She learns of Théodore's decision to abandon her (she is told he marries a rich old widow instead), only through the impersonal agency of a stranger, one of the young man's friends (203/21). She walks ten miles to Honfleur so that she may bid farewell to Victor, whom she never sees again, only to find the gangway to his ship being pulled ashore (211/

34). Devastated by the news that Virginie is dying at her convent, again she arrives too late, learning of the beloved child's death only from the lips of an unfamiliar nun (215/39). The significant point is that she recovers from each of these calamities and always returns to her life of loving, giving, and forgiving. It is a pattern that continues until her death. But although Félicité exhibits unfailing endurance in the face of misery, perhaps the only effectual power of the powerless, we never feel that she suffers in abject aloneness. The fortitude that she fails to derive from human support on these occasions is clearly supplied by the Holy Ghost, one of whose designations, we recall, is Comforter—a term that derives from the Latin *confortare* (to strengthen). The age-old symbol of divine comfort and advocacy for Christians is the Holy Spirit, referred to as a dove in the Gospels and traditionally so depicted, as in the parish church that Félicité attends. When Loulou enters her life, therefore, it should hardly surprise us that Mme. Aubain's domestic, who after all is only an ignorant peasant, should associate her gift of comfort, almost instinctively, with a parrot. The symbolic association itself is a kind of gift—a poignant illustration of how God enters the lives of souls who are willing to receive Him. Félicité's emotional attachment to the parrot therefore becomes for her a way of loving the divine source of her astonishing strength, a commanding example of what Israel-Pelletier sees as her unique wisdom, her innate capacity for living instinctively both inside and outside the Church's theological structure (26).

Félicité's coming to feel the presence of the Holy Ghost in the form of Loulou is gradual, not a sudden or overpowering supernatural experience. The sequence of details is cumulative in effect and finally circular: Félicité's contemplation of the Holy Ghost in the stained-glass window of her local parish (209/29); her love of doves because of their connection with the symbol she has observed in church (209/30); her attraction to Loulou when he is still owned by the Baron de Larsonnière, subprefect of Pont-l'Évêque, because the bird, coming from America, reminds her of Victor (218/44); the passing of the parrot, first into Mme. Aubain's possession, and then into Félicité's (218/44); the disappearance of Loulou, an event from which Félicité never fully recovers and which shows how deep the attachment has become (219/45-46); the passage of three years during which Félicité becomes so deaf that she can hear only the voice of Loulou (219/46); their conversations involving much intimate touching in which the bird becomes for her almost a son or a lover (21920/47); her discovery of the dead bird in his cage, poisoned, as she imagines, by Fabu (220/47); her part-way journey to the taxidermist (she takes Loulou as far as Honfleur herself) and her installation of the stuffed bird in her room (220-21/47-49); finally in completion of the circle her semi-miraculous identification of Loulou with the image of the Paraclete in the church window—this rein-

forced by a colorful picture of Christ's baptism with its attendant dove with "its red wings and emerald-green body," a copy of which she purchases and hangs beside Loulou's perch in her room. Félicité has now come to recognize in these representations "something of the parrot . . . the very image of Loulou" (221-22/50).

Noting the inception and step-by-step development of Félicité's involvement with the parrot, we can see that her symbolic link between Loulou and the third Person of the Trinity has a certain psychological inevitability about it. The only tangible picture of the Holy Ghost that Félicité can appropriate is that of a dove, whether she examines the images in her local parish or listens to the scriptures read at Mass. Fire and breath, the other two traditional symbols, which Flaubert also correctly associates with the Holy Ghost, are ultimately less compelling to her. Félicité is aware that fire and breath are sometimes identified with the Holy Spirit, but she finds these images difficult to imagine, undoubtedly because of their comparative abstractness and impersonality. Consequently she tries to associate them with familiar or natural phenomena—flickering light, wind-driven clouds, the music of bells (209/30). Fire and breath, however, are subtly introduced into the tale in the description of Félicité's death, particularly in the details of the glowing monstrance which is the centerpiece of the altar on which Loulou is enshrined, referred to by Flaubert as a "great shining gold sun," and the incense which the dying figure rapturously breathes in during her final moments (225/56). Someone as childlike as Félicité, free to approach spiritual matters in a natural and spontaneous way, could hardly be expected to apprehend or feel intimate with the Holy Ghost in a form other than that of a dove or at least of a bird. As the narrator instructs us, "to minds like hers the supernatural is a simple matter" (215/39). Moreover this bird can speak, "Hail Mary" being one of his three comic utterances; and, as Andrea Greenbaum observes, the parrot's exoticism "represents something . . . exciting and mysterious, and therefore, to Félicité, divine" (210). Catholic worshipers need visual and tactile symbols of the sacred as aids to devotion, and there is nothing especially inappropriate or unusual about Félicité's requirement in this aspect of her piety. What is noteworthy, however, is Félicité's instinctive connecting of natural phenomena with the holy—her tender love for lambs, for instance, because of their association in her mind with the Lamb of God, and for doves "for the sake of the Holy Ghost" (209/30).

If we are to see **"Un Coeur simple"** as a tale essentially about the operations of the Holy Ghost in a particular life, the timing of Loulou's arrival into Félicité's world becomes highly significant. During her many years of sadness and loss, the ignorant housemaid remains a pillar of strength and basically unchanged. Presumably, the Holy Ghost has made this steadfastness possible. By the time Loulou enters the household and becomes Mme. Aubain's gift to her servant, however, much has altered. Félicité's loved ones have either died or gone away. For instance at Honfleur Victor sails off on a packet boat to a sea-going vessel at Le Havre and ultimately to his death from yellow fever across a wide ocean. Félicité's confusion at the unfamiliar docking area, which she reaches too late to bid her beloved nephew farewell because she has taken a wrong turn at the *"le Calvaire"* or town crucifix, constitutes a kind of emotional crucifixion for a lonely woman who desperately needs to express her love but is prevented by ironic circumstance from doing so (**"Un Coeur simple"** 211-12/33-34). A bleak future awaits her. There remains to her now only the visit of the emotionally dead Paul (appropriately a functionary in the office of Wills and Probates) and his pretentious fiancé; the death of Mme. Aubain; a second visit of the now married couple for the purpose of stripping the house of its possessions; and her own near-blindness and deafness. Félicité now confronts the lack of opportunity and physical stamina to serve others and the absence of any means by which to focus her unselfish feelings and affections. Whereas the Holy Ghost inspires Félicité to right and courageous actions while she is still young, He comes to her now in the unfamiliar form of Loulou as the comfort of her final years. By instinctively embracing the notion that Loulou and her divine Comforter are mystically one, she is able to enter the loneliness of her final years in the assurance of an abiding and transcendent companionship.

The benefits of this recognition are manifold. As Nathaniel Wing remarks, "The ability to imagine the Holy Ghost will await the fortuitous arrival of the parrot Loulou, who furnishes the material component that will eventually enable [Félicité] to assimilate the divine as real" (96). Haig sees the association in an equally positive light: "To the enrichment of Félicité's spiritual life (her deafness and declining eyesight are indices of her absorption into inner existence and slow, but steady passage from the human to the otherworldly) corresponds the decay of Félicité's physical surroundings and her detachment from earthly concerns . . ." (313). The talking bird, a new and special manifestation of the bequest of grace, is a fitting emblem of her faith and long-standing partnership with the Advocate and Comforter. Loulou serves as the type of her reward for a life well lived and provides the promised solace that she now so urgently needs and deserves. It is important to remember that Félicité's life has been marked from the beginning by the presence of the Holy Ghost. The arrival of Loulou and the connection Félicité makes between the parrot and the third Person of the Trinity do, indeed, reinforce and enhance the relationship, but they do not provide it. The Holy Spirit, who has become the essential link between Félicité and the presence of God in her life, has remained her perpetual companion.

Nevertheless her devotion to Loulou, however credulously excessive it may appear to the rationalist eye, enables Félicité to enjoy full communion with the Holy Ghost. In the parrot she has found a verbal partner: "They held conversations with each other, he repeating *ad nauseam* the three phrases in his repertory, she replying with words which were just as disconnected but which came from the heart" (219/47). Loulou also becomes an aid to prayer: "Fixing an anguished look on him as she appealed to the Holy Ghost, she contracted the idolatrous habit of kneeling in front of the parrot to say her prayers" (223/52). We have noted already that among the important functions of the Holy Ghost, as specified in scripture, is mediation between God and humankind with respect to what might otherwise be ineffectual prayer. In her now diminished state of mind, which naturally clings to memories of the past, the association is fond and tender: "Every morning when she awoke, she saw [the parrot] in the light of the dawn, and then she remembered the old days, and the smallest details of insignificant actions, not in sorrow but in absolute tranquillity" (221/50). With Loulou as the outward and visible sign of her divine intermediary, Félicité is enabled to rise above the remembered sufferings of her past, to contemplate them in fresh and broader perspective, and to achieve self-acceptance and spiritual serenity. Old, frail, and solitary, Félicité becomes for us, then, the prototype of a Christian soul finally at peace with herself and with her God. Nor is it surprising that she should erect an emotional and symbolic bridge between Loulou, now a somewhat pathetic stuffed effigy, and the Holy Ghost. Considered from within the framework of her own limited taste and mentality, the decaying stuffed bird need not be regarded as humorous, inappropriate, or pathetically inadequate. As readers, Flaubert asks us to identify imaginatively with Félicité's interior simplicity. It should be noted, however, that this process of nearly romantic identification with the narrator's unsophisticated heroine in no way precludes the absurdity which ironic distance lends to the overall effect.

As Félicité's death approaches, we see Loulou in an advanced state of decay. Owing to blindness, the old woman has been unable to care properly for her icon; and when she offers him up to be used on an altar of repose for the Feast of Corpus Christi, Loulou is infested with worms, broken-winged, and becoming abdominally unstuffed. In the street below the room in which she lies dying, a noisy throng of clergy, church wardens, nuns, and acolytes with thuribles lead the townsfolk and their children in procession. Flaubert partly mutes, indeed even undercuts, the devotional seriousness of the event (signified by the religious singing and the presence of the Blessed Sacrament in its gold monstrance) by his description of the portable altar—an altar overdecorated with garlands and lace flounces, piled high with bric-a-brac (moss, plants, ill-assorted flowers, silver, china, gems, Chinese screens), and high-lighted incongruously by Loulou, his blue poll, which resembles lapis lazuli, emerging from a blanket of roses. To accept that a miracle of faith could occur in this satirically tasteless setting puts even the most devoutly inclined reader to a severe test. Karl Uitti concedes that by placing Loulou on an altar at the end of the tale Flaubert prepares us for the supernatural visitation of the parrot at the moment of Félicité's death; but he regards this supposedly otherworldly experience as the product of mental confusion: "The double contiguity—the holy altar in addition to the banal, even ridiculous, junk accompanying it—helps confer upon Loulou an ambiguous sanctification which comments upon and even authorizes narrationally Félicité's final vision" (162). Even if we accept that Flaubert invites us to entertain the notion that Félicité is a genuine saint and that her parrot symbolizes the divinity that overshadows and inspires the totality of her life, it is not hard to understand the reaction of critics such as Greenbaum: "While using the structural narrative of a saint's life, so genuinely valued by Flaubert, and superimposing the preposterous dimensions of devotional excess, **"Un Coeur simple"** is quite plainly a monumental satire, a 'parrot-dy' of faith, a joke turned in on itself . . ." (211).

But if we focus on the centrality of Félicité's death rather than on the vulgarity of its context, a different mode of perception emerges. For if we grant that the Holy Spirit has attended the dying woman from the beginning of the tale—more noticeably after Loulou's arrival—we cannot but expect that the heavenly force that sustained her throughout her earthly travails would also be present as the comfort of her final hours. Félicité experiences a moment of joy when the priest accepts her offer of the parrot, "the only thing of value she possessed" (223/53), as an altar decoration when she dies. Then in a last embrace she clutches Loulou devotedly, kissing him on the forehead and pressing him against her cheek, before Mère Simon carries him away (224/54). Finally, the last words Félicité speaks on earth reflect passionate concern for Loulou's welfare: "'Is he all right?'—worrying about the parrot" (225/55). As her life ebbs away, the maidservant thinks only of Loulou, who now fills up her emptiness, at once supplying her with something precious to give away and with someone to love and worry about. At Félicité's end, then, we revisit with her and experience vicariously the generosity, love, and peace that have made up the very fabric of her life. The Holy Ghost, now domesticated and made mystically one with a comically disintegrating bird, becomes for her a veritable and intimate member of her own family.

At the moment of Félicité's death, silence overtakes the citizens of Pont-l'Évêque, who kneel in the street outside Mme. Aubain's house. As the incense rises into the room above, Félicité breathes in the vapors "with a mystical sensuous fervour," smiles seraphically, and, as the welcoming clouds part to receive her, believes that she sees a huge Loulou gliding over her: "she thought she could see, in the opening heavens, a gigantic parrot hovering above her head" (225/56). Surely this final climactic moment represents the culminating miracle that had first been adumbrated when Félicité identified her pet with the Holy Ghost in church—a defining miracle traditionally essential to the genre of the saint's life and a clear marker of differentiation from the virtue of mere innocents. Seen in this light, the kneeling assembly in the courtyard below reifies the awe and respect that appropriately characterize witnesses to the departure of a saint from the earth. And Félicité's last smile becomes her ultimate testimonial of the supreme comfort, peace, and happiness that, for believers, only the Holy Ghost can confer.

If, then, we understand the workings of the Holy Spirit as revealed in scripture, accept the universality of His gifts as extending to all, and accord Félicité's life the serious dignity it deserves, at the same time embracing the metonymic relationship she establishes between Loulou and her divine comforter and sustainer, we can do no less than take Flaubert's ending for what it is—a genuinely miraculous vision of supernal love bestowed in rare instances upon the truly holy. Flaubert establishes Félicité's religious dedication in the early pages of his tale, continually reinforcing it in what follows so that we come to understand what a life lived in communion with the Holy Spirit is actually like; then he shows that same life rising in old age and death to mystical unification with the ultimate center of its empowerment. At an important level of the narration too often ignored by critics, we are invited to experience Félicité's spiritual elevation through her own feelings and capacity for faith—a faith that acknowledges the otherworldly and the limits of human rationality. Critics who rightly emphasize Flaubert's ironic mode of narration often stress the bizarre details that attend Félicité's demise—the grotesque improprieties, the superstitious indecorums, and vulgar excesses of the bourgeois culture in which it is embedded. The famous ambiguities of his method, however, are effected largely by the gap that separates this quasi-satiric, omnisciently "objective" stance from the richly subjective interiority of the heroine's profound spirituality, experienced imaginatively by readers as inhabiting her own admittedly artless and untutored consciousness. But the verb *croire* (to believe), positioned so prominently and so crucially in the tale's final sentence, is itself thoroughly *un*ambiguous. The enlarged and inclusively dominant Loulou which Félicité *believes* she sees inspires no scintilla of doubt in her soul and, coinciding precisely with her final breath, exists for her, and for us *through her,* not as a fevered delusion but as a sign of her translation to eternity. As Alexandra Lajoux phrases it,

Although the narrator belittles Félicité's vision by terming it "mere" belief, yet his perspective works once for all to reinforce Félicité's world-view and hence her sanctity. She dies in this instant. The duration of her believed vision is therefore infinite, despite its grammatical status.

(47)[6]

Our argument that in his portrait of Félicité Flaubert occupied himself seriously with the realm of the spiritual can be further supported by reference to the trilogy of which **"Un Coeur simple"** is but the first part. Per Nykrog broke new ground in 1973 by pointing out that each of the three tales deals with a separate manifestation of the Trinity—**"Hérodias"** with God the Father (through the words of Jokanaan in their resemblance to the Old Testament prophets); **"La Légende de Saint Julien"** with Jesus; and **"Un Coeur simple"** with the Holy Ghost, whom the Danish commentator characterizes accurately as "pure immateriality, interiority, and total spirituality" (61).[7] The tendency to belittle Loulou continues, however—even among those who acknowledge the Holy Ghost as Flaubert's central concern in the tale. Frederic Shepler, agreeing with Nykrog that the Trinity is the unifying principle of the three stories, sees "divine hope" in **"Hérodias"** and "the hand of God" in **"La Légende,"** but concludes, with specific reference to Loulou, that "God is moribund in **"Un Coeur simple"** (414).[8] James Mall goes so far as to write that God is "absent" (45) in the tale. But interpreting it as a story of divine grace operating actively in the life of Félicité—grace increasingly embodied in her close attachment to Loulou—helps us to make better sense of continuities among the three stories that their grouping seems intentionally to suggest. For it is hardly likely that Flaubert, notoriously a devotee of formal integrity, would deliberately plan a series of three stories without special attention to their unity and connectedness. It should be recalled that the novelist decided to write **"Un Coeur simple"** immediately after finishing his work on Saint Julian, a tale in which Christ, in the guise of a leper, visits the repentant sinner in his ferry boat and carries him off to heaven; and also that the ending of **"Hérodias"** finds John the Baptist proclaiming the advent of Christ. Both tales conclude on a note of spiritual triumph. To suggest that Flaubert would end his third story on the life and death of Félicité by portraying a merely illusory connection with the divine or a failed and essentially empty belief in a deteriorating parrot—a merely pathetic or inadequate metaphor for the Holy Spirit in the mind of an ignorant servant—would be to convict the author of a jarring inconsistency of tone and theme.

Doubtless the masterfully constructed story of Félicité and her life of faith will continue to be read in a variety of ways as has been the case heretofore. Indeed the richness of Flaubert's art consists partly in the very diversity of interpretive perspectives that the story seems to encourage. Latterly, with the popularity of deconstructivist and linguistically theorized approaches to literary analysis, critics have been turning away from interpretations rooted in Flaubert's biography, especially in his personal resistance to Christian orthodoxy, and have been readier to explore, if not actually to embrace, the transcendent experiences of his fictional characters in a way that allows ontology to balance or even counteract his famous protective irony. But a major obstacle in coming to settled conclusions about what the tale finally offers us is still the huge divide that sunders our sense of Flaubert's personal experiences and beliefs from those of his heroine. George Willenbrink stops short of accusing the author of hostile feelings toward organized religion in **"Un Coeur simple"**: "Religion," he admits, "escapes Flaubert's mockery in this story because his heroine's lack of education permits him to ignore the one aspect of it he found distasteful—dogma" (245). But Willenbrink also observes that Flaubert and Félicité live in entirely different worlds when it comes to matters of spirituality, especially when Loulou enters the equation. Regarding Félicité's deathbed vision of the parrot, he writes: "Not only is it the climax of [her] love, but also its reward—the only reward that Flaubert, in his unbelief, can offer his heroine" (244). Summarizing what he sees as the double role played by Loulou in the story, Brombert speaks of the parrot as being simultaneously a mystical fetish for the character and an instrument of irony for the author (*Chambre,* 80). Following up on Brombert's useful insight, we may affirm, then, that two opposing perspectives are operative in the story. Flaubert would seem to be juxtaposing his well-known disdain for the bourgeoisie with a complex and ambiguous attitude to matters spiritual. This juxtaposition allows him to treat Félicité with the utmost sympathy and to portray her progress to sanctification with a lively sense of her holy calling and peaceful acceptance in a world the author personally detests. It is probable that Flaubert, as skeptic, may have regarded Félicité's final vision of the parrot as a laughable, if not indeed meaningless, hallucination, while, as imaginative participant in the maidservant's inner world, he simultaneously treated it as an authentic apotheosis. Narratalogically speaking, we might even say that the two perspectives exist finally in unresolved tension with each other.

Although scholars have pursued a variety of routes to the deeper significances of **"Un Coeur simple,"** this study has sought to concentrate on Félicité's spiritual odyssey from the viewpoint of her own subjective experience with relation to certain axioms of traditional Christianity. Perhaps the central tenet here is the teaching that all God's children, no matter how naive, unlettered, or intellectually impaired, are eligible for full participation in the kingdom through the constant presence and intervention of the Holy Spirit in their lives;

and a corollary implication is that such interventions may appear incongruous, absurd, or even crazy to observers from outside the sphere of belief. For what is Christianity, after all, but a religion of irony that flies radically in the face of conventional expectations and assumptions, based, as it is, on an outlaw who claims divinity, who preaches unqualified love and the dignity of the poor, who challenges human power-structures, and who is finally put to death for his uncompromising resistance to them? To believe that an important legacy of Christ is comfort offered through companionship with an invisible presence, the Paraclete, has traditionally tested the credulity even of those who claim the gift of faith. It is little wonder, then, that in the proliferation of scholarly commentary on Flaubert's important tale, the most notable omission thus far has been any true understanding of the theological nature and function of the Holy Ghost together with a recognition of His peculiar gifts. As we have seen, however, certain relevant passages from the Bible provide a clearer understanding of such benefits as the Holy Ghost can confer. These include the courage to act rightly in dangerous and difficult circumstances and to allay fear, the hunger to serve others, the power of the defenseless to forgive those who have victimized them, the profoundest kind of spiritual companionship available to the lonely and forgotten of the world, and the fortifying acceptance of divine presence to the dying. Félicité is portrayed as a character on whom these gifts have been liberally bestowed and who, on account of them, lives unusually close to God—especially when she is leaving life on earth. It is within this context that the bizarre prominence of Loulou makes logical sense, becoming, as the bird ultimately does for her, Félicité's tangible proof of her special relationship with her Maker.

Such a reading in no way invalidates the ironic, ambiguous, and at times even acrid or satirical take on Félicité's story that Flaubert perhaps reserved to himself and the more agnostic of his readers. But it has the advantage of allowing interpreters of a narrative that is so often associated with malaise or a jaundiced attitude toward the world of Pont-l'Évêque to cross a "threshold," as Culler puts it, and to find "a kind of order" (210) in which reconciliation between the decomposing carcass of a bird and saintly miracle finally becomes possible. Flaubert invites us into a world where a focus on Félicité's Otherness, the transcendent world of her inner simplicity, can ultimately displace the tale's honest recognition of bourgeois vulgarity, pretension, and superstition. Moreover, a willing entry into this higher, more mystical space can subtly convict the reader of his or her narrowness, self-protective smugness, or intolerant judgmentalism; and this too would seem to have been part of the author's final purpose. Whatever his private reservations might be, Flaubert created in Félicité a character defined and sustained by a rich inner core of unself-conscious spirituality. Among its many other excellences, **"Un Coeur simple"** enables us movingly to share a sense of that inner realm, to enter through Flaubert's subtle manipulations of tone and voice into his heroine's simple heart without equivocation or embarrassment.

Notes

1. Unless otherwise noted, the version of scripture cited throughout is *The New Oxford Annotated Bible.*

2. I must acknowledge at the outset that this essay builds upon assumptions, cogently defended by Christopher Wise, which align Flaubert's religious discourse with the traditional "ontotheological basis of Western thought" rather than with the deconstructionist, post-modern, and materialist approaches of Jacques Derrida, Roland Barthes, and other like-minded critics. By rejecting orthodox belief in the reality of Christ as the Word made flesh, these latter writers "displace ontology in favor of textuality" in their interpretive methodologies and thereby engage in what amounts to "an attack on the Christian faith itself" (Wise 37). I should also like to thank Professor Charles R. Forker of Indiana University, who assisted me materially with the documentation of this article.

3. Page and volume references to Flaubert's correspondence are to the edition in *Oeuvres complètes*; the translations into English are my own. For quotations from and references to "Un Coeur simple," I give first the page number from *Trois Contes,* also in *Oeuvres complètes* (vol. 4), then, separated by a virgule, the page number from Baldick's English translation.

4. I translate here from Chateaubriand's French.

5. See Robert Baldick's introduction to his translation of *Trois Contes,* 9-11. Baldick later points out, for instance, that Flaubert was so wedded to accuracy of representation that he "even borrowed a stuffed parrot from Rouen Museum to serve as a model for Loulou," installing it "in a place of honour" on his "work-table, like Loulou in Félicité's bedroom" (13). Julian Barnes' witty novel, *Flaubert's Parrot* (1984), makes this incident the basis of his title; in its opening chapter the narrator, Geoffrey Braithwaite, perceptively describes Loulou as a "controlled example of the Flaubertian grotesque" and characterizes Félicité's identification of her pet with the Holy Ghost as "neither satirical, sentimental, nor blasphemous" (17). He then goes on to suggest that the talking bird symbolizes not only the Holy Ghost, "the giver of tongues," but also Flaubert's own power of articulation or "voice" (18) as an artist.

6. In analyzing the true meaning of Félicité's vision, we must not forget what the Bible teaches us about the Holy Ghost, namely that, although on one occasion He appeared in the form of a bird, He is ordinarily invisible to human perception. Stoltz-

fus, when he alleges that Félicité's vision is the result merely of "delirium" because she confuses a parrot with a dove (22), betrays a considerable degree of theological naiveté. The Holy Ghost, being an aspect of God, can represent himself in any form He chooses, not excluding a gigantic parrot.

7. I translate here from Nykrog's French.

8. I translate here from Shepler's French.

Works Cited

Baldick, Robert, trans. *Gustave Flaubert: Three Tales.* Harmondsworth: Penguin Books, 1961.

Barnes, Julian. *Flaubert's Parrot.* New York: Vintage Books, 1990.

Bart, Benjamin F. *Flaubert.* Syracuse: Syracuse UP, 1967.

Bidney, Martin. "Parrots, Pictures, Rays, Perfumes: Epiphanies in George Sand and Flaubert." *Studies in Short Fiction* 22.2 (1985): 209-17.

Bouhours, Le R. P., trans. *Le Nouveau Testament de Notre Seigneur Jésus-Christ, Traduit sur L'Ancienne Édition Latine. . . .* Paris: Librairie Écclésiastique de Rusand, 1830.

Brombert, Victor. *The Novels of Flaubert: A Study of Themes and Techniques.* Princeton: Princeton UP, 1966.

———. *"La Chambre de Félicité: bazar ou chapelle?" George Sand et son temps: Hommage à Annarosa Poli.* Ed. Elio Mosele. 3 vols. Geneva: Slatkine, 1994. 1. 73-86.

Butler's Lives of the Saints. Ed. Herbert Thurston, S.J. and Donald Attwater. 4 vols. New York: P. J. Kennedy, 1956.

Chateaubriand, François-René Vicompte de. *Génie du christianisme.* 2 vols. Paris: Garnier-Flammarion, 1966.

Culler, Jonathan. *Flaubert: The Uses of Uncertainty.* Ithaca: Cornell UP, 1974; rev. ed., 1985.

Erickson, Karen L. "Prophetic Utterance and Irony in *Trois Contes." Modernity and Revolution in Late Nineteenth-Century France.* Eds. Barbara T. Cooper and Mary Donaldson-Evans. Newark: U of Delaware P, 1992; London: Associated UPs, 1992. 65-73.

Flaubert, Gustave. *Correspondance. Oeuvres complètes.* Vols. 12-16.

———. *Oeuvres complètes. Édition nouvelle . . . par la Société des Études littéraires françaises.* 16 vols. Paris: Club de l'Honnête Homme, 1971-75.

———. *Trois Contes. Oeuvres complètes.* Vol. 4. 173-277.

Greenbaum, Andrea. "Flaubert's *Un Coeur simple." Explicator* 53.4 (1995): 208-11.

Griffin, Robert. "Flaubert: The Transfiguration of Matter." *French Studies* 44.1 (1990): 18-33.

Haig, Stirling. "The Substance of Illusion in Flaubert's *Un Coeur simple." Stanford French Review* 7.3 (1983): 301-15.

Interpreter's Bible: The Holy Scriptures in the King James and Revised Standard Versions with General Articles and Introduction, Exegesis, Exposition for Each Book of the Bible. Ed. G. A. Buttrick et al. 12 vols. New York: Abingdon, 1951-57.

Israel-Pelletier, Aimée. *Flaubert's Straight and Suspect Saints: The Unity of "Trois Contes."* Philadelphia: John Benjamins Publishing, 1991.

Kran, Paul. "Religion and Representation: The Rhetoric of Faith in Flaubert's '*Hérodias*' and Manet's *Dead Christ with Angels." Proceedings of the Fourth Annual Graduate Student Conference in French and Comparative Literatures March 4-5, 1994.* New York: Columbia UP, 1994. 41-46.

Lajoux, Alexandra Reed. "From Emma to Félicité: The Use of Hagiography in the Works of Gustave Flaubert." *Studies in Medievalism* 2.2 (1983): 35-50.

Mall, James P. "Flaubert's *Un Coeur simple*: Myth and the Genealogy of Religion." *AUMLA* 47 (1977): 39-48.

New Oxford Annotated Bible with the Apocrypha. Revised Standard Version, Ed. Herbert G. May and Bruce M. Metzger. New York: Oxford UP, 1977.

Nykrog, Per. "*Les* Trois Contes *dans l'évolution de la structure thématique chez Flaubert." Romantisme* 6 (1973): 55-66.

Rousseau, Jean-Jacques. *Emile, or Education.* Trans. Barbara Foxley. New York: Dutton, 1911.

Shepler, Frederic J. "*La Mort et la rédemption dans les* Trois Contes *de Flaubert." Neophilologus* 56.4 (1972): 407-16.

Spencer, Philip. *Politics of Belief in Nineteenth-Century France.* New York: Grove Press, 1954.

Starkie, Enid. *Flaubert: The Making of the Master.* London: Weidenfeld and Nicolson, 1967.

———. *Flaubert: The Master.* London: Weidenfeld and Nicolson, 1971.

Stoltzfus, Ben. "Point of View in *Un Coeur simple." French Review* 35.1 (1961): 19-25.

Thibaudet, Albert. *Gustave Flaubert, 1821-1880: Sa Vie, Ses Romans, Son Style.* Paris: Plon-Nourrit, 1922.

Thorlby, Anthony. *Gustave Flaubert and the Art of Realism.* New Haven: Yale UP, 1957.

Uitti, Karl D. "Figures and Fiction: Linguistic Deformation and the Novel." *Kentucky Romance Quarterly* 17.2 (1970): 149-69.

VanderWolk, William. *Flaubert Remembers: Memory and the Creative Experience.* New York: Peter Lang, 1990.

Willenbrink, George A. *The Dossier of Flaubert's "Un Coeur simple."* Amsterdam: Editions Rodopi, 1976.

Wing, Nathaniel. "Reading Simplicity: Flaubert's '*Un Coeur simple.*'" *Nineteenth-Century French Studies* 21.1-2 (Fall-Winter 1992-93): 88-101.

Wise, Christopher. "The Whatness of Loulou: Allegories of Thomism in Flaubert." *Religion & Literature* 25.1 (Spring 1993): 35-49.

FURTHER READING

Criticism

Cervo, Nathan A. "Flaubert's 'Un Coeur Simple.'" *Explicator* 55, no. 2 (winter 1997): 80-1.

Refutes Andrea Greenbaum's argument that "Un Coeur simple" is a satire is incorrect, as it fails to stress Flaubert's theme of "simple love."

Greenbaum, Andrea. "Flaubert's 'Un Coeur Simple.'" *Explicator* 53, no. 4 (summer 1995): 208-11.

States that "Un Coeur simple" is "a monumental satire."

Reynolds, James M. "Flaubert's 'Un Coeur Simple.'" *Explicator* 55, no. 1 (fall 1996): 26-8.

Notes the presence of humor, hyperbolic exaggeration, and satire in "Un Coeur simple."

Stipa, Ingrid. "Desire, Repetition and the Imaginary in Flaubert's 'Un Coeur simple.'" *Studies in Short Fiction* 31, no. 4 (fall 1994): 617-26.

Follows the narrative strategy of irony, repetition, desire, and imaginary reality in "Un Coeur simple."

Additional coverage of Flaubert's life and career is contained in the following sources published by the Gale Group: *Dictionary of Literary Biography,* Vol. 119; *DISCovering Authors: British Edition*; *DISCovering Authors: Canadian Edition*; *DISCovering Authors Modules: Most-studied Authors* and *Novelists*; *DISCovering Authors 3.0*; *European Writers,* Vol. 7; *Exploring Short Stories*; *Guide to French Literature, 1789 to the Present*; *Literature and Its Times,* Vol. 2; *Literature Resource Center*; *Nineteenth-Century Literature Criticism,* Vols. 2, 10, 19, 62, 66; *Novels for Students,* Vol. 14; *Reference Guide to Short Fiction,* Ed. 2; *Reference Guide to World Literature,* Eds. 2, 3; *Short Stories for Students,* Vol. 6; *Short Story Criticism,* Vol. 11; *Twayne's World Authors*; and *World Literature Criticism.*

Thomas Hardy
1840-1928

English short story writer, novelist, poet, and play-wright.

The following entry presents criticism of Hardy's short fiction works from 1989 to 1999. For criticism on Hardy's short fiction career published prior to 1989, see *SSC,* Volume 2.

INTRODUCTION

Widely considered among the greatest novelists in English literature, Hardy is also recognized as an accomplished and compelling short fiction writer. In both genres, he depicted human existence as a tragedy determined by powers beyond the individual's command, in particular the external pressures of society and the internal compulsions of character. In his short stories, Hardy frequently wrote about grotesque situations in the lives of rural characters and made extensive use of irony to demonstrate the lack of control his protagonists hold over their own lives. While his reputation as a seminal figure in the development of the nineteenth-century novel overshadows his achievement in short fiction, several of Hardy's tales, including "The Three Strangers" and "The Distracted Preacher," continue to be read by students and scholars as exemplary works of late Victorian literature.

BIOGRAPHICAL INFORMATION

Hardy was born and raised in the region of Dorsetshire, which he employed in his fiction and poetry as the basis of his Wessex countryside setting. He originally sought recognition as a poet but turned to prose as a more ready means of literary success. His unpublished first novel, *The Poor Man and the Lady,* was rejected as overly satirical by George Meredith, a reader for Chapman & Hall Publishing Company and an influential nineteenth-century literary authority. Having been advised by Meredith to incorporate the plot devices of popular fiction into his work, Hardy wrote *Desperate Remedies* (1871), a novel that defined many of the fundamental characteristics of his emerging style. Because he considered strict realism insufficient to hold readers' attention, Hardy created novels with artificially elaborate plots, extensive use of coincidence, and the characteristic mood of Gothic melodrama. Beginning in the 1870s, Hardy wrote several novels considered among the finest in the English language. When he received harsh criticism for his novels *Tess of the D'Urbervilles* (1891) and *Jude the Obscure* (1895), his response was to cease writing fiction and to devote himself to poetry, which he had composed intermittently throughout his career. Hardy's last major work, *Dynasts: A Drama of the Napoleonic Wars* (1904-08), is an epic historical drama of the Napoleonic wars written in verse which summarizes his philosophy on the forces that influence human existence.

MAJOR WORKS OF SHORT FICTION

Between 1874 and 1900, in addition to writing novels and poetry, Hardy published short fiction in various English and American periodicals. Most of these pieces were later reprinted in Hardy's short story collections. His first such volume, *Wessex Tales* (1888), depicts protagonists in Hardy's standard Wessex country setting who are engaged in situations that Hardy identified in his subtitle as "Strange, Lively, and Commonplace." Ranging in length from the brief vignette to the novella, the stories in *Wessex Tales* also vary widely in tone. For instance, "The Three Strangers" and "The Distracted Preacher" display affection for rural customs and employ country vernacular through good-natured tales involving thievery and smuggling, respectively, while "The Withered Arm" reveals Hardy's interest in the supernatural. "Fellow-Townsmen" and "Interlopers at the Knap" are stories that rely heavily upon irony and circumstance. Hardy's next short story collection, *A Group of Noble Dames* (1891), portrays the lives of ten women as narrated by male members of a "Wessex Field and Antiquarian Club" who are ensconced at an inn after a rainstorm has postponed their outing.

In Hardy's subsequent short story collections, *Life's Little Ironies* (1894) and *A Changed Man* (1913), his dark, cynical outlook is again prevalent. Such stories in *Life's Little Ironies* as "A Tragedy of Two Ambitions" and "On the Western Circuit" display Hardy's despairing view of human existence, while "An Imaginative Woman" possesses a heavily ironic, derisive tone in its examination of human frailties. In the last pieces of *Life's Little Ironies,* however, Hardy's tone changes considerably, as he hearkens back to the portrayals of rustic characters that distinguish the stories in *Wessex Tales* and scenes from several of his novels. *A Changed Man* is generally regarded as a miscellaneous collection that is nevertheless characteristic of Hardy's short fiction. Such stories as "The Grave by the Handpost," "The Waiting Supper," and "A Changed Man" possess a typically mournful atmosphere and an overriding sense of the failure and tragedy of human destiny. Once again, however, Hardy lightens the foreboding tone of his volume with a concluding piece that combines romance, fantasy, and rustic characters.

CRITICAL RECEPTION

Although considered of lesser importance than his novels and poetry, Hardy's short stories are generally regarded as significant additions to his literary output. Several critics have noted that his short fiction is in some ways superior to his novels due to its narrower focus and lack of digressions. The effectiveness of Hardy's pessimistic view of human existence has long been the subject of critical debate; because of the compressed atmosphere of his short stories, many reviewers and scholars have found Hardy's portraits of tragic characters trapped by chance and circumstance to be especially overbearing and unlikely in that genre. Neverthe-

less, Hardy has been universally lauded for his tales, which feature rustic protagonists, pastoral settings, and rural vernacular.

PRINCIPAL WORKS

Short Fiction

Wessex Tales: Strange, Lively, and Commonplace 1888

A Group of Noble Dames 1891

Life's Little Ironies 1894

A Changed Man, The Waiting Supper, and Other Tales 1913

The Short Stories of Thomas Hardy 1928

Old Mrs. Chundle and Other Stories, with The Tragedy of the Famous Queen of Cornwall 1977

An Indiscretion in the Life of an Heiress and Other Stories 1994

The Complete Stories 1997

"The Fiddler of the Reels" and Other Stories 1997

Other Major Works

Desperate Remedies (novel) 1871

Under the Greenwood Tree (novel) 1872

A Pair of Blue Eyes (novel) 1873

Far from the Madding Crowd (novel) 1874

The Hand of Ethelberta (novel) 1876

The Return of the Native (novel) 1878

The Trumpet-Major (novel) 1880

A Laodicean (novel) 1881

Two on a Tower (novel) 1882

The Mayor of Casterbridge (novel) 1886

The Woodlander (novel) 1887

Tess of the D'Urbervilles (novel) 1891

Jude the Obscure (novel) 1895

The Well-Beloved (novel) 1895

Wessex Poems, and Other Verses (poetry) 1898

Poems of the Past and Present (poetry) 1902

The Dynasts: A Drama of the Napoleonic Wars. 3 vols. (drama) 1904-08

Time's Laughingstocks, and Other Verses (poetry) 1909

Satires of Circumstances, Lyrics, and Reveries (poetry) 1914

Winter Words, in Various Moods and Metres (poetry) 1928

CRITICISM

T. R. Wright (essay date 1989)

SOURCE: Wright, T. R. "Diabolical Dames and Grotesque Desires: The Short Stories." In *Hardy and the Erotic*, pp. 89-105. London: Macmillan, 1989.

[*In the following essay, Wright considers the role of the erotic in Hardy's short fiction.*]

Hardy published nearly fifty short stories in a variety of periodicals from 1865 to 1900, collecting the majority of them for republication in four volumes: *Wessex Tales,* a set of rural romances drawn from the folklore of the West Country; *A Group of Noble Dames,* recounting the perverse desires of a number of aristocratic ladies of the seventeenth and eighteenth centuries; *Life's Little Ironies,* a macabre series of illustrations of the tricks fate plays upon loving men and women; and *A Changed Man,* a miscellaneous collection of tales whose central theme is the chaos introduced into human lives by the irresistible dictates of desire. Each of these volumes contributes to Hardy's exploration of the erotic. Like the short stories of Hawthorne and Poe, of which so much has been made by post-structuralist and psychoanalytic critics, they lead beyond the 'normal' characterisation of the realistic novel to consider those areas of the psyche which are abnormal, obsessive and irrational.

Hardy's short stories are often dismissed as melodramatic and clumsy because they are full of such abnormal characters and perverse situations. Even when they have been recognised as instances of his 'interest in psychology, especially in its bizarre and unusual aspects', they have been criticised for their fixation upon single oddities of character at the expense of the 'whole personality' (Sumner, 1981: 18). Yet Hardy can be seen to be challenging the liberal humanist notion of coherent personality, deliberately focusing on the incoherence of human behaviour, in particular the irrationality of desire. The short stories demonstrate a particular interest in the 'uncanny' in Freud's famous definition, 'that class of the frightening which leads back to what is known of old and long familiar', combining the 'strange' with the 'commonplace', breaking down that 'distinction between imagination and reality' upon which sanity is based and shedding doubt on the stable certainties of the rational world (Keys, 1985: 111). The *Wessex Tales* in particular draw on familiar traditions of folklore to undermine any belief in the simplicity of country life (Brady, 1982: 48-9).

WESSEX TALES

At least five of the seven stories written between 1879 and 1888 which were collected as *Wessex Tales* focus on the dreams and illusions of desire. '**The Melancholy Hussar of the German Legion**' tells a familiar tale of infatuation with the exotic and unknown, a local girl finding herself fascinated by the melancholy face of a young German soldier. The language barrier between them speeds the process of her infatuation, for 'the eyes . . . helped out the tongue and . . . the lips helped out the eyes' (*WT* [*Wessex Tales*]: 50). Refusing to see him in the same serious light as someone who spoke the same language,

> She no longer checked her fancy for the Hussar. . . . The young foreign soldier was almost an ideal being to her, with none of the appurtenances of an ordinary house-dweller; one who had descended she knew not whence, and would disappear she knew not whither; the subject of a fascinating dream—no more.
>
> (53)

She is quite shocked when he proposes, for such a 'practical step had not been in her mind in relation to such an unrealistic person as he was' (54). The Hussar is captured and shot for desertion, leaving her to contemplate her unfaithful fiancé's departing gift, 'a very handsome looking-glass in a frame of *repoussé* silverwork' (59). Her self-reflexive desire, it is implied, will no doubt find new objects on which to reshape itself.

'**The Withered Arm**' is the most bizarre of the *Wessex Tales,* concerned as it is with the magical powers of a jealous woman. It has been called 'an essay in the pathology of sexual jealousy, . . . a psychological fable' exploring that uncanny area of strange coincidence determined by the forces beyond our conscious control (Keys, 1985: 106). It begins with a neglected woman sending her son to report on his father's new bride. The lad's 'hard gaze' takes in every ounce of her charm, 'every feature, shade, and contour distinct, from the curve of her little nostril, to the colour of her eyes', lit up by the evening sun. He notices not only how 'nice and red' her mouth is but how her gown 'whewed and whistled' against the pews in church (*WT*: 68-70), culture combining with nature to give a clear indication of her erotic attraction even to the boy.

On the basis of her son's evidence and that of the village gossip, the neglected Rhoda is able to build up 'a mental image' of her rival, as 'realistic as a photograph' and sufficient for a vivid dream in which

> the young wife, in the pale silk dress and white bonnet, but with features shockingly distorted, and wrinkled by age, was sitting upon her chest as she lay . . . the blue eyes peered cruelly into her face, and then the figure thrust forward its left hand mockingly, so as to make the wedding-ring it wore glitter in Rhoda's eyes.
>
> (71)

The dream vision is clearly a reflection of Rhoda's jealousy and its deformity a product of her wish-fulfilment. Her vindictive desires are fulfilled in the following sequence of the dream, in which she seizes the bride's mocking left arm and whirls the spectre on to the floor.

But it is not only in the dream that Rhoda achieves her revenge. On waking in a cold sweat she continues to feel the arm within her grasp while the bride actually suffers the resultant injuries, which grow progressively worse until the conjuror to whom she turns as a last resort recommends the touch of a corpse as the only remedy. The corpse she chooses, however, in another uncanny coincidence, turns out to be Rhoda's son, unjustly condemned to hang for arson. Rhoda catches hold of her bare arm, as in the dream, and causes her instant death. The story baffles its readers, breaking down all certainty about what is real and unreal, conscious and unconscious.

Everything is beyond the control of the unfortunate Mr Barnet, one of the two 'Fellow-Townsmen', who never manages to attain the object of his desire, which remains fixed on his first love, Lucy Saville. He comforts himself during his unhappy marriage to a dominating and wilful woman by meditating on the beauties of Lucy's face, reminding himself of 'the Raffaelesque oval of its contour' by paying her a visit (103) and projecting a 'gaze' of longing on to the curl of smoke which rises from her chimney 'as from a fire new kindled' (117) at the very moment that his wife's body lies believed drowned upon his bed. His wife, however, recovers as a result of his dutiful attentions and proceeds to live just long enough for Lucy to marry the bereaved Mr Downe and thus remain inaccessible to Mr Barnet, who returns after an interval of twenty-one years to find her once more free to marry. She at first refuses him, changing her mind too late to prevent his disappearing for ever unsatisfied. The irony is that Mr Downe is blessed with two marvellous wives whom he takes almost for granted. Possession once more reduces desire, which survives in his fellow-townsman only through perpetual frustration.

Marriage and desire are portrayed throughout the *Wessex Tales* as mutually incompatible. Farmer Charles Darton, for instance, who congratulates himself at the beginning of **'Interlopers at the Knap'** on his resolve to do the sensible thing and marry the good-hearted Sally in place of the superior Helena, the first object of his affections, soon finds his old desire reawakened when he encounters Helena in Sally's house wearing the dress he had bought for Sally to marry in. Sally discovers them with their eyes 'fixed' upon each other, the farmer unable to stop 'looking at Helena's dress and outline, and listening to her voice like a man in a dream' (163-5). None of the three participants in this scene knows, at this stage, how the other two relate to each other. It transpires that Helena has married Sally's brother, who has returned from Australia to die. This, of course, leaves Helena free to marry the farmer, only for him to find the reality of marriage an inevitable disappointment, a pale reflection of the delights of desire.

The last of the *Wessex Tales,* **'The Distracted Preacher'**, plays with the struggle in the mind of a Wesleyan minister between the delights of the erotic and the demands of his conscience. This 'lovable youth, who won upon his female hearers as soon as they saw and heard him' (183), is delighted to find that his widowed landlady, whose first entrance is announced by a provocative 'rustle of garments', is

> a fine and extremely well-made young woman, with dark hair, a wide, sensible, beautiful forehead, eyes that warmed him before he knew it, and a mouth that was in itself a picture to all appreciative souls.
>
> (185)

He does not see much of his 'enkindling landlady' since she limits her availability in the deliberate hope of increasing his interest. But the fact that she refers in a slip of the tongue to her 'first husband' makes it clear even to the minister that she 'had thought pretty frequently of a second' (191). He spends a 'titillating fortnight' being allowed only the occasional glimpse of her 'seductive eyes'. Too often, for his taste, there is 'no Lizzy Newberry and no sweet temptations' (192-4). Excited by the mystery of her night-time absences and an independence of manner which 'would have kept from flagging the passion of a far more mutable man' (203), he eventually discovers that she is involved in smuggling.

The combination of drink, sex and smuggling proves irresistible. It is symbolised in a scene in which the young widow offers to cure the minister's cold by uncovering a secret supply of liquor under the singing-gallery of the church, and they refill the keg with water which he sucks from her 'pretty lips' by means of the pressure produced by alternately squeezing and releasing the keg. He even accompanies her on a mission during which their cheeks come into accidental contact as they peer out at the Customs men from their concealed position. His conscience finally forces him to demand that she cease her smuggling if she is to become his wife. The reader is given alternative endings: that of the magazine, in which she gives up smuggling in order to become a dutiful minister's wife and that, according to a footnote added to the collected version, which 'would have been preferred by the writer', in which she sticks to her smuggling. The latter ending certainly captures the spirit in which the whole story is told, the mischievous delight in the sweetness of sin and the impossibility of reconciling the dutiful and the erotic.

None of these macabre stories is 'realistic' at the level of plot or characterisation. They are not long enough to prepare readers for the melodramatic twists with which they are filled. But in terms of the vagaries of desire, the absence of what conventional criticism would call 'convincing' and 'coherent' characterisation becomes a virtue. Acting upon impulse in response to uncontrollable drives, the protagonists of these tales perform the most extraordinary antics, all of which serve to demonstrate the absurdity and unpredictability of human emotions. Hardy abandons realism for a more complex 'reality' beyond the reach of conscious control.

A GROUP OF NOBLE DAMES

Hardy himself described *A Group of Noble Dames* as 'rather a frivolous piece of work' written 'in a sort of desperation during a fit of low spirits' (*CL* I [*The Collected Letters of Thomas Hardy,* Volume 1]: 239). The stories are supposedly narrated by the ancient male members of the Wessex Antiquarian Club, who seem to regard the subjects of their stories as of little more interest than the stuffed birds, deformed butterflies and prehistoric dung-mixens which form their surroundings. They interrupt from time to time to comment on the subtlety of their 'psychological studies' and on 'the dreamy and impulsive nature of woman' (*GND* [*A Group of Noble Dames*]: 131). But they are clearly unreliable as narrators, providing an ironic reflection of the main themes of the collection, the irrationality of desire and the conflict between passion and convention. The noble dames themselves, so much more vital than the antiquarian members, can be seen as victims of social rules, in particular of marriage. They retain a certain fascination, distanced as they are both by time and by class from most of their lovers and most of their readers (Brady, 1982: 51-3, 93). They also illustrate many of the erotic features noticed in Hardy's earlier work, in particular the perversity of desire, its construction of illusory images which are all too easily displaced.

'**Barbara of the House of Grebe**' is perhaps the best-known of these stories, partly because of the attack launched upon it by T.S. Eliot, who saw it as a vivid illustration of the entry of the diabolic into modern literature (Eliot, 1934: 58). Its heroine, like the archaeologist in Thomas Mann's much-analysed *Gradiva*, falls in love with a statue, that Lacanian symbol of objectified desire. She begins the tale 'a good and pretty girl' but then elopes with the impoverished Edmond Willowes, who has little to recommend him apart from his looks. Sir John and Lady Grebe accept the married couple only on condition that the husband undertake a continental tour to remedy some of the defects of his education and it is on this trip, heroically rescuing others from a fire in Venice, that he becomes so badly disfigured that his wife cannot repress the horror she feels on seeing him, reproach herself though she does for being a 'slave to mere eyesight' (*GND*: 63).

The unwanted husband disappears and dies, only for a statue commissioned on his tour to be sent on to the now remarried Barbara. She falls hopelessly in love all over again, forgetting the 'mutilated features' of the real man in favour of the perfect beauty of his image. 'What are you doing?' demands her second husband, Lord Uplandtowers, discovering her 'lost in reverie' before the statue. 'I am looking at my husb—my statue,' she stammers in parapractic reply (67), for this is the image she married. Enshrining the statue in a secret recess of her boudoir, she steals there in the middle of the night and is seen by her husband

> standing with her arms clasped tightly round the neck of Edmond, and her mouth on his. The shawl which she had thrown round her night-clothes had slipped from her shoulders, and her long white robe and pale face lent her the blanched appearance of a second statue embracing the first.
>
> (69)

Two images intertwine in utterly 'unreal' relationship testifying only to the wife's 'intensity of feeling'. The outraged lord, anticipating the horrors of aversion therapy (Sumner, 1980: 230-1), employs a local artist to disfigure the statue in precisely the same manner as the original, destroying her fantasy but also, as a final irony, reducing her to a clinging dependant without the 'resource' that the 'mental world of her own' had provided (*GND*: 75). Human nature, it is implied, relies upon fantasy and illusion for survival.

Three of the other stories in this collection, while illustrating the perversity of desire, end in apparently happy marriages. '**The First Countess of Wessex**' is initially so eager to escape the embraces of her older husband that she deliberately contracts smallpox before making a dramatic exit through an upstairs window in order to join her handsome young lover. When he rejects her, repelled by her disfigured face, she returns to her husband, whose patience and forbearance she learns to appreciate. '**The Honourable Laura**' reaches a similarly happy conclusion when the husband whom her Italian operatic lover attempted to murder and whom she nursed penitently back to health returns after an absence of twelve years to renew their relationship. '**Anna, Lady Baxby**,' having resolved to leave her Royalist husband for her Parliamentary brother, changes her mind when she is mistaken for her husband, escaping at night in his hat and cloak, by a local wench waiting for a secret assignation. Seeing him as an object of another's desire ironically rekindles her own erotic interest in him.

Most of the marriages depicted in these stories, however, as one might expect, fail to satisfy the demands of these diabolical dames. '**The Marchioness of Stonehenge**' 'perversely and passionately' fixes her affections upon an unremarkable poor man, 'stimulated' by seeing him as the object of another's desire but losing interest once they are married. The plain '**Lady**

Mottisfont' has her illusory marital bliss destroyed by an exotic Italian contessa while the marriages of **'Lady Icenway'** and **'Squire Petrick's Lady'** bear equally disastrous fruit, the former remaining barren in spite of employing her first husband as a gardener to make good the incapacity of her second, the latter managing to convince herself that her legitimate son is really the product of an earlier illicit liaison, which turns out to have been 'a delicate ideal dream' (129), a product of her imagination. **'Lady Penelope'** actually fulfils her mocking promise to marry all three of her suitors in turn, thereby coming under suspicion for murder, while **'The Duchess of Hamptonshire',** a girl of 'extraordinary beauty' (149), becomes enamoured of a local curate with whom she has a 'sweet and secret understanding' (151). She escapes from the duke she is forced to marry, hiding on board the ship on which her lover is emigrating, only to die of fever during the voyage and to be buried at sea, anonymously, in a service conducted by the curate himself, who returns to England, having spent ten years 'dreaming of her', finally to discover the dreadful truth.

Desire, in these stories at least, can only be fulfilled in dreams and illusions. The real world offers at best a contentment attainable only after the death of desire. None of these stories, of course, should be taken very seriously: they represent the mild diversions of a group of cynical old men. But they illustrate, with grim and sometimes grotesque humour, the illusions of reciprocal relationship. None of these noble ladies falls in love with a 'real' object but with a series of objectifications of her desire. The attempt to regulate or control such desire, however, as in the case of the unfortunate curate, meets with little success. There is no moral to be drawn. The whole subject becomes merely a matter for sardonic observation.

LIFE'S LITTLE IRONIES

The illusion of reciprocal relationship is very much at the centre of *Life's Little Ironies,* a series of stories first published between 1882 and 1893 which focus once more on the fascinating but false visions produced by the erotic imagination, the gap between the actual object of desire and the image the lover sees. Hardy's irony in these tales has been seen to combine the tragic and the farcical (Brady, 1982: 156). The results of their illusions, from the viewpoint of the protagonists, tend to be tragic while the attempts made by society to control desire through marriage can only appear absurd to the eyes of a dispassionate observer.

'A Few Crusted Characters', the last story in the book, employs the device of multiple narration as various travellers in a carrier's van bring a returning exile from their village up to date on the comic cycle of courtship and marriage that has taken place in his absence. Two cousins, for example, having become engaged to girls unexcitingly similar to themselves, swap partners on the eve of their wedding with disastrous results. A philanderer ends up playing off three prospective fiancées in the same wagon. Similar tales of illusory and unrequited passion reinforce the notion that desire eludes all attempts at its regulation.

A well-meaning attempt to put right the wrong done to a woman twenty years earlier is the subject of **'For Conscience' Sake',** in which a guilt-ridden bachelor discovers the woman he abandoned passing herself off as a widowed dancing instructor. She is hardly the same person but he persists in his penitential proposal, accidentally putting at risk his daughter's prospect of marriage to a respectable curate who starts to suspect the older couple's 'new' relationship. The bachelor is forced to abandon his mistress for a second time, acknowledging that 'whatever the remedy may be in such a case it is not marriage' (*LLI* [*Life's Little Ironies*]: 57). In **'A Tragedy of Two Ambitions',** two self-righteous sons make an even more dramatic sacrifice of their consciences, allowing their embarrassing drunken father to drown within earshot rather than ruin the marriage prospects of their sister, a 'sylph-like' creature who captivates a wealthy and lecherous local landowner (69-70). Marriage is also seen as a vehicle for upward social mobility by a priggish young clergyman in **'The Son's Veto',** who stands firmly in the way of his mother's remarriage to the gardener she had first loved, preferring to see her pine away and die rather than satisfy such base desires.

The irrational, uncontrollable nature of sexual attraction is conveyed through the metaphor of music in **'The Fiddler of the Reels'.** Car'line, 'a pretty, invocating, weak-mouthed girl', finds herself 'unable to shake off the strange infatuation' she has for Wat Ollamor, a 'woman's man . . . envied for his power over unsophisticated maidenhood' and nicknamed 'Mop' for his abundance of hair (126-9). Even after her marriage to the worthy Ned Hipcroft she cannot resist the sound of Mop's fiddle, dancing fanatically to his music and suffering 'excruciating spasms, a sort of blissful torture' (140-1), which overthrows every conscious concern— even for the welfare of her daughter, whom Mop abducts.

The two stories in this collection which most clearly reveal the illusory nature of desire are those which Hardy took great care in revising. **'An Imaginative Woman'** tells the story of an 'impressionable, palpitating creature' whose husband's 'obtuseness' causes her to let off 'her delicate and ethereal emotions in imaginative occupations, day-dreams, and night-sighs' (1-2). The ill-assorted couple happen, by chance, to rent the seaside rooms of one of her favourite poets, Robert Trewe. Having exposed both her vanity and her Lacanian self-doubt by 'testing the reflecting powers of the mirror in the wardrobe door' (4), she settles down to reread his poems and to luxuriate in his 'circumambient' presence in the room. She even tries on his clothes, and when she hears that there is a photograph of him concealed in a frame in the room she can hardly contain her excitement. She puts off the moment of Trewthe, however, the longer to enjoy the erotic delights of delay:

> After her light dinner Ella idled about the shore with the children till dusk, thinking of the yet uncovered photograph in her room with a serene sense of something ecstatic to come. For, with the subtle luxuriance of fancy in which this young woman was an adept, on learning that her husband was to be absent that night she had refrained from incontinently rushing upstairs and opening the picture-frame, preferring to reserve the inspection till she could be alone, and a more romantic tinge be imparted to the occasion by silence, candles, solemn sea and stars outside, than was afforded by the garish afternoon sunlight.
>
> (11-12)

Everything, in other words, is carefully prepared for a positive orgy of eroticism. As the story develops we learn to read the words 'romantic' and 'imaginative' as synonyms for illusory and unreal.

Eventually Ella goes to bed, where she makes more elaborate 'preparations' for the final gratification of her 'passionate curiosity . . . first getting rid of superfluous garments', erotic defamiliarisation for undressing, before indulging in 'several pages of Trewe's tenderest utterances'. At last she takes out the photograph, which reveals 'a luxuriant black moustache' and 'large dark eyes' and to which she murmurs in her 'lowest, richest, tenderest tones', gazing at it so long that she falls into a reverie before finally kissing it. Such is the swoon into which she then falls 'that it seemed as if his very breath, warm and loving, fanned her cheeks from those walls', walls which bear the sacred imprint of his poetic pencillings (12-13). The poet himself, however, manages to avoid all her attempts to engineer a meeting and eventually commits suicide in despair at never finding the 'unattainable creature' of his dreams, the 'undiscoverable, elusive' inspiration of his last volume, 'Lyrics to a Woman Unknown'. As a final irony, Ella herself dies in giving birth to a child who, by an 'inexplicable trick of nature', bears 'strong traces of resemblance' to the poet (25). There has, of course, been no actual relationship between them. However impossible the final genetic twist may be, the story illustrates how little the erotic need involve relationship with a 'real' object.

Another of *Life's Little Ironies* takes place **'On the Western Circuit'** where a London barrister, eyeing the various 'gyrating personages' flashing 'kaleidoscopically' past on a circus hobby-horse with 'long plate-glass mirrors set at angles', selects with some difficulty 'the prettiest girl out of the several pretty ones revolving' and studies her 'as well as he was able during each of her brief transits across his visual field'. She meanwhile feels herself to be 'the fixed point in an undulating, dazzling, lurid universe' in which he 'loomed forward most prominently' (85-6), a description which is confirmed as a metaphor for the human condition—the impossibility, in particular, of direct undistorted relationship—in a sentence which reads like a parody of Hardy:

> Each time that she approached the half of her orbit that lay nearest him they gazed at each other with smiles, and with that unmistakable expression which means so little at the moment, yet so often leads up to passion, heartache, union, disunion, devotion, overpopulation, drudgery, content, resignation, despair.
>
> (87)

Here, compressed into two lines, are the results of relations between the sexes as Hardy sees them.

This whole performance is observed from a window overlooking the square by a lady of about thirty, 'what is called an interesting creature rather than a handsome woman', who turns out to be the young girl's mistress. She was made a widow for the magazine serial, her husband being restored to her among other changes in the final version (Page, 1977: 128). When she comes to collect her maid, the crowd presses her so close to the barrister that 'his breath fanned her cheek', while he, taking advantage of the situation, clasps her hand, clearly under the impression that it is the girl's, and, finding no resistance, slips 'two of his fingers inside her glove, against her palm' (*LLI*: 89). Fascinated by a combination of his gentlemanly manners and seeming sexual sophistication (she finds him 'very wicked and nice'), she relapses into Bovarine ennui, 'lonely impressionable creature that she was', regretting that she had not married 'a London man who knew the subtleties of love-making as they were evidently known to him who had mistakenly caressed her hand' (91).

The barrister meanwhile indulges his 'violent fancy' for the girl, wins her 'body and soul' and immediately loses interest, returning to London with a sense of relief. Distance and the monotony of his work combine to reawaken his desire but when a letter arrives from the maid he delays opening it, partly for the same erotic reason that the 'Imaginative Woman' postponed her enjoyment of the photograph, but also because he feels his own 'imaginative sentiment' is more likely to satisfy his desire than her writing. It turns out, however, to be 'the most charming little missive he had ever received from woman' (note the generic term) and he enters into a passionate correspondence, unaware that it is not the maid who replies, since she is illiterate, but the mistress, 'possessed to the bottom of her soul with the image of a man to whom she was hardly so much as a name'. His looks, his voice, his 'tender touch' and finally his successful seduction of another woman in a mere two days have an irresistible 'fascination for her as a she-animal' (97). This last 'crowning' attribute, together with a sentence describing the mistress as 'a woman whose deeper nature had never been stirred', does not appear in the manuscript or serial versions of the story, Hardy allowing himself to add such unacceptably explicit recognitions of female sexuality in the final process of revision.

The mistress's 'predilection' for the barrister, she recognises, is 'subtle and imaginative', synonyms again for unreal, but this does not prevent her from living in an 'ecstasy of fancy' (99) until faced with the dilemma of his proposal which she advises the now pregnant maid to accept. After the wedding, aware of his mistake, the barrister extracts one kiss from the mistress, with the injunction: 'If it was all pure invention in those letters, give me your cheek only. If you meant what you said, let it be lips', before he resigns himself to a marriage as 'a galley, in which he . . . was chained to work for the rest of his life' with no compensation but the rereading of 'all those sweet letters . . . signed "Anna"' (105-7). I have refrained from giving any names until now, partly because the story is not about characters in the conventional sense but about erotic images produced by fertile imaginations. The 'Anna' the barrister loves does not exist: she is a combination of the visual image encountered on the hobbyhorse and the signature on the letters.

These last two stories in particular, extravagant though they are in terms of plot, explore with sympathetic irony the irrational world of unsatisfied desire. Clearly unfulfilled by their marriages, the wives throw themselves wholeheartedly into erotic fantasy until it dominates their lives. To call such fantasy 'unreal' is to miss the point that it becomes the most 'real' element in their respective worlds.

A CHANGED MAN

The full title of Hardy's final volume of short stories, *A Changed Man, The Waiting Supper, and Other Tales, Concluding with The Romantic Adventures of a Milkmaid,* has been seen, 'by the absence of any thematic concept', to embody an 'admission that the book has no coherent unifying principle' (Brady, 1982: 157). Yet the same distorting processes of desire, increased by the distance, difference and inaccessibility of its object and diminished by actual contact, can be observed in many of these tales, particularly those included in the title. Other stories, such as **'Enter a Dragoon',** in which a woman treasures her fiancé's memory only to discover his widow tending his grave, illustrate the illusory nature of love, while **'What the Shepherd Saw',** like a machine on a seaside arcade, presents four different

moonlit encounters which are tragically misinterpreted by a jealous husband. Five of the twelve stories, written between 1881 and 1900, warrant more detailed discussion.

'A Changed Man' itself is told from the perspective of a voyeur, a man with an oriel window overlooking the High Street in Casterbridge, who observes a local girl's fascination with the Hussars in general and a handsome captain in particular, a man with 'an attractive hint of wickedness in his manner which was sure to make him adorable with good young women' (*CM* [*A Changed Man, The Waiting Supper, and Other Tales*]: 4). Attending their wedding, he jots in his prayer book a somewhat ominous verse which begins and ends with the lines:

> If hours be years, the twain are blest,
> For now they solace sweet desire.
>
> [8]

But hours are not years, and in the course of time the handsome young captain is transformed into an earnest, dull clergyman who drives his wife into a 'reckless flirtation' with a young lieutenant. When the husband dies in a valiant attempt to combat cholera the lieutenant duly proposes, though 'there was languor in his utterance, hinting at the probability that it was perfunctorily made' (22). They never, in fact, marry, for which the narrator posits a number of possible reasons:

> whether because the obstacle had been the source of love, or from a sense of error, and because Mrs. Maumbry bore a less attractive look as a widow than before, their feelings seemed to decline from their former incandescence to a mere tepid civility.
>
> (23)

Desire, it seems, can die as perversely and unpredictably as it rises.

'The Waiting Supper' begins with an erotic scene typical of Hardy: a young farmer gazing through the lighted window of a manor-house at the object of his desire within. She soon escapes to meet him secretly in the garden, as she has done for the past three years, though she continues to urge him to travel abroad and become a more acceptable suitor in her father's eyes. She explains somewhat tactlessly why his absence would be preferable to his presence for her as well: 'The realities would not stare at us so. You would be a pleasant dream to me, which I would be free to indulge in without reproach to my conscience' (31). She is plainly tiring of the simple farmer who presents a 'romantic object for a woman's dream' only when 'idealised by moonlight, or a thousand miles of distance' (42). Seeing him dance with the dairyman's daughter momentarily rekindles her desire, but when this last flickering of her love subsides the young man decides to leave. He returns fifteen years later to find her abandoned by her explorer-husband, whose possible return prevents their ever marrying. Possession is indefinitely postponed although the farmer visits the object of his desire on a daily basis, moving to a cottage only five hundred yards away, which provides sufficient distance to keep his desire warm without exhausting his energy. Even when the belated discovery of the husband's death leaves them free to marry, the couple decide against it, having found the perfect arrangement for the perpetuation of desire.

'Alicia's Diary' tells a morbid tale of rivalry between two sisters ended only by the suicide by drowning of the object of their desire. The heroine of 'A Mere Interlude' has better luck, though her first husband, married on impulse while waiting for the ferry to take her to an arranged wedding with an older man, is also drowned. As she ponders what to do, 'his image, in her mind's eye, waned curiously, receded far away, grew stranger and stranger, less and less real' (273). So she returns to the older man, goes ahead with the marriage and eventually enjoys a relationship based upon friendship rather than desire. She has to endure a macabre honeymoon, sleeping between her living husband in one room and the corpse of her dead one in the next, but the point is that her short-lived romance becomes a mere 'fantasy' (275) in comparison with the daily routine of her second marriage, which abandons the dangerous currents of desire. The erotic and the everyday are two separate worlds.

The final tale in this volume, 'The Romantic Adventures of a Milkmaid', gives more weight to the attractions of the erotic, the exotic and the unfamiliar. The eponymous milkmaid, engaged though she is to a worthy young lime-burner, cannot reconcile herself to a life of drudgery once she has encountered a mysterious handsome baron whom she accompanies to a ball, for which she undergoes a magic transformation, changing into a magnificent dress in a hollow elm in the centre of a dark wood. The images she imbibes at the ball, 'whirling figures . . . reflected from a glassy floor' (333), continue to occupy her mind, preventing her from paying any attention to her lime-burner until he turns in despair to the baron, who guiltily provides the kind of glamorous furniture to which the milkmaid now aspires. Some magnificent mirrors make her cry with joy, 'I can see myself in a hundred places' (342).

But the lonely baron also dwells on 'her image' (347) and summons her once more to a meeting for which she misses her wedding. The steadfast lime-burner continues nevertheless to pursue her, even courting another woman in an attempt to 'warm' her up. He finally succeeds, in spite of a late bid by the baron to escape with the milkmaid in his yacht. The tale ends with her confessing to her husband the fascination the baron still holds for her. Hardy's own copy of the story contains a note dated 1927 to the effect that 'the ending originally sketched' involved her 'disappearing with the baron in his yacht . . . and being no more heard of in England' (Brady, 1982: 168-9). Either way, it dramatises once more the unpredictability of desire and its undermining of the everyday world. It also illustrates to what extent the erotic is a matter of images, both of the self and of the other, images which are far removed from 'reality'.

Nothing is as it seems in the world of Hardy's short stories. Even the most seemingly innocent among them such as 'Our Exploits at West Poley', ostensibly about some children who succeed in diverting a stream at its secret underground source, turns out to be susceptible to a sexual reading. As the fictitious founder of the Alternative Centre for Thomas Hardy Studies points out, this story reaches its climax

> when the two pre-pubescent males find themselves lost and drowning in the cave, itself screened and fringed by bushes, with nothing to help them but a small supply of inadequate guttering candles.
>
> (Jacobson, 1984: 178)

One of them insists on climbing into an 'arched nook' tantalisingly out of their reach, but the other realises that it would not 'look so wonderful if we got close to it'. The reality of sex, in other words, proves more frightening and less alluring than the delights of the erotic imagination.

None of these stories, it should be noted, concerns itself very deeply with characterisation in the conventional sense, which may explain their relative unpopularity. What they do show, in a complex and often powerful manner, is the perennial perversity of desire: its refusal to accommodate itself to morality, to marriage, to any of the means by which people try to bring their lives under some form of control. The world Hardy depicts in his short stories is anarchic and fundamentally cruel, for desire is seen to bring in its wake suffering, sadness and a total disregard for the conventions by which society struggles to survive. To repress it is dangerous and debilitating, yet to indulge it is to make the everyday world which we call 'real' meaningless and absurd.

Penelope Pether (essay date February 1991)

SOURCE: Pether, Penelope. "Hardy and the Law." *Thomas Hardy Journal* 7, no. 1 (February 1991): 28-41.

[*In the following essay, Pether examines Hardy's use of legal terminology in his stories.*]

In his "Preface" to **Wessex Tales** Hardy wrote, *apropos* of **"The Withered Arm"**:

Since writing this story some years ago I have been reminded by an aged friend who knew "Rhoda Brook" that, in relating her dream, my forgetfulness has weakened the facts out of which the tale grew. In reality it was while lying down on a hot afternoon that the incubus oppressed her and she flung it off, with the results upon the body of the original as described. To my mind the occurrence of such a vision in the daytime is more impressive than if it had happened in a midnight dream. Readers are therefore asked to correct the misrelation, which affords an instance of how our imperfect memories insensibly formalize the fresh originality of living fact—from whose shape they slowly depart, as machine-made castings depart by degrees from the sharp hand-work of the mould.

As this suggests, Hardy displayed a sophisticated awareness of the interplay between his "fictions", his "life" and "history". (Other examples of this characteristic include his elaborate "ghosting" of his wife's "biography" of himself, his periodic ruthless "editing" of his personal papers including his correspondence, and the biography, autobiography and fiction of the *Poems of 1912-13*.)

In her review of Penny Boumelha's *Thomas Hardy and Women: Sexual Ideology and Narrative Form* Merryn Williams exhorts us that "Biography is a dangerous tool for the critic",[1] but like most critics, whether their project be exegetical, exemplary, or evaluative, she proceeds to succumb to the temptation of using it. My argument would be that danger is in the hand of the user: most tools can be dangerous or useful, depending on the degree of skill and care with which they are wielded. In Hardy's case careful attention to biographical material alerts us to a pattern of usage of legal terminology which assists an historicist reading of his canon.

At least one earlier critic, Kristin Brady, has sought to use biographical evidence about Hardy's familiarity with the law.[2] This is done in the context of her reading of **"On the Western Circuit"**: she notes that Hardy's "unobtrusive but deliberate use of legal language throughout the narrative invites the reader to analyse events as though in a court room" and speculates that this "style may result from Hardy's experiences dating from 1884 as a Justice of the Peace and from his observations made while attending the London police courts in 1890 'to get novel padding.'" Her perceptions of the ways in which the usages of the law are manipulated by Hardy in this story are often extremely acute, as in her identification of the locutions of the theatrical style of cross-examination in Charles Raye's questioning of Edith Harnham about the extent of her role as her maid Anna's "amanuensis". Brady also draws attention to the story's "focus" on legal contracts, but does not fully explore the implications of this perception. She sees the significance of the legal language in its dramatisation of the "inadequacy of the legal contracts which give final expression to" the sexual choices of its characters; she

suggests that the story's real point is its ironic presentation of the inability of men and women to integrate ethics and psychological need in sexual relations. Her expression of the unifying theme of the stories in *Life's Little Ironies* focuses on their irony and their contemporaneity as tools for a critique of social conventions, in particular those imposed by Victorian morality. I will go on to suggest that this is an unnecessarily limited historical perspective from which to read the stories, which has led to a critique that is too narrowly focused. Another way of reading Hardy's stories is suggested when the persistence and extent of his interest in and familiarity with the law is identified in biographical and historical sources.

Harold Orel has lamented that even the best of the plethora of Hardy biographies inadequately treats his "work as a J.P. and his service at various assizes".[3] This and the attendance at London courts referred to by Brady do not constitute the extent of his connection with the law, however. That which remains of his correspondence and which has been brought to light in Purdy and Millgate's *Collected Letters* shows that he corresponded with eminent lawyers including Sir Francis Jeune (later Lord St Helier) and Sir Douglas Straight. He was using the London courts as material for "reportage" as early as 1863-4.[4] His knowledge of the laws of copyright and contract was substantial. One of the most revealing of the biographical myths perpetrated by Hardy in the *Life* and at least undermined if not quite exploded[5] by both Gittings and Millgate in their respective biographies, relates to Hardy's ownership of Copinger's *The Law of Copyright in Works of Literature and Art*. Hardy's story was that between agreeing to be paid a paltry £30 for the copyright of *Under the Greenwood Tree* and negotiating a payment of £200 from the same publisher for the serialization and three-volume publication rights (but not the copyright) of *A Pair of Blue Eyes* he acquired a copy of, and a knowledge of, Copinger. He attributes his enhanced bargaining power to this episode of self-instruction in the law. This interest in copyright law continued: on 10 May 1875 he was a member of a deputation to Disraeli seeking an improvement in domestic and international copyright laws.[6] His correspondence provides numerous examples of his firm grasp of copyright principles and practice.[7] His bent for legal autodidacticism extended beyond copyright law, which after all might be presumed to interest the professional writer. In a 7 July 1897 letter to Madeleine Rolland he gives a particularly clear account of the principles of offer and acceptance, essential elements of the law of contract, using them to analyse examples of transactions.

Two stories in which Hardy's familiarity with legal principles is particularly evident are **"An Imaginative Woman"** and **"On the Western Circuit"**. Both come from the 1912 edition of *Life's Little Ironies*, the former having previously been included in **Wessex Tales.** Hardy claimed that the reason for the movement of the story was to do with the story "turning . . . upon a trick of Nature". What seems a more compelling argument for this placement of the story is the period in which it is set. The *Life's Little Ironies* stories are set in the second half of the nineteenth century. They appear to have been written between 1888 annd 1893; all but one of them were written between *Tess* and *Jude*.[8] And they are about the late-nineteenth century bourgeoisie and their age: in **"On the Western Circuit"** the central male character, Charles Raye, is identified as an "end-of-the-age young man". The age in question is described as a "century wherein sordid ambition is the master-passion that seems to be taking the time-honoured place of love" and Raye is not altogether of it. For Hardy Raye is a specimen of the modern, and the age of the modern is described in **"The Fiddler of the Reels"**, the story which is perhaps the keystone of this collection, the pointer to the collection's dramatisation of the clash between an old world and a new. The modern is ushered in by the Great Exhibition of 1851, symbol of "an era of great hope and activity among the nations and industries", if not, as seems implied, for countries and the countryside, places where communities and land and landscape connect. For South Wessex 1851 forms

> . . . in many ways an extraordinary chronological frontier or transit-line, at which there occurred what one might call a precipice in Time. As in a geological "fault", we had presented to us a sudden bringing of ancient and modern into absolute contact, such as probably in no other single year since the Conquest was ever witnessed in this part of the country.

"The Fiddler of the Reels" is a history of the deracination of a people which uses the railways as its symbol of the efficient new inferno of the machine age. Its most trenchant social criticism is perhaps contained in a passage which shows that the poor, and particularly the female poor, are peculiarly at risk in the machine age. While it is true to say that they are vulnerable to the forces of fate and the environment in the Wessex before and beyond the reach of the railways, particularly if they are feckless or improvident, they have a superadded set of environmental dangers to endure in the age of the machine:

> The seats for the humbler class of travellers in these early experiments in steam-locomotion, were open trucks, without any protection whatever from the wind and rain, and damp weather having set in with the afternoon, the unfortunate occupants of these vehicles were, on the train drawing up to the London terminus, found to be in a pitiable condition from their long journey; blue-faced, stiff-necked, sneezing, rain-beaten, chilled to the marrow, many of the men being hatless; in fact, they resembled people who had been out all night in an open boat on a rough sea, rather than inland

excursionists for pleasure. The women had in some degree protected themselves by turning up the skirts of their gowns over their heads, but as by this arrangement they were additionally exposed about the hips, they were all more or less in a sorry plight.

Literally and metaphorically exposed to the elements, they are on a journey from which they cannot escape. The language of this passage is characterised by striking imagistic subtleties which underscore the bleakness of the picture which it paints. This, the image of the fault-line, and the gothic quality of the infernal elements of this tale suggest that Hardy's criticism of the arrival of the machine age in Wessex is as violent as that advent is said to be.

"On the Western Circuit" and **"An Imaginative Woman"**, on the other hand, evoke the fin-de-siècle, scraps of imitation Shelley, the *symboliste* and *décadent,* and "curvilinear and sensuous"-looking young men—and women—"full of latter-day glooms and popular melancholies". Of course, given Hardy's capacity to write an age in its own language and imagery we might expect a more sophisticated and subtle—if you like a more "modern"—encoding of social criticism in these tales.

What we find in these two 'nineties stories is that the language of writing and the language of the law are used in a curiously "modern" way. To explore the first of these phenomena is beyond the scope of this essay, but it is worth remembering that the autodidactic and self-inventing Hardy is writing about the decadent and symbolist movements six years before Arthur Symon's *The Symbolist Movement in Literature*. Further, the contrast between the gothic images of the infernal in **"The Fiddler of the Reels"** and the mirrored, kaleidoscopic, infernal, steam-powered funfair of **"On the Western Circuit"** seems too marked not to be intentional (I imply "intentional" there to have the lawyer's sense of "tending to produce an outcome").

The stories themselves centre respectively on the law and on writing. **"On the Western Circuit"** is about the seduction of Anna, a young woman from the Great Plain of Wessex, maidservant to the Harnhams of Melchester. Her seducer is Charles Bradford Ray, Esq., a young barrister on the Western Circuit. The seduction results in a pregnancy. Raye and Anna correspond after his return to London, and he arranges to marry her after she informs him of her condition. The "irony" is that the letters, whose "deep sensibilities", charm, and "prettiness" move Raye to marry Anna are in fact written by her mistress, Edith Harnham. Edith is unhappily married to a wine merchant many years her senior and Hardy makes explicit the thrill which this vicarious passion brings her.

On the afternoon of the marriage of Anna and Raye he discovers the real identity of his correspondent. A rather melodramatic scene of dénouement is enacted by

Charles and Edith; the "marriage question"—or perhaps rather the "divorce question"—is somewhat crudely evoked by Raye's expression of the conflict between the law (and indeed in this case the fact) and the soul and spirit:

> "Why, you and I are friends—lovers—devoted lovers—by correspondence! . . . More . . . Plainly more. It is no use blinking that. Legally I have married her—God help us both!—in soul and spirit I have married you, and no other woman in the world!"

The pun on "correspondent" seems uncomfortably at odds with the seriousness with which Hardy apparently regards this particular mismatch, as implied at the climax of the plot:

> The simple girl, upheld by the sense that she was indeed married, showed her delight at finding that he was as kind as ever after the disclosure. She did not know that before his eyes he beheld as it were a galley, in which he, the fastidious urban, was chained to work for the remainder of his life, with her, the unlettered peasant, chained to his side.

More subtle and interesting uses of legal language in the story point up the social criticism inherent in it.

In their essay "The Animal, the Madman, and Death" in Foucault's edition of documents relating to a nineteenth-century parricide trial, *I, Pierre Rivière, having slaughtered my mother, my sister, and my brother . . . ,*[9] Jean-Pierre Peter and Jeanne Favret suggest that post-feudalism—which admittedly arrived rather more suddenly in France than in England—was a period when the lower and middle classes, landed or not, saw their new power and equality as a function of the "legal liberation which they believed they had gained: equality of rights, status as citizens". Peter and Favret go on to suggest that the symbol of this perceived new freedom and equality at law was the capacity to enter contracts and that

> Peasant life thereafter was invested in the contract and in the greed for land, governed, satiated, and renewed by the contract.

Their example of the man who wholeheartedly accepted this idea and identified himself as a buyer and lessor of lands, they say, "identified himself with the being of the Contract, alienated himself in it, and lost himself in it". That is, they see the sense of power which embourgeoisement and enfranchisement brought to be expressed in the individual's confidence in his capacity to enter contracts, particularly those relating to real property. They imply that this sense of power is illusory.

George Eliot gave us an English example of the type in Mr Tulliver, and indeed in his twin passions for "learning" and the law, he provides a useful insight into Har-dy's presentation of the relation between the three central characters in **"On the Western Circuit"**. Elsewhere[10] Eliot notes the same phenomenon as Peter and Favret in nineteenth-century Germany. While she locates the origin of the taste for litigation in the peasant's "unreasoning persistency" which she says was developed by and under feudalism, she goes on to claim that the (English) peasant farmer's litigiousness is produced by a pride in the knowledge of the customs of the country. Tulliver's combined hungers for legal recompense for the infringement of his "rights", for entering into the "capitalist" transactions of guarantee and land and chattel mortgage, and for the acquisition of middle-class professional status for his son suggest that she, like Hardy after her, saw in the nineteenth-century tendency for the lower and middle classes to assert their equality at law a site where the vulnerability to *gesellschaft* would be revealed. Given that after the Reform Bills of 1867 and 1884 the extent of franchise upon which Peter and Favret's theory is posited existed in England, it is unsurprising that the attitude to contract which they identify should manifest itself in Hardy's late fiction. Indeed, given the persistence in England of a peculiarly limited class of freehold proprietors of land, it seems reasonable to expect that the focus on contract as the insignia of increasing status would be even more pronounced in England than in France. As Wotton has noted, drawing on Spencer and Balibar,[11] England's landless capitalist class were identified by social organization characterised by the "regime of contract" and by an ideology of progress which manifested itself in a concept of history as "a line of progress with a logic akin to destiny".

In **"On the Western Circuit"** as in **"An Imaginative Woman"** the contract which Hardy focuses on is the marriage contract. Anna and Edith Harnham are representatives of the classes whom the *gesellschaft* world and its characteristic relation, the contract, show to be economically and socially powerless. Both are country girls, from the "Village on the Great Plain". The city and marriage appear to present benefits to both of them—glamour, society, property, status. Anna craves and anticipates "a new hat that cost fifteen and ninepence" and also a marriage which will be the saving of a reputation and—remembering Fanny Robin—perhaps a life. Edith secures the chatelaineship of "a dignified residence of considerable size" and the appurtenances of the wife of a rich wine-merchant; she is spared the stigma of spinsterhood. The women's ambition and materialism are perhaps in themselves signals of their impotence. The text makes this impotence manifest in language which draws attention to their reification: Anna is perceived to be a "select country beauty" by Raye; Edith is "what is called an interesting creature rather than a handsome woman" and is treated with contempt very thinly veiled with politeness by the husband with whom she has "consented" to "contract" under her parents' duress. She then becomes "possessed . . . with the image of a man to whom she was hardly so much as a name". After a letter which hints at Anna's pregnancy puts Raye to flight Edith writes to him in the person of Anna in a tone which emphasizes the incapacity to contract of the woman without "protection", without power, and without money. The description of the letter is uncharacteristically revealing of the text's attitude towards Raye:

> . . . the absence of any word of reproach, the devotion to his interests, the self-sacrifice apparent in every line, all made up a nobility of character that he had never dreamt of finding in womankind.

Raye's response is to call this composite Edith/Anna "a treasure".

Hardy's plays upon legal language and concepts in the story are a measure of its achievement as well as a pointer to the nature of its social criticism. The fair into which Anna, Raye, and Edith plunge is likened to the eighth chasm of Dante's inferno, to which the counsellors of fraud were consigned. When the three are momentarily caught in the crush of the fair and Raye clasps what he thinks is Anna's gloved hand, but is in fact the susceptible Edith's, Hardy writes of "the imprisoned hand". Hardy describes Raye, sitting idly in the courtroom of the county-town next-but-one on the circuit after Melchester, blaming his seduction, deception, and abandonment of Anna as "unpremeditated conduct". Thus by a piece of self-deluding sophistry he is able to remove the *mens rea* from the *actus reus,* and to render his conduct not something worthy of punishment. Anna's "claims" on Raye are called "encumbrances"—clogs on the freedom to deal in property.

Perhaps the most interesting group of legal terminology in the story is that which relates to fiduciary duty. (The most common example of fiduciary duty is that which a trustee owes to the beneficiaries of the trust, say when a trustee administers property for minor children under the will of their parent(s).) The text's attention to Raye's clothing signals that he is at least one of the counsellors of fraud alluded to by the reference to *The Inferno*. Raye meets and ensnares Anna while wearing a "rough pea-jacket and wideawake", clothes which disguise his status and occupation. Edith accurately if incompletely identifies him as "a black-coated man". He truants in Melchester and arrives late at the next-but-one assizes; it is only then that he appears in the identifying garments of the "stuff-gownsman, educated at Wintoncester, called to the bar at Lincoln's Inn", his "gown and gray wig, curled in tiers, in the best fashion of Assyrian bas-reliefs". A further clue to the meaning of this disguise is found in the "partial name" which Raye gives Anna, "Charles Bradford". We are not surprised, then, when he breaches his "fiduciary" duty and defrauds the

artless, inexperienced young woman who "has placed herself unreservedly in his hands" of the consideration which society dictates that she should bring to the contract of marriage. While Raye is perhaps the story's only "wolf" he is not its only Assyrian: Edith, who is also socially and economically superior to Anna, likewise has duties towards her; this is emphasized by Hardy's calling her Anna's "protector" and Anna her "protegée". Her slippage from protector to pander because of her own fascination with Raye leads to a pregnancy which would normally see Anna a Tess or Fanny Robin-like victim of social and economic forces.

It is suggested then that the story's usage of legal language and concepts points up the illusoriness of Edith's and Anna's purporting to contract, symbol of their perception of their capacity to act with a new freedom at the end of the nineteenth century.[12] These women's economic and social powerlessness is if anything exacerbated by the social mobility, the improvement of transport and communications, and the pastoral fantasies which the machine age produced; they are thus made accessible and desirable to men from the metropolis like the seducer-lawyer Raye. The most profound irony of the story perhaps is to be found in the fact that Raye himself is a victim of the age. Middle-class, professional, gentlemanly, educated, he is too romantic, too infatuated by fin-de-siècle pastoral dreams not to be a victim of a century "wherein sordid ambition is the master-passion that seems to be taking the time-honoured place of love". Raye may have access to the privileged language of the law, he is male, (although feminised by the descriptions of his appearance and romanticism) but the text repeatedly draws attention to his poverty. Nowhere is this so tellingly illustrated as in his first meeting with Anna. This takes place before the "pleasure-machine", the infernal steam circus which temporarily masks the uses of the market square which it occupies. Here he embarks on the relation which "so often leads up to passion, heartache, union, disunion, devotion, overpopulation, drudgery, content, resignation, despair" and which in his case leads to the "dreary resignation" of the story's closing sentence. Raye decides to pay for another turn on the "pleasure-machine" for Anna, and the conversational dramatisation of their different understandings warns us that a man like Raye is almost as much a victim of capitalism as is a woman like Anna:

> When the horses slowed anew he stepped to her side and proposed another heat. "Hang the expense for once", he said "I'll pay!".
>
> She laughed till the tears came.
>
> "Why do you laugh, dear?" said he.
>
> "Because—you are so genteel that you must have plenty of money, and only say that for fun!" she returned.

"Ha-ha!" laughed the young man in unison, and gallantly producing his money she was enabled to whirl on again.

The similarities in class and period of characters and setting between this story and **"An Imaginative Woman"** are signalled at the conclusion of the former and beginning of the latter. Charles and Anna leave by train for a brief honeymoon at Knollsea; William and Ella Marchmill are encountered having arrived by train for a holiday at Solentsea. As William Marchmill is a prosperous "gunmaker in a thriving city northwards" it is not unexpected that the Marchmills propose to take an entire house (which revealingly wears the highly symbolic alternative identifiers of **"Coburg House"** and **"Thirteen, New Parade"**) for a month; the Rayes as we might guess propose to spend only a few days at the seaside. William and Ella Marchmill represent the two aspects of the middle class, here shown locked in a fatal mating dance:

> Marchmill considered his wife's likes and inclinations somewhat silly; she considered his sordid and material. The husband's business was that of a gunmaker in a thriving city northwards, and his soul was in that business always; the lady was best characterized by that superannuated phrase of elegance "a votary of the muse".

In negotiating to rent all of the Solentsea house the Marchmills temporarily displace Robert Trewe, a poet who lives in two of the rooms year-round. He moves to the nearby Isle of Wight for the duration of the Marchmills' summer holiday. Ella, a very minor poet with the pseudonym "John Ivy", discovers Trewe's identity only after he has left the house. He has long been her poetic model and more successful rival. She falls in love with him—or rather, never having met him, with his photograph, his poetry, and the romantic idea which they awaken in her "impressionable, palpitating" psyche. She makes several abortive attempts to meet him. After receiving a bad review of his "Lyrics to a Woman Unknown" Trewe suicides in his rooms at "Coburg House", where Ella had mooned in front of a mirror wearing his clothes, and lain with his photograph under her pillow. His suicide note blames his despair on the absence of a woman "tenderly devoted to" him; an "imaginary woman, . . . unrevealed, unmet, unwon", "unattainable, . . . undiscoverable, elusive". In short order, Ella discovers she is pregnant (again) and her husband leaps—or rather is guided by Ella—to the conclusion that Ella and Trewe have been lovers; she denies this. Then, determined to do so, she dies in childbirth. Some years later the remarried William discovers Ella's cache of Trewe memorabilia and decides that the child who

> By a known but inexplicable trick of Nature [bore] undoubtedly strong traces of resemblance to the man Ella had never seen

is Trewe's and rejects it.

Mismatches which blight their participants' lives and those of the next generation are familiar features of the Hardy canon, but this story is noteworthy in that it deals symbolically and specifically with the stresses within the middle class in the late nineteenth century, when the distinction between haute and petite bourgeoisie became more pronounced.[13] The Marchmills are deracinated: we see them on trains, on "the steamboats of the cheap-trippers", in a "jerry-built" house at the seaside, in the suburbs of the midlands city where their grand new house is built; their only connection with the city where they live is that it is the site of William's business. Unusually in the Hardy canon, none of the central characters are connected with a family or a native place. The Marchmills are climbing. Their house stands in "rather extensive grounds" behind gates which are a "fine . . . bit of modern wrought-iron work". Ella has a nursemaid to whom to consign the care of her children and a Bond Street dressmaker, and has a book of poems privately printed at "a ruinous charge" which is matter-of-factly paid by her husband at the same time as the bill for her third confinement.

This story differs from **"On the Western Circuit"** in that the text directs little sympathy towards any of its protagonists. Ella is presented as flirtatious, vain, querulous, pretentious and silly, despising her "commonplace" husband and the "plain-looking" children he has fathered, while revelling in the Bond Street frocks and vanity publishing which are provided by the income from the profession which she so despises. Having hatched a plan to engineer a "surprise" meeting with Trewe in her grand house through the offices of a business friend of her husband's, she is exposed by her variation on the *Song of Solomon*:

> Ella was blithe and buoyant. Her scheme had succeeded, her beloved though as yet unseen one was coming. "Behold, he standeth behind our wall; he looked forth at the windows, showing himself through the lattice", she thought ecstatically. "And, lo, the winter is past, the rain is over and gone, the flowers appear on the earth, the time of the singing birds is come, and the voice of the turtle is heard in our land".

Trewe is as self-pitying and self-indulgent as Ella; William, whose regard for Ella is not "any more than, or even so much as" hers for him, obliges her to stay in the Solentsea lodings while he pursues erotic encounters "on board the steamboats of the cheap-trippers, where there was dancing by moonlight, and where the couples would come suddenly down with a lurch into each other's arms". "He spoke in squarely shaped sentences, and was supremely satisfied with a condition of sublunary things which made weapons a necessity".

The omniscient narrator once speaks of the death of the Marchmill marriage in a way which seems revealingly personal as well as radical, saying that it is the "natural way of passion under the too practical conditions which civilization has devised for its fruition" that love should be extinguished relatively early in marriage. He also seems to imply that possessors of "very living ardours" will require "sustenance of some sort", impliedly outside marriage. However in the context of the collection the story functions not just as a criticism of Victorian marriage, but also of the Victorian middle classes and the way that they live. None of the characters in this story have found a way to live which is both fulfilling and sustaining. Ella's restlessness springs from an internal division and conflict which are paradigms of the division and conflict between her and William:

> . . . though less than a poet of her century, [she] was more than a mere multiplier of her kind.

Despite her poetic sentiments, her behaviour frequently reveals her to be "a pushing tradesman's wife, . . . the mother of three children by a matter-of-fact small arms manufacturer". Her tragedy, and that of the class as well as the sex to which she belongs, is that she cannot resolve these two elements of her life. The conflict between the world of production and the emotional and cultural world blights her life and those of her children. Hardy's usage of legal language in this story emphasizes the ascendancy of capitalism and the way in which heart and mind are rendered insignificant in an age which commodifies all: culture, marriage partners, children, everything. William is Ella's "proprietor" and "possessor", but she is not without complicity in this commodifying process.

We are told that despite her distaste for her husband's occupation

> She had never antecedently regarded [it] as any objection to having him for a husband. Indeed, the necessity of getting life-leased at all cost, a cardinal virtue which all good mothers teach, kept her from thinking of it at all till she had closed with William, had passed the honeymoon, and reached the reflecting stage. Then, like a person who has stumbled upon some object in the dark, she wondered what she had got; mentally walked round it, estimated it; whether it were rare or common; contained gold, silver, or lead; were a clog or a pedestal, everything to her or nothing.

Ella, self-centred and much given to gazing into mirrors, is repeatedly said to "reflect" or "regard" rather than to think or to reason. It seems that Hardy thus implies a pun on consideration, the legal term for the payment, passing from the promisee, which seals the contractual promise. Ella's marrying is void of consideration: void consideration in law condemns a contract, like this marriage, to failure.

"An Imaginative Woman" and **"On the Western Circuit"** use the language of contract and real property to emphasize the difficulties which the *gesellschaft* world

is bringing to the class which sees itself as the inheritor of its riches. The emphasis in **"The Melancholy Hussar of the German Legion"**, from *Wessex Tales,* which was written in 1889[14] but set in the first few years of the nineteenth century, is different. As her name suggests Phyllis Grove belongs to an earlier England than do Ella Marchmill and Edith Harnham. However like them she is *déraciné,* of the middle classes, and occupies a rented house near a fashionable "watering-place". Here the drama of mismatching turns on the fatality of relations negotiated across the lines of class and nationality, as is frequently the case in the earlier and "older" stories of *Wessex Tales* and *A Group of Noble Dames.* Typical of Hardy's heroines, Phyllis is motherless and socially isolated. She lives in a walled, isolated house rented by her reclusive father, formerly a "a professional man", now a distinctly amateur philosopher. She becomes affianced, across class lines, to an "approximately fashionable" member of a county family. The engagement is prolonged, and Phyllis falls in love with a German soldier stationed on the downs near her house. Eventually she agrees to elope with him to his native place—he is homesick for country and family. On the night of the elopement she withdraws from the escapade, having overheard a conversation between her fiancé—returning at last, unannounced—and his travelling companion. In fact Gould, the fiancé, has come to break the engagement: he has "married another". Phyllis's soldier-lover, Matthäus Tina, and his companion are caught, court-martialled for desertion, and shot.

The language of contract is absent from this story: the engagement is expressed in terms of mutual promises, conquests, choices, social stratagems. The branch of law whose language is most used here is the law of tort—civil wrongs which entitle the person wronged to damages. The specific tort evoked by the language of the story is defamation: the text speaks of "imputations" on character, of stories getting abroad which are "most unfavourable to . . . character". There is a manifestation of the justice system familiar in the Hardy canon—execution, although here it is military rather than civilian justice which is being exercised. Hardy also speaks in this tale of natural law, saying specifically that at the time of the story's setting, a marriage across class lines such as that contemplated by Phyllis Grove and Humphrey Gould was regarded "rather as a violation of the laws of nature than as a mere infringement of convention, the more modern view". In his treatment of the relation between marriage, mating and community in *Wessex Tales* and *A Group of Noble Dames* Hardy sets up a Comtean-derived teleological system of natural law which treats the *telos* for all mankind as community; the environment of which community forms a part punishes transgressors against this natural law, that is, those who contract exogamous marriages or sexual unions. The stories show these relations threatening *gemeinschaft* stability; the social changes which characterised the nineteenth century provide conditions in which they are contracted more frequently. The community exacts a penalty on Phyllis Grove: her father's social isolation and the class difference between the Groves and the Goulds make him reluctant to explore the reasons of Gould's dilatoriness in marrying Phyllis and his absence at the King's seaside court at Weymouth; he will not ask anything which might be "deemed an imputation on that bachelor's honour", that is, for fear of defaming him. These two factors also prevent the transmission of information about Gould's activities in Weymouth through gossip, that transmitter and enforcer of *gemeinschaft* values. However Gould is far from socially isolated and news of Phyllis's dalliance with the soldier is transmitted by gossip to him at Weymouth. There is a suggestion that this may be one reason for his long absence. Her reputation ruined, and her heart broken, Phyllis dies unmarried. The community's revenge upon her transgression of endogamy is thorough going.

The sheer quantity of information which biographical material provides about Hardy's knowledge of, interest in, and multifarious connections with the law prompts an altertness to his literary usage of legal language. Following the work of theorists like Peter and Favret—and, indeed, following George Eliot—the different types of legal relations on which stories set in different parts of the nineteenth century focus inform a reading of the stories which illuminates the development of Hardy's social criticism in a century when *gemeinschaft* waned and *gesellschaft* waxed. The stories of **Wessex Tales** and **A Group of Noble Dames** record Hardy's anxieties about the breakdown of the life of country communities: the rupturing of the bonds of community typically ends in death or barrenness, the effect on subsequent generations implied rather than expressed. In stories which deal with the end of the century the focus shifts to what "modern" people make of themselves, the ways in which they "make" themselves, and the illusoriness of machine-age propaganda which suggests that they have the power to do either; that is, of course, unless unlike Hardy you are satisfied with the survival of the "self-made-man", with a "condition of sublunary things" which renders prosperous wine-merchants and gun-manufacturers like Harnham and Marchmill "the fittest".

Notes

1. In Norman Page (ed.), *Thomas Hardy Annual No. 2* (London and Basingstoke: Macmillan, 1984) 249-52, 249.

2. In *The Short Stories of Thomas Hardy* (London and Basingstoke: Macmillan, 1982.)

3. In Norman Page 249-52, 247. Orel has attempted to make good this deficiency in *The Unknown Thomas Hardy* (Brighton: Harvester, 1988.)

4. M. Millgate, *Thomas Hardy* (Oxford: Oxford U.P., 1980) 86.

5. The copy in Hardy's library was not published until the year after the contract for publication of *A Pair of Blue Eyes.*

6. M. Millgate 175.

7. See, for example, his correspondence with Madeleine Rolland in Purdy and Millgate's *Collected Letters.*

8. F. B. Pinion, "Bibliographical Note" to the New Wessex Edition of *Life's Little Ironies* and *"A Changed Man" and Other Tales* (London and Basingstoke: Macmillan, 1977) 493.

9. See M. Foucault (ed.), *I, Pierre Rivière, having slaughtered my mother, my sister, and my brother . . .* (Lincoln and London: University of Nebraska Press, 1982); R. A. Posner, *Law and Literature: A Misunderstood Relation* (Cambridge, Mass. and London: Harvard University Press, 1988); S. Levinson and S. Mailloux (eds.), *Interpreting Law and Literature: A Hermeneutic Reader* (Evanson, Ill: Northwestern University Press, 1988) 175-99.

10. In "The Natural History of German Life: Riehl", in C. L. Lewes (ed.), *The Works of George Eliot, Vol. 12, Essays and Leaves from a Notebook* (London and Edinburgh: Blackwoods, 1885) 188-236, 205, 213-4; see also A. S. Byatt, "Introduction" to George Eliot, *The Mill on the Floss* (Harmondsworth: Penguin, 1979, 1986) 13-14.

11. In *Thomas Hardy: Towards a Materialist Criticism* (Totowa, NJ: Barnes and Noble, 1985) 28.

12. While the Married Women's Property Act was passed in 1882, England did not grant female suffrage until the legislation of 1918 and 1928.

13. D. Bell, in A. Bullock and O. Stallybrass (eds.), *The Fontana Dictionary of Modern Thought* (London: Fontana, 1977) 76.

14. F. B. Pinion, "Bibliographical Note" to the New Wessex Edition of *Wessex Tales* (London and Basingstoke: Macmillan, 1976) 248.

Roger Ebbatson (essay date 1993)

SOURCE: Ebbatson, Roger. "'The Withered Arm' and History." *Critical Survey* 5, no. 2 (1993): 131-35.

[*In the following essay, Ebbatson provides some historical background for "The Withered Arm."*]

'The Withered Arm' has long been acknowledged as one of Hardy's finest short stories. As Kristin Brady points out, its form is close to the folk tale: 'There is an oral quality to its prose style, but it has no actual narrator with a personal motive for telling his story'.[1] This is so even though the tale also refers to nineteenth-century developments such as photography and galvanism. Brady deals ably with the curious admixture here, noting Hardy's reluctance to comply with Leslie Stephen's request that the phenomenon of the withered arm itself be more fully explained to the reader. The story's supernatural aspects are held firmly in place by the social realism of the presentation, as instanced in the opening description of the 'eighty-cow dairy',[2] the size and capitalist structure of which Brady comments upon, adding that the simultaneous continuance of old-style practices makes the dairy 'an emblem of its transitional time'.[3]

I am interested here, not in adding one more literary-critical interpretation, since Brady's is exemplary along these lines, but in briefly furnishing a more material context for **'The Withered Arm'**. Critics of Hardy have often moved all too readily from the social and historical to the plane of a universalising liberal humanism. In seeking to reverse this tendency, I will focus the reader's attention upon the two crucial incidents of the tale, the phenomenon of the withered arm and its treatment, and the hanging of the illegitimate son of Rhoda Brook and Farmer Lodge.

The voice which transmits the narrative of **'The Withered Arm'** is that of a sympathetic observer, a kind of literary folklorist. In his magisterial book, *Literacy and Popular Culture,* David Vincent has noticed how the act of writing places the folklorist 'on the other side of a divide' from those studied, who still accepted superstitious ideas.[4] Certainly, such folklorists uncovered, as one contemporary of Hardy put it, 'a vast mass of superstition holding its ground most tenaciously'[5] against the kind of literate, capitalist structures impregnating even a remote countryside. In the preliterate, communal world of which Rhoda is a denizen, 'the bizarre was commonplace and daily life suffused with the extraordinary'.[6] Discussion in such communities often centres, as a writer noted of West Yorkshire, on 'the powers possessed by some of the neighbours who had an "evil eye" and who could produce bad luck among others by simply wishing it to occur'.[7]

The tale recounts how the beautiful Gertrude Lodge 'visited the supplanted woman in [Rhoda's] dreams', mockingly thrusting her wedding-ring into the milkmaid's face. 'Maddened' and 'nearly suffocated', Rhoda grasps the left arm of her rival, and flings her to the floor in a dream action which leaves her still able to 'feel her antagonist's arm within her grasp', 'the very flesh and bone of it' (*WT* [*Wessex Tales: Strange, Lively, and Commonplace*], p. 63). When, next day, Mrs Lodge makes a charitable visit to the cottage Rhoda is alarmed to perceive 'faint marks of an unhealthy colour' on the 'pink round surface' of the arm (*WT,* p.

65). As the summer progresses, the arm begins to shrivel, 'as if some witch, or the devil himself, had taken hold of me there, and blasted the flesh', as Gertrude pitifully remarks (*WT,* p. 67). The belief system in which Rhoda is embedded demands an extreme sensitivity to all kinds of social conduct, and to every manifestation of the natural world. The common denominators of her culture are orality and the natural rhythm of the seasons, and it is these factors which come into play in the recommendation to her lucklessly pretty rival, Gertrude Lodge, to seek the advice of the white wizard, Conjuror Trendle, in the recesses of Egdon Heath. Gertrude is rendered increasingly desperate by the withering of her arm, and consequent loss of sexual allure. As Vincent observes, 'The more a disease resisted a remedy, the more desperate became the search for alternatives'.[8] Figures such as Conjuror Trendle, or Conjuror Fall whom Henchard consults in *The Mayor of Casterbridge,* 'could formulate the demand for their services into a decent livelihood',[9] though Hardy stresses Trendle's feigned scepticism in his own powers, and his alternative career as a dealer in furze. The word 'trendle' derives from an Anglo-Saxon term for a circle; progressively, in **'The Withered Arm'** and elsewhere in Hardy's Wessex fiction, we see a repetitive, seasonal conception of time replaced by its linear opposite, in a process which Vincent characterises as 'the invasion of the circular, immutable rhythms of nature by the progressive, man-made movement of an historically conscious society'.[10] We see this clearly in the distinction drawn between Mrs Durbeyfield, with her faith in the prophetic powers of *The Compleat Fortune Teller,* and Tess herself, with her schizophrenic ability to speak the 'two languages' of village community and metropolis. In *Tess of the d'Urbervilles,* of course, the invasion is registered and focused by the arrival of the steam-threshing machine. Enlightenment, so-called, resided in the Established Church, and the Anglican pastor often sought to challenge and undermine village credulity during the nineteenth century. The increase in literacy was crucial here, but Vincent interestingly notes the caveat that a printed culture also *preserved* superstition, in the form of fortune-telling, dream books and quack prescriptions of the kind purveyed by Vilbert in *Jude the Obscure.* The 'aged friend' from whom the narrator heard of the curative incident appears to have been Hardy's mother, Jemima. The Dorchester hangman, William Calcraft, was in the habit of selling the rope by the inch after a hanging to customers who believed in its medical efficacy. He was once rebuked by the authorities for allowing a man to come to the scaffold to have a wart touched by the dead man's hand.

The climactic recognition scene, the execution of Rhoda's and Lodge's son for attending a rick-fire, has all too often been read as melodramatic contrivance. I suggest instead that we may contextualise it within a certain historical conjuncture. The serial version of **'The

Withered Arm', published in *Blackwood's Magazine* in January 1888, placed the action in 1833; later versions revised this date, pushing the action back to 1825. This confusion on Hardy's part is of some significance in connection with the kinds of agricultural distress and upheaval which are registered in the execution of the anonymous boy, since the 1830s were, of course, notable in the countryside for the Captain Swing riots of 1830 and subsequent violent outbreaks of social protest. The situation of the workfolk in the period following the Nepoleonic War was extreme. Social control was exerted through poor relief, which proved totally inadequate, and the vestries which administered such relief were dominated by the squire, the parson and the farmer. As a result class antagonism increased and led to the formation of the so-called 'dark' village, mutinous and discontented. Rocketing food prices and plummeting living standards provoked rural protest and crime in a wave of activity which Hobsbawm and Rudé, in their history of the period, characterise as 'a defence against hunger'.[11] Arson, or letters threatening arson, possessed a long history in the story of struggle and deprivation. As one commentator remarks, 'arson gave the labouring community the opportunity to transform an individual act of covert protest into a collective and overt display of hatred against the farmers':[12] the boy thus attends a rick-fire which might be aimed at his own father. The characteristic arsonist was the young labourer responding to his appalling plight, and this response was at its height in the period between 1830 and 1850. Indeed, arson appears to have increased specifically because of the failure of the machine-breaking Swing Riots of 1830. Hardy himself was to recall:

> My father saw four men hung for *being with* some others who had set fire to a rick. Among them was a stripling boy of eighteen . . . with youth's excitement he had rushed to the scene to see the blaze . . . Nothing my father ever said to me drove the tragedy of life so deeply into my mind.[13]

Incendiarists believed that dread of fire would induce farmers to increase wages, and men would repeat the threatening motto, 'Work, money or fire'. Arson peaked in the years 1834-6, 1839-40 and 1843-50. The efflorescence of these activities prompted an Act to amend the law on the burning of farm buildings in 1844, and a concurrently sharp increase in insurance on farming stock. It is possible that, at the age of nineteen, Thomas Hardy attended the hanging in September 1830 in Somerset of the Kenn arsonists. This group of men was convicted on flimsy evidence of setting fire to a corn-rick. Whether or not this was the case, **'The Withered Arm'** certainly seems to recall the hanging of Sylvester Wilkins of Bridport, who was executed for arson at Dorchester Gaol on 30 March 1833. Wilkins was found guilty of setting fire to a combing shop in Bridport, and the fire spread rapidly to adjacent properties. The governor of the gaol provided two lead weights, which may

still be viewed in the Dorset County Museum, each embossed with the word 'mercy', to ensure that the lightly built seventeen-year-old youth should be guaranteed a quick end. Hardy utilised this incident fairly directly in a later story, **'The Winters and the Palmleys',** which appeared in *Life's Little Ironies.*

If we date the action of **'The Withered Arm'** as 1833, therefore, we can fit it more securely within the period of social unrest. In particular, the reader of the tale might profitably ponder the fact that it was the introduction and marketing of the lucifer match in 1830 which rendered the job of the incendiarist much easier. As a magistrate observed in 1851, 'We all know that lucifer matches have become very cheap . . . they are not only in the cottage, but in the pockets of every labourer'.[14] Stealth and speed now enabled the firing of ricks and farm buildings on a scale hitherto unattempted, and the lucifer match meant that the majority of incendiarists were never caught. Hardy may have subliminally recalled this period when, in his 1874 preface to *Far From the Madding Crowd,* he referred to

> a modern Wessex of railways, the penny post, mowing and reaping machines, union workhouses, lucifer matches, labourers who could read and write, and National school children.[15]

The appalling punishment meted out to the luckless youth at the end of Hardy's tale is somewhat displaced for the reader by the spectacular effects of Gertrude's shock and subsequent death. But the lugubrious interview with the hangman, and the execution which ensues, endorse for the attentive reader a central contention of Hobsbawm's and Rudé's seminal study of rural protest:

> Property was its legitimate object, life was not. The labourers' scale of values was thus the diametrical opposite of their betters', for whom property was more precious to the law than life.[16]

It is surely not simply authorial pathos that Farmer Lodge, after the death of his son, gives up his lands and farms, moves to Port-Bredy and declines in 'solitary lodgings' (*WT,* p. 85). He carries with him the guilt of the propertied class. Nor was the boy's punishment exaggerated for the sake of the tale, since every person forming part of the crowd at a rick-fire was liable to punishment. As Hobsbawm and Rudé drily remark, 'the intention was to inspire terror and make an example'.[17] Of the nineteen executions which followed the Swing Riots in southern England, the majority were for the rural crime of arson. As the writers of *Captain Swing* conclude:

> From no other protest movement of the kind—from neither Luddites nor Chartists, nor trade unionists—was such a bitter price exacted.[18]

The supposedly timeless ballad qualities of **'The With-ered Arm'** beloved of so many Hardy commentators need to be balanced by the historical specificity of the 'bitter price' which the tale so dramatically embodies in the lives of Rhoda Brook and her son, victims of a carefully rendered moment of class antagonism in rural England.[19]

Notes

1. Kristin Brady, *The Short Stories of Thomas Hardy* (London: Macmillan, 1982), p. 21.

2. 'The Withered Arm', in *Wessex Tales,* ed. Kathryn R. King (Oxford: Oxford University Press, 1991), p. 57. Subsequent page references are to this edition.

3. Brady, p. 24.

4. David Vincent, *Literacy and Popular Culture* (Cambridge: Cambridge University Press, 1989), p. 57.

5. William Henderson, writing in 1866; cited in Vincent, p. 156.

6. Vincent, p. 159.

7. John Sykes, cited in Vincent, p. 160.

8. Vincent, pp. 162-3.

9. Vincent, p. 172.

10. Vincent, p. 158.

11. E. J. Hobsbawm and George Rudé, *Captain Swing* (Harmondsworth: Penguin Books, 1973), p. 54.

12. J. E. Archer, 'A personal comment on arson in Norfolk and Suffolk', in *Class, Conflict and Protest in the English Countryside 1700-1880,* ed. Mick Reed and Roger Wells (London: Frank Cass, 1990), p. 85.

13. Cited in Brady, p. 28. Hardy also recalled, 'My father knew a man who was hanged for saying to a farmer "it will be a light night"—his ricks being set fire to before the morning'. Cited in W. Rothenstein, *Man and Memories* (New York: Tudor Publishing, n.d.), p. 164.

14. Cited in Reed and Wells, p. 171.

15. *Hardy: Personal Writings,* ed. H. Orel (London: Macmillan, 1966), p. 9.

16. Hobsbawm and Rudé, p. 247.

17. Hobsbawm and Rudé, p. 221.

18. Hobsbawm and Rudé, p. 225.

19. Hardy's interest in hangings and other matters relevant to this article are usefully examined in Charlotte Lindgren's 'Thomas Hardy: Grim Facts and Local Lore', *The Thomas Hardy Journal,* vol. I, no. 3 (October 1985), pp. 18-27.

John Plotz (essay date summer 1996)

SOURCE: Plotz, John. "Motion Slickness: Spectacle and Circulation in Thomas Hardy's 'On the Western Circuit.'" *Studies in Short Fiction* 33, no. 3 (summer 1996): 369-86.

[*In the following essay, Plotz explores the meaning of technical advances and machinery in Hardy's short fiction, particularly the steam roundabout in "On the Western Circuit."*]

> Dreading the moment when the inexorable stoker, grimly lurking behind the rococo-work, should decide that this set of riders had had their pennyworth, and bring the whole concern of steam-engine, horses, mirrors, trumpets, drums, cymbals, and such-like to pause and silence, he waited for her every reappearance.
>
> **("On the Western Circuit"** 246)

The grim stoker, who makes only this one brief appearance in Thomas Hardy's 1891 story, **"On the Western Circuit,"** is the invisible producer of phantasmagoria, embodying all the evils that the steam roundabout's cheery whirl seems to belie. Harmless and beautiful as a ride on the roundabout may seem at first, the reader does not need to have been tutored by **"The Fiddler of the Reels"** or by the ecstatic dancing scenes in *The Return of the Native* to know that such a face-flushing holiday from reality will do neither its riders nor onlookers any good. **"On the Western Circuit"** traces meticulously the consequences of one ill-chosen ride: disaster for a housemaid, Anna; for the admiring onlooker who woos her, Charles Bradford Raye; and for her mistress Edith Harnham, who writes Anna's love letters to the peripatetic Charles and falls in love with him herself.

The love triangle may be old, but roundabout love is new. At the story's base is the arrival of a machine that brings urban worries—and urban illusions—into Hardy's rural Wessex. The presence of "steam circuses, as the roundabouts were called by their owners" (245) creates a phantasmagoric effect that engenders a thoroughly mistaken love at first sight, a sort of love impossible in *ante*industrial Wessex. The steam circuses do not merely conceal some aspect of reality, but create, in a viewer's eye, an illusion that becomes *preferable* to reality. When Charles falls in love with what he thinks he sees of Anna on the roundabout, he sets into motion a chain of events designed to recreate or to perpetuate the phantasmatic desire.[1] Out of children, young men, old people, and three pretty girls spinning by on the roundabout, Charles Bradford Raye creates a girl he loves madly. And out of the revolving images and counterimages she sees while riding the roundabout, Anna deludes herself into believing she has chosen Charles.

Conceived in a whirl, this love has its existence strengthened and sustained by three subsequent evils, all linked causally, but also poetically, to the roundabout's motion: first, Charles's financial ability to pay for Anna to ride again; second, Charles's job moving with the judicial circuit, which keeps him away so that the enchantment does not wear off; third, a series of letters between Charles and Edith, who eventually pursues a full-blown epistolary romance (under Anna's name) with the absent Charles. A whirl of illusions, in other words, follows on the original visual mistake, allowing a queer emotion—that both *is* and *is not* love—to be created. But in the beginning was the image, born of the roundabout.

Hardy's distrust of the modern and of technological innovations is evidenced in every one of his works. His novels sometimes seem an almost Luddite rejection of the forces of urbanization and mechanization (not to mention transportation) that were in his day rapidly replacing "homogeneous piles of medieval architecture" (244) with more homogeneous piles of slag, and greenswards with suburbs.[2] He deploys a variety of techniques to convey that distrust. He is fond of curious juxtapositions, for example, as his repeated use of French exiles, and English or German soldiers quartered in Wessex makes clear. He also lets drop a great many references to the metaphysical "ache of modernism"; "vague latter-day glooms and popular melancholies" (246) often afflict his fashionable youths. And there are more than a few pilgrimages to London, as when Caroline Aspent and Ned Hipcroft travel up to see the Great Exhibition (in the 1893 **"The Fiddler of the Reels"**), or Sam Hobson passes through suburban streets at night with loads of vegetables from the country (in **"The Son's Veto,"** also 1893).

In fact, Hardy's descriptions of a general or *epistemic* break between the old and the new are often unforgettable. Take for instance the marvelous description, in **"The Fiddler of the Reels,"** of the significance of 1851, the year of the Great Exhibition:

> For South Wessex the year formed in many ways an extraordinary chronological frontier or transit-line, at which there occurred what one might call a precipice in Time. As in a geological "fault," we had presented to us a sudden bringing of ancient and modern into absolute contact, such as probably in no other single year since the Conquest was ever witnessed in this part of the country.
>
> (286)

Still, the "excursion trains" that run down into Wessex play a fairly small role in that story—its real center is music's seductive powers. A similar shyness hovers over much of the rest of Hardy's work. Clym Yeobright, for example, is free to go abroad—as long as his experience of Paris is rendered only in a few redolent details. And the city (be it London or Paris) has other ways of coming to those who will not come to it. In *The Hand of Ethelberta,* as Slater points out, "the ten-

tacles of a de-individualising metropolitan culture . . . reach out all over the country" (49); even on the Isle of Slingers, Avice can fall thrall to metropolitan customs, because "those who brought her up [strove] to make her an exact copy of tens of thousands of other people, in whose circumstances there was nothing special, distinctive, or picturesque." But it is rare that there appears any *tangible* avatar of the mobile and mechanical modern age.

What is generally lacking in Hardy, we might say, is any direct representation of those technical advances that bring to outlying counties (as they might to the overseas colonies) a particular object that almost seems dropped from a future age. Guy Debord has aptly named such intrusive objects "star commodities" (45). Debord has in mind things like Coca-Cola in twentieth-century Africa, but a list for the nineteenth century might include striking incursions such as the British railways in India and the telegraph or camera in the French and British African empires. The consequences of such objects pass far beyond their immediate work and function: it is the fact of *discontinuity* implied by their presence that most jars and changes the invaded landscape.

The reader is well warned to look sharp—and well rewarded for doing so—when such an object appears in the work of writers who confronted the approach of modernity with as much mingled dread and curiosity as did Hardy. There are at least two fascinating instances of such an intrusion in Hardy's novels. In *The Mayor of Casterbridge* (1886), Farfrae's glistening sowing machine, "a compound of hornet, grasshopper, and shrimp, magnified enormously" is at once so novel and potentially so useful that "it created about as much sensation in the corn-market as a flying machine would create at Charing Cross" (238). The threshing machine that Tess feeds in *Tess of the D'Urbervilles* (1891) is another, a "portable repository of force, round whose hot blackness the morning air quivered" (319).[3] Like the steam roundabout, it exists on quite another level of reality from its pastoral Wessex surroundings: "in a few seconds, [the engineer] could make the long strap move at an invisible velocity. Beyond its extent the environment might be corn, straw or chaos; it was all the same to him" (320). Earlier in the novel, Tess had stood silhouetted against the London milk train. The passage describing her then applies again now: "no object could have looked more foreign to the gleaming cranks and wheels than this unsophisticated girl, with the round bare arms, the rainy face and hair, the suspended attitude of a friendly leopard at pause" (212).

In these brief passages, one of the great English conservative thinkers confronts directly a systematic, widespread, and terrifying social change that in almost all of his writing he preferred simply to ignore or to combat indirectly. The description of the steam roundabout in

"On the Western Circuit" is no less fascinating, and it has the advantage of being the story's defining moment. The roundabout crystallizes the story's paradigmatic association of whirling motion and London's creeping contamination of England's rural counties. Both *Tess* and *The Mayor* turn quickly away from invasive modern machinery, but in this short story, all of Wessex, like those "revolving" on the roundabout, is trapped somewhere between solid ground and ephemeral rotation.

As its concern with the circulation of goods from an urban core to a rural periphery should suggest, **"On the Western Circuit"** may be able to provide a way to read Hardy's complicated criticism of modernity in relation to Britain's conceptions of its imperial ventures overseas. Literary critics have recently focused a great deal of critical attention on the presence (via representation, allusion, or indirect influence) of Britain's overseas empire in nineteenth-century literature (Said, Sharpe, Suleri). A careful consideration of the place of the star commodity in the circulating systems of outlying regions of England itself suggests, however, that the relationship between the rural counties and "metropolitan" London also has something to tell critics about the advent of modernity, or its *trickle-down* from capital to outskirts.[4] The role that the *inland* literature of the time has to play in broadening our understanding of the relationship between imperialism and modernity, then, may depend not only on the covert colonial references adduced in such writers as Austen, Brontë, Thackeray, and Dickens, but also upon representations of the struggle between a rural, peripheral past and an increasingly intrusive urban present.[5]

To put it another way, **"On the Western Circuit"** benefits by being read through the lens Adorno turned on Wagner:

> Wagner belongs to the first generation to realize that in a world that has been socialized through and through it is not possible for an individual to alter something that is determined over the heads of men. Nevertheless it was not given to him to call the overarching totality by its real name. In consequence it is transformed for him into myth.
>
> (87)

The mythic structure abides in most of Hardy—even in **"On the Western Circuit."** Hardy begins nonetheless to tell the story of the advent of simulations (moving from London to the provinces), which is also the story of the relinquishment of human autonomy and decision-making to a mechanical structure. Hardy finds (or manufactures) in his Wessex a breathing-space, a space from which to confront a modern life that by 1891 had held London in its thrall a full 60 years. In a space where modernity is *dilatory,* where it is late in arriving,

the steam roundabout becomes visible in its full, complicated relationship to other *roundabout* systems of the modern age: to the fiscal system that sends cash to Wessex, and carnivals to gather that cash; to the judicial circuit that wheels Charles through Wessex; and to the postal system that sends letters from Charles to Anna, and from Anna to Edith, and from Edith back to Charles. That same postal system also sends Hardy's manuscripts up to London and his published stories down to subscribers of *The English Illustrated Magazine.* Thomas Hardy himself, the stoker of textual machinery and the "amanuensis" (the book's first title [Manford 95]) of textual lovers, is part of the spin cycle too.

The steam roundabout exists on a slightly different plane of reality from its surroundings: it is "in the agricultural world, but not of it" (*Tess* 319). We might say that it systematically distorts visual stimuli around it. Debord's definition of "spectacle" is relevant here, especially given Thomas Hardy's notable concern with distinguishing between work and play:

> The spectacle is not identifiable with mere gazing even combined with hearing. It is that which escapes the activity of men, that which escapes reconsideration and correction by their work.
>
> (18)[6]

What is seen on the roundabout is disconnected from any of the ordinary *standards* by which any sensory input can be judged. Vision gains some unquantifiable added essence.

The results of the roundabout's visual *plus-power* are enormous, ranging from Charles's paying for (one) young beauty to continue riding the roundabout, to the judicial circuitry wheeling young Charles away at just the right (or wrong) moment, to the eventual entire misguided correspondence. But the salient fact is that all of these later misuses of three entirely different circulatory systems of the world—money, the judicial circuitry, and letter writing—are the results of an initial visual misapprehension. All the subsequent trouble can be indirectly traced back to the original spectacular mistake, the thing seen that not only was not there, but could never even have been *imagined* without the roundabout.

VISION

> The spectacle, as a tendency to make one see the world by means of various specialized mediations (it can no longer be grasped directly) naturally finds vision to be the privileged human sense which the sense of touch was for other epochs. The most abstract, the most mystifiable sense corresponds to the generalized abstraction of present-day society.
>
> (Debord 18)

Vision, by the latter half of the nineteenth century, is credited with almost mystical powers and acknowledged as the site of imponderable occurrences: occurrences, that is, that cannot be weighed against other sensory input. That visual imponderability, or *incommensurability*, and the corresponding rise in fascination with mechanical phantasmagoria, opens up an entire sphere of the world that can neither be "brought back into focus" nor "brought back to earth" (Castle 30). If the fascination of mechanical phantasmagoria partially depended on the knowledge that they were not "real" ghosts but "only" optical illusions, their allure was only heightened by the realization that this merely transplanted the realm of the eerie into the subjective mind: made alchemy psychology.

Jonathan Crary's *Techniques of the Observer* documents the rise of interest in the phantasmagoric and illusionary and the era's increasingly strange and vivid speculations on the science of optics. A chart in Johannes Muller's *Handbuch der Physiologie des Menschen* (1833), for example, lists all the agencies capable of producing the sensation of sight. After mechanical abrasions, electrical influx, chemicals, and blood, photons are ranked a poor fifth, and with this caveat: "although they [photons] may have many other actions than this; for instance they effect chemical changes, and are the means of maintaining the chemical processes in plants" (90). Muller also goes on to document the effects on the other sense that the aforementioned stimuli may have (effects that do not correspond to their effect on vision). What is being created is a world of hermetically riven senses, in which there is no reason that any one sense can serve as standard for another.

The idea that the senses are, or indeed *ought* to be, integrated to each other is related to the notion of an ordered and known social setting. It is reasonable to expect to be able to relate visual and auditory stimuli—to pick the easiest example—when spending one's days in a landscape where every sound and sight is known. There, the song of a bird can be matched up with the appropriate tree, and the tractor on the horizon explains a characteristic buzz. But (and here Hardy tends to desert us, since the modern city is not his usual bailiwick) in man-made and technology-rich realms, there is little hope of integrating the senses or of judging the failings of one sense by reference to another.[7] In an integrated world, neither roundabout nor correspondence would have entered Anna's life. Even if they had, in Hardy's Wessex—a world of continuities and traces of permanence, not intermittent arrivals and departures—most such interruptions (the thresher and the sowing machine) can be shrugged off. In this story, though, they linger, and they matter.

Fragmented or dissociated vision is the explanatory key to the phantasmatic effect in **"On the Western Circuit."** What Charles Bradford Raye and Anna see on the kaleidoscopic roundabout—he watching her ride, she watching him and the world revolve—is a visual phantasm, an irreproducible and finally inexplicable occurrence. The illusion is its own litmus-test, and its own judge. A self-validating vision in a world that has given up holding one sense accountable to the good advices or comparisons other senses could provide.

In fact, the description of Charles watching Anna seems to derive from the experience of watching a "phenakistiscope" (literally "deceptive view"), a device that had been around since the 1830s. As Crary describes it,

> It consisted of a single disc, divided into eight or sixteen equal segments, each of which contained a small slitted opening and a figure, representing one position in a sequence of movement. The side with the figures drawn on it was faced toward a mirror while the viewer stayed immobile as the disc turned. When an opening passed in front of the eye, it allowed one to see the figure on the disc very briefly. The same effect occurs with each of the slits. Because of retinal persistence, a series of images results that appears to be in continuous motion before the eye.

(109-10)

While the scene may not have been written with a phenakistiscope specifically in mind, Hardy certainly intended to convey the idea of rushing pictures forming a continuous gestalt. Charles is described catching glimpses of various country figures spinning by:

> The revolving figures passed before his eyes with an unexpected and quiet grace in a throng whose natural movements did not suggest gracefulness or quietude as a rule. By some contrivance there was imparted to each of the hobby-horses a motion which really was the triumph and perfection of roundabout inventiveness—a galloping rise and fall, so timed that, of each pair of steeds, one was on the spring while the other was on the pitch. The riders were quite fascinated by these equine undulations in this most delightful holiday-game of our times. There were riders as young as six, and as old as sixty years, with every age in between. At first it was difficult to catch a personality, but by and by the observer's eyes centered on the prettiest girl out of the several pretty ones revolving.

(246)

The most obvious comparison of roundabout to phenakistiscope here is in its commercial and voyeuristic potential. The delight afforded here is not the *rider's* sense of speed, but the fact that the London viewer (and the London reader of Hardy's stories as well) can see provincials *slowed down,* "quietized" by the mechanical contraption, a mechanization that paradoxically seems more natural (that is, pleasing in its smooth modulations) to him than their "natural movements." Moreover, the inventiveness that gives a sense of continuity is also clearly an arbitrary mechanical one, caused by the steady progression of pitching and springing horses at just the right rate to please the eye. The multitudes of individuals have become, by stepping onto this roundabout, part of its smooth mechanical function.

Only after its visual pace is established—it is significant that the eye of Charles, trained or overtrained by London, is set to catch that pace quickest of all those present—can one "catch a personality":

> It was not that one with the light frock and light hat whom he had been at first attracted by; no it was the one with the black cape, grey skirt, light gloves and— no, not even she, but the one behind her; she with the crimson skirt, dark jacket, brown hat and brown gloves. Unmistakably that was the prettiest girl.
>
> (246)

The moment of selection rests on a double mistake. She is, literally, the third prettiest girl: he has run through the salient characteristics of each girl, only to settle on the hindmost. While the entire roundabout may not form a single coherent spinning image, it seems clear that these three are visually linked, like the quickly changing but coherent illusion produced by the spinning images (quite often horses) on a phenakistiscope.[8] In Muller's terms, the phantasm of the steam-roundabout has no basis in an enduring reality, but is instead *constitutive* of a new (internal) reality. Charles indeed *sees* a beautiful girl, but only out of manufactured optical effects. And when Anna's eyes "dance" from the motion of the steam roundabout, their "dance" picks out from the world a beautiful young man with whom she exchanges "that unmistakable expression" that is, like anything else in this "undulating, dazzling, lurid universe," manufactured in the eye of the beholder (248).

Only a few more of Charles's observations are pertinent: "Having finally selected her, this idle spectator studied her as well as he was able during each of her brief transits across his visual field" (246). We might say that what he actually studies is the fact of *difference* itself. The three girls with their varying accessories— frocks, capes, hats and skirts—create a set of homogenous differences ("infinite variation within the form") out of which one girl must become, by sheer force of contrast, the "prettiest." In each pass, Charles studies something a good deal more complicated than the lineaments of a single face, an irony that is made yet more obvious by the claim that "he had never seen a fairer product of nature, and at each round she made a deeper mark on his sentiments" (246). What has been constructed here is palpably not a product of nature; and the juxtaposition of the appositive, "his select county beauty" in the line above only reinforces the durability of this whirling simulation: together he, she, and the machine have made a new sort of sensation.

The innovation in sensation is reflected as well in Anna's account of the ride. When she speaks, it is to stress the ride's novelty: "'O yes!' she said, with dancing eyes. 'It has been quite unlike anything I have ever felt in my life before!'" (247). The "dancing eyes" seem

also to be an aftereffect of the spinning. It might even be argued that the constant motion introduced into the text in general—the residuum of the roundabout— makes "dancing" (or dazed) eyes ultimately a prerequisite for the entire story.

Anna's reaction serves to remind us that the mystification of the roundabout is not unidirectional. "The lives of Hardy's characters are as frequently disrupted by their acts of observation as they are by being spied upon" (Levine 537). During her second turn on the roundabout, Anna finds in the young man what he has already found in her: some semantic content for the glorious spectacle, a *locus amoenus* for all the exhilaration of a new sort of visual stimulus:

> Then the pleasure-machine started again, and to the light-hearted girl, the figure of the handsome young man, the market-square with its lights and crowd, the houses beyond, and the world at large, began moving round as before, countermoving in the revolving mirrors on her right hand, she being as it were the fixed point in an undulating, dazzling, lurid universe, in which loomed forward most prominently of all the form of her late interlocutor.
>
> (247-48)

A world of buzzing sensation provides the pleasure that is conveniently deposited in the one nearby site of "legitimate" pleasure: a marriageable young man. All the thrill of the machine has accrued to the benefit of a nearby human host.[9] That the pleasure of motion seems to work to the benefit of that man is one of the deceptions built into the roundabout. The joy that is scaled and supplied by machine can never be accommodated (in Hardy's economy) to the man who seems to be there so conveniently to receive it.

It is true that such female dazzlement occurs elsewhere in Hardy, **"The Fiddler of the Reels"** and the dance scene in *The Return of the Native* being only two of the most prominent examples. But those other intoxications are auditory, and moreover embedded in a long tradition. Adorno is right to speak of the normalizing powers of a myth, and the myth used by Hardy to explain fiddling enchantment is the ecstatic powers of the fairy fiddle.[10] With these new visual phantasmagoria, the consequences are a good deal more serious, and there is no standard myth of visual enchantment around to smooth things over again.

A remarkable event occurs here: the purely intangible, and irreproducible thrill of the world viewed in motion is, for Anna and Charles, solidified in the form of *each other*. They think they are falling in love, but they have actually made the first of many mistaken identifications in this story—they have confused the thrill of motion with the thrill of romance and cut the cloth of their romance to a machine-made form. It is not merely that they are ill-suited to each other, it is that they—or any two human beings, Hardy seems to say—are by nature incapable of bearing the representational burden of living up to an illusory love born on a steam-driven machine, of trying to suit their "live lips to a plummet-measured" ideal. This young couple has been formed, and will unhappily live, in the image of a machined dream. "Machine-made castings depart by degrees from the sharp hand-work of a mould," Hardy writes in his preface to **Wessex Tales,** but no departure is available for these two castoffs of the roundabout—at least, no departure from each other.

CIRCULATION

Circulation is both cyclical and progressive, concerned both with motion *around* and motion *forward.* In **"On the Western Circuit,"** three systems—money, the judicial circuit, and the exchange of letters—become accomplices after the fact to the deceptive simulation engendered at the roundabout. The workings of both fiscal and judicial circulation serve as Hardy's useful introduction to the more complicated and more potentially dangerous postal circulation that perpetuates the triple deceit of Anna, Charles, and Edith.

A. MONEY

Money is there at the roundabout, if not producing then at least sustaining the original blur. When Charles buys Anna a third ride, he seals their flirtation as more than a mere visual *frisson*: the cash sends their relationship into the realm of possible futurity, making it one of those things "that means so little at the moment, yet so often leads up to passion, heart-ache, union, disunion, devotion, overpopulation, drudgery, content, resignation, despair" (248).

"'Ha-ha!' laughed the young man in unison, and gallantly producing his money she was enabled to whirl on again" (248).[11] The fiscal system has been abused here—it is cash that enables Charles to continue the (simulated) pleasure he is taking in her motion, a pleasure that is formed in sending her *away,* not in keeping her near him. Hardy's ethical code might countenance Charles's paying—in the form of sweets, presents, etc.—for the pleasure of her presence, but he is paying instead for the pleasure of her absence, of her reengulfment by the machinery.

This moment bespeaks the contamination of a fiscal system that had managed, prior to the roundabout, to fortify rather than to imperil conventional mores. This fiscal contamination is precisely *not* paradigmatic of Hardy's other work. The ways that money is naturalized in the rest of Hardy are various—when gambling at night takes place by glowworm in *The Return of the Native,* for instance, the gold pieces, dice, and worms are all integrated into a syncretic moment that produces something like a natural casino. And even when money does strike one as noticeably an alien power at work in Hardy, its allure is immediately diminished by the unsympathetic actions it provokes. Consider Donald Farfrae's loss of self-control as he rhapsodizes to Lucetta about his style of profit-making:

> And so by contenting mysel' with small profits frequently repeated, I soon made five hundred pounds—yes!—(bringing down his hand upon the table and quite forgetting where he was)—while the others by keeping theirs in hand made nothing at all!
>
> (122)

Money takes Farfrae, as it were, *far* from the emotional *fray* at this moment. In talking of his profits, Farfrae fails to charm Lucetta. In much of *The Mayor of Casterbridge,* therefore, the fiscal propensities of Farfrae are restrained by his larger desire for concord with the community.

Money used to pay to prolong the spectacle in **"On the Western Circuit,"** however, carves for itself no such benign avenue towards normalization. In its first use, as in the later deployment of the judicial and postal systems, money precisely *alienates* the two who are using it, deferring the conversation (not held till after the wedding) that would undeceive Charles and Anna as to each other's pre-simulation identity.

B. JUSTICE

The judicial circuit too becomes a *post facto* accomplice to deceit and its credibility suffers accordingly. One can easily imagine Hardy finding ways to take the notion of a judicial circuit in stride, to treat it as part of Wessex proper, and not an alien invasion: there are many magistrates in his books, there is some justice done at London, even several royal visits to Wessex that do not imperil social stability. But after the tragically wrong object-choice of affection made by Anna, Edith and Charles (literally an object choice, since the sex appeal rests not in people but in a machine), the judicial circuit too becomes a culpable *machina ex machina.*

We are well warned of its malign nature by the first mention of Charles's place in the grand (vocational) scheme of things:

> Who would have supposed him to be Charles Bradford Raye, Esquire, stuff-gownsman, educated at Wintoncester, called to the bar at Lincoln's-Inn, now going to the Western Circuit, merely detained in Melchester by a small arbitration after his brethren had moved on to the next county-town?
>
> (248)

Charles's work has to date literally been a *career,* from Wintoncester to Lincoln's Inn to Melchester to the Western Circuit, an education and profession formed on the fly. And a life shaped to take advantage of that fact: he reminds himself at one point that romance is completely permissible because his migrations will keep him out of the reach of any girl who wants to track him. (Hardy explains with a wonderful neologism: "the *interspace* of a hundred miles—which to a girl of her limited capabilities was like a thousand—would effectually hinder this summer fancy from greatly encumbering his life" [253].) The reader knows that Charles, like a fiddler of the (urban) reels, can keep himself in exactly the sort of circuitous motion he so loves to see *simulated* (in the "leisure-activity" of which the new age turns out to have a boundless supply) on the roundabout.

The irony here bears stressing, for it bridges the apparent gap between—to borrow Elaine Scarry's terms—play and work (93). Lucetta calls the sowing machine in *The Mayor of Casterbridge* "a sort of agricultural piano" (238), a phrase that captures perfectly the "interspace" it occupies between the worlds of work and of play. The roundabout figures both work and play as well, for in its *purposeless* whirl, the *purposive* movement of Charles on the circuit returns in fetishized form. It is only when Charles sees that whirl served up as a star commodity, as an entertainment, that he can properly taste its delights. The roundabout's aesthetic appeal is founded on a displaced identification with Charles's perpetual circuitousness.[12]

Moreover, the profession in which Charles is firmly entrapped necessitates, it turns out, a wife who will "convey," a wife educated enough to "move" with the times and so keep Charles on his inexorable spiral, out on the circuits and then up into the mobile coils of power.[13] At the story's end, therefore, when Charles imagines himself in a galley, "the fastidious urban . . . chained to work for the remainder of his life, with her, the unlettered peasant, chained to his side" (268), it is the *restricted* mobility that galls him most: how he might have moved with a lettered wife, with that indefinable something her letters had—how little circulation on the circuit he can hope for now.

C. LETTERS

In the gale of mystification and deceit blown outward from the roundabout, even epistolary communication falls under suspicion. All along we have known Charles and Anna were wrong for each other—their forced physical intimacy only a temporary byblow of their whirlwind courtship. Now their mistaken union produces as consequence the most physicalized example of "body and soul" separation: Edith becomes the soul of Anna, writing love letters to help her illiterate servant win back Charles. As Pether puts it, Edith changes from "protector to pander" (35).

Hardy refuses to show the reader any samples of Edith's letters themselves, merely asserting their "inspiration,"

their odd intuition of exactly the right thing to say, their ability to calculate beyond calculation into the heart of Charles.[14] These letters (unlike the many other sorts of documents that Hardy quite freely "extracts from" in other works, among them valentines in *Far from the Madding Crowd* and marmalade-jar slogans or religious slogans painted on rocks in *Tess*) are *irreproducible* on the printed page in exactly the same way that the roundabout experience is. They participate in an economy of *incommensurability,* which only comes into being after the initial incommensurability of the roundabout vision. The *"niceness," "inspiration,"* and *"telepathy"* that Charles and Anna praise in these letters can affect those of us *outside* the charmed circle of the vision as little as a spectacular phantasmatic effect would affect those outside its *camera obscura*. The letters can no more be reproduced as mere words on a page than the vision of Anna or of Charles on that roundabout could be reduced to a series of pictures.[15] **"On the Western Circuit"** asserts that in certain situations—when the characters have gone too far into this realm of simulation and deceit—even verbal creations cannot be recreated verbally.

It is of course true that the difference between the initial ingenuous misreading of the figures on the roundabout and the later intentional deception by mail has substantial ethical weight for Hardy: the blame for the roundabout deception is *diffuse,* while there are clear culprits in this latter affectation of affection. This exchange of letters, however, is *simulation* rather than dissimulation, and this works to make the occurrence at the roundabout and the exchange of "false" letters seem quite closely interrelated. That is, Edith may start out only feigning love in letters, but the continuing correspondence creates the very love (inside her) that it is intended merely to falsify. The mouth-to-mouth kiss that Edith exchanges with Charles just *after* he has married Anna affirms that (267). It is not only that the simulation of letter-writing mimics that simulation of affection that takes place at the roundabout; it is also that this secondary deceit can take place only because the roundabout scene touched off events in the first place.

The turn to epistolary production—the system Hardy would have been most reluctant to admit could be contaminated by the modern and yet clearly the system the *most* affected in this story—returns us inevitably to Hardy himself and to the image this paper started with: the inexorable stoker. As the grim stoker turns the roundabout, as Charles circles from Wintoncester to London to Melchester, as Anna spins on her horse and then spins out an epistolary lie, as Edith circulates false letters, so too the story itself *circles* in a slow spiral progression, leaping forward and then "returning now" (255) to chronicle a past event elsewhere. At the heart of this story is Hardy's desperate fear, and partial conviction, that he too is like that stoker. A man in a machine grimly producing and controlling the pleasures of his riders, supplying the motive force for the whirl, but unable himself to be anything but a wizened precipitate of everything that his images are not: not carefree but careful; not beautiful but ugly; not female (like Hardy's most sympathetic protagonists) but male; not a semi-lettered peasant but an all-too-knowing professional.[16]

Were Hardy to have stayed completely silent on modern technical incursions into a retrograde Wessex, we would be justified in begging the question of authorial moral culpability. But we should feel free to interrogate closely the representations he does give us. **"On the Western Circuit"** is immanently an expression of Hardy's anxiety about his own authorship. A printing press, like a thresher, can make its "long strap move at an invisible velocity" (*Tess* 319) to turn agricultural products into grain for London's greedy maw. Most of the time, Hardy can make himself, like that strap, invisible when he works—but not always. Hardy wrote **"On the Western Circuit"** out of a tortured suspicion that his own act of representation/creation might be part and parcel of the London-based, train-imported modern world he strove so hard to keep away from his Wessex.[17] In circulating stories of that half-*conjured* and half-*represented* Wessex, Hardy takes part in the inherently mendacious modern systems that perpetuate desires—and *stories*—far from their destined, their original, "spots in time." He both craves and dreads to do so.[18]

Notes

1. Guy Debord introduced, and Jean Baudrillard popularized, the notion of the "simulation." If a "dissimulation" conceals what already exists, a "simulation" produces what had not heretofore existed, but in such a way that it obliterates or replaces the no-longer-ascertainable "real" beneath it. An illusion may be dispelled, even phantasmagoria have only a limited temporal duration (Crary, Castle), but a simulation permanently maps mental misapprehension back onto the (seemingly) objective world.

2. It is not, as Manford opines, a "purely stylistic" change when the description of a Gothic cathedral is changed from "perfect medieval ensemble" to "homogeneous pile" in the final manuscript of "On the Western Circuit" (97). The necessary homogeneity of the Wessex past would be dented by the suggestion that it contained an "ensemble."

3. Brooks has also noted the connection: she aptly calls the "inexorable stoker" of "On the Western Circuit" a "brother to the engineer in *Tess*" (146).

4. There have been interesting recent reappraisals of Raymond Williams's work on the country-city binary (Dworkin and Roman, especially Radhakrishnan), while Barrell and Brantlinger

both address, albeit in very different ways, the presence of imperial concerns in canonical English writers.

5. In "On the Western Circuit" we might say that the power of imperious, imperial London is "reflected sharply" into rural Wessex—much as the roar of steam roundabout noise is bounced to Charles's ear off the "homogeneous pile of . . . the Close" in the story's opening paragraph (244). In this analogy, the steam roundabout is the modern world, the "homogeneous pile" is Wessex, the noise is Hardy's stories, and readers are—like Charles—the victims of a roar reflected from the gaudy intrusive circus of the modern age.

6. As Elaine Scarry has argued, Hardy's "deepest sympathies belong to the realm of work rather than the realm of play" (92). Charles's actions, however, are situated somewhere in between. Scarry postulates a world in which work consists of "ongoing activity," but Charles's work as peripatetic clerk is sustained only in its *disentanglement* from its material surroundings—most permanent in its dislocation, and most perfectly accomplished in his departure. Thus, it is entirely apt that he should choose his nightly recreation in the provinces, as he does in the book's opening paragraph, by idly *moving* from "architecture in the dark" to "throbbing humanity in full light" (245).

7. In a nineteenth-century train, for example, even inside a carriage, vision predominates over sound. Moreover both in turn are quite alienated and separable from the bone-jarring "railway shock" that tells the sense of touch that something quite different is occurring from what the sight and hearing report (Schivelbusch 139-49).

8. Angel tells Tess at one point, "The woman I have been loving is not you, but another woman in your shape," suggesting a misfit between an outer shape (pure, presumably) and an inner content (impure). In this story, however, the misprision is all on the surface and all the more thorough for that: three woman and a whirl have produced beauty that is afterward attributed to one woman alone.

9. The arbitrariness of this choice has a series of successors in Modernist literature: for example, in Forster's *Howards End* both Schlegel sisters fall in love with the Wilcoxes as an ensemble and an institution, before either fixes on one particular, *marriageable* Wilcox. Forster is an apt comparison because his writing too, in its not-quite-modernist form, resists what he conceives of as the impending arbitrariness of "something that is determined over the heads of men." Whether that *something* is the power of the Imperial and West

Africa Rubber company to control what the disappearing will of the Schlegels no longer can, or the creation of Helen and Margaret's individual desires in a complicated conglomeration of landscape, action, and family, Forster is as interested as Hardy in isolating the outside influence and at least drawing it to someone's attention—though he cannot stop it.

10. William Butler Yeats's exactly contemporary Red Hanrahan stories contain similar scenes of musical enchantment. That enchantment's time-honored place within the accepted forms and mores of an older era means that seductions or abductions performed under its auspices are less shocking, even less morally egregious, than modern techniques of befuddlement would be.

11. The grammatical oddity of that sentence—there is no originary subject for "gallantly producing"—works to lend further systematic anonymity to the fiduciary transaction.

12. Scarry says of play that it allows "separability" (95). Although Raye is finally unable to dissever himself from the two women he has seduced, the work he takes part in partially justifies a playful indifference to the fate of those he has seen only on the move. The material traces Charles leaves in Wessex—a pregnancy, letters, a marriage and an illicit kiss after marriage—disguise themselves in the story as courtship, but their real implications are also *economic*. That is, courtship certainly takes center stage, but it does so in order to justify and perpetuate a narrative partially *vocational*—what kind of man would take such a itinerant job, what kind of new men is modernity fashioning?—and partially *regional*—what can it mean for an illiterate country woman to forsake the limited certainties of her hometown for "lodgings, newly taken in a new suburb" (265)?

13. Benedict Anderson accurately describes the spiral upward to power in England's empire, the movement through various colonial (or, in this case, provincial) postings necessary for the ambitious young functionary looking eventually to "rise" in London (9-20). By the story's end, Charles and Anna have only made it as far as the suburbs, where they will presumably stick, like several other unhappy characters in *Life's Little Ironies*, the collection in which this story appeared in 1893.

14. There is an additional *explicit* attraction to Edith's letters. They are awash with "self-sacrifice," a sacrifice made easy by the fact that Edith, the actual writer, is "sacrificing" not herself but Anna. That is, Edith is able to find the words to persuade Charles to marry the pregnant Anna because she is writing to him "concerning a corporeal condi-

tion that was not Edith's at all," so that if she writes "from the promptings of her own heart" she also writes out of a calculating understanding of the promptings of Anna's womb as well (261).

15. This is reminiscent of the debate that raged in the late nineteenth and early twentieth century about whether images could be reduced to verbal equivalents, or whether verbal propositions could be turned into pictorial or visual images (Mitchell). Compare also Turner's arresting paintings of angels, which to Crary represent the *im*possibility of signification (143).

16. At the time he wrote these stories, Hardy lived in Dorset but "continued to spend five months [in London] every year" (Hill 14-15)—although he believed that "residence in or near a city tended to force *mechanical* and ordinary productions from his pen" (emphasis added; *The Life and Work of Thomas Hardy* 154).

17. Brooks goes slightly astray in saying that "Charles Raye, Anna and her mistress [whirl] into a merry-go-round of cross-purposes and passions as arbitrary as" the stoker's whim (146). The cross-purposes are all too motivated, the passions all too aptly manufactured out of the visual deceit that Hardy both deplores and employs.

18. Jennifer Raskin, Ivan Kreilkamp, and Elaine Scarry, have improved this article enormously with their careful readings and insightful suggestions. Amy King, Mary Anne Boelskvey, and Neel Choudhury, members of Elaine Scarry's 1992 Hardy seminar, did more than they know; Lisa Hamilton knows exactly how much she has done. All of them deserve my warmest thanks.

Works Cited

Adorno, Theodor. *In Search of Wagner*. Trans. Rodney Livingstone. London: New Left, 1981.

Anderson, Benedict. *Imagined Communities*. London: Verso, 1983.

Barrell, John. *Infection of Thomas De Quincey: A Psychopathology of Imperialism*. New Haven: Yale UP, 1991.

Baudrillard, Jean. *Simulations*. Trans. Paul Foss, Paul Patton, and Philip Beitchman. New York: Semiotext(e), 1983.

Brantlinger, Patrick. *Rule of Darkness: British Literature and Imperialism, 1830-1914*. Ithaca, New York: Cornell UP, 1988.

Brooks, Jean R. *The Poetic Structure*. London: Elek, 1971.

Castle, Terry. "Phantasmagoria: Spectral Technology and the Metaphorics of Modern Reverie." *Critical Inquiry* 15 (1988): 26-61.

Crary, Jonathan. "Spectacle, Attention, Counter-Memory." *October* 50 (1988): 97-107.

———. *Techniques of the Observer.* Cambridge: MIT P, 1990.

Debord, Guy. *Society of the Spectacle.* Rev. ed. Detroit: Red and White, 1977.

Dworkin, Dennis L. and Leslie G. Roman. *Views Beyond the Border Country: Raymond Williams and Cultural Politics.* New York: Routledge, 1993.

Hardy, Thomas. *Far from the Madding Crowd.* New York: Penguin, 1967.

———. "Fiddler of the Reels." [*Life's Little Ironies* (1893)] *The Distracted Preacher and Other Tales.* Ed. Susan Hill. London: Penguin, 1979.

———. *The Life and Work of Thomas Hardy.* Ed. Michael Millgate. London: Macmillan, 1984.

———. *The Mayor of Casterbridge.* London: Penguin, 1978.

———. "On the Western Circuit." [*English Illustrated Magazine* (1891)] *The Distracted Preacher and Other Tales.* Ed. Susan Hill. London: Penguin, 1979.

———. *Return of the Native.* New York: Penguin, 1969.

———. *Tess of the D'Urbervilles.* New York: Penguin, 1971.

Hill, Susan. Introduction. *The Distracted Preacher and Other Tales* by Thomas Hardy. London: Penguin, 1979: 11-33.

Levine, George. "Shaping Hardy's Art: Vision, Class, and Sex." *Columbia History of the British Novel* Ed. John Richetti. New York: Columbia UP, 1994: 534-59.

Manford, Allan. "Life's Little Ironies: The Manchester Manuscripts." *Bulletin of the John Rylands University Library of Manchester* 72 (1990): 89-100.

Mitchell, W. J. T. "What Is an Image?" *New Literary History* 15:3 (1984): 503-37.

Pether, Penelope. "Hardy and the Law." *The Thomas Hardy Journal* 7 (1991): 28-41.

Radhakrishnan, R. "Cultural Theory and the Politics of Location." *Views Beyond the Border Country: Raymond Williams and Cultural Politics.* Ed. Dennis L. Dworkin and Leslie G. Roman. New York and London: Routledge, 1993. 275-94.

Scarry, Elaine, "Work and the Body in Hardy and Other Nineteenth-Century Novelists." *Representations* 3 (1983): 90-123.

Said, Edward. *Culture and Imperialism.* New York: Knopf, 1993.

Schivelbusch, Wolfgang. *The Railway Journey: Trains and Travel in the 19th Century.* Trans. Anselm Hollo. Berkeley: U of California P, 1979.

Sharpe, Jenny. *Allegories of Empire: The Figure of Woman in the Colonial Text.* Minneapolis: U of Minnesota P, 1993.

Slater, Michael. "Hardy and the City." *New Perspectives on Thomas Hardy.* Ed. Charles P. C. Pettit. New York: St. Martin's, 1994. 41-57.

Suleri, Sara. *The Rhetoric of English India.* Chicago: U of Chicago P, 1992.

Angelique Richardson (essay date May 1998)

SOURCE: Richardson, Angelique. "'How I Mismated Myself for Love of You!'[1]: The Biologization of Romance in Hardy's *A Group of Noble Dames*." *Thomas Hardy Journal* 14, no. 2 (May 1998): 59-76.

[*In the following essay, Richardson investigates the impact of science—especially ideas of mating and hereditary—on Hardy's* A Group of Noble Dames.]

> The pedigrees of our county families, arranged in diagrams on the pages of country histories, mostly appear at first sight to be as barren of any touch of nature as a table of logarithms. But given a clue—the faintest tradition of what went on behind the scenes, and this dryness as of dust may be transformed into a palpitating drama.
>
> (*ND* [*A Group of Noble Dames*] preface xi)

In the late nineteenth century, new biological discourses breathed life into dry parchment and bones, transforming genealogy into a bodied, and palpitating, drama. In Hardy's words "dear, delightful Wessex, whose statuesque dynasties are even now only beginning to feel the shaking of the new and strange spirit without, like that which entered the lonely valley of Ezekiel's vision, and made the dry bones move" (*ND* 42). The new spirit was science.

At the turn of the century, middle-class Britain became increasingly preoccupied with national efficiency. Time-hallowed ideas relating to blood descent, inheritance and transmission were recast in an apparently scientific mould as the social and biological quality of future generations became a pressing moral and political issue. Fears for the health of the population converged with concern over the nation's position amidst growing international imperialist rivalry. The birth rate was perceived to be declining (among the middle classes) and the early reverses suffered by British troops in the Boer

War (1899-1902) confirmed apprehension about national health. In this atmosphere of foreboding the discourse of Darwinian sexual selection became increasingly racialized, and Galtonian eugenics, a heavily class-based theory of society that aimed to improve on nature through self-conscious control of human evolution through selective breeding,[2] caught the public mood.[3] By 1906, the eugenist and sexologist Havelock Ellis could declare with conviction and rhetorical deftness "the new St Valentine will be a saint of science rather than of folklore".[4] Romance had met science, and they were bedfellows.

Daniel Pick has contended that, in the aftermath of 1848, the problems of history were displaced into the problem of inheritance;[5] I would add that this displacement intensified at the *fin de siècle* and was clearly visible in the biologization of the romance plot. Charles Darwin's *The Descent of Man and Selection in Relation to Sex* (1871) had placed ideas of mating and heredity in the spotlight of scientific (and social) interest. Sexual selection differed from natural selection (the survival of favoured individuals in the struggle for life, which Herbert Spencer was to term "survival of the fittest") in that it centred on successful breeding and was dependent, therefore, on the advantage which an individual had over others of the same sex and species solely in respect of acquiring a mate and reproducing. Sexual selection explained physical and mental differences between the sexes as advantageous in finding mates; Darwin also believed it to be the key cause of racial differentiation in humans. In *The Descent,* Darwin used sexual selection to explain why competition occurred not simply between but also within species. If natural selection was selection by nature, then sexual selection, highlighting the importance of sexual choice in the process of evolution, invested agency, and agency for change, in individuals. While Darwin himself was ambivalent about eugenics, his arguments were easily appropriated by eugenist social programmes.

In *The Descent,* drawing on ideas of 'artificial selection', into which eugenics easily bled, Darwin declared that man might 'by selection, do something not only for the bodily constitution and frame of his offspring, but for their intellectual and moral qualities. Both sexes ought to refrain from marriage if in any marked degree inferior in body or mind; but such hopes are Utopian and will never be even partially realized until the laws of inheritances are thoroughly known. All do good service who aid towards this end'.[6] Earlier in this work Darwin cited Arthur Schopenhauer: 'the final aim of all love intrigues, be they comic or tragic, is really of more importance than all other ends in human life . . . it is not the weal or woe of any one individual, but that of the human race to come, which is here at stake'.[7] The love-plot, habitual to the Victorian novel, suddenly mattered to evolutionary scientists. In the decades that followed,

ideas of inheritance were increasingly at large in literature, generating new ontological narratives.[8] This paper considers ways in which Hardy's *A Group of Noble Dames* (1891),[9] published at a time when the reputation and writing of fiction was in a state of transition, registers and exploits the encounter between science and romance.

In her sociological account of the ways in which men supplanted women as novelists in the last third of the nineteenth century, Gaye Tuchman, drawing largely on the London archives of Macmillan and Company, documents changing attitudes towards romance on the part of publishers, publishers' readers and an elite male coterie of reviewers.[10] While it is possible to see the hostile review by Henry Knight of Elfride Swancourt's romance (*The Court of King Arthur's Castle: A Romance of Lyonnesse*) in *A Pair of Blue Eyes* (1872-3) as paralleling publishers' and reviewers' treatment of Hardy,[11] Hardy's contention that Knight bore biographical resemblance to himself suggests his perception of his relations with the publishing industry was more complex.[12] Hardy was determined to be part of the literary world and yet sufficiently peripheral (and rebuffed) to be aloof. Tuchman demonstrates how the Macmillan reader John Morley, and his successors, identified men with ideals capable of having an impact upon the mind with activity and the production orientation associated with high culture. In the period of "male invasion" (identified by Tuchman as taking place between 1840 and 1879), "Morley was actively engaged in excluding the romance—that form cultivated by women—from acceptable culture"[13] and as part of this process he redefined the novel "by stressing realism and insistently distinguishing it from the earlier romances associated with women writers".[14]

Lyn Pykett has opened up further the late nineteenth-century debates around fiction. She argues that there was not simply a battle between the sexes, rather "a battle . . . waged on the terrain of gender, it was part of a contest about the meaning of gender and about and by whom gender is to be defined".[15] Pykett demonstrates that Naturalism and the New Realism, two significant areas of innovation in late nineteenth-century fiction, were in part attempts to masculinize the novel, just as Elaine Showalter has argued that the revival of romance by male writers in the 1890s was part of the move to turn the novel into male form, as the heterosexual romance of "courtship, manners and marriage" was replaced with "the masculine and homosocial 'romance' of adventure and quest".[16]

Most recently, Peter McDonald has analysed the material and sociohistorical conditions of "the literary field" in the 1890s.[17] He notes how Edmund Gosse, in lamenting the effects on literature of democracy, and of a readership composed in the main of women (particularly young married women), exempted writers such as Hardy, George Meredith and Henry James from his criticism by arguing that "it is probably to the approval of male readers that most eminent novelists owe that prestige which ultimately makes them favourites of the women". When *Tess of the D'Urbervilles* (1891) came under anonymous fire in the *Saturday Review* he assured Hardy "you have strengthened your position tremendously, among your own confrères and the serious male public".[18]

What these sociological and literary accounts have in common is the identification of a *fin de siècle* flux in fiction. Fiction, historically and culturally bound to romance,[19] was clearly under pressure from a number of directions, as Naturalism, New Realism and Protomodernism competed for textual space. I would stress, also, the role that biology played in broadening the franchise of fictional possibilities at this time—and not simply in terms of a more open treatment of sex, and sexual relations, but in broader portrayals of life, love and heredity. Whether or not Gosse was correct in his assumption that Hardy had a serious, male following, biology was no bad way of acquiring one; like all (male) discourses of science, it was serious stuff.

Romance would have to be rewritten—laced with realism—if it was to rise above the lowly status it had reached in face of new literary prejudice. Hardy's relationship to realism was a complicated one;[20] he was a firm disbeliever in "photographic realism", which he saw as an obstacle to higher truths. Love was his passion, lending itself perhaps more to romance than realism. Nonetheless, it was a passion which, with its affinities both with literary tradition and the new biological discourses on relations between the sexes, he was to turn to considerable advantage. As Havelock Ellis put it, Hardy "is less a story-teller than an artist who has intently studied certain phases of passion, and brings us a simple and faithful report of what he has found".[21] In his first letter to Alexander Macmillan, of 1868, Hardy had declared: "no fiction will considerably interest readers poor or rich unless the passion of love forms a prominent feature in the thread of the story".[22] Biology would provide him with a palatable route to realism, and a novel spin on romance. As he wrote in the *New Review* in 1890, the year in which six of the stories in *A Group of Noble Dames* were first published, "life being a physiological fact, its honest portrayal must be largely concerned with, for one thing, the relations between the sexes, and the substitution for such catastrophes as favour the false colouring best expressed by the regulation finish that 'they married and were happy ever after,' of catastrophes upon sexual relations as it is".[23] In an interview with Raymond Blathwayt in *Black and White* two years later he reiterated the point: "I do feel very strongly that the position of men and women in nature, things which everyone is thinking,

and nobody saying, may be taken up and treated frankly. Until lately novelists have been obliged to arrange situations and dènouements which they knew to be indescribably unreal, but dear to the heart of the amiable library subscriber. See how this ties the hands of a writer who is forced to make his characters act unnaturally, in order that he may produce the spurious effect of their being in harmony with social forms and ordinances."[24]

Hardy's interest in contemporary scientific ideas is undisputed.[25] An attendant at Darwin's funeral in Westminster, he declared himself one of "the earliest acclaimers of the *Origin*".[26] He was quick to see the implications of Darwin's theories beyond the world of science: "Darwinism is as fruitful in its bearing upon sociology as in its bearing upon natural history".[27] Likewise, his interest in genealogy is self-evident, and well-established.[28] However, his interest in eugenic discourses has largely been neglected.[29] Hardy was fascinated by the possibilities of biological determinism, exploiting its creative possibilities. Peter Widdowson has underscored an "obsession" with social class and gender relations in Hardy's "minor" novels which forces these elements in the "major" ones into much greater prominence.[30] This interest in hierarchical relations of class and gender, which predominates in *A Group of Noble Dames,* links the stories to ideas of degeneracy and eugenics which were in the air at the Victorian *fin de siècle*. Romance in *A Group of Noble Dames* is punctuated by ideas of Darwinian sexual selection and concerns about breeding (a conflation of the social and the biological). However, Hardy's ideological position is elusive, both in these tales[31] and in general, and can be seen as exemplified by his poem, "The Pedigree" (1916), which explores the tension between heredity and individual will, without apparently committing itself to either. Publicly conceding biological determinism—"I am merest mimicker and counterfeit"—the speaker privately steels himself against the forces of heredity: "I am I / And what I do I do myself alone". Through the paradox of the poem the possibilities of eugenics are at once acknowledged and resisted.[32]

In *A Group of Noble Dames,* Hardy spices up the romance plot by drawing on evolutionary discourses on love and sex. Unified by a concern with genealogy, the ten (anti-)romances are refracted through a wide range of (male) narrative voices. The first eight tales are located in the seventeenth and eighteenth centuries, and thus enjoy an ostensible distance both from contemporary romance and biologized narratives of sexual selection. By way of contrast, the ninth tale takes place only fifty years previous to, and the tenth is set in, the narrator's present. Elements of absurdity, which run through the collection, are made relatively unobtrusive through the temporal distance of the first eight.[33]

In one sense, *A Group of Noble Dames* takes its place in a long and honourable literary tradition; the use of story-telling as a pretext for a framed narrative harks back to Boccacio's *Decameron*,[34] Chaucer's *Canterbury Tales* and *The Thousand and One Nights*.[35] But the tales gesture equally towards an innovative, framed but fragmented form which repeatedly draws attention to its own oral immediacy and plural status and, like other literary experiments of the 1890s, suggested that the days of the "three-decker novel" were numbered and that the single authorial voice was waning. Hardy had a strong sense of the historical development of literature: "narrative art is neither mature in its artistic aspect, nor in its ethical or philosophical aspect; neither in form nor in substance. To me, at least, the difficulties of perfect presentation in both these kinds appear of such magnitude that the utmost which each generation can be expected to do is to add one or two strokes towards the selection and shaping of a possible ultimate perfection".[36] Writing, self-consciously, in time, Hardy borrows here from the voguish register of natural selection (the progressive spin which he gives it, and which Darwin did not, challenges popular conceptions of Hardy as a pessimist).

By gaining the undivided attention of a socially disparate audience, each story in *A Group of Noble Dames* seems, at least for its duration, to have triumphed in the struggle for expression, but each is met by a chorus of debate from which the next is apparently spontaneously generated, and which, in producing a variation on whatever theme has gone before, has implications for its predecessor.[37] In this way, *A Group of Noble Dames* becomes a microcosm of evolutionary history. Each of the (contemporary) narrators belongs to the Wessex Field and Antiquarian Club, "an inclusive and intersocial" club with broad and broadly scientific interests (*ND* 42; 131);[38] weather-bound for a day, they pass the time in telling stories. At times the tales seem scarcely mediated utterances, but on occasion we are reminded that what follows is "only an approximation" (*ND* 121) or simply the "substance" (*ND* 107) of the original version. However, rather than bringing a disciplining authorial presence to bear, this qualification, by adding a further layer of narration, serves to underscore the multivocality of the collection. This multivocality is brought home by the dialogic relationship which the tales enjoy with each other. For example, child adoption is celebrated in the third tale, **"The Marchioness of Stonehenge"** where emotional ties count for more than economic or biological capital: "flesh and blood's nothing" declares Milly, as her adopted son (he is known only as "Milly's Boy") chooses her in preference to his "corporeal" mother. In **"Lady Mottisfont",** the next tale in the sequence, Dorothy (who was discovered in "a patch of wild oats") happily swaps her adoptive for her biological mother "with a strange and instinctive readiness that intimated the wonderful subtlety of the threads which bind flesh and flesh together" (*ND* 100). But the biological tie gains only temporary ascendance before it falls victim to social law; both parentage and adoption are exposed as unreliable forms of social security. The biological and adoptive mothers of Dorothy reject her when she stands in the way of social ambition, leaving her to be brought up by a "cottage-woman". This was a theme that Hardy took up, and elaborated, in *Jude the Obscure*: when Jude Junior "seems to be wanted by nobody" Jude is provoked to declare "the beggarly question of parentage—what is it, after all? What does it matter, when you come to think of it, whether a child is yours by blood or not? All the little ones of our time are collectively the children of us adults of the time, and entitled to our general care."[39] Adoption, more useful to Hardy for creative than ideological purposes, was a springboard for the exploration of the complex matrix of social, economic and biological ties.

Fittingly narrated by the Old Surgeon, the second tale in *A Group of Noble Dames,* **"Barbara of the House of Grebe",** registers the entry of science (here, Lyellian geology) into the language and, ultimately, the practice, of romance—"a lover's heart after possession being comparable to the earth in its geologic stages, as described to us sometimes by our worthy President; first a hot coal, then a warm one, then a cooling cinder, then chilly—the simile shall be pursued no further" (*ND* 50). Later in the story, when the surgeon describes Edmond Willowes as "metamorphosed to a specimen of another species" (*ND* 61), he borrows from the register of Darwin's evolutionary theory of descent with modification. Scientific imagery pervades the collection; even the Rural Dean talks of passion "electrified back to life" (*ND* 76). Following the sixth tale, **"Squire Petrick's Lady"** (narrated by the Crimson Maltster), the audience exclaim "that such subtle and instructive psychological studies as this (now that psychology was so much in demand) were precisely the tales they desired, as members of a scientific club' (*ND* 131). In this tale, Timothy Petrick 'studied prints of the portraits of [the Dukes of Southwesterland], and then, like a chemist watching a crystallization, began to examine young Rupert's face for the unfolding of those historic curves and shades that the painters Vandyke and Lely had perpetuated on canvas" (*ND* 127-128). The convergence of art and biology promises to inscribe itself on the illegitimate boy's body. But Petrick is disappointed: instead the boy turns out "a fleshly reproduction of a wretched old uncle whose very name he wished to forget!" Biology trumps language: "the boy's Christian name, even, was an imposture and an irony, for it implied hereditary force and brilliancy to which he would plainly never attain" (*ND* 130). Earlier, in **"Lady Mottisfont",** Dorothy's body gradually reveals her pedigree: the eponymous subject "had seen there not only her husband's traits, which she had often beheld before, but others, of the shade, shape, and expression which characterized those of her new neighbour" (*ND* 99). In the ninth tale, **"The Duchess of Hamptonshire"** (narrated by the Quiet Gentleman), the language of evolution resuscitates and animates the Duke of Hamptonshire's pictorial genealogy: he ascends to his picture-gallery with the express aim of spending some time considering "what an important part those *specimens* of womankind had played in the *evolution* of the Saxelby race" (*ND* 151, emphasis added). This interest in the vivid visibility of genealogy occurs elsewhere in Hardy's writing: when Tess encounters portraits of her foremothers we learn "her fine features were unquestionably traceable in these exaggerated forms",[40] and the romance plot of *A Laodicean* (1881) is kindled, and inflamed, in a picture-gallery: "a new and romantic feeling that the De Stancys had stretched out a tentacle from their genealogical tree to seize her by the hand and draw her in to their mass took possession of Paula".[41]

In **"Barbara of the House of Grebe"**, we learn that the eponymous heroine (who at this time was "a good and pretty girl", and "hated other pretty women the very least possible" (*ND* 47)) has no romantic feeling for Lord Uplandtowers; his confidant gives him little cause for hope: "and as for thought of a good match, why, there's no more calculation in her than in a bird" (*ND* 46). Barbara loves and marries a suitor lower down in the social hierarchy: Willowes, "a young fellow of Shottsford-Forum—a widow-woman's son"; "Willowes's father, or grandfather, was the last of the old glass-painters in that place" (*ND* 49). She herself is the daughter of Sir John and Lady Grebe; "Sir John's was a baronetcy created a few years before the breaking out of the Civil War, and his lands were even more extensive than those of Lord Uplandtowers himself" (*ND* 46). The tale initially presents itself as a conventional love-match—"the young married lovers, caring no more about their blood than about ditch-water, were intensely happy" (*ND* 50). But Barbara is won over to selection for breeding: "now too, she was older, and admitted to herself that a man whose ancestor had run scores of Saracens through and through in fighting for the site of the Holy Sepulchre was a more desirable husband, socially considered, than one who could only claim with certainty to know that his father and grandfather were respectable burgesses" (*ND* 65). Following the death ("in a foreign land") of the rejected Willowes, Barbara marries the persistent Lord Uplandtowers (who has exhibited cynical doggedness from the age of nineteen [*ND* 45]) in what is no less than the playing out of a biologically determined drama: "determination was hereditary in the bearers of that escutcheon" (*ND* 45).

However, Barbara retains intense sexual desire for her first husband, towards whom she had cooled socially (and, following his horrific disfigurement in a theatre fire in Venice—where she sent him to up his social credentials—physically), but whose sexual memory she cherishes long after his reported death. Following the arrival from Italy of a life-size statue of Willowes, Up-

landtowers discovers her in her private recess, in a passionate embrace with the statue, "standing with her arms clasped tightly round the neck of Edmond, and her mouth on his" (*ND* 69). Significantly, her feelings of sexual desire thwart her capacity to breed; as Uplandtowers now realizes, it is her sexual passion that threatens to cut off his line: "this is where we evaporate—this is where my hopes of a successor in the title dissolve" (*ND* 69).

As Angus McLaren and Thomas Laqueur have argued, a one-sex model of humanity was gradually succeeded by a two-sex model during the course of the eighteenth century. This was accompanied by the replacement of the desiring female by the passive, undesiring Angel from the eighteenth century onwards.[42] The emergence of preformation theories in the late seventeenth and early eighteenth centuries, both on the Continent and in Britain, attributed to woman a much more passive role than had the previous semence or two-seed theory. A general consensus emerged that the new creation of life required two distinct building blocks. This stress on difference increasingly underplayed the role of pleasure in the woman's procreative contribution. Only when Barbara becomes a dutiful, passive wife to Uplandtowers does she reproduce—she produces "no less than eleven children in the nine following years" (though only one survives premature death) (*ND* 75). Her attachment to him is one of servility, not sexual passion. "Cured" of the "disease" of desire (*ND* 74), Barbara is no longer barren (even if "the cure became so permanent as to be itself a new disease" [*ND* 74]).[43] Recently, Francesco Marroni has explained the deaths of her children as punishment for adultery, and with a man who is not of her class, and for her infatuation with an inanimate object.[44] However, these deaths can equally be seen as symptomatic of her location in the midst of an English aristocracy which was having increasing problems keeping up its numerical end. Round about the same time, Tess was lavishing care on her child, but as a child of the "belated seedling of an effete aristocracy" (*Tess* 302)[45] it stood little chance of surviving: "some such collapse had been probable, so tender and puny was its frame" (*Tess* 42). In similar vein, the partially blue-blooded Elfride in *A Pair of Blue Eyes*, connected to the aristocratic Luxellian family by birth and, later, by marriage too, dies of a miscarriage.[46] And, in the third tale, Lady Caroline's second marriage, to the Marquis of Stonehenge, is desirable socially, but not biologically; it bears no fruit. This was one charge at least which could not be levelled at the parish-clerk's son, from whom she had had a son.

At the end of **"Barbara of the House of Grebe"**, the Dean of Melchester draws attention to a divide between aesthetics and biology, or, more specifically, Willowes' lifeless statue and his earlier, living self, in his condemnation of 'the folly of indulgence in sensual love for a handsome form only' (*ND* 76). However, it is important not to conflate authorial voice with the Dean of Melchester's sermonizing. In an acute, post-structuralist reading of the story, Roger Ebbatson sees Willowes as stepping "out of life into art";[47] I suggest that the intensity of Barbara's sexual feeling for the statue does not simply result from her projecting the memory of her lover onto his aesthetic representation, but is predicated on a proximity between the two which is at one with contemporary ideas on the convergence of biology and aesthetics. Willowes is likened to Adonis and Phoebus-Apollo. His statue unites life and art; it is "a specimen of manhood almost perfect in every line and contour" (*ND* 61; 67). In life, Willowes is "metamorphosed to a specimen of another species" (*ND* 61). He is at once a figure of classical beauty, resurrected in art when disfigured in life, and a redundant figure in a Darwinian narrative. Rather than see the life-force of the artist as "draining away into the aesthetic object", which Ebbatson suggests is being hinted at in this story,[48] I would argue that life, for Hardy (in particular, life in the biological sense) is imbricated with the aesthetic. In *The Well-Beloved,* as I argue elsewhere,[49] Jocelyn Pearson's capacity to love and his artistic creativity (he is a sculptor) come and go together: "the artistic sense had left him, and he could no longer attach a definite sentiment to images of beauty recalled from the past".[50] In *Physiological Aesthetics* (1877, dedicated to Herbert Spencer) the biologist-cum-artist Grant Allen, with whom Hardy corresponded,[51] emphasized the biological impulses which lay behind sculpture, concerned, as it was, almost exclusively with the human body and aiming "at absolute beauty of form"; "every limb must be in proportion, every feature in exquisite harmony".[52] As Allen put it, "the facts on which Mr Darwin bases his theory of sexual selection thus become of the first importance for the aesthetic philosopher, because they are really the only solid evidence for the existence of a love for beauty in the infra-human world".[53]

When Barbara finds the statue which Uplandtowers has mutilated—a moment of Gothic terror—she lets out "a loud prolonged shriek" (*ND* 71); an anti-orgasm. She is repelled from the defaced figure as she was from the disfigured Willowes. While critics have argued that Barbara's failure is her inability to learn that ugliness can become beauty in sexual love,[54] I would argue that her repulsion has as much to do with the story's eugenic subtext as with Barbara's moral blindness. Like the beautiful, the ugly has a part in the evolutionary drama. As Grant Allen put it "the ugly for every kind, in its own eyes, must always be (in the main) the deformed, the aberrant, the weakly, the unnatural, the impotent." He highlighted the eugenic ideology underlying his thesis: "were it ever otherwise—did any race or kind ever habitually prefer the morbid to the sound, that race or kind must be on the highroad to extinction."[55] Lord Uplandtowers, exhibiting on occasion "sculptural repose"

(*ND* 46), inadvertently touches on an emergent eugenic aesthetic when, mutilating Willowes' sculpture, he remarks "a statue should represent a man as he appears in life, and that's as he appeared. Ha ha!" (*ND* 70). The centrality of art, beauty, science and ugliness to **"Barbara of the House of Grebe"** makes it another, albeit sensational, example of the late nineteenth-century biologization of aesthetics. It should come as no surprise that the periodical *Literary Opinion* advised the eugenically unfit against reading *A Group of Noble Dames,* declaring that these are "stories for the reading of healthy and vigorous men and women. For the sickly sentimentalist, or the morbid mental anatomist, this book has not been written."[56]

Love is repeatedly deromanticized in the stories. For example, the narrator of the fifth tale, **"The Lady Icenway"**, holding views somewhat modern for a churchwarden, considers sexual attachments to be neither sinful nor virtuous but merely natural: "a tender feeling (as it is called by the romantic) sprang up between the two young people" (*ND* 112). Likewise, in **"Lady Mottisfont"**, the ironically named "Sentimental Member" refers unromantically to Philippa, the subject of his love-match, as a "supernumerary" (*ND* 92), and to marriage as a "sort of experiment" (*ND* 93). Perhaps the most dramatic instance of the romantic trope's replacement with selection for breeding is found in **"Squire Petrick's Lady"**. Here, after an initial degree of resistance, Squire Petrick's belief that his wife, Anetta, mated with a man of stock socially superior to his own actually increases his love for her. (He has no truck with the notion that the aristocracy itself was a node of degeneracy.) This pronounced and systematic overhaul of romantic love is unprecedented in fiction: "being a man, whatever his faults, of good old beliefs in the divinity of kings and those about 'em, the more he overhauled the case in this light, the more strongly did his poor wife's conduct in improving the blood and breed of the Petrick family win his heart" (*ND* 126).[57] In fact, he romanticizes her eugenic choice: thinking of his own inefficient ancestors "and the probability that some of their bad qualities would have come out in a merely corporeal child of his loins, to give him sorrow in his old age, turn his black hairs gray, his gray hairs white, cut down every stick of timber, and Heaven knows what all, had he not, or rather his good wife, like a skilful gardener, given attention to the art of grafting, and changed the sort; till at length this right-minded man fell down on his knees every night and morning and thanked God that he was not as other meanly descended fathers in such matters" (*ND* 127). Darwin had warned in *The Descent* "it is surprising how soon a want of care, or care wrongly directed, leads to the degeneration of a domestic race".[58] His cousin Francis Galton, founder of eugenics, urged that the principles of good breeding, or artificial selection, be religiously applied to the human race. Squire Petrick imagines his wife to be a moral horticulturist, an apostle of eugenic practice.

This association of human breeding with the cultivation of nature finds expression elsewhere in the stories. In **"The Lady Icenway"** we learn that Anderling had once "taken great interest in tulip-culture, as well as gardening in general"; and that, on returning to England, "he acquired in a few months great skill in horticulture. Waiting till the noble lord, his lady's husband, had room for an under-gardener of a general sort, he offered himself for the place" (*ND* 118). His work turns out to be general indeed: as Lord Icenway's displeasure at the lack of lineal successor increases, it is to the gardener that Lady Icenway turns; the son she previously had with him is corporeal proof that their sexual union will bear fruit. But, dying from Lady Icenway's social rejection, the gardener responds with a faint wan smile to her blushing request that they reanimate their union: "Ah—why did you not say so sooner? Time was . . . but that's past!" (*ND* 120). He is unable to perform the act that would bless Lord Icenway with a son. Anderling, a foreigner (his name signalling "other", as Brady points out),[59] has brought new blood to the failing English aristocracy.[60] That his son should know him only as "the gardener" is, in the Darwinian world which the tales court, not wholly inappropriate. The trade resonates with tropes of creativity.

In the sixth tale, when Petrick learns that his son is in fact biologically his, his wife's confession of extramarital selection having been based on a "a form of hallucination to which [her] mother and grandmother had been subject" (*ND* 129), he finds little consolation in biological fatherhood, wishing instead a son can be "one's own and somebody else's likewise" (*ND* 127). The moment foreshadows Gallia Hamesthwaite's eugenic demand for substitute motherhood in Mènie Muriel Dowie's *Gallia* (1895);[61] she insists that a child should have both a biological and a social parent: "people will see the folly of curing all sorts of ailments that should not have been created, and then they will start at the right end, they will make better people"; "think of this: a man may love woman and marry her; they may be devoted to each other, and long for a child to bring up and to love, but the woman may be too delicate to run the risk. What are they to do? What would be the reasonable thing to do? Sacrifice the poor woman for the sake of a weakly baby? No, of course no, but get in a mother!" (*Gallia* 113).

Through their novels a number of *fin de siècle* writers, such as Sarah Grand, Grant Allen and Emma Frances Brooke, situated themselves in the cross-fire of the cultural debates on heredity. *Gallia* is the most explicitly eugenic of these 1890s novels. Its eponymous heroine refuses to marry the man for whom she feels romantic

or sexual feeling: "when I marry, I shall, of course, marry without love. For that is used up" (*Gallia* 129). She declares her determination to marry "solely with a view to the child I am going to live for" (*Gallia* 129). When the Dark Essex tries (and pushes) his luck by kissing her, and addressing her as "my love—love", we learn "the word, which feeling made sing in the air, had that in it which seemed to cradle Gallia's heart" (*Gallia* 132). But this fleeting association of the heart with love is soon severed. The heart in *Gallia* is brought from its metaphysical plane, as archetypal site of romantic feeling, to a level of physical reality and limitation. Hearts are markers of health, and of hereditary taint. The narrative concludes with the revelation that Gallia made the correct eugenic choice in marrying the healthy Mark Gurdon: Dark Essex turns out to have a dodgy ticker. He is but a 'manifestation of heart-disease' (albeit an "attractive" one) (*Gallia* 200). And, in his own words, "a man with pronounced heart-disease ought not to marry. Nothing is more inevitably hereditary" (*Gallia* 200). The novel ends on a note of eugenic triumph.

Hardy holds his ideological cards much closer to his chest. In **"The Marchioness of Stonehenge"**, Lady Caroline makes the wrong choice in marrying the parish-clerk's son—"a plain-looking young man of humble birth and no position at all" (*ND* 77); he remains unnamed throughout the tale. We learn that "when the first wild warmth of her love had gone off, the Lady Caroline sometimes wondered within herself how she, who might have chosen a peer of the realm, baronet, knight; or if serious-minded, a bishop or judge of the more gallant sort who prefer young wives, could have brought herself to do such a thing so rash as to make this marriage" (*ND* 78-79).

The young and nameless man's bad heart functions as shorthand for his unsuitability as a partner: "he was liable to attacks of heart-disease, one of which, the doctor had informed them, might some day carry him off" (*ND* 79).[62] His declaration "Oh, my heart!", more usually a declaration of love, or love undone, is peculiarly literal, and out of place, in what began as a love story. Luckily for Lady Caroline, if not for the conventions of fiction, it stops, allowing her to make a new, healthier choice—both biologically and socially. The following day, his body having been discovered outside his father's house (Lady Caroline dragged him there by his tied hands), an inquest is held and "syncope from heart-disease was ascertained to be beyond doubt the explanation of his death" (*ND* 81). But, Hardy's position fluctuates. Elsewhere in the collection, the heart is a metonymic figuring of love: Alwyn in **"The Duchess of Hamptonshire"** addresses Emmeline as "dear tender heart" (154); Lady Penelope in the preceding tale suffers from heartsickness (143); Lady Mottisfont's heart "dies" with jealousy (142); Anderling's "withers" within him (115); Betty suffers rejection in love "with a swollen heart" (35). And, by the end of the third tale, when Lady Caroline, now the Marchioness of Stonehenge, is denied the filial love of her biological son, she dies of "a broken heart" (*ND* 90). The romantic narrative reasserts itself; the heart regains its susceptibility to metaphysical disease.

Hardy was not championing eugenics. Nonetheless, close reading of *A Group of Noble Dames* reveals that he exploited its language in his fiction. He coined the verb "mismate", which has its first outing in **"The Marchioness of Stonehenge"**: Lady Caroline (daughter of an earl) apostrophizes her first husband "why not have died in your own cottage if you would die! Then nobody would ever have known of our imprudent union, and no syllable would have been breathed of how I *mismated* myself for love of you!" (*ND* 80).[63] This neologism is emblematic of a new, biologized, romance that was coming to birth at the Victorian *fin de siècle*.

Notes

I would like to thank Laura Marcus, Dorothy Porter and Martin Ray for their comments on a previous draft of this paper.

1. Thomas Hardy, "The Marchioness of Stonehenge" (1890), *A Group of Noble Dames* (1891; Stroud: Alan Sutton Publishing, 1993), 80. This edition includes Hardy's preface of 1896. Subsequent references to this collection of stories (abbreviated as *ND*) appear in the text.

2. Charles Darwin's cousin Francis Galton coined the term "eugenics" in *Inquiries into Human Faculty and its Development* (London: Macmillan, 1883), at 24-25. "Eugenics" the process of artificial selection for reproduction in humans—was from the Greek *eugenes*—"good in stock".

3. See, for example, Gareth Stedman Jones, *Outcast London: A Study in the Relationship between Classes in Victorian Society* (1971; Harmondsworth, Penguin, 1992), 128.

4. Havelock Ellis, "Eugenics and St Valentine", *The Nineteenth Century* 59 (1906), 785. I am grateful to Robert Mighall for this reference.

5. Daniel Pick, *Faces of Degeneration: A European Disorder, c1848—c1918* (Cambridge: Cambridge University Press, 1993), 59.

6. Charles Darwin, *The Descent of Man, and Selection in Relation to Sex* (1871; Chichester: Princeton University Press, 1981) II, 403.

7. Darwin took this quotation from Dr David Asher, "Schopenhauer and Darwinism", *Journal of Anthropology* (January 1871), 323; absent from the first edition of the *Descent*, for which it presum-

ably appeared too late to be included, it is cited in the second edition (London: John Murray, 1874), 586 (Ch. xx).

8. For an example of ways in which "New Woman" texts of the 1890s took up and reworked ideas of Darwinian sexual selection and heredity see my forthcoming paper 'The Morality of Genealogy: Sarah Grand and the Eugenization of Love'.

9. Six of the stories in this collection first appeared in the Christmas issue of the *Graphic* (1890); they were published in book form in May 1991 by Osgood McIlvaine as *A Group of Noble Dames,* with the addition of the first and last three tales, "The First Countess of Wessex", "The Lady Penelope", "The Duchess of Hamptonshire" and "The Honourable Laura"—see James Gibson, *Thomas Hardy: A Literary Life* (London: Macmillan, 1996), 113. See also Millgate, *Thomas Hardy: A Biography* (Oxford: Clarendon Press, 1892), 305 for the *Graphic*'s demand for revisions. For the contemporary reception of *A Group of Noble Dames* see Millgate, *Thomas Hardy: His Career as a Novelist* (1971; Basingstoke: Macmillan, 1994), 289. *A Group of Noble Dames* has largely been neglected by recent criticism: for an interesting exception, see Roger Ebbatson's discussion of "Barbara of the House of Grebe" in *Hardy: The Margin of the Unexpressed* (Sheffield: Sheffield Academic Press, 1993), 92-106; see further below. The fullest general critical appraisal of Hardy's short stories, including *A Group of Noble Dames* is Kristin Brady, *The Short Stories of Thomas Hardy* (London: Macmillan, 1982).

10. Gaye Tuchman with Nina E. Fortin, *Edging Women Out, Victorian Novelists, Publishers, and Social Change* (London: Routledge, 1989), 56.

11. See for example, Thomas Hardy, *The Life of Thomas Hardy* (1928-1930; London: Studio Editions, 1994) II, 40 and Gibson, *Thomas Hardy: A Literary Life,* 34-36, 45.

12. Robert Gittings, *Young Thomas Hardy,* (Harmondsworth: Penguin, 1978), 237.

13. Tuchman, *Edging Women Out,* 81.

14. Tuchman, *Edging Women Out,* 83.

15. Lyn Pykett, *The 'Improper' Feminine: The Women's Sensation Novel and the New Woman Writing* (London and New York: Routledge, 1992), 36. Cf. Ellen Miller Casey, "Edging Women Out?" *Victorian Studies* 39 (1996), 151-171; Casey also argues that the situation was more complex.

16. Elaine Showalter, *Sexual Anarchy: Gender and Culture at the Fin de Siècle* (London: Virago, 1991), 789. For a contemporary discussion of late-

Victorian fiction which comes out in favour of romance, see Andrew Lang, "Realism and Romance", *The Contemporary Review* 52 (1887), 683-693.

17. Peter D. McDonald, *British Literary Culture and Publishing Practice,* 1880-1914 (Cambridge: Cambridge University Press, 1997).

18. Edmund Gosse, "The Tyranny of the Novel", *National Review* (1892) 167-168 and Evan Charteris, *The Life and Letters of Sir Edmund Gosse* (London: Heinemann, 1931), both cited in McDonald, *British Literary Culture and Publishing Practice,* 6. William Algernon Locker, assistant editor of the *Graphic* and son of Arthur Locker, editor of the paper, communicated to Hardy that the stories of *A Group of Noble Dames* were "very suitable and entirely harmless to the robust minds of the Club smoking-room, but not at all suitable for the more delicate imaginations of young girls" (cited in Martin Seymour-Smith, *Hardy* (London, Bloomsbury, 1994), 392). Hardy had perhaps gone too far. W.A. Locker did not think that fathers ("accustomed to read or have read to their family-circles the stories in the *Graphic*") "would approve for this purpose a series of tales almost every one of which turns upon questions of childbirth, and those relations between the sexes over which conventionality is accustomed (wisely or unwisely) to draw a veil" (W.A. Locker to Hardy, 25 June 1890, Dorset County Museum, cited in Millgate, *Thomas Hardy: A Biography,* 305).

19. See, for example, Anthony Giddens, *The Transformation of Intimacy: Sexuality, Love & Eroticism in Modern Societies* (Cambridge: Polity Press, 1992), 40: "the rise of romantic love more or less coincided with the emergence of the novel: the connection was one of newly discovered narrative form". More recently Margaret Anne Doody, in a wide-ranging and lucid account of the history of the novel, argues for locating the origins of the novel and romance in classical times: "the development of sentiment and erotic passion in prose narratives dealing with individual characters—this is a much older literary event that most of us are told about in college" *(The True Story of the Novel,* (London: Harper Collins, 1997), 6). Establishing that romance and imaginative prose share a long history, she collapses the distinction between the romance and the novel on the grounds that the novel is no less likely to employ romance than realism (16). She does not, however, consider the late nineteenth-century gendered debates on realism.

20. See, for example, William J. Hyde, "Hardy's View of Realism: A Key to the Rustic Characters", *Victorian Studies* 11 (1958), 45-59. While Hardy did not consider himself a realist, if realism meant "copyism", the Macmillan reader for *Desperate Remedies* noted that Hardy demonstrated "somewhat in excess the feelings of a realist" (British Library Macmillan Archives 175 Add. MS 55931). In his literary notebooks Hardy recorded Anthony Trollope's assertion that a good novel should be both realistic and sensational and both in the highest degree which perhaps comes closest to his own view of the ideal novel (Lennart A. Björk, ed. *The Literary Notebooks of Thomas Hardy* (London and Basingstoke: Macmillan, 1985) I, 163).

21. Havelock Ellis, "Concerning *Jude the Obscure*", *Savoy* (October 1896; The Ulysses Bookshop, 1931), 9.

22. Thomas Hardy to Alexander Macmillan (25 July 1868) British Library Macmillan Archives 54923 362F 1.

23. Harold Orel, ed. *Thomas Hardy's Personal Writings* (Basingstoke: Macmillan, 1967), 127.

24. "A Chat with the Author of Tess", *Black and White* 4 (August 27 1892), 240.

25. See, for example, Gillian Beer, *Darwin's Plots: Evolutionary Narrative in Darwin, George Eliot and Nineteenth-Century Fiction* (London: Routledge & Kegan Paul, 1983); Roger Ebbatson, *The Evolutionary Self,* and Perry Meisel, Thomas Hardy, *The Return of the Repressed: A Study of the Major Fiction* (New Haven, Conn., and London: Yale University Press, 1972).

26. Hardy, *The Life* I, 198.

27. Hardy, *Literary Notebooks* I, 132.

28. For the most recent treatment of Hardy's interest in genealogy see Tess O'Toole, *Genealogy and Fiction in Hardy: Family Lineage and Narrative Lines* (Basingstoke: Macmillan, 1997). For an exemplary discussion of heredity in *Tess* and *Jude* see William Greenslade, *Degeneration, Culture and the Novel* 1880-1940 (Cambridge: Cambridge University Press, 1994), Chapter 8.

29. Hardy's personal writings evidence his friendship with the eugenist physician Caleb William Saleeby, with whom he corresponded regularly. He also knew scientists such as the eugenist James Crichton-Brown and the degenerationist Ray Lankester (*The Life* I, 18, 24-25, 167-7, 269-73). For Hardy's interest in, and creative use of, eugenics, see my article "'Some Science underlies all Art': The Dramatization of Sexual Selection and Racial Biology in Thomas Hardy's *A Pair of Blue Eyes* and *The Well-Beloved*", *Journal of Victorian Culture* 3.2 (1998).

30. Peter Widdowson, *Hardy in History: A Study in Literary Sociology* (London: Routledge, 1989), 54-55.

31. For a comprehensive account of the cumulative workings of the stories, which argues that they are 'ambivalent exempla', see Brady, chapter 2.

32. Hardy, *The Complete Poems of Thomas Hardy,* ed., James Gibson (1976; London: Macmillan, 1990), 791 2.

33. See George Wing, "*A Group of Noble Dames*: 'Statuesque Dynasties of Delightful Wessex'", *The Thomas Hardy Journal* 7 (May 1991) 27. As Wing points out (27), "The Honourable Laura" appeared as "Benighted Travels" in the *Bolton Weekly Journal* ten years before the original six stories appeared in the *Graphic*; it would seem it was added to the group to make up numbers. For further criticism of the last two tales, see Brady, who argues that they lack the moral coherence and sociological acuity of the rest of the collection (83).

34. A review in *Literary Opinion* 7 (1891) considered *A Group of Noble Dames* to be "a perfectly new departure in the fiction of today, being nothing so much as an English nineteenth-century *Decameron*" (17).

35. Millgate notes that Hardy's main source for the tales was Hutchins' *History and Antiquities of the County of Dorset,* but that Hardy also stressed their relation to oral tradition: Richard Little Purdy, *Thomas Hardy: A Bibliographical Study* (London, 1954), 67; Thomas Hardy to Lord Lytton, 15 July 1891, *Complete Letters* I, 239-40, cited in Millgate, *Thomas Hardy: A Biography,* 316-317. Millgate also notes that the publication of *A Group of Noble Dames* led to a general ostracism of the Hardys, first by the families concerned and then by all levels of local society (317; *One Rare Fair Woman: Thomas Hardy's Letters to Florence Henniker* 1893-1922, ed. Evelyn Hardy and F.B. Pinion [London: Macmillan, 1972] and S. Heath, 'How Thomas Hardy Offended the County Families of Dorset', unpub. TS [Dorset County Museum]).

36. Orel, ed. *Thomas Hardy's Personal Writings,* 116.

37. See Brady 54. For the 1891 book edition, Hardy altered the order of the tales as they had appeared in the *Graphic* the year before; while they are in dialogue with each other in the *Graphic,* their re-arrangement for the first edition underscores their intertextuality, and highlights the variety of interpretative strategies which can be brought to bear on any one theme. For example, in the *Graphic,* the "Marchioness of Stonehenge", as it was finally called, is followed by "Anna, Lady Baxby", but in the first edition "Lady Mottisfont", which was originally the sixth tale, follows "Marchioness of Stonehenge"; both tales are concerned with adoption.

38. As Millgate notes, this was the Dorset Natural History and Antiquarian Field Club, of which Hardy was a member (Millgate, *Thomas Hardy: His Career as a Novelist,* 264). Millgate also records that Hardy had himself delivered a paper before the society: "Some Romano-British Relics Found at Max Gate, Dorchester".

39. *Jude the Obscure* (1895; Harmondsworth: Penguin, 1985) 340-341.

40. *Tess of the D'Urbervilles* (1891; Harmondsworth: Penguin, 1986), 284. Cf. "The Continuity of the Germ Plasm as the Foundation of a Theory of Heredity", Weismann, *On Heredity and Kindred Biological Problems* (Oxford: Clarendon Press, 1889), 165: "how is it that such a single cell can reproduce the *tout ensemble* of the parent with all the faithfulness of a portrait?"

41. Hardy, *A Laodicean* (1881; Oxford: OUP, 1991), 187. See my forthcoming article 'The Desire for "a name, and historic what-do-they-call-it": Narratives of Romance in Hardy's *A Laodicean*'.

42. Angus McLaren, "*The Pleasures of Procreation: Traditional and Biomedical Theories of conception*" in *William Hunter and the Eighteenth-Century Medical World,* ed. W.F. Bynum, and Roy Porter (Cambridge: Cambridge University Press, 1985), 323-341; Thomas Laqueur, *Making Sex: Body and Gender from the Greeks to Freud* (Cambridge, Massachusetts, and London: Harvard University Press, 1990). See also Ornella Moscucci's exemplary study *The Science of Woman, Gynaecology and Gender in England 1800-1929* (Cambridge: Cambridge University Press, 1990) for ways in which woman's "otherness" was intensified at this time through medical discourses.

43. In a rejoinder to Hardy's response to an unfavourable review of the collection, in which he had assumed the hostile critic to be "sensitive and beautiful", a woman, identifying her sex, and herself as "Your Sensitive and Beautiful Reviewer", declared "if my husband, the Earl, were to act like Lord Uplandtowers, I should not bear him eleven idiot children in eight years, but should appeal to Mr Justice Butt to relieve me from the duty of continuing his noble line" (*Pall Mall Gazette* July 10, 1891; Orel, ed. *Personal Writings* 243).

44. Francesco Marroni, "The Negation of Eros in Barbara of the House of Grebe", *The Thomas Hardy Journal* 10 (1994), 39.

45. *A Group of Noble Dames* and *Tess* were composed in the same year; see Gibson, *Thomas Hardy, A Literary Life,* 113.

46. Hardy's revisions of 1912 make it explicit that Elfride died "with a miscarriage" *(A Pair of Blue Eyes* (Oxford: Oxford University Press, 1985), appendix, 308).

47. Ebbatson, *Hardy: The Margin of the Unexpressed,* 100.

48. Ebbatson, *Hardy: The Margin of the Unexpressed,* 101.

49. See my article "'Some Science underlies all Art': The Dramatization of Sexual Selection and Racial Biology in Thomas Hardy's *A Pair of Blue Eyes* and *The Well-Beloved*', *The Journal of Victorian Culture,* 3.2 (1998).

50. *The Well-Beloved* (Oxford: Oxford University Press, 1986), 198.

51. See *The Collected Letters of Thomas Hardy,* eds, Richard Little Purdy and Michael Millgate (Oxford: Clarendon Press, 1978-) I. 277, II. 58, 68, 74, 106.

52. Grant Allen, *Physiological Aesthetics* (London: Henry S. King & Co., 1877), 238.

53. Grant Allen, "Aesthetic Evolution in Man", *Mind* V (1880), 447.

54. Jean R. Brooks, *Thomas Hardy: The Poetic Structure* (London: Paul Elek, 1971) 145-6; Roy Morrell, *Thomas Hardy: The Will and the Way* (Kuala Lumpur: University of Malaya Press, 1965) 114, both cited in Brady 208.

55. Grant Allen, "Aesthetic Evolution in Man", 448, 449. Sander Gilman's concluding words on the link between sexuality and the beautiful fit perfectly Allen's thesis: "the ugly is anti-erotic rather than merely unaesthetic. It is denied the ability to reproduce" (Gilman, *Health and Illness: Images of Difference* (London: Reaktion Books Ltd, 1995), 92).

56. "Hardy's and Black's latest", review of *A Group of Noble Dames, Literary Opinion* 7 (July 1891) 18.

57. For the *Graphic* editor's initial rejection of this tale (along with '*Lady Mottisfont*'), see Millgate, *Thomas Hardy: A Biography,* 305. Simon Gatrell records Hardy's references to "the tyranny of Mrs Grundy" on the altered manuscript of "*Squire Petrick's Lady*"; one leaf (fo. 108) and the versos of the next two of the manuscript for the first edition are marked with a variant of "the above lines were deleted against the author's wish, by compulsion of Mrs Grundy, as were all other pasages marked in blue" (Simon Gatreell, *Hardy the Creator: A Textual Biography*: (Oxford: Clarendon Press, 1988) 84-85; 86). See also Purdy, *Thomas Hardy: A Bibliographical Study,* 65.

58. Darwin, *The Descent* I, 168.

59. Brady 71.

60. The association in "The Lady Icenway" of human reproduction with the cultivation of nature has been overlooked by critics. For example, George Wing dismisses Anderling's enrolment as a gardener as evidence that "he accepts uncaringly the menial job in the nursery hot-houses" (41) while it is clear that the narrator has gone into more than passing detail to establish Anderling's early attraction to, and professional credentials for, gardening.

61. Mènie Muriel Dowie, *Gallia* (1895; London, J.M. Dent, 1995).

62. First edition (London: James R. Osgood, McIlvaine, and Co., 1891), 112. In the Wessex Edition of 1912, "heart-disease" is replaced by "heart-failure" (*ND* 79), perhaps to avoid using the term heart-disease twice; it is used as the findings of the inquest (*ND* 81; first edition, 115).

63. Emphasis added. The *OED* gives this as the first recorded usage of "mismate", a rare verb meaning "to mate or match (oneself) unsuitably"; "unsuitable match" (it was previously in existence only as an adjective).

Jeanette Roberts Shumaker (essay date spring 1999)

SOURCE: Shumaker, Jeanette Roberts. "Abjection and Degeneration in Thomas Hardy's 'Barbara of the House of Grebe.'" *College Literature* 26, no. 2 (spring 1999): 1-17.

[In the following essay, Shumaker asserts that Hardy illustrates the danger of the Victorian myth of degeneration in "Barbara of the House of Grebe."]

Thomas Hardy's Gothic tale, **"Barbara of the House of Grebe"** (1891), dramatizes the horrid consequences of belief in the Victorian myth of degeneration. Only months after writing *Tess of the D'Urbervilles,* Hardy creates another tragedy in the less well-known **"Barbara"**; this time tragedy stems from dread of the lower class and of sexually assertive women of any class.[1] The theory of degeneration situates the hatred of the working class and women seen in **"Barbara"** within the pseudo-scientific debates of the late-Victorian era. Hardy shows how belief in the myth of degeneration could ruin relationships and lives.

Recent studies of degenerationism in history and literature do not discuss Hardy's short stories, but their ideas illuminate **"Barbara."** Degenerationism posited that groups such as the urban poor, the insane, prostitutes, criminals, and homosexuals adapted to immoral, polluted cities by taking on characteristics of their environment; as a result, they became physically stunted and mentally depraved. Degenerates were thought to pass on their flaws to their children through a kind of Lamarckian evolution that increased aberrations with each succeeding generation. Facial and bodily deformities might be warnings of degeneracy. But the most dangerous degenerates carried no marks: these decadent artists and writers might seem free from any "taint," helping them to spread their degenerate thinking to the general population through their works (Spackman 1989, 9).[2] Like a disease, degeneracy was thought to be gradually spreading through late-Victorian societies, imperiling their future. Protection of "the race" against decadence was sought through the ostracism of those who weren't respectable, as well as through vigilance about literature and art.

In the 1850s, French psychiatrist Benedict-Augustin Morel developed the theory of degeneration to explain cretinism. An Italian follower of Morel, Cesare Lombroso, applied degenerationism to criminals in a widely read book (Pick 1989, 178-79). Lombroso argued that the "born criminal" is an atavistic throwback to an earlier, more vicious type of human (Hurley 1996, 93); in a later book, Lombroso drew on other studies written from a degeneratist perspective, linking the prostitute to the Hottentot woman as atavistic types (Gilman 1985, 98). Racism, classism, and sexism intertwined in studies such as Lombroso's: "For the colonial mentality that sees 'natives' as needing control easily shifts that concern to the woman, in particular the prostitute caste" (Gilman 1985, 107). While degenerationism rationalized imperialism, scientific theory helped sell degenerationism to the educated classes. Evolutionary theory, physics, and medicine suggested models of entropy that made degenerationism seem plausible to Victorians (Hurley 1996, 65).

Increasingly, degenerationism made sense to the affluent as there was "a growing sense in the last decades of the century of a lack of synchrony between the rhetoric of progress, the confident prediction by the apostles of *laissez-faire* of ever-increasing prosperity and wealth, and the facts . . . of poverty and degradation at the heart of ever richer empires" (Greenslade 1994, 15).[3] In the 1880s, English psychiatrist Henry Maudsley argued that modern Britain was oscillating between progress and decadence; its development might end up being either regenerative or degenerative (Pick 1989, 209; Hurley 1996, 66). If crowding in cities continued to spread moral and physical degeneration throughout the population, British society might decay rather than evolve.

Maudsley popularized degenerationism for middle-class readers by associating it with both common sense and typical fears (Arata 1996, 16). Through the myth of degeneration, "the conventional and respectable classes could justify and articulate their hostility against the deviant, the diseased, and the subversive" (Greenslade 1994, 2). No longer would the respectable need to feel guilty about the misery of the urban poor. In other words, degenerationism explained poverty and crime in a supposedly scientific manner rather than as ethical problems needing redress (Pick 1989, 10).

Nevertheless, degenerationism was used to justify a variety of middle-class responses to social problems, including philanthropy (Arata 1996, 17). However, the affluent most often used degenerationism to prove that mass democracy and particularly socialism were dangerous (Pick 1989, 218). Dread of democracy and socialism grew from memories of a century of riots and revolutions in Britain, Europe, and America. It was feared that in the future, widespread degeneracy might lead to mob rule under the guise of democracy or socialism, destroying the middle and upper classes.

Widely translated books about degeneration such as Max Nordau's drew heavily upon nineteenth-century literature for examples of degenerates, including aesthetes (Arata 1996, 28-9). Nordau's ideas about fictional degenerates were then used by London journalists, for example, to explain the accusations of homosexuality against Oscar Wilde (Arata 1996, 3). As for fiction itself, degenerationism influenced novelists such as Rider Haggard and Rudyard Kipling (Arata 1996, 13), Bram Stoker and Robert Louis Stevenson (Hurley 1996, 30), and Emile Zola (Pick 1989, 4). Degenerative motifs appear most commonly in Gothic novels, as degenerationism "is a 'gothic' discourse, and as such is a crucial imaginative and narrative source for the fin-de-siecle Gothic" (Hurley 1996, 65). In the case of **"Barbara,"** degenerationism is an imaginative source for Hardy's treatment of disfigurement and wife abuse.

ABJECTION

The popularity of degenerationism during Hardy's era can be explained ahistorically as well as historically. Abjection explains the appeal of degenerationism from the ahistorical perspective of psychoanalysis. *Powers of Horror: An Essay on Abjection* describes the abject as "the not-I" (Kristeva 1982, 2). The abject is associated with moral and physical decline as well as with death. Julia Kristeva's theory of abjection explains racial, class, gender, national, and religious hatreds that recur throughout history in new guises. Degenerationism is one manifestation of the tendency to label "others" as abject; degenerationism was used by some well-heeled Victorians to justify acting upon their hatred of those whom they saw as abject.

Using the developmental perspective that characterizes psychoanalytic approaches like Kristeva's, we can see abjection as a lifelong process. Abjection appears early in human development, as the child struggles to create a sense of identity in the face of his or her fear of death. Repulsion towards the mother as nauseatingly linked to decay and death motivates the child's rejection of her. Her exclusion lets the child deny the threat of death, and it fosters the child's narcissism (Kristeva 1982, 13). Labeling the mother as abjectly "other" helps the child erect a sense of self in spite of his or her dread of death. Throughout the human lifespan, the danger to the psyche posed by awareness of death continues to be dealt with through projecting the abject onto a variety of "others."

Kristeva observes that "There looms, within abjection, one of those violent, dark revolts of being, directed against a threat that seems to emanate from an exorbitant outside or inside, ejected beyond the scope of the possible, the tolerable, the thinkable" (1982, 1). As the potential for decay exists "inside" of the body, bodily fluids, taboo foods, and sexual acts are sometimes viewed as abject; so are symbols of moral decay such as sins. Marginalized groups, too, are labeled abject since they threaten contagion from "outside." Such groups may include women, the homeless, the disabled, and Jews. What or who is labeled abject varies according to the prejudices of those who project the abject onto the "other" to suppress recognition of it inside themselves. Despite the variability of regarding what is categorized as abject, the process of labeling the "other" as abject is both universal and ancient, according to Kristeva.

Hardy's story can be understood through considering the intersection between abjection and degenerationism. Both degenerationism and abjection marginalize "others" to build up the confidence of the fortunate (Hurley 1996, 79). In addition, abjection involves revulsion against that which one associates with decay. In late-Victorian England, the decay that triggers the abjective response takes the forms of moral and physical degeneracy. In Hardy's **"Barbara,"** the abject degenerates are working-class men and upper-class women by turns, as classism and then sexism fortified by belief in degenerationism are critiqued.

THE DEGENERATE WORKING CLASS HERO

"Barbara" is set late in the eighteenth century. Handsome yet poor, Edmond Willowes elopes with a young aristocrat, Barbara Grebe. Barbara's parents had been pressing her to marry rich Lord Uplandtowers; she runs away with Edmond to escape their arguments. But after several weeks of marriage, Barbara begins to regret the match when she grasps its cost in social terms: her friends greet her coldly now that she is the wife of a

nobody. At this point Barbara's disgruntled parents forgive the couple and then send Edmond abroad, as though sensitive to Barbara's growing ambivalence towards him.[4] Barbara guiltily hides her snobbery towards her absent husband for over a year until Edmond is maimed while saving strangers from a fire in Italy. His severe disfigurement horrifies Barbara, causing her to reject him.

Barbara had married Edmond because of his exceptional beauty; once accustomed to that loveliness after marriage, she began to search for the revolting qualities that her prejudices tell her he must have as a working man. Those "low" qualities would give her an excuse for distancing herself from him to avoid "contamination" by his degeneracy. "The biologising of class differences was encouraged by the fear of contagion and infection" (Greenslade 1994, 22). Barbara responds to the maimed Edmond as though she fears "catching" his ugliness like a cold—ugliness that symbolizes his low status that she has already "caught," to a certain extent, as his wife.

Barbara's overreaction to Edmond's disfigurement implies that, as an aristocrat, she had secretly attributed dreaded qualities to Edmond for a long time. Her gradual revulsion is implied through the narrator's mocking description of her declining interest in Edmond after their wedding, and later through her lack of interest in his affectionate letters from Europe. Edmond's disfigurement increases her distaste as his looks prove that her doubts about him are correct. Persecuting groups tend to attribute to their objects of hatred "disabilities and deformities that would reinforce the polarization against the victim, were they real" (Girard 1986, 18).[5] In Barbara's mind, Edmond's repulsive origins are what scar his once lovely face; she projects abjection and degeneracy upon him—poverty, loathsomeness, and death. Barbara "had just that same sense of dismay and fearfulness that she would have had in the presence of an apparition . . . he was metamorphosed to a specimen of another species" (Hardy 1928, 556). Maimed, Edmond is an "apparition" indeed: Barbara's fear that he is a monster has come true. To Barbara, Edmond was of "another species" in the sense of belonging to Disraeli's other, impoverished England even before his accident. As the narrator reminds us at the story's end, Barbara refuses to see that Edmond's nobility of spirit, if not of birth, has been proven by his heroism during the fire. Sadly, his disfigurement causes her to project her fears about the degenerate working class onto him to the point of self-deceit about his character.

For the affluent, degenerationism "offered a displacement and transference of guilt" (Greenslade 1994, 2). By regarding the disfigured Edmond as a degenerate, Barbara transfers her guilt about her dissatisfaction with their marriage onto him. She need not feel guilty about loathing him if his repulsive looks prove that he actually is unworthy of her. During their last interview, Edmond reinforces her opinion by acting as though he agrees with her transference of blame onto him.

In her pitilessness, Barbara denies the implications for herself of Edmond's abjection as a supposed degenerate. To see this truth, Barbara would have to recognize the presence of the abject within herself, rather than projecting it onto Edmond. When one sees abjection inside oneself, one knows that "all abjection is in fact recognition of the want on which any being, meaning, language, or desire is founded" (Kristeva 1982, 5). Barbara is afraid to see an inherent lack or vulnerability in herself, so she cannot accept the embodiment of it in her mutilated husband. Tied to a husband, who signifies entropy and death, she fears that they will take her over. Abjection and the abject are "safeguards" against such fears, that, if acknowledged, may "annihilate" the self (Kristeva 1982, 2). "These body fluids, this defilement, this shit are what life withstands, hardly and with difficulty" (Kristeva 1982, 3). Edmond's burns disrupt the border between the inside and outside of his body, showing his skeleton. This makes him symbolize the erupting bodily fluids that signify the dedifferentiation of death. Kristeva describes the significance of broken skin such as Edmond's as "It is as if the skin, a fragile container, no longer guaranteed the integrity of one's 'own and clean self'" (1982, 53). In seeing Edmond as abjectly degenerate, Barbara refuses to accept that the entropy which she associates with the lower orders will erupt from her too at some unpredictable moment; she avoids seeing that all humans of every class must degenerate into the abject through accident, deprivation, disease, aging, or death.

Barbara as Art Collector, Edmond as Aesthetic Object

Upon his arrival in Italy, Edmond had ordered that a statue of him be made for Barbara. At that time, he gloried in being an admired aesthetic object. After the fire, his depression over losing his looks heightens when he realizes that Barbara valued him for his beauty alone. Edmond had taken a traditional "feminine" position that he comes to regret: "Men look at women. Women watch themselves being looked at. This determines not only most relations between men and women but also the relation of women to themselves" (Berger 1972, 47). What this says about women applies to Edmond too, as the subservient spouse in a cross-class marriage that feminizes him. After the fire, Edmond says to Barbara, "Can you bear such a thing of the charnel-house near you? . . . Your Adonis, your matchless man, has come to this!" (Hardy 1928, 556). Infected by Barbara's prejudice that ties the worth of a working-class husband to beauty, Edmond can't see his own value as a self-sacrificing, scarred hero.

Like the stereotypical upper-class male of her time (and others), Barbara possesses a sense of the erotic that rests on beauty. That is how her class and gender prejudices intersect, causing her to feminize her working-class husband. Barbara's shallowness in desiring a gorgeous consort is consistent with her youth and her babyish facial features that the narrator describes more than once. As the narrator points out, perhaps Barbara's emphasis on a lover's beauty is not that different from how most of us feel; perhaps we would act as cruelly as she does towards a newly ugly spouse whom we hadn't seen for over a year (Hardy 1891, 552). In *Tales of Love,* Kristeva writes, "As soon as the other appears different from myself, it becomes alien, repelled, repugnant, abject—hated" (Kristeva 1987, 222). Hardy dramatizes this process of alienation through the burns that ruin Edmond's face, justifying Barbara's sense that he has always been inadequate.

Years later, when Barbara worships Edmond's statue after marrying Uplandtowers, she compensates for her guilt about having rejected Edmond the living man as abjectly degenerate. Early in her marriage to Edmond, Barbara's guilt had been about her repugnance at her husband's "low" ancestry, but after his accident, it is additionally about her looks and health being much better than his. Her guilt intensifies when, after her remarriage, she finds out that Edmond had been as unhappy after their separation as she had feared, and had died lonely and ill years previously. At that point, his naked statue arrives and her obsession with it starts, perhaps as a result of survivor guilt.

What is unusual is that Barbara is a female aristocrat who collects a male art nude. One reason that Uplandtowers is angry at Barbara's infatuation with Edmond's statue is that she has dared to usurp the aristocratic male position of collector of erotic art. Whereas upper-class men could buy beautiful prostitutes, upper-class women had no such option, nor were they thought to need it. Barbara's possession of Edmond the beautiful man and then of his lovely statue can be seen as extensions of the sexual prerogatives of the upper class male of which Uplandtowers feels robbed.

Usually, nineteenth-century art nudes had provided a way for rich men to objectify and own lower-class women. In such representations of naked women, "the subject is aware of being seen by a spectator" for his pleasure (Berger 1972, 49). This representation creates the reassuring illusion that working-class women like to be dominated by upper-class men. Hardy's story transposes genders, yet otherwise adheres to such a representation.[6] Edmond presumably had hoped that Barbara's love would be solidified through the pleasure of gazing at his statue and imagining that he gazed back in approval of her ownership of him.[7]

But it is not simply Barbara's ambition to experience "masculine" privileges that underlies her obsession with Edmond's statue. Her attachment to the statue is a way to compensate for the lovelessness of her marriage to Uplandtowers: "The Pygmalion-like episode of the statue suggests that an ideal aesthetic image is preferred to a living body, or to the quotidian banality of sexual intercourse" (Ebbatson 1993, 93). That sex with Uplandtowers is not quotidian, but threatening, is suggested by Barbara's fear of him. She can control the statue of her first husband in a way that she cannot control Upland-towers; Barbara is freer to feel sexual pleasure through contemplation of the statue than in the arms of her living husband.

Also pertinent to explaining the statue's appeal for Barbara is the idea that "To seduce is to die as reality and reconstruct oneself as illusion" (Baudrillard 1979, 69). That is what happens when Edmond dies and Barbara replaces him with his perfect image. Edmond's image seduces her as his living beauty once did until it began to become too familiar through marriage. Barbara takes the voyeuristic experience of art ownership to an extreme when she repeatedly kisses Edmond's statue. Reflecting upon the statue, Barbara can revel in her pleasure over her former husband's beauty without having to think about his significance as an abject member of the working class.

It appears that, for Barbara, fixity is the statue's greatest appeal—a permanence available only to art objects such as John Keats's Grecian urn. Such fixity counteracts the horrible inevitability of Barbara's own decline into death that Edmond's disfigurement had conveyed. The statue's seeming invulnerability to decay reassures Barbara that she is safe from mortality's depredations.

Through her macabre interest in the image of a dead spouse, Barbara recalls the duke in Robert Browning's "My Last Duchess." Though Barbara does not kill her spouse directly as the duke does, she does so indirectly by causing that depression which, combined with Edmond's burns, makes him susceptible to death from a slight illness. Both the duke and Barbara thrive on control of their spouses. This means control of the duchess's manner in the duke's case, and of Edmond's looks and demeanor in Barbara's. Such absolute control of a spouse cannot be achieved in life; it is only achievable through manipulating artistic representations of the deceased spouse. Ironically, both the duke and Barbara are much happier in their relationships with images of the dead than they were with their living spouses. Browning's and Hardy's analyses of such relationships reveal the murderous sterility of aristocrats' need for control.[8]

Hardy questions what collecting art means not only for the highborn, but for the middle class of his time and ours. He does this through creating a narrative frame in which a surgeon tells Barbara's tale as one of ten stories within *A Group of Noble Dames.* Told at a dinner of the Antiquarian Society, each of the legends of dead Dames represents an attempt by a different middle-class narrator to know, thus in a sense possess, the ladies involved through tale-telling.[9] What do antiquarians do but collect and study remnants from the past—narrative remnants, in this case, of tragic lives. Because of class barriers, the amateur antiquarians would not be allowed the intimacy with the ladies in actual life that they are allowed through the mediation of art and history. That is also true for the readers of the tales, ourselves, positioned at one further remove from the mythologized ladies.[10] Collecting the ladies' tales voyeuristically, we participate in Hardy's dissection of why people label "others" as abject degenerates.

THE STATUE GAME

Reacting to Barbara's obsession with Edmond's statue, Uplandtowers has the statue defaced and painted in life-like hues so that it mimics the first husband's injuries from the fire. The Earl then places the statue in a wardrobe in front of Barbara's bed, surprising her with it by candlelight. He forces her to view the wrecked image during several successive nights. When the terrorized Barbara finally protests that she no longer loves Edmond but loves her new husband instead, Uplandtowers has the statue removed.

Through the statue game Uplandtowers punishes Barbara for being a degenerate who "fell" twice—in marrying below her to gratify her youthful passion for Edmond, and in being adulterous in that she desires his statue. Through disfiguring Edmond's statue, the Earl revenges himself upon Barbara for her two "falls," and especially for having eloped with Edmond while Uplandtowers was courting her; it offends Uplandtowers that she preferred Edmond's beauty to the Earl's blood. More generally, Uplandtowers hates the female autonomy that such novel preferences as Barbara's demonstrate. In particular, he castigates her for her desire for Edmond as a living and dead man, passion that is forbidden to an upper-class woman.

Even more controlling as a spouse than Barbara was during her marriage to Edmond, Uplandtowers manipulates Barbara through her terror of the disfigured statue. Perhaps Barbara's horror comes in part from the realization that what Uplandtowers did to Edmond's statue, and what she did to Edmond the living man, Uplandtowers may do to her, now that she is the subordinate spouse. In a sense, Uplandtowers does disfigure her through a series of back-to-back pregnancies that eventually kill her. Ultimately, he does reject her, though less definitively than she did Edmond. Her hysterics at the sight of Edmond's mangled statue may come from anticipation of her doom as Upland-towers' consort.

Another reason for Barbara's fear of the maimed statue is that she wishes to deny her guilt over rejecting Edmond when he became disfigured. Paradoxically, she is afraid for a seemingly contradictory reason: though she knows that she should not have rejected Edmond after he lost his looks, she nevertheless continues to feel revolted by the thought of his ugliness that, for her, is a mark of his degenerate background. Uplandtowers shares her contempt for the class into which she "lowered" herself through marriage. The Earl's mockery of her desire for Edmond through the cruel statue game is a kind of private charivari intended to humiliate her into modesty and subservience. Through the Earl's description of the defaced statue in the closet as a "shrine" and through his laughter at Barbara's hysterical reaction to it, Uplandtowers attempts to humble Barbara (Hardy 1891, 568). Viewed through the lens of Kristeva's theory, the Earl's laughter can also be seen as a method of displacing abjection from himself (Kristeva 1982, 8).

The Earl's statue game shifts Barbara's position from victimizer to victim as it grinds her fears about Edmond's degeneracy into her psyche yet again. As the widow of a so-called degenerate, Barbara is one too, in her mind and in the Earl's. Through his defeat of Edmond's statue, the symbol of his dead rival, Uplandtowers "asserts the supremacy of the landowning class" over rebels like Barbara and Edmond (Ebbatson 1993, 103). Just as Edmond the working-class spouse was ruled by an aristocratic wife, so Barbara the aristocrat is manipulated by the crafty Lord whose name connotes his dominance. The narrator describes Barbara's relation to her husband after the statue game as abject, servile, and slavish, emphasizing that she accepts the lowly marital position that Edmond once held. Once Barbara is no longer the collector of art that idealizes members of the lower classes such as Edmond, she becomes an aesthetic object to be collected herself.[11]

The Abjection of Barbara and The Degeneration of Uplandtowers

In her study of female masochism in Gothic novels, Michelle Masse argues that Gothic heroines feel "the cultural, psychoanalytic, and fictional expectation that they should be masochistic if they are 'normal' women" (Masse 1992, 2). Defying this expectation when she weds Edmond and then when she resists the Earl's precedence as her husband, Barbara finally acts masochistic under the rigors of the latter's statue game. That game can be compared to the Gothic beating drama that Masse explores. Masse describes the Gothic dyad of male beater and female victim, in which romance requires female suffering and sacrifice. Surely, the Earl's repeated torments through the statue game are a kind of psychological beating of Barbara that results in her abjection. She learns to seek her beater's attentions, though they torment her. In the light of Masse's analy-

sis, Barbara's sufferings become the expected results of a wife's culturally conditioned "natural" abjection as a "normal" female masochist.

The editors of *The Graphic,* the periodical for which **"Barbara"** was commissioned as part of *A Group of Noble Dames,* forced Hardy to remove the intimate details of physical abuse that dramatized the Earl's cruelty towards Barbara; those details remain absent from the story published in *Noble Dames* the book (Wing 1987, 82, 87).[12] However, George Wing posits that what remains of the brutality of Uplandtowers is "not more than a filament removed from so-called normal posture" (Wing 1987, 89). Wing is referring to an alleged Victorian norm of mild mental abuse of wives; such a "normal posture" may stem from widespread use of the myth of degeneration to justify placing "uppity" women in abject positions.

Like a stereotypical Gothic heroine, Barbara ultimately embraces her role as the Earl's abject victim. She experiences an intense absorption in her abjection that recalls her previous focus upon prostrating herself before Edmond's statue. Kristeva writes of the appeal of abjection that it can create "a jouissance in which the Other, in return, keeps the subject from foundering by making it repugnant. One thus understands why so many victims of the abject are its fascinated victims—if not its submissive and willing ones" (Kristeva 1982, 9). Barbara is fascinated, submissive, and willing when she gives up her autonomy to Uplandtowers. Abjection appeals to her because it will save her from having to make further, perilous decisions that could cause her to feel the intense guilt and pain that she faced after Edmond was maimed. Not only does Barbara accept abjection as her punishment for rejecting Edmond long ago, but because abjection relieves her from the burden of self-determination.

To make Barbara experience herself as abject and degenerate, Uplandtowers takes on the role of the late-Victorian doctor battling the female patient for control of her psyche, a practice discussed in *The Female Malady* (Showalter 1987, 160). It is reassuring for Uplandtowers to pretend that Barbara's interest in Edmond's statue is a sign of mental disease, not the result of her unhappiness in their marriage. One reason she worshipped the statue was to defy the authority of Uplandtowers under the self-righteous guise of a grieving widow rather than the incriminating one of a shrewish wife; Uplandtowers reacts in a similarly sneaky manner to make his tyranny look benevolent. Uplandtowers hopes Barbara will be "cured" of her illicit passion for Edmond by the sight of his ghastly statue (Hardy 1891, 568).

But the "cure" frightens Uplandtowers as well as Barbara, for the sight of Edmond's disfigured statue causes her to experience "an epileptic fit" (Hardy 1891, 569).

Epilepsy was associated with perversion by degenerationists such as Lombroso (Spackman 1989, 30). Barbara's desire for Edmond's statue proves she is unnaturally masculine and perverse, according to the Earl's conservative perspective. Hence, the Earl's "treatment" of Barbara's epilepsy can be seen as coming from a degenerationist point of view. However, the narrator comments that her "cure became so permanent as to be itself a new disease" when describing Barbara's consequent servility towards her husband (Hardy 1891, 570). In calling the "cure" a "disease," the narrator uses black humor to question the discourse of medical mastery that Uplandtowers exploits for his own ends. The narrator sees the Earl's "treatment" of his wife as a sign of his perversion, rather than seeing Barbara's seizure as a sign of hers. A further irony is that the narrator is himself a member of the medical profession. His sarcasm suggests that nonprofessionals like Uplandtowers should avoid usurping the doctor's role. However, the narrator's denunciation of the Earl's homemade psychiatric "treatment" of Barbara may be a way to deflect his audience from criticizing his profession's similarly harsh methods for controlling so-called hysterical women.

Barbara's hysteria when Uplandtowers forces her to view the disfigured statue is her defense against the supposedly improper desire she had felt for Edmond, living and dead. The broken Barbara confesses to the inexorable Uplandtowers, "It fills me with shame—how could I ever be so depraved!" (Hardy 1891, 570). In the nineteenth century, doctors saw modesty as a defense against forbidden sexual knowledge or feelings manifested by the hysteric (Ender 1995, 50). Barbara becomes a stereotypically modest, submissive wife to avoid further hysteria, for hysteria's concomitant is the forbidden desire that marks a woman as a destructive degenerate (Gilman 1985, 105). Barbara cannot tell Uplandtowers what her hysteria means, because, as Ender explains about the hysteric, "she would show what she cannot show," sexual desire that she is not supposed to feel, and sexual experience that she is not supposed to have had (Ender 1995, 19). Were Barbara to betray such desire, Uplandtowers might treat her even more cruelly. Hence, she exhibits the form of sexuality expected from a wife—passive acceptance of her husband's advances resulting in numerous pregnancies. Hysterical women were thought to be prone to miscarriages (Greenslade 1994, 139): Barbara starts to miscarry and to bear fragile infants under the terror of her husband's "cure" of her worship of Edmond's statue (Hardy 1891, 570).

Because of her passivity along with her production of children who are too weak to survive, Barbara could be labeled a neurasthenic as well as an hysteric. In the late nineteenth century, neurasthenia was an amorphous term for combinations of symptoms that eluded standard definitions of mental disease. Neurasthenics' characteristic passivity was thought to result from "a decrease in the wattage of the nervous system" (Gilman 1985, 199) caused by modern "turbulence" (Gilman 1985, 204). Previously, chronic passivity had been thought to result from masturbation (Gilman 1985, 200). However, by the late nineteenth century, "neurasthenia displaced masturbation as the means of presenting the interrelationship of degeneration, sexuality, and society" (Gilman 1985, 204). Neurasthenia thus became the illness "that paradigmatically revealed the degenerative effects of society" (Gilman 1985, 204).

From a Victorian perspective, Barbara's permanent passivity after Uplandtowers humiliates her can be seen not just as symptomatic of neurasthenia, but as the result of her forbidden onanistic pleasure in Edmond's statue. Seen so, her passivity comes from the "turbulence" of ambivalence created by the broken statue: she recalls her guilt over her rejection of the newly maimed Edmond; in addition, the defaced statue triggers her forbidden desire for Edmond simultaneously with her old, contradictory repugnance. Such conflicts that reflect class battles drive Barbara temporarily mad. Despite her degenerationist fear of the lower class, Barbara also suffers from paralyzing self-hatred because she desires one of its members. She finds a refuge from her searing conflicts in the numbness of neurasthenia. However, Hardy shows that Barbara's neurasthenia is caused less by her "degenerate" desire for Edmond than by the Earl's vengeful prodding of her opposing feelings.

Barbara's frequent, failed pregnancies suggest her new, abject status as a disgraced wife. Uplandtowers turns "the once radiant and passionate Barbara into a sickly woman condemned to a cowed life of repeated, unsuccessful pregnancies" (Wing 1987, 88). That all but one of Barbara's eleven babies dies bolsters Hardy's critique of her second marriage as debased. She is now the vehicle of feminine fluids and transformative powers that take her over in the name of patriarchal succession. As Edmond was disfigured as a result of being exiled due to class prejudices, so Barbara is disfigured by gender prejudices that compel her to become a monster of thwarted fertility.

Not only Barbara, but all women may be associated with death because of their "messy" childbearing capabilities (Kristeva 1982, 54). Through repeated bereavement Barbara dramatizes that association, mocking the Earl's attempts to create a dynasty that would make his name last. "Blood" loses again, as it did when Barbara chose Edmond over Uplandtowers. As the artist who tries to memorialize Edmond's beauty for all time through his statue fails, so the Earl fails to gain immortality through continuing his family name; Barbara unintentionally revenges herself upon Uplandtowers by producing a living daughter and dead sons. When Uplandtowers dies, his estate goes to a distant male relative, in another example of gender prejudices stealing from a woman—this time, from Barbara's daughter.

The drama of inheritance by "blood" is played out through the Earl's degenerate sexual pleasures. As well as voyeuristic pleasure, Uplandtowers gains a sadistic sexual pleasure directly from Barbara that is suggested by the number and frequency of her pregnancies. In reflecting upon his sexual satisfaction at Barbara's sufferings, we might consider Kristeva's contention that "The erotization of abjection . . . is an attempt at stopping the hemorrhage: a threshold before death, a halt or a respite?" (Kristeva 1982, 55). Through making Barbara an erotic object of abjection, Uplandtowers can draw thrillingly close to death while denying its threat. Unlike Barbara, whose contorted facial expressions, Gothic screams, fainting spells, and epileptic fits express her fears, Uplandtowers hides his feelings in the style of the stereotypical male aristocrat; we can only speculate that the fear of death motivates his displacement of the abject onto his wife and her dead husband. The Earl's coldness suggests that his fears are in fact so great that they have frozen him. His sexual relationship with Barbara is one of loathing that expresses his fear of sexuality's link with death.

Blood, as an abject bodily fluid associated with death, mingles with "blood" as the vehicle of class to explain how the Earl's prejudices stem from fear. The near sterility of his marriage as well as of his personality proves that his obsession with "blood" breeds the degeneracy in himself that he denies. Kelly Hurley argues that degenerationism creates "a gothic nightmare of heredity" in late-Victorian fiction (Hurley 1996, 67). This nightmare can be seen through the Earl's cruel treatment of his wife that stems from his injured sense of "blood" because she continues to favor a man of no family over him.

ABJECTION, DEGENERACY, AND THE GOTHIC

Hardy's story does not endorse the Earl's definition of Barbara as an abject producer of "unfit" progeny, nor does it support her horror at Edmond's injuries. The old surgeon who narrates the story uses sarcasm to dramatize his disapproval of the two aristocrats' views. Hardy's narrator employs dark humor that distances the reader from Uplandtowers and Barbara, bringing their opinions and actions into question. Wing notes the narrator's "defiant jauntiness" (Wing 1987, 89) and "grim playfulness" (Wing 1987, 81). Mocking his own discomfort with the story, the surgeon considers his tale "a little too professional" (Hardy 1891, 536). Like a surgeon's knife, the narrator's irony dispassionately dissects the twisted aristocratic mentality of Barbara and Uplandtowers.

The use of humor to unveil the meaning of a dark plot is not uncommon in Gothics. Judith Halberstam's ideas about Gothic fiction illuminate Hardy's story, though she does not specifically address it: "Gothic . . . is a textual machine, a technology that transforms class struggle, hostility towards women, and tensions arising out of the emergent ideology of racism into what looks like sexual or psychosexual battles between and within individuals" (Halberstam 1995, 33). Halberstam discusses the creation of monsters in nineteenth-century Gothic fiction as a result of the fear of decay associated with marginalized groups: "in the Gothic, crime is embodied within a specifically deviant form—the monster—that announces itself (de-monstrates) as the place of corruption" (Halberstam 1995, 2). In keeping with the myth of degeneration, "monstrosity was a combination of the features of deviant race, class, and gender" (Halberstam 1995, 4). Citing Franco Moretti, Halberstam sees nineteenth-century monsters as symbols of the proletariat (Halberstam 1995, 30).

Although Edmond symbolizes the danger to the upper classes posed by the proletariat, Hardy shifts our sympathy to him. Whereas Edmond's disfigurement makes him a monster in Barbara's eyes, the narrator's irony brings her perspective into question. Since readers don't have to look at Edmond's apparent monstrosity, we can see his nobility in saving strangers from a fire and in forgiving Barbara for rejecting him. We are also shown enough of the Earl's domestic life to know that Barbara's second husband is the real monster, not her first. The leaking of inner into outer characterizes monsters (Halberstam 1995, 7). Hardy's story moves from the physical leaking of bones into public sight on Edmond's scarred face to the partial unveiling of the Earl's secret cruelty. Through this inversion of expected monstrosities, Hardy questions the myth of working class and "fallen" female degeneration. However, Hardy's questioning is not unique. Some members of the Victorian middle class regarded the upper class as lazy degenerates. Hardy seems to fall into that camp through making Uplandtowers, not Edmond, the actual monster. Rather than abandoning the myth of degeneration, then, Hardy applies it to a powerful group, the aristocracy.[13] This brings Hardy's story into the Gothic tradition of depicting decaying noble "blood" through skeptical middle-class eyes—here, a surgeon's. Perhaps Sade's observation that the rise of the Gothic is associated with the rise of revolution is pertinent both to eighteenth-century Gothic novels (Graham 1989, 260) and to Hardy's late-Victorian story that criticizes dynastic imperatives. Like *Tess*, **"Barbara"** draws upon the Gothic tradition to problematize the Victorian controversy over degenerate "blood."

What Greenslade says of *Tess, Jude the Obscure,* and *The Mayor of Casterbridge* is also true of **"Barbara"**: Hardy's texts "take up the cudgels against the myths of degeneration . . . there is a commitment both to the complexities of human experience and to a concern with those sources of ideological power which shape the possibilities open to individuals: determinisms, not merely of biology, of course, but of money, class, status, education" (Greenslade 1994, 10). **"Barbara"** presents a complex picture of characters' motives, focusing especially upon the simple-minded belief in working-class degeneration shared by Barbara and Uplandtowers, and upon the painful abjection that belief forces onto Edmond and Barbara.

Several generations after Barbara and Uplandtowers die, Edmond's maimed statue is unearthed in their garden. The broken statue surfaces like a decayed corpse that no one recognizes as the symbol of the legions of working class men and of the women from all classes who have been regarded as abject degenerates. In *Jude the Obscure,* the corpses of Sue's and Jude's children, dead due to prejudice against their sexually "degenerate" parents, come to mind.

To me, reading **"Barbara"** over a century after Hardy wrote it, the buried, disfigured statue of Edmond suggests the victims of genocide—victims of the theory of degeneration later put into practice by men even more ruthless than Uplandtowers. Through arbitrarily emphasizing one element in a victim's identity, such men illustrate the workings of abjection and degeneration at their most frightening. Recent studies of degenerationism show that the disparagement of misfits that characterizes both of the Uplandtowers persists through Hardy's time into ours. British degenerationists, including socialists H.G. Wells and Karl Pearson, created the eugenics movement at the turn of the century (Pick 1989, 5). Eugenics fed not only Nazism but also fascist movements in Britain, France, and Italy (Pick 1989, 30, 218). In addition, eugenics was used to justify new laws against immigration in Britain (Pick 1989, 215). Eugenics arguments persuaded some American states to sterilize inmates of asylums and prisons during the first four decades of the twentieth century (Pick 1989, 238). Today a variant of degenerationism underlies the view that American society is decaying due to the influence of non-white immigrants; such fears in California, for example, stimulated the recent passage of laws that eliminated bilingual education and affirmative action. With an extraordinary ability to prophesy the future based on scrutinizing the past, Hardy allegorizes persecutors' attempts to escape the distressing sense of their own mortality through projecting it upon the supposedly degenerate members of the working class and the female gender (or of whatever marginalized race, nation, religion, or disability): ironically, the humiliation and death of the abject cannot save each newly defined "privileged" group from a similar fate.[14]

Notes

1. James F. Scott believes that "Barbara" and "The Doctor's Legend" are Hardy's most Gothic fictions (Scott 1963, 375). Another theme related to Gothicism that fits "Barbara" into the Hardy canon is psychological abuse of a wife by her husband (Wing 1987).

   A third way "Barbara" fits into the Hardy canon is through questioning, as Jules Law says Hardy does in his novels, whether "the ostensible irreversibility of history is a socially or a naturally imposed constraint" (Law 1997, 248). For the working class hero of the story, prejudice conspires with accident to permanently deprive him of his beauty along with his wife's love.

   "Barbara" also fits into the Hardy canon through articulating the concern about gender prejudices seen in *Tess* and the concern about class prejudices later seen in *Jude*. In all three works those prejudices appear through a complex, romantic plot that involves the beloved's abjection.

2. Oscar Wilde's *Portrait of Dorian Gray,* for example, depicts degenerationists' fear of handsome aesthetes who hide their perversions.

3. Poverty and consequent social unrest threatened France and Italy more than Britain; as a result, degenerationism was more influential in France and Italy (Pick 1989, 177).

4. "Edmond's journey is not so much a means of forming his character as a kind of quarantine for a misfit, for a person who is still too uncouth to have access to the refined world of the aristocracy" (Marroni 1994, 35).

5. Girard continues by saying that "This tendency is clearly observable in racist cartoons" (Girard 1986, 18). He also comments that "Sickness, madness, genetic deformities, accidental injuries, and even disabilities in general tend to polarize persecutors" (Girard 1986, 18). Edmond's "accidental injuries" certainly do that with Barbara.

6. The exception is that Edmond is Barbara's spouse, whereas female nude models were generally not the wives of wealthy art collectors.

7. From a commercial perspective, the Italian sculptor of Edmond's statue hopes that it will display his talents to the British aristocracy; then the sculptor could profit from enshrining additional lower-class bodies as sexually charged art objects for wealthy connoisseurs to ponder.

8. George Wing also compares "Barbara" to "My Last Duchess"; however, Wing compares Uplandtowers to Browning's Duke as a fatally controlling spouse, whereas I compare Barbara to Browning's Duke for the same reason (Wing 1987, 89).

9. Francesco Marroni reports that Hardy believed that the strategy of using a surgeon to narrate the story would distance and protect readers from its

horror. On the contrary, Marroni himself believes that strategy makes the story appear more real (Marroni 1994, 33).

10. Albert Guerard argues that Hardy's use of the unseen observer device, seen here through Uplandtowers, reveals the Lord's tendency to voyeurism (Guerard 1966, 115-17). Alexander Fischler connects Uplandtowers' voyeurism to sadism (Fischler 1949, 437). Echoing Uplandtowers, we readers view Barbara's passion for Edmond's statue voyeuristically. Through creating this parallel between the sadistically voyeuristic Uplandtowers and us, Hardy suggests that reading, as a form of mental art collection, may be seen as perverted. The Earl's voyeurism is part of what makes him a moral degenerate, and so we may be as well, in as unacknowledged a sense as he.

In her classic study of film, Laura Mulvey argues that the voyeurism associated with the sadistic male gaze often creates a narrative of punishment and forgiveness for the heroine (Mulvey 1989, 22). Hardy critiques that stereotypical narrative through ruining Barbara rather than saving her.

In an essay deriving from Mulvey's ideas, Judith Mitchell contends that Hardy's novels involve a classic melodrama plot of women torn between two inappropriate men; such plots are "protests against the cultural marginalization of the female" (Mitchell 1993, 185). "Barbara" can be seen in this light to a certain extent, as both Edmond and Uplandtowers are problematic husbands in different ways. However, Edmond becomes problematic due to Barbara's classism rather than his own flaws.

11. The shifting significance of Barbara's gender and class illustrates the discourse of positionality. As described by Susan Stanford Friedman in 1996, this discourse suggests that, depending upon a character's situation, either gender or class may be the more salient attribute.

12. *A Group of Noble Dames* is the only collection of short stories that Hardy wrote for a periodical. *The Graphic* was shocked by Hardy's frank treatment of wife abuse, childbirth, adultery and the dynastic rule of aristocrats; Hardy resented the fact that the magazine forced him to bowdlerize several of his stories, including "Barbara" (Seymour-Smith 1994, 393; Wing 1987, 77).

The critical reception of "Barbara" and its collection was less than enthusiastic, until in recent decades Brady (1982), Wing (1987), Ebbatson (1993), and Marroni (1994) delved deeply into the story's dense meanings. For example, Hardy's fellow novelist George Gissing found the story "coarse," while T.S. Eliot found "Barbara" written "solely to provide a satisfaction for some morbid emotion" (Seymour-Smith 1994, 393).

13. Paradoxically, Hardy enjoyed consorting with the titled and was obsessed with his own family's decayed gentility (Wing 1987, 93).

14. Ursula LeGuin's modern science fiction story, "The Ones Who Walk Away from Omelas," deals with a similar theme of a child who, like Edmond, is seen by his society as a symbol of all that is revolting and degenerate. The child becomes a scapegoat whose abjection enables the happiness of the rest of the people of Omelas, as the abjection of the working class enabled the triumphant joys of the aristocracy in Barbara's England, and as that of third-world workers enables first-world prosperity today.

Works Cited

Arata, Stephen. 1996. *Fictions of Loss in the Victorian fin de siecle.* Cambridge: Cambridge University Press.

Baudrillard, Jean. 1979. *Seduction.* New York: St. Martin's Press.

Berger, John. 1972 *Ways of Seeing.* New York: Penguin.

Brady, Kristin. 1982. *The Short Stories of Thomas Hardy.* New York: St. Martin's Press.

Ebbatson, Roger. 1993. *Hardy: The Margin of the Unexpressed.* Sheffield: Sheffield Academic Press.

Ender, Evelyne. 1995. *Sexing the Mind: Nineteenth-Century Fictions of Hysteria.* Ithaca: Cornell University Press.

Fischler, Alexander. 1966. Theatrical Techniques in Thomas Hardy's Short Stories. *Studies in Short Fiction* 3.4: 435-45.

Friedman, Susan Stanford. 1996. Beyond Gynocriticism and Gynesis: The Geographics of Identity and the Future of Feminist Criticism. *Tulsa Studies in Women's Literature* 15.1: 13-40.

Gilman, Sander. 1985. *Difference and Pathology.* Ithaca: Cornell University Press.

Girard, Rene. 1986. *The Scapegoat.* Trans. Yvonne Freccero. Baltimore: Johns Hopkins University Press.

Graham, Kenneth. 1989. *Gothic Fictions.* New York: AMS Press.

Greenslade, William. 1994. *Degeneration, Culture, and the Novel 1880-1940.* Cambridge: Cambridge University Press.

Guerard, Albert. 1949. *Thomas Hardy.* London: Cambridge University Press.

Halberstam, Judith. 1995. *Skin Shows: Gothic Horror and the Technology of Monsters.* Durham: Duke University Press.

Hardy, Thomas. 1928. Barbara of the house of Grebe. In *The Short Stories of Thomas Hardy.* 1891. Reprint. London: Macmillan. 537-72.

Hurley, Kelly. 1996. *The Gothic Body: Sexuality, Materialism, and Degeneration at the fin de siecle.* Cambridge: Cambridge University Press.

Kristeva, Julia. 1982. *Powers of Horror: An Essay on Abjection.* Trans. Leon S. Roudiez. New York: Columbia University Press.

———. 1987. *Tales of Love.* New York: Columbia University Press.

Law, Jules. 1997. A "Passing Corporeal Blight": Political Bodies in *Tess of the D'Urbervilles. Victorian Studies* 40.2: 245-70.

Marroni, Francesco. 1994. The Negation of Eros in "Barbara of the House of Grebe." *Thomas Hardy Journal* 10.1: 33-41.

Masse, Michelle. 1992. *In the Name of Love: Women, Masochism, and the Gothic.* Ithaca: Cornell University Press.

Mitchell, Judith. 1993. Hardy's Female Reader. In *The Sense of Sex: Perspectives on Hardy,* ed. Margaret Higgonnet. Urbana: University of Illinois Press. 172-87.

Mulvey, Laura. 1989. *Visual and other pleasures.* London: Macmillan.

Pick, Daniel. 1989. Faces of Degeneration: A European Disorder, c. 1848-1918. Cambridge: Cambridge University Press.

Scott, James F. 1963. Thomas Hardy's Use of the Gothic. *Nineteenth-Century Fiction* 17: 363-80.

Seymour-Smith, Martin. 1994. *Hardy: A Biography.* New York: St. Martin's Press.

Showalter, Elaine. 1987. *The Female Malady.* London: Virago.

Spackman, Barbara. 1989. *Decadent Genealogies.* Ithaca: Cornell University Press.

Wing, George. 1987. A Group of Noble Dames: "Statuesque Dynastics of Delightful Wessex." In *Thomas Hardy Annual* No. 5, ed. Norman Page. London: Macmillan. 75-101.

FURTHER READING

Criticism

Gibson, James. *Thomas Hardy: A Literary Life.* London: Macmillan, 1996, 206 p.
  Critical and biographical study.

Ray, Martin. "Thomas Hardy's 'The Son's Veto': A Textual History." *Review of English Studies* 47, no. 188 (November 1996): 542-47.
  Traces the various versions of "The Son's Veto."

Additional coverage of Hardy's life and career is contained in the following sources published by the Gale Group: *British Writers,* Vol. 6; *British Writers Retrospective Supplement,* Vol. 1; *Concise Dictionary of British Literary Biography, 1890-1914; Contemporary Authors,* Vols. 104, 123; *Dictionary of Literary Biography,* Vols. 18, 19, 135; *DISCovering Authors; DISCovering Authors: British Edition; DISCovering Authors: Canadian Edition; DISCovering Authors Modules: Most-studied Authors, Novelists,* and *Poets; DISCovering Authors 3.0; Exploring Novels; Exploring Poetry; Literature and Its Times,* Vol. 2; *Literature Resource Center; Major 20th-Century Writers,* Eds. 1, 2; *Novels for Students,* Vols. 3, 11, 15; *Poetry Criticism,* Vol. 8; *Poetry for Students,* Vols. 3, 4; *Reference Guide to English Literature,* Ed. 2; *Reference Guide to Short Fiction,* Ed. 2; *Short Story Criticism,* Vol. 2; *Twayne's English Authors; Twentieth-Century Literary Criticism,* Vols. 4, 10, 18, 32, 48, 53, 72; *World Literature and Its Times,* Vol. 4; and *World Literature Criticism.*

Franz Kafka
1883-1924

Austro-Czech short story writer, novelist, autobiographer, and diarist.

The following entry presents criticism of Kafka's short fiction works from 1995 to 2001. For criticism on Kafka's short fiction career published prior to 1995, see *SSC*, Volume 5; for discussion of the short story "Ein Hungerkünstler" (1922; "A Hunger Artist"), see *SSC*, Volume 29; and for discussion of the novella *Die Verwandlung* (1915; *The Metamorphosis*), see *SSC*, Volume 35.

INTRODUCTION

One of the most acclaimed and influential twentieth-century writers, Kafka is renowned for prophetic and profoundly enigmatic stories that often portray human degradation and cruelty. In his works, Kafka presents a grotesque vision of the world in which alienated, angst-ridden individuals vainly seek to transcend their condition or pursue some unattainable goal. His fiction derives its power from his use of precise, dispassionate prose and realistic detail to relate bizarre, often absurd events, and from his probing treatment of moral and spiritual problems.

BIOGRAPHICAL INFORMATION

Kafka was born to financially secure Jewish parents in Prague, a prominent provincial capital of the Austro-Hungarian Empire. His father had risen from poverty to success as a businessman, and the family had been assimilated into Prague's Czech community by the time of Kafka's birth. Seeking acceptance into the German-speaking elite of the city, Kafka's father sent him to German rather than Czech schools. Despite this fact, the dichotomy between the German and Czech communities led to Kafka's early feelings of alienation. As the eldest child and only surviving son, Kafka was expected to follow a planned course in life, but beginning in childhood he considered himself a disappointment to his father and felt inadequate when compared with him. Against his own wishes, Kafka studied law at the German University in Prague, earning his doctorate in 1906. Unhappy with the prospect of a legal career, he instead accepted a position with an insurance firm in Prague. He worked there from 1908 until 1922, when the de-

bilitating effects of tuberculosis finally forced him to retire. Kafka spent his remaining years in various sanatoriums, writing fiction until his death in Kierling, Austria, in 1924. In his will, Kafka ordered nearly all of his manuscripts burned, but Max Brod, his friend and literary executor, ignored this request and organized Kafka's writings into several posthumous publications.

MAJOR WORKS OF SHORT FICTION

Kafka was plagued by the discord between his vocation and literary ambitions and by his ambivalence about marriage, which he believed offered the greatest happiness, but which he feared would stifle his creativity. Some considered his relationship with Felice Bauer, to whom he was engaged twice but never married, the catalyst to a fertile period of literary production that began in 1912. During this time Kafka wrote "Das Urteil" (1913; "The Judgement") and *Die Verwandlung* (1915; *The Metamorphosis*). Many critics cite "The Judgement" as Kafka's "breakthrough" story, the one that established his central thematic preoccupation: the conflict between father and son that produces guilt in the younger character and is ultimately reconciled through suffering and expiation. Kafka's next major work, "The Metamorphosis," is one of the most frequently analyzed stories in world literature. This elusive work, which portrays the transformation of Gregor Samsa from a man into an insect, has inspired diverse interpretations. In 1919, Kafka published "In der Strafkolonie" ("In the Penal Colony"), which is a characteristic fantasy of psychological and physical brutality that suggests a variety of readings due to the obscure nature of the events. From 1916 to 1917, Kafka wrote a series of prose pieces, known as the "Country Doctor Cycle," which reflects a sense of decaying order in Europe during World War I. These tales were later collected and published as *Ein Landarzt* (1919; *The Country Doctor*). The stories in the last book published by Kafka during his lifetime, *Ein Hungerkunstler* (1924; *A Hunger Artist*), depict characters whose extreme isolation represents the status of the artist in a modern industrialized world.

CRITICAL RECEPTION

Kafka is ranked among the most important writers of the twentieth century for works that express modern humanity's loss of personal and collective order. His writing has inspired the term "Kafkaesque," which has come to describe situations of psychological, social, political, and metaphysical instability and confusion that defy logical explanation and which typify Kafka's conception of humanity's absurd relationship with the universe. Although Kafka's work has elicited various critical interpretations, he himself characterized his fiction as symbolic manifestations of his "dreamlike inner life" in which he attempted to reconcile feelings of guilt and insecurity. In recent years, some critics have explored Kafka's relationship with Judaism as demonstrated by his texts. For many critics, Kafka's greatness resides in his ability to transform his private torment into universal fables.

PRINCIPAL WORKS

Short Fiction

Betrachtung 1913
Der Heizer: Ein Fragment 1913
Das Urteil: Eine Geschichte [*The Sentence*; also translated as *The Judgement*] 1913

Die Verwandlung [*The Metamorphosis*] 1915
Ein Landarzt: Kleine Erzählungen [*The Country Doctor: A Collection of Fourteen Short Stories*] 1919
In der Strafkolonie [*In the Penal Colony*] 1919
Ein Hungerkunstler: Vier Geschichten [*A Hunger Artist*] 1924
Beim Bau der chinesischen Mauer: Ungedruckte Erzählungen und Prosa aus dem Nachlaß [*The Great Wall of China and Other Pieces*] 1931
*Gesammelte Schriften. 6 vols. 1935-37
The Complete Stories 1946
The Penal Colony: Stories and Short Pieces 1948
Dearest Father: Stories and Other Writings 1954
The Great Wall of China: Stories and Reflections 1970
Stories 1904-1924 1981

Other Major Works

Der Prozeß: Roman [*The Trial*] (novel) 1925
Das Schloß: Roman [*The Castle: A Novel*] (novel) 1926
Amerika: Roman [*America*] (novel) 1927
The Diaries of Franz Kafka 1910-1923 (diaries) 1948
The Diaries of Franz Kafka 1914-1923 (diaries) 1949
Letter to His Father (letters) 1953
Letters to Felice (letters) 1973
I am a Memory Come Alive: Autobiographical Writings by Franz Kafka (autobiography) 1974
Letters to Friends, Family, and Editors (letters) 1977

**This work includes: *Erzählungen und kleine Prosa* (1935; *In the Penal Settlement: Tales and Short Prose Works*) and *Beschreibung eines Kampfes: Novellen, Skizzen, Aphorismen aus dem Nachlaß* (1936; *Description of a Struggle and The Great Wall of China*).

CRITICISM

Evelyn Torton Beck (essay date 1995)

SOURCE: Beck, Evelyn Torton. "Gender, Judaism, and Power: A Jewish Feminist Approach to Kafka." In *Approaches to Teaching Kafka's Short Fiction*, edited by Richard T. Gray, pp. 35-42. New York: The Modern Language Association of America, 1995.

[*In the following essay, Beck, using a Jewish feminist approach, looks at the influence of Yiddish theater on Kafka's short ficiton.*]

> Fiction is like a spider's web, attached ever so lightly perhaps, but still attached to life at all four corners.
>
> —Virginia Woolf, *A Room of One's Own*

Long before I became aware of the significance of gender, my approach to the study of literature was both contextual and integrative. I took it as given that art is not separable from life and that establishing the cultural and biographical contexts of an artist's work is as essential to an understanding of a text as is the analysis of symbol, imagery, and language.

Such an integrated approach is especially essential to Franz Kafka, for the membrane separating the life of this writer from his work is particularly permeable. For this reason, I always begin teaching his texts by establishing his historic realities and the value system of the worlds in which he lived. Students must know from the start that Kafka was multiply a minority. He was a German-speaking Jew living in Prague when anti-Semitism was widespread and the German language associated (by Czech natives) with the hostile ruling class. He was a Jew who despised and rejected his father's superficial way of being Jewish but who could neither believe nor entirely give up belief. He was also a man who had difficulty being sexual with women; who feared the responsibility of marriage, which he associated with the bourgeois life he saw as inimical to the artist in him. But, ironically, he also believed, in accordance with Jewish custom, that a man who did not marry would never be more than half a man. In addition, contemporary social pressure and Jewish mores kept him from ever contemplating the meaning of his sexual revulsion for women (made explicit in his letters and diaries) and perhaps facing his homoerotic attractions, which are amply manifest in accounts of his dreams and fantasies as well as in the homosocial worlds of his fiction and fragments (see Beck, "Kafka's Traffic" and "Kafka's Triple Bind").

These multiple contexts provide a basic framework within which it becomes possible to begin to analyze the stories. Because most students find interpretation of Kafka's fiction so formidable, I first concentrate on demystifying his work by demonstrating the ways in which he transmuted significant elements from Jewish culture and religion and reworked them in his fiction in an abstract way, giving these elements an aura of mystery and terror. In this process I show how Kafka's own method of decontextualizing makes his work so richly layered and open to multiple interpretations.

Becoming more specific, I begin with the influence of Yiddish theater on his work and show the coincidence of Kafka's artistic "breakthrough" in 1912 with the reawakening of his interest in Judaism, brought about by an extended encounter with an eastern European wandering theater troupe that performed Yiddish plays in Prague from 1910 to 1911 (see Beck, *Yiddish Theater* and "Kafka's 'Durchbruch'"). Kafka believed that this impoverished, semiprofessional troupe's repertoire of tragicomic plays, dealing with ancient and contempo-

rary Jewish life, represented a more authentic form of Judaism than he had ever encountered, and for a time they gave him some relief from the pressing existential and familial problems that so troubled him. Kafka also became infatuated with both the leading actor and actress of the troupe. In September 1912, directly following this theater experience, he wrote **"The Judgment,"** the first story to show the characteristic dramatic style that typifies Kafka's mature writing and stands in stark contrast to all his writing before that time (see Beck, *Yiddish Theater* 31-48).

Having established this background, I demonstrate to students how I came to trace not only the style but also the essential themes of Kafka's entire oeuvre to these Yiddish plays. Specifically, these themes are the impossibility of obtaining justice within the machinery of the law, the struggle against authority (both divine and temporal), the relationship between the individual and the "absolute" as well as the community, the cleanliness toward which Kafka's characters strive, the elusive knowledge they seek, the hunger they cannot sate.

Moreover, the effect of power on the Jew (particularly the Jewish male) is central to the Yiddish plays and made concrete in battles of power between fathers and sons within the nuclear family, king and Jew in the nation-state, individual Jew and rabbinic leader in Jewish communal life, and God and subject in the Jewish religious sphere. While heterosexual marriage, procreation, and adherence to Jewish law are offered in these plays as ideals to all Jews, women are also expected to be subservient to men and to sacrifice themselves willingly for the benefit of men. Kafka saw as important the guilt and punishment associated with disobedience of Jewish law and disavowal of Jewish ethics and values; in these plays such defiance inevitably leads to apostasy and abandonment of the community.

Kafka's echo of these themes should make it evident that the influence of Yiddish theater was particularly strong on the short stories under discussion in this volume, stories in which such themes appear in transmuted form without specific reference to Jewish history. The stories also include entire scenes whose origins can be traced to the plays, which Kafka saw several times in the space of a few months just before he wrote **"The Judgment."**[1]

The Yiddish plays themselves were aesthetically uneven and produced on a limited budget in a tiny theater in one of the poorest sections of Prague. Kafka's parents, especially his father, strongly disapproved of his interest in this theater. The plays performed there were written between 1880 and 1907 but remained untouched by the spirit of modernism that was sweeping Europe in those years; rather, they were composed of elements taken from the traditional five-act play, the melodrama, and the burlesque.[2] Because the plays were performed under poor conditions, even the tragic scenes sometimes became comic, as for example when during one performance the dying hero's wig slipped off in the middle of a tragic speech. Kafka recorded such details in his diaries and seemed actually to find such juxtapositions oddly effective.[3] The familiar figure of the wedding jester, whose stylized mocking declamations infused traditional Jewish weddings in the small towns of eastern Europe, also found his way into these plays and, through them, into Kafka's narratives.

To make the relation of Kafka's fiction to Yiddish theater more concrete, I focus on **"The Judgment"** (1913) and **"The Metamorphosis"** (1915), which show the direct influence of three of these plays with particular clarity. The plays in question are Jacob Gordin's *God, Man, and Devil* and *The Savage One* and Abraham Scharkansky's *Kol Nidre; or, The Secret Jews of Spain.* In *Kol Nidre* the overlap of the father-child and God-Jew conflicts is particularly prominent. In *God, Man, and Devil* the father is a retired wedding jester who (under the influence of wine) inappropriately reverts to his public role in the midst of a family gathering. In **"The Judgment"** Georg's father echoes this jester role in a grotesquely comic fashion that quickly becomes menacing when Georg cannot withstanding his father's psychological attack (see Beck, *Yiddish Theater* 70-121).

In both Kafka's story and Gordin's play, a son is at first embarrassed by his father's out-of-control behavior (leaping onto a chair, wild gesticulation, and verbal attacks) but then takes control by carrying the father off to bed, where the old and foolish belong; in both works, however, the father ultimately triumphs over his son. Although the stark simplicity of the action in **"The Judgment"** may seem far removed from the involved plot of *God, Man, and Devil,* many of the story's most bizarre elements, and all the theatrical ones, correspond strikingly to the details of Gordin's play. Both works build up to a scene of trial and judgment, followed by the self-inflicted death of the hero, whose demise marks a return to order. Both fathers accuse their sons of abandoning them in favor of business opportunities and financial success associated with taboo sexual activity.

In each work, however, the father's accusation bears a unique relation to the realities of its respective text, and for this reason a comparison of the two is extremely instructive. While in the Yiddish play the son is truly engaged in an inappropriate, if not outright incestuous, relationship with his niece, in Kafka's story the father's objection to the son's adult sexuality seems so inappropriate as to suggest that it is he and not the son who is off balance.

> "Because she lifted up her skirts!" his father began to flute, "because she lifted her skirts like this, the nasty creature," and mimicking her he lifted his shirt so high

that one could see the scar on his thigh from his war wound, "because she lifted her skirts like this and this you made up to her, and in order to make free with her undisturbed, you have disgraced your mother's memory, betrayed your friend and stuck your father into bed so he can't move. But he can move, or can't he?"

(*CS* 85)

Georg's acceptance of his father's inappropriate judgment suggests that he cannot sustain his newly won independence and has completely internalized the father's voice. A complementary reading suggests that Georg's feelings for the "friend in Russia" (who he posits will be "so upset" by the news of his forthcoming marriage) are homoerotic.[4] "Since your friends are like that, Georg, you shouldn't ever have got engaged at all," his fiancée tells him (*CS* 80). The very different use to which Kafka puts the play's dramatic scene shows that he has taken a theme that was comprehensible in the Yiddish play and deliberately made it less easy to interpret in the context of his fiction.[5]

The startling ending of **"The Judgment,"** in which the son literally carries out his father's verdict—"I sentence you now to death by drowning" (*CS* 87)—originated in Scharkansky's *Kol Nidre.* In that play the head inquisitor is a convert from Judaism who is forced to condemn his own child to death because she is revealed to be living as a secret Jew and she refuses to renounce her Jewish identity when it is exposed. She dies saying the *Shm'a*—"Hear O Israel: the Lord is our God, the Lord is One"—the traditional avowal of allegiance to Judaism recited at least twice daily by Orthodox Jews as part of morning and evening prayers and always recited under life-threatening circumstances. In Kafka's **"The Judgment,"** this speech provides an ironic parallel, for Georg dies vowing loyalty to the very father who has condemned him: "Dearest parents, I have always loved you, all the same" (*CS* 88).

What separates Kafka's fiction from the Yiddish theater is its ambiguity and its creation of a fictional world in which one cannot judge the characters' perception or the accuracy of any accusation. In contrast, the Yiddish play makes clear who is guilty (of what) and when those who accuse are out of control. The Yiddish plays usually offer the possibility of an alternative perspective that bears some relation to a more sane "reality" outside the family or social system. Kafka's narratives present worlds so self-enclosed with characters so self-absorbed that they preclude the possibility of any external commonsense perspective. In this difference lies both the power of Kafka's stories and their frustrating resistance to a single interpretation.

"The Metamorphosis," Kafka's best-known story, illustrates with particular clarity not only the continuing influence of Yiddish theater but also his working method. In theme, characters, structure, and technique, this story reflects the influence of several Yiddish plays, especially *The Savage One,* by Jacob Gordin, whose work deeply impressed Kafka as the most complex in the repertoire. Like **"The Metamorphosis,"** this play also contains a son, Lemekh, who, like Gregor, is in some serious way "defective." Born gentle but retarded, in the course of events Lemekh is taunted and abused by his family and thus becomes the savage of the play's title; his situation closely parallels that of Gregor Samsa (once Gregor's condition has been concretized in insect form). Like the defective son in the play, Gregor is barely tolerated and is looked upon with disgust as an outcast whose very existence shames his family. In different ways the two sons combine the qualities of "thing" and "person." Both are presented as essentially simple, meek, self-effacing persons who become animallike creatures because of a drastic transformation that ends in catastrophe. The two works are also parallel in the number and kinds of characters they portray, down to the family housekeeper, in each tale the only person who does not fear the strange son (see Beck, *Yiddish Theater* 135-46).

The Oedipal conflict and broader theme of incest, presented in blatant and highly exaggerated form in *The Savage One,* are also played out in **"The Metamorphosis."** In both works a son's sexual desire becomes inappropriately lodged in family members and played out in father-son rivalry. Gregor faints when he sees his father and mother embrace, and later he imaginatively projects himself and his sister into his locked room, where he would not only protect her against all "intruders," but also "raise himself to her shoulder and kiss her on the neck" (*CS* 131). In Gordin's play, in a scene with similarly sexual overtones, the hero literally locks himself into a room with his sleeping stepmother and swears to keep her as his own. Gregor's final degradation, startlingly signaled by his crawling around on all fours, finds its parallel in the Yiddish play in Lemekh's loss of rational control, after which he, too, ends up crawling on the floor.

Structurally, Kafka's stories progress like dramas, building through a series of crises to a final denouement. In a given story, the various episodes relate to one another like the separate, self-contained acts in a play. In handling setting, Kafka also adapts the techniques of the stage, limiting the relatively few characters to a small, clearly defined area, accounting for physical details as if they were to be made concrete on a stage. The movements of the characters are recorded with the precision of stage directions, and the exaggerated action often culminates in a grouping of characters that recalls the tableaux of the Yiddish theater. Kafka's language evokes the economy of a stage performance in which words resonate to suggest meaning beyond the literal. While one would never claim that the Yiddish theater experi-

ence was solely responsible for the breakthrough to Kafka's mature style represented in **"The Judgment"** and **"The Metamorphosis,"** it clearly influenced not only his central themes but also his imagery, with which he emphasized gesture, costume, comic pantomime, and stark visual effects.

I completed my research on the impact of Yiddish theater on Kafka's work in the early 1970s and find that it is still valid in the 1990s, although I am now painfully aware that I, like all other Kafka scholars of that time (and most, even today), completely ignored the issue of gender in my analysis. Starting in the mid-1970s I began to reexamine Kafka's writings from a feminist perspective, and in 1978 I made a presentation called "Feminist Criticism and Franz Kafka"; by 1981 I had organized a session at the Modern Language Association convention titled "Kafka's Sexual Politics/at Work/in the Text."[6] Since then I have come to believe that any interpretation of Kafka is seriously impoverished if it does not take gender into account as a factor of analysis.

It is not difficult to show that the question of gender is the single most ignored aspect of Kafka's work yet, at the same time, one of its most outstanding issues. A few observations should suffice to lay the foundation for this conclusion. Kafka's fictional worlds are almost entirely male—homosocial and often homoerotic. Woman is literally absent from many of the texts, and when she is not absent, her presence is obliterated, obscured, or trivialized. Where she is not obscured, she is seen as purely instrumental, as a vehicle or conduit for male activity, specifically for the male quest and the essential power struggles between males that are at the center of Kafka's works. Even in the few stories that have a central female character (e.g., **"Josephine, the Mouse"**), the male narrator speaks for her. Nowhere in Kafka does a woman speak from her own perspective.

More significant, the male heroes organize the text's way of seeing, and as a result, the angle of vision in Kafka's texts is necessarily androcentric. This viewpoint is especially clear when the male eye looks out at women. The narrative eye sees not the "person" of a woman but always an other or the physical body or part of a body. It is therefore no accident that Kafka's heroes have been described in strictly male terms, as Fausts, schlemiels, or even little boys. Woman in Kafka's world is purely instrumental: she can help or hinder the hero, but never can she herself be an active participant in the quest. Moreover, as Kafka represents her, she is incapable of understanding even the impulse to act or its spiritual dimension.

In analyzing Kafka's perception of women's function as nurturers and servicers of men, it is helpful to place his viewpoint within the context of Jewish attitudes toward women. Such attitudes are not essentially different from those of other patriarchal societies but are perhaps experienced more intensely in Jewish communities (and by other oppressed minorities), for whom community survival has always been at risk. As a Jewish male, Kafka saw women as nourishers of men. Given his sexual difficulties with women and the explicit revulsion of heterosexuality repeatedly recorded in his diaries, it is likely that Kafka's own sexual proclivity was toward men. Since this attraction was taboo as an open choice and specifically prohibited by Jewish law, Kafka lived out his life in a self-loathing he did not fully comprehend. When his internalized anti-Semitism is paired with his internalized homophobia, neither of which was speakable or was mentioned by name in his fiction, these submerged themes press upon his texts and give them particular force and intensity.

While Kafka exposed the virtual powerlessness of women in a patriarchy and laid bare the structures that bind them, he nonetheless also perpetuated the patriarchal ideology itself. Even his most disempowered hero seeks domination over women and thinks of them in the language of ownership. Thus, for a woman to read Kafka in the way he pushes us to read him, through the eyes of a Georg or Gregor, Josef K. or K., she must forget that she is a woman, which is what polite society and traditional literary criticism also invite her to do. But such an act of "forgetting" seems contradictory to Kafka's own vision of what a book should be—"the axe for the frozen sea inside us" (*Letters to Friends* 16). Foregrounding the gender of the characters in Kafka's texts and similarly locating the readers of his texts result in a clarifying re-vision that can keep us from mystifying Kafka's works. Such revision also helps modify the hopelessness of his vision, for if we keep the specificity of our own (as well as Kafka's) situation in mind, we need not blindly accept the notion that he describes eternal, existential, universal life conditions. We can more easily see how his vision grows out of his own life experiences, rooted as they are in gender, sexuality, ethnicity, religion, history, and culture. And though his texts may speak to us, they need not speak for us, need not define a limit; his ambivalence need not become ours. If we also begin to recognize that "us" and "ours" are not homogeneous categories, if we can learn to read Kafka "against the grain," we will facilitate this process.[7] Such a reading in no way diminishes Kafka's power as an artist but may fruitfully diminish his hold over us, which often depresses and frightens students. Perhaps if we can help students understand that the origins of Kafka's tragicomic creations lie in the ways he experienced Jewish life at a certain moment in history, they will be able not only to appreciate his humor (as well as his use of it as a coping strategy) but also to understand why his own life so terrified him.

Notes

1. This influence is not limited to the short stories but is also evident in the novels, particularly *The Trial*, whose opening scene—the arrest of an apparently innocent man who has been falsely denounced—is lifted directly from Asher Zelig Faynman's *The Viceroy* (originally translated as *The Vice-King*), a Yiddish play set at the time of the Inquisition, in which a man who has hidden his Judaism is denounced and arrested for continuing the forbidden Jewish practices.

2. For a list of the Yiddish plays and a detailed description of them, see the references in Beck, *Yiddish Theater.*

3. See Kafka's *Diaries, 1910-1913.* Detailed descriptions of the plays and the theater performances are scattered throughout the entries for 1911 and 1912.

4. This reading is substantiated by numerous diary entries, letters, dreams, and fragments as well as other fictional texts in which the erotic male dance is fairly explicit. Among the early works, see, for example, "Description of a Struggle." Numerous examples are documented in Beck, "Kafka's Triple Bind."

5. Another significant parallel in the two works is the father's accusation that his son has betrayed a friend and is therefore a "devilish" human being. In *God, Man, and Devil* this charge is accurate, since the play is a reworking of Goethe's *Faust*; in this version, the hero has literally betrayed his closest friend by striking a bargain with the devil, who takes human shape. In Kafka's story Georg's mysterious "friend in Russia" is modeled on Yitzkhok Levi, the leading actor of whom Kafka's father disapproved violently, perhaps sensing the attraction between the two men. "Whoever lies down with dogs gets up with fleas," Kafka's father reportedly said, referring to his actor friend (*Diaries, 1910-1913* 131).

6. The 1978 session took place at the meeting of the American Association of Teachers of German; the 1981 MLA session also included presentations by Angelika Bammer and Helen Fehervary.

7. The concept of reading against the grain is elaborated on as a strategy of feminist criticism by Judith Fetterley, who rereads Faulkner, Hemingway, and other male writers of the American canon.

Kenneth Hughes (essay date 1995)

SOURCE: Hughes, Kenneth. "A Psychoanalytic Approach to 'The Judgement.'" In *Approaches to Teaching*

Kafka's Short Fiction, edited by Richard T. Gray, pp. 84-93. New York: The Modern Language Association of America, 1995.

[*In the following essay, Hughes employs psychoanalytic theory in his reading of "The Judgement."*]

By definition, the psychoanalytic approach to literature takes as its object some psyche involved at some point of the literary process. The most convenient objects to have offered themselves to date are the mind of the author, the mind of a text's narrator or of a character, and the mind of the reader. This sequence, which recapitulates the natural order of literary mediation (an idea occurs to the author's mind; the author "embodies" the idea in his narrator or in a character; the reader perceives the character's emotion and divines the author's intention as the motivating force behind it), also charts the three-stage historical course of psychoanalytic criticism.

Psychoanalytic theory was initially applied to the creative process by Freud and a number of his colleagues (such as Otto Rank and Karl Abraham), primarily in the decade following the publication in 1905 of Freud's *Wit and Its Relation to the Unconscious.* In the movement's first stage (dominating the 1920s), critics tended to scrutinize literature for clues concerning the personality and psychological profile of the author. Apart from such book-length studies as Axel Uppvall's *August Strindberg: A Psychoanalytic Study,* Katherine Anthony's *Margaret Fuller: A Psychological Biography,* and Edward Carpenter and George Barnefield's *The Psychology of the Poet Shelley,* the pages of the professional journals are full of articles with titles like "Psychopathological Glimpses of . . ." and "Psychoanalysis of . . ." (see Cassity; Dooley), many of which were written under the influence of Freud's chief American champion, G. Stanley Hall, at Clark University, who had sponsored Freud's famous American sojourn in 1909. Not without reason have such studies been called pathographies (see Schrey), and not without reason did they provoke the predictable reaction from defenders of formalism and aestheticism, who were intent on ensuring art a special realm above and beyond the processes of either normal or abnormal human psychology.

Generally superseding the pathography of the author was a second stage, which concentrated more intently than the first on the meanings of texts and did not so exclusively use them merely as tools in the analysis of the psyches of their creators; in this method—as in, for example, Marie Bonaparte's and Joseph Wood Krutch's studies of Poe—critics went beyond using the work as a tool to analyze the author, instead applying psychoanalytic understanding of the author toward a better understanding of the work. This is the manner of psychoanalytic criticism with which we are commonly most

familiar, the manner that has dominated criticism of **"The Judgment"** from the beginning, since this story did not become widely known until the second stage had largely superseded the first.[1]

Clearly, however, there are problems with both methods. First, we can never know enough about an author to construct a convincing psychoanalytic profile: we cannot get that individual on the couch as analysand and allow the free association with the material of the dream work necessary for true analysis, and whatever insights we might think we have into the author's psychic life cannot be verified anyway—so why bother harrowing the text to begin with? Second, literary characters are, inescapably, fictional constructs, and even the most psychologically complex of them do not have, indeed cannot have, as roundly or fully profiled a psyche as that of even the flattest and most uninteresting real-life subject. How then, despite all the analogies that indisputably exist between literary character and real person, can the fictional psyche be profitably scrutinized with the aid of tools developed through analysis of the real minds of living people? And even if analysis were possible, could it be conducted by literary critics lacking the training and experience of the practicing analyst (Hughes, "Psychoanalytic Criticism" 163)?[2]

In the face of such practical impediments, the third stage of psychoanalytic criticism has tended to shift the focus of attention from the mind of an author or a character to the psyche of the reader, the one person in the literary process who is neither inaccessible to analysis (if only self-analysis) nor fictional in character. This manner of criticism is the third referred to by Norman N. Holland in his seminal 1962 essay "Shakespearean Tragedy and the Three Ways of Psychoanalytic Criticism," the manner that forms the basis of the psychoanalytically oriented reader-response criticism on which he elaborates in subsequent studies and that we may consider the third stage in a historical sense. In that essay, Holland appeals to a consideration of the literary work "as a total configuration or *Gestalt,* not as just a single character," as "the showplace of an interior drama in the minds of the playwright or his audience," and concludes that "in treating the work as an indivisible whole the critic assumes that the work of art is to be itself savored as a final reality, not as a filtered version of something else" (210, 211, 213). Holland alludes to (210) but does not cite a point that Freud made in his essay "The Relation of the Poet to Day-dreaming," a point that is of crucial importance in the psychoanalytic approach to **"The Judgment."** Freud wrote of

the tendency of modern writers to split up their ego by self-observation into many component-egos, and in this way to personify the conflicting trends in their own mental life in many heroes . . . in these [works] the person introduced as the hero plays the least active part of anyone, and seems instead to let the actions and sufferings of other people pass him by like a spectator.

(51-52)

These two points, rather than the aspect of reader-response, are what I wish to examine here: the text is a total configuration, a gestalt, an "interior drama," and the apparent "hero" of a literary text may be no more than a passive spectator of a play enacted by the component parts of his own psyche. These two propositions provide us with an important key to understanding **"The Judgment"** as the staging of an oedipal drama in which all the requisite properties and actors (Georg's ego, id, and superego; son, father, and mother; present incidence and recalled memory) are present in some capacity in the text of the story.

Most of the psychoanalytic discussion of **"The Judgment"** has focused on objects and artifacts of the fictional texture (the so-called phallic symbols) and on its chief actors (Georg, the father, and the friend). The critics in question have rarely addressed other elements of fiction, such as metaphor, symbol, or image. But such intrinsic aspects of the text are essential to understanding what happens in the central scene of the story, the one in which Gregor puts his father to bed, and in the ensuing peripeteia, which leads to Georg's sentencing and death. Much of the ambiguity in this scene comes from the father's apparently unstable role: Is he a child, or is he a man? Is he helpless, or is he the dominant one? Heinz Politzer reframes this question in relation to the father's clinging to Georg's watch chain: does the gesture indicate childishness, contempt, weakness, or a firm grip? "The silent gesture . . . remains unexplained," he says (*Parable and Paradox* 57).

But let us recall significant passages of that scene to attempt an explanation. It begins when Georg evades his father's question about whether he "really" has a friend in Saint Petersburg (*CS* 82) and instead suggests making some changes in the father's living conditions:[3]

". . . I'll put you to bed now for a little, I'm sure you need to rest. Come, I'll help you take off your things, you'll see I can do it. . . ."

. . . Georg [lifted] his father from the chair and [slipped] off his dressing gown. . . .

Meanwhile Georg had succeeded in lowering his father down again and carefully taking off the woollen drawers he wore over his linen underpants and his socks. . . .

He carried his father to bed in his arms. It gave him a dreadful feeling to notice that while he took the few steps toward the bed the old man on his breast was playing with his watch chain. . . .

But as soon as he was laid in bed, all seemed well. He covered himself up and even drew the blankets farther than usual over his shoulders. He looked up at Georg with a not unfriendly eye. . . .

"Am I well covered up now?" asked his father, as if he were not able to see whether his feet were properly tucked in or not.

"So you like it in bed," said Georg, and arranged the blankets better around him.

"Am I well covered up?" asked the father once more, and seemed to pay particular attention to the answer.

"Don't worry, you're well covered up."

"No!" cried his father . . .

(*CS* 83-84)

We must question who is being put to bed in this scene. On the most immediate plane of the narration, it is of course the father. All oedipal interpretations of **"The Judgment"** have naturally emphasized the symbolic aspect of Georg's putting his father to bed and "covering him up" as a representation of the son's replacement of the father as head of the household and of the business. And of course this interpretation parallels some biographical evidence in *Letter to His Father,* when Kafka commented, "My writing was all about you; all I did there, after all, was to bemoan what I could not bemoan upon your breast" (87). In this regard, Peter U. Beicken has noted that Kafka's work is "a continuation of the struggle against his father and the principles and values which he represented" (*Kritische Einführung* 206). Observing that before this scene Georg says to himself, "My father is still a giant of a man" (*CS* 81), and that immediately thereafter the father returns to his gigantic stature and sentences Georg, we can see the patriarchally superior and even "gigantic" (*Letter* 41) position of Hermann Kafka opposing the "slave" (29), of which Kafka also wrote in that letter.

But we must note that the father appears in both aspects that Politzer's query above suggests: he has Georg in his grip, yet he also appears in the guise of a child. Moreover, is he being child*ish* or child*like* when he plays with the chain? Walter Sokel ("Perspectives and Truth" 225) and Hartmut Binder (*Kafka-Kommentar* 150) refer this gesture to the father's supposed "senility" or "infantility," respectively, and Claude-Edmonde Magny has trivialized the point by claiming it to be a sign of "insanity" (84). But more important than a precise analysis of the father's mental state in this scene is the role reversal that takes place. According to the dynamics of the oedipal conflict, if the son displaces the father, then the father is automatically put into the position, vis-à-vis the woman, formerly occupied by the son. And since there is no evidence of the father's supposed senility, we must seek for another explanation of what is happening here. In fact, apparently the figure being put to bed is not only the father qua father but also, symbolically, a somewhat reluctant child, who, to prolong the process a bit and register whatever weak protest can be made, catches hold of Georg's watch chain and for a while refuses to let go. This event is completely within the experience of any adult wearing any chain, necklace, or (alas) eyeglasses who has ever tried to put an unwilling infant to bed, and Kafka's journals show us what an astute observer of children he was. Thus the image does not so much indicate the father's childishness or senility as it does his symbolic transformation to childlike behavior.

This interpretation, however, still does not explain why Georg should have witnessed this action with "a dreadful feeling." Here we must recall Freud's explanation of the artistic process. One of the most frequent failings of the psychoanalytic approach to literature is that while it does apply Freud's categories to the work and the writer, it tends to overlook Freud's psychology of creation and what that theory implies about the work itself. Freud states that the work of art is a fulfillment of a wish "in which elements of the recent event *and* the old memory should be discernible" (*Collected Papers* 181). It is to this "old memory" that we can attribute Georg's "dreadful feeling": when his father takes hold of his chain, Georg suddenly comprehends the role reversal this gesture implies. In his father he recognizes the child he himself once was, playing with his father's watch chain, and in himself he recognizes his father putting him to bed. The oedipal conflict is for a moment jolted out of its repression in Georg's subconscious mind, and the old memory to which Freud alludes enters the texture of the fiction along with the recent event.

Only this interpretation, it seems to me, can adequately explain Georg's "dreadful feeling" ("schreckliches Gefühl") and the subsequent characterization of his father as a "dreadful apparition" ("Schreckbild") (*CS* 85). The description of this feeling accords perfectly with Freud's definition of the "uncanny" as "that genre of the *dreadful* which goes back to things long since and intimately known" (*Gesammelte Werke* 231). "This uncanny," Freud tells us, "is really nothing new or unknown, but rather something long familiar to the psychic life but which has become estranged from it through the process of repression" (254). It is particularly appropriate that Georg's uncanny feeling be evoked by his recognition of the role reversal, for precisely in such situations does Freud locate the origin of this feeling: "The uncanny in experience arises when repressed infantile complexes are revived through an impression or when outlived primitive beliefs seem once again confirmed" (263). We may thus conclude that the figure being put to bed here along with the father is not just any representative of childhood but in fact Georg himself as a child.

These two possibilities, however, do not even yet exhaust the purposeful ambiguities of the action. Kafka pays unusually detailed attention to the act of undress-

ing, to the necessary physical motions of standing, seating, and laying down—more attention than is necessary and more than can be justified on the realistic plane of the fiction alone. In fact, the description of this disrobing ritual seems more appropriate to a bedroom seduction scene than to the symbolic undressing of even a reluctant child. Georg's provisionally triumphant statement "So you like it in bed" is obviously not the least of these ambiguities. Nor should we forget that this detailed attention to clothing is charged also with the erotic associations that arise immediately after, when for a moment the father actually plays the role of Georg's bride:

> "Because she lifted up her skirts," his father began to flute, "because she lifted her skirts like this, the nasty creature," and mimicking her he lifted his shirt so high that one could see the scar on his thigh from the war wound, "because she lifted her skirts like this and this you made up to her, and in order to make free with her undisturbed you have disgraced your mother's memory. . . ."
>
> (*CS* 85)

To realize the sexual significance of this scar on the father's upper thigh, one need only recall the rose-colored "wound" on the side of the patient in **"A Country Doctor,"** described in obvious genital association as "dark in the hollows, lighter at the edges, softly granulated, with irregular clots of blood, open as a surface mine to the daylight" (*CS* 223), and narrowly triangular in shape, "cut in an acute angle with two strokes of the hatchet" (*CS* 225).

Further evidence for the presence of a female component in Kafka's representation of the father is provided by his diary entry regarding **"The Judgment"**: "Thoughts of Freud naturally . . . of Werfel's 'Giantess'" (*Diaries, 1910-1913* 276). The reference to Freud, so welcome to psychoanalytic critics, has obscured the even more useful reference to Werfel. What exactly Kafka had in mind we cannot know, but we can see that the entire passage is too sexually charged for the reference to a woman to have been irrelevant to him, and we cannot forget that Georg literally looks up to his father as to a "giant." It seems undeniable, then, that along with the father and the image of Georg as a child, there is yet a third person being put to bed in this scene: a woman, whom Georg's father also represents.

Kafka himself first pointed to the shadowy presence of Georg's bride in this scene. His diary entry of 11 February 1913 refers to "the bride, who lives in the story only through her relationship to the friend, in other words to what is mutual" (*Diaries, 1910-1913* 278-79). She is not merely a "catalyst" (Nagel, *Aspekte* 183); as Sokel has said, she plays a "decisive role" (*Tragik und Ironie* 48). In her absence from the scene as an actor and in the role she plays as an object of contention between Georg and his father, she neatly recapitulates the position of the deceased mother. We might go even farther and note that in accusing Georg of having dishonored his mother's memory through his alliance with Frieda, the father establishes an equivalence—in the sense of a substitution—between these two women. Georg first sees his father sitting in a corner "hung with various mementoes of Georg's dead mother" (*CS* 81), and the old Bendemann constantly reminds us that he and his wife have usually acted as a unit, not the least when he appeals to the mother's symbolic presence: "All by myself I might have had to give way, but your mother has given me so much of her strength . . ." (*CS* 86). But we do not have to dwell on any specific equivalence between mother and bride; in any oedipal situation the beloved reactivates the child's incestuous desire for the mother; the dynamics of the conflict itself create the association, so the image of the mother is always subsumed in the figure of the beloved.

The central scene in **"The Judgment"** thus appears to be a distillation of the oedipal drama, a reduction of the complex interactions of all the characters of the story to a symbolic nuclear familial constellation. Previous attempts to see the scene in the light of the oedipal conflict, concentrating on Georg's desire to do away with his father, have neglected the symbolic presence of the child and the mother and so have unwittingly slighted the aesthetic economy that Kafka achieved here. Naturally, this economy is purchased at the expense of strict psychoanalytic logic, but the "inner truth" of which Kafka spoke in reference to his story (*Letters to Felice* 87) is more important. It is not true, as he wrote to Felice Bauer, that **"The Judgment"** cannot be explained (265), for he himself had rendered a reasonable explanation in his diary (*Diaries, 1910-1913* 278-79) while reading the proofs. What counts is the quality of lyrical association, a suggestive juxtaposition of images: they are the chief ordering principles in this scene. Freud would of course object that to combine father, child, and mother in one person is a distortion of the oedipal situation. And so it is, but Kafka was not interested in a prosaic and unilinear development in his story. He was, rather, aware that an almost alchemical process had been at work in its composition, as he noted in his diary: "how for all, even for the strangest ideas a great fire is prepared, in which they perish and again arise" (*Diaries, 1910-1913* 276). This kaleidoscopic freedom of the images to combine and recombine in the reader's perception is undoubtedly what he had in mind when he insisted to his publisher that the story was "more poem than story . . . more lyric than epic" (*Letters to Friends* 125-26).

Nevertheless, all is not fluid, not even in terms of the oedipal representation. For if we look at the cast of characters in the scene, we find that although they are symbolically telescoped (one is tempted to use Freud's

term *condensed*) into one person, as well as being there in their own behalf, they nonetheless occupy a stage importance commensurate with their importance in the real-life drama. The son is the person most palpably and immediately present: the main perspective on the action is his, just as the oedipal conflict is in the first order a conflict within the son. Kafka seems to have had good reason for initially planning to include the story, along with **"The Stoker"** (from *America*) and **"The Metamorphosis,"** in a volume tentatively to be called *Sons* (*Letters to Friends* 96-97). Confronting the son here is a father who seems somewhat less real than the son himself but who in any case is real enough to be the rival and to emerge as victor and judge in the struggle. This relative unreality is also appropriate, for it is not only the real father who precipitates the oedipal conflict in the son but, equally, the son's image of the father as rival, potential victor, and judge. And the shadowy, symbolic presence of the mother in the text is equally suited to represent her situation in the actual conflict: she is the source of the struggle, the prize to be won, but she need not be physically present; it suffices that her "memory" is alive. Nor is an oedipal drama complete without the child himself. Again, in the conflict situation of the adult Georg Bendemann, the child can be present only symbolically, as representative of the original oedipal situation and, in the present case of an unresolved conflict, as "administrator" of the adult situation.

"Do you know what the final sentence means?" the author asked of Max Brod. "I thought of a strong ejaculation" (Brod, *Biography* 129). Although there is reason to contrast the vital assertiveness of the world in that final sentence with Georg's sexual failure, Kafka probably meant not so much the double entendre of the word *Verkehr* (translated as "traffic" but meaning also "intercourse" in the sexual sense) as he did the precipitous relaxation of tension following on the extraordinary compactness of the preceding scene. That sentence, read as Georg is plunging to his death in the river and after his father has collapsed back onto the bed, is the only one in the story narrated from outside the torments of the oedipal struggle. It is orgasmic and centrifugal, its extreme decompression all the greater in contrast to the compression of the preceding pages. This view is borne out by Kafka's journal entry of the following day: "Only *this way* can one write, only . . . with such complete opening of the body and soul" (*Diaries, 1910-1913* 276). Charles Bernheimer connects Kafka's metaphor of the ejaculation with his later view of the story as having been born of him like an infant "covered with filth and slime" (*Diaries, 1910-1913* 278):

> [T]he ejaculation Kafka associated with the final sentence may have its genesis in the victory he felt his writing act had achieved over the spectre of hostile pa-

ternal narcissism that prevailed in the story's narrative. In the terms in which Kafka metaphorizes his creative process, the feminine experience of release through birth is prior to, and may even trigger, the masculine experience of release through ejaculation. Thus it would seem that, for Kafka, to mother a text is to triumph over that paternal threat of castration which structures the text's signifying function.

(167)

It is gratifying to think of Kafka's resolution of the oedipal situation in this positive light. More immediate to the text, though, is a negative outcome: at the end of the story, there is no one left save the maid, the live woman frozen in fright on the stairs between the two dead oedipal contenders. For dead they both presumably are. Georg's execution of his father's sentence is so powerful that we easily forget the father's fate: "Now he'll lean forward, thought Georg, what if he topples and smashes himself!" (*CS* 86). It seems that precisely this event happens, for when Georg rushes as if pursued from the room, the last thing that he (and the reader) hears of Bendemann Senior is "the crash with which his father fell on the bed behind him" (*CS* 87).

In one painfully utopian passage in *Letter to His Father*, Kafka allows himself to imagine a situation in which both he and his father would overturn their real-life attitudes toward each other, a situation

> so beautiful because then I could be a free, grateful, guiltless, upright son, and you could be an untroubled, untyrannical, sympathetic, contented father. But to this end everything that ever happened would have to be undone, that is, we ourselves should have to be cancelled out.

(115)

The extent to which Kafka's fiction of **"The Judgment"** enacts the sobering realization of that last sentence is truly astonishing: everything that "ever happened" has been, literally, "undone"; the actors themselves have been, literally, "cancelled out." The stage is clear; the set is struck; the house is dark. What remains is the fleetingly envisioned hope for a different play with a less tragic ending, a hope for the unending human movement, over the bridge, to the vernal green of the opposite bank.

Although not everyone agrees with Harold Bloom's appraisal of Sigmund Freud as "the principal writer and the principal thinker of our century," it is difficult to argue against his contention that "we live more than ever in the age of Freud" (*Freud* 1). Many literary critics, however, still object to the psychoanalytic approach as an "extrinsic" method, one essentially foreign to the behests of art and incapable of illuminating the artistic process or of contributing to our aesthetic appreciation of the text. One still hears comments like "[A]n empha-

sis on the oedipal conflict is virtually a psycholiterary cliché. . . . The reader and critic are seduced away from the rich subtleties and cognitive processes within the work" (Lindauer 21). But the latter statement need not be the result of the former, for it is clear from our analysis that by recognizing the oedipal drama underlying the text of **"The Judgment,"** our appreciation of Kafka's enormous artistic economy is enlarged, not diminished. He has brought together all the requisite personnel in mature son, child (memory), father, and mother, and within the narrative he has assigned to each an immediacy and importance commensurate with his or her role in the actual conflict. Kafka has created an unparalleled ambiguity in which Georg's actions apply with equal credibility to child, father, and mother. This scene is aesthetic concentration at its most impressive: the desires for elimination of the father and possession of the mother are ultimately inseparable in the oedipal striving of the child. One can imagine how a lesser writer would have artificially bifurcated these desires by representing them in separate scenes or by putting more actors physically on stage. Thus it seems that our appreciation of the "rich subtleties" of the story is increased when we see it in an oedipal light.

Moreover, the psychoanalytic perspective enables us to recognize that this story, which seems so bizarre, so maverick, and so unique, has venerable literary ancestors all over the world—but especially in the German-language area of Europe. It emerges as nothing less than a variant of the "Godfather Death" tale (Aarne and Thompson, no. 59; see Belmont; Le Roy Ladurie, ch. 14), albeit a variant appropriately peculiar to Kafka, ending as it does not with the protagonist's marriage but with his death.

We gain such insights, it is true, when we bring psychoanalytic theory to bear on the text itself, not on the author or any of the author's fictional characters. In this way, these insights are particularly well suited to complement the perceptions gained through other methods of textual analysis, such as, for example, the application of rhetorical theory to Kafka's works. That perspective has demonstrated well that "the relationships among narrative elements in Kafka's fiction are intimately linked to relationships at the level of the verbal signifier" (Koelb 122). With respect specifically to **"The Judgment,"** Stanley Corngold has argued persuasively that a fundamental aspect of the text is a kind of rhetorical alchemy with the words *Urteil* ("general judgment" *or* "judicial sentence") and *verurteilen* ("to sentence or condemn"): Georg seeks his father's judgment about the letter he has written to his friend, but instead his father sentences him ("ich verurteile dich") to death, so in fact Georg does get an *Urteil*, but it's a sentence instead of a judgment ("Kafka's **'The Judgment'**"). Clayton Koelb has pointed to a specific incident in Kafka's life that may have prepared him for the rhetorical slippage in exactly these words (208-11). "Although it is certainly true that Kafka's pain could have existed in the utter absence of this rhetoric of *Urteile,*" he writes, "it is also true that the particular sort of pain he suffered was formed according to the channels of possibility inherent in the German language" (210). This observation is completely convincing, and it is true that psychoanalysis has had very little to say about style, rhetoric, or the very rhetoricity—the sheer delight in linguistic possibilities—that Koelb has shown as basic to much of Kafka's writing, if not his very incentive and motivation to write. Rhetorical theory has nothing to say, however, about why Kafka's story chooses to exploit the rhetorical possibilities of the word *Urteil* expressly in a context that depends so signally on the properties and cast of the oedipal conflict: judgments and sentences can be about all sorts of things; they don't have to be about fathers, sons, mothers, marriages, and sex. Although the psychoanalytic perspective is not the only fruitful approach that one can adopt toward Kafka's writing, it is apparently capable of insights and explanations that are not within the province of other approaches.

Notes

1. The bibliography of criticism on "The Judgment" is far too extensive to be given even in part here. See Beicken's *Kritische Einführung,* Angel Flores's *Bibliography,* the occasional updates of the literature compiled by Marie Luise Caputo-Mayr and Julius Herz in the *Journal of the Kafka Society of America.*

2. My analysis of the central scene presented here is adapted from that earlier study.

3. I have somewhat emended the translations, here and throughout.

Henry Sussman (essay date 1995)

SOURCE: Sussman, Henry. "The Text That Was Never a Story: Symmetry and Disaster in 'A Country Doctor.'" In *Approaches to Teaching Kafka's Short Fiction,* edited by Richard T. Gray, pp. 123-34. New York: The Modern Language Association of America, 1995.

[*In the following essay, Sussman argues that the structure of "A Country Doctor" creates an extended metaphor, but not a complete story.*]

Although organized, perhaps, by an intense oedipal pain, Kafka's **"A Country Doctor"** never becomes what might be properly called a story. The results are so inconclusive, the characters so blurred as to deny any pretense to narrative cohesion on the part of this brief work. Twice the peasants who receive the doctor's

judgments break out into incantations that, like the music throughout Kafka's writing, exemplified by Josephine's piping, are refrains of fugitive and unfulfilled desire. The doctor may indeed be stripped and placed beside the ailing young patient as the chants exhort, but he is "only a doctor, only a doctor" (*CS* 224). The peasant song, which lends the text the air of an anthropological encounter, declares the limits of its own expectations, as well as those of the patient.

But for all the tale's declared and dramatized inconclusiveness, it is a suggestive allegory of how texts configure themselves. There is no lack of structure here. The text begins and ends in the forbidding winter landscape to which an aging doctor no less harsh and forlorn has been summoned by his vastly inferior clients. The scenic and thematic symmetry of the two scenes constituting the narrative framework is duplicated within the dramatic core. The text dramatizes not one diagnostic scene but two. Only after an initially unsympathetic examination of the sick boy—on the basis of which the doctor concludes that "the boy was quite sound, something a little wrong with his circulation, saturated with coffee by his solicitous mother, but sound"—is the doctor persuaded to admit "that the boy might be ill after all" (*CS* 222, 223). A reexamination, which the doctor undertakes almost whimsically, reveals the extent and nature of the illness as it affects both patient and healer.

At the end of the narrative the doctor sits in the same coach that brought him to his appointment, no longer wearing his coat, perhaps, but facing the same climatic and personal bleakness with which the text began. If anything, the framework and organization of the narrative suggest structure: mirrored endpoints bracketing a doubled scene. And this structural symmetry, at least on the level of the text's widest components, is well suited to the doubling that takes place between characters and that is discussed more fully below. **"A Country Doctor"** is not reticent to admit the place of structure within its own encoding and decoding. Structure, however, does not so much account for or determine the allegory of the text as support or facilitate it. As I show, associations of a far more shifting nature disclose the qualities of this text but within the format that structure provides. The text gathers its resonance at the point where its structure embraces something other, something transformational and anomalous. And here, as throughout Kafka's fiction, the image bonding structure to theme, but precluding the narrative cohesion of a story, is nothing more than a metaphor.

The symmetry that so strikingly frames and colors this story places it in the nexus of Kafka's long-standing interest in doubling—as a narratological, psychological, and even phenomenological feature. Kafka's fascination with doubling, deriving from his most beloved literary sources, among them E. T. A. Hoffmann and Dostoyevsky, transcends the particular uses to which doubling can be put. Kafka began his exploration of this phenomenon in such brief works as **"The Knock on the Manor Gate,"** in which the nearly undefinable guilt of the sister is displaced and irrationally magnified as it rebounds on the brother, and **"A Crossbreed [A Sport],"** in which an uncanny commiseration links the family son to his biologically and logically anomalous legacy. In stories even as late as **"The Burrow,"** Kafka's artistic burrowing rodent projects the image of a predator, his semblable, who stalks him and deprives him of his supplies in the subterranean deep.

The title character in **"A Country Doctor"** finds unlikely doubles in the groom with whom he wages battle over Rose and in the twice-examined, twice-dismissed wounded little boy. The story thus reverberates off Kafka's brief masterpiece of doubling, **"The Judgment,"** which Kafka believed to have been his breakthrough piece of fiction.[1] **"The Judgment"** records and dramatizes the undermining of a son's best-faith narrative of his own achievements, qualities, and prospects by a discourse of the other that turns out to emanate from his uncannily hostile father. The narrative voice is a willing conspirator in this confusion. It subliminally sides with and rationalizes the son's position until the father attacks him—not with heaved apples, as in **"The Metamorphosis,"** but with accusations: that the son tricked the friend in Russia (toward whom he feels condescendingly protective), allowed himself to be seduced by his fiancée, and violated the better interest of the family business.

"The Judgment" resides at a benchmark in the systematicness of the kinds of doubling it entertains. The excruciating dialectical tension between the discourse of the son and the father's debunking cynicism corresponds to the "split consciousness" that for Freud, at the time of Kafka's writing, constituted the very structure of repression (indeed, the vast majority of the manifestations Freud interpreted between 1893 and 1910 were conditions of repression, above all hysteria). In writing so penetratingly on ambivalence, whether Gregor's toward the family that takes his sacrifices so much for granted or the country doctor's toward the groom and the sick boy, Kafka performs Freudian acts of undermining the divisions that segment the divided consciousness. The systematic duplication structuring **"The Judgment"** is narratological and characterological as well. Georg Bendemann watches in horror as the friend in Russia, whom he regards as a subordinate, supplants him as his father's son; indeed, the letters by means of which Georg has attempted to control the relationship are duplicated and disqualified by the counter-correspondence that his father has maintained with his double. With regard to the relentless doubling that structures and informs **"The Judgment," "A Country Doctor"** may well be the countertext sharing the closest affinities.

In the very first episode of **"A Country Doctor,"** we see already the major structural and thematic elements that will serve as a setting for the story's metaphoric transformation. When Rose, the maid who will become the source and object of the doctor's anxiety throughout the text, offers her comment on the scene—"You never know what you're going to find in your own house"—she touches on the narrative's key psychoanalytic and sociological concerns. The well-equipped and generally efficient country doctor—"I had a gig, a light gig with big wheels, exactly right for our country roads"—is in a frustrated rage. He cannot begin a house call to a neighboring village because his horse died the previous night: "Muffled in furs, my bag of instruments in my hand, I was in the courtyard all ready for the journey." The bleak weather in which he waits with impotent anger only reinforces the sense that he is a man without a horse, a man who has lost his horse, or his kingdom for a horse, a victim of his own horse: "but there was no horse to be had, no horse" (*CS* 220).

The motif of psychological repression in this text is reinforced by the dreamlike quality of its movements and transitions. The doctor arrives instantaneously at the remote hamlet he is visiting: "I was already there" (*CS* 221). Just as suddenly, the apparent solutions to his predicament emerge from an abandoned pigsty on his property that he kicks open in his desperation: a man whose open, blue-eyed face is reminiscent of other servants in Kafka's fiction (notably, Barnabas of *The Castle*), and two horses, whose steaming bodies and powerful buttocks evoke a power that contrasts sharply with the doctor's present frailty. The doctor is well conditioned to make optimal use of this unexpected man—and horsepower. He commands Rose to help the groom (*Knecht*) hitch the horses to his wagon (the groom has emerged from the pigsty ready to serve), and he threatens the *Knecht* with whipping when the latter inexorably turns his attentions to Rose. This pugnaciousness turns to anxious despair when it becomes clear to the doctor that Rose is fated to serve the groom's sexual whims, that his own home is to be the setting for the vigorous sexuality figured in the splitting and bursting of the door. The doctor's tormenting vision of the groom's sexual victory over Rose and himself haunts him throughout the text with the force of obsessional thought as Freud defined it.[2] Until the groom declares, "I'm not coming with you anyway, I'm staying with Rose," the doctor has treated her indifferently as "the pretty girl who had lived in [his] house for years almost without [his] noticing her" (*CS* 221, 223). In many senses, then, the narrative's first scene may be said to investigate repression as it operates in psychoanalytic theory. Distinctly sexual beings emerge from a repository on the property, a long-abandoned hiding place. Late-oedipal competition stimulates a previously stunted desire for the girl. The psychological locus of the pigsty is repression in the unconscious.

This first scene is reminiscent of another repression, the sociopolitical sort dramatized and subverted in the section of *Phenomenology of Spirit* that Hegel entitled "Herrschaft und Knechtschaft" ("Lordship and Bondage"; 104-19). The doctor is not oblivious to his bullying and threatening his *Knecht,* even though, as he acknowledges, the groom is "a stranger . . . I did not know where he came from, and . . . of his own free will he was helping me out when everyone else had failed me" (*CS* 221). The groom is described as the sibling of the two horses, which he calls Bruder (Brother) and Schwester (Sister). The groom's conquest of Rose thus completes a series of substitutions set into play by the upheaval of the doctor's authority. The groom's sexual displacement of the doctor results in a deflection of the threatened whipping from the horses to the groom. The ultimate victim in this sequence of power-mongering is Rose, but the narrative, curiously, does not pursue that result.

The quick reversal of the doctor's mastery over his servants signals an ambiguity in characterization. Why does the doctor develop such a sudden, intense attachment to Rose? The contest over her may be between two distinct male characters or, as occurs at other points in Kafka's fiction, may represent a conflict within a single fictive subject, a conflict here between active heterosexual lust and repressive asexuality. More than any other major writer dealing in twentieth-century aesthetics, Kafka exploited the ambiguity between the intra- and intersubjective representations of dramatic interaction.[3] In the context of the intertwining and reversal of roles that will prevail between the doctor and the sick boy, it is perhaps not unreasonable to suggest that the doctor and the *Knecht* also exist as doubles in relation to each other. The doctor's doubling is doubled: he merges with his servants and patients. Doubling in characterization coincides with the doubling already observed in the scenic construction. **"A Country Doctor"** dispenses double medicine, but doubling, as Freud applies it to Hoffmann's tale "The Sandman," is a mark of the uncanny as well as of the familiar.[4] In Kafka's fiction, as in familial relations, it is sometimes difficult to ascertain where one identity begins and another ends. This soft border between fictive subjects becomes a major issue in the doctor's interaction with the peasant family.

For indeed, having arrived instantaneously at his patient's peasant cottage (this immediacy questioning again the status of distance and scale in the narrative), the doctor remains secure in the superiority and authority that have just been battered by the groom's conquest. In deference to the doctor, the patient's sister sets a chair out for his instruments and takes charge of his fur coat. No higher honor does the family pay the doctor than the precious glass of rum the father pours out for him.

Throughout Kafka's fiction siblings are implicated in one another's guilts and torments. The air in the Kafkan familial scene is stifling. Not only can the siblings exchange identities, but the horses get into the act as well, the same horses to which the groom referred as Brother and Sister: "each of them had stuck a head in at a window and, quite unmoved by the startled cries of the family, stood eyeing the patient" (*CS* 222). Throughout **"A Country Doctor,"** but especially in the family setting, identities merge, making totemic distinctions useless. The highly visible horses in this text, at play in every aspect of the country doctor's interaction with the family, belong to a unique category of characters in Kafka's fiction: the mute and reactive figures who do not add to the action but comment on it with their silent gestures.[5] The horses' status as animals in no way impedes their serving this metacritical function. Their siblings in the world of Kafka's writing include K.'s servants, Arthur and Jeremias, in *The Castle*; the astonished villagers in **"The Knock at the Manor Gate"**; and the onlookers who witness Joseph K.'s arrest in *The Trial*.

Yet just as the doctor's mastery is undermined in the opening scene by the groom's (or his own) vibrant sexuality, so too does his encounter with the sick boy dissolve his air of superiority, his clinical detachment, his complacency, and his indifference. Intellectually, the doctor grasps the limits of his position when he thinks, "To write prescriptions is easy, but to come to an understanding with people is hard" (*CS* 223); this formulation, however, is only the weakest form of the lesson that the boy teaches him. During his initial examination of the boy, the doctor vacillates between two postures: contempt for the entire family, buttressed by a kind of self-aggrandizing rationalization, and a compulsive, morbid interest in Rose's current status:

> I am no world reformer and so I let him lie. I was the district doctor and did my duty to the uttermost, to the point where it became almost too much. I was badly paid and yet generous and helpful to the poor. I had still to see that Rose was all right, and then the boy might have his way and I wanted to die too. What was I doing there in that endless winter! My horse was dead, and not a single person in the village would lend me another. I had to get my team out of the pigsty; if they hadn't chanced to be horses I should have had to travel with swine. That was how it was.
>
> (*CS* 222-23)

This passage intertwines the doctor's two roles as aggressor and victim. Having conceded his lack of philanthropic interest, the doctor dramatizes his self-sacrifices to himself in the way that a manipulative parent would attempt to induce guilt in his or her family. The climate is terrible, the pay is not good, he constantly makes concessions to his patients. The humor in the passage is that of uncontrollable self-indulgence. The doctor suggests that if he hadn't found horses to transport him, pigs would have had to do. The doctor thus places himself in the role of a temporary paterfamilias whose bad conscience spurs him on to increasingly outrageous assertions of benevolence. But the doctor's martyrdom would not be real unless he faced some immediate and dire threat. The loss of Rose is not only like death; it is death itself ("I wanted to die"). The form, if not nature, of the doctor's fear is hypochondriacal. What threatens him is not a condition but the self-representation of a condition. It is no accident that he ends up beside his patient. In all this posturing, Kafka does not allow the aggression, bad faith, guiltmongering, and hypochondriacal cries for help to remain implicit: "And I nodded to the family. They knew nothing about it, and, had they known, would not have believed it" (*CS* 223). The doctor protects his posturing by endowing it with the aura of superior knowledge.

Thus far, then, we have a story structured to favor its themes of jealousy, displacement, ambivalence, ambiguity of character, and social conflict. The most prominent themes also lend themselves to interpretation through two readily available models of repression: the psychoanalytic model and the Hegelian undermining of mastery through the more direct relation to material (including words) in labor. Yet only when the doctor, casually and almost by chance, condescends to review his diagnosis does the text crystallize an emblem for its own operation as a text. The text locates its image only as the practitioner concedes some small margin of error. And, just as important, the insignia that the text inscribes upon itself (as the punitive apparatus of **"In the Penal Colony"** writes its sentence on the human body) is the external manifestation of a disease:

> And this time I discovered that the boy was indeed ill. In his right side, near the hip, was an open wound as big as the palm of my hand. Rose-red, in many variations of shade, dark in the hollows, lighter at the edges, softly granulated, with irregular clots of blood, open as a surface mine to the daylight. That was how it looked from a distance. But on a closer inspection there was another complication. I could not help a low whistle of surprise. Worms, as thick and long as my little finger, themselves rose-red and blood-spotted as well, were wriggling from their fastness in the interior of the wound toward the light, with small white heads and many legs. Poor boy, you were past helping. I had discovered your great wound; this blossom in your side was destroying you.
>
> (*CS* 223)

Unapparent during the initial examination, the wound opens itself like a hitherto undisclosed secret, like a groom hiding in a neglected part of one's estate, like the desire for a servant girl that has lain dormant under daily ceremony. The wound announces itself like a secret to the doctor, who discovers it and, as a competent practitioner, examines it both at a distance and in proximity.

Although located on the flank of a local boy, the wound is a metaphor for the secrets that have been disclosed to the doctor about himself. The festering wound, embellished with twisting parasitic worms, is an image of the doctor's own festering sexuality. These worms, for all the revulsion that they might inspire, consummate an intensity of narrative description rare in Kafka's work. Like certain tumors and growths encountered by practicing physicians, the boy's wound radiates a peculiar beauty—in this case, the beauty of vividness.

The wound is a displaced image for the doctor's sexual conflicts. While its color, "Rose," causes some syntactical ambiguity by virtue of its placement at the head of a sentence, the choice of hue relates the wound to the doctor's apparent competition with the groom over Rose. Kafka underscores the incorporation of the source of desire into the wound; he places in relief the inscription of desire as the wound's very nature. The wound is rosy. The doctor describes it explicitly as a flower in the boy's side. The bloody worms have white heads. They thrive on red fluid but are themselves consumptive. In different ways, the doctor and patient are both consumed.

The wound is the flower of desire. Desire here, as in Proust, is a disease. The boy, because he is affected with the festering wound of the doctor's desire, is the doctor's unlikely double. The bystanders are thus not being provincial when they place the two in the same bed, when they connect the doctor to his disease by means of metonymic contiguity. An aging man and an adolescent boy share a longing-sickness.

In the course of the story, then, the doctor is twice doubled, first in relation to the surprising groom, then with the sick boy. The image of the wound is both the mark and the agent of this doubling. It is that which connects the doubled framework to the doubled scene of medical speculation. The wound takes Rose out of the narrative's external shell, where she appears as a semiautonomous bone of contention, and internalizes her within a scene of subjective ambivalence. As Rose passes from exteriority to interiority, so too does the narrative as a linguistic wound fold on and consume itself. This text structures a desire for the resolution between its outside and inside, between its structure and its material. And the binding that it offers for its conflicts is the image of a wound. But a wound is traumatized tissue; it is the locus where the body capitulates to rather than resists dismemberment.

By virtue of its bruised texture, **"A Country Doctor"** may be taken as an instance of that weak cohesion that characterizes a literary work. It demonstrates that what binds texts need not be as tangible as themes, as abstract as ideas, or as systematic as logical schemes. The somewhat crumbly coherence of this text concentrates around the signifier rose, which functions simultaneously as the name of a character, the color of a wound, and the name and color of a flower. The character, wound, and color are depicted within the text's representational field, while the flower hovers beyond the textual margins as a metaphoric icon, insignia, caption, or shorthand for the narrative's "events." The boy's wound becomes allegorical of the text because of the shifting permitted, even solicited, by rose. Rose marks the spot, precisely, where the text's dramatic scenario, structure, semantics, and thematic underpinnings intertwine. By closely implicating a persona, Rose, within the metaphoric economy of a text, Kafka comes as close as any author has to admitting the semiological rather than substantive nature of fictive "characters." Characters do not exist (or even act) so much as play within an ultimately deranged exchange of positions demarcated by Hegel as the speculative limit of the notion of force. They gather and abandon meaning in texts as signifiers pursue chains of displacement in the Lacanian imaginary (see Lacan, *Ecrits* 146-78; *Fundamental Concepts* 42-52).

The overdetermination of the role of rose within the text helps account for the pronounced duplicity of the characterization and thematics. The self-referentiality dramatized by this signifier also serves as a precedent for the allegory of parasitism. A consumptive boy devoured by consumptive worms is a narrative representation of a metaphor that can both consume and fragment itself.

The boy is indeed correct, then, when he asserts, "A fine wound is all I brought into the world; that was my sole endowment" (*CS* 225). For this brief work as well as for the sick character, a wound constitutes the total equipment and production. The wound in the work as well as in the boy constitutes the fissure in the Möbius strip describing the text's configuration. Crowned by a rose, the wound is the site where the text endlessly folds and feeds on itself.

It is therefore no accident that any departure from this domain must be abrupt and arbitrary. If the narrative framework results in an unresolved conflict over a woman between the doctor and his double, then in the core of the text the doctor's link to his second double, the sick boy, is ultimately complicitous:

> "Do you know," said a voice in my ear, "I have very little confidence in you. Why, you were only blown in here, you didn't come on your feet. Instead of helping me, you're cramping me on my deathbed. What I'd like best is to scratch your eyes out." "Right," I said, "it is a shame. And yet I am a doctor. What am I to do? Believe me, it is not too easy for me either." "Am I supposed to be content with this apology?" . . . "My young friend," said I, "your mistake is: you have not a wide enough view . . . and I tell you: your wound is

> not so bad. Done in a tight corner with two strokes of the ax. Many a one proffers his side and can hardly hear the ax in the forest, far less that it is coming nearer to him." "Is that really so, or are you deluding me in my fever?" "It is really so, take the word of honor of an official doctor." And he took it and lay still.

> (*CS* 224-25)

As this consultation commences, the boy has no confidence in the doctor, and the latter shows no sign of deviating from his general contempt for the surroundings. By the end of the interchange, the practitioner has been roused out of his indifference and the patient is calm, reassured, and perhaps prepared for death. The motive for this double reversal of positions may well come from the potentials offered by the ax and its relation to the image of the wound. If the wound figures the ambiguous textual intertwining afforded by the movement of the shifter between structural, thematic, and semantic levels, the ax promises release from the uncertainty by the excision of the function that loosens while it binds. A wound is all the text brings into the world to hold itself together, yet precisely as a function of textuality, the wound marks the side of repression, desire, and internal and external conflict. It delimits the extent of life with surgical precision.

At the end of **"A Crossbreed [A Sport],"** both the marginal kitten-lamb and the narrator, the son for whom the creature and its intellectual conditions are an inescapable legacy, eye the butcher's knife as a possible escape from their despair. The execution of Joseph K. in *The Trial* may be described as the application of a penetrating instrument to the victim after it has playfully shuttled back and forth between the henchmen. In **"A Country Doctor"** as well, a sharp blade holds out the promise of resolution and acquires the thrust of a poignant wish. A double blow of the ax in a tight corner can free the patient from his inherited mark of Cain. Only in conceptually offering this instrument does the country doctor serve as a healer. The prescribed treatment involves, however, not a regeneration of tissue but an amputation. Two decisive strokes of an ax can release the prisoner from his double bind, can free him, perhaps, from the narrow path on which Oedipus meets his father. The ax strikes outward, beyond the confines of a constricting familial space, but, to complete its task, also strikes inward, penetrating the superficial layers of the flesh.

The image of the ax is the sum total of the country doctor's reassurance. The wound is not so severe ("übel"): done ("geschaffen") "with two strokes of the ax," both dispatched and created by the healing-incising ax. The ax is a messiah (or avenging angel) of resolution. Those who offer their sides to it, in reverence, may not hear it in the forest, but eventually its work is done, silently and implicitly ("geschweige"). The silent ax in the forest recalls the falling tree whose status is so crucial to ontology and to the hypothetical status of God. The ax, were there only an ax, would clarify, resolve, amputate, the duplicity and ambiguity whose locus is language and whose form is that of a congenital wound. But the closure provided by the ax may still be described only in terms of inscription: incision, marking, scarring. The poignant wish for a termination of involution and complexity is expressed by several of Kafka's characters; it hovers at the horizon in much of his fiction. This end-wish or wish to end wishes can be articulated only in writing, through the textual economy that writing both promises and renders bankrupt. The ax is only one moment of the wound that is both the flower and disease of writing.

The mere invocation of the ax is sufficient to release the patient from his tension. To terminate a text whose insignia assumes the form of a Möbius strip is, however, not so simple. The country doctor's exit from the narrative stage necessarily takes the form of a desperate escape. Only the fall of an ax can truncate this text. Like his arrival at the patient's house—"as if my patient's farmyard had opened out just before ["unmittelbar"] my courtyard gate, I was already there" (*CS* 221)—the doctor's departure is abrupt. These movements are as sudden as the shifts of location that Freud finds characteristic of dreams, but the doctor's concerns are hardly dreamlike. The narrative ends as the doctor helplessly reaches for his fur coat at the back of his gig. He remains naked, having been stripped by the peasants and placed in bed next to his patient. He despairs of ever reaching home, fears seeing his medical practice collapse as he is usurped by a successor—and, of course, he despairs at the sacrifice of Rose and at the groom's successful rage. "Betrayed! Betrayed!" moans the doctor as the text ends. "A false alarm on the night bell once answered—it cannot be made good, not ever" (*CS* 225). The betrayal that the country doctor suffers is systematic and not merely sexual. Events are simply out of control. The arbitrary truncation of this text is merely one further manifestation of the loss of control that it has embellished. The losses and concerns that the text dramatizes are not to be recuperated. Betrayal cannot be undone. The "false alarms" that will disturb the doctor's sleep forever are the tones of absence whose textual manifestation is the figure of a wound.

Related contrapuntally to the rhythm of the eruption and amputation of ambiguity that may in fact constitute this text's only story is the music that twice breaks forth from the peasants. Although the text provides some psychosocial context for this singing, its very outbreak in the text possesses a shock value that cannot be reduced or assimilated. The peasants' incantations shift the narrative's setting to a world of primitive, obsessive, and ritualistic thought.

A school choir with the teacher at the head of it stood before the house and sang these words to an utterly simple tune:

> "Strip his clothes off, then he'll heal us,
> If he doesn't, kill him dead!
> Only a doctor, only a doctor."

(*CS* 224)

The performative dimension of this chant consists of two imperatives and a judgment. The logic of the exhortations is the simple causality characteristic of infantile obsession. The stripping of the doctor is the initial phase of a sacrificial act. If we prepare the doctor for sacrifice, the logic runs, he will spare our martyr. If this effort fails, we will sacrifice him. The narrative rationalizes the singing in terms of the sociopolitical wish it expresses: to cut the doctor down to size, to strip him, literally, of his authority and paternalism. The song's prescriptions intertwine him with the boy. The doctor will suffer what he fails to cure. Because the doctor has been inscribed within the peasants' obsessive reasoning, the outcome of the boy's case is already fated to be his own condition. The peasant's final incantation celebrates the events that the initial one announces and, with inexorable logic, fulfills: "O be joyful, all you patients, / The doctor's laid in bed beside you" (*CS* 225).

The music in the text not only intensifies the arbitrariness of its events but also breaks free of the thematic networks that would seem to reinforce a sense of cohesion. The gestures celebrated by the music are precisely arbitrary: command, soothsaying, judgment, exaltation. The incantations become a counterpoint of arbitrariness arising from the text but then floating above it with impunity, only tangentially related. The music hovers above the text as the doorbell tone floats beyond the confining domestic setting of "A Fratricide," "right over the town and up to heaven" (*CS* 403). In Kafka's fiction music diacritically annotates the directional aspirations of his writing. Though of the text, the music hovers above it, uncommitted to the apparent trends in which the thematic level has invested. Music underscores the constitutive role played by the metaphor in Kafka's writing: a fleeting refrain that sings of the difference between texts and stories.

Notes

1. In *Diaries, 1910-1913* Kafka writes of "[t]he fearful strain and joy, how the story developed before me, as if I were advancing over water. . . . How everything can be said, how for everything, for the strangest fancies, there awaits a great fire in which they perish and rise up again" (276).

2. A good general introduction to Freud's thought regarding obsessional ideas is to be found in the theoretical section of the "Rat Man" case history (*Standard Edition* 10: 221-49).

3. This ambiguity in characterization may be said to structure such major works as "Description of a Struggle" and "A Hunger Artist." Kafka rehearses its potentials in "First Sorrow." For a full treatment of "Description of a Struggle" as an exercise in scenic construction based on a play between intersubjective and intrasubjective conflict, see Sussman 61-74.

4. Freud develops his notion of the uncanny in a 1919 essay, "The 'Uncanny,'" whose major instance of this phenomenon derives from E. T. A. Hoffmann's "Sandman." Initially, Freud situates the uncanny at the end of primary narcissism, when a child's self-image of benevolent omnipotence is partially eclipsed by its opposite. Freud realizes, however, the inadequacy of a developmental explanation in accounting for the full literary potentials of doubling (*Standard Edition* 17: 232-45).

5. Of all critics, Walter Benjamin provides the best account of the allegorical gestic language in Kafka's fiction, an illustration of his broader notion of shock. For a discussion of Kafka's gestic language, see Benjamin, "Franz Kafka."

Kurt Fickert (essay date fall 1996)

SOURCE: Fickert, Kurt. "An Epiphany in 'Vor dem Gesetz.'?" *Germanic Notes and Reviews* 27, no. 2 (fall 1996): 97-101.

[*In the following essay, Fickert analyzes "Vor dem Gesetz," part of* Der Prozess.]

With some notable exceptions (see below) critics analyzing Kafka's brief prose piece **"Vor dem Gesetz"** have been inclined to neglect its appearance as an independent work while they emphasize the key role the same text plays as a part of the novel *Der Prozeß*.[1] Since Kafka obviously intended **"Vor dem Gesetz"** to have a unique and therefore significant place among the works he held to be publishable and never even contemplated seeing it in print as it had come into being, namely as a spoken passage written for a crucial scene in his (unfinished) manuscript, a close reading of the text which Kafka prepared for publication seems appropriate. The title attests to the legendary character of the tale, for it confronts the reader with the physical presence of an abstraction. **"The Law"** exists, first of all, as a place to be scrutinized, much as one would scrutinize the words one encounters on the printed page. Secondly, the first sentence in the story conjures up a figure who stands in the way of a clear view of the object in sight, with his back to it. He is identified as a doorkeeper, although it remains to be established—and, in

the long run, never is—that the structure (cf. another of Kafka's titles, **"Der Bau,"** which exists as empty space) can be entered or exited through a door. The text immediately identifies the entryway as a "Tor," which suggests a gate or portal, and only at one point, a climactic one, uses the word *Türe* (sic). Nevertheless, the doorkeeper as a term signifying the guardian of access into **"The Law"** dominates the text; *Türhüter* occurs seventeen times (plus a related *dieser*) on the one page or so that encompasses the entire story.

It soon becomes apparent to the reader that the importance assigned to the character of the doorkeeper by the narrator reflects the significance this lowly porter has for the story's protagonist, the third aspect of the triangular basis (narrator—protagonist—doorkeeper) on which the text rests. This "man from the country" is not as unsophisticated as one might infer from this description, for he does not come to his encounter with the law unaware and unprepared: "er (hat) sich für seine Reise mit vielem ausgerüstet."[2] But the kind of foresight he has exhibited has not provided him with the means to deal with the barrier of the doorkeeper's presence. Although the narrator places this character *outside* the law, the doorkeeper immediately makes use of the authority granted him by way of his having been designated as one of the law's functionaries even before the arrival of the man from the country on the scene. By allowing the storyteller to take command of the text in the beginning and thus report: "Zu diesem Türhüter kommt ein Mann vom Lande und bittet um Eintritt in das Gesetz" (120), Kafka has precluded the reader's questioning of *how* the unlearned man from the country could be expected to have anticipated the presence of the doorkeeper and of *why* it would have occurred to this adventuresome man to ask a doorman for permission to enter in the law. As soon as the doorkeeper begins his unmotivated bedeviling of the stranger with a series of meretricious responses and actions (e.g., providing a stool for the man to sit on), the narrator gives way in his storytelling to his protagonist, whose fate now becomes the center of the reader's attention. The shift in perspective is indicated by the inclusion in the text of the man from the country's thinking: "Solche Schwierigkeiten hat der Mann vom Lande nicht erwartet; das Gesetz soll doch jedem und immer zugänglich sein, denkt er . . ." (120).[3]

With the words "Dort sitzt er (der Mann vom Lande) Tage und Jahre" (121), the narrator begins his exposition of the relationship which develops between the protagonist and his "adversary." The length of time involved in their mutually shared interest in admission into the law—a lifetime—sheds some light on the nature of the law itself. It represents under these circumstances a goal, perhaps the attainment of true insight into the human condition, which is irrefutably beyond the reach of those whose live with the knowledge that their lives are foreshortened by their mortality. Thus, the man from the country becomes not only the prototypal protagonist in Kafka's work[4] but also the symbol of the predicament of all human kind.[5] Because **"Vor dem Gesetz"** in its brief compass and with its powerful imagery opens up to exploration the vast unknown within whose confines human life exists, it has garnered many an accolade from critics; Ritchie Robertson has called it "the supreme moment in Kafka's writing."[6] The subtlety of the text in depicting both the central issue of admittance to the law and the viewpoints in this regard of the contending figures of the doorkeeper and the man from the country attests to Kafka's literary craftmanship; he portrays the characters and their thinking by interweaving terse narration and trenchant dialogue. In this fashion the doorkeeper shows himself to be as intimidated by the law as his vis-à-vis is. He reveals that he has had only a tentative relationship with this construct, confessing that the sight of the third (rank of) doorkeeper has overawed him. The thrust of this remark indicates both that his knowledge of the law is scant, almost as wanting as that of the man from the country, and that therefore he can sympathize with the petitioner for admittance, whom he, moreover, has no power to turn away. Another and certainly more significant aspect of his lack of authority involves his assignment as doorkeeper, for this position, his right to which is never authenticated, requires him to play a subordinate role to that of the protagonist. It is clear that the doorkeeper can only react, and then in a limited way, to whatever the man from the country says or does. In addition, the doorkeeper concedes, in a final moment of rebellion, that the entrance he has had the task of guarding has existed for the sake of the man from the country alone; because the owner had made no use of the gate, he must now fulfill the last obligation he has to the law and close it.

The interdependency of the man and the doorkeeper can but suggest to the reader the possibility or probability that the one is but an extention of the other, in effect, the doorkeeper, originally conjured up by the narrator together with the instance of the law which gives him validity, externalizes the protagonist's inner doubts about the meaningfulness of his mission to acquire self-knowledge by breaching the barrier of the guarded doorway. The "not now" uttered by the doorkeeper on the occasion of the man's first attempt to cross the void between the self and the infinite gives expression to the trepidation experienced by the protagonist. Nagel has evaluated the situation in a similar way: "So wird z.B. der Türhüter—an sich eine reine Abstraktion, nämlich die Personalisierung der subalternen, aber raumgreifenden Schwierigkeiten und Hindernisse im Leben des Mannes vom Lande—als eine konkret menschliche Figur vor Augen gestellt. . . ."[7] The narrator, who as the agent of the implied author has fashioned the two characters as well as the contention between them, un-

derscores and ridicules the extreme nature of the man from the country's timidity by depicting his nonsensical behavior in appealing to the fleas in the doorkeeper's fur coat collar for their sympathy. I would also propose that the factor of the man's falling under the spell of the doorkeeper because he has a theatrical appearance—a big, pointed nose, a thin black straggly beard, a fur coat, smacks of satire. Perhaps the principal feature in the story by which the narrator undermines the protagonist's judgment and wisdom concerns the man's failure to seize the moment, to declare his triumph over the doorkeeper, on two occasions. The first occurs at the beginning of his stay outside the portal, the second at the very end. The narrator takes note of this occurrence at the time of the protagonist's arrival on the scene: "Da das Tor zum Gesetz offensteht wie immer und der Türhüter beiseite tritt, *bückt sich* der Mann, um durch das Tor in das Innere zu sehn" (120, my emphasis). Indicating that the protagonist is at the height of his control over the circumstances—he momentarily dominates the scene—and has looked into the nothingness which is the law, the narrator nevertheless allows him to be persuaded by the doorkeeper's tirade to withdraw. The second instance of neartriumph is almost a reversal of the first; near death, the man has, shrunken to a whisk and is almost blind. The storyteller relates: "Er weiß nicht, ob es um ihn wirklich dunkler wird, oder ob ihn nur seine Augen täuschen. Wohl aber erkennt er jetzt im Dunkel einen Glanz, der unverlöschlich aus der Türe des Gesetzes bricht" (121). The use of the indicative verb forms in the latter sentence attests to the reality of his experience: he has seen the mystic glow which characterizes the eternal, and, having seen it, he dies.

The light of eternity or God, which is depicted in Jewish sacred texts as "d(ie) Glorie, d(er) groß(e) Glanz,"[8] represents insight into the nature of human beings who have a brief existence in the physical world while their consciousness (rooted in their individuality) provides them with intimations of immortality. Kafka's text in the case of **"Vor dem Gesetz"** and in many other instances portrays his protagonist (who mirrors the real author) as experiencing a flawed epiphany; the man from the country finds himself on the point of achieving true insight. He dies before he can say "eureka." In like fashion, the journey of the country doctor ends in limbo, and the dying inmates of the penal colony can only briefly sense, yet never know the reason for their death sentence. At this point I can but digress from my topic of interpreting **"Vor dem Gesetz"** without reference to *Der Prozeß* in order to give another, most relevant example of the flawed epiphany in Kafka's work. The doomed Josef K.'s all but last visual perception is that of a window being opened in a distant house ("wie ein Licht aufzuck[end]")[9] to allow a figure to lean out, arms outstretched. K. has no time left to sort out the meaning of this vision.[10] As Jacques Derrida has pointed out in his renowned interpretation of the legend of the doorkeeper and the man from the country, which is based on that text alone without specific reference to its function as a part of *Der Prozeß,* such associations must be considered tentative at best, if not patently specious. Derrida maintains: "The récit **'Before the Law'** does not tell or describe anything but itself as text."[11] In this light Derrida distinguishes between **"Vor dem Gesetz"** and the recitation of the legend, undertaken, together with an explanation, by the prison chaplain in the penultimate chapter of *Der Prozeß.* "From the point of view of literature," Derrida notes, "the same content gives rise to an entirely different work."[12] With a view to this distinction, which is logically valid, an interpretation of the legend can but begin and end with an evaluation of the scene set in the entryway to the law. Furthermore, it cannot be assumed that that concept (the law) may refer to something other than itself. The law exists only as a relationship (a conflict) between the man from the country and the doorkeeper.[13] Guided by the hand of the narrator (a creation of the implied author), the implied (or ideal) reader, that is, the one considered by the author to have the capacity to follow his train of thought most adroitly, is led to accept the point of view espoused by the protagonist. This man from the country finds himself thwarted in his endeavor to reach a goal by giving way to inner doubts—largely the threat of failure—represented as the inhibitions imposed on him by a laughably pompous bogy-man. The purport of the story would seem to be, considering the man from the country's twice enacted surrender on the point of victory, to provide the reader with a cautionary message: "Hier konnte niemand sonst Einlaß erhalten, denn dieser Eingang war nur für dich bestimmt" (121). With this statement the implied author identifies the unraveling of the meaning of his text as a goal set for his readers which they must keep on pursuing.

Notes

1. "Vor dem Gesetz" was first published in the periodical *Selbstwehr* in the issue of September 7, 1915. It next appeared in the book *Vom jüngsten Tag. Ein Almanach neuer Dichtung,* published by Kurt Wolff in 1916. In 1919 it became a part of a collection of short fiction, titled *Ein Landarzt,* with the same publisher.

2. Franz Kafka, *Erzählungen* (Frankfurt am Main: Fischer, 1976), 121. Further references to this text will appear in parentheses in my article.

3. Compare this thought of the man from the country with the assertion made earlier by the narrator: "Da das Tor zum Gesetz offensteht *wie immer* und der Türhüter beiseite tritt, bückt sich der Mann, um durch das Tor in das Innere zu sehn" (120, my emphasis).

4. See Bert Nagel, *Franz Kafka* (Berlin: Erich Schmidt, 1974), 214: "Der Mann vom Lande . . . ist der Prototyp des Kafkaschen Helden überhaupt."

5. See ibid., 224:"Die Parabel endet also mit der pessimistischen Feststellung, daß keiner sein Ziel erreicht, daß Scheitern unausweichlich ist, weil Schuld und Irrtum zu spät erkannt werden und erst im Strafakt des Gerichts der Mensch zur Einsicht in sich selbst gelangt." In reference to what I call the predicament of all human kind, I would not concur with Nagel's reading insofar as it suggests that Kafka considered death to be a punishment (Strafakt) for mortality; to my mind, Kafka's symbolism does not preclude a reading which would hold death to be, in essence, a consequence of mortality. In his aphorisms Kafka has proposed that the explusion from Eden is a misapprehension.

6. Ritchie Robertson, *Kafka: Judaism, Politics, and Literature* (Oxford: Clarendon Press, 1985), 122.

7. Nagel, *Franz Kafka,* 235.

8. See Werner Hoffmann, "Die Kabbala" in *Kafka-Handbuch II* (Stuttgart: Alfred Kröner, 1979), 491.

9. Franz Kafka, *Der Prozeß* (Frankurt am Main: Fischer, 1976), 194.

10. In his discussion of *Der Prozeß,* Richard Lawson raises the question of whether or not Josef K. experiences an epiphany in his last moments and reaches this conclusion: »Then does he experience an epiphany in "The End"? I find it difficult to be convinced of much development, but on the eve of his thirty-first birthday, K. does seem to experience a partial or qualified epiphany,« Richard H. Lawson, *Franz Kafka* (New York: Ungar, 1987), 82.

11. Jacques Derrida, "Devant la Loi" in *Kafka and the Contemporary Critical Performance,* ed. Alan Udoff (Bloomington and Indianapolis: Indiana University Press, 1987), 144. The translation is by Avital Ronell.

12. Ibid., 146.

13. In his article, "Before the Question of the Laws: Kafkan Reflections" in *Kafka and the Contemporary Critical Performance,* Alan Udoff also characterizes the distinct nature of the text as it appears independently and as a part of the novel: "The man from the country, the doorkeeper, and the writings which recount their tale are *before the Law*; K., the Priest, and the commentators are *before the scriptural text*" (204).

Martin Wasserman (essay date spring 1997)

SOURCE: Wasserman, Martin. "Kafka's 'The Animal in the Synagogue': His Marten as a Special Biblical Memory." *Studies in Short Fiction* 34, no. 2 (spring 1997): 241-45.

[*In the following essay, Wasserman posits that the marten-like character in "The Animal in the Synagogue" symbolizes the female prophet Huldah.*]

Exploring the identity of Kafka's marten-like creature in his story, **"The Animal in the Synagogue,"** Marthe Robert speculated that it should be viewed as the memory of something sacred (113-14). Elaborating on Robert's conjecture, I would argue that the marten specifically symbolized the female prophet, Huldah.[1]

Kafka probably wrote **"The Animal in the Synagogue"** in 1923,[2] when he had become quite competent in his understanding of Hebrew. One of his teachers, Jiri Langer—who had been a member of the Hasidic sect and thus would have been highly proficient in Hebrew—said of his student: "Yes, Kafka spoke Hebrew. We always spoke Hebrew in the last times we had together. . . . Unlike the other Prague Zionists, he was speaking fluently" (Oppenheimer 303). Kafka's sound comprehension of his newfound language makes it reasonable to assume that he knew that the Hebrew word, *Huldah,* meant "marten."[3] That Kafka would use his knowledge of Hebrew when writing **"The Animal in the Synagogue"** also seems reasonable if one takes into account his similar approach with *The Castle,* completed only a year earlier. Here, too, he used specific German words in such a way that they took on deeper biblical meanings when translated into Hebrew (Beck 198; Robertson 228).

The storyline of **"The Animal in the Synagogue"** appears, on first glance, quite fantastic. An animal resembling a marten, but blue-green in color, frightens the women in the synagogue by its movements on the latticework above them. The men, on the other hand, have learned to ignore the marten, although they are periodically angered by its actions. When not near the women, the marten climbs down to the curtain of the Ark of the Covenant and hangs from a shining brass rod. The synagogue itself, where the marten has roamed freely for years, is in a state of disrepair, and the marten senses that in the future something terrible might happen to its congregants. The story ends with the beadle's reminiscence of his grandfather's plans to drive the marten out. However, this desire is never translated into action, as Kafka abruptly breaks off his narrative with ellipsis points.[4]

The events in **"The Animal in the Synagogue"** closely approximate much of the available traditions regarding Huldah. Kafka would have had access to this informa-tion either in the his own books on Judaism or those in the library at the *Hochschule für die Wissenschaft des Judentums* (Academy for the Study of Judaism) in Berlin, an institute that trained rabbis and Jewish scholars, and that Kafka had attended in 1923—the same year he apparently wrote **"The Animal in the Synagogue."** Kafka's marten may therefore reasonably be examined with this background in mind.[5]

Examining Kafka's story, one could explain the normally dark brown marten's blue-green appearance in terms of ancient blue-green dye, *tekhalet,* used by both men and women in the kingdom of Judah to dye the fringes of their garments (*Encyclopedia Judaica* 15: 913, 16:1187). This blue-green *tekhalet* would be a particularly appropriate color in Huldah's case because of the seventh century BCE belief that it could bring an individual closer to the "throne of glory." Huldah, as a Mosaic prophet, was recognized as capable of intercession with Yahweh and, thus, would have had a special interest in wearing garments died with *tekhalet* (Wilson 220).

In **"The Animal in the Synagogue,"** Kafka's marten usually stays near the female congregants, communicating through movements that tended to frighten them. These activities would be compatible with Huldah's role, which, in biblical times, would have been to urge women to follow the Mosaic Law they had heard during services (*Jewish Encyclopedia* 6: 488), a task she accomplished by scolding those deviating from Mosaic Law, strongly exhorting them to repent their transgressions. Huldah's threatening approach is reputed to have produced great fear in its hearers (Wilson 221). Huldah and the marten's respective communication with women differs only in that Huldah used words, whereas the marten uses gesture and action.

In Kafka's story, the men's attitude of generally ignoring the marten resembles the traditional male response to Huldah in matters related to religious practice in the First Temple.[6] As a woman, Huldah could function neither as a priest (*Kohen*) nor as an assistant priest (*Levite*), and was therefore ineligible to conduct worship services. Her role in organized worship would have been limited to secondary activities out of view of the male congregants (Shulman 1: 450).

In **"The Animal in the Synagogue,"** the marten, when not at its favorite haunt near the women, situated itself near the Ark of the Covenant, which was a repository for the scrolls containing Mosaic Law. This close connection to Mosaic Law would have made sense for Huldah as well, because, although not allowed to conduct services in the First Temple, she taught Mosaic Law at her schoolhouse in Jerusalem (*Jewish Encyclopedia* 6: 488).

Kafka's narrative describes a synagogue as in a slow state of deterioration, much like that of the First Temple, which was in such a state during most of Huldah's life-time (Wilson 219). Indeed, the great edifice had become so run down that extensive repairs were required during the reign of King Josiah.[7]

Kafka's marten senses that something tragic might happen to the synagogue's congregants: as Kafka expresses it, the marten's terror could be viewed as a "premonition of times to come" (*Parables* 57). Huldah similarly sensed terror when presented a sacred Law Book discovered during the First Temple's restoration. Realizing that the people of Judah had not been obeying the book's dictates, Huldah prophesied that great evil would befall them. This evil is generally taken to have referred to Jerusalem's fall to the Babylonians in 587 BCE, along with the destruction of the First Temple and the exile of almost every important Jewish official (Sawyer 80).

Kafka ends his narrative with the reminiscence about the plans of the beadle's grandfather—also a beadle—to drive away the marten. However, as soon as these plans are stated, the story ends in ellipsis points. This literally elliptical conclusion suggests that neither the beadle nor the marten were defeated: the beadle's position continues through his grandson, and the marten still roams freely throughout the synagogue (Bruce 459). The story's ending suggests another connection to Huldah in her prophetic teaching that individual adversaries who struggle within the synagogue would eventually gain the strength and resolve to guarantee protection from enemies *outside* the synagogue (Bruce 454-55). On this score, the outcome of Huldah's prophecy was neither the destruction of the Jewish people nor eradication of her legacy by the Babylonian conquerors. The future brought not an end to the kingdom of Judah, but, instead, a return of the exiled leaders' grandchildren and the rebuilding of Jerusalem's Second Temple (Sawyer 80).[8] Once again congregants could practice their traditional religion, using an entrance gate that, a century before, had stood in front of the schoolhouse in which Huldah had taught Mosaic Law (*Encyclopedia Judaica* 8: 1063).

In his diaries Kafka described himself as "a memory come alive" (*Memory* 203). Expanding on this description, Harold Bloom characterizes Kafka's works as "a Jewish memory come alive" (15). Such is the case with **"The Animal in the Synagogue,"** in which the memory of the biblical prophet, Huldah, comes alive. Kafka chose the narrative's marten-like creature to symbolize the life of this unique woman and prophet.

Notes

1. Although the dates of Huldah's birth and death are unknown, most of her accomplishments are believed to have coincided with the lifetime of King Josiah (seventh century BCE; Wollman-Tsamir 102, 157).

2. As is the case with many of Kafka's works, it is difficult to establish the precise time of the composition of "Animal in the Synagogue." Kafka's lifelong friend and the executor of his estate, Max Brod puts the date in 1923: he had found this story immediately following "A Hunger Artist" in the same notebook. Brod knew that "Hunger Artist" had been written in 1923 (Kafka, *Dearest Father* 407).

3. See *Webster's New World Hebrew Dictionary* for an English definition of Huldah (651). Kafka wrote in German, in the Hebrew *Huldah* means *Marders* (marten), which was precisely the word Kafka uses in the story.

4. A bilingual text of "Animal in the Synagogue" was published in the 1961 Schocken edition of *Parables and Paradoxes* (48-59).

5. Kafka owned over sixty books and articles on Judaism (Bruce 490-93), including the Old Testament and Old Testament commentaries by the French Talmudic and scriptural scholar, Rashi. Also, although Kafka did not own Jakob Fromer's book on tractates of the *Babylonian Talmud* (a work containing information on Huldah), he indicated that he had read it (Bruce 105, 208-09). Finally, the library of the *Hochschule für die Wissenschaft des Judentums* possessed copies of the *Pesikta Rabbati* and the *Tarqum Jonathon to the Prophets,* both of which include material on Huldah. I am indebted to Diane Spielmann, Public Services and Development Coordinator of the Leo Baeck Institute (New York City), who provided information of the *Hochscule*'s holdings circa 1923.

6. The First Temple in Jerusalem was the major house of worship in the Kingdom of Judah from 950-587 BCE (Gribetz 13, 25).

7. Josiah ruled as King of Judah from 640-609 BCE (Wollman-Tsamir 102).

8. The Second Temple was fully reconstructed and able to receive worshipers in 515 BCE (Gribetz 28).

Works Cited

Beck, Evelyn. *Kafka and the Yiddish Theater: Its Impact on His Work.* Madison: U of Wisconsin P, 1971.

Bloom, Harold. *Franz Kafka.* New York: Chelsea, 1986.

Bruce, Iris M. *A Life of Metamorphosis: Franz Kafka and the Jewish Tradition.* Diss., U of Toronto, 1980. Ann Arbor, Michigan: UMI, 1992. 65968.

Encyclopedia Judaica. 16 vols. Jerusalem: Keter, 1971.

Gribetz, Judah. *The Timetables of Jewish History.* New York: Simon, 1993.

Jewish Encyclopedia. 12 vols. New York: Funk & Wagnalls, 1972.

Kafka, Franz. *Dearest Father.* New York: Schocken, 1954.

—. *I Am a Memory Come Alive.* New York: Schocken, 1974.

—. *Parables and Paradoxes.* New York: Schocken, 1961.

Oppenheimer, Anne. *Franz Kafka's Relation to Judaism.* Diss., Oxford U, 1977.

Robert, Marthe. "Zu Franz Kafka's Fragment 'In unsere Synagogue.'" *Merkur* 2 (1948): 113-14.

Robertson, Ritchie. *Kafka: Judaism, Politics, and Literature.* New York: Oxford UP, 1985.

Sawyer, John F. A. *Prophecy and the Biblical Prophets.* New York: Oxford UP, 1993.

Shulman, Albert M. *Gateway to Judaism.* 2 vols. S. Brunswick, NJ: Thomas Yoseloff, 1971.

Webster's New World Hebrew Dictionary. New York: Prentice, 1992.

Wilson, Robert R. *Prophecy and Society in Ancient Israel.* Philadelphia: Fortress, 1980.

Wollman-Tsamir, Pinchas. *The Graphic History of the Jewish Heritage.* New York: Shengold, 1963.

Michael P. Ryan (essay date spring 1999)

SOURCE: Ryan, Michael P. "Samsa and *Samsara*: Suffering, Death, and Rebirth in 'The Metamorphosis.'" *The German Quarterly* 72, no. 2 (spring 1999): 133-52.

[*In the following essay, Ryan utilizes the eastern philosophy Samsara to explore suffering, death, and rebirth in "The Metamorphosis," and ultimately offers a new interpretation of it.*]

The variety of suffering which plagued the life of Franz Kafka is well documented. The illness which hounded him, relegating him to a life of fitful coughs and extended stays at various sanitariums, is clearly not the least of them. Before dying in Kierling of tuberculosis, Kafka would constantly suffer the most destructive form of reproach a person can endure—his own. Max Brod terms Kafka's disposition as one of "deep pessimism" (48). Such a disposition might be viewed in part responsible for his haunting tales. Considering **"Die Verwandlung,"** William Kluback writes, "we wander into a world of violence, of frightful laughter, and terror"

(92). Similarly, Franz Kempf notes the view that **"Das Urteil"** (**"The Judgment"**) and **"Die Verwandlung"** (**"The Metamorphosis"**) depict the "mercilessness of the world" (11). Probing which method(s) Kafka may have employed to communicate torment (metaphor, analogy, parable) is of considerable importance. Scholars nevertheless might agree that regardless of method, Kafka's writing does indulge pain and suffering.

The apparent misery in Kafka's writing is perhaps what precipitated scholars to compare his works with the philosophy of Arthur Schopenhauer. Erich Heller, for instance, believes Kafka's aphorisms to "read like marginal glosses . . . [of] a text by Schopenhauer" (24). T.J. Reed concurs: "the contents of his notes offer sufficient proof that he was intensively occupied with Schopenhauer" (168). This warrants further investigation into the nature of Schopenhauer's pessimism and its possible influence(s) on Kafka.

For Arthur Schopenhauer, life is what eastern religious philosophy calls *Samsara*: this life of birth, suffering, sickness, lust, craving, old age, death and rebirth. Stanley Corngold, considering the phrase "ungeheueres Ungeziefer," reminds us that "Kafka—reader of etymologies—knew what depth of unbeing underlies this phrase" (32).[1] Perhaps, too, Franz Kafka knew the profundity *Samsara* offered. Like the phrase "ungeheueres Ungeziefer," it presents the opportunity to torture his character(s) not only with circumstance, but with their own etymology. While discussing **"Die Verwandlung"** Kafka declares, "Samsa is not merely Kafka, and nothing else" (Janouch 32). Hence, *Samsara* is very possibly the root word for the family name Samsa in **"Die Verwandlung."** It is the purpose of this essay to explore that possibility. To do so I will first discuss the concept of *Samsara*, and then consider the possible mediators that may have inspired Kafka's use of the name Samsa in **"Die Verwandlung."** This will be followed by a new interpretation of **"Die Verwandlung."**

The term *Samsara* appears for the first time in the Upanishads; by circa 600 B.C. it is a primary tenet of both Hinduism and Buddhism. *Samsara* (also pronounced and written *Sansara*) is this world of craving, lust, suffering, death, rebirth, and disease. Indeed, anything that could be considered objectionable in our lives is a part of *Samsara*. Deliverance from this *Samsaric* world is the responsibility of the individual. This deliverance is contingent upon one's *Karma,* a moral causality, which helps the spiritual-minded justify his own plight. One's situation is a matter of past and present deeds. It is fatalistic in a manner of speaking, yet it is the opposite of fatalism; each individual has the opportunity to shape his own destiny. One can perform deeds which will secure salvation or at least a higher state of existence. *Samsara* has three common translations: *wander, journey,* and *bondage* (which is more a translation of the

Sanskrit term's *effect* rather than the word itself). This endless wandering and its effect of bondage, a pessimistic view which the West has difficulty accepting, strongly influenced the thinking of Arthur Schopenhauer.

Schopenhauer works, in part, from the *Oupnekhat,* a Latin translation of the Upanishads. Throughout his *Sämtliche Werke,* both in text and footnote, one sees the term *Sansara,* as for example in the following passage:

> Nirwana, das Gegenteil von Sansara, welches die Welt der steten Wiedergeburten, des Gelüstes und Verlangens, der Sinnentäuschung und wandelbaren Formen, des Geborenwerdens, Alterns, Erkrankens und Sterbens ist.
>
> ([1894-96] 1:61 n.)

His use of the term is neither surprising nor difficult to explain. The outlines of Schopenhauer's philosophy have a definite counterpart in eastern thought. Like the Hindus, he believes this world to be comprised of pain and suffering; according to Schopenhauer it is a world that should not be. The responsibility of the individual is to deny the *Ding-an-sich,* i.e., the will. The will is the driving force behind everything and causes endless anguish. The intelligent person recognizes this and seeks to deny the will. Propagation of the species is the most powerful manifestation of the will; voluntary abstention, fasting, and non-avoidance of pain should be our goal. Knowledge, i.e., recognizing this world as *Samsara,* is our salvation. Put simply, Schopenhauer uses the term *Samsara* to show that others, an ancient religion in this case, agree with his philosophy. In the *Parerga and Paralipomena* Schopenhauer addresses those who believe that life's pleasures outweigh its suffering; to test this assertion, he suggests they "compare the feelings of an animal that is devouring another with those of that other" (2: 292). For Schopenhauer, nothing is more ridiculous than to call pain negative; he sees it as something positive:

> I know of no greater absurdity than that of most metaphysical systems which declare evil to be something negative; whereas it is precisely that which is positive and makes itself felt. On the other hand, that which is good, in other words, all happiness and satisfaction, is negative, that is, the mere elimination of a desire and the ending of pain
>
> (291-92).

We know Kafka owned and read Schopenhauer's collected works. Kafka may have simply substituted an *m* for an *n* to modify the sound of the word. However, it was probably not from Schopenhauer that he first became acquainted with the concept of *Samsara,* and he may very well have been familiar with both pronunciations and spellings.

It was Oskar Pollak who, according to Brod, "was the man who won a decisive influence over Kafka in his younger days," due probably to the breadth of his interests (56). Pollak's obituary, written by Hugo Bergmann, reads, "the richness of his interests was inexhaustible; but to whatever it might be that got hold of him . . . he devoted himself completely . . . [and] forgot everything else for its sake. . . . In this way he studied the Upanishad" (56). There was almost certainly a running dialogue between Kafka and Pollak concerning what they may have been reading or studying. In a letter to Pollak in November of 1903 Kafka writes that he is reading "Fechner [and] Eckhart . . . [whose] books seem like a key to unfamiliar rooms in one's own castle" (*Letters* 10). Brod informs us that he has deleted about twelve pages of this letter due to an extended criticism of a lecture given by Professor Paul Schulze-Namburg. Regardless of what Brod has deleted, we can nevertheless deduce that Pollak too was open with Kafka about what he was reading, not failing to criticize or praise what he may have found wanting or exhilarating, e.g., within the Upanishads. Given that *Samsara* is important to the Upanishads, we may assume that as Pollak immersed himself in his study, he probably, by letter or in conversation, discussed with Kafka its more interesting components. If nothing else, Kafka's letter to Pollak serves as a clue to when he developed an interest in mystics such as Eckhart.

This interest may have found a home in the Theosophical Society. In Kafka's personal library we find *Populäre Theosophie*[2] and Rudolph Steiner's *Die Erziehung des Kindes vom Gesichtspunkte der Geisteswissenschaft,* which were published in 1897 and 1907 respectively.[3] Curiously, the latter's publication corresponds with Steiner's visit to Czechoslovakia, where he stopped during a lecture tour of Europe. It is not known whether Kafka attended any theosophical lectures this early, but by 1911 he had done so. By his own account, found in a diary entry dated March 1911, he recounts a lecture given by Steiner and their subsequent meeting at the Victoria Hotel on Jungmannstrasse. During this meeting he tells Steiner, "I feel that a great part of my being is striving toward theosophy" (*Diaries* 48). Here we must keep Kafka's temperament in mind: he was not one to confide in just anyone, nor would he ascribe a great part of himself as tending toward any intellectual or religious movement without being familiar with its philosophy or theology. We may therefore confidently rely on the supposition that Kafka was very familiar with Steiner's writing. Steiner was known to use Sanskrit terms both in print and during lectures; like Pollak, he was familiar with the Upanishads and with Indian religions in general. We know too that Kafka was preoccupied with what he tells Steiner are "the clairvoyant states described by you" (48). There is a heavy concentration of dream entries in Kafka's diary from 1911 to 1913. This is, I believe, evidence of Kafka's study of Schopenhauer. Dreams for Schopenhauer can be a dreaming of reality, hence, at certain times, a matter of clairvoyance. For these reasons alone one can assume that Kafka came in contact with the term in question. However, that Kafka was reading works by Steiner, and believed himself to some degree clairvoyant, returns us to Schopenhauer's *Sämtliche Werke.* For it was Steiner who wrote the *Einleitung* for the 1894-96 edition, the edition Kafka owned and referred to in various letters. Steiner, introducing Schopenhauer's philosophy and life, probably seized Kafka's attention with his personal influences and philosophical solutions. Steiner writes:

> Die Erlösungs- und Mitleidslehre Schopenhauers sind hervorgegangen aus seiner Willenslehre unter dem Einflusse indischer Anschauungen: dem Brahmanismus und Buddhismus. . . . Nach dem Buddhismus ist alles Sein mit Schmerz verknüpft. Dieser wäre auch dann nicht vernichtet, wenn es bloß ein einziges Urwesen gäbe. Nur die Vernichtung alles Seins durch Entsagung und Unterdrükkung der Leidenschaften kann zur Erlösung, zum Nirwana, d. h. Vernichtung alles Daseins führen
>
> (1: 25).

Schopenhauer's influence on Kafka's writing has been connected with Kafka as late as *Das Schloß (The Castle)* and as early as **"Das Urteil."** In October of 1902, while attending a lecture on "Schopenhauer and Nietzsche," Kafka met Max Brod who would become his closest friend. When considering the influence that Nietzsche may have had on Kafka, we might keep in mind that Nietzsche was Schopenhauer's student. Furthermore, it was not just Schopenhauer's philosophy but his abilities as a writer that captured Kafka's attention. While discussing the *Bhagavad Gita,* a conversation between Gustav Janouch and Kafka turned to Schopenhauer. Kafka admired Schopenhauer's writing abilities and remarked: "Schopenhauer is an artist in language. That is the source of his thinking. For the language alone, one must not fail to read him" (Janouch 85). According to Walter Jens and Hans Kueng, "[Kafka] read Dostoyevsky to his favorite sister Ottla, along with Schopenhauer and Kleist" (268).

Schopenhauer's pessimism (in addition to his writing abilities) was definitely recognized by Kafka:

> The world, if it were nothing but a peepshow, would really be infinitely beautiful. But unfortunately it is not that; rather this beautiful life in a beautiful world has really to be lived through in every detail of every moment and that is no longer so beautiful, but simply toilsome. That's more or less what Schopenhauer said
>
> (*Letters* 267).

In the wake of such pessimism Brod notes "[Kafka] wants to lump all his literary work together as an 'attempt to get away from my father'" (24). In a letter to his father, Kafka writes:

> My writings were about you, in them I merely poured out the lamentations I could not pour out on your breast. It was a farewell deliberately drawn out, save that, although you, it is true, imposed it, the direction it was given *I* determined
>
> (*Father* 25).

This offers the opportunity to consider alternatives to *Samsara* as Samsa's root word, namely Holland's suggestion of Samson and Weinberg's idea of *sam jesm.*

Weinberg believes that Kafka has formed a phonetic contraction of the Czech "*sam (allein)* and *jsem (ich bin)* = '*ich bin allein*'" (238). This then, according to Weinberg, is "ein Schmerzensschrei, der sowohl den Isolierung des Büßers und ungeheuren Ungeziefers Gregor Samsa, als auch die Einzigartigkeit der von ihm ersehnten Messiasrolle (des eingeborenen Sohnes Gottes) treffend bezeichnet" (238). With Gregor's messianic role, Weinberg ascribes the father's role "als Jahvegestalt, der Mutter als Verkörperung des jüdischen Glaubens und der jüdischen Stammesangehörigkeit, der Schwester als Seelenund Caritas- figur" (236). There is a multitude of possibilities here. Perhaps for instance, Kafka had both *Samsara* and *sam jesm* in mind, if "Samsa is not merely Kafka, and nothing else" (Janouch 32). Maybe Samsa is not simply *Samsara* or *sam jesm,* and nothing else. The malaise of being alone could fit with the idea of *Samsara.*

In Kafka scholarship there is often a tendency toward Judaic and/or Christian interpretation. Adding *Samsara* (Hinduism, Buddhism) to Weinberg's Judaic and Christian mix, might suggest the metamorphosis of world religions. It could be viewed as an ecumenical movement; each religion working in tandem, making its contribution to **"Die Verwandlung."** Kafka's interest in and struggle with "religion" could also emphasize each faith's antagonism toward the other. Gregor's last name, though, passed on from generation to generation, suggests the longevity and prevalence of *Samsara.* If there is to be an overview of the possible world religions in **"Die Verwandlung,"** it might hinge on *Samsara's* emphasis on suffering via transmigration.

Having said that, the question remains: does Kafka actually feel "alone" or does he feel trapped within a horrible cycle? Kafka tells us "my writings were about you" (*Father* 25); thus he may *not* be alone. Quite the contrary, he may be constantly followed, haunted by the oppressive image of his father. Considering Kafka's entire body of works, we are presented with an author who takes the role of something one might term transcendent. **"Die Verwandlung"** serves beautifully as an example; as in so many of his other stories, the main character appears to be Franz Kafka: that is why we have "K" in *Der Prozeß,* Bende-mann in **"Das Urteil,"** and in this case Samsa. Kafka himself considers the similarity between Georg Bendemann's name and his own. He writes, "Georg has the same number of letters as Franz. In Bendemann, 'mann' is a strengthening of 'Bende'. . . . But Bende has exactly the same number of letters as Kafka, and the vowel *e* occurs in the same places as does the vowel *a* in Kafka" (*Diaries* 214). In his works he transcends his existence as merely the author; it is a transmigration of his "soul" into new lives and bodies. He thus watches himself in this new life, his father once again stalking him within, causing suffering and a consequent death, whether by suicide or slow starvation. And as he dies within each story, Kafka views himself reborn in another, whether as a man recalling his "apehood" (Kafka, *Report* 281), a dog in **"Forschungen eines Hundes" ("Investigations of a Dog")**, or vermin in **"Die Verwandlung."** The same torturous cycle then begins once again. This is why *Samsara*, denoting rebirth and suffering, is so fitting: with this term Kafka tells us what Gregor Samsa is atoning for, as **"Das Urteil"** came out of Kafka "like a real birth, covered with filth and slime," and as the brown liquid drips from Gregor Samsa, we know this vermin might be the rebirth of that first slimy conception (*Diaries* 214). It may be Georg Bendemann, also known as Gregor Samsa, atoning for his suicide.

According to Holland, Gregor ("Samson") saves the Samsa family ("the chosen people") from the three boarders ("the Philistines") (148-49). Apart from the story of Samson in Judges, Holland states, "in fact, a good deal of incidental imagery of **'Metamorphosis'** was derived from Isaiah" (149). Reading **"Die Verwandlung,"** however, one does not find much similarity between Gregor and Samson. Samson possesses great strength; Gregor does not have the strength to get out of bed, he must swing "himself out of bed with all his might" (Kafka, **"Metamorphosis"** 125). Moreover, even if Gregor did possess extraordinary strength, unlike Samson there is no long hair to be cut. Similarly, Gregor does not appear to be, like Samson, a judge of Israel. Nor does the family's treatment of Gregor correspond to Samson's familial relationship. Gregor is left in his room with rotten food, and repeatedly driven back into his den of misery by his father. Samson's family is at his disposal: when he wants to marry a particular woman his family is happy to support him. Holland, however, does not suggest that **"Die Verwandlung"** is an inversion of the story of Samson; rather, he draws on an analogy. He writes, "Samson's sacrifice is a traditional analogue to Christ's; in German he is called *Judenchrist*" (149). Weinberg and Holland agree that "Kafka has given Gregor a number of Christ-like attributes" (Holland 147). Weinberg refers to Gregor as "*Christkind*," and surmises that Gregor's metamorphosis is related to his desire to send his sister to the *conservatoire* (237). There does appear to be something ontological about Gregor. Furthermore, *Samsara's* emphasis on suffering and rebirth could allow for such an interpretation; but there are other possibilities. Gregor's savior quality might be explained by eastern philoso-

phy's notion of the *avatar*. This will be discussed in further detail later.

Franz Kafka was probably not a Hindu or Buddhist; however it does appear that he took an interest in their beliefs. One might consider, too, that it is not Samson or *sam jesm*, but *Samsara* that appears to connect all three of the stories within the *Strafen* (**"Das Urteil," "Die Verwandlung,"** and **"In der Strafkolonie"**; Kafka, *Briefe* 147). Kafka tells Gustav Janouch, "words must be exactly and strictly defined . . . otherwise we may fall into entirely unexpected pitfalls" (Janouch 145). It has been suggested that Georg Bendemann (again the *mann* appears only to strengthen *Bende*), is perhaps derived from *Bande* (bonds, shackles, fetters).[4] Here one might note the connection with *Samsara's* translation as bondage. This could be the bondage of Kafka's relationship with his father, and the bondage of metempsychosis. In **"Die Verwandlung,"** Gregor Samsa is a *Reisender*, a traveling salesman, which gives us *Samsara's* second translation as "journey." *Der Reisende*, the main character in **"In der Strafkolonie,"** completes the connection. These three stories may not be separate; they could be viewed as the chapters of one story; shackled together by the concept of metempsychosis. We might even call them "Kafkaesque," in the sense that Kafka is observing himself in various forms, always trying to escape his father. Hence, *Verwandlung* and its etymological connection with the third literal translation of *Samsara*—"*wandern.*" *Samsara* serves the spirit of Kafka's writing, and this spirit is one of evasion, even deceit; Kafka intends for his works to be illusory. He alone stands as the exception to the elusiveness of his writing; it is *his* "escape" (Brod 25), and, playing the role of a fugitive, it is therefore fitting that only he, at the time of conception, knows the tunnels by which he absconds.

I believe it is clear that each of Kafka's works has its own secrets, and that in the case of the *Strafen* there exists a common secret. In a letter to Kurt Wolff in April of 1913, Kafka tells him that:

> "The Stoker," "The Metamorphosis" . . . and "The Judgment" belong together, both inwardly and outwardly. There is an obvious connection among the three and, even more important, a secret one, for which reason I would be reluctant to forgo the chance of having them published together in a book, which might be called *The Sons*
>
> (*Letters* 96).

This letter was written before Kafka had written **"In der Strafkolonie."** It may be the case that Kafka intended **"In der Strafkolonie"** to continue his secret connection; this is why the *Reisender* is again the main character. This is not to suggest however, that the *only* reason Kafka wrote **"In der Strafkolonie"** was to continue this connection, but rather, that it may not be beyond Kafka to include such intentions with any other ideas for the story. A diary entry concerning **"Der Heizer"** and **"In der Strafkolonie"** further supports such a supposition. In 1915 Kafka writes, "if the two elements—most pronounced in **'The Stoker'** and **'In the Penal Colony'**—do not combine, I am finished" (*Diaries* 330). Kafka apparently considered the creation and continuation of such connections somewhat important; this is perhaps why he wants **"Das Urteil," "Die Verwandlung,"** and **"In der Strafkolonie"** to appear under the common title of *Strafen*. Kafka is clear that **"Die Verwandlung"** must accompany **"Das Urteil"** and **"In der Strafkonlonie"** if they are to appear together. He tells Kurt Wolff, **"[The] Metamorphosis"** might still mediate between them, but without that story you would have two alien heads knocking violently at each other" (*Letters* 126). If Wolff had wanted to publish **"Der Heizer"** and **"Das Urteil"** together without **"Die Verwandlung"** to mediate between them, Kafka probably would have made the same assertion. All the stories may stand alone; when combining them, however, they must be assembled completely and correctly: **"Die Verwandlung"** must be the middle story.

"Die Verwandlung" is probably the connector among these three stories. It is the middle point of atonement, suffering by force of transmigration. Gregor Samsa suffers Georg Bendemann's actions, and in **"In der Strafkolonie"** Gregor Samsa is born yet again, in yet another story, and suffers yet another life. Schopenhauer writes:

> Um allezeit einen sichern Kompaß, zur Orientierung im Leben, bei der Hand zu haben, und um dasselbe, ohne je irre zu werden, stets im richtigen Lichte zu erblicken, ist nichts tauglicher, als dass man sich angewöhne, diese Welt zu betrachten als einen Ort der Buße, also gleichsam als eine Strafanstalt, a penal colony
>
> (*Sämtliche Werke* [1894-96] 10: 288).

On the same page, Schopenhauer makes clear why this world is a penal colony:

> Dies ist Sansara: die Welt des Gelüstes und Verlangens, und daher die Welt der Geburt, der Krankheit, des Alterns und Sterbens: es ist die Welt, welche nicht sein sollte. Und dies hier ist die Bevölkerung der Sansara
>
> ([1894-96] 10: 288 n.).

It is important to note that Schopenhauer writes *penal colony* rather than *Strafkolonie*, which probably served to capture Kafka's attention. The etymology of "Strafkolonie" continues his theme of movement or transmigration. Georg Bendemann begins the series, his name representing the bondage of *Samsara*; in keeping with that, our next two characters are each a *Reisender. Verwandlung* is connected with *wandern*, and *Strafen*

provides our collective title. Finally then, the connection between *Kolonie* and *Ansiedler* suggests movement, travel, and thus the punishment quality of transmigration (Kluge 463).

The connection between **"Das Urteil"** and **"Die Verwandlung"** has been well documented. Corngold in his excellent analysis of Kafka's "writing" observes, "the hero of **'The Metamorphosis'** is **'The Judgment'**" (36). Kurz Gerhard writes, "Gregor Samsa *ist der im Namen 'östlich' akzentuierte Georg Bendemann"*(172). For Corngold **"Die Verwandlung"** is the story of a "metamorphosed metaphor"(27). Both of these connections might be extended to **"In der Strafkolonie."** For those who disagree with the idea that the *Strafen* tell the story of a character's transmigrating soul, there are other alternatives. For instance, an interesting substitution might be the transmigration of metaphor; the "soul" of a metaphor. After all, why wouldn't Kafka torture Georg Bendemann, Gregor Samsa, and *der Reisende* with their apparent connection to *Samsara*?

One might therefore be inclined to believe (1) that Kafka related to Schopenhauer's pessimism; (2) that Schopenhauer's writing ability only further enticed Kafka; (3) that he was attracted to his essays on dreams, and their relation to his own experience; (4) that Kafka took note of Schopenhauer's use of *Samsara,* the Sanskrit term with which he was probably already familiar; (5) that *Samsara,* properly understood as wandering, journeying, and bondage, uncovers the secret connection among the *Strafen*. This leads us to a new interpretation of **"Die Verwandlung."**

Kafka's interest in Judaic and Christian theologies has been well probed in various interpretations. The interpretation which follows, on the other hand, attempts to stress another possible path. This approach makes use of Schopenhauerian and Indian metaphysics. It is based on the concept of *Samsara,* while keeping in mind that Schopenhauer, for Kafka at least, was probably the mediator of this term. Thus, what may have been taken from Indian philosophy by Kafka, could have been coupled with Schopenhauer's philosophy or vice versa. Schopenhauer believed his philosophy to be akin to eastern metaphysics, although he was quick to point out that he was unaware of its tenets prior to the conception of his philosophy. Through the lens of Schopenhauerian metaphysics and Indian philosophy, Franz Kafka's **"Die Verwandlung"** requires immediate immersion in the text. Kafka gives so much information on the first page that the horror of the situation confronts the reader. Even the main character has difficulty coming to grips with his predicament: "Als Gregor Samsa eines Morgens aus unruhigen Träumen erwachte, fand er sich in seinem Bett zu einem ungeheueren Ungeziefer verwandelt" (Kafka, **"Verwandlung"** 96). Here Gregor Samsa is immediately enveloped by the slimy birth which is

Kafka's **"Das Urteil."** It seems that Kafka is acutely aware of the literal translations of *Samsara,* and therefore, after introducing his character by his full name, the narrator uses only Gregor thereafter, with one exception, on the first page: "—Samsa war Reisender—" (96). Kafka is perhaps saying that Gregor is not only in terms of *Samsara* a *Reisender,* traveling from one existence to another, but he is also saying that Gregor *is Samsara;* he embodies rebirth and its consequent suffering.

His soul is stained and he is caught in a vicious cycle, each life is a curse as a result of past transgressions, and these transgressions have the father entwined in the same fate. For Gregor's father is also a Samsa and therefore a *Reisender:* In keeping with that, Georg's father has also been reborn, and Gregor suffers as a result of his rebirth. This is to suggest that the father judges his son and sentences him to death in **"Das Urteil,"** tortures his son in **"Die Verwandlung,"** and then defends (as the officer), the entire process in **"In der Strafkolonie."** The instrument of torture may be a metaphor for the doctrine of metempsychosis: it performs a slow, drawnout process, we never know our crime, yet our transgression is written indelibly on our soul. Our world is a penal system, our lives like Georg's friend in **"Das Urteil"** are repeatedly spent in this "colony" (Kafka, **"Judgment"** 58). Hence, Gregor does not hear the "voice of merely one father," but the voices of many fathers from many lives (Kafka, **"Metamorphosis"** 139). Viewing Gregor in his new form, Mr. Samsa "[wept] so hard that his powerful chest began to quake" (133). The father is irate and possessed by the anger he feels at the way he was neglected in his past life; although probably not fully aware why, "the father charge[s] pitilessly, spewing hisses like a savage" (138). This is definitely frightening for Gregor, but it is also a saving grace, "a true deliverance" (139). The torture Gregor endures at his father's hands will speed up his deliverance from this transient life. One must keep in mind, though, that Gregor's father played a devilish role in **"Das Urteil."** Seeing his son, the product of his love for his wife, in such a loathsome state, makes the metamorphosis on some level a punishment for him as well. Both father and son are engaged in a process of atonement.

Within **"Die Verwandlung"** there is perhaps, like **"Das Urteil"** and **"In der Strafkolonie,"** an emphasis on the idea of atonement. This is why, with the exception cited above, the narrator refers to the young Samsa as "Gregor." The name Gregor is used to more closely delineate Kafka's use of *Samsara,* which can mean *all* the sufferings of the world, i.e., disease, old age, and so on. This is to suggest that the use of Gregor accentuates the process of atonement within metempsychosis. Gregor's first name is probably taken from *Papst Gregor der Große,* who was brought to Kafka's attention and put

into the context of *Samsara* by Arthur Schopenhauer. A brief examination of the context will be helpful. In his essay, "On Religion," Schopenhauer lashes out at both Jews and Christians, pointing out in his usual fashion what he finds wanting or altogether offensive. Of the latter, the doctrine of predestination is something that Schopenhauer finds particularly atrocious:

> Springing from the combination of the Old and New Testaments, . . . among other things, . . . [is] the Christian doctrine of predestination and grace. . . . [T]he offensive springs . . . merely from the Old Testament assumption that man is the work of another's will and is thereby created out of nothing
>
> (*Parerga* 2: 364).

Schopenhauer believes that Hinduism's and Buddhism's doctrine of metempsychosis is far superior. The advantages that one man has over another at birth is a result of his good deeds in a past life and not "another's gift of grace" (2: 364). Schopenhauer is confident that the doctrine of metempsychosis has over time become readily accepted by almost the entire human race, that is, he points out, with the exception of the Jews. However (and this is what probably inspired Kafka's use of Gregor), in the case of the Catholic Church Schopenhauer writes:

> Eben um den hieraus entspringenden kolossalen Übelstand zu beseitigen und das Empörende des Dogmas zu mildern hat, im 6. Jahrhundert, Papst Gregor I., sehr weislich, die Lehre vom Purgatorio, welche im wesentlichen sich schon beim Origenes . . . findet, ausgebildet und dem Kirchenglauben förmlich einverleibt, wodurch die Sache sehr gemildert und die Metempsychose einigermassen ersetzt wird; da das eine wie das andere einen Läuterungsprozess gibt
>
> (*Sämtliche Werke* [1894-96] 11: 50).

Kafka often portrayed Christian characters, and he most likely knew that his audience was predominantly Christian. He probably used the name Gregor because (as Schopenhauer points out) purgatory, like metempsychosis, offers a process of purification. Furthermore, besides having the spelling of "Georg" within the spelling of "Gregor," and Gregor's job being the name of the character in **"In der Strafkolonie,"** this theme of purgatory deepens the connection between **"Das Urteil," "Die Verwandlung,"** and **"In der Strafkolonie."** Certainly they are all stories of punishment, but Kafka wrote **"Das Urteil"** on the eve of Yom Kippur, the Jewish day of atonement, and Kafka now utilizes *Gregor der Große* to further reflect in **"Die Verwandlung"** the idea of his characters' atonement. Considering **"In der Strafkolonie"** and *"The Trial,"* Max Brod writes, "they are documents of literary self punishment, imaginative rites of atonement" (146). This is perhaps brought to a head by the traveling salesman's criticism of the entire process; the criticism that ultimately incites the officer's suicide, therefore inverting the father and son's role in **"Das Urteil."** It is now the son (*der Reisende*) who forces the father (*der Offizier*) to take his own life. Here we might also see the accentuation of cyclicality in the *Strafen.* In **"Die Verwandlung"** Gregor's life is a purgatory, an atonement for the crimes upon his soul. Georg Bendemann's failure to take adequate care of his elderly father is one of those crimes, for "Georg reproached himself for neglecting his father" (Kafka, **"Judgment"** 66). Moreover, as Kafka told Kurt Wolff, "'The Metamorphosis' is the mediator of these three stories: it resides in between **'The Judgment'** and **'In the Penal Colony,'** just as purgatory lies somewhere in between heaven and hell."

Kafka may be portraying a reality in which death is not a curse, but a goal. He retells a story from that "tremendous world" inside his head (*Diaries* 222); **"Die Verwandlung"** was probably formed within his "dreamlike inner life" (302). Kafka, like everyone else, enters his nightmares unwillingly; and this may be the precise locale of Gregor's purgatory—the nightmare of reality. Schopenhauer remarks that a dream "like the outside world, forces itself on us without our intervention and even against our will" (*Parerga* 1: 230). It is also possible that the dream aspect of **"Die Verwandlung"** refers to what in eastern philosophy is called *Maya.* Quoting Indian philosophy, Schopenhauer writes:

> It is *Maya,* the veil of deception, which covers the eyes of mortals, and causes them to see a world which one cannot say either that it is or that it is not; for it is like a dream, like the sunshine on the sand which the traveler from a distance takes to be water, or like the piece of rope on the ground which he regards as a snake
>
> (qtd. in *World as Will* 1: 8).

The journey Gregor Samsa embarks on in order to escape life may very well be what Kafka views as his own fate. True, Kafka tells the story in the past tense, but only because it was a dream he had prior to his writing the story. Throughout the *Strafen* Kafka is haunted by his father: sometimes when Kafka writes, he is trying to empty his head and escape the suffering of his own notion of inferiority in comparison to his father. Nevertheless, in spite of authoring new existences in various forms, his father still follows through each tale, but this is not a chase:

> Gregor scooted away, stopping only when the father halted, and skittering forward again the instant the father moved. In this way they circled the room several times with nothing decisive happening; in fact, because of its slow tempo, the whole business did not even resemble a chase.
>
> (**"Metamorphosis"** 163).

Kafka's writing appears to lament that his father deals with him with "the utmost severity" (163). However, this is what Kafka and Gregor want, for they are "tor-

tured by self-rebukes and worries" (161). Life is a punishment, the metamorphosis is part of life's cruelty, but in **"Die Verwandlung"** it turns out to be a possible means of salvation both for Gregor and his family. Subsequently, this vermin could be viewed as exhibiting the qualities of a savior.

What Kafka may depict in **"Die Verwandlung"** is Gregor within his room continuing his pathetic existence and the theme of "in-betweens." Even the metamorphosis itself is an "in-between"; Kafka toys with the idea of rebirth and transmigration. By combining *Gregor der Große* and *Samsara,* he makes the statement that this is a story not only of a punishment, but of atonement, and that this atonement, this process of purification, is performed through the transmigration of souls. Yet the metamorphosis itself is so abrupt that it seems somewhat incomplete. Gregor is in this state as a result of past evil deeds, and his state is such that it resembles being caught between two fates. Gregor is neither totally human nor is he totally an animal. In addition, although his actions "during his travels" belong to his soul, they do not belong to Gregor himself (121). There is something terribly unfair about this doctrine of metempsychosis. Metaphorically this verminous creation might be Georg Bendemann's **"Judgment,"** "covered with filth and slime" (Kafka, *Diaries* 214). Gregor is trapped, he suffers the bondage of *Samsara,* and is condemned for a crime that he, in the strictest terms of his present personality, did not *actually* commit. He is like a man sentenced who has no remembrance of the crime he has committed (like K. in *Der Prozeß*), nor any recollection of the ensuing trial. In fact, he has no opportunity to offer a defense. Gregor does not remember what he did as Georg, he doesn't remember **"Das Urteil"**; therefore, in a manner of speaking, this punishment is not fully his. The unfairness of the doctrine of metempsychosis could be viewed as being more clearly criticized in **"In der Strafkolonie."** *Der Reisende* asks, "he doesn't know his own judgment . . . he does not know that he has been condemned?" (Kafka, **"Colony"** 198). Smiling, the officer replies, "no" (198). The reason why Gregor is unable to control his own physical faculties may be that he does not remember his crime. Gregor is unable to control the punishment; "his many legs, wretchedly thin, . . . dance helplessly before his eyes" (Kafka, **"Metamorphosis"** 117): "If he tried to bend a leg, it first straightened out; and if he finally succeeded in taking charge of it, the other legs meanwhile all kept carrying on, as if emancipated, in extreme and painful agitation" (122).

This may bemoan the lack of power Gregor has over his punishment, and the fact of every human being's existence. Try as we may, we cannot control the circumstances under which we are born, and in this life we can not control other people's actions. Sometimes we succeed in taking charge of our lives; Gregor "straightens out a leg"; nevertheless, just as one leg obeys, Gregor's other legs "all kept carrying on" (122). We order our lives in a fashion we are pleased with, but the people around us interfere, and they affect our plans and progress in life. This was certainly the case for Franz Kafka; he wished to write and quench the compulsion he felt to his art. However his family, especially his father, would interfere. In deference to his familial duty, his duty to his inspiration was often forced to suffer and wait. Kafka writes:

> Recently, when I told you that nothing coming from outside could disturb my writing now . . . , I was thinking only of how my mother whimpers to me almost every evening that I really should look in on the factory. . . . I [realize] with perfect clarity now only two possibilities remain open to me, either to jump out of the window . . . or in the next two weeks to go daily to the factory . . .

> (*Letters* 89).

Apparently Kafka's family could interrupt his writing, to such a degree, in fact, that he would consider suicide. Under the pressure of duty to his family, Kafka sees only two alternatives, to die or to appease his parents. Similarly Gregor feels the same confinement to two options. However, it is not the interruption of Gregor's writing for the sake of familial obligation, but suicide itself.

Early in the story Kafka portrays Gregor as planning to quit his job. In reference to his job he cries, "to hell with it all," if it were not for his family he "would have given notice long ago" (118-19). Living in this *Samsaric* world, the agonies of life and transmigration are too much for Gregor. He is not deciding to quit his job when he says "to hell with it all"; he is deciding to commit suicide. For "Dies ist Samsara: die Welt des Gelüstes und Verlangens . . . es ist die Welt, welche nicht sein sollte" (*Sämtliche Werke* [1960-65] 5: 356 n.). Hence, it is a life that should not be, Gregor's job in this life *is* life, it is pain: he is planning a suicide in order to avoid this torture and avoid his process of atonement. He calls out to the heavens, "God Almighty!" (Kafka, **"Metamorphosis"** 119). With the clock glaring at him, he thinks of his family once again, in contrast to Georg's lack of concern for his family. Gregor resolves to provide for his family and then "go through with it no matter what. I'll make a big clean break!" (119). This is, however, not simply a firm resolution, but a matter of hope: "well, I haven't abandoned all hope" (119). Gregor's greatest consolation in this life is the future "hope" of suicide (119). Gregor's consideration of suicide appears to reflect Kafka's own thoughts of suicide. In October of 1912, just before writing **"Die Verwandlung,"** he writes in a letter to Brod:

> I stood for a long time at the window and pressed against the pane, and there were many moments when it would have suited me to alarm the toll collector on the bridge by my fall. . . . Dearest Max I am putting this whole thing before you . . . not for your opinion, . . . but since I was firmly determined to jump . . .

> (*Letters* 90).

Gregor and the author wish to make a break from life and all its anxiety. *Samsara* is suffering, life is suffering, and this is a story of suffering. Kafka tries to live his life, he tries to work during the day for a few hours and to come home at night and write. Life however will not allow it.

Here we get to the crux of the issue in **"Die Verwandlung."** To be sure the metamorphosis itself is part of the punishment. However, waking to find himself a vermin is only a part of the greater punishment, which is waking itself—life. That Gregor was ever (re)born is the real punishment: as he must suffer the "agonies of traveling" (118). Gerhard Kurz on the other hand, views Gregor's metamorphosis as *"ein neues Leben"* (173). For Kurz, Gregor's metamorphosis is a saving grace, "kein blindes oder tragisches Opfer, . . . sondern eine Befreiung, eine Neugeburt" (173). Even with the opportunity for atonement, I propose that Gregor suffers a torturous rebirth, rather than a new lease on life. I think Gerhard Kurz's view is compatible with this idea, since he suggests,

> der Schrecken ist nicht der Tod, sondern die Existenz; der Tod, wie noch der zweideutige Tod Gregors, Georgs und des Offiziers der "Strafkolonie" ex negativo sagt, ist Erlösung, Befreiung, Gnade, Rückkehr ins Paradies

> (177).

Kurz, enlisting existence as suffering, suggests that whether vermin or human, Gregor's goal is death. *Samsara*, with its emphasis on life as pain, supports this view; but it also suggests the possibility of rebirth, rather than an automatic place in Paradise.

In order for Gregor to escape his situation, he must first accept it: he must accept his punishment so as to begin his atonement. By not getting out of bed and facing the world, he runs the risk of perpetuating the ordeal, consequently suffering the same fate in life after life. He tells himself "just don't dawdle in bed," for he must get up (Kafka, **"Metamorphosis"** 122-23). Arising from the bed, which seems to have him paralyzed and trapped, might signify his resolution to face, accept, and atone for his past conduct. For most of the first chapter Gregor will not, cannot, accept his punishment. Gregor wishes to escape this course of atonement; he first contemplates suicide, then decides to postpone it, and ultimately dismisses the idea completely (with the qualification of a "hope"), resolving that he is "condemned" and must suffer (125).

Although condemned to life, "condemned" to working and suffering, through reflection, "indeed the calmest reflection was far superior to desperate resolves," Gregor decides he must get out of bed (123). With getting Gregor out of bed, Kafka positions him to suffer within his purgatory. By living through the reproaches of his life and family, and by denying suicide, he may have the opportunity to escape the cycle of transmigration. Gregor would rather not get out of bed and open the door to his family. To do so, he believes he deserves support, even applause. In keeping with that, while attempting to open the bedroom door, "everyone should have cheered him on . . . 'attaboy, Gregor . . .' they should have shouted" (132).

Again Schopenhauerian and eastern metaphysics might be taken into consideration. Gregor has traveled from one life to the next, the father always close behind. Now that Gregor has tossed himself from the bed, he is better situated to foresee the species of his punishment for he "[does] possess such foresight" (135). More to the point, he is preparing to *try* and suffer his punishment properly; he wants to attain an escape that will be *permanent.* Near the end of the first chapter Gregor knows his "final recovery from all sufferings [is] at hand" (136). By remaining in his wretched state, avoiding suicide, leading an existence which resembles that of an ascetic, and restoring his family to a dutiful order, he can hopefully achieve his salvation—a permanent death.

Gregor is desperate that the director be made aware that he has extracted himself from the bed. Even while being attacked by his father, Gregor is most concerned with the disposition of his job or life (which his job represents), so much so that he "had no time for his parents: the office manager was already on the stairs" (137). If the job represents life for Kafka, the director is probably an ontological figure, the office manager his intermediary, and Gregor, like the errand boy, "[is] the director's creature" (120). Sitting above everyone, the director "talks down to the employees from his great height" (119). He judges everyone's conduct, thus Gregor is "deeply obligated to the director" (134). It is of the utmost importance to Gregor that the office manager "report all this accurately," for the director is easily "swayed against an employee" (134). Kafka has created a punishing God, one who is hasty with His judgments. He could be nothing else but punishing, having sentenced his children to this *Samsaric* world: again and again we live in a pathetic state, suffering disease, rebirth, and the reproach of our creator; we are a creation that "can so easily fall victim to gossip, coincidences, and unwarranted complaints" (134). Nevertheless, even though Gregor's life and sentence are not understood, he must face the world of wandering and accept its bondage. To do so the world of transmigration offers a recipe.

Kafka seems to utilize the outlines of Schopenhauer's remedy for the will-to-live, this blind driving force

which is the author of our pain. It is through quelling the desire to live that we emancipate ourselves. This emancipation is death:

> Death says: You are the product of an act that ought not to have taken place; therefore, to wipe it out, you must die. To die willingly, to die gladly, to die cheerfully, is the prerogative of the resigned, of him who gives up and denies the will-to-live
>
> (*World as Will* 1: 507-08).

According to eastern philosophy Gregor can exhibit such willingness by conducting himself as an ascetic. Schopenhauer believes that one must abstain from sexual activity, there must be non-avoidance of injury or degradation from others, fasting, and even self-torture. Out of this discomfort, Gregor will grasp what will hopefully lead him toward salvation, i.e., death. This is not to suggest, however, that suicide is an option; for Schopenhauer "suicide is a phenomenon of the will's strong affirmation" (1: 398).

So in a great way acceptance is the answer to all of Gregor's problems. Because his problems are so egregious, Gregor continuously balks in his efforts at self denial. He has gotten himself out of bed, thereby affirming a degree of willingness, but he shies away from his decision. This is demonstrated by his consumption of food, which is an affirmation of the will-to-live, although one could deem this consumption too as a form of punishment. The food Gregor eats is putrid: compiled of "half-rotten vegetables, some bones . . . coated with a solidified white sauce, . . . [and]some cheese that Gregor had declared inedible two days ago" (Kafka, **"Metamorphosis"** 145). Kafka seems to make every natural act an act of suffering. In Kafka's eyes *Samsara* and purgatory require the utmost misery *if only because they are both religious terms.* Kafka tells Gustav Janouch that "illness, pain [and]suffering are the most important sources of religious feeling" (Janouch 100). Certainly Kafka has taken every measure to intensify Gregor's plight. Even the help Gregor receives from Grete causes "him great suffering" (**"Metamorphosis"** 152). Not in keeping with so many of his other stories (e.g., **"Forschungen eines Hundes," "Bericht für eine Akademie," "Ein Hungerkünstler"**), Kafka did not choose an animal with fur, which is odd, since for Kafka fur appears to cause and represent misery. He tells us this in a letter to a friend: "white dresses and sympathy become you best of all, whereas furs conceal the timid girl . . . and cause suffering" (*Letters* 29).

Instead he chooses the form of an insect, which turns out to be for good reason. By giving him the form of vermin, Kafka burdens Gregor with a fervent will. The greater the will-to-live, the more potent the torture. It is difficult for Gregor to deny his will; for instance, he experiences the "tremendous urge" to shoot out from under the settee, and "beg" for food (Kafka, **"Metamorphosis"** 144). The will-to-live has varying degrees within various species. A human being, for example, will cut off his arm to save his life, but a hurt insect will simply engage in its most immediate act. That is to say that an insect, as Schopenhauer points out, will continue to eat "when the back part of the body is nearly torn off and hangs by a mere thread of gut" (*Parerga* 2: 298). This is the case, because the degree to which an animal feels pain is contingent on its degree of knowledge or intelligence. An insect being very low on the evolutionary scale would feel less pain than, say, a dog. Not so, however, with Gregor; his will is that of an insect, but his intellect is that of a man. This makes for a will that is all the more powerful and torturous; it is, like **"Die Verwandlung,"** a hybrid made for pain. Schopenhauer writes: "the will is the string, . . . knowledge the sounding board, and pain the tone" (2: 298). It should be noted that these ruminations and their connection to Schopenhauer are not arbitrary; both quotes are taken from an essay that would have captured Kafka's attention, "Doctrine of Suffering of the World."

So Gregor is "repeatedly yanked awake by his hunger"; and if it's not hunger, it is his "fretting amid vague hopes" (Kafka, **"Metamorphosis"** 143). The street lamps create light on the ceiling of his room, but where Gregor resides "it [is] dark" (141). Just as Georg's father had been left in an "unbearably dark" room (Kafka, **"Judgment"** 63), so, too, does Gregor live in darkness. Grete would in the meantime sweep out the leftovers in Gregor's room. This, however, is probably not just food. No one is really taking care of Gregor; this dismal room is not just full of rotten food, but probably Gregor's feces and urine. Grete upon entering the room races "over to the window, . . . yank[s] it open . . . , lingering there briefly no matter how chilly the weather and inhale[s] deeply" (Kafka, **"Metamorphosis"** 152). This is where Gregor "received his food every day" (146).

Gregor experiences ignominy throughout the story. The sight and probably stench of Gregor is so repulsive that the maid "implore[s] the mother on bended knees to dismiss her" (147). Gregor soon begins again to accept his only recourse. After succumbing to his hunger in the beginning of the second chapter, Grete later reports that "now once again nothing's been touched" of Gregor's daily fare (147). Gregor experiences moments when his resolve to die overtakes his desire to live: eating now "[gives] him no pleasure whatsoever" (154). Beginning once again to accept this judgment as his own allows him to "more effectively" control his body (155). Nevertheless, even in the midst of all his misery and the prospect of an unending cycle of rebirths, Gregor once again falters. This time, though, it is a violent reaction and therefore all the more pathetic.

While the mother and sister rest, having just moved some of Gregor's furniture, Gregor scurries to decide what he will save for himself. Gregor is again racing back towards life, and all its horror. "He quickly scrambled . . . and squeezed" against himself the picture of the woman in fur (159). This fur may represent suffering, the torment found in life. In spite of all life's despair, Gregor, like us, covets it. Similar to a man on his death bed, even what was once considered horrible does not appear so bad in the face of death. At the brink of death we often long for even the hardships in life. In a peculiar way, this is the self-torture Schopenhauer demands of someone who is to achieve extinction. For clearly Gregor isn't clinging to the happiness in life, but the misery which the fur represents. "He clung to his picture," and his life, "refusing to surrender it"; he does this even though his life is no more than the stains he leaves on the walls (160).

After causing his mother to faint (the sight of Gregor is just too disgusting), Gregor then races out of his room for a second time. Hence, "they circled the room several times" (163). Here Kafka might be alluding to the cyclicality of the father-son relationship. This is the relationship that in so many of Kafka's stories is portrayed over and over, i.e., the father is represented literally or metaphorically as the author of punishment. Time and time again the image of Kafka's father follows him in his stories of anguish. Gregor's father "fill[s] his pockets with fruit . . . hurling apple after apple" (164). One apple digs "right into [Gregor's] back" (164). Although this is probably a literary play on Kafka's Judaic heritage, this "red" apple might also be viewed as a representation of desire, in terms of eastern philosophy, the desire to live (164). This persistent craving has embedded itself in Gregor throughout **"Die Verwandlung"** and is now thrown at him by his father. Gregor lumbers around with what "reminded even the father that Gregor . . . was a member of the family" (165). Here Kafka might mean that Gregor still possesses the will-to-live, that which is common to all humanity.

In the third chapter, as Gregor's condition worsens, the family decides "to swallow their repulsion and endure" (165). In the meantime, Gregor for the most part denies his urges: he "was now eating next to nothing" (171). In the third chapter Kafka tells us what species of vermin Gregor is. The charwoman screams at Gregor, "'you old dung beetle!'" (171). It is difficult to deny that this vermin is a scarab. A dung beetle, whether written in English or in German ("*Mistkäfer*"), *is* a scarab. Kafka could have surmised this simply by glancing in his dictionary. Moreover, in the light of *Samsara*, perhaps connecting all three of the *Strafen*, setting forth a theme of transmigration, this must be a sacred scarab: resurrection fits with Kafka's theme of transmigration. When Gregor covers himself with his "sheet," Kafka is alluding to this scarab's sacredness; he enshrouds Gregor (153). Furthermore, the metamorphosis is so abrupt that it resembles a resurrection. Apparently, Kafka knowingly utilized the insect which in Egyptian lore is the symbol for resurrection.

There has been over time a considerable amount of attention lent to Kafka's wish that Gregor, in his state as vermin, never be drawn. Kafka pleads that it not be drawn on the grounds that it would "restrict him" (*Letters* 114). Scholars for the most part have interpreted what Kafka tells Wolff as suggesting that this vermin, if drawn, would cause the restriction of his meaning. I disagree. Of course, it could very well be the case that the restriction of meaning is that the depiction of Gregor as anything other than a scarab restricts him to **"Die Verwandlung,"** which does not allow him to move from story to story. However, Kafka is not making an argument; in a state of panic he makes a plea: "Not that, please not that!" (114). He is not worried that Gregor's meaning will be restricted: he is frightened that, by disclosing Gregor's actual species, a scarab, the secret connection among the *Strafen* will be discovered. The themes of resurrection, transmigration, purgatory, and suffering would no longer belong to him alone.

Gregor's function within the story appears at times to correspond to the characteristics of a savior. Gregor provides not so much the metamorphosis of the family, but the restoration of the family, which elicits further consideration of Kafka's sources. Perhaps there is something else of eastern origin in Gregor's function. The father's situation invites such consideration, for he certainly has been restored to a position of duty, causing one to wonder if Kafka, continuing his probable use of eastern philosophy and religion, had the notion of an *avatar* in mind. Again he would have run across this term via Schopenhauer: "The New Testament . . . must somehow be of Indian origin, as is testified by its thoroughly Indian ethics which carries morality to the point of asceticism, by its pessimism and its avatar" (*Parerga* 2: 380). An *avatar,* also spelled *avatara,* is an incarnation of God. Jesus Christ and Krishna alike would be considered *avatars*; both appear in order to restore *dharma* or duty. Krishna, for instance, says "whenever there is fall of *dharma,* . . . then I create myself, to establish *dharma* I appear in age after age" (qtd. in Chandola 31). The notion that Gregor is an *avatar* might explain part of Gregor's effect on the family. There is, it appears, the erosion of duty within Gregor's family. Krishna in the *Bhagavad-Gita* warns; "For when the family decays, the eternal family-*dharma* dies; unrighteousness overcometh all the family, when *dharma* dies" (qtd. in Thadani 6).

Because of Gregor's metamorphosis, Gregor's father "who had not done a lick of work in five years," begins to work again (Kafka, **"Metamorphosis"** 150). Even though in the beginning of the second chapter we are told that "he had grown very fat, becoming rather clumsy" (151). By the end of the same chapter:

> The father stood quite steady in a snug blue uniform with gold buttons, . . . his heavy double chin unfurled over the high stiff collar of the jacket. . . . [His] black eyes gazed fresh and alert the once disheveled hair was now glossy, combed down, and meticulously parted
>
> (162-63).

Mr. Samsa stands erect like a general or the officer who would later appear in **"In der Strafkolonie."** Meanwhile the sister has gone through her own restoration. She is at first portrayed as dutifully taking care of Gregor, showing concern for his eating habits, intuitively attending to Gregor's likes and dislikes, even demonstrating "self control" (153), whereas earlier the parents "had often been cross with her for being, they felt, a somewhat useless girl" (153-54). As she shows less and less regard for Gregor, ("she certainly saw the dirt . . . but she had simply made up her mind to leave it there"), her concern for her own future rises (170). "The sister, having found a job as a salesgirl, was studying shorthand and French every evening in hopes of . . . eventually obtaining a better position" (166). Even the mother, who was in the first two chapters protected by the family, is now more independent and efficient. Barring what the charwomen would attend to, "everything else was taken care of by the mother along with her great amount of needlework" (168). In order to secure more money the entire family takes the initiative to take boarders into the house, and they work together in order to do so. Gregor has restored them to proper duty and self sufficiency: as opposed to being the leeches of his work as a salesman they exhibit responsibility. In the end, as a result of Gregor's eventual death, the sun comes out, and a family excursion ensues. The family then realizes that their jobs "[are] . . . exceedingly advantageous and also promising" (188). They now have a future; life has meaning.

This is not to suggest that a happy ending ensues, it is actually (unbeknownst to the family) exceedingly tragic. Prior to the father, who like a general, barks the order for the three tenants to "leave my home at once!" (185). Gregor foresees that his pains will "ultimately vanish altogether" (182). He is inspired to this realization by his sister and her music. He appears to grasp that, not just suffering, but the acceptance of his death is his ultimate solution. Schopenhauer is once again indispensable to our interpretation.

Schopenhauerian metaphysics includes the metaphysics of music. Schopenhauer views music as a "copy of the will itself" (*World as Will* 2: 257). Furthermore, Schopenhauer proposes that we, through music, seize the *actual* shape of our emotions. Music does not represent the feelings of the artist, but is in a manner of speaking without content; emotion stands naked before us. Schopenhauer writes:

> [M]usic does not express this or that particular and definite pleasure, this or that affliction, pain, sorrow, horror, gaiety, merriment, or peace of mind, but joy, pain, sorrow, horror, gaiety, merriment, peace of mind *themselves,* to a certain extent in the abstract, their essential nature, without any accessories, and so also without the motives for them
>
> (1: 261).

Music, too, can quiet the will-to-live; it leaves it for the moment docile. From "the sound of the violin," Gregor sees in the deepest recesses of the self what he really needs—death (Kafka, **"Metamorphosis"** 174). While Grete plays, "he felt as if he were being shown the path to the unknown food he was yearning for" (176). Some have suggested that Gregor experiences incestuous impulses toward Grete.[5] Although the pain of an incestuous relationship could fit within the idea of *Samsara,* perhaps in this instance, he is acceding to death, i.e., the "food" he longs for is a permanent demise (177). Interestingly, Kafka authors not just the sister, but the entire family, as a result of their new-found solidarity, working together to kill Gregor, thus saving him from his present state of suffering. "The father arrived with the music stand, the mother with the sheet music, and the sister with the violin" (174). Having restored the family to good order, Gregor is thereby provided with the inspiration to allow "his final breath [to leave] from his nostrils" (182). As discussed, the apple in Gregor's back represents the desire to live. This apple now decays in Gregor's back, and the desire to live is rotting. He no longer resists death, he accepts it.

Kafka first hints that Gregor will be emancipated, and then seems to state that Gregor's final goal was not reached. Kafka may allude to this with the aid of the mother and sister, both of whom have great meaning for Gregor. They represent the precise means of Mr. Samsa's and Gregor's torture; both women may symbolize (re)birth. In the first chapter, "Gregor could not help snapping his jaws a few times at the sight of the flowing coffee" (137). In the company of his mother, the flowing coffee reminds Gregor of birth; it might represent a woman's water breaking. Unconsciously, nothing has more of an unsettling affect on Gregor than the thought of (re)birth. The rage of countless past lives wells up inside him, and he cannot help but snap his jaws. In the third chapter the mother, in the presence of Gregor, "stretch[ed] out her legs and press[ed] them together" (181). This suggests that the cycle of births is coming to an end. Even Gregor foresees his "pains . . . ultimately vanish[ing]" (182). Kafka, though, sentences Gregor to yet another life of suffering. For in the end:

> As they were conversing, both Mr. and Mrs. Samsa, upon seeing the daughter becoming more and more vivacious, realized almost in unison that lately, despite all the sorrows that had left her cheeks pale, she had blossomed into a lovely and shapely girl. Lapsing into silence and communicating almost unconsciously with their eyes, they reflected that it was high time they found a decent husband for her
>
> (188).

Grete is fertile, ready now in the eyes of the mother, father, and Kafka to start a family. She will continue the cycle of (re)birth. Unlike the mother, she does not clamp her legs together; she "stretch[es] her young body out," suggesting that her legs are allowed to rest open, alluding to the eventual rebirth of Georg and Gregor. Kafka appears to make the statement that Gregor is reborn, for our character in **"In der Strafkolonie"** is a *Reisender.* Perhaps there has been movement up the ladder of rebirth; Gregor is still a traveling salesman, but he is no longer vermin. *Samsara,* this world of suffering, in endless cyclic motion, supports this interpretation. *Der Reisende* sits in judgment of the doctrine of metempsychosis, and the father (*der Offizier*) desperately needs his approval. Beyond the suicide of the father figure, there appears to be another inversion of roles: where Kafka had sought the approval of his father, in **"In der Strafkolonie,"** it is now the father who seeks the approval of the son. Our hero, however, does not approve; he refuses to support the "judicial procedure" of metempsychosis (**"Colony"** 200). Even though he, like Schopenhauer, recognizes that this world is "a penal colony, [and] that unusual measures [are] needed here" (200).

It is inspiration which Kafka said he "dread[s] rather than long[s] for" (Brod 90). With **"Die Verwandlung,"** however, I suggest that Gregor's demise is a matter produced by a moment of inspiration. It is Grete's violin, the sound of musical notes, which quiets Gregor's passion for life and inspires him to allow "his final breath" to exit (**"Metamorphosis"** 182). Max Brod writes, "thus, [for Kafka] art serves the religious principle of giving a meaning to life" (Brod 97-98). In the end I agree with Brod; however, I believe Kafka offers "meaning" as a goal which is found through a process, the search for inspiration. Gregor searches for inspiration, and finds it through the music of Grete. This I think is Schopenhauerian with a Kafkaesque twist. Inspired to die, Gregor "[is] so moved . . . [that] he felt as if he were being shown the path to the unknown food he was yearning for" (Kafka, **"Metamorphosis"** 176). The rebirth of Georg Bendemann, the suffering of Gregor Samsa, and his transmigration as *Reisender,* suggests that Gregor could not break the cycle of transmigration, Therefore, Kafka tortures his hero with yet another life in this *Samsaric* world. An eastern influence such as the idea of *Samsara* calls perhaps for a redefinition of what we mean by the term Kafkaesque. In light of the "secret connection" among the *Strafen,* it is not sufficient that Kafkaesque should merely arouse im-

ages of the grotesque or the unjustly accused and perse-
cuted (Kafka, *Letters* 96). If one accepts Samsa as *Samsara*; and if *Samsara* "connects" **"Die Verwandlung"**
with **"Das Urteil"** and **"In der Strafkolonie,"** further
review of the two corner stories, in this context, might
be justified. Knowing that Kafka believed **"Das Urteil"**
to be his breakthrough provides the possibility that *Samsara* was an element of Kafka's development; therefore
a part of what Kafka might view as Kafkaesque. Kafka's work should not merely be *compared* to eastern
philosophy, but viewed as being in part *made* of eastern
philosophy. Furthermore, this approach might warrant
another examination of Kafka's historical personage.
This could begin with further scrutiny of what Kafka
meant by the word *dream*. The concept of *Samsara*
suggests that Kafka's works contain a quality which
goes beyond that of the ordinary dream. This quality,
which is probably the result of a Schopenhauerian metaphysical influence, an influence which is itself *comprised* of eastern philosophy, culminates in a propensity
towards eastern born art and philosophy. Beyond the
works by Rudolf Steiner which Kafka owned and which
have their own eastern elements, and in addition to the
twelve volumes of Schopenhauer's *Sämtliche Werke*,
Kafka's personal library holds yet more eastern works.
Die letzen Tage Gotamo Buddhos might top the list,[6]
and Joo-Dong Lee in his study *Taoistische Weltanschauung im Werke Franz Kafkas,* counts no less than 25
books concerning Chinese philosophy, religion, and literature.[7]

This might be considered evidence of a continuing,
even a growing interest in eastern philosophy. Kafka's
personal library supports the idea of *Samsara*, which I
have endeavored to present as a viable alternative to the
theories of Samson and *jsemsam*. Both become less
likely as one considers that: Kafka points to Schopenhauer as "an artist in language" (Janouch 85); *Samsara*
may connect the *Strafen* etymologically; and the narrator refers to Gregor almost exclusively by his first name
with the exception of the statement "Samsa war Reisender" (**"Verwandlung"** 96). In other words, and in
keeping with one of *Samsara's* most common translations—Samsa is *Samsara*.

Notes

This article owes a deep debt of gratitude to David H.
Chisholm, Professor of German Studies, University of
Arizona, for his invaluable insight, editing, and scholarly criticism. I also thank Elisabeth Neiss Cobbs, University of Arizona, for her patient editing, and *The German Quarterly's* reviewers for their thought-provoking
suggestions.

1. See also Weinberg 316-17.

2. Eduard Hermann, *Populäre Theosophie* (Leipzig:
   Verlag von Wilhelm Friedrich, 1897).

3. Rudolf Steiner, *Die Erziehung des Kindes vom
   Gesichtspunkte der Geisteswissenschaft* (Berlin: In
   Kommission "Besant-Zweig" der "Theosoph. Ge-
   sellschaft," Berlin W., Motzstr. 17 1907).

4. See, for instance, Brod 130.

5. See, for instance, Holland 149.

6. Karl Eugen Neumann, *Die letzten Tage Gotamo
   Buddhos*. Ed. and Trans. Karl Eugene Neumann
   (Munich: Piper, 1911).

7. Joo-Dong Lee, Taoistische Weltanschauung im
   Werke Franz Kafkas (New York: Plang, 1985).

Works Cited

Brod, Max. *Franz Kafka: A Biography*. Ed. and Trans.
G. Humphreys Roberts (Ch. I-VII) and Richard Winston (Ch. VIII). New York: Da Capo Press, 1965.

Chandola, Anoop. *The Way to True Worship: A Popular
Story of Hinduism*. Lanham, MD: UP of America, 1991.

Corngold, Stanley. *The Commentator's Despair: The
Interpretation of Kafka's Metamorphosis*. Ed. Eugene
Goodheart. Port Washington: Kennikat, 1973.

Heller, Erich. *Franz Kafka: Modern Masters*. Ed. Frank
Kermode. New York: Viking, 1975.

Holland, Norman. "Realism and Unrealism: Kafka's
'Metamorphosis'" *Modern Fiction Studies* 6 (1958):
143-50.

Janouch, Gustav. *Conversations with Kafka*. Ed. and
Trans. Goronwy Rees. New York: New Directions,
1971.

Jens, Walter, and Hans Kueng. *Literature and Religion*.
Ed. and Trans. Peter Heinegg. New York: Paragon,
1991.

Kafka, Franz. *Franz Kafka: Briefe*. Ed. Max Brod. New
York: Schocken, 1958.

—. *Dearest Father: Stories and Other Writings*. Ed.
and Trans. Ernst Kaiser and Eithne Wilkins. New York:
Schocken, 1954.

—. *Franz Kafka: The Diaries 1910-1923*. Ed. Max
Brod. Trans. Joseph Kresh (1910-13) and Martin Green-
berg with the cooperation of Hannah Arendt (1914-23).
New York: Schocken, 1976.

—. "Forschungen eines Hundes." *Franz Kafka: Die
Erzählungen und andere ausgewählte Prosa*. Ed. Roger
Hermes. Frankfurt am Main: Fischer, 1996. 411-55.

—. "Der Heizer." *Franz Kafka: Die Erzählungen und
andere ausgewählte Prosa*. Ed. Roger Hermes. Frankfurt am Main: Fischer, 1996. 61-95.

—. "In der Strafkolonie." *Franz Kafka: Die Erzählungen und andere ausgewählte Prosa*. Ed. Roger Hermes.
Frankfurt am Main: Fischer, 1996. 164-98.

—. "Das Urteil." *Franz Kafka: Die Erzählungen und andere ausgewählte Prosa.* Ed. Roger Hermes. Frankfurt am Main: Fischer, 1996. 47-60.

—. "Die Verwandlung." *Franz Kafka: Die Erzählungen und andere ausgewählte Prosa.* Ed. Roger Hermes. Frankfurt am Main: Fischer, 1996. 96-161.

—. "Investigations of a Dog." *Selected Short Stories of Franz Kafka.* Trans. Willa and Edwin Muir. Intro. Philip Rahv. New York: Modern Library, 1993. 214-70.

—. "The Judgment." *The Great Short Works of Franz Kafka: The Metamorphosis, In the Penal Colony and Other Stories.* Trans. Joachim Neugroschel. New York: Simon and Schuster, 1995. 57-72.

—. "The Metamorphosis." *The Great Short Works of Franz Kafka: The Metamorphosis, In the Penal Colony and Other Stories.* Trans. Joachim Neugroschel. New York: Simon and Schuster, 1995. 117-88. References follow this text.

—. "In the Penal Colony." *The Great Short Works of Franz Kafka: The Metamorphosis, In the Penal Colony and Other Stories.* Trans. Joachim Neugroschel. New York: Simon and Schuster, 1995. 191-229. References follow this text.

—. "Report for an Academy." *The Great Short Works of Franz Kafka: The Metamorposis, In the Penal Colony and Other Stories.* Trans. Joachim Neugroschel. New York: Simon and Schuster, 1995. 281-93. References follow this text.

—. *Franz Kafka: Letters to Friends, Family, and Editors.* Ed. and Trans. Richard and Clara Winston. New York: Schocken, 1977. References follow this text.

Kempf, Franz. *Everyone's Darling: Kafka and The Critics of His Short Fiction.* Columbia, SC: Camden, 1994.

Kluback, William. *Franz Kafka: Challenges and Confrontations.* New York: Peter Lang, 1993.

Kluge, Friedrich. *Etymologisches Wörterbuch der deutschen Sprache.* Adapt. Elmar Seebold. Berlin: de Gruyter, 1995.

Kurz, Gerhard. *Traum-Schrecken: Kafkas literarische Existenzanalyse.* Stuttgart: Metzler, 1980.

Reed, T.J.. "Kafka und Schopenhauer: Philisophisches Denken und dichterisches Bild" *Euphorion* 59 (1965): 160-72.

Schopenhauer, Arthur. *Arthur Schopenhauers Sämtliche Werke in fünf Bänden.* Stuttgart: Cotta-Insel, 1960-65.

—. *Arthur Schopenhauers Sämtliche Werke in zwölf Bänden: Mit einer Einleitung von Dr. Rudolf Steiner.* Stuttgart: Cotta'schen, O.J. [1894-96].

—. *Parerga and Paralipomena: Short Philisophical Essays.* Ed. and Trans. E.F.J. Payne. 2 vols. Oxford: Clarendon, 1974.

—. *The World as Will and Representation.* Ed. and Trans. E.F.J. Payne. 2 vols. New York: Dover, 1966.

Thadani, N.V.. *Bhagavad Gita.* Ed. Preet Chablani and Jivat Thadani Trans. N.V. Thandani. New Delhi: Munshiram Manoharlal, 1990.

Weinberg, Kurt. *Kafkas Dichtungen: Die Travestien des Mythos.* Berne: Francke, 1963.

Leena Eilittä (essay date 1999)

SOURCE: Eilittä, Leena. "Kierkegaardian Redefinition of Identity: *Erstes Leid* (1921), *Ein Hungerkünstler* (1922), *Josefine, die Sängerin oder das Volk der Mäuse* (1924)." In *Approaches to Personal Identity in Kafka's Short Fiction: Freud, Darwin, Kierkegaard,* pp. 149-208. Finland: Academia Scientiarum Fennica, 1999.

[In the following essay, Eilittä explores the influence of Kierkegaard's religious-existential philosophy on Kafka's attempts through short fiction to regard the notion of identity.]

Kafka's relationship with Søren Kierkegaard's (1813-1855) philosophical ideas has been a source of constant controversy in Kafka criticism during the past decades. As with Freudian critiques, the critical discussion of Kafka and Kierkegaard has shifted radically from one view to another: some critics have maintained that Kafka's work bears significant resemblances to Kierkegaard's philosophy whereas other critics have suggested that Kierkegaard did not influence Kafka.

Those critics who have emphasised Kierkegaard's influence on Kafka's fiction have often drawn attention to the fact that Kafka knew Kierkegaard's works. He was well read in Kierkegaard's philosophy and his library included some of Kierkegaard's major works which were available in German translations during his lifetime, including *Der Begriff der Angst, Die Krankheit zum Tode, Der Pfahl im Fleisch,* and *Stadien auf dem Lebensweg.* On the other hand, the critics who have claimed that Kierkegaard was an unimportant figure for Kafka have drawn attention to Kafka's often critical remarks on Kierkegaard's philosophy in his letters and diaries. Typical of both views is a tendency to interpret Kafka's work allegorically and to look for literary translations of Kierkegaard's ideas in his works. To date, critics have paid less attention to how Kafka might have assimilated Kierkegaardian ideas to his own views.

In order to analyse Kafka's attitude towards Kierkegaard I will begin by presenting a detailed survey of his often contradictory references to Kierkegaard's philosophy in his diary and letters. Since Kierkegaard's influence on Kafka has been such a controversial topic in critical discussion, I continue by undertaking an analysis of these interpretations and during this analysis I intend to indicate some major shifts in this critical discussion during the past seventy years. And in the last part of this chapter I will finally analyse how Kafka appropriated some central concepts from Kierkegaard's philosophy and adapted them to his view about existential questions in his last stories **"Erstes Leid," "Ein Hungerkünstler"** and **"Josefine, die Sängerin oder das Volk der Mäuse."**

1. KAFKA'S REFERENCES TO KIERKEGAARD

Judging by Kafka's remarks in his diaries and letters his preoccupation with Kierkegaard goes through two phases. First, around the years 1913-1916, Kafka was interested in Kierkegaard's personal life and looked for parallels between Kierkegaard's difficulties with his fiancée Regina Olsen and those that he himself was at that time going through with Felice. During the year 1913 Kafka complained repeatedly in his diary of his solitary situation within his own family and reflected on his relationship with Felice, whom he had known by that time for a year. When reading in August 1913 a collection of extracts from Kierkegaard's diaries, *Das Buch des Richters,* Kafka was struck by the similarities between the difficulties that Kierkegaard had over Regina Olsen and those that he was having with Felice.[1] Because of the consoling resemblances between their situations, Kafka calls Kierkegaard his friend:

> Ich habe heute Kierkegaards Buch des Richters bekommen. Wie ich es ahnte, ist sein Fall trotz wesentlicher Unterschiede dem meinen sehr ähnlich, zumindest liegt er auf der gleichen Seite der Welt. Er bestätigt mich wie ein Freund.
>
> (T 578)

Kafka mentions Kierkegaard again in his diary three years later after his unsuccessful meeting with Felice in the Bohemian holiday resort of Marienbad. In this diary entry, written in August 1916, Kafka regrets his inability to cope with his difficulties with Felice and compares his passivity with Kierkegaard's courage to take the initiative in a similar situation.

> Laß auch den unsinnigen Irrtum, daß du Vergleiche anstellst, etwa mit Flaubert, Kierkegaard, Grillparzer. Das ist durchaus Knabenart. Als Glied in der Kette der Berechnungen sind die Beispiele gewiß zu brauchen oder vielmehr mit den ganzen Berechnugen unbrauchbar, einzeln in Vergleich gesetzt sind sie aber schon von vornherein unbrauchbar. Flaubert und Kierkegaard wußten ganz genau, wie es mit ihnen stand, hatten den geraden Willen, das war nicht Berechnung, sondern Tat. Bei Dir aber eine ewige Folge von Berechnungen ein ungeheuerlicher Wellengang von 4 Jahren.
>
> (T 803)

More important than the above remarks reflecting Kafka's problems with Felice are, however, for the present study the remarks which Kafka wrote on Kierkegaard's philosophy in his letters between November 1917 and March 1918. At this time Kafka was on sick-leave in Zürau after the diagnosis of his acute tuberculosis in September of the same year. In spite of his worsening illness Kafka found himself in an intensely active spiritual and intellectual state. He not only read in Zürau many of Kierkegaard's major works, *Furcht und Zittern, Entweder-Oder,* and *Widerholung,* but he also wrote there a large number of letters and notes in which he commented on Kierkegaard's Abraham figure.[2]

Kafka's first brief reference to Kierkegaard from Zürau is in a letter written in October 1917 to his friend Oskar Baum. Although by this time Kafka had read only Kierkegaard's *Furcht und Zittern* he mentions Kierkegaard's name admiringly and encourages Baum in his readings of Kierkegaard:

> Kierkegaard ist ein Stern, aber über einer mir fast unzugänglichen Gegend, es freut mich, daß du ihn jetzt lesen wirst, ich kenne nur "Furcht und Zittern".
>
> (Br, 190)

Only a few weeks after this, in November 1917, Kafka mentions his further readings of Kierkegaard in the letter to Max Brod, which starts a vivid and polemical discussion about Kierkegaard's philosophy between Kafka and Brod. Kafka's brief reference to Kierkegaard at this point suggests that he was looking for a new means of exploring his inner world in the solitary and sensitive state brought on by illness and separation from the social world:

> Da es aber nicht mehr so ist, ich ja gar nicht schreibe, mich vor mäuseloser beleuchteter Abend- und Nachtruhe zwar nicht fürchten würde, aber auch nicht auf sie abziele, die freien Vormittage im Bett [. . .], die paar Augenblicke beim Buch (jetzt Kierkegaard), gegen Abend ein Spaziergang auf der Landstraße, mir als Alleinsein genügen und nur immer voller erfüllt sein wollten, ist äußerlich keine Klage nötig.
>
> (Br 2, 199)

At the beginning of 1918 Kafka's interest in Kierkegaard intensified after Oskar Baum had paid him a few days' visit in Zürau. But as he writes to Brod, his first reading of *Entweder-Oder* had resulted in disappointment and a revulsion against Kierkegaard's style:[3]

> Richtig und genau sind sie und "Entweder-Oder" besonders ist mit allerspitzigster Feder geschrieben [. . .], aber sie sind zum Verzweifeln und wenn man vor ihnen einmal, wie es bei gespanntem Lesen vorkommen kann, unbewußt das Gefühl hat, es seien die einzigen Bücher auf der Welt, muß auch der gesündesten Lunge fast der Atem ausgehn. [. . .] Es sind Bücher, die sowohl geschrieben als auch gelesen werden können nur in der Weise, daß man wenigstens eine Spur wirklicher Überlegenheit über sie hat. So aber wächst mir ihre Abscheulichkeit unter den Händen.
>
> (Br 2, 228)

In his response Brod writes about his readings of *Stadien auf dem Lebensweg* in which Kierkegaard tells about his dissolved engagement with Regina Olsen and compares his own marital problems with those of Kierkegaard. Brod concludes, however, that Kafka's difficulties with Felice had been, if only superficially, more similar to those of Kierkegaard than his own:

> Nachdem ich längere Zeit an Kierkegaard herumgeschleckt, bald dies, bald jenes begonnen habe, ohne recht Wurzel zu fassen, bin ich auf eine Arbeit von ihm gestoßen, die mir repräsentativ scheint. Sie steht im Band "Stadien auf dem Lebensweg" und heißt: "Schuldig - Unschuldig? Eine Leidensgeschichte". - Hier scheint er so ziemlich ohne Verkleidung seine eigene Verlobungsgeschichte zu erzählen. - So weit ich es bis jetzt urteilen kann, hat er mir aber nichts zu geben. Denn sein Fall ist von dem meinen grundverschieden. Die Ähnlichkeit mit deinem Schicksal ist wohl auffallend, aber doch mehr im Äußerlichen.

> (Br 2, 237)

When reflecting upon the differences between Kierkegaard's and Kafka's personal situations, Brod turns this into a religious question. He suggests that their differing attitudes in respect of their personal problems might have had a religious origin revealing, as he defines it, the 'negativity' of Christianity and the 'positivity' of Judaism. He maintains that Kierkegaard's refusal to marry reflected merely his resigned Christianity whereas Kafka was looking for positive alternatives when making his decision not to marry:

> [. . .] das Grundmotiv des Bruches ist bei ihm, wenn er sich recht erkennt, etwas Negatives, nämlich seine Schwermut. Du dagegen berufst dich auf positive Möglichkeiten. Sollte das auf den Gegensatz christlich: jüdisch hinauslaufen? - Was ihn von mir distanziert, ist die Merkwürdigkeit, daß er sich zwar als tadellos Liebender, aber als zur Ehe ungeeignet fühlt. Während bei mir die Sache umgekehrt liegt. Zumindest ist mir seine Skepsis, daß vollkommene Liebe nicht zur vollkommenen Ehe ausreichen soll, gänzlich fremd.

> (Br 2, 237-238)

Kafka suggests in his response to Brod that Kierkegaard's Christianity is not merely negative. He maintains in contrast that Kierkegaard's description of Abraham in *Fear and Trembling* is very positive when portraying Abraham as somebody whose faith in God is so vast that he is willing to sacrifice his own son. Kafka, however, suggests that Kierkegaard's philosophy is exclusive, since only exceptional figures, such as Abraham, may reach the religious stage which is precluded for common people:

> Aber nur negativ kann man ihn gewiß weder hier noch dort nennen, in "Furcht und Zittern" z.B. (das Du jetzt lesen solltest) geht seine Positivität ins Ungeheuerliche und macht erst vor einem gewöhnlichen Steuereinnehmer halt, wenn es nicht eben ein Einwand - so meine

> ich es - gegen die Positivität wäre, daß sie sich zu hoch versteigt; den gewöhnlichen Menschen (mit dem er übrigens merkwürdigerweise so gut sich zu unterhalten verstand) sieht er nicht und malt den ungeheueren Abraham in die Wolken.

> (Br 2, 240)

In his following letter to Kafka on 19 March Brod reflects further on Kierkegaard's religious development which led him to sacrifice his life and commit himself to God in suffering. He maintains that this Kierkegaardian inwardness, where a human being finds his way to God only through painful and solitary development, is a negative understanding of God. He concludes therefore that Kierkegaard's definition of God entails not positive qualities but pain and fear:

> Ein anderer Einwand gegen seine Haltung betrifft den Grund der Auflösung des Verlöbnisses. Diesen Grund gibt er in den "Stadien" sehr rational an. Er war "verschlossen" und sie verstand ihn nicht. Daher Ehe unmöglich. - Gleichzeitig aber deutet er an, daß seiner "Verschlossenheit" jedes Verständnis, jedes Sich-Anvertrauen prinzipiell fernbleiben muß. - Denn diese Verschlossenheit ist sein Schmerz und nur durch diesen Schmerz hindurch kann er zu Gott. - Da liegt das Negative. Daß sein Gott nur ein Gott der Schmerzen ist, ein Gott der Furcht, der Schrecknisse.

> (Br 2, 244)

When reflecting on Kierkegaard's concept of God, Brod compares Kierkegaard's Christianity with Judaism. He maintains that Kierkegaard's concept of God differentiates between religion and physicality, whereas Judaism does not. Brod suggests therefore that Kierkegaard's resigned Christianity leads to misunderstandings about the role of the religious person in life:

> K. hatte also den Weg, daß er dadurch, daß er sich Schmerzen zufügte, seines Gottes sicher wurde. Und das ist das Negative. Wie viel schwerer hat es einer, dessen Gott will, daß man lebe und Leben schaffe. Er kann seines Gottes nicht so leicht gewiß werden. Denn dieser Gott schlägt sich nur manchmal, nicht unbedingt auf die Seite, wo keine Freude, keine Sinnlichkeit lockt. Dieser positive Gott kann eventuell mit Sinnlichkeit parallel gehen und verlangt von seinem Bekenner, daß er diese parallelen Strähne zu sondern wisse.

> (Br 2, 244-245)

In his following letter to Brod Kafka emphasises again that Kierkegaard's concept of God is not negative as Brod had suggested but eludes any definition. He suggests that in Kierkegaard's philosophy the religiosity of a human being is decided only after his death ('eine Frage des jüngsten Gerichts') so that his present religious state cannot be estimated:

> Denn das Verhältnis zum Göttlichen entzieht sich zunächst für Kierkegaard jeder fremden Beurteilung, vielleicht so sehr, daß selbst Jesus nicht urteilen dürfte,

wie weit derjenige gekommen ist, der ihm nachfolgt. Es scheint das für Kierkegaard gewissermaßen eine Frage des jüngsten Gerichts zu sein, also beantwortbar - sofern eine Antwort noch nötig ist - nach Beendigung dieser Welt. Darum hat das gegenwärtige Außenbild des religiösen Verhältnisses keine Bedeutung.

(Br 2, 247-248)

Kafka stresses that in Kierkegaard's philosophy the religious person finds himself in a contradictory situation since his religiosity looks for ways to express itself, which is impossible in this world. The religious part of his spiritual life is therefore in constant opposition with the world and always threatened by it. In order to emphasise the severe opposition of a religious person with the world Kafka uses the word 'vergewaltigen':

> Nun will sich allerdings das religiöse Verhältnis offenbaren, kann das aber nicht in dieser Welt, darum muß der strebende Mensch sich gegen sie stellen, um das Göttliche in sich zu retten oder, was das gleiche ist, das Göttliche stellt ihn gegen die Welt, um sich zu retten. So muß die Welt vergewaltigt werden von Dir wie von Kierkegaard.

(Br 2, 248)

Kafka emphasises his admiration for Kierkegaard's religious person by quoting a long passage from *Das Buch des Richters*. In this passage Kierkegaard describes the unique relationship of a religious person to his surroundings as well as the ability of a religious person to overcome obstacles through his faith, through his 'originality'. Kierkegaard suggests here that a religious person may overcome the limits of the empirical world through his spiritual capacities:

> "Sobald ein Mensch kommt, der etwas Primitives mit sich bringt, so daß er also nicht sagt: Man muß die Welt nehmen wie sie ist (dieses Zeichen das man als Stichling frei passiert), sondern der sagt: Wie die Welt auch ist, ich bleibe bei einer Ursprünglichkeit, die ich nicht nach dem Gutbefinden der Welt zu verändern gedenke: im selben Augenblick, als dieses Wort gehört wird, geht im ganzen Dasein eine Verwandlung vor sich. Wie im Märchen, wenn das Wort gesagt wird, sich das seit hundert Jahren verzauberte Schloß öffnet und alles Leben wird: so wird das Dasein lauter Aufmerksamkeit. Die Engel bekommen zu tun und sehen neugierig zu, was daraus werden wird, denn dies beschäftigt sie. Auf der andern Seite: finstere, unheimliche Dämonen, die lange untätig dagesessen und an ihren Fingern genagt haben, springen auf und recken die Glieder, denn, sagen sie, hier, worauf sie lange gewartet haben, gibts etwas für uns u.s.w."

(Br 2, 239)

This letter, which was written towards the end of March 1918, finishes Kafka's and Brod's correspondence on Kierkegaard's philosophy.[4] In the notes which Kafka wrote in Zürau in February 1918 and which were later published as *Oktavhefte* Kafka continues his reflections

on Kierkegaard's Abraham figure. These remarks on Abraham stand in sharp contrast to his enthusiasm for Kierkegaard's conception of the religious person as expressed in his letters to Brod. In these often very sarcastic remarks Kafka repeatedly mocks Abraham's mental faculties and motivations. Kafka first suggests that Kierkegaard's Abraham is merely a greedy character who is not in harmony with his spiritual world. He describes Abraham ironically as somebody for whom the everyday world is not enough but who does not possess enough spiritual capacity to enter the realm of spirit and therefore he remains stuck with his possessions on the way there:

> Die vergängliche Welt reicht für A's Vorsorglichkeit nicht aus, deshalb beschließt er mit ihr in die Ewigkeit auszuwandern. Sei es aber, daß das Ausgangs-, sei es daß das Eingangstor zu eng ist, er bringt den Möbelwagen nicht durch. Die Schuld schreibt er der Schwäche seiner kommandierenden Stimme zu. Es ist die Qual seines Lebens.

(N2, 104)

Kafka claims that due to his mental poverty Abraham remains caught between the material and spiritual realms. He does not like this world which appears to him as boring but he does not possess the capacity to experience the plurality of the world. Kafka concludes, therefore, that Abraham's complaints about the world reveal his lack of involvement with the richness of this world:

> A. ist in folgender Täuschung begriffen: Die Einförmigkeit dieser Welt kann er nicht ertragen. Nun ist aber die Welt bekanntlich ungemein mannigfaltig, was jederzeit nachzuprüfen ist, indem man eine Handvoll Welt nimmt und näher ansieht. Die Klage über die Einförmigkeit der Welt ist also eigentlich eine Klage über nicht genügend tiefe Vermischung mit der Mannigfaltigkeit der Welt.

(N2, 104-105)

A few years later, in June 1921, Kafka returned to the Abraham legend in a letter to Robert Klopstock. As in his earlier remarks, Kafka ironically attributes to his Abraham such materialism that when Abraham is supposed to leave his house and sacrifice his son, he cannot obey God's order since his house is not finished:

> Ich könnte mir einen andern Abraham denken, der - freilich würde er es nicht bis zum Erzvater bringen, nicht einmal bis zum Altkleiderhändler - der die Forderung des Opfers sofort, bereitwillig wie ein Kellner zu erfüllen bereit wäre, der das Opfer aber doch nicht zustandebrächte, weil er von zuhause nicht fort kann, er ist unentbehrlich, die Wirtschaft benötigt ihn, immerfort ist noch etwas anzuordnen, das Haus ist nicht fertig, aber ohne daß sein Haus fertig ist, ohne diesen Rückhalt kann er nicht fort.

(Br, 333)

When reflecting upon Abraham's mental faculties Kafka questions the very basic assumptions of Kierkegaard's interpretation of the Abraham legend. He doubts if Abraham's development, in which he is led into a higher stage by sacrificing something of his own life, was based on a leap of faith. Kafka also imagines other Abraham figures who are commanded to sacrifice their sons even though they do not have any and are too old to become fathers. Kafka maintains ironically that these men are cowards who do not finish their houses on purpose and escape instead into ancient biblical legends which save them from confronting reality. Towards the end of his letter Kafka draws his last ironical portrayal of Abraham. This imaginary Abraham, who is 'ein widerlicher Alter' and whose son Isaac is 'der schmutzige Junge' might not lack faith, but he does lack the self-assurance to believe that he is the chosen one of God:

> Aber ein anderer Abraham. Einer, der durchaus richtig opfern will und überhaupt die richtige Witterung für die ganze Sache hat, aber nicht glauben kann, daß er gemeint ist, er, der widerliche alte Mann und sein Kind, der schmutzige Junge. Ihm fehlt nicht der wahre Glaube, diesen Glauben hat er, er würde in der richtigen Verfassung opfern, wenn er nur glauben könnte, daß er gemeint ist.

(Br, 333-334)

Kafka therefore concludes in his letter to Klopstock that the Abraham legend belongs to 'alte Geschichten, nicht mehr der Rede wert'. (Br, 333)[5]

As we have seen above, Kafka's comments on Kierkegaard's ideas are obviously extremely contradictory. In his letters to Brod he is interested in Kierkegaard's description of the religious person, whereas in his further comments on the Abraham figure he ironizes these same ideas. In the following part of this study I will analyse how the critics so far have interpreted Kafka's contradictory comments on Kierkegaard and Kafka's reception of Kierkegaardian ideas in his fictional works.

2. PREVIOUS INTERPRETATIONS OF KIERKEGAARD'S INFLUENCE ON KAFKA

2.1. EARLY ALLEGORICAL INTERPRETATIONS

Max Brod was the first critic to suggest that Kierkegaard's philosophy influenced Kafka's fiction. In his introduction to the first edition of *Das Schloß* in 1926 Brod wrote a Kierkegaardian interpretation of the novel, in which he suggests that Kierkegaard's thought had an enormous influence on Kafka's treatment of philosophical and religious issues in this novel.

In his analysis Brod claims that the castle of the novel, with its unattainability and its hierarchic character, represents Kierkegaard's concept of the divine, to which the protagonist of the novel, K., is looking in vain for access. Brod also reads the Amalia-Sortini episode of the novel in Kierkegaardian terms. He suggests that this episode is a parallel to the episode in Kierkegaard's *Fear and Trembling* where God orders Abraham to sacrifice his son. But Brod emphasises that Kafka's interpretation of the 'teleological suspension of the ethical' in the novel is quite different from Kierkegaard's philosophy. In contrast to Kierkegaard's Abraham, Kafka's K. lacks the faith to overcome the discrepancy between the finite world and divinity and does not receive mercy in the Kierkegaardian sense. Brod concludes therefore that in *Das Schloß* the human and divine worlds remain entirely separate:

> Die Inkommensurabilität irdischen und religiösen Tuns: das führt direkt ins Zentrum von Kafkas Roman. Wobei nicht zu übersehen ist, daß Kierkegaard, der Christ, von diesem Konflikt der Inkommensurabilität aus in späteren Werken immer deutlicher zum Verzicht auf das Diesseitsleben gelangt, während Franz Kafkas Held hartnäckig und bis zur Erschöpfung darauf beharrt, sein Leben gemäß den Weisungen des "Schlosses" einzurichten, wiewohl er von allen Schloßbeauftragten geradezu grob und handbegreiflich zurückgestoßen wird.[6]

In his interpretation Brod translates *Das Schloß* allegorically into Kierkegaardian terms and assumes that certain of its characters and episodes illustrate Kierkegaard's philosophical ideas. Brod's early views about Kierkegaard's influence on Kafka spread rapidly to the critical discussion. Herbert Tauber's Kierkegaardian interpretation of *Das Schloß*, written in 1948, is obviously influenced by Brod's ideas.[7] Similarly to Brod, Tauber suggests that the castle of the novel represents Kierkegaardian divinity and that the village symbolises the worldly reality. He maintains that K.'s striving throughout the novel reflects his attempt to come to terms with the divine which is totally separated from the finite world. Tauber's interpretation of *Das Schloß* develops the ideas of Brod's allegorical interpretation to the point where the novel seems like Kafka's retranslation of Kierkegaardian ideas into fiction. He thereby draws attention to the powerful contrast between the finite and infinite worlds in the novel, the loyalty of officials to the divine and how it affects their behaviour, as well as to the melancholy that possesses the characters when they become aware of their powerlessness. But Tauber claims that when Kafka makes his protagonist look for the divine in the temporal realm he intentionally misinterprets Kierkegaard, whose major point was to show how the gap between the divine and finite worlds could be overcome.

In his interpretation of *Der Proceß* of 1940 John Kelly uses a similar Kierkegaardian approach although he does not take into consideration that Kafka wrote the novel before the period of his most intensive preoccupation with Kierkegaard. Kelly suggests that the novel reflects not only Kierkegaard's religious ideas but that Kafka's approach to religious questions in the novel is similar to those of Kierkegaard's disciple Karl Barth, and he also refers to Calvin's theology. In his allegorical readings of the novel Kelly analyses Josef K.'s development in theological terms by stressing the incommensurability of the human and the divine worlds. According to Kelly's analysis, Josef K. becomes aware of his primordial guilt through his arrest, and his development demonstrates the futility of human endeavour to remove this primordial guilt. Kelly suggests that although Josef K. is going through an existential crisis he paradoxically experiences his salvation at the end of the novel by sacrificing his own life. His execution, Kelly claims, corresponds to the Kierkegaardian 'teleological suspension of the ethical' during which he is confronted with the divine:

> So far there is at least a negative case to be made out in favour of Joseph K.'s salvation; and the signs that he is a man about to undergo a frightful doom may be read in an entirely different light. The doom may be really his salvation, his peculiar call from the Absolute. This view is made certain, when the nature of his death is inspected. In his death Joseph K. makes what is considered by Kierkegaard the greatest gesture toward salvation it is within the power of man to make. This gesture is the famous "teleological suspension of the ethical".[8]

2.2. FRENCH EXISTENTIALIST CRITICS

Instead of retranslating Kierkegaard allegorically into Kafka's works like the earlier critics, the French critics of the 1940s started to relate Kafka's Kierkegaardian ideas to the existentialist philosophy. Martha Robert has suggested that this influence, which Kafka exercised on French Existentialism, reflects more generally Kafka's position in the intellectual discussion in France. In France the critics often had very little information about Kafka's background and circumstances and they considered him therefore as an author without any specific social or national roots and easily adaptable to different periods and modes of thought:

> Kafka trat als Angehöriger irgendeines "Niemanlandes" hervor, als Einsamer, dem nichts voranging und von dem man nicht einmal genau wußte, in welcher Sprache er sein Werk verfaßt hatte. Da er scheinbar frei von jeglichen historischen und geographischen Bindungen dastand, wurde er ohne Bedenken adoptiert, ja man möchte fast sagen "naturalisiert", denn es war wirklich etwas wie ein Naturalisierungsprozeß, bei dem ein neuer, französischer, dem wahren allerdings weit genug entfernter Kafka entstand.[9]

Robert suggests that for the French existentialist authors and critics, such as Camus and Sartre, Kafka's work represented a state of absolute exile which acted as a starting-point from which to explore their existentialist ideas. According to Robert, Kafka's fiction attracted Existentialists' attention to Kierkegaard's ideas whose philosophy, along with that of Hegel and Heidegger, was one of their major sources:

> [. . .] Kafka wurde in einem Zuge mit den Philosophen - Kierkegaard, Hegel, Heidegger - genannt, die zur Zeit das existentialistische Denken beherrschten. Er war nicht nur einer der ihren, sondern er trug auch dazu bei, das Interesse für ihre Werke zu wecken.[10]

The first French critic to analyse similarities between Kafka and Kierkegaard was J.C. Daniel-Rops. In his article "L'Univers désespéré de Franz Kafka" in 1937 he writes briefly about Kafka's background and makes comparisons between Kafka's works and those of E.T.A. Hoffmann, Edgar Allan Poe, Marcel Proust and James Joyce. In his analysis Daniel-Rops pays attention to the conditions of modern existence in Kafka's fiction and suggests that Kafka's descriptions were profoundly influenced by Kierkegaard's philosophy:

> Cette âme qu'a dominée la passion de l'absolu, était vraiment un fils spirituel de Kierkegaard, qui, jusqu'au coeur de la pire angoisse, accepte la condition humaine et tire de sa souffrance l'élément fondamental de sa grandeur.[11]

Jean Wahl explored in detail Kafka's relationship to Kierkegaard in his article "Kafka et Kierkegaard: Commentaires".[12] In his article Wahl examines Kafka's interpretation of the Abraham figure in the *Oktavhefte*. He suggests that Kafka's interpretation not only of the Abraham figure but also that of the ethical mode of existence differs profoundly from Kierkegaard's. The ethical mode of existence, which in Kierkegaard's philosophy offers stable norms and values, becomes in Kafka's interpretation of it ambiguous and incommunicable. Wahl maintains therefore that in the *Oktavhefte* Kafka seems to construct a Kierkegaardian world of his own, which is paradoxical and somewhat confusing. In Kafka's interpretation of Abraham his lack of participation in the earthly world leads to the need for another world and his spiritual weakness helps him to concentrate but simultaneously makes it difficult to use this concentration. Moreover, in Kafka's interpretation Kierkegaard's spiritual richness allows a union between the irrational and dialectics but simultaneously leads to their deterioration into negative theology. Wahl concludes therefore that in his critical remarks Kafka rejects Kierkegaard's ethical and religious states and aims at an ethical stage of his own:

> La question se poserait alors de savoir si le stade éthique tel qu'il le conçoit appartient (pour prendre la terminologie kierkegaardienne), à la première éthique, celle d'avant la religion, ou à la seconde éthique, celle que l'on atteint après avoir traversé le religieux et qui est une éthique transfigurée.[13]

In order to demonstrate Kafka's own unique religiosity Wahl analyses some of Kafka's aphorisms and suggests that Kafka's concept of the absolute in these aphorisms is incommensurable with human life. The divine in Kafka's works appears cruel and inhuman when compared to human logic which is inadequate to approach it. But Wahl suggests that Kafka's concern with religious issues in his fiction demonstrates his Jewish belief in the unity of God and humanity. Wahl suggests therefore that Kafka's fiction describes the reverse of his religious ideals by showing the absurdity of life, its insignificant details and frightening aspects. But Wahl concludes that Kafka's work carries a hope that is available for a human being if he knows how to resist the unbearable logic described in his works through the will to live:

> La délivrance sera pour nous si nous conservons la foi dans l'indéstructible, bien que sur cet indéstructible nous ne puissions rien formuler. Sie malgré les horreurs que nous présente Kafka, nous conservons notre courage, si nous pensons toujours: Je serai délivré demain, nous serons purifiés; le châtiment injuste sera devenue justice et purification. Aujourd'hui plus que jamais une telle pensée parâit proche de nous.[14]

In Wahl's view Kafka's comments on the Abraham figure formed a starting point for him from which to explore his own cultural and religious background. Wahl describes Kierkegaard's influence on Kafka in existential terms by emphasising in his interpretation some central ideas of French existentialism such as the absurdity of life and hope available for a man.

In his essay "L'espoir et l'absurde dans l'oeuvre de Franz Kafka" (1942) Albert Camus draws parallels between Kierkegaard's thought and Kafka's fiction with regard to some central existentialist ideas.[15] In his interpretation of *Das Schloß,* Camus presents similar views about the discrepancy between the ethical and the divine that Brod had done earlier. Camus suggests that K.'s ultimate task in the novel is to find his way to this divinity which is not represented by ethical categories but is hidden and appears to the protagonist as emptiness, indifference, injustice and hate. But in contrast to those earlier religious interpretations which had suggested that Kafka's treatment of religious questions ends in resignation, Camus argues that Kafka's description of disillusionment and tragedy paradoxically anticipates hope. Camus describes this development in Kierkegaardian terms by saying that hope and divinity are introduced into the existence of a human being at the moment when he accepts the absurdity of existence and renounces his finite life:

> Ils[16] embrassent le Dieu qui les dévore. C'est par l'humilité que l'espoir s'introduit. Car l'absurde de cette existence les assure un peu plus de la réalité surnaturelle. Si le chemin de cette vie aboutit à Dieu, il y a donc une issue. Et la persévérance, l'entêtement avec lesquels Kierkegaard, Chestov et les héros de Kafka répètent leurs itinéraires sont un garant singulier du pouvoir exaltant de cette certitude.[17]

Maja Goth explores further parallels between Kafka and French Existentialism in her study *Franz Kafka et les lettres françaises 1928-1955* (1956) in which she makes comparisons between Kafka's and Sartre's reception of Kierkegaard's existentialist ideas. Goth argues that Kafka's and Sartre's works describe the absurdity of modern existence in a situation where there is no longer any religious authority or the awareness of tradition. In this situation a man is left alone facing the emptiness of existence and has to solve the question of his existence and undergo a second birth, which is a spiritual one. Goth analyses the notion of existentialist birth in Sartre's and Kafka's works and compares their existentialist definitions of the human condition to that of Kierkegaard. She suggests that Kafka's understanding of existentialist birth is even more profoundly Kierkegaardian than that of Sartre since in his work the possibility of creating a successful existence depends on the possibility that an individual is able to confront his guilt through personal faith:

> Ce parallèle entre Kierkegaard et Kafka éclaire l'affinité de Sartre avec l'auteur du *Procès*: le néant existentiel en tant que condition de la liberté et du choix constitue le rapport entre Sartre et Kafka, rapport qui se base sur Kierkegaard. Mais, à part ce parallélisme, Sartre diffère par l'absence de tout élément religieux dans sa pensée. Il dévie donc de la conception kierkegaardienne sur l'un des points ou Kafka y reste fidèle.[18]

Goth also shows that Sartre's and Kafka's understanding of existentialist choice is similar to that of Kierkegaard. When comparing their descriptions of existentialist choice she suggests again that Kafka is more profoundly Kierkegaardian than Sartre. According to Goth, Kafka relates the choice to divine transcendence and in his fiction the choice is therefore based on faith, which for Kafka eventually forms the basis of authentic existence:

> Mais il y a pourtant un point essentiel où la liberté de Kafka diffère de celle de Sartre. Être soi, c'est se choisir coupable, disions-nous au sujet de Kafka. Or la notion de culpabilité renvoie à une autorité de laquelle dépend le jugement du bien et du mal, à une Loi. Le choix de moimême ne pourra donc s'effectuer indépendamment de la Loi: dès que je pose mon essence, ja me place en rapport avec cette dernière instance dont la validité absolue existe en-dehors de moi. L'être-soi se fonde sur ce rapport.[19]

Goth suggests that Kafka's description of faith in the novel resembles Kierkegaard's concept of faith by condemning all rationalistic approaches to God. Goth maintains, however, that Kafka's description of faith in the novel as well as his remarks in the *Oktavhefte* reveal that he lacks the passion of Kierkegaard's original concept. Goth suggest therefore that Kafka does not believe that a human being may attain a private, passionate relationship with God which would place him beyond the ethical code. Thus, Goth's conclusion seems to be that although Kafka's description of existentialist questions is more Kierkegaardian than that of Sartre's, he does not ultimately reach the point of Kierkegaard's religious state:

> Kafka reste donc plus attaché au général que Kierkegaard. Mais il place pourtant la notion de choix au premier plan comme l'a fait Kierkegaard et comme le fera Sartre. Or le choix de Sartre diffère de celui de Kierkegaard dans la mesure où son choix c'est le choix absolu de moimême par moi alors que Kafka reste kierkegaardien aussi dans le fait que son choix de moi-même par moi est, comme celui de Kierkegaard, un choix de moi comme choisi par l'Absolu qui équivaut à un choix de l'Absolu par moi.[20]

Eduard Grangier stressed in his article of 1950 the differences between Kafka's and Kierkegaard's understanding of existential and religious questions. He claims that Kafka's criticism of the Abraham figure in the *Oktavhefte* reveals his complete distrust of Kierkegaard's religious categories. Grangier argues that Kafka's notes on the Abraham figure reveal that he fails to understand the transformation of Abraham's consciousness before and after the events at Mount Moriah.[21] In Kafka's criticism Abraham degenerates into a common man who loses himself to the details of everyday life, to materialism and dishonesty. Grangier contends that Kafka's Abraham is more similar to the protagonists of his own works than the original Abraham figure and he concludes therefore that Kafka seems to be reading Kierkegaard through his own prejudices. Grangier suggests that lacking Kierkegaard's belief in the leap of faith, Kafka's remarks in the *Oktavhefte* reveal that he can imagine merely unsuccessful, ridiculous or grotesque attempts at it.

Pierre de Boisdeffre also argues in his analysis of 1955 that Kafka's and Kierkegaard's approach to spiritual questions and biographical problems were radically different. He maintains that Kierkegaard's resignation from earthly life led him to spiritual freedom and made him a religious thinker, whereas Kafka's decision led him to such a level of isolation and scepticism that he no longer believed in any religion:

> Kierkegaard est passé du stade esthétique au stade éthique, puis au stade religieux qui s'exprime dans *la Maladie mortelle* et *le Concept d'Angoisse*. Il savait très bien qu'en quittant Régine, il avait "choisi la mort": le ciel terrestre lui était désormais fermé. Mais il se rendait ainsi libre pour une expérience spirituelle plus profonde. [. . .] Kafka, au contraire, a cessé de croire à la Terre Promise.[22]

Maurice Blanchot, too, claims that Kierkegaard's and Kafka's situations when making their personal sacrifices were different. Kierkegaard abandoned the ethical life when making this sacrifice but reached the reli-

gious, whereas Kafka's sacrifice of the ethical, his renunciation of marriage, meant the sacrifice of his religiosity as well because it placed him outside the Jewish law:

> Mais Kafka, s'il abandonne le bonheur terrestre d'une vie normale, abandonne aussi la fermeté d'une vie juste, se met hors de la loi, se prive du sol et de l'assise dont il a besoin pour être et, dans une certaine mesure, en prive la loi. C'est l'éternelle question d'Abraham. Ce qui est demandé à Abraham, ce n'est pas seulement de scrifier son fils, mais Dieu lui-même: le fils est l'avenir de Dieu sur terre, car c'est le temps qui est, en vérité, la Terre Promise, le vrai, le seul séjour du peuple élu et de Dieu en son peuple.[23]

The existentialist critics in France whose comments on Kafka I have surveyed analysed in detail Kierkegaard's influence on Kafka in terms of issues central to existentialist thought. Although the critics identified considerable differences between their ideas, they highlighted Kierkegaard's significant influence on the way Kafka described existential issues in his works. For such critics as Wahl, Camus and Sartre, Kafka's work involved central existentialist issues, such as the absurdity of the world, existential choice, and the hope which is available for a human being. When relating existentialist ideas to Kafka's works they succeeded in detaching themselves from the mere surface level of Kafka's fiction and thereby succeeded in avoiding the allegorical approach of earlier critics.

In contrast, the later critics in France, who started to write around 1950, such as Eduard Grangier, Pierre de Boisdeffre and Maurice Blanchot, stressed the crucial differences between Kierkegaard's and Kafka's religious views. This seems to be the starting-point for the new and more dominant line of criticism in Kafka's reception of Kierkegaard's thought.

2.3. CRITICISM FROM THE 1960s ONWARDS

When we come to the critical discussion in the German- and English-speaking world starting in the 1960s we note a growing tendency among the critics to dissociate Kafka from Kierkegaard's ideas. From then onwards the critics no longer look for similarities between Kafka's and Kierkegaard's views but tend to identify their differences over existential and religious issues.

Fritz Schaufelberger, who published two articles on Kafka and Kierkegaard in *Reformatio*, suggests that although Kierkegaard's philosophy was an inspiration for Kafka when approaching existentialist questions, the solutions he found to these questions involved considerable differences. Schaufelberger begins by analysing Kafka's and Kierkegaard's differences in respect of their personal problems. He suggests that Kierkegaard succeeded in resolving his personal problems through his religion whereas Kafka failed because he did not possess religious faith. He also suggests that Kafka's protagonists are in the constant state of suffering due to their guilt, and that this suffering is Kafka's equivalent to the concept of repentance in Kierkegaard's philosophy. But he maintains that in contrast to Kierkegaard's conception of repentance as a free choice made by human beings, suffering belongs inevitably to human existence in Kafka's fiction. Schaufelberger draws evidence for his argument about Kafka's disbelief in Kierkegaard's religious categories from Kafka's criticism of Abraham. He suggests, however, that Kafka's criticism of Kierkegaard's religious ideas should be understood as his criticism not only of Christian but also of Jewish religiosity:

> In diesem Gedanken liegt Kafkas eindeutige Distanzierung vom christlichen wie vom jüdischen Entweder-Oder, das den Menschen um des Göttlichen Willen zwingt, sich gegen die Welt zu stellen und sie zu vergewaltigen - diesen Vorwurf erhebt er gegen Kierkegaard.[24]

Fritz Billeter draws comparisons between Kafka and Kierkegaard in his study *Das Dichterische bei Kafka und Kierkegaard* in which he also compares their literary qualities which are otherwise neglected in the critical discussion.[25] Billeter's starting-point in his study is, however, that both Kierkegaard and Kafka considered art and being an artist as something inferior to ethical life. He suggests that where Kierkegaard overcame his earlier aestheticism through faith, Kafka remained in the aesthetic stage. Billeter also compares Kafka's and Kierkegaard's treatment of style and language, their concepts of suffering, guilt and fear as well as the mystical tendencies that they both possess. In the second part of his study Billeter analyses Kafka and Kierkegaard as mystical authors who aim to overcome the discrepancy between the finite world and infinity and focuses on similarities in Kafka's and Kierkegaard's style, especially their use of metaphor, allegory, and parable as well as dialectics.[26]

Brian F.M. Edwards and Wiebrecht Ries have analysed Kierkegaard's and Kafka's relationship from the psychological point of view. Edwards attempts to show in his article that Kierkegaard's example was psychologically significant for Kafka when coping with his personal problems. According to Edwards, Kierkegaard offered Kafka the means to cope with the 'spiritual masochism' and 'selfdestructive urges' within his own personality. Edwards claims that although Kierkegaard's religious ideas influenced Kafka's description of his early protagonists his understanding of Kierkegaardian ideas is ultimately irreligious. When looking for further evidence for Kierkegaard's influence on Kafka, Edwards suggests that later in his life, around 1917, Kafka began to relate Kierkegaard's religious ideas to the pathological side of his personality. Edwards claims that Kafka was at that time obsessed with his own sin-

fulness and was looking for confirmation of the overwhelming sense of guilt which in his aphorisms he broadens to include the guilt of mankind:

> Kafka approaches religion with neither faith nor belief, and extracts from it a mandate whose execution, without faith, is unethical, irreligious (even to Kierkegaard) and diseased. He makes upon himself religious demands and applies to himself religious criteria of guilt and punishment, but without being religious. [. . .] Neither in the marriage-question, nor in his religious thought can one say that Kafka was 'influenced' by Kierkegaard. The new-found religious zeal which appears to dominate the years 1917-19 is neither a new nor a truly religious phenomenon, but rather a new and more general formulation of an old theme. Kafka moves from 'I am guilty' to 'Mankind is guilty and therefore I am guilty', and that is really no progress at all.[27]

Wiebrecht Ries also attempts to show parallels between Kafka's and Kierkegaard's personalities in his study *Transzendenz als Terror* (1977). He suggests that in his work Kafka undertook a criticism of Kierkegaard's religious ideas by describing the negative side of Kierkegaard's absolute paradox which leads him to stress sin and guilt. From this point of view Ries offers a new interpretation of the Amalia-Sortini episode of *Das Schloß* in which he suggests that Sortini represents pure power and aggression whereas Amalia, 'die kühnste Metamorphose Abrahams', has undertaken a courageous decision not to submit passively to a humiliating power. Ries suggests therefore that Kafka radically reversed Kierkegaard's religious ideas into his criticism of power structures:

> Denn nicht als Erbe, sondern als Kritiker hat Kafka die Motti aus Kierkegaards "Furcht und Zittern" übernommen, jene verkappten Abbreviaturen eines theologischen Absolutismus der Macht, dessen Sirenenton in der Amalia-Episode aus den Trompeten des "Schlosses" erklingt. Pflegt ihm menschliches Dasein zu erliegen, so soll doch nicht widerstandslos Ergebung verklärt werden. In der Amalia-Figur, der kühnsten Metamorphose Abrahams, kündigt sich die sich vollziehende Revision dieses Erliegens also Sabotage der ihm eingeschriebenen Theodizee an.[28]

Reed Merrill and Wolfgang Lange attempted to relate Kafka's works to Kierkegaard's concept of irony and thereby show the difference between Kafka's and Kierkegaard's views. Merrill compared in his article the concepts of irony held by Socrates, Kierkegaard and Kafka. He suggests that Kierkegaard introduced his concept of passionate faith in order to avoid Socrates's unresolvable ironic attitude and irony is, for Kierkegaard, only a guide to higher knowledge and belief. Merrill illustrates Kafka's use of irony by analysing some short passages from his fiction, and in his analysis he maintains that Kafka's position differs from that of both Socrates and Kierkegaard since irony, for Kafka, is no longer a means but an end in itself, reflecting the basic relativity of his world. He criticises Brod's early religious interpretation, arguing that in Kafka's work a reaching-out for metaphysical unity only results in ironic despair and humour. Although Merrill suggests that Kafka was preoccupied with the same passionate certitude as Kierkegaard, he draws the conclusion that in Kafka's work the spiritual quests of his protagonists lead only to frustration:

> Kierkegaard and Kafka recognised the same division of truth and illusion. Kierkegaard described the conditions for faith, while Kafka could only stand on the brink describing the logical impossibilities of faith, yet hoping for a sign, a metaphoric discloser which would miraculously unite truth and illusion. [. . .] However, where it is evident that Kierkegaard attained a kind of self-mastery, or at least a distancing from the frustrations of pluralistic existence, Kafka succumbed to that pluralism, making it into a topsy-turvy ontology rather than a transitional system which could lead to unity of man and God.[29]

Wolfgang Lange analysed in his article Kafka's aphorisms in which he aims to demonstrate Kierkegaard's influence on Kafka's irony. According to Lange, both Kierkegaard's and Kafka's attitude towards all religious, scientific and political discourses is profoundly ironic: they use these discourses selectively and interpret them in the light of their own experiences. Lange claims that through the freedom of irony they both aim at the constructive destruction of their worlds. But he also emphasises that Kafka's aims when doing this differ significantly from Kierkegaard's. In contrast to Kierkegaard who aimed at breaking the objective world through his irony and arriving at the moment of absolute paradox, for Kafka the irony became an end in itself and subjectivity, which irony brought forth, the only truth:

> Vielmehr sind diese Aphorismen die Trümmer, die übrigblieben, als Kafka sich daran machte, den Kerker in seinem Innern aufzubrechen, als er begann, jenes kulturelle Netzwerk von Diskursen und Praktiken, das uns bis tief in die *physis* hinein durchdringt und stabilisiert, von innen her aufzusprengen, mit dem Ziel, eine Souveränität zu erfahren, die nur in der Überschreitung, im Sprung, im "Ansturm gegen die letzte Grenze" aufleuchtet.[30]

When we approach the critical discussion of Kafka's reception of Kierkegaard which appeared in the 1980s, the critics start to question Kierkegaard's importance for Kafka in general, and many suggest that Kierkegaard was an irrelevant figure for Kafka's thought and literary works.

Claude David analysed Kafka's remarks on Abraham in his article "Die Geschichte Abrahams: Zu Kafkas Auseinandersetzung mit Kierkegaard", in which he interprets these remarks as the formation of Kafka's criticism of Kierkegaard's ethical and religious mode of be-

ing. David suggests that Kafka criticises Kierkegaard for his attempt to mediate the paradox of faith since faith cannot be mediated or even known by someone who possesses it. As Jean Wahl had suggested earlier, David stresses that Kafka understood Kierkegaard's view of the ethical as problematic since the ethical does not reveal itself immediately. David finds evidence for Kafka's problematic understanding of the ethical by referring to his biography. He maintains that Kafka's attitude towards his life shows that the peace and harmony which Kierkegaard linked with the ethical mode of existence are to be found only in death.

David also suggests that Kafka's remarks on the Abraham figure reveal that Kafka does not believe in Kierkegaard's leap of faith either, where the barrier between the ethical and the religious is overcome. Kafka's Abraham is portrayed as someone who is merely caught in the illusion of faith but lives in a spiritual vacuum. David argues therefore that Kafka's comments on Abraham reveal that religious faith becomes an attempt to escape from the richness of this world so that Abraham's faith is ultimately only a weak person's attempt to escape from the world. David also maintains that Kafka's analysis of Kierkegaard's style shows that there is a danger of degenerating into the aesthetic mode of existence and that Kafka accuses Kierkegaard of an intellectual dishonesty.

When analysing Kafka's remarks on Kierkegaard in the *Oktavhefte,* David emphasises Kafka's subjectivity. By referring to Kafka's letter to Robert Klopstock, David maintains that Kafka has created an Abraham of his own which has no resemblance to the original one:

> Wir sind diesmal sehr weit von Kierkegaard. Diese letzte Wendung ist die trostloseste. Die Betrachtungen über Abraham enden in dem Brief an Robert Klopstock mit den Worten: "Schreckliche Dinge - genug."[31]

Ritchie Robertson also addresses Kafka's remarks on the Abraham figure in his study and when analysing these remarks he focuses on Kafka's ambivalence towards Kierkegaard's conception of a private, individualistic, asocial faith. Robertson refers to Kafka's early fascination with Kierkegaard's religiousness in his letters and contrasts these remarks with Kafka's later criticism of the Abraham figure. He suggests that in his isolation Abraham fails to enter human society and is therefore excluded from the rest of the community. He maintains, furthermore, that Kafka shows his critical attitude to Abraham by accusing him of lacking an awareness of the problems of living and therefore of being arrogant and tyrannical. Robertson concludes therefore that Kafka's ideals were totally different from those of Kierkegaard, and that there is no evidence for Brod's early views about Kierkegaard's influence on Kafka:

> Thus Kafka's meditations on *Furcht und Zittern* have led him to a conclusion opposite to Kierkegaard's. [. . .] Altogether, there seems to be only the slenderest

of evidence for Max Brod's famous and influential assertion that Kafka drew heavily on Kierkegaard and
worked his doctrine of the incommensurability of divine and human law into *Das Schloß*.[32]

Richard Sheppard discusses Kierkegaard's influence on
Kafka in his recent article in which he pays attention to
the similarities between their biography, style and treatment of metaphysical questions. He points out Kafka's
selective reception of Kierkegaard's ideas and he demonstrates his views by offering a new interpretation of
Kafka's comments in the *Oktavhefte*. Sheppard suggests
that Kafka's remarks on the Abraham figure reveal that
the revelation of Abraham's false pride can lead to a
dialectical reversal whereby a right way and a sense of
peace are eventually discovered:

> [. . .] Kafka recognises the possibility of 'Ruhe' ('rest',
> 'peace', 'response'); sees that someone like Kierkeg-
> aard's Abraham can acknowledge his pride as a delu-
> sion and use that realization as a 'springboard into the
> world'; and arrives at the concept of a 'constructive de-
> struction of the world'. Far from being a straightfor-
> ward critique of Kierkegaard's Abraham, the nine para-
> graphs of H124-6 transcribe Kafka's dawning, and
> never very confident awareness that someone whose
> life is heading up a metaphysical or existential cul-de-
> sac can, by colliding with its end wall, undergo a dia-
> lectical reversal which may enable him or her to dis-
> cover the right way and issue in a sense of peace.[33]

Sheppard backs up his argument about the hope available for man by drawing attention to Kafka's concept
of the nature of man and authentic existence, which he
derives from Kafka's more positive statements on Kierkegaard in his letters. He maintains that due to Kierkegaard's influence Kafka's remarks reveal a metaphysical tension between the nature of man and
authentic existence. According to Sheppard, Kafka's remarks express a belief in a dynamic power inherent in
human beings which allows them to live authentically
even though they would otherwise remain in a state of
tension with the world:

> [. . .] that there is an essential and dynamic power in
> human nature which can, at least in some instances, en-
> able the individual to live authentically while remain-
> ing, paradoxically, in a state of tension with and accep-
> tance of the world.[34]

Sheppard suggests that Kierkegaard's positive influence
on Kafka is manifested as early as in *Der Proceß*, a
novel which was written before Kafka's intensive preoccupation with Kierkegaard had started. He maintains
that towards the end of his trial Josef K. achieves some
of the positive qualities deprived of him earlier, a development which according to Sheppard shows Kierkegaard's influence on Kafka. Sheppard suggests that Kierkegaard's influence becomes even more obvious in
the portrayal of K. in *Das Schloß*. Due to K.'s activity
and ability to communicate Sheppard thinks that he ac-

quires during the novel Kierkegaardian 'inwardness'
and achieves a more positive relationship with the
castle. Sheppard draws the conclusion that Kierkegaard
contributed to Kafka's more positive view of human
nature and his conception of the world in general.

The above discussion of Kierkegaardian interpretations
of Kafka's work has demonstrated that Kierkegaard's
influence on Kafka has been a lively and controversial
topic among critics over the past decades. The early
critics (Tauber, Kelly) were influenced by Brod's allegorical interpretation of *Das Schloß* and retranslated
Kafka's works into Kierkegaardian religious ideas. The
French existentialist critics (Camus, Sartre) looked instead in Kafka's work for those Kierkegaardian ideas
which corresponded to their view about the existential
situation of human beings. At an early stage the critics
started to pay attention to differences between Kafka's
and Kierkegaard's treatment of religious issues. Some
critics (Wahl, Blanchot) stressed thereby Kafka's Judaism and some suggested that Kafka's approach to religious questions reveals his indifference towards religion
in general (Grangier, de Boisdeffre).

This tendency to disassociate Kafka from Kierkegaard's
religious thought became more and more obvious in the
1960s and 1970s (Schaufelberger, Ries) when critics
found instead similarities between Kierkegaard's and
Kafka's attitude towards their personal problems on a
psychological level (Ries, Edwards), in their concept of
irony (Merrill, Lange) and in the role that art played for
them (Billeter). Most of these more recent critics
(including Claude David and Ritchie Robertson) emphasised the difference between Brod's early religious
interpretation and their own views.

3. KIERKEGAARD'S THEOLOGY AND KAFKA'S AESTHETIC VIEWS

Although the critical discussion has by now overcome
the phase where Kafka's works have been read as re-
translations of Kierkegaard's religious ideas, the question concerning Kierkegaard's influence on Kafka has
quite obviously not been settled. So far the critics have
agreed that Kierkegaard's example was important for
Kafka to cope with his personal problems but his contradictory remarks on Kierkegaard's religious person
have remained largely unresolved. In the following part
of this study I will suggest that although Kafka's criticism on the Abraham figure shows that he rejected Kierkegaard's religious views as such, these same ideas
gave him inspiration to form his own views about existential questions. To start with I will describe how Kierkegaard presented some central ideas about existential
questions in his philosophy.

3.1. KIERKEGAARD'S VIEW OF HUMAN EXISTENCE

In his philosophy Kierkegaard distinguishes between
three different modes of existence: the aesthetic, the
ethical and the religious.[35] In the lowest mode of exist-

ence, the aesthetic state, the human being lives 'ins Blaue hinein', in the state of 'Either/Or' where he explores all the possibilities of life without committing himself to any biding decisions about life. As Kierkegaard describes his soul is 'like a plot of ground in which all sorts of herbs are planted' and he is only able to make immediate choices about his life which are not an expression of his personality but 'a mere letting go'. Kierkegaard emphasises that 'the act of choosing is essentially a proper and stringent expression of the ethical' and a human being who has reached the ethical state consciously wills his own development. As a result, his actions are no longer determined by outer circumstances or passing moments like those of an aesthetic individual but he understands his life in terms of fulfilling duties. When entering the highest state, the religious state, a human being makes the most significant choice possible, since in the religious state he chooses himself, his true and essential self.

Kierkegaard describes this spiritual development through stages in *Either/Or* as a gradual transformation of a person, in which he divides himself into two selves. One of these selves is the typical, imperfect self, a 'shadow' which the person during spiritual 'journey'[36] eventually rejects, and the other is the actual self which remains:

> In the morning he casts a shadow in front of him, at noon it goes beside him almost unnoticed, and in the evening it falls behind him.[37]

According to Kierkegaard human existence is in a constant process of becoming, from lower modes of existence towards the higher forms. As Jean Wahl has pointed out, in Kierkegaard's understanding the existence of a human being is in constant change and eventually reaches authentic existence in the religious state: '[. . .] l'existent reculera, remontera vers son origine, vers sa nouveauté éternelle, au-dessus du temps, et s'efforcera du plus en plus de coincider avec elle.'[38]

Kierkegaard stresses the mental energy and passion which a person needs in order to make the choice which eventually leads to authentic existence. He emphasises that in the proper choosing it is less a question of the contents of this choice as 'of the energy, the earnestness, the pathos with which one chooses'.[39]

But Kierkegaard stresses that when making this existential choice a person not only enters into a new and more profound relationship with himself, but he also enters into a relationship with the transcendence:

> For inasmuch as the choice is undertaken with all the personality's inwardness, his nature is purified and he himself is brought into immediate relation to the eternal power whose omnipresence interpenetrates the whole of existence.[40]

Edward Mooney has described this Kierkegaardian choosing on the one hand as self-choice and on the other hand as self-receptivity.[41] Mooney's idea of self-choice stresses the ethical aspect of this choice, in which a human being relates himself to the moral values of his surroundings. The idea of self-receptivity emphasises the humility which this choice demands when a human being enters into a relationship with the transcendental God. In *Either/Or* Kierkegaard describes this moment of choice as a sudden moment of revelation in which a person simultaneously finds his own true personality and is able to relate himself to the God:

> When around me all has become still, solemn as a star-lit night, when the soul is all alone in the world, there appears before it not a distinguished person, but the eternal power itself. It is as though the heavens parted, and the I chooses itself - or, more correctly, it accepts itself. The soul has then seen the highest, which no mortal eye can see and which never can be forgotten. The personality receives the accolade of knighthood which ennobles it for an eternity. He does not become someone other than he was before, he becomes himself; consciousness unites.[42]

Before a person is able to make such a successful choice he has to fulfil two preconditions. The first of these is a resignation, which does not mean a mere passive surrender to existence but a state in which a person actively renounces temporal things with a view to eternity. In the state of resignation a person may achieve 'peace and rest and comfort in pain' whereby he grows to understand his 'eternal validity, and only then can one speak of grasping existence by virtue of faith'. When resigning from the temporal world a person achieves his spiritual validity which eventually leads to the most advanced spiritual state, based on religious faith:

> Infinite resignation is the last stage before faith, so that anyone who has not made this movement does not have faith, for only in infinite resignation do I become conscious of my eternal validity, and only then can one speak of grasping existence by virtue of faith.[43]

Kierkegaard describes this act of resignation in *Fear and Trembling* by drawing a portrayal of 'the knight of infinite resignation', a young man who enters a hopeless love-affair and must give up his beloved. His desire for the girl, which he cannot actualise in the love relationship, is turned into an inward feeling, and at that moment the man is able to grasp his love in the eternal sense. In this infinite resignation from temporal needs and desires the man finds peace and comfort in pain since he has been able to reconcile himself with existence:

> In infinite resignation there is peace and rest; every person who wills it, who has not debased himself by self-disdain - which is still more dreadful than being too proud - can discipline himself to make this movement, which in its pain reconciles one to existence.[44]

The second prerequisite for choosing oneself is despair. Kierkegaard stresses that the despair which leads to spiritual development concerns the whole personality of a human being in contrast to the aesthetic person who lives in danger of despairing over something particular: 'Only a man who despairs over something particular suffers a break, but that is due precisely to the fact that he does not fully despair.' When analysing his idea of despair in spiritual development Kierkegaard draws a distinction between despair and doubt. He stresses that doubt concerns only the intellectual part of a human being, whereas despair, which always involves a profound choice about one's existence, concerns the whole personality:

> So then choose despair, since despair is itself a choice, for one can doubt without choosing to, but despair one cannot without choosing to do so. And when one despairs one chooses again, and what then does one choose? One chooses oneself, not in one's immediacy, not as this contingent individual, one chooses oneself in one's eternal validity.[45]

The search for authentic existence in Kierkegaard's philosophy is a development leading towards new subjectivity in which a person via absolute isolation reaches spiritual 'inwardness' in the religious stage. The subjective truth which a human being achieves in this development is in Kierkegaard's view not communicable and no other human being may assist in this development. This inward state is a silent and a hidden state in which a touch with the transcendental God gives a religious person an aura of grace.[46] In contrast to an ethical person, who looks for a balance between exteriority and interiority in his life, a religious person possesses a spiritual inwardness which does not find expression in the exterior world:

> Thus in the ethical view of life, it is the task of the single individual to strip himself of the qualification of interiority and to express this in something external. Every time the individual shrinks from it, every time he witholds himself in or slips down again into the qualifications of feeing, mood, etc. that belong to interiority, he trespasses, he is immersed in spiritual trial. The paradox of faith is that there is an interiority that is incommensurable with exteriority, an interiority that is not identical, please note, with the first but is a new interiority.[47]

Kierkegaard maintains that the singularity of a religious person is the precondition for his religious state since as soon as he reveals himself by expressing his faith explicitly he loses his singularity and is outside the paradox of faith:

> The knight of faith, however, is kept in a state of sleeplessness, for he is constantly being tested, and at every moment there is the possibility of his returning penitently to the universal, and this possibility may be a spiritual trial as well as the truth. He cannot get any information on that from any man, for in that case he is outside the paradox.[48]

A person who reaches a religious state is therefore first led into a solitary state in which he has renounced his finite existence. Kierkegaard, however, posits the possibility of regaining one's finite existence through an idea which he calls repetition, 'gjentagelsen'[49]. As Gouwens has suggested, the idea of repetition posits the notion of forward-looking hope in Kierkegaard's religious philosophy, which is grounded in God as the source of endless possibility.[50] Repetition does not therefore mean the mere recurrence of what has been earlier but is a religious experience involving personal choice whereby something that existed earlier continues as something new. In Kierkegaard's view repetition may occur when all human certainty is abandoned and a human being receives his spiritual salvation and regains his finite existence via an irrational 'leap of faith' into the unknown.

Kierkegaard describes his idea of repetition in *Fear and Trembling* by retelling the biblical myth of Abraham who obeys God's order to sacrifice his son Isaac. When called to sacrifice his son, Abraham voluntarily gives up his ethical life, his duties as husband and father, and undertakes in solitary silence a voyage to the mountain of Moriah where he is to sacrifice his little son. As Edward Mooney has suggested, God's command does not express any general or universal requirement but is God's utterly private demand upon Abraham.[51] The precondition for this religious experience is the suspension of ethical norms upon which, until now, Abraham's existence had depended. His spiritual development is possible only after he has succeeded in breaking the ethical norms which have so far ruled his life, i.e., his duties as husband and father. As Jean Wahl pointed out, it is the suspension of ethical norms which is the precondition for religious experience:

> [. . .] c'est le péché qui est la condition de l'existence religieuse la plus profonde. Par le péché la séparation d'avec l'immanence devient absolue. L'individu s'est retranché d'elle. [. . .] Mais cette séparation sera la condition de sa réunion avec lui; et la conscience malheureuse est une bénédiction.[52]

Wahl describes this suspension of ethical order as an irrational moment when a human being enters voluntarily into uncertainty, accepts absurdity of existence and renounces all worldly values. It is this confrontation with absurdity which allows Abraham to experience the miracle of faith and perform the Kierkegaardian 'leap of faith':

> Risquons notre pensée, faisons le sacrifice de ce que nous avons de plus cher, car nous sacrifions notre entendement, fermons les yeux, croyons contre l'entendement, abandonnons-nous à la force de l'absurde et croyons par sa force. On voit l'absurde, et, par la force de l'absurde, on croit en lui. Le miracle de la grâce rend possible la foi au miracle.[53]

God's inhuman order to sacrifice Isaac expresses this absurdity in which Abraham is brought to face the emptiness of existence. It is only through his endless trust in God that Abraham is able to regain his existence and receive his son Isaac again. Abraham's finite life is eventually enriched by this irrational leap into the unknown, made possible because he possesses spiritual courage and infinite confidence. This Kierkegaardian 'leap of faith' means the acceptance of the paradox of God, which comes about by the fact that the infinite and eternal God reveals itself as finite and in temporal existence.

3.2. PARALLELS BETWEEN KAFKA'S AESTHETIC VIEWS AND KIERKEGAARD'S THEOLOGY

Although critics have made several attempts to relate Kierkegaard's views to Kafka, they have paid very little attention to the similarities between Kierkegaard's theological views and Kafka's aesthetics.[54] In the following I will suggest that although Kierkegaard's philosophy may not have had any influence on Kafka's religious views as such, it nonetheless gave him philosophical ideas with which to formulate his views about art and being an artist.

In his personal remarks Kafka, throughout his life, described his attitude towards literature in similar terms to those in which Kierkegaard talked about religion. As early as August 1913 the thirty-year-old Kafka wrote in his diary that his deep devotion to literature makes him find everything else unsatisfying:

> Mein Posten ist mir unerträglich, weil er meinem einzigen Verlangen und meinem einzigen Beruf das ist der Litteratur widerspricht. Da ich nichts anderes bin als Litteratur und nichts anderes sein kann und will, so kann mich mein Posten niemals zu sich reißen, wohl aber kann er mich gänzlich zerrütten.
>
> (T 579)

In this early remark Kafka implies that for him literature was a conscious choice for his life. His statement reveals that his decision to choose literature was as determined and as self-evident as it was for Kierkegaard to look for religious dimension in life. In August 1913 Kafka further stressed the overriding importance of literature for him in his letter to Felice Bauer's father in which he explains his difficulties in deciding to marry. Here he says that literature is such an essential part of him that if he were separated from it he would not exist any more:

> Mein ganzes Wesen ist auf Literatur gerichtet, die Richtung habe ich bis zu meinem 30sten Jahr genau festgehalten; wenn ich sie einmal verlasse, lebe ich eben nicht mehr. Alles was ich bin und nicht bin, folgert daraus.
>
> (Br F, 456)

In several later remarks Kafka also emphasises the passion that he feels about writing and adds that if he had to stop writing his entire existence would lose its mean-

ing. In August 1914 he wrote in his diary that only after he has started to write again does his otherwise empty life find meaning and fulfilment:

> Ich schreibe seit ein Paar Tagen, möchte es sich halten. So ganz geschützt und in die Arbeit eingekrochen, wie ich es vor 2 Jahren war, bin ich heute nicht, immerhin habe ich doch einen Sinn bekommen, mein regelmäßiges, leeres, irrsinniges junggesellenmäßiges Leben hat eine Rechtfertigung. Ich kann wieder ein Zwiegespräch mit mir führen und starre nicht so in vollständige Leere. Nur auf diesem Wege gibt es für mich eine Besserung.
>
> (T 548-549)

The passion that Kafka felt for writing led him to renounce the worldly life just as Kierkegaard had done when he devoted himelf to the religious life. But it was not only marriage that Kafka had to renounce when devoting himself to literature. He recalled in a diary entry from as early as January 1912 that when it became clear for him that he was made for literature and writing, he took an immediate decision to reject everything else in his life. In this following remark Kafka suggests that he was willing to renounce his whole finite existence when making his choice to concentrate on literature:

> Als es in meinem Organismus klar geworden war, daß das Schreiben die ergiebigste Richtung meines Wesens sei, drängte sich alles hin und ließ alle Fähigkeiten stehn, die sich auf die Freuden des Geschlechtes, des Essens, des Trinkens, des philosophischen Nachdenkens der Musik zu allererst, richteten. Ich magerte nach allen diesen Richtungen ab.
>
> (T 341)

Moreover, in his diary entry of July 1913 where Kafka reflects on the positive and negative consequences of his possible marriage, he underlines not only his lack of interest in anything else except literature but also his growing distaste for everything else:

> 4 Alles, was sich nicht auf Litteratur bezieht, hasse ich, es langweilt mich Gespräche zu führen (selbst wenn sie sich auf Litteratur beziehn), es langweilt mich, Besuche zu machen, Leiden und Freuden meiner Verwandten langweilen mich in die Seele hinein.
>
> (T 569)

The inner life which writing allowed Kafka to explore made him repeatedly neglect everything else in his life to the extent that everyday life started to lose its value for him. Kafka's following entry, which he wrote in August 1914, reveals how self-evident the renunciation of finite existence was for him when he made his choice to concentrate on literature:

> Der Sinn für die Darstellung meines traumhaften innern Lebens hat alles andere ins Nebensächliche gerückt und es ist in einer schrecklichen Weise verkümmert und hört nicht auf zu verkümmern. Nichts anderes kann mich jemals zufrieden stellen.
>
> (T 546)

And in the late letter to Robert Klopstock, Kafka underlined the importance of writing for him as well as the loneliness that writing demands:

> Und darum halte ich das Schreiben in zitternder Angst vor jeder Störung umfangen und nicht nur das Schreiben, sondern auch das dazu gehörige Alleinsein.
>
> (Br, 431)

But although Kafka's remarks show that writing was a conscious choice for him and led him to reject everything else in life, they do not yet reveal the religious implications of literature for him. In contrast, Kafka's following comments show that he regarded writing in very similar terms to those in which Kierkegaard regarded religious life. Perhaps Kafka's most revealing remark on this subject is in an aphorism in which Kafka equates writing with praying:

> Schreiben als Form des Gebetes.
>
> (N 2, 354)

When Kafka talked about the poetic inspiration which allowed him to write, he often expressed himself in images derived from the religious realm. Fritz Billeter has suggested that when writing Kafka experienced a moment of divine grace that was the equivalent of Kierkegaard's concept of grace. This moment of grace allowed him to experience salvation not in the religious experience but in the form of poetic inspiration:

> Kafka erlebte den Augenblick nicht streng theologisch als bekehrende Gnadenfunktion, sondern als 'Gnade' dichterischer Inspiration. Strukturell ist jedoch sein Augenblick derselbe wie der Kierkegaards, nämlich ein das Leben bestimmendes Moment, eine zwar schlagartige, aber über die Zeit hingetragende und darum 'ewige' innere Erhebung.[55]

Billeter has also compared Kafka's and Kierkegaard's ideas about spiritual development and found similar parallels. He maintains that Kierkegaard's idea of 'Selbstwerdung', in which a person, through spiritual development, eventually reaches his origins and the transcendence in the religious state, corresponds to Kafka's idea of 'das Unzerstörbare' in a human being which has to be liberated.[56] In several remarks Kafka discusses his idea of 'das Unzerstörbare' in religious terms. He first defines 'das Unzerstörbare' as the object of one's continuous trust in something unbroken and hidden in oneself which enables one to live:

> Der Mensch kann nicht leben ohne ein dauerndes Vertrauen zu etwas Unzerstörbarem in sich, wobei sowohl das Unzerstörbare als auch das Vertrauen ihm dauernd verborgen bleiben können. Eine der Ausdrucksmöglichkeiten dieses Verborgen-Bleibens ist der Glaube an einen persönlichen Gott.
>
> (N 2, 124)

Kafka maintains that 'das Unzerstörbare' is something which is possessed by every single individual and is simultaneously shared by all mankind:

> Das Unzerstörbare ist eines: jeder einzelne Mensch ist es und gleichzeitig ist es allen gemeinsam, daher die beispiellos untrennbare Verbindung der Menschen.
>
> (N 2, 128)

Moreover, he stresses that 'das Unzerstörbare' is always present in human being so that one does not need to strive towards it but only to believe in it:

> Theoretisch gibt es eine vollkommene Glücksmöglichkeit: An das Unzerstörbare in sich glauben und nicht zu ihm streben.
>
> (N 2, 128)

Kafka stated above that one way of expressing the belief in 'das Unzerstör bare' is to believe in a personal God. Many critics have suggested that Kafka himself did not possess a belief in God so for Kafka, 'das Unzerstörbare' expresses itself probably not in any religious categories but in the aesthetic realm, through literature and writing. Billeter has suggested that writing allowed Kafka to find his way to 'das Unzerstörbare' since only writing allowed him to experience inner truth.[57] When describing his relationship to his writing, Kafka also talks about inner powers that he possesses, probably referring thereby to his concept of 'das Unzerstörbare'. He confessed in a letter to Felice from June 1913 that these inherent powers have to be liberated first and that this liberation takes place through writing:

> Das einzige, was ich habe, sind irgendwelche Kräfte, die sich in einer im normalen Zustand gar nicht erkennbaren Tiefe zur Literatur koncentrieren.
>
> (Br F, 400)

A further significant similarity between Kierkegaard's theology and Kafka's aesthetic ideas concerns the idea of a leap.[58] In his diaries and letters Kafka often described his thinking symbolically with the image of a leap. He reports the imaginative leaps which he had experienced while writing in the letter to Felice of June 1913 in which he complains about his difficulties in thinking and emphasies that it is only via leaps of thought that he can achieve new ideas:

> Ich kann nicht denken, in meinem Denken stoße ich immerfort an Grenzen, im Sprung kann ich noch einzelweise manches erfassen, zusammenhängendes, entwicklungsmäßiges Denken ist mir ganz unmöglich.
>
> (Br F, 400)

Kafka's description of this leap implies that such an imaginative leap was a part of his creative process and allowed him to leave the limits of everyday life. Kafka's following description of such a leap in his diary in January 1922 resembles the Kierkegaardian 'leap of faith' through which a human being after having abandoned his finite existence may gain a higher spiritual level:

> Merkwürdiger, geheimnisvoller, vielleicht gefährlicher, vielleicht erlösender Trost des Schreibens: das Hinausspringen aus der Totschlägerreihe Tat—Beobachtung, Tat—Beobachtung, indem eine höhere Art der Beobachtung geschaffen wird, eine höhere, keine schärfere, und je höher sie ist, je unerreichbarer von der 'Reihe' aus, desto unabhängiger wird sie, desto mehr eigenen Gesetzen der Bewegung folgend, desto unberechenbarer, freudiger, steigender ihr Weg.
>
> (T 892)

Kafka's description of the artist's existence also resembles Kierkegaard's view of the religious person as being outside ethical life. He confesses in the letter to Brod written in July 1922 that writing for him is an enjoyable 'Teufelsdienst' which allows him to approach the dark, unconscious powers within himself of which he would otherwise remain unaware:

> Das Schreiben ist ein süßer wunderbarer Lohn, aber wofür? In der Nacht war es mir mit der Deutlichkeit kindlichen Anschauungsunterrichtes klar, daß es der Lohn für Teufelsdienst ist. Dieses Hinabgehn zu den dunklen Mächten, diese Entfesselung von Natur aus gebundener Geister, fragwürdige Umarmungen und was alles noch unten vor sich gehen mag, von dem man oben nichts mehr weiß, wenn man im Sonnenlicht Geschichten schreibt.
>
> (Br 2, 377-378)

Kafka further emphasies the writer's irrational powers by defining himself as a 'Sündenbock' of mankind who allows other people to enjoy sin innocently:

> Er ist der Sündenbock der Menschheit, er erlaubt den Menschen, eine Sünde schuldlos zu genießen, fast schuldlos.
>
> (Br 2, 380)

As for Kierkegaard, Kafka's devotion to the aesthetic life meant not only the renunciation of worldly life, but sometimes even conscious destruction of oneself and therefore to suffer in the world. Kafka emphasised this suffering as an essential part of writing in the following diary entry, written in June 1913, in which he states that when writing his aim is to liberate his creative potential and, if necessary, even voluntarily destroy himself in the process:

> Die ungeheure Welt, die ich im Kopf habe. Aber wie mich befreien und sie befreien, ohne zu zerreißen. Und tausendmal lieber zerreißen, als sie in mir zurückhalten oder begraben. Dazu bin ich ja hier.
>
> (T 562)

The above analysis has shown that throughout his life Kafka expressed in his personal remarks similar ideas in relation to literature as Kierkegaard had done in relation to religion. Kafka's comments reveal that he felt a similar passion for literature as Kierkegaard had for religion, and that choosing literature was a conscious choice of his life resembling Kierkegaard's choosing of one in the religious mode of existence. In the following part of this chapter I will analyse how Kierkegaard's views influenced Kafka's description of the artistic realm and the artist's existence in his very last stories.

4. THE KIERKEGAARDIAN REDEFINITION OF IDENTITY: *ERSTES LEID* (1921), *EIN HUNGERKÜNSTLER* (1922) AND *JOSEFINE, DIE SÄNGERIN ODER DAS VOLK DER MÄUSE* (1924)

Although Kafka had addressed in his personal remarks throughout his life the questions what it means to be an artist and create art, it was not until in his last stories that he approached these questions in fictional form. Kafka wrote these stories within the two last years of his life and they were published together for the first time in the collection *Ein Hungerkünstler,* along with the short story "Eine kleine Frau," soon after his death in 1924. Kafka's late stories have, in earlier Kafka criticism, scarcely been addressed in Kierkegaardian terms, even though Sokel suggested more than thirty years ago that Kafka's late figures embody Kierkegaard's 'religious person'.[59]

To start with I will analyse how Kafka turns Kierkegaard's ideas about spiritual inwardness and the passionate attitude towards religious life into artistic inwardness and a passionate attitude towards art in these stories. Secondly, I will show how the devotion that these artists feel towards their art leads to their solitude and how their lives reflect suffering, doubt and despair which is similar to Kierkegaard's description of religious suffering. And in the last section of this chapter I will finally relate the Kierkegaardian idea of repetition to the aesthetic lives of these artists.

4.1. PASSION, INWARDNESS AND ART

The devotion that the trapeze artist feels towards his art in "Erstes Leid" is so complete that when engaged by a company he stays on his trapeze throughout the day and night.[60] His devotion shows that he has undertaken a conscious choice about his life which places art beyond anything else:

> Ein Trapezkünstler [. . .] hatte, zuerst nur aus dem Streben nach Vervollkommnung, später auch aus tyrannisch gewordener Gewohnheit sein Leben derart eingerichtet, daß er, solange er im gleichen Unternehmen arbeitete, Tag und Nacht auf dem Trapeze blieb.
>
> (D 317)

The trapeze artist is most satisfied when he is high up on the trapeze on his own and practising his art, through which he achieves a silent and hidden state resembling Kierkegaardian 'inwardness' in which other people and outer circumstances have ceased to have any meaning for him:

> Doch war es oben auch sonst gesund, und wenn in der wärmeren Jahreszeit in der ganzen Runde der Wölbung die Seitenfenster aufgeklappt wurden und mit der frischen Luft die Sonne mächtig in den dämmernden Raum eindrang, dann war es dort sogar schön.

> (D 318)

Throughout the story the performance of the trapeze artist breaks through as a light and easy, almost non-physical chain of movements. The narrator of the story implies the metaphysical nature of his art by stressing the unusual involvement it demands from the artist:

> Bekanntlich ist diese hoch in den Kuppeln der großen Varietébühnen ausgeübte Kunst eine der schwierigsten unter allen, Menschen erreichbaren.

> (D 317)

In **"Ein Hungerkünstler"** Kafka describes an artist whose devotion towards his art is equally passionate. The hunger artist is such a passionate starver that he cares about nothing but those long starvation periods during which he spends forty consecutive days in his small cage. While starving, the hunger artist nearly dies away from the rest of the world, takes no notice of his surroundings, and sinks utterly into himself:

> [. . .] dann aber wieder ganz in sich selbst versank, um niemanden sich kümmerte, nicht einmal um den für ihn so wichtigen Schlag der Uhr, die das einzige Möbelstück des Käfigs war, sondern nur vor sich hinsah mit fast geschlossenen Augen und hie und da aus einem winzigen Gläschen Wasser nippte, um sich die Lippen zu feuchten.

> (D 334)

The hunger artist's starvation shows are watched over by guards but the narrator knows that this is unnecessary since during his starvation periods the hunger artist would never eat, not even if forced. The passionate self-oblivion of the hunger artist results in masochism when, after having entertained his alert guards throughout the night by telling them stories and jokes, he enjoys observing them eating the breakfast that is brought to them in the morning. The pleasure that the hunger artist finds in starving seems to be endless and for his passion he is willing to pay any price. When the hunger artist is forced to stop his periods of starvation and show his emaciated body to the public, his reaction is neither relief nor satisfaction but a constant desire to starve further:

> Warum gerade jetzt nach vierzig Tagen aufhören? Er hätte es noch lange, unbeschränkt lange ausgehalten; warum gerade jetzt aufhören, wo er im besten, ja noch

> nicht einmal im besten Hungern war? Warum wollte man ihn des Ruhmes berauben, weiter zu hungern, nicht nur der größte Hungerkünstler aller Zeiten zu werden, der er ja wahrscheinlich schon war, aber auch noch sich selbst zu übertreffen bis ins Unbegreifliche, denn für seine Fähigkeit zu hungern fühlte er keine Grenzen.

> (D 338-339)

When describing the art of public fasting in this story Kafka portrayed a form of entertainment that still existed during his life-time and which had a long tradition in the Western culture.[61] The story takes place during the unspecified time when the interest in the starvation art is diminishing and this gradually affects the hunger artist's position and eventually leads to his death. The narrator of the story repeatedly deplores this change and reflects, sometimes melancholically, upon the past golden age when the starvation art was highly appreciated. He speculates about the causes of this change by addressing it melancholically as a historical turning point when the interest of the public is gradually attracted by other shows. When looking back, however, the narrator remembers that the change was after all not so sudden and unpredictable as it first appeared. He maintains that even earlier some orders had been introduced which made it more difficult for the hunger artists to continue their art and which were not taken seriously enough:

> Denn inzwischen war jener erwähnte Umschwung eingetreten; fast plötzlich war das geschehen; es mochte tiefere Gründe haben, aber wem lag daran, sie aufzufinden; jedenfalls sah sich eines Tages der verwöhnte Hungerkünstler von der vergnügungssüchtigen Menge verlassen, die lieber zu anderen Schaustellungen strömte.

> (D 342)

Much of the critical discussion concerning this story has sought to define the starvation art and the period described in the story. It would be tempting to see starvation art as a symbol of modern art, as has been suggested, by Frederick Krotz and Gerhard Kurz in their interpretations of the story. Krotz has compared Kafka's story to several other modern works and suggests that Kafka's description of art in this story resembles the ambition of modern art to attain a new transcendence.[62] Kurz, on the other hand, suggests that Kafka has undertaken an ideological criticism of the modern artist in this story by stressing his pathological sides.[63] Kurz fails therefore to see the value of the hunger artist's unique performance, and although Krotz succeeds in relating hunger art to modernist ideas about art he nevertheless fails to explain why art of fasting had been so popular earlier.

It seems therefore that the starvation art refers not to something radically new but, on the contrary, to something ancient with which the public of the story is confronted and wants to reject. Some earlier critics of the story have taken this into account in their interpretations of the story. As early as 1936 Harry Steinhauer suggested that the change described in the story reflects a cultural change in which religion gradually loses its meaning and society enters an atheistic phase.[64] As he maintains the hunger artist is therefore comparable to an ascetic saint who is confronted by an age without religion.

In his last story **"Josefine, die Sängerin oder das Volk der Mäuse"** Kafka depicts a singing female mouse, Josefine, who in her passion for her art surpasses the earlier protagonists.[65] While singing Josefine is able to forget her physical surroundings entirely so that it is as if she had died away from this world:

> [. . .] wie sich ihre Lippe kräuselt, zwischen den niedlichen Vorderzähnen die Luft ausstößt, in Bewunderung der Töne, die sie selbst hervorbringt, erstirbt und dieses Hinsinken benützt, um sich zu neuer, ihr immer unverständlicher werdender Leistung anzufeuern.
>
> (D 366)

These short moments of mystical absorption, 'Hinsinken', always encourage her to achieve better results and give her strength to overcome the difficulties and obstacles which she confronts. Her passion towards her art is limitless and she shows her deep devotion by putting her artistic ambition always higher:

> Sie greift nach dem höchsten Kranz, nicht, weil er im Augenblick gerade ein wenig tiefer hängt, sondern weil es der höchste ist; wäre es in ihrer Macht, sie würde ihn noch höher hängen.
>
> (D 372)

The narrator of the story speculates upon Josefine's unique singing in detail during the story, beginning by questioning whether it should be called singing or mere squeaking:

> Ist es denn überhaupt Gesang? Ist es nicht vielleicht doch nur ein Pfeifen?
>
> (D 351)

But despite expressing doubts about Josefine's song, the narrator recounts that when listening to her song the otherwise unmusical mice are so captivated that they, too, enter a trance-like state:

> Schon tauchen auch wir in das Gefühl der Menge, die warm, Leib an Leib, scheu atmend horcht.
>
> (D 356)

The narrator explains the fascination that this people feels towards Josefine's singing by suggesting that it is able to capture the essence of her nation. The situation of the mice nation throughout the story is described as being extremely difficult, being surrounded by enemies and constantly in danger.[66] But the narrator tells that she succeeds not only in consoling but also in protecting them during these difficult times:

> Etwas von der armen kurzen Kindheit ist darin, etwas von verlorenem, nie wieder aufzufindendem Glück, aber auch etwas vom tätigen heutigen Leben ist darin, von seiner kleinen, unbegreiflichen und dennoch bestehenden und nicht zu ertötenden Munterkeit.
>
> (D 366-367)

Sokel has explained the nature of Josefine's song and its meaning for her people with reference to Nietzsche's idea of the Dionysiac spirit of music. Sokel suggests that Josefine's song symbolises the vital spirit of Dionysos that can restore the original unity of Josefine's nation which would otherwise lose its coherence as a nation. Sokel emphasises the metaphysical value of Josefine's song for her people, who are, while listening to her song, able to reach their origins and thereby the absolute, which Josefine's song transmits:

> Man vergleiche damit die Funktion, die der dionysische Geist der Musik, der dithyrambische Chor, bei Nietzsche spielt. In einem Dasein, das durch den Fluch der Individuation zu dauerndem Kampf um Selbsterhaltung, Mühsal und Not verurteilt ist, kommt die dithyrambische Musik des Chors als Wiederbeschwörung der ursprünglichen Einheit in die zerklüftete Welt. In ihr fühlt der von der Not der Endlichkeit bedrängte Einzelne zum unendlichen Leben der Gesamtheit zurück.[67]

As we have seen, Kafka's protagonists in his last stories **"Erstes Leid," "Ein Hungerkünstler"** and **"Josefine, die Sängerin"** possess similar qualities to those Kierkegaard entitled to a religious person. All these artists have chosen art to be the most valuable part of their lives and they implement their decisions with devotion and passion that is similar to the religious life in Kierkegaard's philosophy. In these stories Kafka's description of art shows further similarities to Kierkegaard's ideas about religion when he stresses that art may surpass the limits of empirical reality and give a metaphysical dimension to existence.

4.2. Solitude and suffering

When Kafka describes the involvement that these artists have with their art he simultaneously shows that this involvement cuts them off from the rest of the world. Like the religious persons in Kierkegaard's philosophy, Kafka's artists renounce their finite lives in order to be able to devote themselves entirely to their artistic activity.

In **"Erstes Leid"** the trapeze artist's longing for solitude is so extensive that he insists on staying on his own high up on the trapeze when others are performing. His only social contacts, except for his impressario, are his servants and a few colleagues who occasionally visit him on the trapeze:

> Freilich, sein menschlicher Verkehr war eingeschränkt, nur manchmal kletterte auf der Strickleiter ein Turnerkollege zu ihm hinauf, dann saßen sie beide auf dem Trapez, lehnten rechts und links an den Haltestricken und plauderten, oder es verbesserten Bauarbeiter das Dach und wechselten einige Worte mit ihm durch ein offenes Fenster, oder es überprüfte der Feuerwehrmann die Notbeleuchtung auf der obersten Galerie und rief ihm etwas Respektvolles, aber wenig Verständliches zu. Sonst blieb es um ihn still.

> (D 318)

The trapeze artist's need for solitude is described in the latter part of the story, when he is forced to leave his trapeze and start travelling in order to perform. When he has to come down from his trapeze and enter the world, the trapeze artist falls into a state of despair. While travelling from one city to another, the impressario makes every possible concession in order to meet the trapeze artist's demand for solitude. In order to avoid the painful contact with the common world the trapeze artist travels either during the night or in the early hours of the morning; he uses the fastest car available; and when travelling by train he feels comfortable only when he can stay high up in the luggage-rack, which resembles his trapeze. And when he arrives at the theatre where he is to perform, everything possible is done so that he can concentrate on his performance: the trapeze has been set up a while ago, the doors leading to the theatre are wide open and the corridors are reserved for the trapeze artist only. But despite these careful preparations, the trapeze artist's devotion to his art is deeply disturbed by travelling:

> So viele Reisen nun auch schon dem Impresario geglückt waren, jede neue war ihm doch wieder peinlich, denn die Reisen waren, von allem anderen abgesehen, für die Nerven des Trapezkünstlers jedenfalls zerstörend.

> (D 319)

The hunger artist's devotion to his art has similarly separated him totally from the rest of the world and made him alien to worldly life. His only social contact, except with his public, is with his guards who frequently consider him a fool and suspect him of betrayal while fasting. Moreover, the sympathy that his public shows towards him after periods of starvation when he shows his emaciated body to his audience is superficial. What appears to the mass of spectators as friendliness is from his point of view cruelty. His feeling of unease among the drinking and chattering public which has gathered to greet him results in his deep dissatisfaction, since he is forced to re-enter the profane world:

> Dann kam das Essen, von dem der Impresario dem Hungerkünstler während eines ohnmachtähnlichen Halbschlafes ein wenig einflößte, unter lustigem Plaud-

ern, das die Aufmerksamkeit vom Zustand des Hungerkünstlers ablenken sollte; dann wurden noch ein Trinkspruch auf das Publikum ausgebracht, welcher dem Impresario angeblich vom Hungerkünstler zugeflüstert worden war; das Orchester bekräftigte alles durch einen großen Tusch, man ging auseinander, und niemand hatte das Recht, mit dem Gesehenen unzufrieden zu sein, niemand, nur der Hungerkünstler, immer nur er.

> (D 340-341)

In contrast to the trapeze artist the mental state of the hunger artist is unbalanced and doubt and despair are often mingled with his passionate devotion. The narrator hints at the hunger artist's dissatisfaction at the very beginning of the story by suggesting that the hunger artist had lost so much weight only because he was so dissatisfied with his situation. The narrator tells that the major reason for the hunger artist's dissatisfaction is his public's negative attitude towards him and contempt for his art which becomes more and more evident towards the end of the story:

> So lebte er mit regelmäßigen kleinen Ruhepausen viele Jahre, in scheinbarem Glanz, von der Welt geehrt, bei alledem aber meist in trüber Laune, die immer noch trüber wurde dadurch, daß niemand sie ernst zu nehmen verstand.

> (D 341)

This growing lack of understanding on the part of his public deepens the hunger artist's despair and eventually makes him defensive and openly aggressive. When somebody from his audience doubts that his melancholy state may be caused by fasting he loses his temper and starts to rebel like an animal. His state of despair deepens even more towards the end of the story, when he is removed to the circus where he has to continue his starvation shows not among other human beings but among the animal cages. After his removal his mental state becomes so unbalanced that he eventually becomes frightened of his public and begins to stare absentmindedly into the far distance. When the crowds push to see not the hunger artist but the animal cages, the hunger artist no longer even tries to attract their interest but is pleased at being left on his own:

> In der ersten Zeit hatte er die Vorstellungspausen kaum erwarten können; entzückt hatte er der sich heranwälzenden Menge entgegengesehn, bis er sich nur zu bald - auch die hartnäckigste, fast bewußte Selbsttäuschung hielt den Erfahrungen nicht stand - davon überzeugte, daß es zumeist der Absicht nach, immer wieder, ausnahmslos, lauter Stallbesucher waren. Und dieser Anblick von der Ferne blieb noch immer der schönste.

> (D 345)

It also seems that in this state of resignation the hunger artist does not know how to make use of the new interest in his art which might be already developing. The narrator suggests towards the end of the story that the children attending the circus with their parents show a renewed interest in the art of starvation which might lead to the revival of his art in the future:[68]

> Und es war kein allzu häufiger Glücksfall, daß ein Familienvater mit seinen Kindern kam, mit dem Finger auf den Hungerkünstler zeigte, ausführlich erklärte, um was es sich hier handelte, von früheren Jahren erzählte, wo er bei ähnlichen, aber unvergleichlich großartigeren Vorführungen gewesen war, um was es sich hier handelte, und dann die Kinder, wegen ihrer ungenügenden Vorbereitung von Schule und Leben her, zwar immer noch verständnislos blieben - was war ihnen Hungern? - aber doch in dem Glanz ihrer forschenden Augen etwas von neuen, kommenden, gnädigeren Zeiten verrieten.
>
> (D 346)

In his last story Kafka portrays the situation of his heroine, Josefine, as equally solitary. Although Josefine receives support from her faithful friends, the public constantly threatens her and doubts the value of her singing. In spite of a certain admiration for Josefine the narrator also repeatedly addresses her critically. The narrator also tells that there is an organised opposition to Josefine's art among her people which aims at devaluing her art and depriving her of the privileges that she has succeeded in achieving. The public's constant dissatisfaction with her privileges strengthens towards the end of the story when the public starts to demand that she participate more actively in the daily work of her people. Josefine's reasons for being freed from work, that work would harm her voice so that she would be unable to achieve the best results, are dismissed as excuses.

But this constant threat from her public only strengthens Josefine's devotion to her art even though it also makes her more and more solitary. This situation forces her into a defensive position in which, in her own opinion, she sings to deaf ears, and she does not even search any more for a true understanding of her art. When unfair comparisons are made between her artistic song and the squeaking produced by the members of her people, she shows her superiority by an arrogant laugh which causes further irritation among her people:

> Ich war einmal zugegen, als sie jemand, wie dies natürlich öfters geschieht, auf das allgemeine Volkspfeifen aufmerksam machte, und zwar nur ganz bescheiden, aber für Josefine war es schon zu viel. Ein so freches, hochmütiges Lächeln, wie sie es damals aufsetzte, habe ich noch nicht einmal gesehn; sie, die äußerlich eigentlich vollendete Zartheit ist, auffallend zart selbst in unserem an solchen Frauengestalten reichen Volk, erschien damals geradezu gemein; sie mochte es übrigens in ihrer großen Empfindlichkeit auch gleich selbst fühlen und faßte sich. Jedenfalls leugnet sie also jeden Zusammenhang zwischen ihrer Kunst und dem Pfeifen. Für die, welche gegenteiliger Meinung sind, hat sie nur Verachtung und wahrscheinlich uneingestandenen Haß.
>
> (D 353-354)

The narrator of the story refers to Josefine's exceptional position among her folk by addressing it as though in explicitly Kierkegaardian terms. When describing Josefine's privileges and critically examining her exceptional position, the narrator maintains that Josefine seems to be outside the law, beyond the ethical norms and codes that govern the life of her people. The narrator's characterisation of Josefine's position at this point resembles Kierkegaard's definition of a religious person as being outside the ethical life and forced at times to suspend the ethical norms of his surroundings. Although the people think that Josefine's song protects them so that they therefore gather in huge meetings when threatened by their enemy, the narrator suggests that it might in fact be Josefine's song which has attracted the enemy to the people in the first place. But even this doubt does not affect Josefine's position or diminish the value of her singing for her, as the narrator regretfully admits. Therefore the narrator draws the conclusion that in relation to her people Josefine is almost outside the law and that she may do whatever she wishes without taking the consequences of her actions into consideration:

> Daraus könnte man schließen, daß Josefine fast außerhalb des Gesetzes steht, daß sie tun darf, was sie will, selbst wenn es die Gesamtheit gefährdet, und daß ihr alles verziehen wird.
>
> (D 368)

Kafka's late artists are quite obviously solitary and unsociable figures who sometimes consciously trangress the laws and norms of their surroundings. In this sense their similarity is more than obvious to Kierkegaard's 'religious person' who, as we recall, not only suffers in the finite world but finds himself often in the opposition with the world. After analysing how Kafka's late artistic figures resemble Kierkegaard's 'religious person', I will now explore how these devoted artists relate to the question of repetition which is the ultimate trial of religiousness in Kierkegaard's philosophy.

4.3. THE POSSIBILITY OF REPETITION

In **"Erstes Leid"** the trapeze artist's relation to his surroundings seemed harmonious since the artist had been allowed an exceptional position and had a mutual understanding with his impressario. Towards the end of the story this harmonious relationship breaks down and the artist falls into an increasing state of despair. This happens during one of his strenuous trips when the trapeze artist, who is by this point exhausted and nervous, starts insistently to ask for a second trapeze for his performances. Although the impressario responds immediately to his demands the trapeze artist remains in a confused state and as a result of this incident loses his trust in his impressario:

> Der Trapezkünstler sagte, die Lippen beißend, er müsse jetzt für sein Turnen, statt des bisherigen einen, immer zwei Trapeze haben, zwei Trapeze einander gegenüber.

Der Impresario war damit sofort einverstanden. Der Trapezkünstler aber, so als wolle er zeigen, daß hier die Zustimmung des Impresario ebenso bedeutungslos sei, wie es etwa sein Widerspruch wäre, sagte, daß er nun niemals mehr und unter keinen Umständen nur auf einem Trapez turnen werde.

(D 320)

The impressario eventually succeeds in calming the artist down but this incident has more lasting consequences than at first appears. After consoling the artist, the impressario expresses his fear that the trapeze artist's anxiety may threaten his whole existence. The impressario also observes that the artist now has some wrinkles on his forehead, symbolising the despair which has entered his life permanently:

So gelang es dem Impresario, den Trapezkünstler langsam zu beruhigen, und er konnte wieder zurück in seine Ecke gehen. Er selbst aber war nicht beruhight, mit schwerer Sorge betrachtete er heimlich über das Buch hinweg den Trapezkünstler. Wenn ihn einmal solche Gedanken zu quälen begannen, konnten sie je gänzlich aufhören? Mußten sie sich nicht immerfort steigern? Waren sie nicht existenzbedrohend? Und wirklich glaubte der Impresario zu sehn, wie jetzt im scheinbar ruhigen Schlaf, in welchen das Weinen geendet hatte, die ersten Falten auf des Trapezkünstlers glatter Kinderstirn sich einzuzeichnen begannen.

(D 321)

This brief incident at the end of the story implies that the trapeze artist is no longer able to form a renewed relationship with his art but remains in a desperate state. His suffering in the world becomes permanent and by falling into a state of deep despair he gradually loses his capacity to form a renewed relationship with his art. It seems therefore that in this resigned state the trapeze artist is not able to undertake a Kierkegaardian 'leap of faith' and to form a renewed relationship with his art. In this story Kafka therefore describes something by which he constantly felt threatened: namely that an artist in his willingness to take risks and confront the absurdity of being may be destroyed by his art.

In **"Ein Hungerkünstler"** we can see a similar development with even more tragic consequences. As mentioned above, throughout the story the hunger artist's passionate devotion to his art is mingled with doubt and despair. After being deprived of the chance to continue his art, he himself eventually loses touch with his art. This tragic development is revealed towards the end of the story when a guard from the circus discovers his nearly invisible but still living body among the straw. When discovered by the guard, the hunger artist begs for forgiveness for himself and his profession, asks not be admired for his art and suddenly confesses that he had been starving only because he could not find anything suitable to eat, and not for any higher reasons:

"Verzeiht mir alle", flüsterte der Hungerkünstler; nur der Aufseher, der das Ohr ans Gitter hielt, verstand ihn. "Gewiß", sagte der Aufseher und legte den Finger an die Stirn, um damit den Zustand des Hungerkünstlers dem Personal anzudeuten, "wir verzeihen dir". "Immerfort wollte ich, daß ihr mein Hungern bewundert", sagte der Hungerkünstler. "Wir bewundern es auch", sagte der Aufseher entgegenkommend. "Ihr solltet es aber nicht bewundern", sagte der Hungerkünstler. "Nun, dann bewundern wir es also nicht", sagte der Aufseher, "warum sollen wir es denn nicht bewundern?" "Weil ich hungern muß, ich kann nicht anders", sagte der Hungerkünstler. "Da sieh mal einer", sagte der Aufseher, "warum kannst du denn nicht anders?" "Weil ich", sagte der Hungerkünstler, hob das Köpfchen ein wenig und sprach mit wie zum Kuß gespitzten Lippen gerade in das Ohr des Aufsehers hinein, damit nichts verloren ginge, "weil ich nicht die Speise finden konnte, die mir schmeckt. Hätte ich sie gefunden, glaube mir, ich hätte kein Aufsehen gemacht und mich vollgegessen wie du und alle".

(D 348-349)

When making this confession the hunger artist reveals that he has lost faith in his art and, moreover, that he has become deprived of the contact with the absolute. Richard Sheppard has suggested that the hunger artist, in spite of his proximity to salvation, is ultimately incapable of making the leap of faith.[69] In his interpretation Sheppard refers to Kierkegaard's portrayal of the despairing personality in *The Sickness unto Death* and suggests that the hunger artist suffers from a false self-image similar to that of a despairing person and is therefore not capable of coping with the world around him. I have drawn attention to the humiliating circumstances of the hunger artist's surroundings, which Sheppard in his analysis overlooks and claims instead that while starving the hunger artist 'never seriously tried to communicate anything intelligible'.[70]

After the hunger artist's death his body is immediately removed and the cage is occupied by a young panther whose arrival indicates that the cultural decline described in the story is complete. In the original manuscript version of the story, which Kafka rejected, this contrast between the dying spirit and brutal vitality is sharpened by a coarse, offensive cannibal who was introduced in the last scene of the story.[71] Through this dramatic change the world described in this story enters another, lower and more brutal cultural period in which starvation art has lost the means to capture the attention of this pleasure-seeking public. This dull public is so captivated by this vigorous animal that it cannot tear itself away from the cage, which it ignored when it was occupied by the hunger artist:

"Nun macht aber Ordnung!" sagte der Aufseher, und man begrub den Hungerkünstler samt dem Stroh. In den Käfig gab man einen jungen Panther. Es war eine selbst dem stumpfsten Sinn fühlbare Erholung, in dem so lange öden Käfig dieses wilde Tier sich herumwerfen zu sehn. Ihm fehlte nichts. Die Nahrung, die ihm schmeckte, brachten ihm ohne langes Nachdenken die Wächter; nicht einmal die Freiheit schien er zu vermissen; dieser edle, mit allem Nötigen bis knapp zum Zerreißen ausgestattete Körper schien auch die Freiheit mit sich herumzutragen; irgendwo im Gebiß schien sie zu stecken; und die Freude am Leben kam mit derart starker Glut aus seinem Rachen, daß es für die Zuschauer nicht leicht war, ihr standzuhalten. Aber sie überwanden sich, umdrängten den Käfig und wollten sich gar nicht fortrühren.

(D 349)

This dramatic conclusion has received much attention in the critical discussion concerning the story. Meno Spann suggested in his interpretation that the arrival of the panther is a positive conclusion for the story.[72] H.M. Waidson criticised his interpretation and suggested that in contrast to Kafka's earlier heroes the hunger artist 'dies a martyr's death'.[73] Spann defended his position further by claiming that with the panther 'Kafka has shown this creature in full possession of all the life values the hunger artist lacked'.[74] He also maintained that the butchers guarding the hunger artist express the same vitality as the panther and, in contrast to the hunger artist, lead an 'authentic existence'.[75] This line of criticism which attacks the hunger artist and his art has been continued by many later critics. Helmut Richter contrasted the hunger artist's alienation from society and his meaningless art with the panther who, Richter claims, represents 'die ganze, vollwertige Existenz'.[76] Peter Waldeck has suggested that the 'hunger artist must be annihilated, totally extinguished in order that health and vitality can return to their worlds'.[77] Sheppard also questioned the hunger artist and his art and Fritz Billeter maintained that by his portrayal of artistic figures Kafka in his late stories criticises his own artistic activity.[78]

When emphasising the negative sides of the hunger artist's life the critics have failed to see the value of his unique performance and the humiliating attitude of his surroundings. It is obvious that the hunger artist is not able to form a renewed relationship with his art anymore but collapses into resignation and despair. He ultimately lacks the ability to undertake the 'leap of faith' in the Kierkegaardian sense which would give him a renewed sense of his art.

The hunger artist's tragic development throughout the story shows that he gradually loses touch not only with his art but with his life. Kafka's description of the hunger artist in the latter part of the story reveals that the will to die gradually invades his personality and he no longer reaches towards life but towards death, as his absent-mindedness and passivity earlier in the story also indicated. It becomes obvious towards the end of the story that the hunger artist's instinctual energies, which he had earlier directed towards his art, transform themselves into the death instinct.

Freud differentiates in his later theory between the life instincts and the death instincts, 'Lebenstriebe' and 'Todestriebe'. In Freud's psychoanalytic understanding dying means that the instinctual energies which in earlier life supported living change into destructive death instincts which aim at transforming life into an inorganic state. In *Jenseits des Lustprinzips* (1920) Freud reflects upon the possibility that the destructive death impulse may always be present in human life. He observes that the sexual impulses of a human being include not only positive but also negative impulses:

> Wir haben von jeher eine sadistische Komponente des Sexualtriebes anerkannt; sie kann sich, wie wir wissen, selbständig machen und als Perversion das gesamte Sexualstreben der Person beherrschen. Sie tritt auch in einer der von mir sogenannten "prägenitalen Organisationen" als dominierender Partialtrieb hervor. Wie soll man aber den sadistischen Trieb, der auf die Schädigung des Objekts zielt, vom lebenserhaltenden Eros ableiten können? Liegt da nicht die Annahme nahe, daß dieser Sadismus eigentlich ein Todestrieb ist, der durch den Einfluß der narzißtischen Libido vom Ich abgedrängt wurde, so daß er erst am Objekt zum Vorschein kommt?[79]

Freud also suggests that the regressive nature of human instinctual life may support the idea of the presence of death impulses throughout the life.[80]

Kafka's description of the hunger artist's life resembles Freud's psychoanalytic understanding of life as a transformation from life instincts to death instincts in which the hunger artist's instinctual energies are gradually directed towards dying. the hunger artist no longer succeeds in approaching life through his art but voluntarily submits himself to the dominance of death instincts. Kafka might also have pointed to the presence of death instincts in **"Erstes Leid"** where, at the end of the story, the trapeze artist starts growing old. His first wrinkles on the forehead suggest symbolically that he, too, is approaching death.

In Josefine's case the question of repetition is more difficult to define since we must rely on the information given by the narrator of the story whose point of view is much more limited and distanced than in **"Erstes Leid"** and **"Ein Hungerkünstler."** During the story the narrator describes Josefine's singing career as a continuously declining one in which Josefine eventually disappears, and at the end of the story the narrator refers to her possible death. It seems therefore that Josefine's end would be equally tragic as those of the trapeze artist and the hunger artist and that she, too, in spite of her devotion, eventually loses touch with her art. But a careful examination of the narrator of the story shows that this is not necessarily the case, since we cannot infer Josefine's whole story from the narrator's remarks nor can we rely completely on the information that the narrator transmits. By analysing the narrator of the story I will suggest in what follows that the conclusion of this, Kafka's last story is more ambivalent than those of his earlier stories.

To start with, the narrator addresses Josefine quite positively by calling her 'our own singer' and by stressing the value of her song for her people:

> Unsere Sängerin heißt Josefine. Wer sie nicht gehört hat, kennt nicht die Macht des Gesanges. Es gibt niemanden, den ihr Gesang nicht fortreißt, was um so höher zu bewerten ist, als unser Geschlecht im ganzen Musik nicht liebt.

(D 350)

But in spite of these admiring remarks at the beginning of the story, the narrator soon enters on a long and, I would suggest, contradictory reflection about Josefine and the value of her singing. Moreover, the narrator asks what the effect of Josefine's song is on her people, and when reflecting on this the narrator gives several contradictory reasons:

> Was treibt das Volk dazu, sich für Josefine so zu bemühen? Eine Frage, nicht leichter zu beantworten als die nach Josefines Gesang; mit der sie ja auch zusammenhängt. Man könnte sie streichen und gänzlich mit der zweiten Frage vereinigen, wenn sich etwa behaupten ließe, daß das Volk wegen des Gesanges Josefine bedingungslos ergeben ist. Dies ist aber eben nicht der Fall.

(D 358)

Michel Dentan has studied the narrator's style in the story and suggested that throughout the story the narrator takes the role of an objective observer, a man of science, who aims at an exhaustive analysis of apparent facts.[81] This aim manifests itself in the narrator's style so that the narrator poses questions, makes hypotheses, rejects unsuitable ones and eventually draws some conclusions. The vocabulary of the narration reflects this attitude when the narrator tries to convey precision and logic by often using expressions like 'meiner Meinung nach', 'daraus könnte man schließen', 'nun ist es ja klar' etc. This mixture of quasi-scientific style and pedantic attitude results in involuntary parody and shows the narrator's inadequacy to the object of narration.

I would claim, however, that the narrator's attitude towards Josefine and her art expresses not only his inability to approach the artistic realm, as Dentan has suggested, but also a conscious wish to devalue Josefine's art and perhaps even to abolish her. When carefully analysed it becomes clear that the narration becomes more openly hostile towards Josefine at the latter part of the story when the narrator starts to describe Josefine's demands to be freed from the daily work of her people. When relating Josefine's fierce struggle with

her people the narrator aims to describe Josefine as unrealistic and childish by blaming her for her privileges and her arrogant attitude towards her people:

> Schon seit langer Zeit, vielleicht schon seit Beginn ihrer Künstlerlaufbahn, kämpft Josefine darum, daß sie mit Rücksicht auf ihren Gesang von jeder Arbeit befreit werde; man solle ihr also die Sorge um das tägliche Brot und alles, was sonst mit unserem Existenzkampf verbunden ist, abnehmen und es - wahrscheinlich - auf das Volk als Ganzes überwälzen. Ein schnell Begeisterter - es fanden sich auch solche - könnte schon allein aus der Sonderbarkeit dieser Forderung, aus der Geistesverfassung, die eine solche Forderung auszudenken imstande ist, auf deren innere Berechtigung schließen.

(D 368-369)

Throughout this negative characterisation, however, the narrator of the story often slips involuntarily into a positive characterisation of Josefine's song and her personality. He points out Josefine's arrogance by saying that while singing she is in a nervous state and, moreover, seems blinded by her self-consciousness. But when portraying Josefine as somebody who aims for boundless admiration, the narrator also admits that admiration itself means nothing to her and that her actions are caused by inner logic, not exterior circumstances:

> Wenn sie etwas fordert, so wird sie nicht durch äußere Dinge, sondern durch innere Folgerichtigkeit dazu gebracht.

(D 372)

The question to be answered when analysing the narrator's ambivalent or negative attitude towards Josefine is what might be its motivation. Walter H. Sokel has offered a possible explanation in pointing to the exceptional status of this story within Kafka's entire work. Sokel suggests that in this story Kafka for the first time shows the reversal of power, its decline and also its tragedy. He maintains that, in contrast to Kafka's earlier works, where power was always contrasted with weak protagonists and seen through their eyes, in Kafka's last story the heroine Josefine is seen through the eyes of the declining power:

> Wir sehen die Macht nicht mehr durch die zweifelnden Augen des Ich-Helden, sondern den Helden durch die Augen der Macht. Nicht der innere Zustand des Helden, sondern der der Macht ist uns durch einen ihrer sinnierenden Teilhaber zugänglich.[82]

I would suggest that Josefine's position throughout the story reflects this situation. The narrator approaches her with judgments that reveal his ignorance and possibly also a consciously hostile attitude towards her which indicates that the narrator belongs to the declining power of nation of mice, who feel threatened by the qualities that Josefine's singing transmits.

The question now arises about the essence of Josefine's singing which the narrator addresses so doubtfully. At the beginning of the story the narrator compares Josefine's singing to nut-cracking and maintains that it expresses something quite common but that she succeeds in making something different out of it:

> Ein Nuß aufknacken ist wahrhaftig keine Kunst, deshalb wird es auch niemand wagen, ein Publikum zusammenzurufen und vor ihm, um es zu unterhalten, Nüsse knacken. Tut er es dennoch und gelingt seine Absicht, dann kann es sich eben doch nicht nur um bloßes Nüsseknacken handeln. Oder es handelt sich um Nüsseknacken, aber es stellt sich heraus, daß wir über diese Kunst hinweggesehen haben, weil wir sie glatt beherrschten und daß uns dieser neue Nußknacker erst ihr eigentliches Wesen zeigt, wobei es dann für die Wirkung sogar nützlich sein könnte, wenn er etwas weniger tüchtig im Nüsseknacken ist als die Mehrzahl von uns. Vielleicht verhält es sich ähnlich mit Josefines Gesang.
>
> (D 353)

The narrator also repeatedly points to the minimalist nature of Josefine's song—remarks which imply that Josefine's song is not traditional art but modernistic. The narrator's doubts about Josefine and her singing might express, therefore, the prejudices against modern art and the artist which were still a commonplace in the 1920s when the story was written.

Most earlier critics of the story have, however, not paid attention to this narrative possibility but have instead assumed that the narrator is reliable. James Rolleston calls him a 'skeptical narrator' whose 'efforts to extract a permanent "meaning" from the situation are equally frustrated by the heroine's sheer quirkiness'.[83] The exceptions to this major line of criticism are Ursula Mahlendorf's psychoanalytical account of the story and Ruth Gross's feminist interpretation of the narration.[84]

After the above analysis it should be clear that we should address the narrator's revelations about Josefine with extreme scepticism and, in fact, doubt whether his speculations about her death at the end of the story are true. He seems to be satisfied by the idea that she might have died, stresses her tragical fate, and maintains unrealistically that the future of the nation of mice will be harmonious and peaceful after Josefine's disappearance:

> Sonderbar, wie falsch sie rechnet, die Kluge, so falsch, daß man glauben sollte, sie rechne gar nicht, sondern werde nur weiter getrieben von ihrem Schicksal, das in unserer Welt nur ein sehr trauriges werden kann. Selbst entzieht sie sich dem Gesang, selbst zerstört sie die Macht, die sie über die Gemüter erworben hat. Wie konnte sie nur diese Macht erwerben, da sie diese Gemüter so wenig kennt. Sie versteckt sich und singt nicht, aber das Volk, ruhig, ohne sichtbare Enttäuschung, herrisch, eine in sich ruhende Masse, die förmlich, auch wenn der Anschein dagegen spricht, Geschenke nur geben, niemals empfangen kann, auch von Josefine nicht, dieses Volk zieht weiter seines Weges.
>
> (D 376)

Although Margot Norris has suggested that when rejecting Josefine the mice folk performs a counter-evolutionary act by surrendering to their animal instinctuality,[85] most critics have again taken the narrator's words here as reliable comments on Josefine and her people. Wilhelm Emrich suggested that in his portrayal of Josefine, 'Kafka setzt sich entschieden ab gegen die Genieverherrlichung der Vergangenheit'.[86] Klaus Hermsdorf has similarly claimed that the nation of mice is 'weise' and 'eine Gemeinschaft nüchterner und auf menschliche Weise urteilender Wesen'.[87]

I would argue that the narrator's unintentional revelations about Josefine have, on the contrary, pointed to the fact that Josefine possesses infinite artistic powers and is able to overcome any difficulties which are put in her way. Despite these difficulties Josefine's relationship with her art remains undisturbed, as the narrator involuntarily reveals many times and especially towards the end of the story. It seems therefore that Josefine's resolute attitude towards her art knows no real doubt or continuous despair. When confronted by the hostility of her surroundings Josefine gives up her singing only temporarily and is soon after able to form a renewed relationship with her art, as the narrator recounts:

> Die Abweisung ist manchmal so hart, daß selbst Josefine stutzt, sie scheint sich zu fügen, arbeitet wie sich's gehört, singt so gut sie kann, aber das alles nur eine Weile, dann nimmt sie den Kampf mit neuen Kräften - dafür scheint sie unbeschränkt viele zu haben - wieder auf.
>
> (D 369)

It is therefore difficult to imagine that Josefine would have completely given up her singing and no reason is given in the text for Josefine's sudden death. On the contrary, the narrator always stresses Josefine's vitality and her powers:

> Für sie gibt es kein Altern und keine Schwächen ihrer Stimme.
>
> (D 372)

It seems much more likely that Josefine's disappearance at the end of the story refers not to her death, about which the narrator also is not sure, but to her escape from the threatening circumstances which she has left behind.

I would therefore suggest that in his last story Kafka approaches the question of repetition when applied to artistic creativity more positively than in his earlier artistic stories. His portrayal of Josefine implies that in spite of difficulties, an artist is able to form a renewed relationship with her art. And even if Josefine had died at the end of the story her end would have been different from that of the hunger artist, who denied the value of his art, or the trapeze artist who remained in a state of doubt. It seems therefore that in Josefine Kafka portrays a truly Kierkegaardian figure whose devotion leads her to trust her art endlessly, to move easily beyond the ethical code and to preserve her trust with her art and life. In spite of the doubts that Kafka addresses to Josefine through the narrator, which might express Kafka's own doubts about his art, he eventually portrays Josefine as an artist who remains in touch with her art and knows no fear in approaching the absurdity of existence.

Notes

1. Kierkegaard confesses in his diary: 'Sie (Regina Olsen) hat mich vielleicht eigentlich nie so sehr geliebt, als sie mich bewundert hat, und ich habe sie vielleicht nie so im erotischen Sinne geliebt, als ich mit Wahrheit sagen kann, daß das liebenswürdige Kind mich im schönsten Sinne gerührt hat.' Kierkegaard, S., *Das Buch des Richters* (Jena and Leipzig, 1905), 38.

2. He also read in Zürau a selection from Kierkegaard's papers entitled "Sören Kierkegaard und sein Verhältnis zu 'ihr'", and a biography by O.P. Monrad. See Robertson, ibid., 191.

3. Kafka is here referring also to Martin Buber's two books, *Die Rede, die Lehre und das Lied* and *Ereignisse und Bewegungen*. See Robertson, ibid., 191.

4. Max Brod commented further on Kierkegaard's Abraham figure in his study *Heidentum, Christentum, Judentum: Ein Bekenntnisbuch* (1922) where he analyses how paganism, Christianity and Judaism approach religious questions. Brod maintains that paganism is an ideology of 'Diesseitsfortsetzung' according to which divinity is a continuation of the material world. He suggests that Christianity is in contrast a religion of 'Diesseitsverneinung' because it stresses the unimportance of a finite world in contrast to divinity. Brod argues that Judaism is the only religion which does not fit into this dualistic division. He defines therefore Judaism as a religion of 'Diesseitswunder', where the divinity comes into being in the finite world. When Brod describes this idea of 'Diesseitswunder' in Jewish religion, he refers to Kierkegaard's philosophy, maintaining that Kierkegaard's retelling of the Abraham myth in *Fear and Trembling* clearly expresses this Jewish idea: "Der Begriff des 'Diesseitswunders', wie ich ihn als Kern des jüdischen Weltgefühls fasse, ist nirgends so klar, nirgends so erlebt formuliert wie in Kierkegaards Schrift 'Furcht und Zittern'." Brod, M., *Heidentum, Judentum, Christentum: Ein Bekenntnisbuch* (Leipzig, 1922), 284.

5. There is only one brief reference to Kierkegaard later in Kafka's personal remarks and this is to be found in his diary towards the end of his life. Despite his earlier criticism, Kierkegaard's philosophy seems to have retained its hold over Kafka, for he started to read *Either/Or* once more only a year and a half before his death, in December 1922: "18. Dezember. Die ganze Zeit über im Bett. Gestern *Entweder-Oder.*" (T 925)

6. Brod, M., *Nachwort*, in: Kafka, F., *Das Schloß* (Munich, 1926), 500-501.

7. Tauber, H., *Franz Kafka: An Interpretation of His Works* (London, 1948). See particularly 138-142.

8. Kelly, J., "Franz Kafka's *Trial* and the Theology of Crisis", *The Southern Review,* 5 (1940), 763.

9. Robert, M., "Kafka in Frankreich", *Akzente,* 13 (1966), 310.

10. Robert, ibid., 317.

11. Daniel-Rops, J.C., "L'Univers désespéré de Franz Kafka", *Les Cahiers du Sud* (1937), 172-173.

12. Wahl's article was first published in *L'Arbalète* in 1942.

13. Wahl, J., *Petite historie de l'existentialisme* (Paris, 1947), 105-106, 108-109.

14. Wahl, ibid., 130-131.

15. Camus's essay was first published in *L'Arbalète* in 1942 and appeared in the collection *Le Mythe de Sisyphe* in 1948. See Grenier, R., *Album Camus* (Paris, 1982), 112: "'*Le Mythe de Sisyphe* est publié en octobre, chez Gallimard, le numéro XII de la collection 'Les Essais'. Par crainte de la censure nazie, le chapitre sur Kafka avait été supprimé et remplacé par une étude sur Kirilov, le héros de Dostoievski. *L'Espoir et l'absurde dans l'oeuvre de Franz Kafka* parut en 1942, à Lyon, dans la revue *L'Arbalète,* avant d'être réinséré dans *Le Mythe de Sisyphe* en 1948."

16. Camus refers here also to Russian author and philosopher Lev Shestov.

17. Camus, A., "L'espoir et l'absurde dans l'oeuvre de Franz Kafka", in: *Oeuvres complètes d'Albert Camus* (Paris, 1983), 249.

18. Goth, M., *Franz Kafka et les lettres françaises 1928-1955* (Paris, 1956), 162-164.

19. Goth, ibid., 204-205.

20. Goth, ibid., 217.

21. Grangier, E., "Abraham, oder Kierkegaard, wie Kafka und Sartre ihn sehen", *Zettschrift für Philosophische Forschung,* 4 (1950), 414-415.

22. Boisdeffre, P., "Kierkegaard et Kafka", *Revue de Paris,* July (1955), 142.

23. Blanchot, M., *De Kafka à Kafka* (Paris, 1981), 100.

24. Schaufelberger, F., "Kafka und Kierkegaard", *Reformatio,* 8 (1959), 456.

25. Billeter, F., *Das Dichterische bei Kafka und Kierkegaard* (Winterthur, 1965).

26. In the following section of this chapter I will analyze in detail Billeter's ideas on the similarities between Kierkegaard's theological and Kafka's aesthetic views.

27. Edwards, B., "Kafka and Kierkegaard: A Reassessment", *GLL,* 20 (1966-67), 224.

28. Ries, W., *Transzendenz als Terror: Eine religionsgeschichtliche Studie über Franz Kafka* (Heidelberg, 1977), 64.

29. Merrill, R., "Infinite Absolute Negativity: Irony in Socrates, Kierkegaard and Kafka", *Comparative Literature Studies,* 16 (1979), 232, 234.

30. Lange, W., "Über Kafka Kierkegaard-Lektüre und einige damit zusammenhängende Gegenstände", *DVjs* 60 (1986), 303-304.

31. David, C., "Die Geschichte Abrahams: Zu Kafkas Auseinandersetzung mit Kierkegaard", in: *Bild und Gedanke* (Munich, 1980), 89.

32. Robertson, *Kafka - Judaism, Politics, and Literature,* 193, 195.

33. Sheppard, R., "Kafka, Kierkegaard and the K's: Theology, Psychology and Fiction", *Journal of Literature and Theology,* 5 (1991), 280-281.

34. Sheppard, ibid., 283.

35. This analysis of Kierkegaard's existentialist views is based on his early works *Either/Or* (1843), particularly on the essay "Equilibrium between the Aesthetic and the Ethical" and *Fear and Trembling* (1843) and *Repetition* (1843). When writing this analysis I have been informed by the following studies on Kierkegaard's philosophy: Gouwens, D.J., *Kierkegaard as Religious Thinker* (Cambridge, 1996), Mooney, E., *Selves in Discord and Resolve: Kierkegaard's Moral-Religious Psychology from Either/Or to Sickness unto Death* (New York and London, 1996), Nordentoft, K., *Kierkegaard's Psychology* (Pittsburgh, 1978) and Wahl, J., *Études Kierkegaardiennes* (Paris, 1937).

36. The self is in Kierkegaard's philosophy variously described as a 'wanderer', a 'wayfarer' or a 'pilgrim', a 'traveller', and as a 'seeker'. Kierkegaard visualizes human existence as a 'journey' or a 'way'. Gouwens, *Kierkegaard as Religious Thinker,* 91.

37. Kierkegaard, S., *Either/Or: A Fragment of Life* (London, 1992), 550.

38. Wahl, *Études Kierkegaardiennes,* 262.

39. The emphasis which Kierkegaard lays on the emotional life of a human being, in contrast to his rational faculties, separates Kierkegaard's philosophy from the major line of thought in the Western philosophy, which Kierkegaard considered to have underrated the emotional side of human life. See Gouwens, ibid., 77.

40. Kierkegaard, ibid., 486.

41. Mooney, *Selves in Discord and Resolve,* 12, 21.

42. Kierkegaard, *Either/Or,* 491.

43. Kierkegaard, S., *Fear and Trembling* (Princeton, New Jersey, 1983), 46.

44. Kierkegaard, ibid., 45.

45. Kierkegaard, *Either/Or,* 513.

46. Jean Wahl has described the solitude, silence and hiddenness of a religious person as follows: "L'idée d'être 'devant Dieu' est liée par Kierkegaard à l'idée de solitude. [. . .] Être décidé, être sûr de soi, c'est être silencieux. Être croyant, c'est être caché." Wahl, *Études Kierkegaardiennes,* 273.

47. Kierkegaard, *Fear and Trembling,* 69.

48. Kierkegaard, ibid., 78.

49. This original word for repetition in Danish means taking possession of something again that one had had earlier.

50. Gouwens, *Kierkegaard as Religious Thinker,* 160-161.

51. Mooney, *Selves in Discord and Resolve,* 57.

52. Wahl, *Études Kierkegaardiennes,* 329-330.

53. Wahl, ibid., 334.

54. The only critic who has so far related Kierkegaard's ideas to Kafka's aesthetic views is Fritz Billeter in his book *Das Dichterische bei Kafka und Kierkegaard* to which I referred earlier when commenting on the Kierkegaardian reception of Kafka's works. There is, however, much more evidence for Kierkegaard's influence on Kafka's aesthetic views than Billeter provides.

55. Billeter, F., *Das Dichterische bei Kafka und Kierkegaard: Ein typologischer Vergleich* (Winterthur, 1965), 89.

56. Billeter, ibid., 92.

57. Billeter, ibid., 96.

58. Billeter, ibid., 87.

59. Sokel, *Franz Kafka: Tragik und Ironie,* 521. Sokel also claimed in his interpretation that Kafka's approach to Kierkegaard's religiosity was merely ironical in these stories, a view the following interpretation should correct.

60. When choosing to describe the life of a trapeze artist in *Erstes Leid* Kafka might have recalled his own earlier interest in circus performers. See Bauer-Wabnegg, W.H., "Monster und Maschinen, Artisten und Technik in Franz Kafkas Werk", in: Neumann, G. and Kittler, W., *Franz Kafka: Schriftverkehr* (Freiburg, 1990), 316.

61. Neumann, G., "Hungerkünstler und Menschenfresser", in: Neumann and Kittler, *Franz Kafka: Ein Schriftverkehr,* 405-408.

62. Krotz, F., "Franz Kafka: Ein Hungerkünstler", *Modern Austrian Literature,* 5 (1972), 104-114.

63. Kurz, *Traum-Schrecken: Kafkas literarische Existenzanalyse,* 79.

64. Steinhauer, H., "Hungering Artist", in: *Die Deutsche Novelle* (New York, 1936), 33-38.

65. Hartmut Binder has suggested that Kafka might have thought of Else Lasker-Schüler while portraying Josefine. See Binder, H., "Else Lasker-Schüler in Prag: Zur Vorgeschichte von Kafkas Josefine-Erzählung", *Wirkendes Wort* 44 (1944), 232.

66. Max Brod was the first to suggest that the people of the story represent Jewish people and their difficulties throughout history. Brod, M., *Franz Kafka: Eine Biographie* (Frankfurt, 1954), 234. Ritchie Robertson has also suggested that the mice represent Jewish people. See Robertson, *Kafka - Judaism, Politics, and Literature,* 281-284.

67. Sokel, *Franz Kafka: Tragik und Ironie,* 574.

68. Benno von Wiese has suggested that "Im Staunen der Kinder lag ja schon zu Beginn der Erzählung eine wenn auch nur leise angedeutete Ahnung echten Verstehens", von Wiese, B., *Die Deutsche Novelle von Goethe bis Kafka* (Düsseldorf, 1962), 338.

69. Sheppard, R., "Kafka's *Ein Hungerkünstler*: A Reconsideration", *German Quarterly,* 46 (1973), 229.

70. Sheppard, ibid., 231.

71. Pasley, J.M.S., "Ascetism and Cannibalism: Notes on an Unpublished Kafka Text", *Oxford German Studies,* 1 (1966), 104.

72. Spann, M., "The Starvation Artist and the Leopard", *Germanic Review,* 34 (1959), 262-269.

73. Waidson, H.M., "The Starvation Artist and the Leopard", *Germanic Review,* 35 (1960), 266.

74. Spann, M., "Don't hurt the Jackdaw", *Germanic Review,* 36 (1962), 74-75.

75. Spann, ibid., 75.

76. Richter, H., *Franz Kafka* (Berlin, 1962), 243-245.

77. Waldeck, P., "Kafka's 'Die Verwandlung' and 'Ein Hungerkünstler' as influenced by Leopold von Sacher-Masoch", *Monatshefte,* 64 (1972), 151.

78. Billeter, *Das Dichterische bei Kafka und Kierkegaard,* 11.

79. Freud, S., "Jenseits des Lustprinzips", in: *Gesammelte Werke* 13 (London, 1940), 58.

80. Freud, ibid., 64.

81. Dentan, M., *Humour et création littéraire dans l'oeuvre de Kafka* (Geneva and Paris, 1961), 154-155.

82. Sokel, *Franz Kafka: Tragik und Ironie,* 576.

83. Rolleston, J., *Kafka's Narrative Theater,* 131-132, 136-137. Roy Pascal maintains that he is 'a medium that must be transparent and utterly reliable'. Pascal, *Kafka's Narrators,* 220.

84. Mahlendorf's article "Kafka's Josephine, the Singer or the Mousefolk: Art at the Edge of Nothingness" appeared in *Modern Austrian Literature,* 11 (1978) and Ruth Gross's article "Of Mice and Women" in *The Germanic Review,* 60 (1985).

85. Norris, M., "Kafka's Josephine", *Modern Language Notes,* 98 (1983), 378.

86. Emrich, *Franz Kafka,* 170. Helmut Richter argues similarily in his Marxist interpretation of the story. Richter, H., *Franz Kafka* (Berlin, 1962), 249.

87. Hermsdorf, K., "Künstler und Kunst bei Franz Kafka", in: *Franz Kafka aus Prager Sicht,* edited by E. Goldstücker (Berlin, 1963), 98-99.

Bibliography

1. KAFKA'S WORKS CITED

Briefe 1902-1924 (B), edited by Max Brod (Frankfurt, 1958)

Briefe an Felice und andere Korrespondenz aus der Verlobungszeit (BF), edited by Erich Heller and Jürgen Born (Frankfurt, 1967)

Briefe an Milena (BM), edited by Jürgen Born and Michael Müller (Frankfurt, 1994)

Der Proceß, edited by Malcolm Pasley (Frankfurt, 1990)

Drucke zu Lebzeiten (D), edited by Wolf Kittler, Hans-Gerd Koch and Gerhard Neumann (Frankfurt, 1994)

Max Brod - Franz Kafka Eine Freundschaft: Briefwechsel (Br 2), edited by Malcolm Pasley (Frankfurt, 1989)

Nachgelassene Schriften und Fragmente I (N1), edited by Malcolm Pasley (Frankfurt, 1993)

Nachgelassene Schriften und Fragmente I, Apparatband, edited by Malcolm Pasley (Frankfurt, 1993)

Nachgelassene Schriften und Fragmente II (N2), edited by Jost Schillemeit (Frankfurt, 1992)

Tagebücher in der Fassung der Handschrift (T), edited by Hans-Gerd Koch, Michael Müller and Malcolm Pasley (Frankfurt, 1990)

2. SECONDARY KAFKA LITERATURE

Anderson, Mark, *Kafka's Clothes: Ornament and Aestheticism in the Habsburg Fin de Siècle* (Oxford, 1992)

"Kafka, Homosexuality and the Aesthetics of 'Male Culture'", in: Robertson, Ritchie and Timms, Edward (eds), *Gender and Politics in Austrian Fiction,* Austrian Studies 7 (Edinburgh, 1996), 79-99

———. Bartels, Martin, "Der Kampf um den Freund - die psychoanalytische Sinneinheit im 'Urteil'", *DVjs* 56 (1982), 225-258

Bauer-Wabnegg, Walter, "Monster und Maschinen, Artisten und Technik in Franz Kafkas Werk", in: Kittler, Wolfgang and Neumann, Gerhard (eds), *Franz Kafka: Schriftverkehr* (Freiburg, 1990)

Beicken, Peter, *Franz Kafka - Eine kritische Einführung in die Forschung* (Frankfurt, 1974)

Bernheimer, Charles, *Flaubert and Kafka: Studies in Psychopoetic Structure* (New Haven and London, 1982)

Billeter, Fritz, *Das Dichterische bei Kafka und Kierkegaard: Ein typologischer Vergleich* (Winterthur, 1965)

Binder, Hartmut, *Motiv und Gestaltung bei Franz Kafka* (Bonn, 1966)

———. *Kafka-Handbuch,* volume 2 (Stuttgart, 1979)

———. "Else Lasker-Schüler in Prag: Zur Vorgeschichte von Kafkas 'Josefine' - Erzählung", *Wirkendes Wort* 44 (1994), 229-241

Blanchot, Maurice, *De Kafka à Kafka,* Collection Idées (Paris, 1981)

Bloom, Harold (ed.), *Franz Kafka's Metamorphosis: Modern Critical Interpretations* (New York, 1988)

Boa, Elizabeth, *Kafka: Gender, Class, and Race in the Letters and Fictions* (Oxford, 1996)

Boisdeffre, Pierre de, "Kierkegaard et Kafka", *La Revue de Paris,* July (1955), 38-42

Bridgwater, Patrick, "Rotpeters Ahnherren oder der gelehrte Affe in der deutschen Dichtung", *DVjs* 56 (1982), 447-462

Brod, Max, Nachwort, in: Kafka, Franz, *Das Schloß* (Munich, 1926), 492-503

———. *Franz Kafka: A Biography* (New York, 1947)

———. *Franz Kafka: Eine Biographie,* Dritte, erweiterte Auflage (Frankfurt, 1954)

Camus, Albert, "L'espoir et l'absurde dans l'oeuvre de Franz Kafka", in: *Oeuvres complètes d'Albert Camus* I, edited by Roger Grenier (Paris, 1983), 241-252

Cersowsky, Peter, *"Mein ganzes Wesen ist auf Literatur gerichtet": Franz Kafka im Kontext der literarischen Dekadenz* (Würzburg, 1983)

Daniel-Rops, J.C., "L'Univers désespéré de Franz Kafka", *Les Cahiers du Sud* (1937), 161-176

David, Claude,"Die Geschichte Abrahams: Zu Kafkas Auseinandersetzung mit Kierkegaard", in: *Bild und Gedanke: Festschrift für Gerhart Baumann zum 60. Geburtstag,* edited by Günter Schnitzler (Munich, 1980), 79-90

Dentan, Michel, *Humour et création littéraire dans l'oeuvre de Kafka* (Geneva and Paris, 1961)

Edwards, Brian F.M., "Kafka and Kierkegaard: A Reassessment", *German Life and Letters,* 20 (1966-67), 218-225

Emrich, Wilhelm, *Franz Kafka* (Bonn, 1958)

Falke, Rita, "Biographisch-literarische Hintergründe von Kafkas 'Das Urteil'", *GRM* 10 (1960), 164-180

Fickert, K.J., "Fatal knowledge: Kafka's 'Ein Landarzt'", *Monatschefte,* 78 (1970), 381-386

Flores, Angel and Swander, Homer (eds), *Franz Kafka Today* (Madison, 1964) *The Kafka Debate: New perspectives for our time* (New York, 1977)

Goldstein, Bluma, "Franz Kafka's 'Ein Landarzt': A Study in Failure", *DVjs* 42 (1968), 745-759

Goth, Maja, *Franz Kafka et les lettres françaises 1928-1955* (Paris, 1956)

Grangier, Eduard, "Abraham, oder Kierkegaard, wie Kafka und Sartre ihn sehen", *Zeitschrift für Philosophische Forschung,* 4 (1950), 412-421

Gray, Ronald, *Franz Kafka* (Cambridge, 1973)

Gross, Ruth V., "Of Mice and Women: Reflections on a Discourse in Kafka's *Josefine, die Sängerin oder Das Volk der Mäuse*", *The Germanic Review,* 60 (1985), 59-67

Heidsieck, Arnold, *The Intellectual Contexts of Kafka's Fiction: Philosophy, Law, Religion* (Columbia, 1994)

Heller, Paul, *Franz Kafka: Wissenschaft und Wissenschaftskritik* (Tübingen, 1989)

Hermsdorf, Klaus, "Künstler und Kunst bei Franz Kafka", in: *Franz Kafka aus Prager Sicht,* edited by Eduard Goldstücker (Berlin, 1963), 95-106

Hiebel, Hans Helmut, *Franz Kafka: "Ein Landarzt"* (Munich, 1984)

Kelly, John, "Franz Kafka's *Trial* and the Theology of Crisis", *The Southern Review,* 5 (1940), 748-766

Koblinkg, Hartmut, "Zum Verständnis der Schuld in Kafkas Erzählungen 'Die Verwandlung' und 'Das Urteil'", *WW* 32 (1982), 391-405

Koelb, Clayton, *Kafka's Rhetoric: The Passion of Reading* (Ithaca, 1989)

Krotz, Frederick W., "Franz Kafka: *Ein Hungerkünstler* - Eine Interpretation", *Modern Austrian Literature,* 5 (1972), 93-119

Kurz, Gerhard, *Traum - Schrecken: Kafkas literarische Existenzanalyse* (Stuttgart, 1980)

(ed.), *Der junge Kafka* (Frankfurt, 1984)

Lange, Wolfgang, "Über Kafkas Kierkegaard-Lektüre und einige damit zusammenhängende Gegenstände", *DVjs* 60 (1986), 286-308

Mahlendorf, Ursula R., "Kafka's *Josephine, the Singer or the Mousefolk*: Art at the Edge of Nothingness", *Modern Austrian Literature,* 11 (1978), 199-241

Marson, Eric and Leopold, Keith, "Kafka, Freud and 'Ein Landarzt'", *The German Quarterly,* 59 (1964), 146-160

Merrill, Reed, "Infinite Absolute Negativity: Irony in Socrates, Kierkegaard and Kafka", *Comparative Literature Studies,* 16 (1979), 222-236

Möbus, Frank, *Sünden-Fälle: Die Geschlechtlichkeit in Erzählungen Franz Kafkas* (Göttingen, 1994)

Nagel, Bert, *Franz Kafka: Aspekte zur Interpretation und Wertung* (Berlin, 1974)

Neider, Charles, *The Frozen Sea: A Study of Franz Kafka* (New York, 1948)

Neumann, Gerhard, "'Ein Bericht für eine Akademie'. Erwägungen zum 'Mimesis'-Charakter Kafkascher Texte", *DVjs* 49 (1975), 166-183

———. "Hungerkünstler und Menschenfresser. Zum Verhältnis von Kunst und kulturellem Ritual im Werk Franz Kafkas", in: Kittler, Wolfgang and Neumann, Gerhard (eds), *Franz Kafka: Schriftverkehr* (Freiburg, 1990), 399-432

Norris, Margot, "Darwin, Nietzsche, Kafka, and the Problem of Mimesis", *MLN* 95 (1980), 1232-1253

———. "Kafka's Josephine: The Animal as the Negative Site of Narration", *Modern Language Notes,* 98 (1983), 366-383

———. *Beasts of the Modern Imagination: Darwin, Nietzsche, Kafka, Ernst and Lawrence* (Baltimore and London, 1985)

Pascal, Roy, *Kafka's Narrators: A Study of his Stories and Sketches* (Cambridge, 1982)

Pasley, J.M.S., "Asceticism and Cannibalism: Notes on an Unpublished Kafka Text", *Oxford German Studies,* 1 (1966), 102-114

Politzer, Heinz, *Franz Kafka: Parable and Paradox* (Ithaca, 1962)

———. *Franz Kafka: der Künstler* (Frankfurt, 1965)

———(ed.). *Das Kafka-Buch: Eine innere Biographie in Selbstzeugnissen* (Frankfurt, 1966)

Richter, Helmut, *Franz Kafka,* Neue Beiträge zur Literaturwissenschaft, Band 14 (Berlin, 1962)

Ries, Wiebrecht, *Transzendenz als Terror: Eine religionsgeschichtliche Studie über Franz Kafka* (Heidelberg, 1977)

Robert, Martha, "Kafka in Frankreich", *Akzente,* 13 (1966), 310-320

Robertson, Ritchie, *Kafka - Judaism, Politics, and Literature* (Oxford, 1985)

———. "In Search of the Historical Kafka: A Selective Review of Research, 1980-1982", *Modern Language Review,* 89 (1994), 107-137

Rolleston, James, *Kafka's Narrative Theater* (University Park, Pennsylvania, and London, 1974)

Rubinstein, William C., "Franz Kafka: A Hunger Artist", *Monatshefte,* 44 (1952), 13-19

Ryan, Judith, "Die zwei Fassungen der 'Beschreibung eines Kampfes': Zur Entwicklung von Kafkas Erzähltechnik", in: *Jb. d. Dt. Schillergesellschaft,* 14 (1970), 546-572

———. *The Vanishing Subject: Early Psychology and Literary Modernism* (Chicago and London, 1991)

Ryan, Lawrence, "'Zum letztenmal Psychologie': Zur psychologischen Deutbarkeit der Werke Franz Kafkas'", in: Paulsen, Wolfgang (ed.), *Psychologie in der Literaturwissenschaft, Viertes Amherster Kolloqium zur modernen deutschen Literatur* (Heidelberg, 1970), 157-173

Schaufelberger, Fritz, "Kafka und Kierkegaard", *Reformatio* 7, 8 (1959), 387-400, 451-456

Schulz-Behrend, G., "Kafka's 'Ein Bericht für eine Akademie", *Monatshefte,* 55 (1963), 1-6

Seidler, Ingo, "*Das Urteil*: 'Freud natürlich?'", in: Paulsen, Wolfgang (ed.), *Psychologie in der Literaturwissenschaft, Viertes Amherster Kolloqium zur modernen deutschen Literatur* (Heidelberg, 1970), 174-190

Sheppard, Richard, "Kafka's *Ein Hungerkünstler*: A Reconsideration", *The German Quarterly,* 46 (1973), 219-233

———. "Kafka, Kierkegaard and the K's: Theology, Psychology and Fiction", *Journal of Literature and Theology,* 5 (1991), 277-296

Sokel, Walter, *Franz Kafka: Tragik und Ironie: zur Struktur seiner Kunst* (Munich and Vienna, 1964)

Spann, Meno, "The Starvation Artist and the Leopard", *Germanic Review,* 34 (1959), 262-269

———. "Don't hurt the Jackdaw", *Germanic Review,* 36 (1962), 68-78

Steinhauer, Harry, "Hungering Artist or Artist in Hungering: Kafka's A Hunger Artist", in: *Die Deutsche Novelle 1880-1933* (New York, 1936), 28-43

Stölzl, Christoph, *Kafkas böses Böhmen: Zur Sozialgeschichte eines Prager Juden* (Munich, 1973)

Storr, Anthony, "Kafka's Sense of Identity", in: Stern, J.P. and White, J.J. (eds), *Paths and Labyrinths: Nine Papers from a Kafka Symposium* (London, 1985), 1-24

Tauber, Herbert, *Franz Kafka: An Interpretation of His Works,* translated by G. Humphreys Roberts and Roger Senhouse (London, 1948)

Timms, Edward, "Kafka's Expanded Metaphors: A Freudian Approach to *Ein Landarzt*", in: Stern, J.P. and White, J.J. (eds), *Paths and Labyrinths: Nine Papers from a Kafka Symposium* (London, 1985), 66-79

Wagenbach, Klaus, *Franz Kafka: Eine Biographie seiner Jugend 1883-1912* (Bern, 1958)

Wahl, Jean, "Kafka et Kierkegaard: Commentaires", in: *Petite histoire de l'existentialisme,* (Paris, 1947), 103-131

Waidson, H.M., "The Starvation Artist and the Leopard", *Germanic Review,* 35 (1960), 262-269

Waldeck, Peter B., "Kafka's 'Die Verwandlung' and 'Ein Hungerkünstler' as influenced by Leopold von Sacher-Masoch", *Monatshefte,* 44 (1972), 147-151

Weinstein, Leo, "Kafka's ape: heel or hero?", *MFS* 8 (1962), 75-79

White, John J., "Franz Kafka's 'Das Urteil' - an Interpretation", *DVjs* 38 (1964), 208-229

Wiese, Benno von, *Die Deutsche Novelle vom Goethe bis Kafka: Interpretationen,* volume 2 (Düsseldorf, 1962)

Witt, Ann-Marie, "Confinement in *Die Verwandlung* and *Les Séquestrés d'Altona*", *Comparative Literature,* 23 (1971), 32-44

3. GENERAL

Anderson, Harriet, *Utopian Feminism: Women's Movements in fin-de-siècle Vienna* (New Haven and London, 1992)

Andreas-Salomé, Lou, "Narzissmus als Doppelrichtung", *Imago: Zeitschrift für Anwendung der Psychoanalyse auf die Geisteswissenschaften,* 7.4 (1921), 361-386

Anz, Thomas, *Literatur der Existenz: Literarische Psychopathographie und ihre soziale Bedeutung im Frühexpressionismus* (Stuttgart, 1977)

Bahr, Hermann, *Zur Überwindung des Naturalismus,* (Stuttgart, 1968)

Beller, Steven, *Vienna and the Jews, 1867-1938. A Cultural History* (Cambridge, 1989)

Broch, Hermann, *Hofmannsthal und seine Zeit* (Tübingen, 1964)

Brod, Max, *Heidentum, Judentum, Christentum: Ein Bekenntnisbuch,* volume 1 (Leipzig, 1922)

Darwin, Charles, *The Origin of Species by Means of Natural Selection or The Preservation of Favoured Races in The Struggle for Life,* first published in 1859, edited with an Introduction by J.W. Burrow (London, 1985) *The Portable Darwin,* edited by Duncan M. Porter and Peter W. Graham (London, 1993)

Erikson, Erik H., *Identity and the Life Cycle* (New York and London, 1979)

Ferguson, Harvie, *Melancholy and the Critique of Modernity: Søren Kierkegaard's Religious Psychology* (London and New York, 1995)

Ferguson, Harvie, *The Lure of Dreams: Sigmund Freud and the Construction of Modernity* (London and New York, 1996)

Fischer, Jens Malte, *Fin de Siècle: Kommentar zu einer Epoche* (Munich, 1978)

Freud, Sigmund, "Die Inzestscheu der Wilden", *Pan,* 21 (1912), 624-629 "Schluss", *Pan,* 21 (1912), 653-655

———. "Die Verdrängung", *Gesammelte Werke* 10 (London, 1940), 248-261

———. "Zur Einführung des Narzißmus", *Gesammelte Werke* 10 (London, 1940), 138-170

———. *Totem und Tabu, Gesammelte Werke* 11 (London, 1940)

———. "Geschichtspunkte der Entwicklung und Regression", *Gesammelte Werke* 11, 351-371

———., *Jenseits des Lustprinzips, Gesammelte Werke* 13 (London, 1940)

———. "Über einige neurotische Mechanismen bei Eifersucht, Paranoia und Homosexualität", *Gesammelte Werke* 13 (London, 1940), 195-207

———., "Psychoanalyse und Libidotheorie", *Gesammelte Werke* 13 (London, 1940), 211-233

———., "Der Untergang des Ödipuskomplexes", *Gesammelte Werke* 13 (London, 1940), 396-402

Gouwens, David J., *Kierkegaard as Religious Thinker* (Cambridge, 1996)

Grenier, Roger (ed.), *Album Camus,* Bibliothèque de la Pléiade (Paris, 1982)

Haeckel, Ernst, *Die Welträtsel: Gemeinverständliche Studien über Monistische Philosophie* (Bonn, 1899)

Hellpach, Wilhelm, "Psycho-Analyse", *Die Neue Rundschau,* 21 (1910), 1653-1659

Hessen, Robert, "Nervenschwäche", *Die Neue Rundschau,* 21 (1910), 1531-1543

Hirschlaff, Leo, "Suggestivtherapie", *Die Neue Rundschau,* 20 (1911), 692-700

Hofmannsthal, Hugo von, *Gedichte und kleine Dramen,* edited by Herbert Steiner (Frankfurt, 1966)

Hume, David, *A Treatise of Human Nature: An Attempt to introduce the experimental Method of Reasoning into Moral Subjects,* first published in 1739 (Oxford, 1949)

Janik, Allan and Toulmin, Stephen, *Wittgenstein's Vienna* (New York, 1973)

Jones, Ernst, *Sigmund Freud: Life and Work,* 3 vols (London, 1955, 1957, 1959)

Kelly, Alfred, *The Descent of Darwin: The Popularization of Darwinism in Germany, 1860-1914* (Chapel Hill, 1981)

Kierkegaard, Søren, *Das Buch des Richters*: Seine Tagebücher 1833-1855, edited by Hermann Gottsched (Jena and Leipzig, 1905)

Kierkegaard, Søren, *Either/Or: A Fragment of Life,* edited by Victor Eremita, translated by Alastair Hannay, first published in 1843 (London, 1992)

Kierkegaard, Søren, *Fear and Trembling, Repetition,* edited and translated by Howard V. Hong and Edna H. Hong, first published in 1843 (New Jersey, 1983)

Kierkegaard, Søren, *Enten-Eller: Et Livs-Fragment,* Samlade Vaerker 1-2, edited by U.B. Drachmann, J.L. Heiberg and D. Lange (Copenhagen, 1920)

Kierkegaard, Søren, *Utten opbyggelige Taler,* Samlade Vaerker 3, edited by U.B. Drachmann, J.L. Heiberg and D. Lange (Copenhagen, 1921)

Kropotkin, Peter, "Der philosophische Versuch Herbert Spencers", *Die Aktion,* 24 (1911), 750-752

Laing, R.D., *The Divided Self: An Existential Study in Sanity and Madness* (London, 1960)

Laplanche, Jean and Pontalis J.-B., *Vocabulaire de la Psychanalyse* (Paris, 1967) Mach, Ernst, *Die Analyse der Empfindungen und das Verhältnis des Physischen zum Psychischen,* first published in 1886 (Darmstadt, 1987)

Michaels, Jennifer, *Anarchy and Eros: Otto Gross' impact on German expressionist writers* (New York, 1983)

Mooney, Edward, *Selves in Discord and Resolve: Kierkegaard's Moral-Religious Psychology from Either/Or to Sickness unto Death* (New York and London, 1996)

Nordentoft, Kresten, *Kierkegaard's Psychology,* translated from Danish by Bruce H. Kirmmse (Pittsburgh, 1978)

Ploetz, Alfred, *Grundlinien einer Rassenhygiene, 1. Theil. Die Tüchtigkeit unserer Rasse und der Schutz der Schwachen. Ein Versuch über Rassenhygiene und ihr Verhältnis zu den humanen Ideen, besonders zum Sozialismus* (Berlin, 1895)

Popper-Lynkeus, Joseph, *Die allgemeine Nährpflicht als Lösung der sozialen Frage,* im Auftrag des Verfassers nach seinem Tode herausgegeben von Margit Ornstein (Vienna, 1923)

Pynsent, Robert, (ed.): *Decadence and Innovation: Austro-Hungarian Life and Art at the Turn of the Century* (London, 1989)

Rank, Otto, "Der Inzest", *Pan,* 34 (1912), 952-963

Reik, Theodor, "Flauberts Jugenderregungen", *Pan,* 4 (1911), 75-84

Reik, Theodor, "Der liebende Flaubert", *Pan,* 5 (1911), 101-114

Reik, Theodor, "Dichtung und Psychoanalyse", *Pan,* 18 (1911), 519-526

Reik, Theodor, "Arthur Schnitzler vor dem Anatol", *Pan,* 32 (1911), 899-905

Le Rider, Jacques, *Modernity and Crises of Identity: Culture and Society in Fin-de-Siècle Vienna,* translated by Rosemary Morris (New York, 1993)

Ritvo, Lucille B., *Darwin's Influence on Freud* (New Haven and London, 1990)

Roazen, Paul, *Freud and his Followers* (London, 1976)

Schorske, Carl E., *Fin-de-Siècle Vienna: Politics and Culture* (New York, 1980)

Sonnenfeld, Marion (ed.), *Stefan Zweig: The World of Yesterday's Humanist Today,* Proceedings of the Stefan Zweig Symposium (Albany, 1983)

Stekel, Wilhelm, *Störungen des Trieb-und Affektlebens* II, third edition, first published in 1917 (Berlin, 1923)

Uexküll, Jakob von, "Das Tropenaquarium", *Die Neue Rundschau,* 19 (1908), 694-706

"Die Umwelt", *Die Neue Rundschau,* 21 (1910), 638-664

Wahl, Jean, *Études Kierkegaardiennes* (Paris, 1937)

Wilson, Edmund, *The Wound and the Bow: Seven Studies in Literature* (London, 1952)

Wollheim, Richard (ed.), *Philosophical essays on Freud* (Cambridge, 1982)

Zweig, Stefan, *Die Welt von Gestern: Erinnerungen eines Europäers,* first published in 1944 (Hamburg, 1981)

Rochelle Tobias (essay date spring 2000)

SOURCE: Tobias, Rochelle. "A Doctor's Odyssey: Sickness and Health in Kafka's 'Ein Landarzt.'" *The Germanic Review* 75, no. 2 (spring 2000): 120-31.

[*In the following essay, Tobias examines the character of the doctor in "Ein Landarzt" in order to analyze his purpose of and the question of to whose sickbed is he called.*]

Of all the accusations made against the country doctor in Kafka's tale by the same name, none seems more harsh than the one the patient whispers as the doctor is laid next to him in bed: "[Du] kommst nicht auf eigenen Füßen."[1] While this observation would scarcely seem to compare with the usual charges made against the doctor—he has been accused, for example, of selfishness, passivity, and inconsiderateness[2]—it nonetheless is more condemning, because it is based on the simple fact that the doctor does not arrive at the sickbed by his own means. Rather, he is transported there by "unearthly horses" which materialize out of thin air; they at least appear unexpectedly on his property from a pigsty that he had not used in years. The gift of the horses enables the doctor to travel to his patient. But his trip no longer takes the form of a late-night house call once he grabs hold of the reins of the horses, which appear "durch die Kraft der Wendungen ihres Rumpfes" (DL 253), through a turn of their rumps which suggests a "Redewendung" or turn of phrase as well. Once the doctor latches on to these mythical horses, he is drawn into a mythical realm where he is forced to make a sacrifice in order to accomplish what he calls sardonically holy aims, "heilige Zwecke" (DL 259).

These holy aims might simply be the achievement of peace or rest. In a diary entry written in 1922, when Kafka's tuberculosis had advanced to a critical state,

Kafka recalls the story **"Ein Landarzt"** which he completed in 1917.[3] In a somewhat paradoxical formulation he argues that rest cannot be neglected but must be attained through the mobilization of new forces which exceed the forces that one has available. He then cites the appearance of the horses in **"Ein Landarzt"** as one of those rare occasions where help was granted to one who had reached the limit of his resources: "Hier allerdings gibt es Überraschungen, das muß der trostloseste Mensch zugeben, es kann erfahrungsgemäß aus Nichts etwas kommen, aus dem verfallenen Schweinestall der Kutscher mit den Pferden kriechen" (T 892). Kafka's characterization of the horses as a stroke of good fortune would seem to run counter to his tale—a tale in which the doctor is not only undressed and laid in bed with the sick but finally sentenced to perpetual wandering when his horses refuse to take him home or bring him back to his own bed. But his insistence that this gift alone is what enables the "most despondent of men" to rest calls into question what it is that the doctor is supposed to accomplish in this work.

His visit to his patient would at first seem to be in the service of "heilige Zwecke," holy aims, since nothing is more holy than the aim of the medical profession: to cure the ill, to save them from death. To achieve that, however, the doctor must himself be in possession of health; that is, he must be able to travel to the sickbed on his own two feet to restore another to health. The doctor's health is the condition for the realization of his aim, since his calling is what he incarnates each time he rescues another from death. He becomes what he calls in a scarcely veiled allusion to Christ "ein Weltverbesserer" (DL 256) each time he helps another escape the threat of death. In this tale, however, there is no "Weltverbesserer." The doctor introduces the term only to explain, "Ich bin kein Weltverbesserer" (DL 256).

What ends the doctor then serves will be the focus of this paper. To whose sickbed is he called? And what, finally, can he do as one who must rely on figurative feet and metaphoric horses to travel to the ill and infirm? The doctor's means of transport are by no means incidental in this work, since if the doctor is a figure for the writer, as so many critics have suggested, it is these very means (tropes, turns, and figures) that link them in their nighttime labors.

Three times in this short work, the doctor asks what it is that he does. The question first arises as he thinks of Rose, his loyal servant, whom he left behind in the hands of a predatory horse groom: "Was tue ich, wie rette ich sie?" (DL 256); it comes up again as he establishes that his patient is healthy and his visit unnecessary: "Was tue ich hier in diesem endlosen Winter!" (DL 257); it arises one final time as the doctor is laid next to the patient in bed who, it ends up, is suffering from a fatal wound to the hip: "Was soll ich tun?" (DL

260). The question is striking given the doctor's initial certainty that he has important business to do which cannot be delayed. Delayed, of course, it is, from his opening statement: "Ich war in großer Verlegenheit: eine dringende Reise stand mir bevor; ein Schwerkranker wartete auf mich in einem zehn Meilen entfernten Dorfe; . . . aber das Pferd fehlte, das Pferd" (DL 252). What detains the doctor, according to this statement, is the absence of a means to take him toward his end, a patient in a distant village. His horse, he tells us, died the night before "as a result of overexertion." Without a second horse, he cannot travel to his patient; he is caught in a terrible dilemma.

This is at least the doctor's predicament, as he understands it. He is prepared in every respect to travel, with the exception of a horse, a vehicle. Nonetheless, insofar as this one circumstance prevents him from answering the call he has received, it calls into question his ability to be a country doctor, the one name we have for him. As such a doctor, he is required to answer requests for help, although on this occasion he cannot despite his best intentions. This occasion, consequently, represents both a starting and a stopping point, a point at which he may renew his title as doctor, and one at which he may lose it if he cannot attend to his patient tonight. Both possibilities are written into the doctor's posture; he stands, as he puts it, "reisefertig schon auf dem Hofe" (DL 252), ready to embark on a journey and finished with journeying, done with his work as a country doctor.

If the doctor is, as I suspect, finished with his work, it is because of an injury he sustains, one which is represented in this text through the death of his horse but which extends beyond this one circumstance. For a horse alone can be replaced; the doctor himself admits as much when he later claims, "wären es nicht zufällig Pferde, müßte ich mit Säuen fahren" (DL 257). What is irreplaceable is the mobility the doctor loses, the fitness to exercise his trade which is represented through the vehicle of his horse, but which finally has the doctor's health or well-being as its tenor. For this reason, the consequences of this loss are so grave for the doctor's person. If he cannot attend to his patient, if he cannot venture from his yard, he cannot be a country doctor. He is stripped of his raison d'être: "Immer mehr vom Schnee überhäuft, immer unbeweglicher werdend, stand ich zwecklos da" (DL 253).

The doctor's admission that he stands "zwecklos" in his own courtyard would at first glance seem to refer to the mere fact that he does nothing; he does not even help his servant Rose find out if a neighbor might lend him a horse. But the admission refers to his peculiar standstill as well which prevents him from making the movement necessary to reaffirm his purpose or "Zweck." This movement is dialectical, requiring a means through which the doctor can return to the aims or ends ("Zwecke") defining him. These ends take the form of the doctor's calling or trade; he must attend to the patient who has called him to renew his calling as his own, as that which he embodies. From the outset, he stands deficient vis-à-vis this end, since only he has received this call; "[es] war nur für ihn bestimmt," as the gatekeeper in "Before the Law" might say (DL 269). This demand pertains only to him, for only he has elected for himself the task of curing the ill, of saving them from death. It is this purpose which in fact awakens him at night, calling him to a distant village to rescue someone. The doctor would not feel motivated—or mobilized—to answer this request if he did not already define himself as someone who serves this end. But in choosing this end as his exclusive measure, he also condemns himself to falling short of his determination in his immobility. Without a horse, without means, the doctor cannot reach the end he has set for himself as a human being. To this extent, then, he stands "zwecklos" in his courtyard. Once he can no longer move toward his end, what remains of him is what cannot be put to work, what serves no purpose.

Insofar as the doctor cannot leave his house he fails to live up to his determination. Although he is trapped in the proper—namely, his property—he cannot rise to the calling that supposedly defines him. Something hinders him in progressing toward the end that is not only his livelihood, but life itself. In one of the few readings attentive to the religious dynamics in this work, Bluma Goldstein contends that the doctor must be a medium for a spiritual life to rescue others from sickness and death.[4] As a model for such a process, she points to the rabbis of Hasidic legend, in particular the Zaddikim who, because of their extreme piety, were endowed with the gift of performing miracles. Goldstein argues that several aspects of Kafka's story parallel the legends of the Zaddikim recorded in Alexander Eliasberg's *Sagen polnischer Juden,* a popular anthology of Hasidic folklore that Kafka is known to have possessed.[5] However compelling these examples may be, they are nonetheless of secondary importance in her reading. Her primary concern is to show that the Zaddik represents the ideal, against which the country doctor is measured. The Zaddik heals, she points out, in drawing out the divine sparks in the individual. These sparks stem from the act of creation, when the vessels containing divine light burst and were dispersed throughout the world.[6] The sparks nonetheless represent a unity: the unity of divine light or even divine substance. In releasing the sparks in others as well as in himself, the Zaddik brings forth a spiritual life that inheres in both and which transcends their mere physical existence.

The country doctor may, as Goldstein contends, fail to be a Zaddik, but only because he cannot be a Christ, who heals the ill and raises the dead in a manner surprisingly similar to her account of the Zaddik. Indeed, what Goldstein argues is the unequivocally Jewish strain in this work bears a striking resemblance to the figure of Christ, as Kafka understood it. In an earlier version of his now famous aphorism, "Der Messias wird erst kommen, wenn er nicht mehr nötig sein wird" (NgS 2. 56-7), Kafka addresses the Christian notion of the redeemer directly:

> Der Messias wird kommen, bis der zügelloseste Individualismus des Glaubens möglich ist, niemand diese Möglichkeit vernichtet, niemand die Vernichtung duldet, also die Gräber sich öffnen. Das ist vielleicht auch die christliche Lehre, sowohl in der tatsächlichen Aufzeigung des Beispieles dem nachgefolgt werden soll, eines individualistischen Beispieles, als auch in der symbolischen Aufzeigung der Auferstehung des Mittlers im einzelnen Menschen.
>
> (NgS 2. 55)

The first sentence of this aphorism requires some explanation. Kafka uses the term "bis" in lieu of "wenn," as was apparently customary in Austro-Hungarian dialect; in one diary entry, he even notes that he was prone to confuse the two terms.[7] This aphorism, then, like the later one, is primarily concerned with the condition for the coming of the Messiah, the prerequisite for his advent. Christian doctrine, according to Kafka, illuminates this condition in two respects: First, it offers an example of someone who rose from the grave; and secondly it offers a symbol of the resurrection that can occur in each individual.

It is in this latter function that Christian doctrine bears on the healing process. Christ as "ein einzelner Mensch," a single human being, is subject to death. What enables him to transcend his finite existence is the "Mittler," the intermediary of a spiritual life resurrected in him. Although Christ is often identified as this intermediary, Kafka refrains from doing so here in order to distinguish between Christ the individual and Christ the supposed savior; in other words, he distinguishes between Christ as an example of someone who was saved and Christ as the symbol of the intermediary who can save every human being. As such a symbol, Christ is in fact compelled to save, for only in saving others does he simultaneously save himself; that is, he can demonstrate that he is a vehicle for a life victorious over death only if he repeatedly delivers others to this life, which is also the consummate state of health. For this reason, the priests who follow in his image are sometimes referred to as well as "doctors of the soul," particularly in their pastoral mission. In administering the sacraments, they elevate the souls of their parishioners to a spiritual life which they incarnate, at least for the moment of the ritual.

"Ein Landarzt" invokes this model of healing on more than one occasion. The doctor even invites the comparison with priests when he complains that the people in his region are always asking the impossible of him. They demand that he heal them ("heilen"), which in German has the added connotation of redeeming or saving, as indicated by the number of words based on this root, including sacred ("heilig"), salvation ("Heil"), and savior ("Heiland"). They turn to the doctor, as he puts it, because they have "lost the old faith." For this reason, the local priest sits at home unraveling his vestments, whereas he is summoned to the deathbed, as if to administer the last rites, which mark not only the end of life on earth, but also the beginning of an everlasting life in heaven. Several critics have argued that Kafka understood the task of the writer in a similar vein, in part because of one diary entry where he states that although work such as **"Ein Landarzt"** brings him occasional satisfaction, he will only find happiness if he can transform the world "ins Reine, Wahre, Unveränderliche" (T 838)[8]. But it is precisely this end which the doctor fails to attain, since he himself has been touched by sickness, or even death, inasmuch as he cannot rise to his own designation. In other words, he is wounded, perhaps in the rump or hip, because he cannot incarnate the calling that supposedly sustains him.

His one means of sustenance in his predicament is, in fact, his sickness, which reveals to him more than he knew he had in his house, the metonymy for his wounded body or infirm person. Confined to his courtyard, the doctor starts pacing around its perimeter and in a moment of distraction and frustration ("zerstreut, gequält" [DL 253]) kicks the door of a pigsty he had not used in years. To his astonishment, he discovers there both the smell of horses and an individual who offers to bring him to his patient: "'Soll ich anspannen?' fragte er auf allen Vieren hervorkriechend" (DL 253). The offer is ambivalent, inasmuch as it is unclear who or what should be yoked up, either the still-invisible horses, suspected of being there only because of the smell, or the man who, crouched on all fours, could be said to be volunteering himself as a horse for the purposes of the trip; that is, a man whose "Bestimmung" or "Zweck" would be being a horse, a means toward an end. The doctor's and Rose's response to this man would only underscore his degradation to the extent that they identify him as a thing found by chance on the property: "'Man weiß nicht, was für Dinge man im eigenen Hause vorrätig hat,' sagte es [das Dienstmädchen], und wir beide lachten" (DL 253). Laugh the two may, for in the heart of the proper (das "eigene Haus") they discover what they had not known and what they cannot appropriate. Although these "things" are found on the doctor's property, they do not belong entirely to him; he does not recognize them as his own, as part of his own person. For this reason, perhaps, Kafka referred to the horses and horse groom in the story as the appearance of "something out of nothing," which suggests as well the appearance of what till now had been a lack, a deficit hindering the doctor's realization. This deficit, however, now becomes the doctor's means. It opens a space for him to figure what he would need to make the dialectical movement toward his own completion. All this in a figure.

Horses are by no means an unusual figure in Kafka's work. In "Wunsch, Indianer zu werden," Kafka's one-sentence meditation, a horse provides the running start for a flight that eventually exceeds it; what remains is simply the flight in the absence of any means.[9] In **"Ein Landarzt,"** by contrast, the horses that are introduced do not disappear, since what makes them figurative is not the flight they launch, but their mere appearance as replacements:

> "Hollah, Bruder, hollah, Schwester!" rief der Pferde-knecht, und zwei Pferde, mächtige flankenstarke Tiere schoben sich hintereinander, die Beine eng am Leib, die wohlgeformten Köpfe wie Kamele senkend, nur durch die Kraft der Wendungen ihres Rumpfes aus dem Türloch, das sie restlos ausfüllten. Aber gleich standen sie aufrecht, hochbeinig, mit dicht ausdampfendem Körper.

(DL 253-4)

The horses emerge through the door as if they were being born into the world; indeed, the way in which they enter the courtyard—head first, rear last, limbs packed close to the chest—all suggests birth.[10] This birth, however, has an element of the uncanny as well, since the horses that come to be rapidly outsize the pigsty in which they had been held; that is, they inflate in passing through the door into almost mythical creatures, creatures whose strength and size recall "homerische Gestalten" (T 842), the term Kafka coined to describe the horses he saw in the country in 1917. They acquire this stature, however, only by virtue of a series of "turns" which push them from inside to outside and set them in the world. These turns are not visible to the eye; indeed, the horses they eject through the door effectively conceal them. They are nonetheless the condition for the visibility of the animals, as they are first and foremost "Redewendungen." What the text describes as the repetitive turnings of the horses' buttocks are in fact the turns of phrase, which the text deploys at this very moment to create the means the doctor lacks. In other words, the text refers, "durch die Kraft der Wendungen," to the work it does, turning out phrases that turn nothing into something; in short, storytelling. What makes this coincidence significant—a coincidence in which the text speaks of what it does—is that it simultaneously catapults the story, which had reached an impasse in the doctor's stasis.[11] It brings or pulls the story from the doctor's yard to the bedside of his patient in a village ten miles off. This space, however, cannot be seen as a continuation of the former one, as what renders it accessible is a "Redewendung" that creates something out of nothing.

THE ALLEGORY OF THE WOUND

The mobility that the doctor gains thus does not come without a cost. He himself names the price for his trip to his patient when he yells at the groom accompanying the horses: "Es fällt mir nicht ein, dir für die Fahrt das Mädchen als Kaufpreis hinzugeben" (DL 254). The exchange the doctor did not envision nonetheless occurs, insofar as he is whisked off to the sickbed; whereas Rose, the girl in the above quote, is left behind with the horse groom, who intends to rape her. Marianne Schuller argues that this exchange is but the final one in a series, in which Rose's body is "marked" and replaced by the signs signifying it.[12] The first of these exchanges occurs as the horse groom bites Rose on the cheek, a location which is not entirely incidental given that the patient's wound will later be found in the right buttock or cheek: "[D]as willige Mädchen eilte, dem Knecht das Geschirr des Wagens zu reichen. Doch kaum war es bei ihm, umfaßt es der Knecht und schlägt sein Gesicht an ihres" (DL 254). The second occurs as he names the servant, who had till now been anonymous: "'Kutschieren werde aber ich, du kennst nicht den Weg,' sage ich. 'Gewiß,' sagt er, 'ich fahre gar nicht mit, ich bleibe bei Rose'" (DL 254). These two incidents, biting and naming, first determine Rose as a sexual being, the object of someone else's desire in Schuller's reading. Indeed, as she points out, the servant is in grammatical terms a genderneutral being ("*das* Mädchen" or simply "es"), until the horse groom announces her name, which establishes her as female.[13] Rose can be a sexual object, however, only insofar as she is absent in the flesh. Schuller's reading depends on this reversal, whereby the signs that signify the body simultaneously negate it, in order to claim that what propels the remainder of the story is a desire: the desire to fill the vacancy in the name "Rose."

If this desire is indeed what drives the story, then the story's end is, as Schuller argues, certain. The doctor is taken to his patient and discovers in the patient's side a sign of the life he has forsaken to fulfill his mission as a doctor.[14] But the mere fact that this story continues, even after the patient's wound is found, indicates that the sacrifice the doctor makes is not merely physical, but metaphysical as well. The price he pays for his trip, in other words, is not only Rose in her pure physical state prior to her representation in signs, but a life that cannot be embodied, as it is infinite and everlasting. The doctor forsakes this metaphysical life the moment he takes a seat in his carriage and grabs hold of the reins of horses that do not exist, which only figure what he lacks. As soon as he grabs hold of the reins, he is drawn into an "unearthly" realm; that is, into an allegorical drama, in which the life that he pursued as a doctor returns in its negation and perversion as an emblem.

This emblem is precisely the patient's wound. Although the doctor is initially convinced that his patient is healthy, he agrees to examine him again and this time discovers a fatal wound to the hip, which he describes in lurid detail:

> In seiner rechten Seite, in der Hüftengegend hat sich eine handtellergroße Wunde aufgetan. Rose, in vielen Schattierungen, dunkel in der Tiefe, hellwerdend zu den Rändern, zartkörnig, mit ungleichmäßig sich aufsammelndem Blut, offen wie ein Bergwerk obertags. So aus der Entfernung. In der Nähe zeigt sich noch eine Erschwerung . . . Würmer, an Stärke und Länge meinem kleinen Finger gleich, rosig aus eigenem und außerdem blutbespritzt, winden sich, im Innern der Wunde festgehalten, mit weißen Köpfchen, mit vielen Beinchen ans Licht. Armer Junge, dir ist nicht zu helfen. Ich habe deine große Wunde aufgefunden; an dieser Blume in deiner Seite gehst du zugrunde.
>
> (DL 258)

To the extent that Rose is imprinted or emblazoned in this wound, she returns from the dead or at least from the site of her brutal rape at the hands of the horse groom. Her return, however, is simultaneously an act of revenge, insofar as she appears in the wound as a sign of the life that the doctor sacrifices for the sake of his profession. Although this life is undeniably Rose's, it is the doctor's as well to the extent that it is the physical or sexual life he might have shared with Rose, had he not devoted himself so exclusively to his work. The doctor at least intimates that such a life was a possibility in the same breath in which he acknowledges that this possibility no longer exists for him: "[D]ieses schöne Mädchen, das jahrelang, von mir kaum beachtet, in meinem Hause lebte - dieses Opfer ist zu groß" (DL 257). In lieu of this life, the doctor consistently chose death—"[I]ch [bin] schon in allen Krankenstuben, weit und breit, gewesen" (DL 260)—to affirm another life that he would embody as a healer or even savior. In this wound, however, he discovers that he cannot attain this end. He cannot be a medium for a spiritual life because he cannot cure this sickness unto death.

The wound he discovers in his patient's side thus simultaneously wounds or injures him. It reveals the limits of his power to transform the world "ins Reine, Wahre und Unveränderliche," to borrow Kafka's phrase again. This power to transform, however, is itself called into question by the very figurative nature of the wound, its status as an emblem. As emblem of another wound not accessible to sight, the wound is not affixed to the body of the patient or to that of the doctor. Rather it joins these two apparently separate persons in and under one sign: the sign "Rose," which not only refers to the doctor's servant, but also to the flower. The rose is among other things a traditional symbol for the wound in Christ's heart; that is, a symbol of the wound Christ suffers as a man and that he overcomes as a Messiah.[16]

Thus it brings together what would otherwise stand apart: life and death, sickness and health, patient and doctor.

Such is at least the significance of the rose as it pertains to Christ, himself a symbolic figure who unifies opposites (man and God). In this text, however, the rose cannot symbolically unify opposites, since there is no essential difference between the doctor and the patient. Or their difference is one in appearance only. Ostensibly, there is a patient suffering from a terrible wound and a doctor called to heal him. But to the extent the wound is incurable, it cripples them both; it reveals both as mortal. Both, in other words, are subject to this incurable disease, which has no proper expression in the world, no expression that is "pure, true and immutable." The one suitable expression for this illness, consequently, is an emblem which does not purport to be anything but a sign or, put otherwise, which does not claim to embody anything. In the rose, the symbol of Christ's wound, the text finds such an emblem. It takes the symbol of the wound that Christ overcame and converts it into the emblem of a wound that no one can outlive.

No one can survive the wound, since no one is a Messiah. If the text consistently alludes to Christ, it is only to question his validity as a model for the healer ("Heiler") as well as for the savior ("Heiland"). Both the doctor and the patient are depicted in terms clearly borrowed from the representation of Christ. The patient's wound is, as I have noted, in his right side, like Christ's. Both wounds, moreover, are identified with flowers, if toward different ends, as I discussed above. But none of these examples would suffice as a critique of the model of healing epitomized in Christ if the text did not also invoke Christ's death on the cross. It does so in the scene immediately following the discovery of the wound. To appease the villagers, who expect him to perform miracles, the doctor agrees to let them use him for sacred ends: "[V]erbraucht ihr mich zu heiligen Zwecken, lasse ich auch das mit mir geschehen" (DL 259). What follows is a ritual resembling Christ's sacrifice. The doctor is undressed, before being laid in bed with the sick, as Christ was undressed before being crucified. He is then sung to by a chorus of schoolchildren, who taunt him to show his healing powers, as Christ was taunted on the cross to show that he was the Messiah: "'Entkleidet ihn, dann wird er heilen, / Und heilt er nicht, so tötet ihn? / 'Sist nur ein Arzt, 'sist nur ein Arzt" (DL 259). However crude the song may be, it nonetheless reveals a fundamental premise of this text; namely, that the doctor must be a medium for a spiritual life if he is to rescue others from death. Only if he is such a medium, such an incarnation of everlasting life, can he also turn the "Wunde" into a "Wunder," which, I suspect, is one of the unwritten puns of this text.

Something else happens, though, as the doctor and the patient are laid next to one another in bed and left in an empty room, which recalls the tomb in which Christ was buried. The two separate figures blend into one, conjoined at the hip or in the wound, which extends to them both: "Zur Mauer, an die Seite der Wunde legen sie mich" (DL 259). Whose wound this line speaks of remains ambiguous, as the wound is treated independently of the body or person bearing it. It could be the patient's wound in his side; but it could just as well be the doctor's wound as a mortal man. Because this wound cannot be localized, it cannot be healed. The healing process depends on the appearance of an illness in its proper form, so that it can be eradicated for good. Christ essentially does so for those who believe in him. He eliminates the threat of death in dying and then rising from the grave. But in this wound, he, too, might reach the limit of his powers to heal, since this wound has no proper form, which determines what it is. The worms twisting in its interior attest to its constant change; that is, its ability to vary its appearance (shape, size, color, etc.) and even to appear as something else. No healer, consequently, can eliminate this wound, since nowhere is it present as itself, as that which it truly is. Whenever and wherever it appears, it appears as something else, which is not to say it is without consequence. This wound kills, precisely because it has no essence. It lives in sucking off life, in depleting a person's resources. But as an exclusively negative phenomenon, which lives only in robbing life, the wound makes the sacrifice that defines the healing process utterly futile. One cannot suffer this wound and come out the other side. One cannot make it the means for one's own redemption, as it is nowhere embodied.

In the final paragraph of the story, the question is thus raised if there is in fact a patient, a boy who embodies this fatal sickness. After the alleged patient dies, the doctor prepares to leave the scene; a mob of angry patients suddenly appears out of nowhere and threatens to kill him. In his haste to escape them, he jumps half-naked into his carriage and orders his horses to leave. Although the horses first brought him to the house at lightning speed, this time they refuse to do more than amble aimlessly. The story ends with the doctor being driven around a wintry landscape without any hope of return to his home or to his bed. He cries out in the last line of the text: "Betrogen. Betrogen! Einmal dem Fehlläuten der Nachtglocke gefolgt—es ist niemals gutzumachen" (DL 261). The doctor cannot "make good" on the call he obeyed, since as a false alarm it deprives him of the patient he would need to draw a profit or a return. The reward of his trip would presumably be his return to himself as a doctor, who in the image of Christ delivers the ill from death. But in the absence of a patient the doctor no longer has any means to restore and redeem himself as a healer. What remains is simply his body, immobilized by death, or more precisely, his body

immobilized *and* errant, because it cannot arrive at any end. The doctor never returns to the house that he in some respects never left, since, already on his deathbed, he cannot reach his "Zweck."

The doctor does nonetheless complete one thing in this tale, even if he fails on every other count. He tells the sick boy a story as he is laid next to him in bed:

> Deine Wunde ist so übel nicht. Im spitzen Winkel mit zwei Hieben der Hacke geschaffen. Viele bieten ihre Seite an und hören kaum die Hacke im Forst, geschweige denn, daß sie ihnen näher kommt.
>
> (DL 260)

On the basis of this story the boy is able to surrender to his illness. He takes "das Ehrenwort eines Amtarztes mit hinüber" (DL 260), to a place outside the world. If the doctor can be said to accomplish something here, where all efforts at healing are in vain, it is to help this boy die through the power of his words. He figures death as a forester, the swinging of an axe in order to let this boy know that he has been touched by death. Death does not touch; it is neither an axe nor a scythe. These are figures, emblems, or turns of phrase invented to explain something which otherwise is not manifest. Because death has no proper form in which to appear, improper expressions, such as allegories and stories, are necessary to announce its onset and its work. The call that provides the pretext for this text is a figure for the arrival of death. The call or plea that the story directs to its reader is to let the doctor know who has come to visit him. It asks the reader to write a fable, just as the doctor did for his patient whose first words were, "Doktor, laß mich sterben" (DL 255).

What healing becomes in this respect is help to alleviate the pain of dying, which for Kafka was neither a natural nor a finite process. Indeed, the doctor in this story is exposed to what Kafka called "die ewigen Qualen des Sterbens" (T 546), precisely because he does not know what has hit him, what saps his strength. In this state of seeming oblivion, he mistakes death for life, thereby intensifying and extending the torment of dying. For example, he mistakes two "unearthly" horses for earthly ones, and mistakes his own injuries for a wound in his patient's side. These mistakes reveal the danger of storytelling, which can create something out of nothing and thus replace life with a simulation. At the same time, however, storytelling belongs to the healing and restoration process, for the wound it figures is the one that will be lifted when the Messiah comes. In the unfinished text that Kafka wrote for Isaak Löwy on the Yiddish theater, he explains the aim of his account in the following fashion: "Meine Absicht ist ganz einfach . . . den Vorhang zu heben und die Wunde zu zeigen. Nur nach Erkenntnis der Krankheit läßt sich ein Heilmittel finden und möglicherweise das wahre jüdische Theater schaffen" (NgS 1.430). In this text, I would say, Kafka does more than raise the curtain. He creates the forum in which the wound can be seen: an allegorical drama or, in his words, "[ein] wahres jüdisches Theater."

Notes

1. Franz Kafka, "Ein Landarzt," in *Drucke zu Lebzeiten,* eds. Wolf Kittler, Hans-Gerd Koch and Gerhard Neumann, in *Franz Kafka. Schriften Tagebücher Briefe. Kritische Ausgabe,* ed. Jürgen Born et al. (Frankfurt a.M.: Fischer, 1994), 260. All subsequent references to Kafka's work are to the critical edition, unless otherwise indicated. The following abbreviations will be used to indicate the volumes of the edition: DL for *Drucke zu Lebzeiten*; T for *Tagebücher,* eds. Hans-Gerd Koch, Michael Müller and Malcolm Pasley (Frankfurt a.M.: Fischer, 1990); NgS for *Nachgelassene Schriften und Fragmente,* 2 vols., ed. Malcolm Pasley (Frankfurt a.M.: Fischer, 1993). Volume and page number for all citations will be listed in the text.

2. See, for example, Walter Sokel's analysis of the doctor's character in Walter H. Sokel, *Franz Kafka - Tragik und Ironie. Zur Struktur seiner Kunst* (Munich: Albert Langen Georg Müller Verlag, 1964), 270-81.

3. According to the critical edition, "Ein Landarzt" was written sometime between December 1916 and January 1917. See *Drucke zu Lebzeiten,* Vol. 2 (Apparatband), 286-32.

4. Bluma Goldstein, "Franz Kafka's 'Ein Landarzt': A Study in Failure," in *Deutsche Vierteljahrsschrift für Literaturwissenschaft und Geistesgeschichte* 42 (1968), 745-59.

5. Alexander Eliasberg, *Sagen polnischer Juden* (Munich: Georg Müller, 1916). It is unclear whether Kafka would have been familiar with this anthology at the time he was working on "Ein Landarzt," given that the anthology was published in 1916, the same year that Kafka presumably wrote the story. Even if he had not yet read this volume, he would have been familiar with the legends of the Zaddikim through the writings of Martin Buber and Micha Josef bin Gorion as well as numerous others. Hartmut Binder confirms that Kafka owned a copy of Eliasberg's anthology. See H. Binder, *Kafka-Handbuch in zwei Bänden,* Vol. 1: Der Mensch und seine Zeit (Stuttgart: Alfred Kröner Verlag, 1979), 472.

6. For reasons of brevity, I have had to abbreviate Goldstein's far more nuanced account of the Kabbalistic creation myth adopted by the Hasidim. See Goldstein, 746-49. For a more detailed account of the notion of God's contraction (Zimzum) and the breaking of the vessels (Shehirath haKelim) see Gershom Scholem, *Die jüdische Mystik in ihren Hauptströmungen* (Frankfurt a.M.: Alfred Metzner Verlag, 1957), 285-314.

7. The diary entry is from 24 January 1915. Kafka mentions that Felice Bauer corrected him for ordering a waiter, "Bringen Sie die Zeitung, *bis* sie ausgelesen ist" (T 722).

8. Sokel, *Tragik und Ironie,* 261; Kurt J. Fickert, "Fatal Knowledge: Kafka's 'Ein Landarzt,'" in *Monatshefte* 66 (1974), 385-6.

9. The text of this meditation reads: "Wenn man doch ein Indianer wäre, gleich bereit, und auf dem rennenden Pferde, schief in der Luft, immer wieder kurz erzitterte über dem zitternden Boden, bis man die Sporen ließ, bis man die Zügel wegwarf, denn es gab keine Zügel, und kaum das Land vor sich als glatt gemähte Heide sah, schon ohne Pferdehals und Pferdekopf" (DL 32-3).

10. Frank Möbus argues likewise that the horses' appearance resembles a birth. See Möbus, *Sünden-Fälle: Die Geschlechtlichkeit in Erzählungen Franz Kafkas* (Göttingen: Wallenstein Verlag, 1994), 130.

11. Marianne Schuller underscores the ways in which the text performs its own narration. Her reading first drew my attention to the forces at work in the text that bring the story from its initial stasis to its rapid movement in the second half. In her view, desire is what rips the narrative from its initial stasis. While I agree with her reading for the most part, I would place the impulse for the sudden shift in the narration elsewhere, as I discuss in the section that follows. See M. Schuller, "Wunde und Körperbild: Zur Behandlung des Wunden Motivs bei Goethe und Kafka," in *BildKörper. Verwandlungen des Menschen zwischen Medium und Medizin* (Hamburg: Lit, 1998), 35-8.

12. Schuller, 38.

13. Schuller, 38; Möbus, *Sünden-Fälle,* 131.

14. In recent years, "Ein Landarzt" has been interpreted almost exclusively as an allegory of desire. Josef Vogl argues, like Marianne Schuller, that the exchange of Rose for two horses involves the replacement of Rose with signs in J. Vogl, *Ort der Gewalt. Kafkas literarische Ethik* (Munich: Fink Verlag, 1990), 124-6. Henry Sussman likewise claims that the wound is a mark or sign of the doctor's desire in H. Sussman, "The Text that Never was a Story: Symmetry and Disaster in 'A Country Doctor,'" in *Approaches to Teaching Kafka's Short Fiction,* ed. Richard T. Gray (New

York: Modern Language Assoc. of America, 1995), 123-34. My objection concerning this reading is that it takes only one aspect of this story into account. The doctor's desire is at least two-fold in this work: for Rose and for his calling as doctor, for flesh as well as spirit.

15. Claudine Raboin remarks that Kafka interpreted his sickness as the "revenge of the unlived life," in C. Raboin, "'Ein Landarzt' und die Erzählungen aus den Blauen Oktavheften 1916-1918," in *Text + Kritik,* VII (1994), 150. Raboin's observation seems particularly apt in the connection with the wound in "Ein Landarzt" whose autobiographical dimensions are unmistakable. The two poles that the doctor is caught between (Rose and his patient) reflect Kafka's constant torment between marriage and writing, family and a solitary existence. Kafka believed that in the wound in this story he predicted his own tuberculosis, as indicated in a letter to Max Brod from September 1917, "Auch habe ich es selbst vorausgesagt. Erinnerst Du Dich an die Blutwunde im 'Landarzt'." See Max Brod/Franz Kafka. *Eine Freundschaft.,* Vol. II *Briefwechsel,* ed. Malcolm Pasley (Frankfurt a.M.: Fischer, 1959), 160. Of greater relevance to the current reading was Kafka's description of the wound in his lung as an emblem, bearing the name Felice for his twice-finacée Felice Bauer, whom he could not marry: "Ist die Lungenwunde nur ein Sinnbild, wie Du behauptest, Sinnbild der Wunde, deren Entzündung Felice und deren Tiefe Rechtfertigung heißt, ist dies so, dann sind auch die ärztlichen Ratschläge (Licht Luft Sonne Ruhe) Sinnbild. Fasse dieses Sinnbild an" (T 831).

16. For reasons of brevity, I have had to limit my discussion of the symbolic significance of the rose to this one aspect. It is worth noting, however, that the rose is also associated with the Virgin Mary, in particular with her love for her son. For a fuller account of the iconographic significance of the rose, see Wilhelm Molsdorf, *Christliche Symbolik der mittelalterlichen Kunst* (Leipzig: Verlag Karl. W. Hiersemann, 1926), 142-3 and Gerhart B. Ladner, *Handbuch der frühchristlichen Symbolik. Gott Kosmos Mensch* (Stuttgart/Zurich: Belser Verlag, 1992), 138-44. Bluma Goldstein notes that Angelus Silesius refers to Christ's wound as a rose in a poem whose refrain is, "Laß meine Seel ein Bienlein / Auff deinen Rosen-Wunden seyn," in Goldstein, "Franz Kafka's 'Ein Landarzt,'" 755-6. One possible biblical precedent for the symbol of the rose is *Ecclesiasticus* 24: 13-14: "There I grew like a cedar of Lebanon, like a cypress on the slopes of Hermon, like a date palm at Enged, like roses at Jericho." The rose of Jericho is also called the Resurrection Rose (in German "die Auferstehungsrose") because the flower is normally curled in a tight ball, except when wet, when its petals open in the shape of a Greek cross. The opening of the wound in this text, it seems to me, resembles the opening of the Resurrection Rose when placed in water. What is at stake in this text, however, is whether resurrection is possible.

Kurt J. Fickert (essay date fall 2001)

SOURCE: Fickert, Kurt J. "The Failed Epiphany in Kafka's 'In der Strafkolonie.'" *Germanic Notes and Reviews* 32, no. 2 (fall 2001): 153-59.

[In the following essay, Fickert investigates the dramatic epiphany that occurs in "In the Penal Colony" and compares it to other works by Kafka.]

The literary device of the "epiphany" or moment of inner revelation has been put to use in the early work of Franz Kafka with remarkable subtlety and, in the case of his **"In der Strafkolonie"** (written in 1914, published in 1919), with dramatic intensity. Although Kafka makes no reference to the celebrated concept of the epiphany that James Joyce put to use in his autobiographical writings during the century's first decade, there can be no doubt that he was familiar with a similar trope developed contemporaneously in European literature. It, too, had its origin in the effort of authors to find the means to express truth in their works, in particular truth about the self. The poems and prose narratives of Hugo von Hofmannsthal, a fellow Austrian whom Kafka held in high esteem, represented for the novice writer an achievement that he could but strive to emulate. In Hofmannsthal's evocation of the crisis he had undergone in his literary pursuits, vividly portrayed in his "Lord Chandos Brief," Kafka encountered an experience similar to his own in his pursuit of an identity as a writer. Kafka's inner conflict, arising from his need to write despite his need first to fulfill his obligations to his family lies at the root of his fiction. Kafka's struggle to express the truth in regard to this aspect of his life and work is the theme that he embellishes with episodes of an epiphany in the quasi-allegorical stories he wrote, beginning with **"Das Urteil"** and reaching a high point with **"In the Penal Colony."**[1]

That Kafka, while aspiring to become an author, first undertook to write poetry is an aspect of his literary career often overlooked. Although the poems themselves were never published, references to them (e.g., by Max Brod) are enlightening and provocative. Interpreters of Kafka's early work stress Hofmannsthal's influence on both his prose and poetry. Thus Mark Anderson notes: "Several passages in 'Description of a Struggle' (1904-

06) [. . .] are almost literal quotations from Hofmannsthal and reveal the 'young Kafka' in a phase of literary experimentation and self-searching."[2] In reference to Kafka's poems, Hartmut Binder not only contends that Hofmannsthal's poetic credo "Über Gedichte" (1903) characterizes the poem itself as constituting the description of an epiphanic moment but also ventures to conclude: "Kafkas Gedichte sind zweifellos Versuche, Epiphanien zu schaffen" (*Kafka-Handbuch II*, 403).[3] The literary movement of Romanticism brought the epiphany into the everyday world, giving the commonplace a symbolic value and associating it with a revelation.[4] As an inheritor of this tradition of the profundity of verse, Hofmannsthal in an autobiographical essay, the "Lord Chandos Letter," confesses his inability to continue to write poetry in the face of the awesome nature of the simplest aspects of life. He testifies that he has been rendered inarticulate by the sight of a wheelbarrow in the sun. Hofmannsthal's confession of the urgency of his need to write and his inability to satisfy that need can but have resonated in the similarly conflicted mind of Franz Kafka. In a conversation with Max Brod, Kafka attested to his reverence for Hofmannsthal by citing a phrase from Hofmannsthal's work which one can readily associate with an impetus to experience an epiphany: "Der Geruch nasser Steine in einem Hausflur."[5]

Kafka's pithy sentences and short prose pieces which likewise seem to move toward some kind of revelation are aptly exemplified by the sketch **"Der Kreisel"** ("The [Spinning] Top"), written late in his life (1920) and first published in 1933. It describes Kafka's attempt to capture in words the moment when true insight[6] regarding an aspect of human nature emerges. The anecdote depicts the author, who seeks to find the answer to the riddle of life by interrupting children at play with a top by attempting to pick up the toy from their midst. The intrusion of the outsider represents the disruption caused by the writer, intent upon analyzing the phenomenon of the spinning top (viz., the world). Since the intruder never succeeds in holding the top without stopping its motion, he has failed, so he concludes, to give expression to the meaning of an ordinary incident in human life. The tale of the spinning top testifies to the inadequacy of language in describing the creative process. In more general terms, Richard Thieberger associates **"Der Kreisel"** with the dilemma that every writer confronts: "Leben läßt sich mit Beobachtung des Lebens nicht vereinbaren" (*Kafka-Handbuch II*, 375).

Dissatisfied with his early efforts to portray his life in the form of fiction, Kafka labeled as his first true literary achievement his story **"Das Urteil,"** written in a single night in 1912. The primary study of his tension-ridden relationship with his father, Kafka's narrative has at its climax a fatal encounter between father and son. In depicting this scene, Kafka puts aside straight-forward narration and enters into a realm of the fantastic.[7] The frail father becomes a vengeful and merciless Jehovah, who condemns the protagonist to death by drowning. The "guilty" son immediately carries out his self-execution by lowering himself over the railing of a bridge over a river and plunging to his death. The climactic moment before he drowns affords him insight into the justice embodied in his suicidal act. In the last words of **"Das Urteil,"**: "In diesem Augenblick ging über die Brücke ein geradezu unendlicher Verkehr," the protagonist envisions (too late) an utopian kind of communication.[8] The epiphanic nature of this experience is derived from the unique nature of this flash of insight. In his *Epiphany in the Modern Novel*, Morris Beja has aptly characterized an epiphany of this kind as being "a frozen tableau" (23). Furthermore, Beja credits Kafka with being particularly deft in employing the epiphanic moment in his writing. He proposes: "Few writers convey the strange, dreamlike universe of temporal (and spatial) relativity so hauntingly as Franz Kafka" (63). Notably, in all of Kafka's moments of epiphany or mental awakening, true insight fades quickly into darkness and doubt.

A second narrative that makes use of the epiphany, written in 1912, is **"Die Verwandlung."** It begins by describing the aftermath of one epiphany and ends with an extended account of another.[9] During a night of troubled sleep, the protagonist Gregor Samsa spontaneously comes to the realization that as a family member and salesman in the business world he exists only in the form of a monstrous and repulsive insect.[10] Throughout the story, however, his perceptions remain those of a human being. The work relates what the effect of this horrific transfiguration would be, if his employers and family were to accept his moment of insight, his epiphany, as their own. Like the guilty son in **"Das Urteil,"** the story's protagonist Gregor determines, but less abruptly, to die.[11] Gradually, Gregor (a variant of "Georg") realizes that his business associates and relatives, and even his sister, although with great reluctance, regard him as a monster and come to welcome his demise. She tries, nevertheless, to pacify the boarders in the family apartment, who are revolted by suddenly catching sight of the monstrous insect, by playing the violin for them. Under the epiphany-like spell of the music Gregor accepts the truth which his transformation has made evident and resolves no longer to resist the progress of his desiccation. The moment of Gregor's death occurs in the first light of day. Framed by the halo of dawn, he is reconciled to his death sentence. "An seine Familie dachte er mit Rührung und Liebe zurück" (*Erzählungen*, 103), the narrator reports about his last moment.

The aftermath of Gregor's satisfaction with the outcome of his fatal transformation, the salvation of his family's peace of mind and bourgeois way of life, is revealed in the final pages of **"Die Verwandlung."** The narrator gives an account of the happiness of the bereaved Samsas. Notably, Kafka expressed his dissatisfaction with the shift in viewpoint; in his journal he lamented: "Unlesbares Ende."[12] In contrast to the epiphanic moment he described so tersely and proficiently at the end of **"Das Urteil,"** his overly elaborate account of the result of Gregor Samsa's intense experience can but be supererogatory. The same flaw, an inability on Kafka's part to write or perhaps even to conceive of a denouement to his story, characterizes **"In der Strafkolonie"** and explains the unfinished state of his novels.

The interrelationship between the three stories, **"Das Urteil," "Die Verwandlung"** and **"In der Strafkolonie,"** is self-evident. Kafka himself acknowledged the correlation and proposed to his publisher that all three should appear in one volume. For this he suggested the title *Strafen* (*Punishments*). Pointedly, the theme of punishment (again, a death sentence) plays a major role in **"In der Strafkolonie."** Walter Sokel has proposed that **"In der Strafkolonie"** presents a direct critique (*Auseinandersetzung*) of the bourgeois values espoused in the earlier two.[13] The key figure in the story of the penal colony is a scientist, who, like Darwin, is making a tour of the world. His views diverge to a large extent from those of the other characters in the narrative who are markedly similar to personages in the two earlier tales. The judgmental father in **"Das Urteil"** and **"Die Verwandlung"** reappears as both the Old Commandant, the inventor of the execution machine, which inflicts the torment of a slow and brutal death on its victims while bringing to light their human failings. Another returning character, the Commandant's self-appointed accomplice, the officer in charge of the execution, has a principal role as the Commandant's advocate. The visiting observer in the penal colony constitutes a different aspect of the dilemma that haunted Kafka, namely, his inability to choose between obedience to paternal hegemony and resistance to it. Both the nameless prisoner condemned to death on a facetious basis at the beginning of **"In the Penal Colony"** and the officer of the execution are victims of the same paternalistic system that condemned to death Georg in **"Das Urteil"** and Gregor Samsa in **"Die Verwandlung."** However, conflict occurs in **"In the Penal Colony"** since the officer of the execution and the observer hold two diametrically opposite points of view in the matter of crime and punishment. The crime for which the lowly soldier in the penal colony is about to be executed, neglect of duty in a paternally oriented world, is a blatantly exaggerated version of Kafka's rebellion against the rigidity of the rules in his father's world. In effect, death upon the execution machine demonstrates the extreme nature of the conflict between the world of the writer Kafka and the business world of his father. The orthodoxy of the Old Commandant and his successor, the officer of

the execution, and the qualms their adversary, the reluctant witness to the execution, has in regard to the cause they espouse are at the root of the conflict in the story. To the concept of the torture machine, which Kafka may well have borrowed from Octave Mirbeau's *Le Jardin des Supplices,* he gave new significance by adding the element of the torture's epiphanic climax and its deadly association with the act of writing. Undoubtedly, Kafka was also aware of the French penal colony on Devil's Island and its celebrated onetime prisoner Alfred Dreyfus. (The warders of Kafka's colony speak French.) The machine's significance in the story, however, is totally Kafka's invention. The similarity between the Old Commandant and the father figure in **"Das Urteil"** is implicit rather than deliberate. In regard to **"Die Verwandlung,"** on the other hand, the paterfamilias Samsa is unambiguously given the role of the creator of Eden who sends the disobedient Adam out of Paradise, while throwing apples at him. A piece of an apple, caught under the insect's scale, causes an infection that brings about the vermin's death. Thus, the moment of illumination that overcomes Gregor as he listens to his sister playing the violin, points him not only in the direction of insight into the conflict that threatens his life but also in the direction of his problem's insolubility.

A new factor in **"In der Strafkolonie"** is the wavering role assigned to the scientist-observer, the visitor to the penal colony. Kafka has made him a foil for the officer of the execution, the dutiful son figure. The author Kafka thereby becomes more closely related to the objective observer. Although the traveler seems to reject the concept of society as a patrimony, he is willing to consider the validity of the rules of the one in which he finds himself confined for the moment. Under these circumstances, the motif of the voluntary death or suicide of one of the story's key figures can recur in **"In der Strafkolonie"** when the officer of the execution in the stead of the condemned man becomes the machine's next and final victim. The officer dies in order to convince the skeptical observer that at the sixth hour, the hour of death, the condemned man is afforded a moment of true insight into the nature of his "crime." In other words, each victim experiences an epiphany. With the expectation of achieving the state of complete apprehension of the self, the officer has previously proclaimed: "Wie nahmen wir alle den Ausdruck der Verklärung von dem gemarterten Gesicht, wie hielten wir unsere Wangen in den Schein dieser endlich erreichten und schon vergehenden Gerechtigkeit."[14] Since the visitor to the colony has suspended his disbelief in the possibility of experiencing any such fleeting prescience, the officer can but seize the moment and take the place of the pitiful condemned man on the execution machine. In consequence he dies with his expectation still unfulfilled that the occurrence of an epiphany, a moment of self-discovery, will justify the torment inflicted by the writing machine. In this way Kafka has made plain the relevance to himself of the officer's devotion to the machine. With the machine's failure he can demonstrate his realization that he can never express *adequately* the truth about himself.[15] His writing, he concedes, is inadequate as a vehicle that justifies his abandoning his familial life. In particular, as his father's only (living) son[16] he had placed his ambitions to be a writer above his father's aspiration to continue the family line. In this frame of reference, the story's turning point, the foiling of the officer's attempt to reach the heights of true insight effected by the breakdown of the machine, emphasizes the negativity of the story's climactic moment. The epiphany loses its value, since Kafka can but realize that words are but an imitation of reality. Nagel describes the situation in this way: "So war es nur konsequent, daß ihm (dem Offizier) bei seiner eigenen Exekution auch das Erlebnis der Erleuchtung [. . .] nicht zuteil werden konnte."[17] Significant in relationship to the failed epiphany is the sentence which the machine has decreed to be the message that it will imprint on the officer's back at the (epiphanic) moment of his death: "Sei gerecht!" "Be just" pertains ironically to Kafka, the writer, who must admit to himself that his epiphany is a failed one since he cannot envision a reconciliation between father and son. Malcolm Pasley has described the situation in these words: "Recurrently, the puritan artist laid his natural, all-too-human self on the torture machine, while a third splinter of his personality—the observer—stood by with helplessly ambivalent feelings.[18] The escape of the traveler from the scene of the crime with its collapsed instrument of torture can provide only an anticlimax to the events already depicted. Here another similarity among the three stories under discussion makes itself manifest: the failed ending of the epiphany, the insufficiency of the moment of true insight, which prevails in each instance. In the case of **"In der Strafkolonie,"** the traveler's attempted but never executed escape from his dilemma subtly duplicates Kafka's vain effort to remove himself from the family circle and live (and write) on his own. Thus the scientist is shown visiting the tomb of the Old Commandant in an inn. He finds it hidden under a table and reads imprinted on the tombstone a prophecy that predicts the return of the tyrant. This tacked-on (and incomplete) ending is only a repetition of the previous occurrence of a failed epiphany. As an unintended addendum to this trio of narratives and others that deal with a foiled epiphany, e.g., "Vor dem Gesetz," Kafka wrote what must be considered the most direct account of his relationship with his father: a forty-page letter addressed to him, describing his son's dilemma. According to J. B. Honegger, Kafka's letter to his father contains the most direct and intensive portrayal of the power and, as its partner, the fear, which constitute the basis of Kafka's work.[19] Kafka's use of the metaphor or literary device which James Joyce named "epiphany"

was an intuitive response to the urgency of his need to address the central problem in his life and work: the father-and-son relationship. His achievement of insight into his troubled life as a writer and his failure to resolve the personal conflict between being a writer and being a family member resulted in the production of a body of literature that attempts to light up with its blaze life's hidden depths.

Notes

1. Hartmut Binder contends that, because Kafka wrote in the German language for a small provincial audience, he did not envision a readership well-schooled in the classical literary tradition and did not follow academic models, such as the allegory. See Hartmut Binder, *Kafka-Handbuch II* (Stuttgart: Alfred Kröner, 1979) 56: "(D)ie in der Allegorie notwendigen begrifflich-eindeutigen Zuordnungen entsprechen weder seiner Denkweise noch seiner Weltsicht." Compare also in the *Kafka-Handbuch,* the comment of Ingeborg Henel: "(*In der Strafkolonie*) ist die einzige Allegorie, die Kafka geschrieben hat, und vertritt als solche den extremen Pol seiner Neigung zum Abstrakten" (229). Bert Nagel writes: "Gewiß ist die Strafkolonie *auch* ein allegorisches Märchen, aber nicht nur" in *Franz Kafka* (Berlin: Erich Schmidt, 1974) 240.

2. Mark Anderson, "Introduction," *Reading Kafka* (New York: Schocken, 1989) 13.

3. See Thomas Wagenbaur, *The Moment: A History, Typology and Theory of the Moment in Philosophy and Literature* (Frankfurt/M, etc.: Peter Lang, 1993) 16 and 47.

4. See Morris Beja, *Epiphany in the Modern Novel* (Seattle: Univ. of Washington Press, 1971) 75: "We cannot identify epiphany with symbolism either, for epiphany involves not merely representation but revelation as well."

5. Max Brod, *Franz Kafka* (New York: Schocken, 1975) 44.

6. Judith Ryan in *The Vanishing Subject* (Chicago and London: Univ. of Chicago Press, 1991) uses the terms "daylight mysticism" and "special moments of ecstasy" in referring to the presence of epiphanic moments in the work of Robert Musil. In his book on the epiphany (see above) Morris Beja quotes the phrase used by the character Dr. Krokowski in Thomas Mann's *The Magic Mountain* to describe the phenomenon: "an orgasm of the brain" (Beja, 42).

7. See Franz R. Kempf, *Everyone's Darling: Kafka and the Critics of his Short Fiction* (Columbia, SC: Camden House, 1994): "With his contemporary Gustav Meyrink, Kafka has in common the fantastic" (10).

8. Franz Kafka, *Erzählungen* Frankfurt/M: Fischer, 1976) 53.

9. See Thomas Wagenbaur's *The Moment* for a definition of the term relevant to Gregor Samsa's moment of insight which precedes the opening of the story: "'Epiphany' has become the standard term for the description . . . of the sudden flare into revelation of an ordinary object or scene" (53).

10. See Martin Greenberg, "Gregor Samsa's Modern Spirituality" in *Franz Kafka's The Metamorphosis,* ed. Harold Blum (New York, Philadelphia: Chelsea House, 1988): "(Gregor's) metamorphosis is indeed no dream (meaning something unreal) but a revelation of the truth" (20).

11. "Seine Meinung (war), daß er verschwinden müsse" (*Erzählungen* 103).

12. Franz Kafka: Dichter über ihre Dichtungen, ed. Erich Heller & Joachim Beug (München: Heimeran, 1969) 57.

13. See Walter Sokel, *Franz Kafka, Tragik und Ironie: Zur Struktur seiner Kusnt* (München, Wien: Albert Langen, George Müller, 1964) 107.

14. Note the conclusion of the officer's explanation: ". . . how we turned our cheeks toward the light of this (instance of) justice, finally attained, *but already on the wane*" (my translation).

15. See Ramon G. Mendosa, *Outside Humanity: A Study of Kafka's Fiction* (Lanham, N.Y., London: University Press of America, 1986) 106f.: "Should we accept the instrument of torture to be the unequivocal symbol of the author's writing, it seems that we would have a suitable, indeed almost compelling interpretation of *In the Penal Colony*".

16. Kafka's two younger brothers died in infancy; one was named Georg.

17. Nagel 248.

18. Malcolm Paseley, "In the Penal Colony" in *The Kafka Debate: New Perspectives or our Time,* ed. Angel Flores (New York: Gordian Press, 1977) 299.

19. Christoph Stöltzl, "Nichtepische Arbeiten und Lebenszeugnisse" in *Kafka-Handbuch II,* 528.

Larry Vaughan (essay date 2001)

SOURCE: Vaughan, Larry. "Franz Kafka's 'Eine kaiserliche Botschaft' through an Hasidic Prism." *Germanisch-Romanische Monatsschrift* 51, no. 2 (2001): 151-58.

[*In the following essay, Vaughan employs Hasidic tales to come to an understanding of Kafka's parable "Eine kaiserliche Botschaft."*]

Das stärkste Mittel, auf die himmlischen
Sphären einzuwirken, ist das Gebet.

Alexander Eliasberg[1]

Schreiben als Form des Gebets

Franz Kafka[2]

Faith was fire [for the Ba'al Shem Tov], not sediment.

Abraham Joshua Heschel[3]

I am undertaking the illumination of Kafka's **"Eine kaiserliche Botschaft,"**[4] suggesting shared elements with the Hasidic tales of Alexander Eliasberg's collection, *Sagen polnischer Juden,*[5] that Kafka held in his library and that evinced "Gebrauchsspuren,"[6]; and also particularly elements shared with and disparate to a parable and tales from Martine Buber's two collections, *Die Legende des Baalschem* and *Die Geschichte des Rabbi Nachman, ihm nacherzählt,*[7] indicated critically, hence knowledgeably, in a letter by Kafka, four years before he wrote his parable, and six years before it was published.[8] Hasidic tales appropriate the tradition of Jewish folk tales and are the form in which the trenchant, the sacred, the true—in a word, hope—appeared and fueled the popular movement of Hasidism. My presentation looks in good part to and through Hasidic tales, attempting to come to terms with Kafka's parable.

Kafka begins **"Eine kaiserliche Botschaft"** with the emperor, who, as any emperor, represents state power and embodies spiritual authority, and the immediately following narrator's reference to one to whom the emperor sends a message: "Dir, dem Einzelnen, den jämmerlichen Untertanen, dem winzig vor der kaiserlichen Sonne in die fernste Ferne geflüchteten Schatten, gerade Dir". The emperor, on his deathbed summons the messenger to whom he whispers the message. We are never told its contents, but we know its importance from the fact that the emperor has the message repeated in his ear. And the message takes on an even greater importance by the fact that all obstructing walls are broken down to reveal the grandees of the empire, in a ring around the emperor, on rising open staircases, almost as a (celestial) host, before whom, among others, he dispatches his messenger.

In *Die Geschichte von dem Klugen und dem Einfältigen,*[9] from the stories of Rabbi Nachman, the great-grandson of the Ba'al Shem Tov—the latter who founded the Hasidic movement in the mid-18th century in Eastern Europe—"die Botschaft des Königs" directly reaches its designated recipients, which is different from the Kafka parable, as we shall see, but the story strikes a similar chord to the narrator's "directly you" ("gerade Dir"), by the self-characterization of the Clever One: "Was bin ich, daß ein mächtiger König meiner begehrt? . . . Hat er nicht genug der edelen Vasallen und der tiefsinnigen Berater an seinem Hofe, daß er mich kleinen und unwürdigern Mann zu sich bescheiden sollte?"[10]

The inner expanse of Kafka's parable, after the messenger sets out on his way, after the preamble, as it were, lies within the (im)possible human connection between the emperor and his most distant subject, mediated by the messenger, or more specifically, it concerns the way itself travelled by the imperial message. At first, when the messenger sets out, he makes progress through the multitude; "ein kraftiger, ein unermündlicher Mann"; if he encounters resistance, he bears the sign of the imperial sun on his chest. "Aber": and here is a dialectical "hinge"; here is where the parable begins to turn, and the subjunctive mood enters the picture. "Aber": a second negation, a second hinge; and the parable turns. "Aber die Menge ist so groß. . . . Öffnete sich freies Feld, wie würde er fliegen . . .". There follows a long series (11) of semicolons—not full stops—picking up steam and lending the parable a staccato rhythm (short bursts of energy): "die Gemächer des innersten Palastes; niemals wird er sie überwinden; und gelänge ihm dies, nichts wäre gewonnen; die Treppen hinab müßte er sich kämpfen; und gelänge ihm dies, nichts wäre gewonnen." The messenger encounters seemingly insurmountable obstacles, which he "overcomes" in the subjunctive mood: chambers, steps, courts, another palace; "und so weiter durch Jahrtausende. . . ."

An oft-cited parable, the parable of barriers (to approaching the king),[11]—recorded from the Ba'al Shem Tov, the Besht, and brought in one version by Buber in the volume Kafka mentions in his letter—though it moves in the opposite direction from Kafka's parable, it is nonetheless instructive. The king built a palace "mit zahlosen Gemächtern,"[12] and summoned all his princes to appear before him. "Aber als sie eintraten, sahen sie: da waren Türen offen nach allen Seiten, von denen führten gewundene Gänge in die Ferne, und da waren weider Türen und wieder Gänge, und kein Ende stand vor dem verwirrten Augen."[13] The son came and saw that the confusion was a matter of reflection. In other words, the endless series was illusory, though the King's palace did have "countless chambers." In any event, the princes were in fact hindered by the seeming infinitude of doors and hallways. So on the one hand, in Kafka's parable, we have obstacles "overcome"—but not transcended—in the subjunctive mood, on the other, in the Besht's parable from Buber, the seeming obstacles are "transcended" (from confusion to clarity, darkness to light), and the son saw his father sitting before him in the grand hall. The Hasidic parable, moves toward resolution on a higher plane: *Devekut*: cleaving to God. And although *Devekut* is the desired goal,[14] attained it is said (if momentarily) by Hasidic masters, in the paragraph immediately following the Besht's parable, Buber puts a different spin on the matter, one that brings to mind the almost unimaginable stretch of spatial time before the messenger in Kafka's parable ("und weiter durch Jahrtausende"). Buber writes, "Das Geheimnis der Gnade ist nicht zu deuten. Zwischen Suchen und Fin-

den liegt die Spannung eines Menschenlebens, ja tausendfacher Wiederkehr der wandernde Seele."[15] The magnitude of the two ways, wandering or striving, resonate on an existential continuum.

Writing on *Rabbi Nachman und die jüdische Mystik,* prior to the stories he brings, Buber evokes the notion of the "shell" (die "Schale").[16] To elaborate, from another source, Rabbi Nachman addresses "the evil" that "surrounds holiness." According to him, "to pray and to speak to God," one must "split the barriers and screens [shells or husks] which surround him." This is achieved by following the level of truth at which one is.[17] The *kelipot* or shells belong to a constellation of myths central to Lurianic Kabbalah (shared, if given an axial turn toward the category of popular existence and ethics, by Hasidism), myths - as shared structures of meaning to organize experience of the world -[18] which have to do with a catastrophe of cosmic proportions: the "breaking of the vessels." The vessels of heavy light, or emanations of divine attributes (*sefirot*), were shattered under the force or weight of a ray of divine light meant to cleanse them of their residue of *kelipot* to bring the *kelipot* together in one place. Holy sparks were cast everywhere over the lower worlds,[19] where the shells came together for the first time to form their own realm. Now, the shells gather around the holy sparks, imprison them and derive their vitality from them; the shells constitute the "Other Side," the dark side, the *sefirot* on the left. In one of the introductory pieces to his collection of stories from Rabbi Nachman, which Kafka referred to in his letter cited above, Buber captures the nature of the *kelipah*: "Was wir das Böse nennen, ist kein Wesen, sondern ein Mangel, es ist "Gottes Exil" . . . es ist—in der Sprache der alten Kabbala—die 'Schale', die das Wesen der Dinge umgibt und verhüllt."[20] Indeed, the shells surround and conceal the holy sparks. To elaborate in line with the Hasidic masters, the sparks are everywhere, in all things and acts, sustaining them. They can be extracted and elevated from concealment through the recharged traditional Rabbinic paths of the study of Torah (Pentatuch) and the performance of *mitzvot* (Commandments), but also through repentence, and especially through (contemplative) prayer, as well as through the proper (sanctifying) manner of eating, conversing, transacting business, and other matters: viz. here the novel notion of linking the celestial with the mundane, of doing everything with enthusiasm and attachment to God.[21] The liberation of the holy sparks is meant to restore a harmonious world—*tikkun olam*—not Tikkun write large, as under Lurianic Kabbalah (mid-16th century Safed, Palestine), which aimed at repairing the balance of the universe.[22]

To return to **"Eine kaiserliche Botschaft,"** although we have never left it, or it has never left us, were the messenger to finally burst through the outermost gate of the palaces, he would be confronted by "die Residenzstadt," the great divide of the world, "die Mitte der Welt." Prior to the imperial capital, the obstacles are temporal in character, negations of the messenger's striving—"niemals," and finally, most emphatically, "niemals, niemals"—without transcendence or reconciliation. But before the imperial capital the negative dialectic,[23] empowered by the resistance of the obstacles themselves—if in the subjunctive mood which, however, always canceled overtaken impossibilities—stops dead in its tracks. Now the parable speaks in terms of an abstract yet concrete personal term: "Niemand." The imperial capital looms before the messenger; and: "Niemand dringt hier durch. . . ." Definitive. There can be no resolution of confusion, no passage from darkness to light (awareness), as in the Besht's parable, as related by Buber above - for that was a different age, albeit with its *Judenverfolgung,* from fiscal extortion to pogroms - the imperial capital is not transparent but opaque, "hochgeschüttet voll ihres Bodensatzes." It is an inverted city whose ground defines its heights. That the negative dialectical movement of the message cannot determinately negate this last obstacle, means that it cannot draw its power from it, for the sedimentary city embodies anti-existence, I would put forth, which is the nature of the *kelipot,* they draw their existence from that which they surround; in other words the imperial city may be seen as a gigantic "shell"; or, a mass of compressed shells, that imprison the holy sparks of existence. And, as Gershom Scholem writes, it is in the nature of the "shells" to "dam up and choke life."[24] The imperial capital, highly congested with its own sediment, imprisons the holy sparks (for all—linear—time). There is no dialectical cancelation here; it is rather something whose sound would be "ein einiges Getön von ungeheurem Weh" that surrounded the Besht's camp one night on his aborted journey to Jerusalem.[25] However, outside spatial time (reified time)—in an age-old sound perhaps—there is still the note of transcendence and the hope of redemption: "Denn die Zeit ist kein festes Ding . . .".[26]

To repeat, the world is inverted, topsy-turvy; *Boden*satz no longer just lies at the ground level but has risen to the top of the imperial capital. It is as if a monstrous shell, or a monstrosity of shells, encases the city and imprisons the holy sparks within. If one could proceed directly: "Er [der Widersacher: biblical, the Adversary] ist die Schale die du zerschlagen sollst."[27] At the world divide, the messenger stands face to face with an impenetrable concreteness. Here it is not just a matter of (urban decay! or) the urban masses, since the messenger has already vigorously overcome the multitude, "die Menge," and its endless domiciles, in a dialectical leap as it were. No mortal person, not even a well-rested and powerful, mythological messenger (as the Messiah is God's messenger), could see his way clear through the city, the seat of the imperium, crammed full of its own

residue. There follows a brief declarative sentence made up of two parts: "Niemand dringt hier durch und gar mit der Botschaft eines Toten." That little "gar" in the second part of the compound sentence, in a reversal of the meaning of the first half of the sentence, intimates that one could just perhaps see one's way clear, and it brings to mind the liberation of the trapped holy sparks.

In *Beim Bau der Chinesischen Mauer,* in which the parable was originally embedded,[28] two sentences prior to the parable, it reads: "Das Kaisertum ist unsterblich, aber der einzelne Kaiser fällt und stürtzt ab . . .".[29] Such a statement would seem to break the spell of the parable, crack it open to reveal light on another level perhaps (the Hasidic master's goal); in any event, there are layers of meaning in the parable; and one layer does not exclude the other. Still, does the dead emperor—as the penultimate sentence slips this fact in—validate Nietzsche's famous comment, namely that "God is dead"? Heinz Politzer implies that it does.[30] Perhaps the anthropocentric sky-God, but not the God within, as Hasidism would have it; or, the ineffable, unknowable *Ein-Sof,* without beginning, "Without End": "from eternity to eternity. . . ." (Psalms 90:2) Yet, and yet, I would venture that it might not matter: Perhaps the road taken by the message—*Eine kaiserliche Botschaft*—or the striving messenger, or the striving itself, against all odds, are what matter here. Perhaps the emperor is just that—an emperor. There is an interplay of levels here.

The message must be powerful enough to drive the messenger ever onward, even if he could not penetrate the silted-up imperial capital (though he overcame other impossibilities along the way). We can speculate endlessly on the contents of the message; in any case, it is conveyed further through dreaming. And the parable turns again, this time toward the personal, on the final hinge of "Du aber. . . ." You sit at your window—window, a liminal place between inner and outer;[31] and dream the message—in a state of sleeping while awake: another liminal point; when the night falls—thus dusk: the third threshold state. The message is conveyed—in an overdetermined manner—but the emperor is dead. A message for "you" (representationally, but intimately)—historically kept underfoot—far from the sources of power. To borrow an apt alternative by the narrator after the end of the parable within *Beim Bau der Chinesischen Mauer,* which concerns how "unser Volk" perceives the Emperor, one which may fit here: "hoffungslos und hoffnungsvoll."[32] Though they are alternatives, they are not an empty to-and-fro; but perhaps it is a matter of the messenger moving within the force field of a negative dialectic, which takes its driving power from the obstacle or ideology it engages, and engenders hope, as it strives toward truth, through negating the barriers, be they internal or external.

The importance of dreaming, which comes over, or overcomes one, can be seen in a tale from the Eliasberg collection that Kafka possessed; and where the dreaming process is repeated, its power doubled so to speak: "Eines Tages schlief ich bei mir zu Hause ein, und es träumte mir, daß ich auf einer Reise sei: denn ich bin ja gewohnt in meinen Geschäften zu reisen. Und es träumte mir. . . ."[33] And dreaming affects the highest born as well the merchant; even kings can dream potent dreams.[34] Dreaming comes up often in Hasidic tales. Dreaming involves a sinking into oneself, so that one can rise into upper regions: the transcending movement lifts the barrier between upper and lower realms—and reveals the truth of the outer world.

The final words of Kafka's parable are: "wenn der Abend kommt." In contradistinction to this placement, the English translators of the parable make them the penultimate words, which give the parable an *uplift,* when there is none in a conventional sense. "But you sit at your window when night falls and dream it [the message] to yourself."[35] In the process the translators omit the comma (or the invisible hand of English usage does it)—as beforehand they omitted the dash that sets the sentence off, yet binds it inextricably to the previous one. "Niemand dringt hier durch und gar mit der Botschaft eines Toten.—Du aber sitzt an Deinem Fenster und erträumst sie Dir, wenn der Abend kommt." But the last sentence is not the final thought of the parable, for in its threefold movement, it sparks the recollection of possibilities, deep within the dialectic of the text. One hundred years after the publication of the Stories of Rabbi Nachman, Kafka evinced the impossiblity of redemption, while he dreamed its possibility.

Notes

1. Einleitung, *Sagen polnischer Juden,* selected and trans. Alexander Eliasberg (München: Müller, 1916), p. 16.

2. Cited by W[erner] Kraft, *Das Religiöse bei Kafka,* in E.E. Urbach et al., *Studies in Mysticism and Religion* (Presented to Gershom Scholem on his Seventieth Birthday) (Jerusalem: Magnes, 1967), p. 171.

3. Abraham Joshua Heschel, *A Passion for Truth* (New York: Farrah, Straus and Giroux, 1973), p. 47. Quoted by Rabbi Burt Jacobson in a public lecture, *The Ba'al Shem Tov and the Renewal of the Jewish Soul,* May 2000. I am deeply grateful to Rabbi Jacobson for reading a draft of this article and offering his comments and especially his encouragement; he also suggested further readings which proved helpful.

4. In: Franz Kafka, *Sämtliche Erzählungen,* ed. Paul Raabe (Frankfurt am Main: Fischer, 1981), pp. 138-39. Citations are from this text, and are easy to follow. The parable was probably written March/April 1917, and it was first published in Die Selbstwehr, Prag, September 24, 1919. Raabe, "Zu den Texten", p. 400. The parable first appears about three-fifths of the way through *Beim Bau der Chinesischen Mauer,* p. 296 (commas instead of dashes set off "so heißt es") evidently incomplete and published in 1954. See Raabe, p. 404.

5. See note 1 above.

6. Julius Born et al., *Kafkas Bibliothek: Ein beschreibendes Verzeichnis* (Frankfurt am Main: S. Fischer, 1990), p. 81.

7. Martin Buber, *Die Legende des Baalschem* (Frankfurt am Main: Rütten and Loening, 1908); I use a latter edition (1916). Martin Buber, *Die Geschichten des Rabbi Nachman, ihm nacherzählt* (Frankfurt am Main: Rütten und Loening, 1906): "Ich war bemüht, alle Elemente der originalen Fabeln . . . unberührt zu erhalten und den Grundton einer jeden . . . zu wahren." Ibid., p. 1.

8. Franz Kafka, *Briefe an Felice und andere Korrespondenz aus der Verlobungszeit,* ed. Erich Heller und Jürgen Born, *Gesammelte Werke,* ed. Max Born (Frankfurt am Main: S. Fischer, 1967), vol. 10, vom 20. zum 21.I.13, p. 260 and note 2.

9. Buber, *Die Geschichten des Rabbi Nachman,* pp. 63-82.

10. Ibid., p. 77. This citation is a shorter, less potent version of the original, *The Sophisticate and the Simpleton,* in: *Rabbi Nachman's Stories (Sippurey Ma'asioth),* trans. Rabbi Aryeh Kaplan, *The Stories of Rabbi Nachman of Breslov* (Jerusalem, Israel: The Breslov Research Institute, 1983), p. 184. See Arnold J. Band, trans., *Nahman of Bratslav: The Tales* (New York and Mahwah, N.J.: Paulist Press, 1978), p. 154.

11. So characterized straightway, without the implied parenthetical addition, in: Yoran Jacobson, *Hasidic Thought,* trans. from the Hebrew, Jonathan Chipman (Tel-Aviv: MOD Press, 1998), p. 21.

12. Buber, *Die Legende des Baalschem,* p. 10.

13. Ibid., pp. 10-11.

14. "[D]evekut is Hasidism's chief and most characteristic religious value." Norman Lamm, *The Religious Thought of Hasidism: Text and Commentary* (New York: Yeshva University Press, 1999), ch. 5, *"Devekut"* Introduction, p. 133. "In Hasidism . . . man's highest religious vocation is devekut, the attempt to commune with God." Ibid., ch. 5, no. 19, *"Devekut* No Miracle," Introduction, p. 160.

15. Buber, *Die Legende des Baalschem,* p. 11. See Buber, *Die Geschichten des Rabbi Nachman, Worte des Rabbi Nachman,* "Glaube", p. 34.

16. Buber, *Die Geschichten des Rabbi Nachman,* pp. 15-16.

17. Alan Untermann, trans. *The Wisdom of the Jewish Mystics* (New York: New Directions, 1976), pp. 77-78, CXVII.,,When you wish to ascend [to the upper worlds], you will first see what seems to be the image of a man and the images of dogs; these are the *kelipot* that exist throughout the world of Asiyah ["action" or "making"]. Be strong and do not fear." [first bracket Lamm's, second mine] Source: Besht, *Likkutim Yekarim,* p. 9b, no. 49, in: Lamm, *The Religious Thought of Hasidism,* ch. 5, no. 14, "Ascending in Stages," p. 155.

18. Niel Gillman, *Philosophy and Tradition,* in: *The State of Jewish Studies,* ed. Shaye J.D. Cohen and Edward L. Greenstein (Detroit: Wayne State University Press, 1990), p. 219.

19. The Ba'al Shem Tov accepted this cataclysmic cosmic theory, while R. Dov Ber, *The Maggid of Mezerith,* who organized Hasidism after the death of the Besht (1760), said that "a breaking was necessary so that the light [of his Lordship] could be acknowledged." Source: R. Dov Ber, *The Maggid of Mezeritch,* Or ha-Emet, p. 4 11c, in: Lamm, *The Religious Thought of Hasidism,* ch. 1, "God and Providence," no.6, "The Descent of God and the Ascent of Man," p. 46. See Buber, *Das Leben der Chassidim: von der Intention,* in: *Die Legende des Baalschem,* p. 25.

20. Buber, *Rabbi Nachman und die jüdische Mystik: Die jüdische Mystik,* in: *Die Geschichten des Rabbi Nachman,* pp.15-16. For a thumbnail sketch of the *kelipot,* see Gershom Scholem, *Major Trends in Jewish Mysticism* (New York: Schocken, 1941; 1974), pp. 266-67.

21. Lamm, *The Religious Thought of Hasidism,* ch. 10, "Repentance," no. 6, *Repentence as Elevation of Sparks,* p. 347; Source: Besht, *Keter Shem Tov,* pt. 1, no. 53. Jacobson, *Hasidic Thought,* pp. 61, 181. Rachel Elior,,,*Hasidism - Historical Continuity and Spiritual Change,* in: Gershom Scholem's *Major Trends in Jewish Mysticism* 50 Year After, Proceedings of the Sixth International Conference on the History of Jewish Mysticism, ed. Peter Schäfer and Joseph Dan (Tübingen: Mohr, 1993), p. 317.

22. See *Die Geschichte von dem Königssohn und dem Sohn der Magd,* in: Buber, *Die Geschichten des Rabbi Nachmann,* p. 99. See Buber, *Kawwana: von der Intention,* in: *Die Legende des Baalschem,* p. 23: "wirken kann der Mensch an der Erlösung der Welt."

23. Theodor W. Adorno, *Negative Dialektik* (Frankfurt am Main: Suhrkamp, 1966).

24. Gerschom Scholem, *Toward an Understanding of the Messianic Idee,* trans., Michael A. Meyer, in: *The Messianic Idea in Judaism and Other Essays on Jewish Spirituality* (New York: Schocken, 1971), p. 23.

25. *Jerusalem,* in: Buber, *Die Legende des Baalschem,* p. 81.

26. *Die Geschichte von den sieben Bettlern,* in: Buber, *Die Geschichten des Rabbi Nachman,* p. 142.

27. *Der Werwolf,* in: Buber, *Die Legende des Baalschem,* p. 46.

28. Paul Raabe speaks of "dieser für Kafka so zentralen Geschichte . . .". In: Kafka, *Sämtliche Erzählungen,* "Nachwort," p. 404, no. 7. And see note 4 above.

29. Kafka, *Beim Bau der Chinesischen Mauer,* in: Ibid., p. 296.

30. Heinz Politzer, *Franz Kafka: Der Künstler* (Frankfurt am Main: Suhrkamp, 1965; 1978), p. 147. Originally: *Frank Kafka: Parable and Paradox* (Ithaca, N.Y.: Cornell University Press, 1962).

31. I owe this crucial insight to Professor Emeritus Bluma Goldstein; and her article of some three decades ago still serves as a pathfinder for anyone studying Kafka's relation to Hasidism. *Franz Kafka's 'Ein Landsarzt': A Study in Failure,* DVjs 42 (1968): 745-59. Also, I am indeed grateful for her close reading of a draft of my article and her sagacious observations.

32. Kafka, *Beim Bau,* in: *Sämtliche Erzählungen,* p. 296.

33. *Eine Bekehrung,* in: Eliasberg, *Sagen polnischer Juden,* p. 159.

34. *Die Geschichte von Stier und Widder,* in: Buber, *Die Geschichten des Rabbi Nachman,* p. 49.

35. Franz Kafka, *An Imperial Message,* trans. Willa and Edwin Muir, in: *Franz Kafka: The Complete Stories,* ed. Nahum N. Glatzer (New York: Schocken, 1971), p. 5.

FURTHER READING

Criticism

Whitlark, James S. "Kafka's Parodies of Sexual Homicide." *Journal of the Kafka Society of America* 22, no. 1-2 (June/December 1998): 70-80.

Examines the theme of sexual homicide in Kafka's works.

Wiley, David. "Divinity and Denial in Franz Kafka's 'The Metamorphosis' and *The Complete Fiction of*

Bruno Schulz." Canadian-American Slavic Studies 31, no. 2 (summer 1997): 171-176.

Investigates oblivion to divinity in characters of "The Metamorphosis" and *The Complete Fiction of Bruno Schulz.*

Additional coverage of Kafka's life and career is contained in the following sources published by the Gale Group: *Authors and Artists for Young Adults,* Vol. 31; *Beacham's Encyclopedia of Popular Fiction: Biography & Resources,* Vol. 2; *Concise Dictionary of World Literary Biography,* Vol. 2; *Contemporary Authors,* Vols. 105, 126; *Dictionary of Literary Biography,* Vol. 81; *DISCovering Authors; DISCovering Authors: British Edition; DISCovering Authors: Canadian Edition; DISCovering Authors Modules: Most-studied Authors* and *Novelists; DISCovering Authors 3.0; European Writers,* Vol. 9; *Exploring Short Stories; Literature Resource Center; Major 20th-Century Writers,* Eds. 1, 2; *Novels for Students,* Vol. 7; *Reference Guide to Short Fiction,* Ed. 2. *Reference Guide to World Literature,* Eds. 2, 3; *St. James Guide to Science Fiction Writers,* Ed. 4;*Short Stories for Students,* Vols. 3, 7, 12; *Short Story Criticism,* Vols. 5, 29, 35; *Twayne's World Authors; Twentieth-Century Literary Criticism,* Vols. 2, 6, 13, 29, 47, 53, 112; and *World Literature Criticism.*

The Shawl: A Story and a Novella

Cynthia Ozick

(Also wrote under the pseudonym Trudie Vosce) American short fiction writer, novelist, essayist, and playwright.

The following entry presents criticism of Ozick's short fiction collection *The Shawl: A Story and a Novella* (1989). For discussion of Ozick's complete short fiction career, see *SSC,* Volume 15.

INTRODUCTION

One of Ozick's most critically acclaimed works, *The Shawl: A Story and a Novella* (1989), consisting of the short story "The Shawl" and the novella *Rosa,* provides a devastating picture of the Holocaust and a survivor's life after it. Considered a departure from Ozick's previously cerebral and ironic tone, the fierceness and immediacy of *The Shawl* make it one of her most powerful works. The focus of these narratives is a woman who idolatrously worships the memory of her infant daughter who was murdered in a Nazi concentration camp.

PLOT AND MAJOR CHARACTERS

The Shawl tells the story of Rosa Lublin's life, both during the Holocaust and her existence afterwards in Florida. "The Shawl," which first appeared in the *New Yorker* on May 26, 1980, depicts the death of Rosa's fifteen-month-old daughter, Magda, in a concentration camp and the shawl that sustained her when Rosa's breasts could not. *Rosa,* originally published in the *New Yorker* on March 23, 1983, is set some thirty years later in Florida, where Rosa has moved after burning down her store in New York. The torment Rosa still feels from her experience in the concentration camp can be seen through her interactions with Stella, a niece who shared her experience in the camp and now supports Rosa from New York, and Rosa's interactions with people in her immediate surroundings including Dr. Tree, who would like her to join a study on people who have been incarcerated and malnourished. The effects of Rosa's horrifying experience can be seen through her memories and her active imagination. Throughout the story, she brings her daughter back to life in order to invent different lives for her, which serve to allow the

reader to see the intense psychological and emotional effects of having lived through such an odious event. It is only through a friendship she begins to forge with the unrelenting Simon Persky, also originally from Warsaw, that she may be able to escape the torment of her own experiences.

MAJOR THEMES

Although the Holocaust serves as a touchstone in much of Ozick's short fiction, for the most part her works examine the dilemma of being Jewish in modern Western society, particularly the United States. However, "The Shawl" focuses on the experience and the horror of the Holocaust itself. Despite its brevity, Ozick vividly conveys the unspeakable atrocities that occurred in the concentration camps. *Rosa* then focuses on the aftereffects of such an experience on Rosa. The loss of her daughter and Rosa's obsession with the shawl that Magda carried until just prior to her death come to symbolize one of the strongest themes of the collection, the extreme losses suffered by the Holocaust survivors. The shawl also points to a second theme that does not appear until the very end of the text, that of recovery. It is only when Rosa is finally reunited with Magda's shawl that the reader can see the possibility of Rosa letting go of the past and focusing on the present.

CRITICAL RECEPTION

Since the publication of her first novel *Trust* (1966), Ozick has garnered critical acclaim for her attention to language and thought-provoking arguments about Jewish American culture. Reviews of *The Shawl* commend the powerful manner in which Ozick portrays the brutality of the Holocaust both in the camps themselves and in its aftereffects. Both "The Shawl" and *Rosa* won first prize in the O. Henry Prize Stories and were chosen for Best American Short Stories. Much of the criticism of Ozick's works focuses on her identity as a Jewish woman and her representations of Jewish people in her texts. Although many critics are quick to find somewhat simplistic interpretations of both works, many others point to the complexity of the characters and situations created by Ozick. Ozick herself has warned against reducing her work to oversimplified themes; instead, readers need to examine the intricacies and accept the contradictions. Many scholars have focused their criticism on one of Ozick's major recurring themes—the contradiction between writing fiction and obeying Jewish law which forbids the creation of idols. The critical reaction to Ozick's argument that art can act as a form of idolatry has been sharply mixed.

PRINCIPAL WORKS

Short Fiction

The Pagan Rabbi and Other Stories 1971
Bloodshed and Three Novellas 1976
Levitation: Five Fictions 1982
*The Shawl: A Story and a Novella 1989
Puttermesser Papers 1997

Other Major Works

Trust (novel) 1966
Art and Ardor (essays) 1983
The Cannibal Galaxy (novel) 1983

The Messiah of Stockholm (novel) 1987
Fame and Folly: Essays (essays) 1989
Metaphor and Memory: Essays (essays) 1989
What Henry James Knew and Other Essays on Writers (essays) 1993
Blue Light (play) 1994
Portrait of the Artist as a Bad Character and Other Essays on Writing (essays) 1996
Quarrel and Quandary (essays) 2000

*Includes the short story "The Shawl" and the novella *Rosa*, which is also termed a story by some critics.

CRITICISM

Elaine M. Kauver (essay date 1993)

SOURCE: Kauver, Elaine M. "The Magic Shawl." In *Cynthia Ozick's Fiction: Tradition and Invention*, pp. 179-202. Bloomington: Indiana University Press, 1993.

[*In the following essay, Kauver investigates how themes from Ozick's earlier writings both reoccur and change in* The Shawl.]

A writer who resists finality is a writer whose imagination is given over to a habit of many sidedness and multiplicity. Having concluded *The Cannibal Galaxy* and **"The Laughter of Akiva"** in Miami, Florida, with Joseph Brill and Reuben Karpov inhabiting at the end of their lives a metaphoric hell of their own devising, Ozick begins **"The Shawl"** and **"Rosa,"** which she wrote during the same period, with Rosa Lublin first in the demonic hell of the Nazi death camps and then in the continuing hell of their aftermath. Initially published separately—**"The Shawl"** in 1980 and **"Rosa"** in 1983—before they appeared in a single volume in 1989, the two stories are wed thematically, yoked by corresponding images, and unified by a commanding metaphor; the tales flow seamlessly together. Ozick duplicates their imagery, pairs their events, and then allows them to coalesce so as to see them with double sight. In its emphasis on the relationship between mother and daughter, in its engagement with the significance of silence, in its involvement with the idea of cannibalism, *The Shawl* bears marked resemblances to *The Cannibal Galaxy* and **"The Laughter of Akiva."** But *The Shawl* turns their concerns inside out: "every notion owns a double face." Manifesting the storyteller's practice of shaping related tales into fictions that unfold alternate positions, *The Shawl* opens a perspective unlike the one Cynthia Ozick developed in her second novel.

I

Hidden in the cellar of a convent, Joseph Brill escaped the butchery of the death camps; incarcerated in one of them, Rosa Lublin experienced its horrors and witnessed a demonic world of unparalleled proportions. In *The Shawl* Ozick not only instances with piercing intensity the brutality common to the German hell but reveals how it continued to torment its victims and perpetuated the work of the victimizers. For the first time in her fiction, she tells a tale directly from the consciousness of a Holocaust survivor, enshrining her as a spokeswoman for the truth. To Holocaust literature *The Shawl* is undeniably of huge importance: the events in the German abattoir become searingly real as their effects emerge in Rosa Lublin's thoughts, which record the torment the survivor endured and so "rescue the suffering . . . from dreadful anonymity" (Appelfeld 92). Ozick's achievement does not end there, however, for incorporating into the tales facts gleaned from history and events derived from memoirs, the storyteller lays bare the intricacies of the human mind. As she has from the very beginning of her career, Cynthia Ozick penetrates the individual psyche by apprehending the historical occurrences that shaped it. If **"The Shawl"** and **"Rosa"** expose the anguish inflicted by radical evil, they affirm the courage displayed by human beings in their efforts to vanquish the powers of darkness.

Interwoven in **"The Shawl"** are allusions to Elie Wiesel's *Night,* to which Ozick refers in "A Mercenary," and to Primo Levi's *Survival in Auschwitz.* What memoirs contain are facts; and facts, as Enoch Vand and Stanislav Lushinski avow, constitute "what really happened." Facts register the "Real." The unfathomable reality of the German hell, the harrowing events reported by Wiesel and Levi, are evoked in *The Shawl* and lend to it the configurations of biography. It is to the interrelatedness of biography and fiction that Ozick increasingly turns; yoking the two forms, she implies they yield a key to the world's design. But the linear time of biography is radically dislocated in **"The Shawl"** and replaced by the terrifying feeling of timelessness, the sense that for the victims of the death camps "history had stopped" (Levi 107). For that reason, the beginning of **"The Shawl,"** which recounts events from Rosa's point of view, affords neither orientation in time nor clarification of place. Instead, the tale opens with the elliptical, "Stella, cold, cold, the coldness of hell." What follows unfolds the effects of that hell on the three people imprisoned in it. Not until the second paragraph, when she mentions the yellow Star of David sewn into Rosa's coat, does Ozick reveal that Rosa, Stella, and Magda are Jews on a march whose destination is a Nazi concentration camp.

The stars, which in *The Cannibal Galaxy* represent the heights to which Joseph Brill once aspired, have in **"The Shawl"** become ominous signs of exclusion and doom. And they are buttressed by Rosa's description of Stella: "Her knees were tumors on sticks, her elbows chicken bones" (3). In **"Levitation"** flight signals the direction toward which the Jews soar to recover Covenant; for Joseph Brill, height points to success. But in **"The Shawl"** the dichotomy between the air and the ground marks the distinction between the innocent and the evil: "Rosa did not feel hunger; she felt light, not like someone walking but like someone in a faint, in trance, arrested in a fit, someone who is already a floating angel, alert and seeing everything, but in the air, not there, not touching the road" (3-4). Of separating the victims of the Holocaust from its perpetrators Ozick has written:

> The Holocaust happened *to* its victims. It did not happen *in* them. The victims were not the participants. The event swept over them, but they were separate from it. That is why they are "sanctified"—because they did not perform evil. . . . And if there is one notion we need to understand more than any other, it is this principle of separation. The people for whom the Holocaust "happened" were the people who made it happen. The perpetrators *are* the Holocaust; the victims stand apart.
>
> ("Roundtable" 284)

The metaphor of flight in **"The Shawl"** does not link Rosa to Feingold in **"Levitation,"** nor does it attribute to her the ability "to overcome history" (Berger 53). Rosa is in the air because she does not partake of evil. She is divided from desecration.

That intensifies Rosa's struggle to conceal Magda from the Nazis, which in turn increases the conflicts with a fourteen-year-old's jealousy and makes more fierce the battle Rosa must wage to stay alive. She judges her niece—Stella's relationship to Rosa is divulged in the following story—the epitome of coldness, her envy the prelude to cannibalism. Wanting "to be wrapped in a shawl, hidden away, asleep, rocked by the march, a baby, a round infant in arms," Stella, Rosa thinks, is "waiting for Magda to die" (3, 5). But it is Stella who studies the blueness of the baby's eyes, gazes at the roundness of its face, stares at the yellowness of its hair, and declares Magda an Aryan. In fact, Magda appears to be "one of *their* babies," the child, Ozick intimates, born of an S.S. officer in a concentration camp (4).

The implied connection between Rosa and a German recalls **"The Suitcase"** and **"A Mercenary"**—the relationship between Genevieve Lewin and Gottfried Hencke and the one between Stanislav Lushinski and his mistress Lulu. Imagery from those stories, as well as from *Trust,* reappears in **"The Shawl."** At first associating yellow with Europe and then with Tilbeck, Ozick ultimately joins the aestheticism that produced the Final Solution to paganism. Yellow is the color to which Mr.

Hencke is "susceptible": buttercups remind him of his past in Germany, and the color suffuses the dream he has of his niece lying dead on a turntable in the nave, her body covered only by her yellow hair (PR 105). In *Trust,* however, a baby plays with a spool of yellow thread, an emblem of what is to come. Catching up those implications, Magda's yellow hair connects the infant to the color of Germany and to the baby in *Trust* who, like Magda, is an augury of the future. To the paganism conjured up by yellow in **"The Shawl"** Ozick adds roundness, a reminder of Lushinski's adopted and pagan country. That mourning is associated with roundness in **"A Mercenary"** suggests the "round infant" in **"The Shawl,"** its tooth an "elfin tombstone of white marble," will be the reason for her mother's grief (4). Although Rosa shares with Lushinski's parents the impulse to give their child away, she can neither save her infant nor spare herself the horror of being a witness to her daughter's death. That is the event toward which **"The Shawl"** inexorably moves.

It is the event the shawl delays. To the main metaphor of **"The Shawl"** and **"Rosa,"** Ozick attaches antithetical pairs of images—sound and silence, darkness and light. Wrapped in the shawl in the "place without pity," Magda is safe because quiet. The substitute for her mother's teat, its "duct crevice extinct, a dead volcano, blind eye, chill hole," the shawl is "guarded" by Magda: "No one could touch it; only Rosa could touch it. Stella was not allowed. The shawl was Magda's own baby, her pet, her little sister" (4, 6). Robbed of the shawl, Magda breaks the long silence that enabled Rosa to hide the baby in the barracks or to disguise the infant as the "shivering mound" of her mother's breasts. Because of its capacity to nourish an "infant for three days and three nights," Rosa believes the shawl is magic; because Stella took the shawl away, Rosa thinks her niece "made Magda die." But the reason Magda died had little to do with her lost shawl and less to do with her cries; Magda died because "the historical necessity of killing the children of Jews was self-demonstrative to the Germans" (Levi 16).

Even magic could not have saved Magda from those murderers. Bereft of her shawl, she toddles into the "roll-call arena" where her mouth spills a "long viscous rope of clamor," forcing her mother to decide whether to rush into the arena and grab the "howling" baby or to run back to the barracks, recover the shawl, and silence her grieving daughter (8). Having fetched the magical object she believes will preserve her infant's life, Rosa emerges from the dark barracks into the "perilous sunlight of the arena" only to glimpse her baby far away, "high up, elevated, riding someone's shoulder" (8, 9). It is the shoulder from which Magda is hurled against the electrified fence. If the absence of the shawl contributes to Magda's death, the shawl helps keep Stella and Rosa alive. Hidden under the shawl after she steals it from Magda, Stella sleeps safely in the barracks while Magda is being murdered. Juxtaposing those events, Ozick doubles Magda's milking the shawl at the beginning of the story with Rosa's stuffing the shawl into her mouth at the end of the story. Forced to watch Magda fall "from her flight against the electrified fence," Rosa knows that to cry out or to dash to her dead child is to be shot: the shawl, which once nourished the infant, now stifles its mother's screams—the "wolf's screech" that will bring instant death. The antithesis between sound and silence, between speech and muteness, pervades the story, recalls the role accorded to silence in *The Cannibal Galaxy,* and reinforces the shawl's significance. **"The Shawl"** begins with Magda's scream on the road to the camp and ends with Rosa's suppressed cry. Throughout the tale, it is silence that saves: "Everyday Magda was silent, and so she did not die" (7). But it is her infant's quietness that induces Rosa to believe that "Magda was defective, without a voice; perhaps she was deaf; there might be something amiss with her intelligence" (7).

Rosa's anxieties about Magda revive Brill's conclusions about Beulah Lilt: the principal regards her reticence as evidence of her stupidity, the sign of failure. In Ozick's second novel, the absence of language signals potential, the kind of silence André Neher accords to the "boundary event in the human history of silence"—Auschwitz (137). That silence—the stilling of "human sound," the muteness before the incomprehensibility of madness—counters the "curt, barbaric barking of Germans in command" in the description Levi provides of his journey to Auschwitz (15). In his memoir Wiesel tells of the silence of God, the "nocturnal silence" that robbed him "of the desire to live"; but in **"The Shawl,"** it is silence and darkness which offer a chance for survival (Wiesel 31-32). The "grainy sad voices," which Rosa hears in the fence and which Stella says are "only an imagining," at first direct the mother to "hold up the shawl, high" to lure her child back and then turning "mad in their growling," the voices urge Rosa to rush to Magda. To obey the "lamenting voices," the voices she has internalized, would invite certain death and so Rosa "took Magda's shawl, and filled her mouth with it." Stifling her screams, she remains alive while her child dies in the sunlit arena.[1] In the pitiless world of the death camps, the sun's ordinary benefits were transformed into omens of danger: "it seemed," Primo Levi writes, "as though the new sun rose as an ally of our enemies to assist in our destruction" (12). It is the dark gloom of the barracks that conceals and protects in **"The Shawl"**; "in the perilous sunlight of the arena" Magda is detected and murdered (4).

Against the innocent "sunheat" which "murmured of another life, of butterflies in summer" Ozick juxtaposes the sunlit roll-call arena (8). Above the arena, separate from the evil perpetrated in it, or beyond the fence, where "green meadows speckled with dandelions and deep-colored violets" thrive, the light "was placid, mellow" (8). That light promotes bloom. But in the roll-call arena the harsh sunlight exposes Magda's murderer, his glinting helmet "tapped" by the light that "sparkled" the helmet "into a goblet" (9). To the opposing kinds of light, Ozick adds the competing round heads—the helmeted murderer's head, reminiscent of Morris Ngambe's "forehead, perfectly rounded, like a goblet," and the round, vulnerable infant's head. The contrasting images divide good from evil; but Magda's eyes, innocent of evil, are "horribly alive, like blue tigers." Magda's eyes reflect the fierceness born of deprivation. Outside the fence, nourished by nature's plenitude, grow "innocent tiger lilies, tall, lifting their orange bonnets" (8). Emblems of the life struggled for inside the fence and the life flourishing outside it, the tiger eyes and the tiger lilies divide the world of the death camp from the world that surrounds it.

Images of life vie with images of death as Ozick evokes the chilling events common to the death camps in almost unbearably moving terms. Because of its perfect narrative art, **"The Shawl"** manages to celebrate the power to imagine another life, the human endeavor to survive. The voices in the fence and the magic of the shawl are imaginings; when they direct Rosa to unfurl the shawl to attract Magda, the voices represent the saving power of the imagination. But the power to preserve coexists in the imagination alongside the power to destroy, as the "electrified voices" demonstrate when they begin "to chatter wildly" and command Rosa to die (9). The magic she attributes to the shawl is for the narrator of "Usurpation" forbidden, but in **"The Shawl"** Rosa owes her life to the shawl's magic. And Magda, her saliva redolent of cinnamon and almond—part of the sacred anointing oil in Scripture and a biblical symbol of divine approval—becomes for Rosa a holy babe capable of being sustained for three days and three nights as if by magic.

Indeed, Rosa's belief in the magic forbidden by Judaism is more accurately linked to paganism. More importantly, the three days and three nights the magic shawl keeps Magda alive conjure in her mother the infant Jesus Christ; and the allusion to Christ in context of the Holocaust recalls Lucy Feingold equating it with the Crucifixion. That alive the baby "flopped onward with her little pencil legs scribbling this way and that," that the child "swimming through the air" resembles a "butterfly touching a silver vine"—these are images which sever Magda from the evildoers in the camp, it is true. But the images are not evidence of Rosa's covenantal belief; they foreshadow the miraculous realm of the imagination to which Rosa will be forced to consign her beloved dead child and its magical shawl.[2] Although the child journeys "through loftiness," her flight ends in a fall against the electrified fence (9). Magda's

fate is not Sheindel's. In employing the image of the butterfly by placing it first in the context of life and then in the context of death, Ozick summons up the doubleness with which she has endowed her image. Present at the conclusion of *The Cannibal Galaxy* as a sign of Beulah Lilt's aestheticism, the butterfly is a pagan emblem, one appropriate to the pagan act from which Magda was born. Seeing her fall to her death, Rosa envisions her child as Psyche's emblem. Yet at the end of **"The Shawl,"** despite the imaginary voices urging her like sirens to follow them to the fence where she will be shot, Rosa contravenes what she imagines. Her will to live triumphs over her imagination, over rushing to her infant's remains, over her maternal instincts. The insupportable pain arising in the wake of such an experience constitutes part of the terrible cost of surviving the German hell.

II

What follows in its aftermath becomes achingly apparent in **"Rosa,"** which takes place, though Ozick does not immediately divulge it, over thirty years after **"The Shawl."** Instead of presenting the events of Rosa's life directly, Ozick begins her novella evocatively: "Rosa Lublin, a madwoman and a scavenger, gave up her store—she smashed it up herself—and moved to Miami." The reasons she was driven to destroy her store emerge later in the tale, not in the chronology of biography but in the associations made by the psyche. In the sequel to **"The Shawl"** Ozick continues to disclose the linear past the way it appears in the consciousness of her character, but in **"Rosa"** the storyteller also employs the epistolary form to set forth the events in Rosa's life. Like Allegra Vand, Rosa Lublin recounts her history in the letters she writes. Whether imaginary or real, letters illuminate the workings of a mind, and letters occupy a prominent place in Ozick's fiction: they constitute chapters of people's lives. If in **"The Shawl"** the consequences of what Rosa has undergone are registered in her thoughts, in **"Rosa"** she refashions her history in the act of letterwriting. More than the portrayal of Rosa's psyche adjoins **"The Shawl"** to **"Rosa,"** however. They are connected by common thematic concerns, unified by a mutual metaphor, linked by shared imagery; the tales are consanguineous. Doubling actions and images in **"The Shawl"** and **"Rosa,"** Ozick penetrates the multiple significations inhering in all experience.

Not only are **"The Shawl"** and **"Rosa"** reflections of each other, they mirror the themes that obsess *The Cannibal Galaxy*. Haunting all three fictions is the idea of hell. At the beginning of Ozick's second novel, Joseph Brill envisions the Middle as a particular kind of hell; at the beginning of **"The Shawl,"** Rosa Lublin ponders the coldness of hell in the death camp; but in **"Rosa,"** under the blaze of Miami's sun, she "felt she was in hell" (14). In late middle age, the fifty-eight-year-old schoolmaster and the fifty-eight-year-old woman are melancholics, counters of losses, worshipers at altars of death. Bearing similarities to Joseph Brill, Rosa Lublin recalls Hester Lilt as well. Her relationship with Beulah, one the schoolmaster judges analogous to that between Madame de Sévigné and her daughter, is echoed and extended in the relationship between Rosa and Magda. If the kinship between mother and daughter provides, as it did for Madame de Sévigné, a muse for Hester Lilt and Rosa Lublin, the bond leaves Beulah Lilt an orphan of the future and turns Rosa Lublin into an idolator of the past. Sharing with *Trust* a concern for the relations between mothers and daughters, *The Cannibal Galaxy* and **"The Shawl"** are tied to Ozick's first novel by the issue of a mysterious paternity. But the puzzle of Beulah's paternity remains unresolved, that of Magda's only dimly perceived. Wholly disparate, the three tales are nonetheless harnessed by kindred themes and paired motifs. In fact, **"Rosa,"** which is set in Miami and which begins where **"The Laughter of Akiva"** and *The Cannibal Galaxy* end, becomes a kind of sequel to them as well as to **"The Shawl."** Although the novella's three parts duplicate the number prominent in **"The Shawl,"** they extend—they do not merely repeat—the significance of the number three. Matching images and related events occur throughout **"Rosa,"** as Ozick doubles episodes within the novella and between it and the story to connect existence in the camp to life after it, to distinguish truth from illusion, to reflect emotional conflict, to measure psychic change. In evidence from the very beginning of **"Rosa,"** doubling is the organizing principle of the novella.

In Miami Rosa lives "in a dark hole, a single room in a 'hotel'" that recalls the dark barracks of the camp (13). There she was starved; in her room she starves herself. She exists on "toast with a bit of sour cream and half a sardine, or a small can of peas heated in a Pyrex mug" or, like Zindel, on "two bites of a hard-boiled egg" (13, 14). Imagining the hot streets are a "furnace, the sun, an executioner," she aligns them to the sunheat in the arena, to Moloch to whom children were sacrificed (14). In the darkness of her room, Rosa Lublin re-enacts the horrors she lived through in the past. But the scraps of food she eats—some fish, a bit of egg—augur fertility, betoken the renewal of life. On her writing board, Rosa composes letters to Magda in Polish and writes to Stella in English. Her letters set forth feelings about a daughter whose death Rosa often does not acknowledge and about her niece whom she addresses "Angel . . . for the sake of peace," but privately thinks is the "Angel of Death" (15). Rosa's description of Stella, "already nearly fifty years old," reveals that the novella takes place almost thirty-five years after **"The Shawl,"** when Stella was only fourteen and when Rosa was convinced her niece made her daughter die (15). And Stella's "round . . . doll's eyes" and "buttercup lips" recall

Magda as Rosa describes her in **"The Shawl"** (15). Attributing to them twin traits, Ozick implies that for Rosa Magda and Stella are opposing selves. In the death camp Rosa believed the fourteen-year-old girl had thoughts of cannibalizing the baby; in Miami Rosa has "cannibal dreams about Stella" (15). It is as if Rosa has revived the past in the present, for the "killing" sun in Florida—a "murdering sunball" which "fried" the elderly "scarecrows"—conjures up the perilous sunlight in the arena and its emaciated victims (15, 16). Over three decades later, even Florida is awash with reminders of the torment she endured in the German hell.

Ruminating over the past, Rosa gazes at her dirty sheets and knows she must wash them; at the laundromat an "old man sat cross-legged beside her, fingering a newspaper" (17). He speaks Yiddish, but she does not, and her mother's mockery of Yiddish explains why. Their mutual birthplaces in Warsaw, their inability to speak English fluently—these bring Rosa and Persky together, but she separates herself from him, lamenting her "lost and kidnapped Polish" the way Edelshtein mourns "in English the death of Yiddish" (*Shawl* 20; PR 43). The "Warsaw of her girlhood" is juxtaposed against the "thieves who took her life," and Warsaw survives "behind her eyes": a "bright field flashed; then a certain shadowy corridor. . . , Once, walking there, she was conscious of the coursing of her own ecstasy" (20). Of the "house of her girlhood" she recalls a "thousand books. Polish, German, French; her father's Latin books"; in that house she read the Polish poet Julian Tuwim (21). Hers was a family proud of its assimilation.

Born of middle-class Jewish parents, the Polish poet came from a background strikingly parallel to Rosa's. Not only do his allegiances clarify Rosa's, they signal the presence of another theme in the novella—the obsessions of the writer. Like Rosa Lublin's, Julian Tuwim's mother was an assimilationist who instilled in her son a devoted Polish spirit. The Polish poet's pervasive use of the word "blood," as Adam Gillon explains, "fits neatly into Tuwim's pantheistic view of the world, according to which everything can be deified, everything constitutes an element of God" (Gillon 10). Scorning the elderly in Florida for being bourgeois, preoccupied with fabrics, the "meals they used to cook," their hair, Rosa resembles Tuwim and his hatred of "Philistines . . . for their lack of imagination" (*Shawl* 20; Gömöri 51). In his poems he celebrated the sacredness of poetry, often alluding to Christ and even producing litanies.[3] An émigré in New York in 1944, Tuwim loved Poland ardently, but he was savaged by its antisemitic critics.[4] Out of his experience came "We the Jews of Poland," wherein Tuwim declared the "only binding ties those based on . . . the blood of martyrs, spilled by villains" (Markish 41). Tuwim's article became the manifesto of assimilated Jewry throughout Europe, and at the end of his life, the Polish poet gave his support to Israel. His path augurs Rosa's.

To her new acquaintance Simon Persky, a "third cousin to Shimon Peres, the Israeli politician," Rosa speaks of Warsaw, the model of "Cultivation, old civilization, beauty, history!" (22, 21). A "great light" illuminated Warsaw and its gardens; murderous sunlight burns the "perpetual garden of Florida" (21, 16). Doubling the gardens, Ozick dramatizes the way in which Rosa keeps the memory of Warsaw alive in Florida. That she calls herself "Lublin, Rosa" reveals her attachment to Poland; that Ozick chose the name Lublin stresses the fate of Rosa's assimilation. Originally planned as a reservation for the concentration of Jews by the Nazis, Lublin became one of the centers for mass extermination and was the site of a prisoner of war camp for Jews who had served in the Polish army. The Nazis made no distinction between Jews who abandoned their Jewishness and Jews who celebrated it: religious Jews were murdered alongside assimilated ones. Rosa's and Lushinski's histories accentuate the fundamental futility of the Jew in hiding.[5] Though they resemble each other in denying their identities, Rosa and Lushinski are opposites. Where Lushinski runs from the roil of Europe and masters the language of Africa, Rosa remains mainly ignorant of English and wants to return to her girlhood in Poland.

To gainsay any similarity to the Jew Persky, Rosa reiterates the distinction between her Warsaw and his. But Persky, "proud of being a flirt," is not easily discouraged. Instinctively sensing the reason she lives like a hermit, he admonishes her, "'You can't live in the past.'" Before the window of the kosher cafeteria to which her new acquaintance leads her, Rosa descries a "ragged old bird with worn feathers, Skinny, a stork" (23). Of the reason the stork is deemed impure by Jewish law, Hester Lilt writes: "She hopes only for the distinction of the little one under her heart. She will not cherish the stranger's young" (CG 158). The window, like the mirrors in *Trust,* **"Envy,"** and **"The Doctor's Wife,"** throws back an image of the truth: Rosa cares only for Magda. Other facts emerge in the conversation Rosa and Persky have as they sit at a round table, a counterpart to the table in Rosa's room. His son, whom Persky supports, forced his father to sell the factory where he made buttons and accessories; Rosa, whom Stella supports, specialized in antique mirrors until she destroyed her own store. Their careers establish their differences: an unexceptional man, Persky wanted to make new and ordinary buttons. He sought to join things together, but treasuring a former time, Rosa detached herself from others. Without even a pocket mirror now—a reminder of her lost daughter's "pocket mirror of a face"—Rosa revived the past in her antique mirrors. But her missing button not only separates her from Persky, it is an emblem of the hell she crawled

out of. Part of the hell of Auschwitz, Primo Levi observed, had to do with the "infinite and senseless" rites of the camp such as the "control of buttons on one's jacket, which had to be five" (29). And later in his memoir, the absence of buttons becomes a sign of the helplessness and vulnerability of those who were forced to leave the camp's infirmary, "naked and almost always insufficiently cured," and had to adapt to a new Block and a new *Kommando* (51). Finding herself in another hell three decades after the German one, Rosa, Ozick implies, is as ill-equipped for "human contact" as the partially healed man Levi describes in his memoirs (51).

Rosa's psychic wounds have not healed, for the "thieves" who wrested her life from her left Rosa no alternative save to retreat to a life "inside her eyes" (20-21). And so she toils away from a new human contact to withdraw to her room. On Miami's scalding streets, she thinks, "Summer without end, a mistake!" (28). Her reflection conjures up Joseph Brill's grim apprehension of perpetuity and alludes to E. B. White's essay, "Once More to the Lake." Revisiting the summer camp of his childhood with his son, the father witnessed the perdurability of nature, the "pattern of life indelible, the fadeproof lake, the woods unshatterable, the pasture with the sweetfern and the juniper forever and ever, summer without end" (200). The distinction between himself, his father, and his son blurred, White felt that "there had been no years," that the generations were linked "in a strong indestructible chain" (199, 202). But in the wake of that perception comes a more chilling one—his sudden awareness of the swift and inexorable passage of time, a glimpse of his own mortality. In Miami where her memories of the death camp are continually awakened, Rosa is racked not by her own mortality but by her daughter's death, not by the congruence of the generations but by their disjunction, not by the ravages of time but by "time at the fix."

The mirrored lobby yields up a reflection of the hotel's residents and Rosa sees they believe "in the seamless continuity of the body," in the eternal sameness of life, in permanence: "In these mirrors the guests appeared to themselves as they used to be" (28, 29). Forgetful of their children and their grandchildren, the aged grow "significant to themselves" (29). What is important to them is insignificant to Rosa, for she looks forward to finding her child's shawl delivered in the day's mail. Turning the box "round and round" in her room as if to mimic the shape of Magda's face, Rosa recollects her child's smell, the "holy fragrance of the lost babe. Murdered. Thrown against the fence, barbed, thorned, electrified; grid and griddle; a furnace; the child on fire!" (31). The bed covers "knotted together like an umbilical cord" link the mother's dreams in Miami to the infant who died in Germany. Of the ritual that accompanies Rosa's memories Stella writes:

It's thirty years, forty, who knows, give it a rest. It isn't as if I don't know just exactly how you do it, what it's like. What a scene, disgusting! You'll open the box and take it out and cry, and you'll kiss it like a crazy person. Making holes in it with kisses. You're like those people in the Middle Ages who worshiped a piece of the True Cross, a splinter from some old outhouse as far as anybody knew, or else they fell down in front of a single hair supposed to be some saint's.

(31-32)

And in Stella's comparison of Rosa's idolatry to the worship of the Cross, Ozick affirms what she implies in **"The Shawl"**—that the child who was kept alive for three days and three nights is for its mother an image of the infant Christ. It is an image that renders Rosa unable to relinquish the past and incapable of resuming her life. To face the truth of Stella's remarks is to sacrifice illusion and to suffer further loss. The Angel of Death who made Magda die wants to shatter Rosa's idol.

In a remarkably deft association, Ozick joins Stella's urging Rosa to live her life, her memory of the thieves who robbed her of her life, and her missing a pair of underpants. That loss, ostensibly a trivial one, symbolizes a loss of such magnitude that to confront it directly would be intolerable. Untangling a blue-striped dress, Stella's birthday present, from the bedsheets the way Persky had unwound her laundry, Rosa recalls the striped uniforms worn in the death camps: "Stripes, never again anything on her body with stripes!" (33). And she condemns Stella for buying the dress, denounces her for forgetting her past—"As if innocent, as if ignorant, as if *not there*"—and for becoming "indistinguishable" from "ordinary" Americans who cannot "guess what hell she had crawled out of" (33). The memory of that hell prompts Rosa to remember Magda's shawl, which she means "to crush . . . in her mouth" the way she did when she witnessed her baby murdered (35). As if to receive communion, "She tidied all around. . . . She spread jelly on three crackers and deposited a Lipton's tea bag on the Welch's lid. It was grape jelly" (34). But the idea that Persky "had her underpants in his pocket" distracts her from her ritual and revives memories of a painful sexual experience: "The shame. Pain in the loins. Burning" (34). Ozick forges the links among the events indirectly, the way they appear in consciousness when ordinary sights and objects evoke deeper and more disturbing thoughts from which the mind turns in wincing pain.

Rather than remember the brute who violated her, Rosa makes Persky into the culprit: a "sex maniac, a wife among the insane, his parts starved" (34). That Stella believes her aunt belongs with the insane and has the power to put Rosa in a mental hospital, as Persky has his wife, induces Rosa to imagine herself with Mrs. Persky learning about "Persky's sexual habits" and telling her, a "woman with children," about Magda (35). In this manner, Ozick doubles the kinds of madness in order to distinguish them: she separates mental pathology from the madness brought about by war.[6] The intricacy of the consciousness Ozick has produced emerges in the letters Rosa writes and in her responses to the letters of others. Letters afford entry into Rosa's consciousness; they furnish the fragments of a history that must be fit together like the pieces of a puzzle. Vacillating between remembering her baby's death and denying it, Rosa bears testimony to the extent of her suffering. Of such agony Dr. James W. Tree from the "Department of Clinical Social Pathology at the University of Kansas-Iowa" knows little. His "university letter," which arrived along with Stella's letter, reduces Rosa's anguish to sociological jargon, conjuring up the mechanistic predictions of the psychologists against whom Hester Lilt inveighs and the pompous platitudes of the famous critic whom Ozick satirizes in **"The Suitcase."**

The recipient of funds from "the Minew Foundation of the Kansas-Iowa Institute for Humanitarian Context," Dr. James W. Tree finds "remarkable" the persistence in survivors' lives of "neurological residues" and "hormonal changes" (36). What "particularly engages" him is the "'metaphysical' side of Repressed Animation (R.A)," a theory he believes accounts for survivors' responses to the death camps: "It begins to be evident that prisoners gradually came to Buddhist positions. They gave up craving and began to function in terms of non-functioning, i.e., non-attachment. . . . Non-attachment is attained through the Eightfold Path, the highest stage of which is the cessation of human craving, the loftiest rapture, one might say, of consummated indifference" (37, 38). Rosa considers the "special word . . . *survivor*" the way Lushinski protests Lulu's exclusion of the Jews from mankind: "A name like a number—counted apart from the ordinary swarm. Blue digits on the arm, what difference?" (36). To Tree's request that she invite him to study her "survivor syndroming within the natural setting" Rosa cries, "Home. Where, where?" (38). Of his opinion that she is "ideally circumstanced to make a contribution to [the] R-S study" she thinks, "Drop in a hole! Disease! . . . this is the cure for the taking of a life" (38-39). And setting his letter afire, she throws it in the sink, consigning Tree to a dark void like her hotel room and submitting his letter to a fate like Magda's. But she revives Magda by writing to her, and imagining her daughter a "professor of Greek philosophy at Columbia University," Rosa invents a life for her child the way a storyteller brings a character into being.

Her letter—part biography, part fiction—chronicles the tale of three generations. The daughter of a father who "had the instincts of a natural nobleman" and "was never a Zionist," Rosa saved Stella from being "shipped . . . with a boatload of orphans to Palestine, to become

God knows what, to live God knows how. A field worker jabbering Hebrew" (40). The scorn Rosa has for such a fate parallels her derision of Yiddish and bears the imprint of her family. Similarly, her belief, "like the Catholics, in mystery" stems from her mother's desire to convert: attracted to Christianity, her mother "let the maid keep a statue of the Virgin and the Child in the corner of the kitchen" (41). From motherhood, Rosa tells Magda, comes the ability "To pass on a whole genetic system"; from her mother, a poetess who "was not afraid to call herself a 'symbolist,'" comes Rosa's capacity to imagine other lives. Replicating traits of parents in their children, Ozick instances the continuity between generations.

If Rosa tells the truth about her own upbringing, she fabricates one for Magda. Claiming for her child parents who had "respectable, gentle, cultivated, lives," Rosa then reveals that she was not married to Andrzej but "engaged to be married" to him (43). Nonetheless, she denies "Stella's accusations," for they furnish a less than gentle account of Magda's father: "your father was not a German. I was forced by a German, it's true, and more than once, but I was too sick to conceive. Stella has a naturally pornographic mind, she can't resist dreaming up a dirty sire for you, an S.S. man! Stella was with me the whole time, she knows just what I know" (43). The suggestion in **"The Shawl"** that Magda could belong to a German and was born in a camp, the memory Rosa has of the degrading pain in her loins, the admission that she was raped by Germans several times—these revelations identify Magda's father as the S.S. man who raped Rosa. They are recollections too painful to face, they motivate the accusation that Stella "thieves all the truth"; they spur Rosa to create another history (43). Called a "parable-maker" by Stella, Rosa is one of Ozick's artists:

> What a curiosity it was to hold a pen—nothing but a small pointed stick, after all, oozing its hieroglyphic puddles: a pen that speaks, miraculously, Polish. A lock removed from the tongue. Otherwise the tongue is chained to the teeth and the palate. An immersion into the living language: all at once this cleanliness, this capacity, this power to make a history, to tell, to explain. To retrieve, to reprieve!
>
> To lie.
>
> (44)

That Magda will become her mother's muse is hinted at in **"The Shawl"** when Rosa considers her baby's "pencil legs" as they scribble into the arena and likens her daughter to a butterfly as she flutters through the air to her death. That Rosa calls Magda a "yellow lioness"—an allusion to the last three lines of Tuwim's poem, "Draw Blood with the Word"—attaches the child to writing: "O words! Sharp and Golden! / Pouncing words of prey, / Like lions! Like lions!" (Gillon 33).

Oozing puddles, the pen recalls the volcanic typewriter in "Usurpation"; releasing lies, the pen is an instrument for mendacity as well as for veracity.

The "routine" Rosa practices after receiving "university letters" counters the ritual she engages in with Magda's shawl: in those acts she divides her rage from her grief. Dressed in "good shoes" and a "nice dress," Rosa mounts the "bed on her knees," as if kneeling before an altar (44). In that position she ruminates, like Joseph Brill, for hours on the "pitiless tableaux" of her past, worshiping like James's Stransom at an altar of loss (45). The word "pitiless" matches the triple repetition of the phrase, the "place without pity" in **"The Shawl"** and determines the provenance of the tableaux—the death camp where Magda was murdered. In the tableaux there are "Darkened cities, tombstones, colorless garlands, a black fire in a gray field, brutes forcing the innocent, women with their mouths stretched and their arms wild, her mother's voice calling" (44-45). In the newspaper after Rosa demolished her store there was a "big photograph, Stella standing near with her mouth stretched and her arms wild" (18). Bringing together the tombstones in the tableaux with Magda's "tombstone tooth," the violated women with the distraught Stella, Ozick links the rapists to the infant, a self-destructive act to a savage one, and makes Rosa's niece a witness to both. Absorbed by such recollections until late afternoon, Rosa becomes "certain that whoever put her underpants in his pocket was a criminal capable of every base act. Humiliation. Degradation. Stella's pornography!" (45). In those linked associations is the significance of the lost underpants: they symbolize Rosa's sexual organs which the rape violated and desecrated, dirtied like the "stains in the crotch [that] are nobody's business" (34).

Wanting "to retrieve, to reprieve," powers she accords to her pen, Rosa leaves the box she believes holds Magda's shawl on the table and goes in search of her underpants. Grieved by her loss of them, she is driven into the streets of Miami as once, bereft of her shawl, Magda toddled into the perilous roll-call arena, where she died. Like the arena, the streets are scalded by the "murdering sunball" during the day; toward dusk a "scarlet sun, round and brilliant as a blooded egg yolk" hangs in the sky. Reminiscent of Rosa's hard-boiled egg, the fertilized egg in **"Puttermesser and Xanthippe,"** and the cosmic egg in *Trust*, the egg alludes to the primordial egg from which Eros sprang, a symbol of the repetition of the primeval act. At the end of the long road, Ozick suggests, lies a new world, the possibility of a future. Oppressive by day, at night the streets "are clogged with wanderers and watchers; everyone in search, bedouins with no fixed paths" (45). Unlike the roll-call arena, the streets are an arena in which to reclaim life. Just as Puttermesser's "long introspective stride" up Lexington Avenue uncovers the lawyer's motives for creating a golem, Rosa's peregrination of Miami un-earths the reasons the survivor must recover her under-pants. And Rosa's impression of the sand is the first of several associations leading to the meaning of the "lost laundry": the "sand never at rest, always churning, al-ways inhabited; copulation under blankets at night, be-neath neon-radiant low horizons" (46). Her subsequent ideas of the underpants "smoldering in an ash heap" or in "conflagrations of old magazines" invoke the death camp and connect it to the underpants (46). To imagine "what a weight of sand would feel like in the crotch of her pants, wet heavy sand, still hot from the day" is to wonder what it would feel like to have the trunk of her body buried (47). Walking "unconnected to anything," seeing "everything, but as if out of invention, out of imagination," Rosa retreats to a landscape behind her eyes (47).

The one before them is littered with "so many double mounds," bodies in the sand which conjure up a photo-graph of Pompeii (48). Among the pictures taken of the fields of ash that preserved the shapes of corpses within a mold of a void, were casts of lovers "who fell to-gether, side by side, mingling their last breath" (Brion 37). Ozick's reference to those photographs supplies the connection Rosa makes between her lost laundry and the fate of the buried lovers: "Her pants were under the sand; or else packed hard with sand, like a piece of torso, a broken statue, the human groin detached, the whole soul gone, only the loins left for kicking by strangers" (48). From that alliance emerges the reason she cares more for her underwear than for her store: it was only a "cave of junk" (21). But the theft of her pants left her broken like one of those shells Brill sees on the beach of the Phlegethon, the "life in them cleaned out, scooped, eaten, decomposed" (CG 86). Amid the "lovers plugged into a kiss," Rosa considers stepping "cleanly into the sea," a suicidal impulse like murder-ing "her business with her own hands" (48). As she does at the end of **"The Shawl,"** Rosa rejects the pull toward death, the ease with which she could enter the "horizontal tunnel," for the "unpredictable"—for life (48). Double acts of self-preservation compete against double impulses to self-destruction: they manifest the way victimizers manage to perpetuate torment in their victims long after victimizing them. His oppressors drove Lushinski to murder his own soul, to appropriate another identity, to end in desolation. To overcome the desolation Rosa must repossess her soul.

On the beach she encounters a pair of homosexual lov-ers; their mockery elicits her hissing response, "So-dom," and Ozick establishes the chain of Rosa's asso-ciations—Pompeii, Sodom and Gomorrah, the death camps. In connecting those places, Rosa unites their history of sexual perversion, and the storyteller yokes the wicked biblical cities destroyed by the fire of heaven, the immoral pagan city buried by an eruption,

and the modern country whose ferocious evil annihi-lated an entire civilization. Derided by the homosexu-als' laughter and "locked behind" the "barbed wire" of the fence encircling the private beach, Rosa trembles in remembrance; but she is no longer in the place without pity, the place with the murderous fence (49). Although they conjure in her memories of sexual perversion and Nazi paganism, the homosexual lovers are not bent on killing her but on ignoring her: "They hated women. Or else they saw she was a Jew, they hated Jews; but no, she had noticed the circumcision, like a jonquil, in the dim sand. . . . No one knew who she was; what had happened to her; where she came from" (49). The jon-quil parallels the buttercup to which she compares Stel-la's lips, the "harmless containers" in which the "blood-sucker comes," and both flowers bring back the innocent tiger lilies growing outside the fence at the end of **"The Shawl"** (15). Then Rosa could only gaze beyond the fence and dream of another life; in Miami the fence leads her to "light" and to freedom.

Free, she accosts the manager in the hotel lobby: "'Only Nazis,'" she tells him, "'catch innocent people behind barbed wire'" (51). Judging the way he runs his hotel evidence of Finkelstein's indifference to the Holocaust, Rosa is enraged. Whereas silence had been her savior in the camp, noise became her redeemer after she was liberated: "They had trapped her, nearly caught her; but she knew how to escape. Speak up, yell. The same way she saved Stella, when they were pressing to take her on the boat to Palestine" (52). Unlike the survivors in Ozick's other fiction—Sheindel in **"The Pagan Rabbi,"** the rebbe in **"Bloodshed,"** the refugee in **"Levita-tion"**—Rosa has inherited from her parents a "certain contempt" for Jews, whom she regards as "primitive" and common (52, 53). Finkelstein's red wig reminds her of Persky's red wig: "Florida was glutted with fake fire, burning false hair! Everyone a piece of imposter" (50). In Warsaw, she regarded the "swarm" of Jews as "shut off from the grandeur of the true world"; in Mi-ami, she protests Tree's word, "survivor," because it ex-cludes Jews from the "ordinary swarm" (52-53, 36). But she divides herself from both groups of Jews and leaves the Hotel Marie Louise "Irradiated, triumphant, cleansed" (52). To complete her victory, Rosa must find her underpants: she must reclaim her soul.

Like the trek to the laundromat, Rosa's walk culminates in a meeting with Persky. In her room, "miraculously ready: tidy, clarified," their differences become more apparent (55). Persky judges her room "cozy"; Rosa finds it "cramped." One seeks a good "way of describ-ing," the other calls that a way of lying (56). Hugging the box she presumes contains Magda's shawl, Rosa feels as if "someone had cut out her life-organs and given them to her to hold," had removed her soul (56). Aware she has "to work things through," Persky advises her to "'adjust,'" to become a "'regular person,'" to forget the past so as "'to get something out of life'" (57, 58). What Persky, an American Jew, cannot fathom and has no right to judge is her enduring memory of the Holocaust, and so Rosa shames him with her account of the survivor's three lives: "'The life after is now. The life before is our *real* life, at home, where we was born. . . . Before is a dream. After is a joke. Only during stays. And to call it a life is a lie'" (58). For the rebbe in **"Bloodshed,"** a man who believes in "turnings," the life after holds possibility, potential, hope. On one thing, however, the rebbe and Rosa agree: the importance of remembering the past, and that conviction is fundamental to Ozick's thought, especially with regard to the Holocaust. In a discussion about writing and the Holocaust published in 1988, five years after **"Rosa,"** Ozick anticipates the objections to her own "act of memorial," her steadfast refusal ever to visit Germany: "What can be done about it now? Let bygones be bygones. Choose erasure. Wipe out memory" ("Roundtable" 283). In Ozick's novella, it is Rosa who complains that Stella "wants to wipe out memory," but her aunt's "act of memorial" results in an obsession, in idolatrous worship of the dead—a pagan ritual.

To include Persky in that ritual is to yield to a stranger "what her own hands longed to do." It is "to prove herself pure: a madonna" (59). But the box shelters not Magda's shawl but houses Hidgeson's book, *Repressed Animation: A Theory of the Biological Ground of Survival,* the study of survivors Tree extolled in the letter Rosa burned in the sink. Enraged by Tree's note directing her to read Chapter Six, "Defensive Group Formation: The Way of the Baboons," Rosa hurls the book at the ceiling, the way she smashed up her store; and Ozick separates a melancholic self-destructive impulse from an angry and healthy one. Attempting to wreck Tree for his indifference to human suffering, Rosa adds to her first outburst of fury with Finkelstein a second erruption of rage against Tree and a third one against Persky. Connecting him to the researchers who have equated the human struggle to survive the inhuman conditions in the death camps with the habits of baboons, Rosa cries: "'I'm not your button, Persky! I'm nobody's button, not even if they got barbed wire everywhere!'" (61). That she accuses him of being a "thief"—the name she calls the person who took her life—reveals she has projected onto Persky feelings about someone else. He has become in her mind the tormentor from her past. To her allegation Persky responds, "'I can see I'm involved in a mistake,'" and Rosa discovers her mistake the next day when she finds the missing underpants "curled inside a towel" (61).

Unfolding from her character's consciousness the events that ultimately led to intense rage, Ozick instances the sorrows of Jewish history and brings them into sharp relief by depicting their grave effects on one woman's life. At the same time, the storyteller explores with acute and compassionate insight the way the human psyche can turn against itself, transforming rage into guilt and guilt into grief which, at its most extreme, can develop into the melancholia that abrogates interest in the outside world. That it is necessary for Rosa "to prove herself pure" attests to a deeper emotional demand: the need to deny the history of Magda's creation, to metamorphose her infant into a holy babe brought forth not from a violent rape but from an immaculate conception. The shawl's magical capacity to nurture a child for three days and three nights testifies to that psychic requirement. Three is a preponderant number in **"Rosa."** At first establishing an affinity in **"The Shawl"** between Magda and the infant Christ, the number three becomes in **"Rosa"** an insistent reminder of the death camps: under the Third Reich, one-third of the Jewish people were murdered. The three lives survivors possess, the three cups Rosa owns, the three crackers she prepares for her ritual, the three steps she takes to the bed, the three "bloodsuckers" she counts, and the three members of her family who she tells Persky remained alive after the Holocaust—these signal indelible memories of the German hell for which three is a symbol.

Nonetheless, Rosa delays writing to Magda and decides instead to reconnect her telephone. Ozick converts the electrified wire of the camp's fence from which Rosa heard "grainy sad voices" urging her to die into ordinary telephone wire empowering her to live. That she has begun to emerge from the landscape behind her eyes is suggested by her indifference to Magda's shawl. Once redolent of the holy fragrance of the murdered child, the shawl now "lay like an old bandage, a discarded sling," its "faint saliva smell . . . more nearly imagined than smelled" (62). Rather than engage in her ritual, Rosa telephones Stella who grimly tells her aunt to end her "morbidness," to recuperate, not to call "long *dis*tance" (64). On that phrase, "Magda sprang to life" and Rosa puts the shawl "over the knob of the receiver," transforming it into a "little doll's head," a reminder of Stella's round "doll's" eyes (64). But the shawl chokes off Rosa's conversation the way it once stifled Rosa's screams and revives the memory of the child lighting on the electrified fence like a butterfly on a silver vine.

The mother recoils from that memory and imagines her daughter at sixteen dressed in a "sky-colored dress," one of "Rosa's dresses from high school" (64). Beginning "to resemble Rosa's father," Magda begins to become Rosa, but she is bewildered by her daughter's "other strain": "The other strain was ghostly, even dangerous. It was as if the peril hummed out from the filaments of Magda's hair, those narrow bright wires" (65-66). In the imagery with which Rosa limns the girl is a clue to Magda's other strain. Reminiscent of the "lamenting voices" in the camp's fence, Magda's hair recalls the sirens' songs. If the daughter's "sky-filled" eyes are like the mother's blue dress, Magda's buttercup yellow hair is the color of the yellow badges issued in Nazi Germany. Inherited from "idolatrous Germans," Magda's "other strain" is the dangerous strain inhering in the imagination—the propensity for paganism (A& A 235). In calling Magda a butterfly and in choosing butterfly pins for Beulah Lilt's hair, Ozick makes the two girls, who are their mother's muses, symbols of the imagination in its capacity to invent idols. If Hester Lilt produces an aesthete who forgets her past, Rosa Lublin bears a daughter whose death anchors her mother in the past; if the painter escapes into a nimbus, the letter-writer retreats into her thoughts. Behind her eyes Rosa envisions various lives for Magda, fancies her a professor of Greek philosophy, pictures her a painter or a musician, conceives her history, writes her story.

The power of the imagination to remove a lock from the tongue, to impel the pen "to tell, to explain"—the imagination's crowning act of splendor—is illustrated in the second and imaginary letter Rosa writes to Magda. A kind of parable, the letter recounts the history of Rosa's family and doubles events from the past in each of Rosa's three lives. Despite their ability to enunciate "Polish . . . with the most precise articulation," despite their assimilation into Polish life, despite their denial of a Jewish identity, Rosa and her family were confined in a ghetto "with teeming Mockowiczes and Rabinowiczes and Perskys and Finkelsteins . . . old Jew peasants worn out from their rituals and superstitions" (68, 66, 67). Including Persky and Finkelstein among the Warsaw Jews, Rosa renders them indistinguishable from American Jews. But all the Jews in Warsaw were separated from other Polish citizens by the wall built around the ghetto, and the memory of the tramcar that "came right through the middle of the ghetto" was one Rosa used to share with her customers as testimony to the evils she had witnessed. The bridge constructed to prevent the Jews from escaping into the "other side of the wall" kept them crowded together in a "terrible slum" while ordinary Poles traveled through the ghetto daily and witnessed the Jews' misery without protesting. In the death camp the wall of the ghetto was replaced by the fence, the overhead electric wire of the tramcar by the fence's electrified wires.

After she was liberated, Rosa remembered the woman she had seen with a head of lettuce protruding from her shopping sack: that plain, working-class woman was considered a Pole, better than Rosa and her well-educated family. That woman remained silent and unresponsive to the suffering around her. In New York Rosa "became like the woman with the lettuce": a witness, but one who spoke up "to the deaf" in her store (69). Impassive and indifferent like the Polish citizens the tramcar carried through the ghetto, Rosa's customers reignited the rage of abandonment Rosa experienced in the ghetto, the rage the tormented feels against the tormentor, the rage that later propelled Rosa to wreck her

store. But in Miami Rosa met a former vegetable-store owner whose reminiscences of romaine lettuce revived the painful event she endured over thirty years ago in the Warsaw Ghetto. Her suffering there—the salivary glands that ached at the sight of the lettuce—became excitement for others: "They let their mouths water up. . . . Consider also the special word they used: *survivor*. . . . Even when your bones get melted into the grains of the earth, still they'll forget *human being*. Survivor and survivor and survivor; always and always. Who made up these words, parasites on the throat of suffering!" (36-37). Pairing events from the past and the present, Cynthia Ozick dramatizes their persistence.

If the witness who recounts the Nazis' atrocities to unconcerned Americans speaks English the way the uneducated woman in Warsaw spoke Polish, it is not because Rosa is uncultivated: "They, who couldn't read one line of Tuwim, never mind Virgil, and my father, who knew nearly the whole half of the *Aeneid* by heart" (69). Having lived in a house filled with art—"replicas of Greek vases" and "wonderful ink drawings"—Rosa has inherited a "whole genetic system," the legacy of classicism (68). To that tradition belong her ritual with Magda's shawl, her belief in mystery, her idolatry. But the imaginary letter, the ones she writes "inside a blazing flying current, a terrible beak of light bleeding out a kind of cuneiform on the underside of her brain," fatigues her and augurs change (69). In matching Magda's disappearance at the end of **"Rosa"**—the "blue of her dress" becoming "only a speck in Rosa's eye"— with Rosa's vision of the "speck of Magda" before she was thrown against the fence, Ozick doubles Rosa's losses (69, 9). The first is brought by Magda's death, the second by the collapse of Rosa's illusion. That is the illusion the imagination fashions: it can transform a telephone into a "little grimy silent god" akin to the "black baal" in *The Cannibal Galaxy,* an idol that founders before reality—"Voices, sounds, echoes, noise" (69). The silence that pervades **"The Shawl"** is broken in **"Rosa"** where the ringing phone heralds the arrival of Persky—the ordinary button, the shatterer of illusion, the harbinger of renewal. Accepting Persky, Rosa abandons her father's aversion for Jews.

In *Trust* Ozick alludes to the *Odyssey* as she charts the quest to recover a father; in **"Rosa"** the storyteller adverts to the *Aeneid* as she chronicles the need for separation from the father. To unlock the secret of her father's identity, the narrator of *Trust* must enter hell, the room where William apprises her of her illegitimacy. If "every story has its Charon," several of Ozick's tales have their hells. Referring to Edom in **"A Mercenary,"** Ozick implies that Lushinski ends in a kind of hell; Joseph Brill and Rosa Lublin proclaim hell their habitations. Where Brill ends is where Rosa begins. Images from the *Aeneid* thread their way through **"Rosa,"** but the parallels Ozick draws between Aeneas's journey to the underworld and Rosa's symbolic descent into the past broadens the meaning of the novella, lending to its revelations universal truth. From the very beginning of **"Rosa,"** Ozick establishes resemblances between Rosa and Aeneas: survivors of wars which are moral tragedies and which result in exile, Rosa and Aeneas are aligned to Venus, Aeneas's mother, whose sacred flower, the rose, and whose emblem, the star, are alluded to in the names Rosa and Stella. In Ozick's novella and Virgil's poem, a slain daughter is a grim foreboding of a return, the sacrifice of Iphigenia to appease the gods a counterpart to the brutally irrational murder of Magda. Aeneas, whom Virgil likens to a wolf—the poet's symbol of "birth" and "violence"—must make his way into the particular hell of Troy's fall even as Rosa must stifle her "wolf's screech" and make her way into a private hell, the hell of the persistent "during" (Putnam 148; Virgil 2.383). Aeneas and Rosa both grieve over dead families, desire to die, and are forced to wander.

Ozick merges in **"Rosa"** episodes and motifs from several books of the *Aeneid*. Rosa's madness conjures up the madness which accompanies the fall of Troy in Virgil's poem, which like the novella possesses a "pattern of madness suppressed and released" (Putnam 16). The madness of the survivor is induced by the madness of war and is not madness at all. To have been forced to witness the murder of her own child is, as the dying Priam cries out angrily after watching the murder of his son Polites, the "worst pollution" (2.563). Small wonder, then, that Rosa in her grief must continue, like Andromache, to call Magda's "ghost to the place which she had hallowed / With double altars, a green and empty tomb" (3.304-5). The injustice, the horror, the madness of war—these point to the central question of the *Aeneid*: "What divinity can demand the righteous suffer and why?" (Medcalf 306). It is the question asked by Job; it is the question many raised in the aftermath of the Holocaust, and it is the unspoken question at the heart of **"Rosa."** Which is to say, the question has no answer. The triumphant experience Rosa has at the Hotel Marie Louise attests not to her discovery of saving truths in the Holocaust, for "no promise, no use, no restitution and no redemption can come out of the suffering and destruction of one-third of the Jewish people," but to her ultimate refusal to become someone's button, to surrender her soul, to die ("Roundtable" 279). Hers is a victory of the human spirit.

But it is a victory with its own demands. To possess a future Rosa and Aeneas must return to the past, liberate themselves from its shackles, master their grief. If Aeneas drives his fleet "To Cumae's coast-line" to begin his descent to the underworld, Rosa moves to the peninsula of Florida and writes to her niece, "'Where I put myself is in hell'" (14). Throughout her novella, Ozick alludes to the first six books of the *Aeneid*; conflating episodes from it, invoking its imagery, rearranging its

events, she summons up the Virgilian hell in Miami, Florida, to illuminate Rosa Lublin's harrowing experience in the German hell. At the beginning of her walk on the shore, the sun and the moon, "Two strange competing lamps . . . hung simultaneously at either end of the long road"; they are reminders of Cumae, of Apollo's temple and Diana's grove, of the Sibyl's dwelling place (45). In the Sibyl's dusky cave the Trojan learns how to cross the Styx, to find his father, whom Aeneas carried out of Troy on his shoulders. Less loving shoulders dispatched Magda to her death. Driven like Aeneas and frenzied like the Sibyl in her cavern, Rosa resides in a "dark hole" in Miami, in a Sibylline cave.

In the *Aeneid* Apollo's temple stands near the priestess's cave, and its doors, carved by Daedalus, portray scenes akin to Rosa's experiences. "On a trip to Crete," Rosa's father discovered a Greek vase, a reminder of the urn on the temple doors, the urn from which lots were drawn to determine the children "For sacrifice each year" (*Shawl* 68; Virgil 6.23). The "land of Crete," to which Rosa's father traveled and from which Daedalus fled, rises out of the picture the artisan chiseled on the doors, which display "The mongrel Minotaur, half man, half monster, / The proof of lust unspeakable" (6.28-29). His overwhelming grief prevented Daedalus from including his son Icarus in the picture. The "souls of infants" who died "Before their share of living," the doomed youth Marcellus—these dead children, the children Aeneas sees in the underworld, are in **"Rosa"** versions of Magda, the murdered babe, proof of unspeakable lust (6.455, 457).

After that horror Rosa believed herself "used to everything"; thinking "no form of trouble . . . Is new, or unexpected," Aeneas begs the Sibyl to open the portals barring the way to his father. For Rosa as for Aeneas

> . . . the portals of dark Dis
> Stand open: it is easy, the descending
> Down to Avernus
> But to climb again,
> To trace the footsteps back to the air above,
> There lies the task, the toil.
>
> (6.144-148)

Entering the gates to the private beach of the Hotel Marie Louise, the "threshold of the wicked," Rosa sees "Vague forms in lonely darkness," unearths "matters buried deep in earth and darkness" (6.583,285,284). Just as Aeneas must confront his past in his descent, so Rosa must confront hers. But before Aeneas can see the Stygian kingdoms, he has to prepare Misenus for burial. Washing him from water in "Bronze caldrons," the men perform the rites required for admittance to Dis's portals; watching the "round porthole of the washing machine," where her underwear is "slapped . . . against the pane," her dress "against the caldron's metal sides,"

Rosa readies herself to conquer her furies (19). Then approaching their respective gates, Aeneas and Rosa brave their pasts.

On the beach, Rosa envisions her lost underpants "like a piece of torso" detached from the loins and Ozick summons up Priam's terrible death: "a nameless body, on the shore, / Dismembered, huge, the head torn from the shoulders" (2.581-82). Rending Priam's head from his shoulders, Pyrrhus leaves the proud ruler nameless, unidentifiable; forcibly desecrating her genitals, the Nazi wrested from his victim her very soul. To discharge her fury at Finkelstein is to force the deaf customers to hear what she witnessed, to redirect the rage that impelled her to a kind of suicide, to reclaim the "loins" the S.S. man "left for kicking" (48). It is "to trace the footsteps back to the air above." As Aeneas's two encounters with Palinurus and Dido precede the third and most important one with Anchises, so Rosa's conflicts with the homosexual couple and Finkelstein herald a vision of Magda.

And she is evoked by Stella's word "long *dis* stance." The god of the lower world, Dis is offered "An altar in the night," an altar such as the one Rosa prepares in her room (6.270). In its power to provide nourishment for three days and three nights, in its ability to save a mother from death, in its capacity to afford contact with the dead, Magda's shawl stands as a counterpart to the golden bough, which was sacred to Persephone, queen of the underworld. It is to that maiden Ozick alludes in Rosa's imaginary letter. Unlike the first letter, which Rosa begins, "Magda, My Soul's Blessing," the salutation of the second letter implies that Magda is a symbolic Persephone: "My Gold, my Wealth, My Treasure, my Hidden Sesame, my Paradise, my Yellow Flower, my Magda! Queen of Bloom and Blossom!" (39, 66). And Magda, in whom a ghostly, perilous strain runs has, like Persephone, "two aspects, girl-like daughter of the Corn Goddess and Mistress of the Dead" (Burkert 159). Attaching to Magda's hair "two barrettes, in the shape of cornets," emblems of Persephone's attribute, the cornucopia, Ozick joins Magda to Persephone as well as to Beulah Lilt, to whose hair the storyteller fastens symbols of the imagination.

The union of the three girls holds tightly together, their various strands of significance gathering in the fabric of Ozick's art into an intricate knot. If the imagination yields new bloom, it is bound to the world of the dead: as long as Demeter wanders through the world "fasting, with her hair untied, carrying flaming torches . . . propelled by pain and anger . . . in mourning, a reversal of normal life takes place" (Burkert 160). The lost child halts germination, arrests growth; even as her return ushers in the cycle of vegetation, the revival of life, she introduces into it the presence of death. Yoked to Madame de Sévigné and Françoise Marguerite, to Allegra

Vand and her daughter, to Hester and Beulah Lilt, Rosa Lublin and Magda raise the Demeter and Persephone myth into a parable about art, into historical truth. The motive force for the survivor's anguish and the pivot of Rosa's creativity, the death of Magda differs from the loss of Persephone.

Abducted and raped by Hades, Persephone returns periodically, and mother and daughter come together again. Only in Rosa's imagination can mother and child be reunited. If Persephone's marriage to Hades is a "common" metaphor "for death," if "[a]t bottom, the myth does not speak of a cycle either" but of how "things will never be the same as they were before the rape," Rosa's Hades speaks of history's reality, history's evil (Burkert 161). In *Trust* Ozick incorporates the myth of Demeter and Poseidon into the origins of the narrator's history; watching the intercourse between Stephanie and Tilbeck, the narrator of *Trust,* a symbolic Persephone, "witnessed the very style of [her] creation" and is initiated into the mysteries of her existence (*Trust* 598). In **"Rosa"** Ozick integrates the myth of Demeter and Persephone, the basis for the mysteries of Eleusis and its initiation rites, into the brutal events of Jewish history. A victim of them, Rosa Lublin becomes another kind of witness, a witness to the very style of destruction, and is initiated into the evils of existence. The narrator of *Trust* must recover her history to make a future; Rosa must overcome her history to have a future. Theirs are separate journeys.

Like Aeneas's final encounter with Anchises in the underworld, Rosa's imagined experience with Magda leads ultimately to an engagement not with death but with life. Although Magda "did not even stay to claim her letter" and runs from Persky, Rosa's unspoken words reveal her reluctance to sever her ties to Magda forever: "Butterfly, I am not ashamed of your presence: only come to me, come to me again, if no longer now, then later, always come" (69). It is a temporary farewell. Magda's "head as bright as a lantern" recalls the lamps at the beginning of Rosa's journey, conjures up Apollo, and aligns the brightness of Magda's head with the nimbus into which Beulah Lilt escapes (70). Present at the end of *The Cannibal Galaxy* and **"Rosa"** are signs of paganism along with emblems of the imagination. Yet the two hotels in which Rosa works through the anguish of the past, her own hotel a "parody of a real hotel . . . the Marie Louise," suggest her as a visitor, not an inhabitant, of hell—the way at Duneacres the narrator of *Trust* is a tourist, not a tenant, of the ruined abbey (70).

Doubling the hotels, Ozick doubles as well Rosa's experiences in those hotels. At seventeen the "future Marie Curie" felt the "coursing of her own ecstasy" as she walked to the "laboratory-supplies closet"; at fifty-eight, after forty-one years of wandering in the wilderness her life became, Rosa marches triumphantly "through the emerald glitter" at the Hotel Marie Louise and away from "its fountains, its golden thrones, its thorned wire, its burning Tree" (20, 52, 70). The "shadowy corridor" leading to the supply closet ultimately becomes the "hall of a palace," the hotel's lobby. There the "thorned wire" revives the "thorned" fence, the "burning Tree," the "child on fire"—the memories Rosa relives in her hotel room and which have placed an embargo on her life. But she prevails amidst the "golden babble" at the Marie Louise: she transforms the "frivolous" into the momentous, the trivializing term, "Repressed Animation," into healthy fury, the Tree of the Buddha's Awakening, which the narrator of *Trust* envisioned in the swamp at Duneacres, into the tree of the sociologist's undoing (50). And Ozick, as she does in *Trust,* endows the tree in **"Rosa"** with multiple meanings. If Dr. Tree occasions Rosa's rage and elicits her mockery of his "Buddhist positions," the burning tree also conjures up the burning bush from which God spoke to Moses and the golden thrones in Ezekiel's description of God's appearance on His throne surrounded by fire. That her mind returns to the scene at the Marie Louise as Rosa awaits Persky's arrival implies that her liberation arises from her acceptance of the world of the Jews. The target of her catharsis, Finkelstein is the opposite of Persky, the dispeller of illusion, the agent of regeneration. But the journey toward renewal, the exit from hell, has persisted for over thirty years. Though she completes that journey, Rosa, in late middle age, faces a shrinking future. The thieves who took her life own most of it.

Invoking the Roman poet's hell in her novella, the storyteller becomes a kind of "Virgil of the German hell," a guide into the subterranean world of a survivor. In 1988, five years after the publication of **"Rosa,"** Ozick wrote of Primo Levi, "He has been a Darwin of the death camps: not the Virgil of the German hell but its scientific investigator" (M& M 37). Her review of the last book Levi wrote, *The Drowned and the Saved,* before committing suicide revives the powerful electrical imagery in **"The Shawl"** and **"Rosa,"** uncovers the consequence of Levi's famous and widely praised detachment, and affords a striking parallel to the psychic truths disclosed in Cynthia Ozick's own novella. Rather than merely accept the appearance of tranquility in Levi's books, Ozick exposes, in images that conjure up those in **"The Shawl"** and **"Rosa,"** the "deadly anger" that saturates "Levi's final testimony": "Gradually, cumulatively, rumble by rumble, it ["the change of tone"] leads to disclosure, exposure—one can follow the sizzle flying along the fuse. . . . It may be cruel; but it is Levi's own hand that tears away the veil and sets the fuse. The fuse is ignited almost instantly, in the Preface" (M& M 41). Withholding his rage, Levi, Ozick reveals, achieved "not detachment" but the "slow accretion of an insurmountable pressure," a pressure that imploded in "a convulsion: self-destruction" (47). Con-

scious of the furies propelling Rosa to destroy her store, Ozick chronicles the catharsis that releases Rosa from the rage that led Primo Levi, more than forty years after Auschwitz, to commit suicide so as to escape the horrors of an endless "during." In her fiction and in her essay, Ozick probes the historical and psychic forces that drive human beings to turn rage into self-destruction. Hers is a vision that encompasses in its breadth historical veracity and emotional verity. To limit **"Rosa"** to "authentic Jewish response to catastrophe" or to "Holocaust melancholia," therefore, is to deny the painful truths of "Primo Levi's Suicide Note" (Berger 126, 127).

From the sadists who elicited the note from Levi, Rosa discovers a painful truth: their absolute idea of the Jew, traditional or assimilated. Disdainful of the Jewishness her father taught her to shun, Rosa Lublin ultimately comes to acknowledge as her own the identity he disavowed. In moving toward the Yiddish-speaking Persky, in welcoming him into her life, she separates herself from her father, from his Hellenism, and moves closer to Hebraism. That she removes the shawl from the phone, that its clamor, "animated at will, ardent with its cry," replaces Magda with Persky suggests Rosa's acceptance of the Jews she once resented being "billeted with" (70, 67). That Magda runs from Persky, that she is only "away" implies her eventual return. The ending of the tale bears its teller's elusive and inconclusive mark—the uncertain note on which Ozick closes her fiction from *Trust* onward.

Recurring to the concerns central to her first novel, Ozick inverts and augments them. What the narrator of *Trust* searches for, Rosa owns; what the girl celebrates, Rosa is forced to question. The one must discover her father's legacy, the other must repudiate it. And the storyteller's allusions to the *Odyssey* and to the *Aeneid* buttress Ozick's overarching concern with the father. The roles of the fathers in the two epics diverge, the fathers' fates part, the sons' paths fork. If Telemachos and the narrator of *Trust* must find their fathers, Aeneas and Rosa must detach themselves from theirs, must emerge from Virgil's hell, not encounter, as the girl does at Duneacres, the "Virgil of the Eclogues" (*Trust* 531). If the girl and Rosa have unlike quests, Tilbeck, Allegra Vand, and Rosa's parents are yoked by a reverence for Ancient Greece and Sacred Beauty, the idyllic vision of nature. In *Trust* the daughter compares her mother's idea of nature to an art object: a "vase with its dark dread hole kept secret and small . . . and the whole to be held to the light for an unimaginable and always absent flaw . . . as though nature had no bloody underside, and grief had no ugliness, and fact had no dirt in it" (*Trust* 422). Like the Greek jars Tilbeck collects, the Greek vase unearthed by Rosa's father testifies to a similar notion: the vase "was all pieced together, and the missing parts, which broke up the design of a warrior with a javelin, filled in with reddish clay" (68). In their veneration of Ancient Greece, the parents overlook the "tragic grain of nature," the savagery of war. Linked by their illegitimacy, the narrator of *Trust* and Magda are related to Beulah Lilt, whose father is unknown. The finding of the father, the fate of the fatherless, the farewell to the father—these evince an abiding interest in a figure to whom Ozick accords a further dimension in *The Messiah of Stockholm,* her third novel.

Notes

1. Berger remarks that "the dialectical movement between silence and speech as authentic responses to the catastrophe" is "curiously absent from Ozick's literary interpretation" of the Holocaust (58-59).

2. See Berger (53) and Lowin (109) for interpretations that attempt to join Rosa to Covenant.

3. This is a summary taken from Gillon (10-11).

4. Conflated from Gillon (10-11) and Markish (41-42).

5. Berger comments that Ozick uses Lublin and Warsaw to link the "fate of religious and assimilationist Jews" and claims that despite her religious attitudes, Rosa "exemplifies a specifically Jewish determination to survive and testify" (121).

6. To limit, as Berger does, Rosa's madness to "Wieselian moral madness," which is "anchored in the prophetic strain of Judaism," is to deny the significance of the Christian imagery in the story (122).

Works Cited

Appelfeld, Aharon. "After the Holocaust." In Lang, *Writing* 83-92.

Brion, Marcel. *Pompeii and Herculaneum: The Glory and the Grief.* New York: Crown, 1960.

Burkert, Walter. *Greek Religion.* Trans. John Raffan. Cambridge, Mass.: Harvard UP, 1985.

Gillon, Adam, ed. *The Dancing Socrates and Other Poems,* by Julian Tuwim. New York: Twayne, 1968.

Gömöri, George. *Polish and Hungarian Poetry, 1945-1956.* London: Oxford UP, 1966.

Levi, Primo. *Survival in Auschwitz.* New York: Macmillan, 1961.

Medcalf, Stephen. "Virgil's 'Aeneid.'" *The Classical World.* Ed. David Daiches and Anthony Thorlby. London: Aldus, 1972. 297-326.

Ozick, Cynthia. *Art & Ardor.* 1983. Reprint. New York: Dutton, 1984.

———. *The Cannibal Galaxy.* New York: Knopf, 1983.

———. *Metaphor & Memory.* New York: Knopf, 1989.

———. *The Shawl.* New York: Knopf, 1989.

———. *Trust.* 1966. Reprint. New York: Dutton, 1983.

Virgil. *The Aeneid.* Trans. Rolfe Humphries. New York: Scribner's, 1951.

Wiesel, Elie. *Night.* New York: Bantam, 1982.

Andrew Gordon (essay date 1994)

SOURCE: Gordon, Andrew. "Cynthia Ozick's 'The Shawl' and the Transitional Object." *Literature and Psychology* 40, nos. 1 and 2 (1994): 1-9.

[*In the following essay, Gordon examines the shawl as a transitional object, as defined by D.W. Winnicott, and as the focus of the conflict in "The Shawl."*]

Cynthia Ozick's **"The Shawl"** (1980) is a Holocaust story about a mother struggling heroically but in vain to save her baby in a death camp. Brief and poetically compressed—two thousand words, just two pages in its original publication in *The New Yorker*—it has a shattering impact. Ozick manages to avoid the common pitfalls of Holocaust fiction: on the one hand, she does not sentimentalize, but on the other, she does not numb the reader with a succession of horrifying events.[1] She works largely through metaphor, "indirection and concentration" (Lowin 107). For example, the words "Jew," "Nazi," "concentration camp," or even "war" are never mentioned; these would arouse the kind of immediate, unearned responses Ozick eschews. We do not know what year it is or what country. As the story opens, we only know that three female characters—Rosa, her fifteen-month-old baby Magda, and a fourteen-year-old girl named Stella (only in a sequel story, **"Rosa"** [1983], do we learn that Stella is Rosa's niece)—are being marched, exhausted and starving, toward an unknown destination.[2] Two details—the word "Aryan" and the mention of yellow stars sewn into their coats—allow us to fill in the rest. The historical and political context disappears, and the focus narrows to the feelings of three characters as they struggle to survive moment by moment in extreme circumstances: "They were in a place without pity" (**"Shawl"** 33). Rosa, the central character, could be any mother who wants to keep her baby alive against impossible odds. This is a story about the oppression of women: there is no mention of Magda's father, and the only male referred to is the guard who murders Magda, a faceless monster described in terms of a helmet, "a black body like a domino and a pair of black boots" (34).

I want to consider the central symbol of the story, the shawl in which Magda is wrapped, which I believe functions in a way similar to what D.W. Winnicott would call a "transitional object." But the shawl serves not only as a transitional object for the infant in the story but also as the focus of the conflict, and while it passes from hand to hand among the three characters, it becomes a totem or fetish for the teenage Stella and the mother Rosa as well.[3] The shawl suggests the necessity for illusion, for magical thinking as a defense against anxiety in traumatic circumstances, but also the ways in which healthy illusion can easily shift into unhealthy delusion. As Winnicott writes, "I am therefore studying the substance of *illusion,* that which is allowed to the infant, and which in adult life is inherent in art and religion, and yet becomes a hallmark of madness . . ." (*Playing and Reality* 3). Rosa, Stella, and Magda form a group on the basis of their shared illusion concerning the "magic shawl" (**"Shawl"** 33). Although the infant's use of the shawl is understandable, Rosa and Stella's belief in it is a sign of desperation, of regression and the breakdown of rationality in the face of extreme deprivation and loss. Transitional phenomena, Winnicott explains, eventually become diffused and spread "over the whole cultural field," including such generally healthy activities as play, art, and religion, but also such neurotic manifestations as "fetishism" and "the talisman of obsessional rituals" (5). The shawl in Ozick's story, I believe, functions as a transitional object which later changes into an infantile fetish for the baby, and for the teenager and the mother it definitely becomes a fetish or magical talisman.

The transitional object, Winnicott explains, is the infant's "first 'not-me' possession," (1) something which is both found and created, both inner and outer, and stands in for the breast. The object, which may be a bit of cloth or a security blanket, comes at an intermediate stage of development between thumb-sucking and attachment to a toy or doll. It exists in an intermediate area "between the subjective and that which is objectively perceived" (3). "The object represents the infant's transition from a state of being merged with the mother to a state of being in relation with the mother as something outside and separate" (14).

If the transitional object is a form of defense against the loss of the breast and separation from the mother (Wright 93), then all three characters in **"The Shawl"**—the baby, the teenager, and the mother—in their need to possess the shawl can be considered as infants suffering extreme oral deprivation and in need of a mother. Here is the opening paragraph:

> Stella, cold, cold, the coldness of hell. How they walked on the roads together, Rosa with Magda curled up between sore breasts. Magda wound up in the shawl. Sometimes Stella carried Magda. But she was jealous of Magda. A thin girl of fourteen, too small, with thin breasts of her own. Stella wanted to be wrapped in a shawl, hidden away, asleep, rocked by the march, a baby, a round infant in arms. Magda took Rosa's nipple,

> and Rosa never stopped walking, a walking cradle. There was not enough milk; sometimes Magda sucked air; then she screamed. Stella was ravenous. Her knees were tumors on sticks, her elbows chicken bones.

> (**"Shawl"** 33)

The keynotes of oral deprivation, inadequate mothering, and the desire to revert to infancy are established in this opening: Rosa is defined as a mother with sore breasts who can no longer adequately feed her infant. Magda is suffering from forced weaning. Stella too is starving—she has been turned into a thing resembling sticks or the skeleton of a chicken. Stella, a teenager, "in a stage between childhood and adulthood" (Martin 31), longs to revert to infancy, symbolized by her desire to be wrapped in and mothered by the shawl that protects Magda.

By the second paragraph, Rosa's milk has entirely dried up and Magda has relinquished the breast and turned to the shawl as a surrogate breast: "The duct crevice extinct, a dead volcano, blind eye, chill hole, so Magda took the corner of the shawl and milked it instead" (**"Shawl"** 33). At the same time, Stella moves from desiring the shawl to seeming to want to devour Magda: "Stella gazed at Magda like a young cannibal . . . it sounded to Rosa as if Stella had said 'Let us devour her'. . . . She was sure that Stella was waiting for Magda to die so she could put her teeth into the little thighs" (33).

While the ravenous Stella regresses to a stage of oral sadism, the starving Rosa also seems to regress to infancy: "she learned from Magda how to drink the taste of a finger in one's mouth" (33). The shawl becomes Magda's means of survival: "It was a magic shawl, it could nourish an infant for three days and three nights" (33). Magda grows silent and guarded: she stops crying and never seems to sleep. Her silence and the shawl keep her alive: "Rosa knew Magda was going to die very soon; she should have been dead already, but she had been buried away deep inside the magic shawl, mistaken there for the shivering mound of Rosa's breasts" (33). But Rosa fears that Magda has become a deaf-mute from the experience.

For Magda, this shawl has become everything: mother, food, clothing, and shelter.

> She watched like a tiger. She guarded her shawl. No one could touch it; only Rosa could touch it. Stella was not allowed. The shawl was Magda's own baby, her pet, her little sister. She tangled herself up in it and sucked on one of the corners when she wanted to be very still.

> (33)

At this point, it is appropriate to ask whether this shawl is truly a transitional object for Magda or instead an infantle fetish. According to Phyllis Greenacre, the transitional object is an aid to growth that results from healthy development when the child has a goodenough mother. But the infantile fetish results from a disturbance in development, when the mothering is not good enough or "the infant has suffered unusually severe deprivation" (447). The fetish "grows out of early inadequate object relations and, through its crystallization, tends to constrict their further development" (450). It has some similarities to "the fetish in adult perversion" (449). Considering the trauma that Magda has suffered—a terrorized mother, exposure to a hostile, constantly life-threatening environment, premature weaning and starvation—and the hysterical mutism that she develops, her attachment to the shawl seems to partake more of the neurotic fetish than of the healthy transitional object.

Greenacre mentions that fetishistic phenomena usually appear after weaning at the end of the first year, which corresponds to Magda's case. The fetish begins "at about the time that the transitional object may be adopted by infants most of whom seem less disturbed. The fetish here seems to represent the feeding function even more strongly than is true of the transitional object" (448), which also holds in Magda's case: because she is starving, she has practically nothing to feed on but the shawl. Greenacre mentions an instance of infantile fetishism which strongly resembles Magda's behavior, in which a blanket was "of great magical effectiveness in quieting severe disturbances of infantile separation anxiety and even of physical pain" (448). When head lice and body lice bite Magda and "crazed her so that she became as wild as one of the big rats that plundered the barracks . . . , she rubbed and scratched and kicked and bit and rolled without a whimper" ("Shawl" 33-34). Her silence is abnormal behavior for an infant, just as her relationship to the shawl seems far more intense than the healthy connection of a baby to a transitional object.

But one sunny afternoon, Stella appropriates the shawl for herself and goes to sleep beneath it in the barracks. She wants some of the mothering power associated with the shawl. "Thus, by losing her magical shawl, Magda loses the magical charm that apparently protects her from death for so long" (Martin 34).

Rosa is outside and sees Magda toddling into the sunlight, howling for the lost shawl, screaming "'Maaaa—'" ("Shawl" 34). It is the first sound she has made since Rosa's milk dried up, and the only word she speaks in the story. It seems a cry for both shawl and mother, which for her have become synonymous. "Magda was going to die, and at the same time a fearful joy ran in Rosa's two palms" (33): the joy comes from realizing that her baby can speak, the fear from the ironic fact that the noise has doomed Magda (Martin 34). Only her continued silence would have saved her.

Rosa finds the shawl and tears it away from Stella: the object of struggle has now passed among all three characters. Then, under the influence of "voices" she imagines she hears in the electrified fence (one can take this as another sign of her derangement, although a critic reads these voices as symbolic of the Jewish dead [Lowin 109]), Rosa runs outside again and waves the shawl like a flag to attract Magda's attention. The shawl is now a banner representing life and faith and hope. But it is too late: a guard has already seized the baby, carries her off, and abruptly tosses her to her death against the fence.

The few minutes leading up to Magda's destruction take up over half the narrative. The murder is described in slow motion and beautiful metaphors to intensify both the suspense and the horror. Magda's arms reach out to the shawl and to her mother, but she recedes into the distance, becoming a "speck" and "no bigger than a moth" ("Shawl" 34). When she is hurled at the fence, she turns into a floating angel: "All at once Magda was swimming through the air. The whole of Magda traveled through loftiness. She looked like a butterfly touching a silver vine" (34).

Through metaphor, the moment of death becomes a moment of magical transfiguration. As she watches her baby murdered, there is nothing further Rosa can do without endangering her own life. The voices of the fence urge her to run to Magda. But "Rosa's instinct for self-preservation overcomes both her maternal instincts and any heroic urges she may have had" (Lowin 109). The final sentence of the story (which, for the sake of emphasis, is also its longest sentence) shows the shawl now becoming a transitional object for Rosa:

> She only stood, because if she ran they would shoot, and if she tried to pick up the sticks of Magda's body they would shoot, and if she let the wolf's screech ascending now through the ladder of her skeleton break out, they would shoot; so she took Magda's shawl and filled her own mouth with it, stuffed it in and stuffed it in, until she was swallowing up the wolf's screech and tasting the cinnamon and almond depth of Magda's saliva; and Rosa drank Magda's shawl until it dried.
>
> ("Shawl" 34)

By stifling her screams, the shawl becomes a means of survival for Rosa, as it had been for Magda (Lowin 109). And the shawl nurtures her, filling her mouth, just as it had done for Magda. Finally, as the shawl had become a surrogate mother for Magda, so it becomes a surrogate baby for Rosa. "Magda's cinnamon and almond breath has permeated her shawl, which now become synonymous with her spirit." In drinking the shawl, she is devouring her dead infant (Scrafford 14), although this is a symbolic cannibalism, unlike the butchery of the death camps or the lethal selfishness of Stella. To put it another way, Rosa is attempting to reincorporate Magda in order to mourn her.

Thus I read **"The Shawl"** as a story about delusion as a defense against an overwhelming reality, against loss of control, and against traumatic loss. I see it as a story about separation, isolation, death, and thwarted mourning. The three characters are together, yet each suffers alone: Stella separates herself by her selfishness and Magda by withdrawing into the substitute womb of her shawl. Magda dies alone, and Rosa is powerless either to prevent her death or even to embrace her dead baby or mourn aloud her loss. In this environment, simply being human can condemn you to death, so you must suppress your humanity. The isolation and separation are also expressed metaphorically. Characters are never seen whole but reduced to body parts or things: Rosa is "sore breasts" and "a walking cradle," Stella has elbows like "chicken bones," Magda shows "one mite of a toothtip . . . an elfin tombstone of white marble" (33), and the guard is merely a helmet, "a black body like a domino and a pair of black boots" (34).[4] This is a vivid, terrifying world of part objects and fetish objects which never approaches the world of whole object relations.

Any infant is in a condition of helplessness and absolute dependence; through attachment to the transitional object, it begins to come to terms with reality and with the separateness of the mother as an object in her own right. If the mothering is insufficient or the environment hostile, the infant may instead latch onto a fetish object. As prisoners of the Holocaust, the teenage Stella and the grown Rosa are thrust back into the helplessness of infants, infants with a monster parent. The Nazi state becomes a cannibal, annihilating and devouring its offspring. Finally, to survive such intolerable circumstances, these desperately needful characters resort to magical thinking. Each seizes upon Magda's shawl as a magical object, a substitute for the good mother, the only thing on which an assurance of survival or a sense of identity can be grounded. And for all three characters, the transitional object shades over into a fetish object and a healthy *illusion* becomes instead a neurotic *delusion*.

In 1983, Ozick wrote a sequel to **"The Shawl"** entitled **"Rosa."** This story takes place in Miami Beach thirty years after the events of **"The Shawl"**; Rosa has survived the Holocaust but is mentally unstable. She denies her daughter's death and fantasizes that Magda is a married woman, a successful doctor or professor. And she now worships as a religious relic the only object left from her daughter: the shawl. As Greenacre writes, "The relation of illusion to the fixed delusion might be roughly compared to that of the transitional object to the fetish" (452).

Notes

1. Not every critic was pleased with "The Shawl." Suzanne Klingenstein was troubled by "being forced into such distressing intimacy and into voy-

eurism" and says, "I considered it unethical to make up fictions about the Shoah. For me 'Holocaust fiction' is an intolerable concept" (166).

2. The two stories, "The Shawl" and "Rosa," originally published in *The New Yorker* in 1980 and 1983 respectively, were reprinted together under the title *The Shawl* (NY: Knopf, 1989). My page references, however, are to the original *New Yorker* version of "The Shawl."

3. Critics have read the symbolic shawl in many ways. For example, Alan Berger (54) and S. Lielian Kremer compare it to the Jewish prayer shawl: "The garment is the narrative's primary Jewish symbol of the sacredness of life" (Kremer 153). In an interview with Kremer, however, Ozick denied she had this in mind when she wrote the story (Kremer 161). Suzanne Klingenstein says the shawl functions in place of speech for both infant and mother (166) and also as a kind of umbilical cord between the two characters (167). Again, Ozick denies having this in mind, writing Klingenstein that "'The Shawl' is *about*—no, is (symbolically) the Nazi murders. . . . No pop psychology. No mothers and daughters. Mothers-and-daughters is NOT my theme, here or elsewhere" (172). Nevertheless, despite Ozick's resistance to the critics and denial of any interest in psychology or mother-daughter relationships, hers cannot be the final word in interpreting her story.

4. S. Lillian Kremer notes the "Jewish/German dichotomies" in the story, so that Jews try to preserve life while Germans destroy it. Thus the mother and daughter are referred to metonymically by body parts but the Nazi guard is only "helmet" and "boots" (153). I agree, but also think it interesting that *all* the characters in the story are seen metonymically, as parts rather than wholes.

Works Cited

Berger, Alan. *Crisis and Covenant: The Holocaust in American Jewish Fiction.* Albany: SUNY Press, 1985.

Greenacre, Phyllis. "The Transitional Object and the Fetish With Reference to the Role of Illusion." *International Journal of Psycho-Analysis* 51 (1970): 447-56.

Klingenstein, Suzanne. "Destructive Intimacy: The Shoah Between Mother and Daughter in Fictions by Cynthia Ozick, Norma Rosen, and Rebecca Goldstein." *Studies in American Jewish Literature* 11.2 (Fall 1992): 162-73.

Kremer, S. Lielian. "Holocaust-Wrought Women: Portraits by Four American Writers." *Studies in American Jewish Literature* 11.2 (Fall 1992): 150-61.

Lowin, Joseph. *Cynthia Ozick.* Boston: Twayne, 1988.

Martin, Margot. "The Theme of Survival in Cynthia Ozick's 'The Shawl.'" *RE: Artes Liberales* 14.1 (Spring-Fall 1988): 31-36.

Ozick, Cynthia. "The Shawl." *The New Yorker* 26 May 1980: 33-34.

—"Rosa." *The New Yorker* 21 March 1983: 38-71.

Scrafford, Barbara. "Nature's Silent Scream: A Commentary on Cynthia Ozick's 'The Shawl.'" *Critique* 31.1 (Fall 1989): 11-15.

Winnicott, D.W. *Playing and Reality*. London: Tavistock, 1971.

Wright, Elizabeth. *Psychoanalytic Criticism: Theory in Practice*. London: Methuen, 1984.

S. Lillian Kremer (essay date 1995)

SOURCE: Kremer, S. Lillian. "The Holocaust and the Witnessing Imagination." In *Violence, Silence, and Anger: Women's Writing as Transgression*, edited by Deirdre Lashgari, pp. 231-46. Charlottesville: University Press of Virginia, 1995.

[*In the following essay, Kremer compares* The Shawl *to* Touching Evil *by Jewish American writer Norma Rosen, while exploring the violence brought upon Jewish women in the Holocaust.*]

Writing by Jewish American women focusing on women's Holocaust experience portrays Jewish women doubly cursed in the Nazi universe as racial pariahs and sexual victims, brutalized while the world remained silent. Although the primary motives of the Nazis' commitment to the destruction of the Jewish people were rooted in political, racial, and religious beliefs, women experienced the Holocaust in ways unique to their gender. Beyond the starvation, disease, hard labor, and physical violence endured by all victims, women were subject to gender-based suffering and degradation. They were sexually abused and subjected to medical experiments; pregnant women were killed or forced to undergo abortions; infants were systematically destroyed at birth; and young mothers were routinely murdered with their children rather than selected for slave labor. When the survivors returned to civilization, silence about their experience was often both internally and externally imposed. Some sought to still their voices to hasten recovery and quicken their adjustment to postwar society. Others, ready to testify, encountered indifference and at times hostility from those who did not want to know, from those who chose to evade the truth because of what it implied about the human condition, and from those who shrank from facing their own complicity. In the succeeding decades as Holocaust history

and literature became more readily available, the experiences and perceptions of Jewish women were often obscured or absorbed into accounts and interpretations of male experience. However, significant writing by women survivors, scholars, and artists has appeared that gives voice to the experience of Jewish women under Nazi rule as well as to the postwar reactions of women survivors.

American novelists Cynthia Ozick and Norma Rosen had no direct Holocaust experience. They nevertheless felt compelled to write about the event that altered conventional thought about humanity, divinity, and social and political structure. In "Toward a New Yiddish," Ozick advocates an indigenous American Jewish literature, "centrally Jewish in its concerns."[1] Jewish history and the Holocaust, as the orienting event of the twentieth century, are moral and artistic imperatives for such a literature. Psychological, political, and theological consequences of the catastrophe find expression throughout Ozick's work.[2] The short story and novella collected in *The Shawl* focus on a woman who endures the agony of watching a guard murder her child in a Nazi camp and spends ensuing decades trapped by that memory. Norma Rosen, Ozick's colleague and friend, was profoundly moved by Emmanuel Ringelblum's *Notes from the Warsaw Ghetto* and by eyewitness testimony at the Eichmann trial. Rosen professes to be a "witness-through-the-imagination," a "documenter of the responses of those who 'had heard the terrible news.'"[3] Because the Holocaust is "the central occurrence of the twentieth-century . . . the central human occurrence," Rosen wrote *Touching Evil* to explore "what might happen to people who truly took into consciousness the fact of the Holocaust . . . the meaning to human life and aspiration of the knowledge that human beings—in great numbers—could do what had been done."[4] Both *The Shawl* and *Touching Evil* explore the violence perpetrated against Jewish women during the Holocaust, the responses of the victims and those who remember them, and the problematics of Holocaust transmission.

The title story of *The Shawl* marks the first instance in which Ozick locates her fiction directly in the lice-infested, disease-ridden, death-dominated world of the concentration camp. Its sequel, *Rosa,* chronicles the postwar survivor syndrome of the title character nearly four decades after the events recounted in the first story. Unlike **"The Shawl,"** Rosen's *Touching Evil* is removed in time and place from the historic concentration camp universe. The present tense of the novel is 1961, during the Eichmann trial; the place America; the major characters neither Jewish nor survivors of the Holocaust. Because Rosen perceives the Holocaust as a human rather than a Jewish problem, Jews appear only as the ghostly shadows of the documentaries, a somber reminder of the enormity of the Final Solution. The central characters of the novel are two gentile American women who learn of the horror through newspaper photographs of concentration camps and television coverage of the Eichmann trial. Their friendship is initiated and sustained by exposure to the concentration camp universe as they meet each day to view the trial. Past and present collide and merge as the novel alternates between 1944, the year Jean learned of the death camps, and 1961, the year of the Eichmann trial, which is the catalyst both for her rediscovery of the Holocaust's central significance to her life and for Hattie's initial Holocaust encounter. Moments of consciousness impinge on one another, varying in intensity from the fleeting to the all-consuming, and extend to penetrate the emotions and intellects of both women.

"The Shawl" begins dramatically with the central characters, Rosa, a young mother and her infant, Magda, and Rosa's fourteen-year-old niece, Stella, struggling to survive a death march to a concentration camp. Rosa confronts the choice many Jewish mothers suffered, whether to entrust her child to a stranger's goodwill or try to preserve its life herself. She considers passing her baby to a woman along the road, a choice fraught with danger for mother and child, since the penalty for stepping out of the line of march is death. There are other risks, too: the unexpected transfer might so startle the stranger that she would drop the bundle and injure the child, or if the stranger understood the Jewish woman's intentions, she might reject the child and denounce the mother.

Throughout the march and in the concentration camp, Ozick invests the shawl, which covers mother and child, with mystical power as an agent of its bearer's survival. The shawl provides Magda shelter, concealment, and nourishment. Ozick conveys the nurturing capacity of the shawl by juxtaposing the natural world with the unnatural Nazi universe. She describes the shawl-swaddled infant as "a squirrel in a nest"; the shawl forms a "little house" that hides her in the barracks when her mother stands outdoors for roll call.[5]

Ozick foreshadows the child's death by inverting normally joyous childhood milestones. The infant Magda's first tooth is described as "an elfin tombstone of white marble" (4), and her first steps are but a new source of terror for Rosa, who fears that a mobile but uncomprehending infant will stray into the sight of a German guard. When Stella usurps the shawl to warm her own frozen body, Magda toddles into the roll call area crying, uttering her first sounds since Rosa's breasts dried up. Uncertain whether to run for the shawl or to retrieve Magda without it and chance her continued screaming, Rosa runs for the shawl. But she is too late. As Magda reaches toward mother and shawl, a German guard sweeps her up and tosses her onto the electrified fence. The novelist gives life metonymically to the en-

dangered Jewish woman and dead child by enumerating human parts, arms, legs, head, belly, to signify the valued lives. For the Nazis, she uses such metonyms as "helmet" and "boots," signifying their callousness and their disregard for Jewish life.

Nature imagery, pointedly contrasting Nazi-Jewish dichotomies, drawing attention to the discrepancy between the natural order and its German perversion, sharply heightens the intensity of the death scene. Ozick counterpoints plant and flower imagery suggestive of the world beyond the barbed wire with images of the human desecration of nature to convey the environment of the concentration camp and the transitory quality of life for the Jewish prisoners. Even the infant's journey to death is symbolically imbued with life as we follow her "swimming through the air . . . like a butterfly touching a silver vine" (9). The unnatural morbidity of the Nazi system and its environment is evoked in the humming of the electric fence and the "ash-stippled wind" (7). Butterflies yield to electrified fence as the Jewish reverence for life succumbs to the technologically charged carnage of the Nazis.

The text compounds the impact of the mother's pain by revealing her need to endure silently. With the electricity buzzing, Rosa suppresses her maternal instinct to scream and run to her child. She stifles the instinctive "wolf's screech" (10) ascending through her body. She must deny her body to save it; she must still her despairing voice and mute her grief, and she must stop her legs from running to the still child. Instead, she honors the survival instinct. To shriek and retrieve her baby's charred corpse would invite her own murder. As women have often responded to male violence with silence, so Rosa muffles her cry in the shawl, now *her* life preserver.

Although scenes of mothers witnessing the suffering and murder of their young children are a central feature of women's Holocaust writing, they are virtually absent in male Holocaust fiction, because children were segregated with women. Engaging reader sympathy through the evocation of the victimization of mothers and children is an essential feature in *Touching Evil* as well as in *The Shawl*. Norma Rosen's American women empathize with the women of the Holocaust: Jean, who expresses solidarity with the victims by remaining childless, and the pregnant Hattie, who identifies with women she learned of through the Eichmann trial: a pregnant woman on a forced march and another woman giving birth in typhus-lice-infested straw. Unlike the immediacy of the Holocaust universe in "The Shawl," Norma Rosen composes an indirect encounter, in which the characters witness the Holocaust through a fusion of documentary and art. Desire for respite from Eichmann trial testimony about the murder of mothers and children has brought the childless Jean and pregnant Hattie to the Museum of Modern Art to look at visions of holiness, statues of serene mothers surrounded by healthy, exuberant children. While the expectant mother gazes at the marble mother, a testament to human creative genius, she begins to read from a newspaper clipping covering trial testimony that shares with Ozick's portrait images of nurturing women trying, in vain, to bring some measure of relief to doomed children: "The children were covered with sores. They had diarrhea. They screamed and wept all night in the empty rooms where they had been put. There was nothing in the rooms but filthy mats full of vermin. Before dawn, our women crept among the children, trying to comfort and clean them. But there were no clean cloths, the water was icy cold. Terror had overcome them. The halls were a madhouse. When the orders were given to take the children to Auschwitz, it was as if they sensed what was in store. Then the police would go up and the children, screaming with terror, would be carried kicking and struggling to the courtyard."[6] Complementing the reported cries of the captive children is Jean's imagined hearing of a sound something like a great scream filling the silent sculpture hall and her imagined vision of the great goddesses "on broken toes with hands severed at the wrists" (223) suddenly struck blind, petrified by the testimony of human degradation. The children clinging to the mutilated marble figures now evoke Holocaust mothers and children. Rosen's integration of documentary detail and artistic empathy fuses the destructive and creative impulses of the twentieth century.

Both Ozick and Rosen make use of diction and image patterns to emphasize the gender-related suffering of the characters and their ways of coping. Ozick uses breast imagery to emphasize the female nature of women's Holocaust experience: Rosa, no longer able to nurse because of malnutrition, agonizes over her incapacity to provide nourishment for her infant. Anxiety about Magda's danger from starvation or electrocution is conveyed through references to teat and nipple: "Magda relinquished Rosa's teats . . . both were cracked, not a sniff of milk. The duct-crevice extinct, a dead volcano, blind eye, chill hole, so Magda took the corner of the shawl and milked it instead" (4) And when Magda walks into the roll call area, "A tide of commands hammered in Rosa's nipples" (8). Rosen's propensity for mixing Holocaust images with those of procreation and sexuality earned her Edward Alexander's condemnation for having "a womb's eye view" of the Holocaust and being "diverted by the temptations of analogy, of heavy symbolism, and feminist topicality."[7] Far from distracting, this rhetoric provides the authentic voice by which Rosen's women understand and claim the Holocaust. It is, indeed, through feminine language and imagery that Jean and Hattie connect humanely and elementally to their concentration camp sisters.

Like a number of other American writers who have not experienced the Holocaust directly, Rosen delineates the Holocaust sphere indirectly. Her American women respond to the victims' experiences through their own experience of pain. Hattie's childbirth and Jean's rape provide them with a means to imagine the pain and violation European Jewry suffered. Although Rosen deliberately removes her novel from the place and time of the Holocaust, the event is intended to be an experience that is felt, not an abstraction. Her language with its emphasis on sexuality and biology is intrinsic to her female characters' will to remember the suffering of women in the Holocaust. To suggest, as Nora Sayre does, that Rosen is making a feminist assertion that hospitals, or labor rooms in particular, are like concentration camps, is to ignore their role as objective correlative, as Hattie's postwar referent for the helplessness and vulnerability of the camp inmate.[8] Hattie's commiseration with a helpless patient subjected to the cruel indifference of an overworked inner-city hospital intern gains significance because it provides another connection with the Jewish woman who was completely powerless and humiliated, giving birth in a prison barrack beneath the gaze of a booted soldier of the "master race." The American patient's "unsightly genitals, bleeding, gaping, oozing" in the presence of and at the mercy of unsympathetic white, urban medical personnel in starched uniforms are Hattie's postwar link with the Eichmann trial account of the woman "who squeezed her baby out into a world of concrete, straw, and lice" (252). And it is Hattie's acknowledgment of the Holocaust legacy that is the source of her scream of outrage: "Cursed be the booted feet. Cursed be the legs that stood on them . . . Curse the Hun heart that shit on this grace" (252-53). In this cry, Hattie gives voice to the sexist nature of Nazi persecution of Jewish women and becomes a witness for the millions of Jewish women who did not live to testify to the devastation.

The violence the fictional women endure, whether Rosa's encounter with radical evil in the concentration camp or the emotional assault that the American women experience upon exposure to Holocaust history, becomes a constant element of their consciousness. In a sense, the American women, too, are survivors: Rosa is a physical survivor, but the Americans are psychological survivors. *Rosa,* the long sequel to **"The Shawl,"** deals with the title character at fifty-eight, decades after the events recounted in the first story, as it explores the long-term effects of Holocaust trauma. Measuring time and life by the Holocaust, Rosa identifies three ages of human experience: "The life before, the life during, the life after. . . . The life after is now. The life before is our *real* life, at home, where we was born" (58). "During" is, of course, the Nazi era. For Rosa, "Before is a dream. After is a joke. Only during stays and to call it a life is a lie" (58). Rosa is unable either to repress or to express Holocaust memories, and mourns perpetually for her lost child. Unlike parents who lose their children to natural causes or accident and are granted time to withdraw temporarily from routine activities, to grieve and express their anguish, Holocaust victims were imprisoned in silence.

Ozick dramatizes the severity of Rosa's lasting torment by contrasting her continued suffering with Stella's apparent recovery. Although Stella has no dramatic role in the narrative, she functions as Rosa's psychological foil. We do not know whether Stella is free of Holocaust trauma because she is kept offstage and we do not enter her thoughts and dreams, but we do get an inkling of her post-Holocaust adjustment in her letters to Rosa and in Rosa's commentary on them. In contrast to Rosa's fixation on the past, Stella focuses on school, career plans, and personal goals. Emblematic of their antithetical attitudes is Stella's gift of a striped dress to Rosa. Rosa, baffled and pained, concludes that Stella is acting "as if innocent, as if ignorant, as if *not there*" (33). To Stella, the dress is only an attractive garment; to Rosa, it is a direct link to the hated camp uniforms. Equally illustrative of their differences is Stella's embrace of English and Rosa's stubborn clinging to Polish. Rosa's faulty English, with its syntactical misstructuring and fragmentation, evokes the Holocaust-wrought ruptures she endured. Increasingly tormented by the remembered loss of her child and frustrated by her customers' indifference on the rare occasions when she tries to communicate her feelings about the Holocaust, Rosa destroys her antique shop and is sent by Stella to recuperate in Florida. Her violent behavior abates, but there is little evidence of significant healing during the Florida respite. Mourning Magda's loss is Rosa's major preoccupation.

Rosa and Stella perceive each other as mentally ill. Their understanding of the shawl and of Magda's death could hardly be more different. For Rosa, the shawl is a holy emblem of her child; for Stella, it is Rosa's "trauma," "fetish," "idol," and she compares Rosa's adulation of the shawl to that of a benighted medieval worshiper of a false relic. Rosa pretends to accept Magda's death to appease Stella and convince her that she is sane. Yet her behavior reveals her delusion that Magda lives. Stella knows Rosa is trapped in the Holocaust and urges her to emerge from her self-imposed prison: "It's thirty years, forty . . . give it a rest" (31). In her letter chastising Rosa for worshiping the shawl, she warns, "One more public outburst puts you in the bughouse" (32-33). Stella's harsh words reinforce Rosa's charge of heartlessness, except in her last sentence, where she urges Rosa, "Live your life!" (33).

Rosa and Stella represent antithetical survivor roles. Rosa resembles survivors in the psychiatric literature who are plagued by associations and memories in their waking hours and by nightmares during sleep. Her survival is bitter: the hell of failed communication both with those who evade her Holocaust testimony and with those who would exploit her history; the hell of lost family, lost aspirations, lost language, lost life. Separated from the family she loved, the culture she loved, the language she loved, Rosa views life as a chain of dismal encounters that differ only in degree. She says, "Once I thought the worst was the worst, after that nothing could be the worst. But now I see, even after the worst there's still more" (14). From Rosa's perspective, Stella is free of Holocaust memories and anxieties because she consciously represses them and believes in the possibility of a new world. Rosa repudiates Stella's attitudes. In letters to the daughter she imagines is still alive, and in conversations with her Florida acquaintance, Persky, Rosa charges that "Stella is self-indulgent. She wants to wipe out memory" (58).

Ozick illustrates the survivor's tendency to experience postwar life through the Holocaust prism in a scene in which Rosa strays onto a private beach surrounded by a barbed wire fence. Rosa, like other survivors, experiences terror when encountering images that trigger Holocaust memories. She rebukes the hotel manager, insisting that barbed wire fences are inappropriate in American society. "'Only Nazis,'" she charges, "'catch innocent people behind barbed wire'" (51). When the manager treats her as a nuisance, she asks, "'Where were you when we was there?'" (51), challenging his ethics and, by implication, challenging others guilty of complicity whether by omission or commission.

Rosa's room and personal appearance reflect her unhealed trauma. She lives temporarily in a sparsely furnished unkempt hotel room described as "a dark hole" (13). The bed is unmade, "covers knotted together like an umbilical cord" (30) and the room smells of fish. A disconnected telephone attests to her alienation. Rather than taking meals at the oak table, she eats in bed or standing at the sink. Her diet, visually unappetizing and far from nutritious, is emblematic of self-imposed deprivation motivated by survivor guilt or remembrance of those who perished from starvation. Rosa's physical appearance complements her room and signifies her diminished interest in life. Hair askew, button missing from her dress, she is "the reflection of a ragged old bird with worn feathers. Skinny, a stork" (22). Ozick dramatically contrasts Rosa's usually slovenly room and disheveled personal appearance to her frenzied, yet deliberate, cleaning of the room and donning of freshly laundered clothing in anticipation of a package from Stella containing Magda's shawl, behavior evocative of the sacred attitude she assumes toward her martyred child. That Rosa exists in the present but lives in the past is conveyed in letters to Magda and rare conversations with living acquaintances. "Without a life," Rosa says, "a person lives where they can. If all they got is thoughts, that's where they live" (27-28). Rosa's suffering may be related to Robert Jay Lifton's connection between survivor guilt and "death guilt." He argues that the guilt is a response to the question "Why did I survive, while others died?" Lifton contends: "Part of the survivors' sense of horror is the memory of their own inactivation—helplessness—within the death imagery, of their inability to act in a way they would ordinarily have thought appropriate (save people, resist the victimizers, etc.) or even feel the appropriate emotions. . . . Death guilt begins, then, in the gap between that physical and psychic inactivation and what one feels called upon to do and feel. That is one reason why the imagery keeps recurring, in dreams and in waking life.'"[9] Ozick's survivor portrait also embodies the findings of Jack Terry, who identifies unresolved mourning as a characteristic of traumatic Holocaust experience: "In concentration camps, mourning would have been impossible even if it had been permitted. Grief in itself threatens the integrity of the ego, and under circumstances in which the intensity of the affect is too great or the ego has been so weakened—both of which were the case in the Holocaust—mourning cannot take place. Thus, the attachment to the lost object remains unresolved."[10]

Henry Krystal's explanation of survivors engaging in "various forms of denial, idealization, and . . . 'walling off'" in response to inability to mourn the loss of a child finds expression in Ozick's Rosa.[11] Self-preservation demanded silence at the time of Magda's murder, and Rosa suffers the trauma of her infant's death decades later. Her denial of Magda's death and her invention of a mature Magda with a prosperous adult life epitomize the behavior chronicled in the psychiatric literature. In letters addressing Magda as "snow queen," "yellow blossom," "cup of sun," and "soul's blessing," vibrant language negating her child's terrible death, Rosa supplants reality with imagination. Three such restoration reveries reveal her desire for the life that should have been. She imagines Magda as a lovely young girl of sixteen at the threshold of adulthood; at thirty-one, a physician married to another physician with a large house in a New York suburb; and as a professor of Greek philosophy at a prestigious university. Because Magda's imagined lives are more real to Rosa than her death, Stella's insistence on Magda's death seems aberrant. But to placate Stella, Rosa "pretends" that Magda is dead. Her imagined constructions simultaneously address her need to deny Magda's murder and provide herself, in the imagined living daughter, with a nonjudgmental confidante to whom she can express post-Holocaust despair.

Psychological and psychiatric literature identify paranoia, suspicion, and emotional isolation and distance manifested by unwillingness to forge emotional connections as symptoms of survivor syndrome. Ozick dramatizes these responses by contrasting her survivor with a pre-Holocaust immigrant foil, Mr. Persky, whom Rosa meets in a Miami laundromat. Mr. Persky is socially engaged, trusting, at ease with his peers. Rosa has felt separate from Miami Jews, historically and socially alienated, convinced that, "Everything stayed the same for them: intentions, actions, even expectations" (28). Painfully aware of the gulf separating her from Persky, who emigrated from Warsaw decades before the Holocaust, she tells him, "'My Warsaw isn't your Warsaw'" (19). Not having known Poland in wartime, he cannot share Holocaust memories. Moreover, because his experience is limited to escape from nongenocidal Polish anti-Semitism and a circumscribed standard of living, he fails to understand the magnitude of Rosa's trauma. He exclaims: "'You ain't in a camp. It's finished. Long ago it's finished'" (58). But for Rosa it is not finished. Her pain endures. Profound lack of understanding, like Persky's, leads some survivors to fashion their own psychological prison, isolating themselves among their own kind, suspicious and distrusting of nonsurvivors.

Ozick, who believes in *t'shuva*, the redemptive Judaic faith in the individual's capacity to change, dramatizes in Rosa a dawning sense of this regenerative possibility. Herein lies our hope for Rosa. When Rosa discovers that she has wrongly suspected Persky of stealing her underpants in the laundromat, she forgoes detachment in favor of communication and begins to tell him her Holocaust history. Emblematic of Rosa's new trust is her order to reconnect her telephone, her call to Stella about returning to New York, and her reception of Persky as her guest. These small gestures suggest a turning point. More certain signs that healing is under way are Rosa's diminished interest in the shawl when it finally comes, and her realization that she is perpetuating a fantasy. When Persky arrives at her hotel, "Magda was not there. Shy, she ran from Persky. Magda was away" (70). Earlier in the novella, Rosa would have dismissed Persky rather than delay her imagined encounter with Magda. By the narrative's end, although she invites Magda's return, she responds to the immediate presence of the living. And in her willing social association with a person she had earlier disdained, she is on the road to a more complete recovery.

Jean, Norma Rosen's protagonist, is a survivor of a different sort, a psychological survivor who discovers that her life is radically altered by Holocaust knowledge: "Nothing of her life would, after she learned of the existence of the death camps, be as before."[12] For a considerable time, the mere mention of the words "concentration camps" was, Jean testifies, occasion for desolation. "My body and soul emptied out. I was ready to faint, to fall down. I marveled at anyone who remained standing" (77). At the end of the war, when others sought to return to prewar pursuits, Jean elected sacrifice: refusal to generate life in a universe of death. Marriage and motherhood no longer had meaning for her. That Jean's Holocaust epiphany occurred while making love and that her response is refusal to bear children is illustrative of her feminist political rebuttal to Holocaust history. Confronted by the reality of human evil, by the millions of gassed and burned bodies, the American woman shares the position of some survivors who refused to bring children into a Holocaust-corrupted world. In rejecting the maternal role for herself, Jean allies herself with her European sisters who lost their children and testifies to humanity's loss of Jewish progeny. Through this politically symbolic act, Jean makes the catastrophe her own.

The Eichmann trial serves as catalyst for Jean's re-evaluation of her acceptance of the Holocaust as her own personal catastrophe. Despite considerable temporal distance from the event, she discovers that, contrary to expectations of release from Holocaust obsession, she is forcefully reclaimed by history. Sharing the trial with Hattie is for Jean a reiteration of her initial Holocaust despair. Her mind and heart are violated once more. Almost two decades after the initial trauma, Jean still feels surrounded by corpses. The horrors reappear, not instantaneously in a unified photographic composition, but piecemeal in daily doses of devastation: "machine guns punching bullet holes," "clubs beating against bone" (209), visions of the starving and screaming, bodies forever falling, piercing the psyches of heretofore immune Americans.

The Holocaust's continuing effect on future generations is conveyed through the fact that Hattie, too, becomes absorbed in the trial. As the trial progresses, the pregnant Hattie is at once physical foil and emotional double to the intentionally childless Jean. Astonished by the trial revelations, Hattie concurs with Jean's judgment that the Nazis defiled life itself, and she too expresses reservations about propagating the species. The trial is Hattie's initial Holocaust exposure, Jean's second exposure, and the author's affirmation that the Holocaust must not be conveniently put to rest for any of us.

An early title for this novel, *Heart's Witness,* reflects the importance Rosen assigns to the attestor role of the women. They are witnesses observing other witnesses who have come forward to testify in the Eichmann trial. Hattie's response to the television coverage of the trial echoes Jean's earlier reaction to postwar newspaper pictures of the camps. The younger woman absorbs the Holocaust experience, takes it thoroughly into her consciousness, into her body. "Hattie drinks in the words . . . sucks up the images . . . Her shoulders watch, her knees watch. Her fetus thrusts forward to watch" (68). For the Hatties and Jeans of the world, suffering will not heal with time; the dead will not depart from their thoughts, but burrow in.

Repudiation of God or, at the very least, anger for divine passivity in the face of absolute evil, is a charac-

teristic response in Holocaust literature. Like the protesting Jews in the works of Elie Wiesel and I. B. Singer, Rosen's non-Jews agonize over God's responsibility for the six million. Jean Lamb offers vitriolic denunciation of the merciless God of Auschwitz: "God of the medical-experiment cell block . . . God of the common lime pit grave . . . God of chopped fingers . . . of blinded eyes, God of electrodes attached at one end to a jeep battery and at the other to the genitals of political prisoners" (233). Countercommentary is used by Jewish writers to parallel liturgical and Holocaust disruption. Rosen echoes this technique with a prayer parody that replaces the traditional divine attributes of mercy and justice with diction connoting divine passivity in the face of Holocaust crimes. Hattie's transformation to nonbeliever is charted in her reactions in response to the trial: first personal relief, then an expression of doubt, and finally her identification with Holocaust horror: *"There but for the grace of God and there is no grace of God, we see that there is none—so I go sideslipping into the life of that woman who gave birth in the typhus-infected straw"* (131). And when Hattie asks whether God sees us, the older initiate responds, "It seems irrelevant . . . Isn't it enough that we see each other? Witnessing and being witnessed without end?" (238).

Both Ozick and Rosen are concerned with the problems related to Holocaust remembrance and transmission. Expression of Holocaust memories and thoughts is difficult not only for its physical victims but also for those who choose to examine its relevance to the human condition. Sidney Bolkosky says that one problem that interviewers regularly encounter is the survivor's inability to find "proper words to express unimaginable and exhausting memories"; they describe the "paralyzing, dumbfounding difficulty: the poverty of language to convey emotion and unreal reality": "At the semantic . . . level lurk deeply hidden or repressed meanings; at the narrative level, the tone and style conceal complex emotions, memories, and associations. In the end, we must be resigned to the human inability to duplicate or assimilate those meanings and memories."[13] Sensitive to these difficulties, Cynthia Ozick dramatizes Rosa's reluctance and incapacity to communicate her Holocaust experience to strangers. The survivor knows that even those who invite her to speak are without the frame of reference to understand what she says. People sympathetic to survivors distress Rosa, for she believes that they perceive her one-dimensionally, as a refugee, "like a number—counted apart from the ordinary swarm. Blue digits on the arm" (36). Rosa's initial response to an American Jew's invitation to unburden herself is silence. She cannot communicate the incommunicable. Poverty of language is at the heart of Rosa's inexpressiveness. No satisfactory analogy exists. Driven inward, Rosa's authentic voice emerges in her Polish letters to her daughter conveying pre-Holocaust pleasure and plenty, Holocaust era deprivation and degradation, and post-Holocaust angst and anger.

Convinced that writers should make moral judgments, Ozick asserts the continuity of immorality by linking Polish disregard for Jewish suffering during the Holocaust with postwar American Holocaust amnesia. Rosa remembers, "The most ordinary citizens going from one section of Warsaw to another, ran straight into the place of our misery. Every day, and several times a day, we had these witnesses" (68). Similarly, American indifference to Holocaust history prompts Rosa to observe: "I wanted to tell everybody . . . Nobody knew anything. This amazed me, that nobody remembered what happened only a little while ago" (66).

That the Holocaust legacy continues is evidenced in Rosen's portrayal of characters immersed in the Eichmann trial two decades after the atrocities were committed, and in Hattie's bequeathing of this inheritance to her daughter and to her readers. In the scenario for the play she is writing, Hattie casts her daughter as the reincarnation of an infant victim among other young victims: "New children. . . . New births. . . . New joys. . . . Centuries and centuries and centuries of joyful births and terrible deaths" (237). Thus, the pattern of transmission is established for another generation; as it has been passed down from Jean to Hattie, so it will be from Hattie to her daughter. Each woman bears witness creatively, Jean in her diary-letters and Hattie in manuscripts for a play, a memoir, a novel. Hattie's writing, incorporated as long italicized interludes in Jean's letters, becomes the life force of Jean's childless existence.

Holocaust images and references permeate the lives of Jean and Hattie, and Holocaust associations inform their thinking and their speech. Contemporary events, people, and conditions are correlated with Holocaust categories and definitions. A personal betrayal is "like telling the police where Anne Frank is hiding" (60); a person of ignoble behavior is described as "a gold tooth salvager" (60), or "an informer" (60). A skeletal Chinese laundryman is likened to "the near-corpses of last evening's televised trial" (43), and seen, in the mind's eye, stretched out on the freezing shelves with camp inmates whose will to live had been destroyed. Characteristic of Rosen's powerful merging of present experience with Holocaust perception is Jean's walk through the urban renewal project. As she stumbles over broken pavement, the trial legacy floods her consciousness and the walker through rubble becomes the digger through corpses. In this fleeting moment of free association, Rosen portrays the pervasive impact of the Holocaust on post-Holocaust sensibility. Jean, for whom the 1944 image of American soldiers evacuating "stick bodies, two and three to an armful" (78) initiated new consciousness, is the woman for whom the Vietnam era

confirms that the evil of Nazism continues as an ever present specter.

That the Holocaust alarms so few people profoundly distresses Jean and her author as it does Ozick's Rosa. Jean had expected the Holocaust to evoke general horror comparable to that expressed in Picasso's *Guernica.* Instead, she discovered that there was virtual indifference to the destruction of European Jewry on her college campus, when the school president spoke of "troubled times," and campus life proceeded as usual. Representative of the larger world's apathy are the attitudes of the men most closely associated with Jean and Hattie. Hattie's husband, Ezra, is a photographer aesthetically distanced from flesh and blood, devoted instead to pleasing patterns. Jean's absent lover, Loftus, is (as his name suggests) above these concerns. When Hattie turns to him for an explanation of evil in the world, he brings the two women together to enable Hattie to get through the trial. Loftus, like most people who had lived through the Holocaust era, does not comprehend it any better as it is reiterated in the course of the Eichmann trial. His anxiety is not for the victims but for the sensibilities of a student who just might lose her joie de vivre if she succumbs to "the horrors of the monster's cave" (28). Yet it is, of course, through the clouded lens of the Holocaust that Ozick and Rosen insist we now must view human existence and measure radical evil.

Rosen forces her readers to consider the implications of the Holocaust for all of us. Like Jean before her, Hattie refuses to be lulled to indifference, to dismiss the Holocaust from her mind because it happened to other people. For Hattie, and others like her, the philosophical implications of the Holocaust remain. One cannot simply curse the Nazis and forget them: "Their possibilities are always with us" (84). Rosen poses the crucial question of our time: since the Nazis "passed for human beings, what does that say about human beings?" (84). Rosen's charge to her readers is that succeeding generations must encounter the consequences of Germany's legacy of shame: "A poison went into the atmosphere. Just as when an atomic bomb explodes. Each generation in turn will be sickened, poisoned with disgust for the human race" (84).

The moral injunction to remember collective history, central to Jewish thinking, is also central to Ozick's *Rosa.* She not only confirms appropriate memory in Rosa's legitimate anger and healing sequences, but extends her commentary on Holocaust transmission and scholarship to condemn inappropriate transmittal. To convey the latter, she constructs a scathing satiric portrait of an unethical scholar who wants "to observe survivor syndroming within the natural setting" (38). In a jargon-strewn letter to Rosa, void of any sympathetic sensibility, Dr. Tree describes his interest in Rosa's camp experience for use in his study on repressed animation. Rosa sees him as a parasite and is offended at being addressed as a lab specimen. She is fully aware that Dr. Tree views her merely as a figure with "blue digits on the arm," and she condemns his intent to exploit her pain and is outraged by his assertion that he plans to write the definitive work on the subject, "to close the books so to speak on this lamentable subject" (36, 37). Tree's letter shows him to be insufferably arrogant, intellectually misguided, and insensitive. Although Rosa clearly wished to have an audience for her testimony, she refuses to dishonor that testimony by offering it to an inappropriate recorder whose misappropriation of Holocaust memory would be a disservice to history and Holocaust victims.

Holocaust transmission is a secondary theme in *Rosa,* but it is of primary importance in *Touching Evil.* Rosen's narrative gives voice to Holocaust victims through survivor trial testimony and writing by American surrogate witnesses, Jean's letters and diary entries, and Hattie's journals, plays, and novel. The passage between receiving the news and making it one's own, between listening and telling, is traversed as Jean's memory is sparked by trial testimony. Acting both as Jean's foil and as her double, Hattie formally assumes the task of Holocaust transmission to the next generation. Transferal of the appalling tale leads to Rosen's narrative design of manuscript within manuscript within manuscript as readers experience Hattie's diary entries and writing strategies through the medium of Jean's letters.

A generation after the Holocaust, we possess a body of imaginative literature that struggles to comprehend an unparalleled evil. Cynthia Ozick and Norma Rosen have made significant contributions to that endeavor by demonstrating how lives are changed by the knowledge of Holocaust evil: Ozick through the survivor's voice and Rosen through the creation of American women who choose to bear "witness through the imagination."[14]

Notes

1. Cynthia Ozick, "Toward a New Yiddish," 174.

2. For a full analysis of Ozick's Holocaust works, aside from *The Shawl,* see S. Lillian Kremer, "The Dybbuk of All the Lost Dead."

3. Norma Rosen, "The Holocaust and the American-Jewish Novelist," 58.

4. Ibid., 57, 59. The Rosen sections of this essay are derived from S. Lillian Kremer, "The Holocaust in Our Time: Norma Rosen's *Touching Evil.*"

5. Cynthia Ozick, "The Shawl," *The Shawl* (New York: Knopf, 1989), 4. Subsequent references to the two works in this collection will be given in parentheses in the text.

6. Norma Rosen, *Touching Evil* (New York: Harcourt, Brace, and World, 1969, rpt. Wayne State Univ. Press, 1990), 224. Subsequent references in the text are to the 1969 edition. This passage has much in common with a description of young French Jewish orphans being prepared for deportation from Drancy to Auschwitz in the historic account of the fate of French Jewry under Nazi occupation. See Claude Levy and Paul Tillard, *Betrayal at the Vel d'Hiv,* 157.

7. Edward Alexander, *The Resonance of Dust,* 132.

8. Nora Sayre, review of *Touching Evil,* 26.

9. Robert Jay Lifton, "The Concept of the Survivor," quoted in George Kren, "The Holocaust Survivor and Psychoanalysis," 70.

10. Jack Terry, "The Damaging Effects of the 'Survivor Syndrome,'" 145.

11. Henry Krystal, "Integration and Self-Healing in Post-traumatic States," 125.

12. Rosen, "The Holocaust," 58.

13. Sidney M. Bolkosky, "Interviewing Victims Who Survived," 34.

14. Rosen, "The Holocaust," 58.

Joseph Alkana (essay date winter 1997)

SOURCE: Alkana, Joseph. "'Do We Not Know the Meaning of Aesthetic Gratification?': Cynthia Ozick's *The Shawl,* The Akedah, and the Ethics of Holocaust Literary Aesthetics." *Modern Fiction Studies* 43, no. 4 (winter 1997): 963-90.

[*In the following essay, Alkana argues that Ozick presents a "more complex post-Holocaust literary aesthetic" than previous authors writing of the Holocaust have offered.*]

For American Jewish writers, the Holocaust remains a compelling subject for fiction; and their work constitutes an ongoing reply to Theodor Adorno's famous claim "that it is barbaric to continue to write poetry after Auschwitz" (87). The task of telling Holocaust stories has involved a recognition that beyond the fundamental value of presenting witness and survivor accounts, whether in nonfictional or fictional forms, there is value in telling more stories, particularly stories of life after Auschwitz. A work such as Art Spiegelman's *Maus* features a self-conscious narrative style that addresses this as an imperative while highlighting the sense that conventional literary forms may be inadequate to the task. Such anxiety is evident in the trajectory of American Jewish literary attitudes toward the Holocaust, and the career of Philip Roth exemplifies changing literary responses to the Holocaust.

The characteristic American Jewish response during the years following the Holocaust, when not omission, took the form of allusion in place of direct commentary.[1] This strategy is evident in one of Roth's better known early pieces, "Defender of the Faith." In this story, the problematic status of allegiances and cohesion within a group of American Jewish soldiers is given added dramatic and moral weight by the Holocaust, the one principal event that is cited only obliquely and, at that, by a self-serving Jewish soldier in a manipulative plea for ethnic unity. Roth's work since that time has displayed more explicit and sustained interest in the Holocaust and its consequences. For example, he facilitated the American publication of Bruno Schulz and Jírí Weil, Jewish writers who remained in Europe during the Holocaust. And more recently, in *Operation Shylock,* Roth centered his reflections on identity around such related things as the Holocaust crimes trial of John Demjanjuk, an interview with Aharon Appelfeld, the Israeli writer of Holocaust novels, and the notion of "Diasporism," a bitterly comic reflection on the possibility of a Jewish return to post-Holocaust Europe. Between the silences of "Defenders" and the articulations of *Shylock,* Roth offered a serious questioning of Holocaust literature in *The Ghost Writer,* which critiqued the American Jewish reception of Anne Frank's *Diary,* particularly its adaptation for the stage. The elevation to iconic status of Anne Frank by American Jews during the 1950s led Roth to suggest that through excessive sentimentality and a lack of historical consciousness, Jews of that era not only failed to come to terms with the Holocaust—to the extent that such a thing is possible—but too often were relying on successes in the United States to justify their complacency after the Holocaust. Roth emblematically transforms Anne Frank into Anne Franklin as part of his satire on upper-middle-class materialism and a concomitant American exceptionalist ideology that reinforced the sense of the foreignness of the Holocaust.

Roth's satire of sentimentality about victimization and his insistence on the historical specificity of Holocaust suffering are two characteristics of much recent work on the Holocaust. The clearest attempt by an American fiction writer to move beyond these negative, though necessary, steps of rejecting sentimentalism and universalism and toward the development of a more complex post-Holocaust literary aesthetic is offered by Cynthia Ozick's *The Shawl.*[2]

The Shawl is neither Ozick's first nor her most recent fictional reflection on the Holocaust. Earlier short pieces, such as **"Bloodshed"** and **"The Pagan Rabbi,"** and her lengthy first novel, *Trust,* dramatize predicaments posed by the Holocaust and its consequences.

Her most recent novels, *The Cannibal Galaxy* and *The Messiah of Stockholm,* directly treat the Holocaust as the central event in twentieth-century Jewish consciousness. *The Shawl,* a pair of related stories that appeared individually in 1980 and 1983 and were published together in 1989, resembles Ozick's other fiction insofar as it deals with a theme Ozick's critics agree is one of her primary concerns, the tension between Jewish and non-Jewish cultures.[3] But unlike her other writings on the Holocaust, the very form of the two stories that constitute *The Shawl* issues a challenge to conventional aesthetics, a challenge that also touches upon questions of history and of theology.

The two stories of *The Shawl,* **"The Shawl"** and **"Rosa,"** are presented in historical sequence: **"The Shawl"** describes in an elliptical, impressionistic manner the concentration camp captivity of Rosa, her perceptions of her niece, Stella, and the death of her infant daughter, Magda; **"Rosa,"** set approximately four decades later in Miami Beach, tells of how Rosa feels radically isolated and remains preoccupied with her murdered daughter. The historical circumstances these two stories describe, the moments of crisis faced by the protagonist, and the language used to convey Rosa's character in the two stories are deeply interrelated, each feature serving to expand on and to complicate the others.

In the lengthier **"Rosa,"** the reader is furnished with a character portrait that reveals the protagonist to be both alienated and alienating, someone who through bizarre and self-righteous judgments globally repels the sympathies of others. The early action of the story unfolds as a reflection of her character: we are introduced to Rosa Lublin, described in the first sentence as a "madwoman and a scavenger" (13), a woman who for no apparent reason had destroyed her small used-furniture shop and moved from New York to Miami, thus becoming financially dependent on her niece. In a rare venture from her filthy room, which is cluttered with letters written in Polish to her dead daughter, whom she imagines "a professor of Greek philosophy at Columbia University" (39), Rosa goes to a laundromat, where she meets a garrulous retired button manufacturer, Simon Persky. Rebuffing with sarcasm Persky's advances, Rosa indicates her alienation from Jewish culture and from humanity in general. Her wholesale rejection of people, even those who might be inclined to commiserate with her, may well be an understandable result of her Holocaust experiences, but it also marks her as someone with whom most people would prefer to sympathize from a distance.

By sculpting such a sharply edged protagonist, Ozick does more than create the premise for a story; she also takes a stance against a tendency that she along with other Jewish writers have found vexatious—universalism, the tendency to level human suffering under the general heading of an all-inclusive existential or theological quandary. As Ozick herself noted in an essay, when distinguishing between death camp victims,

> Those who suffered at Auschwitz suffered with an absolute equality, and the suffering of no one victimized group or individual weighs more in human anguish than that of any other victimized group or individual. But note: Catholic Poland, for instance (language, culture, land), continues, while European Jewish civilization (language, culture, institutions) was wiped out utterly—and that, for Jewish history, is the different and still more central meaning of Auschwitz.

(*Metaphor* 43)

Ozick here takes issue with the approach to Holocaust suffering that focuses on personal experience, an approach that all too readily can feed into a universalist interpretation, by choosing to highlight distinctions based on group histories. Ozick's own focus on group identity is inverted by Rosa, who continues to evade any self-definition that groups her with other Jews. Rosa thus rejects Persky's overtures, attempting to spoil his excitement at discovering that they both came from the same city by insisting, "'My Warsaw isn't your Warsaw'" (19). And Rosa substantiates this by proudly claiming that she knows no Yiddish, preferring instead the "most excellent literary Polish" (14) with which she composes her letters to Magda. Rosa thereby sets herself apart as one who rejects a Yiddish-speaking Jewish identity in favor of kinship with a secularized Polish-Jewish community which "was wiped out utterly."

The remainder of **"Rosa"** dramatizes the difficulties created by her rejection of the living in favor of both a dead daughter and an inhospitable pre-Holocaust Polish culture. She spends her time holding off the persistent and pesky Persky, searching through the streets and the beach in a grotesquely comic manner for a pair of underwear she suspects him of stealing from her laundry and, finally, succumbing to his insistent sociality by inviting him up to her room over her newly reconnected telephone. Rosa's obsession with her underwear parallels her obsession with another garment, the shawl in which she had wrapped the infant Magda. Through much of **"Rosa,"** she awaits the arrival of the shawl, promised to her by Stella, who accuses her of acting crazily: "You're like those people in the Middle Ages who worshiped a piece of the True Cross" (31-32). Rosa's worshipful stance mirrors a fundamental predicament within Ozick's work, a dilemma she believes inevitably confronts the Jewish artist. Janet Handler Burstein summarizes the critical consensus when she observes, "Ozick's conviction that art is idolatrous for Jews announces itself in essay after essay" (85).[4] Ozick's vision of the Jewish artist's conflicted state parallels Rosa's obsession with her past, as indicated by the epithet with which Stella labels Rosa, "parable-

maker" (41). It is as a parable maker, one who keeps recalling the past but recalling it in an altered manner, that Rosa undertakes the problematic yet necessary task of Jewish authors who write about the Holocaust.

Although Rosa's rejection of her Jewish contemporaries and her strangely anachronistic assimilationist attitude may be troublesome from Ozick's perspective, Rosa's refusal to forget the past signifies her importance. Unlike the niece whom she ridicules for forgetfulness ("'Stella is self-indulgent. She wants to wipe out memory'" [58]) and American exceptionalism ("Stella Columbus! She thinks there's such a thing as the New World" [42]), Rosa continually finds reminders in her surroundings: the stripes of a dress summon forth a camp uniform, and the clinically detached language of a midwestern professor researching Holocaust victims resembles dehumanizing Nazi rhetoric. When the environment fails to trigger associations, she deliberately sets out to remember. In a letter to Magda, she tells of physical privations in the Warsaw Ghetto and the loss of her secularized, urban Polish-Jewish identity, as expressed in the outrage of her family, who had affirmed Enlightenment ideals, at being treated like "these old Jew peasants worn out from their rituals and superstitions" (67). But Rosa also fashions a new past for herself and Magda, one with which she rejects Stella's seemingly more accurate memory: "Your father was not a German. I was forced by a German, it's true, and more than once, but I was too sick to conceive. Stella has a naturally pornographic mind, she can't resist dreaming up a dirty sire for you, an S.S. man!" (43). Rosa recalls being raped in a Nazi brothel, yet she detaches Magda from these memories, instead substituting the image of a Polish Gentile husband and father to Magda, "respectable, gentle, cultivated" (43).[5]

Rosa's invented lineage for Magda coupled with her monologues directed toward a fictive adult daughter denote her madness, yet they also link her to the writer's work. A writer's tendency toward obsession and madness motivates **"Envy,"** and a more general connection between madness and the imagination may be found in "The Pagan Rabbi"; but, unlike these early Ozick stories, *The Shawl* specifies the Holocaust as the source of a disruptive yet recuperative imagination. Rosa's obstinate inventiveness certainly reflects a Holocaust survivor mentality insofar as it manifests an amalgam of guilt, shame, fear of not being believed, and an inability to accept powerlessness in the face of deadly force. As if to compensate for this powerlessness, Rosa invents, and this outrages Stella and elicits the label "parable-maker." It is the making of parables about the Holocaust, the rules to guide or limit a post-Holocaust aesthetic, that *The Shawl* dramatizes and questions.

Ozick's critics have offered commentaries and insights on the symbolism and the ethical import of *The Shawl*, but they generally have displayed only passing interest

in the aesthetic implications of juxtaposing its two sty-
listically dissimilar component pieces.[6] In part this no
doubt reflects the tendency in Ozick's own essays to diminish the significance of aesthetic issues in favor of
the ethical. Critics have followed Ozick's lead when
tracing the progress of her career from the Jamesian
convolutions of her first novel, *Trust*, to her most recent
works, which, despite Jamesian overtones (such as the
similarly compulsive searches for manuscripts in *The
Messiah of Stockholm* and **"The Aspern Papers"**), assert the primacy of the ethical. Alone among scholars
writing on **The Shawl**, Joseph Lowin has focused on
the relationship between the utterly disparate styles of
its two stories, suggesting that the elaboration in **"Rosa"**
on the sparse language of **"The Shawl,"** which fills a
mere seven pages, amounts to a midrashic commentary.
Lowin's observation, however, would seem to contra-
dict Ozick's own assertion, regarding the need to negotiate between traditional Jewish and Western Enlightenment aesthetic forms, that "Such a project cannot be
answered with a proposal to 'compose *midrashim*,' by
which is usually meant a literature of parable"
(*Metaphor* 238). Midrashic parable, though perhaps not
constitutive of **The Shawl** in the straightforward manner that Lowin suggests, does furnish the basis from
which Ozick attempts to elaborate a way of telling post-
Holocaust stories, of exploring the relationship between
dominant Western fictional forms and this traditionally
Jewish one.

The inclusion within the past decade of *midrash* among
the arsenal of terms available to literary theorists has
brought to the foreground the debate over definitions
and descriptions of the methodologies of midrash. This
debate, which like midrash itself does not lend itself to
summary without loss, nevertheless yields several points
useful to a discussion of the aesthetics and argument of
The Shawl. Although it primarily concerns itself with
the exegesis of sacred texts, midrashic activity frequently takes the form of fiction, especially didactic fiction. These fictions focus on textual gaps, which may
be regarded in two ways. Midrash as textual exegesis
attempts to render comprehensible fissured or otherwise
perplexing biblical passages. A second, related function
of midrash is that which brings about interpretations
consistent with contemporary religious beliefs and circumstances. Thus the didactic or moralistic aspects of
midrash work to cast contemporary intellectual and
ethical dilemmas as extensions of tradition. This process of mediating the intellectual distances between sacred scripture and a present largely constituted by relationships with non-Jewish cultures locates for itself
space within an otherwise canonically foreclosed past
by identifying interpretive problems in sacred texts.[7]

It is with the first sense of midrash in mind, the act of
filling textual gaps, that Lowin discovers a midrashic
quality in **"Rosa,"** which elaborates and explains much

of the earlier story. **"The Shawl"** provides little more
than the most essential information for the construction
of a narrative: the names of the three characters, descriptions without explanations of their deprivations,
sketchy accounts of their journey on foot to a camp,
Rosa's act of hiding the silent Magda in her shawl, and,
finally, a depiction of how Magda, deprived of the shawl
by Stella, comes out crying into the roll call area where
a helmeted guard throws her against an electrified fence.
The only dialogue reported is Stella's response to her
study of Magda's face ("Aryan" [5]) and her explanation of why she took Magda's shawl ("I was cold" [6]).
The lack of explanation, the omissions in this brief
story, recalls Daniel Boyarin's succinct description of
midrashic exegesis: "The biblical narrative is gapped
and dialogical. The role of the midrash is to fill in the
gaps" (17).

"Rosa" might be considered the equivalent of a supplementary or exegetic commentary on **"The Shawl"** were
it not for the complexity of their relationship: **"Rosa"**
delivers an account of a survivor's life that ultimately
refutes the lesson learned from **"The Shawl,"** seeking
to displace it rather than merely elaborate on it. From
the perspective suggested by the later story, **"The
Shawl"** resembles less a primary and sacred text that
needs to be interpreted than it does a potential obstacle
to understanding. **"The Shawl"** describes how Rosa is
brutalized, and to these events she reacts with a tangled
set of inconsistent beliefs that include the importance of
remembering history, the distortions of her own and
Magda's histories, and a sense of alienation from others
in her community. Rosa's feeling of alienation from
other Jews did not begin with the Holocaust—"Her father, like her mother, mocked at Yiddish; there was not
a particle of the ghetto left in him, not a grain of rot"
(21)—but her experiences would appear to have reinforced it. By the conclusion of the second story, however, a shift in her attitude has appeared, one that induces Rosa to become more social and to diminish the
imaginary role of her daughter in her life. The need for
this final change in attitude, for this reconfiguration of
"The Shawl" by **"Rosa,"** becomes apparent when we
observe that **"The Shawl"** *itself* appears to be a midrashic commentary on a biblical story, a midrashic
commentary of the second type, one that seeks to reconcile the Bible with recent history.

The midrashic dimensions of **"The Shawl"** emerge
upon a comparison with what Jewish commentators
typically treat as the preeminent episode in Genesis,
Abraham's binding of Isaac, an episode referred to
among midrashic writers by the Hebrew word for *binding, Akedah*.[8] The Akedah features a series of basic plot
elements and symbols that are refracted through Ozick's
reconfiguration in **"The Shawl."** The sparsely worded
biblical account begins with God calling to Abraham
and summoning him to travel to Moriah and, once there,

to prepare Isaac for a burnt sacrifice. In contrast to, for example, his extended debate with God over the fate of Sodom and Gomorrah, Abraham responds without question to the instructions, and, accompanied by Isaac and two others, he travels for three days. He then takes Isaac alone to prepare an altar, and he binds Isaac as for a sacrifice. At this point, an angel intercedes, commanding Abraham to not harm Isaac. After Abraham sacrifices a ram, the story concludes with God's final iteration of the promise to Abraham that his descendants will be plentiful and have strength against their enemies.

The parallels between the two stories are sufficiently striking to make **"The Shawl"** seem like a female version of the Akedah.[9] Each story features a parent of the same gender as the imperiled child traveling through unnamed territories, the biblical wilderness and the ironically equivalent wilderness of World War II Europe. And the children resemble each other in that both were conceived in unlikely circumstances: Isaac is born to the postmenopausal Sarah, and, as Rosa states in the second story, she thought she was "too sick to conceive." The children are greatly loved by their parents; the prominence of parental love is indicated in the Akedah by God's initial words to Abraham, in which Isaac is identified as the son "whom you love" (Genesis 22: 2), coincidentally the first biblical use of the word *love*.[10] Correspondingly, Rosa makes clear her devotion to Magda throughout both **"Rosa,"** as her ongoing conversation with her daughter suggests, and **"The Shawl,"** in which she hides the fifteen-month old at obvious peril to herself.[11] In their journeys to the places where their children are threatened with death and burning, the protagonists are accompanied by companions of the same gender who are not actually present when the final actions occur. The protagonists' minimal speech is balanced against the surveillance over both sets of actors by largely silent powers with control over life and death. The binding of the two children, of Isaac in preparation for a sacrifice and of Magda with the shawl to keep her hidden and silent, furnishes each story with its name and serves as the single most prominent symbolic point at which the two stories converge.

But why should Ozick have chosen the Akedah as the occasion for a midrash? An answer to this question needs to take into account the attitude of God as it frequently has been explained by Jewish commentators. The Akedah typically has been understood to display God's abhorrence of human sacrifice and preference for spiritual dedication. In a direct commentary on the Akedah, Ozick uses this reading as the grounds for her interpretation of the episode, citing its insistence on "Judaism's first social task, so to speak. The story of Abraham and Isaac announces, in the voice of divinity

itself, the end of human sacrifice forever. The binding of Isaac represents and introduces the supreme scriptural valuation of innocent life" (*Metaphor* 274).[12]

Ozick thus interprets the Akedah as God's unambiguous rejection of human sacrifice, a rejection that reveals not merely some distinction from other deities—Ozick characteristically juxtaposes the Jewish deity against those of the Greeks—but an imperative that helps make the Akedah a defining episode. Her view of the ethical centrality of the Akedah harmonizes with the midrashic understanding that the Akedah refers not merely to Abraham but to the entire nation of Israel as well. In his remarks on the midrashic commentary *Genesis Rabbah*, Jacob Neusner summarizes the traditional attitude, asserting that "the testing of Abraham stands for the trials of Israel" (269). Abraham thus proves himself worthy of God's blessing, the promise to protect Abraham's descendants: "I will make your seed many, yes, many, like the stars of the heavens and like the sand that is on the shore at the sea; your seed shall inherit the gate of their enemies" (Genesis 22: 17).

This final point creates the need for a midrash—not an exegetical midrash that seeks to bridge scriptural gaps but an attempt to resolve the tension between a biblical story and human history. The circumstances of death camp victims test God's promise to Abraham, and the deaths of children pose some of the most intense psychological and theological problems to writers on the Holocaust. Elie Wiesel's *Night,* itself largely organized around the relationship between a son and his father, presents perhaps the paradigmatic dramatic enactment of this situation when it tells of how three inmates implicated in an act of sabotage were publicly hanged. The two adult victims shouted, "'Long live liberty'" (61), and they quickly died, but the one child among them died slowly and silently. Wiesel recounts that he heard a man behind him repeatedly asking,

> "Where is God now?"
>
> And I heard a voice within me answer him:
>
> "Where is He? Here He is—He is hanging there on this gallows. . . ."

> (62)

The question asked by Wiesel's fellow inmate is one implied by Ozick in **"The Shawl."** This question is accusatory, as is so much Holocaust writing, and in Ozick's story, which ultimately offers a different response than the one supplied by Wiesel, it takes the form of a midrashic problem because of the dramatic link between her story and that of Abraham and Isaac.

The differences between the Akedah and **"The Shawl"** signal Ozick's attempt to make salient the tension between sacred scripture and human history. The most consequential difference between the two stories is the nature of supreme power: in the Akedah, the power over life and death ultimately resides in God, while in the camps a human power prevails, and from this all other distinctions devolve. The sites are themselves infused with the characters of each type of power: Rosa marches to a slave labor camp, whereas Genesis identifies Abraham's destination as Mount Moriah, the future location of the Temple.[13] The way by which the protagonists submit themselves to power reflects basic differences: although Rosa has the most limited range of choice, which she exercises in her attempt to preserve Magda, Abraham and, according to midrashic tradition, Isaac voluntarily submit to God's command. Moreover, the vastly differing conclusions characterize the two types of power: Abraham elicits words of blessing and the promise of life, while by contrast Magda dies, and Rosa, to maintain the secret of her motherhood and thus her own life, smothers a scream by stuffing the shawl into her mouth. The words of an angel direct Abraham to spare Isaac's life, but the only sound accompanying Magda's murder by a silent guard is the incomprehensible chatter of the electric wires.

Despite the differing relationships between speech and silences (or incomprehensibility) in the two stories, silences structure the actions in both, the lapses of speech, not surprisingly, also denoting distinctive moral responses and responsibilities. Unlike Rosa's silence and secretive preservation of Magda, an enactment of her maternal devotion, Abraham's wordless acceptance of God's command signals a detachment from both his paternal bond and his relationship with Sarah, who presumably would challenge his intention. Abraham's withdrawal from his family leads Jacques Derrida to speculate that silence and secrecy are essential to our understanding of Abraham's action and *in*action: "He doesn't speak, he doesn't tell his secret to his loved ones. . . . Abraham is a witness of the absolute faith that cannot and must not witness before men. He must keep his secret" (73). Abraham's commitment to secrecy and his silence most tellingly elides the "paradox, scandal and aporia" that Derrida locates between an ethics that would prioritize Abraham's ordinary allegiances to family and his devotion to a transcendent deity. From Derrida's perspective, the eruption of the paradoxical and the scandalous in the Akedah, which calls into question the function of morality and moral judgment, would seemingly highlight by contrast Rosa's silent preservation of Magda; for despite the question of Magda's paternity, Rosa's silence and actions coalesce in an unambiguous devotion to family that on its face comports with normative ethics. Yet when we juxtapose the silences of **"The Shawl"** against the speech of **"Rosa,"** we may find, if not the aporia of the Akedah, both paradox and scandal; once again we en-

counter the unseemliness and impropriety of Holocaust fiction, particularly that which attempts to restore speech to the camps, a realm that its creators treated as secret.

The speech of **"Rosa"** fills many textual gaps left by **"The Shawl,"** but speech also functions in its own right as an obsessional focus for Rosa, one that ultimately and ironically isolates her. Rosa treats her language as essential to her being. When she tells Persky, "My Warsaw isn't your Warsaw" (19) and, again, "Your Warsaw isn't my Warsaw" (22), her point is obviously less geographical or temporal than it is linguistic, cultural, and, in the final instance, constitutive of her identity. She took her cue from her parents, who eschewed Yiddish and instead "enunciated Polish in soft calm voices with the most precise articulation" (68). It is this memory of language that anchors Rosa in a family network, as she rhapsodizes in one of her letters to Magda: "A pleasure, the deepest pleasure, *home* bliss, to speak in our own language" (40; emphasis added). Now that her immediate family is gone and she lives in the United States, her Polish language remains as her home.

Rosa's sense of a linguistic home is challenged by the instrumentalist vision of language Persky reveals when conversing with Rosa in her room:

> ". . . this is very nice, cozy. You got a cozy place, Lublin."
>
> "Cramped," Rosa said.
>
> "I work from a different theory. For everything there's a bad way of describing, also a good way. You pick the good way, you get along better."
>
> "I don't like to give myself lies," Rosa said.
>
> "Life is short, we all got to lie."
>
> (56)

To Persky's conventional sensibilities, what matters is getting along, and any epistemological or aesthetic orientation in language-use should at most be secondary. Hence, when describing his "loiterer" son, who is what Rosa wishes Magda to be, a philosopher, he bluntly opines, "Too much education makes fools" (25). But Rosa the parable maker labels Persky's use of language "lies," and she resists the notion that one can find a "good way" to describe her experiences, metaphorically speaking to Persky of her three lives, "The life before, the life during, the life after" (58). Persky, with the embarrassment of a Jew who had spent the Holocaust years in the United States, nevertheless echoes the ordinary advice given to one who has experienced loss: "it's over. . . . You went through it, now you owe yourself something" (58). Persky here professes the wisdom of a button manufacturer, his belief that gaps exist to be spanned and veiled with cloth, an outlook he initially displays when professionally observing a missing button at Rosa's waist: "A shame. That kind's hard to match, as far as I'm concerned we stopped making them around a dozen years ago" (25).

Despite his commonplace advice to the obsessed Rosa, Persky seems attracted to Rosa's display of a loss for which no compensation is available; if Persky cannot answer Rosa's demand for a wisdom or a language commensurate with her loss, then what he offers is relationship. Relationship is paramount to Rosa's idea of a "mother tongue" (57) that connects her to a literary tradition ("For literature you need a mother tongue" [57]) and that also, and more significantly, forms the basis of her "home bliss," her bond not only to her parents but to the language that constitutes her own ongoing sense of motherhood and being. Her roomful of letters to Magda in a "lost and kidnapped Polish" (20) would bond her with Stella as well, "but her niece had forgotten Polish" (14). Rosa's fervor for her language isolates her and structures the devotional posture Stella criticizes as idolatrous; yet her fantasy of Magda as a professor at *Columbia* University, which approximates the epithet "Stella Columbus," brings these two relatives into at least a lexical relationship. The tension between Magda and Stella, a competition that began even before Stella took Magda's shawl in the camp, is suggestive of Rosa's inevitably fractured worldview.

The most basic of Rosa's contradictions is between her private idolatry and her public role as an idol breaker. Rosa's foremost public act, her moment of American fame, was, according to newspaper headlines, as the destroyer of her second-hand furniture store: "WOMAN AXES OWN BIZ" (18). Rosa's bizarre action remains unexplained until late in the narrative when she recalls in a letter to Magda some of the humiliations and privations of everyday ghetto life, experiences she had tried to relate to uncomprehending or unsympathetic customers. As she ruefully remarks, even when she tried to pare down the enormity of her loss to some particular item, "no one understood" (67). The customers "were in a hurry" (67), too great a hurry to hear of her history and, presumably, too averse to the painful stories of an obsessed woman. Her destruction of the items within her shop would serve to enact her criticism of their misplaced attention; more pointedly yet, her destruction of her own store is a mute critique of the American iconization of business.

In her role as a destroyer of American icons, Rosa once more recalls Abraham, specifically the Abraham of midrashic stories who had to depart his homeland after smashing the idols in his father's shop.[14] Rosa's rescue and subsequent emigration to the United States may not quite parallel Abraham's leave-taking from home nor his destination, but her willingness to mark herself as an outcast by wrecking things and images that others prize, but which she considers meaningless diversions,

complicates Stella's accusation that Rosa is an idol worshipper. This complication serves to thematize a pair of related problems entailed by the worship of lifeless things (whether physical objects or language itself). First, the silence of idols demands explanatory speech, such as Abraham's provocative story to his father that the idols had destroyed one another or Rosa's own provocations, her making of parables. And second, an isolating engagement with something that cannot reply, like the shawl, may displace dialogue with those who can. The dramatizations and structurings of silences, unanswered speech, and interpretive elaborations in *The Shawl* link it to another text that considers the Akedah: Erich Auerbach's comparison of Hebraic with Hellenic modes of literary representation in the opening chapter of *Mimesis*.

The relationship between the need for textual interpretation and the Akedah has been prominent to literary theorists since Auerbach chose the Akedah as his representative biblical text, a choice that seems as deliberate as Ozick's when we recall that he wrote *Mimesis* between 1942 and 1945 while at the Turkish State University at Istanbul. (In 1935 Auerbach had been forced to leave his professorship at the University of Marburg as a result of Aryanization policies and the Nuremberg laws.) Most relevant to the coincidental choice of biblical texts are questions about interpretation and the Akedah, and the relationship of Ozick's ideas about aesthetics with Auerbach's. In his comparison between the relative clarity of the Homeric and the biblical, which in its textual sparseness relies on a dense background of motivation and history, Auerbach insists that radically differing modes of interpretation, and thus cognition, are both assumed and demanded; and this insistence entails for Auerbach—as for Ozick—extensive ethical and political consequences.

These consequences result from the particular method by which the biblical works to intrude on its readers' lives: it attempts to propel itself, through mediating interpretive processes, into the historical realm. By contrast, the Homeric, characterized by a "procession of phenomena [that] takes place in the foreground" (7), a "legendary" style (18), and static, unvarying characters, assumes a uniformity of explicative strategies and an ideal of hierarchical social stasis, the latter understood to reflect an immutable underlying order resistant to historical change. When confronted with the Homeric, the job of the critic is to analyze, for Homer presents "no teaching"; and because there is no underlying stratum, "he cannot be interpreted" (13). The danger of the Homeric, with its implied rejection of historical complexity, leads Auerbach to ask his reader to "think of the history which we ourselves are witnessing; anyone who, for example, evaluates the behavior of individual men and groups of men at the time of the rise of National Socialism in Germany" (19) will understand how ahistorical legend defies the complexities of history; Auerbach feels no need to elaborate on the problems that such simplifications entail. Although the more historically oriented Hebrew writings also lend themselves at times to such simplification, for the most part they demand a more complex interpretive mode, one outlined in Auerbach's essay "Figura."

In "Figura," first published in 1944, Auerbach conveys the sense of crisis over National Socialism that pervades *Mimesis.* "Figura" elaborates on the interpretive processes briefly described in the opening of *Mimesis,* and Auerbach here identifies interpretation as a site where history, ethics, and aesthetics intersect. Figural interpretation, unlike the "symbolic" interpretations he associates with "magic power," "must always be historical" (57). The historical dimension of figural interpretation derives from its method: "Figural interpretation establishes a connection between two events or persons, the first of which signifies not only itself but also the second, while the second encompasses or fulfills the first. The two poles of the figure are separate in time, but both, being real events or figures, are within time, within the stream of historical life" (53). As Geoffrey Green points out, Auerbach's insistence on historically oriented interpretation serves his refutation of Nazi mysticism and aestheticism in both a direct manner and in an indirect one as well. Auerbach painstakingly describes in "Figura" the development of the historicized figural method as a foundation for Christian interpretation and theology. Without commenting on the analogies with certain midrashic interpretative methods, he effectively tethers the Christian to the Jewish as he attempts to drive a theoretical wedge between Nazism and Christianity.[15]

When Auerbach affixes Christian to Jewish interpretive traditions, we confront the distance of four decades that separates his from Ozick's work; the crisis of survival facing Auerbach, and thus the need to cultivate potential allies by stressing the cultural affinities of Christians and Jews while casting Nazism as essentially anti-Christian, no longer has relevance. Contemporary American Jewish writers accordingly tend to stress the complicity of Christianity with Nazism rather than seek distinctions.[16] This sort of pointed assessment may be found in one of Ozick's essays, "Of Christian Heroism," which distinguishes between heroic rescuers of Holocaust victims, victimizers, the victims themselves, and the bystanders who, "taken together," she judges to be "culpable" (*Fame and Folly* 201). Attention to such distinctions is typical of Ozick as an essayist who prizes clarity and moral judgment, yet Ozick's fiction reveals greater tension and ambiguity, as in her presentation of Rosa as simultaneously an idolater and an iconoclast. This kind of ambiguity, which suggests a continuity be-

tween her reasoning and Auerbach's coupling of the Christian with the Jewish, pervades *The Shawl* from its opening pages.

The Shawl begins with an epigraph taken from Paul Celan's "Todesfuge": "*dein goldenes Haar Margarete / dein aschenes Haar Sulamith.*" Celan's Holocaust poem uses these two phrases as a kind of refrain; he routinely returns to the distinction between the Jews and the Germans with his apostrophic lines, "your golden hair Margarete" and "your ashen hair Shulamith" (Celan 63). The distinction between Margarete and Shulamith, between the golden and the ashen, appears to be an odd one for Ozick to emphasize, for, while both Celan's poem and her story respond to the Holocaust, she blurs Celan's distinction. Blue-eyed Magda, whom Rosa addresses in her letters as "my gold" (66), "my yellow lioness" (39), is the subject of Rosa's and Stella's scrutiny during their forced march in **"The Shawl"**; and Stella, with an observation that sets Magda apart, calls her "Aryan" (5), adjudicating Magda's status based on her presumptive paternity.[17] Rosa obviously rejects Stella's desire to make the kind of exclusionary racial appraisal that replicates those of the Nazis, and her own steadfastness toward Magda points out a different irony, the fact that Judaic matrilineal law would lead both Jews and Nazis to recognize the golden, blue-eyed Magda as a Jew. Thus Celan's distinction between the golden and the ashen is effaced by Ozick in a move that suggests her valuing of categorical purity or distinctions operates, like Auerbach's, as a secondary element of some larger strategy.[18]

Ozick's stories may offer a greater degree of aesthetic complexity than the stark dichotomy outlined in Celan's brief poem, yet this should not obscure her skepticism toward aestheticist demands, a skepticism as profound as Auerbach's. Auerbach's distrust of aestheticism pervades his historicist, philological methodology, while Ozick's repeatedly emerges in her essays. Her position is apparent, for example, in her 1970 criticism of contemporary fictional trends, as opposed to the tradition of the densely historical nineteenth-century novel whose ethical concerns she more clearly values: "Now it is the novel that has been aestheticized, poeticized, and thereby paganized. . . . The most flagrant point is this: the nineteenth-century novel has been declared dead" (*Art* 164). For both Ozick and Auerbach, the turn toward historical understanding is primary, and the story of the binding of Isaac provides the two with an occasion to raise questions about interpretation and to affirm an ethical imperative: a rejection of appeals to higher authorities and causes that diminish the quotidian world of human sociality and history. In a discussion of the Holocaust, Ozick declared "that Nazism was an *aesthetic* idea. . . . Let us have a beautiful and harmonious society, said the aesthetics of Nazism; let us get rid of this ugly dark spot, the Jew, the smear on the surface of our glorious dream. Do we not know the meaning of aesthetic gratification?" ("Roundtable" 280). The price of aesthetic consistency that Ozick raises in this question is the issue central to *The Shawl* and Ozick's Holocaust literary aesthetics.

Ozick's Holocaust literature has thematized invariably unsuccessful attempts at accommodating cultural fissures. Joseph Brill's "dual curriculum" in *The Cannibal Galaxy,* a juxtaposition of Jewish and European classics, and Lars Andemening's attempt in *The Messiah of Stockholm* to retrieve a manuscript lost during the Holocaust—gestures aimed at relieving the historical and cultural tensions either deepened or precipitated by the Holocaust—are, in Ozick's fictions, doomed. The midrashic dimensions of *The Shawl,* by contrast, convey inescapable and irreconcilable tensions. "The Shawl," with its retelling of the Akedah in a world where no angel arrives to save the child, presents a story understood by its protagonist as a model for human relations, a story that overshadows the original biblical promise of rescue and life. Rosa is left with nothing but contempt and anger toward the living, an alienation that by the conclusion of the second story begins to yield. "Rosa" thus attempts a midrashic displacement of "The Shawl," just as "The Shawl" had rewritten the Akedah; and, in so doing, "Rosa" restores the primacy of the Akedah. But this restoration does not blot out the memories of "The Shawl." Rather, as Rosa's mental image of Magda recedes yet does not disappear when she accepts Persky's visit at the conclusion, the memories of Holocaust deaths do not disappear, nor can they simply be assimilated into life afterwards.

This failure to assimilate Holocaust experiences into the everyday serves as a defense against Adorno's challenge to a post-Holocaust literary aesthetic. If fiction may properly operate in a kind of productive tension with history, then the central fantasy of "Rosa," her ongoing relationship with her dead daughter, may be understood to preserve the memory and experience that history or the well-meaning, therapeutic sociality of a Simon Persky could well occlude. The ending of *The Shawl* sees Rosa reunited with the magical shawl that brings with it the memory of Magda, allowing Magda briefly to live again within Rosa's altered memory. Rosa's defiance of her own history is hardly unique to Holocaust literature. In Jˇirí Weil's *Life With a Star,* the narrator routinely addresses his lover, a woman whose death was triumphantly announced over loudspeakers in Prague. And still more similar to *The Shawl* is Sandra Brand's account of survival that concludes, after her arrival in the United States, "For me, my child has remained alive. He is with me whenever I want him. . . . 'Bruno, you are the only child I have ever had,' I murmur fiercely to a little boy that only I can see. 'Nothing can come between us any more!'" (204). The line of demarcation between the living and the dead appears in

such accounts to soften momentarily, but the limits of language and literature to compensate for loss remain intact. In Primo Levi's words, "the injury cannot be healed" (24).

If the promise of healing is compromised by the almost inevitable accompaniment of sentimentality—"to give myself lies," as Rosa might put it—nevertheless a nonremedial intervention may plausibly constitute a central feature of a post-Holocaust aesthetic. In *The Shawl,* the preservation of invention and parable is maintained despite a wariness toward universalizing myth and the dangers of emotional appeals. Notwithstanding the ways that personal experience might be sacrificed by attention to common history, the most efficacious gesture remains the return to the historical and social realm advised by Auerbach and enacted with difficulty by Rosa. The return to the social and historical as well as the desire to preserve personal experience may furnish the clearest intellectual response to the Holocaust, but it is Rosa's posture of wariness that may prove most telling. Derrida's discussion of the Akedah, a discussion that more than once slides into the topic of the Holocaust, begins by referring to Kierkegaard's *Fear and Trembling*; Derrida observes that the trembling associated with the Akedah "suggests that violence is going to break out again" (54). The unpredictability of the Akedah is its salient feature here: the fantastic and unprecedented directive to Abraham with its implied threat comes against all rational expectation and without warning (as does the timely angelic intercession and appearance of the ram); similarly, it is not unreasonable to adduce from experience that the more general threat of political, possibly genocidal, violence may apparently diminish but persists in the world. For the traumatized Rosa, who, when faced with an uncooperative hotel manager, summons forth the accusation, "Finkelstein, you S. S., admit it!" (52), the Holocaust remains a paradigmatic experience. Yet the excesses of her interpretations and responses to the world, her avoidances and distortions of reality, call into question the uses of rather than the need for her Holocaust remembrances.

The issue facing Rosa is one that, in a somewhat attenuated form, faces those in the United States who attempt to memorialize the Holocaust: how does one build museums, commemorative structures, or archives without turning away from the present moment? In the case of narrative structures, a turning away from the present generally devolves into the kind of sentimentality and universalist interpretations that have accompanied Anne Frank's story. Obverse to these evasions are such moments as the confrontation in *Operation Shylock* between Roth's ghostly cousin Apter, a Holocaust survivor with an extraordinarily difficult person: "Cousin Philip, I understood what I was up against. I said to her, 'Madam, which camp?' 'All of them!' she cried, and then she spat in my face" (58). The fury she broadcasts, like Rosa's, may be understandable, but her unsocial behavior renders her less than the ideal victim, one who should be ennobled by suffering. The "useless violence" of the Holocaust analyzed by Primo Levi or what Emmanuel Levinas has termed "the paradigm of gratuitous suffering" (162) may not generate sympathetic victims receptive to Persky's prescription of conventionality; yet it is interesting to note how Persky's intercession dramatizes the interpersonal focus of Levinas, for whom the interpersonal in ethics has a philosophical and metaphysical priority.

The measured advocacy of the interpersonal realm offered in *The Shawl* comports with Ozick's characterization elsewhere of the Jewish "Lord of History" (*Metaphor* 253), yet it presents less a developed ethical or theological position than it does the grounds for an aesthetic tension. While Ozick the essayist is quite ready to argue forcefully in favor of or against artistic and social agendas, her fiction, particularly *The Shawl,* maintains greater equanimity. Such balance is, of course, not suggested by Rosa's definitions of her life in terms of dichotomies: either Magda or Stella, either the assimilationist view of her parents or the separatism of Yiddish speaking or Zionist Jews, either full speech in her language or a partial, circumscribed, inadequate English. Like the logic of God's initial directive in the Akedah, which presents Abraham with a stark choice of allegiances, Rosa's logic has remained exclusionary, reminiscent of those times the Holocaust has been sentimentalized or memorialized in opposition to a present historical moment. But Rosa's uneasy acquiescence to sociality, as suggested by her concluding decisions to restore her telephone and to invite Persky to her room in which the ghostly presence of Magda remains, reveals a departure from her either/or mentality, a departure for which fidelity to Holocaust experience does not necessarily overwhelm sociality. Like the angelic intercession of the Akedah, which preserves Abraham's metaphysical and familial allegiances, *The Shawl* maintains the two basic categories as defined by the moments of the two constituent stories. Yet the irreconcilable tensions of *The Shawl* reinforce Primo Levi's insistence that there are wounds without the promise of healing, experiences without the offer of positive significance. Those who seek such a positive significance reveal their own desire for a happy ending more than anything else, for unlike acts of martyrdom or victimizing, either of which reveals moral choice, there is no moral stance implicit in being a victim.

Notes

1. As recently as 1974, Norma Rosen deplored the fact that although "the Holocaust is the central occurrence of the twentieth century . . . by and large, American Jewish writers have omitted it from their work" (8-9). S. Lillian Kremer speaks

of the Eichmann trial and the 1967 Arab-Israeli War as events that spurred American Jewish writers to examine the Holocaust ("Post-Alienation" 576). To this I would add that increasing attention to the importance of recording the testimony of aging survivors may have enhanced Jewish writers' sense of urgency about the topic during the past decade.

2. Sidra DeKoven Ezrahi describes the problem dramatized by Roth: "In America a kind of sentimentality has covered the victims with a thick haze dispelled only by the pious formulas of popular culture, while a certain indulgent fascination with the potential for evil in Everyman has largely replaced the outrage and empathy that suffering traditionally commands. All the facts of human behavior are admissible in a kind of neutral effort to classify all the news that's fit to print" (217-18). Elaine Kauver expresses a similar concern about the translation of the Holocaust into a figure for general human suffering ("Some Reflections" 344-47), but James E. Young warns that the alternative "is to risk excluding it altogether from public consciousness. And this seems to be too high a price to pay for saving it from those who would abuse its memory in inequitable metaphor" (133). S. Lillian Kremer distinguishes between Jewish American Holocaust literature and that of Europeans and Israelis, noting that American writers focus less on survival experiences and are more enclined to attend to post-Holocaust survivor trauma (*Witness* 19-20). This may represent an unspoken recognition of what Naomi Diamont has described as the "cruel paradox facing the survivor—the inadequacy of language to bear witness as against the imperative of testimony" (97). Along similar lines, Lawrence L. Langer has expressed the concern that literary structure "can deflect our attention from the 'dreadful familiarity' of the event itself" (*Holocaust Testimonies* xii-xiii). A similar desire for experiential immediacy informs Patterson's and Roskies's studies, though they also explore potential relationships to older Jewish traditions.

3. Elaine Kauver describes "the themes that obsess Ozick's fiction—the battle between Hebraism and Hellenism, the lure of paganism and the dangers of idolatry, the implications and consequences of assimilation, the perplexities of the artist and the besetting dangers of art" (*Ozick's Fiction* xii). Victor Strandberg's study of Ozick concentrates on these and other bifurcations in Ozick's writings (as the title of his book indicates). Lawrence Friedman similarly describes the underlying tension in Ozick's work as the struggle between a Jewish-historical consciousness versus romantic-ahistorical religions (11-12). Sarah Blacher Cohen approaches this tension in Ozick's work through

form, finding in the comic genre a means for Ozick to explore moral questions. Michael Greenstein calls Ozick's actuating tension a postmodern combination of polemical essay and fiction. In an interview, Ozick bluntly identifies her own position: "Pagans excel at art; Hebrews (as Matthew Arnold and George Eliot understood) engage themselves in deed" (Rainwater and Scheick 260).

4. Louis Harap describes this conflict between morality and art: "She interprets the Mosaic commandment against idolatry to mean not only to reject worship of material objects or images, but also not to pursue anything for its own sake apart from moral or religious status. Thus literature enjoyed for its own sake as an aesthetic object is 'idolatry'" (167). Sanford Pinsker similarly poses Ozick's question: "In what way—sometimes subtle, sometimes not—was the writer a usurper of God, a maker of idols?" (2).

5. Joel Shatzky, discussing *The Pawnbroker*'s image of a Jewish woman in an S. S. brothel, claims that because the Nuremberg laws illegalized sexual relations between German officers and Jewish women, such contact could not have been institutionalized. Chaim A. Kaplan's Warsaw Ghetto diary recounts an incident that seems to support Shatzky: "When the Nazis confiscated our apartment, they permitted our Christian maid to remain. Since she is exempt from the Nuremberg Laws, they raped her" (46). Susan Fromberg Schaeffer's *Anya* accordingly features a Jewish woman who fears her non-Jewish appearance creates the threat of enslavement in a German army brothel. Yet it seems difficult to rule out the possibility that camp brothel administrators failed to scrupulously avoid potential violations of the Nuremberg laws, particularly when the enslaved women were as highly assimilated as Rosa Lublin. For a discussion of sexual abuses in Holocaust literature, see Heinemann, 27-33.

6. In her meticulous reading of *The Shawl,* which treats the pairing of the two stories as a reflection of the antitheses and tensions that inform Ozick's writings, Elaine Kauver comments on the significance of doubling; she perceives the dislocated style of the first story to reflect the understanding that to its victims the Holocaust does not end (*Ozick's Fiction* 185). Lawrence Langer insightfully observes that the second story challenges easy notions of recovery from the loss and trauma outlined in "The Shawl" ("Myth and Truth"). Lawrence Friedman finds in the temporal relation of the two stories a progression from death to rebirth.

7. A concise, lucid introduction to midrash is presented by Barry Holtz, who notes that the rabbis believed "God would foresee the need for new interpretations; all interpretations, therefore, are already in the Torah text" (185). From this assumption, it logically follows that midrashic writers felt justified in bridging gaps between history and Torah. The relationship between midrash and contemporary literary theory necessarily must take into account the goals of midrash; accordingly, Daniel Boyarin frames his densely theoretical discussion of midrash by attempting to mediate between the positions that midrash manifests the desire "to take a position on the burning questions of the day" and interpretive impulses that are less ideological and more concerned with textual problems in scripture (3-5). On the relationship between contemporary theory and midrash, also see Stern and Kermode. For differing understandings of the history and goals of rabbinic midrash, see Kugel and Neusner (*What Is Midrash?* 43-51).

8. The liturgy for the Jewish New Year reflects the centrality of the Akedah: the traditional Torah reading for the first day of the New Year, from Genesis 21, recounts the birth of Isaac; the reading for the second day is from Genesis 22, the Akedah. The authoritative scholarly work on the midrashic literature associated with the Akedah is Shalom Spiegel's *The Last Trial.*

9. Ozick earlier had transformed a traditional Jewish story though gender exchange: in "Puttermesser and Xanthippe," Ruth Puttermesser, a lawyer working in New York's municipal government, substitutes for Rabbi Judah Loew of sixteenth-century Prague as one who brings to life a golem. A provocative feminist interpretation of the Akedah is offered by Nancy Jay, who understands the retraction of Abraham's knife as a patriarchal displacement according to which Isaac "received his life not by birth from his mother but from the hand of his father as directed by God" (102).

10. Everett Fox's translation of Genesis is used in this essay.

11. Barbara Scrafford centers her discussion of "The Shawl" on Rosa's heroic affirmation of motherhood as a contrast to the reality of the death camps.

12. Ozick offers her traditional interpretation as a conscious repudiation of what she describes as "current anthropology" (*Metaphor* 273), which suggests that since human sacrifice was not customary in ancient times her traditional interpretation of the episode, as a rejection of religions that practiced such sacrifice, has no basis. Nahum Sarna offers a brief exposition of the view with which Ozick is in accord, claiming that "Such an understanding of the narrative [of the Akedah] cannot

be supported either by history or by biblical tradition" (392-93).

13. The one other biblical reference to Mount Moriah may be found in 2 Chronicles 3.1, in which the building of the temple under Solomon is described.

14. In response to the silence of the biblical account with respect to Abraham's early life, midrash supplies motivation for his sudden departure from the land of Terah, Abraham's father, as well as the initial blessing conveyed in Genesis 12. According to legend, Abraham destroyed Terah's smaller idols, placed a hatchet in the hand of the largest, and then told his distressed father that the largest idol had broken the others while fighting for the food set before them. When Terah insisted this was not possible, Abraham responded by asking how one could worship a powerless idol, and, the legend continues, Abraham was brought before the Babylonian ruler, Nimrod, who had him imprisoned and then sentenced to death. Abraham's miraculous rescue from the fire by an angel rewards him for his faith, a faith that brought about his departure from home and elicited the initial, seemingly arbitrary, blessing in Genesis. For traditional stories of Abraham's iconoclasm, see Ginzberg, 193-217.

15. Auerbach emphasizes this by asserting. "We may say roughly that the figural method in Europe goes back to Christian influences, while the allegorical method derives from ancient pagan sources, and also that the one is applied primarily to Christian, the other to pagan materials" (63). Green regards "Figura" as Auerbach's attempt to restore Jewish scripture within a Judeo-Christian tradition, thus foregrounding Nazi discomfort with the Jewish sections of the Christian Bible (26-35). Interestingly, the difference between Jewish midrashic and Christian figural interpretations of the Akedah may have affected the English translation of *Mimesis,* which renders the German word "Opfer" as "sacrifice" (e.g., "the sacrifice of Isaac" [8]). This translation implies a typological understanding of the Akedah as a prefiguration of Christ's death. Had "Opfer" been translated as "offering," the more traditionally Jewish understanding of the Akedah that the incomplete nature of the act signified God's rejection of such sacrifice would have been connoted.

16. See, for example, Kremer's *Witness,* 17-18.

17. Distinctions are blurred still further when Rosa ironically opens a letter to her niece with the words, "Golden and beautiful Stella" (14).

18. In a midrash on the Book of Ruth, Ozick considers the situation of Ruth, a Moabite—against whom stood a biblical proscription against intermarriage, for her people had been among the most abhorred of the Israelites' enemies (see Deuteronomy 23: 4-5). Ozick clearly is fascinated with the integration of historical enemies in this story, albeit one based on Ruth's acceptance of the Hebrew god, for which Ozick offers the highest commendation: "one can almost imagine her a kind of Abraham" (*Metaphor* 259). Ozick asks a question that resonates with the situation she outlines in *The Shawl*: "The Book of Ruth . . . is sown in desertion, bereavement, barrenness, death, loss, displacement, destitution. What can sprout from such ash?" (*Metaphor* 264). For Ozick, the answer will lie in a covenantal theology.

Works Cited

Adorno, Theodor. *Notes to Literature.* Trans. Shierry Weber Nicholsen. Vol. 2. New York: Columbia UP, 1992. 2 vols.

Auerbach, Erich. *Mimesis: The Representation of Reality in Western Literature.* Trans. Willard R. Trask. Princeton: Princeton UP, 1953.

———. "Figura." *Scenes from the Drama of European Literature.* Trans. Ralph Mannheim. Minneapolis: U of Minnesota P, 1984. 11-76.

Boyarin, Daniel. *Intertextuality and the Reading of Midrash.* Bloomington: Indiana UP, 1990.

Brand, Sandra. *I Dare to Live.* New York: Shengold, 1978.

Burstein, Janet Handler, "Cynthia Ozick and the Transgressions of Art." *American Literature* 59 (1987): 85-101.

Celan, Paul. *Poems of Paul Celan.* Trans. Michael Hamburger. New York: Persea, 1989.

Cohen, Sarah Blacher: *Cynthia Ozick's Comic Art: From Levity to Liturgy.* Bloomington: Indiana UP, 1994.

Diamont, Naomi. "Writing the Holocaust: Canons and Contexts." *Prooftexts* 11 (1991): 96-106.

Derrida, Jacques. *The Gift of Death.* Trans. David Wills. Chicago: U of Chicago P, 1995.

Ezrahi, Sidra DeKoven. *By Words Alone: The Holocaust in Literature.* Chicago: U of Chicago P, 1980.

Fox, Everett, trans. *In the Beginning: A New English Rendition of the Book of Genesis.* New York: Shocken, 1983.

Friedman, Lawrence S. *Understanding Cynthia Ozick.* Columbia: U of South Carolina P, 1991.

Ginzberg, Louis. *The Legends of the Jews.* Trans. Henrietta Szold. Vol. 1. Philadelphia: Jewish Publication Society, 1968. 7 vols. 1909-38.

Green, Geoffrey. *Literary Criticism and the Structures of History: Erich Auerbach and Leo Spitzer.* Lincoln: U of Nebraska P, 1982.

Greenstein, Michael. "The Muse and the Messiah: Cynthia Ozick's Aesthetics." *Studies in Jewish American Literature* 8.1 (1989): 50-65.

Harap, Louis. *In the Mainstream: The Jewish Presence in Twentieth-Century American Literature, 1950s-1980s.* New York: Greenwood, 1987.

Heinemann, Marlene. *Gender and Destiny: Women Writers and the Holocaust.* New York: Greenwood, 1986.

Holtz, Barry W. "Midrash." *Back to the Sources: Reading the Classic Jewish Texts.* Ed. Barry W. Holtz. New York: Summit, 1984. 177-211.

Jay, Nancy. *Throughout Your Generations Forever: Sacrifice, Religion, and Paternity.* Chicago: U of Chicago P, 1992.

Kaplan, Chaim A. *Scroll of Agony: The Warsaw Diary of Chaim A. Kaplan.* Trans. and ed. Abraham Katsch. New York: Collier, 1973.

Kauver, Elaine. *Cynthia Ozick's Fiction: Tradition and Innovation.* Bloomington: Indiana UP, 1993.

———. "Some Reflections on Contemporary Jewish American Culture." *Contemporary Literature* 34 (1993): 337-57.

Kermode, Frank. "The Plain Sense of Things." *Midrash and Literature.* Ed. Geoffrey Hartman and Sanford Budick. New Haven: Yale UP, 1986. 179-94.

Kremer, S. Lillian. "Post-Alienation: Recent Directions in Jewish-American Literature." *Contemporary Literature* 34 (1993): 571-91.

———. *Witness Through the Imagination: Jewish American Holocaust Literature.* Detroit: Wayne State UP, 1989.

Kugel, James L. "Two Introductions to Midrash." *Midrash and Literature.* Ed. Geoffrey Hartman and Sanford Budick. New Haven: Yale UP, 1986. 77-103.

Langer, Lawrence L. *Holocaust Testimonies: The Ruins of Memory.* New Haven: Yale UP, 1991.

———. "Myth and Truth in Cynthia Ozick's 'The Shawl' and 'Rosa.'" *Admitting the Holocaust: Collected Essays.* New York: Oxford, 1995. 139-44.

Levi, Primo. *The Drowned and the Saved.* Trans. Raymond Rosenthal. New York: Vintage, 1989.

Levinas, Emmanuel. "Useless Suffering." *The Provocation of Levinas: Rethinking the Other.* Ed. Robert Bernasconi and David Wood. New York: Routledge, 1988. 156-67.

Lowin, Joseph. *Cynthia Ozick.* Boston: Twayne, 1988.

Neusner, Jacob, trans. *Genesis Rabbah: The Judaic Commentary to the Book of Genesis, A New American Translation.* Vol. 2. Atlanta: Scholars P, 1985. 3 vols.

———. *What is Midrash?* Philadelphia: Fortress, 1987.

Ozick, Cynthia. *Art and Ardor.* New York: Knopf, 1983.

———. *Fame and Folly.* New York: Knopf, 1996.

———. *Metaphor and Memory: Essays.* New York: Knopf, 1989.

———. "Roundtable Discussion." *Writing and the Holocaust.* Ed. Berel Lang. New York: Holmes and Meier, 1988. 277-84.

———. *The Shawl.* New York: Knopf, 1989.

Patterson, David. *The Shriek of Silence: A Phenomenology of the Holocaust Novel.* Lexington: UP of Kentucky, 1992.

Pinsker, Sanford. *The Uncompromising Fictions of Cynthia Ozick.* Columbia: U of Missouri P, 1987.

Rainwater, Catherine, and William J. Scheick. "An Interview with Cynthia Ozick." *Texas Studies in Literature and Language* 25 (1983): 255-65.

Rosen, Norma. *Accidents of Influence: Writing as a Woman and a Jew in America.* Albany: State U of New York P, 1992.

Roskies, David G. *Against the Apocalypse: Responses to Catastrophe in Modern Jewish Culture.* Cambridge: Harvard UP, 1984.

Roth, Philip. *Operation Shylock: A Confession.* New York: Random House, 1993.

Sarna, Nahum M. Commentary. *The JPS Torah Commentary: Genesis.* Philadelphia: Jewish Publication Society, 1989.

Scrafford, Barbara. "Nature's Silent Scream: A Commentary on Cynthia Ozick's 'The Shawl.'" *Critique: Studies in Contemporary Fiction* 31 (1989): 11-15.

Shatzky, Joel. "Creating an Aesthetic for Holocaust Literature." *Studies in Jewish American Literature* 10.1 (1991): 104-14.

Spiegel, Shalom. *The Last Trial: On the Legends and Lore of the Command to Abraham to Offer Isaac as a Sacrifice: The Akedah.* Trans. Judah Goldin. 1950. Woodstock, VT: Jewish Lights, 1993.

Stern, David. "The Rabbinic Parable and the Narrative of Interpretation." *The Midrashic Imagination: Jewish Exegesis, Thought, and History.* Ed. Michael Fishbane. Albany: State U of New York P, 1993. 78-95.

Strandberg, Victor. *Greek Mind/Jewish Soul: The Conflicted Art of Cynthia Ozick.* Madison: U of Wisconsin P, 1994.

Wiesel, Elie. *Night*. Trans. Stella Rodway. New York: Bantam, 1982.

Young, James E. *Writing and Rewriting the Holocaust: Narrative and the Consequences of Interpretation.* Bloomington: Indiana UP, 1988.

Hana Wirth-Nesher (essay date 1998)

SOURCE: Wirth-Nesher, Hana. "The Languages of Memory: Cynthia Ozick's *The Shawl*." In *Multilingual America: Transnationalism, Ethnicity, and the Languages of American Literature,* edited by Werner Sollors, pp. 313-26. New York: New York University Press, 1998.

[*In the following essay, Wirth-Nesher examines how fiction acts as collective memory and the specific instance in* The Shawl *of the fictional account of a Holocaust survivor's remembrance.*]

> There is One God, and the Muses are not Jewish but Greek.
>
> —Cynthia Ozick

> Since the coming forth from Egypt five millenia ago, mine is the first generation to think and speak and write wholly in English.
>
> —Cynthia Ozick

The first of Cynthia Ozick's epigraphic assertions concerns the relationship between Judaism and artistic representation; the second concerns the means of representation and of communication within Jewish civilization. The first concerns what Jews may say; the second, how they say it. It is clear in the first statement that there is an ethical imperative, that certain forms of representation are antithetical to Judaism. Ozick has repeatedly argued that invented fictional worlds are forms of idolatry, reenactments of paganism. Ozick's only recourse out of the paradox of inventing fictions that defy her own dictum is to seek forms that will require continuity, that will make literature liturgical in that it evokes the texts of Jewish civilization. What this means is that "liturgy" becomes a dynamic concept, one that requires reexamination within Jewish culture, and that English as a monolingual rupture with the past must be recontextualized within the many languages that have made up that Jewish culture for millenia.

To test her ideas within her own represented and invented worlds, Ozick sets up the most extreme case imaginable: she writes a novella about the Holocaust, one in which a mother is witness to the murder of her own child. The main character's loss and her subsequent idolizing and fetishizing of the child's shawl is at the center of a text that is itself a weaving together of texts in many languages that constitute one version of the fabric of Jewish civilization. *The Shawl* as a work of literature tests its readers both in terms of the idolatry of placing Holocaust representation at the center of Jewish civilization and in terms of recognizing the strands of textuality, beyond English, that comprise Jewish history and culture and that defy translation. It is as if the injunction not to create idols is ameliorated by the presence of many languages and many texts. One of the lessons of Babel so appealing to modern readers is its denial of the rational transparency of monolingualism.[1] If the idolized shawl at the center of the text is the temptation of idolatry, then the text of *The Shawl* itself, crosshatched with the languages of Jewish civilization, requires historicity and collective memory, thereby making Ozick's work a continuous part of that civilization. "When a Jew in Diaspora leaves liturgy . . . literary history drops him and he does not last."[2] Intertextuality restores Jewish fiction to its Aggadic role.[3]

In this chapter, I will be concerning myself with fiction as a means of collective memory, and more specifically with an American Jewish writer's invented account of a Holocaust survivor's act of remembrance. In choosing Cynthia Ozick's work **"The Shawl,"** I am interested in two aspects of this act of remembering: (1) the role played by different languages in both the invented world of the characters and the historical context of the writer, and (2) the role of language itself in the representation of mother-child bonding. Although *The Shawl* evokes and partially reproduces a multilingual world, it is written almost entirely in English. And like other works of minority discourse, it appears to be alienated from the language of which it is constituted, estranged from its own linguistic matrix. In *The Shawl* this is compounded by its subject matter, for it is the story of the murder of a child at the very moment that she is making her entry into the world of language and the prolonged grieving of the surviving mother, who denies the loss by addressing and enveloping her phantom daughter in lost languages.

I am reading Ozick's work, then, from two main points of departure: as an example of Holocaust literature in America, and as an example of Jewish-American ethnic literature to the extent that such a literature "remembers" a pre-American and non-English Jewish past. These categories dovetail in *The Shawl* in that the main character is depicted first in a concentration camp and then as an immigrant to the United States. Here, the Old World is not simply lost through the act of emigrating; it is completely annihilated physically but is present as a phantom for the survivor.

Since the early part of the century, Jewish-American writing has often located itself between languages, primarily because it was an immigrant literature.[4] The writers who actually had some knowledge of an alternative Jewish literary tradition, in Hebrew or in Yiddish, located their own works between two traditions, the English and the Yiddish, the Christian and the Jewish. This has expressed itself not only in linguistic borrowings by incorporation of phrases from the other language but also by allusions to the other traditions, or to the borrowing of models and types from the other canon.[5] Just as Yiddish poets in America placed themselves in the line of Whitman and Emerson, so writers like Henry Roth, Abraham Cahan, Saul Bellow, and Delmore Schwartz, composing in the English language, often drew on quotations from Jewish sources, interspersed Yiddish words, and turned their characters into types between two different frames of reference.[6] The extent to which Cynthia Ozick engages with such material is evident in her story **"Envy—or Yiddish in America,"** in which the imminent extinction of Yiddish language and culture is the very subject of the story because the Yiddish writer is left wholly dependent on translation to ensure some precarious survival.

As for the category of Holocaust literature, Jewish-American writers have felt the need to incorporate the subject of the Holocaust into their fiction, often with results that reflect their discomfort in presuming to give voice to survivors.[7] Philip Roth, for example, has abstained from even taking that step as he focuses, instead, on the Jewish-American *response* to the Holocaust, and not the historical trauma itself. His character Zuckerman is haunted by his mother's deathbed legacy to him, a scrap of paper with the word *Holocaust* on it, a legacy that paralyzes him as an artist. Earlier, Roth gave us the fantasy of Anne Frank as Holocaust survivor in *The Ghost Writer* and the Holocaust survivor as the last remaining embodiment of authentic Jewishness for the Jewish-American community in "Eli the Fanatic." It is precisely this collapse of Jewish identity into Holocaust remembrance, with its dangers of mystification and sanctification, that has produced Bellow's antisentimental character Sammler, who shares many traits with Ozick's Rosa. Products of the Polish-Jewish upper class, of an assimilated and urbane world, Sammler and Rosa find themselves in an American urban nightmare that has embittered them further.

Let me turn to the work itself. The acknowledgment page of *The Shawl* refers to the "two stories that comprise this work" as having been previously published in the *New Yorker.*[8] It is a deceptively simple statement, for it suggests that these two separate stories are now two parts of one artistic whole, and the relation between them is left for the reader to determine. The only connecting devices offered by the author are the title, which gives preference to the first story in the sequence, **"The Shawl,"** and the German epigraph from Paul Celan's "Todesfuge": "Dein goldenes Haar Margarete / dein aschenes Haar Sulamith," to which I shall return.

What connects these two narratives remains the central question before the reader not merely as a problem in aesthetics but as a moral problem in the representation of the Holocaust by an American author for an American audience. I believe that in this work Ozick has to date provided the most self-conscious and challenging fictional work in the Jewish-American repertoire on the subject of Holocaust representation in language.

Tying the two stories together is the assumption that there is continuity in biography, and that the narrative of two episodes in the life of one individual is sufficient to insure coherence and unity. In this particular case, the individual is a Holocaust survivor by the name of Rosa Lublin. The first story is an account of the death of her baby daughter at the hands of the Nazis in a concentration camp; the second story is a series of incidents in her life more than forty years later in Florida. The former records the child's first utterance; the latter is a fall into a babel of languages, as Rosa belatedly and compulsively communicates with her dead child. To what extent the second story can be understood only in the context of the first is Ozick's main concern and eventually ours. And if we hastily conclude that it is "necessary" to read **"The Shawl"** first, what does that mean? and what exactly does it explain?

In a failed attempt to protect her infant daughter from detection by Nazi guards in **"The Shawl,"** Rosa Lublin also denies her child's entrance into speech, into the symbolic order. The sound uttered by the one-year-old Magda that betrays her to the Nazis, "Maaaa," is a cry provoked by the loss of her shawl, but within Ozick's text as filtered through the mind of the mother, it is the first syllable of "maamaa," later hummed wildly by the electric wires against which the girl is hurled. Having retrieved the shawl too late to quiet her daughter's wail, Rosa stuffs it into her own mouth to prevent her outcry and detection by the Nazis after they have already murdered her child. Swallowing the "wolf's screech" and tasting the "cinnamon and almond depth of Magda's saliva," she internalizes both the child's cry and the child's muteness. In **"Rosa,"** the sequel **"The Shawl,"** and the second part of the divided text—*The Shawl*—Rosa Lublin writes letters in Polish to her imaginary adult daughter in an attempt to connect the two parts of her life, before and after the Holocaust, and to give her daughter a life in her own fantasies. The first part of the combined work, then, as an American author's account of a Holocaust experience, is the context for reading the multilingual narrative that follows.

What distinguishes Ozick's treatment of this issue from those of her fellow Jewish-American authors is the degree of her self-consciousness about the inadequacy of language to render these experiences and her choice of a female character so that the narrative circles around maternity and the woman's relation to language and loss.[9] Let me return to that moment in **"The Shawl"** when the one-year-old child whom Rosa has been successfully hiding from the Nazis wanders into the open square of the concentration camp and screams as soon as she discovers that she has lost the shawl that has hidden, enveloped, and nurtured her from birth. Up to that point,

> Magda had been devoid of any syllable; Magda was mute. Even the laugh that came when the ash stippled wind made a clown out of Magda's shawl was only the air-blown showing of her teeth. . . . But now Magda's mouth was spilling a long viscous rope of clamor.
>
> "Maaaa—"
>
> It was the first noise Magda had ever sent out from her throat since the drying of Rosa's nipples.
>
> "Maaaa . . . aaa!"
>
> . . . She saw that Magda was grieving for the loss of her shawl, she saw that Magda was going to die. A tide of commands hammered in Rosa's nipples: Fetch, get, bring! But she did not know which to go after first, Magda or the shawl. If she jumped out into the arena to snatch Magda up, the howling would not stop, because Magda would still not have the shawl; but if she ran back into the barracks to find the shawl, and if she found it, and if she came after Magda holding it and shaking it, then she would get Magda back, Magda would put the shawl in her mouth and turn dumb again.
>
> (8)

Rosa at first chooses to hear the one syllable cry "Maaa" as an expression of pain for the baby's separation from the shawl. But when she fails to save the child from death, Rosa hears the electric voices of the fence chatter wildly, "Maamaa, maaamaaa," a reproach to her—for if the outcry was the girl's first act of communication rather than merely a wail, if she called out to her mother, then her mother failed her.

The verbal development of the infant, according to Lacan, begins as "a demand addressed to the mother, out of which the entire verbal universe is spun."[10] This moment in **"The Shawl"** is left suspended between sound and language, between undirected pain and an appeal to the mother, the beginning of a dialogue the price of which is death. Rosa's response to that cry for the rest of her life is to answer it obsessively in the most articulate language known to her, to write eloquent letters to her dead daughter in Polish.

Her letter writing is both a repeated recognition of her child's tragic entry into language and a denial of the war that murdered her, for Rosa's letters to a daughter whom she imagines as a professor of classics, specifically a professor of Greek—a dead language (and an indecipherable one for Rosa)—are primarily elegies for the lost world before the war, a world of elegant turns of phrase, of literature and art. Magda becomes for her

the self that has been stolen from her, the self that she might have become. Rosa grieves as much for herself as lost daughter as she does for herself as lost mother.

Before I take a closer look at the languages that serve as various substitutes for the shawl, I want to turn to the shawl itself. What sort of language is it? For Rosa it signifies the preverbal bond between mother and daughter, as it becomes an extension of the mother's body for the infant Magda, a miracle of maternity that appears to nurture the sucking child after the mother's breasts are dry, "it could nourish an infant three days and three nights." Yet it also seems to serve as a denial of maternity, the means whereby Magda's presence is denied to the rest of the world.[11] Denial of Magda's birth is Rosa's way of protecting her and herself. After Magda's death, Rosa stuffs the shawl into her own mouth, an act that muffles her cries and that, metonymically, devours her daughter and returns her to the womb. Thus, the shawl is both mother to the child and child to the mother, their prenatal inseparability. The choice before Rosa when she spies her unprotected daughter whose cries are bound to reveal her presence to the Nazi guards is to retrieve the child or retrieve the shawl for the child. Rosa does not do the first because she believes that Magda cannot be comforted by her actual mother, that her only comfort is the shawl, metonym for womb and breast. Yet when the girl is murdered, Rosa believes that the child had actually cried out to *her,* that the pause between the utterances was not the interval of a repeated and meaningless wail but, rather, Magda's first word, "Maamaa."

Attempting to swallow that sign of maternity while also becoming that lost child in the act of sucking it—this image marks the end of the account of Magda's death and the end of the first text, **"The Shawl."** The second text, **"Rosa,"** is made up of a series of discourses and languages that are responses to the traumatic events of **"The Shawl"**: the responses of Rosa to her past and the responses of the American community of which Ozick is a part.

First, there is English, the language of the novella *The Shawl,* the language that Rosa shuns, "Why should I learn English? I didn't ask for it, I got nothing to do with it." Much of the English expression that surrounds Rosa seems to mock her and her past, primarily the lingo of advertising, journalism, and psychology. Kollins Kosher Cameo in Miami appeals to nostalgia to lure clients into the restaurant. "Remembrances of New York and the Paradise of your Maternal Kitchen." Aimed at an American-born clientele, the sign is read by Rosa knowing that she left New York because it drove her mad and that her own daughter never experienced the "paradise of a maternal kitchen." The accumulated grief and despair that drove her to destroy her own livelihood in New York is recorded in the newspaper as "Woman Axes Own Biz," an account of her action that never refers to her traumatic past. This is **"Rosa"** without **"The Shawl."** The most humiliating English discourse for Rosa, however, is that of clinical psychology's language of disease for Holocaust victims. The letters that she receives from Dr. Tree, who is applying a model of "Repressed Animation" to his study of "Survivor Syndrome," offer a catalogue of terms—"survivor," "refugee," "derangement," "neurological residue"—but never, Rosa is quick to observe, the term "human being." In short, English in this novella is represented as a language of parody, a fall from some authentic primary language. It is the place of Rosa's exile, a maimed language that distorts and perverts her experiences.

Rosa seeks her protection in languages that are never represented mimetically in the text but are there either in translation, as is the case for Polish, or by allusion, as in Latin and Greek. They represent oases of cultivation. Her father, she recalls, "knew nearly the whole first half of the *Aeneid* by heart"; her imaginary adult daughter Magda is a professor of Greek philosophy.[12] She writes to her daughter "in the most excellent literary Polish." If Magda is killed in the moment of her entry into speech, then she will be forever associated with eloquence, language cut off from the flow of life around Rosa. "A pleasure, the deepest pleasure, home bliss, to speak in our own language. Only to you." Just as the shawl signifies the prespeech bond between mother and child, these languages cut off from community—Polish, Latin, and Greek—become the medium of intimacy between Rosa and her Magda, as if they envelope Rosa in a world of her wishing. But they are not the languages of dialogue; they are the languages of the dead.

Rosa's letters to her imaginary daughter are conveyed in apostrophe, which always "calls up and animates the absent, the lost, and the dead."[13] Addressing her child as "Butterfly," she continues, "I am not ashamed of your presence; only come to me, come to me again, if no longer now, then later, always come" or elsewhere, "in me the strength of your being consumes my joy." Magda's imaginary future in America, as projected by Rosa, is an extension of Rosa's past—a non-Jewish world of intellect and aesthetics. The apostrophe to a Polish-speaking daughter who is a professor of classics is a denial of the Jewish identity that marked both mother and daughter as enemies of that European civilization by Polish and German anti-Semites responsible for her murder.

The only other language actually represented in the novella apart from English is Yiddish, much despised by Rosa and her assimilated family. "Her father, like her mother, mocked at Yiddish: there was not a particle of ghetto left in him, not a grain of rot" (21). In *The Shawl*, Yiddish is associated in the past with Rosa's grand-

mother, and in the present with Simon Persky, the Eastern European immigrant to America, former manufacturer, and retired widower in Miami who takes a romantic interest in her and gently admonishes her, "You can't live in the past." Rosa looks condescendingly at his Yiddish newspaper in the laundromat where he makes his first move.

> "Excuse me, I notice you speak with an accent."
>
> Rosa flushed. "I was born somewhere else, not here."
>
> "I was also born somewhere else. You're a refugee? Berlin?"
>
> "Warsaw."
>
> "I'm also from Warsaw! 1920 I left. 1906 I was born."
>
> "Happy birthday," Rosa said."
>
> (18)
>
> "Imagine this," he said. "Two people from Warsaw meet in Miami, Florida."
>
> "My Warsaw isn't your Warsaw," Rosa said.
>
> (18)

Rosa is intent on distinguishing her Warsaw from Persky's on two grounds, one prewar and one postwar:

The prewar difference is based on rank, for Rosa's denial of any knowledge of Yiddish is her badge of honor in terms of social class. Rosa stems from an affluent assimilated Warsaw home, where the family spoke eloquent Polish and was steeped in Polish culture. Her parents, she recalls, enunciated Polish "in soft calm voices with the most precise articulation, so that every syllable struck its target" (68). Considering the fate of these parents, the trope of Polish syllables striking their target works against Rosa's intense nostalgia. In America, she is deeply offended by the homogenizing of the Old World that places her in the same category with Persky. "The Americans couldn't tell her apart from this fellow with his false teeth and his dewlaps and his rakehell reddish toupee bought God knows when and where—Delancey Street, the Lower East Side. A dandy." Rosa's continuing denial of her Jewishness and her romanticizing of her Polishness results in this peculiar misplaced rage. The American tendency to ignore differences among Jews seems to her a benign repetition of European racism. "Warsaw!" Rosa argues in her mind. "What did he know? In school she had read Tuwim: such delicacy, such loftiness, such *Polishness*" (20).

The irony of Rosa's evocation of pure Polishness in the poetry of Julian Tuwim is that he was a Polish-Jewish poet who wrote in New York in 1944, "So it is with mourning pride that we shall wear this rank, exceeding all others—the rank of the Polish Jew—we, the survivors by miracle or chance. With pride? shall we say, rather, with pangs of conscience and biting shame." The man who served Rosa as the embodiment of quintessential Polishness eventually reached the conclusion that "I shall deem it the highest prize if a few of my Polish poems survive me, and their memory shall be tied to my name—the name of a Polish Jew."[14]

The postwar difference dividing them is that Persky, who left well before the Second World War, has no firsthand experience of the ghetto, the transports, the death camps. As she says to the hotel manager whom she accosts for the presence of barbed wire on the Florida beaches, "Where were you when we was there?"

When asked her name by Persky, Ozick's character replies, "Lublin, Rosa." "A pleasure," he said. "Only why backwards? I'm an application form? Very good. You apply, I accept." Despite Persky's amusement at her self-naming, we recognize that this is not backwards at all, that Rosa first associates herself with Lublin, with her Polishness, and only secondly with Rosa, her Jewishness.[15] In her last letter to Magda she reminds her daughter of their aristocratic background, injured by the social leveling of the Warsaw Ghetto: "[I]magine confining *us* with teeming Mockowiczes and Rabinowiczes and Perskys and Finkelsteins, with all their bad-smelling grandfathers and their hordes of feeble children!" But it is only Persky with his Yiddish paper and his garbled English who has the power to separate her from her Polish phantom child and bring her back to the land of the living.

Despite Rosa's rebuff, Persky persists in his attempt to engage her in conversation:

> "You read Yiddish?" the old man said.
>
> "No."
>
> "You can speak a few words, maybe?"
>
> "No." My Warsaw isn't your Warsaw.

At the very moment that she denies any knowledge of Yiddish, in her mind she recalls her grandmother's "cradle-croonings," and Ozick adds the Yiddish words in transliteration, a rupture in the text because it is the only instance of a language other than English actually represented in the work. "*Unter Reyzls vigele shteyt a klorvays tsigele,*" the first words of the popular Yiddish lullabye "*Rozhinkes mit Mandlen*" (Raisins and almonds). In this lullabye a little goat sets out on a journey from which it will bring raisins and almonds to the sleeping child who is destined to be a merchant of raisins and almonds himself but is now urged to sleep in his cradle. The cradle rhymes with the little goat; it rocks the child to sleep while the goat under his cradle is an ambassador of far-off lands of sweets, the Eastern European Jewish equivalent of sugar-plum fairies. In the story **"Rosa,"** the almonds hark back to the previous text, **"The Shawl,"** and to the "cinnamon and al-

mond depth of Magda's saliva" that Rosa drank from the shawl after her child's death.[16] The clear little white goat under Rosa's cradle is merged in her own mind with the little innocent child, uncradled, to whom she writes in Polish to keep her pure of the Yiddish world that marked her as a Jew, but whom she also links with her grandmother, cradle-crooner in that tongue.

The choice of "*Rozhinkes mit Mandlen*" as the only Yiddish intertext in **The Shawl** adds further to both the gender and historical dimensions of the work. The first stanza of the lullabye, taken from the 1880 operetta by Abraham Goldfaden entitled *Shulamis* (Shulamith), frames the account of the baby and the goat by depicting the following scene:

> In a corner of a room in the Holy Temple [in Jerusalem],
>
> a widow named Daughter of Zion sits all alone
>
> —and as she rocks her only son to sleep,
>
> she sings him a little song.[17]

Within the masculine setting of the Holy Temple itself, a small corner has been domesticated, appropriated by mother and child. And in this woman's space the kid that is traditionally offered for sacrifice, or that takes the community's sins upon itself, has been transformed into the sustaining and nurturing creature who provides raisins and almonds. During the Second World War, the lullabye was adapted to conditions under the Nazis— one ghetto version being "In the Slobodka yeshiva an old sexton is reading his will. . . . When you will be free, tell your children of our suffering and murder, show them the graves and inscriptions of our extermination."[18]

While Rosa reminisces about a home comprising only Polish, Latin, and Greek, she shies away from any image of home that contains Yiddish. But in Miami decades later it is Persky, the Yiddish speaker, who tells her in fractured English, "Wherever is your home is my direction that I'm going anyhow."

Perhaps American-Jewish authors writing in English have invented cultivated and assimilated Holocaust survivors like Rosa and Mr. Artur Sammler as their main protagonists for in their prewar lives these characters inhabited a linguistic world as far removed from the Jewish languages of Hebrew and Yiddish as the authors themselves. Beauty, cultivation—civilization itself appears to be synonymous with the languages of their assimilation. For many American-Jewish authors and readers, such as Philip Roth, Yiddish is a language frozen socially and historically, embedded forever in a milieu of poverty, parochialism, and salty vernacular. Regardless of the historical facts that testify to a variegated Yiddish cultural and literary world before the Second

World War, for the American-Jewish writer, product of immigrant parents or grandparents, Yiddish has tended to signify a maternal embrace, a home long since outgrown. For her or him, the lure of Yiddish seems to lie in its inarticulateness, in the rusty and homespun English of its translation.[19] In *The Shawl* the route to Rosa's grandmother's lullabye and to her own cradle is through social decline, through dialogue with the likes of a Persky. It is as if the well-crafted English of the Jewish-American fictional text is kept in its place by the admonition of the lost mother culture evident only in the scrappy sentences of non-English speakers.

No surprise then that the epigraph is in German, taken from a poem entitled "Death Fugue" by Paul Celan, a Rumanian-Jewish Holocaust survivor who chose to write in the language of his people's murderers. For most well-educated or assimilated Jews in Europe, Yiddish was scorned as a corrupt form of German, frequently dubbed a bastard or stepchild born of writers unfaithful to the legitimate language, Hebrew.[20] Because Yiddish did evolve from Middle German, while retaining the Hebrew alphabet, it is indeed a joining of these two languages. The Yiddish words of a lullabye in a book recounting the murder of a Jewish child constitute the opposite pole to the words of the epigraph, which also connect German and Hebrew. That Magda herself may be the product of rape by a Nazi adds a further grotesque dimension to the linguistic and historic analogues in *The Shawl.*

> Death is a master from Germany his eyes are blue
> he strikes you with leaden bullets his aim is true
> a man lives in the house your golden hair Margarete
> he sets his pack on to us he grants us a grave in the
>   air,
> he plays with the serpents and daydreams death is a
>   master from Germany
>   your golden hair Margarete
>   your ashen hair Shulamith[21]

Margarete's golden hair is close enough to be that of Magda's, child of a romanticized (for Rosa) non-Jewish world that aimed to be Judenrein; as the object of desire of Goethe's *Faust,* Margarete is the incarnation of German romantic love. Shulamith, a "female emblem of beauty and desire celebrated in The Song of Songs, is an incarnation of Jewish biblical and literary yearnings. But there is a bitter difference and shocking irony in the echoing resemblance."[22] One is the fair-haired maiden of the Aryan ideal, the other the darker, ashen features of the Semitic woman. Moreover, the figurative ashen hair is brutally undercut by its literal allusion to Shulamith's burnt hair reduced to ashes. In fact, this may be the source for the ash-stippled wind that encircles Magda in the concentration camp. Shulamith is associated with the "Rose of Sharon" in the biblical text, in Hebrew "Shoshana," and hence with Rosa.[23] Just as Rosa's series of letters to her dead daughter are

apostrophic, so too these lines in the poem are apostrophic, animating what is lost and dead, both the language of Goethe, contaminated by Nazi Germany, and Jewish civilization in Europe. But it also implicates Goethe's language, implying that the idealization of Margarete's golden hair leads inevitably to the ashes of Shulamith's hair. To add a tragic ironic twist to this entanglement of languages and texts, Goethe translated the Song of Songs from Hebrew into German, and in the Walpurgis Night scene in *Faust,* the young witch's lewd remarks to Faust echo some of the most sensuous lines of the biblical text. Earlier, Mephistopheles mocks Faust's love of Margarete by his sexual jests about her body that allude to the Songs of Songs as well, particularly to the often-quoted lines likening Shulamith's breasts to two fawns feeding among the lilies (4:5), which Goethe translated more accurately as among the roses ("*shoshanim*"). Margarete's being identified with Shulamith as mediated through Geothe's romanticism makes her signification as the antithesis of all that is Judaic particularly striking. Celan's poem severs Shulamith from Margarete, recovering the former for Semitic civilization and implicating the latter in anti-Semitic atrocity. He sunders the German-Jewish symbiosis that yielded rich cultural products, among them the first German-language periodical for Jews, significantly called *Sulamith.*[24] Clean explained his own loyalty to the German language by insisting that "only in one's mother tongue can one express one's own truth. In a foreign language, the poet lies."[25] Bonded then to the language of the murderers of his own parents, Celan seeks "to annihilate his own annihilation in it."[26]

As the work of a Holocaust survivor poet, Celan's epigraph lends the authority of testimony to Ozick's novella, as well as the legitimacy of rendering this subject matter in art. The link to Celan, and through Celan to Goethe, is striking in two other respects. (1) In 1943 while a prisoner in a labor camp, Celan wrote a poem originally entitled "Mutter" and then retitled "Black Flakes" ("Schwarze Flocken") in which his mother addresses him: "Oh for a cloth, child / to wrap myself when it's flashing with helmets / . . . hooves crushing the Song of Cedar / . . . [sic] A shawl, just a thin shawl." In his reply to her envisioned plea a few lines later, he offers her his poem as shawl: "I sought out my heart so it might weep, I found—oh the summer's breath, / it was like you. / Then came my tears. I wove the shawl." Ozick's *Shawl* is a response and continuation of the one woven by Celan. An apostrophe to his dead mother, who instilled in him the love of Goethe, his poem mirrors the apostrophic letters of Ozick's Rosa to her daughter and her fixation on her shawl. (2) In *Faust,* the imprisoned near-insane Margarete raves about her dead child as if it were alive and pleads to be allowed to nurse it. Margarete is thus not only the incarnation of German romantic love, she is also a female victim of male brutality and a child murderer haunted by her deed. Associated with the Song of Songs, victimized by forces of evil, and finally reduced to infanticide and madness, Margarete could appear to be a parallel of Rosa as well as her antithesis, were it not for the decisive and colossal difference dividing myth from history, metaphor from victim.

The medium for the coexistence of Margaret and Shulamith, Magda and Rosa, is Paul Celan's German, the medium for the story of *The Shawl* is English, and the medium for Rosa's reentry into the world of the living is Yiddish, through Perksy's gentle insistence and her grandmother's voice. And the medium for prespeech bonding is the shawl itself, not the masculine prayer shawl that it evokes by association but the feminine wimple of the cradle, the swaddling clothes that, like the tallit, also serve as a shroud. As a Jewish-American woman writer, Ozick creates a common ground in her book for her audience and her subjects, for the American readers and the Holocaust survivor protagonists, through a barely remembered mother tongue, Yiddish, and woman's translation of the tallit into the maternal wimple. Stemming from the same Persian root, the word "shawl" is used in German, English, and Yiddish for the same garment. Moreover, the word "shawlgoat," occasionally used interchangeably for "shawl" in earlier periods, refers to a goat that furnishes the wool for shawls. The "tsigele," then, the pure-white little goat in the Yiddish lullabye, can be the source of "the shawl," mother for both Rosa and Magda, and finally, not a child merchant, after all, but a provider of shawls as well as of milk.

And this brings me to my final observation about Ozick's work, namely, the dimension that she brings to this material as a woman writer. Although by now the literature of the Holocaust is voluminous, Elie Wiesel's testimony in *Night* of the murder of a child in Auschwitz remains central in any discussion of this subject, in part because it is witnessed by a child and in part because the adult who remembers interprets this atrocity as the equivalent of the death of God. No image conveys the unspeakable horror more than the murder of children. Wiesel speaks with the authority of the eyewitness; Ozick, moved to write literature about the Holocaust, must do what every fiction writer does—act the ventriloquist for characters of her own making. Faced with an ethical dilemma, the fiction writer must choose either to abstain from all fictional portrayals of the Holocaust (as Philip Roth does repeatedly by invoking the subject and then backing off), or to find a means of conveying Holocaust experience that at the same time conveys awareness of the debate on the subject. D. M. Thomas's deliberate retreat from fictionality in the Babi Yar scene of his novel *The White Hotel,* in which he substitutes the testimony of a survivor of the massacre recorded in Kuznetzov's documentary report, is, according to Thomas, his reluctance to place his own

words in the mouth of a character.[27] Ozick's *The Shawl* is clearly a work informed by this debate, and by the indictment of poetic language in Adorno's by now declaration-turned-axiom "After Auschwitz, it is no longer possible to write poems."[28]

Ozick begins by placing before the reader that searing moment of the death of a child: the death of a daughter witnessed by the mother. The reader is positioned with the mother, sharing the mother's excruciating decision as to which strategy will offer more protection, and then witnessing the failure to protect. The mother, and reader, are left with the first wail of a mute child, that demand addressed to the mother from which the entire verbal universe is spun, the demand for a presence that stems from the first sensibility of absence. The silence preceding the wail, the silence of mother-child preverbal inseparability is transformed, by that one utterance of pain, into the self-inflicted silence of Adorno's dictum, as Rosa muffles her own voice and attempts to swallow her daughter back into her own body by taking the child's muteness into herself. The babel of languages in the second part, the weaving together of a text that offers a variety of languages, each with its own claim to solace or heal, does not displace the wail in Part I. Rosa's spinning out of the letters to Magda stems from her guilt-ridden decision to hear Magda's cry as the moment of her entry into language, thereby intensifying the pain of her failure to save her, and also treating that moment as the first verbal communication of her child addressed to her, which requires a lifetime of reply and denial. The Yiddish lullabye, the maternal legacy denied to Magda, is the melody (and it is as much song as it is lyrics) of the mother tongue that cannot soothe away Magda's wail. By placing us within ear's range of the child's cry and with the shattered mother, Ozick insists on demetaphorizing the language of Holocaust literature. If her subsequent evocation of a Yiddish lullabye, in what is by now nearly a dead language, in a work of Holocaust literature written by an American seems sentimental, it is also a means for that community of readers, two or three generations removed from Eastern Europe, to identify with the Old World culture that was destroyed. And if her evocation of European Jewry's entanglement in the languages and cultures of their annihilators appears to blur the lines dividing Jewish from non-Jewish culture (as in Celan's poetry), it also provides American Jewish readers with another face of that community that is no more. "Then came my tears. I wove the shawl."

Notes

1. For the paradoxes inherent in the Babel story and the double-edged effects of multilingualism, see Jacques Derrida, "Des Tours de Babel," in *Difference in Translation,* ed. Joseph F. Graham (Ithaca: Cornell University Press, 1985).

2. Cynthia Ozick, "America: Toward Yavne," *Judaism* (Summer, 1970), reprinted in *What Is Jewish Literature?*, ed. Hana Wirth-Nesher (Philadelphia: Jewish Publcation Society, 1994), p. 28.

3. For a discussion of Ozick's struggle for historicity and her relation to Jewish memory, see Norman Finkelstein, *The Ritual of New Creation: Jewish Tradition and Contemporary Literature* (Albany: State University of New York Press, 1992).

4. Both Baal-Makhshoves (Isidore Elyashev) and Shmuel Niger have argued that bi- and multilingualism have been intrinsic features of Jewish literature in all periods. See Baal-Makhshoves, "One Literature in Two Languages," trans. Hana Wirth-Nesher and reprinted in *What Is Jewish Literature?* and Niger, *Bilingualism in the History of Jewish Literature,* trans. Joshua Fogel (New York: University Press of America, 1990).

5. For an analysis of poetic strategies of translation within narrative, see Meir Sternberg, "Polylingualism as Reality and Translation as Mimesis," *Poetics Today* 2 (1981), pp. 225-232.

6. Benjamin Harshav has argued that the work of many Yiddish poets in America should be considered a branch of American literature in the introduction to *American Yiddish Poetry: A Bilingual Anthology,* ed. Benjamin and Barbara Harshav (Berkeley: University of California Press, 1986). For discussions of the multilingual aspects of the writings of Henry Roth and of Saul Bellow, see Hana Wirth-Nesher, "Between Mother Tongue and Native Language: Multilingualism in *Call It Sleep*," *Prooftexts: A Journal of Jewish Literary History* 10 (1990), pp. 297-312, and Hana Wirth-Nesher, "'Who's he when he's at home?': Saul Bellow's Translations," in *New Essays on Seize the Day,* ed. Michael Kramer (Cambridge: Cambridge University Press, 1998).

7. Among the many works on this subject, the following have had a significant influence on my own writing: Sidra DeKoven Ezrahi, *By Words Alone: The Holocaust in Literature* (Chicago: University of Chicago Press, 1980); Lawrence Langer, *The Holocaust and the Literary Imagination* (New Haven: Yale University Press, 1975); Alan Mintz, *Hurban: Responses to Catastrophe in Hebrew Literature* (New York: Columbia University Press, 1984); Alvin Rosenfeld, *A Double Dying: Reflections on Holocaust Literature* (Bloomington: Indiana University Press, 1980); David Roskies, *Against the Apocalypse: Responses to Catastrophe in Modern Jewish Culture* (Cambridge: Harvard University Press, 1984).

8. Cynthia Ozick, *The Shawl* (New York: Random House, 1990), copyright page. All further page numbers will be cited in the text.

9. Ozick's sensitivity about representing the sufferings of Holocaust victims is evident in her letter to a survivor reprinted in Sarah Blacher Cohen, *Cynthia Ozick's Comic Art* (Bloomington: Indiana University Press, 1994), p. 148.

Every Jew should feel as if he himself came out of Egypt . . . The Exodus took place 4000 years ago, and yet the Haggadah enjoins me to incorporate it into my own mind and flesh, to so act as if it happened directly and intensely to me, not as mere witness but as participant. Well, if I am enjoined to belong to an event that occurred 4000 years ago, how much more strongly am I obliged to belong to an event that occurred only 40 years ago.

10. Barbara Johnson, "Apostrophe, Animation, and Abortion," in *A World of Difference* (Baltimore: Johns Hopkins University Press, 1987), p. 198.

11. Sarah Blacher Cohen traces the source of this to the account of a devastating narrative of the denial of the maternal instinct in Tadeusz Borowski, *This Way for the Gas, Ladies and Gentlemen,* trans. Barbara Vedder (New York: Penguin, 1976), p. 43.

12. For a detailed analysis of the *Aeneid* as a central intertext in *The Shawl,* see Elaine Kauver, "The Magic Shawl," in *Cynthia Ozick's Fiction* (Bloomington: Indiana University Press, 1993), pp. 197-199.

13. Johnson, p. 187.

14. Julian Tuwim, "We, the Polish Jews . . ." (Fragments) in *Poems of the Ghetto: A Testament of Lost Men,* ed. and with introduction by Adam Gillon (New York: Twayne, 1969), p. 83.

15. Kauver notes that the choice of the name Lublin stresses the fate of Rosa's assimilation. "Originally planned as a reservation for the concentration of Jews by the Nazis, Lublin became one of the centers for mass extermination and was the site of a prisoner of war camp for Jews who had served in the Polish army. The Nazis made no distinction between Jews who abandoned their Jewishness and Jews who celebrated it" (187).

16. Berger suggests that the cinnamon-and-almond flavor evokes the scent of the spices in the decorative box used for the Havdalah service marking the end of the Sabbath; it thereby signifies liturgy as spiritually invigorating. Kauver associates cinnamon and almond with the sacred anointing oil in Scripture and a biblical symbol of divine approval, so that Magda becomes a holy babe for Rosa. I believe that two intertexts are evoked in these two scents: the almonds are obviously an allusion to the Yiddish lullabye "Raisins and Almonds"; the cinnamon is a reference to "The Cin-

namon Shops" by the Polish-Jewish writer Bruno Shultz, murdered by the Nazis and the inspiration for Ozick's novel *Messiah of Stockholm.*

17. Abraham Goldfaden, *Shulamis: oder Bat Yerushalayim* (New York: Hebrew Publishing Company), p. 10 (my translation).

18. Introductory notes for "Rozhinkes mit Mandlen," in *Mir Trogn A Gezang: The New Book of Yiddish Songs,* 4th ed. (New York: Workmen's Circle Education Department, 1982).

19. While Ozick is aware of this tendency in American-Jewish culture generally, her excellent translations of the works of Jacob Glatstein, Chaim Grade, and Dovid Einhorn are proof of her knowledge of and commitment to Yiddish literature. See also her essays on Yiddish literature and on the problems of translation, "Sholem Aleichem's Revolution" and "A Translator's Monologue," in *Metaphor and Memory* (New York: Knopf, 1989), pp. 173-198; 199-208.

20. For an excellent discussion of Celan's multilingual upbringing and its cultural resonances see, "Loss and the Mother Tongue," in John Felstiner, *Paul Celan: Poet, Survivor, Jew* (New Haven: Yale University Press, 1995), pp. 3-22. The cultural significance of linguistic choice in Eastern European Jewish civilization is explored at length in Dan Miron, *A Traveler Disguised: A Study in the Rise of Modern Yiddish Fiction* (New York: Schocken, 1973).

21. Paul Celan, "Death Fugue," Michael Hamburger's translation, in Paul Celan, *Poems,* selected, translated and introduced by Michael Hamburger (New York: Persea Books, 1980), p. 53.

22. Shoshana Felman, *Testimony: Crises of Witnessing in Literature, Psychoanalysis, and History* (New York: Routledge, 1992), p. 32.

23. Cynthia Ozick's Hebrew name is Shoshana. The Hebrew original of "I am the rose of Sharon, the lily of the valleys" is "Ani havazellet hasharon, shoshonat ha'amakim."

24. Felstiner, p. 298.

25. Israel Chalfen, *Einer Biographie seiner Jugend,* 1979, quoted in Katherine Washburn's introduction to *Paul Celan: Last Poems* (San Francisco: North Point Press, 1986), p. vii.

26. Felman, p. 27.

27. For a discussion of this issue, see Hana Wirth-Nesher, "The Ethics of Narration in D. M. Thomas's *White Hotel,*" *Journal of Narrative Technique* (Winter 1985).

28. Theodor Adorno, "After Auschwitz," in *Negative Dialectics,* trans. E. B. Ashton (New York: Continuum, 1973), p. 362. As Langer has noted, "Adorno never intended it to be taken literally as his own elaborations of the principle demonstrate" (see pp. 1-3).

Meisha Rosenberg (essay date spring 1999)

SOURCE: Rosenberg, Meisha. "Cynthia Ozick's Post-Holocaust Fiction: Narration and Morality in the Midrashic Mode." *Journal of the Short Story in English* 32 (spring 1999): 113-27.

[*In the following essay, Rosenberg investigates how Ozick's use of the midrashic mode, which finds its origins in "to search" or "to inquire," allows her to approach the topic of the Holocaust.*]

Cynthia Ozick's writings can be viewed in light of a midrashic mode by virtue of her need to sustain Jewish tradition in the wake of great devastation—the Holocaust. What is the proper mode of representation for an event that is arguably unprecedented, not only in the history of the Jews, but in the history of humankind? Figurative discourse about the Holocaust has experienced considerable objections,[1] haunted as it still is by Theodor Adorno's famous pronouncement that to write poetry after Auschwitz is barbaric. This despite the fact that Adorno later qualified his statement.[2] Writers and artists today are still wary about approaching the subject, for fear that works classified as fiction about the Holocaust will only fuel the arguments of the all-too-prevalent Holocaust deniers.[3] Fiction and art that is not rooted to historical reality can create distortion, saccharin morality tales about the "triumph of the human spirit", and at the worst, obfuscation and denial. One has to be suspect of, for example, a film about the Holocaust titled *Life Is Beautiful.* Life was distinctly *not* beautiful for the great majority of Jewish children that were gassed immediately as they arrived in the concentration camps, if they even made it that far.

However, extreme insistence on historicization is dangerous because it blocks imaginative entry into the event. This insistence privileges survivor testimony over the unwritten works of the dead; this can lead to another, more subtle kind of distortion in which all the stories we hear are from the perspective of those who miraculously lived through the horrors.[4] It is easy to be shuttled emotionally between wanting to stay true to the reality of the Holocaust on the one hand—perhaps limiting one's intake of Holocaust representation to only a select few works of a documentary nature, for example those by Primo Levi, Anne Frank, and Elie Wiesel—and to desire on the other hand departures from the strictures of conventional narrative that confront us with the extreme disjuncture of the Holocaust, for example the highly creative and disturbing cartoon *Maus* by Art Spiegelman.

Arguments on the side of artistic freedom do not necessarily oppose faithfulness to historicity, and it is my goal to point out how the two can and should dovetail. Furthermore, as the number of survivors dwindles, figurative representation becomes an even more important way of continuing to "bear witness"[5]. Fiction about the Holocaust can fill a void in the Jewish literary community left by the millions of stories completely lost to the genocide. Fiction about the Holocaust can go where history cannot, paying tribute to the personal experiences that have been silenced by mass murder.

However, narratives of any kind about the Holocaust—both fiction and nonfiction are susceptible—must not become blind to the realities of the genocide. Ozick's use of the midrashic mode allows her in **The Shawl,** a short book that consists of two linked stories, to fictionally approach the subject of the Holocaust while never forgetting its historical reality.

Ozick's works, in their blending of literature and law, return to a traditional form of Jewish literary and religious inquiry known as midrash. The meaning of the root for the word midrash is "to search" or "to inquire"[6]. Midrash encompasses a vast body of text of distinct periods, beginning about the first to second centuries C.E., when it was transmitted orally by the rabbis in sermons or public teachings. It was only later written down, compiled at different periods and by different editors.[7] Some writings are halakhic (having to do with Jewish civil law and ritual) and others aggadic (meaning allegory, exhortation, legend—in short, figurative expression).[8] Midrash is usually in some way interpretation of Torah, whether it is direct exegesis, homily, or the more creative narrative. The midrashists' project was to create a body of text that could guide the Diaspora after the destruction of the Temple in 70 C.E.

What was created, however, was not a didactic reinscription of Torah, but rather a chorus of rabbinical voices debating, raising questions, and delighting in linguistic play. Because the midrashists could read Torah in Hebrew,[9] they could create linguistically based interpretations in ways that later Christians—because they were dealing with once- or twice-translated text—could not. This allows for, beyond multiplicity of meaning, an almost infinite universe of interpretive departures, all stemming from the intimate interstices of words, letters, even the musical and numerical values of text. In addition, midrash is a practice in which fantasy and figuration are inseparable from context, history, and morality, and it is this nonoppositional approach that is essential in narrating the Holocaust. Daniel Boyarin has done

much to argue that midrash simultaneously breaks and reinscribes tradition through strategies such as quotation—which both interrupts and bridges the source text—and a self-conscious intertextuality[10] that stems from the interpretive philosophy that no text, including the Torah, is created *ex nihilo* by a "self-identical" subject.

In her essay "Bialik's Hint" Ozick explicitly entertains midrash as a way to create a new Jewish literature. She interprets a statement of Chaim Bialik's to mean that aggadah and halachah, the two components of midrash, are fused together,

> The value of Aggadah," he asserts, "is that it issues in Halachah. Aggadah that does not bring Halachah in its train is ineffective." If we pause to translate Aggadah as tale and lore, and Halachah as consensus and law, or Aggadah as the realm of the fancy, and Halachah as the court of duty, then what Bialik proposes next is astonishing. Contrariwise, he says, Halachah can bring Aggadah in its train. Restraint the begetter of poetry? "Is she not"—and now Bialik is speaking of the Sabbath—"a source of life and holiness to a whole nation, and a fountain of inspiration to its singers and poets?"[11]

This statement is central to an understanding of Ozick. She believes that law and morality inspire the imagination. Normally, one would think of "restraint" and law as antithetical to the anomie of creativity, but Ozick asserts the opposite. Like the rabbis who composed midrashim, Ozick allows for what might seem paradoxes to the contemporary mind to flourish.

Some scholars have proposed that **The Shawl** be considered literally as midrash. Joseph Lowin reads **"Rosa"** as a midrashic commentary or gloss on **"The Shawl"**[12]. Joseph Alkana, in an enlightening paper, argues that **The Shawl** is actually a midrash on the story of Abraham's near-sacrifice of Isaac.[13] These readings are insightful and important in adding to our understanding of Ozick's text and the possibilities of post-Holocaust fiction. However, Ozick herself has said that, when it comes to creating a contemporary Jewish literature, midrash alone is not enough, because of its "dependence on a single form." Midrash, she says, usually means "a literature of parable".[14] However, I'd like to propose that we look at midrash not as a single limiting form that demands we read texts as literal midrashim or as parables, but rather as a mode, a way in to a Jewish literature that thrives on dialectics and multiple interpretations.

Midrash is unique in its all-encompassing array of topics—from what one is to do when Pesach falls on the Sabbath and how many goats one man might owe another, to profound questions about suffering. Midrash, in its ability to take in minutiae as well as epistemology, is especially useful as an approach to thinking and writing about the Holocaust, which must be regarded as a historical as well as a philosophical and a personal cataclysm.

The Shawl was actually written in 1977—Ozick said it was her fear of making art out of the Holocaust that prevented her from publishing it.[15] *The Shawl* is a slender book that contains two stories, one titled **"The Shawl,"** the other, **"Rosa,"** both concerning the same character, Rosa Lublin. Already in the fact that the two stories present two different views of the same life we have a midrashic mode of writing.

Ozick tackles the challenge of representing the Holocaust in several ways characteristic of midrash. (1) She uses a compressed narrative voice in **"The Shawl,"** the first of the two stories, that invites the reader, as an active participant, into the text; (2) she draws inspiration from the uncovering of neglected historical perspectives, a move characteristic of midrash, which fuses history and lore; (3) she draws attention to silence as a metaphor, thus allowing for the alternate, radical discourse possibilities that reside outside of her narrative; (4) she creates a symbol, the shawl, that stands for figuration itself and provides a vehicle for the question of how one can figuratively represent the Holocaust; and (5) she narrates the moment of horror in **"The Shawl"**, the first story, from the very human point of view of Rosa, the main character, as a way of simultaneously showing the necessity and the impossibility of portraying the terrors of the Holocaust.

First, as part of her midrashic, liturgical approach[16] Ozick collapses narrative distance in **"The Shawl,"** the first story of the pair, placing the reader inside the experience. Scholar Berel Lang has called for "intransitive writing", a concept of Roland Barthes, in the representation of the Holocaust, a modernist form that attempts to close up the distance between reader, writer, and characters. Lang uses the Passover Haggadah—large parts of which are actually midrash—as an example of intransitive writing. In the Haggadah Jews are called upon to retell the events of the Exodus as though they had been there themselves.

As with the intransitive voice, in **"The Shawl"** the reader finds herself plunged into the very real, harsh world of the camps without a friendly interpreter. This is how it should be. The lack of verbs and severely elliptical structure[17] creates an overwhelming feeling of powerlessness. The first sentences of the story are not complete sentences and are posed as an unasked question:

> Stella, cold, cold, the coldness of hell. How they walked on the roads together, Rosa with Magda curled up between sore breasts, Magda wound up in the shawl.[18]

The asyndeton of the first sentence is followed by the periodic phrase "how they walked on", which, contrary to expectation, does not end with a question mark. The

question of how they walked on—and how they suffered—can barely be asked and cannot be answered. The midrash Lamentations Rabbah relates that three important prophets began prophesies with the word "how": Moses, Isaiah, and Jeremiah.[19] This is a very important word used to address the people of Israel in times of crisis. The very first word of the book of Lamentations is "how," in Hebrew, *Eikhah,* which Chaim Raphael points out has a "mournful ring, like 'alack,' or 'woe.'"[20] The first line of the book of Lamentations reads, "How lonely sits the city that was full of people!" (Lam. 1:1.) Raphael also notes that the first word of a book of Torah is often referred to by its first word, so in this case, "How" stands in synechdochally for the entire book of Lamentations. In the Midrash on Lamentations, it is written that "R. Eleazar said, 'The word is made up of two syllables, which read individually mean 'where is the 'thus'?'"[21] If we pause at R. Eleazar's contribution, we gain considerable insight into Ozick's use of the word. It mourns and asks the ultimate question, "where is the 'thus?'"; in other words, where is the meaning to this horror? Simply: Why did this happen?

The rhetorical device of periodicity in **"The Shawl"** causes the reader to anticipate this unanswerable question. **"The Shawl"** is marked by incomplete sentences, as in "One mite of a tooth tip sticking up in the bottom gum, how shining, an elfin tombstone of white marble gleaming there" and "The little round head. Such a good child, she gave up screaming, and sucked now only for the taste of the drying nipple itself".[22] The narrative of **"The Shawl"** is also marked by a verbless poetic rhythm punctuated by the occasional exclamation.[23] "Staccato phrases"[24] are joined by semicolons in a chainlike construction that is more like constriction, as in the line "There was not enough milk; sometimes Magda sucked air; then she screamed."[25]

"The Shawl" may well approximate Lang's definition of the "intransitive voice"; however, there are problems with this approach. Even assuming **"The Shawl"** is an example of the intransitive voice, how does this, or a midrashically informed literature for that matter, ensure a moral, non-mythopoeticizing[26] literature of the Holocaust? One can't help thinking that, while Jews in America were reciting Haggadah—an example of Midrash and of intransitive writing—in Europe the very kind of thing this recitation admonishes against was occurring. Intransitive writing, indeed any prescribed literary form, is no guarantee that the reader will avoid the mistakes of "mytho-poeticization" and immorality. Many writers and critics have expressed dismay at the fact that the Holocaust occurred in one of the most literate cultures of the time.[27]

Rather than adhering to a formula for representation, one must, as a writer of Holocaust literature, insist on bringing to light the contradictions of language itself.

What comes close to describing how Ozick does this in "The Shawl" is Jean-François Lyotard's description of the warping of language that occurred as a result of the concentration camps' denial of the pronoun "we." The command given by the Nazis to the Jews "to die", he says, did not allow for any comprehensible relationship between addressee and addressor. The assumptions of discourse have been challenged at their foundations.

Indeed: "where is the 'thus'?" Therefore, as we grapple with the Holocaust we must struggle in the realm of language and representation. Lyotard defends the position that the Holocaust, in addition to being a historical reality, must be considered an "experience of language." One cannot write about the Holocaust adequately without addressing the instabilities of language.

In "The Shawl," to use Lyotard's phrase, "Auschwitz has no name." There are no last names in the story, no direct references to the Holocaust as such, nor mentions of German or Jew. But, as Lyotard also says, "One must . . . speak"[28], and this is the tragic paradox of victims of the Holocaust, for whom it often feels impossible to speak of their experience at the same time that it is essential.[29]

The second, and a crucial tactic Ozick uses to represent the Holocaust without mytho-poeticizing is to stay true to the historical facts.[30] She wrote *The Shawl* upon reading a historical work: William Shirer's *Rise and Fall of the Third Reich,* which described the Nazi practice of throwing babies against electrical fences. Another source was a conversation with Jerzy Kozinski, in which the two writers discussed the reality of those assimilated Jews who were not "shtetl Jews" yet suffered the same fate. In this way, the genesis of the pair of stories results from bringing to light historical reality.

Further, Ozick places the two stories chronologically—first is "The Shawl" and World War II, and then "Rosa" in contemporary Miami. This is a choice that emphasizes historicity and creates tension with Rosa's need, in "Rosa" for the creation of an elaborate fantasy life in which she imagines Magda still alive. One might argue that the two stories stand dialectically opposed, because while "The Shawl," with its spare narrative style and minimalist use of language and detail might stand for historical representation, "Rosa", with its more colorful array of characters, place, fantasy, and allusions, could stand for figurative representation.

However the two stories are too intertwined for such a simplistic assignment. One could also argue, conversely, that because the story "Rosa" takes place in an identifiable time and culture, it stands for historicity, while "The Shawl", with its abbreviated structure and poetically informed disruptive tropes stands for figuration.

In actuality, each story contains within its center—like a mother with child—the other story. Rosa does not admit to herself the story of "The Shawl" until the end of "Rosa", the second story. In this way, we as readers are left, not with "Rosa", but with the first story, "The Shawl", and the Holocaust. So it is not a linear, evolutionary history we are left with. The two stories inform one another in a narrative circle, and thus emphasize that the Holocaust, while it must first and foremost be remembered as history, must also allow for figuration.

In a third midrashic strategy, Ozick uses silence and muteness to symbolize the unspeakability of the crimes of the Holocaust. By pointing a textual arrow to silence, Ozick allows for the radical unspeakability of suffering that lies outside her text.[31] The matter of silence and speech is a leitmotif in *The Shawl,* as in midrash, where rabbis confront the silences to Torah. Rosa is preoccupied by her baby Magda's muteness, and the child's expression when she can't find her shawl is a primal scream. Her wail is the ultimate, prelingual expression of the horrors of the Holocaust. Ozick makes this inarticulate cry Magda's only direct speech by way of entertaining the possibility that this is the only true way to represent the horror of the premeditated genocide. At the end of the story, Rosa stifles her own scream using Magda's shawl, leaving us with a deafening silence.

The shawl itself is, as a physical object for stifling cries, a chronic reminder of silence in both its harmful and its comforting manifestations. Using the shawl as her central symbol is the fourth, and most straightforwardly midrashic, strategy, because the object of the shawl comes to resemble the signifiers of so many Jewish traditions.

For Rosa the shawl is a "magic" shawl, reminiscent of the miraculous oil of the *hannukiah,* because it could "nourish an infant for three days and three nights." It smells of Magda's "cinnamon and almond" saliva, perhaps a reference to "the *besamim* which Jews sniff at the end of the Sabbath"[32]. The "cinnamon and almond" smell is also a midrashic link to a famous Yiddish song, *Rozhinkes mit Mandlen* (Raisins and Almonds) that in referenced in the story "Rosa"[33]. The shawl additionally represents the Jewish prayer shawl, or *tallis.* So in this way, the shawl now also takes on the extra-heavy weight of signifying belief in God, or at least a wish to believe in God. As Magda's transitional object, it represents the child's first attempt to project self onto the world outside the mother. As such, the shawl represents the child's first imaginative act.[34] The shawl is additionally a fake shroud for Magda, and a symbol for the death all around them. Because the shawl is a conduit for so many, contradictory symbols, it begins to stand for figuration itself. It is through her creation of a symbol for figuration that Ozick is able to engage the question of how to represent the Holocaust.

Magda is hidden underneath the shawl and doubly hidden under Rosa's clothing. She is additionally hidden in her "Aryan" features. When Rosa stops lactating, Magda turns to the shawl, also a symbol for the breast, which she "milks"[35]. The shawl is like the placenta, a powerful image of motherhood's sole creative power. Rosa, distancing herself from fellow Jews, begins to see herself as a kind of Virgin Mary and Magda as the child of an immaculate conception, although as we learn later Rosa was raped by a Nazi.

Because of the illogical and inflated symbolism enforced by the Nazis, the shawl obtains a too-powerful control over Magda's fate. It is at this point that Ozick deals with the most difficult task of representing the Holocaust: that of directly showing her readers the horror of the genocide. In my argument, her fifth strategy is to narrate this charged moment through Rosa's point of view, and thereby show us two alternate pictures of the atrocity. Ozick deliberately problematizes this moment. For a Holocaust representation not to become a soothing story of the "triumph of the human spirit" the artist must, within the work itself, raise and confront the question of how one can represent unimaginable atrocity.

When Magda runs out to find the shawl that Stella, Rosa's neice, has stolen, Rosa is faced with an impossible decision. Rosa decides to do the only thing she can do; she tries to retrieve the shawl and then find Magda. When Magda totters out in search of her stolen shawl, she is seen by an SS guard, who is described only in metonyms:

> But the shoulder that carried Magda was not coming toward Rosa and the shawl, it was drifting away, the speak of Magda was moving more and more into the smoky distance. Above the shoulder a helmet glinted. The light tapped the helmet and sparkled it into a goblet. Below the helmet a black body like a domino and a pair of black boots hurled themselves in the direction of the electrified fence. The electric voices began to chatter wildly.[36]

Magda's actual moment of death is described in the passive voice. The Nazi is signified by a helmet. The sun turns the helmet into a goblet—a primitive drinking vessel. A goblet is also a religious item, and here we see Rosa begin to aestheticize this horrifying moment. The black boots "hurled themselves." German agency in the Holocaust is a medusa, impossible to look directly in the face. The most disturbing and powerful element of the story is the following description of Magda's death:

> All at once Magda was swimming through the air. The whole of Magda traveled through loftiness. She looked like a butterfly touching a silver vine.[37]

This is the moment of horror in "The Shawl." Is the description "a butterfly" an aestheticization of the Holocaust? Or does it describe an ascension to heaven? This moment is suspended in the text as Magda is suspended above ground. Human comprehension cannot pass beyond this moment of suspension. We know that Magda cannot possibly fit into this image because of the con-

sciously mixed metaphor, "swimming" through "air." Rosa, as we begin to see, is flawed, that is to say, she is a human being, who imagines, instead of death, that her daughter has become a butterfly.[38] It is this emphasis on the failure of human comprehension that returns us to a midrashic mode in which Jews are constantly striving and yet never succeeding at apprehending God.[39]

We do not find out in **"The Shawl"** whether or not Rosa will die, and this is an important omission. As at least one possible "ending" for the story cycle, **"The Shawl"** leaves us with the possibility of death or worse than death for its main character, and this—as well as the undeniable presence of silence as a force in the story—makes a strong argument for fiction that represents the experiences of those who didn't survive, or those who survived too damaged to tell their own stories.[40]

Although I do not have the space here to discuss **"Rosa"**, the second story of the volume, in full, I will say that it continues to operate in the midrashic mode, yet by way of entirely differing narrative strategies. Departing from the elliptical style of **"The Shawl"**, Rosa is given, to borrow a phrase from Isaac Bashevis Singer, an "address"—a place in time and culture. **"Rosa"** operates midrashically by constructing a dialogue between Rosa and Simon Persky, who take the sides of alternately, "truth" and "lying," or "history", and "fiction."

In conclusion, Ozick uses many midrashic techniques in order to tackle the task of representing the Holocaust figuratively. The Holocaust presents a radical loss and disjunction from Judaic theology, culture, traditions, and language itself. Attempting to rebuild a shattered culture, writers like Ozick and others must reach back to traditions like midrash, which, because it is open-ended, invites us into its infinite world of interpretations, profound questionings, and paradox.

Notes

1. Lawrence Langer's book *Preempting the Holocaust* still maintains a position of strict adherence to "literalist," unsentimentalized treatments of the Holocaust. As well he should, he argues vociferously against the works of Judy Chicago and Tzvetan Todorov, among others, who attempt to draw out of the Holocaust a watered-down moral lesson that caters to a contemporary American fad of victimization. Langer insists that, to try to comprehend the Holocaust, one must "start with an unbuffered collision with its starkest crimes." Langer, Lawrence, *Preempting the Holocaust* (New Haven: Yale University Press, 1999) 1. Langer's tactic is to present the reader with the most horrific details told by survivors, in order to strike home his point that no "ideals" can be supported by atrocities such as a German ripping a baby in half in front of its mother, or Jews being boiled alive in acid.

I fully support Langer's criticism of those who use the Holocaust to support an agenda of political correctness or universalism that *departicularizes* suffering. However, there is a danger in insisting, so forcefully as Langer does, decontextualized narratives of atrocity on the reader. Such a tactic threatens to 1) rob documentary narratives of their full implications and context and 2) duplicate the cruelty of the Nazis without providing a foundation of morality from which to condemn their crimes. As Jurek Becker, a survivor and fiction writer says, "What is the reason for meeting and remembering that fifty years ago the Nazis burned books? Just for remembrance? That's not enough for me. I am not interested in these memories; they are not so great—I can imagine better memories. . . . The only important and good reason to remember is to ask ourselves what attitude was behind that happening, and where do we find that attitude today?" From *Art out of Agony,* Lewis, Stephen (Toronto: CBC Enterprises, 1984) 101-102.

Berel Lang, another scholar wary of figurative representation, insists on "deference to the conventions of historical discourse as a literary means" (*Act and Idea in the Nazi Genocide* (Chicago: University of Chicago Press, 1990) 135) in representation of the Holocaust. He posits that historical chronology is the "point zero" of narrative, both historical and figurative, recognizing that in most all historical representations—even chronologies—lie elements of figuration and narrative. "The Representation of Limits," in *Probing the Limits of Representation,* ed. Saul Friedlander (Cambridge: Harvard University Press, 1992) 307.

Hayden White modifies Lang's position, arguing that "What all this suggests is that modernist modes of representation may offer possiblities of representing the reality of both the Holocaust and the experience of it that no other version of realism could do." From "Historical Emplotment and the Problem of Truth," in *Probing the Limits of Representation,* ed. Saul Friedlander. While I agree with White that to construct an artificial opposition between history and figuration is problematic, I find his solution (that is, modernist writing in the "intransitive" or "middle" voice) equally troubling, because insisting on modernism, a particularly secular, Western creation, still limits Holocaust representation. I start from the other end of the argument—why *begin* with the assumption that limitations on representation are necessary? I take White's inclusion of fiction into Lang's model further to suggest that figurative language fulfills a particular task in representation unfulfilled by "objective" historical representation.

2. Lang, "The Representation of Limits," 317.

3. Sara R. Horowitz notes that "To protect their respective projects from the kind of assaults mounted by historical deniers, and to assert the truth claims of their work to an uninitiated readership, [Art] Spiegelman [author of the cartoon/documentary *Maus*] and [Claude] Lanzmann [filmmaker of *Shoah*] insist upon the "nonfictionality" of Holocaust art." Horowitz, Sara R., *Voicing the Void: Muteness and Memory in Holocaust Fiction* (Albany: State University of New York Press, 1997) 12.

4. Of course, there also exist works that somehow survived that were authored by those who did not, in the most obvious example, the *Diary of Anne Frank.* However the fact remains that once she was deported her voice was silenced. As I later suggest, perhaps this loud silence is the most powerful tribute to the dead.

5. Alan L. Berger makes an important distinction between "witnessing" and "bearing witness": "[Elie] Wiesel, the best known and most widely read witnessing writer, now emphasizes that the next generation must bear witness." "Bearing Witness: Theological Implications of Second-Generation Literature in America," in *Breaking Crystal: Writing and Memory after Auschwitz,* ed. Efraim Sicher (Urbana: University of Illinois Press, 1998) 259.

6. Hartman, Geoffrey H., and Budick, Sanford, eds., *Midrash and Literature,* (New Haven: Yale University Press, 1986) 363.

7. Midrash, as Barry W. Holtz points out, is usually seen as falling under three categories: the exegetical (interpretive), the homiletical (based on sermons), and the narratival (the most creative category, often stories or "re-written" Torah). There is no one "Midrash," as Holtz relates, but rather collections of midrashim compiled over the centuries, beginning as early as the second century C.E. The "flowering" of midrash is considered to have been from 400 to 1200 C.E. From Holtz, Barry W., "Midrash," in *Back to the Sources: Reading the Classic Jewish Texts,* ed. Barry W. Holtz (New York: Summit Books, 1984) 177-211.

8. Hartman and Budick, 363.

9. Dan, Joseph, "Midrash and the Dawn of Kabbalah," *Midrash and Literature,* ed. Geoffrey H. Hartman and Sanford Budick (New Haven: Yale University Press, 1986) 128. Joseph Dan points out that the rabbis used, as tools for interpretation, the shapes, sounds, musical signs, decorative flourishes, frequency, and the numerical values of letters and words, among many other non-ideonic exegetical techniques.

10. Boyarin, Daniel, Intertextuality and the Reading of Midrash (Bloomington: Indiana University Press, 1990).

11. Ozick, Cynthia, "Bialik's Hint," Metaphor and Memory (New York: Alfred A. Knopf, 1989) 228.

12. Lowin, Joseph, *Cynthia Ozick* (Boston: G. K. Hall & Co., 1988) 109.

13. Alkana, Joseph, "'Do We Not Know the Meaning of Aesthetic Gratification?': Cynthia Ozick's The Shawl, The Akedah, and the Ethics of Holocaust Literary Aesthetics," *Modern Fiction Studies* 43:4 (1997) 963-990.

14. Ozick, "Bialik's Hint," 238.

15. Heron, Kim, "'I Required a Dawning,'" *New York Times Book Review*, 1989.

16. For discussions of the liturgical nature of Ozick's writing, see Gottfried, Amy, "Fragmented Art and the Liturgical Community of the Dead in Cynthia Ozick's *The Shawl*," *Studies in American Jewish Literature*, 13 (1994) 39-51; Rose, Elisabeth, "Cynthia Ozick's Liturgical Postmodernism: *The Messiah of Stockholm*," *Studies in American Jewish Literature*, 9:1 (1990) 93-107; and by Ozick herself, "Toward a New Yiddish," in *Art and Ardor*, (New York: E. P. Dutton, 1983) 151-177.

17. Kauvar, Elaine, *Cynthia Ozick's Fiction: Tradition and Invention* (Bloomington: Indiana University Press, 1993) 180.

18. Ozick, Cynthia, "The Shawl," *The Shawl* (New York: Random House, Inc., 1990) 1.

19. *Lamentations Rabbah: An Analytical Translation,* ed. Neusner, Jacob (Atlanta: Scholars Press, 1989) Lamentations I:1, Parashah XXXV.i. A, p. 108.

20. Raphael, Chaim, *The Walls of Jerusalem: An Excursion into Jewish History* (New York: Alfred A. Knopf, 1968) 92.

21. *Lamentations Rabbah,* ed. Neusner, Parashah XXXV.ii.B, p. 109.

22. Ozick, "The Shawl," 4. Later in the text is another example of a period phrase, or sentence, prefaced by the word "how": "How far Magda was from Rosa now, across the whole square, past a dozen barracks, all the way on the other side!" In this case, the question mark has been replaced by an exclamation mark, meant to denote the extremity of her distance and her situation.

23. Examples of these exclamations are "Again!" (8); also Magda's utterance, "'Maaaa . . . aaa!'" (8) Ozick, *The Shawl.*

24. Klingenstein, Susanne, "Destructive Intimacy: The Shoah between Mother and Daughter in Fictions by Cynthia Ozick, Norma Rosen, and Rebecca Goldstein," *Studies in American Jewish Literature* 11:2 (1992) 162-173. Klingenstein points out how the incomplete sentences and thought fragments in "Rosa," when Rosa receives the shawl and recalls her dead daughter, taken together, form a poem.

25. Ozick, "The Shawl," 1. For another example of these asyndetonic, chainlike sentences, see especially Rosa's interior monologue when she comes close to what might almost be hope as Magda utters her first sound in a long time: "Rosa believed that something had gone wrong with her vocal cords, her windpipe, with the cave of her larynx; Magda was defective, without a voice; perhaps she was deaf; there might be something amiss with her intelligence; Magda was dumb." Ozick, "The Shawl," 7.

26. Kim Heron.

27. Sara Horowitz points out that "The flourishing of atrocity among a highly literate people particularly disturbs [George] Steiner, undermining his trust altogether in the literary endeavor." *Voicing the Void,* 19.

28. Lyotard, Jean-François, "Discussions, or Phrasing, After Auschwitz," *The Lyotard Reader,* ed. Andrew Benjamin (Cambridge, MA: Basil Blackwell, Inc., 1989) 1.

29. Primo Levi has spoken of this; and Elie Wiesel, despite his dedication to bearing witness, has expressed its impossibility. See *A Double Dying: Reflections on Holocaust Literature,* Alvin H. Rosenfeld (Bloomington: Indiana University Press, 1980) 14, 28. Sara Horowitz sums it up well: "At the heart of Holocaust narrative resides an essential contradiction: an impossibility to express the experience, coupled with a psychological and moral obligation to do so." Horowitz, 16.

30. That Ozick draws on historical references is not to say that she privileges historicity, as Berel Lang does (interpreting it to mean realism and therefore morality), over figuration. "For me," says Ozick, deconstructing this opposition between morality and imagination, "with certain rapturous exceptions, literature *is* the moral life." "Innovation and Redemption: What Literature Means," *Art and Ardor,* (New York: E. P. Dutton, 1983) 245.

31. Horowitz writes that Holocaust fiction has been marked by a "tropological muteness." (29) She is also one of the few critical voices to argue outright for the necessity of fiction about the Holocaust, saying "For it is the absent story made present by radical imagining that confronts the mass murder." (14) She also notes that in some ways, fictional representation is ahead of critical discourse when it comes to apprehending issues of Holocaust representation. (29)

32. Berger, Alan, *Crisis and Covenant: The Holocaust in American Jewish Fiction,* quoted in Gottfried, Amy, "Fragmented Art and the Liturgical Community of the Dead in Cynthia Ozick's The Shawl," *Studies in American Jewish Literature* 13 (1994) 46.

33. Wirth-Nesher, Hana, "The Languages of Memory: Cynthia Ozick's *The Shawl*," in *Multilingual America: Transnationalism, Ethnicity, and the Languages of American Literature,* ed. Werner Sollors (New York: New York University Press, 1998) 320. Wirth-Nesher points out a fascinating link between, among other texts, "Todesfuge," by Paul Celan (the epigraph of *The Shawl)* and *Rozhinkes mit Mandlen.* This would further suggest that there exists an intertextual and therefore midrashic relationship between Ozick's *The Shawl* and many other, primarily Jewish-centered narratives. One might posit that the lines of Celan's poem that appear as epigraph serve as the proof-text for Ozick's midrash.

34. Drawing on theories of Lacan, Wirth-Nesher has pointed out that Magda's first words, ""Maaaa—" constitute the ultimate demand the child makes to the mother "out of which the entire verbal universe is spun." Lacan as quoted by Wirth-Nesher, "The Languages of Memory," 317.

35. Wirth-Nesher among others identifies the shawl as shroud (323), and by extension, death. The shawl stands for both life and death.

36. Ozick, "The Shawl," 9.

37. Ozick, "The Shawl," 9.

38. Ozick, "The Shawl," 8.

39. This is arguably the central tenet of the Jewish religion, i.e., that human beings cannot apprehend God in any direct manner; hence the need for an infinity of interpretation.

40. Documentary testimonies are crucial, and in fact there would be little fictional representation worth mentioning without them. Some liken documentary testimonies to Torah and, by extension, "second-generation" literature, to midrash. To be sure, the story "The Shawl" is midrashically linked to documentary narratives like those of Primo Levi and Aharon Appelfeld. However, to ascribe sacredness to texts that document atrocity is to invite sacralization of the Holocaust itself, a dangerous proposition indeed. Instead of sacralizing Rosa's experience in the camp, *The Shawl* points to the flawed humanness of Rosa as a character, and thereby negates our ability to mythologize her or commit idolatry. Humanizing her also prevents the dangerous opposition we might pose between "strong" survivor and "weak" victim, an ideological system too closely linked with Nazi hierarchies. Any figurative representation that does not somehow pay tribute to documentary narratives and/or problematize the relationship between documentary and artistic representation is liable to stumble into the murky waters of denial.

Darryl Hattenhauer, Shay McCool, and P. K. McMahon (essay date summer 1999)

SOURCE: Hattenhauer, Darryl, Shay McCool, and P. K. McMahon. "Ozick's *The Shawl*." *The Explicator* 57, no. 4 (summer 1999): 238-9.

[*In the following essay, Hattenhauer, McCool, and McMahon, in a close reading of the "The Shawl"'s conclusion, suggest that a complex reading is more appropriate than a simplistic one.*]

Critics have pondered the indeterminate plot resolution of Cynthia Ozick's **"The Shawl,"** which ends with a Nazi throwing an infant onto an electrified fence. Many critics contend that the murder is affirmative because the infant's death somehow surmounts the suffering of the Holocaust—that her death saves the infant Magda from further suffering, or that her death delivers others from suffering. For example Amy Gottfried claims that Ozick "grants the most powerless of victims a final moment of transcendence [. . .]" (42).

Indeed, some of the air imagery suggests transcendence. Rosa, Magda's mother, seems like an angel. She feels "light, like someone in a faint [. . .] someone who is already a floating angel [. . .] in the air" (33). When Rosa chases after the wandering Magda, Rosa is so light that she can fly: "Rosa [. . .] flew—she could fly, she was only air—into the arena" (34). Magda is even more angelic. With her blonde hair, blue eyes, and fair skin, she is the typical image of an angel. Her hair is like feathers, and her breath smells like almonds and cinnamon. The narrator repeatedly compares Magda to a butterfly and a moth.

But all of this imagery is bitterly ironic. A butterfly has already gone through its metamorphosis. And like a moth, she is headed for a flame. Much of the air imagery indicates that the prisoners will end up in a crematorium. For example, the air of the camp is an "ash-stippled wind" carrying "a bitter fatty floating smoke." But more important, the air imagery symbolizes starvation. Women and children are drying up and floating away. Rosa and Stella are "slowly turning into air" (33). The starving Magda's belly is "balloonish," "air-fed," and "fat with air" (33-34). Because of malnutrition—or rather no nutrition at all—Magda's laugh is silent, "only the air-blown showing of her teeth" (33).

The arguments in favor of the murder as transcendent simply deflect its horror. For example, Margot Martin claims that "as Magda hits the fence, in a sense the soldier has freed her from her bondage to enjoy immortality [. . .] and possibly to cross into that beautiful world beyond the fence" (35). But to speak of Magda as immortal or transformed is to subscribe to an extreme idealism in both the philosophical and ordinary sense. Whereas in Flannery O'Connor's fiction the murdered are not victims because their killers inadvertently transform their victims and thereby save them for everlasting life, Magda may go to heaven, but not because of her victimization. In an argument similar to Martin's, Gottfried claims that Ozick "centers her text upon a transformative motif [. . .]" (42) and wonders if "Magda's metaphoric transformation into a butterfly [is] a gift of redemption for those who suffered in the Holocaust" (43). Perhaps some of those who survived the Holocaust can, in some sense, be redeemed. But in what sense could the death of one more infant redeem the others? Gottfried goes on to say, "This graceful death signifies an instant of transcendence." But the gracefulness is in Ozick's prose. The scene is hideous, with no gracefulness to be found. How can an infant be graceful when being electrocuted? Gottfried adds that "Ozick creates a character who refuses to be 'assimilated' into the role of Holocaust victim [. . .]" (43). But to imply that anyone, much less an infant, can refuse to be victimized by the Holocaust is to vaporize the Holocaust into thin air.

Elsewhere Ozick writes, "The so-called 'affirmative' is simpleminded, single-minded, crudely explicit; it belongs either to journalism or to piety or to 'uplift.' It is the enemy of literature and the friend of coercion" ("Lesson" 295). Ozick's statement characterizes her story's attitude toward anti-Semitism, the Holocaust, and infanticide.

Works Cited

Gottfried, Amy. "Fragmented Art and the Liturgical Community of the Dead in Cynthia Ozick's *The Shawl*." *Studies in American Jewish Literature* 13 (1994): 39-51.

Martin, Margot L. "The Themes of Survival in Cynthia Ozick's 'The Shawl.'" *Re Artes: Liberales* 14 (1988): 31-36.

Ozick, Cynthia. "The Lesson of the Master." *Art and Ardor: Essays.* 1983. New York: Dutton, 1984.

———. "The Shawl." *The New Yorker* 26 (May 1980): 33-34.

FURTHER READING

Criticism

Friedman, Lawrence S. "*Bloodshed and Three Novellas* and *The Shawl: A Story and a Novella*." In *Understanding Cynthia Ozick,* pp. 88-121. Columbia: University of South Carolina Press, 1991.
    Investigates Holocaust imagery and representations of Holocaust survivors.

Rosen, Alan. "The Specter of Eloquence: Reading the Survivor's Voice." In *Celebrating Elie Wiesel: Stories, Essays, Reflections,* edited by Alan Rosen, pp. 41-56. Notre Dame: University of Notre Dame Press, 1998.
    Rosen compares the use of early and late testimony in Art Spiegelman's *Maus* to Ozick's *Rosa*.

Yalom, Marilyn. "Cynthia Ozick's Paradoxical Wisdom." In *People of the Book: Thirty Scholars Reflect on Their Jewish Identity,* edited by Jeffrey Rubin-Dorsky and Shelley Fisher Fishkin, pp. 427-38. Madison: University of Wisconsin Press, 1996.
    Yalom examines the complexity of Ozick's representation of the Jewish experience.

Additional coverage of Ozick's life and career is contained in the following sources published by the Gale Group: *American Writers Supplement,* Vol. 5; *Bestsellers,* 1990:1; *Contemporary Authors,* Vols. 17-20R; *Contemporary Authors New Revision Series,* Vols. 23, 58; *Contemporary Literary Criticism,* Vols. 3, 7, 28, 62, 155; *Contemporary Novelists,* Ed. 7; *Contemporary Popular Writers*; *Dictionary of Literary Biography,* Vols. 28, 152; *Dictionary of Literary Biography Yearbook,* 1982; *DISCovering Authors Modules: Novelists* and *Popular Fiction and Genre Authors*; *DISCovering Authors 3.0;Exploring Short Stories*; *Literature Resource Center*; *Major 20th-Century Writers,* Eds. 1, 2; *Reference Guide to American Literature,* Ed. 4; *Reference Guide to Short Fiction,* Ed. 2; *Short Stories for Students,* Vols. 3, 12; and *Short Story Criticism,* Vol. 15.

How to Use This Index

CMW = *St. James Guide to Crime & Mystery Writers*
CN = *Contemporary Novelists*
CP = *Contemporary Poets*
CPW = *Contemporary Popular Writers*
CSW = *Contemporary Southern Writers*
CWD = *Contemporary Women Dramatists*
CWP = *Contemporary Women Poets*
CWRI = *St. James Guide to Children's Writers*
CWW = *Contemporary World Writers*
DA = *DISCovering Authors*
DA3 = *DISCovering Authors 3.0*
DAB = *DISCovering Authors: British Edition*
DAC = *DISCovering Authors: Canadian Edition*
DAM = *DISCovering Authors: Modules*
   DRAM: Dramatists Module; MST: Most-studied Authors Module;
   MULT: Multicultural Authors Module; NOV: Novelists Module;
   POET: Poets Module; POP: Popular Fiction and Genre Authors Module
DFS = *Drama for Students*
DLB = *Dictionary of Literary Biography*
DLBD = *Dictionary of Literary Biography Documentary Series*
DLBY = *Dictionary of Literary Biography Yearbook*
DNFS = *Literature of Developing Nations for Students*
EFS = *Epics for Students*
EXPN = *Exploring Novels*
EXPP = *Exploring Poetry*
EXPS = *Exploring Short Stories*
EW = *European Writers*
FANT = *St. James Guide to Fantasy Writers*
FW = *Feminist Writers*
GFL = *Guide to French Literature,* Beginnings to 1789, 1798 to the Present
GLL = *Gay and Lesbian Literature*
HGG = *St. James Guide to Horror, Ghost & Gothic Writers*
HW = *Hispanic Writers*
IDFW = *International Dictionary of Films and Filmmakers: Writers and Production Artists*
IDTP = *International Dictionary of Theatre: Playwrights*
LAIT = *Literature and Its Times*
LAW = *Latin American Writers*
JRDA = *Junior DISCovering Authors*
MAICYA = *Major Authors and Illustrators for Children and Young Adults*
MAICYAS = *Major Authors and Illustrators for Children and Young Adults Supplement*
MAWW = *Modern American Women Writers*
MJW = *Modern Japanese Writers*
MTCW = *Major 20th-Century Writers*
NCFS = *Nonfiction Classics for Students*
NFS = *Novels for Students*
PAB = *Poets: American and British*
PFS = *Poetry for Students*
RGAL = *Reference Guide to American Literature*
RGEL = *Reference Guide to English Literature*
RGSF = *Reference Guide to Short Fiction*
RGWL = *Reference Guide to World Literature*
RHW = *Twentieth-Century Romance and Historical Writers*
SAAS = *Something about the Author Autobiography Series*
SATA = *Something about the Author*
SFW = *St. James Guide to Science Fiction Writers*
SSFS = *Short Stories for Students*
TCWW = *Twentieth-Century Western Writers*
WLIT = *World Literature and Its Times*
WP = *World Poets*
YABC = *Yesterday's Authors of Books for Children*
YAW = *St. James Guide to Young Adult Writers*

Literary Criticism Series
Cumulative Author Index

Author Index

Berger, Thomas (Louis) 1924- .. **CLC 3, 5, 8, 11, 18, 38**
See also BPFB 1; CA 1-4R; CANR 5, 28, 51; CN 7; DAM NOV; DLB 2; DLBY 1980; EWL 3; FANT; INT CANR-28; MTCW 1, 2; RHW; TCWW 2

Bergman, (Ernst) Ingmar 1918- ...... **CLC 16, 72**
See also CA 81-84; CANR 33, 70; DLB 257; MTCW 2

Bergson, Henri(-Louis) 1859-1941 . **TCLC 32**
See also CA 164; EW 8; EWL 3; GFL 1789 to the Present

Bergstein, Eleanor 1938- .... **CLC 4**
See also CA 53-56; CANR 5

Berkeley, George 1685-1753 .... **LC 65**
See also DLB 31, 101, 252

Berkoff, Steven 1937- .... **CLC 56**
See also CA 104; CANR 72; CBD; CD 5

Berlin, Isaiah 1909-1997 .... **TCLC 105**
See also CA 162; 85-88

Bermant, Chaim (Icyk) 1929-1998 ... **CLC 40**
See also CA 57-60; CANR 6, 31, 57, 105; CN 7

Bern, Victoria
See Fisher, M(ary) F(rances) K(ennedy)

Bernanos, (Paul Louis) Georges
1888-1948 .... **TCLC 3**
See also CA 130; 104; CANR 94; DLB 72; EWL 3; GFL 1789 to the Present; RGWL 2, 3

Bernard, April 1956- .... **CLC 59**
See also CA 131

Berne, Victoria
See Fisher, M(ary) F(rances) K(ennedy)

Bernhard, Thomas 1931-1989 ..... **CLC 3, 32, 61; DC 14**
See also CA 127; 85-88; CANR 32, 57; CD-WLB 2; DLB 85, 124; EWL 3; MTCW 1; RGWL 2, 3

Bernhardt, Sarah (Henriette Rosine)
1844-1923 .... **TCLC 75**
See also CA 157

Bernstein, Charles 1950- .... **CLC 142,**
See also CA 129; CAAS 24; CANR 90; CP 7; DLB 169

Berriault, Gina 1926-1999 .... **CLC 54, 109; SSC 30**
See also CA 185; 129; 116; CANR 66; DLB 130; SSFS 7,11

Berrigan, Daniel 1921- .... **CLC 4**
See also CA 33-36R; CAAE 187; CAAS 1; CANR 11, 43, 78; CP 7; DLB 5

Berrigan, Edmund Joseph Michael, Jr.
1934-1983
See Berrigan, Ted
See also CA 110; 61-64; CANR 14, 102

Berrigan, Ted .... **CLC 37**
See Berrigan, Edmund Joseph Michael, Jr.
See also DLB 5, 169; WP

Berry, Charles Edward Anderson 1931-
See Berry, Chuck
See also CA 115

Berry, Chuck .... **CLC 17**
See Berry, Charles Edward Anderson

Berry, Jonas
See Ashbery, John (Lawrence)
See also GLL 1

Berry, Wendell (Erdman) 1934- ... **CLC 4, 6, 8, 27, 46; PC 28**
See also AITN 1; AMWS 10; ANW; CA 73-76; CANR 50, 73, 101; CP 7; CSW; DAM POET; DLB 5, 6, 234, 275; MTCW 1

Berryman, John 1914-1972 ... **CLC 1, 2, 3, 4, 6, 8, 10, 13, 25, 62**
See also AMW; CA 33-36R; 13-16; CABS 2; CANR 35; CAP 1; CDALB 1941-1968; DAM POET; DLB 48; EWL 3; MTCW 1, 2; PAB; RGAL 4; WP

Bertolucci, Bernardo 1940- ..... **CLC 16, 157**
See also CA 106

Berton, Pierre (Francis Demarigny)
1920- .... **CLC 104**
See also CA 1-4R; CANR 2, 56; CPW; DLB 68; SATA 99

Bertrand, Aloysius 1807-1841 .... **NCLC 31**
See Bertrand, Louis oAloysiusc

Bertrand, Louis oAloysiusc
See Bertrand, Aloysius
See also DLB 217

Bertran de Born c. 1140-1215 .... **CMLC 5**

Besant, Annie (Wood) 1847-1933 ..... **TCLC 9**
See also CA 185; 105

Bessie, Alvah 1904-1985 .... **CLC 23**
See also CA 116; 5-8R; CANR 2, 80; DLB 26

Bethlen, T. D.
See Silverberg, Robert

Beti, Mongo .... **BLC 1; CLC 27**
See Biyidi, Alexandre
See also AFW; CANR 79; DAM MULT; EWL 3; WLIT 2

Betjeman, John 1906-1984 ...... **CLC 2, 6, 10, 34, 43**
See also BRW 7; CA 112; 9-12R; CANR 33, 56; CDBLB 1945-1960; DA3; DAB; DAM MST, POET; DLB 20; DLBY 1984; EWL 3; MTCW 1, 2

Bettelheim, Bruno 1903-1990 .... **CLC 79**
See also CA 131; 81-84; CANR 23, 61; DA3; MTCW 1, 2

Betti, Ugo 1892-1953 .... **TCLC 5**
See also CA 155; 104; EWL 3; RGWL 2, 3

Betts, Doris (Waugh) 1932- ..... **CLC 3, 6, 28; SSC 45**
See also CA 13-16R; CANR 9, 66, 77; CN 7; CSW; DLB 218; DLBY 1982; INT CANR-9; RGAL 4

Bevan, Alistair
See Roberts, Keith (John Kingston)

Bey, Pilaff
See Douglas, (George) Norman

Bialik, Chaim Nachman
1873-1934 .... **TCLC 25**
See also CA 170; EWL 3

Bickerstaff, Isaac
See Swift, Jonathan

Bidart, Frank 1939- .... **CLC 33**
See also CA 140; CANR 106; CP 7

Bienek, Horst 1930- .... **CLC 7, 11**
See also CA 73-76; DLB 75

Bierce, Ambrose (Gwinett)
1842-1914(?) ..... **SSC 9; TCLC 1, 7, 44; WLC**
See also AMW; BYA 11; CA 139; 104; CANR 78; CDALB 1865-1917; DA; DA3; DAC; DAM MST; DLB 11, 12, 23, 71, 74, 186; EWL 3; EXPS; HGG; LAIT 2; RGAL 4; RGSF 2; SSFS 9; SUFW 1

Biggers, Earl Derr 1884-1933 .... **TCLC 65**
See also CA 153; 108

Billiken, Bud
See Motley, Willard (Francis)

Billings, Josh
See Shaw, Henry Wheeler

Billington, (Lady) Rachel (Mary)
1942- .... **CLC 43**
See also AITN 2; CA 33-36R; CANR 44; CN 7

Binchy, Maeve 1940- .... **CLC 153**
See also BEST 90:1; BPFB 1; CA 134; 127; CANR 50, 96; CN 7; CPW; DA3; DAM POP; INT CA-134; MTCW 1; RHW

Binyon, T(imothy) J(ohn) 1936- .... **CLC 34**
See also CA 111; CANR 28

Bion 335B.C.-245B.C. .... **CMLC 39**

Bioy Casares, Adolfo 1914-1999 ... **CLC 4, 8, 13, 88; HLC 1; SSC 17**
See Casares, Adolfo Bioy; Miranda, Javier; Sacastru, Martin
See also CA 177; 29-32R; CANR 19, 43, 66; DAM MULT; DLB 113; EWL 3; HW 1, 2; LAW; MTCW 1, 2

Birch, Allison .... **CLC 65**

Bird, Cordwainer
See Ellison, Harlan (Jay)

Bird, Robert Montgomery
1806-1854 .... **NCLC 1**
See also DLB 202; RGAL 4

Birkerts, Sven 1951- .... **CLC 116**
See also CA 133, 176; 128; CAAE 176; CAAS 29; INT 133

Birney, (Alfred) Earle 1904-1995 .. **CLC 1, 4, 6, 11**
See also CA 1-4R; CANR 5, 20; CP 7; DAC; DAM MST, POET; DLB 88; MTCW 1; PFS 8; RGEL 2

Biruni, al 973-1048(?) .... **CMLC 28**

Bishop, Elizabeth 1911-1979 ..... **CLC 1, 4, 9, 13, 15, 32; PC 3, 34; TCLC 121**
See also AMWR 2; AMWS 1; CA 89-92; 5-8R; CABS 2; CANR 26, 61, 108; CDALB 1968-1988; DA; DA3; DAC; DAM MST, POET; DLB 5, 169; EWL 3; GLL 2; MAWW; MTCW 1, 2; PAB; PFS 6, 12; RGAL 4; SATA-Obit 24; TUS; WP

Bishop, John 1935- .... **CLC 10**
See also CA 105

Bishop, John Peale 1892-1944 ..... **TCLC 103**
See also CA 155; 107; DLB 4, 9, 45; RGAL 4

Bissett, Bill 1939- .... **CLC 18; PC 14**
See also CA 69-72; CAAS 19; CANR 15; CCA 1; CP 7; DLB 53; MTCW 1

Bissoondath, Neil (Devindra)
1955- .... **CLC 120**
See also CA 136; CN 7; DAC

Bitov, Andrei (Georgievich) 1937- ... **CLC 57**
See also CA 142

Biyidi, Alexandre 1932-
See Beti, Mongo
See also BW 1, 3; CA 124; 114; CANR 81; DA3; MTCW 1, 2

Bjarme, Brynjolf
See Ibsen, Henrik (Johan)

Bjoernson, Bjoernstjerne (Martinius)
1832-1910 .... **TCLC 7, 37**
See also CA 104

Black, Robert
See Holdstock, Robert P.

Blackburn, Paul 1926-1971 .... **CLC 9, 43**
See also BG 2; CA 33-36R; 81-84; CANR 34; DLB 16; DLBY 1981

Black Elk 1863-1950 .... **NNAL; TCLC 33**
See also CA 144; DAM MULT; MTCW 1; WP

Black Hawk 1767-1838 .... **NNAL**

Black Hobart
See Sanders, (James) Ed(ward)

Blacklin, Malcolm
See Chambers, Aidan

Blackmore, R(ichard) D(oddridge)
1825-1900 .... **TCLC 27**
See also CA 120; DLB 18; RGEL 2

Blackmur, R(ichard) P(almer)
1904-1965 .... **CLC 2, 24**
See also AMWS 2; CA 25-28R; 11-12; CANR 71; CAP 1; DLB 63; EWL 3

Black Tarantula
See Acker, Kathy

Blackwood, Algernon (Henry)
1869-1951 .... **TCLC 5**
See also CA 150; 105; DLB 153, 156, 178;
HGG; SUFW 1

Blackwood, Caroline 1931-1996 .... **CLC 6, 9, 100**
See also CA 151; 85-88; CANR 32, 61, 65;
CN 7; DLB 14, 207; HGG; MTCW 1

Blade, Alexander
See Hamilton, Edmond; Silverberg, Robert

Blaga, Lucian 1895-1961 .... **CLC 75**
See also CA 157; DLB 220; EWL 3

Blair, Eric (Arthur) 1903-1950 .... **TCLC 123**
See Orwell, George
See also CA 132; 104; DA; DA3; DAB;
DAC; DAM MST, NOV; MTCW 1, 2;
SATA 29

Blair, Hugh 1718-1800 .... **NCLC 75**

Blais, Marie-Claire 1939- .... **CLC 2, 4, 6, 13, 22**
See also CA 21-24R; CAAS 4; CANR 38,
75, 93; DAC; DAM MST; DLB 53; EWL
3; FW; MTCW 1, 2; TWA

Blaise, Clark 1940- .... **CLC 29**
See also AITN 2; CA 53-56; CAAS 3;
CANR 5, 66, 106; CN 7; DLB 53; RGSF
2

Blake, Fairley
See De Voto, Bernard (Augustine)

Blake, Nicholas
See Day Lewis, C(ecil)
See also DLB 77; MSW

Blake, Sterling
See Benford, Gregory (Albert)

Blake, William 1757-1827 .... **NCLC 13, 37, 57; PC 12; WLC**
See also AAYA 47; BRW 3; BRWR 1; CD-
BLB 1789-1832; CLR 52; DA; DA3;
DAB; DAC; DAM MST, POET; DLB 93,
163; EXPP; MAICYA 1, 2; PAB; PFS 2,
12; SATA 30; TEA; WCH; WLIT 3; WP

Blanchot, Maurice 1907- .... **CLC 135**
See also CA 144; 117; DLB 72; EWL 3

Blasco Ibanez, Vicente 1867-1928 . **TCLC 12**
See also BPFB 1; CA 131; 110; CANR 81;
DA3; DAM NOV; EW 8; EWL 3; HW 1,
2; MTCW 1

Blatty, William Peter 1928- .... **CLC 2**
See also CA 5-8R; CANR 9; DAM POP;
HGG

Bleeck, Oliver
See Thomas, Ross (Elmore)

Blessing, Lee 1949- .... **CLC 54**
See also CAD; CD 5

Blight, Rose
See Greer, Germaine

Blish, James (Benjamin) 1921-1975 . **CLC 14**
See also BPFB 1; CA 57-60; 1-4R; CANR
3; DLB 8; MTCW 1; SATA 66; SCFW 2;
SFW 4

Bliss, Reginald
See Wells, H(erbert) G(eorge)

Blixen, Karen (Christentze Dinesen)
1885-1962
See Dinesen, Isak
See also CA 25-28; CANR 22, 50; CAP 2;
DA3; DLB 214; MTCW 1, 2; SATA 44

Bloch, Robert (Albert) 1917-1994 .... **CLC 33**
See also AAYA 29; CA 146; 5-8R, 179;
CAAE 179; CAAS 20; CANR 5, 78;
DA3; DLB 44; HGG; INT CANR-5;
MTCW 1; SATA 12; SATA-Obit 82; SFW
4; SUFW 1, 2

Blok, Alexander (Alexandrovich)
1880-1921 .... **PC 21; TCLC 5**
See also CA 183; 104; EW 9; EWL 3;
RGWL 2, 3

Blom, Jan
See Breytenbach, Breyten

Bloom, Harold 1930- .... **CLC 24, 103**
See also CA 13-16R; CANR 39, 75, 92;
DLB 67; EWL 3; MTCW 1; RGAL 4

Bloomfield, Aurelius
See Bourne, Randolph S(illiman)

Blount, Roy (Alton), Jr. 1941- .... **CLC 38**
See also CA 53-56; CANR 10, 28, 61;
CSW; INT CANR-28; MTCW 1, 2

Blowsnake, Sam 1875-(?) .... **NNAL**

Bloy, Leon 1846-1917 .... **TCLC 22**
See also CA 183; 121; DLB 123; GFL 1789
to the Present

Blue Cloud, Peter (Aroniawenrate)
1933- .... **NNAL**
See also CA 117; CANR 40; DAM MULT

Bluggage, Oranthy
See Alcott, Louisa May

Blume, Judy (Sussman) 1938- .... **CLC 12, 30**
See also AAYA 3, 26; BYA 1, 8, 12; CA 29-
32R; CANR 13, 37, 66; CLR 2, 15, 69;
CPW; DA3; DAM NOV, POP; DLB 52;
JRDA; MAICYA 1, 2; MAICYAS 1;
MTCW 1, 2; SATA 2, 31, 79; WYA; YAW

Blunden, Edmund (Charles)
1896-1974 .... **CLC 2, 56**
See also BRW 6; CA 45-48; 17-18; CANR
54; CAP 2; DLB 20, 100, 155; MTCW 1;
PAB

Bly, Robert (Elwood) 1926- .... **CLC 1, 2, 5, 10, 15, 38, 128; PC 39**
See also AMWS 4; CA 5-8R; CANR 41,
73; CP 7; DA3; DAM POET; DLB 5;
EWL 3; MTCW 1, 2; PFS 17; RGAL 4

Boas, Franz 1858-1942 .... **TCLC 56**
See also CA 181; 115

Bobette
See Simenon, Georges (Jacques Christian)

Boccaccio, Giovanni 1313-1375 ... **CMLC 13, 57; SSC 10**
See also EW 2; RGSF 2; RGWL 2, 3; TWA

Bochco, Steven 1943- .... **CLC 35**
See also AAYA 11; CA 138; 124

Bode, Sigmund
See O'Doherty, Brian

Bodel, Jean 1167(?)-1210 .... **CMLC 28**

Bodenheim, Maxwell 1892-1954 .... **TCLC 44**
See also CA 187; 110; DLB 9, 45; RGAL 4

Bodenheimer, Maxwell
See Bodenheim, Maxwell

Bodker, Cecil 1927-
See Bodker, Cecil

Bodker, Cecil 1927- .... **CLC 21**
See also CA 73-76; CANR 13, 44, 111;
CLR 23; MAICYA 1, 2; SATA 14, 133

Boell, Heinrich (Theodor)
1917-1985 ..... **CLC 2, 3, 6, 9, 11, 15, 27, 32, 72; SSC 23; WLC**
See Boll, Heinrich
See also CA 116; 21-24R; CANR 24; DA;
DA3; DAB; DAC; DAM MST, NOV;
DLB 69; DLBY 1985; MTCW 1, 2; TWA

Boerne, Alfred
See Doeblin, Alfred

Boethius c. 480-c. 524 .... **CMLC 15**
See also DLB 115; RGWL 2, 3

Boff, Leonardo (Genezio Darci)
1938- .... **CLC 70; HLC 1**
See also CA 150; DAM MULT; HW 2

Bogan, Louise 1897-1970 .... **CLC 4, 39, 46, 93; PC 12**
See also AMWS 3; CA 25-28R; 73-76;
CANR 33, 82; DAM POET; DLB 45, 169;
EWL 3; MAWW; MTCW 1, 2; RGAL 4

Bogarde, Dirk
See Van Den Bogarde, Derek Jules Gaspard
Ulric Niven
See also DLB 14

Bogosian, Eric 1953- .... **CLC 45, 141**
See also CA 138; CAD; CANR 102; CD 5

Bograd, Larry 1953- .... **CLC 35**
See also CA 93-96; CANR 57; SAAS 21;
SATA 33, 89; WYA

Boiardo, Matteo Maria 1441-1494 .... **LC 6**

Boileau-Despreaux, Nicolas 1636-1711 . **LC 3**
See also DLB 268; EW 3; GFL Beginnings
to 1789; RGWL 2, 3

Boissard, Maurice
See Leautaud, Paul

Bojer, Johan 1872-1959 .... **TCLC 64**
See also CA 189; EWL 3

Bok, Edward W. 1863-1930 .... **TCLC 101**
See also DLB 91; DLBD 16

Boland, Eavan (Aisling) 1944- .. **CLC 40, 67, 113**
See also BRWS 5; CA 143; CAAE 207;
CANR 61; CP 7; CWP; DAM POET;
DLB 40; FW; MTCW 2; PFS 12

Boll, Heinrich
See Boell, Heinrich (Theodor)
See also BPFB 1; CDWLB 2; EW 13; EWL
3; RGSF 2; RGWL 2, 3

Bolt, Lee
See Faust, Frederick (Schiller)

Bolt, Robert (Oxton) 1924-1995 .... **CLC 14**
See also CA 147; 17-20R; CANR 35, 67;
CBD; DAM DRAM; DFS 2; DLB 13,
233; EWL 3; LAIT 1; MTCW 1

Bombal, Maria Luisa 1910-1980 .... **HLCS 1; SSC 37**
See also CA 127; CANR 72; EWL 3; HW
1; LAW; RGSF 2

Bombet, Louis-Alexandre-Cesar
See Stendhal

Bomkauf
See Kaufman, Bob (Garnell)

Bonaventura .... **NCLC 35**
See also DLB 90

Bond, Edward 1934- .... **CLC 4, 6, 13, 23**
See also BRWS 1; CA 25-28R; CANR 38,
67, 106; CBD; CD 5; DAM DRAM; DFS
3,8; DLB 13; EWL 3; MTCW 1

Bonham, Frank 1914-1989 .... **CLC 12**
See also AAYA 1; BYA 1, 3; CA 9-12R;
CANR 4, 36; JRDA; MAICYA 1, 2;
SAAS 3; SATA 1, 49; SATA-Obit 62;
TCWW 2; YAW

Bonnefoy, Yves 1923- .... **CLC 9, 15, 58**
See also CA 85-88; CANR 33, 75, 97;
CWW 2; DAM MST, POET; DLB 258;
EWL 3; GFL 1789 to the Present; MTCW
1, 2

Bonner, Marita .... **HR 2**
See Occomy, Marita (Odette) Bonner

Bonnin, Gertrude 1876-1938 .... **NNAL**
See Zitkala-Sa
See also CA 150; DAM MULT

Bontemps, Arna(ud Wendell)
1902-1973 ..... **BLC 1; CLC 1, 18; HR 2**
See also BW 1; CA 41-44R; 1-4R; CANR
4, 35; CLR 6; CWRI 5; DA3; DAM
MULT, NOV, POET; DLB 48, 51; JRDA;
MAICYA 1, 2; MTCW 1, 2; SATA 2, 44;
SATA-Obit 24; WCH; WP

Booth, Martin 1944- .... **CLC 13**
See also CA 93-96; CAAE 188; CAAS 2;
CANR 92

Booth, Philip 1925- .... **CLC 23**
See also CA 5-8R; CANR 5, 88; CP 7;
DLBY 1982

Booth, Wayne C(layson) 1921- .... **CLC 24**
See also CA 1-4R; CAAS 5; CANR 3, 43,
117; DLB 67

Borchert, Wolfgang 1921-1947 .... **TCLC 5**
See also CA 188; 104; DLB 69, 124; EWL
3

Borel, Petrus 1809-1859 .... **NCLC 41**
  See also DLB 119; GFL 1789 to the Present
Borges, Jorge Luis 1899-1986 ... **CLC 1, 2, 3, 4, 6, 8, 9, 10, 13, 19, 44, 48, 83; HLC 1; PC 22, 32; SSC 4, 41; TCLC 109; WLC**
  See also AAYA 26; BPFB 1; CA 21-24R; CANR 19, 33, 75, 105; CDWLB 3; DA; DA3; DAB; DAC; DAM MST, MULT; DLB 113; DLBY 1986; DNFS 1, 2; EWL 3; HW 1, 2; LAW; LMFS 2; MSW; MTCW 1, 2; RGSF 2; RGWL 2, 3; SFW 4; SSFS 17; TWA; WLIT 1
Borowski, Tadeusz 1922-1951 .... **SSC 48; TCLC 9**
  See also CA 154; 106; CDWLB 4; DLB 215; EWL 3; RGSF 2; RGWL 3; SSFS 13
Borrow, George (Henry)
  1803-1881 .... **NCLC 9**
  See also DLB 21, 55, 166
Bosch (Gaviño), Juan 1909-2001 ..... **HLCS 1**
  See also CA 204; 151; DAM MST, MULT; DLB 145; HW 1, 2
Bosman, Herman Charles
  1905-1951 .... **TCLC 49**
  See Malan, Herman
  See also CA 160; DLB 225; RGSF 2
Bosschere, Jean de 1878(?)-1953 ... **TCLC 19**
  See also CA 186; 115
Boswell, James 1740-1795 ... **LC 4, 50; WLC**
  See also BRW 3; CDBLB 1660-1789; DA; DAB; DAC; DAM MST; DLB 104, 142; TEA; WLIT 3
Bottomley, Gordon 1874-1948 ..... **TCLC 107**
  See also CA 192; 120; DLB 10
Bottoms, David 1949- .... **CLC 53**
  See also CA 105; CANR 22; CSW; DLB 120; DLBY 1983
Boucicault, Dion 1820-1890 .... **NCLC 41**
Boucolon, Maryse
  See Conde, Maryse
Bourget, Paul (Charles Joseph)
  1852-1935 .... **TCLC 12**
  See also CA 196; 107; DLB 123; GFL 1789 to the Present
Bourjaily, Vance (Nye) 1922- .... **CLC 8, 62**
  See also CA 1-4R; CAAS 1; CANR 2, 72; CN 7; DLB 2, 143
Bourne, Randolph S(illiman)
  1886-1918 .... **TCLC 16**
  See also AMW; CA 155; 117; DLB 63
Bova, Ben(jamin William) 1932- ...... **CLC 45**
  See also AAYA 16; CA 5-8R; CAAS 18; CANR 11, 56, 94, 111; CLR 3; DLBY 1981; INT CANR-11; MAICYA 1, 2; MTCW 1; SATA 6, 68, 133; SFW 4
Bowen, Elizabeth (Dorothea Cole)
  1899-1973 . **CLC 1, 3, 6, 11, 15, 22, 118; SSC 3, 28**
  See also BRWS 2; CA 41-44R; 17-18; CANR 35, 105; CAP 2; CDBLB 1945-1960; DA3; DAM NOV; DLB 15, 162; EWL 3; EXPS; FW; HGG; MTCW 1, 2; NFS 13; RGSF 2; SSFS 5; SUFW 1; TEA; WLIT 4
Bowering, George 1935- .... **CLC 15, 47**
  See also CA 21-24R; CAAS 16; CANR 10; CP 7; DLB 53
Bowering, Marilyn R(uthe) 1949- .... **CLC 32**
  See also CA 101; CANR 49; CP 7; CWP
Bowers, Edgar 1924-2000 .... **CLC 9**
  See also CA 188; 5-8R; CANR 24; CP 7; CSW; DLB 5
Bowers, Mrs. J. Milton 1842-1914
  See Bierce, Ambrose (Gwinett)
Bowie, David .... **CLC 17**
  See Jones, David Robert

Bowles, Jane (Sydney) 1917-1973 ..... **CLC 3, 68**
  See Bowles, Jane Auer
  See also CA 41-44R; 19-20; CAP 2
Bowles, Jane Auer
  See Bowles, Jane (Sydney)
  See also EWL 3
Bowles, Paul (Frederick) 1910-1999 . **CLC 1, 2, 19, 53; SSC 3**
  See also AMWS 4; CA 186; 1-4R; CAAS 1; CANR 1, 19, 50, 75; CN 7; DA3; DLB 5, 6, 218; EWL 3; MTCW 1, 2; RGAL 4; SSFS 17
Bowles, William Lisle 1762-1850 . **NCLC 103**
  See also DLB 93
Box, Edgar
  See Vidal, Gore
  See also GLL 1
Boyd, James 1888-1944 .... **TCLC 115**
  See also CA 186; DLB 9; DLBD 16; RGAL 4; RHW
Boyd, Nancy
  See Millay, Edna St. Vincent
  See also GLL 1
Boyd, Thomas (Alexander)
  1898-1935 .... **TCLC 111**
  See also CA 183; 111; DLB 9; DLBD 16
Boyd, William 1952- .... **CLC 28, 53, 70**
  See also CA 120; 114; CANR 51, 71; CN 7; DLB 231
Boyle, Kay 1902-1992 .... **CLC 1, 5, 19, 58, 121; SSC 5**
  See also CA 140; 13-16R; CAAS 1; CANR 29, 61, 110; DLB 4, 9, 48, 86; DLBY 1993; EWL 3; MTCW 1, 2; RGAL 4; RGSF 2; SSFS 10, 13, 14
Boyle, Mark
  See Kienzle, William X(avier)
Boyle, Patrick 1905-1982 .... **CLC 19**
  See also CA 127
Boyle, T. C.
  See Boyle, T(homas) Coraghessan
  See also AMWS 8
Boyle, T(homas) Coraghessan
  1948- .... **CLC 36, 55, 90; SSC 16**
  See Boyle, T. C.
  See also AAYA 47; BEST 90:4; BPFB 1; CA 120; CANR 44, 76, 89; CN 7; CPW; DA3; DAM POP; DLB 218, 278; DLBY 1986; EWL 3; MTCW 2; SSFS 13
Boz
  See Dickens, Charles (John Huffam)
Brackenridge, Hugh Henry
  1748-1816 .... **NCLC 7**
  See also DLB 11, 37; RGAL 4
Bradbury, Edward P.
  See Moorcock, Michael (John)
  See also MTCW 2
Bradbury, Malcolm (Stanley)
  1932-2000 .... **CLC 32, 61**
  See also CA 1-4R; CANR 1, 33, 91, 98; CN 7; DA3; DAM NOV; DLB 14, 207; EWL 3; MTCW 1, 2
Bradbury, Ray (Douglas) 1920- .... **CLC 1, 3, 10, 15, 42, 98; SSC 29, 53; WLC**
  See also AAYA 15; AITN 1, 2; AMWS 4; BPFB 1; BYA 4, 5, 11; CA 1-4R; CANR 2, 30, 75; CDALB 1968-1988; CN 7; CPW; DA; DA3; DAB; DAC; DAM MST, NOV, POP; DLB 2, 8; EXPN; EXPS; HGG; LAIT 3, 5; MTCW 1, 2; NFS 1; RGAL 4; RGSF 2; SATA 11, 64, 123; SCFW 2; SFW 4; SSFS 1; SUFW 1, 2; TUS; YAW
Braddon, Mary Elizabeth
  1837-1915 .... **TCLC 111**
  See also BRWS 8; CA 179; 108; CMW 4; DLB 18, 70, 156; HGG
Bradford, Gamaliel 1863-1932 .... **TCLC 36**
  See also CA 160; DLB 17

Bradford, William 1590-1657 .... **LC 64**
  See also DLB 24, 30; RGAL 4
Bradley, David (Henry), Jr. 1950- .... **BLC 1; CLC 23, 118**
  See also BW 1, 3; CA 104; CANR 26, 81; CN 7; DAM MULT; DLB 33
Bradley, John Ed(mund, Jr.) 1958- . **CLC 55**
  See also CA 139; CANR 99; CN 7; CSW
Bradley, Marion Zimmer
  1930-1999 .... **CLC 30**
  See Chapman, Lee; Dexter, John; Gardner, Miriam; Ives, Morgan; Rivers, Elfrida
  See also AAYA 40; BPFB 1; CA 185; 57-60; CAAS 10; CANR 7, 31, 51, 75, 107; CPW; DA3; DAM POP; DLB 8; FANT; FW; MTCW 1, 2; SATA 90; SATA-Obit 116; SFW 4; SUFW 2; YAW
Bradshaw, John 1933- .... **CLC 70**
  See also CA 138; CANR 61
Bradstreet, Anne 1612(?)-1672 ...... **LC 4, 30; PC 10**
  See also AMWS 1; CDALB 1640-1865; DA; DA3; DAC; DAM MST, POET; DLB 24; EXPP; FW; PFS 6; RGAL 4; TUS; WP
Brady, Joan 1939- .... **CLC 86**
  See also CA 141
Bragg, Melvyn 1939- .... **CLC 10**
  See also BEST 89:3; CA 57-60; CANR 10, 48, 89; CN 7; DLB 14, 271; RHW
Brahe, Tycho 1546-1601 .... **LC 45**
Braine, John (Gerard) 1922-1986 . **CLC 1, 3, 41**
  See also CA 120; 1-4R; CANR 1, 33; CDBLB 1945-1960; DLB 15; DLBY 1986; EWL 3; MTCW 1
Braithwaite, William Stanley (Beaumont)
  1878-1962 .... **BLC 1; HR 2**
  See also BW 1; CA 125; DAM MULT; DLB 50, 54
Bramah, Ernest 1868-1942 .... **TCLC 72**
  See also CA 156; CMW 4; DLB 70; FANT
Brammer, William 1930(?)-1978 ...... **CLC 31**
  See also CA 77-80
Brancati, Vitaliano 1907-1954 .... **TCLC 12**
  See also CA 109; DLB 264; EWL 3
Brancato, Robin F(idler) 1936- .... **CLC 35**
  See also AAYA 9; BYA 6; CA 69-72; CANR 11, 45; CLR 32; JRDA; MAICYA 2; MAICYAS 1; SAAS 9; SATA 97; WYA; YAW
Brand, Max
  See Faust, Frederick (Schiller)
  See also BPFB 1; TCWW 2
Brand, Millen 1906-1980 .... **CLC 7**
  See also CA 97-100; 21-24R; CANR 72
Branden, Barbara .... **CLC 44**
  See also CA 148
Brandes, Georg (Morris Cohen)
  1842-1927 .... **TCLC 10**
  See also CA 189; 105
Brandys, Kazimierz 1916-2000 .... **CLC 62**
  See also EWL 3
Branley, Franklyn M(ansfield)
  1915-2002 .... **CLC 21**
  See also CA 207; 33-36R; CANR 14, 39; CLR 13; MAICYA 1, 2; SAAS 16; SATA 4, 68, 136
Brant, Beth (E.) 1941- .... **NNAL**
  See also CA 144; FW
Brathwaite, Edward Kamau
  1930- .... **BLCS; CLC 11**
  See also BW 2, 3; CA 25-28R; CANR 11, 26, 47, 107; CDWLB 3; CP 7; DAM POET; DLB 125; EWL 3
Brathwaite, Kamau
  See Brathwaite, Edward Kamau

Author Index

Chona, Maria 1845(?)-1936 .... **NNAL**
See also CA 144

Chopin, Kate ..... **SSC 8; TCLC 127; WLCS**
See Chopin, Katherine
See also AAYA 33; AMWR 2; AMWS 1;
CDALB 1865-1917; DA; DAB; DLB 12,
78; EXPN; EXPS; FW; LAIT 3; MAWW;
NFS 3; RGAL 4; RGSF 2; SSFS 17; TUS

Chopin, Katherine 1851-1904
See Chopin, Kate
See also CA 122; 104; DA3; DAC; DAM
MST, NOV

Chretien de Troyes c. 12th cent. - . **CMLC 10**
See also DLB 208; EW 1; RGWL 2, 3;
TWA

Christie
See Ichikawa, Kon

Christie, Agatha (Mary Clarissa)
1890-1976 .. **CLC 1, 6, 8, 12, 39, 48, 110**
See also AAYA 9; AITN 1, 2; BPFB 1;
BRWS 2; CA 61-64; 17-20R; CANR 10,
37, 108; CBD; CDBLB 1914-1945; CMW
4; CPW; CWD; DA3; DAB; DAC; DAM
NOV; DFS 2; DLB 13, 77, 245; MSW;
MTCW 1, 2; NFS 8; RGEL 2; RHW;
SATA 36; TEA; YAW

Christie, Philippa .... **CLC 21**
See Pearce, Philippa
See also BYA 5; CANR 109; CLR 9; DLB
161; MAICYA 1; SATA 1, 67, 129

Christine de Pizan 1365(?)-1431(?) .... **LC 9**
See also DLB 208; RGWL 2, 3

Chuang Tzu c. 369B.C.-c.
286B.C. .... **CMLC 57**

Chubb, Elmer
See Masters, Edgar Lee

Chulkov, Mikhail Dmitrievich
1743-1792 .... **LC 2**
See also DLB 150

Churchill, Caryl 1938- .... **CLC 31, 55, 157;
DC 5**
See also BRWS 4; CA 102; CANR 22, 46,
108; CBD; CWD; DFS 12, 16; DLB 13;
EWL 3; FW; MTCW 1; RGEL 2

Churchill, Charles 1731-1764 .... **LC 3**
See also DLB 109; RGEL 2

Churchill, Sir Winston (Leonard Spencer)
1874-1965 .... **TCLC 113**
See also BRW 6; CA 97-100; CDBLB
1890-1914; DA3; DLB 100; DLBD 16;
LAIT 4; MTCW 1, 2

Chute, Carolyn 1947- .... **CLC 39**
See also CA 123

Ciardi, John (Anthony) 1916-1986 . **CLC 10,
40, 44, 129**
See also CA 118; 5-8R; CAAS 2; CANR 5,
33; CLR 19; CWRI 5; DAM POET; DLB
5; DLBY 1986; INT CANR-5; MAICYA
1, 2; MTCW 1, 2; RGAL 4; SAAS 26;
SATA 1, 65; SATA-Obit 46

Cibber, Colley 1671-1757 .... **LC 66**
See also DLB 84; RGEL 2

Cicero, Marcus Tullius
106B.C.-43B.C. .... **CMLC 3**
See also AW 1; CDWLB 1; DLB 211;
RGWL 2, 3

Cimino, Michael 1943- .... **CLC 16**
See also CA 105

Cioran, E(mil) M. 1911-1995 .... **CLC 64**
See also CA 149; 25-28R; CANR 91; DLB
220; EWL 3

Cisneros, Sandra 1954- .. **CLC 69, 118; HLC
1; SSC 32**
See also AAYA 9; AMWS 7; CA 131;
CANR 64; CWP; DA3; DAM MULT;
DLB 122, 152; EWL 3; EXPN; FW; HW
1, 2; LAIT 5; MAICYA 2; MTCW 2; NFS
2; RGAL 4; RGSF 2; SSFS 3, 13; WLIT
1; YAW

Cixous, Helene 1937- .... **CLC 92**
See also CA 126; CANR 55; CWW 2; DLB
83, 242; EWL 3; FW; GLL 2; MTCW 1,
2; TWA

Clair, Rene .... **CLC 20**
See Chomette, Rene Lucien

Clampitt, Amy 1920-1994 .... **CLC 32; PC 19**
See also AMWS 9; CA 146; 110; CANR
29, 79; DLB 105

Clancy, Thomas L., Jr. 1947-
See Clancy, Tom
See also CA 131; 125; CANR 62, 105;
DA3; INT CA-131; MTCW 1, 2

Clancy, Tom .... **CLC 45, 112**
See Clancy, Thomas L., Jr.
See also AAYA 9; BEST 89:1, 90:1; BPFB
1; BYA 10, 11; CMW 4; CPW; DAM
NOV, POP; DLB 227

Clare, John 1793-1864 .. **NCLC 9, 86; PC 23**
See also DAB; DAM POET; DLB 55, 96;
RGEL 2

Clarin
See Alas (y Urena), Leopoldo (Enrique
Garcia)

Clark, Al C.
See Goines, Donald

Clark, (Robert) Brian 1932- .... **CLC 29**
See also CA 41-44R; CANR 67; CBD; CD
5

Clark, Curt
See Westlake, Donald E(dwin)

Clark, Eleanor 1913-1996 .... **CLC 5, 19**
See also CA 151; 9-12R; CANR 41; CN 7;
DLB 6

Clark, J. P.
See Clark Bekederemo, J(ohnson) P(epper)
See also CDWLB 3; DLB 117

Clark, John Pepper
See Clark Bekederemo, J(ohnson) P(epper)
See also AFW; CD 5; CP 7; RGEL 2

Clark, M. R.
See Clark, Mavis Thorpe

Clark, Mavis Thorpe 1909-1999 ...... **CLC 12**
See also CA 57-60; CANR 8, 37, 107; CLR
30; CWRI 5; MAICYA 1, 2; SAAS 5;
SATA 8, 74

Clark, Walter Van Tilburg
1909-1971 .... **CLC 28**
See also CA 33-36R; 9-12R; CANR 63,
113; DLB 9, 206; LAIT 2; RGAL 4;
SATA 8

Clark Bekederemo, J(ohnson) P(epper)
1935- .... **BLC 1; CLC 38; DC 5**
See Clark, J. P.; Clark, John Pepper
See also BW 1; CA 65-68; CANR 16, 72;
DAM DRAM, MULT; DFS 13; EWL 3;
MTCW 1

Clarke, Arthur C(harles) 1917- .... **CLC 1, 4,
13, 18, 35, 136; SSC 3**
See also AAYA 4, 33; BPFB 1; BYA 13;
CA 1-4R; CANR 2, 28, 55, 74; CN 7;
CPW; DA3; DAM POP; DLB 261; JRDA;
LAIT 5; MAICYA 1, 2; MTCW 1, 2;
SATA 13, 70, 115; SCFW; SFW 4; SSFS
4; YAW

Clarke, Austin 1896-1974 .... **CLC 6, 9**
See also CA 49-52; 29-32; CAP 2; DAM
POET; DLB 10, 20; EWL 3; RGEL 2

Clarke, Austin C(hesterfield) 1934- .. **BLC 1;
CLC 8, 53; SSC 45**
See also BW 1; CA 25-28R; CAAS 16;
CANR 14, 32, 68; CN 7; DAC; DAM
MULT; DLB 53, 125; DNFS 2; RGSF 2

Clarke, Gillian 1937- .... **CLC 61**
See also CA 106; CP 7; CWP; DLB 40

Clarke, Marcus (Andrew Hislop)
1846-1881 .... **NCLC 19**
See also DLB 230; RGEL 2; RGSF 2

Clarke, Shirley 1925-1997 .... **CLC 16**
See also CA 189

Clash, The
See Headon, (Nicky) Topper; Jones, Mick;
Simonon, Paul; Strummer, Joe

Claudel, Paul (Louis Charles Marie)
1868-1955 .... **TCLC 2, 10**
See also CA 165; 104; DLB 192, 258; EW
8; EWL 3; GFL 1789 to the Present;
RGWL 2, 3; TWA

Claudian 370(?)-404(?) .... **CMLC 46**
See also RGWL 2, 3

Claudius, Matthias 1740-1815 .... **NCLC 75**
See also DLB 97

Clavell, James (duMaresq)
1925-1994 .... **CLC 6, 25, 87**
See also BPFB 1; CA 146; 25-28R; CANR
26, 48; CPW; DA3; DAM NOV, POP;
MTCW 1, 2; NFS 10; RHW

Clayman, Gregory .... **CLC 65**

Cleaver, (Leroy) Eldridge
1935-1998 .... **BLC 1; CLC 30, 119**
See also BW 1, 3; CA 167; 21-24R; CANR
16, 75; DA3; DAM MULT; MTCW 2;
YAW

Cleese, John (Marwood) 1939- .... **CLC 21**
See Monty Python
See also CA 116; 112; CANR 35; MTCW 1

Cleishbotham, Jebediah
See Scott, Sir Walter

Cleland, John 1710-1789 .... **LC 2, 48**
See also DLB 39; RGEL 2

Clemens, Samuel Langhorne 1835-1910
See Twain, Mark
See also CA 135; 104; CDALB 1865-1917;
DA; DA3; DAB; DAC; DAM MST, NOV;
DLB 12, 23, 64, 74, 186, 189; JRDA;
MAICYA 1, 2; NCFS 4; SATA 100; SSFS
16; YABC 2

Clement of Alexandria
150(?)-215(?) .... **CMLC 41**

Cleophil
See Congreve, William

Clerihew, E.
See Bentley, E(dmund) C(lerihew)

Clerk, N. W.
See Lewis, C(live) S(taples)

Cliff, Jimmy .... **CLC 21**
See Chambers, James
See also CA 193

Cliff, Michelle 1946- .... **BLCS; CLC 120**
See also BW 2; CA 116; CANR 39, 72; CD-
WLB 3; DLB 157; FW; GLL 2

Clifford, Lady Anne 1590-1676 .... **LC 76**
See also DLB 151

Clifton, (Thelma) Lucille 1936- .... **BLC 1;
CLC 19, 66, 162; PC 17**
See also AFAW 2; BW 2, 3; CA 49-52;
CANR 2, 24, 42, 76, 97; CLR 5; CP 7;
CSW; CWP; CWRI 5; DA3; DAM MULT,
POET; DLB 5, 41; EXPP; MAICYA 1, 2;
MTCW 1, 2; PFS 1, 14; SATA 20, 69,
128; WP

Clinton, Dirk
See Silverberg, Robert

Clough, Arthur Hugh 1819-1861 ... **NCLC 27**
See also BRW 5; DLB 32; RGEL 2

Clutha, Janet Paterson Frame 1924-
See Frame, Janet
See also CA 1-4R; CANR 2, 36, 76; MTCW
1, 2; SATA 119

Clyne, Terence
See Blatty, William Peter

Cobalt, Martin
See Mayne, William (James Carter)

Cobb, Irvin S(hrewsbury)
1876-1944 .... **TCLC 77**
See also CA 175; DLB 11, 25, 86

Author Index

Cobbett, William 1763-1835 .... **NCLC 49**
See also DLB 43, 107, 158; RGEL 2

Coburn, D(onald) L(ee) 1938- .... **CLC 10**
See also CA 89-92

Cocteau, Jean (Maurice Eugene Clement)
1889-1963 ...... **CLC 1, 8, 15, 16, 43; DC
17; TCLC 119; WLC**
See also CA 25-28; CANR 40; CAP 2; DA;
DA3; DAB; DAC; DAM DRAM, MST,
NOV; DLB 65, 258; EW 10; EWL 3; GFL
1789 to the Present; MTCW 1, 2; RGWL
2, 3, TWA

Codrescu, Andrei 1946- .... **CLC 46, 121**
See also CA 33-36R; CAAS 19; CANR 13,
34, 53, 76; DA3; DAM POET; MTCW 2

Coe, Max
See Bourne, Randolph S(illiman)

Coe, Tucker
See Westlake, Donald E(dwin)

Coen, Ethan 1958- .... **CLC 108**
See also CA 126; CANR 85

Coen, Joel 1955- .... **CLC 108**
See also CA 126

The Coen Brothers
See Coen, Ethan; Coen, Joel

Coetzee, J(ohn) M(ichael) 1940- ...... **CLC 23,
33, 66, 117, 161, 162**
See also AAYA 37; AFW; BRWS 6; CA 77-
80; CANR 41, 54, 74, 114; CN 7; DA3;
DAM NOV; DLB 225; EWL 3; LMFS 2;
MTCW 1, 2; WLIT 2

Coffey, Brian
See Koontz, Dean R(ay)

Coffin, Robert P(eter) Tristram
1892-1955 .... **TCLC 95**
See also CA 169; 123; DLB 45

Cohan, George M(ichael)
1878-1942 .... **TCLC 60**
See also CA 157; DLB 249; RGAL 4

Cohen, Arthur A(llen) 1928-1986 ...... **CLC 7,
31**
See also CA 120; 1-4R; CANR 1, 17, 42;
DLB 28

Cohen, Leonard (Norman) 1934- ...... **CLC 3,
38**
See also CA 21-24R; CANR 14, 69; CN 7;
CP 7; DAC; DAM MST; DLB 53; EWL
3; MTCW 1

Cohen, Matt(hew) 1942-1999 .... **CLC 19**
See also CA 187; 61-64; CAAS 18; CANR
40; CN 7; DAC; DLB 53

Cohen-Solal, Annie 19(?)- .... **CLC 50**

Colegate, Isabel 1931- .... **CLC 36**
See also CA 17-20R; CANR 8, 22, 74; CN
7; DLB 14, 231; INT CANR-22; MTCW
1

Coleman, Emmett
See Reed, Ishmael

Coleridge, Hartley 1796-1849 .... **NCLC 90**
See also DLB 96

Coleridge, M. E.
See Coleridge, Mary E(lizabeth)

Coleridge, Mary E(lizabeth)
1861-1907 .... **TCLC 73**
See also CA 166; 116; DLB 19, 98

Coleridge, Samuel Taylor
1772-1834 ...... **NCLC 9, 54, 99, 111; PC
11, 39; WLC**
See also BRW 4; BRWR 2; BYA 4; CD-
BLB 1789-1832; DA; DA3; DAB; DAC;
DAM MST, POET; DLB 93, 107; EXPP;
PAB; PFS 4, 5; RGEL 2; TEA; WLIT 3;
WP

Coleridge, Sara 1802-1852 .... **NCLC 31**
See also DLB 199

Coles, Don 1928- .... **CLC 46**
See also CA 115; CANR 38; CP 7

Coles, Robert (Martin) 1929- .... **CLC 108**
See also CA 45-48; CANR 3, 32, 66, 70;
INT CANR-32; SATA 23

Colette, (Sidonie-Gabrielle)
1873-1954 .... **SSC 10; TCLC 1, 5, 16**
See Willy, Colette
See also CA 131; 104; DA3; DAM NOV;
DLB 65; EW 9; EWL 3; GFL 1789 to the
Present; MTCW 1, 2; RGWL 2, 3; TWA

Collett, (Jacobine) Camilla (Wergeland)
1813-1895 .... **NCLC 22**

Collier, Christopher 1930- .... **CLC 30**
See also AAYA 13; BYA 2; CA 33-36R;
CANR 13, 33, 102; JRDA; MAICYA 1,
2; SATA 16, 70; WYA; YAW 1

Collier, James Lincoln 1928- .... **CLC 30**
See also AAYA 13; BYA 2; CA 9-12R;
CANR 4, 33, 60, 102; CLR 3; DAM POP;
JRDA; MAICYA 1, 2; SAAS 21; SATA 8,
70; WYA; YAW 1

Collier, Jeremy 1650-1726 .... **LC 6**

Collier, John 1901-1980 . **SSC 19; TCLC 127**
See also CA 97-100; 65-68; CANR 10;
DLB 77, 255; FANT; SUFW 1

Collier, Mary 1690-1762 .... **LC 86**
See also DLB 95

Collingwood, R(obin) G(eorge)
1889(?)-1943 .... **TCLC 67**
See also CA 155; 117; DLB 262

Collins, Hunt
See Hunter, Evan

Collins, Linda 1931- .... **CLC 44**
See also CA 125

Collins, Tom
See Furphy, Joseph
See also RGEL 2

Collins, (William) Wilkie
1824-1889 .... **NCLC 1, 18, 93**
See also BRWS 6; CDBLB 1832-1890;
CMW 4; DLB 18, 70, 159; MSW; RGEL
2; RGSF 2; SUFW 1; WLIT 4

Collins, William 1721-1759 .... **LC 4, 40**
See also BRW 3; DAM POET; DLB 109;
RGEL 2

Collodi, Carlo .... **NCLC 54**
See Lorenzini, Carlo
See also CLR 5; WCH

Colman, George
See Glassco, John

Colonna, Vittoria 1492-1547 .... **LC 71**
See also RGWL 2, 3

Colt, Winchester Remington
See Hubbard, L(afayette) Ron(ald)

Colter, Cyrus J. 1910-2002 .... **CLC 58**
See also BW 1; CA 205; 65-68; CANR 10,
66; CN 7; DLB 33

Colton, James
See Hansen, Joseph
See also GLL 1

Colum, Padraic 1881-1972 .... **CLC 28**
See also BYA 4; CA 33-36R; 73-76; CANR
35; CLR 36; CWRI 5; DLB 19; MAICYA
1, 2; MTCW 1; RGEL 2; SATA 15; WCH

Colvin, James
See Moorcock, Michael (John)

Colwin, Laurie (E.) 1944-1992 .... **CLC 5, 13,
23, 84**
See also CA 139; 89-92; CANR 20, 46;
DLB 218; DLBY 1980; MTCW 1

Comfort, Alex(ander) 1920-2000 .... **CLC 7**
See also CA 190; 1-4R; CANR 1, 45; CP 7;
DAM POP; MTCW 1

Comfort, Montgomery
See Campbell, (John) Ramsey

Compton-Burnett, I(vy)
1892(?)-1969 .... **CLC 1, 3, 10, 15, 34**
See also BRW 7; CA 25-28R; 1-4R; CANR
4; DAM NOV; DLB 36; EWL 3; MTCW
1; RGEL 2

Comstock, Anthony 1844-1915 ...... **TCLC 13**
See also CA 169; 110

Comte, Auguste 1798-1857 .... **NCLC 54**

Conan Doyle, Arthur
See Doyle, Sir Arthur Conan
See also BPFB 1; BYA 4, 5, 11

Conde (Abellan), Carmen
1901-1996 .... **HLCS 1**
See also CA 177; DLB 108; EWL 3; HW 2

Conde, Maryse 1937- ..... **BLCS; CLC 52, 92**
See also BW 2, 3; CA 110; CAAE 190;
CANR 30, 53, 76; CWW 2; DAM MULT;
EWL 3; MTCW 1

Condillac, Etienne Bonnot de
1714-1780 .... **LC 26**

Condon, Richard (Thomas)
1915-1996 .... **CLC 4, 6, 8, 10, 45, 100**
See also BEST 90:3; BPFB 1; CA 151;
1-4R; CAAS 1; CANR 2, 23; CMW 4;
CN 7; DAM NOV; INT CANR-23;
MTCW 1, 2

Confucius 551B.C.-479B.C. .... **CMLC 19;
WLCS**
See also DA; DA3; DAB; DAC; DAM
MST

Congreve, William 1670-1729 ... **DC 2; LC 5,
21; WLC**
See also BRW 2; CDBLB 1660-1789; DA;
DAB; DAC; DAM DRAM, MST, POET;
DFS 15; DLB 39, 84; RGEL 2; WLIT 3

Conley, Robert J(ackson) 1940- .... **NNAL**
See also CA 41-44R; CANR 15, 34, 45, 96;
DAM MULT

Connell, Evan S(helby), Jr. 1924- . **CLC 4, 6,
45**
See also AAYA 7; CA 1-4R; CAAS 2;
CANR 2, 39, 76, 97; CN 7; DAM NOV;
DLB 2; DLBY 1981; MTCW 1, 2

Connelly, Marc(us Cook) 1890-1980 . **CLC 7**
See also CA 102; 85-88; CANR 30; DFS
12; DLB 7; DLBY 1980; RGAL 4; SATA-
Obit 25

Connor, Ralph .... **TCLC 31**
See Gordon, Charles William
See also DLB 92; TCWW 2

Conrad, Joseph 1857-1924 . **SSC 9; TCLC 1,
6, 13, 25, 43, 57; WLC**
See also AAYA 26; BPFB 1; BRW 6;
BRWC 1; BRWR 2; BYA 2; CA 131; 104;
CANR 60; CDBLB 1890-1914; DA; DA3;
DAB; DAC; DAM MST, NOV; DLB 10,
34, 98, 156; EWL 3; EXPN; EXPS; LAIT
2; MTCW 1, 2; NFS 2, 16; RGEL 2;
RGSF 2; SATA 27; SSFS 1, 12; TEA;
WLIT 4

Conrad, Robert Arnold
See Hart, Moss

Conroy, (Donald) Pat(rick) 1945- ... **CLC 30,
74**
See also AAYA 8; AITN 1; BPFB 1; CA
85-88; CANR 24, 53; CPW; CSW; DA3;
DAM NOV, POP; DLB 6; LAIT 5;
MTCW 1, 2

Constant (de Rebecque), (Henri) Benjamin
1767-1830 .... **NCLC 6**
See also DLB 119; EW 4; GFL 1789 to the
Present

Conway, Jill K(er) 1934- .... **CLC 152**
See also CA 130; CANR 94

Conybeare, Charles Augustus
See Eliot, T(homas) S(tearns)

Cook, Michael 1933-1994 .... **CLC 58**
See also CA 93-96; CANR 68; DLB 53

Cook, Robin 1940- .... **CLC 14**
See also AAYA 32; BEST 90:2; BPFB 1;
CA 111; 108; CANR 41, 90, 109; CPW;
DA3; DAM POP; HGG; INT CA-111

Cook, Roy
See Silverberg, Robert

Deighton, Len .... **CLC 4, 7, 22, 46**
    See Deighton, Leonard Cyril
    See also AAYA 6; BEST 89:2; BPFB 1; CD-
      BLB 1960 to Present; CMW 4; CN 7;
      CPW; DLB 87

Deighton, Leonard Cyril 1929-
    See Deighton, Len
    See also CA 9-12R; CANR 19, 33, 68;
      DA3; DAM NOV, POP; MTCW 1, 2

Dekker, Thomas 1572(?)-1632 ..... **DC 12; LC
  22**
    See also CDBLB Before 1660; DAM
      DRAM; DLB 62, 172; RGEL 2

de Laclos, Pierre Ambroise Franois
    See Laclos, Pierre Ambroise Francois

Delafield, E. M. .... **TCLC 61**
    See Dashwood, Edmee Elizabeth Monica
      de la Pasture
    See also DLB 34; RHW

de la Mare, Walter (John)
    1873-1956 . **SSC 14; TCLC 4, 53; WLC**
    See also CA 163; CDBLB 1914-1945; CLR
      23; CWRI 5; DA3; DAB; DAC; DAM
      MST, POET; DLB 19, 153, 162, 255;
      EWL 3; EXPP; HGG; MAICYA 1, 2;
      MTCW 1; RGEL 2; RGSF 2; SATA 16;
      SUFW 1; TEA; WCH

de Lamartine, Alphonse (Marie Louis Prat)
    See Lamartine, Alphonse (Marie Louis Prat)
      de

Delaney, Franey
    See O'Hara, John (Henry)

Delaney, Shelagh 1939- .... **CLC 29**
    See also CA 17-20R; CANR 30, 67; CBD;
      CD 5; CDBLB 1960 to Present; CWD;
      DAM DRAM; DFS 7; DLB 13; MTCW 1

Delany, Martin Robison
    1812-1885 .... **NCLC 93**
    See also DLB 50; RGAL 4

Delany, Mary (Granville Pendarves)
    1700-1788 .... **LC 12**

Delany, Samuel R(ay), Jr. 1942- .... **BLC 1;
  CLC 8, 14, 38, 141**
    See also AAYA 24; AFAW 2; BPFB 1; BW
      2, 3; CA 81-84; CANR 27, 43, 115, 116;
      CN 7; DAM MULT; DLB 8, 33; FANT;
      MTCW 1, 2; RGAL 4; SATA 92; SCFW;
      SFW 4; SUFW 2

De la Ramee, Marie Louise (Ouida)
    1839-1908
    See Ouida
    See also CA 204; SATA 20

de la Roche, Mazo 1879-1961 .... **CLC 14**
    See also CA 85-88; CANR 30; DLB 68;
      RGEL 2; RHW; SATA 64

De La Salle, Innocent
    See Hartmann, Sadakichi

de Laureamont, Comte
    See Lautreamont

Delbanco, Nicholas (Franklin)
    1942- .... **CLC 6, 13, 167**
    See also CA 17-20R; CAAE 189; CAAS 2;
      CANR 29, 55, 116; DLB 6, 234

del Castillo, Michel 1933- .... **CLC 38**
    See also CA 109; CANR 77

Deledda, Grazia (Cosima)
    1875(?)-1936 .... **TCLC 23**
    See also CA 205; 123; DLB 264; EWL 3;
      RGWL 2, 3

Deleuze, Gilles 1925-1995 .... **TCLC 116**

Delgado, Abelardo (Lalo) B(arrientos)
    1930- .... **HLC 1**
    See also CA 131; CAAS 15; CANR 90;
      DAM MST, MULT; DLB 82; HW 1, 2

Delibes, Miguel .... **CLC 8, 18**
    See Delibes Setien, Miguel
    See also EWL 3

Delibes Setien, Miguel 1920-
    See Delibes, Miguel
    See also CA 45-48; CANR 1, 32; HW 1;
      MTCW 1

DeLillo, Don 1936- ..... **CLC 8, 10, 13, 27, 39,
  54, 76, 143**
    See also AMWS 6; BEST 89:1; BPFB 1;
      CA 81-84; CANR 21, 76, 92; CN 7; CPW;
      DA3; DAM NOV, POP; DLB 6, 173;
      EWL 3; MTCW 1, 2; RGAL 4; TUS

de Lisser, H. G.
    See De Lisser, H(erbert) G(eorge)
    See also DLB 117

De Lisser, H(erbert) G(eorge)
    1878-1944 .... **TCLC 12**
    See de Lisser, H. G.
    See also BW 2; CA 152; 109

Deloire, Pierre
    See Peguy, Charles (Pierre)

Deloney, Thomas 1543(?)-1600 .... **LC 41**
    See also DLB 167; RGEL 2

Deloria, Ella (Cara) 1889-1971(?) ..... **NNAL**
    See also CA 152; DAM MULT; DLB 175

Deloria, Vine (Victor), Jr. 1933- ...... **CLC 21,
  122; NNAL**
    See also CA 53-56; CANR 5, 20, 48, 98;
      DAM MULT; DLB 175; MTCW 1; SATA
      21

del Valle-Inclan, Ramon (Maria)
    See Valle-Inclan, Ramon (Maria) del

Del Vecchio, John M(ichael) 1947- .. **CLC 29**
    See also CA 110; DLBD 9

de Man, Paul (Adolph Michel)
    1919-1983 .... **CLC 55**
    See also CA 111; 128; CANR 61; DLB 67;
      MTCW 1, 2

DeMarinis, Rick 1934- .... **CLC 54**
    See also CA 57-60, 184; CAAE 184; CAAS
      24; CANR 9, 25, 50; DLB 218

de Maupassant, (Henri Rene Albert) Guy
    See Maupassant, (Henri Rene Albert) Guy
      de

Dembry, R. Emmet
    See Murfree, Mary Noailles

Demby, William 1922- .... **BLC 1; CLC 53**
    See also BW 1, 3; CA 81-84; CANR 81;
      DAM MULT; DLB 33

de Menton, Francisco
    See Chin, Frank (Chew, Jr.)

Demetrius of Phalerum c.
    307B.C.- .... **CMLC 34**

Demijohn, Thom
    See Disch, Thomas M(ichael)

De Mille, James 1833-1880 .... **NCLC 123**
    See also DLB 99, 251

Deming, Richard 1915-1983
    See Queen, Ellery
    See also CA 9-12R; CANR 3, 94; SATA 24

Democritus c. 460B.C.-c. 370B.C. . **CMLC 47**

de Montaigne, Michel (Eyquem)
    See Montaigne, Michel (Eyquem) de

de Montherlant, Henry (Milon)
    See Montherlant, Henry (Milon) de

Demosthenes 384B.C.-322B.C. ...... **CMLC 13**
    See also AW 1; DLB 176; RGWL 2, 3

de Musset, (Louis Charles) Alfred
    See Musset, (Louis Charles) Alfred de

de Natale, Francine
    See Malzberg, Barry N(athaniel)

de Navarre, Marguerite 1492-1549 ..... **LC 61**
    See Marguerite d'Angouleme; Marguerite
      de Navarre

Denby, Edwin (Orr) 1903-1983 .... **CLC 48**
    See also CA 110; 138

de Nerval, Gerard
    See Nerval, Gerard de

Denham, John 1615-1669 .... **LC 73**
    See also DLB 58, 126; RGEL 2

Denis, Julio
    See Cortazar, Julio

Denmark, Harrison
    See Zelazny, Roger (Joseph)

Dennis, John 1658-1734 .... **LC 11**
    See also DLB 101; RGEL 2

Dennis, Nigel (Forbes) 1912-1989 ...... **CLC 8**
    See also CA 129; 25-28R; DLB 13, 15, 233;
      EWL 3; MTCW 1

Dent, Lester 1904(?)-1959 .... **TCLC 72**
    See also CA 161; 112; CMW 4; SFW 4

De Palma, Brian (Russell) 1940- ...... **CLC 20**
    See also CA 109

De Quincey, Thomas 1785-1859 ..... **NCLC 4,
  87**
    See also BRW 4; CDBLB 1789-1832; DLB
      110, 144; RGEL 2

Deren, Eleanora 1908(?)-1961
    See Deren, Maya
    See also CA 111; 192

Deren, Maya .... **CLC 16, 102**
    See Deren, Eleanora

Derleth, August (William)
    1909-1971 .... **CLC 31**
    See also BPFB 1; BYA 9, 10; CA 29-32R;
      1-4R; CANR 4; CMW 4; DLB 9; DLBD
      17; HGG; SATA 5; SUFW 1

Der Nister 1884-1950 .... **TCLC 56**
    See Nister, Der

de Routisie, Albert
    See Aragon, Louis

Derrida, Jacques 1930- .... **CLC 24, 87**
    See also CA 127; 124; CANR 76, 98; DLB
      242; EWL 3; MTCW 1; TWA

Derry Down Derry
    See Lear, Edward

Dersonnes, Jacques
    See Simenon, Georges (Jacques Christian)

Desai, Anita 1937- .... **CLC 19, 37, 97**
    See also BRWS 5; CA 81-84; CANR 33,
      53, 95; CN 7; CWRI 5; DAB; DAM
      NOV; DLB 271; DNFS 2; EWL 3; FW;
      MTCW 1, 2; SATA 63, 126

Desai, Kiran 1971- .... **CLC 119**
    See also CA 171

de Saint-Luc, Jean
    See Glassco, John

de Saint Roman, Arnaud
    See Aragon, Louis

Desbordes-Valmore, Marceline
    1786-1859 .... **NCLC 97**
    See also DLB 217

Descartes, Rene 1596-1650 .... **LC 20, 35**
    See also DLB 268; EW 3; GFL Beginnings
      to 1789

De Sica, Vittorio 1901(?)-1974 .... **CLC 20**
    See also CA 117

Desnos, Robert 1900-1945 .... **TCLC 22**
    See also CA 151; 121; CANR 107; DLB
      258; EWL 3

Destouches, Louis-Ferdinand
    1894-1961 .... **CLC 9, 15**
    See Celine, Louis-Ferdinand
    See also CA 85-88; CANR 28; MTCW 1

de Tolignac, Gaston
    See Griffith, D(avid Lewelyn) W(ark)

Deutsch, Babette 1895-1982 .... **CLC 18**
    See also BYA 3; CA 108; 1-4R; CANR 4,
      79; DLB 45; SATA 1; SATA-Obit 33

Devenant, William 1606-1649 .... **LC 13**

Devkota, Laxmiprasad 1909-1959 . **TCLC 23**
    See also CA 123

De Voto, Bernard (Augustine)
    1897-1955 .... **TCLC 29**
    See also CA 160; 113; DLB 9, 256

De Vries, Peter 1910-1993 ..... **CLC 1, 2, 3, 7, 10, 28, 46**
See also CA 142; 17-20R; CANR 41; DAM NOV; DLB 6; DLBY 1982; MTCW 1, 2

Dewey, John 1859-1952 .... **TCLC 95**
See also CA 170; 114; DLB 246, 270; RGAL 4

Dexter, John
See Bradley, Marion Zimmer
See also GLL 1

Dexter, Martin
See Faust, Frederick (Schiller)
See also TCWW 2

Dexter, Pete 1943- .... **CLC 34, 55**
See also BEST 89:2; CA 131; 127; CPW; DAM POP; INT 131; MTCW 1

Diamano, Silmang
See Senghor, Leopold Sedar

Diamond, Neil 1941- .... **CLC 30**
See also CA 108

Diaz del Castillo, Bernal
1496-1584 .... **HLCS 1; LC 31**
See also LAW

di Bassetto, Corno
See Shaw, George Bernard

Dick, Philip K(indred) 1928-1982 ... **CLC 10, 30, 72; SSC 57**
See also AAYA 24; BPFB 1; BYA 11; CA 106; 49-52; CANR 2, 16; CPW; DA3; DAM NOV, POP; DLB 8; MTCW 1, 2; NFS 5; SCFW; SFW 4

Dickens, Charles (John Huffam)
1812-1870 .... **NCLC 3, 8, 18, 26, 37, 50, 86, 105, 113; SSC 17, 49; WLC**
See also AAYA 23; BRW 5; BRWC 1; BYA 1, 2, 3, 13, 14; CDBLB 1832-1890; CMW 4; DA; DA3; DAB; DAC; DAM MST, NOV; DLB 21, 55, 70, 159, 166; EXPN; HGG; JRDA; LAIT 1, 2; MAICYA 1, 2; NFS 4, 5, 10, 14; RGEL 2; RGSF 2; SATA 15; SUFW 1; TEA; WCH; WLIT 4; WYA

Dickey, James (Lafayette)
1923-1997 .... **CLC 1, 2, 4, 7, 10, 15, 47, 109; PC 40**
See also AITN 1, 2; AMWS 4; BPFB 1; CA 156; 9-12R; CABS 2; CANR 10, 48, 61, 105; CDALB 1968-1988; CP 7; CPW; CSW; DA3; DAM NOV, POET, POP; DLB 5, 193; DLBD 7; DLBY 1982, 1993, 1996, 1997, 1998; EWL 3; INT CANR-10; MTCW 1, 2; NFS 9; PFS 6, 11; RGAL 4; TUS

Dickey, William 1928-1994 .... **CLC 3, 28**
See also CA 145; 9-12R; CANR 24, 79; DLB 5

Dickinson, Charles 1951- .... **CLC 49**
See also CA 128

Dickinson, Emily (Elizabeth)
1830-1886 ... **NCLC 21, 77; PC 1; WLC**
See also AAYA 22; AMW; AMWR 1; CDALB 1865-1917; DA; DA3; DAB; DAC; DAM MST, POET; DLB 1, 243; EXPP; MAWW; PAB; PFS 1, 2, 3, 4, 5, 6, 8, 10, 11, 13, 16; RGAL 4; SATA 29; TUS; WP; WYA

Dickinson, Mrs. Herbert Ward
See Phelps, Elizabeth Stuart

Dickinson, Peter (Malcolm) 1927- .. **CLC 12, 35**
See also AAYA 9; BYA 5; CA 41-44R; CANR 31, 58, 88; CLR 29; CMW 4; DLB 87, 161, 276; JRDA; MAICYA 1, 2; SATA 5, 62, 95; SFW 4; WYA; YAW

Dickson, Carr
See Carr, John Dickson

Dickson, Carter
See Carr, John Dickson

Diderot, Denis 1713-1784 .... **LC 26**
See also EW 4; GFL Beginnings to 1789; RGWL 2, 3

Didion, Joan 1934- . **CLC 1, 3, 8, 14, 32, 129**
See also AITN 1; AMWS 4; CA 5-8R; CANR 14, 52, 76; CDALB 1968-1988; CN 7; DA3; DAM NOV; DLB 2, 173, 185; DLBY 1981, 1986; EWL 3; MAWW; MTCW 1, 2; NFS 3; RGAL 4; TCWW 2; TUS

Dietrich, Robert
See Hunt, E(verette) Howard, (Jr.)

Difusa, Pati
See Almodovar, Pedro

Dillard, Annie 1945- .... **CLC 9, 60, 115**
See also AAYA 6, 43; AMWS 6; ANW; CA 49-52; CANR 3, 43, 62, 90; DA3; DAM NOV; DLB 275, 278; DLBY 1980; LAIT 4, 5; MTCW 1, 2; NCFS 1; RGAL 4; SATA 10; TUS

Dillard, R(ichard) H(enry) W(ilde)
1937- .... **CLC 5**
See also CA 21-24R; CAAS 7; CANR 10; CP 7; CSW; DLB 5, 244

Dillon, Eilis 1920-1994 .... **CLC 17**
See also CA 147; 9-12R, 182; CAAE 182; CAAS 3; CANR 4, 38, 78; CLR 26; MAICYA 1, 2; MAICYAS 1; SATA 2, 74; SATA-Essay 105; SATA-Obit 83; YAW

Dimont, Penelope
See Mortimer, Penelope (Ruth)

Dinesen, Isak .... **CLC 10, 29, 95; SSC 7**
See Blixen, Karen (Christentze Dinesen)
See also EW 10; EWL 3; EXPS; FW; HGG; LAIT 3; MTCW 1; NCFS 2; NFS 9; RGSF 2; RGWL 2, 3; SSFS 3, 6, 13; WLIT 2

Ding Ling .... **CLC 68**
See Chiang, Pin-chin
See also RGWL 3

Diphusa, Patty
See Almodovar, Pedro

Disch, Thomas M(ichael) 1940- ... **CLC 7, 36**
See also AAYA 17; BPFB 1; CA 21-24R; CAAS 4; CANR 17, 36, 54, 89; CLR 18; CP 7; DA3; DLB 8; HGG; MAICYA 1, 2; MTCW 1, 2; SAAS 15; SATA 92; SCFW; SFW 4; SUFW 2

Disch, Tom
See Disch, Thomas M(ichael)

d'Isly, Georges
See Simenon, Georges (Jacques Christian)

Disraeli, Benjamin 1804-1881 ... **NCLC 2, 39, 79**
See also BRW 4; DLB 21, 55; RGEL 2

Ditcum, Steve
See Crumb, R(obert)

Dixon, Paige
See Corcoran, Barbara (Asenath)

Dixon, Stephen 1936- .... **CLC 52; SSC 16**
See also AMWS 12; CA 89-92; CANR 17, 40, 54, 91; CN 7; DLB 130

Doak, Annie
See Dillard, Annie

Dobell, Sydney Thompson
1824-1874 .... **NCLC 43**
See also DLB 32; RGEL 2

Doblin, Alfred .... **TCLC 13**
See Doeblin, Alfred
See also CDWLB 2; EWL 3; RGWL 2, 3

Dobroliubov, Nikolai Aleksandrovich
See Dobrolyubov, Nikolai Alexandrovich
See also DLB 277

Dobrolyubov, Nikolai Alexandrovich
1836-1861 .... **NCLC 5**
See Dobroliubov, Nikolai Aleksandrovich

Dobson, Austin 1840-1921 .... **TCLC 79**
See also DLB 35, 144

Dobyns, Stephen 1941- .... **CLC 37**
See also CA 45-48; CANR 2, 18, 99; CMW 4; CP 7

Doctorow, E(dgar) L(aurence)
1931- .... **CLC 6, 11, 15, 18, 37, 44, 65, 113**
See also AAYA 22; AITN 2; AMWS 4; BEST 89:3; BPFB 1; CA 45-48; CANR 2, 33, 51, 76, 97; CDALB 1968-1988; CN 7; CPW; DA3; DAM NOV, POP; DLB 2, 28, 173; DLBY 1980; EWL 3; LAIT 3; MTCW 1, 2; NFS 6; RGAL 4; RHW; TUS

Dodgson, Charles L(utwidge) 1832-1898
See Carroll, Lewis
See also CLR 2; DA; DA3; DAB; DAC; DAM MST, NOV, POET; MAICYA 1, 2; SATA 100; YABC 2

Dodson, Owen (Vincent) 1914-1983 .. **BLC 1; CLC 79**
See also BW 1; CA 110; 65-68; CANR 24; DAM MULT; DLB 76

Doeblin, Alfred 1878-1957 .... **TCLC 13**
See Doblin, Alfred
See also CA 141; 110; DLB 66

Doerr, Harriet 1910- .... **CLC 34**
See also CA 122; 117; CANR 47; INT 122

Domecq, H(onorio Bustos)
See Bioy Casares, Adolfo

Domecq, H(onorio) Bustos
See Bioy Casares, Adolfo; Borges, Jorge Luis

Domini, Rey
See Lorde, Audre (Geraldine)
See also GLL 1

Dominique
See Proust, (Valentin-Louis-George-Eugene-)Marcel

Don, A
See Stephen, Sir Leslie

Donaldson, Stephen R(eeder)
1947- .... **CLC 46, 138**
See also AAYA 36; BPFB 1; CA 89-92; CANR 13, 55, 99; CPW; DAM POP; FANT; INT CANR-13; SATA 121; SFW 4; SUFW 1, 2

Donleavy, J(ames) P(atrick) 1926- .... **CLC 1, 4, 6, 10, 45**
See also AITN 2; BPFB 1; CA 9-12R; CANR 24, 49, 62, 80; CBD; CD 5; CN 7; DLB 6, 173; INT CANR-24; MTCW 1, 2; RGAL 4

Donnadieu, Marguerite
See Duras, Marguerite
See also CWW 2

Donne, John 1572-1631 ..... **LC 10, 24; PC 1, 43; WLC**
See also BRW 1; BRWC 1; BRWR 2; CD-BLB Before 1660; DA; DAB; DAC; DAM MST, POET; DLB 121, 151; EXPP; PAB; PFS 2, 11; RGEL 2; TEA; WLIT 3; WP

Donnell, David 1939(?)- .... **CLC 34**
See also CA 197

Donoghue, P. S.
See Hunt, E(verette) Howard, (Jr.)

Donoso (Yanez), Jose 1924-1996 ... **CLC 4, 8, 11, 32, 99; HLC 1; SSC 34; TCLC 133**
See also CA 155; 81-84; CANR 32, 73; CD-WLB 3; DAM MULT; DLB 113; EWL 3; HW 1, 2; LAW; LAWS 1; MTCW 1, 2; RGSF 2; WLIT 1

Donovan, John 1928-1992 .... **CLC 35**
See also AAYA 20; CA 137; 97-100; CLR 3; MAICYA 1, 2; SATA 72; SATA-Brief 29; YAW

Don Roberto
See Cunninghame Graham, Robert (Gallnigad) Bontine

Doolittle, Hilda 1886-1961 . **CLC 3, 8, 14, 31, 34, 73; PC 5; WLC**
See H. D.
See also AMWS 1; CA 97-100; CANR 35; DA; DAC; DAM MST, POET; DLB 4, 45; EWL 3; FW; GLL 1; LMFS 2; MAWW; MTCW 1, 2; PFS 6; RGAL 4

Doppo, Kunikida .... **TCLC 99**
See Kunikida Doppo

Dorfman, Ariel 1942- .... **CLC 48, 77; HLC 1**
See also CA 130; 124; CANR 67, 70; CWW 2; DAM MULT; DFS 4; EWL 3; HW 1, 2; INT CA-130; WLIT 1

Dorn, Edward (Merton)
1929-1999 .... **CLC 10, 18**
See also CA 187; 93-96; CANR 42, 79; CP 7; DLB 5; INT 93-96; WP

Dor-Ner, Zvi .... **CLC 70**

Dorris, Michael (Anthony)
1945-1997 .... **CLC 109; NNAL**
See also AAYA 20; BEST 90:1; BYA 12; CA 157; 102; CANR 19, 46, 75; CLR 58; DA3; DAM MULT, NOV; DLB 175; LAIT 5; MTCW 2; NFS 3; RGAL 4; SATA 75; SATA-Obit 94; TCWW 2; YAW

Dorris, Michael A.
See Dorris, Michael (Anthony)

Dorsan, Luc
See Simenon, Georges (Jacques Christian)

Dorsange, Jean
See Simenon, Georges (Jacques Christian)

Dos Passos, John (Roderigo)
1896-1970 ... **CLC 1, 4, 8, 11, 15, 25, 34, 82; WLC**
See also AMW; BPFB 1; CA 29-32R; 1-4R; CANR 3; CDALB 1929-1941; DA; DA3; DAB; DAC; DAM MST, NOV; DLB 4, 9, 274; DLBD 1, 15; DLBY 1996; EWL 3; MTCW 1, 2; NFS 14; RGAL 4; TUS

Dossage, Jean
See Simenon, Georges (Jacques Christian)

Dostoevsky, Fedor Mikhailovich
1821-1881 .. **NCLC 2, 7, 21, 33, 43, 119; SSC 2, 33, 44; WLC**
See Dostoevsky, Fyodor
See also AAYA 40; DA; DA3; DAB; DAC; DAM MST, NOV; EW 7; EXPN; NFS 3, 8; RGSF 2; RGWL 2, 3; SSFS 8; TWA

Dostoevsky, Fyodor
See Dostoevsky, Fedor Mikhailovich
See also DLB 238; LMFS 2

Doughty, Charles M(ontagu)
1843-1926 .... **TCLC 27**
See also CA 178; 115; DLB 19, 57, 174

Douglas, Ellen .... **CLC 73**
See Haxton, Josephine Ayres; Williamson, Ellen Douglas
See also CN 7; CSW

Douglas, Gavin 1475(?)-1522 .... **LC 20**
See also DLB 132; RGEL 2

Douglas, George
See Brown, George Douglas
See also RGEL 2

Douglas, Keith (Castellain)
1920-1944 .... **TCLC 40**
See also BRW 7; CA 160; DLB 27; EWL 3; PAB; RGEL 2

Douglas, Leonard
See Bradbury, Ray (Douglas)

Douglas, Michael
See Crichton, (John) Michael

Douglas, (George) Norman
1868-1952 .... **TCLC 68**
See also BRW 6; CA 157; 119; DLB 34, 195; RGEL 2

Douglas, William
See Brown, George Douglas

Douglass, Frederick 1817(?)-1895 ..... **BLC 1; NCLC 7, 55; WLC**
See also AFAW 1, 2; AMWC 1; AMWS 3; CDALB 1640-1865; DA; DA3; DAC; DAM MST, MULT; DLB 1, 43, 50, 79, 243; FW; LAIT 2; NCFS 2; RGAL 4; SATA 29

Dourado, (Waldomiro Freitas) Autran
1926- .... **CLC 23, 60**
See also CA 25-28R; 179; CANR 34, 81; DLB 145; HW 2

Dourado, Waldomiro Autran
See Dourado, (Waldomiro Freitas) Autran
See also CA 179

Dove, Rita (Frances) 1952- . **BLCS; CLC 50, 81; PC 6**
See also AAYA 46; AMWS 4; BW 2; CA 109; CAAS 19; CANR 27, 42, 68, 76, 97; CDALBS; CP 7; CSW; CWP; DA3; DAM MULT, POET; DLB 120; EWL 3; EXPP; MTCW 1; PFS 1, 15; RGAL 4

Doveglion
See Villa, Jose Garcia

Dowell, Coleman 1925-1985 .... **CLC 60**
See also CA 117; 25-28R; CANR 10; DLB 130; GLL 2

Dowson, Ernest (Christopher)
1867-1900 .... **TCLC 4**
See also CA 150; 105; DLB 19, 135; RGEL 2

Doyle, A. Conan
See Doyle, Sir Arthur Conan

Doyle, Sir Arthur Conan
1859-1930 .... **SSC 12; TCLC 7; WLC**
See Conan Doyle, Arthur
See also AAYA 14; BRWS 2; CA 122; 104; CDBLB 1890-1914; CMW 4; DA; DA3; DAB; DAC; DAM MST, NOV; DLB 18, 70, 156, 178; EXPS; HGG; LAIT 2; MSW; MTCW 1, 2; RGEL 2; RGSF 2; RHW; SATA 24; SCFW 2; SFW 4; SSFS 2; TEA; WCH; WLIT 4; WYA; YAW

Doyle, Conan
See Doyle, Sir Arthur Conan

Doyle, John
See Graves, Robert (von Ranke)

Doyle, Roddy 1958(?)- .... **CLC 81**
See also AAYA 14; BRWS 5; CA 143; CANR 73; CN 7; DA3; DLB 194

Doyle, Sir A. Conan
See Doyle, Sir Arthur Conan

Dr. A
See Asimov, Isaac; Silverstein, Alvin; Silverstein, Virginia B(arbara Opshelor)

Drabble, Margaret 1939- ...... **CLC 2, 3, 5, 8, 10, 22, 53, 129**
See also BRWS 4; CA 13-16R; CANR 18, 35, 63, 112; CDBLB 1960 to Present; CN 7; CPW; DA3; DAB; DAC; DAM MST, NOV, POP; DLB 14, 155, 231; EWL 3; FW; MTCW 1, 2; RGEL 2; SATA 48; TEA

Drapier, M. B.
See Swift, Jonathan

Drayham, James
See Mencken, H(enry) L(ouis)

Drayton, Michael 1563-1631 .... **LC 8**
See also DAM POET; DLB 121; RGEL 2

Dreadstone, Carl
See Campbell, (John) Ramsey

Dreiser, Theodore (Herman Albert)
1871-1945 .... **SSC 30; TCLC 10, 18, 35, 83; WLC**
See also AMW; AMWR 2; CA 132; 106; CDALB 1865-1917; DA; DA3; DAC; DAM MST, NOV; DLB 9, 12, 102, 137; DLBD 1; EWL 3; LAIT 2; LMFS 2; MTCW 1, 2; NFS 17; RGAL 4; TUS

Drexler, Rosalyn 1926- .... **CLC 2, 6**
See also CA 81-84; CAD; CANR 68; CD 5; CWD

Dreyer, Carl Theodor 1889-1968 ...... **CLC 16**
See also CA 116

Drieu la Rochelle, Pierre(-Eugene)
1893-1945 .... **TCLC 21**
See also CA 117; DLB 72; EWL 3; GFL 1789 to the Present

Drinkwater, John 1882-1937 .... **TCLC 57**
See also CA 149; 109; DLB 10, 19, 149; RGEL 2

Drop Shot
See Cable, George Washington

Droste-Hulshoff, Annette Freiin von
1797-1848 .... **NCLC 3**
See also CDWLB 2; DLB 133; RGSF 2; RGWL 2, 3

Drummond, Walter
See Silverberg, Robert

Drummond, William Henry
1854-1907 .... **TCLC 25**
See also CA 160; DLB 92

Drummond de Andrade, Carlos
1902-1987 .... **CLC 18**
See Andrade, Carlos Drummond de
See also CA 123; 132; LAW

Drummond of Hawthornden, William
1585-1649 .... **LC 83**
See also DLB 121, 213; RGEL 2

Drury, Allen (Stuart) 1918-1998 .... **CLC 37**
See also CA 170; 57-60; CANR 18, 52; CN 7; INT CANR-18

Dryden, John 1631-1700 ..... **DC 3; LC 3, 21; PC 25; WLC**
See also BRW 2; CDBLB 1660-1789; DA; DAB; DAC; DAM DRAM, MST, POET; DLB 80, 101, 131; EXPP; IDTP; RGEL 2; TEA; WLIT 3

Duberman, Martin (Bauml) 1930- ..... **CLC 8**
See also CA 1-4R; CAD; CANR 2, 63; CD 5

Dubie, Norman (Evans) 1945- .... **CLC 36**
See also CA 69-72; CANR 12, 115; CP 7; DLB 120; PFS 12

Du Bois, W(illiam) E(dward) B(urghardt)
1868-1963 ..... **BLC 1; CLC 1, 2, 13, 64, 96; HR 2; WLC**
See also AAYA 40; AFAW 1, 2; AMWC 1; AMWS 2; BW 1, 3; CA 85-88; CANR 34, 82; CDALB 1865-1917; DA; DA3; DAC; DAM MST, MULT, NOV; DLB 47, 50, 91, 246; EWL 3; EXPP; LAIT 2; LMFS 2; MTCW 1, 2; NCFS 1; PFS 13; RGAL 4; SATA 42

Dubus, Andre 1936-1999 ..... **CLC 13, 36, 97; SSC 15**
See also AMWS 7; CA 177; 21-24R; CANR 17; CN 7; CSW; DLB 130; INT CANR-17; RGAL 4; SSFS 10

Duca Minimo
See D'Annunzio, Gabriele

Ducharme, Rejean 1941- .... **CLC 74**
See also CA 165; DLB 60

Duchen, Claire .... **CLC 65**

Duclos, Charles Pinot- 1704-1772 .... **LC 1**
See also GFL Beginnings to 1789

Dudek, Louis 1918- .... **CLC 11, 19**
See also CA 45-48; CAAS 14; CANR 1; CP 7; DLB 88

Duerrenmatt, Friedrich 1921-1990 ... **CLC 1, 4, 8, 11, 15, 43, 102**
See Durrenmatt, Friedrich
See also CA 17-20R; CANR 33; CMW 4; DAM DRAM; DLB 69, 124; MTCW 1, 2

Duffy, Bruce 1953(?)- .... **CLC 50**
See also CA 172

Author Index

Faludy, Gyoergy
See Faludy, George
Fanon, Frantz 1925-1961 .... **BLC 2; CLC 74**
See also BW 1; CA 89-92; 116; DAM
MULT; LMFS 2; WLIT 2
Fanshawe, Ann 1625-1680 .... **LC 11**
Fante, John (Thomas) 1911-1983 ..... **CLC 60**
See also AMWS 11; CA 109; 69-72; CANR
23, 104; DLB 130; DLBY 1983
Farah, Nuruddin 1945- ...... **BLC 2; CLC 53,
137**
See also AFW; BW 2, 3; CA 106; CANR
81; CDWLB 3; CN 7; DAM MULT; DLB
125; EWL 3; WLIT 2
Fargue, Leon-Paul 1876(?)-1947 .... **TCLC 11**
See also CA 109; CANR 107; DLB 258;
EWL 3
Farigoule, Louis
See Romains, Jules
Farina, Richard 1936(?)-1966 .... **CLC 9**
See also CA 25-28R; 81-84
Farley, Walter (Lorimer)
1915-1989 .... **CLC 17**
See also BYA 14; CA 17-20R; CANR 8,
29, 84; DLB 22; JRDA; MAICYA 1, 2;
SATA 2, 43, 132; YAW
Farmer, Philip Jose 1918- .... **CLC 1, 19**
See also AAYA 28; BPFB 1; CA 1-4R;
CANR 4, 35, 111; DLB 8; MTCW 1;
SATA 93; SCFW 2; SFW 4
Farquhar, George 1677-1707 .... **LC 21**
See also BRW 2; DAM DRAM; DLB 84;
RGEL 2
Farrell, J(ames) G(ordon)
1935-1979 .... **CLC 6**
See also CA 89-92; 73-76; CANR 36; DLB
14, 271; MTCW 1; RGEL 2; RHW; WLIT
4
Farrell, James T(homas) 1904-1979 . **CLC 1,
4, 8, 11, 66; SSC 28**
See also AMW; BPFB 1; CA 89-92; 5-8R;
CANR 9, 61; DLB 4, 9, 86; DLBD 2;
EWL 3; MTCW 1, 2; RGAL 4
Farrell, Warren (Thomas) 1943- ...... **CLC 70**
See also CA 146
Farren, Richard J.
See Betjeman, John
Farren, Richard M.
See Betjeman, John
Fassbinder, Rainer Werner
1946-1982 .... **CLC 20**
See also CA 106; 93-96; CANR 31
Fast, Howard (Melvin) 1914-2003 .. **CLC 23,
131**
See also AAYA 16; BPFB 1; CA 1-4R, 181;
CAAE 181; CAAS 18; CANR 1, 33, 54,
75, 98; CMW 4; CN 7; CPW; DLB NOV;
DLB 9; INT CANR-33; MTCW 1; RHW;
SATA 7; SATA-Essay 107; TCWW 2;
YAW
Faulcon, Robert
See Holdstock, Robert P.
Faulkner, William (Cuthbert)
1897-1962 .... **CLC 1, 3, 6, 8, 9, 11, 14,
18, 28, 52, 68; SSC 1, 35, 42; WLC**
See also AAYA 7; AMW; AMWR 1; BPFB
1; BYA 5; CA 81-84; CANR 33; CDALB
1929-1941; DA; DA3; DAB; DAC; DAM
MST, NOV; DLB 9, 11, 44, 102; DLBD
2; DLBY 1986, 1997; EWL 3; EXPN;
EXPS; LAIT 2; LMFS 2; MTCW 1, 2;
NFS 4, 8, 13; RGAL 4; RGSF 2; SSFS 2,
5, 6, 12; TUS
Fauset, Jessie Redmon
1882(?)-1961 .. **BLC 2; CLC 19, 54; HR
2**
See also AFAW 2; BW 1; CA 109; CANR
83; DAM MULT; DLB 51; FW; LMFS 2;
MAWW

Faust, Frederick (Schiller)
1892-1944(?) .... **TCLC 49**
See Austin, Frank; Brand, Max; Challis,
George; Dawson, Peter; Dexter, Martin;
Evans, Evan; Frederick, John; Frost, Fred-
erick; Manning, David; Silver, Nicholas
See also CA 152; 108; DAM POP; DLB
256; TUS
Faust, Irvin 1924- .... **CLC 8**
See also CA 33-36R; CANR 28, 67; CN 7;
DLB 2, 28, 218, 278; DLBY 1980
Fawkes, Guy
See Benchley, Robert (Charles)
Fearing, Kenneth (Flexner)
1902-1961 .... **CLC 51**
See also CA 93-96; CANR 59; CMW 4;
DLB 9; RGAL 4
Fecamps, Elise
See Creasey, John
Federman, Raymond 1928- .... **CLC 6, 47**
See also CA 17-20R; CAAE 208; CAAS 8;
CANR 10, 43, 83, 108; CN 7; DLBY
1980
Federspiel, J(uerg) F. 1931- .... **CLC 42**
See also CA 146
Feiffer, Jules (Ralph) 1929- ...... **CLC 2, 8, 64**
See also AAYA 3; CA 17-20R; CAD; CANR
30, 59; CD 5; DAM DRAM; DLB 7, 44;
INT CANR-30; MTCW 1; SATA 8, 61,
111
Feige, Hermann Albert Otto Maximilian
See Traven, B.
Feinberg, David B. 1956-1994 .... **CLC 59**
See also CA 147; 135
Feinstein, Elaine 1930- .... **CLC 36**
See also CA 69-72; CAAS 1; CANR 31,
68; CN 7; CP 7; CWP; DLB 14, 40;
MTCW 1
Feke, Gilbert David .... **CLC 65**
Feldman, Irving (Mordecai) 1928- ..... **CLC 7**
See also CA 1-4R; CANR 1; CP 7; DLB
169
Felix-Tchicaya, Gerald
See Tchicaya, Gerald Felix
Fellini, Federico 1920-1993 .... **CLC 16, 85**
See also CA 143; 65-68; CANR 33
Felsen, Henry Gregor 1916-1995 ..... **CLC 17**
See also CA 180; 1-4R; CANR 1; SAAS 2;
SATA 1
Felski, Rita .... **CLC 65**
Fenno, Jack
See Calisher, Hortense
Fenollosa, Ernest (Francisco)
1853-1908 .... **TCLC 91**
Fenton, James Martin 1949- .... **CLC 32**
See also CA 102; CANR 108; CP 7; DLB
40; PFS 11
Ferber, Edna 1887-1968 .... **CLC 18, 93**
See also AITN 1; CA 25-28R; 5-8R; CANR
68, 105; DLB 9, 28, 86, 266; MTCW 1,
2; RGAL 4; RHW; SATA 7; TCWW 2
Ferdowsi, Abu'l Qasem 940-1020 . **CMLC 43**
See also RGWL 2, 3
Ferguson, Helen
See Kavan, Anna
Ferguson, Niall 1964- .... **CLC 134**
See also CA 190
Ferguson, Samuel 1810-1886 .... **NCLC 33**
See also DLB 32; RGEL 2
Fergusson, Robert 1750-1774 .... **LC 29**
See also DLB 109; RGEL 2
Ferling, Lawrence
See Ferlinghetti, Lawrence (Monsanto)
Ferlinghetti, Lawrence (Monsanto)
1919(?)- ..... **CLC 2, 6, 10, 27, 111; PC 1**
See also CA 5-8R; CANR 3, 41, 73;
CDALB 1941-1968; CP 7; DA3; DAM
POET; DLB 5, 16; MTCW 1, 2; RGAL 4;
WP

Fern, Fanny
See Parton, Sara Payson Willis
Fernandez, Vicente Garcia Huidobro
See Huidobro Fernandez, Vicente Garcia
Fernandez-Armesto, Felipe .... **CLC 70**
Fernandez de Lizardi, Jose Joaquin
See Lizardi, Jose Joaquin Fernandez de
Ferre, Rosario 1938- ...... **CLC 139; HLCS 1;
SSC 36**
See also CA 131; CANR 55, 81; CWW 2;
DLB 145; EWL 3; HW 1, 2; LAWS 1;
MTCW 1; WLIT 1
Ferrer, Gabriel (Francisco Victor) Miro
See Miro (Ferrer), Gabriel (Francisco
Victor)
Ferrier, Susan (Edmonstone)
1782-1854 .... **NCLC 8**
See also DLB 116; RGEL 2
Ferrigno, Robert 1948(?)- .... **CLC 65**
See also CA 140
Ferron, Jacques 1921-1985 .... **CLC 94**
See also CA 129; 117; CCA 1; DAC; DLB
60; EWL 3
Feuchtwanger, Lion 1884-1958 .... **TCLC 3**
See also CA 187; 104; DLB 66; EWL 3
Feuillet, Octave 1821-1890 .... **NCLC 45**
See also DLB 192
Feydeau, Georges (Leon Jules Marie)
1862-1921 .... **TCLC 22**
See also CA 152; 113; CANR 84; DAM
DRAM; DLB 192; EWL 3; GFL 1789 to
the Present; RGWL 2, 3
Fichte, Johann Gottlieb
1762-1814 .... **NCLC 62**
See also DLB 90
Ficino, Marsilio 1433-1499 .... **LC 12**
Fiedeler, Hans
See Doeblin, Alfred
Fiedler, Leslie A(aron) 1917-2003 ..... **CLC 4,
13, 24**
See also CA 9-12R; CANR 7, 63; CN 7;
DLB 28, 67; EWL 3; MTCW 1, 2; RGAL
4; TUS
Field, Andrew 1938- .... **CLC 44**
See also CA 97-100; CANR 25
Field, Eugene 1850-1895 .... **NCLC 3**
See also DLB 23, 42, 140; DLBD 13; MAI-
CYA 1, 2; RGAL 4; SATA 16
Field, Gans T.
See Wellman, Manly Wade
Field, Michael 1915-1971 .... **TCLC 43**
See also CA 29-32R
Field, Peter
See Hobson, Laura Z(ametkin)
See also TCWW 2
Fielding, Helen 1959(?)- .... **CLC 146**
See also CA 172; DLB 231
Fielding, Henry 1707-1754 .... **LC 1, 46, 85;
WLC**
See also BRW 3; BRWR 1; CDBLB 1660-
1789; DA; DA3; DAB; DAC; DAM
DRAM, MST, NOV; DLB 39, 84, 101;
RGEL 2; TEA; WLIT 3
Fielding, Sarah 1710-1768 .... **LC 1, 44**
See also DLB 39; RGEL 2; TEA
Fields, W. C. 1880-1946 .... **TCLC 80**
See also DLB 44
Fierstein, Harvey (Forbes) 1954- ..... **CLC 33**
See also CA 129; 123; CAD; CD 5; CPW;
DA3; DAM DRAM, POP; DFS 6; DLB
266; GLL
Figes, Eva 1932- .... **CLC 31**
See also CA 53-56; CANR 4, 44, 83; CN 7;
DLB 14, 271; FW
Filippo, Eduardo de
See de Filippo, Eduardo
Finch, Anne 1661-1720 .... **LC 3; PC 21**
See also DLB 95

Forten, Charlotte L. 1837-1914 .... **BLC 2; TCLC 16**
See Grimke, Charlotte L(ottie) Forten
See also DLB 50, 239

Fortinbras
See Grieg, (Johan) Nordahl (Brun)

Foscolo, Ugo 1778-1827 .... **NCLC 8, 97**
See also EW 5

Fosse, Bob .... **CLC 20**
See Fosse, Robert Louis

Fosse, Robert Louis 1927-1987
See Fosse, Bob
See also CA 123; 110

Foster, Hannah Webster
1758-1840 .... **NCLC 99**
See also DLB 37, 200; RGAL 4

Foster, Stephen Collins
1826-1864 .... **NCLC 26**
See also RGAL 4

Foucault, Michel 1926-1984 . **CLC 31, 34, 69**
See also CA 113; 105; CANR 34; DLB 242;
EW 13; EWL 3; GFL 1789 to the Present;
GLL 1; MTCW 1, 2; TWA

Fouque, Friedrich (Heinrich Karl) de la Motte 1777-1843 .... **NCLC 2**
See also DLB 90; RGWL 2, 3; SUFW 1

Fourier, Charles 1772-1837 .... **NCLC 51**

Fournier, Henri-Alban 1886-1914
See Alain-Fournier
See also CA 179; 104

Fournier, Pierre 1916- .... **CLC 11**
See Gascar, Pierre
See also CA 89-92; CANR 16, 40

Fowles, John (Robert) 1926- . **CLC 1, 2, 3, 4, 6, 9, 10, 15, 33, 87; SSC 33**
See also BPFB 1; BRWS 1; CA 5-8R;
CANR 25, 71, 103; CDBLB 1960 to
Present; CN 7; DA3; DAB; DAC; DAM
MST; DLB 14, 139, 207; EWL 3; HGG;
MTCW 1, 2; RGEL 2; RHW; SATA 22;
TEA; WLIT 4

Fox, Paula 1923- .... **CLC 2, 8, 121**
See also AAYA 3, 37; BYA 3, 8; CA 73-76;
CANR 20, 36, 62, 105; CLR 1, 44; DLB
52; JRDA; MAICYA 1, 2; MTCW 1; NFS
12; SATA 17, 60, 120; WYA; YAW

Fox, William Price (Jr.) 1926- .... **CLC 22**
See also CA 17-20R; CAAS 19; CANR 11;
CSW; DLB 2; DLBY 1981

Foxe, John 1517(?)-1587 .... **LC 14**
See also DLB 132

Frame, Janet .. **CLC 2, 3, 6, 22, 66, 96; SSC 29**
See Clutha, Janet Paterson Frame
See also CN 7; CWP; EWL 3; RGEL 2;
RGSF 2; TWA

France, Anatole .... **TCLC 9**
See Thibault, Jacques Anatole Francois
See also DLB 123; EWL 3; GFL 1789 to
the Present; MTCW 1; RGWL 2, 3;
SUFW 1

Francis, Claude .... **CLC 50**
See also CA 192

Francis, Dick 1920- .... **CLC 2, 22, 42, 102**
See also AAYA 5, 21; BEST 89:3; BPFB 1;
CA 5-8R; CANR 9, 42, 68, 100; CDBLB
1960 to Present; CMW 4; CN 7; DA3;
DAM POP; DLB 87; INT CANR-9;
MSW; MTCW 1, 2

Francis, Robert (Churchill)
1901-1987 .... **CLC 15; PC 34**
See also AMWS 9; CA 123; 1-4R; CANR
1; EXPP; PFS 12

Francis, Lord Jeffrey
See Jeffrey, Francis
See also DLB 107

Frank, Anne(lies Marie)
1929-1945 .... **TCLC 17; WLC**
See also AAYA 12; BYA 1; CA 133; 113;
CANR 68; DA; DA3; DAB; DAC; DAM
MST; LAIT 4; MAICYA 2; MAICYAS 1;
MTCW 1, 2; NCFS 2; SATA 87; SATA-
Brief 42; WYA; YAW

Frank, Bruno 1887-1945 .... **TCLC 81**
See also CA 189; DLB 118; EWL 3

Frank, Elizabeth 1945- .... **CLC 39**
See also CA 126; 121; CANR 78; INT 126

Frankl, Viktor E(mil) 1905-1997 ...... **CLC 93**
See also CA 161; 65-68

Franklin, Benjamin
See Hasek, Jaroslav (Matej Frantisek)

Franklin, Benjamin 1706-1790 .... **LC 25; WLCS**
See also AMW; CDALB 1640-1865; DA;
DA3; DAB; DAC; DAM MST; DLB 24,
43, 73, 183; LAIT 1; RGAL 4; TUS

Franklin, (Stella Maria Sarah) Miles (Lampe) 1879-1954 .... **TCLC 7**
See also CA 164; 104; DLB 230; FW;
MTCW 2; RGEL 2; TWA

Fraser, (Lady) Antonia (Pakenham)
1932- .... **CLC 32, 107**
See also CA 85-88; CANR 44, 65; CMW;
DLB 276; MTCW 1, 2; SATA-Brief 32

Fraser, George MacDonald 1925- ...... **CLC 7**
See also CA 45-48, 180; CAAE 180; CANR
2, 48, 74; MTCW 1; RHW

Fraser, Sylvia 1935- .... **CLC 64**
See also CA 45-48; CANR 1, 16, 60; CCA
1

Frayn, Michael 1933- .... **CLC 3, 7, 31, 47**
See also BRWS 7; CA 5-8R; CANR 30, 69,
114; CBD; CD 5; CN 7; DAM DRAM,
NOV; DLB 13, 14, 194, 245; FANT;
MTCW 1, 2; SFW 4

Fraze, Candida (Merrill) 1945- .... **CLC 50**
See also CA 126

Frazer, Andrew
See Marlowe, Stephen

Frazer, J(ames) G(eorge)
1854-1941 .... **TCLC 32**
See also BRWS 3; CA 118

Frazer, Robert Caine
See Creasey, John

Frazer, Sir James George
See Frazer, J(ames) G(eorge)

Frazier, Charles 1950- .... **CLC 109**
See also AAYA 34; CA 161; CSW

Frazier, Ian 1951- .... **CLC 46**
See also CA 130; CANR 54, 93

Frederic, Harold 1856-1898 .... **NCLC 10**
See also AMW; DLB 12, 23; DLBD 13;
RGAL 4

Frederick, John
See Faust, Frederick (Schiller)
See also TCWW 2

Frederick the Great 1712-1786 .... **LC 14**

Fredro, Aleksander 1793-1876 .... **NCLC 8**

Freeling, Nicolas 1927- .... **CLC 38**
See also CA 49-52; CAAS 12; CANR 1,
17, 50, 84; CMW 4; CN 7; DLB 87

Freeman, Douglas Southall
1886-1953 .... **TCLC 11**
See also CA 195; 109; DLB 17; DLBD 17

Freeman, Judith 1946- .... **CLC 55**
See also CA 148; DLB 256

Freeman, Mary E(leanor) Wilkins
1852-1930 .... **SSC 1, 47; TCLC 9**
See also CA 177; 106; DLB 12, 78, 221;
EXPS; FW; HGG; MAWW; RGAL 4;
RGSF 2; SSFS 4, 8; SUFW 1; TUS

Freeman, R(ichard) Austin
1862-1943 .... **TCLC 21**
See also CA 113; CANR 84; CMW 4; DLB
70

French, Albert 1943- .... **CLC 86**
See also BW 3; CA 167

French, Antonia
See Kureishi, Hanif

French, Marilyn 1929- .... **CLC 10, 18, 60**
See also BPFB 1; CA 69-72; CANR 3, 31;
CN 7; CPW; DAM DRAM, NOV, POP;
FW; INT CANR-31; MTCW 1, 2

French, Paul
See Asimov, Isaac

Freneau, Philip Morin 1752-1832 .. **NCLC 1, 111**
See also AMWS 2; DLB 37, 43; RGAL 4

Freud, Sigmund 1856-1939 .... **TCLC 52**
See also CA 133; 115; CANR 69; EW 8;
EWL 3; MTCW 1, 2; NCFS 3; TWA

Freytag, Gustav 1816-1895 .... **NCLC 109**
See also DLB 129

Friedan, Betty (Naomi) 1921- .... **CLC 74**
See also CA 65-68; CANR 18, 45, 74; DLB
246; FW; MTCW 1, 2

Friedlander, Saul 1932- .... **CLC 90**
See also CA 130; 117; CANR 72

Friedman, B(ernard) H(arper)
1926- .... **CLC 7**
See also CA 1-4R; CANR 3, 48

Friedman, Bruce Jay 1930- ...... **CLC 3, 5, 56**
See also CA 9-12R; CAD; CANR 25, 52,
101; CD 5; CN 7; DLB 2, 28, 244; INT
CANR-25

Friel, Brian 1929- .... **CLC 5, 42, 59, 115; DC 8**
See also BRWS 5; CA 21-24R; CANR 33,
69; CBD; CD 5; DFS 11; DLB 13; EWL
3; MTCW 1; RGEL 2; TEA

Friis-Baastad, Babbis Ellinor
1921-1970 .... **CLC 12**
See also CA 134; 17-20R; SATA 7

Frisch, Max (Rudolf) 1911-1991 ... **CLC 3, 9, 14, 18, 32, 44; TCLC 121**
See also CA 134; 85-88; CANR 32, 74; CD-
WLB 2; DAM DRAM, NOV; DLB 69,
124; EW 13; EWL 3; MTCW 1, 2; RGWL
2, 3

Fromentin, Eugene (Samuel Auguste)
1820-1876 .... **NCLC 10**
See also DLB 123; GFL 1789 to the Present

Frost, Frederick
See Faust, Frederick (Schiller)
See also TCWW 2

Frost, Robert (Lee) 1874-1963 .. **CLC 1, 3, 4, 9, 10, 13, 15, 26, 34, 44; PC 1, 39; WLC**
See also AAYA 21; AMW; AMWR 1; CA
89-92; CANR 33; CDALB 1917-1929;
CLR 67; DA; DA3; DAB; DAC; DAM
MST, POET; DLB 54; EWL 3;
EXPP; MTCW 1, 2; PAB; PFS 1, 2, 3, 4,
5, 6, 7, 10, 13; RGAL 4; SATA 14; TUS;
WP; WYA

Froude, James Anthony
1818-1894 .... **NCLC 43**
See also DLB 18, 57, 144

Froy, Herald
See Waterhouse, Keith (Spencer)

Fry, Christopher 1907- .... **CLC 2, 10, 14**
See also BRWS 3; CA 17-20R; CAAS 23;
CANR 9, 30, 74; CBD; CD 5; CP 7; DAM
DRAM; DLB 13; EWL 3; MTCW 1, 2;
RGEL 2; SATA 66; TEA

Frye, (Herman) Northrop
1912-1991 .... **CLC 24, 70**
See also CA 133; 5-8R; CANR 8, 37; DLB
67, 68, 246; EWL 3; MTCW 1, 2; RGAL
4; TWA

Fuchs, Daniel 1909-1993 .... **CLC 8, 22**
See also CA 142; 81-84; CAAS 5; CANR
40; DLB 9, 26, 28; DLBY 1993

Garner, Alan 1934- .... **CLC 17**
See also AAYA 18; BYA 3, 5; CA 73-76, 178; CAAE 178; CANR 15, 64; CLR 20; CPW; DAB; DAM POP; DLB 161, 261; FANT; MAICYA 1, 2; MTCW 1, 2; SATA 18, 69; SATA-Essay 108; SUFW 1, 2; YAW

Garner, Hugh 1913-1979 .... **CLC 13**
See Warwick, Jarvis
See also CA 69-72; CANR 31; CCA 1; DLB 68

Garnett, David 1892-1981 .... **CLC 3**
See also CA 103; 5-8R; CANR 17, 79; DLB 34; FANT; MTCW 2; RGEL 2; SFW 4; SUFW 1

Garos, Stephanie
See Katz, Steve

Garrett, George (Palmer) 1929- .. **CLC 3, 11, 51; SSC 30**
See also AMWS 7; BPFB 2; CA 1-4R; CAAE 202; CAAS 5; CANR 1, 42, 67, 109; CN 7; CP 7; CSW; DLB 2, 5, 130, 152; DLBY 1983

Garrick, David 1717-1779 .... **LC 15**
See also DAM DRAM; DLB 84, 213; RGEL 2

Garrigue, Jean 1914-1972 .... **CLC 2, 8**
See also CA 37-40R; 5-8R; CANR 20

Garrison, Frederick
See Sinclair, Upton (Beall)

Garro, Elena 1920(?)-1998 .... **HLCS 1**
See also CA 169; 131; CWW 2; DLB 145; EWL 3; HW 1; LAWS 1; WLIT 1

Garth, Will
See Hamilton, Edmond; Kuttner, Henry

Garvey, Marcus (Moziah, Jr.)
1887-1940 .... **BLC 2; HR 2; TCLC 41**
See also BW 1; CA 124; 120; CANR 79; DAM MULT

Gary, Romain .... **CLC 25**
See Kacew, Romain
See also DLB 83

Gascar, Pierre .... **CLC 11**
See Fournier, Pierre
See also EWL 3

Gascoyne, David (Emery)
1916-2001 .... **CLC 45**
See also CA 200; 65-68; CANR 10, 28, 54; CP 7; DLB 20; MTCW 1; RGEL 2

Gaskell, Elizabeth Cleghorn
1810-1865 .... **NCLC 5, 70, 97; SSC 25**
See also BRW 5; CDBLB 1832-1890; DAB; DAM MST; DLB 21, 144, 159; RGEL 2; RGSF 2; TEA

Gass, William H(oward) 1924- . **CLC 1, 2, 8, 11, 15, 39, 132; SSC 12**
See also AMWS 6; CA 17-20R; CANR 30, 71, 100; CN 7; DLB 2, 227; EWL 3; MTCW 1, 2; RGAL 4

Gassendi, Pierre 1592-1655 .... **LC 54**
See also GFL Beginnings to 1789

Gasset, Jose Ortega y
See Ortega y Gasset, Jose

Gates, Henry Louis, Jr. 1950- ... **BLCS; CLC 65**
See also BW 2, 3; CA 109; CANR 25, 53, 75; CSW; DA3; DAM MULT; DLB 67; EWL 3; MTCW 1; RGAL 4

Gautier, Theophile 1811-1872 .. **NCLC 1, 59; PC 18; SSC 20**
See also DAM POET; DLB 119; EW 6; GFL 1789 to the Present; RGWL 2, 3; SUFW; TWA

Gawsworth, John
See Bates, H(erbert) E(rnest)

Gay, John 1685-1732 .... **LC 49**
See also BRW 3; DAM DRAM; DLB 84, 95; RGEL 2; WLIT 3

Gay, Oliver
See Gogarty, Oliver St. John

Gay, Peter (Jack) 1923- .... **CLC 158**
See also CA 13-16R; CANR 18, 41, 77; INT CANR-18

Gaye, Marvin (Pentz, Jr.)
1939-1984 .... **CLC 26**
See also CA 112; 195

Gebler, Carlo (Ernest) 1954- .... **CLC 39**
See also CA 133; 119; CANR 96; DLB 271

Gee, Maggie (Mary) 1948- .... **CLC 57**
See also CA 130; CN 7; DLB 207

Gee, Maurice (Gough) 1931- .... **CLC 29**
See also AAYA 42; CA 97-100; CANR 67; CLR 56; CN 7; CWRI 5; EWL 3; MAICYA 2; RGSF 2; SATA 46, 101

Geiogamah, Hanay 1945- .... **NNAL**
See also CA 153; DAM MULT; DLB 175

Gelbart, Larry (Simon) 1928- .... **CLC 21, 61**
See Gelbart, Larry
See also CA 73-76; CANR 45, 94

Gelbart, Larry 1928-
See Gelbart, Larry (Simon)
See also CAD; CD 5

Gelber, Jack 1932- .... **CLC 1, 6, 14, 79**
See also CA 1-4R; CAD; CANR 2; DLB 7, 228

Gellhorn, Martha (Ellis)
1908-1998 .... **CLC 14, 60**
See also CA 164; 77-80; CANR 44; CN 7; DLBY 1982, 1998

Genet, Jean 1910-1986 .. **CLC 1, 2, 5, 10, 14, 44, 46; TCLC 128**
See also CA 13-16R; CANR 18; DA3; DAM DRAM; DFS 10; DLB 72; DLBY 1986; EW 13; EWL 3; GFL 1789 to the Present; GLL 1; LMFS 2; MTCW 1, 2; RGWL 2, 3; TWA

Gent, Peter 1942- .... **CLC 29**
See also AITN 1; CA 89-92; DLBY 1982

Gentile, Giovanni 1875-1944 .... **TCLC 96**
See also CA 119

Gentlewoman in New England, A
See Bradstreet, Anne

Gentlewoman in Those Parts, A
See Bradstreet, Anne

Geoffrey of Monmouth c.
1100-1155 .... **CMLC 44**
See also DLB 146; TEA

George, Jean
See George, Jean Craighead

George, Jean Craighead 1919- .... **CLC 35**
See also AAYA 8; BYA 2, 4; CA 5-8R; CANR 25; CLR 1; 80; DLB 52; JRDA; MAICYA 1, 2; SATA 2, 68, 124; WYA; YAW

George, Stefan (Anton) 1868-1933 . **TCLC 2, 14**
See also CA 193; 104; EW 8; EWL 3

Georges, Georges Martin
See Simenon, Georges (Jacques Christian)

Gerhardi, William Alexander
See Gerhardie, William Alexander

Gerhardie, William Alexander
1895-1977 .... **CLC 5**
See also CA 73-76; 25-28R; CANR 18; DLB 36; RGEL 2

Gerson, Jean 1363-1429 .... **LC 77**
See also DLB 208

Gersonides 1288-1344 .... **CMLC 49**
See also DLB 115

Gerstler, Amy 1956- .... **CLC 70**
See also CA 146; CANR 99

Gertler, T. .... **CLC 34**
See also CA 121; 116

Gertsen, Aleksandr Ivanovich
See Herzen, Aleksandr Ivanovich

Ghalib .... **NCLC 39, 78**
See Ghalib, Asadullah Khan

Ghalib, Asadullah Khan 1797-1869
See Ghalib
See also DAM POET; RGWL 2, 3

Ghelderode, Michel de 1898-1962 ..... **CLC 6, 11; DC 15**
See also CA 85-88; CANR 40, 77; DAM DRAM; EW 11; EWL 3; TWA

Ghiselin, Brewster 1903-2001 .... **CLC 23**
See also CA 13-16R; CAAS 10; CANR 13; CP 7

Ghose, Aurabinda 1872-1950 .... **TCLC 63**
See Ghose, Aurobindo
See also CA 163

Ghose, Aurobindo
See Ghose, Aurabinda
See also EWL 3

Ghose, Zulfikar 1935- .... **CLC 42**
See also CA 65-68; CANR 67; CN 7; CP 7; EWL 3

Ghosh, Amitav 1956- .... **CLC 44, 153**
See also CA 147; CANR 80; CN 7

Giacosa, Giuseppe 1847-1906 .... **TCLC 7**
See also CA 104

Gibb, Lee
See Waterhouse, Keith (Spencer)

Gibbon, Lewis Grassic .... **TCLC 4**
See Mitchell, James Leslie
See also RGEL 2

Gibbons, Kaye 1960- .... **CLC 50, 88, 145**
See also AAYA 34; AMWS 10; CA 151; CANR 75; CSW; DA3; DAM POP; MTCW 1; NFS 3; RGAL 4; SATA 117

Gibran, Kahlil 1883-1931 .. **PC 9; TCLC 1, 9**
See also CA 150; 104; DA3; DAM POET, POP; EWL 3; MTCW 2

Gibran, Khalil
See Gibran, Kahlil

Gibson, William 1914- .... **CLC 23**
See also CA 9-12R; CAD 2; CANR 9, 42, 75; CD 5; DA; DAB; DAC; DAM DRAM, MST; DFS 2; DLB 7; LAIT 2; MTCW 2; SATA 66; YAW

Gibson, William (Ford) 1948- ... **CLC 39, 63; SSC 52**
See also AAYA 12; BPFB 2; CA 133; 126; CANR 52, 90, 106; CN 7; CPW; DA3; DAM POP; DLB 251; MTCW 2; SCFW 2; SFW 4

Gide, Andre (Paul Guillaume)
1869-1951 ..... **SSC 13; TCLC 5, 12, 36; WLC**
See also CA 124; 104; DA; DA3; DAB; DAC; DAM MST, NOV; DLB 65; EW 8; EWL 3; GFL 1789 to the Present; MTCW 1, 2; RGSF 2; RGWL 2, 3; TWA

Gifford, Barry (Colby) 1946- .... **CLC 34**
See also CA 65-68; CANR 9, 30, 40, 90

Gilbert, Frank
See De Voto, Bernard (Augustine)

Gilbert, W(illiam) S(chwenck)
1836-1911 .... **TCLC 3**
See also CA 173; 104; DAM DRAM, POET; RGEL 2; SATA 36

Gilbreth, Frank B(unker), Jr.
1911-2001 .... **CLC 17**
See also CA 9-12R; SATA 2

Gilchrist, Ellen (Louise) 1935- .. **CLC 34, 48, 143; SSC 14**
See also BPFB 2; CA 116; 113; CANR 41, 61, 104; CN 7; CPW; CSW; DAM POP; DLB 130; EWL 3; EXPS; MTCW 1, 2; RGAL 4; RGSF 2; SSFS 9

Giles, Molly 1942- .... **CLC 39**
See also CA 126; CANR 98

Gill, Eric 1882-1940 .... **TCLC 85**
See Gill, (Arthur) Eric (Rowton Peter Joseph)

Gombrowicz, Witold 1904-1969 .... **CLC 4, 7, 11, 49**
See also CA 25-28R; 19-20; CANR 105; CAP 2; CDWLB 4; DAM DRAM; DLB 215; EW 12; EWL 3; RGWL 2, 3; TWA

Gomez de Avellaneda, Gertrudis
1814-1873 .... **NCLC 111**
See also LAW

Gomez de la Serna, Ramon
1888-1963 .... **CLC 9**
See also CA 116; 153; CANR 79; EWL 3; HW 1, 2

Goncharov, Ivan Alexandrovich
1812-1891 .... **NCLC 1, 63**
See also DLB 238; EW 6; RGWL 2, 3

Goncourt, Edmond (Louis Antoine Huot) de
1822-1896 .... **NCLC 7**
See also DLB 123; EW 7; GFL 1789 to the Present; RGWL 2, 3

Goncourt, Jules (Alfred Huot) de
1830-1870 .... **NCLC 7**
See also DLB 123; EW 7; GFL 1789 to the Present; RGWL 2, 3

Gongora (y Argote), Luis de
1561-1627 .... **LC 72**
See also RGWL 2, 3

Gontier, Fernande 19(?)- .... **CLC 50**

Gonzalez Martinez, Enrique
1871-1952 .... **TCLC 72**
See also CA 166; CANR 81; EWL 3; HW 1, 2

Goodison, Lorna 1947- .... **PC 36**
See also CA 142; CANR 88; CP 7; CWP; DLB 157; EWL 3

Goodman, Paul 1911-1972 ..... **CLC 1, 2, 4, 7**
See also CA 37-40R; 19-20; CAD; CANR 34; CAP 2; DLB 130, 246; MTCW 1; RGAL 4

Gordimer, Nadine 1923- ...... **CLC 3, 5, 7, 10, 18, 33, 51, 70, 123, 160, 161; SSC 17; WLCS**
See also AAYA 39; AFW; BRWS 2; CA 5-8R; CANR 3, 28, 56, 88; CN 7; DA; DA3; DAB; DAC; DAM MST, NOV; DLB 225; EWL 3; EXPS; INT CANR-28; MTCW 1, 2; NFS 4; RGEL 2; RGSF 2; SSFS 2, 14; TWA; WLIT 2; YAW

Gordon, Adam Lindsay
1833-1870 .... **NCLC 21**
See also DLB 230

Gordon, Caroline 1895-1981 . **CLC 6, 13, 29, 83; SSC 15**
See also AMW; CA 103; 11-12; CANR 36; CAP 1; DLB 4, 9, 102; DLBD 17; DLBY 1981; EWL 3; MTCW 1, 2; RGAL 4; RGSF 2

Gordon, Charles William 1860-1937
See Connor, Ralph
See also CA 109

Gordon, Mary (Catherine) 1949- .... **CLC 13, 22, 128; SSC 59**
See also AMWS 4; BPFB 2; CA 102; CANR 44, 92; CN 7; DLB 6; DLBY 1981; FW; INT CA-102; MTCW 1

Gordon, N. J.
See Bosman, Herman Charles

Gordon, Sol 1923- .... **CLC 26**
See also CA 53-56; CANR 4; SATA 11

Gordone, Charles 1925-1995 .. **CLC 1, 4; DC 8**
See also BW 1, 3; CA 150; 93-96; 180; CAAE 180; CAD; CANR 55; DAM DRAM; DLB 7; INT 93-96; MTCW 1

Gore, Catherine 1800-1861 .... **NCLC 65**
See also DLB 116; RGEL 2

Gorenko, Anna Andreevna
See Akhmatova, Anna

Gorky, Maxim .... **SSC 28; TCLC 8; WLC**
See Peshkov, Alexei Maximovich
See also DAB; DFS 9; EW 8; EWL 3; MTCW 2; TWA

Goryan, Sirak
See Saroyan, William

Gosse, Edmund (William)
1849-1928 .... **TCLC 28**
See also CA 117; DLB 57, 144, 184; RGEL 2

Gotlieb, Phyllis Fay (Bloom) 1926- .. **CLC 18**
See also CA 13-16R; CANR 7; DLB 88, 251; SFW 4

Gottesman, S. D.
See Kornbluth, C(yril) M.; Pohl, Frederik

Gottfried von Strassburg fl. c.
1170-1215 .... **CMLC 10**
See also CDWLB 2; DLB 138; EW 1; RGWL 2, 3

Gotthelf, Jeremias 1797-1854 .... **NCLC 117**
See also DLB 133; RGWL 2, 3

Gottschalk, Laura Riding
See Jackson, Laura (Riding)

Gould, Lois 1932(?)-2002 .... **CLC 4, 10**
See also CA 208; 77-80; CANR 29; MTCW 1

Gould, Stephen Jay 1941-2002 .... **CLC 163**
See also AAYA 26; BEST 90:2; CA 205; 77-80; CANR 10, 27, 56, 75; CPW; INT CANR-27; MTCW 1, 2

Gourmont, Remy(-Marie-Charles) de
1858-1915 .... **TCLC 17**
See also CA 150; 109; GFL 1789 to the Present; MTCW 2

Govier, Katherine 1948- .... **CLC 51**
See also CA 101; CANR 18, 40; CCA 1

Gower, John c. 1330-1408 .... **LC 76**
See also BRW 1; DLB 146; RGEL 2

Goyen, (Charles) William
1915-1983 .... **CLC 5, 8, 14, 40**
See also AITN 2; CA 110; 5-8R; CANR 6, 71; DLB 2, 218; DLBY 1983; EWL 3; INT CANR-6

Goytisolo, Juan 1931- .... **CLC 5, 10, 23, 133; HLC 1**
See also CA 85-88; CANR 32, 61; CWW 2; DAM MULT; EWL 3; GLL 2; HW 1, 2; MTCW 1, 2

Gozzano, Guido 1883-1916 .... **PC 10**
See also CA 154; DLB 114; EWL 3

Gozzi, (Conte) Carlo 1720-1806 .... **NCLC 23**

Grabbe, Christian Dietrich
1801-1836 .... **NCLC 2**
See also DLB 133; RGWL 2, 3

Grace, Patricia Frances 1937- .... **CLC 56**
See also CA 176; CN 7; EWL 3; RGSF 2

Gracian y Morales, Baltasar
1601-1658 .... **LC 15**

Gracq, Julien .... **CLC 11, 48**
See Poirier, Louis
See also CWW 2; DLB 83; GFL 1789 to the Present

Grade, Chaim 1910-1982 .... **CLC 10**
See also CA 107; 93-96; EWL 3

Graduate of Oxford, A
See Ruskin, John

Grafton, Garth
See Duncan, Sara Jeannette

Grafton, Sue 1940- .... **CLC 163**
See also AAYA 11; BEST 90:3; CA 108; CANR 31, 55, 111; CMW 4; CPW; CSW; DA3; DAM POP; DLB 226; FW; MSW

Graham, John
See Phillips, David Graham

Graham, Jorie 1951- .... **CLC 48, 118**
See also CA 111; CANR 63; CP 7; CWP; DLB 120; EWL 3; PFS 10, 17

Graham, R(obert) B(ontine) Cunninghame
See Cunninghame Graham, Robert (Gallnigad) Bontine
See also DLB 98, 135, 174; RGEL 2; RGSF 2

Graham, Robert
See Haldeman, Joe (William)

Graham, Tom
See Lewis, (Harry) Sinclair

Graham, W(illiam) S(idney)
1918-1986 .... **CLC 29**
See also BRWS 7; CA 118; 73-76; DLB 20; RGEL 2

Graham, Winston (Mawdsley)
1910- .... **CLC 23**
See also CA 49-52; CANR 2, 22, 45, 66; CMW 4; CN 7; DLB 77; RHW

Grahame, Kenneth 1859-1932 .... **TCLC 64**
See also BYA 5; CA 136; 108; CANR 80; CLR 5; CWRI 5; DA3; DAB; DLB 34, 141, 178; FANT; MAICYA 1, 2; MTCW 2; RGEL 2; SATA 100; TEA; WCH; YABC 1

Granger, Darius John
See Marlowe, Stephen

Granin, Daniil .... **CLC 59**

Granovsky, Timofei Nikolaevich
1813-1855 .... **NCLC 75**
See also DLB 198

Grant, Skeeter
See Spiegelman, Art

Granville-Barker, Harley
1877-1946 .... **TCLC 2**
See Barker, Harley Granville
See also CA 204; 104; DAM DRAM; RGEL 2

Granzotto, Gianni
See Granzotto, Giovanni Battista

Granzotto, Giovanni Battista
1914-1985 .... **CLC 70**
See also CA 166

Grass, Guenter (Wilhelm) 1927- ... **CLC 1, 2, 4, 6, 11, 15, 22, 32, 49, 88; WLC**
See also BPFB 2; CA 13-16R; CANR 20, 75, 93; CDWLB 2; DA; DA3; DAB; DAC; DAM MST, NOV; DLB 75, 124; EW 13; EWL 3; MTCW 1, 2; RGWL 2, 3; TWA

Gratton, Thomas
See Hulme, T(homas) E(rnest)

Grau, Shirley Ann 1929- .... **CLC 4, 9, 146; SSC 15**
See also CA 89-92; CANR 22, 69; CN 7; CSW; DLB 2, 218; INT CA-89-92, CANR-22; MTCW 1

Gravel, Fern
See Hall, James Norman

Graver, Elizabeth 1964- .... **CLC 70**
See also CA 135; CANR 71

Graves, Richard Perceval
1895-1985 .... **CLC 44**
See also CA 65-68; CANR 9, 26, 51

Graves, Robert (von Ranke)
1895-1985 .. **CLC 1, 2, 6, 11, 39, 44, 45; PC 6**
See also BPFB 2; BRW 7; BYA 4; CA 117; 5-8R; CANR 5, 36; CDBLB 1914-1945; DA3; DAB; DAC; DAM MST, POET; DLB 20, 100, 191; DLBD 18; DLBY 1985; EWL 3; MTCW 1, 2; NCFS 2; RGEL 2; RHW; SATA 45; TEA

Graves, Valerie
See Bradley, Marion Zimmer

Gray, Alasdair (James) 1934- .... **CLC 41**
See also CA 126; CANR 47, 69, 106; CN 7; DLB 194, 261; HGG; INT CA-126; MTCW 1, 2; RGSF 2; SUFW 2

Gray, Amlin 1946- .... **CLC 29**
See also CA 138

Gray, Francine du Plessix 1930- ..... **CLC 22, 153**
See also BEST 90:3; CA 61-64; CAAS 2; CANR 11, 33, 75, 81; DAM NOV; INT CANR-11; MTCW 1, 2

Gray, John (Henry) 1866-1934 ...... **TCLC 19**
See also CA 162; 119; RGEL 2

Gray, Simon (James Holliday) 1936- .... **CLC 9, 14, 36**
See also AITN 1; CA 21-24R; CAAS 3; CANR 32, 69; CD 5; DLB 13; EWL 3; MTCW 1; RGEL 2

Gray, Spalding 1941- ..... **CLC 49, 112; DC 7**
See also CA 128; CAD; CANR 74; CD 5; CPW; DAM POP; MTCW 2

Gray, Thomas 1716-1771 .... **LC 4, 40; PC 2; WLC**
See also BRW 3; CDBLB 1660-1789; DA; DA3; DAB; DAC; DAM MST; DLB 109; EXPP; PAB; PFS 9; RGEL 2; TEA; WP

Grayson, David
See Baker, Ray Stannard

Grayson, Richard (A.) 1951- .... **CLC 38**
See also CA 85-88; CANR 14, 31, 57; DLB 234

Greeley, Andrew M(oran) 1928- ...... **CLC 28**
See also BPFB 2; CA 5-8R; CAAS 7; CANR 7, 43, 69, 104; CMW 4; CPW; DA3; DAM POP; MTCW 1, 2

Green, Anna Katharine 1846-1935 .... **TCLC 63**
See also CA 159; 112; CMW 4; DLB 202, 221; MSW

Green, Brian
See Card, Orson Scott

Green, Hannah
See Greenberg, Joanne (Goldenberg)

Green, Hannah 1927(?)-1996 .... **CLC 3**
See also CA 73-76; CANR 59, 93; NFS 10

Green, Henry .... **CLC 2, 13, 97**
See Yorke, Henry Vincent
See also BRWS 2; CA 175; DLB 15; EWL 3; RGEL 2

Green, Julian (Hartridge) 1900-1998
See Green, Julien
See also CA 169; 21-24R; CANR 33, 87; DLB 4, 72; MTCW 1

Green, Julien .... **CLC 3, 11, 77**
See Green, Julian (Hartridge)
See also EWL 3; GFL 1789 to the Present; MTCW 2

Green, Paul (Eliot) 1894-1981 .... **CLC 25**
See also AITN 1; CA 103; 5-8R; CANR 3; DAM DRAM; DLB 7, 9, 249; DLBY 1981; RGAL 4

Greenaway, Peter 1942- .... **CLC 159**
See also CA 127

Greenberg, Ivan 1908-1973
See Rahv, Philip
See also CA 85-88

Greenberg, Joanne (Goldenberg) 1932- .... **CLC 7, 30**
See also AAYA 12; CA 5-8R; CANR 14, 32, 69; CN 7; SATA 25; YAW

Greenberg, Richard 1959(?)- .... **CLC 57**
See also CA 138; CAD; CD 5

Greenblatt, Stephen J(ay) 1943- ...... **CLC 70**
See also CA 49-52; CANR 115

Greene, Bette 1934- .... **CLC 30**
See also AAYA 7; BYA 3; CA 53-56; CANR 4; CLR 2; CWRI 5; JRDA; LAIT 4; MAICYA 1, 2; NFS 10; SAAS 16; SATA 8, 102; WYA; YAW

Greene, Gael .... **CLC 8**
See also CA 13-16R; CANR 10

Greene, Graham (Henry) 1904-1991 .... **CLC 1, 3, 6, 9, 14, 18, 27, 37, 70, 72, 125; SSC 29; WLC**
See also AITN 2; BPFB 2; BRWR 2; BRWS 1; BYA 3; CA 133; 13-16R; CANR 35, 61; CBD; CDBLB 1945-1960; CMW 4; DA; DA3; DAB; DAC; DAM MST, NOV; DLB 13, 15, 77, 100, 162, 201, 204; DLBY 1991; EWL 3; MSW; MTCW 1, 2; NFS 16; RGEL 2; SATA 20; SSFS 14; TEA; WLIT 4

Greene, Robert 1558-1592 .... **LC 41**
See also BRWS 8; DLB 62, 167; IDTP; RGEL 2; TEA

Greer, Germaine 1939- .... **CLC 131**
See also AITN 1; CA 81-84; CANR 33, 70, 115; FW; MTCW 1, 2

Greer, Richard
See Silverberg, Robert

Gregor, Arthur 1923- .... **CLC 9**
See also CA 25-28R; CAAS 10; CANR 11; CP 7; SATA 36

Gregor, Lee
See Pohl, Frederik

Gregory, Lady Isabella Augusta (Persse) 1852-1932 .... **TCLC 1**
See also BRW 6; CA 184; 104; DLB 10; IDTP; RGEL 2

Gregory, J. Dennis
See Williams, John A(lfred)

Grekova, I. .... **CLC 59**

Grendon, Stephen
See Derleth, August (William)

Grenville, Kate 1950- .... **CLC 61**
See also CA 118; CANR 53, 93

Grenville, Pelham
See Wodehouse, P(elham) G(renville)

Greve, Felix Paul (Berthold Friedrich) 1879-1948
See Grove, Frederick Philip
See also CA 141, 175; 104; CANR 79; DAC; DAM MST

Greville, Fulke 1554-1628 .... **LC 79**
See also DLB 62, 172; RGEL 2

Grey, Zane 1872-1939 .... **TCLC 6**
See also BPFB 2; CA 132; 104; DA3; DAM POP; DLB 9, 212; MTCW 1, 2; RGAL 4; TCWW 2; TUS

Grieg, (Johan) Nordahl (Brun) 1902-1943 .... **TCLC 10**
See also CA 189; 107; EWL 3

Grieve, C(hristopher) M(urray) 1892-1978 .... **CLC 11, 19**
See MacDiarmid, Hugh; Pteleon
See also CA 85-88; 5-8R; CANR 33, 107; DAM POET; MTCW 1; RGEL 2

Griffin, Gerald 1803-1840 .... **NCLC 7**
See also DLB 159; RGEL 2

Griffin, John Howard 1920-1980 ..... **CLC 68**
See also AITN 1; CA 101; 1-4R; CANR 2

Griffin, Peter 1942- .... **CLC 39**
See also CA 136

Griffith, D(avid Lewelyn) W(ark) 1875(?)-1948 .... **TCLC 68**
See also CA 150; 119; CANR 80

Griffith, Lawrence
See Griffith, D(avid Lewelyn) W(ark)

Griffiths, Trevor 1935- .... **CLC 13, 52**
See also CA 97-100; CANR 45; CBD; CD 5; DLB 13, 245

Griggs, Sutton (Elbert) 1872-1930 .... **TCLC 77**
See also CA 186; 123; DLB 50

Grigson, Geoffrey (Edward Harvey) 1905-1985 .... **CLC 7, 39**
See also CA 118; 25-28R; CANR 20, 33; DLB 27; MTCW 1, 2

Grile, Dod
See Bierce, Ambrose (Gwinett)

Grillparzer, Franz 1791-1872 .... **DC 14; NCLC 1, 102; SSC 37**
See also CDWLB 2; DLB 133; EW 5; RGWL 2, 3; TWA

Grimble, Reverend Charles James
See Eliot, T(homas) S(tearns)

Grimke, Angelina (Emily) Weld 1880-1958 .... **HR 2**
See Weld, Angelina (Emily) Grimke
See also BW 1; CA 124; DAM POET; DLB 50, 54

Grimke, Charlotte L(ottie) Forten 1837(?)-1914
See Forten, Charlotte L.
See also BW 1; CA 124; 117; DAM MULT, POET

Grimm, Jacob Ludwig Karl 1785-1863 .... **NCLC 3, 77; SSC 36**
See also DLB 90; MAICYA 1, 2; RGSF 2; RGWL 2, 3; SATA 22; WCH

Grimm, Wilhelm Karl 1786-1859 .. **NCLC 3, 77; SSC 36**
See also CDWLB 2; DLB 90; MAICYA 1, 2; RGSF 2; RGWL 2, 3; SATA 22; WCH

Grimmelshausen, Hans Jakob Christoffel von
See Grimmelshausen, Johann Jakob Christoffel von
See also RGWL 2, 3

Grimmelshausen, Johann Jakob Christoffel von 1621-1676 .... **LC 6**
See Grimmelshausen, Hans Jakob Christoffel von
See also CDWLB 2; DLB 168

Grindel, Eugene 1895-1952
See Eluard, Paul
See also CA 193; 104

Grisham, John 1955- .... **CLC 84**
See also AAYA 14, 47; BPFB 2; CA 138; CANR 47, 69, 114; CMW 4; CN 7; CPW; CSW; DA3; DAM POP; MSW; MTCW 2

Grossman, David 1954- .... **CLC 67**
See also CA 138; CANR 114; CWW 2; EWL 3

Grossman, Vasilii Semenovich
See Grossman, Vasily (Semenovich)
See also DLB 272

Grossman, Vasily (Semenovich) 1905-1964 .... **CLC 41**
See Grossman, Vasilii Semenovich
See also CA 130; 124; MTCW 1

Grove, Frederick Philip .... **TCLC 4**
See Greve, Felix Paul (Berthold Friedrich)
See also DLB 92; RGEL 2

Grubb
See Crumb, R(obert)

Grumbach, Doris (Isaac) 1918- . **CLC 13, 22, 64**
See also CA 5-8R; CAAS 2; CANR 9, 42, 70; CN 7; INT CANR-9; MTCW 2

Grundtvig, Nicolai Frederik Severin 1783-1872 .... **NCLC 1**

Grunge
See Crumb, R(obert)

Grunwald, Lisa 1959- .... **CLC 44**
See also CA 120

Guare, John 1938- .... **CLC 8, 14, 29, 67; DC 20**
See also CA 73-76; CAD; CANR 21, 69; CD 5; DAM DRAM; DFS 8, 13; DLB 7, 249; EWL 3; MTCW 1, 2; RGAL 4

Gubar, Susan (David) 1944- .... **CLC 145**
See also CA 108; CANR 45, 70; FW; MTCW 1; RGAL 4

Gudjonsson, Halldor Kiljan 1902-1998
See Laxness, Halldor
See also CA 164; 103; CWW 2

Guenter, Erich
See Eich, Gunter

Guest, Barbara 1920- .... **CLC 34**
  See also BG 2; CA 25-28R; CANR 11, 44,
  84; CP 7; CWP; DLB 5, 193
Guest, Edgar A(lbert) 1881-1959 ... **TCLC 95**
  See also CA 168; 112
Guest, Judith (Ann) 1936- .... **CLC 8, 30**
  See also AAYA 7; CA 77-80; CANR 15,
  75; DA3; DAM NOV, POP; EXPN; INT
  CANR-15; LAIT 5; MTCW 1, 2; NFS 1
Guevara, Che .... **CLC 87; HLC 1**
  See Guevara (Serna), Ernesto
Guevara (Serna), Ernesto
  1928-1967 .... **CLC 87; HLC 1**
  See Guevara, Che
  See also CA 111; 127; CANR 56; DAM
  MULT; HW 1
Guicciardini, Francesco 1483-1540 ..... **LC 49**
Guild, Nicholas M. 1944- .... **CLC 33**
  See also CA 93-96
Guillemin, Jacques
  See Sartre, Jean-Paul
Guillen, Jorge 1893-1984 . **CLC 11; HLCS 1;**
  PC 35
  See also CA 112; 89-92; DAM MULT,
  POET; DLB 108; EWL 3; HW 1; RGWL
  2, 3
Guillen, Nicolas (Cristobal)
  1902-1989 .... **BLC 2; CLC 48, 79; HLC**
  1; PC 23
  See also BW 2; CA 129; 125; 116; CANR
  84; DAM MST, MULT, POET; EWL 3;
  HW 1; LAW; RGWL 2, 3; WP
Guillen y Alvarez, Jorge
  See Guillen, Jorge
Guillevic, (Eugene) 1907-1997 .... **CLC 33**
  See also CA 93-96; CWW 2
Guillois
  See Desnos, Robert
Guillois, Valentin
  See Desnos, Robert
Guimaraes Rosa, Joao 1908-1967 .... **HLCS 2**
  See also CA 175; LAW; RGSF 2; RGWL 2,
  3
Guiney, Louise Imogen
  1861-1920 .... **TCLC 41**
  See also CA 160; DLB 54; RGAL 4
Guinizelli, Guido c. 1230-1276 ...... **CMLC 49**
Guiraldes, Ricardo (Guillermo)
  1886-1927 .... **TCLC 39**
  See also CA 131; EWL 3; HW 1; LAW;
  MTCW 1
Gumilev, Nikolai (Stepanovich)
  1886-1921 .... **TCLC 60**
  See Gumilyov, Nikolay Stepanovich
  See also CA 165
Gumilyov, Nikolay Stepanovich
  See Gumilev, Nikolai (Stepanovich)
  See also EWL 3
Gunesekera, Romesh 1954- .... **CLC 91**
  See also CA 159; CN 7; DLB 267
Gunn, Bill .... **CLC 5**
  See Gunn, William Harrison
  See also DLB 38
Gunn, Thom(son William) 1929- .. **CLC 3, 6,**
  18, 32, 81; PC 26
  See also BRWS 4; CA 17-20R; CANR 9,
  33, 116; CDBLB 1960 to Present; CP 7;
  DAM POET; DLB 27; INT CANR-33;
  MTCW 1; PFS 9; RGEL 2
Gunn, William Harrison 1934(?)-1989
  See Gunn, Bill
  See also AITN 1; BW 1, 3; CA 128; 13-
  16R; CANR 12, 25, 76
Gunn Allen, Paula
  See Allen, Paula Gunn
Gunnars, Kristjana 1948- .... **CLC 69**
  See also CA 113; CCA 1; CP 7; CWP; DLB
  60

Gunter, Erich
  See Eich, Gunter
Gurdjieff, G(eorgei) I(vanovich)
  1877(?)-1949 .... **TCLC 71**
  See also CA 157
Gurganus, Allan 1947- .... **CLC 70**
  See also BEST 90:1; CA 135; CANR 114;
  CN 7; CPW; CSW; DAM POP; GLL 1
Gurney, A. R.
  See Gurney, A(lbert) R(amsdell), Jr.
  See also DLB 266
Gurney, A(lbert) R(amsdell), Jr.
  1930- .... **CLC 32, 50, 54**
  See Gurney, A. R.
  See also AMWS 5; CA 77-80; CAD; CANR
  32, 64; CD 5; DAM DRAM; EWL 3
Gurney, Ivor (Bertie) 1890-1937 ... **TCLC 33**
  See also BRW 6; CA 167; DLBY 2002;
  PAB; RGEL 2
Gurney, Peter
  See Gurney, A(lbert) R(amsdell), Jr.
Guro, Elena 1877-1913 .... **TCLC 56**
Gustafson, James M(oody) 1925- ... **CLC 100**
  See also CA 25-28R; CANR 37
Gustafson, Ralph (Barker)
  1909-1995 .... **CLC 36**
  See also CA 21-24R; CANR 8, 45, 84; CP
  7; DLB 88; RGEL 2
Gut, Gom
  See Simenon, Georges (Jacques Christian)
Guterson, David 1956- .... **CLC 91**
  See also CA 132; CANR 73; MTCW 2;
  NFS 13
Guthrie, A(lfred) B(ertram), Jr.
  1901-1991 .... **CLC 23**
  See also CA 134; 57-60; CANR 24; DLB 6,
  212; SATA 62; SATA-Obit 67
Guthrie, Isobel
  See Grieve, C(hristopher) M(urray)
Guthrie, Woodrow Wilson 1912-1967
  See Guthrie, Woody
  See also CA 93-96; 113
Guthrie, Woody .... **CLC 35**
  See Guthrie, Woodrow Wilson
  See also LAIT 3
Gutierrez Najera, Manuel
  1859-1895 .... **HLCS 2**
  See also LAW
Guy, Rosa (Cuthbert) 1925- .... **CLC 26**
  See also AAYA 4, 37; BW 2; CA 17-20R;
  CANR 14, 34, 83; CLR 13; DLB 33;
  DNFS 1; JRDA; MAICYA 1, 2; SATA 14,
  62, 122; YAW
Gwendolyn
  See Bennett, (Enoch) Arnold
H. D. .... **CLC 3, 8, 14, 31, 34, 73; PC 5**
  See Doolittle, Hilda
H. de V.
  See Buchan, John
Haavikko, Paavo Juhani 1931- .. **CLC 18, 34**
  See also CA 106; EWL 3
Habbema, Koos
  See Heijermans, Herman
Habermas, Juergen 1929- .... **CLC 104**
  See also CA 109; CANR 85; DLB 242
Habermas, Jurgen
  See Habermas, Juergen
Hacker, Marilyn 1942- . **CLC 5, 9, 23, 72, 91**
  See also CA 77-80; CANR 68; CP 7; CWP;
  DAM POET; DLB 120; FW; GLL 2
Hadrian 76-138 .... **CMLC 52**
Haeckel, Ernst Heinrich (Philipp August)
  1834-1919 .... **TCLC 83**
  See also CA 157
Hafiz c. 1326-1389(?) .... **CMLC 34**
  See also RGWL 2, 3

Haggard, H(enry) Rider
  1856-1925 .... **TCLC 11**
  See also BRWS 3; BYA 4, 5; CA 148; 108;
  CANR 112; DLB 70, 156, 174, 178;
  FANT; MTCW 2; RGEL 2; RHW; SATA
  16; SCFW 4; SFW 4; SUFW 1; WLIT 4
Hagiosy, L.
  See Larbaud, Valery (Nicolas)
Hagiwara, Sakutaro 1886-1942 .... **PC 18;**
  TCLC 60
  See Hagiwara Sakutaro
  See also CA 154; RGWL 3
Hagiwara Sakutaro
  See Hagiwara, Sakutaro
  See also EWL 3
Haig, Fenil
  See Ford, Ford Madox
Haig-Brown, Roderick (Langmere)
  1908-1976 .... **CLC 21**
  See also CA 69-72; 5-8R; CANR 4, 38, 83;
  CLR 31; CWRI 5; DLB 88; MAICYA 1,
  2; SATA 12
Haight, Rip
  See Carpenter, John (Howard)
Hailey, Arthur 1920- .... **CLC 5**
  See also AITN 2; BEST 90:3; BPFB 2; CA
  1-4R; CANR 2, 36, 75; CCA 1; CN 7;
  CPW; DAM NOV, POP; DLB 88; DLBY
  1982; MTCW 1, 2
Hailey, Elizabeth Forsythe 1938- ..... **CLC 40**
  See also CA 93-96; CAAE 188; CAAS 1;
  CANR 15, 48; INT CANR-15
Haines, John (Meade) 1924- .... **CLC 58**
  See also AMWS 12; CA 17-20R; CANR
  13, 34; CSW; DLB 5, 212
Hakluyt, Richard 1552-1616 .... **LC 31**
  See also DLB 136; RGEL 2
Haldeman, Joe (William) 1943- .... **CLC 61**
  See Graham, Robert
  See also AAYA 38; CA 53-56, 179; CAAE
  179; CAAS 25; CANR 6, 70, 72; DLB 8;
  INT CANR-6; SCFW 2; SFW 4
Hale, Janet Campbell 1947- .... **NNAL**
  See also CA 49-52; CANR 45, 75; DAM
  MULT; DLB 175; MTCW 2
Hale, Sarah Josepha (Buell)
  1788-1879 .... **NCLC 75**
  See also DLB 1, 42, 73, 243
Halevy, Elie 1870-1937 .... **TCLC 104**
Haley, Alex(ander Murray Palmer)
  1921-1992 .... **BLC 2; CLC 8, 12, 76**
  See also AAYA 26; BPFB 2; BW 2, 3; CA
  136; 77-80; CANR 61; CDALBS; CPW;
  CSW; DA; DA3; DAB; DAC; DAM MST,
  MULT, POP; DLB 38; LAIT 5; MTCW
  1, 2; NFS 9
Haliburton, Thomas Chandler
  1796-1865 .... **NCLC 15**
  See also DLB 11, 99; RGEL 2; RGSF 2
Hall, Donald (Andrew, Jr.) 1928- ...... **CLC 1,**
  13, 37, 59, 151
  See also CA 5-8R; CAAS 7; CANR 2, 44,
  64, 106; CP 7; DAM POET; DLB 5;
  MTCW 1; RGAL 4; SATA 23, 97
Hall, Frederic Sauser
  See Sauser-Hall, Frederic
Hall, James
  See Kuttner, Henry
Hall, James Norman 1887-1951 ..... **TCLC 23**
  See also CA 173; 123; LAIT 1; RHW 1;
  SATA 21
Hall, (Marguerite) Radclyffe
  1880-1943 .... **TCLC 12**
  See also BRWS 6; CA 150; 110; CANR 83;
  DLB 191; MTCW 2; RGEL 2; RHW
Hall, Rodney 1935- .... **CLC 51**
  See also CA 109; CANR 69; CN 7; CP 7

MTCW 1, 2; PAB; PFS 1, 3, 6, 10, 15;
RGAL 4; RGSF 2; SATA 4, 33; SSFS 4,
7; TUS; WCH; WP; YAW
Hughes, Richard (Arthur Warren)
1900-1976 .... **CLC 1, 11**
See also CA 65-68; 5-8R; CANR 4; DAM
NOV; DLB 15, 161; EWL 3; MTCW 1;
RGEL 2; SATA 8; SATA-Obit 25
Hughes, Ted 1930-1998 . **CLC 2, 4, 9, 14, 37,
119; PC 7**
See Hughes, Edward James
See also BRWR 2; BRWS 1; CA 171; 1-4R;
CANR 1, 33, 66, 108; CLR 3; CP 7;
DAB; DAC; DLB 40, 161; EWL 3; EXPP;
MAICYA 1, 2; MTCW 1, 2; PAB; PFS 4;
RGEL 2; SATA 49; SATA-Brief 27;
SATA-Obit 107; TEA; YAW
Hugo, Richard
See Huch, Ricarda (Octavia)
Hugo, Richard F(ranklin)
1923-1982 .... **CLC 6, 18, 32**
See also AMWS 6; CA 108; 49-52; CANR
3; DAM POET; DLB 5, 206; EWL 3; PFS
17; RGAL 4
Hugo, Victor (Marie) 1802-1885 .... **NCLC 3,
10, 21; PC 17; WLC**
See also AAYA 28; DA; DA3; DAB; DAC;
DAM DRAM, MST, NOV, POET; DLB
119, 192, 217; EFS 2; EW 6; EXPN; GFL
1789 to the Present; LAIT 1, 2; NFS 5;
RGWL 2, 3; SATA 47; TWA
Huidobro, Vicente
See Huidobro Fernandez, Vicente Garcia
See also EWL 3; LAW
Huidobro Fernandez, Vicente Garcia
1893-1948 .... **TCLC 31**
See Huidobro, Vicente
See also CA 131; HW 1
Hulme, Keri 1947- .... **CLC 39, 130**
See also CA 125; CANR 69; CN 7; CP 7;
CWP; EWL 3; FW; INT 125
Hulme, T(homas) E(rnest)
1883-1917 .... **TCLC 21**
See also BRWS 6; CA 203; 117; DLB 19
Hume, David 1711-1776 .... **LC 7, 56**
See also BRWS 3; DLB 104, 252; TEA
Humphrey, William 1924-1997 .... **CLC 45**
See also AMWS 9; CA 160; 77-80; CANR
68; CN 7; CSW; DLB 6, 212, 234, 278;
TCWW 2
Humphreys, Emyr Owen 1919- .... **CLC 47**
See also CA 5-8R; CANR 3, 24; CN 7;
DLB 15
Humphreys, Josephine 1945- ..... **CLC 34, 57**
See also CA 127; 121; CANR 97; CSW;
INT 127
Huneker, James Gibbons
1860-1921 .... **TCLC 65**
See also CA 193; DLB 71; RGAL 4
Hungerford, Hesba Fay
See Brinsmead, H(esba) F(ay)
Hungerford, Pixie
See Brinsmead, H(esba) F(ay)
Hunt, E(verette) Howard, (Jr.)
1918- .... **CLC 3**
See also AITN 1; CA 45-48; CANR 2, 47,
103; CMW 4
Hunt, Francesca
See Holland, Isabelle (Christian)
Hunt, Howard
See Hunt, E(verette) Howard, (Jr.)
Hunt, Kyle
See Creasey, John
Hunt, (James Henry) Leigh
1784-1859 .... **NCLC 1, 70**
See also DAM POET; DLB 96, 110, 144;
RGEL 2; TEA
Hunt, Marsha 1946- .... **CLC 70**
See also BW 2, 3; CA 143; CANR 79

Hunt, Violet 1866(?)-1942 .... **TCLC 53**
See also CA 184; DLB 162, 197
Hunter, E. Waldo
See Sturgeon, Theodore (Hamilton)
Hunter, Evan 1926- .... **CLC 11, 31**
See McBain, Ed
See also AAYA 39; BPFB 2; CA 5-8R;
CANR 5, 38, 62, 97; CMW 4; CN 7;
CPW; DAM POP; DLBY 1982; INT
CANR-5; MSW; MTCW 1; SATA 25;
SFW 4
Hunter, Kristin 1931-
See Lattany, Kristin (Elaine Eggleston)
Hunter
Hunter, Mary
See Austin, Mary (Hunter)
Hunter, Mollie 1922- .... **CLC 21**
See McIlwraith, Maureen Mollie Hunter
See also AAYA 13; BYA 6; CANR 37, 78;
CLR 25; DLB 161; JRDA; MAICYA 1,
2; SAAS 7; SATA 54, 106; WYA; YAW
Hunter, Robert (?)-1734 .... **LC 7**
Hurston, Zora Neale 1891-1960 ...... **BLC 2;
CLC 7, 30, 61; DC 12; HR 2; SSC 4;
TCLC 121, 131; WLCS**
See also AAYA 15; AFAW 1, 2; AMWS 6;
BW 1, 3; BYA 12; CA 85-88; CANR 61;
CDALBS; DA; DA3; DAC; DAM MST,
MULT, NOV; DFS 6; DLB 51, 86; EWL
3; EXPN; EXPS; FW; LAIT 3; LMFS 2;
MAWW; MTCW 1, 2; NFS 3; RGAL 4;
RGSF 2; SSFS 1, 6, 11; TUS; YAW
Husserl, E. G.
See Husserl, Edmund (Gustav Albrecht)
Husserl, Edmund (Gustav Albrecht)
1859-1938 .... **TCLC 100**
See also CA 133; 116
Huston, John (Marcellus)
1906-1987 .... **CLC 20**
See also CA 123; 73-76; CANR 34; DLB
26
Hustvedt, Siri 1955- .... **CLC 76**
See also CA 137
Hutten, Ulrich von 1488-1523 .... **LC 16**
See also DLB 179
Huxley, Aldous (Leonard)
1894-1963 .... **CLC 1, 3, 4, 5, 8, 11, 18,
35, 79; SSC 39; WLC**
See also AAYA 11; BPFB 2; BRW 7; CA
85-88; CANR 44, 99; CDBLB 1914-1945;
DA; DA3; DAB; DAC; DAM MST, NOV;
DLB 36, 100, 162, 195, 255; EWL 3;
EXPN; LAIT 5; MTCW 1, 2; NFS 6;
RGEL 2; SATA 63; SCFW 2; SFW 4;
TEA; YAW
Huxley, T(homas) H(enry)
1825-1895 .... **NCLC 67**
See also DLB 57; TEA
Huysmans, Joris-Karl 1848-1907 ... **TCLC 7,
69**
See also CA 165; 104; DLB 123; EW 7;
GFL 1789 to the Present; RGWL 2, 3
Hwang, David Henry 1957- .. **CLC 55; DC 4**
See also CA 132; 127; CAD; CANR 76;
CD 5; DA3; DAM DRAM; DFS 11; DLB
212, 228; INT CA-132; MTCW 2; RGAL
4
Hyde, Anthony 1946- .... **CLC 42**
See Chase, Nicholas
See also CA 136; CCA 1
Hyde, Margaret O(ldroyd) 1917- ..... **CLC 21**
See also CA 1-4R; CANR 1, 36; CLR 23;
JRDA; MAICYA 1, 2; SAAS 8; SATA 1,
42, 76
Hynes, James 1956(?)- .... **CLC 65**
See also CA 164; CANR 105
Hypatia c. 370-415 .... **CMLC 35**
Ian, Janis 1951- .... **CLC 21**
See also CA 187; 105

Ibanez, Vicente Blasco
See Blasco Ibanez, Vicente
Ibarbourou, Juana de 1895-1979 ..... **HLCS 2**
See also HW 1; LAW
Ibarguengoitia, Jorge 1928-1983 ...... **CLC 37**
See also CA 113; 124; EWL 3; HW 1
Ibn Battuta, Abu Abdalla
1304-1368(?) .... **CMLC 57**
See also WLIT 2
Ibsen, Henrik (Johan) 1828-1906 .... **DC 2;
TCLC 2, 8, 16, 37, 52; WLC**
See also AAYA 46; CA 141; 104; DA; DA3;
DAB; DAC; DAM DRAM, MST; DFS 1,
6, 8, 10, 11, 15, 16; EW 7; LAIT 2;
RGWL 2, 3
Ibuse, Masuji 1898-1993 .... **CLC 22**
See Ibuse Masuji
See also CA 141; 127; MJW; RGWL 3
Ibuse Masuji
See Ibuse, Masuji
See also DLB 180; EWL 3
Ichikawa, Kon 1915- .... **CLC 20**
See also CA 121
Ichiyo, Higuchi 1872-1896 .... **NCLC 49**
See also MJW
Idle, Eric 1943-2000 .... **CLC 21**
See Monty Python
See also CA 116; CANR 35, 91
Ignatow, David 1914-1997 .... **CLC 4, 7, 14,
40; PC 34**
See also CA 162; 9-12R; CAAS 3; CANR
31, 57, 96; CP 7; DLB 5; EWL 3
Ignotus
See Strachey, (Giles) Lytton
Ihimaera, Witi 1944- .... **CLC 46**
See also CA 77-80; CN 7; RGSF 2
Ilf, Ilya .... **TCLC 21**
See Fainzilberg, Ilya Arnoldovich
See also EWL 3
Illyes, Gyula 1902-1983 .... **PC 16**
See also CA 109; 114; CDWLB 4; DLB
215; EWL 3; RGWL 2, 3
Immermann, Karl (Lebrecht)
1796-1840 .... **NCLC 4, 49**
See also DLB 133
Ince, Thomas H. 1882-1924 .... **TCLC 89**
See also IDFW 3, 4
Inchbald, Elizabeth 1753-1821 ...... **NCLC 62**
See also DLB 39, 89; RGEL 2
Inclan, Ramon (Maria) del Valle
See Valle-Inclan, Ramon (Maria) del
Infante, G(uillermo) Cabrera
See Cabrera Infante, G(uillermo)
Ingalls, Rachel (Holmes) 1940- .... **CLC 42**
See also CA 127; 123
Ingamells, Reginald Charles
See Ingamells, Rex
Ingamells, Rex 1913-1955 .... **TCLC 35**
See also CA 167; DLB 260
Inge, William (Motter) 1913-1973 ..... **CLC 1,
8, 19**
See also CA 9-12R; CDALB 1941-1968;
DA3; DAM DRAM; DFS 1, 5, 8; DLB 7,
249; EWL 3; MTCW 1, 2; RGAL 4; TUS
Ingelow, Jean 1820-1897 .... **NCLC 39, 107**
See also DLB 35, 163; FANT; SATA 33
Ingram, Willis J.
See Harris, Mark
Innaurato, Albert (F.) 1948(?)- ... **CLC 21, 60**
See also CA 122; 115; CAD; CANR 78;
CD 5; INT CA-122
Innes, Michael
See Stewart, J(ohn) I(nnes) M(ackintosh)
See also DLB 276; MSW
Innis, Harold Adams 1894-1952 .... **TCLC 77**
See also CA 181; DLB 88
Insluis, Alanus de
See Alain de Lille

Kawabata, Yasunari 1899-1972 ..... **CLC 2, 5, 9, 18, 107; SSC 17**
  See Kawabata Yasunari
  See also CA 33-36R; 93-96; CANR 88; DAM MULT; MJW; MTCW 2; RGSF 2; RGWL 2, 3

Kawabata Yasunari
  See Kawabata, Yasunari
  See also DLB 180; EWL 3

Kaye, M(ary) M(argaret) 1909- .... **CLC 28**
  See also CA 89-92; CANR 24, 60, 102; MTCW 1, 2; RHW; SATA 62

Kaye, Mollie
  See Kaye, M(ary) M(argaret)

Kaye-Smith, Sheila 1887-1956 .... **TCLC 20**
  See also CA 203; 118; DLB 36

Kaymor, Patrice Maguilene
  See Senghor, Leopold Sedar

Kazakov, Yuri Pavlovich 1927-1982 . **SSC 43**
  See Kazakov, Yury
  See also CA 5-8R; CANR 36; MTCW 1; RGSF 2

Kazakov, Yury
  See Kazakov, Yuri Pavlovich
  See also EWL 3

Kazan, Elia 1909- .... **CLC 6, 16, 63**
  See also CA 21-24R; CANR 32, 78

Kazantzakis, Nikos 1883(?)-1957 .... **TCLC 2, 5, 33**
  See also BPFB 2; CA 132; 105; DA3; EW 9; EWL 3; MTCW 1, 2; RGWL 2, 3

Kazin, Alfred 1915-1998 ..... **CLC 34, 38, 119**
  See also AMWS 8; CA 1-4R; CAAS 7; CANR 1, 45, 79; DLB 67; EWL 3

Keane, Mary Nesta (Skrine) 1904-1996
  See Keane, Molly
  See also CA 151; 114; 108; CN 7; RHW

Keane, Molly .... **CLC 31**
  See Keane, Mary Nesta (Skrine)
  See also INT 114

Keates, Jonathan 1946(?)- .... **CLC 34**
  See also CA 163

Keaton, Buster 1895-1966 .... **CLC 20**
  See also CA 194

Keats, John 1795-1821 ...... **NCLC 8, 73, 121; PC 1; WLC**
  See also BRW 4; BRWR 1; CDBLB 1789-1832; DA; DA3; DAB; DAC; DAM MST, POET; DLB 96, 110; EXPP; PAB; PFS 1, 2, 3, 9, 16; RGEL 2; TEA; WLIT 3; WP

Keble, John 1792-1866 .... **NCLC 87**
  See also DLB 32, 55; RGEL 2

Keene, Donald 1922- .... **CLC 34**
  See also CA 1-4R; CANR 5

Keillor, Garrison .... **CLC 40, 115**
  See Keillor, Gary (Edward)
  See also AAYA 2; BEST 89:3; BPFB 2; DLBY 1987; EWL 3; SATA 58; TUS

Keillor, Gary (Edward) 1942-
  See Keillor, Garrison
  See also CA 117; 111; CANR 36, 59; CPW; DA3; DAM POP; MTCW 1, 2

Keith, Carlos
  See Lewton, Val

Keith, Michael
  See Hubbard, L(afayette) Ron(ald)

Keller, Gottfried 1819-1890 .... **NCLC 2; SSC 26**
  See also CDWLB 2; DLB 129; EW; RGSF 2; RGWL 2, 3

Keller, Nora Okja 1965- .... **CLC 109**
  See also CA 187

Kellerman, Jonathan 1949- .... **CLC 44**
  See also AAYA 35; BEST 90:1; CA 106; CANR 29, 51; CMW 4; CPW; DA3; DAM POP; INT CANR-29

Kelley, William Melvin 1937- .... **CLC 22**
  See also BW 1; CA 77-80; CANR 27, 83; CN 7; DLB 33; EWL 3

Kellogg, Marjorie 1922- .... **CLC 2**
  See also CA 81-84

Kellow, Kathleen
  See Hibbert, Eleanor Alice Burford

Kelly, M(ilton) T(errence) 1947- ...... **CLC 55**
  See also CA 97-100; CAAS 22; CANR 19, 43, 84; CN 7

Kelly, Robert 1935- .... **SSC 50**
  See also CA 17-20R; CAAS 19; CANR 47; CP 7; DLB 5, 130, 165

Kelman, James 1946- .... **CLC 58, 86**
  See also BRWS 5; CA 148; CANR 85; CN 7; DLB 194; RGSF 2; WLIT 4

Kemal, Yashar 1923- .... **CLC 14, 29**
  See also CA 89-92; CANR 44; CWW 2

Kemble, Fanny 1809-1893 .... **NCLC 18**
  See also DLB 32

Kemelman, Harry 1908-1996 .... **CLC 2**
  See also AITN 1; BPFB 2; CA 155; 9-12R; CANR 6, 71; CMW 4; DLB 28

Kempe, Margery 1373(?)-1440(?) ... **LC 6, 56**
  See also DLB 146; RGEL 2

Kempis, Thomas a 1380-1471 .... **LC 11**

Kendall, Henry 1839-1882 .... **NCLC 12**
  See also DLB 230

Keneally, Thomas (Michael) 1935- ... **CLC 5, 8, 10, 14, 19, 27, 43, 117**
  See also BRWS 4; CA 85-88; CANR 10, 50, 74; CN 7; CPW; DA3; DAM NOV; EWL 3; MTCW 1, 2; NFS 17; RGEL 2; RHW

Kennedy, Adrienne (Lita) 1931- .... **BLC 2; CLC 66; DC 5**
  See also AFAW 2; BW 2, 3; CA 103; CAAS 20; CABS 3; CANR 26, 53, 82; CD 5; DAM MULT; DFS 9; DLB 38; FW

Kennedy, John Pendleton 1795-1870 .... **NCLC 2**
  See also DLB 3, 248, 254; RGAL 4

Kennedy, Joseph Charles 1929-
  See Kennedy, X. J.
  See also CA 1-4R; CAAE 201; CANR 4, 30, 40; CP 7; CWRI 5; MAICYA 2; MAICYAS 1; SATA 14, 86; SATA-Essay 130

Kennedy, William 1928- ... **CLC 6, 28, 34, 53**
  See also AAYA 1; AMWS 7; BPFB 2; CA 85-88; CANR 14, 31, 76; CN 7; DA3; DAM NOV; DLB 143; DLBY 1985; EWL 3; INT CANR-31; MTCW 1, 2; SATA 57

Kennedy, X. J. .... **CLC 8, 42**
  See Kennedy, Joseph Charles
  See also CAAS 9; CLR 27; DLB 5; SAAS 22

Kenny, Maurice (Francis) 1929- ..... **CLC 87; NNAL**
  See also CA 144; CAAS 22; DAM MULT; DLB 175

Kent, Kelvin
  See Kuttner, Henry

Kenton, Maxwell
  See Southern, Terry

Kenyon, Robert O.
  See Kuttner, Henry

Kepler, Johannes 1571-1630 .... **LC 45**

Ker, Jill
  See Conway, Jill K(er)

Kerkow, H. C.
  See Lewton, Val

Kerouac, Jack 1922-1969 ...... **CLC 1, 2, 3, 5, 14, 29, 61; TCLC 117; WLC**
  See Kerouac, Jean-Louis Lebris de
  See also AAYA 25; AMWC 1; AMWS 3; BG 3; BPFB 2; CDALB 1941-1968; CPW; DLB 2, 16, 237; DLBD 3; DLBY 1995; EWL 3; GLL 1; LMFS 2; MTCW 2; NFS 8; RGAL 4; TUS; WP

Kerouac, Jean-Louis Lebris de 1922-1969
  See Kerouac, Jack
  See also AITN 1; CA 25-28R; 5-8R; CANR 26, 54, 95; DA; DA3; DAB; DAC; DAM MST, NOV, POET, POP; MTCW 1, 2

Kerr, Jean 1923- .... **CLC 22**
  See also CA 5-8R; CANR 7; INT CANR-7

Kerr, M. E. .... **CLC 12, 35**
  See Meaker, Marijane (Agnes)
  See also AAYA 2, 23; BYA 1, 7, 8; CLR 29; SAAS 1; WYA

Kerr, Robert .... **CLC 55**

Kerrigan, (Thomas) Anthony 1918- .. **CLC 4, 6**
  See also CA 49-52; CAAS 11; CANR 4

Kerry, Lois
  See Duncan, Lois

Kesey, Ken (Elton) 1935-2001 ... **CLC 1, 3, 6, 11, 46, 64; WLC**
  See also AAYA 25; BG 3; BPFB 2; CA 204; 1-4R; CANR 22, 38, 66; CDALB 1968-1988; CN 7; CPW; DA; DA3; DAB; DAC; DAM MST, NOV, POP; DLB 2, 16, 206; EWL 3; EXPN; LAIT 4; MTCW 1, 2; NFS 2; RGAL 4; SATA 66; SATA-Obit 131; TUS; YAW

Kesselring, Joseph (Otto) 1902-1967 .... **CLC 45**
  See also CA 150; DAM DRAM, MST

Kessler, Jascha (Frederick) 1929- ...... **CLC 4**
  See also CA 17-20R; CANR 8, 48, 111

Kettelkamp, Larry (Dale) 1933- .... **CLC 12**
  See also CA 29-32R; CANR 16; SAAS 3; SATA 2

Key, Ellen (Karolina Sofia) 1849-1926 .... **TCLC 65**
  See also DLB 259

Keyber, Conny
  See Fielding, Henry

Keyes, Daniel 1927- .... **CLC 80**
  See also AAYA 23; BYA 11; CA 17-20R, 181; CAAE 181; CANR 10, 26, 54, 74; DA; DA3; DAC; DAM MST, NOV; EXPN; LAIT 4; MTCW 2; NFS 2; SATA 37; SFW 4

Keynes, John Maynard 1883-1946 .... **TCLC 64**
  See also CA 162, 163; 114; DLBD 10; MTCW 2

Khanshendel, Chiron
  See Rose, Wendy

Khayyam, Omar 1048-1131 ... **CMLC 11; PC 8**
  See Omar Khayyam
  See also DA3; DAM POET

Kherdian, David 1931- .... **CLC 6, 9**
  See also AAYA 42; CA 21-24R; CAAE 192; CAAS 2; CANR 39, 78; CLR 24; JRDA; LAIT 3; MAICYA 1, 2; SATA 16, 74; SATA-Essay 125

Khlebnikov, Velimir .... **TCLC 20**
  See Khlebnikov, Viktor Vladimirovich
  See also EW 10; EWL 3; RGWL 2, 3

Khlebnikov, Viktor Vladimirovich 1885-1922
  See Khlebnikov, Velimir
  See also CA 117

Khodasevich, Vladislav (Felitsianovich) 1886-1939 .... **TCLC 15**
  See also CA 115; EWL 3

Kielland, Alexander Lange 1849-1906 .... **TCLC 5**
  See also CA 104

Kiely, Benedict 1919- ... **CLC 23, 43; SSC 58**
  See also CA 1-4R; CANR 2, 84; CN 7; DLB 15

Kogawa, Joy Nozomi 1935- ...... **CLC 78, 129**
See also AAYA 47; CA 101; CANR 19, 62;
CN 7; CWP; DAC; DAM MST, MULT;
FW; MTCW 2; NFS 3; SATA 99

Kohout, Pavel 1928- .... **CLC 13**
See also CA 45-48; CANR 3

Koizumi, Yakumo
See Hearn, (Patricio) Lafcadio (Tessima Carlos)

Kolmar, Gertrud 1894-1943 .... **TCLC 40**
See also CA 167; EWL 3

Komunyakaa, Yusef 1947- .. **BLCS; CLC 86, 94**
See also AFAW 2; CA 147; CANR 83; CP
7; CSW; DLB 120; EWL 3; PFS 5; RGAL
4

Konrad, George
See Konrad, Gyorgy
See also CWW 2

Konrad, Gyorgy 1933- .... **CLC 4, 10, 73**
See Konrad, George
See also CA 85-88; CANR 97; CDWLB 4;
CWW 2; DLB 232; EWL 3

Konwicki, Tadeusz 1926- .... **CLC 8, 28, 54, 117**
See also CA 101; CAAS 9; CANR 39, 59;
CWW 2; DLB 232; EWL 3; IDFW 3;
MTCW 1

Koontz, Dean R(ay) 1945- .... **CLC 78**
See also AAYA 9, 31; BEST 89:3, 90:2; CA
108; CANR 19, 36, 52, 95; CMW 4;
CPW; DA3; DAM NOV, POP; HGG;
MTCW 1; SATA 92; SFW 4; SUFW 2;
YAW

Kopernik, Mikolaj
See Copernicus, Nicolaus

Kopit, Arthur (Lee) 1937- ...... **CLC 1, 18, 33**
See also AITN 1; CA 81-84; CABS 3; CD
5; DAM DRAM; DFS 7, 14; DLB 7;
MTCW 1; RGAL 4

Kopitar, Jernej (Bartholomaus)
1780-1844 .... **NCLC 117**

Kops, Bernard 1926- .... **CLC 4**
See also CA 5-8R; CANR 84; CBD; CN 7;
CP 7; DLB 13

Kornbluth, C(yril) M. 1923-1958 .... **TCLC 8**
See also CA 160; 105; DLB 8; SFW 4

Korolenko, V. G.
See Korolenko, Vladimir Galaktionovich

Korolenko, Vladimir
See Korolenko, Vladimir Galaktionovich

Korolenko, Vladimir G.
See Korolenko, Vladimir Galaktionovich

Korolenko, Vladimir Galaktionovich
1853-1921 .... **TCLC 22**
See also CA 121; DLB 277

Korzybski, Alfred (Habdank Skarbek)
1879-1950 .... **TCLC 61**
See also CA 160; 123

Kosinski, Jerzy (Nikodem)
1933-1991 .... **CLC 1, 2, 3, 6, 10, 15, 53, 70**
See also AMWS 7; BPFB 2; CA 134; 17-
20R; CANR 9, 46; DA3; DAM NOV;
DLB 2; DLBY 1982; EWL 3; HGG;
MTCW 1, 2; NFS 12; RGAL 4; TUS

Kostelanetz, Richard (Cory) 1940- .. **CLC 28**
See also CA 13-16R; CAAS 8; CANR 38,
77; CN 7; CP 7

Kostrowitzki, Wilhelm Apollinaris de
1880-1918
See Apollinaire, Guillaume
See also CA 104

Kotlowitz, Robert 1924- .... **CLC 4**
See also CA 33-36R; CANR 36

Kotzebue, August (Friedrich Ferdinand) von
1761-1819 .... **NCLC 25**
See also DLB 94

Kotzwinkle, William 1938- ..... **CLC 5, 14, 35**
See also BPFB 2; CA 45-48; CANR 3, 44,
84; CLR 6; DLB 173; FANT; MAICYA
1, 2; SATA 24, 70; SFW 4; SUFW 2;
YAW

Kowna, Stancy
See Szymborska, Wislawa

Kozol, Jonathan 1936- .... **CLC 17**
See also AAYA 46; CA 61-64; CANR 16,
45, 96

Kozoll, Michael 1940(?)- .... **CLC 35**

Kramer, Kathryn 19(?)- .... **CLC 34**

Kramer, Larry 1935- .... **CLC 42; DC 8**
See also CA 126; 124; CANR 60; DAM
POP; DLB 249; GLL 1

Krasicki, Ignacy 1735-1801 .... **NCLC 8**

Krasinski, Zygmunt 1812-1859 .... **NCLC 4**
See also RGWL 2, 3

Kraus, Karl 1874-1936 .... **TCLC 5**
See also CA 104; DLB 118; EWL 3

Kreve (Mickevicius), Vincas
1882-1954 .... **TCLC 27**
See also CA 170; DLB 220; EWL 3

Kristeva, Julia 1941- .... **CLC 77, 140**
See also CA 154; CANR 99; DLB 242;
EWL 3; FW

Kristofferson, Kris 1936- .... **CLC 26**
See also CA 104

Krizanc, John 1956- .... **CLC 57**
See also CA 187

Krleza, Miroslav 1893-1981 .... **CLC 8, 114**
See also CA 105; 97-100; CANR 50; CD-
WLB 4; DLB 147; EW 11; RGWL 2, 3

Kroetsch, Robert 1927- .. **CLC 5, 23, 57, 132**
See also CA 17-20R; CANR 8, 38; CCA 1;
CN 7; CP 7; DAC; DAM POET; DLB 53;
MTCW 1

Kroetz, Franz
See Kroetz, Franz Xaver

Kroetz, Franz Xaver 1946- .... **CLC 41**
See also CA 130; EWL 3

Kroker, Arthur (W.) 1945- .... **CLC 77**
See also CA 161

Kropotkin, Peter (Aleksieevich)
1842-1921 .... **TCLC 36**
See Kropotkin, Petr Alekseevich
See also CA 119

Kropotkin, Petr Alekseevich
See Kropotkin, Peter (Aleksieevich)
See also DLB 277

Krotkov, Yuri 1917-1981 .... **CLC 19**
See also CA 102

Krumb
See Crumb, R(obert)

Krumgold, Joseph (Quincy)
1908-1980 .... **CLC 12**
See also BYA 1, 2; CA 101; 9-12R; CANR
7; MAICYA 1, 2; SATA 1, 48; SATA-Obit
23; YAW

Krumwitz
See Crumb, R(obert)

Krutch, Joseph Wood 1893-1970 ..... **CLC 24**
See also ANW; CA 25-28R; 1-4R; CANR
4; DLB 63, 206, 275

Krutzch, Gus
See Eliot, T(homas) S(tearns)

Krylov, Ivan Andreevich
1768(?)-1844 .... **NCLC 1**
See also DLB 150

Kubin, Alfred (Leopold Isidor)
1877-1959 .... **TCLC 23**
See also CA 149; 112; CANR 104; DLB 81

Kubrick, Stanley 1928-1999 .... **CLC 16; TCLC 112**
See also AAYA 30; CA 177; 81-84; CANR
33; DLB 26

Kueng, Hans 1928-
See Kung, Hans
See also CA 53-56; CANR 66; MTCW 1, 2

Kumin, Maxine (Winokur) 1925- ..... **CLC 5, 13, 28, 164; PC 15**
See also AITN 2; AMWS 4; ANW; CA
1-4R; CAAS 8; CANR 1, 21, 69, 115; CP
7; CWP; DA3; DAM POET; DLB 5;
EWL 3; EXPP; MTCW 1, 2; PAB; SATA
12

Kundera, Milan 1929- . **CLC 4, 9, 19, 32, 68, 115, 135; SSC 24**
See also AAYA 2; BPFB 2; CA 85-88;
CANR 19, 52, 74; CDWLB 4; CWW 2;
DA3; DAM NOV; DLB 232; EW 13;
EWL 3; MTCW 1, 2; RGSF 2; RGWL 3;
SSFS 10

Kunene, Mazisi (Raymond) 1930- ... **CLC 85**
See also BW 1, 3; CA 125; CANR 81; CP
7; DLB 117

Kung, Hans .... **CLC 130**
See Kueng, Hans

Kunikida Doppo 1869(?)-1908
See Doppo, Kunikida
See also DLB 180; EWL 3

Kunitz, Stanley (Jasspon) 1905- .. **CLC 6, 11, 14, 148; PC 19**
See also AMWS 3; CA 41-44R; CANR 26,
57, 98; CP 7; DA3; DLB 48; INT CANR-
26; MTCW 1, 2; PFS 11; RGAL 4

Kunze, Reiner 1933- .... **CLC 10**
See also CA 93-96; CWW 2; DLB 75; EWL
3

Kuprin, Aleksander Ivanovich
1870-1938 .... **TCLC 5**
See Kuprin, Alexandr Ivanovich
See also CA 182; 104

Kuprin, Alexandr Ivanovich
See Kuprin, Aleksander Ivanovich
See also EWL 3

Kureishi, Hanif 1954(?)- .... **CLC 64, 135**
See also CA 139; CANR 113; CBD; CD 5;
CN 7; DLB 194, 245; GLL 2; IDFW 4;
WLIT 4

Kurosawa, Akira 1910-1998 ..... **CLC 16, 119**
See also AAYA 11; CA 170; 101; CANR
46; DAM MULT

Kushner, Tony 1957(?)- .... **CLC 81; DC 10**
See also AMWS 9; CA 144; CAD; CANR
74; CD 5; DA3; DAM DRAM; DFS 5;
DLB 228; EWL 3; GLL 1; LAIT 5;
MTCW 2; RGAL 4

Kuttner, Henry 1915-1958 .... **TCLC 10**
See also CA 157; 107; DLB 8; FANT;
SCFW 2; SFW 4

Kutty, Madhavi
See Das, Kamala

Kuzma, Greg 1944- .... **CLC 7**
See also CA 33-36R; CANR 70

Kuzmin, Mikhail 1872(?)-1936 ...... **TCLC 40**
See also CA 170; EWL 3

Kyd, Thomas 1558-1594 .... **DC 3; LC 22**
See also BRW 1; DAM DRAM; DLB 62;
IDTP; RGEL 2; TEA; WLIT 3

Kyprianos, Iossif
See Samarakis, Antonis

L. S.
See Stephen, Sir Leslie

Labrunie, Gerard
See Nerval, Gerard de

La Bruyere, Jean de 1645-1696 .... **LC 17**
See also DLB 268; EW 3; GFL Beginnings
to 1789

Lacan, Jacques (Marie Emile)
1901-1981 .... **CLC 75**
See also CA 104; 121; EWL 3; TWA

Marques, Rene 1919-1979 .. **CLC 96; HLC 2**
See also CA 85-88; 97-100; CANR 78;
DAM MULT; DLB 113; EWL 3; HW 1,
2; LAW; RGSF 2

Marquez, Gabriel (Jose) Garcia
See Garcia Marquez, Gabriel (Jose)

Marquis, Don(ald Robert Perry)
1878-1937 .... **TCLC 7**
See also CA 166; 104; DLB 11, 25; RGAL
4

Marquis de Sade
See Sade, Donatien Alphonse Francois

Marric, J. J.
See Creasey, John
See also MSW

Marryat, Frederick 1792-1848 .... **NCLC 3**
See also DLB 21, 163; RGEL 2; WCH

Marsden, James
See Creasey, John

Marsh, Edward 1872-1953 .... **TCLC 99**

Marsh, (Edith) Ngaio 1899-1982 .. **CLC 7, 53**
See also CA 9-12R; CANR 6, 58; CMW 4;
CPW; DAM POP; DLB 77; MSW;
MTCW 1, 2; RGEL 2; TEA

Marshall, Garry 1934- .... **CLC 17**
See also AAYA 3; CA 111; SATA 60

Marshall, Paule 1929- .. **BLC 3; CLC 27, 72;
SSC 3**
See also AFAW 1, 2; AMWS 11; BPFB 2;
BW 2, 3; CA 77-80; CANR 25, 73; CN 7;
DA3; DAM MULT; DLB 33, 157, 227;
EWL 3; MTCW 1, 2; RGAL 4; SSFS 15

Marshallik
See Zangwill, Israel

Marsten, Richard
See Hunter, Evan

Marston, John 1576-1634 .... **LC 33**
See also BRW 2; DAM DRAM; DLB 58,
172; RGEL 2

Martha, Henry
See Harris, Mark

Marti (y Perez), Jose (Julian)
1853-1895 .... **HLC 2; NCLC 63**
See also DAM MULT; HW 2; LAW; RGWL
2, 3; WLIT 1

Martial c. 40-c. 104 .... **CMLC 35; PC 10**
See also AW 2; CDWLB 1; DLB 211;
RGWL 2, 3

Martin, Ken
See Hubbard, L.(afayette) Ron(ald)

Martin, Richard
See Creasey, John

Martin, Steve 1945- .... **CLC 30**
See also CA 97-100; CANR 30, 100;
MTCW 1

Martin, Valerie 1948- .... **CLC 89**
See also BEST 90:2; CA 85-88; CANR 49,
89

Martin, Violet Florence 1862-1915 .. **SSC 56;
TCLC 51**

Martin, Webber
See Silverberg, Robert

Martindale, Patrick Victor
See White, Patrick (Victor Martindale)

Martin du Gard, Roger
1881-1958 .... **TCLC 24**
See also CA 118; CANR 94; DLB 65; EWL
3; GFL 1789 to the Present; RGWL 2, 3

Martineau, Harriet 1802-1876 .... **NCLC 26**
See also DLB 21, 55, 159, 163, 166, 190;
FW; RGEL 2; YABC 2

Martines, Julia
See O'Faolain, Julia

Martinez, Enrique Gonzalez
See Gonzalez Martinez, Enrique

Martinez, Jacinto Benavente y
See Benavente (y Martinez), Jacinto

Martinez de la Rosa, Francisco de Paula
1787-1862 .... **NCLC 102**
See also TWA

Martinez Ruiz, Jose 1873-1967
See Azorin; Ruiz, Jose Martinez
See also CA 93-96; HW 1

Martinez Sierra, Gregorio
1881-1947 .... **TCLC 6**
See also CA 115; EWL 3

Martinez Sierra, Maria (de la O'LeJarraga)
1874-1974 .... **TCLC 6**
See also CA 115; EWL 3

Martinsen, Martin
See Follett, Ken(neth Martin)

Martinson, Harry (Edmund)
1904-1978 .... **CLC 14**
See also CA 77-80; CANR 34; DLB 259;
EWL 3

Martyn, Edward 1859-1923 .... **TCLC 131**
See also CA 179; DLB 10; RGEL 2

Marut, Ret
See Traven, B.

Marut, Robert
See Traven, B.

Marvell, Andrew 1621-1678 .... **LC 4, 43; PC
10; WLC**
See also BRW 2; BRWR 2; CDBLB 1660-
1789; DA; DAB; DAC; DAM MST,
POET; DLB 131; EXPP; PFS 5; RGEL 2;
TEA; WP

Marx, Karl (Heinrich)
1818-1883 .... **NCLC 17, 114**
See also DLB 129; TWA

Masaoka, Shiki -1902 .... **TCLC 18**
See Masaoka, Tsunenori
See also RGWL 3

Masaoka, Tsunenori 1867-1902
See Masaoka, Shiki
See also CA 191; 117; TWA

Masefield, John (Edward)
1878-1967 .... **CLC 11, 47**
See also CA 25-28R; 19-20; CANR 33;
CAP 2; CDBLB 1890-1914; DAM POET;
DLB 10, 19, 153, 160; EWL 3; EXPP;
FANT; MTCW 1, 2; PFS 5; RGEL 2;
SATA 19

Maso, Carole 19(?)- .... **CLC 44**
See also CA 170; GLL 2; RGAL 4

Mason, Bobbie Ann 1940- ... **CLC 28, 43, 82,
154; SSC 4**
See also AAYA 5, 42; AMWS 8; BPFB 2;
CA 53-56; CANR 11, 31, 58, 83;
CDALBS; CN 7; CSW; DA3; DLB 173;
DLBY 1987; EWL 3; EXPS; INT CANR-
31; MTCW 1, 2; NFS 4; RGAL 4; RGSF
2; SSFS 3,8; YAW

Mason, Ernst
See Pohl, Frederik

Mason, Hunni B.
See Sternheim, (William Adolf) Carl

Mason, Lee W.
See Malzberg, Barry N(athaniel)

Mason, Nick 1945- .... **CLC 35**

Mason, Tally
See Derleth, August (William)

Mass, Anna .... **CLC 59**

Mass, William
See Gibson, William

Massinger, Philip 1583-1640 .... **LC 70**
See also DLB 58; RGEL 2

Master Lao
See Lao Tzu

Masters, Edgar Lee 1868-1950 ...... **PC 1, 36;
TCLC 2, 25; WLCS**
See also AMWS 1; CA 133; 104; CDALB
1865-1917; DA; DAC; DAM MST,
POET; DLB 54; EWL 3; EXPP; MTCW
1, 2; RGAL 4; TUS; WP

Masters, Hilary 1928- .... **CLC 48**
See also CA 25-28R; CANR 13, 47, 97; CN
7; DLB 244

Mastrosimone, William 19(?)- .... **CLC 36**
See also CA 186; CAD; CD 5

Mathe, Albert
See Camus, Albert

Mather, Cotton 1663-1728 .... **LC 38**
See also AMWS 2; CDALB 1640-1865;
DLB 24, 30, 140; RGAL 4; TUS

Mather, Increase 1639-1723 .... **LC 38**
See also DLB 24

Matheson, Richard (Burton) 1926- .. **CLC 37**
See also AAYA 31; CA 97-100; CANR 88,
99; DLB 8, 44; HGG; INT 97-100; SCFW
2; SFW 4; SUFW 2

Mathews, Harry 1930- .... **CLC 6, 52**
See also CA 21-24R; CAAS 6; CANR 18,
40, 98; CN 7

Mathews, John Joseph 1894-1979 .. **CLC 84;
NNAL**
See also CA 142; 19-20; CANR 45; CAP 2;
DAM MULT; DLB 175

Mathias, Roland (Glyn) 1915- .... **CLC 45**
See also CA 97-100; CANR 19, 41; CP 7;
DLB 27

Matsuo Basho 1644-1694 .... **LC 62; PC 3**
See Basho, Matsuo
See also DAM POET; PFS 2, 7

Mattheson, Rodney
See Creasey, John

Matthews, (James) Brander
1852-1929 .... **TCLC 95**
See also DLB 71, 78; DLBD 13

Matthews, Greg 1949- .... **CLC 45**
See also CA 135

Matthews, William (Procter III)
1942-1997 .... **CLC 40**
See also AMWS 9; CA 162; 29-32R; CAAS
18; CANR 12, 57; CP 7; DLB 5

Matthias, John (Edward) 1941- .... **CLC 9**
See also CA 33-36R; CANR 56; CP 7

Matthiessen, F(rancis) O(tto)
1902-1950 .... **TCLC 100**
See also CA 185; DLB 63

Matthiessen, Peter 1927- ... **CLC 5, 7, 11, 32,
64**
See also AAYA 6, 40; AMWS 5; ANW;
BEST 90:4; BPFB 2; CA 9-12R; CANR
21, 50, 73, 100; CN 7; DA3; DAM NOV;
DLB 6, 173, 275; MTCW 1, 2; SATA 27

Maturin, Charles Robert
1780(?)-1824 .... **NCLC 6**
See also BRWS 8; DLB 178; HGG; RGEL
2; SUFW

Matute (Ausejo), Ana Maria 1925- .. **CLC 11**
See also CA 89-92; EWL 3; MTCW 1;
RGSF 2

Maugham, W. S.
See Maugham, W(illiam) Somerset

Maugham, W(illiam) Somerset
1874-1965 .. **CLC 1, 11, 15, 67, 93; SSC
8; WLC**
See also BPFB 2; BRW 6; CA 25-28R;
5-8R; CANR 40; CDBLB 1914-1945;
CMW 4; DA; DA3; DAB; DAC; DAM
DRAM, MST, NOV; DLB 10, 36, 77, 100,
162, 195; EWL 3; LAIT 3; MTCW 1, 2;
RGEL 2; RGSF 2; SATA 54; SSFS 17

Maugham, William Somerset
See Maugham, W(illiam) Somerset

Maupassant, (Henri Rene Albert) Guy de
1850-1893 .... **NCLC 1, 42, 83; SSC 1;
WLC**
See also BYA 14; DA; DA3; DAB; DAC;
DAM MST; DLB 123; EW 7; EXPS; GFL
1789 to the Present; LAIT 2; RGSF 2;
RGWL 2, 3; SSFS 4; SUFW; TWA

McManus, Declan Patrick Aloysius
See Costello, Elvis

McMillan, Terry (L.) 1951- . **BLCS; CLC 50, 61, 112**
See also AAYA 21; BPFB 2; BW 2, 3; CA 140; CANR 60, 104; CPW; DA3; DAM MULT, NOV, POP; MTCW 2; RGAL 4; YAW

McMurtry, Larry (Jeff) 1936- .. **CLC 2, 3, 7, 11, 27, 44, 127**
See also AAYA 15; AITN 2; AMWS 5; BEST 89:2; BPFB 2; CA 5-8R; CANR 19, 43, 64, 103; CDALB 1968-1988; CN 7; CPW; CSW; DA3; DAM NOV, POP; DLB 2, 143, 256; DLBY 1980, 1987; EWL 3; MTCW 1, 2; RGAL 4; TCWW 2

McNally, T. M. 1961- .... **CLC 82**

McNally, Terrence 1939- .... **CLC 4, 7, 41, 91**
See also CA 45-48; CAD; CANR 2, 56, 116; CD 5; DA3; DAM DRAM; DFS 16; DLB 7, 249; EWL 3; GLL 1; MTCW 2

McNamer, Deirdre 1950- .... **CLC 70**

McNeal, Tom .... **CLC 119**

McNeile, Herman Cyril 1888-1937
See Sapper
See also CA 184; CMW 4; DLB 77

McNickle, (William) D'Arcy
1904-1977 .... **CLC 89; NNAL**
See also CA 85-88; 9-12R; CANR 5, 45; DAM MULT; DLB 175, 212; RGAL 4; SATA-Obit 22

McPhee, John (Angus) 1931- .... **CLC 36**
See also AMWS 3; ANW; BEST 90:1; CA 65-68; CANR 20, 46, 64, 69; CPW; DLB 185, 275; MTCW 1, 2; TUS

McPherson, James Alan 1943- . **BLCS; CLC 19, 77**
See also BW 1, 3; CA 25-28R; CAAS 17; CANR 24, 74; CN 7; CSW; DLB 38, 244; EWL 3; MTCW 1, 2; RGAL 4; RGSF 2

McPherson, William (Alexander)
1933- .... **CLC 34**
See also CA 69-72; CANR 28; INT CANR-28

McTaggart, J. McT. Ellis
See McTaggart, John McTaggart Ellis

McTaggart, John McTaggart Ellis
1866-1925 .... **TCLC 105**
See also CA 120; DLB 262

Mead, George Herbert 1863-1931 . **TCLC 89**
See also DLB 270

Mead, Margaret 1901-1978 .... **CLC 37**
See also AITN 1; CA 81-84; 1-4R; CANR 4; DA3; FW; MTCW 1, 2; SATA-Obit 20

Meaker, Marijane (Agnes) 1927-
See Kerr, M. E.
See also CA 107; CANR 37, 63; INT 107; JRDA; MAICYA 1, 2; MAICYAS 1; MTCW 1; SATA 20, 61, 99; SATA-Essay 111; YAW

Medoff, Mark (Howard) 1940- .... **CLC 6, 23**
See also AITN 1; CA 53-56; CAD; CANR 5; CD 5; DAM DRAM; DFS 4; DLB 7; INT CANR-5

Medvedev, P. N.
See Bakhtin, Mikhail Mikhailovich

Meged, Aharon
See Megged, Aharon

Meged, Aron
See Megged, Aharon

Megged, Aharon 1920- .... **CLC 9**
See also CA 49-52; CAAS 13; CANR 1; EWL 3

Mehta, Ved (Parkash) 1934- .... **CLC 37**
See also CA 1-4R; CANR 2, 23, 69; MTCW 1

Melanter
See Blackmore, R(ichard) D(oddridge)

Meleager c. 140B.C.-c. 70B.C. ...... **CMLC 53**

Melies, Georges 1861-1938 .... **TCLC 81**

Melikow, Loris
See Hofmannsthal, Hugo von

Melmoth, Sebastian
See Wilde, Oscar (Fingal O'Flahertie Wills)

Melo Neto, Joao Cabral de
See Cabral de Melo Neto, Joao
See also EWL 3

Meltzer, Milton 1915- .... **CLC 26**
See also AAYA 8, 45; BYA 2, 6; CA 13-16R; CANR 38, 92, 107; CLR 13; DLB 61; JRDA; MAICYA 1, 2; SAAS 1; SATA 1, 50, 80, 128; SATA-Essay 124; WYA; YAW

Melville, Herman 1819-1891 ..... **NCLC 3, 12, 29, 45, 49, 91, 93, 123; SSC 1, 17, 46; WLC**
See also AAYA 25; AMW; AMWR 1; CDALB 1640-1865; DA; DA3; DAB; DAC; DAM MST, NOV; DLB 3, 74, 250, 254; EXPN; EXPS; LAIT 1, 2; NFS 7, 9; RGAL 4; RGSF 2; SATA 59; SSFS 3; TUS

Members, Mark
See Powell, Anthony (Dymoke)

Membreno, Alejandro .... **CLC 59**

Menander c. 342B.C.-c. 293B.C. .... **CMLC 9, 51; DC 3**
See also AW 1; CDWLB 1; DAM DRAM; DLB 176; RGWL 2, 3

Menchu, Rigoberta 1959- .. **CLC 160; HLCS 2**
See also CA 175; DNFS 1; WLIT 1

Mencken, H(enry) L(ouis)
1880-1956 .... **TCLC 13**
See also AMW; CA 125; 105; CDALB 1917-1929; DLB 11, 29, 63, 137, 222; EWL 3; MTCW 1, 2; NCFS 4; RGAL 4; TUS

Mendelsohn, Jane 1965- .... **CLC 99**
See also CA 154; CANR 94

Menton, Francisco de
See Chin, Frank (Chew, Jr.)

Mercer, David 1928-1980 .... **CLC 5**
See also CA 102; 9-12R; CANR 23; CBD; DAM DRAM; DLB 13; MTCW 1; RGEL 2

Merchant, Paul
See Ellison, Harlan (Jay)

Meredith, George 1828-1909 ... **TCLC 17, 43**
See also CA 153; 117; CANR 80; CDBLB 1832-1890; DAM POET; DLB 18, 35, 57, 159; RGEL 2; TEA

Meredith, William (Morris) 1919- .... **CLC 4, 13, 22, 55; PC 28**
See also CA 9-12R; CAAS 14; CANR 6, 40; CP 7; DAM POET; DLB 5

Merezhkovsky, Dmitry Sergeevich
See Merezhkovsky, Dmitry Sergeyevich
See also EWL 3

Merezhkovsky, Dmitry Sergeyevich
1865-1941 .... **TCLC 29**
See Merezhkovsky, Dmitry Sergeevich
See also CA 169

Merimee, Prosper 1803-1870 ... **NCLC 6, 65; SSC 7**
See also DLB 119, 192; EW 6; EXPS; GFL 1789 to the Present; RGSF 2; RGWL 2, 3; SSFS 8; SUFW

Merkin, Daphne 1954- .... **CLC 44**
See also CA 123

Merlin, Arthur
See Blish, James (Benjamin)

Mernissi, Fatima 1940- .... **CLC 171**
See also CA 152; FW

Merrill, James (Ingram) 1926-1995 .. **CLC 2, 3, 6, 8, 13, 18, 34, 91; PC 28**
See also AMWS 3; CA 147; 13-16R; CANR 10, 49, 63, 108; DA3; DAM POET; DLB 5, 165; DLBY 1985; EWL 3; INT CANR-10; MTCW 1, 2; PAB; RGAL 4

Merriman, Alex
See Silverberg, Robert

Merriman, Brian 1747-1805 .... **NCLC 70**

Merritt, E. B.
See Waddington, Miriam

Merton, Thomas (James)
1915-1968 . **CLC 1, 3, 11, 34, 83; PC 10**
See also AMWS 8; CA 25-28R; 5-8R; CANR 22, 53, 111; DA3; DLB 48; DLBY 1981; MTCW 1, 2

Merwin, W(illiam) S(tanley) 1927- ... **CLC 1, 2, 3, 5, 8, 13, 18, 45, 88; PC 45**
See also AMWS 3; CA 13-16R; CANR 15, 51, 112; CP 7; DA3; DAM POET; DLB 5, 169; EWL 3; INT CANR-15; MTCW 1, 2; PAB; PFS 5, 15; RGAL 4

Metcalf, John 1938- .... **CLC 37; SSC 43**
See also CA 113; CN 7; DLB 60; RGSF 2; TWA

Metcalf, Suzanne
See Baum, L(yman) Frank

Mew, Charlotte (Mary) 1870-1928 .. **TCLC 8**
See also CA 189; 105; DLB 19, 135; RGEL 2

Mewshaw, Michael 1943- .... **CLC 9**
See also CA 53-56; CANR 7, 47; DLBY 1980

Meyer, Conrad Ferdinand
1825-1905 .... **NCLC 81**
See also DLB 129; EW; RGWL 2, 3

Meyer, Gustav 1868-1932
See Meyrink, Gustav
See also CA 190; 117

Meyer, June
See Jordan, June (Meyer)

Meyer, Lynn
See Slavitt, David R(ytman)

Meyers, Jeffrey 1939- .... **CLC 39**
See also CA 73-76; CAAE 186; CANR 54, 102; DLB 111

Meynell, Alice (Christina Gertrude Thompson) 1847-1922 .... **TCLC 6**
See also CA 177; 104; DLB 19, 98; RGEL 2

Meyrink, Gustav .... **TCLC 21**
See Meyer, Gustav
See also DLB 81; EWL 3

Michaels, Leonard 1933- .... **CLC 6, 25; SSC 16**
See also CA 61-64; CANR 21, 62; CN 7; DLB 130; MTCW 1

Michaux, Henri 1899-1984 .... **CLC 8, 19**
See also CA 114; 85-88; DLB 258; EWL 3; GFL 1789 to the Present; RGWL 2, 3

Micheaux, Oscar (Devereaux)
1884-1951 .... **TCLC 76**
See also BW 3; CA 174; DLB 50; TCWW 2

Michelangelo 1475-1564 .... **LC 12**
See also AAYA 43

Michelet, Jules 1798-1874 .... **NCLC 31**
See also EW 5; GFL 1789 to the Present

Michels, Robert 1876-1936 .... **TCLC 88**

Michener, James A(lbert)
1907(?)-1997 .. **CLC 1, 5, 11, 29, 60, 109**
See also AAYA 27; AITN 1; BEST 90:1; BPFB 2; CA 161; 5-8R; CANR 21, 45, 68; CN 7; CPW; DA3; DAM NOV, POP; DLB 6; MTCW 1, 2; RHW

Mickiewicz, Adam 1798-1855 . **NCLC 3, 101; PC 38**
See also EW 5; RGWL 2, 3

Molnar, Ferenc 1878-1952 .... **TCLC 20**
See also CA 153; 109; CANR 83; CDWLB
4; DAM DRAM; DLB 215; EWL 3;
RGWL 2, 3

Momaday, N(avarre) Scott 1934- ...... **CLC 2,**
19, 85, 95, 160; NNAL; PC 25; WLCS
See also AAYA 11; AMWS 4; ANW; BPFB
2; CA 25-28R; CANR 14, 34, 68;
CDALBS; CN 7; CPW; DA; DA3; DAB;
DAC; DAM MST, MULT, NOV, POP;
DLB 143, 175, 256; EWL 3; EXPP; INT
CANR-14; LAIT 4; MTCW 1, 2; NFS 10;
PFS 2, 11; RGAL 4; SATA 48; SATA-
Brief 30; WP; YAW

Monette, Paul 1945-1995 .... **CLC 82**
See also AMWS 10; CA 147; 139; CN 7;
GLL 1

Monroe, Harriet 1860-1936 .... **TCLC 12**
See also CA 204; 109; DLB 54, 91

Monroe, Lyle
See Heinlein, Robert A(nson)

Montagu, Elizabeth 1720-1800 .... **NCLC 7,**
117
See also FW

Montagu, Mary (Pierrepont) Wortley
1689-1762 .... **LC 9, 57; PC 16**
See also DLB 95, 101; RGEL 2

Montagu, W. H.
See Coleridge, Samuel Taylor

Montague, John (Patrick) 1929- ..... **CLC 13,**
46
See also CA 9-12R; CANR 9, 69; CP 7;
DLB 40; EWL 3; MTCW 1; PFS 12;
RGEL 2

Montaigne, Michel (Eyquem) de
1533-1592 .... **LC 8; WLC**
See also DA; DAB; DAC; DAM MST; EW
2; GFL Beginnings to 1789; RGWL 2, 3;
TWA

Montale, Eugenio 1896-1981 ... **CLC 7, 9, 18;**
PC 13
See also CA 104; 17-20R; CANR 30; DLB
114; EW 11; EWL 3; MTCW 1; RGWL
2, 3; TWA

Montesquieu, Charles-Louis de Secondat
1689-1755 .... **LC 7, 69**
See also EW 3; GFL Beginnings to 1789;
TWA

Montessori, Maria 1870-1952 ...... **TCLC 103**
See also CA 147; 115

Montgomery, (Robert) Bruce 1921(?)-1978
See Crispin, Edmund
See also CA 104; 179; CMW 4

Montgomery, L(ucy) M(aud)
1874-1942 .... **TCLC 51**
See also AAYA 12; BYA 1; CA 137; 108;
CLR 8; DA3; DAC; DAM MST; DLB 92;
DLBD 14; JRDA; MAICYA 1, 2; MTCW
2; RGEL 2; SATA 100; TWA; WCH;
WYA; YABC 1

Montgomery, Marion H., Jr. 1925- .... **CLC 7**
See also AITN 1; CA 1-4R; CANR 3, 48;
CSW; DLB 6

Montgomery, Max
See Davenport, Guy (Mattison, Jr.)

Montherlant, Henry (Milon) de
1896-1972 .... **CLC 8, 19**
See also CA 37-40R; 85-88; DAM DRAM;
DLB 72; EW 11; EWL 3; GFL 1789 to
the Present; MTCW 1

Monty Python
See Chapman, Graham; Cleese, John
(Marwood); Gilliam, Terry (Vance); Idle,
Eric; Jones, Terence Graham Parry; Palin,
Michael (Edward)
See also AAYA 7

Moodie, Susanna (Strickland)
1803-1885 .... **NCLC 14, 113**
See also DLB 99

Moody, Hiram (F. III) 1961-
See Moody, Rick
See also CA 138; CANR 64, 112

Moody, Minerva
See Alcott, Louisa May

Moody, Rick .... **CLC 147**
See Moody, Hiram (F. III)

Moody, William Vaughan
1869-1910 .... **TCLC 105**
See also CA 178; 110; DLB 7, 54; RGAL 4

Mooney, Edward 1951-
See Mooney, Ted
See also CA 130

Mooney, Ted .... **CLC 25**
See Mooney, Edward

Moorcock, Michael (John) 1939- ...... **CLC 5,**
27, 58
See Bradbury, Edward P.
See also AAYA 26; CA 45-48; CAAS 5;
CANR 2, 17, 38, 64; CN 7; DLB 14, 231,
261; FANT; MTCW 1, 2; SATA 93;
SCFW 2; SFW 4; SUFW 1, 2

Moore, Brian 1921-1999 ... **CLC 1, 3, 5, 7, 8,**
19, 32, 90
See Bryan, Michael
See also CA 174; 1-4R; CANR 1, 25, 42,
63; CCA 1; CN 7; DAB; DAC; DAM
MST; DLB 251; EWL 3; FANT; MTCW
1, 2; RGEL 2

Moore, Edward
See Muir, Edwin
See also RGEL 2

Moore, G. E. 1873-1958 .... **TCLC 89**
See also DLB 262

Moore, George Augustus
1852-1933 .... **SSC 19; TCLC 7**
See also BRW 6; CA 177; 104; DLB 10,
18, 57, 135; EWL 3; RGEL 2; RGSF 2

Moore, Lorrie .... **CLC 39, 45, 68**
See Moore, Marie Lorena
See also AMWS 10; DLB 234

Moore, Marianne (Craig)
1887-1972 .... **CLC 1, 2, 4, 8, 10, 13, 19,**
47; PC 4; WLCS
See also AMW; CA 33-36R; 1-4R; CANR
3, 61; CDALB 1929-1941; DA; DA3;
DAB; DAC; DAM MST, POET; DLB 45;
DLBD 7; EWL 3; EXPP; MAWW;
MTCW 1, 2; PAB; PFS 14, 17; RGAL 4;
SATA 20; TUS; WP

Moore, Marie Lorena 1957- .... **CLC 165**
See Moore, Lorrie
See also CA 116; CANR 39, 83; CN 7; DLB
234

Moore, Thomas 1779-1852 .... **NCLC 6, 110**
See also DLB 96, 144; RGEL 2

Moorhouse, Frank 1938- .... **SSC 40**
See also CA 118; CANR 92; CN 7; RGSF
2

Mora, Pat(ricia) 1942- .... **HLC 2**
See also CA 129; CANR 57, 81, 112; CLR
58; DAM MULT; DLB 209; HW 1, 2;
MAICYA 2; SATA 92, 134

Moraga, Cherrie 1952- .... **CLC 126**
See also CA 131; CANR 66; DAM MULT;
DLB 82, 249; FW; GLL 1; HW 1, 2

Morand, Paul 1888-1976 .... **CLC 41; SSC 22**
See also CA 69-72; 184; DLB 65; EWL 3

Morante, Elsa 1918-1985 .... **CLC 8, 47**
See also CA 117; 85-88; CANR 35; DLB
177; EWL 3; MTCW 1, 2; RGWL 2, 3

Moravia, Alberto .... **CLC 2, 7, 11, 27, 46;**
SSC 26
See Pincherle, Alberto
See also DLB 177; EW 12; EWL 3; MTCW
2; RGSF 2; RGWL 2, 3

More, Hannah 1745-1833 .... **NCLC 27**
See also DLB 107, 109, 116, 158; RGEL 2

More, Henry 1614-1687 .... **LC 9**
See also DLB 126, 252

More, Sir Thomas 1478(?)-1535 .... **LC 10, 32**
See also BRWC 1; BRWS 7; DLB 136;
RGEL 2; TEA

Moreas, Jean .... **TCLC 18**
See Papadiamantopoulos, Johannes
See also GFL 1789 to the Present

Moreton, Andrew Esq.
See Defoe, Daniel

Morgan, Berry 1919-2002 .... **CLC 6**
See also CA 208; 49-52; DLB 6

Morgan, Claire
See Highsmith, (Mary) Patricia
See also GLL 1

Morgan, Edwin (George) 1920- .... **CLC 31**
See also CA 5-8R; CANR 3, 43, 90; CP 7;
DLB 27

Morgan, (George) Frederick 1922- .. **CLC 23**
See also CA 17-20R; CANR 21; CP 7

Morgan, Harriet
See Mencken, H(enry) L(ouis)

Morgan, Jane
See Cooper, James Fenimore

Morgan, Janet 1945- .... **CLC 39**
See also CA 65-68

Morgan, Lady 1776(?)-1859 .... **NCLC 29**
See also DLB 116, 158; RGEL 2

Morgan, Robin (Evonne) 1941- .... **CLC 2**
See also CA 69-72; CANR 29, 68; FW;
GLL 2; MTCW 1; SATA 80

Morgan, Scott
See Kuttner, Henry

Morgan, Seth 1949(?)-1990 .... **CLC 65**
See also CA 132; 185

Morgenstern, Christian (Otto Josef
Wolfgang) 1871-1914 .... **TCLC 8**
See also CA 191; 105; EWL 3

Morgenstern, S.
See Goldman, William (W.)

Mori, Rintaro
See Mori Ogai
See also CA 110

Moricz, Zsigmond 1879-1942 .... **TCLC 33**
See also CA 165; DLB 215; EWL 3

Morike, Eduard (Friedrich)
1804-1875 .... **NCLC 10**
See also DLB 133; RGWL 2, 3

Mori Ogai 1862-1922 .... **TCLC 14**
See Ogai
See also CA 164; DLB 180; EWL 3; RGWL
3; TWA

Moritz, Karl Philipp 1756-1793 .... **LC 2**
See also DLB 94

Morland, Peter Henry
See Faust, Frederick (Schiller)

Morley, Christopher (Darlington)
1890-1957 .... **TCLC 87**
See also CA 112; DLB 9; RGAL 4

Morren, Theophil
See Hofmannsthal, Hugo von

Morris, Bill 1952- .... **CLC 76**

Morris, Julian
See West, Morris L(anglo)

Morris, Steveland Judkins 1950(?)-
See Wonder, Stevie
See also CA 111

Morris, William 1834-1896 .... **NCLC 4**
See also BRW 5; CDBLB 1832-1890; DLB
18, 35, 57, 156, 178, 184; FANT; RGEL
2; SFW 4; SUFW

Morris, Wright 1910-1998 .. **CLC 1, 3, 7, 18,**
37; TCLC 107
See also AMW; CA 167; 9-12R; CANR 21,
81; CN 7; DLB 2, 206, 218; DLBY 1981;
EWL 3; MTCW 1, 2; RGAL 4; TCWW 2

Mussolini, Benito (Amilcare Andrea)
1883-1945 .... TCLC 96
See also CA 116
My Brother's Brother
See Chekhov, Anton (Pavlovich)
Myers, L(eopold) H(amilton)
1881-1944 .... TCLC 59
See also CA 157; DLB 15; EWL 3; RGEL
2
Myers, Walter Dean 1937- .. BLC 3; CLC 35
See also AAYA 4, 23; BW 2; BYA 6, 8, 11;
CA 33-36R; CANR 20, 42, 67, 108; CLR
4, 16, 35; DAM MULT, NOV; DLB 33;
INT CANR-20; JRDA; LAIT 5; MAICYA
1, 2; MAICYAS 1; MTCW 2; SAAS 2;
SATA 41, 71, 109; SATA-Brief 27; WYA;
YAW
Myers, Walter M.
See Myers, Walter Dean
Myles, Symon
See Follett, Ken(neth Martin)
Nabokov, Vladimir (Vladimirovich)
1899-1977 .... CLC 1, 2, 3, 6, 8, 11, 15,
23, 44, 46, 64; SSC 11; TCLC 108;
WLC
See also AAYA 45; AMW; AMWC 1;
AMWR 1; BPFB 2; CA 69-72; 5-8R;
CANR 20, 102; CDALB 1941-1968; DA;
DA3; DAB; DAC; DAM MST, NOV;
DLB 2, 244, 278; DLBD 3; DLBY 1980,
1991; EWL 3; EXPS; MTCW 1, 2; NCFS
4; NFS 9; RGAL 4; RGSF 2; SSFS 6, 15;
TUS
Naevius c. 265B.C.-201B.C. .... CMLC 37
See also DLB 211
Nagai, Kafu .... TCLC 51
See Nagai, Sokichi
See also DLB 180
Nagai, Sokichi 1879-1959
See Nagai, Kafu
See also CA 117
Nagy, Laszlo 1925-1978 .... CLC 7
See also CA 112; 129
Naidu, Sarojini 1879-1949 .... TCLC 80
See also EWL 3; RGEL 2
Naipaul, Shiva(dhar Srinivasa)
1945-1985 .... CLC 32, 39
See also CA 116; 112; 110; CANR 33;
DA3; DAM NOV; DLB 157; DLBY 1985;
EWL 3; MTCW 1, 2
Naipaul, V(idiadhar) S(urajprasad)
1932- .... CLC 4, 7, 9, 13, 18, 37, 105;
SSC 38
See also BPFB 2; BRWS 1; CA 1-4R;
CANR 1, 33, 51, 91; CDBLB 1960 to
Present; CDWLB 3; CN 7; DA3; DAB;
DAC; DAM MST, NOV; DLB 125, 204,
207; DLBY 1985, 2001; EWL 3; MTCW
1, 2; RGEL 2; RGSF 2; TWA; WLIT 4
Nakos, Lilika 1899(?)- .... CLC 29
Narayan, R(asipuram) K(rishnaswami)
1906-2001 . CLC 7, 28, 47, 121; SSC 25
See also BPFB 2; CA 196; 81-84; CANR
33, 61, 112; CN 7; DA3; DAM NOV;
DNFS 1; EWL 3; MTCW 1, 2; RGEL 2;
RGSF 2; SATA 62; SSFS 5
Nash, (Fredric) Ogden 1902-1971 . CLC 23;
PC 21; TCLC 109
See also CA 29-32R; 13-14; CANR 34, 61;
CAP 1; DAM POET; DLB 11; MAICYA
1, 2; MTCW 1, 2; RGAL 4; SATA 2, 46;
WP
Nashe, Thomas 1567-1601(?) .... LC 41
See also DLB 167; RGEL 2
Nathan, Daniel
See Dannay, Frederic
Nathan, George Jean 1882-1958 .... TCLC 18
See Hatteras, Owen
See also CA 169; 114; DLB 137

Natsume, Kinnosuke
See Natsume, Soseki
Natsume, Soseki 1867-1916 .... TCLC 2, 10
See Natsume Soseki; Soseki
See also CA 195; 104; RGWL 2, 3; TWA
Natsume Soseki
See Natsume, Soseki
See also DLB 180; EWL 3
Natti, (Mary) Lee 1919-
See Kingman, Lee
See also CA 5-8R; CANR 2
Navarre, Marguerite de
See de Navarre, Marguerite
Naylor, Gloria 1950- ..... BLC 3; CLC 28, 52,
156; WLCS
See also AAYA 6, 39; AFAW 1, 2; AMWS
8; BW 2, 3; CA 107; CANR 27, 51, 74;
CN 7; CPW; DA; DA3; DAC; DAM
MST, MULT, NOV, POP; DLB 173; EWL
3; FW; MTCW 1, 2; NFS 4, 7; RGAL 4;
TUS
Neff, Debra .... CLC 59
Neihardt, John Gneisenau
1881-1973 .... CLC 32
See also CA 13-14; CANR 65; CAP 1; DLB
9, 54, 256; LAIT 2
Nekrasov, Nikolai Alekseevich
1821-1878 .... NCLC 11
See also DLB 277
Nelligan, Emile 1879-1941 .... TCLC 14
See also CA 204; 114; DLB 92; EWL 3
Nelson, Willie 1933- .... CLC 17
See also CA 107; CANR 114
Nemerov, Howard (Stanley)
1920-1991 .... CLC 2, 6, 9, 36; PC 24;
TCLC 124
See also AMW; CA 134; 1-4R; CABS 2;
CANR 1, 27, 53; DAM POET; DLB 5, 6;
DLBY 1983; EWL 3; INT CANR-27;
MTCW 1, 2; PFS 10, 14; RGAL 4
Neruda, Pablo 1904-1973 .. CLC 1, 2, 5, 7, 9,
28, 62; HLC 2; PC 4; WLC
See also CA 45-48; 19-20; CAP 2; DA;
DA3; DAB; DAC; DAM MST, MULT,
POET; DNFS 2; EWL 3; HW 1; LAW;
MTCW 1, 2; PFS 11; RGWL 2, 3; TWA;
WLIT 1; WP
Nerval, Gerard de 1808-1855 ... NCLC 1, 67;
PC 13; SSC 18
See also DLB 217; EW 6; GFL 1789 to the
Present; RGSF 2; RGWL 2, 3
Nervo, (Jose) Amado (Ruiz de)
1870-1919 .... HLCS 2; TCLC 11
See also CA 131; 109; EWL 3; HW 1; LAW
Nesbit, Malcolm
See Chester, Alfred
Nessi, Pio Baroja y
See Baroja (y Nessi), Pio
Nestroy, Johann 1801-1862 .... NCLC 42
See also DLB 133; RGWL 2, 3
Netterville, Luke
See O'Grady, Standish (James)
Neufeld, John (Arthur) 1938- .... CLC 17
See also AAYA 11; CA 25-28R; CANR 11,
37, 56; CLR 52; MAICYA 1, 2; SAAS 3;
SATA 6, 81; SATA-Essay 131; YAW
Neumann, Alfred 1895-1952 .... TCLC 100
See also CA 183; DLB 56
Neumann, Ferenc
See Molnar, Ferenc
Neville, Emily Cheney 1919- .... CLC 12
See also BYA 2; CA 5-8R; CANR 3, 37,
85; JRDA; MAICYA 1, 2; SAAS 2; SATA
1; YAW
Newbound, Bernard Slade 1930-
See Slade, Bernard
See also CA 81-84; CANR 49; CD 5; DAM
DRAM

Newby, P(ercy) H(oward)
1918-1997 .... CLC 2, 13
See also CA 161; 5-8R; CANR 32, 67; CN
7; DAM NOV; DLB 15; MTCW 1; RGEL
2
Newcastle
See Cavendish, Margaret Lucas
Newlove, Donald 1928- .... CLC 6
See also CA 29-32R; CANR 25
Newlove, John (Herbert) 1938- .... CLC 14
See also CA 21-24R; CANR 9, 25; CP 7
Newman, Charles 1938- .... CLC 2, 8
See also CA 21-24R; CANR 84; CN 7
Newman, Edwin (Harold) 1919- ...... CLC 14
See also AITN 1; CA 69-72; CANR 5
Newman, John Henry 1801-1890 . NCLC 38,
99
See also BRWS 7; DLB 18, 32, 55; RGEL
2
Newton, (Sir) Isaac 1642-1727 ...... LC 35, 53
See also DLB 252
Newton, Suzanne 1936- .... CLC 35
See also BYA 7; CA 41-44R; CANR 14;
JRDA; SATA 5, 77
New York Dept. of Ed. .... CLC 70
Nexo, Martin Andersen
1869-1954 .... TCLC 43
See also CA 202; DLB 214; EWL 3
Nezval, Vitezslav 1900-1958 .... TCLC 44
See also CA 123; CDWLB 4; DLB 215;
EWL 3
Ng, Fae Myenne 1957(?)- .... CLC 81
See also CA 146
Ngema, Mbongeni 1955- .... CLC 57
See also BW 2; CA 143; CANR 84; CD 5
Ngugi, James T(hiong'o) .... CLC 3, 7, 13
See Ngugi wa Thiong'o
Ngugi wa Thiong'o
See Ngugi wa Thiong'o
See also DLB 125; EWL 3
Ngugi wa Thiong'o 1938- .... BLC 3; CLC 36
See Ngugi, James T(hiong'o); Ngugi wa
Thiong'o
See also AFW; BRWS 8; BW 2; CA 81-84;
CANR 27, 58; CDWLB 3; DAM MULT,
NOV; DNFS 2; MTCW 1, 2; RGEL 2
Niatum, Duane 1938- .... NNAL
See also CA 41-44R; CANR 21, 45, 83;
DLB 175
Nichol, B(arrie) P(hillip) 1944-1988 . CLC 18
See also CA 53-56; DLB 53; SATA 66
Nicholas of Cusa 1401-1464 .... LC 80
See also DLB 115
Nichols, John (Treadwell) 1940- .... CLC 38
See also CA 9-12R; CAAE 190; CAAS 2;
CANR 6, 70; DLBY 1982; TCWW 2
Nichols, Leigh
See Koontz, Dean R(ay)
Nichols, Peter (Richard) 1927- .... CLC 5, 36,
65
See also CA 104; CANR 33, 86; CBD; CD
5; DLB 13, 245; MTCW 1
Nicholson, Linda ed. .... CLC 65
Ni Chuilleanain, Eilean 1942- .... PC 34
See also CA 126; CANR 53, 83; CP 7;
CWP; DLB 40
Nicolas, F. R. E.
See Freeling, Nicolas
Niedecker, Lorine 1903-1970 ..... CLC 10, 42;
PC 42
See also CA 25-28; CAP 2; DAM POET;
DLB 48
Nietzsche, Friedrich (Wilhelm)
1844-1900 .... TCLC 10, 18, 55
See also CA 121; 107; CDWLB 2; DLB
129; EW 7; RGWL 2, 3; TWA

Nievo, Ippolito 1831-1861 .... **NCLC 22**
Nightingale, Anne Redmon 1943-
    See Redmon, Anne
    See also CA 103
Nightingale, Florence 1820-1910 ... **TCLC 85**
    See also CA 188; DLB 166
Nijo Yoshimoto 1320-1388 .... **CMLC 49**
    See also DLB 203
Nik. T. O.
    See Annensky, Innokenty (Fyodorovich)
Nin, Anais 1903-1977 ..... **CLC 1, 4, 8, 11, 14,
    60, 127; SSC 10**
    See also AITN 2; AMWS 10; BPFB 2; CA
    69-72; 13-16R; CANR 22, 53; DAM
    NOV, POP; DLB 2, 4, 152; EWL 3; GLL
    2; MAWW; MTCW 1, 2; RGAL 4; RGSF
    2
Nisbet, Robert A(lexander)
    1913-1996 .... **TCLC 117**
    See also CA 153; 25-28R; CANR 17; INT
    CANR-17
Nishida, Kitaro 1870-1945 .... **TCLC 83**
Nishiwaki, Junzaburo
    See Nishiwaki, Junzaburo
    See also CA 194
Nishiwaki, Junzaburo 1894-1982 .... **PC 15**
    See Nishiwaki, Junzaburo; Nishiwaki
    Junzaburo
    See also CA 107; 194; MJW; RGWL 3
Nishiwaki Junzaburo
    See Nishiwaki, Junzaburo
    See also EWL 3
Nissenson, Hugh 1933- .... **CLC 4, 9**
    See also CA 17-20R; CANR 27, 108; CN
    7; DLB 28
Nister, Der
    See Der Nister
    See also EWL 3
Niven, Larry .... **CLC 8**
    See Niven, Laurence Van Cott
    See also AAYA 27; BPFB 2; BYA 10;
    CAAE 207; DLB 8; SCFW 2
Niven, Laurence Van Cott 1938-
    See Niven, Larry
    See also CA 21-24R; CAAS 12; CANR 14,
    44, 66, 113; CPW; DAM POP; MTCW 1,
    2; SATA 95; SFW 4
Nixon, Agnes Eckhardt 1927- .... **CLC 21**
    See also CA 110
Nizan, Paul 1905-1940 .... **TCLC 40**
    See also CA 161; DLB 72; EWL 3; GFL
    1789 to the Present
Nkosi, Lewis 1936- .... **BLC 3; CLC 45**
    See also BW 1, 3; CA 65-68; CANR 27,
    81; CBD; CD 5; DAM MULT; DLB 157,
    225
Nodier, (Jean) Charles (Emmanuel)
    1780-1844 .... **NCLC 19**
    See also DLB 119; GFL 1789 to the Present
Noguchi, Yone 1875-1947 .... **TCLC 80**
Nolan, Christopher 1965- .... **CLC 58**
    See also CA 111; CANR 88
Noon, Jeff 1957- .... **CLC 91**
    See also CA 148; CANR 83; DLB 267;
    SFW 4
Norden, Charles
    See Durrell, Lawrence (George)
Nordhoff, Charles (Bernard)
    1887-1947 .... **TCLC 23**
    See also CA 108; DLB 9; LAIT 1; RHW 1;
    SATA 23
Norfolk, Lawrence 1963- .... **CLC 76**
    See also CA 144; CANR 85; CN 7; DLB
    267
Norman, Marsha 1947- .... **CLC 28; DC 8**
    See also CA 105; CABS 3; CAD; CANR
    41; CD 5; CSW; CWD; DAM DRAM;
    DFS 2; DLB 266; DLBY 1984; FW

Normyx
    See Douglas, (George) Norman
Norris, (Benjamin) Frank(lin, Jr.)
    1870-1902 .... **SSC 28; TCLC 24**
    See also AMW; BPFB 2; CA 160; 110;
    CDALB 1865-1917; DLB 12, 71, 186;
    LMFS 2; NFS 12; RGAL 4; TCWW 2;
    TUS
Norris, Leslie 1921- .... **CLC 14**
    See also CA 11-12; CANR 14, 117; CAP 1;
    CP 7; DLB 27, 256
North, Andrew
    See Norton, Andre
North, Anthony
    See Koontz, Dean R(ay)
North, Captain George
    See Stevenson, Robert Louis (Balfour)
North, Captain George
    See Stevenson, Robert Louis (Balfour)
North, Milou
    See Erdrich, Louise
Northrup, B. A.
    See Hubbard, L(afayette) Ron(ald)
North Staffs
    See Hulme, T(homas) E(rnest)
Northup, Solomon 1808-1863 ...... **NCLC 105**
Norton, Alice Mary
    See Norton, Andre
    See also MAICYA 1; SATA 1, 43
Norton, Andre 1912- .... **CLC 12**
    See Norton, Alice Mary
    See also AAYA 14; BPFB 2; BYA 4, 10,
    12; CA 1-4R; CANR 68; CLR 50; DLB
    8, 52; JRDA; MAICYA 2; MTCW 1;
    SATA 91; SUFW 1, 2; YAW
Norton, Caroline 1808-1877 .... **NCLC 47**
    See also DLB 21, 159, 199
Norway, Nevil Shute 1899-1960
    See Shute, Nevil
    See also CA 93-96; 102; CANR 85; MTCW
    2
Norwid, Cyprian Kamil
    1821-1883 .... **NCLC 17**
    See also RGWL 3
Nosille, Nabrah
    See Ellison, Harlan (Jay)
Nossack, Hans Erich 1901-1978 .... **CLC 6**
    See also CA 85-88; 93-96; DLB 69; EWL 3
Nostradamus 1503-1566 .... **LC 27**
Nosu, Chuji
    See Ozu, Yasujiro
Notenburg, Eleanora (Genrikhovna) von
    See Guro, Elena
Nova, Craig 1945- .... **CLC 7, 31**
    See also CA 45-48; CANR 2, 53
Novak, Joseph
    See Kosinski, Jerzy (Nikodem)
Novalis 1772-1801 .... **NCLC 13**
    See also CDWLB 2; DLB 90; EW 5; RGWL
    2, 3
Novick, Peter 1934- .... **CLC 164**
    See also CA 188
Novis, Emile
    See Weil, Simone (Adolphine)
Nowlan, Alden (Albert) 1933-1983 ... **CLC 15**
    See also CA 9-12R; CANR 5; DAC; DAM
    MST; DLB 53; PFS 12
Noyes, Alfred 1880-1958 ...... **PC 27; TCLC 7**
    See also CA 188; 104; DLB 20; EXPP;
    FANT; PFS 4; RGEL 2
Nugent, Richard Bruce 1906(?)-1987 ... **HR 3**
    See also BW 1; CA 125; DLB 51; GLL 2
Nunn, Kem .... **CLC 34**
    See also CA 159

Nwapa, Flora (Nwanzuruaha)
    1931-1993 .... **BLCS; CLC 133**
    See also BW 2; CA 143; CANR 83; CD-
    WLB 3; CWRI 5; DLB 125; EWL 3;
    WLIT 2
Nye, Robert 1939- .... **CLC 13, 42**
    See also CA 33-36R; CANR 29, 67, 107;
    CN 7; CP 7; CWRI 5; DAM NOV; DLB
    14, 271; FANT; HGG; MTCW 1; RHW;
    SATA 6
Nyro, Laura 1947-1997 .... **CLC 17**
    See also CA 194
Oates, Joyce Carol 1938- .. **CLC 1, 2, 3, 6, 9,
    11, 15, 19, 33, 52, 108, 134; SSC 6;
    WLC**
    See also AAYA 15; AITN 1; AMWS 2;
    BEST 89:2; BPFB 2; BYA 11; CA 5-8R;
    CANR 25, 45, 74, 113, 113; CDALB
    1968-1988; CN 7; CP 7; CPW; CWP; DA;
    DA3; DAB; DAC; DAM MST, NOV,
    POP; DLB 2, 5, 130; DLBY 1981; EWL
    3; EXPS; FW; HGG; INT CANR-25;
    LAIT 4; MAWW; MTCW 1, 2; NFS 8;
    RGAL 4; RGSF 2; SSFS 17; SUFW 2;
    TUS
O'Brian, E. G.
    See Clarke, Arthur C(harles)
O'Brian, Patrick 1914-2000 .... **CLC 152**
    See also CA 187; 144; CANR 74; CPW;
    MTCW 2; RHW
O'Brien, Darcy 1939-1998 .... **CLC 11**
    See also CA 167; 21-24R; CANR 8, 59
O'Brien, Edna 1936- ..... **CLC 3, 5, 8, 13, 36,
    65, 116; SSC 10**
    See also BRWS 5; CA 1-4R; CANR 6, 41,
    65, 102; CDBLB 1960 to Present; CN 7;
    DA3; DAM NOV; DLB 14, 231; EWL 3;
    FW; MTCW 1, 2; RGSF 2; WLIT 4
O'Brien, Fitz-James 1828-1862 ..... **NCLC 21**
    See also DLB 74; RGAL 4; SUFW
O'Brien, Flann .... **CLC 1, 4, 5, 7, 10, 47**
    See O Nuallain, Brian
    See also BRWS 2; DLB 231; EWL 3;
    RGEL 2
O'Brien, Richard 1942- .... **CLC 17**
    See also CA 124
O'Brien, (William) Tim(othy) 1946- . **CLC 7,
    19, 40, 103**
    See also AAYA 16; AMWS 5; CA 85-88;
    CANR 40, 58; CDALBS; CN 7; CPW;
    DA3; DAM POP; DLB 152; DLBD 9;
    DLBY 1980; MTCW 2; RGAL 4; SSFS
    5, 15
Obstfelder, Sigbjoern 1866-1900 .... **TCLC 23**
    See also CA 123
O'Casey, Sean 1880-1964 .... **CLC 1, 5, 9, 11,
    15, 88; DC 12; WLCS**
    See also BRW 7; CA 89-92; CANR 62;
    CBD; CDBLB 1914-1945; DA3; DAB;
    DAC; DAM DRAM, MST; DLB 10;
    EWL 3; MTCW 1, 2; RGEL 2; TEA;
    WLIT 4
O'Cathasaigh, Sean
    See O'Casey, Sean
Occom, Samson 1723-1792 .... **LC 60; NNAL**
    See also DLB 175
Ochs, Phil(ip David) 1940-1976 .... **CLC 17**
    See also CA 65-68; 185
O'Connor, Edwin (Greene)
    1918-1968 .... **CLC 14**
    See also CA 25-28R; 93-96
O'Connor, (Mary) Flannery
    1925-1964 .... **CLC 1, 2, 3, 6, 10, 13, 15,
    21, 66, 104; SSC 1, 23; TCLC 132;
    WLC**
    See also AAYA 7; AMW; AMWR 2; BPFB
    3; CA 1-4R; CANR 3, 41; CDALB 1941-
    1968; DA; DA3; DAB; DAC; DAM MST,

Parshchikov, Aleksei .... **CLC 59**
Parson, Professor
    See Coleridge, Samuel Taylor
Parson Lot
    See Kingsley, Charles
Parton, Sara Payson Willis
    1811-1872 .... **NCLC 86**
    See also DLB 43, 74, 239
Partridge, Anthony
    See Oppenheim, E(dward) Phillips
Pascal, Blaise 1623-1662 .... **LC 35**
    See also DLB 268; EW 3; GFL Beginnings
    to 1789; RGWL 2, 3; TWA
Pascoli, Giovanni 1855-1912 .... **TCLC 45**
    See also CA 170; EW 7; EWL 3
Pasolini, Pier Paolo 1922-1975 .. **CLC 20, 37,
    106; PC 17**
    See also CA 61-64; 93-96; CANR 63; DLB
    128, 177; EWL 3; MTCW 1; RGWL 2, 3
Pasquini
    See Silone, Ignazio
Pastan, Linda (Olenik) 1932- .... **CLC 27**
    See also CA 61-64; CANR 18, 40, 61, 113;
    CP 7; CSW; CWP; DAM POET; DLB 5;
    PFS 8
Pasternak, Boris (Leonidovich)
    1890-1960 ...... **CLC 7, 10, 18, 63; PC 6;
    SSC 31; WLC**
    See also BPFB 3; CA 116; 127; DA; DA3;
    DAB; DAC; DAM MST, NOV, POET;
    EW 10; MTCW 1, 2; RGSF 2; RGWL 2,
    3; TWA; WP
Patchen, Kenneth 1911-1972 .... **CLC 1, 2, 18**
    See also BG 3; CA 33-36R; 1-4R; CANR
    3, 35; DAM POET; DLB 16, 48; EWL 3;
    MTCW 1; RGAL 4
Pater, Walter (Horatio) 1839-1894 . **NCLC 7,
    90**
    See also BRW 5; CDBLB 1832-1890; DLB
    57, 156; RGEL 2; TEA
Paterson, A(ndrew) B(arton)
    1864-1941 .... **TCLC 32**
    See also CA 155; DLB 230; RGEL 2; SATA
    97
Paterson, Banjo
    See Paterson, A(ndrew) B(arton)
Paterson, Katherine (Womeldorf)
    1932- .... **CLC 12, 30**
    See also AAYA 1, 31; BYA 1, 2, 7; CA 21-
    24R; CANR 28, 59, 111; CLR 7, 50;
    CWRI 5; DLB 52; JRDA; LAIT 4; MAI-
    CYA 1, 2; MAICYAS 1; MTCW 1; SATA
    13, 53, 92, 133; WYA; YAW
Patmore, Coventry Kersey Dighton
    1823-1896 .... **NCLC 9**
    See also DLB 35, 98; RGEL 2; TEA
Paton, Alan (Stewart) 1903-1988 ...... **CLC 4,
    10, 25, 55, 106; WLC**
    See also AAYA 26; AFW; BPFB 3; BRWS
    2; BYA 1; CA 125; 13-16; CANR 22;
    CAP 1; DA; DA3; DAB; DAC; DAM
    MST, NOV; DLB 225; DLBD 17; EWL
    3; EXPN; LAIT 4; MTCW 1, 2; NFS 3,
    12; RGEL 2; SATA 11; SATA-Obit 56;
    TWA; WLIT 2
Paton Walsh, Gillian 1937- .... **CLC 35**
    See Paton Walsh, Jill; Walsh, Jill Paton
    See also AAYA 11; CANR 38, 83; CLR 2,
    65; DLB 161; JRDA; MAICYA 1, 2;
    SAAS 3; SATA 4, 72, 109; YAW
Paton Walsh, Jill
    See Paton Walsh, Gillian
    See also AAYA 47; BYA 1, 8
Patterson, (Horace) Orlando (Lloyd)
    1940- .... **BLCS**
    See also BW 1; CA 65-68; CANR 27, 84;
    CN 7

Patton, George S(mith), Jr.
    1885-1945 .... **TCLC 79**
    See also CA 189
Paulding, James Kirke 1778-1860 ... **NCLC 2**
    See also DLB 3, 59, 74, 250; RGAL 4
Paulin, Thomas Neilson 1949-
    See Paulin, Tom
    See also CA 128; 123; CANR 98; CP 7
Paulin, Tom .... **CLC 37**
    See Paulin, Thomas Neilson
    See also DLB 40
Pausanias c. 1st cent. - .... **CMLC 36**
Paustovsky, Konstantin (Georgievich)
    1892-1968 .... **CLC 40**
    See also CA 25-28R; 93-96; DLB 272;
    EWL 3
Pavese, Cesare 1908-1950 .... **PC 13; SSC 19;
    TCLC 3**
    See also CA 169; 104; DLB 128, 177; EW
    12; EWL 3; RGSF 2; RGWL 2, 3; TWA
Pavic, Milorad 1929- .... **CLC 60**
    See also CA 136; CDWLB 4; CWW 2; DLB
    181; EWL 3; RGWL 3
Pavlov, Ivan Petrovich 1849-1936 . **TCLC 91**
    See also CA 180; 118
Payne, Alan
    See Jakes, John (William)
Paz, Gil
    See Lugones, Leopoldo
Paz, Octavio 1914-1998 . **CLC 3, 4, 6, 10, 19,
    51, 65, 119; HLC 2; PC 1; WLC**
    See also CA 165; 73-76; CANR 32, 65, 104;
    CWW 2; DA; DA3; DAB; DAC; DAM
    MST, MULT, POET; DLBY 1990, 1998;
    DNFS 1; EWL 3; HW 1, 2; LAW; LAWS
    1; MTCW 1, 2; RGWL 2, 3; SSFS 13;
    TWA; WLIT 1
p'Bitek, Okot 1931-1982 ..... **BLC 3; CLC 96**
    See also AFW; BW 2, 3; CA 107; 124;
    CANR 82; DAM MULT; DLB 125; EWL
    3; MTCW 1, 2; RGEL 2; WLIT 2
Peacock, Molly 1947- .... **CLC 60**
    See also CA 103; CAAS 21; CANR 52, 84;
    CP 7; CWP; DLB 120
Peacock, Thomas Love
    1785-1866 .... **NCLC 22**
    See also BRW 4; DLB 96, 116; RGEL 2;
    RGSF 2
Peake, Mervyn 1911-1968 .... **CLC 7, 54**
    See also CA 25-28R; 5-8R; CANR 3; DLB
    15, 160, 255; FANT; MTCW 1; RGEL 2;
    SATA 23; SFW 4
Pearce, Philippa
    See Christie, Philippa
    See also CA 5-8R; CANR 4, 109; CWRI 5;
    FANT; MAICYA 2
Pearl, Eric
    See Elman, Richard (Martin)
Pearson, T(homas) R(eid) 1956- .... **CLC 39**
    See also CA 130; 120; CANR 97; CSW;
    INT 130
Peck, Dale 1967- .... **CLC 81**
    See also CA 146; CANR 72; GLL 2
Peck, John (Frederick) 1941- .... **CLC 3**
    See also CA 49-52; CANR 3, 100; CP 7
Peck, Richard (Wayne) 1934- .... **CLC 21**
    See also AAYA 1, 24; BYA 1, 6, 8, 11; CA
    85-88; CANR 19, 38; CLR 15; INT
    CANR-19; JRDA; MAICYA 1, 2; SAAS
    2; SATA 18, 55, 97; SATA-Essay 110;
    WYA; YAW
Peck, Robert Newton 1928- .... **CLC 17**
    See also AAYA 3, 43; BYA 1, 6; CA 81-84,
    182; CAAE 182; CANR 31, 63; CLR 45;
    DA; DAC; DAM MST; JRDA; LAIT 3;
    MAICYA 1, 2; SAAS 1; SATA 21, 62,
    111; SATA-Essay 108; WYA; YAW

Peckinpah, (David) Sam(uel)
    1925-1984 .... **CLC 20**
    See also CA 114; 109; CANR 82
Pedersen, Knut 1859-1952
    See Hamsun, Knut
    See also CA 119; 104; CANR 63; MTCW
    1, 2
Peeslake, Gaffer
    See Durrell, Lawrence (George)
Peguy, Charles (Pierre)
    1873-1914 .... **TCLC 10**
    See also CA 193; 107; DLB 258; EWL 3;
    GFL 1789 to the Present
Peirce, Charles Sanders
    1839-1914 .... **TCLC 81**
    See also CA 194; DLB 270
Pellicer, Carlos 1900(?)-1977 .... **HLCS 2**
    See also CA 69-72; 153; EWL 3; HW 1
Pena, Ramon del Valle y
    See Valle-Inclan, Ramon (Maria) del
Pendennis, Arthur Esquir
    See Thackeray, William Makepeace
Penn, William 1644-1718 .... **LC 25**
    See also DLB 24
PEPECE
    See Prado (Calvo), Pedro
Pepys, Samuel 1633-1703 ... **LC 11, 58; WLC**
    See also BRW 2; CDBLB 1660-1789; DA;
    DA3; DAB; DAC; DAM MST; DLB 101,
    213; NCFS 4; RGEL 2; TEA; WLIT 3
Percy, Thomas 1729-1811 .... **NCLC 95**
    See also DLB 104
Percy, Walker 1916-1990 .... **CLC 2, 3, 6, 8,
    14, 18, 47, 65**
    See also AMWS 3; BPFB 3; CA 131; 1-4R;
    CANR 1, 23, 64; CPW; CSW; DA3;
    DAM NOV, POP; DLB 2; DLBY 1980,
    1990; EWL 3; MTCW 1, 2; RGAL 4;
    TUS
Percy, William Alexander
    1885-1942 .... **TCLC 84**
    See also CA 163; MTCW 2
Perec, Georges 1936-1982 .... **CLC 56, 116**
    See also CA 141; DLB 83; EWL 3; GFL
    1789 to the Present; RGWL 3
Pereda (y Sanchez de Porrua), Jose Maria
    de 1833-1906 .... **TCLC 16**
    See also CA 117
Pereda y Porrua, Jose Maria de
    See Pereda (y Sanchez de Porrua), Jose
    Maria de
Peregoy, George Weems
    See Mencken, H(enry) L(ouis)
Perelman, S(idney) J(oseph)
    1904-1979 .. **CLC 3, 5, 9, 15, 23, 44, 49;
    SSC 32**
    See also AITN 1, 2; BPFB 3; CA 89-92;
    73-76; CANR 18; DAM DRAM; DLB 11,
    44; MTCW 1, 2; RGAL 4
Peret, Benjamin 1899-1959 .... **PC 33; TCLC
    20**
    See also CA 186; 117; GFL 1789 to the
    Present
Peretz, Isaac Leib 1851(?)-1915
    See Peretz, Isaac Loeb
    See also CA 201
Peretz, Isaac Loeb 1851(?)-1915 ...... **SSC 26;
    TCLC 16**
    See Peretz, Isaac Leib
    See also CA 109
Peretz, Yitzkhok Leibush
    See Peretz, Isaac Loeb
Perez Galdos, Benito 1843-1920 ..... **HLCS 2;
    TCLC 27**
    See Galdos, Benito Perez
    See also CA 153; 125; EWL 3; HW 1;
    RGWL 2, 3

Quincey, Thomas de
 See De Quincey, Thomas
Quinn, Martin
 See Smith, Martin Cruz
Quinn, Peter 1947- .... **CLC 91**
 See also CA 197
Quinn, Simon
 See Smith, Martin Cruz
Quintana, Leroy V. 1944- ...... **HLC 2; PC 36**
 See also CA 131; CANR 65; DAM MULT;
 DLB 82; HW 1, 2
Quiroga, Horacio (Sylvestre)
 1878-1937 .... **HLC 2; TCLC 20**
 See also CA 131; 117; DAM MULT; HW
 1; LAW; MTCW 1; RGSF 2; WLIT 1
Quoirez, Francoise 1935- .... **CLC 9**
 See Sagan, Francoise
 See also CA 49-52; CANR 6, 39, 73; CWW
 2; MTCW 1, 2; TWA
Raabe, Wilhelm (Karl) 1831-1910 . **TCLC 45**
 See also CA 167; DLB 129
Rabe, David (William) 1940- .. **CLC 4, 8, 33;
 DC 16**
 See also CA 85-88; CABS 3; CAD; CANR
 59; CD 5; DAM DRAM; DFS 3, 8, 13;
 DLB 7, 228
Rabelais, Francois 1494-1553 .... **LC 5, 60;
 WLC**
 See also DA; DAB; DAC; DAM MST; EW
 2; GFL Beginnings to 1789; RGWL 2, 3;
 TWA
Rabinovitch, Sholem 1859-1916
 See Aleichem, Sholom
 See also CA 104
Rabinyan, Dorit 1972- .... **CLC 119**
 See also CA 170
Rachilde
 See Vallette, Marguerite Eymery
Racine, Jean 1639-1699 .... **LC 28**
 See also DA3; DAB; DAM MST; DLB 268;
 EW 3; GFL Beginnings to 1789; RGWL
 2, 3; TWA
Radcliffe, Ann (Ward) 1764-1823 ... **NCLC 6,
 55, 106**
 See also DLB 39, 178; HGG; RGEL 2;
 SUFW; WLIT 3
Radclyffe-Hall, Marguerite
 See Hall, (Marguerite) Radclyffe
Radiguet, Raymond 1903-1923 ...... **TCLC 29**
 See also CA 162; DLB 65; GFL 1789 to the
 Present; RGWL 2, 3
Radnoti, Miklos 1909-1944 .... **TCLC 16**
 See also CA 118; CDWLB 4; DLB 215;
 RGWL 2, 3
Rado, James 1939- .... **CLC 17**
 See also CA 105
Radvanyi, Netty 1900-1983
 See Seghers, Anna
 See also CA 110; 85-88; CANR 82
Rae, Ben
 See Griffiths, Trevor
Raeburn, John (Hay) 1941- .... **CLC 34**
 See also CA 57-60
Ragni, Gerome 1942-1991 .... **CLC 17**
 See also CA 134; 105
Rahv, Philip .... **CLC 24**
 See Greenberg, Ivan
 See also DLB 137
Raimund, Ferdinand Jakob
 1790-1836 .... **NCLC 69**
 See also DLB 90
Raine, Craig (Anthony) 1944- .. **CLC 32, 103**
 See also CA 108; CANR 29, 51, 103; CP 7;
 DLB 40; PFS 7
Raine, Kathleen (Jessie) 1908- ..... **CLC 7, 45**
 See also CA 85-88; CANR 46, 109; CP 7;
 DLB 20; MTCW 1; RGEL 2
Rainis, Janis 1865-1929 .... **TCLC 29**
 See also CA 170; CDWLB 4; DLB 220

Rakosi, Carl .... **CLC 47**
 See Rawley, Callman
 See also CAAS 5; CP 7; DLB 193
Ralegh, Sir Walter
 See Raleigh, Sir Walter
 See also BRW 1; RGEL 2; WP
Raleigh, Richard
 See Lovecraft, H(oward) P(hillips)
Raleigh, Sir Walter 1554(?)-1618 .... **LC 31,
 39; PC 31**
 See Ralegh, Sir Walter
 See also CDBLB Before 1660; DLB 172;
 EXPP; PFS 14; TEA
Rallentando, H. P.
 See Sayers, Dorothy L(eigh)
Ramal, Walter
 See de la Mare, Walter (John)
Ramana Maharshi 1879-1950 .... **TCLC 84**
Ramoacn y Cajal, Santiago
 1852-1934 .... **TCLC 93**
Ramon, Juan
 See Jimenez (Mantecon), Juan Ramon
Ramos, Graciliano 1892-1953 .... **TCLC 32**
 See also CA 167; HW 2; LAW; WLIT 1
Rampersad, Arnold 1941- .... **CLC 44**
 See also BW 2, 3; CA 133; 127; CANR 81;
 DLB 111; INT 133
Rampling, Anne
 See Rice, Anne
 See also GLL 2
Ramsay, Allan 1686(?)-1758 .... **LC 29**
 See also DLB 95; RGEL 2
Ramsay, Jay
 See Campbell, (John) Ramsey
Ramuz, Charles-Ferdinand
 1878-1947 .... **TCLC 33**
 See also CA 165
Rand, Ayn 1905-1982 ...... **CLC 3, 30, 44, 79;
 WLC**
 See also AAYA 10; AMWS 4; BPFB 3;
 BYA 12; CA 105; 13-16R; CANR 27, 73;
 CDALBS; CPW; DA; DA3; DAC; DAM
 MST, NOV, POP; DLB 227, 279; MTCW
 1, 2; NFS 10, 16; RGAL 4; SFW 4; TUS;
 YAW
Randall, Dudley (Felker) 1914-2000 . **BLC 3;
 CLC 1, 135**
 See also BW 1, 3; CA 189; 25-28R; CANR
 23, 82; DAM MULT; DLB 41; PFS 5
Randall, Robert
 See Silverberg, Robert
Ranger, Ken
 See Creasey, John
Rank, Otto 1884-1939 .... **TCLC 115**
Ransom, John Crowe 1888-1974 .. **CLC 2, 4,
 5, 11, 24**
 See also AMW; CA 49-52; 5-8R; CANR 6,
 34; CDALBS; DA3; DAM POET; DLB
 45, 63; EXPP; MTCW 1, 2; RGAL 4;
 TUS
Rao, Raja 1909- .... **CLC 25, 56**
 See also CA 73-76; CANR 51; CN 7; DAM
 NOV; MTCW 1, 2; RGEL 2; RGSF 2
Raphael, Frederic (Michael) 1931- ... **CLC 2,
 14**
 See also CA 1-4R; CANR 1, 86; CN 7;
 DLB 14
Ratcliffe, James P.
 See Mencken, H(enry) L(ouis)
Rathbone, Julian 1935- .... **CLC 41**
 See also CA 101; CANR 34, 73
Rattigan, Terence (Mervyn)
 1911-1977 .... **CLC 7; DC 18**
 See also BRWS 7; CA 73-76; 85-88; CBD;
 CDBLB 1945-1960; DAM DRAM; DFS
 8; DLB 13; IDFW 3, 4; MTCW 1, 2;
 RGEL 2
Ratushinskaya, Irina 1954- .... **CLC 54**
 See also CA 129; CANR 68; CWW 2

Raven, Simon (Arthur Noel)
 1927-2001 .... **CLC 14**
 See also CA 197; 81-84; CANR 86; CN 7;
 DLB 271
Ravenna, Michael
 See Welty, Eudora (Alice)
Rawley, Callman 1903-
 See Rakosi, Carl
 See also CA 21-24R; CANR 12, 32, 91
Rawlings, Marjorie Kinnan
 1896-1953 .... **TCLC 4**
 See also AAYA 20; AMWS 10; ANW;
 BPFB 3; BYA 3; CA 137; 104; CANR 74;
 CLR 63; DLB 9, 22, 102; DLBD 17;
 JRDA; MAICYA 1, 2; MTCW 2; RGAL
 4; SATA 100; WCH; YABC 1; YAW
Ray, Satyajit 1921-1992 .... **CLC 16, 76**
 See also CA 137; 114; DAM MULT
Read, Herbert Edward 1893-1968 ..... **CLC 4**
 See also BRW 6; CA 25-28R; 85-88; DLB
 20, 149; PAB; RGEL 2
Read, Piers Paul 1941- .... **CLC 4, 10, 25**
 See also CA 21-24R; CANR 38, 86; CN 7;
 DLB 14; SATA 21
Reade, Charles 1814-1884 .... **NCLC 2, 74**
 See also DLB 21; RGEL 2
Reade, Hamish
 See Gray, Simon (James Holliday)
Reading, Peter 1946- .... **CLC 47**
 See also BRWS 8; CA 103; CANR 46, 96;
 CP 7; DLB 40
Reaney, James 1926- .... **CLC 13**
 See also CA 41-44R; CAAS 15; CANR 42;
 CD 5; CP 7; DAC; DAM MST; DLB 68;
 RGEL 2; SATA 43
Rebreanu, Liviu 1885-1944 .... **TCLC 28**
 See also CA 165; DLB 220
Rechy, John (Francisco) 1934- ...... **CLC 1, 7,
 14, 18, 107; HLC 2**
 See also CA 5-8R; CAAE 195; CAAS 4;
 CANR 6, 32, 64; CN 7; DAM MULT;
 DLB 122, 278; DLBY 1982; HW 1, 2;
 INT CANR-6; RGAL 4
Redcam, Tom 1870-1933 .... **TCLC 25**
Reddin, Keith .... **CLC 67**
 See also CAD
Redgrove, Peter (William) 1932- . **CLC 6, 41**
 See also BRWS 6; CA 1-4R; CANR 3, 39,
 77; CP 7; DLB 40
Redmon, Anne .... **CLC 22**
 See Nightingale, Anne Redmon
 See also DLBY 1986
Reed, Eliot
 See Ambler, Eric
Reed, Ishmael 1938- ..... **BLC 3; CLC 2, 3, 5,
 6, 13, 32, 60**
 See also AFAW 1, 2; AMWS 10; BPFB 3;
 BW 2, 3; CA 21-24R; CANR 25, 48, 74;
 CN 7; CP 7; CSW; DA3; DAM MULT;
 DLB 2, 5, 33, 169, 227; DLBD 8; MSW;
 MTCW 1, 2; PFS 6; RGAL 4; TCWW 2
Reed, John (Silas) 1887-1920 .... **TCLC 9**
 See also CA 195; 106; TUS
Reed, Lou .... **CLC 21**
 See Firbank, Louis
Reese, Lizette Woodworth 1856-1935 . **PC 29**
 See also CA 180; DLB 54
Reeve, Clara 1729-1807 .... **NCLC 19**
 See also DLB 39; RGEL 2
Reich, Wilhelm 1897-1957 .... **TCLC 57**
 See also CA 199
Reid, Christopher (John) 1949- .... **CLC 33**
 See also CA 140; CANR 89; CP 7; DLB 40
Reid, Desmond
 See Moorcock, Michael (John)

Reid Banks, Lynne 1929-
See Banks, Lynne Reid
See also CA 1-4R; CANR 6, 22, 38, 87;
CLR 24; CN 7; JRDA; MAICYA 1, 2;
SATA 22, 75, 111; YAW
Reilly, William K.
See Creasey, John
Reiner, Max
See Caldwell, (Janet Miriam) Taylor
(Holland)
Reis, Ricardo
See Pessoa, Fernando (Antonio Nogueira)
Remarque, Erich Maria 1898-1970 . **CLC 21**
See also AAYA 27; BPFB 3; CA 29-32R;
77-80; CDWLB 2; DA; DA3; DAB;
DAC; DAM MST, NOV; DLB 56; EXPN;
LAIT 3; MTCW 1, 2; NFS 4; RGWL 2, 3
Remington, Frederic 1861-1909 ..... **TCLC 89**
See also CA 169; 108; DLB 12, 186, 188;
SATA 41
Remizov, A.
See Remizov, Aleksei (Mikhailovich)
Remizov, A. M.
See Remizov, Aleksei (Mikhailovich)
Remizov, Aleksei (Mikhailovich)
1877-1957 .... **TCLC 27**
See also CA 133; 125
Renan, Joseph Ernest 1823-1892 .. **NCLC 26**
See also GFL 1789 to the Present
Renard, Jules(-Pierre) 1864-1910 .. **TCLC 17**
See also CA 202; 117; GFL 1789 to the
Present
Renault, Mary .... **CLC 3, 11, 17**
See Challans, Mary
See also BPFB 3; BYA 2; DLBY 1983;
GLL 1; LAIT 1; MTCW 2; RGEL 2;
RHW
Rendell, Ruth (Barbara) 1930- .. **CLC 28, 48**
See Vine, Barbara
See also BPFB 3; CA 109; CANR 32, 52,
74; CN 7; CPW; DAM POP; DLB 87,
276; INT CANR-32; MSW; MTCW 1, 2
Renoir, Jean 1894-1979 .... **CLC 20**
See also CA 85-88; 129
Resnais, Alain 1922- .... **CLC 16**
Revard, Carter (Curtis) 1931- .... **NNAL**
See also CA 144; CANR 81; PFS 5
Reverdy, Pierre 1889-1960 .... **CLC 53**
See also CA 89-92; 97-100; DLB 258; GFL
1789 to the Present
Rexroth, Kenneth 1905-1982 .... **CLC 1, 2, 6,
11, 22, 49, 112; PC 20**
See also BG 3; CA 107; 5-8R; CANR 14,
34, 63; CDALB 1941-1968; DAM POET;
DLB 16, 48, 165, 212; DLBY 1982; INT
CANR-14; MTCW 1, 2; RGAL 4
Reyes, Alfonso 1889-1959 .... **HLCS 2; TCLC
33**
See also CA 131; HW 1; LAW
Reyes y Basoalto, Ricardo Eliecer Neftali
See Neruda, Pablo
Reymont, Wladyslaw (Stanislaw)
1868(?)-1925 .... **TCLC 5**
See also CA 104
Reynolds, Jonathan 1942- .... **CLC 6, 38**
See also CA 65-68; CANR 28
Reynolds, Joshua 1723-1792 .... **LC 15**
See also DLB 104
Reynolds, Michael S(hane)
1937-2000 .... **CLC 44**
See also CA 189; 65-68; CANR 9, 89, 97
Reznikoff, Charles 1894-1976 .... **CLC 9**
See also CA 61-64; 33-36; CAP 2; DLB 28,
45; WP
Rezzori (d'Arezzo), Gregor von
1914-1998 .... **CLC 25**
See also CA 167; 136; 122

Rhine, Richard
See Silverstein, Alvin; Silverstein, Virginia
B(arbara Opshelor)
Rhodes, Eugene Manlove
1869-1934 .... **TCLC 53**
See also CA 198; DLB 256
R'hoone, Lord
See Balzac, Honore de
Rhys, Jean 1894(?)-1979 ...... **CLC 2, 4, 6, 14,
19, 51, 124; SSC 21**
See also BRWS 2; CA 85-88; 25-28R;
CANR 35, 62; CDBLB 1945-1960; CD-
WLB 3; DA3; DAM NOV; DLB 36, 117,
162; DNFS 2; MTCW 1, 2; RGEL 2;
RGSF 2; RHW; TEA
Ribeiro, Darcy 1922-1997 .... **CLC 34**
See also CA 156; 33-36R
Ribeiro, Joao Ubaldo (Osorio Pimentel)
1941- .... **CLC 10, 67**
See also CA 81-84
Ribman, Ronald (Burt) 1932- .... **CLC 7**
See also CA 21-24R; CAD; CANR 46, 80;
CD 5
Ricci, Nino 1959- .... **CLC 70**
See also CA 137; CCA 1
Rice, Anne 1941- .... **CLC 41, 128**
See Rampling, Anne
See also AAYA 9; AMWS 7; BEST 89:2;
BPFB 3; CA 65-68; CANR 12, 36, 53,
74, 100; CN 7; CPW; CSW; DA3; DAM
POP; GLL 2; HGG; MTCW 2; SUFW 2;
YAW
Rice, Elmer (Leopold) 1892-1967 ...... **CLC 7,
49**
See also CA 25-28R; 21-22; CAP 2; DAM
DRAM; DFS 12; DLB 4, 7; MTCW 1, 2;
RGAL 4
Rice, Tim(othy Miles Bindon)
1944- .... **CLC 21**
See also CA 103; CANR 46; DFS 7
Rich, Adrienne (Cecile) 1929- ... **CLC 3, 6, 7,
11, 18, 36, 73, 76, 125; PC 5**
See also AMWR 2; AMWS 1; CA 9-12R;
CANR 20, 53, 74; CDALBS; CP 7; CSW;
CWP; DA3; DAM POET; DLB 5, 67;
EXPP; FW; MAWW; MTCW 1, 2; PAB;
PFS 15; RGAL 4; WP
Rich, Barbara
See Graves, Robert (von Ranke)
Rich, Robert
See Trumbo, Dalton
Richard, Keith .... **CLC 17**
See Richards, Keith
Richards, David Adams 1950- .... **CLC 59**
See also CA 93-96; CANR 60, 110; DAC;
DLB 53
Richards, I(vor) A(rmstrong)
1893-1979 .... **CLC 14, 24**
See also BRWS 2; CA 89-92; 41-44R;
CANR 34, 74; DLB 27; MTCW 2; RGEL
2
Richards, Keith 1943-
See Richard, Keith
See also CA 107; CANR 77
Richardson, Anne
See Roiphe, Anne (Richardson)
Richardson, Dorothy Miller
1873-1957 .... **TCLC 3**
See also CA 192; 104; DLB 36; FW; RGEL
2
**Richardson (Robertson), Ethel Florence
Lindesay** 1870-1946
See Richardson, Henry Handel
See also CA 190; 105; DLB 230; RHW
Richardson, Henry Handel .... **TCLC 4**
See Richardson (Robertson), Ethel Florence
Lindesay
See also DLB 197; RGEL 2; RGSF 2

Richardson, John 1796-1852 .... **NCLC 55**
See also CCA 1; DAC; DLB 99
Richardson, Samuel 1689-1761 ..... **LC 1, 44;
WLC**
See also BRW 3; CDBLB 1660-1789; DA;
DAB; DAC; DAM MST, NOV; DLB 39;
RGEL 2; TEA; WLIT 3
Richardson, Willis 1889-1977 .... **HR 3**
See also BW 1; CA 124; DLB 51; SATA 60
Richler, Mordecai 1931-2001 .... **CLC 3, 5, 9,
13, 18, 46, 70**
See also AITN 1; CA 201; 65-68; CANR
31, 62, 111; CCA 1; CLR 17; CWRI 5;
DAC; DAM MST, NOV; DLB 53; MAI-
CYA 1, 2; MTCW 1, 2; RGEL 2; SATA
44, 98; SATA-Brief 27; TWA
Richter, Conrad (Michael)
1890-1968 .... **CLC 30**
See also AAYA 21; BYA 2; CA 25-28R;
5-8R; CANR 23; DLB 9, 212; LAIT 1;
MTCW 1, 2; RGAL 4; SATA 3; TCWW
2; TUS; YAW
Ricostranza, Tom
See Ellis, Trey
Riddell, Charlotte 1832-1906 .... **TCLC 40**
See Riddell, Mrs. J. H.
See also CA 165; DLB 156
Riddell, Mrs. J. H.
See Riddell, Charlotte
See also HGG; SUFW
Ridge, John Rollin 1827-1867 ...... **NCLC 82;
NNAL**
See also CA 144; DAM MULT; DLB 175
Ridgeway, Jason
See Marlowe, Stephen
Ridgway, Keith 1965- .... **CLC 119**
See also CA 172
Riding, Laura .... **CLC 3, 7**
See Jackson, Laura (Riding)
See also RGAL 4
Riefenstahl, Berta Helene Amalia 1902-
See Riefenstahl, Leni
See also CA 108
Riefenstahl, Leni .... **CLC 16**
See Riefenstahl, Berta Helene Amalia
Riffe, Ernest
See Bergman, (Ernst) Ingmar
Riggs, (Rolla) Lynn
1899-1954 .... **NNAL; TCLC 56**
See also CA 144; DAM MULT; DLB 175
Riis, Jacob A(ugust) 1849-1914 ..... **TCLC 80**
See also CA 168; 113; DLB 23
Riley, James Whitcomb
1849-1916 .... **TCLC 51**
See also CA 137; 118; DAM POET; MAI-
CYA 1, 2; RGAL 4; SATA 17
Riley, Tex
See Creasey, John
Rilke, Rainer Maria 1875-1926 .... **PC 2;
TCLC 1, 6, 19**
See also CA 132; 104; CANR 62, 99; CD-
WLB 2; DA3; DAM POET; DLB 81; EW
9; MTCW 1, 2; RGWL 2, 3; TWA; WP
Rimbaud, (Jean Nicolas) Arthur
1854-1891 .... **NCLC 4, 35, 82; PC 3;
WLC**
See also DA; DA3; DAB; DAC; DAM
MST, POET; DLB 217; EW 7; GFL 1789
to the Present; RGWL 2, 3; TWA; WP
Rinehart, Mary Roberts
1876-1958 .... **TCLC 52**
See also BPFB 3; CA 166; 108; RGAL 4;
RHW
Ringmaster, The
See Mencken, H(enry) L(ouis)
Ringwood, Gwen(dolyn Margaret) Pharis
1910-1984 .... **CLC 48**
See also CA 112; 148; DLB 88

Author Index

Scoppettone, Sandra 1936- .... **CLC 26**
  See Early, Jack
    See also AAYA 11; BYA 8; CA 5-8R;
    CANR 41, 73; GLL 1; MAICYA 2; MAI-
    CYAS 1; SATA 9, 92; WYA; YAW

Scorsese, Martin 1942- .... **CLC 20, 89**
  See also AAYA 38; CA 114; 110; CANR
  46, 85

Scotland, Jay
  See Jakes, John (William)

Scott, Duncan Campbell
    1862-1947 .... **TCLC 6**
    See also CA 153; 104; DAC; DLB 92;
    RGEL 2

Scott, Evelyn 1893-1963 .... **CLC 43**
  See also CA 112; 104; CANR 64; DLB 9,
  48; RHW

Scott, F(rancis) R(eginald)
    1899-1985 .... **CLC 22**
    See also CA 114; 101; CANR 87; DLB 88;
    INT CA-101; RGEL 2

Scott, Frank
  See Scott, F(rancis) R(eginald)

Scott, Joan .... **CLC 65**

Scott, Joanna 1960- .... **CLC 50**
  See also CA 126; CANR 53, 92

Scott, Paul (Mark) 1920-1978 ...... **CLC 9, 60**
  See also BRWS 1; CA 77-80; 81-84; CANR
  33; DLB 14, 207; MTCW 1; RGEL 2;
  RHW

Scott, Sarah 1723-1795 .... **LC 44**
  See also DLB 39

Scott, Sir Walter 1771-1832 .... **NCLC 15, 69,**
    110; PC 13; SSC 32; WLC
    See also AAYA 22; BRW 4; BYA 2; CD-
    BLB 1789-1832; DA; DAB; DAC; DAM
    MST, NOV, POET; DLB 93, 107, 116,
    144, 159; HGG; LAIT 1; RGEL 2; RGSF
    2; SSFS 10; SUFW 1; TEA; WLIT 3;
    YABC 2

Scribe, (Augustin) Eugene 1791-1861 . **DC 5;**
    NCLC 16
    See also DAM DRAM; DLB 192; GFL
    1789 to the Present; RGWL 2, 3

Scrum, R.
  See Crumb, R(obert)

Scudery, Georges de 1601-1667 .... **LC 75**
  See also GFL Beginnings to 1789

Scudery, Madeleine de 1607-1701 .. **LC 2, 58**
  See also DLB 268; GFL Beginnings to 1789

Scum
  See Crumb, R(obert)

Scumbag, Little Bobby
  See Crumb, R(obert)

Seabrook, John
  See Hubbard, L(afayette) Ron(ald)

Sealy, I(rwin) Allan 1951- .... **CLC 55**
  See also CA 136; CN 7

Search, Alexander
  See Pessoa, Fernando (Antonio Nogueira)

Sebastian, Lee
  See Silverberg, Robert

Sebastian Owl
  See Thompson, Hunter S(tockton)

Sebestyen, Igen
  See Sebestyen, Ouida

Sebestyen, Ouida 1924- .... **CLC 30**
  See also AAYA 8; BYA 7; CA 107; CANR
  40, 114; CLR 17; JRDA; MAICYA 1, 2;
  SAAS 10; SATA 39; WYA; YAW

Secundus, H. Scriblerus
  See Fielding, Henry

Sedges, John
  See Buck, Pearl S(ydenstricker)

Sedgwick, Catharine Maria
    1789-1867 .... **NCLC 19, 98**
    See also DLB 1, 74, 183, 239, 243, 254;
    RGAL 4

Seelye, John (Douglas) 1931- .... **CLC 7**
  See also CA 97-100; CANR 70; INT 97-
  100; TCWW 2

Seferiades, Giorgos Stylianou 1900-1971
  See Seferis, George
    See also CA 33-36R; 5-8R; CANR 5, 36;
    MTCW 1

Seferis, George .... **CLC 5, 11**
  See Seferiades, Giorgos Stylianou
    See also EW 12; RGWL 2, 3

Segal, Erich (Wolf) 1937- .... **CLC 3, 10**
  See also BEST 89:1; BPFB 3; CA 25-28R;
  CANR 20, 36, 65, 113; CPW; DAM POP;
  DLBY 1986; INT CANR-20; MTCW 1

Seger, Bob 1945- .... **CLC 35**

Seghers, Anna -1983 .... **CLC 7**
  See Radvanyi, Netty
    See also CDWLB 2; DLB 69

Seidel, Frederick (Lewis) 1936- .... **CLC 18**
  See also CA 13-16R; CANR 8, 99; CP 7;
  DLBY 1984

Seifert, Jaroslav 1901-1986 .. **CLC 34, 44, 93**
  See also CA 127; CDWLB 4; DLB 215;
  MTCW 1, 2

Sei Shonagon c. 966-1017(?) .... **CMLC 6**

Sejour, Victor 1817-1874 .... **DC 10**
  See also DLB 50

Sejour Marcou et Ferrand, Juan Victor
  See Sejour, Victor

Selby, Hubert, Jr. 1928- .... **CLC 1, 2, 4, 8;**
    SSC 20
    See also CA 13-16R; CANR 33, 85; CN 7;
    DLB 2, 227

Selzer, Richard 1928- .... **CLC 74**
  See also CA 65-68; CANR 14, 106

Sembene, Ousmane
  See Ousmane, Sembene
    See also AFW; CWW 2; WLIT 2

Senancour, Etienne Pivert de
    1770-1846 .... **NCLC 16**
    See also DLB 119; GFL 1789 to the Present

Sender, Ramon (Jose) 1902-1982 ...... **CLC 8;**
    HLC 2
    See also CA 105; 5-8R; CANR 8; DAM
    MULT; HW 1; MTCW 1; RGWL 2, 3

Seneca, Lucius Annaeus c. 4B.C.-c.
    65 .... **CMLC 6; DC 5**
    See also AW 2; CDWLB 1; DAM DRAM;
    DLB 211; RGWL 2, 3; TWA

Senghor, Leopold Sedar 1906-2001 ... **BLC 3;**
    CLC 54, 130; PC 25
    See also AFW; BW 2; CA 203; 125; 116;
    CANR 47, 74; DAM MULT, POET;
    DNFS 2; GFL 1789 to the Present;
    MTCW 1, 2; TWA

Senna, Danzy 1970- .... **CLC 119**
  See also CA 169

Serling, (Edward) Rod(man)
    1924-1975 .... **CLC 30**
    See also AAYA 14; AITN 1; CA 57-60; 162;
    DLB 26; SFW 4

Serna, Ramon Gomez de la
  See Gomez de la Serna, Ramon

Serpieres
  See Guillevic, (Eugene)

Service, Robert
  See Service, Robert W(illiam)
    See also BYA 4; DAB; DLB 92

Service, Robert W(illiam)
    1874(?)-1958 .... **TCLC 15; WLC**
    See Service, Robert
    See also CA 140; 115; CANR 84; DA;
    DAC; DAM MST, POET; PFS 10; RGEL
    2; SATA 20

Seth, Vikram 1952- .... **CLC 43, 90**
  See also CA 127; 121; CANR 50, 74; CN
  7; CP 7; DA3; DAM MULT; DLB 120,
  271; INT 127; MTCW 2

Seton, Cynthia Propper 1926-1982 .. **CLC 27**
  See also CA 108; 5-8R; CANR 7

Seton, Ernest (Evan) Thompson
    1860-1946 .... **TCLC 31**
    See also ANW; BYA 3; CA 204; 109; CLR
    59; DLB 92; DLBD 13; JRDA; SATA 18

Seton-Thompson, Ernest
  See Seton, Ernest (Evan) Thompson

Settle, Mary Lee 1918- .... **CLC 19, 61**
  See also BPFB 3; CA 89-92; CAAS 1;
  CANR 44, 87; CN 7; CSW; DLB 6; INT
  89-92

Seuphor, Michel
  See Arp, Jean

Sevigne, Marie (de Rabutin-Chantal)
    1626-1696 .... **LC 11**
    See Sevigne, Marie de Rabutin Chantal
    See also GFL Beginnings to 1789; TWA

Sevigne, Marie de Rabutin Chantal
  See Sevigne, Marie (de Rabutin-Chantal)
    See also DLB 268

Sewall, Samuel 1652-1730 .... **LC 38**
  See also DLB 24; RGAL 4

Sexton, Anne (Harvey) 1928-1974 ..... **CLC 2,**
    4, 6, 8, 10, 15, 53, 123; PC 2; WLC
    See also AMWS 2; CA 53-56; 1-4R; CABS
    2; CANR 3, 36; CDALB 1941-1968; DA;
    DA3; DAB; DAC; DAM MST, POET;
    DLB 5, 169; EXPP; FW; MAWW;
    MTCW 1, 2; PAB; PFS 4, 14; RGAL 4;
    SATA 10; TUS

Shaara, Jeff 1952- .... **CLC 119**
  See also CA 163; CANR 109

Shaara, Michael (Joseph, Jr.)
    1929-1988 .... **CLC 15**
    See also AITN 1; BPFB 3; CA 125; 102;
    CANR 52, 85; DAM POP; DLBY 1983

Shackleton, C. C.
  See Aldiss, Brian W(ilson)

Shacochis, Bob .... **CLC 39**
  See Shacochis, Robert G.

Shacochis, Robert G. 1951-
  See Shacochis, Bob
    See also CA 124; 119; CANR 100; INT 124

Shaffer, Anthony (Joshua)
    1926-2001 .... **CLC 19**
    See also CA 200; 116; 110; CBD; CD 5;
    DAM DRAM; DFS 13; DLB 13

Shaffer, Peter (Levin) 1926- .. **CLC 5, 14, 18,**
    37, 60; DC 7
    See also BRWS 1; CA 25-28R; CANR 25,
    47, 74; CBD; CD 5; CDBLB 1960 to
    Present; DA3; DAB; DAM DRAM, MST;
    DFS 5, 13; DLB 13, 233; MTCW 1, 2;
    RGEL 2; TEA

Shakespeare, William 1564-1616 .... **WLC**
  See also AAYA 35; BRW 1; CDBLB Be-
  fore 1660; DA; DA3; DAB; DAC; DAM
  DRAM, MST, POET; DLB 62, 172, 263;
  EXPP; LAIT 1; PAB; PFS 1, 2, 3, 4, 5, 8,
  9; RGEL 2; TEA; WLIT 3; WP; WS;
  WYA

Shakey, Bernard
  See Young, Neil

Shalamov, Varlam (Tikhonovich)
    1907(?)-1982 .... **CLC 18**
    See also CA 105; 129; RGSF 2

Shamlu, Ahmad 1925-2000 .... **CLC 10**
  See also CWW 2

Shammas, Anton 1951- .... **CLC 55**
  See also CA 199

Shandling, Arline
  See Berriault, Gina

Shange, Ntozake 1948- ... **BLC 3; CLC 8, 25,**
    38, 74, 126; DC 3
    See also AAYA 9; AFAW 1, 2; BW 2; CA
    85-88; CABS 3; CAD; CANR 27, 48, 74;
    CD 5; CP 7; CWD; CWP; DA3; DAM
    DRAM, MULT; DFS 2, 11; DLB 38, 249;
    FW; LAIT 5; MTCW 1, 2; NFS 11;
    RGAL 4; YAW

Silkin, Jon 1930-1997 .... CLC 2, 6, 43
See also CA 5-8R; CAAS 5; CANR 89; CP
7; DLB 27

Silko, Leslie (Marmon) 1948- .... CLC 23, 74,
114; NNAL; SSC 37; WLCS
See also AAYA 14; AMWS 4; ANW; BYA
12; CA 122; 115; CANR 45, 65; CN 7;
CP 7; CPW 1; CWP; DA; DA3; DAC;
DAM MST, MULT, POP; DLB 143, 175,
256, 275; EXPP; EXPS; LAIT 4; MTCW
2; NFS 4; PFS 9, 16; RGAL 4; RGSF 2;
SSFS 4, 8, 10, 11

Sillanpaa, Frans Eemil 1888-1964 ... CLC 19
See also CA 93-96; 129; MTCW 1

Sillitoe, Alan 1928- .. CLC 1, 3, 6, 10, 19, 57,
148
See also AITN 1; BRWS 5; CA 9-12R;
CAAE 191; CAAS 2; CANR 8, 26, 55;
CDBLB 1960 to Present; CN 7; DLB 14,
139; MTCW 1, 2; RGEL 2; RGSF 2;
SATA 61

Silone, Ignazio 1900-1978 .... CLC 4
See also CA 81-84; 25-28; CANR 34; CAP
2; DLB 264; EW 12; MTCW 1; RGSF 2;
RGWL 2, 3

Silone, Ignazione
See Silone, Ignazio

Silva, Jose Asuncion
See da Silva, Antonio Jose
See also LAW

Silver, Joan Micklin 1935- .... CLC 20
See also CA 121; 114; INT 121

Silver, Nicholas
See Faust, Frederick (Schiller)
See also TCWW 2

Silverberg, Robert 1935- .... CLC 7, 140
See also AAYA 24; BPFB 3; BYA 7, 9; CA
1-4R, 186; CAAE 186; CAAS 3; CANR
1, 20, 36, 85; CLR 59; CN 7; CPW; DAM
POP; DLB 8; INT CANR-20; MAICYA
1, 2; MTCW 1, 2; SATA 13, 91; SATA-
Essay 104; SCFW 2; SFW 4; SUFW 2

Silverstein, Alvin 1933- .... CLC 17
See also CA 49-52; CANR 2; CLR 25;
JRDA; MAICYA 1, 2; SATA 8, 69, 124

Silverstein, Virginia B(arbara Opshelor)
1937- .... CLC 17
See also CA 49-52; CANR 2; CLR 25;
JRDA; MAICYA 1, 2; SATA 8, 69, 124

Sim, Georges
See Simenon, Georges (Jacques Christian)

Simak, Clifford D(onald) 1904-1988 . CLC 1,
55
See also CA 125; 1-4R; CANR 1, 35; DLB
8; MTCW 1; SATA-Obit 56; SFW 4

Simenon, Georges (Jacques Christian)
1903-1989 .... CLC 1, 2, 3, 8, 18, 47
See also BPFB 3; CA 129; 85-88; CANR
35; CMW 4; DA3; DAM POP; DLB 72;
DLBY 1989; EW 12; GFL 1789 to the
Present; MSW; MTCW 1, 2; RGWL 2, 3

Simic, Charles 1938- .... CLC 6, 9, 22, 49, 68,
130
See also AMWS 8; CA 29-32R; CAAS 4;
CANR 12, 33, 52, 61, 96; CP 7; DA3;
DAM POET; DLB 105; MTCW 2; PFS 7;
RGAL 4; WP

Simmel, Georg 1858-1918 .... TCLC 64
See also CA 157

Simmons, Charles (Paul) 1924- .... CLC 57
See also CA 89-92; INT 89-92

Simmons, Dan 1948- .... CLC 44
See also AAYA 16; CA 138; CANR 53, 81;
CPW; DAM POP; HGG; SUFW 2

Simmons, James (Stewart Alexander)
1933- .... CLC 43
See also CA 105; CAAS 21; CP 7; DLB 40

Simms, William Gilmore
1806-1870 .... NCLC 3
See also DLB 3, 30, 59, 73, 248, 254;
RGAL 4

Simon, Carly 1945- .... CLC 26
See also CA 105

Simon, Claude (Henri Eugene)
1913-1984 .... CLC 4, 9, 15, 39
See also CA 89-92; CANR 33, 117; DAM
NOV; DLB 83; EW 13; GFL 1789 to the
Present; MTCW 1

Simon, Myles
See Follett, Ken(neth Martin)

Simon, (Marvin) Neil 1927- ... CLC 6, 11, 31,
39, 70; DC 14
See also AAYA 32; AITN 1; AMWS 4; CA
21-24R; CANR 26, 54, 87; CD 5; DA3;
DAM DRAM; DFS 2, 6, 12; DLB 7, 266;
LAIT 4; MTCW 1, 2; RGAL 4; TUS

Simon, Paul (Frederick) 1941(?)- ..... CLC 17
See also CA 153; 116

Simonon, Paul 1956(?)- .... CLC 30

Simonson, Rick ed. .... CLC 70

Simpson, Harriette
See Arnow, Harriette (Louisa) Simpson

Simpson, Louis (Aston Marantz)
1923- .... CLC 4, 7, 9, 32, 149
See also AMWS 9; CA 1-4R; CAAS 4;
CANR 1, 61; CP 7; DAM POET; DLB 5;
MTCW 1, 2; PFS 7, 11, 14; RGAL 4

Simpson, Mona (Elizabeth) 1957- ... CLC 44,
146
See also CA 135; 122; CANR 68, 103; CN
7

Simpson, N(orman) F(rederick)
1919- .... CLC 29
See also CA 13-16R; CBD; DLB 13; RGEL
2

Sinclair, Andrew (Annandale) 1935- . CLC 2,
14
See also CA 9-12R; CAAS 5; CANR 14,
38, 91; CN 7; DLB 14; FANT; MTCW 1

Sinclair, Emil
See Hesse, Hermann

Sinclair, Iain 1943- .... CLC 76
See also CA 132; CANR 81; CP 7; HGG

Sinclair, Iain MacGregor
See Sinclair, Iain

Sinclair, Irene
See Griffith, D(avid Lewelyn) W(ark)

Sinclair, Mary Amelia St. Clair 1865(?)-1946
See Sinclair, May
See also CA 104; HGG; RHW

Sinclair, May .... TCLC 3, 11
See Sinclair, Mary Amelia St. Clair
See also CA 166; DLB 36, 135; RGEL 2;
SUFW

Sinclair, Roy
See Griffith, D(avid Lewelyn) W(ark)

Sinclair, Upton (Beall) 1878-1968 ..... CLC 1,
11, 15, 63; WLC
See also AMWS 5; BPFB 3; BYA 2; CA
25-28R; 5-8R; CANR 7; CDALB 1929-
1941; DA; DA3; DAB; DAC; DAM MST,
NOV; DLB 9; INT CANR-7; LAIT 3;
MTCW 1, 2; NFS 6; RGAL 4; SATA 9;
TUS; YAW

Singe, (Edmund) J(ohn) M(illington)
1871-1909 .... WLC

Singer, Isaac
See Singer, Isaac Bashevis

Singer, Isaac Bashevis 1904-1991 .. CLC 1, 3,
6, 9, 11, 15, 23, 38, 69, 111; SSC 3, 53;
WLC
See also AAYA 32; AITN 1, 2; AMW;
AMWR 2; BPFB 3; BYA 1, 4; CA 134;
1-4R; CANR 1, 39, 106; CDALB 1941-
1968; CLR 1; CWRI 5; DA; DA3; DAB;
DAC; DAM MST, NOV; DLB 6, 28, 52,
278; DLBY 1991; EXPS; HGG; JRDA;
LAIT 3; MAICYA 1, 2; MTCW 1, 2;
RGAL 4; RGSF 2; SATA 3, 27; SATA-
Obit 68; SSFS 2, 12, 16; TUS; TWA

Singer, Israel Joshua 1893-1944 .... TCLC 33
See also CA 169

Singh, Khushwant 1915- .... CLC 11
See also CA 9-12R; CAAS 9; CANR 6, 84;
CN 7; RGEL 2

Singleton, Ann
See Benedict, Ruth (Fulton)

Singleton, John 1968(?)- .... CLC 156
See also BW 2, 3; CA 138; CANR 67, 82;
DAM MULT

Sinjohn, John
See Galsworthy, John

Sinyavsky, Andrei (Donatevich)
1925-1997 .... CLC 8
See Tertz, Abram
See also CA 159; 85-88

Sirin, V.
See Nabokov, Vladimir (Vladimirovich)

Sissman, L(ouis) E(dward)
1928-1976 .... CLC 9, 18
See also CA 65-68; 21-24R; CANR 13;
DLB 5

Sisson, C(harles) H(ubert) 1914- .... CLC 8
See also CA 1-4R; CAAS 3; CANR 3, 48,
84; CP 7; DLB 27

Sitting Bull 1831(?)-1890 .... NNAL
See also DA3; DAM MULT

Sitwell, Dame Edith 1887-1964 ..... CLC 2, 9,
67; PC 3
See also BRW 7; CA 9-12R; CANR 35;
CDBLB 1945-1960; DAM POET; DLB
20; MTCW 1, 2; RGEL 2; TEA

Siwaarmill, H. P.
See Sharp, William

Sjoewall, Maj 1935- .... CLC 7
See Sjowall, Maj
See also CA 65-68; CANR 73

Sjowall, Maj
See Sjoewall, Maj
See also BPFB 3; CMW 4; MSW

Skelton, John 1460(?)-1529 ..... LC 71; PC 25
See also BRW 1; DLB 136; RGEL 2

Skelton, Robin 1925-1997 .... CLC 13
See Zuk, Georges
See also AITN 2; CA 160; 5-8R; CAAS 5;
CANR 28, 89; CCA 1; CP 7; DLB 27, 53

Skolimowski, Jerzy 1938- .... CLC 20
See also CA 128

Skram, Amalie (Bertha)
1847-1905 .... TCLC 25
See also CA 165

Skvorecky, Josef (Vaclav) 1924- ...... CLC 15,
39, 69, 152
See also CA 61-64; CAAS 1; CANR 10,
34, 63, 108; CDWLB 4; DA3; DAC;
DAM NOV; DLB 232; MTCW 1, 2

Slade, Bernard .... CLC 11, 46
See Newbound, Bernard Slade
See also CAAS 9; CCA 1; DLB 53

Slaughter, Carolyn 1946- .... CLC 56
See also CA 85-88; CANR 85; CN 7

Slaughter, Frank G(ill) 1908-2001 ... CLC 29
See also AITN 2; CA 197; 5-8R; CANR 5,
85; INT CANR-5; RHW

Slavitt, David R(ytman) 1935- ..... CLC 5, 14
See also CA 21-24R; CAAS 3; CANR 41,
83; CP 7; DLB 5, 6

Slesinger, Tess 1905-1945 .... TCLC 10
See also CA 199; 107; DLB 102

Slessor, Kenneth 1901-1971 .... CLC 14
See also CA 89-92; 102; DLB 260; RGEL
2

Slowacki, Juliusz 1809-1849 .... NCLC 15
See also RGWL 3

Smart, Christopher 1722-1771 . **LC 3; PC 13**
See also DAM POET; DLB 109; RGEL 2

Smart, Elizabeth 1913-1986 .... **CLC 54**
See also CA 118; 81-84; DLB 88

Smiley, Jane (Graves) 1949- ...... **CLC 53, 76, 144**
See also AMWS 6; BPFB 3; CA 104; CANR 30, 50, 74, 96; CN 7; CPW 1; DA3; DAM POP; DLB 227, 234; INT CANR-30

Smith, A(rthur) J(ames) M(arshall)
1902-1980 .... **CLC 15**
See also CA 102; 1-4R; CANR 4; DAC; DLB 88; RGEL 2

Smith, Adam 1723(?)-1790 .... **LC 36**
See also DLB 104, 252; RGEL 2

Smith, Alexander 1829-1867 .... **NCLC 59**
See also DLB 32, 55

Smith, Anna Deavere 1950- .... **CLC 86**
See also CA 133; CANR 103; CD 5; DFS 2

Smith, Betty (Wehner) 1904-1972 .... **CLC 19**
See also BPFB 3; BYA 3; CA 33-36R; 5-8R; DLBY 1982; LAIT 3; RGAL 4; SATA 6

Smith, Charlotte (Turner)
1749-1806 .... **NCLC 23, 115**
See also DLB 39, 109; RGEL 2; TEA

Smith, Clark Ashton 1893-1961 .... **CLC 43**
See also CA 143; CANR 81; FANT; HGG; MTCW 2; SCFW 2; SFW 4; SUFW

Smith, Dave .... **CLC 22, 42**
See Smith, David (Jeddie)
See also CAAS 7; DLB 5

Smith, David (Jeddie) 1942-
See Smith, Dave
See also CA 49-52; CANR 1, 59; CP 7; CSW; DAM POET

Smith, Florence Margaret 1902-1971
See Smith, Stevie
See also CA 29-32R; 17-18; CANR 35; CAP 2; DAM POET; MTCW 1, 2; TEA

Smith, Iain Crichton 1928-1998 .... **CLC 64**
See also CA 171; 21-24R; CN 7; CP 7; DLB 40, 139; RGSF 2

Smith, John 1580(?)-1631 .... **LC 9**
See also DLB 24, 30; TUS

Smith, Johnston
See Crane, Stephen (Townley)

Smith, Joseph, Jr. 1805-1844 .... **NCLC 53**

Smith, Lee 1944- .... **CLC 25, 73**
See also CA 119; 114; CANR 46; CSW; DLB 143; DLBY 1983; INT CA-119; RGAL 4

Smith, Martin
See Smith, Martin Cruz

Smith, Martin Cruz 1942- .. **CLC 25; NNAL**
See also BEST 89:4; BPFB 3; CA 85-88; CANR 6, 23, 43, 65; CMW 4; CPW; DAM MULT, POP; HGG; INT CANR-23; MTCW 2; RGAL 4

Smith, Patti 1946- .... **CLC 12**
See also CA 93-96; CANR 63

Smith, Pauline (Urmson)
1882-1959 .... **TCLC 25**
See also DLB 225

Smith, Rosamond
See Oates, Joyce Carol

Smith, Sheila Kaye
See Kaye-Smith, Sheila

Smith, Stevie .... **CLC 3, 8, 25, 44; PC 12**
See Smith, Florence Margaret
See also BRWS 2; DLB 20; MTCW 2; PAB; PFS 3; RGEL 2

Smith, Wilbur (Addison) 1933- .... **CLC 33**
See also CA 13-16R; CANR 7, 46, 66; CPW; MTCW 1, 2

Smith, William Jay 1918- .... **CLC 6**
See also CA 5-8R; CANR 44, 106; CP 7; CSW; CWRI 5; DLB 5; MAICYA 1, 2; SAAS 22; SATA 2, 68

Smith, Woodrow Wilson
See Kuttner, Henry

Smith, Zadie 1976- .... **CLC 158**
See also CA 193

Smolenskin, Peretz 1842-1885 .... **NCLC 30**

Smollett, Tobias (George) 1721-1771 ... **LC 2, 46**
See also BRW 3; CDBLB 1660-1789; DLB 39, 104; RGEL 2; TEA

Snodgrass, W(illiam) D(e Witt)
1926- .... **CLC 2, 6, 10, 18, 68**
See also AMWS 6; CA 1-4R; CANR 6, 36, 65, 85; CP 7; DAM POET; DLB 5; MTCW 1, 2; RGAL 4

Snorri Sturluson 1179-1241 .... **CMLC 56**
See also RGWL 2, 3

Snow, C(harles) P(ercy) 1905-1980 ... **CLC 1, 4, 6, 9, 13, 19**
See also BRW 7; CA 101; 5-8R; CANR 28; CDBLB 1945-1960; DAM NOV; DLB 15, 77; DLBD 17; MTCW 1, 2; RGEL 2; TEA

Snow, Frances Compton
See Adams, Henry (Brooks)

Snyder, Gary (Sherman) 1930- . **CLC 1, 2, 5, 9, 32, 120; PC 21**
See also AMWS 8; ANW; BG 3; CA 17-20R; CANR 30, 60; CP 7; DA3; DAM POET; DLB 5, 16, 165, 212, 237, 275; MTCW 2; PFS 9; RGAL 4; WP

Snyder, Zilpha Keatley 1927- .... **CLC 17**
See also AAYA 15; BYA 1, 16; CA 9-12R; CANR 38; CLR 31; JRDA; MAICYA 1, 2; SAAS 2; SATA 1, 28, 75, 110; SATA-Essay 112; YAW

Soares, Bernardo
See Pessoa, Fernando (Antonio Nogueira)

Sobh, A.
See Shamlu, Ahmad

Sobol, Joshua 1939- .... **CLC 60**
See Sobol, Yehoshua
See also CA 200; CWW 2

Sobol, Yehoshua 1939-
See Sobol, Joshua
See also CWW 2

Socrates 470B.C.-399B.C. .... **CMLC 27**

Soderberg, Hjalmar 1869-1941 ...... **TCLC 39**
See also DLB 259; RGSF 2

Soderbergh, Steven 1963- .... **CLC 154**
See also AAYA 43

Sodergran, Edith (Irene) 1892-1923
See Soedergran, Edith (Irene)
See also CA 202; DLB 259; EW 11; RGWL 2, 3

Soedergran, Edith (Irene)
1892-1923 .... **TCLC 31**
See Sodergran, Edith (Irene)

Softly, Edgar
See Lovecraft, H(oward) P(hillips)

Softly, Edward
See Lovecraft, H(oward) P(hillips)

Sokolov, Raymond 1941- .... **CLC 7**
See also CA 85-88

Sokolov, Sasha .... **CLC 59**

Solo, Jay
See Ellison, Harlan (Jay)

Sologub, Fyodor .... **TCLC 9**
See Teternikov, Fyodor Kuzmich

Solomons, Ikey Esquir
See Thackeray, William Makepeace

Solomos, Dionysios 1798-1857 .... **NCLC 15**

Solwoska, Mara
See French, Marilyn

Solzhenitsyn, Aleksandr I(sayevich)
1918- .. **CLC 1, 2, 4, 7, 9, 10, 18, 26, 34, 78, 134; SSC 32; WLC**
See also AITN 1; BPFB 3; CA 69-72; CANR 40, 65, 116; DA; DA3; DAB; DAC; DAM MST, NOV; EW 13; EXPS; LAIT 4; MTCW 1, 2; NFS 6; RGSF 2; RGWL 2, 3; SSFS 9; TWA

Somers, Jane
See Lessing, Doris (May)

Somerville, Edith Oenone
1858-1949 .... **SSC 56; TCLC 51**
See also CA 196; DLB 135; RGEL 2; RGSF 2

Somerville & Ross
See Martin, Violet Florence; Somerville, Edith Oenone

Sommer, Scott 1951- .... **CLC 25**
See also CA 106

Sondheim, Stephen (Joshua) 1930- . **CLC 30, 39, 147**
See also AAYA 11; CA 103; CANR 47, 67; DAM DRAM; LAIT 4

Sone, Monica 1919- .... **AAL**

Song, Cathy 1955- .... **AAL; PC 21**
See also CA 154; CWP; DLB 169; EXPP; FW; PFS 5

Sontag, Susan 1933- .... **CLC 1, 2, 10, 13, 31, 105**
See also AMWS 3; CA 17-20R; CANR 25, 51, 74, 97; CN 7; CPW; DA3; DAM POP; DLB 2, 67; MAWW; MTCW 1, 2; RGAL 4; RHW; SSFS 10

Sophocles 496(?)B.C.-406(?)B.C. .... **CMLC 2, 47, 51; DC 1; WLCS**
See also AW 1; CDWLB 1; DA; DA3; DAB; DAC; DAM DRAM, MST; DFS 1, 4, 8; DLB 176; LAIT 1; RGWL 2, 3; TWA

Sordello 1189-1269 .... **CMLC 15**

Sorel, Georges 1847-1922 .... **TCLC 91**
See also CA 188; 118

Sorel, Julia
See Drexler, Rosalyn

Sorokin, Vladimir .... **CLC 59**

Sorrentino, Gilbert 1929- .. **CLC 3, 7, 14, 22, 40**
See also CA 77-80; CANR 14, 33, 115; CN 7; CP 7; DLB 5, 173; DLBY 1980; INT CANR-14

Soseki
See Natsume, Soseki
See also MJW

Soto, Gary 1952- ... **CLC 32, 80; HLC 2; PC 28**
See also AAYA 10, 37; BYA 11; CA 125; 119; CANR 50, 74, 107; CLR 38; CP 7; DAM MULT; DLB 82; EXPP; HW 1, 2; INT CA-125; JRDA; MAICYA 2; MAIC-YAS 1; MTCW 2; PFS 7; RGAL 4; SATA 80, 120; WYA; YAW

Soupault, Philippe 1897-1990 .... **CLC 68**
See also CA 131; 147; 116; GFL 1789 to the Present

Souster, (Holmes) Raymond 1921- .... **CLC 5, 14**
See also CA 13-16R; CAAS 14; CANR 13, 29, 53; CP 7; DA3; DAC; DAM POET; DLB 88; RGEL 2; SATA 63

Southern, Terry 1924(?)-1995 .... **CLC 7**
See also AMWS 11; BPFB 3; CA 150; 1-4R; CANR 1, 55, 107; CN 7; DLB 2; IDFW 3, 4

Southey, Robert 1774-1843 .... **NCLC 8, 97**
See also BRW 4; DLB 93, 107, 142; RGEL 2; SATA 54

Southworth, Emma Dorothy Eliza Nevitte
1819-1899 .... **NCLC 26**
See also DLB 239

Stephens, James 1882(?)-1950 .... **SSC 50; TCLC 4**
See also CA 192; 104; DLB 19, 153, 162; FANT; RGEL 2; SUFW

Stephens, Reed
See Donaldson, Stephen R(eeder)

Steptoe, Lydia
See Barnes, Djuna
See also GLL 1

Sterchi, Beat 1949- .... **CLC 65**
See also CA 203

Sterling, Brett
See Bradbury, Ray (Douglas); Hamilton, Edmond

Sterling, Bruce 1954- .... **CLC 72**
See also CA 119; CANR 44; SCFW 2; SFW 4

Sterling, George 1869-1926 .... **TCLC 20**
See also CA 165; 117; DLB 54

Stern, Gerald 1925- .... **CLC 40, 100**
See also AMWS 9; CA 81-84; CANR 28, 94; CP 7; DLB 105; RGAL 4

Stern, Richard (Gustave) 1928- ... **CLC 4, 39**
See also CA 1-4R; CANR 1, 25, 52; CN 7; DLB 218; DLBY 1987; INT CANR-25

Sternberg, Josef von 1894-1969 .... **CLC 20**
See also CA 81-84

Sterne, Laurence 1713-1768 .... **LC 2, 48; WLC**
See also BRW 3; BRWC 1; CDBLB 1660-1789; DA; DAB; DAC; DAM MST, NOV; DLB 39; RGEL 2; TEA

Sternheim, (William Adolf) Carl
1878-1942 .... **TCLC 8**
See also CA 193; 105; DLB 56, 118; RGWL 2, 3

Stevens, Mark 1951- .... **CLC 34**
See also CA 122

Stevens, Wallace 1879-1955 . **PC 6; TCLC 3, 12, 45; WLC**
See also AMW; AMWR 1; CA 124; 104; CDALB 1929-1941; DA; DA3; DAB; DAC; DAM MST, POET; DLB 54; EXPP; MTCW 1, 2; PAB; PFS 13, 16; RGAL 4; TUS; WP

Stevenson, Anne (Katharine) 1933- .. **CLC 7, 33**
See also BRWS 6; CA 17-20R; CAAS 9; CANR 9, 33; CP 7; CWP; DLB 40; MTCW 1; RHW

Stevenson, Robert Louis (Balfour)
1850-1894 ...... **NCLC 5, 14, 63; SSC 11, 51; WLC**
See also AAYA 24; BPFB 3; BRW 5; BRWC 1; BRWR 1; BYA 1, 2, 4, 13; CD-BLB 1890-1914; CLR 10, 11; DA; DA3; DAB; DAC; DAM MST, NOV; DLB 18, 57, 141, 156, 174; DLBD 13; HGG; JRDA; LAIT 1, 3; MAICYA 1, 2; NFS 11; RGEL 2; RGSF 2; SATA 100; SUFW; TEA; WCH; WLIT 4; WYA; YABC 2; YAW

Stewart, J(ohn) I(nnes) M(ackintosh)
1906-1994 .... **CLC 7, 14, 32**
See Innes, Michael
See also CA 147; 85-88; CAAS 3; CANR 47; CMW 4; MTCW 1, 2

Stewart, Mary (Florence Elinor)
1916- .... **CLC 7, 35, 117**
See also AAYA 29; BPFB 3; CA 1-4R; CANR 1, 59; CMW 4; CPW; DAB; FANT; RHW; SATA 12; YAW

Stewart, Mary Rainbow
See Stewart, Mary (Florence Elinor)

Stifle, June
See Campbell, Maria

Stifter, Adalbert 1805-1868 .. **NCLC 41; SSC 28**
See also CDWLB 2; DLB 133; RGSF 2; RGWL 2, 3

Still, James 1906-2001 .... **CLC 49**
See also CA 195; 65-68; CAAS 17; CANR 10, 26; CSW; DLB 9; DLBY 01; SATA 29; SATA-Obit 127

Sting 1951-
See Sumner, Gordon Matthew
See also CA 167

Stirling, Arthur
See Sinclair, Upton (Beall)

Stitt, Milan 1941- .... **CLC 29**
See also CA 69-72

Stockton, Francis Richard 1834-1902
See Stockton, Frank R.
See also CA 137; 108; MAICYA 1, 2; SATA 44; SFW 4

Stockton, Frank R. .... **TCLC 47**
See Stockton, Francis Richard
See also BYA 4, 13; DLB 42, 74; DLBD 13; EXPS; SATA-Brief 32; SSFS 3; SUFW; WCH

Stoddard, Charles
See Kuttner, Henry

Stoker, Abraham 1847-1912
See Stoker, Bram
See also CA 150; 105; DA; DA3; DAC; DAM MST, NOV; HGG; SATA 29

Stoker, Bram .... **TCLC 8; WLC**
See Stoker, Abraham
See also AAYA 23; BPFB 3; BRWS 3; BYA 5; CDBLB 1890-1914; DAB; DLB 36, 70, 178; RGEL 2; SUFW; TEA; WLIT 4

Stolz, Mary (Slattery) 1920- .... **CLC 12**
See also AAYA 8; AITN 1; CA 5-8R; CANR 13, 41, 112; JRDA; MAICYA 1, 2; SAAS 3; SATA 10, 71, 133; YAW

Stone, Irving 1903-1989 .... **CLC 7**
See also AITN 1; BPFB 3; CA 129; 1-4R; CAAS 3; CANR 1, 23; CPW; DA3; DAM POP; INT CANR-23; MTCW 1, 2; RHW; SATA 3; SATA-Obit 64

Stone, Oliver (William) 1946- .... **CLC 73**
See also AAYA 15; CA 110; CANR 55

Stone, Robert (Anthony) 1937- ... **CLC 5, 23, 42**
See also AMWS 5; BPFB 3; CA 85-88; CANR 23, 66, 95; CN 7; DLB 152; INT CANR-23; MTCW 1

Stone, Zachary
See Follett, Ken(neth Martin)

Stoppard, Tom 1937- ... **CLC 1, 3, 4, 5, 8, 15, 29, 34, 63, 91; DC 6; WLC**
See also BRWC 1; BRWR 2; BRWS 1; CA 81-84; CANR 39, 67; CBD; CD 5; CD-BLB 1960 to Present; DA; DA3; DAB; DAC; DAM DRAM, MST; DFS 2, 5, 8, 11, 13, 16; DLB 13, 233; DLBY 1985; MTCW 1, 2; RGEL 2; TEA; WLIT 4

Storey, David (Malcolm) 1933- . **CLC 2, 4, 5, 8**
See also BRWS 1; CA 81-84; CANR 36; CBD; CD 5; CN 7; DAM DRAM; DLB 13, 14, 207, 245; MTCW 1; RGEL 2

Storm, Hyemeyohsts 1935- ... **CLC 3; NNAL**
See also CA 81-84; CANR 45; DAM MULT

Storm, (Hans) Theodor (Woldsen)
1817-1888 .... **NCLC 1; SSC 27**
See also DLB 129; EW; RGWL 3

Storm, Theodor 1817-1888 .... **SSC 27**
See also CDWLB 2; RGSF 2; RGWL 2

Storni, Alfonsina 1892-1938 . **HLC 2; PC 33; TCLC 5**
See also CA 131; 104; DAM MULT; HW 1; LAW

Stoughton, William 1631-1701 .... **LC 38**
See also DLB 24

Stout, Rex (Todhunter) 1886-1975 ..... **CLC 3**
See also AITN 2; BPFB 3; CA 61-64; CANR 71; CMW 4; MSW; RGAL 4

Stow, (Julian) Randolph 1935- ... **CLC 23, 48**
See also CA 13-16R; CANR 33; CN 7; DLB 260; MTCW 1; RGEL 2

Stowe, Harriet (Elizabeth) Beecher
1811-1896 .... **NCLC 3, 50; WLC**
See also AMWS 1; CDALB 1865-1917; DA; DA3; DAB; DAC; DAM MST, NOV; DLB 1, 12, 42, 74, 189, 239, 243; EXPN; JRDA; LAIT 2; MAICYA 1, 2; NFS 6; RGAL 4; TUS; YABC 1

Strabo c. 64B.C.-c. 25 .... **CMLC 37**
See also DLB 176

Strachey, (Giles) Lytton
1880-1932 .... **TCLC 12**
See also BRWS 2; CA 178; 110; DLB 149; DLBD 10; MTCW 2; NCFS 4

Strand, Mark 1934- .... **CLC 6, 18, 41, 71**
See also AMWS 4; CA 21-24R; CANR 40, 65, 100; CP 7; DAM POET; DLB 5; PAB; PFS 9; RGAL 4; SATA 41

Stratton-Porter, Gene(va Grace) 1863-1924
See Porter, Gene(va Grace) Stratton
See also ANW; CA 137; DLB 221; DLBD 14; MAICYA 1, 2; SATA 15

Straub, Peter (Francis) 1943- ... **CLC 28, 107**
See also BEST 89:1; BPFB 3; CA 85-88; CANR 28, 65, 109; CPW; DAM POP; DLBY 1984; HGG; MTCW 1, 2; SUFW 2

Strauss, Botho 1944- .... **CLC 22**
See also CA 157; CWW 2; DLB 124

Streatfeild, (Mary) Noel
1897(?)-1986 .... **CLC 21**
See also CA 120; 81-84; CANR 31; CLR 17, 83; CWRI 5; DLB 160; MAICYA 1, 2; SATA 20; SATA-Obit 48

Stribling, T(homas) S(igismund)
1881-1965 .... **CLC 23**
See also CA 107; 189; CMW 4; DLB 9; RGAL 4

Strindberg, (Johan) August
1849-1912 ... **DC 18; TCLC 1, 8, 21, 47; WLC**
See also CA 135; 104; DA; DA3; DAB; DAC; DAM DRAM, MST; DFS 4, 9; DLB 259; EW 7; IDTP; LMFS 2; MTCW 2; RGWL 2, 3; TWA

Stringer, Arthur 1874-1950 .... **TCLC 37**
See also CA 161; DLB 92

Stringer, David
See Roberts, Keith (John Kingston)

Stroheim, Erich von 1885-1957 ..... **TCLC 71**

Strugatskii, Arkadii (Natanovich)
1925-1991 .... **CLC 27**
See also CA 135; 106; SFW 4

Strugatskii, Boris (Natanovich)
1933- .... **CLC 27**
See also CA 106; SFW 4

Strummer, Joe 1953(?)- .... **CLC 30**

Strunk, William, Jr. 1869-1946 ...... **TCLC 92**
See also CA 164; 118

Stryk, Lucien 1924- .... **PC 27**
See also CA 13-16R; CANR 10, 28, 55, 110; CP 7

Stuart, Don A.
See Campbell, John W(ood, Jr.)

Stuart, Ian
See MacLean, Alistair (Stuart)

Stuart, Jesse (Hilton) 1906-1984 ... **CLC 1, 8, 11, 14, 34; SSC 31**
See also CA 112; 5-8R; CANR 31; DLB 9, 48, 102; DLBY 1984; SATA 2; SATA-Obit 36

Stubblefield, Sally
See Trumbo, Dalton

Sturgeon, Theodore (Hamilton)
1918-1985 .... CLC 22, 39
See Queen, Ellery
See also BPFB 3; BYA 9, 10; CA 116; 81-
84; CANR 32, 103; DLB 8; DLBY 1985;
HGG; MTCW 1, 2; SCFW; SFW 4;
SUFW
Sturges, Preston 1898-1959 .... TCLC 48
See also CA 149; 114; DLB 26
Styron, William 1925- .... CLC 1, 3, 5, 11, 15,
60; SSC 25
See also AMW; BEST 90:4; BPFB 3; CA
5-8R; CANR 6, 33, 74; CDALB 1968-
1988; CN 7; CPW; CSW; DA3; DAM
NOV, POP; DLB 2, 143; DLBY 1980;
INT CANR-6; LAIT 2; MTCW 1, 2;
NCFS 1; RGAL 4; RHW; TUS
Su, Chien 1884-1918
See Su Man-shu
See also CA 123
Suarez Lynch, B.
See Bioy Casares, Adolfo; Borges, Jorge
Luis
Suassuna, Ariano Vilar 1927- .... HLCS 1
See also CA 178; HW 2; LAW
Suckert, Kurt Erich
See Malaparte, Curzio
Suckling, Sir John 1609-1642 . LC 75; PC 30
See also BRW 2; DAM POET; DLB 58,
126; EXPP; PAB; RGEL 2
Suckow, Ruth 1892-1960 .... SSC 18
See also CA 113; 193; DLB 9, 102; RGAL
4; TCWW 2
Sudermann, Hermann 1857-1928 .. TCLC 15
See also CA 201; 107; DLB 118
Sue, Eugene 1804-1857 .... NCLC 1
See also DLB 119
Sueskind, Patrick 1949- .... CLC 44
See Suskind, Patrick
Sukenick, Ronald 1932- .... CLC 3, 4, 6, 48
See also CA 25-28R; CAAS 8; CANR 32,
89; CN 7; DLB 173; DLBY 1981
Suknaski, Andrew 1942- .... CLC 19
See also CA 101; CP 7; DLB 53
Sullivan, Vernon
See Vian, Boris
Sully Prudhomme, Rene-Francois-Armand
1839-1907 .... TCLC 31
See also GFL 1789 to the Present
Su Man-shu .... TCLC 24
See Su, Chien
Summerforest, Ivy B.
See Kirkup, James
Summers, Andrew James 1942- .... CLC 26
Summers, Andy
See Summers, Andrew James
Summers, Hollis (Spurgeon, Jr.)
1916- .... CLC 10
See also CA 5-8R; CANR 3; DLB 6
Summers, (Alphonsus Joseph-Mary
Augustus) Montague
1880-1948 .... TCLC 16
See also CA 163; 118
Sumner, Gordon Matthew .... CLC 26
See Police, The; Sting
Sun Tzu c. 400B.C.-c. 320B.C. ...... CMLC 56
Surtees, Robert Smith 1805-1864 .. NCLC 14
See also DLB 21; RGEL 2
Susann, Jacqueline 1921-1974 .... CLC 3
See also AITN 1; BPFB 3; CA 53-56; 65-
68; MTCW 1, 2
Su Shi
See Su Shih
See also RGWL 2, 3
Su Shih 1036-1101 .... CMLC 15
See Su Shi
Suskind, Patrick
See Sueskind, Patrick
See also BPFB 3; CA 145; CWW 2

Sutcliff, Rosemary 1920-1992 .... CLC 26
See also AAYA 10; BYA 1, 4; CA 139;
5-8R; CANR 37; CLR 1, 37; CPW; DAB;
DAC; DAM MST, POP; JRDA; MAICYA
1, 2; MAICYAS 1; RHW; SATA 6, 44,
78; SATA-Obit 73; WYA; YAW
Sutro, Alfred 1863-1933 .... TCLC 6
See also CA 185; 105; DLB 10; RGEL 2
Sutton, Henry
See Slavitt, David R(ytman)
Suzuki, D. T.
See Suzuki, Daisetz Teitaro
Suzuki, Daisetz T.
See Suzuki, Daisetz Teitaro
Suzuki, Daisetz Teitaro
1870-1966 .... TCLC 109
See also CA 111; 121; MTCW 1, 2
Suzuki, Teitaro
See Suzuki, Daisetz Teitaro
Svevo, Italo .... SSC 25; TCLC 2, 35
See Schmitz, Aron Hector
See also DLB 264; EW 8; RGWL 2, 3
Swados, Elizabeth (A.) 1951- .... CLC 12
See also CA 97-100; CANR 49; INT 97-
100
Swados, Harvey 1920-1972 .... CLC 5
See also CA 37-40R; 5-8R; CANR 6; DLB
2
Swan, Gladys 1934- .... CLC 69
See also CA 101; CANR 17, 39
Swanson, Logan
See Matheson, Richard (Burton)
Swarthout, Glendon (Fred)
1918-1992 .... CLC 35
See also CA 139; 1-4R; CANR 1, 47; LAIT
5; SATA 26; TCWW 2; YAW
Sweet, Sarah C.
See Jewett, (Theodora) Sarah Orne
Swenson, May 1919-1989 ...... CLC 4, 14, 61,
106; PC 14
See also AMWS 4; CA 130; 5-8R; CANR
36, 61; DA; DAB; DAC; DAM MST,
POET; DLB 5; EXPP; GLL 2; MTCW 1,
2; PFS 16; SATA 15; WP
Swift, Augustus
See Lovecraft, H(oward) P(hillips)
Swift, Graham (Colin) 1949- ...... CLC 41, 88
See also BRWS 5; CA 122; 117; CANR 46,
71; CN 7; DLB 194; MTCW 2; RGSF 2
Swift, Jonathan 1667-1745 .. LC 1, 42; PC 9;
WLC
See also AAYA 41; BRW 3; BRWC 1;
BRWR 1; BYA 5, 14; CDBLB 1660-1789;
CLR 53; DA; DA3; DAB; DAC; DAM
MST, NOV, POET; DLB 39, 95, 101;
EXPN; LAIT 1; NFS 6; RGEL 2; SATA
19; TEA; WCH; WLIT 3
Swinburne, Algernon Charles
1837-1909 ... PC 24; TCLC 8, 36; WLC
See also BRW 5; CA 140; 105; CDBLB
1832-1890; DA; DA3; DAB; DAC; DAM
MST, POET; DLB 35, 57; PAB; RGEL 2;
TEA
Swinfen, Ann .... CLC 34
See also CA 202
Swinnerton, Frank Arthur
1884-1982 .... CLC 31
See also CA 108; DLB 34
Swithen, John
See King, Stephen (Edwin)
Sylvia
See Ashton-Warner, Sylvia (Constance)
Symmes, Robert Edward
See Duncan, Robert (Edward)
Symonds, John Addington
1840-1893 .... NCLC 34
See also DLB 57, 144

Symons, Arthur 1865-1945 .... TCLC 11
See also CA 189; 107; DLB 19, 57, 149;
RGEL 2
Symons, Julian (Gustave)
1912-1994 .... CLC 2, 14, 32
See also CA 147; 49-52; CAAS 3; CANR
3, 33, 59; CMW 4; DLB 87, 155; DLBY
1992; MSW; MTCW 1
Synge, (Edmund) J(ohn) M(illington)
1871-1909 .... DC 2; TCLC 6, 37
See also BRW 6; BRWR 1; CA 141; 104;
CDBLB 1890-1914; DAM DRAM; DLB
10, 19; RGEL 2; TEA; WLIT 4
Syruc, J.
See Milosz, Czeslaw
Szirtes, George 1948- .... CLC 46
See also CA 109; CANR 27, 61, 117; CP 7
Szymborska, Wislawa 1923- ..... CLC 99; PC
44
See also CA 154; CANR 91; CDWLB 4;
CWP; CWW 2; DA3; DLB 232; DLBY
1996; MTCW 2; PFS 15; RGWL 3
T. O., Nik
See Annensky, Innokenty (Fyodorovich)
Tabori, George 1914- .... CLC 19
See also CA 49-52; CANR 4, 69; CBD; CD
5; DLB 245
Tacitus c. 55-c. 117 .... CMLC 56
See also AW 2; CDWLB 1; DLB 211;
RGWL 2, 3
Tagore, Rabindranath 1861-1941 .... PC 8;
SSC 48; TCLC 3, 53
See also CA 120; 104; DA3; DAM DRAM,
POET; MTCW 1, 2; RGEL 2; RGSF 2;
RGWL 2, 3; TWA
Taine, Hippolyte Adolphe
1828-1893 .... NCLC 15
See also EW 7; GFL 1789 to the Present
Talayesva, Don C. 1890-(?) .... NNAL
Talese, Gay 1932- .... CLC 37
See also AITN 1; CA 1-4R; CANR 9, 58;
DLB 185; INT CANR-9; MTCW 1, 2
Tallent, Elizabeth (Ann) 1954- .... CLC 45
See also CA 117; CANR 72; DLB 130
Tallmountain, Mary 1918-1997 .... NNAL
See also CA 161; 146; DLB 193
Tally, Ted 1952- .... CLC 42
See also CA 124; 120; CAD; CD 5; INT
124
Talvik, Heiti 1904-1947 .... TCLC 87
Tamayo y Baus, Manuel
1829-1898 .... NCLC 1
Tammsaare, A(nton) H(ansen)
1878-1940 .... TCLC 27
See also CA 164; CDWLB 4; DLB 220
Tam'si, Tchicaya U
See Tchicaya, Gerald Felix
Tan, Amy (Ruth) 1952- . AAL; CLC 59, 120,
151
See also AAYA 9; AMWS 10; BEST 89:3;
BPFB 3; CA 136; CANR 54, 105;
CDALBS; CN 7; CPW 1; DA3; DAM
MULT, NOV, POP; DLB 173; EXPN;
FW; LAIT 3, 5; MTCW 2; NFS 1, 13, 16;
RGAL 4; SATA 75; SSFS 9; YAW
Tandem, Felix
See Spitteler, Carl (Friedrich Georg)
Tanizaki, Jun'ichiro 1886-1965 ... CLC 8, 14,
28; SSC 21
See Tanizaki Jun'ichiro
See also CA 25-28R; 93-96; MJW; MTCW
2; RGSF 2; RGWL 2
Tanizaki Jun'ichiro
See Tanizaki, Jun'ichiro
See also DLB 180
Tanner, William
See Amis, Kingsley (William)
Tao Lao
See Storni, Alfonsina

Thomas, R(onald) S(tuart)
1913-2000 .... **CLC 6, 13, 48**
See also CA 189; 89-92; CAAS 4; CANR
30; CDBLB 1960 to Present; CP 7; DAB;
DAM POET; DLB 27; MTCW 1; RGEL
2

Thomas, Ross (Elmore) 1926-1995 .. **CLC 39**
See also CA 150; 33-36R; CANR 22, 63;
CMW 4

Thompson, Francis (Joseph)
1859-1907 .... **TCLC 4**
See also BRW 5; CA 189; 104; CDBLB
1890-1914; DLB 19; RGEL 2; TEA

Thompson, Francis Clegg
See Mencken, H(enry) L(ouis)

Thompson, Hunter S(tockton)
1937(?)- .... **CLC 9, 17, 40, 104**
See also AAYA 45; BEST 89:1; BPFB 3;
CA 17-20R; CANR 23, 46, 74, 77, 111;
CPW; CSW; DA3; DAM POP; DLB 185;
MTCW 1, 2; TUS

Thompson, James Myers
See Thompson, Jim (Myers)

Thompson, Jim (Myers)
1906-1977(?) .... **CLC 69**
See also BPFB 3; CA 140; CMW 4; CPW;
DLB 226; MSW

Thompson, Judith .... **CLC 39**
See also CWD

Thomson, James 1700-1748 .... **LC 16, 29, 40**
See also BRWS 3; DAM POET; DLB 95;
RGEL 2

Thomson, James 1834-1882 .... **NCLC 18**
See also DAM POET; DLB 35; RGEL 2

Thoreau, Henry David 1817-1862 .. **NCLC 7,
21, 61; PC 30; WLC**
See also AAYA 42; AMW; ANW; BYA 3;
CDALB 1640-1865; DA; DA3; DAB;
DAC; DAM MST; DLB 1, 183, 223, 270;
LAIT 2; NCFS 3; RGAL 4; TUS

Thorndike, E. L.
See Thorndike, Edward L(ee)

Thorndike, Edward L(ee)
1874-1949 .... **TCLC 107**
See also CA 121

Thornton, Hall
See Silverberg, Robert

Thubron, Colin (Gerald Dryden)
1939- .... **CLC 163**
See also CA 25-28R; CANR 12, 29, 59, 95;
CN 7; DLB 204, 231

Thucydides c. 455B.C.-c. 395B.C. . **CMLC 17**
See also AW 1; DLB 176; RGWL 2, 3

Thumboo, Edwin Nadason 1933- .... **PC 30**
See also CA 194

Thurber, James (Grover)
1894-1961 .. **CLC 5, 11, 25, 125; SSC 1,
47**
See also AMWS 1; BPFB 3; BYA 5; CA
73-76; CANR 17, 39; CDALB 1929-1941;
CWRI 5; DA; DA3; DAB; DAC; DAM
DRAM, MST, NOV; DLB 4, 11, 22, 102;
EXPS; FANT; LAIT 3; MAICYA 1, 2;
MTCW 1, 2; RGAL 4; RGSF 2; SATA
13; SSFS 1, 10; SUFW; TUS

Thurman, Wallace (Henry)
1902-1934 .... **BLC 3; HR 3; TCLC 6**
See also BW 1, 3; CA 124; 104; CANR 81;
DAM MULT; DLB 51

Tibullus c. 54B.C.-c. 18B.C. .... **CMLC 36**
See also AW 2; DLB 211; RGWL 2, 3

Ticheburn, Cheviot
See Ainsworth, William Harrison

Tieck, (Johann) Ludwig
1773-1853 .... **NCLC 5, 46; SSC 31**
See also CDWLB 2; DLB 90; EW 5; IDTP;
RGSF 2; RGWL 2, 3; SUFW

Tiger, Derry
See Ellison, Harlan (Jay)

Tilghman, Christopher 1948(?)- .... **CLC 65**
See also CA 159; CSW; DLB 244

Tillich, Paul (Johannes)
1886-1965 .... **CLC 131**
See also CA 25-28R; 5-8R; CANR 33;
MTCW 1, 2

Tillinghast, Richard (Williford)
1940- .... **CLC 29**
See also CA 29-32R; CAAS 23; CANR 26,
51, 96; CP 7; CSW

Timrod, Henry 1828-1867 .... **NCLC 25**
See also DLB 3, 248; RGAL 4

Tindall, Gillian (Elizabeth) 1938- ...... **CLC 7**
See also CA 21-24R; CANR 11, 65, 107;
CN 7

Tiptree, James, Jr. .... **CLC 48, 50**
See Sheldon, Alice Hastings Bradley
See also DLB 8; SCFW 2; SFW 4

Tirone Smith, Mary-Ann 1944- .... **CLC 39**
See also CA 136; 118; CANR 113

Tirso de Molina 1580(?)-1648 .... **DC 13;
HLCS 2; LC 73**
See also RGWL 2, 3

Titmarsh, Michael Angelo
See Thackeray, William Makepeace

Tocqueville, Alexis (Charles Henri Maurice
Clerel Comte) de 1805-1859 .. **NCLC 7,
63**
See also EW 6; GFL 1789 to the Present;
TWA

Toffler, Alvin 1928- .... **CLC 168**
See also CA 13-16R; CANR 15, 46, 67;
CPW; DAM POP; MTCW 1, 2

Toibin, Colm
See Toibin, Colm
See also DLB 271

Toibin, Colm 1955- .... **CLC 162**
See Toibin, Colm
See also CA 142; CANR 81

Tolkien, J(ohn) R(onald) R(euel)
1892-1973 .... **CLC 1, 2, 3, 8, 12, 38;
WLC**
See also AAYA 10; AITN 1; BPFB 3;
BRWS 2; CA 45-48; 17-18; CANR 36;
CAP 2; CDBLB 1914-1945; CLR 56;
CPW 1; CWRI 5; DA; DA3; DAB; DAC;
DAM MST, NOV, POP; DLB 15, 160,
255; EFS 2; FANT; JRDA; LAIT 1; MAI-
CYA 1, 2; MTCW 1, 2; NFS 8; RGEL 2;
SATA 2, 32, 100; SATA-Obit 24; SFW 4;
SUFW; TEA; WCH; WYA; YAW

Toller, Ernst 1893-1939 .... **TCLC 10**
See also CA 186; 107; DLB 124; RGWL 2,
3

Tolson, M. B.
See Tolson, Melvin B(eaunorus)

Tolson, Melvin B(eaunorus)
1898(?)-1966 .... **BLC 3; CLC 36, 105**
See also AFAW 1, 2; BW 1, 3; CA 89-92;
124; CANR 80; DAM MULT, POET;
DLB 48, 76; RGAL 4

Tolstoi, Aleksei Nikolaevich
See Tolstoy, Alexey Nikolaevich

Tolstoi, Lev
See Tolstoy, Leo (Nikolaevich)
See also RGSF 2; RGWL 2, 3

Tolstoy, Aleksei Nikolaevich
See Tolstoy, Alexey Nikolaevich
See also DLB 272

Tolstoy, Alexey Nikolaevich
1882-1945 .... **TCLC 18**
See Tolstoy, Aleksei Nikolaevich
See also CA 158; 107; SFW 4

Tolstoy, Leo (Nikolaevich)
1828-1910 . **SSC 9, 30, 45, 54; TCLC 4,
11, 17, 28, 44, 79; WLC**
See Tolstoi, Lev
See also CA 123; 104; DA; DA3; DAB;
DAC; DAM MST, NOV; DLB 238; EFS
2; EW 7; EXPS; IDTP; LAIT 2; NFS 10;
SATA 26; SSFS 5; TWA

Tolstoy, Count Leo
See Tolstoy, Leo (Nikolaevich)

Tomalin, Claire 1933- .... **CLC 166**
See also CA 89-92; CANR 52, 88; DLB
155

Tomasi di Lampedusa, Giuseppe 1896-1957
See Lampedusa, Giuseppe (Tomasi) di
See also CA 111; DLB 177

Tomlin, Lily .... **CLC 17**
See Tomlin, Mary Jean

Tomlin, Mary Jean 1939(?)-
See Tomlin, Lily
See also CA 117

Tomline, F. Latour
See Gilbert, W(illiam) S(chwenck)

Tomlinson, (Alfred) Charles 1927- .... **CLC 2,
4, 6, 13, 45; PC 17**
See also CA 5-8R; CANR 33; CP 7; DAM
POET; DLB 40

Tomlinson, H(enry) M(ajor)
1873-1958 .... **TCLC 71**
See also CA 161; 118; DLB 36, 100, 195

Tonson, Jacob fl. 1655(?)-1736 .... **LC 86**
See also DLB 170

Toole, John Kennedy 1937-1969 ..... **CLC 19,
64**
See also BPFB 3; CA 104; DLBY 1981;
MTCW 2

Toomer, Eugene
See Toomer, Jean

Toomer, Eugene Pinchback
See Toomer, Jean

Toomer, Jean 1892-1967 .. **BLC 3; CLC 1, 4,
13, 22; HR 3; PC 7; SSC 1, 45; WLCS**
See also AFAW 1, 2; AMWS 3, 9; BW 1;
CA 85-88; CDALB 1917-1929; DA3;
DAM MULT; DLB 45, 51; EXPP; EXPS;
LMFS 2; MTCW 1, 2; NFS 11; RGAL 4;
RGSF 2; SSFS 5

Toomer, Nathan Jean
See Toomer, Jean

Toomer, Nathan Pinchback
See Toomer, Jean

Torley, Luke
See Blish, James (Benjamin)

Tornimparte, Alessandra
See Ginzburg, Natalia

Torre, Raoul della
See Mencken, H(enry) L(ouis)

Torrence, Ridgely 1874-1950 .... **TCLC 97**
See also DLB 54, 249

Torrey, E(dwin) Fuller 1937- .... **CLC 34**
See also CA 119; CANR 71

Torsvan, Ben Traven
See Traven, B.

Torsvan, Benno Traven
See Traven, B.

Torsvan, Berick Traven
See Traven, B.

Torsvan, Berwick Traven
See Traven, B.

Torsvan, Bruno Traven
See Traven, B.

Torsvan, Traven
See Traven, B.

Tourneur, Cyril 1575(?)-1626 .... **LC 66**
See also BRW 2; DAM DRAM; DLB 58;
RGEL 2

Tournier, Michel (Edouard) 1924- .... **CLC 6,
23, 36, 95**
See also CA 49-52; CANR 3, 36, 74; DLB
83; GFL 1789 to the Present; MTCW 1,
2; SATA 23

Tournimparte, Alessandra
See Ginzburg, Natalia

Towers, Ivar
See Kornbluth, C(yril) M.

Towne, Robert (Burton) 1936(?)- ..... **CLC 87**
See also CA 108; DLB 44; IDFW 3, 4

Townsend, Sue .... **CLC 61**
See Townsend, Susan Lilian
See also AAYA 28; CA 127; 119; CANR
65, 107; CBD; CD 5; CPW; CWD; DAB;
DAC; DAM MST; DLB 271; INT 127;
SATA 55, 93; SATA-Brief 48; YAW

Townsend, Susan Lilian 1946-
See Townsend, Sue

Townshend, Pete
See Townshend, Peter (Dennis Blandford)

Townshend, Peter (Dennis Blandford)
1945- .... **CLC 17, 42**
See also CA 107

Tozzi, Federigo 1883-1920 .... **TCLC 31**
See also CA 160; CANR 110; DLB 264

Tracy, Don(ald Fiske) 1905-1970(?)
See Queen, Ellery
See also CA 176; 1-4R; CANR 2

Trafford, F. G.
See Riddell, Charlotte

Traill, Catharine Parr 1802-1899 .. **NCLC 31**
See also DLB 99

Trakl, Georg 1887-1914 .... **PC 20; TCLC 5**
See also CA 165; 104; EW 10; LMFS 2;
MTCW 2; RGWL 2, 3

Tranquilli, Secondino
See Silone, Ignazio

Transtroemer, Tomas Gosta
See Transtromer, Tomas (Goesta)

Transtromer, Tomas
See Transtromer, Tomas (Goesta)

Transtromer, Tomas (Goesta)
1931- .... **CLC 52, 65**
See also CA 129; 117; CAAS 17; CANR
115; DAM POET; DLB 257

Transtromer, Tomas Gosta
See Transtromer, Tomas (Goesta)

Traven, B. 1882(?)-1969 .... **CLC 8, 11**
See also CA 25-28R; 19-20; CAP 2; DLB
9, 56; MTCW 1; RGAL 4

Trediakovsky, Vasilii Kirillovich
1703-1769 .... **LC 68**
See also DLB 150

Treitel, Jonathan 1959- .... **CLC 70**
See also DLB 267

Trelawny, Edward John
1792-1881 .... **NCLC 85**
See also DLB 110, 116, 144

Tremain, Rose 1943- .... **CLC 42**
See also CA 97-100; CANR 44, 95; CN 7;
DLB 14, 271; RGSF 2; RHW

Tremblay, Michel 1942- .... **CLC 29, 102**
See also CA 128; 116; CCA 1; CWW 2;
DAC; DAM MST; DLB 60; GLL 1;
MTCW 1, 2

Trevanian .... **CLC 29**
See Whitaker, Rod(ney)

Trevor, Glen
See Hilton, James

Trevor, William .. **CLC 7, 9, 14, 25, 71, 116;**
SSC 21, 58
See Cox, William Trevor
See also BRWS 4; CBD; CD 5; CN 7; DLB
14, 139; MTCW 2; RGEL 2; RGSF 2;
SSFS 10

Trifonov, Iurii (Valentinovich)
See Trifonov, Yuri (Valentinovich)
See also RGWL 2, 3

Trifonov, Yuri (Valentinovich)
1925-1981 .... **CLC 45**
See Trifonov, Iurii (Valentinovich)
See also CA 103; 126; MTCW 1

Trilling, Diana (Rubin) 1905-1996 . **CLC 129**
See also CA 154; 5-8R; CANR 10, 46; INT
CANR-10; MTCW 1, 2

Trilling, Lionel 1905-1975 .... **CLC 9, 11, 24**
See also AMWS 3; CA 61-64; 9-12R;
CANR 10, 105; DLB 28, 63; INT CANR-
10; MTCW 1, 2; RGAL 4; TUS

Trimball, W. H.
See Mencken, H(enry) L(ouis)

Tristan
See Gomez de la Serna, Ramon

Tristram
See Housman, A(lfred) E(dward)

Trogdon, William (Lewis) 1939-
See Heat-Moon, William Least
See also CA 119; 115; CANR 47, 89; CPW;
INT CA-119

Trollope, Anthony 1815-1882 .... **NCLC 6, 33,**
101; SSC 28; WLC
See also BRW 5; CDBLB 1832-1890; DA;
DA3; DAB; DAC; DAM MST, NOV;
DLB 21, 57, 159; RGEL 2; RGSF 2;
SATA 22

Trollope, Frances 1779-1863 .... **NCLC 30**
See also DLB 21, 166

Trotsky, Leon 1879-1940 .... **TCLC 22**
See also CA 167; 118

Trotter (Cockburn), Catharine
1679-1749 .... **LC 8**
See also DLB 84, 252

Trotter, Wilfred 1872-1939 .... **TCLC 97**

Trout, Kilgore
See Farmer, Philip Jose

Trow, George W. S. 1943- .... **CLC 52**
See also CA 126; CANR 91

Troyat, Henri 1911- .... **CLC 23**
See also CA 45-48; CANR 2, 33, 67, 117;
GFL 1789 to the Present; MTCW 1

Trudeau, G(arretson) B(eekman) 1948-
See Trudeau, Garry B.
See also CA 81-84; CANR 31; SATA 35

Trudeau, Garry B. .... **CLC 12**
See Trudeau, G(arretson) B(eekman)
See also AAYA 10; AITN 2

Truffaut, Francois 1932-1984 ... **CLC 20, 101**
See also CA 113; 81-84; CANR 34

Trumbo, Dalton 1905-1976 .... **CLC 19**
See also CA 69-72; 21-24R; CANR 10;
DLB 26; IDFW 3, 4; YAW

Trumbull, John 1750-1831 .... **NCLC 30**
See also DLB 31; RGAL 4

Trundlett, Helen B.
See Eliot, T(homas) S(tearns)

Truth, Sojourner 1797(?)-1883 .... **NCLC 94**
See also DLB 239; FW; LAIT 2

Tryon, Thomas 1926-1991 .... **CLC 3, 11**
See also AITN 1; BPFB 3; CA 135; 29-32R;
CANR 32, 77; CPW; DA3; DAM POP;
HGG; MTCW 1

Tryon, Tom
See Tryon, Thomas

Ts'ao Hsueh-ch'in 1715(?)-1763 .... **LC 1**

Tsushima, Shuji 1909-1948
See Dazai Osamu
See also CA 107

Tsvetaeva (Efron), Marina (Ivanovna)
1892-1941 .... **PC 14; TCLC 7, 35**
See also CA 128; 104; CANR 73; EW 11;
MTCW 1, 2; RGWL 2, 3

Tuck, Lily 1938- .... **CLC 70**
See also CA 139; CANR 90

Tu Fu 712-770 .... **PC 9**
See Du Fu
See also DAM MULT; TWA; WP

Tunis, John R(oberts) 1889-1975 ..... **CLC 12**
See also BYA 1; CA 61-64; CANR 62; DLB
22, 171; JRDA; MAICYA 1, 2; SATA 37;
SATA-Brief 30; YAW

Tuohy, Frank .... **CLC 37**
See Tuohy, John Francis
See also DLB 14, 139

Tuohy, John Francis 1925-
See Tuohy, Frank
See also CA 178; 5-8R; CANR 3, 47; CN

Turco, Lewis (Putnam) 1934- ..... **CLC 11, 63**
See also CA 13-16R; CAAS 22; CANR 24
51; CP 7; DLBY 1984

Turgenev, Ivan (Sergeevich)
1818-1883 ..... **DC 7; NCLC 21, 37, 122;**
SSC 7, 57; WLC
See also DA; DAB; DAC; DAM MST,
NOV; DFS 6; DLB 238; EW 6; NFS 16;
RGSF 2; RGWL 2, 3; TWA

Turgot, Anne-Robert-Jacques
1727-1781 .... **LC 26**

Turner, Frederick 1943- .... **CLC 48**
See also CA 73-76; CAAS 10; CANR 12,
30, 56; DLB 40

Turton, James
See Crace, Jim

Tutu, Desmond M(pilo) 1931- .. **BLC 3; CLC**
80
See also BW 1, 3; CA 125; CANR 67, 81;
DAM MULT

Tutuola, Amos 1920-1997 ..... **BLC 3; CLC 5,**
14, 29
See also AFW; BW 2, 3; CA 159; 9-12R;
CANR 27, 66; CDWLB 3; CN 7; DA3;
DAM MULT; DLB 125; DNFS 2; MTCW
1, 2; RGEL 2; WLIT 2

Twain, Mark .. **SSC 34; TCLC 6, 12, 19, 36,**
48, 59; WLC
See Clemens, Samuel Langhorne
See also AAYA 20; AMW; AMWC 1; BPFB
3; BYA 2, 3, 11, 14; CLR 58, 60, 66; DLB
11; EXPN; EXPS; FANT; LAIT 2; NFS
1, 6; RGAL 4; RGSF 2; SFW 4; SSFS 1,
7; SUFW; TUS; WCH; WYA; YAW

Tyler, Anne 1941- . **CLC 7, 11, 18, 28, 44, 59,**
103
See also AAYA 18; AMWS 4; BEST 89:1;
BPFB 3; BYA 12; CA 9-12R; CANR 11,
33, 53, 109; CDALBS; CN 7; CPW;
CSW; DAM NOV, POP; DLB 6, 143;
DLBY 1982; EXPN; MAWW; MTCW 1,
2; NFS 2, 7, 10; RGAL 4; SATA 7, 90;
SSFS 17; TUS; YAW

Tyler, Royall 1757-1826 .... **NCLC 3**
See also DLB 37; RGAL 4

Tynan, Katharine 1861-1931 .... **TCLC 3**
See also CA 167; 104; DLB 153, 240; FW

Tyutchev, Fyodor 1803-1873 .... **NCLC 34**

Tzara, Tristan 1896-1963 ..... **CLC 47; PC 27**
See also CA 89-92; 153; DAM POET;
MTCW 2

Uchida, Yoshiko 1921-1992 .... **AAL**
See also AAYA 16; BYA 2, 3; CA 139; 13-
16R; CANR 6, 22, 47, 61; CDALBS;
CLR 6, 56; CWRI 5; JRDA; MAICYA 1,
2; MTCW 1, 2; SAAS 1; SATA 1, 53;
SATA-Obit 72

Udall, Nicholas 1504-1556 .... **LC 84**
See also DLB 62; RGEL 2

Uhry, Alfred 1936- .... **CLC 55**
See also CA 133; 127; CAD; CANR 112;
CD 5; CSW; DA3; DAM DRAM, POP;
DFS 15; INT CA-133

Ulf, Haerved
See Strindberg, (Johan) August

Ulf, Harved
See Strindberg, (Johan) August

Ulibarri, Sabine R(eyes) 1919- .... **CLC 83;**
HLCS 2
See also CA 131; CANR 81; DAM MULT;
DLB 82; HW 1, 2; RGSF 2

Unamuno (y Jugo), Miguel de
1864-1936 . **HLC 2; SSC 11; TCLC 2, 9**
See also CA 131; 104; CANR 81; DAM
MULT, NOV; DLB 108; EW 8; HW 1, 2;
MTCW 1, 2; RGSF 2; RGWL 2, 3; TWA

Literary Criticism Series
Cumulative Topic Index

This index lists all topic entries in Gale's *Classical and Medieval Literature Criticism* (CMLC), *Contemporary Literary Criticism* (CLC), *Drama Criticism* (DC), *Literature Criticism from 1400 to 1800* (LC), *Nineteenth-Century Literature Criticism* (NCLC), *Short Story Criticism* (SSC), and *Twentieth-Century Literary Criticism* (TCLC). The index also lists topic entries in the Gale Critical Companion Collection, which includes the following publications: *The Beat Generation* (BG), and *Harlem Renaissance* (HR).

Topic Index

Topic Index

SSC Cumulative Nationality Index

Nationality Index

SSC-60 **Title Index**

ISBN 0-7876-7017-0

90000